The Oxford German Minidictionary

Third edition

GERMAN–ENGLISH
ENGLISH–GERMAN

DEUTSCH–ENGLISCH
ENGLISCH–DEUTSCH

OXFORD
UNIVERSITY PRESS

OXFORD
UNIVERSITY PRESS

Great Clarendon Street, Oxford OX2 6DP

Oxford University Press is a department of the University of Oxford.
It furthers the University's objective of excellence in research,
scholarship, and education by publishing worldwide in

Oxford New York

Auckland Bangkok Buenos Aires
Cape Town Chennai Dar es Salaam Delhi Hong Kong Istanbul
Karachi Kolkata Kuala Lumpur Madrid Melbourne Mexico City Mumbai
Nairobi São Paulo Shanghai Singapore Taipei Tokyo Toronto Warsaw

with an associated company in Berlin

First edition published 1993
Second edition published 1997
This edition published 2002

British Library Cataloguing in Publication Data
Data available

Library of Congress Cataloging in Publication Data
Data available

ISBN 0-19-860468-8

10 9 8 7 6 5 4 3 2 1

Typeset by Morton Word Processing Ltd
Printed by Charles Letts & Co Ltd, Dalkeith, Scotland

Contents

Preface

This new edition of the Oxford German Minidictionary provides a handy and up-to-date reference work for tourists, students, and business people. It fully reflects recent changes to the spelling of German.

The dictionary also includes a unique Phrasefinder, which groups together all the essential phrases you will need for everyday conversation. The section is thematically arranged and covers 8 key topics: going places, keeping in touch, food and drink, places to stay, shopping and money, sports and leisure, time and dates, and conversion charts.

List of contributors

First Edition

Editors

Gunhild Prowe
Jill Schneider

Second Edition

Editors

Roswitha Morris
Robin Sawers

Supplementary Material

Robin Sawers
Neil and Roswitha Morris
Valerie Grundy
Eva Vennebusch

Data Capture

Susan Wilkin
Anne McConnell
Anna Cotgreave

Proof-reading

Andrew Hodgson

Third Edition

Editors

Gunhild Prowe
Jill Schneider

Introduction

The text of this dictionary reflects recent changes to the spelling of German ratified in July 1996. The symbol * has been introduced to refer from the old spelling to the new, preferred one:

As* *nt* **-ses, -se** *s.* **Ass**
dasein* *vi sep (sein)* **da sein,** *s.* **da**
Schiffahrt* *f s.* **Schifffahrt**

Where both the old and new forms are valid, an equals sign = is used to refer to the preferred form:

aufwändig *a* = **aufwendig**
Tunfisch *m* = **Thunfisch**

When such forms follow each other alphabetically, they are given with commas, with the preferred form in first place:

Panther, Panter *m* **-s, -** panther

In phrases, *od* (oder) is used:

...**deine(r,s)** *poss pron* yours;
die D~en *od* **d~en** *pl* your family *sg*

On the English–German side, only the preferred German form is given.

- A swung dash ~ represents the headword or that part of the headword preceding a vertical bar |. The initial letter of a German headword is given to show whether or not it is a capital.
- The vertical bar | follows the part of the headword which is not repeated in compounds or derivatives.
- Square brackets [ ] are used for optional material.
- Angled brackets < > are used after a verb translation to indicate the object; before a verb translation to indicate the subject; before an adjective to indicate a typical noun which it qualifies.

- Round brackets ( ) are used for field or style labels (see list on pages xiii–xv), and for explanatory matter.
- A box □ indicates a new part of speech within an entry.
- *od* (oder) and *or* denote that words or portions of a phrase are synonymous. An oblique stroke / is used where there is a difference in usage or meaning.
- ≈ is used where no exact equivalent exists in the other language.
- A dagger † indicates that a German verb is irregular and that the parts can be found in the verb table on pages 597–603. Compound verbs are not listed there as they follow the pattern of the basic verb.
- The stressed vowel is marked in a German headword by ̠ (long) or ̣ (short). A phonetic transcription is only given for words which do not follow the normal rules of pronunciation. These rules can be found on pages ix–x.
- Phonetics are given for all English headwords and for derivatives where there is a change of pronunciation or stress. In blocks of compounds, if no stress is shown, it falls on the first element.
- A change in pronunciation or stress shown within a block of compounds applies only to that particular word (subsequent entries revert to the pronunciation and stress of the headword).
- German headword nouns are followed by the gender and, with the exception of compound nouns, by the genitive and plural. These are only given at compound nouns if they present some difficulty. Otherwise the user should refer to the final element.
- Nouns that decline like adjectives are entered as follows: **-e(r)** *m/f*, **-e(s)** *nt*.
- Adjectives which have no undeclined form are entered in the feminine form with the masculine and neuter in brackets **-e(r,s)**.
- The reflexive pronoun **sich** is accusative unless marked (*dat*).

Proprietary terms

This dictionary includes some words which are, or are asserted to be, proprietary names or trademarks. Their inclusion does not imply that they have acquired for legal purposes a non-proprietary or general significance, nor is any other judgement implied concerning their legal status. In cases where the editor has some evidence that a word is used as a proprietary name or trademark this is indicated by the letter (P), but no judgement concerning the legal status of such words is made or implied thereby.

Phonetic symbols used for German words

a	Hand	hant	ŋ	lang	laŋ
a:	Bahn	ba:n	o	Moral	mo'ra:l
ɐ	Ober	'o:bɐ	o:	Boot	bo:t
ɐ̯	Uhr	u:ɐ̯	o̯	loyal	lo̯a'ja:l
ã	Conférencier	kõferã'si̯e:	õ	Konkurs	kõ'kʊrs
ã:	Abonnement	abɔnə'mã:	õ:	Ballon	ba'lõ:
ai̯	weit	vai̯t	ɔ	Post	pɔst
au̯	Haut	hau̯t	ø	Ökonom	øko'no:m
b	Ball	bal	ø:	Öl	ø:l
ç	ich	ɪç	œ	göttlich	'gœtlɪç
d	dann	dan	ɔy̆	heute	'hɔy̆tə
d͡ʒ	Gin	d͡ʒɪn	p	Pakt	pakt
e	Metall	me'tal	r	Rast	rast
e:	Beet	be:t	s	Hast	hast
ɛ	mästen	'mɛstən	ʃ	Schal	ʃa:l
ɛ:	wählen	'vɛ:lən	t	Tal	ta:l
ɛ̃	Cousin	ku'zɛ̃:	t͡s	Zahl	t͡sa:l
ə	Nase	'na:zə	t͡ʃ	Couch	kau̯t͡ʃ
f	Faß	fas	u	Kupon	ku'põ:
g	Gast	gast	u:	Hut	hu:t
h	haben	'ha:bən	u̯	aktuell	ak'tu̯ɛl
i	Rivale	ri'va:lə	ʊ	Pult	pʊlt
i:	viel	fi:l	v	was	vas
i̯	Aktion	ak't͡si̯o:n	x	Bach	bax
ɪ	Birke	'bɪrkə	y	Physik	fy'zi:k
j	ja	ja:	y:	Rübe	'ry:bə
k	kalt	kalt	y̆	Nuance	'ny̆ã:sə
l	Last	last	ʏ	Fülle	'fʏlə
m	Mast	mast	z	Nase	'na:zə
n	Naht	na:t	ʒ	Regime	re'ʒi:m

ˀ Glottal stop, e.g. Koordination / koˀɔrdina't͡si̯o:n /.

: length sign after a vowel, e.g. Chrom / kro:m /.

' Stress mark before stressed syllable, e.g. Balkon / bal'kõ:/.

Guide to German pronunciation

Consonants

Produced as in English with the following exceptions:

b	as	p	*at the end of a word or syllable*
d	as	t	
g	as	k	
ch	as in Scottish lo<u>ch</u>		*after a, o, u, au*
	like an exaggerated h as in <u>h</u>uge		*after i, e, ä, ö, ü, eu, ei*
-chs	as	x	(as in bo<u>x</u>)
-ig	as	-ich / ıç /	*when a suffix*
j	as	y	(as in <u>y</u>es)
ps			the p is pronounced
pn			
qu	as	k + v	
s	as	z	(as in <u>z</u>ero) *at the beginning of a word*
	as	s	(as in bu<u>s</u>) *at the end of a word or syllable, before a consonant, or when doubled*
sch	as	sh	
sp	as	shp	*at the beginning of a word*
st	as	sht	*at the beginning of a word*
v	as	f	(as in <u>f</u>or)
	as	v	(as in <u>v</u>ery) *within a word*
w	as	v	(as in <u>v</u>ery)
z	as	ts	

Vowels

Approximately as follows:

a	short	as	u	(as in b<u>u</u>t)
	long	as	a	(as in c<u>a</u>r)
e	short	as	e	(as in p<u>e</u>n)
	long	as	a	(as in p<u>a</u>per)
i	short	as	i	(as in b<u>i</u>t)
	long	as	ee	(as in qu<u>ee</u>n)
o	short	as	o	(as in h<u>o</u>t)
	long	as	o	(as in p<u>o</u>pe)
u	short	as	oo	(as in f<u>oo</u>t)
	long	as	oo	(as in b<u>oo</u>t)

Vowels are always short before a double consonant, and long when followed by an h or when double

ie	is pronounced	ee	(as in k<u>ee</u>p)

Diphthongs

au	as	ow	(as in h<u>ow</u>)
ei ai	as	y	(as in m<u>y</u>)
eu äu	as	oy	(as in b<u>oy</u>)

Die für das Englische verwendeten Zeichen der Lautschrift

ɑ:	barn	bɑ:n	l	lot	lɒt
ɑ̃	nuance	'nju:ɑ̃s	m	mat	mæt
æ	fat	fæt	n	not	nɒt
æ̃	lingerie	'læ̃ʒərɪ	ŋ	sing	sɪŋ
aɪ	fine	faɪn	ɒ	got	gɒt
aʊ	now	naʊ	ɔ:	paw	pɔ:
b	bat	bæt	ɔɪ	boil	bɔɪl
d	dog	dɒg	p	pet	pet
dʒ	jam	dʒæm	r	rat	ræt
e	met	met	s	sip	sɪp
eɪ	fate	feɪt	ʃ	ship	ʃɪp
eə	fairy	'feərɪ	t	tip	tɪp
əʊ	goat	gəʊt	tʃ	chin	tʃɪn
ə	ago	ə'gəʊ	θ	thin	θɪn
ɜ:	fur	fɜ:(r)	ð	the	ðə
f	fat	fæt	u:	boot	bu:t
g	good	gʊd	ʊ	book	bʊk
h	hat	hæt	ʊə	tourism	'tʊərɪzm
ɪ	bit, happy	bɪt, 'hæpɪ	ʌ	dug	dʌg
ɪə	near	nɪə(r)	v	van	væn
i:	meet	mi:t	w	win	wɪn
j	yet	jet	z	zip	zɪp
k	kit	kɪt	ʒ	vision	'vɪʒn

: bezeichnet Länge des vorhergehenden Vokals, z. B. boot [bu:t].

' Betonung, steht unmittelbar vor einer betonten Silbe, z. B. ago [ə'gəʊ].

(r) Ein „r" in runden Klammern wird nur gesprochen, wenn im Textzusammenhang ein Vokal unmittelbar folgt, z. B. fire /'faɪə(r)/; fire at /'faɪər æt/.

Pronunciation of the alphabet/ Ausspreche des Alphabets

English/Englisch		*German/Deutsch*
eɪ	a	a:
bi:	b	be:
si:	c	t͜se:
di:	d	de:
i:	e	e:
ef	f	ɛf
dʒi:	g	ge:
eɪtʃ	h	ha:
aɪ	i	i:
dʒeɪ	j	jɔt
keɪ	k	ka:
el	l	ɛl
em	m	ɛm
en	n	ɛn
əʊ	o	o:
pi:	p	pe:
kju:	q	ku:
a:(r)	r	ɛr
es	s	ɛs
ti:	t	te:
ju:	u	u:
vi:	v	fau
'dʌblju:	w	ve:
eks	x	ɪks
waɪ	y	'ʏpsilɔn
zed	z	tsɛt
eɪ umlaut	ä	ɛ:
əʊ umlaut	ö	ø:
ju: umlaut	ü	y:
es'zed	ß	ɛs'tsɛt

Abbreviations/ Abkürzungen

adjective	*a*	Adjektiv
abbreviation	*abbr*	Abkürzung
accusative	*acc*	Akkusativ
Administration	*Admin*	Administration
adverb	*adv*	Adverb
American	*Amer*	amerikanisch
Anatomy	*Anat*	Anatomie
Archaeology	*Archaeol*	Archäologie
Architecture	*Archit*	Architektur
Astronomy	*Astr*	Astronomie
attributive	*attrib*	attributiv
Austrian	*Aust*	österreichisch
Motor vehicles	*Auto*	Automobil
Aviation	*Aviat*	Luftfahrt
Biology	*Biol*	Biologie
Botany	*Bot*	Botanik
Chemistry	*Chem*	Chemie
collective	*coll*	Kollektivum
Commerce	*Comm*	Handel
conjunction	*conj*	Konjunktion
Cookery	*Culin*	Kochkunst
dative	*dat*	Dativ
definite article	*def art*	bestimmter Artikel
demonstrative	*dem*	Demonstrativ-
dialect	*dial*	Dialekt
Electricity	*Electr*	Elektrizität
something	*etw*	etwas
feminine	*f*	Femininum
figurative	*fig*	figurativ
genitive	*gen*	Genitiv
Geography	*Geog*	Geographie
Geology	*Geol*	Geologie
Geometry	*Geom*	Geometrie
Grammar	*Gram*	Grammatik
Horticulture	*Hort*	Gartenbau
impersonal	*impers*	unpersönlich
indefinite article	*indef art*	unbestimmter Artikel

indefinite pronoun	*indef pron*	unbestimmtes Pronomen
infinitive	*inf*	Infinitiv
inseparable	*insep*	untrennbar
interjection	*int*	Interjektion
invariable	*inv*	unveränderlich
irregular	*irreg*	unregelmäßig
someone	*jd*	jemand
someone	*jdm*	jemandem
someone	*jdn*	jemanden
someone's	*jds*	jemandes
Journalism	*Journ*	Journalismus
Law	*Jur*	Jura
Language	*Lang*	Sprache
literary	*liter*	dichterisch
masculine	*m*	Maskulinum
Mathematics	*Math*	Mathematik
Medicine	*Med*	Medizin
Meteorology	*Meteorol*	Meteorologie
Military	*Mil*	Militär
Mineralogy	*Miner*	Mineralogie
Music	*Mus*	Musik
noun	*n*	Substantiv
Nautical	*Naut*	nautisch
North German	*N Ger*	Norddeutsch
nominative	*nom*	Nominativ
neuter	*nt*	Neutrum
or	*od*	oder
Proprietary term	*P*	Warenzeichen
pejorative	*pej*	abwertend
Photography	*Phot*	Fotografie
Physics	*Phys*	Physik
plural	*pl*	Plural
Politics	*Pol*	Politik
possessive	*poss*	Possessiv-
past participle	*pp*	zweites Partizip
predicative	*pred*	prädikativ
prefix	*pref*	Präfix
preposition	*prep*	Präposition
present	*pres*	Präsens
present participle	*pres p*	erstes Partizip
pronoun	*pron*	Pronomen

Psychology	*Psych*	Psychologie
past tense	*pt*	Präteritum
Railway	*Rail*	Eisenbahn
reflexive	*refl*	reflexiv
regular	*reg*	regelmäßig
relative	*rel*	Relativ-
Religion	*Relig*	Religion
see	*s.*	siehe
School	*Sch*	Schule
separable	*sep*	trennbar
singular	*sg*	Singular
South German	*S Ger*	Süddeutsch
someone	*s.o.*	jemand
something	*sth*	etwas
Technical	*Techn*	Technik
Telephone	*Teleph*	Telefon
Textiles	*Tex*	Textilien
Theatre	*Theat*	Theater
Television	*TV*	Fernsehen
Typography	*Typ*	Typographie
University	*Univ*	Universität
auxiliary verb	*v aux*	Hilfsverb
intransitive verb	*vi*	intransitives Verb
reflexive verb	*vr*	reflexives Verb
transitive verb	*vt*	transitives Verb
vulgar	*vulg*	vulgär
Zoology	*Zool*	Zoologie
familiar	[!]	familiär
slang	⊠	Slang
old spelling	*	alte Schreibung

Aa

Aal *m* **-[e]s, -e** eel
Aas *nt* **-es** carrion; ☒ swine
ạb *prep (+ dat)* from ● *adv* off; *(weg)* away; *(auf Fahrplan)* departs; **ab und zu** now and then; **auf und ab** up and down
ạbändern *vt sep* alter; *(abwandeln)* modify
Ạbbau *m* dismantling; *(Kohlen-)* mining. **a~en** *vt sep* dismantle; mine <*Kohle*>
ạbbeißen† *vt sep* bite off
ạbbeizen *vt sep* strip
ạbberufen† *vt sep* recall
ạbbestellen *vt sep* cancel; **jdn a~** put s.o. off
ạbbiegen† *vi sep (sein)* turn off; **[nach] links a~** turn left
Ạbbildung *f* **-, -en** illustration
ạbblättern *vi sep (sein)* flake off
ạbblend|en *vt/i sep (haben)* **[die Scheinwerfer] a~en** dip one's headlights. **A~licht** *nt* dipped headlights *pl*
ạbbrechen† *v sep* ● *vt* break off; *(abreißen)* demolish; *(Computer)* cancel ● *vi (sein/haben)* break off
ạbbrennen† *v sep* ● *vt* burn off; *(niederbrennen)* burn down ● *vi (sein)* burn down
ạbbringen† *vt sep* dissuade (**von** from)
Ạbbruch *m* demolition; *(Beenden)* breaking off
ạbbuchen *vt sep* debit
ạbbürsten *vt sep* brush down; *(entfernen)* brush off
ạbdanken *vi sep (haben)* resign; <*Herrscher:*> abdicate
ạbdecken *vt sep* uncover; *(abnehmen)* take off; *(zudecken)* cover; **den Tisch a~** clear the table
ạbdichten *vt sep* seal
ạbdrehen *vt sep* turn off
Ạbdruck *m (pl* **⸚e**) impression. **a~en** *vt sep* print
ạbdrücken *vt/i sep (haben)* fire; **sich a~** leave an impression
Abend *m* **-s, -e** evening; **am A~** in the evening; **heute A~** this evening, tonight; **gestern A~** yesterday evening, last night. **A~brot** *nt* supper. **A~essen** *nt* dinner; *(einfacher)* supper. **A~mahl** *nt (Relig)* [Holy] Communion. **a~s** *adv* in the evening
Abenteuer *nt* **-s,-** adventure; *(Liebes-)* affair. **a~lich** *a* fantastic
aber *conj* but; **oder a~** or else ● *adv (wirklich)* really
Abẹr|glaube *m* superstition. **a~gläubisch** *a* superstitious
ạbfahr|en† *v sep* ● *vi (sein)* leave; <*Auto:*> drive off ● *vt* take away; *(entlangfahren)* drive along; use <*Fahrkarte*>; **abgefahrene Reifen** worn tyres. **A~t** *f* departure; *(Talfahrt)* descent; *(Piste)* run; *(Ausfahrt)* exit
Ạbfall *m* refuse, rubbish; *(auf der Straße)* litter; *(Industrie-)* waste
ạbfallen† *vi sep (sein)* drop, fall; *(übrig bleiben)* be left (**für** for); *(sich neigen)* slope away. **a~d** *a* sloping
Ạbfallhaufen *m* rubbish-dump
ạbfällig *a* disparaging
ạbfangen† *vt sep* intercept

abfärben *vi sep* (*haben*) <*Farbe*:> run; <*Stoff*:> not be colour-fast

abfassen *vt sep* draft

abfertigen *vt sep* attend to; (*zollamtlich*) clear; **jdn kurz a~** [!] give s.o. short shrift

abfeuern *vt sep* fire

abfind|en† *vt sep* pay off; (*entschädigen*) compensate; **sich a~en mit** come to terms with. **A~ung** *f* -, **-en** compensation

abfliegen† *vi sep* (*sein*) fly off; (*Aviat*) take off

abfließen† *vi sep* (*sein*) drain *or* run away

Abflug *m* (*Aviat*) departure

Abfluss *m* drainage; (*Öffnung*) drain. **A~rohr** *nt* drain-pipe

abfragen *vt sep* **jdn** *od* **jdm Vokabeln a~** test s.o. on vocabulary

Abfuhr *f* - removal; (*fig*) rebuff

abführ|en *vt sep* take *or* lead away. **A~mittel** *nt* laxative

abfüllen *vt sep* **auf** *od* **in Flaschen a~** bottle

Abgase *ntpl* exhaust fumes

abgeben† *vt sep* hand in; (*abliefern*) deliver; (*verkaufen*) sell; (*zur Aufbewahrung*) leave; (*Fußball*) pass; (*ausströmen*) give off; (*abfeuern*) fire; (*verlauten lassen*) give; cast <*Stimme*>; **jdm etw a~** give s.o. a share of sth

abgehen† *v sep* ● *vi* (*sein*) leave; (*Theat*) exit; (*sich lösen*) come off; (*abgezogen werden*) be deducted ● *vt* walk along

abgehetzt *a* harassed. **abgelegen** *a* remote. **abgeneigt** *a* **etw** (*dat*) **nicht abgeneigt sein** not be averse to sth. **abgenutzt** *a* worn. **Abgeordnete(r)** *m/f* deputy; (*Pol*) Member of Parliament. **abgepackt** *a* pre-packed

abgeschieden *a* secluded

abgeschlossen *a* (*fig*) complete; <*Wohnung*> self-contained. **abgesehen** *prep* apart (from **von**). **abgespannt** *a* exhausted. **abgestanden** *a* stale. **abgestorben** *a* dead; <*Glied*> numb. **abgetragen** *a* worn. **abgewetzt** *a* threadbare

abgewinnen† *vt sep* win (**jdm** from s.o.); **etw** (*dat*) **Geschmack a~** get a taste for sth

abgewöhnen *vt sep* **jdm/sich das Rauchen a~** cure s.o. of/ give up smoking

abgießen† *vt sep* pour off; drain <*Gemüse*>

Abgott *m* idol

abgöttisch *adv* **a~ lieben** idolize

abgrenz|en *vt sep* divide off; (*fig*) define. **A~ung** *f* - demarcation

Abgrund *m* abyss; (*fig*) depths *pl*

abgucken *vt sep* [!] copy

Abguss *m* cast

abhacken *vt sep* chop off

abhaken *vt sep* tick off

abhalten† *vt sep* keep off; (*hindern*) keep, prevent (**von** from); (*veranstalten*) hold

abhanden *adv* **a~ kommen** get lost

Abhandlung *f* treatise

Abhang *m* slope

abhängen[1] *vt sep* (*reg*) take down; (*abkuppeln*) uncouple

abhäng|en[2]† *vi sep* (*haben*) depend (**von** on). **a~ig** *a* dependent (**von** on). **A~igkeit** *f* - dependence

abhärten *vt sep* toughen up

abheben† *v sep* ● *vt* take off; (*vom Konto*) withdraw; **sich a~** stand out (**gegen** against) ● *vi* (*haben*) (*Cards*) cut [the cards]; (*Aviat*) take off; <*Rakete*:> lift off

abheften *vt sep* file

Abhilfe *f* remedy

abholen *vt sep* collect

abhör|en *vt sep* listen to; (*überwachen*) tap; **jdn** *od* **jdm**

Vokabeln a~en test s.o. on vocabulary. **A~gerät** *nt* bugging device
Abitur *nt* **-s** ≈ A levels *pl*
abkaufen *vt sep* buy (*dat* from)
abklingen† *vi sep* (*sein*) die away; (*nachlassen*) subside
abkochen *vt sep* boil
abkommen† *vi sep* (*sein*) **a~ von** stray from; (*aufgeben*) give up. **A~** *nt* **-s,-** agreement
Abkömmling *m* **-s, -e** descendant
abkratzen *vt sep* scrape off
abkühlen *vt/i sep* (*sein*) cool; **sich a~** cool [down]
Abkunft *f* **-** origin
abkuppeln *vt sep* uncouple
abkürz|en *vt sep* shorten; abbreviate <*Wort*>. **A~ung** *f* short cut; (*Wort*) abbreviation
abladen† *vt sep* unload
Ablage *f* shelf; (*für Akten*) tray
ablager|n *vt sep* deposit. **A~ung** *f* **-, -en** deposit
ablassen† *vt sep* drain [off]; let off <*Dampf*>
Ablauf *m* drain; (*Verlauf*) course; (*Ende*) end; (*einer Frist*) expiry. **a~en**† *v sep* ● *vi* (*sein*) run *or* drain off; (*verlaufen*) go off; (*enden*) expire; <*Zeit:*> run out; <*Uhrwerk:*> run down ● *vt* walk along; (*absuchen*) scour (**nach** for)
ableg|en *v sep* ● *vt* put down; discard <*Karte*>; (*abheften*) file; (*ausziehen*) take off; sit, take <*Prüfung*>; **abgelegte Kleidung** cast-offs *pl* ● *vi* (*haben*) take off one's coat; (*Naut*) cast off. **A~er** *m* **-s,-** (*Bot*) cutting; (*Schössling*) shoot
ablehn|en *vt sep* refuse; (*missbilligen*) reject. **A~ung** *f* **-, -en** refusal; rejection
ableit|en *vt sep* divert; **sich a~en** be derived (**von/aus** from). **A~ung** *f* derivation; (*Wort*) derivative
ablenk|en *vt sep* deflect; divert <*Aufmerksamkeit*>. **A~ung** *f* **-, -en** distraction
ablesen† *vt sep* read
ablicht|en *vt sep* photocopy. **A~ung** *f* photocopy
abliefern *vt sep* deliver
ablös|en *vt sep* detach; (*abwechseln*) relieve; **sich a~en** come off; (*sich abwechseln*) take turns. **A~ung** *f* relief
abmach|en *vt sep* remove; (*ausmachen*) arrange; (*vereinbaren*) agree. **A~ung** *f* **-, -en** agreement
abmager|n *vi sep* (*sein*) lose weight. **A~ungskur** *f* slimming diet
abmelden *vt sep* cancel; **sich a~** (*im Hotel*) check out; (*Computer*) log off
abmessen† *vt sep* measure
abmühen (sich) *vr sep* struggle
Abnäher *m* **-s,-** dart
abnehm|en† *v sep* ● *vt* take off, remove; pick up <*Hörer*>; **jdm etw a~en** take/(*kaufen*) buy sth from s.o. ● *vi* (*haben*) decrease; (*nachlassen*) decline; <*Person:*> lose weight; <*Mond:*> wane. **A~er** *m* **-s,-** buyer
Abneigung *f* dislike (**gegen** of)
abnorm *a* abnormal
abnutz|en *vt sep* wear out. **A~ung** *f* **-** wear [and tear]
Abon|nement /abɔnəˈmã:/ *nt* **-s, -s** subscription. **A~nent** *m* **-en, -en** subscriber. **a~nieren** *vt* take out a subscription to
Abordnung *f* **-, -en** deputation
abpassen *vt sep* wait for; **gut a~** time well
abraten† *vi sep* (*haben*) **jdm von etw a~** advise s.o. against sth
abräumen *vt/i* (*haben*) clear away

ạbrechn|en *v sep* ● *vt* deduct ● *vi* (*haben*) settle up. **A~ung** *f* settlement; (*Rechnung*) account

Ạbreise *f* departure. **a~n** *vi sep* (*sein*) leave

ạbreißen† *v sep* ● *vt* tear off; (*demolieren*) pull down ● *vi* (*sein*) come off

ạbrichten *vt sep* train

Ạbriss *m* demolition; (*Übersicht*) summary

ạbrufen† *vt sep* call away; (*Computer*) retrieve

ạbrunden *vt sep* round off

ạbrüst|en *vi sep* (*haben*) disarm. **A~ung** *f* disarmament

ạbrutschen *vi sep* (*sein*) slip

Ạbsage *f* **-, -n** cancellation; (*Ablehnung*) refusal. **a~n** *v sep* ● *vt* cancel ● *vi* (*haben*) **[jdm] a~n** cancel an appointment [with s.o.]; (*auf Einladung*) refuse [s.o.'s invitation]

Ạbsatz *m* heel; (*Abschnitt*) paragraph; (*Verkauf*) sale

ạbschaffen *vt sep* abolish; get rid of <*Auto, Hund*>

ạbschalten *vt/i sep* (*haben*) switch off

Ạbscheu *m* **-** revulsion

abscheulich *a* revolting

ạbschicken *vt sep* send off

Ạbschied *m* **-[e]s, -e** farewell; (*Trennung*) parting; **A~ nehmen** say goodbye (**von** to)

ạbschießen† *vt sep* shoot down; (*abfeuern*) fire; launch <*Rakete*>

ạbschirmen *vt sep* shield

ạbschlagen† *vt sep* knock off; (*verweigern*) refuse

Ạbschlepp|dienst *m* breakdown service. **a~en** *vt sep* tow away. **A~seil** *nt* tow-rope

ạbschließen† *v sep* ● *vt* lock; (*beenden, abmachen*) conclude; make <*Wette*>; balance <*Bücher*> ● *vi* (*haben*) lock up; (*enden*) end. **a~d** *adv* in conclusion

Ạbschluss *m* conclusion. **A~zeugnis** *nt* diploma

ạbschmecken *vt sep* season

ạbschmieren *vt sep* lubricate

ạbschneiden† *v sep* ● *vt* cut off ● *vi* (*haben*) **gut/schlecht a~** do well/badly

Ạbschnitt *m* section; (*Stadium*) stage; (*Absatz*) paragraph

ạbschöpfen *vt sep* skim off

ạbschrauben *vt sep* unscrew

ạbschreck|en *vt sep* deter; (*Culin*) put in cold water <*Ei*>. **a~end** *a* repulsive. **A~ungsmittel** *nt* deterrent

ạbschreib|en† *v sep* ● *vt* copy; (*Comm & fig*) write off ● *vi* (*haben*) copy. **A~ung** *f* (*Comm*) depreciation

Ạbschrift *f* copy

Ạbschuss *m* shooting down; (*Abfeuern*) firing; (*Raketen-*) launch

ạbschüssig *a* sloping; (*steil*) steep

ạbschwellen† *vi sep* (*sein*) go down

ạbseh|bar *a* **in a~barer Zeit** in the foreseeable future. **a~en**† *vt/i sep* (*haben*) copy; (*voraussehen*) foresee; **a~en von** disregard; (*aufgeben*) refrain from

ạbseits *adv* apart; (*Sport*) offside ● *prep* (+ *gen*) away from. **A~** *nt* **-** (*Sport*) offside

ạbsend|en† *vt sep* send off. **A~er** *m* sender

ạbsetzen *v sep* ● *vt* put *or* set down; (*ablagern*) deposit; (*abnehmen*) take off; (*abbrechen*) stop; (*entlassen*) dismiss; (*verkaufen*) sell; (*abziehen*) deduct ● *vi* (*haben*) pause

Ạbsicht *f* **-, -en** intention; **mit A~** intentionally, on purpose

absịchtlich *a* intentional

absitzen† *v sep* ● *vi (sein)* dismount ● *vt* [!] serve <*Strafe*>
absolut *a* absolute
absolvieren *vt* complete; (*bestehen*) pass
absonder|n *vt sep* separate; (*ausscheiden*) secrete. **A∼ung** *f* **-, -en** secretion
absorbieren *vt* absorb
abspeisen *vt sep* fob off (**mit** with)
absperr|en *vt sep* cordon off; (*abstellen*) turn off; (*SGer*) lock. **A∼ung** *f* **-, -en** barrier
abspielen *vt sep* play; (*Fußball*) pass; **sich a∼** take place
Absprache *f* agreement
absprechen† *vt sep* arrange; **sich a∼** agree
abspringen† *vi sep* (*sein*) jump off; (*mit Fallschirm*) parachute; (*abgehen*) come off
Absprung *m* jump
abspülen *vt sep* rinse
abstamm|en *vi sep* (*haben*) be descended (**von** from). **A∼ung** *f* **-** descent
Abstand *m* distance; (*zeitlich*) interval; **A∼ halten** keep one's distance
abstatten *vt sep* **jdm einen Besuch a∼** pay s.o. a visit
Abstecher *m* **-s,-** detour
abstehen† *vi sep* (*haben*) stick out
absteigen† *vi sep* (*sein*) dismount; (*niedersteigen*) descend; (*Fußball*) be relegated
abstell|en *vt sep* put down; (*lagern*) store; (*parken*) park; (*abschalten*) turn off. **A∼gleis** *nt* siding. **A∼raum** *m* box-room
absterben† *vi sep* (*sein*) die; (*gefühllos werden*) go numb
Abstieg *m* **-[e]s, -e** descent; (*Fußball*) relegation
abstimm|en *v sep* ● *vi* (*haben*) vote (**über** + *acc* on) ● *vt* coordinate (**auf** + *acc* with). **A∼ung** *f* vote
Abstinenzler *m* **-s, -** teetotaller
abstoßen† *vt sep* knock off; (*verkaufen*) sell; (*fig: ekeln*) repel. **a∼d** *a* repulsive
abstreiten† *vt sep* deny
Abstrich *m* (*Med*) smear
abstufen *vt sep* grade
Absturz *m* fall; (*Aviat*) crash
abstürzen *vi sep* (*sein*) fall; (*Aviat*) crash
absuchen *vt sep* search
absurd *a* absurd
Abszess *m* **-es, -e** abscess
Abt *m* **-[e]s,⸚e** abbot
abtasten *vt sep* feel; (*Techn*) scan
abtauen *vt/i sep* (*sein*) thaw; (*entfrosten*) defrost
Abtei *f* **-, -en** abbey
Abteil *nt* compartment
Abteilung *f* **-, -en** section; (*Admin, Comm*) department
abtragen† *vt sep* clear; (*einebnen*) level; (*abnutzen*) wear out
abträglich *a* detrimental (*dat* to)
abtreib|en† *vt sep* (*Naut*) drive off course; **ein Kind a∼en lassen** have an abortion. **A∼ung** *f* **-, -en** abortion
abtrennen *vt sep* detach; (*abteilen*) divide off
Abtreter *m* **-s,-** doormat
abtrocknen *vt/i sep* (*haben*) dry; **sich a∼** dry oneself
abtropfen *vi sep* (*sein*) drain
abtun† *vt sep* (*fig*) dismiss
abwägen† *vt sep* (*fig*) weigh
abwandeln *vt sep* modify
abwarten *v sep* ● *vt* wait for ● *vi* (*haben*) wait [and see]
abwärts *adv* down[wards]
Abwasch *m* **-[e]s** washing-up; (*Geschirr*) dirty dishes *pl*.
a∼en† *v sep* ● *vt* wash; wash up <*Geschirr*>; (*entfernen*) wash off

● *vi* (*haben*) wash up. **A~lappen** *m* dishcloth

Abwasser *nt* **-s,**⸚ sewage. **A~kanal** *m* sewer

abwechseln *vi/r sep* (*haben*) **[sich] a~** alternate; <*Personen:*> take turns. **a~d** *a* alternate

Abwechslung *f* **-, -en** change; **zur A~** for a change

abwegig *a* absurd

Abwehr *f* **-** defence; (*Widerstand*) resistance; (*Pol*) counter-espionage. **a~en** *vt sep* ward off. **A~system** *nt* immune system

abweich|en† *vi sep* (*sein*) deviate/(*von Regel*) depart (**von** from); (*sich unterscheiden*) differ (**von** from). **a~end** *a* divergent; (*verschieden*) different. **A~ung** *f* **-, -en** deviation

abweis|en† *vt sep* turn down; turn away <*Person*>. **a~end** *a* unfriendly. **A~ung** *f* rejection

abwenden† *vt sep* turn away; (*verhindern*) avert

abwerfen† *vt sep* throw off; throw <*Reiter*>; (*Aviat*) drop; (*Kartenspiel*) discard; shed <*Haut, Blätter*>; yield <*Gewinn*>

abwert|en *vt sep* devalue. **A~ung** *f* **-, -en** devaluation

Abwesenheit *f* **-** absence; absent-mindedness

abwickeln *vt sep* unwind; (*erledigen*) settle

abwischen *vt sep* wipe

abzahlen *vt sep* pay off

abzählen *vt sep* count

Abzahlung *f* instalment

Abzeichen *nt* badge

abzeichnen *vt sep* copy

Abzieh|bild *nt* transfer. **a~en**† *v sep* ● *vt* pull off; take off <*Laken*>; strip <*Bett*>; (*häuten*) skin; (*Phot*) print; run off <*Kopien*>; (*zurückziehen*) withdraw; (*abrechnen*) deduct ● *vi* (*sein*) go away, <*Rauch:*> escape

Abzug *m* withdrawal; (*Abrechnung*) deduction; (*Phot*) print (*Korrektur-*) proof; (*am Gewehr*) trigger; (*A~söffnung*) vent; **A~̈e** *pl* deductions

abzüglich *prep* (+ *gen*) less

Abzugshaube *f* [cooker] hood

abzweig|en *v sep* ● *vi* (*sein*) branch off ● *vt* divert. **A~ung** *f* **-, -en** junction; (*Gabelung*) fork

ach *int* oh; **a~ je!** oh dear! **a~ so** I see

Achse *f* **-, -n** axis; (*Rad-*) axle

Achsel *f* **-, -n** shoulder. **A~höhle** *f* armpit. **A~zucken** *nt* **-s** shrug

acht *inv a*, **A~** *f* **-, -en** eight

Acht *f* **A~ geben** be careful; **A~ geben auf** (+ *acc*) look after; **außer A~ lassen** disregard; **sich in A~ nehmen** be careful

acht|e(r,s) *a* eighth. **a~eckig** *a* octagonal. **A~el** *nt* **-s,-** eighth

achten *vt* respect ● *vi* (*haben*) **a~ auf** (+ *acc*) pay attention to; (*aufpassen*) look after

Achterbahn *f* roller-coaster

achtlos *a* careless

achtsam *a* careful

Achtung *f* **-** respect (**vor** + *dat* for); **A~!** look out!

acht|zehn *inv a* eighteen. **a~zehnte(r,s)** *a* eighteenth. **a~zig** *a inv* eighty. **a~zigste(r,s)** *a* eightieth

Acker *m* **-s,**⸚ field. **A~bau** *m* agriculture. **A~land** *nt* arable land

addieren *vt/i* (*haben*) add

Addition /-ˈt͡si̯oːn/ *f* **-, -en** addition

ade *int* goodbye

Adel *m* **-s** nobility

Ader *f* **-, -n** vein

Adjektiv *nt* **-s, -e** adjective

Adler *m* **-s,-** eagle

adlig *a* noble. **A~e(r)** *m* nobleman
Administration /-'tsio:n/ *f* - administration
Admiral *m* -s,¨-e admiral
adop|tieren *vt* adopt. **A~tion** /-'tsio:n/ *f* -, **-en** adoption. **A~tiveltern** *pl* adoptive parents. **A~tivkind** *nt* adopted child
Adrenalin *nt* **-s** adrenalin
Adres|se *f* -, **-n** address. **a~sieren** *vt* address
Adria *f* - Adriatic
Adverb *nt* **-s, -ien** /-iən/ adverb
Affäre *f* -, **-n** affair
Affe *m* **-n, -n** monkey; (*Menschen-*) ape
affektiert *a* affected
affig *a* affected; (*eitel*) vain
Afrika *nt* **-s** Africa
Afrikan|er(in) *m* **-s,-** (*f* **-, -nen**) African. **a~isch** *a* African
After *m* **-s,-** anus
Agen|t(in) *m* **-en, -en** (*f* **-, -nen**) agent. **A~tur** *f* -, **-en** agency
Aggres|sion *f* -, **-en** aggression. **a~siv** *a* aggressive
Agnostiker *m* **-s,-** agnostic
Ägypt|en /ɛ'gʏptən/ *nt* **-s** Egypt. **Ä~er(in)** *m* **-s,-** (*f* **-, -nen**) Egyptian. **ä~isch** *a* Egyptian
ähneln *vi* (*haben*) (+ *dat*) resemble; **sich ä~** be alike
ahnen *vt* have a presentiment of; (*vermuten*) suspect
Ahnen *mpl* ancestors. **A~forschung** *f* genealogy
ähnlich *a* similar; **jdm ä~ sehen** resemble s.o. **Ä~keit** *f* -, **-en** similarity; resemblance
Ahnung *f* -, **-en** premonition; (*Vermutung*) idea, hunch
Ahorn *m* **-s, -e** maple
Ähre *f* -, **-n** ear [of corn]
Aids /e:ts/ *nt* - Aids
Airbag /'ɛ:ɐbɛk/ *m* **-s, -s** (*Auto*) air bag

Akademie *f* -, **-n** academy
Akadem|iker(in) *m* **-s,-** (*f* **-, -nen**) university graduate. **a~isch** *a* academic
akklimatisieren (sich) *vr* become acclimatized
Akkord *m* **-[e]s, -e** (*Mus*) chord. **A~arbeit** *f* piece-work
Akkordeon *nt* **-s, -s** accordion
Akkumulator *m* **-s, -en** /-'to:rən/ (*Electr*) accumulator
Akkusativ *m* **-s, -e** accusative. **A~objekt** *nt* direct object
Akrobat|(in) *m* **-en, -en** (*f* **-, -nen**) acrobat. **a~isch** *a* acrobatic
Akt *m* **-[e]s, -e** act; (*Kunst*) nude
Akte *f* -, **-n** file; **A~n** documents. **A~ntasche** *f* briefcase
Aktie /'aktsiə/ *f* -, **-n** (*Comm*) share. **A~ngesellschaft** *f* joint-stock company
Aktion /ak'tsio:n/ *f* -, **-en** action. **A~är** *m* **-s, -e** shareholder
aktiv *a* active
aktuell *a* topical; (*gegenwärtig*) current
Akupunktur *f* - acupuncture
Akustik *f* - acoustics *pl*
akut *a* acute
Akzent *m* **-[e]s, -e** accent
akzept|abel *a* acceptable. **a~ieren** *vt* accept
Alarm *m* **-s** alarm; (*Mil*) alert. **a~ieren** *vt* alert; (*beunruhigen*) alarm
Albdruck *m* nightmare
albern *a* silly ● *vi* (*haben*) play the fool
Albtraum *m* nightmare
Album *nt* **-s, -ben** album
Algebra *f* - algebra
Algen *fpl* algae
Algerien /-iən/ *nt* **-s** Algeria
Alibi *nt* **-s, -s** alibi
Alimente *pl* maintenance *sg*
Alkohol *m* **-s** alcohol. **a~frei** *a* non-alcoholic

Alkoholiker(in) *m* **-s,-** (*f* **-, -nen**) alcoholic. **a~isch** *a* alcoholic

all *inv pron* **all das/mein Geld** all the/my money; **all dies** all this

All *nt* **-s** universe

alle *pred a* finished

all|e(r,s) *pron* all; (*jeder*) every; **a~es** everything, all; (*alle Leute*) everyone; **a~e** *pl* all; **a~es Geld** all the money; **a~e beide** both [of them/us]; **a~e Tage** every day; **a~e drei Jahre** every three years; **ohne a~en Grund** without any reason; **vor a~em** above all; **a~es in a~em** all in all; **a~es aussteigen!** all change!

Allee *f* **-, -n** avenue

allein *adv* alone; (*nur*) only; **a~ stehend** single; **a~ der Gedanke** the mere thought; **von a~[e]** of its/<*Person*> one's own accord; (*automatisch*) automatically ● *conj* but. **A~erziehende(r)** *m/f* single parent. **a~ig** *a* sole. **A~stehende** *pl* single people

allemal *adv* every time; (*gewiss*) certainly

allenfalls *adv* at most; (*eventuell*) possibly

aller|beste(r,s) *a* very best; **am a~besten** best of all. **a~dings** *adv* indeed; (*zwar*) admittedly. **a~erste(r,s)** *a* very first

Allergie *f* **-, -n** allergy

allergisch *a* allergic (**gegen** to)

Aller|heiligen *nt* **-s** All Saints Day. **a~höchstens** *adv* at the very most. **a~lei** *inv a* all sorts of ● *pron* all sorts of things. **a~letzte(r,s)** *a* very last. **a~liebste(r,s)** *a* favourite ● *adv* **am a~liebsten** for preference; **am a~liebsten haben** like best of all. **a~meiste(r,s)** *a* most ● *adv* **am a~meisten** most of all. **A~seelen** *nt* **-s** All Souls Day. **a~wenigste(r,s)** *a* very least ● *adv* **am a~wenigsten** least of all

allgemein *a* general, *adv* -ly; **im A~en (a~en)** in general. **A~heit** *f* **-** community; (*Öffentlichkeit*) general public

Allianz *f* **-, -en** alliance

Alligator *m* **-s, -en** /-ˈto:rən/ alligator

alliiert *a* allied; **die A~en** *pl* the Allies

all|jährlich *a* annual. **a~mählich** *a* gradual

Alltag *m* working day; **der A~** (*fig*) everyday life

alltäglich *a* daily; (*gewöhnlich*) everyday; <*Mensch*> ordinary

alltags *adv* on weekdays

allzu *adv* [far] too; **a~ oft** all too often; **a~ vorsichtig** over-cautious

Alm *f* **-, -en** alpine pasture

Almosen *ntpl* alms

Alpdruck *m* = **Albdruck**

Alpen *pl* Alps

Alphabet *nt* **-[e]s, -e** alphabet. **a~isch** *a* alphabetical, *adv* -ly

Alptraum *m* = **Albtraum**

als *conj* as; (*zeitlich*) when; (*mit Komparativ*) than; **nichts als** nothing but; **als ob** as if *or* though

also *adv & conj* so; **a~ gut** all right then; **na a~!** there you are!

alt *a* old; (*gebraucht*) second-hand; (*ehemalig*) former; **alt werden** grow old

Alt *m* **-s** (*Mus*) contralto

Altar *m* **-s,¨-e** altar

Alt|e(r) *m/f* old man/woman; **die A~en** old people. **A~eisen** *nt* scrap iron. **A~enheim** *nt* old people's home

Alter *nt* **-s,-** age; (*Bejahrtheit*) old age; **im A~ von** at the age of

älter *a* older; **mein ä~er Bruder** my elder brother

altern *vi* (*sein*) age

Alternative *f* **-, -n** alternative

Alters|grenze *f* age limit. **A~heim** *nt* old people's home. **A~rente** *f* old-age pension. **a~schwach** *a* old and infirm

Alter|tum *nt* **-s,¨er** antiquity. **a~tümlich** *a* old; (*altmodisch*) old-fashioned

altklug *a* precocious

alt|modisch *a* old-fashioned. **A~papier** *nt* waste paper. **A~warenhändler** *m* second-hand dealer

Alufolie *f* [aluminium] foil

Aluminium *nt* **-s** aluminium, (*Amer*) aluminum

am *prep* = **an dem; am Montag** on Monday; **am Morgen** in the morning; **am besten** [the] best

Amateur /-'tøːɐ̯/ *m* **-s, -e** amateur

Ambition /-'t͡si̯oːn/ *f* **-, -en** ambition

Amboss *m* **-es, -e** anvil

ambulan|t *a* out-patient ... ● *adv* **a~t behandeln** treat as an out-patient. **A~z** *f* **-, -en** out-patients' department

Ameise *f* **-, -n** ant

amen *int*, **A~** *nt* **-s** amen

Amerika *nt* **-s** America

Amerikan|er(in) *m* **-s,-** (*f* **-, -nen**) American. **a~isch** *a* American

Ammoniak *nt* **-s** ammonia

Amnestie *f* **-, -n** amnesty

amoralisch *a* amoral

Ampel *f* **-, -n** traffic lights *pl*

Amphitheater *nt* amphitheatre

Amput|ation /-'t͡si̯oːn/ *f* **-, -en** amputation. **a~ieren** *vt* amputate

Amsel *f* **-, -n** blackbird

Amt *nt* **-[e]s,¨er** office; (*Aufgabe*) task; (*Teleph*) exchange. **a~lich** *a* official. **A~szeichen** *nt* dialling tone

Amulett *nt* **-[e]s, -e** [lucky] charm

amüs|ant *a* amusing. **a~ieren** *vt* amuse; **sich a~ieren** be amused (**über** + *acc* at); (*sich vergnügen*) enjoy oneself

an

● *preposition (+ dative)*

! Note that **an** plus **dem** can become **am**

····► (*räumlich*) on; (*Gebäude, Ort*) at. **an der Wand** on the wall. **Frankfurt an der Oder** Frankfurt on [the] Oder. **an der Ecke** at the corner. **am Bahnhof** at the station. **an ... vorbei** past

····► (*zeitlich*) on. **am Montag** on Monday. **an jedem Sonntag** every Sunday. **am 24. Mai** on May 24th

····► (*sonstige Verwendungen*) **arm/reich an Vitaminen** low/rich in vitamins. **jdn an etw erkennen** recognize s.o. by sth. **an etw leiden** suffer from sth. **an einer Krankheit sterben** die of a disease. **an [und für] sich** actually

● *preposition (+ accusative)*

! Note that **an** plus **das** can become **ans**

····► to. **schicke es an deinen Bruder** send it to your brother. **er ging ans Fenster** he went to the window

····► (*auf, gegen*) on. **etw an die Wand hängen** to hang sth on the wall. **lehne es an den Baum** lean it on *or* against the tree

····► (*sonstige Verwendungen*) **an etw/jdn glauben** believe in sth/s.o. **an etw denken** think of sth. **sich an etw erinnern** remember sth

● *adverb*

····► (*auf Fahrplan*) **Köln an: 9.15** arriving Cologne 09.15

····➤ (*angeschaltet*) on. **die Waschmaschine/der Fernseher/das Licht/das Gas ist an** the washing machine/ television/light/gas is on
····➤ (*ungefähr*) around; about. **an [die] 20 000 DM** around *or* about 20,000 DM
····➤ (*in die Zukunft*) **von heute an** from today (onwards)

analog *a* analogous; (*Computer*) analog. **A~ie** *f* **-, -n** analogy
Analphabet *m* **-en, -en** illiterate person. **A~entum** *nt* **-s** illiteracy
Analy|se *f* **-, -n** analysis. **a~sieren** *vt* analyse. **A~tiker** *m* **-s,-** analyst. **a~tisch** *a* analytical
Anämie *f* **-** anaemia
Ananas *f* **-, -[se]** pineapple
Anatomie *f* **-** anatomy
Anbau *m* cultivation; (*Gebäude*) extension. **a~en** *vt sep* build on; (*anpflanzen*) cultivate, grow
anbei *adv* enclosed
anbeißen† *v sep* ● *vt* take a bite of ● *vi* (*haben*) <*Fisch:*> bite
anbeten *vt sep* worship
Anbetracht *m* **in A~** (+ *gen*) in view of
anbieten† *vt sep* offer; **sich a~** offer (**zu** to)
anbinden† *vt sep* tie up
Anblick *m* sight. **a~en** *vt sep* look at
anbrechen† *v sep* ● *vt* start on; break into <*Vorräte*> ● *vi* (*sein*) begin; <*Tag:*> break; <*Nacht:*> fall
anbrennen† *v sep* ● *vt* light ● *vi* (*sein*) burn
anbringen† *vt sep* bring [along]; (*befestigen*) fix
Anbruch *m* (*fig*) dawn; **bei A~ des Tages/der Nacht** at daybreak/nightfall

Andacht *f* **-, -en** reverence; (*Gottesdienst*) prayers *pl*
andächtig *a* reverent; (*fig*) rapt
andauern *vi sep* (*haben*) last; (*anhalten*) continue. **a~d** *a* persistent; (*ständig*) constant
Andenken *nt* **-s,-** memory; (*Souvenir*) souvenir
ander|e(r,s) *a* other; (*verschieden*) different; (*nächste*) next; **ein a~er, eine a~e** another ● *pron* **der a~e/die a~en** the other/others; **ein a~er** another [one]; (*Person*) someone else; **kein a~er** no one else; **einer nach dem a~en** one after the other; **alles a~e/nichts a~es** everything/nothing else; **unter a~em** among other things. **a~enfalls** *adv* otherwise. **a~erseits** *adv* on the other hand. **a~mal** *adv* **ein a~mal** another time
ändern *vt* alter; (*wechseln*) change; **sich ä~** change
andernfalls *adv* otherwise
anders *pred a* different; **a~ werden** change ● *adv* differently; <*riechen, schmecken*> different; (*sonst*) else; **jemand a~** someone else
anderseits *adv* on the other hand
andersherum *adv* the other way round
anderthalb *inv a* one and a half; **a~ Stunden** an hour and a half
Änderung *f* **-, -en** alteration; (*Wechsel*) change
andeut|en *vt sep* indicate; (*anspielen*) hint at. **A~ung** *f* **-, -en** indication; hint
Andrang *m* rush (**nach** for); (*Gedränge*) crush
androhen *vt sep* **jdm etw a~** threaten s.o. with sth
aneignen *vt sep* **sich** (*dat*) **a~** appropriate; (*lernen*) learn

aneinạnder *adv & pref* together; <*denken*> of one another; **a~ vorbei** past one another; **a~ geraten** quarrel
Anekdọte *f* **-, -n** anecdote
ạnerkannt *a* acknowledged
ạnerkenn|en† *vt sep* acknowledge, recognize; (*würdigen*) appreciate. **a~end** *a* approving. **A~ung** *f* - acknowledgement, recognition; appreciation
ạnfahren† *v sep* ● *vt* deliver; (*streifen*) hit ● *vi* (*sein*) start
Ạnfall *m* fit, attack. **a~en**† *v sep* ● *vt* attack ● *vi* (*sein*) arise; <*Zinsen:*> accrue
ạnfällig *a* susceptible (**für** to); (*zart*) delicate
Ạnfang *m* **-s,⸚e** beginning, start; **zu** *od* **am A~** at the beginning; (*anfangs*) at first. **a~en**† *vt/i sep* (*haben*) begin, start; (*tun*) do
Ạnfänger(in) *m* **-s,-** (*f* **-, -nen**) beginner
ạnfangs *adv* at first. **A~buchstabe** *m* initial letter. **A~gehalt** *nt* starting salary
ạnfassen *vt sep* touch; (*behandeln*) treat; tackle <*Arbeit*>; **sich a~** hold hands
ạnfechten† *vt sep* contest
ạnfertigen *vt sep* make
ạnfeuchten *vt sep* moisten
ạnflehen *vt sep* implore, beg
Ạnflug *m* (*Avia*) approach
ạnforder|n *vt sep* demand; (*Comm*) order. **A~ung** *f* demand
Ạnfrage *f* enquiry. **a~n** *vi sep* (*haben*) enquire, ask
ạnfreunden (sich) *vr sep* make friends (**mit** with)
ạnfügen *vt sep* add
ạnfühlen *vt sep* feel; **sich weich a~** feel soft
ạnführ|en *vt sep* lead; (*zitieren*) quote; (*angeben*) give. **A~er** *m* leader. **A~ungszeichen** *ntpl* quotation marks
Ạngabe *f* statement; (*Anweisung*) instruction; (*Tennis*) service; **nähere A~n** particulars
ạngeb|en† *v sep* ● *vt* state; give <*Namen, Grund*>; (*anzeigen*) indicate; set <*Tempo*> ● *vi* (*haben*) (*Tennis*) serve; ([!] *protzen*) show off. **A~er(in)** *m* **-s,-** (*f* **-, -nen**) [!] show-off. **A~erei** *f* - [!] showing-off
ạngeblich *a* alleged
ạngeboren *a* innate; (*Med*) congenital
Ạngebot *nt* offer; (*Auswahl*) range; **A~ und Nachfrage** supply and demand
ạngebracht *a* appropriate
ạngeheiratet *a* <*Onkel, Tante*> by marriage
ạngeheitert *a* [!] tipsy
ạngehen† *v sep* ● *vi* (*sein*) begin, start; <*Licht, Radio:*> come on; (*anwachsen*) take root; **a~ gegen** fight ● *vt* attack; tackle <*Arbeit*>; (*bitten*) ask (**um** for); (*betreffen*) concern
ạngehör|en *vi sep* (*haben*) (+ *dat*) belong to. **A~ige(r)** *m/f* relative
Ạngeklagte(r) *m/f* accused
Ạngel *f* **-, -n** fishing-rod; (*Tür-*) hinge
Ạngelegenheit *f* matter
Ạngel|haken *m* fish-hook. **a~n** *vi* (*haben*) fish (**nach** for); **a~n gehen** go fishing ● *vt* (*fangen*) catch. **A~rute** *f* fishing-rod
ạngelsächsisch *a* Anglo-Saxon
ạngemessen *a* commensurate (*dat* with); (*passend*) appropriate
ạngenehm *a* pleasant; (*bei Vorstellung*) **a~!** delighted to meet you!
ạngeregt *a* animated
ạngesehen *a* respected; <*Firma*> reputable

angesichts *prep* (+ *gen*) in view of

angespannt *a* intent; <*Lage*> tense

Angestellte(r) *m/f* employee

angewandt *a* applied

angewiesen *a* dependent (**auf** + *acc* on); **auf sich selbst a~** on one's own

angewöhnen *vt sep* **jdm etw a~** get s.o. used to sth; **sich** (*dat*) **etw a~** get into the habit of doing sth

Angewohnheit *f* habit

Angina *f* - tonsillitis

angleichen† *vt sep* adjust (*dat* to)

anglikanisch *a* Anglican

Anglistik *f* - English [language and literature]

Angorakatze *f* Persian cat

angreif|en† *vt sep* attack; tackle <*Arbeit*>; (*schädigen*) damage. **A~er** *m* **-s,-** attacker; (*Pol*) aggressor

angrenzen *vi sep* (*haben*) adjoin (**an etw** *acc* sth). **a~d** *a* adjoining

Angriff *m* attack; **in A~ nehmen** tackle. **a~slustig** *a* aggressive

Angst *f* **-,¨e** fear; (*Psych*) anxiety; (*Sorge*) worry (**um** about); **A~ haben** be afraid (**vor** + *dat* of); (*sich sorgen*) be worried (**um** about); **jdm A~ machen** frighten s.o.

ängstigen *vt* frighten; (*Sorge machen*) worry; **sich ä~** be frightened; be worried (**um** about)

ängstlich *a* nervous; (*scheu*) timid; (*verängstigt*) frightened, scared; (*besorgt*) anxious

angucken *vt sep* [!] look at

angurten (sich) *vr sep* fasten one's seat-belt

anhaben† *vt sep* have on; **er/es kann mir nichts a~** (*fig*) he/it cannot hurt me

anhalt|en† *v sep* ● *vt* stop; hold <*Atem*>; **jdn zur Arbeit a~en** urge s.o. to work ● *vi* (*haben*) stop; (*andauern*) continue. **a~end** *a* persistent. **A~er(in)** *m* **-s,-** (*f* **-, -nen**) hitchhiker; **per A~er fahren** hitchhike. **A~spunkt** *m* clue

anhand *prep* (+ *gen*) with the aid of

Anhang *m* appendix

anhängen[1] *vt sep* (*reg*) hang up; (*befestigen*) attach

anhäng|en[2]† *vi* (*haben*) be a follower of. **A~er** *m* **-s,-** follower; (*Auto*) trailer; (*Schild*) [tie-on] label; (*Schmuck*) pendant. **A~erin** *f* **-, -nen** follower. **a~lich** *a* affectionate

anhäufen *vt sep* pile up

Anhieb *m* **auf A~** straight away

Anhöhe *f* hill

anhören *vt sep* listen to; **sich gut a~** sound good

animieren *vt* encourage (**zu** to)

Anis *m* **-es** aniseed

Anker *m* **-s,-** anchor; **vor A~ gehen** drop anchor. **a~n** *vi* (*haben*) anchor; (*liegen*) be anchored

anketten *vt sep* chain up

Anklage *f* accusation; (*Jur*) charge; (*Ankläger*) prosecution. **A~bank** *f* dock. **a~n** *vt sep* accuse (*gen* of); (*Jur*) charge (*gen* with)

Ankläger *m* accuser; (*Jur*) prosecutor

anklammern *vt sep* clip on; **sich a~** cling (**an** + *acc* to)

ankleben *v sep* ● *vt* stick on ● *vi* (*sein*) stick (**an** + *dat* to)

anklicken *vt sep* click on

anklopfen *vi sep* (*haben*) knock

anknipsen *vt sep* [!] switch on

ankommen† *vi sep* (*sein*) arrive; (*sich nähern*) approach; **gut a~** arrive safely; (*fig*) go down well (**bei** with); **nicht a~ gegen** (*fig*) be no match for; **a~ auf** (+ *acc*) depend on; **das kommt darauf an** it [all] depends

ankreuzen *vt sep* mark with a cross

ankündig|en *vt sep* announce. **A~ung** *f* announcement

Ankunft *f* - arrival

ankurbeln *vt sep* (*fig*) boost

anlächeln *vt sep* smile at

anlachen *vt sep* smile at

Anlage *f* -, **-n** installation; (*Industrie-*) plant; (*Komplex*) complex; (*Geld-*) investment; (*Plan*) layout; (*Beilage*) enclosure; (*Veranlagung*) aptitude; (*Neigung*) predisposition; **[öffentliche] A~n** [public] gardens; **als A~** enclosed

Anlass *m* **-es,¨-e** reason; (*Gelegenheit*) occasion; **A~ geben zu** give cause for

anlass|en† *vt sep* (*Auto*) start; [!] leave on <*Licht*>; keep on <*Mantel*>. **A~er** *m* **-s,-** starter

anlässlich *prep* (+ *gen*) on the occasion of

Anlauf *m* (*Sport*) run-up; (*fig*) attempt. **a~en**† *v sep* ● *vi* (*sein*) start; (*beschlagen*) mist up; <*Metall:*> tarnish; **rot a~en** blush ● *vt* (*Naut*) call at

anlegen *v sep* ● *vt* put (**an** + *acc* against); put on <*Kleidung, Verband*>; lay back <*Ohren*>; aim <*Gewehr*>; (*investieren*) invest; (*ausgeben*) spend (**für** on); draw up <*Liste*>; **es darauf a~** (*fig*) aim (**zu** to) ● *vi* (*haben*) <*Schiff:*> moor; **a~ auf** (+ *acc*) aim at

anlehnen *vt sep* lean (**an** + *acc* against); **sich a~** lean (**an** + *acc* on)

Anleihe *f* -, **-n** loan

anleit|en *vt sep* instruct. **A~ung** *f* instructions *pl*

anlernen *vt sep* train

Anliegen *nt* **-s,-** request; (*Wunsch*) desire

anlieg|en† *vi sep* (*haben*) **[eng] a~en** fit closely; **[eng] a~end** close-fitting. **A~er** *mpl* residents; **'A~er frei'** 'access for residents only'

anlügen† *vt sep* lie to

anmachen *vt sep* [!] fix; (*anschalten*) turn on; dress <*Salat*>

anmalen *vt sep* paint

Anmarsch *m* (*Mil*) approach

anmeld|en *vt sep* announce; (*Admin*) register; **sich a~en** say that one is coming; (*Admin*) register; (*Sch*) enrol; (*im Hotel*) check in; (*beim Arzt*) make an appointment; (*Computer*) log on. **A~ung** *f* announcement; (*Admin*) registration; (*Sch*) enrolment; (*Termin*) appointment

anmerk|en *vt sep* mark; **sich** (*dat*) **etw a~en lassen** show sth. **A~ung** *f* -, **-en** note

Anmut *f* - grace; (*Charme*) charm

anmutig *a* graceful

annähen *vt sep* sew on

annäher|nd *a* approximate. **A~ungsversuche** *mpl* advances

Annahme *f* -, **-n** acceptance; (*Adoption*) adoption; (*Vermutung*) assumption

annehm|bar *a* acceptable. **a~en**† *vt sep* accept; (*adoptieren*) adopt; acquire <*Gewohnheit*>; (*sich zulegen, vermuten*) assume; **angenommen, dass** assuming that. **A~lichkeiten** *fpl* comforts

Anno *adv* **A~ 1920** in the year 1920

Annon|ce /a'nõ:sə/ *f* **-, -n** advertisement. **a~cieren** /-'si:-/ *vt/i* (*haben*) advertise

annullieren *vt* annul; cancel

Anomalie *f* **-, -n** anomaly

anonym *a* anonymous

Anorak *m* **-s, -s** anorak

anordn|en *vt sep* arrange; (*befehlen*) order. **A~ung** *f* arrangement; order

anorganisch *a* inorganic

anormal *a* abnormal

anpass|en *vt sep* try on; (*angleichen*) adapt (*dat* to); **sich a~** adapt (*dat* to). **A~ung** *f* - adaptation. **a~ungsfähig** *a* adaptable. **A~ungsfähigkeit** *f* adaptability

Anpfiff *m* (*Sport*) kick-off

Anprall *m* **-[e]s** impact. **a~en** *vi sep* (*sein*) strike (**an etw** *acc* sth)

anpreisen† *vt sep* commend

Anprob|e *f* fitting. **a~ieren** *vt sep* try on

anrechnen *vt sep* count (**als** as); (*berechnen*) charge for; (*verrechnen*) allow <*Summe*>

Anrecht *nt* right (**auf** + *acc* to)

Anrede *f* [form of] address. **a~n** *vt sep* address; speak to

anreg|en *vt sep* stimulate; (*ermuntern*) encourage (**zu** to); (*vorschlagen*) suggest. **a~end** *a* stimulating. **A~ung** *f* stimulation; (*Vorschlag*) suggestion

Anreise *f* journey; (*Ankunft*) arrival. **a~n** *vi sep* (*sein*) arrive

Anreiz *m* incentive

Anrichte *f* **-, -n** sideboard. **a~n** *vt sep* (*Culin*) prepare; (*garnieren*) garnish (**mit** with); (*verursachen*) cause

anrüchig *a* disreputable

Anruf *m* call. **A~beantworter** *m* **-s,-** answering machine. **a~en**† *v sep* ● *vt* call to; (*bitten*) call on (**um** for); (*Teleph*) ring ● *vi* (*haben*) ring (**bei jdm** s.o.)

anrühren *vt sep* touch; (*verrühren*) mix

ans *prep* = **an das**

Ansage *f* announcement. **a~n** *vt sep* announce

ansamm|eln *vt sep* collect; (*anhäufen*) accumulate; **sich a~eln** collect; (*sich häufen*) accumulate; <*Leute:*> gather. **A~lung** *f* collection; (*Menschen-*) crowd

ansässig *a* resident

Ansatz *m* beginning; (*Versuch*) attempt

anschaffen *vt sep* [**sich** *dat*] **etw a~** acquire/(*kaufen*) buy sth

anschalten *vt sep* switch on

anschau|en *vt sep* look at. **a~lich** *a* vivid, *adv* -ly. **A~ung** *f* **-, -en** (*fig*) view

Anschein *m* appearance. **a~end** *adv* apparently

anschirren *vt sep* harness

Anschlag *m* notice; (*Vor-*) estimate; (*Überfall*) attack (**auf** + *acc* on); (*Mus*) touch; (*Techn*) stop. **a~en**† *v sep* ● *vt* put up <*Aushang*>; strike <*Note, Taste*>; cast on <*Masche*>; (*beschädigen*) chip ● *vi* (*haben*) strike/(*stoßen*) knock (**an** + *acc* against); (*wirken*) be effective ● *vi* (*sein*) knock (**an** + *acc* against)

anschließen† *v sep* ● *vt* connect (**an** + *acc* to); (*zufügen*) add; **sich a~ an** (+ *acc*) (*anstoßen*) adjoin; (*folgen*) follow; (*sich anfreunden*) become friendly with; **sich jdm a~** join s.o. ● *vi* (*haben*) **a~ an** (+ *acc*) adjoin; (*folgen*) follow. **a~d** *a* adjoining; (*zeitlich*) following ● *adv* afterwards

Anschluss *m* connection; (*Kontakt*) contact; **A~ finden** make friends; **im A~ an** (+ *acc*) after

anschmiegsam *a* affectionate

anschmieren *vt sep* smear
anschnallen *vt sep* strap on; **sich a~** fasten one's seat-belt
anschneiden† *vt sep* cut into; broach <*Thema*>
anschreiben† *vt sep* write (**an** + *acc* on); (*Comm*) put on s.o.'s account; (*sich wenden*) write to
Anschrift *f* address
anschuldig|en *vt sep* accuse. **A~ung** *f* **-, -en** accusation
anschwellen† *vi sep* (*sein*) swell
ansehen† *vt sep* look at; (*einschätzen*) regard (**als** as); [**sich** *dat*] **etw a~** look at sth; (*TV*) watch sth. **A~** *nt* **-s** respect; (*Ruf*) reputation
ansehnlich *a* considerable
ansetzen *v sep* ● *vt* join (**an** + *acc* to); (*veranschlagen*) estimate ● *vi* (*haben*) (*anbrennen*) burn; **zum Sprung a~** get ready to jump
Ansicht *f* view; **meiner A~ nach** in my view; **zur A~** (*Comm*) on approval. **A~s[post]karte** *f* picture postcard. **A~ssache** *f* matter of opinion
ansiedeln (sich) *vr sep* settle
ansonsten *adv* apart from that
anspannen *vt sep* hitch up; (*anstrengen*) strain; tense <*Muskel*>
Anspielung *f* **-, -en** allusion; hint
Anspitzer *m* **-s,-** pencil-sharpener
Ansprache *f* address
ansprechen† *v sep* ● *vt* speak to; (*fig*) appeal to ● *vi* (*haben*) respond (**auf** + *acc* to)
anspringen† *v sep* ● *vt* jump at ● *vi* (*sein*) (*Auto*) start
Anspruch *m* claim/(*Recht*) right (**auf** + *acc* to); **A~ haben** be entitled (**auf** + *acc* to); **in A~ nehmen** make use of; (*erfordern*) demand; take up <*Zeit*>; occupy <*Person*>; **hohe A~e stellen** be very demanding. **a~slos** *a* undemanding. **a~svoll** *a* demanding; (*kritisch*) discriminating; (*vornehm*) upmarket
anstacheln *vt sep* (*fig*) spur on
Anstalt *f* **-, -en** institution
Anstand *m* decency; (*Benehmen*) [good] manners *pl*
anständig *a* decent; (*ehrbar*) respectable; (*richtig*) proper
anstandslos *adv* without any trouble
anstarren *vt sep* stare at
anstatt *conj & prep* (+ *gen*) instead of
ansteck|en *v sep* ● *vt* pin (**an** + *acc* to/on); put on <*Ring*>; (*anzünden*) light; (*in Brand stecken*) set fire to; (*Med*) infect; **sich a~en** catch an infection (**bei** from) ● *vi* (*haben*) be infectious. **a~end** *a* infectious. **A~ung** *f* **-, -en** infection
anstehen† *vi sep* (*haben*) queue
anstelle *prep* (+ *gen*) instead of
anstell|en *vt sep* put, stand (**an** + *acc* against); (*einstellen*) employ; (*anschalten*) turn on; (*tun*) do; **sich a~en** queue [up]. **A~ung** *f* employment; (*Stelle*) job
Anstieg *m* **-[e]s, -e** climb; (*fig*) rise
anstiften *vt sep* cause; (*anzetteln*) instigate
Anstoß *m* (*Anregung*) impetus; (*Stoß*) knock; (*Fußball*) kick-off; **A~ erregen** give offence (**an** + *dat* at). **a~en**† *v sep* ● *vt* knock; (*mit dem Ellbogen*) nudge ● *vi* (*sein*) knock (**an** + *acc* against) ● *vi* (*haben*) adjoin (**an etw** *acc* sth); **a~en auf** (+ *acc*) drink to; **mit der Zunge a~en** lisp
anstößig *a* offensive
anstrahlen *vt sep* floodlight
anstreichen† *vt sep* paint; (*anmerken*) mark

anstreng|en *vt sep* strain; (*ermüden*) tire; **sich a~en** exert oneself; (*sich bemühen*) make an effort (**zu** to). **a~end** *a* strenuous; (*ermüdend*) tiring. **A~ung** *f* **-, -en** strain; (*Mühe*) effort

Anstrich *m* coat [of paint]

Ansturm *m* rush; (*Mil*) assault

Ansuchen *nt* **-s,-** request

Antarktis *f* **-** Antarctic

Anteil *m* share; **A~ nehmen** take an interest (**an** + *dat* in). **A~nahme** *f* **-** interest (**an** + *dat* in); (*Mitgefühl*) sympathy

Antenne *f* **-, -n** aerial

Anthologie *f* **-, -n** anthology

Anthrax *m* **-** anthrax

Anthropologie *f* **-** anthropology

Anti|alkoholiker *m* teetotaller. **A~biotikum** *nt* **-s, -ka** antibiotic

antik *a* antique. **A~e** *f* **-** [classical] antiquity

Antikörper *m* antibody

Antilope *f* **-, -n** antelope

Antiquariat *nt* **-[e]s, -e** antiquarian bookshop

Antiquitäten *fpl* antiques. **A~händler** *m* antique dealer

Antrag *m* **-[e]s,¨-e** proposal; (*Pol*) motion; (*Gesuch*) application. **A~steller** *m* **-s,-** applicant

antreffen† *vt sep* find

antreten† *v sep* ● *vt* start; take up <*Amt*> ● *vi* (*sein*) line up

Antrieb *m* urge; (*Techn*) drive; **aus eigenem A~** of one's own accord

Antritt *m* start; **bei A~ eines Amtes** when taking office

antun† *vt sep* **jdm etw a~** do sth to s.o.; **sich** (*dat*) **etwas a~** take one's own life

Antwort *f* **-, -en** answer, reply (**auf** + *acc* to). **a~en** *vt/i* (*haben*) answer (**jdm** s.o.)

anvertrauen *vt sep* entrust/ (*mitteilen*) confide (**jdm** to s.o.)

Anwalt *m* **-[e]s,¨-e**, **Anwältin** *f* **-, -nen** lawyer; (*vor Gericht*) counsel

Anwandlung *f* **-, -en** fit (**von** of)

Anwärter(in) *m(f)* candidate

anweis|en† *vt sep* assign (*dat* to); (*beauftragen*) instruct. **A~ung** *f* instruction; (*Geld-*) money order

anwend|en *vt sep* apply (**auf** + *acc* to); (*gebrauchen*) use. **A~ung** *f* application; use

anwerben† *vt sep* recruit

Anwesen *nt* **-s,-** property

anwesen|d *a* present (**bei** at); **die A~den** those present. **A~heit** *f* **-** presence

anwidern *vt sep* disgust

Anwohner *mpl* residents

Anzahl *f* number

anzahl|en *vt sep* pay a deposit on. **A~ung** *f* deposit

anzapfen *vt sep* tap

Anzeichen *nt* sign

Anzeige *f* **-, -n** announcement; (*Inserat*) advertisement; **A~ erstatten gegen jdn** report s.o. to the police. **a~n** *vt sep* announce; (*inserieren*) advertise; (*melden*) report [to the police]; (*angeben*) indicate

anzieh|en† *vt sep* ● *vt* attract; (*festziehen*) tighten; put on <*Kleider, Bremse*>; (*ankleiden*) dress; **sich a~en** get dressed. **a~end** *a* attractive. **A~ungskraft** *f* attraction; (*Phys*) gravity

Anzug *m* suit

anzüglich *a* suggestive

anzünden *vt sep* light; (*in Brand stecken*) set fire to

anzweifeln *vt sep* question

apart *a* striking

Apathie *f* **-** apathy

apathisch *a* apathetic

Aperitif *m* **-s, -s** aperitif
Apfel *m* **-s,⁻** apple
Apfelsine *f* **-, -n** orange
Apostel *m* **-s,-** apostle
Apostroph *m* **-s, -e** apostrophe
Apothek|e *f* **-, -n** pharmacy. **A~er(in)** *m* **-s,-** (*f* **-, -nen**) pharmacist, [dispensing] chemist
Apparat *m* **-[e]s, -e** device; (*Phot*) camera; (*Radio, TV*) set; (*Teleph*) telephone; **am A~!** speaking!
Appell *m* **-s, -e** appeal; (*Mil*) roll-call. **a~ieren** *vi* (*haben*) appeal (**an** + *acc* to)
Appetit *m* **-s** appetite; **guten A~!** enjoy your meal! **a~lich** *a* appetizing
Applaus *m* **-es** applause
Aprikose *f* **-, -n** apricot
April *m* **-[s]** April
Aquarell *nt* **-s, -e** water-colour
Aquarium *nt* **-s, -ien** aquarium
Äquator *m* **-s** equator
Ära *f* **-** era
Araber(in) *m* **-s,-** (*f* **-, -nen**) Arab
arabisch *a* Arab; (*Geog*) Arabian; <*Ziffer*> Arabic
Arbeit *f* **-, -en** work; (*Anstellung*) employment, job; (*Aufgabe*) task; (*Sch*) [written] test; (*Abhandlung*) treatise; (*Qualität*) workmanship; **sich an die A~ machen** set to work; **sich** (*dat*) **viel A~ machen** go to a lot of trouble. **a~en** *v sep* ● *vi* (*haben*) work (**an** + *dat* on) ● *vt* make. **A~er(in)** *m* **-s,-** (*f* **-, -nen**) worker; (*Land-, Hilfs-*) labourer. **A~erklasse** *f* working class
Arbeit|geber *m* **-s,-** employer. **A~nehmer** *m* **-s,-** employee
Arbeits|amt *nt* employment exchange. **A~erlaubnis, A~genehmigung** *f* work permit. **A~kraft** *f* worker. **a~los** *a* unemployed; **~los sein** be out of work. **A~lose(r)** *m/f* unemployed person; **die A~losen** the unemployed *pl*. **A~losenunterstützung** *f* unemployment benefit. **A~losigkeit** *f* **-** unemployment
arbeitsparend *a* labour-saving
Arbeitsplatz *m* job
Archäo|loge *m* **-n, -n** archaeologist. **A~logie** *f* **-** archaeology
Arche *f* **- die A~ Noah** Noah's Ark
Architek|t(in) *m* **-en, -en** (*f* **-, -nen**) architect. **a~tonisch** *a* architectural. **A~tur** *f* **-** architecture
Archiv *nt* **-s, -e** archives *pl*
Arena *f* **-, -nen** arena
arg *a* bad; (*groß*) terrible
Argentin|ien /-iən/ *nt* **-s** Argentina. **a~isch** *a* Argentinian
Ärger *m* **-s** annoyance; (*Unannehmlichkeit*) trouble. **ä~lich** *a* annoyed; (*leidig*) annoying; **ä~lich sein** be annoyed. **ä~n** *vt* annoy; (*necken*) tease; **sich ä~n** get annoyed (**über jdn/etw** with s.o./ about sth). **Ä~nis** *nt* **-ses, -se** annoyance; **öffentliches Ä~nis** public nuisance
Arglist *f* **-** malice
arglos *a* unsuspecting
Argument *nt* **-[e]s, -e** argument. **a~ieren** *vi* (*haben*) argue (**dass** that)
Arie /ˈa:riə/ *f* **-, -n** aria
Aristo|krat *m* **-en, -en** aristocrat. **A~kratie** *f* **-** aristocracy. **a~kratisch** *a* aristocratic
Arkt|is *f* **-** Arctic. **a~isch** *a* Arctic
arm *a* poor
Arm *m* **-[e]s, -e** arm; **jdn auf den Arm nehmen** [!] pull s.o.'s leg
Armaturenbrett *nt* instrument panel; (*Auto*) dashboard

Armband *nt* (*pl* **-bänder**) bracelet; (*Uhr-*) watch-strap. **A~uhr** *f* wrist-watch
Arm|e(r) *m/f* poor man/woman; **die A~en** the poor *pl*
Armee *f* **-, -n** army
Ärmel *m* **-s,-** sleeve. **Ä~kanal** *m* [English] Channel. **ä~los** *a* sleeveless
Arm|lehne *f* arm. **A~leuchter** *m* candelabra
ärmlich *a* poor; (*elend*) miserable
armselig *a* miserable
Armut *f* **-** poverty
Arran|gement /arãʒəˈmã:/ *nt* **-s, -s** arrangement. **a~gieren** /-ˈʒi:rən/ *vt* arrange
arrogant *a* arrogant
Arsch *m* **-[e]s,¨e** (*vulg*) arse
Arsen *nt* **-s** arsenic
Art *f* **-, -en** manner; (*Weise*) way; (*Natur*) nature; (*Sorte*) kind; (*Biol*) species; **auf diese Art** in this way
Arterie /-iə/ *f* **-, -n** artery
Arthritis *f* **-** arthritis
artig *a* well-behaved
Artikel *m* **-s,-** article
Artillerie *f* **-** artillery
Artischocke *f* **-, -n** artichoke
Arznei *f* **-, -en** medicine
Arzt *m* **-[e]s,¨e** doctor
Ärzt|in *f* **-, -nen** [woman] doctor. **ä~lich** *a* medical
As* *nt* **-ses, -se** *s.* **Ass**
Asbest *m* **-[e]s** asbestos
Asche *f* **-** ash. **A~nbecher** *m* ashtray. **A~rmittwoch** *m* Ash Wednesday
Asiat|(in) *m* **-en, -en** (*f* **-, -nen**) Asian. **a~isch** *a* Asian
Asien /ˈa:ziən/ *nt* **-s** Asia
asozial *a* antisocial
Aspekt *m* **-[e]s, -e** aspect
Asphalt *m* **-[e]s** asphalt. **a~ieren** *vt* asphalt
Ass *nt* **-es, -e** ace
Assistent(in) *m* **-en, -en** (*f* **-, -nen**) assistant
Ast *m* **-[e]s,¨e** branch
ästhetisch *a* aesthetic
Asth|ma *nt* **-s** asthma. **a~matisch** *a* asthmatic
Astro|loge *m* **-n, -n** astrologer. **A~logie** *f* **-** astrology. **A~naut** *m* **-en, -en** astronaut. **A~nomie** *f* **-** astronomy
Asyl *nt* **-s, -e** home; (*Pol*) asylum. **A~ant** *m* **-en, -en** asylum-seeker
Atelier /-ˈlie:/ *nt* **-s, -s** studio
Atem *m* **-s** breath. **a~los** *a* breathless. **A~zug** *m* breath
Atheist *m* **-en, -en** atheist
Äther *m* **-s** ether
Äthiopien /-iən/ *nt* **-s** Ethiopia
Athlet|(in) *m* **-en, -en** (*f* **-, -nen**) athlete. **a~isch** *a* athletic
Atlant|ik *m* **-s** Atlantic. **a~isch** *a* Atlantic; **der A~ische Ozean** the Atlantic Ocean
Atlas *m* **-lasses, -lanten** atlas
atmen *vt/i* (*haben*) breathe
Atmosphäre *f* **-, -n** atmosphere
Atmung *f* **-** breathing
Atom *nt* **-s, -e** atom. **A~bombe** *f* atom bomb. **A~krieg** *m* nuclear war
Atten|tat *nt* **-[e]s, -e** assassination attempt. **A~täter** *m* assassin
Attest *nt* **-[e]s, -e** certificate
Attrak|tion /-ˈtsio:n/ *f* **-, -en** attraction. **a~tiv** *a* attractive
Attribut *nt* **-[e]s, -e** attribute
ätzen *vt* corrode; (*Med*) cauterize; (*Kunst*) etch. **ä~d** *a* corrosive; <*Spott*> caustic
au *int* ouch; **au fein!** oh good!
Aubergine /obɛrˈʒi:nə/ *f* **-, -n** aubergine
auch *adv & conj* also, too; (*außerdem*) what's more; (*selbst*) even; **a~ wenn** even if; **sie weiß es a~ nicht** she doesn't know

either; **wer/wie/was a~ immer** whoever/however/whatever

Audienz *f* **-, -en** audience

audiovisuell *a* audio-visual

Auditorium *nt* **-s, -ien** (*Univ*) lecture hall

auf

● *preposition (+ dative)*

····➤ (*nicht unter*) on. **auf dem Tisch** on the table. **auf Deck** on deck. **auf der Erde** on earth. **auf der Welt** in the world. **auf der Straße** in the street

····➤ (*bei Institution, Veranstaltung usw.*) at; (*bei Gebäude, Zimmer*) in. **auf der Schule/Uni** at school/university. **auf einer Party/Hochzeit** at a party/wedding. **Geld auf der Bank haben** have money in the bank. **sie ist auf ihrem Zimmer** she's in her room. **auf Urlaub** on holiday

● *preposition (+ accusative)*

····➤ (*nicht unter*) on[to]. **er legte das Buch auf den Tisch** he laid the book on the table. **auf eine Mauer steigen** climb onto a wall. **auf die Straße gehen** go [out] into the street

····➤ (*bei Institution, Veranstaltung usw.*) to. **auf eine Party/die Toilette gehen** go to a party/the toilet. **auf die Schule/Uni gehen** go to school/university. **auf Urlaub schicken** send on holiday

····➤ (*bei Entfernung*) **auf 10 km [Entfernung] zu sehen/hören** visible/audible for [a distance of] 10 km

····➤ (*zeitlich*) (*wie lange*) for; (*bis*) until; (*wann*) on. **auf Jahre [hinaus]** for years [to come]. **auf ein paar Tage** for a few days. **etw auf nächsten Mittwoch verschieben** postpone sth until next Wednesday. **das fällt auf einen Montag** it falls on a Monday

····➤ (*Art und Weise*) in. **auf diese [Art und] Weise** in this way. **auf Deutsch/Englisch** in German/English

····➤ (*aufgrund*) **auf Wunsch** on request. **auf meine Bitte** on *or* at my request. **auf Befehl** on command

····➤ (*Proportion*) to. **ein Teelöffel auf einen Liter Wasser** one teaspoon to one litre of water. **auf die Sekunde/den Millimeter [genau]** [precise] to the nearest second/millimetre

····➤ (*Toast*) to. **auf deine Gesundheit!** your health!

● *adverb*

····➤ (*aufgerichtet, aufgestanden*) up. **auf!** (*steh auf!*) up you get! **auf und ab** (*hin und her*) up and down

····➤ (*aufsetzen*) **Helm/Hut/Brille auf!** helmet/hat/glasses on!

····➤ (*geöffnet, offen*) open. **Fenster/Mund auf!** open the window/your mouth!

aufatmen *vi sep* (*haben*) heave a sigh of relief

aufbahren *vt sep* lay out

Aufbau *m* construction; (*Struktur*) structure. **a~en** *v sep* ● *vt* construct, build; (*errichten*) erect; (*schaffen*) build up; (*arrangieren*) arrange; **sich a~en** (*fig*) be based (**auf** + *dat* on) ● *vi* (*haben*) be based (**auf** + *dat* on)

aufbauschen *vt sep* puff out; (*fig*) exaggerate

aufbekommen† *vt sep* get open; (*Sch*) be given [as homework]

aufbessern *vt sep* improve; (*erhöhen*) increase

aufbewahr|en *vt sep* keep; (*lagern*) store. **A~ung** *f* - safe

keeping; storage; (*Gepäck-*) left-luggage office
aufblas|bar *a* inflatable. **a~en**† *vt sep* inflate
aufbleiben† *vi sep* (*sein*) stay open; <*Person:*> stay up
aufblenden *vt/i sep* (*haben*) (*Auto*) switch to full beam
aufblühen *vi sep* (*sein*) flower
aufbocken *vt sep* jack up
aufbrauchen *vt sep* use up
aufbrechen† *v sep* ● *vt* break open ● *vi* (*sein*) <*Knospe:*> open; (*sich aufmachen*) set out, start
aufbringen† *vt sep* raise <*Geld*>; find <*Kraft*>
Aufbruch *m* start, departure
aufbrühen *vt sep* make <*Tee*>
aufbürden *vt sep* **jdm etw a~** (*fig*) burden s.o. with sth
aufdecken *vt sep* (*auflegen*) put on; (*abdecken*) uncover; (*fig*) expose
aufdrehen *vt sep* turn on
aufdringlich *a* persistent
aufeinander *adv* one on top of the other; <*schießen*> at each other; <*warten*> for each other; **a~ folgend** successive; <*Tage*> consecutive.
Aufenthalt *m* stay; **10 Minuten A~ haben** <*Zug:*> stop for 10 minutes. **A~serlaubnis, A~sgenehmigung** *f* residence permit. **A~sraum** *m* recreation room; (*im Hotel*) lounge
Auferstehung *f* - resurrection
aufessen† *vt sep* eat up
auffahr|en† *vi sep* (*sein*) drive up; (*aufprallen*) crash, run (**auf** + *acc* into). **A~t** *f* drive; (*Autobahn-*) access road, slip road; (*Bergfahrt*) ascent
auffallen† *vi sep* (*sein*) be conspicuous; **unangenehm a~** make a bad impression
auffällig *a* conspicuous
auffangen† *vt sep* catch; pick up
auffass|en *vt sep* understand; (*deuten*) take. **A~ung** *f* understanding; (*Ansicht*) view
aufforder|n *vt sep* ask; (*einladen*) invite. **A~ung** *f* request; invitation
auffrischen *v sep* ● *vt* freshen up; revive <*Erinnerung*>; **seine Englischkenntnisse a~** brush up one's English
aufführ|en *vt sep* perform; (*angeben*) list; **sich a~en** behave. **A~ung** *f* performance
auffüllen *vt sep* fill up
Aufgabe *f* task; (*Rechen-*) problem; (*Verzicht*) giving up; **A~n** (*Sch*) homework *sg*
Aufgang *m* way up; (*Treppe*) stairs *pl*; (*Astr*) rise
aufgeben† *v sep* ● *vt* give up; post <*Brief*>; send <*Telegramm*>; place <*Bestellung*>; register <*Gepäck*>; put in the paper <*Annonce*>; **jdm eine Aufgabe a~** set s.o. a task; **jdm Suppe a~** serve s.o. with soup ● *vi* (*haben*) give up
Aufgebot *nt* contingent (**an** + *dat* of); (*Relig*) banns *pl*
aufgedunsen *a* bloated
aufgehen† *vi sep* (*sein*) open; (*sich lösen*) come undone; <*Teig, Sonne:*> rise; <*Saat:*> come up; (*Math*) come out exactly; **in Flammen a~** go up in flames
aufgelegt *a* **gut/schlecht a~ sein** be in a good/bad mood
aufgeregt *a* excited; (*erregt*) agitated
aufgeschlossen *a* (*fig*) openminded
aufgeweckt *a* (*fig*) bright
aufgießen† *vt sep* pour on; (*aufbrühen*) make <*Tee*>
aufgreifen† *vt sep* pick up; take up <*Vorschlag, Thema*>
aufgrund *prep* (+ *gen*) on the strength of
Aufguss *m* infusion

aufhaben† *v sep* ● *vt* have on; **den Mund a~** have one's mouth open; **viel a~** (*Sch*) have a lot of homework ● *vi* (*haben*) be open

aufhalten† *vt sep* hold up; (*anhalten*) stop; (*abhalten*) keep; (*offenhalten*) hold open; hold out <*Hand*>; **sich a~** stay; (*sich befassen*) spend one's time (**mit** on)

aufhäng|en *vt/i sep* (*haben*) hang up; (*henken*) hang; **sich a~en** hang oneself. **A~er** *m* **-s,-** loop

aufheben† *vt sep* pick up; (*hochheben*) raise; (*aufbewahren*) keep; (*beenden*) end; (*rückgängig machen*) lift; (*abschaffen*) abolish; (*Jur*) quash <*Urteil*>; repeal <*Gesetz*>; (*ausgleichen*) cancel out; **gut aufgehoben sein** be well looked after

aufheitern *vt sep* cheer up; **sich a~** <*Wetter:*> brighten up

aufhellen *vt sep* lighten; **sich a~** <*Himmel:*> brighten

aufhetzen *vt sep* incite

aufholen *v sep* ● *vt* make up ● *vi* (*haben*) catch up; (*zeitlich*) make up time

aufhören *vi sep* (*haben*) stop

aufklappen *vt/i sep* (*sein*) open

aufklär|en *vt sep* solve; **jdn a~en** enlighten s.o.; **sich a~en** be solved; <*Wetter:*> clear up. **A~ung** *f* solution; enlightenment; (*Mil*) reconnaissance; **sexuelle A~ung** sex education

aufkleb|en *vt sep* stick on. **A~er** *m* **-s,-** sticker

aufknöpfen *vt sep* unbutton

aufkochen *v sep* ● *vt* bring to the boil ● *vi* (*sein*) come to the boil

aufkommen† *vi sep* (*sein*) start; <*Wind:*> spring up; <*Mode:*> come in

aufkrempeln *vt sep* roll up

aufladen† *vt sep* load; (*Electr*) charge

Auflage *f* impression; (*Ausgabe*) edition; (*Zeitungs-*) circulation

auflassen† *vt sep* leave open; leave on <*Hut*>

Auflauf *m* crowd; (*Culin*) ≈ soufflé

auflegen *v sep* ● *vt* apply (**auf** + *acc* to); put down <*Hörer*>; **neu a~** reprint ● *vi* (*haben*) ring off

auflehn|en (sich) *vr sep* (*fig*) rebel. **A~ung** *f* - rebellion

auflesen† *vt sep* pick up

aufleuchten *vi sep* (*haben*) light up

auflös|en *vt sep* dissolve; close <*Konto*>; **sich a~en** dissolve; <*Nebel:*> clear. **A~ung** *f* dissolution; (*Lösung*) solution

aufmach|en *v sep* ● *vt* open; (*lösen*) undo; **sich a~en** set out (**nach** for) ● *vi* (*haben*) open; **jdm a~en** open the door to s.o. **A~ung** *f* **-, -en** get-up

aufmerksam *a* attentive; **a~ werden auf** (+ *acc*) notice; **jdn a~ machen auf** (+ *acc*) draw s.o.'s attention to. **A~keit** *f* **-, -en** attention; (*Höflichkeit*) courtesy

aufmuntern *vt sep* cheer up

Aufnahme *f* **-, -n** acceptance; (*Empfang*) reception; (*in Klub, Krankenhaus*) admission; (*Einbeziehung*) inclusion; (*Beginn*) start; (*Foto*) photograph; (*Film-*) shot; (*Mus*) recording; (*Band-*) tape recording. **a~fähig** *a* receptive. **A~prüfung** *f* entrance examination

aufnehmen† *vt sep* pick up; (*absorbieren*) absorb; take <*Nahrung, Foto*>; (*fassen*) hold; (*annehmen*) accept; (*leihen*) borrow; (*empfangen*) receive; (*in Klub, Krankenhaus*) admit; (*beherbergen, geistig erfassen*) take in; (*einbeziehen*) include;

(*beginnen*) take up; (*niederschreiben*) take down; (*filmen*) film, shoot; (*Mus*) record; **auf Band a~** tape[-record]
aufopfer|n *vt sep* sacrifice; **sich a~n** sacrifice oneself. **A~ung** *f* - self-sacrifice
aufpassen *vi sep* (*haben*) pay attention; (*sich vorsehen*) take care; **a~ auf** (+ *acc*) look after
Aufprall *m* **-[e]s** impact. **a~en** *vi sep* (*sein*) **a~en auf** (+ *acc*) hit
aufpumpen *vt sep* pump up, inflate
aufputsch|en *vt sep* incite. **A~mittel** *nt* stimulant
aufquellen† *vi sep* (*sein*) swell
aufraffen *vt sep* pick up; **sich a~** pick oneself up; (*fig*) pull oneself together
aufragen *vi sep* (*sein*) rise [up]
aufräumen *vt/i sep* (*haben*) tidy up; (*wegräumen*) put away
aufrecht *a & adv* upright. **a~erhalten**† *vt sep* (*fig*) maintain
aufreg|en *vt* excite; (*beunruhigen*) upset; (*ärgern*) annoy; **sich a~en** get excited; (*sich erregen*) get worked up. **a~end** *a* exciting. **A~ung** *f* excitement
aufreiben† *vt sep* chafe; (*fig*) wear down. **a~d** *a* trying
aufreißen† *v sep* ● *vt* tear open; dig up <*Straße*>; open wide <*Augen, Mund*> ● *vi* (*sein*) split open
aufrichtig *a* sincere. **A~keit** *f* - sincerity
aufrollen *vt sep* roll up; (*entrollen*) unroll
aufrücken *vi sep* (*sein*) move up; (*fig*) be promoted
Aufruf *m* appeal (**an** + *dat* to). **a~en**† *vt sep* call out <*Namen*>; **jdn a~en** call s.o.'s name
Aufruhr *m* **-s, -e** turmoil; (*Empörung*) revolt
aufrühr|en *vt sep* stir up. **A~er** *m* **-s,-** rebel. **a~erisch** *a* inflammatory; (*rebellisch*) rebellious
aufrunden *vt sep* round up
aufrüsten *vi sep* (*haben*) arm
aufsagen *vt sep* recite
aufsässig *a* rebellious
Aufsatz *m* top; (*Sch*) essay
aufsaugen† *vt sep* soak up
aufschauen *vi sep* (*haben*) look up (**zu** at/(*fig*) to)
aufschichten *vt sep* stack up
aufschieben† *vt sep* slide open; (*verschieben*) put off, postpone
Aufschlag *m* impact; (*Tennis*) service; (*Hosen-*) turn-up; (*Ärmel-*) upturned cuff; (*Revers*) lapel; (*Comm*) surcharge. **a~en**† *v sep* ● *vt* open; crack <*Ei*>; (*hochschlagen*) turn up; (*errichten*) put up; (*erhöhen*) increase; cast on <*Masche*>; **sich** (*dat*) **das Knie a~en** cut [open] one's knee ● *vi* (*haben*) hit (**auf etw** *acc/dat* sth); (*Tennis*) serve; (*teurer werden*) go up
aufschließen† *v sep* ● *vt* unlock ● *vi* (*haben*) unlock the door
aufschlussreich *a* revealing; (*lehrreich*) informative
aufschneiden† *v sep* ● *vt* cut open; (*in Scheiben*) slice ● *vi* (*haben*) [!] exaggerate
Aufschnitt *m* sliced sausage, cold meat [and cheese]
aufschrauben *vt sep* screw on; (*abschrauben*) unscrew
Aufschrei *m* [sudden] cry
aufschreiben† *vt sep* write down; **jdn a~** <*Polizist:*> book s.o.
Aufschrift *f* inscription; (*Etikett*) label
Aufschub *m* delay; (*Frist*) grace
aufschürfen *vt sep* **sich** (*dat*) **das Knie a~** graze one's knee

aufschwingen† **(sich)** *vr sep* find the energy (**zu** for)
Aufschwung *m* (*fig*) upturn
aufsehen† *vi sep* (*haben*) look up (**zu** at/(*fig*) to). **A~** *nt* **-s A~ erregen** cause a sensation; **A~ erregend** sensational
Aufseher(in) *m* **-s,-** (*f* **-, -nen**) supervisor; (*Gefängnis-*) warder
aufsetzen *vt sep* put on; (*verfassen*) draw up; (*entwerfen*) draft; **sich a~** sit up
Aufsicht *f* supervision; (*Person*) supervisor. **A~srat** *m* board of directors
aufsperren *vt sep* open wide
aufspielen *v sep* ● *vi* (*haben*) play ● *vr* **sich a~** show off
aufspießen *vt sep* spear
aufspringen† *vi sep* (*sein*) jump up; (*aufprallen*) bounce; (*sich öffnen*) burst open
aufspüren *vt sep* track down
aufstacheln *vt sep* incite
Aufstand *m* uprising, rebellion
aufständisch *a* rebellious
aufstehen† *vi sep* (*sein*) get up; (*offen sein*) be open; (*fig*) rise up
aufsteigen† *vi sep* (*sein*) get on; <*Reiter:*> mount; <*Bergsteiger:*> climb up; (*hochsteigen*) rise [up]; (*fig: befördert werden*) rise (**zu** to); (*Sport*) be promoted
aufstell|en *vt sep* put up; (*Culin*) put on; (*postieren*) post; (*in einer Reihe*) line up; (*nominieren*) nominate; (*Sport*) select <*Mannschaft*>; make out <*Liste*>; lay down <*Regel*>; make <*Behauptung*>; set up <*Rekord*>. **A~ung** *f* nomination; (*Liste*) list
Aufstieg *m* **-[e]s, -e** ascent; (*fig*) rise; (*Sport*) promotion
Aufstoßen *nt* **-s** burping
aufstrebend *a* (*fig*) ambitious
Aufstrich *m* [sandwich] spread
aufstützen *vt sep* rest (**auf** + *acc* on); **sich a~** lean (**auf** + *acc* on)
Auftakt *m* (*fig*) start
auftauchen *vi sep* (*sein*) emerge; (*fig*) turn up; <*Frage:*> crop up
auftauen *vt/i sep* (*sein*) thaw
aufteil|en *vt sep* divide [up]. **A~ung** *f* division
auftischen *vt sep* serve [up]
Auftrag *m* **-[e]s,¨e** task; (*Kunst*) commission; (*Comm*) order; **im A~** (+ *gen*) on behalf of. **a~en**† *vt sep* apply; (*servieren*) serve; (*abtragen*) wear out; **jdm a~en** instruct s.o. (**zu** to). **A~geber** *m* **-s,-** client
auftrennen *vt sep* unpick, undo
auftreten† *vi sep* (*sein*) tread; (*sich benehmen*) behave, act; (*Theat*) appear; (*die Bühne betreten*) enter; (*vorkommen*) occur
Auftrieb *m* buoyancy; (*fig*) boost
Auftritt *m* (*Theat*) appearance; (*auf die Bühne*) entrance; (*Szene*) scene
aufwachen *vi sep* (*sein*) wake up
aufwachsen† *vi sep* (*sein*) grow up
Aufwand *m* **-[e]s** expenditure; (*Luxus*) extravagance; (*Mühe*) trouble; **A~ treiben** be extravagant
aufwändig *a* = **aufwendig**
aufwärmen *vt sep* heat up; (*fig*) rake up; **sich a~** warm oneself; (*Sport*) warm up
Aufwartefrau *f* cleaner
aufwärts *adv* upwards; (*bergauf*) uphill; **es geht a~ mit jdm/etw** s.o./sth is improving
Aufwartung *f* **-** cleaner
aufwecken *vt sep* wake up
aufweichen *v sep* ● *vt* soften ● *vi* (*sein*) become soft
aufweisen† *vt sep* have, show
aufwend|en† *vt sep* spend; **Mühe a~en** take pains. **a~ig** *a* lavish; (*teuer*) expensive

aufwert|en *vt sep* revalue. **A~ung** *f* revaluation

aufwickeln *vt sep* roll up; (*auswickeln*) unwrap

Aufwiegler *m* **-s,-** agitator

aufwisch|en *vt sep* wipe up; wash <*Fußboden*>. **A~lappen** *m* floorcloth

aufwühlen *vt sep* churn up

aufzähl|en *vt sep* enumerate, list. **A~ung** *f* list

aufzeichn|en *vt sep* record; (*zeichnen*) draw. **A~ung** *f* recording; **A~ungen** notes

aufziehen† *v sep* ● *vt* pull up; hoist <*Segel*>; (*öffnen*) open; draw <*Vorhang*>; (*großziehen*) bring up; rear <*Tier*>; mount <*Bild*>; thread <*Perlen*>; wind up <*Uhr*>; (🄸 *necken*) tease ● *vi* (*sein*) approach

Aufzug *m* hoist; (*Fahrstuhl*) lift, (*Amer*) elevator; (*Prozession*) procession; (*Theat*) act

Augapfel *m* eyeball

Auge *nt* **-s, -n** eye; (*Punkt*) spot; **vier A~n werfen** throw a four; **gute A~n** good eyesight; **unter vier A~n** in private; **im A~ behalten** keep in sight; (*fig*) bear in mind

Augenblick *m* moment; **A~!** just a moment! **a~lich** *a* immediate; (*derzeitig*) present ● *adv* immediately; (*derzeit*) at present

Augen|braue *f* eyebrow. **A~höhle** *f* eye socket. **A~licht** *nt* sight. **A~lid** *nt* eyelid

August *m* **-[s]** August

Auktion /-ˈt̮si̯oːn/ *f* **-, -en** auction

Aula *f* **-, -len** (*Sch*) [assembly] hall

Au-pair-Mädchen /oˈpɛːr-/ *nt* aupair

aus *prep* (+ *dat*) out of; (*von*) from; (*bestehend*) [made] of; **aus Angst** from *or* out of fear; **aus Spaß** for fun ● *adv* out; <*Licht, Radio*> off; **aus sein auf** (+ *acc*) be after; **aus und ein** in and out; **von sich aus** of one's own accord; **von mir aus** as far as I'm concerned

ausarbeiten *vt sep* work out

ausarten *vi sep* (*sein*) degenerate (**in** + *acc* into)

ausatmen *vt/i sep* (*haben*) breathe out

ausbauen *vt sep* remove; (*vergrößern*) extend; (*fig*) expand

ausbedingen† *vt sep* **sich** (*dat*) **a~** insist on; (*zur Bedingung machen*) stipulate

ausbesser|n *vt sep* mend, repair. **A~ung** *f* repair

ausbeulen *vt sep* remove the dents from; (*dehnen*) make baggy

ausbild|en *vt sep* train; (*formen*) form; (*entwickeln*) develop; **sich a~en** train (**als/zu** as); (*entstehen*) develop. **A~ung** *f* training; (*Sch*) education

ausbitten† *vt sep* **sich** (*dat*) **a~** ask for; (*verlangen*) insist on

ausblasen† *vt sep* blow out

ausbleiben† *vi sep* (*sein*) fail to appear/ <*Erfolg:*> materialize; (*nicht heimkommen*) stay out

Ausblick *m* view

ausbrech|en† *vi sep* (*sein*) break out; <*Vulkan:*> erupt; (*fliehen*) escape; **in Tränen a~en** burst into tears. **A~er** *m* runaway

ausbreit|en *vt sep* spread [out]. **A~ung** *f* spread

Ausbruch *m* outbreak; (*Vulkan-*) eruption; (*Wut-*) outburst; (*Flucht*) escape, break-out

ausbrüten *vt sep* hatch

Ausdauer *f* perseverance; (*körperlich*) stamina. **a~nd** *a* persevering; (*unermüdlich*) untiring

ausdehnen *vt sep* stretch; (*fig*) extend; **sich a~** stretch; (*Phys & fig*) expand; (*dauern*) last

ausdenken† *vt sep* **sich** (*dat*) **a~** think up; (*sich vorstellen*) imagine

Ausdruck *m* expression; (*Fach-*) term; (*Computer*) printout. **a~en** *vt sep* print

ausdrücken *vt sep* squeeze out; squeeze <*Zitrone*>; stub out <*Zigarette*>; (*äußern*) express

ausdrucks|los *a* expressionless. **a~voll** *a* expressive

auseinander *adv* apart; (*entzwei*) in pieces; **a~ falten** unfold; **a~ gehen** part; <*Linien, Meinungen:*> diverge; <*Ehe:*> break up; **a~ halten** tell apart; **a~ nehmen** take apart *or* to pieces; **a~ setzen** explain (**jdm** to s.o.); **sich a~ setzen** sit apart; (*sich aussprechen*) have it out (**mit jdm** with s.o.); come to grips (**mit einem Problem** with a problem). **A~setzung** *f* **-, -en** discussion; (*Streit*) argument

auserlesen *a* select, choice

Ausfahrt *f* drive; (*Autobahn-, Garagen-*) exit

Ausfall *m* failure; (*Absage*) cancellation; (*Comm*) loss. **a~en**† *vi sep* (*sein*) fall out; (*versagen*) fail; (*abgesagt werden*) be cancelled; **gut/schlecht a~en** turn out to be good/poor

ausfallend, ausfällig *a* abusive

ausfertig|en *vt sep* make out. **A~ung** *f* **-, -en in doppelter A~ung** in duplicate

ausfindig *a* **a~ machen** find

Ausflug *m* excursion, outing

Ausflügler *m* **-s,-** [day-]tripper

Ausfluss *m* outlet; (*Abfluss*) drain; (*Med*) discharge

ausfragen *vt sep* question

Ausfuhr *f* **-, -en** (*Comm*) export

ausführ|en *vt sep* take out; (*Comm*) export; (*erklären*) explain. **a~lich** *a* detailed ● *adv* in detail. **A~ung** *f* execution; (*Comm*) version; (*äußere*) finish; (*Qualität*) workmanship; (*Erklärung*) explanation

Ausgabe *f* issue; (*Buch-*) edition; (*Comm*) version

Ausgang *m* way out, exit; (*Flugsteig*) gate; (*Ende*) end; (*Ergebnis*) outcome. **A~spunkt** *m* starting-point. **A~ssperre** *f* curfew

ausgeben† *vt sep* hand out; issue <*Fahrkarten*>; spend <*Geld*>; **sich a~ als** pretend to be

ausgebildet *a* trained

ausgebucht *a* fully booked; <*Vorstellung*> sold out

ausgefallen *a* unusual

ausgefranst *a* frayed

ausgeglichen *a* [well-]balanced

ausgeh|en† *vi sep* (*sein*) go out; <*Haare:*> fall out; <*Vorräte, Geld:*> run out; (*verblassen*) fade; **gut/schlecht a~en** end well/badly; **davon a~en, dass** assume that. **A~verbot** *nt* curfew

ausgelassen *a* high-spirited

ausgemacht *a* agreed

ausgenommen *conj* except; **a~ wenn** unless

ausgeprägt *a* marked

ausgeschlossen *pred a* out of the question

ausgeschnitten *a* low-cut

ausgesprochen *a* marked ● *adv* decidedly

ausgestorben *a* extinct; **[wie] a~** <*Straße:*> deserted

Ausgestoßene(r) *m/f* outcast

ausgezeichnet *a* excellent

ausgiebig *a* extensive; (*ausgedehnt*) long; **a~ Gebrauch machen von** make full use of

ausgießen† *vt sep* pour out

Ausgleich *m* **-[e]s** balance; (*Entschädigung*) compensation. **a~en**† *v sep* ● *vt* balance; even out <*Höhe*>; (*wettmachen*) compensate for; **sich a～en** balance out ● *vi* (*haben*) (*Sport*) equalize. **A～streffer** *m* equalizer

ausgrab|en† *vt sep* dig up; (*Archaeol*) excavate. **A～ung** *f* **-, -en** excavation

Ausguss *m* [kitchen] sink

aushaben† *vt sep* have finished <*Buch*>

aushalten† *vt sep* bear, stand; hold <*Note*>; (*Unterhalt zahlen für*) keep; **nicht auszuhalten, nicht zum A～** unbearable

aushändigen *vt sep* hand over

aushängen[1] *vt sep* (*reg*) display; take off its hinges <*Tür*>

aushäng|en[2]† *vi sep* (*haben*) be displayed. **A～eschild** *nt* sign

ausheben† *vt sep* excavate

aushecken *vt sep* (*fig*) hatch

aushelfen† *vi sep* (*haben*) help out (**jdm** s.o.)

Aushilf|e *f* [temporary] assistant; **zur A～e** to help out. **A～skraft** *f* temporary worker. **a～sweise** *adv* temporarily

aushöhlen *vt sep* hollow out

auskennen† **(sich)** *vr sep* know one's way around; **sich mit/in etw** (*dat*) **a～** know all about sth

auskommen† *vi sep* (*sein*) manage (**mit/ohne** with/without); (*sich vertragen*) get on (**gut** well)

auskugeln *vt sep* **sich** (*dat*) **den Arm a～** dislocate one's shoulder

auskühlen *vt/i sep* (*sein*) cool

auskundschaften *vt sep* spy out

Auskunft *f* **-,¨e** information; (*A～sstelle*) information desk/ (*Büro*) bureau; (*Teleph*) enquiries *pl*; **eine A～** a piece of information

auslachen *vt sep* laugh at

Auslage *f* [window] display; **A～n** expenses

Ausland *nt* **im/ins A～** abroad

Ausländ|er(in) *m* **-s,-** (*f* **-, -nen**) foreigner. **a～isch** *a* foreign

Auslandsgespräch *nt* international call

auslass|en† *vt sep* let out; let down <*Saum*>; (*weglassen*) leave out; (*versäumen*) miss; (*Culin*) melt; (*fig*) vent <*Ärger*> (**an** + *dat* on). **A～ungszeichen** *nt* apostrophe

Auslauf *m* run. **a～en**† *vi sep* (*sein*) run out; <*Farbe:*> run; (*Naut*) put to sea; <*Modell:*> be discontinued

ausleeren *vt sep* empty [out]

ausleg|en *vt sep* lay out; display <*Waren*>; (*auskleiden*) line (**mit** with); (*bezahlen*) pay; (*deuten*) interpret. **A～ung** *f* **-, -en** interpretation

ausleihen† *vt sep* lend; **sich** (*dat*) **a～** borrow

Auslese *f* **-** selection; (*fig*) pick; (*Elite*) elite

ausliefer|n *vt sep* hand over; (*Jur*) extradite. **A～ung** *f* handing over; (*Jur*) extradition; (*Comm*) distribution

ausloggen *vi sep* log off *or* out

auslosen *vt sep* draw lots for

auslös|en *vt sep* set off, trigger; (*fig*) cause; arouse <*Begeisterung*>; (*einlösen*) redeem; pay a ransom for <*Gefangene*>. **A～er** *m* **-s,-** trigger; (*Phot*) shutter release

Auslosung *f* draw

auslüften *vt/i sep* (*haben*) air

ausmachen *vt sep* put out; (*abschalten*) turn off; (*abmachen*) arrange; (*erkennen*) make out; (*betragen*) amount to; (*wichtig sein*) matter

Ausmaß *nt* extent; **A～e** dimensions

Ausnahm|e *f* **-, -n** exception. **A～ezustand** *m* state of emergency. **a～slos** *adv* without exception. **a~sweise** *adv* as an exception

ausnehmen† *vt sep* take out; gut <*Fisch*>; **sich gut a~** look good. **a~d** *adv* exceptionally

ausnutz|en, ausnütz|en *vt sep* exploit. **A~ung** *f* exploitation

auspacken *vt sep* unpack; (*auswickeln*) unwrap

ausplaudern *vt sep* let out, blab

ausprobieren *vt sep* try out

Auspuff *m* **-s** exhaust [system]. **A~gase** *ntpl* exhaust fumes. **A~rohr** *nt* exhaust pipe

auspusten *vt sep* blow out

ausradieren *vt sep* rub out

ausrauben *vt sep* rob

ausräuchern *vt sep* smoke out; fumigate <*Zimmer*>

ausräumen *vt sep* clear out

ausrechnen *vt sep* work out

Ausrede *f* excuse. **a~n** *v sep* ● *vi* (*haben*) finish speaking ● *vt* **jdm etw a~n** talk s.o. out of sth

ausreichen *vi sep* (*haben*) be enough. **a~d** *a* adequate

Ausreise *f* departure. **a~n** *vi sep* (*sein*) leave the country. **A~visum** *nt* exit visa

ausreißen† *v sep* ● *vt* pull *or* tear out ● *vi* (*sein*) ! run away

ausrenken *vt sep* dislocate

ausrichten *vt sep* align; (*bestellen*) deliver; (*erreichen*) achieve; **jdm a~** tell s.o. (**dass** that); **ich soll Ihnen Grüße von X a~** X sends [you] his regards

ausrotten *vt sep* exterminate; (*fig*) eradicate

Ausruf *m* exclamation. **a~en**† *vt sep* exclaim; call out <*Namen*>; (*verkünden*) proclaim; **jdn a~en lassen** have s.o. paged. **A~ezeichen** *nt* exclamation mark

ausruhen *vt/i sep* (*haben*) rest; **sich a~** have a rest

ausrüst|en *vt sep* equip. **A~ung** *f* equipment; (*Mil*) kit

ausrutschen *vi sep* (*sein*) slip

Aussage *f* **-, -n** statement; (*Jur*) testimony, evidence; (*Gram*) predicate. **a~n** *vt/i sep* (*haben*) state; (*Jur*) give evidence, testify

ausschalten *vt sep* switch off

Ausschank *m* sale of alcoholic drinks; (*Bar*) bar

Ausschau *f* **- A~ halten nach** look out for

ausscheiden† *vi sep* (*sein*) leave; (*Sport*) drop out; (*nicht in Frage kommen*) be excluded

ausschenken *vt sep* pour out

ausscheren *vi sep* (*sein*) (*Auto*) pull out

ausschildern *vt sep* signpost

ausschimpfen *vt sep* tell off

ausschlafen† *vi/r sep* (*haben*) **[sich] a~** get enough sleep; (*morgens*) sleep late

Ausschlag *m* (*Med*) rash; **den A~ geben** (*fig*) tip the balance. **a~gebend** *a* decisive

ausschließ|en† *vt sep* lock out; (*fig*) exclude; (*entfernen*) expel. **a~lich** *a* exclusive

ausschlüpfen *vi sep* (*sein*) hatch

Ausschluss *m* exclusion; expulsion; **unter A~ der Öffentlichkeit** in camera

ausschneiden† *vt sep* cut out

Ausschnitt *m* excerpt, extract; (*Zeitungs-*) cutting; (*Hals-*) neckline

ausschöpfen *vt sep* ladle out; (*Naut*) bail out; exhaust <*Möglichkeiten*>

ausschreiben† *vt sep* write out; (*ausstellen*) make out; (*bekanntgeben*) announce; put out to tender <*Auftrag*>

Ausschreitungen *fpl* riots; (*Exzesse*) excesses

Ausschuss *m* committee; (*Comm*) rejects *pl*

ausschütten *vt sep* tip out; (*verschütten*) spill; (*leeren*) empty

aussehen† *vi sep* (*haben*) look; **wie sieht er/es aus?** what does he/it look like? **A~** *nt* **-s** appearance

außen *adv* [on the] outside; **nach a~** outwards. **A~bordmotor** *m* outboard motor. **A~handel** *m* foreign trade. **A~minister** *m* Foreign Minister. **A~politik** *f* foreign policy. **A~seite** *f* outside. **A~seiter** *m* **-s,-** outsider; (*fig*) misfit. **A~stände** *mpl* outstanding debts

außer *prep* (+ *dat*) except [for], apart from; (*außerhalb*) out of; **a~ sich** (*fig*) beside oneself ● *conj* except; **a~ wenn** unless. **a~dem** *adv* in addition, as well ● *conj* moreover

äußer|e(r,s) *a* external; <*Teil, Schicht*> outer. **Ä~e(s)** *nt* exterior; (*Aussehen*) appearance

außer|ehelich *a* extramarital. **a~gewöhnlich** *a* exceptional. **a~halb** *prep* (+ *gen*) outside ● *adv* **a~halb wohnen** live outside town

äußer|lich *a* external; (*fig*) outward. **ä~n** *vt* express; **sich ä~n** comment; (*sich zeigen*) manifest itself

außerordentlich *a* extraordinary

äußerst *adv* extremely

äußerste|(r,s) *a* outermost; (*weiteste*) furthest; (*höchste*) utmost, extreme; (*letzte*) last; (*schlimmste*) worst. **Ä~(s)** *nt* **das Ä~** the limit; (*Schlimmste*) the worst; **sein Ä~s tun** do one's utmost; **aufs Ä~** extremely

Äußerung *f* **-, -en** comment; (*Bemerkung*) remark

aussetzen *v sep* ● *vt* expose (*dat* to); abandon <*Kind*>; launch <*Boot*>; offer <*Belohnung*>; **etwas auszusetzen haben an** (+ *dat*) find fault with ● *vi* (*haben*) stop; <*Motor:*> cut out

Aussicht *f* **-, -en** view/(*fig*) prospect (**auf** + *acc* of); **weitere A~en** (*Meteorol*) further outlook *sg*. **a~slos** *a* hopeless

ausspannen *v sep* ● *vt* spread out; unhitch <*Pferd*> ● *vi* (*haben*) rest

aussperren *vt sep* lock out

ausspielen *v sep* ● *vt* play <*Karte*>; (*fig*) play off (**gegen** against) ● *vi* (*haben*) (*Kartenspiel*) lead

Aussprache *f* pronunciation; (*Gespräch*) talk

aussprechen† *vt sep* pronounce; (*äußern*) express; **sich a~** talk; come out (**für/gegen** in favour of/against)

Ausspruch *m* saying

ausspucken *v sep* ● *vt* spit out ● *vi* (*haben*) spit

ausspülen *vt sep* rinse out

ausstatt|en *vt sep* equip. **A~ung** *f* **-, -en** equipment; (*Innen-*) furnishings *pl*; (*Theat*) scenery and costumes *pl*

ausstehen† *v sep* ● *vt* suffer; **Angst a~** be frightened; **ich kann sie nicht a~** I can't stand her ● *vi* (*haben*) be outstanding

aussteigen† *vi sep* (*sein*) get out; (*aus Bus, Zug*) get off; **alles a~!** all change!

ausstell|en *vt sep* exhibit; (*Comm*) display; (*ausfertigen*) make out; issue <*Pass*>. **A~ung** *f* exhibition; (*Comm*) display

aussterben† *vi sep* (*sein*) die out; (*Biol*) become extinct

Aussteuer *f* trousseau

Ausstieg *m* **-[e]s, -e** exit

ausstopfen *vt sep* stuff

ausstoßen† *vt sep* emit; utter <*Fluch*>; heave <*Seufzer*>; (*ausschließen*) expel

ausstrahl|en *vt/i sep (sein)* radiate, emit; (*Radio, TV*) broadcast. **A~ung** *f* radiation

ausstrecken *vt sep* stretch out; put out <*Hand*>

ausstreichen† *vt sep* cross out

ausströmen *v sep* ● *vi (sein)* pour out; (*entweichen*) escape ● *vt* emit; (*ausstrahlen*) radiate

aussuchen *vt sep* pick, choose

Austausch *m* exchange. **a~bar** *a* interchangeable. **a~en** *vt sep* exchange; (*auswechseln*) replace

austeilen *vt sep* distribute

Auster *f* **-, -n** oyster

austragen† *vt sep* deliver; hold <*Wettkampf*>; play <*Spiel*>

Austral|ien /-iən/ *nt* **-s** Australia. **A~ier(in)** *m* **-s,-** (*f* **-, -nen**) Australian. **a~isch** *a* Australian

austreiben† *vt sep* drive out; (*Relig*) exorcize

austreten† *v sep* ● *vt* stamp out; (*abnutzen*) wear down ● *vi (sein)* come out; (*ausscheiden*) leave (**aus etw** sth); **[mal] a~** [!] go to the loo

austrinken† *vt/i sep (haben)* drink up; (*leeren*) drain

Austritt *m* resignation

austrocknen *vt/i sep (sein)* dry out

ausüben *vt sep* practise; carry on <*Handwerk*>; exercise <*Recht*>; exert <*Druck, Einfluss*>

Ausverkauf *m* [clearance] sale. **a~t** *a* sold out

Auswahl *f* choice, selection; (*Comm*) range; (*Sport*) team

auswählen *vt sep* choose, select

Auswander|er *m* emigrant. **a~n** *vi sep (sein)* emigrate. **A~ung** *f* emigration

auswärt|ig *a* non-local; (*ausländisch*) foreign. **a~s** *adv* outwards; (*Sport*) away. **A~sspiel** *nt* away game

auswaschen† *vt sep* wash out

auswechseln *vt sep* change; (*ersetzen*) replace; (*Sport*) substitute

Ausweg *m* (*fig*) way out

ausweichen† *vi sep (sein)* get out of the way; **jdm/etw a~en** avoid/ (*sich entziehen*) evade s.o./ sth

Ausweis *m* **-es, -e** pass; (*Mitglieds-, Studenten-*) card. **a~en†** *vt sep* deport; **sich a~en** prove one's identity. **A~papiere** *ntpl* identification papers. **A~ung** *f* deportation

auswendig *adv* by heart

auswerten *vt sep* evaluate

auswickeln *vt sep* unwrap

auswirk|en (sich) *vr sep* have an effect (**auf** + *acc* on). **A~ung** *f* effect; (*Folge*) consequence

auswringen *vt sep* wring out

auszahlen *vt sep* pay out; (*entlohnen*) pay off; (*abfinden*) buy out; **sich a~** (*fig*) pay off

auszählen *vt sep* count; (*Boxen*) count out

Auszahlung *f* payment

auszeichn|en *vt sep* (*Comm*) price; (*ehren*) honour; (*mit einem Preis*) award a prize to; (*Mil*) decorate; **sich a~en** distinguish oneself. **A~ung** *f* honour; (*Preis*) award; (*Mil*) decoration; (*Sch*) distinction

ausziehen† *v sep* ● *vt* pull out; (*auskleiden*) undress; take off <*Mantel, Schuhe*> ● *vi (sein)* move out; (*sich aufmachen*) set out

Auszug *m* departure; (*Umzug*) move; (*Ausschnitt*) extract; (*Bank-*) statement

Auto *nt* **-s, -s** car; **A~ fahren** drive; (*mitfahren*) go in the car. **A~bahn** *f* motorway

Autobiographie *f* autobiography

Auto|bus *m* bus. **A~fahrer(in)** *m(f)* driver, motorist. **A~fahrt** *f* drive

Autogramm *nt* **-s, -e** autograph

Automat *m* **-en, -en** automatic device; (*Münz-*) slot-machine; (*Verkaufs-*) vending-machine; (*Fahrkarten-*) machine; (*Techn*) robot. **A~ik** *f* **-** automatic mechanism; (*Auto*) automatic transmission

automatisch *a* automatic

Autonummer *f* registration number

Autopsie *f* **-, -n** autopsy

Autor *m* **-s, -en** /-'to:rən/ author

Auto|reisezug *m* Motorail. **A~rennen** *nt* motor race

Autorin *f* **-, -nen** author[ess]

Autori|sation /-'tsio:n/ *f* **-** authorization. **A~tät** *f* **-, -en** authority

Auto|schlosser *m* motor mechanic. **A~skooter** /-sku:tɐ/ *m* **-s,-** dodgem. **A~stopp** *m* **-s per A~stopp fahren** hitch-hike. **A~verleih** *m* car hire [firm]. **A~waschanlage** *f* car wash

autsch *int* ouch

Axt *f* **-,¨e** axe

Bb

B, b /be:/ *nt* **-** (*Mus*) B flat

Baby /'be:bi/ *nt* **-s, -s** baby. **B~ausstattung** *f* layette. **B~-sitter** /-sɪtɐ/ *m* **-s,-** babysitter

Bach *m* **-[e]s,¨e** stream

Backbord *nt* **-[e]s** port [side]

Backe *f* **-, -n** cheek

backen *vt/i*† (*haben*) bake; (*braten*) fry

Backenzahn *m* molar

Bäcker *m* **-s,-** baker. **B~ei** *f* **-, -en, B~laden** *m* baker's shop

Back|obst *nt* dried fruit. **B~ofen** *m* oven. **B~pfeife** *f* [!] slap in the face. **B~pflaume** *f* prune. **B~pulver** *nt* baking-powder. **B~stein** *m* brick

Bad *nt* **-[e]s,¨er** bath; (*Zimmer*) bathroom; (*Schwimm-*) pool; (*Ort*) spa

Bade|anstalt *f* swimming baths *pl*. **B~anzug** *m* swim-suit. **B~hose** *f* swimming trunks *pl*. **B~kappe** *f* bathing-cap. **B~mantel** *m* bathrobe. **b~n** *vi* (*haben*) have a bath; (*im Meer*) bathe ● *vt* bath; (*waschen*) bathe. **B~ort** *m* seaside resort. **B~wanne** *f* bath. **B~zimmer** *nt* bathroom

Bagger *m* **-s,-** excavator; (*Nass-*) dredger. **B~see** *m* flooded gravel-pit

Bahn *f* **-, -en** path; (*Astr*) orbit; (*Sport*) track; (*einzelne*) lane; (*Rodel-*) run; (*Stoff-*) width; (*Eisen-*) railway; (*Zug*) train; (*Straßen-*) tram. **b~brechend** *a* (*fig*) pioneering. **B~hof** *m* [railway] station. **B~steig** *m* **-[e]s, -e** platform. **B~übergang** *m* level crossing

Bahre *f* **-, -n** stretcher

Baiser /bɛ'ze:/ *nt* **-s, -s** meringue

Bake *f* **-, -n** (*Naut, Aviat*) beacon

Bakterien /-iən/ *fpl* bacteria

Balanc|e /ba'lã:sə/ *f* **-** balance. **b~ieren** *vt/i* (*haben/sein*) balance

bald *adv* soon; (*fast*) almost

Baldachin /-xi:n/ *m* **-s, -e** canopy

bald|ig *a* early; <*Besserung*> speedy. **b~möglichst** *adv* as soon as possible

Balg *nt & m* **-[e]s,¨er** 🄸 brat
Balkan *m* **-s** Balkans *pl*
Balken *m* **-s,-** beam
Balkon /bal'kõ:/ *m* **-s, -s** balcony; (*Theat*) circle
Ball¹ *m* **-[e]s,¨e** ball
Ball² *m* **-[e]s,¨e** (*Tanz*) ball
Ballade *f* **-, -n** ballad
Ballast *m* **-[e]s** ballast. **B~stoffe** *mpl* roughage *sg*
Ballen *m* **-s,-** bale; (*Anat*) ball of the hand/(*Fuß-*) foot; (*Med*) bunion
Ballerina *f* **-, -nen** ballerina
Ballett *nt* **-s, -e** ballet
Ballon /ba'lõ:/ *m* **-s, -s** balloon
Balsam *m* **-s** balm
Balt|ikum *nt* **-s** Baltic States *pl*. **b~isch** *a* Baltic
Bambus *m* **-ses, -se** bamboo
banal *a* banal
Banane *f* **-, -n** banana
Banause *m* **-n, -n** philistine
Band¹ *nt* **-[e]s,¨er** ribbon; (*Naht-, Ton-, Ziel-*) tape; **am laufenden B~** 🄸 non-stop
Band² *m* **-[e]s,¨e** volume
Band³ *nt* **-[e]s, -e** (*fig*) bond
Band⁴ /bɛnt/ *f* **-, -s** [jazz] band
Bandag|e /ban'da:ʒə/ *f* **-, -n** bandage. **b~ieren** *vt* bandage
Bande *f* **-, -n** gang
bändigen *vt* control, restrain; (*zähmen*) tame
Bandit *m* **-en, -en** bandit
Band|maß *nt* tape-measure. **B~scheibe** *f* (*Anat*) disc. **B~wurm** *m* tapeworm
Bang|e *f* **B~e haben** be afraid; **jdm B~e machen** frighten s.o. **b~en** *vi* (*haben*) fear (**um** for)
Banjo *nt* **-s, -s** banjo
Bank¹ *f* **-,¨e** bench
Bank² *f* **-, -en** (*Comm*) bank. **B~einzug** *m* direct debit
Bankett *nt* **-s, -e** banquet
Bankier /baŋ'kie:/ *m* **-s, -s** banker
Bankkonto *nt* bank account
Bankrott *m* **-s, -s** bankruptcy. **b~** *a* bankrupt
Bankwesen *nt* banking
Bann *m* **-[e]s, -e** (*fig*) spell. **b~en** *vt* exorcize; (*abwenden*) avert; **[wie] gebannt** spellbound
Banner *nt* **-s,-** banner
bar *a* (*rein*) sheer; <*Gold*> pure; **b~es Geld** cash; **[in] bar bezahlen** pay cash
Bar *f* **-, -s** bar
Bär *m* **-en, -en** bear
Baracke *f* **-, -n** (*Mil*) hut
Barb|ar *m* **-en, -en** barbarian. **b~arisch** *a* barbaric
bar|fuß *adv* barefoot. **B~geld** *nt* cash
barmherzig *a* merciful
barock *a* baroque. **B~** *nt & m* **-[s]** baroque
Barometer *nt* **-s,-** barometer
Baron *m* **-s, -e** baron. **B~in** *f* **-, -nen** baroness
Barren *m* **-s,-** (*Gold-*) bar, ingot; (*Sport*) parallel bars *pl*. **B~gold** *nt* gold bullion
Barriere *f* **-, -n** barrier
Barrikade *f* **-, -n** barricade
barsch *a* gruff
Barsch *m* **-[e]s, -e** (*Zool*) perch
Bart *m* **-[e]s,¨e** beard; (*der Katze*) whiskers *pl*
bärtig *a* bearded
Barzahlung *f* cash payment
Basar *m* **-s, -e** bazaar
Base¹ *f* **-, -n** [female] cousin
Base² *f* **-, -n** (*Chem*) alkali, base
Basel *nt* **-s** Basle
basieren *vi* (*haben*) be based (**auf** + *dat* on)
Basilikum *nt* **-s** basil
Basis *f* **-,Basen** base; (*fig*) basis
basisch *a* (*Chem*) alkaline
Bask|enmütze *f* beret. **b~isch** *a* Basque
Bass *m* **-es,¨e** bass

Bassin /ba'sɛ̃ː/ *nt* **-s, -s** pond; (*Brunnen-*) basin; (*Schwimm-*) pool

Bassist *m* **-en, -en** bass player; (*Sänger*) bass

Bast *m* **-[e]s** raffia

basteln *vt* make ● *vi* (*haben*) do handicrafts

Batterie *f* **-, -n** battery

Bau[1] *m* **-[e]s, -e** burrow; (*Fuchs-*) earth

Bau[2] *m* **-[e]s, -ten** construction; (*Gebäude*) building; (*Auf-*) structure; (*Körper-*) build; (*B~stelle*) building site. **B~arbeiten** *fpl* building work *sg*; (*Straßen-*) road-works

Bauch *m* **-[e]s, Bäuche** abdomen, belly; (*Magen*) stomach; (*Bauchung*) bulge. **b~ig** *a* bulbous. **B~nabel** *m* navel. **B~redner** *m* ventriloquist. **B~schmerzen** *mpl* stomach-ache *sg*. **B~speicheldrüse** *f* pancreas

bauen *vt* build; (*konstruieren*) construct ● *vi* (*haben*) build (**an etw** *dat* sth); **b~ auf** (+ *acc*) (*fig*) rely on

Bauer[1] *m* **-s, -n** farmer; (*Schach*) pawn

Bauer[2] *nt* **-s,-** [bird]cage

bäuerlich *a* rustic

Bauern|haus *nt* farmhouse. **B~hof** *m* farm

bau|fällig *a* dilapidated. **B~genehmigung** *f* planning permission. **B~gerüst** *nt* scaffolding. **B~jahr** *nt* year of construction. **B~kunst** *f* architecture. **b~lich** *a* structural

Baum *m* **-[e]s, Bäume** tree

baumeln *vi* (*haben*) dangle

bäumen (sich) *vr* rear [up]

Baum|schule *f* [tree] nursery. **B~wolle** *f* cotton

Bausch *m* **-[e]s, Bäusche** wad; **in B~ und Bogen** (*fig*) wholesale. **b~en** *vt* puff out

Bau|sparkasse *f* building society. **B~stein** *m* building brick. **B~stelle** *f* building site; (*Straßen-*) roadworks *pl*. **B~unternehmer** *m* building contractor

Bayer|(in) *m* **-s, -n** (*f* **-, -nen**) Bavarian. **B~n** *nt* **-s** Bavaria

bay[e]risch *a* Bavarian

Bazillus *m* **-, -len** bacillus

beabsichtig|en *vt* intend. **b~t** *a* intended; intentional

beacht|en *vt* take notice of; (*einhalten*) observe; (*folgen*) follow; **nicht b~en** ignore. **b~lich** *a* considerable. **B~ung** *f* **-** observance; **etw** (*dat*) **keine B~ung schenken** take no notice of sth

Beamte(r) *m*, **Beamtin** *f* **-, -nen** official; (*Staats-*) civil servant; (*Schalter-*) clerk

beanspruchen *vt* claim; (*erfordern*) demand

beanstand|en *vt* find fault with; (*Comm*) make a complaint about. **B~ung** *f* **-, -en** complaint

beantragen *vt* apply for

beantworten *vt* answer

bearbeiten *vt* work; (*weiter-*) process; (*behandeln*) treat (**mit** with); (*Admin*) deal with; (*redigieren*) edit; (*Theat*) adapt; (*Mus*) arrange

Beatmungsgerät *nt* ventilator

beaufsichtig|en *vt* supervise. **B~ung** *f* **-** supervision

beauftragen *vt* instruct; commission <*Künstler*>

bebauen *vt* build on; (*bestellen*) cultivate

beben *vi* (*haben*) tremble

Becher *m* **-s,-** beaker; (*Henkel-*) mug; (*Joghurt-, Sahne-*) carton

Becken *nt* **-s,-** basin; pool; (*Mus*) cymbals *pl*; (*Anat*) pelvis
bedacht *a* careful; **darauf b~** anxious (**zu** to)
bedächtig *a* careful; slow
bedanken (sich) *vr* thank (**bei jdm** s.o.)
Bedarf *m* **-s** need/(*Comm*) demand (**an** + *dat* for); **bei B~** if required. **B~shaltestelle** *f* request stop
bedauer|lich *a* regrettable. **b~licherweise** *adv* unfortunately. **b~n** *vt* regret; (*bemitleiden*) feel sorry for; **bedaure**! sorry! **b~nswert** *a* pitiful; (*bedauerlich*) regrettable
bedeckt *a* covered; <*Himmel*> overcast
bedenken† *vt* consider; (*überlegen*) think over. **B~** *pl* misgivings; **ohne B~** without hesitation
bedenklich *a* doubtful; (*verdächtig*) dubious; (*ernst*) serious
bedeut|en *vi* (*haben*) mean. **b~end** *a* important; (*beträchtlich*) considerable. **B~ung** *f* **-, -en** meaning; (*Wichtigkeit*) importance. **b~ungslos** *a* meaningless; (*unwichtig*) unimportant. **b~ungsvoll** *a* significant; (*vielsagend*) meaningful
bedien|en *vt* serve; (*betätigen*) operate; **sich [selbst] b~en** help oneself. **B~ung** *f* **-, -en** service; (*Betätigung*) operation; (*Kellner*) waiter; (*Kellnerin*) *f* waitress. **B~ungsgeld** *nt* service charge
Bedingung *f* **-, -en** condition; **B~en** conditions; (*Comm*) terms. **b~slos** *a* unconditional
bedroh|en *vt* threaten. **b~lich** *a* threatening. **B~ung** *f* threat
bedrücken *vt* depress
bedruckt *a* printed
bedürf|en† *vi* (*haben*) (+ *gen*) need. **B~nis** *nt* **-ses, -se** need
Beefsteak /'bi:fste:k/ *nt* **-s, -s** steak; **deutsches B~** hamburger
beeilen (sich) *vr* hurry; hasten (**zu** to)
beeindrucken *vt* impress
beeinflussen *vt* influence
beeinträchtigen *vt* mar; (*schädigen*) impair
beengen *vt* restrict
beerdig|en *vt* bury. **B~ung** *f* **-, -en** funeral
Beere *f* **-, -n** berry
Beet *nt* **-[e]s, -e** (*Hort*) bed
Beete *f* **-, -n rote B~** beetroot
befähig|en *vt* enable; (*qualifizieren*) qualify. **B~ung** *f* **-** qualification; (*Fähigkeit*) ability
befahrbar *a* passable
befallen† *vt* attack; <*Angst:*> seize
befangen *a* shy; (*gehemmt*) self-conscious; (*Jur*) biased. **B~heit** *f* **-** shyness; self-consciousness; bias
befassen (sich) *vr* concern oneself/(*behandeln*) deal (**mit** with)
Befehl *m* **-[e]s, -e** order; (*Leitung*) command (**über** + *acc* of). **b~en**† *vt* **jdm etw b~en** order s.o. to do sth ● *vi* (*haben*) give the orders. **B~sform** *f* (*Gram*) imperative. **B~shaber** *m* **-s,-** commander
befestigen *vt* fasten (**an** + *dat* to); (*Mil*) fortify
befeuchten *vt* moisten
befinden† **(sich)** *vr* be. **B~** *nt* **-s** [state of] health
beflecken *vt* stain
befolgen *vt* follow
beförder|n *vt* transport; (*im Rang*) promote. **B~ung** *f* **-, -en** transport; promotion
befragen *vt* question

befrei|en *vt* free; (*räumen*) clear (**von** of); (*freistellen*) exempt (**von** from); **sich b~en** free oneself. **B~er** *m* **-s,-** liberator. **B~ung** *f* **-** liberation; exemption

befreunden (sich) *vr* make friends; **befreundet sein** be friends

befriedig|en *vt* satisfy. **b~end** *a* satisfying; (*zufrieden stellend*) satisfactory. **B~ung** *f* **-** satisfaction

befrucht|en *vt* fertilize. **B~ung** *f* **-** fertilization; **künstliche B~ung** artificial insemination

Befugnis *f* **-, -se** authority

Befund *m* result

befürcht|en *vt* fear. **B~ung** *f* **-, -en** fear

befürworten *vt* support

begab|t *a* gifted. **B~ung** *f* **-, -en** gift, talent

begeben† **(sich)** *vr* go; **sich in Gefahr b~** expose oneself to danger

begegn|en *vi* (*sein*) **jdm/etw b~en** meet s.o./sth. **B~ung** *f* **-, -en** meeting

begehr|en *vt* desire. **b~t** *a* sought-after

begeister|n *vt* **jdn b~n** arouse s.o.'s enthusiasm. **b~t** *a* enthusiastic; (*eifrig*) keen. **B~ung** *f* **-** enthusiasm

Begierde *f* **-, -n** desire

Beginn *m* **-s** beginning. **b~en**† *vt/i* (*haben*) start, begin

beglaubigen *vt* authenticate

begleichen† *vt* settle

begleit|en *vt* accompany. **B~er** *m* **-s, -** companion; (*Mus*) accompanist. **B~ung** *f* **-, -en** company; (*Mus*) accompaniment

beglück|en *vt* make happy. **b~wünschen** *vt* congratulate (**zu** on)

begnadig|en *vt* (*Jur*) pardon. **B~ung** *f* **-, -en** (*Jur*) pardon

begraben† *vt* bury

Begräbnis *n* **-ses, -se** burial; (*Feier*) funeral

begreif|en† *vt* understand; **nicht zu b~en** incomprehensible. **b~lich** *a* understandable

begrenz|en *vt* form the boundary of; (*beschränken*) restrict. **b~t** *a* limited. **B~ung** *f* **-, -en** restriction; (*Grenze*) boundary

Begriff *m* **-[e]s, -e** concept; (*Ausdruck*) term; (*Vorstellung*) idea

begründ|en *vt* give one's reason for. **b~et** *a* justified. **B~ung** *f* **-, -en** reason

begrüß|en *vt* greet; (*billigen*) welcome. **b~enswert** *a* welcome. **B~ung** *f* **-** greeting; welcome

begünstigen *vt* favour

begütert *a* wealthy

behaart *a* hairy

behäbig *a* portly

behag|en *vi* (*haben*) please (**jdm** s.o.). **B~en** *nt* **-s** contentment; (*Genuss*) enjoyment. **b~lich** *a* comfortable. **B~lichkeit** *f* **-** comfort

behalten† *vt* keep; (*sich merken*) remember

Behälter *m* **-s,-** container

behand|eln *vt* treat; (*sich befassen*) deal with. **B~lung** *f* treatment

beharr|en *vi* (*haben*) persist (**auf** + *dat* in). **b~lich** *a* persistent

behaupt|en *vt* maintain; (*vorgeben*) claim; (*sagen*) say; (*bewahren*) retain; **sich b~en** hold one's own. **B~ung** *f* **-, -en** assertion; claim; (*Äußerung*) statement

beheben† *vt* remedy

behelf|en† **(sich)** *vr* make do (**mit** with). **b~smäßig** *a* makeshift ● *adv* provisionally

beherbergen *vt* put up

beherrsch|en *vt* rule over; (*dominieren*) dominate; (*meistern, zügeln*) control; (*können*) know. **b~t** *a* self-controlled. **B~ung** *f* - control

beherzigen *vt* heed

behilflich *a* **jdm b~ sein** help s.o.

behinder|n *vt* hinder; (*blockieren*) obstruct. **b~t** *a* handicapped; (*schwer*) disabled. **B~te(r)** *m/f* handicapped/ disabled person. **B~ung** *f* **-, -en** obstruction; (*Med*) handicap; disability

Behörde *f* **-, -n** [public] authority

behüte|n *vt* protect. **b~t** *a* sheltered

behutsam *a* careful; (*zart*) gentle

bei

- *preposition (+ dative)*

! Note that **bei** plus **dem** can become **beim**

····➤(*nahe*) near; (*dicht an, neben*) by; (*als Begleitung*) with. **wer steht da bei ihm?** who is standing there next to *or* with him? **etw bei sich haben** have sth with *or* on one. **bleiben Sie beim Gepäck/bei den Kindern** stay with the luggage/the children. **war heute ein Brief für mich bei der Post?** was there a letter for me in the post today?

····➤(*an*) by. **jdn bei der Hand nehmen** take s.o. by the hand

····➤(*in der Wohnung von*) at ...'s home *or* house/flat. **bei mir [zu Hause]** at my home *or* **!** place. **bei seinen Eltern leben** live with one's parents. **wir sind bei Ulrike eingeladen** we have been invited to Ulrike's. **bei Schmidt** at the Schmidts'; (*Geschäft*) at Schmidts'; (*auf Briefen*) c/o Schmidt. **bei jdm/einer Firma arbeiten** work for s.o./a firm. **bei uns tut man das nicht** we don't do that where I come from.

····➤(*gegenwärtig*) at; (*verwickelt*) in. **bei einer Hochzeit/einem Empfang** at a wedding/reception. **bei einem Unfall** in an accident

····➤(*im Falle von*) in the case of, with; (*bei Wetter*) in. **wie bei den Römern** as with the Romans. **bei Nebel** in fog, if there is fog. **bei dieser Hitze** in this heat

····➤(*angesichts*) with; (*trotz*) in spite of. **bei deinen guten Augen** with your good eyesight. **bei all seinen Bemühungen** in spite of *or* despite all his efforts

····➤(*Zeitpunkt*) at, on. **bei diesen Worten errötete er** he blushed at this *or* on hearing this. **bei seiner Ankunft** on his arrival. **bei Tag/Nacht** by day/night.

····➤(*Gleichzeitigkeit, mit Verbalsubstantiv*) **beim ...en** while *or* when ...ing. **beim Spazierengehen im Walde** while walking in the woods. **beim Überqueren der Straße** when crossing the road. **sie war beim Lesen** she was reading. **wir waren beim Frühstück** we were having breakfast

beibehalten† *vt sep* keep

beibringen† *vt sep* **jdm etw b~** teach s.o. sth; (*mitteilen*) break sth to s.o.; (*zufügen*) inflict sth on s.o.

Beicht|e *f* **-, -n** confession. **b~en** *vt/i* (*haben*) confess. **B~stuhl** *m* confessional

beide *a & pron* both; **b~s** both; **dreißig b~** (*Tennis*) thirty all. **b~rseitig** *a* mutual. **b~rseits** *adv & prep* (+ *gen*) on both sides (of)

beieinander *adv* together

Beifahrer(in) *m(f)* [front-seat] passenger; (*Motorrad*) pillion passenger

Beifall *m* **-[e]s** applause; (*Billigung*) approval; **B~ klatschen** applaud

beifügen *vt sep* add; (*beilegen*) enclose

beige /bɛːʒ/ *inv a* beige

beigeben† *vt sep* add

Beihilfe *f* financial aid; (*Studien-*) grant; (*Jur*) aiding and abetting

Beil *nt* **-[e]s, -e** hatchet, axe

Beilage *f* supplement; (*Gemüse*) vegetable

beiläufig *a* casual

beilegen *vt sep* enclose; (*schlichten*) settle

Beileid *nt* condolences *pl*. **B~sbrief** *m* letter of condolence

beiliegend *a* enclosed

beim *prep* = **bei dem; b~ Militär** in the army; **b~ Frühstück** at breakfast

beimessen† *vt sep* (*fig*) attach (*dat* to)

Bein *nt* **-[e]s, -e** leg; **jdm ein B~ stellen** trip s.o. up

beinah[e] *adv* nearly, almost

Beiname *m* epithet

beipflichten *vi sep* (*haben*) agree (*dat* with)

Beirat *m* advisory committee

beisammen *adv* together; **b~ sein** be together

Beisein *nt* presence

beiseite *adv* aside; (*abseits*) apart; **b~ legen** put aside; (*sparen*) put by

beisetz|en *vt sep* bury. **B~ung** *f* **-, -en** funeral

Beispiel *nt* example; **zum B~** for example. **b~sweise** *adv* for example

beißen† *vt/i* (*haben*) bite; (*brennen*) sting; **sich b~** <*Farben:*> clash

Bei|stand *m* **-[e]s** help. **b~stehen**† *vi sep* (*haben*) **jdm b~stehen** help s.o.

beistimmen *vi sep* (*haben*) agree

Beistrich *m* comma

Beitrag *m* **-[e]s,¨e** contribution; (*Mitglieds-*) subscription; (*Versicherungs-*) premium; (*Zeitungs-*) article. **b~en**† *vt/i sep* (*haben*) contribute

bei|treten† *vi sep* (*sein*) (+ *dat*) join. **B~tritt** *m* joining

Beize *f* **-, -n** (*Holz-*) stain

beizeiten *adv* in good time

beizen *vt* stain <*Holz*>

bejahen *vt* answer in the affirmative; (*billigen*) approve of

bejahrt *a* aged, old

bekämpf|en *vt* fight. **B~ung** *f* fight (*gen* against)

bekannt *a* well-known; (*vertraut*) familiar; **jdn b~ machen** introduce s.o.; **etw b~ machen** *od* **geben** announce sth; **b~ werden** become known. **B~e(r)** *m/f* acquaintance; (*Freund*) friend. **B~gabe** *f* announcement. **b~lich** *adv* as is well known. **B~machung** *f* **-, -en** announcement; (*Anschlag*) notice. **B~schaft** *f* **-** acquaintance; (*Leute*) acquaintances *pl*; (*Freunde*) friends *pl*

bekehr|en *vt* convert. **B~ung** *f* **-, -en** conversion

bekenn|en† *vt* confess, profess <*Glauben*>; **sich [für] schuldig b~en** admit one's guilt. **B~tnis** *nt* **-ses, -se** confession; (*Konfession*) denomination

beklag|en *vt* lament; (*bedauern*) deplore; **sich b~en** complain. **b~enswert** *a* unfortunate. **B~te(r)** *m/f* (*Jur*) defendant

bekleid|en *vt* hold <*Amt*>. **B~ung** *f* clothing

Beklemmung *f* **-, -en** feeling of oppression

bekommen† *vt* get; have <*Baby*>; catch <*Erkältung*> ● *vi* (*sein*) **jdm gut b~** do s.o. good; <*Essen*:> agree with s.o.

beköstig|en *vt* feed. **B~ung** *f* - board; (*Essen*) food

bekräftigen *vt* reaffirm

bekreuzigen (sich) *vr* cross oneself

bekümmert *a* troubled; (*besorgt*) worried

bekunden *vt* show

Belag *m* **-[e]s,⸚e** coating; (*Fußboden-*) covering; (*Brot-*) topping; (*Zahn-*) tartar; (*Brems-*) lining

belager|n *vt* besiege. **B~ung** *f* **-, -en** siege

Belang *m* **von B~** of importance; **B~e** *pl* interests. **b~los** *a* irrelevant; (*unwichtig*) trivial

belassen† *vt* leave; **es dabei b~** leave it at that

belasten *vt* load; (*fig*) burden; (*beanspruchen*) put a strain on; (*Comm*) debit; (*Jur*) incriminate

belästigen *vt* bother; (*bedrängen*) pester; (*unsittlich*) molest

Belastung *f* **-, -en** load; (*fig*) strain; (*Comm*) debit. **B~smaterial** *nt* incriminating evidence. **B~szeuge** *m* prosecution witness

belaufen† **(sich)** *vr* amount (**auf** + *acc* to)

belauschen *vt* eavesdrop on

beleb|en *vt* (*fig*) revive; (*lebhaft machen*) enliven. **b~t** *a* lively; <*Straße*> busy

Beleg *m* **-[e]s, -e** evidence; (*Beispiel*) instance (**für** of); (*Quittung*) receipt. **b~en** *vt* cover/(*garnieren*) garnish (**mit** with); (*besetzen*) reserve; (*Univ*) enrol for; (*nachweisen*) provide evidence for; **den ersten Platz b~en** (*Sport*) take first place. **B~schaft** *f* **-, -en** work-force. **b~t** *a* occupied; <*Zunge*> coated; <*Stimme*> husky; **b~te Brote** open sandwiches

belehren *vt* instruct

beleidig|en *vt* offend; (*absichtlich*) insult. **B~ung** *f* **-, -en** insult

belesen *a* well-read

beleucht|en *vt* light; (*anleuchten*) illuminate. **B~ung** *f* **-, -en** illumination

Belg|ien /-iən/ *nt* **-s** Belgium. **B~ier(in)** *m* **-s,-** (*f* **-, -nen**) Belgian. **b~isch** *a* Belgian

belicht|en *vt* (*Phot*) expose. **B~ung** *f* - exposure

Belieb|en *nt* **-s nach B~en** [just] as one likes. **b~ig** *a* **eine b~ige Zahl** any number you like ● *adv* **b~ig oft** as often as one likes. **b~t** *a* popular. **B~theit** *f* - popularity

bellen *vi* (*haben*) bark

belohn|en *vt* reward. **B~ung** *f* **-, -en** reward

belustig|en *vt* amuse. **B~ung** *f* **-, -en** amusement

bemalen *vt* paint

bemängeln *vt* criticize

bemannt *a* manned

bemerk|bar *a* **sich b~bar machen** attract attention. **b~en** *vt* notice; (*äußern*) remark. **b~enswert** *a* remarkable. **B~ung** *f* **-, -en** remark

bemitleiden *vt* pity

bemüh|en *vt* trouble; **sich b~en** try (**zu** to; **um etw** to get sth); (*sich kümmern*) attend (**um** to); **b~t sein** endeavour (**zu** to). **B~ung** *f* **-, -en** effort

benachbart *a* neighbouring

benachrichtig|en *vt* inform; (*amtlich*) notify. **B~ung** *f* **-, -en** notification

benachteiligen *vt* discriminate against; (*ungerecht sein*) treat unfairly

benehmen† **(sich)** *vr* behave. **B~** *nt* **-s** behaviour

beneiden *vt* envy (**um etw** sth)

Bengel *m* **-s,-** boy; (*Rüpel*) lout

benötigen *vt* need

benutz|en, (*SGer*) **benütz|en** *vt* use; take <*Bahn*>. **B~er** *m* **-s, -** user. **b~freundlich** *a* user-friendly. **B~ung** *f* use

Benzin *nt* **-s** petrol

beobacht|en *vt* observe. **B~er** *m* **-s,-** observer. **B~ung** *f* **-, -en** observation

bequem *a* comfortable; (*mühelos*) easy; (*faul*) lazy. **b~en (sich)** *vr* deign (**zu** to). **B~lichkeit** *f* **-, -en** comfort; (*Faulheit*) laziness

berat|en† *vt* advise; (*überlegen*) discuss; **sich b~en** confer ● *vi* (*haben*) discuss (**über etw** *acc* sth); (*beratschlagen*) confer. **B~er(in)** *m* **-s,-,** (*f* **-, -nen**) adviser. **B~ung** *f* **-, -en** guidance; (*Rat*) advice; (*Besprechung*) discussion; (*Med, Jur*) consultation

berechn|en *vt* calculate; (*anrechnen*) charge for; (*abfordern*) charge. **B~ung** *f* calculation

berechtig|en *vt* entitle; (*befugen*) authorize; (*fig*) justify. **b~t** *a* justified, justifiable. **B~ung** *f* **-, -en** authorization; (*Recht*) right; (*Rechtmäßigkeit*) justification

bered|en *vt* talk about; **sich b~en** talk. **B~samkeit** *f* **-** eloquence

beredt *a* eloquent

Bereich *m* **-[e]s, -e** area; (*fig*) realm; (*Fach-*) field

bereichern *vi* enrich

bereit *a* ready. **b~en** *vt* prepare; (*verursachen*) cause; give <*Überraschung*>. **b~halten**† *vt sep* have/(*ständig*) keep ready. **b~legen** *vt sep* put out [ready]. **b~machen** *vt sep* get ready. **b~s** *adv* already

Bereitschaft *f* **-, -en** readiness; (*Einheit*) squad. **B~sdienst** *m* **B~sdienst haben** (*Mil*) be on stand-by; <*Arzt*:> be on call. **B~spolizei** *f* riot police

bereit|stehen† *vi sep* (*haben*) be ready. **b~stellen** *vt sep* put out ready; (*verfügbar machen*) make available. **B~ung** *f* **-** preparation. **b~willig** *a* willing

bereuen *vt* regret

Berg *m* **-[e]s, -e** mountain; (*Anhöhe*) hill; **in den B~en** in the mountains. **b~ab** *adv* downhill. **B~arbeiter** *m* miner. **b~auf** *adv* uphill. **B~bau** *m* **-[e]s** mining

bergen† *vt* recover; (*Naut*) salvage; (*retten*) rescue

Berg|führer *m* mountain guide. **b~ig** *a* mountainous. **B~kette** *f* mountain range. **B~mann** *m* (*pl* **-leute**) miner. **B~steiger(in)** *m* **-s,-** (*f* **-, -nen**) mountaineer, climber

Bergung *f* **-** recovery; (*Naut*) salvage; (*Rettung*) rescue

Berg|wacht *f* mountain rescue service. **B~werk** *nt* mine

Bericht *m* **-[e]s, -e** report; (*Reise-*) account. **b~en** *vt/i* (*haben*) report; (*erzählen*) tell (**von** of). **B~erstatter(in)** *m* **-s,-** (*f* **-, -nen**) reporter

berichtigen *vt* correct

beriesel|n *vt* irrigate. **B~ungsanlage** *f* sprinkler system

Berlin *nt* **-s** Berlin

Bernstein *m* amber

berüchtigt *a* notorious

berücksichtig|en *vt* take into consideration. **B~ung** *f* **-** consideration

Beruf *m* profession; (*Tätigkeit*) occupation; (*Handwerk*) trade. **b~en**† *vt* appoint; **sich b~en**

refer (**auf** + *acc* to); (*vorgeben*) plead (**auf etw** *acc* sth); ● *a* competent; **b~en sein** be destined (**zu** to). **b~lich** *a* professional; <*Ausbildung*> vocational ● *adv* professionally; **b~lich tätig sein** work, have a job. **B~sberatung** *f* vocational guidance. **b~smäßig** *adv* professionally. **B~sschule** *f* vocational school. **B~ssoldat** *m* regular soldier. **b~stätig** *a* working; **b~stätig sein** work, have a job. **B~stätige(r)** *m/f* working man/woman. **B~ung** *f* -, **-en** appointment; (*Bestimmung*) vocation; (*Jur*) appeal; **B~ung einlegen** appeal. **B~ungsgericht** *nt* appeal court

beruhen *vi* (*haben*) be based (**auf** + *dat* on)

beruhig|en *vt* calm [down]; (*zuversichtlich machen*) reassure. **b~end** *a* calming; (*tröstend*) reassuring; (*Med*) sedative. **B~ung** *f* - calming; reassurance; (*Med*) sedation. **B~ungsmittel** *nt* sedative; (*bei Psychosen*) tranquillizer

berühmt *a* famous. **B~heit** *f* -, **-en** fame; (*Person*) celebrity

berühr|en *vt* touch; (*erwähnen*) touch on. **B~ung** *f* -, **-en** touch; (*Kontakt*) contact

besänftigen *vt* soothe

Besatz *m* **-es,¨-e** trimming

Besatzung *f* -, **-en** crew; (*Mil*) occupying force

beschädig|en *vt* damage. **B~ung** *f* -, **-en** damage

beschaffen *vt* obtain, get ● *a* **so b~ sein, dass** be such that. **B~heit** *f* - consistency

beschäftig|en *vt* occupy; <*Arbeitgeber:*> employ; **sich b~en** occupy oneself. **b~t** *a* busy; (*angestellt*) employed (**bei** at). **B~ung** *f* -, **-en** occupation; (*Anstellung*) employment

beschämt *a* ashamed; (*verlegen*) embarrassed

beschatten *vt* shade; (*überwachen*) shadow

Bescheid *m* **-[e]s** information; **jdm B~ sagen** *od* **geben** let s.o. know; **B~ wissen** know

bescheiden *a* modest. **B~heit** *f* - modesty

bescheinen† *vt* shine on; **von der Sonne beschienen** sunlit

bescheinig|en *vt* certify. **B~ung** *f* -, **-en** [written] confirmation; (*Schein*) certificate

beschenken *vt* give a present/ presents to

Bescherung *f* -, **-en** distribution of Christmas presents

beschildern *vt* signpost

beschimpf|en *vt* abuse, swear at. **B~ung** *f* -, **-en** abuse

beschirmen *vt* protect

Beschlag *m* **in B~ nehmen** monopolize. **b~en**† *vt* shoe ● *vi* (*sein*) steam *or* mist up ● *a* steamed *or* misted up. **B~nahme** *f* -, **-n** confiscation; (*Jur*) seizure. **b~nahmen** *vt* confiscate; (*Jur*) seize

beschleunig|en *vt* hasten; (*schneller machen*) speed up <*Schritt*> ● *vi* (*haben*) accelerate. **B~ung** *f* - acceleration

beschließen† *vt* decide; (*beenden*) end ● *vi* (*haben*) decide (**über** + *acc* about)

Beschluss *m* decision

beschmutzen *vt* make dirty

beschneid|en† *vt* trim; (*Hort*) prune; (*Relig*) circumcise. **B~ung** *f* - circumcision

beschnüffeln *vt* sniff at

beschönigen *vt* (*fig*) gloss over

beschränken *vt* limit, restrict; **sich b~ auf** (+ *acc*) confine oneself to

beschrankt *a* <*Bahnübergang*> with barrier[s]
beschränk|t *a* limited; (*geistig*) dull-witted. **B~ung** *f* **-, -en** limitation, restriction
beschreib|en† *vt* describe. **B~ung** *f* **-, -en** description
beschuldig|en *vt* accuse. **B~ung** *f* **-, -en** accusation
beschummeln *vt* [!] cheat
Beschuss *m* (*Mil*) fire; (*Artillerie-*) shelling
beschütz|en *vt* protect. **B~er** *m* **-s,-** protector
Beschwer|de *f* **-, -n** complaint; **B~den** (*Med*) trouble *sg*. **b~en** *vt* weight down; **sich b~en** complain. **b~lich** *a* difficult
beschwindeln *vt* cheat (**um** out of); (*belügen*) lie to
beschwipst *a* [!] tipsy
beseitig|en *vt* remove. **B~ung** *f* **-** removal
Besen *m* **-s,-** broom
besessen *a* obsessed (**von** by)
besetz|en *vt* occupy; fill <*Posten*>; (*Theat*) cast <*Rolle*>; (*verzieren*) trim (**mit** with). **b~t** *a* occupied; <*Toilette, Leitung*> engaged; <*Zug, Bus*> full up; **der Platz ist b~t** this seat is taken. **B~tzeichen** *nt* engaged tone. **B~ung** *f* **-, -en** occupation; (*Theat*) cast
besichtig|en *vt* look round <*Stadt*>; (*prüfen*) inspect; (*besuchen*) visit. **B~ung** *f* **-, -en** visit; (*Prüfung*) inspection; (*Stadt-*) sightseeing
besiedelt *a* **dünn/dicht b~** sparsely/densely populated
besiegen *vt* defeat
besinn|en† **(sich)** *vr* think, reflect; (*sich erinnern*) remember (**auf jdn/etw** s.o./sth). **B~ung** *f* **-** reflection; (*Bewusstsein*) consciousness; **bei/ohne B~ung** conscious/unconscious. **b~ungslos** *a* unconscious
Besitz *m* possession; (*Eigentum, Land-*) property; (*Gut*) estate. **b~en**† *vt* own, possess; (*haben*) have. **B~er(in)** *m* **-s,-** (*f* **-, -nen**) owner; (*Comm*) proprietor
besoffen *a* [x] drunken; **b~ sein** be drunk
besonder|e(r,s) *a* special; (*bestimmt*) particular; (*gesondert*) separate. **b~s** *adv* [e]specially, particularly; (*gesondert*) separately
besonnen *a* calm
besorg|en *vt* get; (*kaufen*) buy; (*erledigen*) attend to; (*versorgen*) look after. **b~t** *a* worried/ (*bedacht*) concerned (**um** about). **B~ung** *f* **-, -en** errand; **B~ungen machen** do shopping
bespitzeln *vt* spy on
besprech|en† *vt* discuss; (*rezensieren*) review. **B~ung** *f* **-, -en** discussion; review; (*Konferenz*) meeting
besser *a* & *adv* better. **b~n** *vt* improve; **sich b~n** get better. **B~ung** *f* **-** improvement; **gute B~ung!** get well soon!
Bestand *m* **-[e]s,¨e** existence; (*Vorrat*) stock (**an** + *dat* of)
beständig *a* constant; <*Wetter*> settled; **b~ gegen** resistant to
Bestand|saufnahme *f* stocktaking. **B~teil** *m* part
bestätig|en *vt* confirm; acknowledge <*Empfang*>; **sich b~en** prove to be true. **B~ung** *f* **-, -en** confirmation
bestatt|en *vt* bury. **B~ung** *f* **-, -en** funeral
Bestäubung *f* **-** pollination
bestaunen *vt* gaze at in amazement; (*bewundern*) admire
best|e(r,s) *a* best; **b~en Dank!** many thanks! **B~e(r,s)** *m/f/nt* best; **sein B~es tun** do one's best
bestech|en† *vt* bribe; (*bezaubern*) captivate. **b~end** *a*

captivating. **b~lich** *a* corruptible. **B~ung** *f* - bribery. **B~ungsgeld** *nt* bribe

Besteck *nt* **-[e]s, -e** [set of] knife, fork and spoon; (*coll*) cutlery

bestehen† *vi* (*haben*) exist; (*fortdauern*) last; (*bei Prüfung*) pass; **~ aus** consist/(*gemacht sein*) be made of; **~ auf** (+ *dat*) insist on ● *vt* pass <*Prüfung*>

besteig|en† *vt* climb; (*aufsteigen*) mount; ascend <*Thron*>. **B~ung** *f* ascent

bestell|en *vt* order; (*vor-*) book; (*ernennen*) appoint; (*bebauen*) cultivate; (*ausrichten*) tell; **zu sich b~en** send for; **b~t sein** have an appointment; **kann ich etwas b~en?** can I take a message? **B~schein** *m* order form. **B~ung** *f* order; (*Botschaft*) message; (*Bebauung*) cultivation

besteuer|n *vt* tax. **B~ung** *f* - taxation

Bestie /ˈbɛsti̯ə/ *f* **-, -n** beast

bestimm|en *vt* fix; (*entscheiden*) decide; (*vorsehen*) intend; (*ernennen*) appoint; (*ermitteln*) determine; (*definieren*) define; (*Gram*) qualify ● *vi* (*haben*) be in charge (**über** + *acc* of). **b~t** *a* definite; (*gewiss*) certain; (*fest*) firm. **B~ung** *f* fixing; (*Vorschrift*) regulation; (*Ermittlung*) determination; (*Definition*) definition; (*Zweck*) purpose; (*Schicksal*) destiny. **B~ungsort** *m* destination

Bestleistung *f* (*Sport*) record

bestraf|en *vt* punish. **B~ung** *f* **-, -en** punishment

Bestrahlung *f* radiotherapy

Bestreb|en *nt* **-s** endeavour; (*Absicht*) aim. **B~ung** *f* **-, -en** effort

bestreiten† *vt* dispute; (*leugnen*) deny; (*bezahlen*) pay for

bestürz|t *a* dismayed; (*erschüttert*) stunned. **B~ung** *f* - dismay, consternation

Bestzeit *f* (*Sport*) record [time]

Besuch *m* **-[e]s, -e** visit; (*kurz*) call; (*Schul-*) attendance; (*Gast*) visitor; (*Gäste*) visitors *pl*; **B~ haben** have a visitor/visitors; **bei jdm zu** *od* **auf B~ sein** be staying with s.o. **b~en** *vt* visit; (*kurz*) call on; (*teilnehmen*) attend; go to <*Schule, Ausstellung*>. **B~er(in)** *m* **-s,-** (*f* **-, -nen**) visitor; caller. **B~szeit** *f* visiting hours *pl*

betagt *a* aged, old

betätig|en *vt* operate; **sich b~en** work (**als** as). **B~ung** *f* **-, -en** operation; (*Tätigkeit*) activity

betäub|en *vt* stun; <*Lärm:*> deafen; (*Med*) anaesthetize; (*lindern*) ease; deaden <*Schmerz*>; **wie b~t** dazed. **B~ung** *f* - daze; (*Med*) anaesthesia. **B~ungsmittel** *nt* anaesthetic

Bete *f* **-, -n Rote B~** beetroot

beteilig|en *vt* give a share to; **sich b~en** take part (**an** + *dat* in); (*beitragen*) contribute (**an** + *dat* to). **b~t** *a* **b~t sein** take part/(*an Unfall*) be involved/ (*Comm*) have a share (**an** + *dat* in); **alle B~ten** all those involved. **B~ung** *f* **-, -en** participation; involvement; (*Anteil*) share

beten *vi* (*haben*) pray

Beton /beˈtɔŋ/ *m* **-s** concrete

betonen *vt* stressed, emphasize

beton|t *a* stressed; (*fig*) pointed. **B~ung** *f* **-, -en** stress

Betracht *m* **in B~ ziehen** consider; **außer B~ lassen** disregard; **nicht in B~ kommen** be out of the question. **b~en** *vt* look at; (*fig*) regard (**als** as)

beträchtlich *a* considerable

Betrachtung *f* **-, -en** contemplation; (*Überlegung*) reflection

Betrag *m* **-[e]s,¨-e** amount. **b~en**† *vt* amount to; **sich b~en** behave. **B~en** *nt* **-s** behaviour; (*Sch*) conduct

betreff|en† *vt* affect; (*angehen*) concern. **b~end** *a* relevant. **b~s** *prep* (+ *gen*) concerning

betreiben† *vt* (*leiten*) run; (*ausüben*) carry on

betreten† *vt* step on; (*eintreten*) enter; '**B~ verboten**' 'no entry'; (*bei Rasen*) 'keep off [the grass]'

betreu|en *vt* look after. **B~er(in)** *m* **-s,-** (*f* **-, -nen**) helper; (*Kranken-*) nurse. **B~ung** *f* **-** care

Betrieb *m* business; (*Firma*) firm; (*Treiben*) activity; (*Verkehr*) traffic; **außer B~** not in use; (*defekt*) out of order

Betriebs|anleitung, B~anweisung *f* operating instructions *pl*. **B~ferien** *pl* firm's holiday. **B~leitung** *f* management. **B~rat** *m* works committee. **B~störung** *f* breakdown

betrinken† **(sich)** *vr* get drunk

betroffen *a* disconcerted; **b~ sein** be affected (**von** by)

betrüb|en *vt* sadden. **b~t** *a* sad

Betrug *m* **-[e]s** deception; (*Jur*) fraud

betrüg|en† *vt* cheat, swindle; (*Jur*) defraud; (*in der Ehe*) be unfaithful to. **B~er(in)** *m* **-s,-** (*f* **-, -nen**) swindler. **B~erei** *f* **-, -en** fraud

betrunken *a* drunken; **b~ sein** be drunk. **B~e(r)** *m* drunk

Bett *nt* **-[e]s, -en** bed. **B~couch** *f* sofa-bed. **B~decke** *f* blanket; (*Tages-*) bedspread

Bettel|ei *f* **-** begging. **b~n** *vi* (*haben*) beg

Bettler(in) *m* **-s,-** (*f* **-, -nen**) beggar

Bettpfanne *f* bedpan

Betttuch (**Bettuch**) *nt* sheet

Bett|wäsche *f* bed linen. **B~zeug** *nt* bedding

betupfen *vt* dab (**mit** with)

beug|en *vt* bend; (*Gram*) decline; conjugate <*Verb*>; **sich b~en** bend; (*lehnen*) lean; (*sich fügen*) submit (*dat* to). **B~ung** *f* **-, -en** (*Gram*) declension; conjugation

Beule *f* **-, -n** bump; (*Delle*) dent

beunruhig|en *vt* worry; **sich b~en** worry. **B~ung** *f* **-** worry

beurlauben *vt* give leave to

beurteil|en *vt* judge. **B~ung** *f* **-, -en** judgement; (*Ansicht*) opinion

Beute *f* **-** booty, haul; (*Jagd-*) bag; (*eines Raubtiers*) prey

Beutel *m* **-s,-** bag; (*Tabak-* & *Zool*) pouch. **B~tier** *nt* marsupial

Bevölkerung *f* **-, -en** population

bevollmächtigen *vt* authorize

bevor *conj* before; **b~ nicht** until

bevormunden *vt* treat like a child

bevorstehen† *vi sep* (*haben*) approach; (*unmittelbar*) be imminent. **b~d** *a* approaching, forthcoming; **unmittelbar b~d** imminent

bevorzug|en *vt* prefer; (*begünstigen*) favour. **b~t** *a* privileged; <*Behandlung*> preferential

bewachen *vt* guard

Bewachung *f* **-** guard; **unter B~** under guard

bewaffn|en *vt* arm. **b~et** *a* armed. **B~ung** *f* **-** armament; (*Waffen*) arms *pl*

bewahren *vt* protect (**vor** + *dat* from); (*behalten*) keep; **die Ruhe b~** keep calm

bewähren (sich) *vr* prove one's/<*Ding:*> its worth; (*erfolgreich sein*) prove a success

bewähr|t *a* reliable; (*erprobt*) proven. **B~ung** *f* - (*Jur*) probation. **B~ungsfrist** *f* [period of] probation. **B~ungsprobe** *f* (*fig*) test

bewältigen *vt* cope with; (*überwinden*) overcome

bewässer|n *vt* irrigate. **B~ung** *f* - irrigation

bewegen¹ *vt* (*reg*) move; **sich b~** move; (*körperlich*) take exercise

bewegen²† *vt* **jdn dazu b~, etw zu tun** induce s.o. to do sth

Beweg|grund *m* motive. **b~lich** *a* movable, mobile; (*wendig*) agile. **B~lichkeit** *f* - mobility; agility. **B~ung** *f* **-, -en** movement; (*Phys*) motion; (*Rührung*) emotion; (*Gruppe*) movement; **körperliche B~ung** physical exercise. **b~ungslos** *a* motionless

Beweis *m* **-es, -e** proof; (*Zeichen*) token; **B~e** evidence *sg*. **b~en†** *vt* prove; (*zeigen*) show; **sich b~en** prove oneself/<*Ding:*> itself. **B~material** *nt* evidence

bewerb|en† (sich) *vr* apply (**um** for; **bei** to). **B~er(in)** *m* **-s,-** (*f* **-, -nen**) applicant. **B~ung** *f* **-, -en** application

bewerten *vt* value; (*einschätzen*) rate; (*Sch*) mark, grade

bewilligen *vt* grant

bewirken *vt* cause; (*herbeiführen*) bring about

bewirt|en *vt* entertain. **B~ung** *f* - hospitality

bewohn|bar *a* habitable. **b~en** *vt* inhabit, live in. **B~er(in)** *m* **-s,-** (*f* **-, -nen**) resident, occupant; (*Einwohner*) inhabitant

bewölk|en (sich) *vr* cloud over; **b~t** cloudy. **B~ung** *f* - clouds *pl*

bewunder|n *vt* admire. **b~nswert** *a* admirable. **B~ung** *f* - admiration

bewusst *a* conscious (*gen* of); (*absichtlich*) deliberate. **b~los** *a* unconscious. **B~losigkeit** *f* - unconsciousness; **B~sein** *nt* **-s** consciousness; (*Gewissheit*) awareness; **bei B~sein** conscious

bezahl|en *vt/i* (*haben*) pay; pay for <*Ware, Essen*>. **B~fernsehen** *nt* pay television; pay TV. **B~ung** *f* - payment; (*Lohn*) pay

bezaubern *vt* enchant

bezeichn|en *vt* mark; (*bedeuten*) denote; (*beschreiben, nennen*) describe (**als** as). **b~end** *a* typical. **B~ung** *f* marking; (*Beschreibung*) description (**als** as); (*Ausdruck*) term; (*Name*) name

bezeugen *vt* testify to

bezichtigen *vt* accuse (*gen* of)

bezieh|en† *vt* cover; (*einziehen*) move into; (*beschaffen*) obtain; (*erhalten*) get; (*in Verbindung bringen*) relate (**auf** + *acc* to); **sich b~en** (*bewölken*) cloud over; **sich b~en auf** (+ *acc*) refer to; **das Bett frisch b~en** put clean sheets on the bed. **B~ung** *f* **-, -en** relation; (*Verhältnis*) relationship; (*Bezug*) respect; **B~ungen haben** have connections. **b~ungsweise** *adv* respectively; (*vielmehr*) or rather

Bezirk *m* **-[e]s, -e** district

Bezug *m* cover; (*Kissen-*) case; (*Beschaffung*) obtaining; (*Kauf*) purchase; (*Zusammenhang*) reference; **B~̈e** *pl* earnings; **B~ nehmen** refer (**auf** + *acc* to); **in B~ auf** (+ *acc*) regarding

bezüglich *prep* (+ *gen*) regarding ● *a* relating (**auf** + *acc* to)

bezwecken *vt* (*fig*) aim at

bezweifeln *vt* doubt

BH /be:ˈha:/ *m* **-[s], -[s]** bra

Bibel *f* **-, -n** Bible

Biber *m* **-s,-** beaver

Biblio|thek *f* **-, -en** library. **B~thekar(in)** *m* **-s,-** (*f* **-, -nen**) librarian

biblisch *a* biblical

bieg|en† *vt* bend; **sich b~en** bend ● *vi* (*sein*) curve (**nach** to); **um die Ecke b~en** turn the corner. **b~sam** *a* flexible, supple. **B~ung** *f* **-, -en** bend

Biene *f* **-, -n** bee. **B~nstock** *m* beehive. **B~nwabe** *f* honeycomb

Bier *nt* **-s, -e** beer. **B~deckel** *m* beer-mat. **B~krug** *m* beer-mug

bieten† *vt* offer; (*bei Auktion*) bid

Bifokalbrille *f* bifocals *pl*

Bigamie *f* **-** bigamy

bigott *a* over-pious

Bikini *m* **-s, -s** bikini

Bilanz *f* **-, -en** balance sheet; (*fig*) result; **die B~ ziehen** (*fig*) draw conclusions (**aus** from)

Bild *nt* **-[e]s, -er** picture; (*Theat*) scene

bilden *vt* form; (*sein*) be; (*erziehen*) educate

Bild|erbuch *nt* picture-book. **B~fläche** *f* screen. **B~hauer** *m* **-s,-** sculptor. **b~lich** *a* pictorial; (*figurativ*) figurative. **B~nis** *nt* **-ses, -se** portrait. **B~schirm** *m* (*TV*) screen. **B~schirmgerät** *nt* visual display unit, VDU. **b~schön** *a* very beautiful

Bildung *f* **-** formation; (*Erziehung*) education; (*Kultur*) culture

Billard /ˈbɪljart/ *nt* **-s** billiards *sg*. **B~tisch** *m* billiard table

Billett /bɪlˈjɛt/ *nt* **-[e]s, -e** & **-s** ticket

Milliarde

Billiarde *f* **-, -n** thousand million million

billig *a* cheap; (*dürftig*) poor; **recht und b~** right and proper. **b~en** *vt* approve. **B~ung** *f* **-** approval

Billion /bɪˈlio:n/ *f* **-, -en** million million, billion

Bimsstein *m* pumice stone

Binde *f* **-, -n** band; (*Verband*) bandage; (*Damen-*) sanitary towel. **B~hautentzündung** *f* conjunctivitis. **b~n**† *vt* tie (**an** + *acc* to); make <*Strauß*>; bind <*Buch*>; (*fesseln*) tie up; (*Culin*) thicken; **sich b~n** commit oneself. **B~strich** *m* hyphen. **B~wort** *nt* (*pl* **-wörter**) (*Gram*) conjunction

Bind|faden *m* string. **B~ung** *f* **-, -en** (*fig*) tie; (*Beziehung*) relationship; (*Verpflichtung*) commitment; (*Ski-*) binding; (*Tex*) weave

binnen *prep* (+ *dat*) within. **B~handel** *m* home trade

Bio- *pref* organic

Bio|chemie *f* biochemistry. **b~dynamisch** *m* organic. **B~graphie, B~grafie** *f* **-, -n** biography

Bio|hof *m* organic farm. **B~laden** *m* health-food store

Biolog|e *m* **-n, -n** biologist. **B~ie** *f* **-** biology. **b~isch** *a* biological; **b~ischer Anbau** organic farming; **b~isch angebaut** organically grown

Bioterrorismus *m* bioterrorism

Birke *f* **-, -n** birch [tree]

Birm|a *nt* **-s** Burma

Birn|baum *m* pear-tree. **B~e** *f* **-, -n** pear; (*Electr*) bulb

bis *prep* (+ *acc*) as far as, [up] to; (*zeitlich*) until, till; (*spätestens*) by; **bis zu** up to; **bis auf** (+ *acc*) (*einschließlich*) [down] to; (*ausgenommen*) except [for]; **drei bis vier Mark** three to four marks; **bis morgen!** see you tomorrow! ● *conj* until

Bischof *m* **-s,¨e** bishop

bisher *adv* so far, up to now

Biskuit|rolle /bɪs'kvi:t-/ *f* Swiss roll. **B~teig** *m* sponge mixture

Biss *m* **-es, -e** bite

bisschen *inv pron* **ein b~** a bit, a little; **kein b~** not a bit

Biss|en *m* **-s,-** bite, mouthful. **b~ig** *a* vicious; (*fig*) caustic

bisweilen *adv* from time to time

bitt|e *adv* please; (*nach Klopfen*) come in; (*als Antwort auf 'danke'*) don't mention it, you're welcome; **wie b~e?** pardon? **B~e** *f* **-, -n** request/(*dringend*) plea (**um** for). **b~en**† *vt/i* (*haben*) ask/(*dringend*) beg (**um** for); (*einladen*) invite, ask. **b~end** *a* pleading

bitter *a* bitter. **B~keit** *f* **-** bitterness. **b~lich** *adv* bitterly

Bittschrift *f* petition

bizarr *a* bizarre

bläh|en *vt* swell; <*Vorhang, Segel*:> billow ● *vi* (*haben*) cause flatulence. **B~ungen** *fpl* flatulence *sg*, [!] wind *sg*

Blamage /bla'ma:ʒə/ *f* **-, -n** humiliation; (*Schande*) disgrace

blamieren *vt* disgrace; **sich b~** disgrace oneself; (*sich lächerlich machen*) make a fool of oneself

blanchieren /blã'ʃi:rən/ *vt* (*Culin*) blanch

blank *a* shiny. **B~oscheck** *m* blank cheque

Blase *f* **-, -n** bubble; (*Med*) blister; (*Anat*) bladder. **b~n**† *vt/i* (*haben*) blow; play <*Flöte*>. **B~nentzündung** *f* cystitis

Blas|instrument *nt* wind instrument. **B~kapelle** *f* brass band

blass *a* pale; (*schwach*) faint

Blässe *f* **-** pallor

Blatt *nt* **-[e]s,¨er** (*Bot*) leaf; (*Papier*) sheet; (*Zeitung*) paper

Blattlaus *f* greenfly

blau *a*, **B~** *nt* **-s,-** blue; **b~er Fleck** bruise; **b~es Auge** black eye; **b~ sein** [!] be tight; **Fahrt ins B~e** mystery tour. **B~beere** *f* bilberry. **B~licht** *nt* blue flashing light

Blech *nt* **-[e]s, -e** sheet metal; (*Weiß-*) tin; (*Platte*) metal sheet; (*Back-*) baking sheet; (*Mus*) brass; ([!] *Unsinn*) rubbish. **B~schaden** *m* (*Auto*) damage to the bodywork

Blei *nt* **-[e]s** lead

Bleibe *f* **-** place to stay. **b~n**† *vi* (*sein*) remain, stay; (*übrig-*) be left; **ruhig b~n** keep calm; **bei etw b~n** (*fig*) stick to sth; **b~n Sie am Apparat** hold the line; **etw b~n lassen** not to do sth. **b~nd** *a* permanent; (*anhaltend*) lasting

bleich *a* pale. **b~en**† *vi* (*sein*) bleach; (*ver-*) fade ● *vt* (*reg*) bleach. **B~mittel** *nt* bleach

blei|ern *a* leaden. **b~frei** *a* unleaded. **B~stift** *m* pencil. **B~stiftabsatz** *m* stiletto heel. **B~stiftspitzer** *m* **-s,-** pencil sharpener

Blende *f* **-, -n** shade, shield; (*Sonnen-*) [sun] visor; (*Phot*) diaphragm; (*Öffnung*) aperture; (*an Kleid*) facing. **b~n** *vt* dazzle, blind

Blick *m* **-[e]s, -e** look; (*kurz*) glance; (*Aussicht*) view; **auf den ersten B~** at first sight. **b~en** *vi* (*haben*) look/(*kurz*) glance (**auf** + *acc* at). **B~punkt** *m* (*fig*) point of view

blind *a* blind; (*trübe*) dull; **b~er Alarm** false alarm; **b~er Passagier** stowaway. **B~darm** *m* appendix. **B~darmentzündung** *f* appendicitis. **B~e(r)** *m/f* blind man/woman; **die B~en** the blind *pl*. **B~enhund** *m* guidedog. **B~enschrift** *f* braille.

B~gänger *m* **-s,-** (*Mil*) dud. **B~heit** *f* - blindness
blink|en *vi* (*haben*) flash; (*funkeln*) gleam; (*Auto*) indicate. **B~er** *m* **-s,-** (*Auto*) indicator. **B~licht** *nt* flashing light
blinzeln *vi* (*haben*) blink
Blitz *m* **-es, -e** [flash of] lightning; (*Phot*) flash. **B~ableiter** *m* lightning-conductor. **b~artig** *a* lightning ... ● *adv* like lightning. **b~en** *vi* (*haben*) flash; (*funkeln*) sparkle; **es hat geblitzt** there was a flash of lightning. **B~licht** *nt* (*Phot*) flash. **b~sauber** *a* spick and span. **b~schnell** *a* lightning ... ● *adv* like lightning
Block *m* **-[e]s,¨e** block ● **-[e]s, -s** & **¨e** pad; (*Häuser-*) block
Blockade *f* **-, -n** blockade
Blockflöte *f* recorder
blockieren *vt* block; (*Mil*) blockade
Blockschrift *f* block letters *pl*
blöd[e] *a* feeble-minded; (*dumm*) stupid
Blödsinn *m* **-[e]s** idiocy; (*Unsinn*) nonsense
blöken *vi* (*haben*) bleat
blond *a* fair-haired; <*Haar*> fair
bloß *a* bare; (*alleinig*) mere ● *adv* only, just
bloß|legen *vt sep* uncover. **b~stellen** *vt sep* compromise
Bluff *m* **-s, -s** bluff. **b~en** *vt/i* (*haben*) bluff
blühen *vi* (*haben*) flower; (*fig*) flourish. **b~d** *a* flowering; (*fig*) flourishing, thriving
Blume *f* **-, -n** flower; (*vom Wein*) bouquet. **B~nbeet** *nt* flower-bed. **B~ngeschäft** *nt* flower-shop, florist's. **B~nkohl** *m* cauliflower. **B~nmuster** *nt* floral design. **B~nstrauß** *m* bunch of flowers. **B~ntopf** *m* flowerpot; (*Pflanze*) pot plant. **B~nzwiebel** *f* bulb
blumig *a* (*fig*) flowery
Bluse *f* **-, -n** blouse
Blut *nt* **-[e]s** blood. **b~arm** *a* anaemic. **B~bahn** *f* bloodstream. **B~bild** *nt* blood count. **B~druck** *m* blood pressure. **b~dürstig** *a* bloodthirsty
Blüte *f* **-, -n** flower, bloom; (*vom Baum*) blossom; (*B~zeit*) flowering period; (*Baum-*) blossom time; (*Höhepunkt*) peak, prime
Blut|egel *m* **-s,-** leech. **b~en** *vi* (*haben*) bleed
Blüten|blatt *nt* petal. **B~staub** *m* pollen
Blut|er *m* **-s,-** haemophiliac. **B~erguss** *m* bruise. **B~gefäß** *nt* blood-vessel. **B~gruppe** *f* blood group. **b~ig** *a* bloody. **B~körperchen** *nt* **-s,-** corpuscle. **B~probe** *f* blood test. **b~rünstig** *a* (*fig*) bloody, gory. **B~schande** *f* incest. **B~spender** *m* blood donor. **B~sturz** *m* haemorrhage. **B~transfusion, B~übertragung** *f* blood transfusion. **B~ung** *f* **-, -en** bleeding; (*Med*) haemorrhage; (*Regel-*) period. **b~unterlaufen** *a* bruised; <*Auge*> bloodshot. **B~vergiftung** *f* blood-poisoning. **B~wurst** *f* black pudding
Bö *f* **-, -en** gust; (*Regen-*) squall
Bob *m* **-s, -s** bob[-sleigh]
Bock *m* **-[e]s,¨e** buck; (*Ziege*) billy goat; (*Schaf*) ram; (*Gestell*) support. **b~ig** *a* [!] stubborn. **B~springen** *nt* leap-frog
Boden *m* **-s,¨** ground; (*Erde*) soil; (*Fuß-*) floor; (*Grundfläche*) bottom; (*Dach-*) loft, attic. **B~satz** *m* sediment. **B~schätze** *mpl* mineral deposits. **B~see (der)** Lake Constance

Bogen *m* **-s,-** & ¨ curve; (*Geom*) arc; (*beim Skilauf*) turn; (*Archit*) arch; (*Waffe, Geigen-*) bow; (*Papier*) sheet; **einen großen B~ um jdn/etw machen** [!] give s.o./sth a wide berth. **B~schießen** *nt* archery

Bohle *f* **-, -n** [thick] plank

Böhm|en *nt* **-s** Bohemia. **b~isch** *a* Bohemian

Bohne *f* **-, -n** bean; **grüne B~n** French beans

bohner|n *vt* polish. **B~wachs** *nt* floor-polish

bohr|en *vt/i* (*haben*) drill (**nach** for); drive <*Tunnel*>; sink <*Brunnen*>; <*Insekt:*> bore. **B~er** *m* **-s,-** drill. **B~insel** *f* [offshore] drilling rig. **B~turm** *m* derrick

Boje *f* **-, -n** buoy

Böllerschuss *m* gun salute

Bolzen *m* **-s,-** bolt; (*Stift*) pin

bombardieren *vt* bomb; (*fig*) bombard (**mit** with)

Bombe *f* **-, -n** bomb. **B~nangriff** *m* bombing raid. **B~nerfolg** *m* huge success

Bon /bɔŋ/ *m* **-s, -s** voucher; (*Kassen-*) receipt

Bonbon /bɔŋˈbɔŋ/ *m* & *nt* **-s, -s** sweet

Bonus *m* **-[sses], -[sse]** bonus

Boot *nt* **-[e]s, -e** boat. **B~ssteg** *m* landing stage

Bord[1] *nt* **-[e]s, -e** shelf

Bord[2] *m* (*Naut*) **an B~** aboard, on board; **über B~** overboard. **B~buch** *nt* log[-book]

Bordell *nt* **-s, -e** brothel

Bordkarte *f* boarding-pass

borgen *vt* borrow; **jdm etw b~** lend s.o. sth

Borke *f* **-, -n** bark

Börse *f* **-, -n** purse; (*Comm*) stock exchange. **B~nmakler** *m* stockbroker

Borst|e *f* **-, -n** bristle. **b~ig** *a* bristly

Borte *f* **-, -n** braid

Böschung *f* **-, -en** embankment

böse *a* wicked, evil; (*unartig*) naughty; (*schlimm*) bad; (*zornig*) cross; **jdm** *od* **auf jdn b~ sein** be cross with s.o.

bos|haft *a* malicious, spiteful. **B~heit** *f* **-, -en** malice; spite; (*Handlung*) spiteful act/ (*Bemerkung*) remark

böswillig *a* malicious

Botani|k *f* **-** botany. **B~ker(in)** *m* **-s,-** (*f* **-, -nen**) botanist

Bot|e *m* **-n, -n** messenger. **B~engang** *m* errand. **B~schaft** *f* **-, -en** message; (*Pol*) embassy. **B~schafter** *m* **-s,-** ambassador

Bouillon /bʊlˈjɔŋ/ *f* **-, -s** clear soup. **B~würfel** *m* stock cube

Bowle /ˈboːlə/ *f* **-, -n** punch

Box *f* **-/-en** box; (*Pferde-*) loose box; (*Lautsprecher-*) speaker; (*Autorennen*) pit

box|en *vi* (*haben*) box ● *vt* punch. **B~en** *nt* **-s** boxing. **B~er** *m* **-s,-** boxer

brachliegen† *vi sep* (*haben*) lie fallow

Branche /ˈbrãːʃə/ *f* **-, -n** [line of] business. **B~nverzeichnis** *nt* (*Teleph*) classified directory

Brand *m* **-[e]s,¨e** fire; (*Med*) gangrene; (*Bot*) blight; **in B~ geraten** catch fire; **in B~ setzen** *od* **stecken** set on fire. **B~bombe** *f* incendiary bomb

Brand|stifter *m* arsonist. **B~stiftung** *f* arson

Brandung *f* **-** surf

Brand|wunde *f* burn. **B~zeichen** *nt* brand

Branntwein *m* spirit; (*coll*) spirits *pl*. **B~brennerei** *f* distillery

bras|ilianisch *a* Brazilian. **B~ilien** /-iən/ *nt* **-s** Brazil
Brat|apfel *m* baked apple. **b~en**† *vt/i* (*haben*) roast; (*in der Pfanne*) fry. **B~en** *m* **-s,-** roast; (*B~stück*) joint. **b~fertig** *a* oven-ready. **B~hähnchen** *nt* roasting chicken. **B~kartoffeln** *fpl* fried potatoes. **B~pfanne** *f* frying-pan
Bratsche *f* **-, -n** (*Mus*) viola
Bratspieß *m* spit
Brauch *m* **-[e]s,Bräuche** custom. **b~bar** *a* usable; (*nützlich*) useful. **b~en** *vt* need; (*ge-, verbrauchen*) use; take <*Zeit*>; **er b~t es nur zu sagen** he only has to say
Braue *f* **-, -n** eyebrow
brau|en *vt* brew. **B~er** *m* **-s,-** brewer. **B~erei** *f* **-, -en** brewery
braun *a*, **B~** *nt* **-s,-** brown; **b~ werden** <*Person:*> get a tan; **b~ [gebrannt] sein** be [sun]tanned
Bräune *f* **-** [sun]tan. **b~n** *vt/i* (*haben*) brown; (*in der Sonne*) tan
Braunschweig *nt* **-s** Brunswick
Brause *f* **-, -n** (*Dusche*) shower; (*an Gießkanne*) rose; (*B~limonade*) fizzy drink
Braut *f* **-, Bräute** bride; (*Verlobte*) fiancée
Bräutigam *m* **-s, -e** bridegroom; (*Verlobter*) fiancé
Brautkleid *nt* wedding dress
Brautpaar *nt* bridal couple; (*Verlobte*) engaged couple
brav *a* good; (*redlich*) honest ● *adv* dutifully; (*redlich*) honestly
bravo *int* bravo!
BRD *abbr* (**Bundesrepublik Deutschland**) FRG
Brech|eisen *nt* jemmy; (*B~stange*) crowbar. **b~en**† *vt* break; (*Phys*) refract <*Licht*>; (*erbrechen*) vomit; **sich b~en** <*Wellen:*> break; <*Licht:*> be refracted; **sich** (*dat*) **den Arm b~en** break one's arm ● *vi* (*sein*) break ● *vi* (*haben*) vomit, be sick. **B~reiz** *m* nausea. **B~stange** *f* crowbar
Brei *m* **-[e]s, -e** paste; (*Culin*) purée; (*Hafer-*) porridge
breit *a* wide; <*Schultern, Grinsen*> broad. **B~e** *f* **-, -n** width; breadth; (*Geog*) latitude. **b~en** *vt* spread (**über** + *acc* over). **B~engrad** *m* [degree of] latitude. **B~enkreis** *m* parallel
Bremse[1] *f* **-, -n** horsefly
Bremse[2] *f* **-, -n** brake. **b~n** *vt* slow down; (*fig*) restrain ● *vi* (*haben*) brake
Bremslicht *nt* brake-light
brenn|bar *a* combustible; **leicht b~bar** highly [in]flammable. **b~en**† *vi* (*haben*) burn; <*Licht:*> be on; <*Zigarette:*> be alight; (*weh tun*) smart, sting ● *vt* burn; (*rösten*) roast; (*im Brennofen*) fire; (*destillieren*) distil. **b~end** *a* burning; (*angezündet*) lighted; (*fig*) fervent **B~erei** *f* **-, -en** distillery
Brennessel* *f s.* **Brennnessel**
Brenn|holz *nt* firewood. **B~ofen** *m* kiln. **B~nessel** *f* stinging nettle. **B~punkt** *m* (*Phys*) focus. **B~spiritus** *m* methylated spirits. **B~stoff** *m* fuel
Bretagne /bre'tanjə/ **(die) -** Brittany
Brett *nt* **-[e]s, -er** board; (*im Regal*) shelf; **schwarzes B~** notice board. **B~spiel** *nt* board game
Brezel *f* **-, -n** pretzel
Bridge /brɪtʃ/ *nt* **-** (*Spiel*) bridge
Brief *m* **-[e]s, -e** letter. **B~beschwerer** *m* **-s,-** paperweight. **B~freund(in)** *m(f)* penfriend. **B~kasten** *m* letter-box. **B~kopf** *m* letter-head. **b~lich** *a & adv* by letter.

B~marke *f* [postage] stamp. **B~öffner** *m* paper-knife. **B~papier** *nt* notepaper. **B~tasche** *f* wallet. **B~träger** *m* postman. **B~umschlag** *m* envelope. **B~wahl** *f* postal vote. **B~wechsel** *m* correspondence

Brikett *nt* **-s, -s** briquette

Brillant /brɪl'jant/ *m* **-en, -en** [cut] diamond

Brille *f* **-, -n** glasses *pl*, spectacles *pl*; (*Schutz-*) goggles *pl*; (*Klosett-*) toilet seat

bringen† *vt* bring; (*fort-*) take; (*ein-*) yield; (*veröffentlichen*) publish; (*im Radio*) broadcast; show <*Film*>; **ins Bett b~** put to bed; **jdn nach Hause b~** take/ (*begleiten*) see s.o. home; **um etw b~** deprive of sth; **jdn dazu b~, etw zu tun** get s.o. to do sth; **es weit b~** (*fig*) go far

Brise *f* **-, -n** breeze

Brit|e *m* **-n, -n**, **B~in** *f* **-, -nen** Briton. **b~isch** *a* British

Bröck|chen *nt* **-s,-** (*Culin*) crouton. **b~elig** *a* crumbly; <*Gestein*> friable. **b~eln** *vt/i* (*haben/sein*) crumble

Brocken *m* **-s,-** chunk; (*Erde, Kohle*) lump

Brokat *m* **-[e]s, -e** brocade

Brokkoli *pl* broccoli *sg*

Brombeere *f* blackberry

Bronchitis *f* **-** bronchitis

Bronze /'brõ:sə/ *f* **-, -n** bronze

Brosch|e *f* **-, -n** brooch. **b~iert** *a* paperback. **B~üre** *f* **-, -n** brochure; (*Heft*) booklet

Brösel *mpl* (*Culin*) breadcrumbs

Brot *n* **-[e]s, -e** bread; **ein B~** a loaf [of bread]; (*Scheibe*) a slice of bread

Brötchen *n* **-s,-** [bread] roll

Brotkrümel *m* breadcrumb

Bruch *m* **-[e]s,⸚e** break; (*Brechen*) breaking; (*Rohr-*) burst; (*Med*) fracture; (*Eingeweide-*) rupture, hernia; (*Math*) fraction; (*fig*) breach; (*in Beziehung*) break-up

brüchig *a* brittle

Bruch|landung *f* crash-landing. **B~rechnung** *f* fractions *pl*. **B~stück** *nt* fragment. **B~teil** *m* fraction

Brücke *f* **-, -n** bridge; (*Teppich*) rug

Bruder *m* **-s,⸚** brother

brüderlich *a* brotherly, fraternal

Brügge *nt* **-s** Bruges

Brüh|e *f* **-, -n** broth, stock. **B~würfel** *m* stock cube

brüllen *vt/i* (*haben*) roar

brumm|eln *vt/i* (*haben*) mumble. **b~en** *vi* (*haben*) <*Insekt:*> buzz; <*Bär:*> growl; <*Motor:*> hum; (*murren*) grumble **B~er** *m* **-s,-** [!] bluebottle. **b~ig** *a* [!] grumpy

brünett *a* dark-haired

Brunnen *m* **-s,-** well; (*Spring-*) fountain; (*Heil-*) spa water

brüsk *a* brusque

Brüssel *nt* **-s** Brussels

Brust *f* **-,⸚e** chest; (*weibliche, Culin: B~stück*) breast. **B~bein** *nt* breastbone

brüsten (sich) *vr* boast

Brust|fellentzündung *f* pleurisy. **B~schwimmen** *nt* breaststroke

Brüstung *f* **-, -en** parapet

Brustwarze *f* nipple

Brut *f* **-, -en** incubation

brutal *a* brutal

brüten *vi* (*haben*) sit (*on eggs*); (*fig*) ponder (**über** + *dat* over)

Brutkasten *m* (*Med*) incubator

brutto *adv*, **B~-** *pref* gross

BSE *f* **-** BSE

Bub *m* **-en, -en** (*SGer*) boy. **B~e** *m* **-n, -n** (*Karte*) jack, knave

Buch *nt* **-[e]s,⸚er** book; **B~ führen** keep a record (**über** + *acc* of); **die B~̈er führen** keep the accounts

Buche *f* **-, -n** beech
buchen *vt* book; (*Comm*) enter
Bücherei *f* **-, -en** library
Bücherregal *nt* bookcase, bookshelves *pl*. **B~schrank** *m* bookcase
Buchfink *m* chaffinch
Buch|führung *f* bookkeeping. **B~halter(in)** *m* **-s,-** (*f* **-, -nen**) bookkeeper, accountant. **B~haltung** *f* bookkeeping, accountancy; (*Abteilung*) accounts department. **B~handlung** *f* bookshop
Büchse *f* **-, -n** box; (*Konserven-*) tin, can
Buch|stabe *m* **-n, -n** letter. **b~stabieren** *vt* spell [out]. **b~stäblich** *adv* literally
Bucht *f* **-, -en** (*Geog*) bay
Buchung *f* **-, -en** booking, reservation; (*Comm*) entry
Buckel *m* **-s,-** hump; (*Beule*) bump; (*Hügel*) hillock
bücken (sich) *vr* bend down
bucklig *a* hunchbacked
Bückling *m* **-s, -e** smoked herring
Buddhis|mus *m* **-** Buddhism. **B~t(in)** *m* **-en, -en** (*f* **-, -nen**) Buddhist. **b~tisch** *a* Buddhist
Bude *f* **-, -n** hut; (*Kiosk*) kiosk; (*Markt-*) stall; ([!] *Zimmer*) room
Budget /bʏˈdʒeː/ *nt* **-s, -s** budget
Büfett *nt* **-[e]s, -e** sideboard; (*Theke*) bar; **kaltes B~** cold buffet
Büffel *m* **-s,-** buffalo
Bügel *m* **-s,-** frame; (*Kleider-*) coathanger; (*Steig-*) stirrup; (*Brillen-*) sidepiece. **B~brett** *nt* ironing-board. **B~eisen** *nt* iron. **B~falte** *f* crease. **b~frei** *a* non-iron. **b~n** *vt/i* (*haben*) iron
Bühne *f* **-, -n** stage. **B~nbild** *nt* set. **B~neingang** *m* stage door
Buhrufe *mpl* boos
Bukett *nt* **-[e]s, -e** bouquet
Bulgarien /-iən/ *nt* **-s** Bulgaria
Bull|auge *nt* (*Naut*) porthole. **B~dogge** *f* bulldog. **B~dozer** /-do:zɐ/ *m* **-s,-** bulldozer. **B~e** *m* **-n, -n** bull; ([x] *Polizist*) cop
Bumme|l *m* **-s,-** [!] stroll. **B~lei** *f* **-** [!] dawdling
bummel|ig *a* [!] slow; (*nachlässig*) careless. **b~n** *vi* (*sein*) [!] stroll • *vi* (*haben*) [!] dawdle. **B~streik** *m* go-slow. **B~zug** *m* [!] slow train
Bums *m* **-es, -e** [!] bump, thump
Bund[1] *nt* **-[e]s, -e** bunch
Bund[2] *m* **-[e]s,¨-e** association; (*Bündnis*) alliance; (*Pol*) federation; (*Rock-, Hosen-*) waistband; **der B~** the Federal Government
Bündel *nt* **-s,-** bundle. **b~n** *vt* bundle [up]
Bundes|- *pref* Federal. **B~genosse** *m* ally. **B~kanzler** *m* Federal Chancellor. **B~land** *nt* [federal] state; (*Aust*) province. **B~liga** *f* German national league. **B~rat** *m* Upper House of Parliament. **B~regierung** *f* Federal Government. **B~republik** *f* **die B~republik Deutschland** the Federal Republic of Germany. **B~tag** *m* Lower House of Parliament. **B~wehr** *f* [Federal German] Army
bünd|ig *a & adv* **kurz und b~ig** short and to the point. **B~nis** *nt* **-sses, -sse** alliance
Bunker *m* **-s,-** bunker; (*Luftschutz-*) shelter
bunt *a* coloured; (*farbenfroh*) colourful; (*grell*) gaudy; (*gemischt*) varied; (*wirr*) confused; **b~e Platte** assorted cold meats. **B~stift** *m* crayon
Bürde *f* **-, -n** (*fig*) burden
Burg *f* **-, -en** castle

Bürge *m* **-n, -n** guarantor. **b~n** *vi* (*haben*) **b~n für** vouch for; (*fig*) guarantee

Bürger|(in) *m* **-s,-** (*f* **-, -nen**) citizen. **B~krieg** *m* civil war. **b~lich** *a* civil; <*Pflicht*> civic; (*mittelständisch*) middle-class. **B~liche(r)** *m/f* commoner. **B~meister** *m* mayor. **B~rechte** *npl* civil rights. **B~steig** *m* **-[e]s, -e** pavement

Bürgschaft *f* **-, -en** surety

Burgunder *m* **-s,-** (*Wein*) Burgundy

Büro *nt* **-s, -s** office. **B~angestellte(r)** *m/f* office-worker. **B~klammer** *f* paper-clip. **B~kratie** *f* **-, -n** bureaucracy. **b~kratisch** *a* bureaucratic

Bursche *m* **-n, -n** lad, youth

Bürste *f* **-, -n** brush. **b~n** *vt* brush. **B~nschnitt** *m* crew cut

Bus *m* **-ses, -se** bus; (*Reise-*) coach

Busch *m* **-[e]s,⸚e** bush

Büschel *nt* **-s,-** tuft

buschig *a* bushy

Busen *m* **-s,-** bosom

Bussard *m* **-s, -e** buzzard

Buße *f* **-, -n** penance; (*Jur*) fine

Bußgeld *nt* (*Jur*) fine

Büste *f* **-, -n** bust; (*Schneider-*) dummy. **B~nhalter** *m* **-s,-** bra

Butter *f* **-** butter. **B~blume** *f* buttercup. **B~brot** *nt* slice of bread and butter. **B~milch** *f* buttermilk. **b~n** *vt* butter

b.w. *abbr* (**bitte wenden**) P.T.O.

Cc

ca. *abbr* (**circa**) about

Café /ka'fe:/ *nt* **-s, -s** café

Camcorder /'kamkɔrdɐ/ *m* **-s, -** camcorder

camp|en /'kɛmpən/ *vi* (*haben*) go camping. **C~ing** *nt* **-s** camping. **C~ingplatz** *m* campsite

Caravan /'ka[:]ravan/ *m* **-s, -s** (*Auto*) caravan; (*Kombi*) estate car

CD /t͡seː'de:/ *f* **-, -s** compact disc, CD. **CD-ROM** /t͡se:de:'rɔm/ *f* **-, -(s)** CD-ROM

Cell|ist(in) /tʃɛ'lɪst(ɪn)/ *m* **-en, -en** (*f* **-, -nen**) cellist. **C~o** /'tʃɛlo/ *nt* **-, -los & -li** cello

Celsius /'t͡sɛlzi̯ʊs/ *inv* Celsius, centigrade

Cent /t͡sɛnt/ *m* **-[s], -[s]** cent

Champagner /ʃam'panjɐ/ *m* **-s** champagne

Champignon /'ʃampɪnjɔŋ/ *m* **-s, -s** [field] mushroom

Chance /'ʃã:s[ə]/ *f* **-, -n** chance

Chaos /'ka:ɔs/ *nt* **-** chaos

Charakter /ka'raktɐ/ *m* **-s, -e** /-'te:rə/ character. **c~isieren** *vt* characterize. **c~istisch** *a* characteristic (**für** of)

charm|ant /ʃar'mant/ *a* charming. **C~e** /ʃarm/ *m* **-s** charm

Charter|flug /'tʃ-, 'ʃartɐ-/ *m* charter flight. **c~n** *vt* charter

Chassis /ʃa'si:/ *nt* **-,-** /-'si:[s], -'si:s/ chassis

Chauffeur /ʃɔ'fø:ɐ/ *m* **-s, -e** chauffeur; (*Taxi-*) driver

Chauvinist /ʃovi'nɪst/ *m* **-en, -en** chauvinist

Chef /ʃɛf/ *m* **-s, -s** head; ⓘ boss
Chemie /çe'mi:/ *f* - chemistry
Chem|iker(in) /'çe:-/ *m* **-s,-** (*f* **-, -nen**) chemist. **c~isch** *a* chemical; **c~ische Reinigung** dry-cleaning; (*Geschäft*) dry-cleaner's
Chicorée /'ʃɪkore:/ *m* **-s** chicory
Chiffre /'ʃɪfɐ, 'ʃɪfrə/ *f* **-, -n** cipher
Chile /'çi:le/ *nt* **-s** Chile
Chin|a /'çi:na/ *nt* **-s** China. **C~ese** *m* **-n, -n, C~esin** *f* **-, -nen** Chinese. **c~esisch** *a* Chinese. **C~esisch** *nt* **-[s]** (*Lang*) Chinese
Chip /tʃɪp/ *m* **-s, -s** [micro]chip. **C~s** *pl* crisps
Chirurg /çi'rʊrk/ *m* **-en, -en** surgeon. **C~ie** /-'gi:/ *f* - surgery
Chlor /klo:ɐ̯/ *nt* **-s** chlorine
Choke /tʃo:k/ *m* **-s, -s** (*Auto*) choke
Cholera /'ko:lera/ *f* - cholera
cholerisch /ko'le:rɪʃ/ *a* irascible
Cholesterin /ço-, kolɛste'ri:n/ *nt* **-s** cholesterol
Chor /ko:ɐ̯/ *m* **-[e]s,¨e** choir
Choreographie, Choreografie /koreogra'fi:/ *f* **-, -n** choreography
Christ /krɪst/ *m* **-en, -en** Christian. **C~baum** *m* Christmas tree. **C~entum** *nt* **-s** Christianity **c~lich** *a* Christian
Christus /'krɪstʊs/ *m* **-ti** Christ
Chrom /kro:m/ *nt* **-s** chromium
Chromosom /kromo'zo:m/ *nt* **-s, -en** chromosome
Chronik /'kro:nɪk/ *f* **-, -en** chronicle
chronisch /'kro:nɪʃ/ *a* chronic
Chrysantheme /krʏzan'te:mə/ *f* **-, -n** chrysanthemum
circa /'t͡sɪrka/ *adv* about
Clique /'klɪkə/ *f* **-, -n** clique
Clou /klu:/ *m* **-s, -s** highlight, ⓘ high spot
Clown /klau̯n/ *m* **-s, -s** clown
Club /klʊp/ *m* **-s, -s** club
Cocktail /'kɔkte:l/ *m* **-s, -s** cocktail
Code /'ko:t/ *m* **-s, -s** code
Comic-Heft /'kɔmɪk-/ *nt* comic
Computer /kɔm'pju:tɐ/ *m* **-s,-** computer. **c~isieren** *vt* computerize. **C~spiel** *nt* computer game
Conférencier /kõ'ferã'si̯e:/ *m* **-s,-** compère
Cord /kɔrt/ *m* **-s**, **C~samt** *m* corduroy
Couch /kau̯tʃ/ *f* **-, -es** settee
Cousin /ku'zɛ̃:/ *m* **-s, -s** [male] cousin. **C~e** /-'zi:nə/ *f* **-, -n** [female] cousin
Creme /kre:m/ *f* **-s, -s** cream; (*Speise*) cream dessert
Curry /'kari, 'kœri/ *nt & m* **-s** curry powder ● *nt* **-s, -s** (*Gericht*) curry
Cursor /'kø:ɐ̯sɐ/ *m* **-s, -** cursor
Cyberspace /'sai̯bɐspe:s/ *m* - cyberspace

Dd

da *adv* there; (*hier*) here; (*zeitlich*) then; (*in dem Fall*) in that case; **von da an** from then on; **da sein** be there/(*hier*) here; (*existieren*) exist; **wieder da sein** be back ● *conj* as, since
dabei (*emphatic*: **dabei**) *adv* nearby; (*daran*) with it; (*eingeschlossen*) included; (*hinsichtlich*) about it; (*währenddem*) during this; (*gleichzeitig*) at the same time; (*doch*) and yet; **dicht d~** close

by; **d~ sein** be present; (*mitmachen*) be involved; **d~ sein, etw zu tun** be just doing sth

Dach *nt* **-[e]s,¨er** roof. **D~boden** *m* loft. **D~luke** *f* skylight. **D~rinne** *f* gutter

Dachs *m* **-es, -e** badger

Dachsparren *m* **-s,-** rafter

Dackel *m* **-s,-** dachshund

dadurch (*emphatic:* **dadurch**) *adv* through it/them; (*Ursache*) by it; (*deshalb*) because of that; **d~, dass** because

dafür (*emphatic:* **dafür**) *adv* for it/them; (*anstatt*) instead; (*als Ausgleich*) but [on the other hand]; **d~, dass** considering that; **ich kann nichts dafür** it's not my fault

dagegen (*emphatic:* **dagegen**) *adv* against it/them; (*Mittel, Tausch*) for it; (*verglichen damit*) by comparison; (*jedoch*) however; **hast du was d~?** do you mind?

daheim *adv* at home

daher (*emphatic:* **daher**) *adv* from there; (*deshalb*) for that reason; **das kommt d~, weil** that's because ● *conj* that is why

dahin (*emphatic:* **dahin**) *adv* there; **bis d~** up to there; (*bis dann*) until/(*Zukunft*) by then; **jdn d~bringen, dass er etw tut** get s.o. to do sth

dahinten *adv* back there

dahinter (*emphatic:* **dahinter**) *adv* behind it/them; **d~ kommen** (*fig*) get to the bottom of it

Dahlie /-iə/ *f* **-, -n** dahlia

dalassen† *vt sep* leave there

daliegen† *vi sep* (*haben*) lie there

damalig *a* at that time; **der d~e Minister** the then minister

damals *adv* at that time

Damast *m* **-es, -e** damask

Dame *f* **-, -n** lady; (*Karte, Schach*) queen; (*D~spiel*) draughts *sg*. **d~nhaft** *a* ladylike

damit (*emphatic:* **damit**) *adv* with it/them; (*dadurch*) by it; **hör auf d~!** stop it! ● *conj* so that

Damm *m* **-[e]s,¨e** dam

dämmer|ig *a* dim. **D~licht** *nt* twilight. **d~n** *vi* <haben> <Morgen:> dawn; **es d~t** it is getting light/(*abends*) dark. **D~ung** *f* dawn; (*Abend-*) dusk

Dämon *m* **-s, -en** /-ˈmoːnən/ demon

Dampf *m* **-es,¨e** steam; (*Chem*) vapour. **d~en** *vi* (*haben*) steam

dämpfen *vt* (*Culin*) steam; (*fig*) muffle <*Ton*>; lower <*Stimme*>

Dampf|er *m* **-s,-** steamer. **D~kochtopf** *m* pressure-cooker. **D~maschine** *f* steam engine. **D~walze** *f* steamroller

danach (*emphatic:* **danach**) *adv* after it/them; <*suchen*> for it/them; <*riechen*> of it; (*später*) afterwards; (*entsprechend*) accordingly; **es sieht d~ aus** it looks like it

Däne *m* **-n, -n** Dane

daneben (*emphatic:* **daneben**) *adv* beside it/them; (*außerdem*) in addition; (*verglichen damit*) by comparison

Dän|emark *nt* **-s** Denmark. **D~in** *f* **-, -nen** Dane. **d~isch** *a* Danish

Dank *m* **-es** thanks *pl*; **vielen D~!** thank you very much! **d~** *prep* (+ *dat or gen*) thanks to. **d~bar** *a* grateful; (*erleichtert*) thankful; (*lohnend*) rewarding. **D~barkeit** *f* - gratitude. **d~e** *adv* **d~e [schön** *od* **sehr]!** thank you [very much]! **d~en** *vi* (*haben*) thank (**jdm** s.o.); (*ablehnen*) decline; **nichts zu d~en!** don't mention it!

dann *adv* then; **selbst d~, wenn** even if

darạn (*emphatic:* **daran**) *adv* on it/them; at it/them; <*denken*> of it; **nahe d∼** on the point (**etw zu tun** of doing sth). **d∼setzen** *vt sep* **alles d∼setzen** do one's utmost (**zu** to)

darauf (*emphatic:* **darauf**) *adv* on it/them; <*warten*> for it; <*antworten*> to it; (*danach*) after that; (*d∼hin*) as a result. **d∼hịn** *adv* as a result

daraus (*emphatic:* **daraus**) *adv* out of *or* from it/them; **er macht sich nichts d∼** he doesn't care for it

darlegen *vt sep* expound; (*erklären*) explain

Darlehen *nt* **-s,-** loan

Dạrm *m* **-[e]s,¨e** intestine

darstell|en *vt sep* represent; (*bildlich*) portray; (*Theat*) interpret; (*spielen*) play; (*schildern*) describe. **D∼er** *m* **-s,-** actor. **D∼erin** *f* **-, -nen** actress. **D∼ung** *f* representation; interpretation; description

darüber (*emphatic:* **darüber**) *adv* over it/them; (*höher*) above it/them; <*sprechen, lachen, sich freuen*> about it; (*mehr*) more; **d∼ hinaus** beyond [it]; (*dazu*) on top of that

darụm (*emphatic:* **darum**) *adv* round it/them; <*bitten, kämpfen*> for it; (*deshalb*) that is why; **d∼, weil** because

darụnter (*emphatic:* **darunter**) *adv* under it/them; (*tiefer*) below it/them; (*weniger*) less; (*dazwischen*) among them

dạs *def art & pron s.* **der**

dasein* *vi sep* (*sein*) **da sein**, *s.* **da. D∼** *nt* **-s** existence

dạss *conj* that

dạsselbe *pron s.* **derselbe**

Daten|sichtgerät *nt* visual display unit, VDU. **D∼verarbeitung** *f* data processing

datieren *vt/i* (*haben*) date

Dativ *m* **-s, -e** dative. **D∼objekt** *nt* indirect object

Dạttel *f* **-, -n** date

Datum *nt* **s, -ten** date; **Daten** dates; (*Angaben*) data

Dauer *f* **-** duration, length; (*Jur*) term; **auf die D∼** in the long run. **D∼auftrag** *m* standing order. **d∼haft** *a* lasting, enduring; (*fest*) durable. **D∼karte** *f* season ticket. **d∼n** *vi* (*haben*) last; **lange d∼n** take a long time. **d∼nd** *a* lasting; (*ständig*) constant. **D∼welle** *f* perm

Daumen *m* **-s,-** thumb; **jdm den D∼ drücken** *od* **halten** keep one's fingers crossed for s.o.

Daunen *fpl* down *sg*. **D∼decke** *f* [down-filled] duvet

davọn (*emphatic:* **davon**) *adv* from it/them; (*dadurch*) by it; (*damit*) with it/them; (*darüber*) about it; (*Menge*) of it/them; **das kommt d∼!** it serves you right! **d∼kommen**† *vi sep* (*sein*) escape (**mit dem Leben** with one's life). **d∼laufen**† *vi sep* (*sein*) run away. **d∼machen** (**sich**) *vr sep* [!] make off. **d∼tragen**† *vt sep* carry off; (*erleiden*) suffer; (*gewinnen*) win

davor (*emphatic:* **davor**) *adv* in front of it/them; <*sich fürchten*> of it; (*zeitlich*) before it/them

dazu (*emphatic:* **dazu**) *adv* to it/them; (*damit*) with it/them; (*dafür*) for it; **noch d∼** in addition to that; **jdn d∼ bringen, etw zu tun** get s.o. to do sth; **ich kam nicht d∼** I didn't get round to [doing] it. **d∼kommen**† *vi sep* (*sein*) arrive [on the scene]; (*hinzukommen*) be added. **d∼rechnen** *vt sep* add to it/them

dazwịschen (*emphatic:* **dazwischen**) *adv* between them;

in between; (*darunter*) among them. **d~kommen**† *vi sep* (*sein*) (*fig*) crop up; **wenn nichts d~kommt** if all goes well

Debat|te *f* **-, -n** debate; **zur D~te stehen** be at issue. **d~tieren** *vt/i* (*haben*) debate

Debüt /de'by:/ *nt* **-s, -s** début

Deck *nt* **-[e]s, -s** (*Naut*) deck; **an D~** on deck. **D~bett** *nt* duvet

Decke *f* **-, -n** cover; (*Tisch-*) table-cloth; (*Bett-*) blanket; (*Reise-*) rug; (*Zimmer-*) ceiling; **unter einer D~stecken** [!] be in league

Deckel *m* **-s,-** lid; (*Flaschen-*) top; (*Buch-*) cover

decken *vt* cover; tile <*Dach*>; lay <*Tisch*>; (*schützen*) shield; (*Sport*) mark; meet <*Bedarf*>; **jdn d~** (*fig*) cover up for s.o.; **sich d~** (*fig*) cover oneself (**gegen** against); (*übereinstimmen*) coincide

Deckname *m* pseudonym

Deckung *f* **-** (*Mil*) cover; (*Sport*) defence; (*Mann-*) marking; (*Boxen*) guard; (*Sicherheit*) security; **in D~ gehen** take cover

defin|ieren *vt* define. **D~ition** /-'tsio:n/ *f* **-, -en** definition

Defizit *nt* **-s, -e** deficit

deformiert *a* deformed

deftig *a* [!] <*Mahlzeit*> hearty; <*Witz*> coarse

Degen *m* **-s,-** sword; (*Fecht-*) épée

degeneriert *a* (*fig*) degenerate

degradieren *vt* (*Mil*) demote; (*fig*) degrade

dehn|bar *a* elastic. **d~en** *vt* stretch; lengthen <*Vokal*>; **sich d~en** stretch

Deich *m* **-[e]s, -e** dike

dein *poss pron* your. **d~e(r,s)** *poss pron* yours; **die D~en** *od* **d~en** *pl* your family *sg*. **d~erseits** *adv* for your part. **d~etwegen** *adv* for your sake; (*wegen dir*) because of you, on your account. **d~etwillen** *adv* **um d~etwillen** for your sake. **d~ige** *poss pron* **der/die/das d~ige** yours. **d~s** *poss pron* yours

Dekan *m* **-s, -e** dean

Deklin|ation /-'tsio:n/ *f* **-, -en** declension. **d~ieren** *vt* decline

Dekolleté, Dekolletee /dekɔl'te:/ *nt* **-s, -s** low neckline

Dekor *m* & *nt* **-s** decoration. **D~ateur** /-'tø:ɐ̯/ *m* **-s, -e** interior decorator; (*Schaufenster-*) window-dresser. **D~ation** /-'tsio:n/ *f* **-, -en** decoration; (*Schaufenster-*) window-dressing; (*Auslage*) display. **d~ativ** *a* decorative. **d~ieren** *vt* decorate; dress <*Schaufenster*>

Deleg|ation /-'tsio:n/ *f* **-, -en** delegation. **D~ierte(r)** *m/f* delegate

delikat *a* delicate; (*lecker*) delicious; (*taktvoll*) tactful. **D~essengeschäft** *nt* delicatessen

Delikt *nt* **-[e]s, -e** offence

Delinquent *m* **-en, -en** offender

Delle *f* **-, -n** dent

Delphin *m* **-s, -e** dolphin

Delta *nt* **-s, -s** delta

dem *def art & pron s.* **der**

dementieren *vt* deny

dem|entsprechend *a* corresponding; (*passend*) appropriate ● *adv* accordingly; (*passend*) appropriately. **d~nächst** *adv* soon; (*in Kürze*) shortly

Demokrat *m* **-en, -en** democrat. **D~ie** *f* **-, -n** democracy. **d~isch** *a* democratic

demolieren *vt* wreck

Demonstr|ant *m* **-en, -en** demonstrator. **D~ation** /-'tsio:n/ *f* **-, -en** demonstration. **d~ieren** *vt/i* (*haben*) demonstrate

demontieren *vt* dismantle

Demoskopie *f* - opinion research
Demut *f* - humility
den *def art & pron s.* **der. d~en** *pron s.* **der**
denk|bar *a* conceivable. **d~en**† *vt/i* (*haben*) think (**an** + *acc* of); (*sich erinnern*) remember (**an etw** *acc* sth); **das kann ich mir d~en** I can imagine [that]; **ich d~e nicht daran** I have no intention of doing it. **D~mal** *nt* memorial; (*Monument*) monument. **d~würdig** *a* memorable
denn *conj* for; **besser/mehr d~ je** better/more than ever ● *adv* **wie/wo d~?** but how/where? **warum d~ nicht?** why ever not? **es sei d~ [, dass]** unless
dennoch *adv* nevertheless
Denunz|iant *m* **-en, -en** informer. **d~ieren** *vt* denounce
Deodorant *nt* **-s, -s** deodorant
deplaciert, deplatziert /-'tsi:ɐt/ *a* (*fig*) out of place
Deponie *f* **-, -n** dump. **d~ren** *vt* deposit
deportieren *vt* deport
Depot /de'po:/ *nt* **-s, -s** depot; (*Lager*) warehouse; (*Bank-*) safe deposit
Depression *f* **-, -en** depression
deprimieren *vt* depress

der, die, das, *pl* **die**
● *definite article*
(*acc* **den, die, das,** *pl* **die**; *gen* **des, der, des,** *pl* **der**; *dat* **dem, der, dem,** *pl* **den**)
····➤ the. **der Mensch** the person; (*als abstrakter Begriff*) man. **die Natur** nature. **das Leben** life. **das Lesen/Tanzen** reading/dancing. **sich** (*dat*) **das Gesicht/die Hände waschen** wash one's face/hands. **5 Mark das Pfund** 5 marks a pound
● *pronoun*
(*acc* **den, die, das,** *pl* **die**; *gen* **dessen, deren, dessen,** *pl* **deren**; *dat* **dem, der, dem,** *pl* **denen**)
● *demonstrative pronoun*
····➤ that; (*pl*) those
····➤ (*attributiv*) **der Mann war es** it was 'that man
····➤ (*substantivisch*) he, she, it; (*pl*) they. **der war es** it was 'him. **die da** (*person*) that woman/girl; (*thing*) that one
● *relative pronoun*
····➤ (*Person*) who. **der Mann, der/dessen Sohn hier arbeitet** the man who/whose son works here. **die Frau, mit der ich Tennis spiele** the woman with whom I play tennis, the woman I play tennis with. **das Mädchen, das ich gestern sah** the girl I saw yesterday
····➤ (*Ding*) which, that. **ich sah ein Buch, das mich interessierte** I saw a book that interested me. **die CD, die ich mir anhöre** the CD I am listening to. **das Auto, mit dem wir nach Deutschland fahren** the car we are going to Germany in *or* in which we are going to Germany

derb *a* tough; (*kräftig*) strong; (*grob*) coarse; (*unsanft*) rough
deren *pron s.* **der**
dergleichen *inv a* such ● *pron* such a thing/such things
der-/die-/dasselbe, *pl* **dieselben** *pron* the same; **ein- und dasselbe** one and the same thing
derzeit *adv* at present
des *def art s.* **der**
Desert|eur /-'tø:ɐ/ *m* **-s, -e** deserter. **d~ieren** *vi* (*sein/haben*) desert
desgleichen *adv* likewise ● *pron* the like

deshalb *adv* for this reason; (*also*) therefore
Designer(in) /di'zainɐ, -nərın/ *m* **-s,-** (*f* **-, -nen**) designer
Desin|fektion /dɛsʔınfɛk'tsio:n/ *f* disinfecting. **D~fektionsmittel** *nt* disinfectant. **d~fizieren** *vt* disinfect
dessen *pron s.* **der**
Destill|ation /-'tsio:n/ *f* - distillation. **d~ieren** *vt* distil
desto *adv* **je mehr d~ besser** the more the better
deswegen *adv* = **deshalb**
Detektiv *m* **-s, -e** detective
Deton|ation /-'tsio:n/ *f* **-, -en** explosion. **d~ieren** *vi* (*sein*) explode
deut|en *vt* interpret; predict <*Zukunft*> ● *vi* (*haben*) point (**auf** + *acc* at/(*fig*) to). **d~lich** *a* clear; (*eindeutig*) plain
deutsch *a* German. **D~** *nt* **-[s]** (*Lang*) German; **auf D~** in German. **D~e(r)** *m/f* German. **D~land** *nt* **-s** Germany
Deutung *f* **-, -en** interpretation
Devise *f* **-, -n** motto. **D~n** *pl* foreign currency *or* exchange *sg*
Dezember *m* **-s,-** December
dezent *a* unobtrusive; (*diskret*) discreet
Dezernat *nt* **-[e]s, -e** department
Dezimalzahl *f* decimal
d.h. *abbr* (*das heißt*) i.e.
Dia *nt* **-s, -s** (*Phot*) slide
Diabet|es *m* - diabetes. **D~iker** *m* **-s,-** diabetic
Diadem *nt* **-s, -e** tiara
Diagnose *f* **-, -n** diagnosis
diagonal *a* diagonal. **D~e** *f* **-, -n** diagonal
Diagramm *nt* **-s, -e** diagram; (*Kurven-*) graph
Diakon *m* **-s, -e** deacon
Dialekt *m* **-[e]s, -e** dialect
Dialog *m* **-[e]s, -e** dialogue
Diamant *m* **-en, -en** diamond
Diapositiv *nt* **-s, -e** (*Phot*) slide
Diaprojektor *m* slide projector
Diät *f* **-, -en** (*Med*) diet; **D~ leben** be on a diet
dich *pron* (*acc of* **du**) you; (*refl*) yourself
dicht *a* dense; (*dick*) thick; (*undurchlässig*) airtight; (*wasser-*) watertight ● *adv* densely; (*nahe*) close (**bei** to). **D~e** density. **d~en¹** *vt* make watertight
dicht|en² *vi* (*haben*) write poetry. ● *vt* write. **D~er(in)** *m* **-s,-** (*f* **-, -en**) poet. **d~erisch** *a* poetic. **D~ung¹** *f* **-, -en** poetry; (*Gedicht*) poem
Dichtung² *f* **-, -en** seal; (*Ring*) washer; (*Auto*) gasket
dick *a* thick; (*beleibt*) fat; (*geschwollen*) swollen; (*fam; eng*) close; **d~ machen** be fattening. **d~flüssig** *a* thick; (*Phys*) viscous. **D~kopf** *m* 🅸 stubborn person; **einen D~kopf haben** be stubborn
die *def art & pron s.* **der**
Dieb|(in) *m* **-[e]s, -e** (*f* **-, -nen**) thief. **d~isch** *a* thieving; <*Freude*> malicious. **D~stahl** *m* **-[e]s,-e** theft
Diele *f* **-, -n** floorboard; (*Flur*) hall
dien|en *vi* (*haben*) serve. **D~er** *m* **-s,-** servant; (*Verbeugung*) bow. **D~erin** *f* **-, -nen** maid, servant
Dienst *m* **-[e]s, -e** service; (*Arbeit*) work; (*Amtsausübung*) duty; **außer D~** off duty; (*pensioniert*) retired; **D~ haben** work; <*Soldat, Arzt:*> be on duty
Dienstag *m* Tuesday. **d~s** *adv* on Tuesdays
Dienst|bote *m* servant. **d~frei** *a* **d~freier Tag** day off; **d~frei haben** have time off; <*Soldat, Arzt:*> be off duty. **D~grad** *m* rank. **D~leistung** *f* service. **d~lich** *a* official ● *adv* **d~lich verreist** away on business.

D~mädchen *nt* maid. **D~reise** *f* business trip. **D~stelle** *f* office. **D~stunden** *fpl* office hours

dies *inv pron* this. **d~bezüglich** *a* relevant ● *adv* regarding this matter. **d~e(r,s)** *pron* this; (*pl*) these; (*substantivisch*) this [one]; (*pl*) these; **d~e Nacht** tonight; (*letzte*) last night

dieselbe *pron s.* **derselbe**

Dieselkraftstoff *m* diesel [oil]

diesmal *adv* this time

Dietrich *m* **-s, -e** skeleton key

Diffamation /-'tsio:n/ *f* **-** defamation

Differential* /-'tsia:l/ *nt* **-s, -e** *s.* **Differenzial**

Differenz *f* **-, -en** difference. **D~ial** *nt* **-s, -e** differential. **d~ieren** *vt/i* (*haben*) differentiate (**zwischen** + *dat* between)

digital *a* digital

Digital- *pref* digital. **D~kamera** *f* digital camera. **D~uhr** *f* digital clock/watch

Dikt|at *nt* **-[e]s, -e** dictation. **D~ator** *m* **-s, -en** /-'to:rən/ dictator. **D~atur** *f* **-, -en** dictatorship. **d~ieren** *vt/i* (*haben*) dictate

Dimension *f* **-, -en** dimension

Ding *nt* **-[e]s, -e** & ⊡ **-er** thing; **guter D~e sein** be cheerful; **vor allen D~en** above all

Dinosaurier /-iɐ/ *m* **-s,-** dinosaur

Diözese *f* **-, -n** diocese

Diphtherie *f* **-** diphtheria

Diplom *nt* **-s, -e** diploma; (*Univ*) degree

Diplomat *m* **-en, -en** diplomat. **d~isch** *a* diplomatic

dir *pron* (*dat of* **du**) [to] you; (*refl*) yourself; **ein Freund von dir** a friend of yours

direkt *a* direct ● *adv* directly; (*wirklich*) really. **D~ion** /-'tsio:n/ *f* **-** management; (*Vorstand*) board of directors. **D~or** *m* **-s, -en** /-'to:rən/, **D~orin** *f* **-, -nen** director; (*Bank-, Theater-*) manager; (*Sch*) head; (*Gefängnis*) governor. **D~übertragung** *f* live transmission

Dirig|ent *m* **-en, -en** (*Mus*) conductor. **d~ieren** *vt* direct; (*Mus*) conduct

Dirndl *nt* **-s,-** dirndl [dress]

Diskette *f* **-, -n** floppy disc

Disko *f* **-, -s** ⊡ disco. **D~thek** *f* **-, -en** discothèque

diskret *a* discreet

Diskus *m* **-, -se** & **Disken** discus

Disku|ssion *f* **-, -en** discussion. **d~tieren** *vt/i* (*haben*) discuss

disponieren *vi* (*haben*) make arrangements; **d~ [können] über** (+ *acc*) have at one's disposal

Disqualifi|kation /-'tsio:n/ *f* disqualification. **d~zieren** *vt* disqualify

Dissertation /-'tsio:n/ *f* **-, -en** dissertation

Dissident *m* **-en, -en** dissident

Distanz *f* **-, -en** distance. **d~ieren (sich)** *vr* dissociate oneself (**von** from). **d~iert** *a* aloof

Distel *f* **-, -n** thistle

Disziplin *f* **-, -en** discipline. **d~arisch** *a* disciplinary. **d~iert** *a* disciplined

dito *adv* ditto

diverse *attrib a pl* various

Divid|ende *f* **-, -en** dividend. **d~ieren** *vt* divide (**durch** by)

Division *f* **-, -en** division

DJH *abbr* (**Deutsche Jugendherberge**) [German] youth hostel

DM *abbr* (**Deutsche Mark**) DM

doch *conj & adv* but; (*dennoch*) yet; (*trotzdem*) after all; **wenn d~ ...!** if only ...! **nicht d~!** don't!
Docht *m* **-[e]s, -e** wick
Dock *nt* **-s, -s** dock. **d~en** *vt/i* (*haben*) dock
Dogge *f* **-, -n** Great Dane
Dogm|a *nt* **-s, -men** dogma. **d~atisch** *a* dogmatic
Dohle *f* **-, -n** jackdaw
Doktor *m* **-s, -en** /-'to:rən/ doctor. **D~arbeit** *f* [doctoral] thesis
Dokument *nt* **-[e]s, -e** document. **D~arbericht** *m* documentary. **D~arfilm** *m* documentary film
Dolch *m* **-[e]s, -e** dagger
Dollar *m* **-s,-** dollar
dolmetsch|en *vt/i* (*haben*) interpret. **D~er(in)** *m* **-s,-** (*f* **-, -nen**) interpreter
Dom *m* **-[e]s, -e** cathedral
Domino *nt* **-s, -s** dominoes *sg*. **D~stein** *m* domino
Dompfaff *m* **-en, -en** bullfinch
Donau *f* **-** Danube
Donner *m* **-s** thunder. **d~n** *vi* (*haben*) thunder
Donnerstag *m* Thursday. **d~s** *adv* on Thursdays
doof *a* [!] stupid
Doppel *nt* **-s,-** duplicate; (*Tennis*) doubles *pl*. **D~bett** *nt* double bed. **D~decker** *m* **-s,-** doubledecker [bus]. **d~deutig** *a* ambiguous. **D~gänger** *m* **-s,-** double. **D~kinn** *nt* double chin. **d~klicken** *vi* (*haben*) double-click (**auf** + *acc* on). **D~name** *m* double-barrelled name. **D~punkt** *m* (*Gram*) colon. **D~stecker** *m* two-way adaptor. **d~t** *a* double; <*Boden*> false; **in d~ter Ausfertigung** in duplicate; **die d~te Menge** twice the amount ● *adv* doubly; (*zweimal*) twice; **d~t so viel** twice as much. **D~zimmer** *nt* double room
Dorf *nt* **-[e]s,¨er** village. **D~bewohner** *m* villager
dörflich *a* rural
Dorn *m* **-[e]s, -en** thorn. **d~ig** *a* thorny
Dorsch *m* **-[e]s, -e** cod
dort *adv* there. **d~ig** *a* local
Dose *f* **-, -n** tin, can
dösen *vi* (*haben*) doze
Dosen|milch *f* evaporated milk. **D~öffner** *m* tin *or* can opener
dosieren *vt* measure out
Dosis *f* **-, Dosen** dose
Dot-com-Firma *f* dot-com (company)
Dotter *m & nt* **-s,-** [egg] yolk
Dozent(in) *m* **-en, -en** (*f* **-, -nen**) (*Univ*) lecturer
Dr. *abbr* (**Doktor**) Dr
Drache *m* **-n, -n** dragon. **D~n** *m* **-s,-** kite. **D~nfliegen** *nt* hang-gliding
Draht *m* **-[e]s,¨e** wire; **auf D~** [!] on the ball. **D~seilbahn** *f* cable railway
Dram|a *nt* **-s, -men** drama. **D~atik** *f* **-** drama. **D~atiker** *m* **-s,-** dramatist. **d~atisch** *a* dramatic
dran *adv* [!] = **daran; gut/schlecht d~ sein** be well off/in a bad way; **ich bin d~** it's my turn
Drang *m* **-[e]s** urge; (*Druck*) pressure
drängeln *vt/i* (*haben*) push; (*bedrängen*) pester. **d~en** *vt* push; (*bedrängen*) urge; **sich d~en** crowd (**um** round) ● *vi* (*haben*) push; (*eilen*) be urgent; **d~en auf** (+ *acc*) press for
dran|halten† **(sich)** *vr sep* hurry. **d~kommen**† *vi sep* (*sein*) have one's turn
drauf *adv* [!] = **darauf**; **d~ und dran sein** be on the point (**etw zu tun** of doing sth). **D~gänger** *m* **-s,-** daredevil

draußen *adv* outside; (*im Freien*) out of doors

drechseln *vt* (*Techn*) turn

Dreck *m* **-s** dirt; (*Morast*) mud

Dreh *m* **-s** [!] knack; **den D~ heraushaben** have got the hang of it. **D~bank** *f* lathe. **D~bleistift** *m* propelling pencil. **D~buch** *nt* screenplay, script. **d~en** *vt* turn; (*im Kreis*) rotate; (*verschlingen*) twist; roll <*Zigarette*>; shoot <*Film*>; **lauter/leiser d~en** turn up/down; **sich d~en** turn; (*im Kreis*) rotate; (*schnell*) spin; <*Wind:*> change; **sich d~en um** revolve around; (*sich handeln*) be about ● *vi* (*haben*) turn; <*Wind:*> change; **an etw** (*dat*) **d~en** turn sth. **D~stuhl** *m* swivel chair. **D~tür** *f* revolving door. **D~ung** *f* **-, -en** turn; (*im Kreis*) rotation. **D~zahl** *f* number of revolutions

drei *inv a*, **D~** *f* **-, -en** three; (*Sch*) ≈ pass. **D~eck** *nt* **-[e]s, -e** triangle. **d~eckig** *a* triangular. **d~erlei** *inv* a three kinds of ● *pron* three things. **d~fach** *a* triple. **d~mal** *adv* three times. **D~rad** *nt* tricycle

dreißig *inv a* thirty. **d~ste(r,s)** *a* thirtieth

dreiviertel* *inv a* **drei viertel**, *s.* **viertel**. **D~stunde** *f* three-quarters of an hour

dreizehn *inv a* thirteen **d~te(r,s)** *a* thirteenth

dreschen† *vt* thresh

dress|ieren *vt* train. **D~ur** *f* - training

dribbeln *vi* (*haben*) dribble

Drill *m* **-[e]s** (*Mil*) drill. **d~en** *vt* drill

Drillinge *mpl* triplets

dringlich *a* urgent

Drink *m* **-[s], -s** [alcoholic] drink

drinnen *adv* inside

dritt *adv* **zu d~** in threes; **wir waren zu d~** there were three of us. **d~e(r,s)** *a* third; **ein D~er** a third person. **d~el** *inv a* third. **D~el** *nt* **-s,-** third. **d~ens** *adv* thirdly. **d~rangig** *a* third-rate

Drog|e *f* **-, -n** drug. **D~enabhängige(r)** *m/f* drug addict. **D~erie** *f* **-, -n** chemist's shop. **D~ist** *m* **-en, -en** chemist

drohen *vi* (*haben*) threaten (**jdm** s.o.)

dröhnen *vi* (*haben*) resound; (*tönen*) boom

Drohung *f* **-, -en** threat

drollig *a* funny; (*seltsam*) odd

Drops *m* **-,-** [fruit] drop

Drossel *f* **-, -n** thrush

drosseln *vt* (*Techn*) throttle; (*fig*) cut back

drüben *adv* over there

Druck[1] *m* **-[e]s,¨-e** pressure; **unter D~ setzen** (*fig*) pressurize

Druck[2] *m* **-[e]s, -e** printing; (*Schrift, Reproduktion*) print. **D~buchstabe** *m* block letter

drucken *vt* print

drücken *vt/i* (*haben*) press; (*aus-*) squeeze; <*Schuh:*> pinch; (*umarmen*) hug; **Preise d~** force down prices; (*an Tür*) **d~** push; **sich d~** [!] make oneself scarce; **sich d~ vor** (+ *dat*) [!] shirk. **d~d** *a* heavy; (*schwül*) oppressive

Drucker *m* **-s,-** printer

Druckerei *f* **-, -en** printing works

Druck|fehler *m* misprint. **D~knopf** *m* press-stud. **D~luft** *f* compressed air. **D~sache** *f* printed matter. **D~schrift** *f* type; (*Veröffentlichung*) publication; **in D~schrift** in block letters *pl*

Druckstelle *f* bruise

Drüse *f* **-, -n** (*Anat*) gland

Dschungel *m* **-s,-** jungle

du *pron* (*familiar address*) you; **auf Du und Du** on familiar terms
Dübel *m* **-s,-** plug
Dudelsack *m* bagpipes *pl*
Duell *nt* **-s, -e** duel
Duett *nt* **-s, -e** [vocal] duet
Duft *m* **-[e]s,¨-e** fragrance, scent; (*Aroma*) aroma. **d~en** *vi* (*haben*) smell (**nach** of)
dulden *vt* tolerate; (*erleiden*) suffer ● *vi* (*haben*) suffer
dumm *a* stupid; (*unklug*) foolish; (🅸 *lästig*) awkward; **wie d~!**. **d~erweise** *adv* stupidly; (*leider*) unfortunately. **D~heit** *f* **-, -en** stupidity; (*Torheit*) foolishness; (*Handlung*) folly. **D~kopf** *m* 🅸 fool.
dumpf *a* dull
Düne *f* **-, -n** dune
Dung *m* **-s** manure
Dünge|mittel *nt* fertilizer. **d~en** *vt* fertilize. **D~er** *m* **-s,-** fertilizer
dunk|el *a* dark; (*vage*) vague; (*fragwürdig*) shady; **d~les Bier** brown ale; **im D~eln** in the dark
Dunkel|heit *f* **-** darkness. **D~kammer** *f* dark-room. **d~n** *vi* (*haben*) get dark
dünn *a* thin; <*Buch*> slim; (*spärlich*) sparse; (*schwach*) weak
Dunst *m* **-es,¨-e** mist, haze; (*Dampf*) vapour
dünsten *vt* steam
dunstig *a* misty, hazy
Duo *nt* **-s, -s** [instrumental] duet
Duplikat *nt* **-[e]s, -e** duplicate
Dur *nt* **-** (*Mus*) major [key]
durch *prep* (+ *acc*) through; (*mittels*) by; **[geteilt] d~** (*Math*) divided by ● *adv* **die Nacht d~** throughout the night; **d~ und d~ nass** wet through
durchaus *adv* absolutely; **d~ nicht** by no means
durchblättern *vt sep* leaf through
durchblicken *vi sep* (*haben*) look through; **d~ lassen** (*fig*) hint at
Durchblutung *f* circulation
durchbohren *vt insep* pierce
durchbrechen[1]† *vt/i sep* (*haben*) break [in two]
durchbrechen[2]† *vt insep* break through; break <*Schallmauer*>
durchbrennen† *vi sep* (*sein*) burn through; <*Sicherung:*> blow
Durchbruch *m* breakthrough
durchdrehen *v sep* ● *vt* mince ● *vi* (*haben/sein*) 🅸 go crazy
durchdringen† *vi sep* (*sein*) penetrate; (*sich durchsetzen*) get one's way. **d~d** *a* penetrating; <*Schrei*> piercing
durcheinander *adv* in a muddle; <*Person*> confused; **d~ bringen** muddle [up]; confuse <*Person*>; **d~ geraten** get mixed up; **d~ reden** all talk at once. **D~** *nt* **-s** muddle
durchfahren *vi sep* (*sein*) drive through; <*Zug:*> go through
Durchfahrt *f* journey/drive through; **auf der D~** passing through; **'D~ verboten'** 'no thoroughfare'
Durchfall *m* diarrhoea. **d~en**† *vi sep* (*sein*) fall through; (🅸 *versagen*) flop; (*bei Prüfung*) fail
Durchfuhr *f* **-** (*Comm*) transit
durchführ|bar *a* feasible. **d~en** *vt sep* carry out
Durchgang *m* passage; (*Sport*) round; **'D~ verboten'** 'no entry'. **D~sverkehr** *m* through traffic
durchgeben† *vt sep* pass through; (*übermitteln*) transmit; (*Radio, TV*) broadcast
durchgebraten *a* **gut d~** well done
durchgehen† *vi sep* (*sein*) go through; (*davonlaufen*) run away; <*Pferd:*> bolt; **jdm etw d~ lassen** let s.o. get away with sth. **d~d** *a* continuous; **d~d**

geöffnet open all day; **d~der Zug** through train

durchgreifen† *vi sep* (*haben*) reach through; (*vorgehen*) take drastic action. **d~d** *a* drastic

durchhalte|n† *v sep* (*fig*) ● *vi* (*haben*) hold out ● *vt* keep up. **D~vermögen** *nt* stamina

durchkommen† *vi sep* (*sein*) come through; (*gelangen, am Telefon*) get through

durchlassen† *vt sep* let through

durchlässig *a* permeable; (*undicht*) leaky

Durchlauferhitzer *m* **-s,-** geyser

durchlesen† *vt sep* read through

durchleuchten *vt insep* X-ray

durchlöchert *a* riddled with holes

durchmachen *vt sep* go through; (*erleiden*) undergo

Durchmesser *m* **-s,-** diameter

durchnässt *a* wet through

durchnehmen† *vt sep* (*Sch*) do

durchnummeriert *a* numbered consecutively

durchpausen *vt sep* trace

durchqueren *vt insep* cross

Durchreiche *f* **-, -n** hatch

Durchreise *f* journey through; **auf der D~** passing through. **d~n** *vi sep* (*sein*) pass through

durchreißen† *vt/i sep* (*sein*) tear

Durchsage *f* **-, -n** announcement. **d~n** *vt sep* announce

Durchschlag *m* carbon copy; (*Culin*) colander. **d~en**† *v sep* ● *vt* (*Culin*) rub through a sieve; **sich d~en** (*fig*) struggle through ● *vi* (*sein*) <*Sicherung:*> blow. **d~end** *a* (*fig*) effective; <*Erfolg*> resounding

durchschneiden† *vt sep* cut

Durchschnitt *m* average; **im D~** on average. **d~lich** *a* average ● *adv* on average. **D~s-** *pref* average

Durchschrift *f* carbon copy

durchsehen† *v sep* ● *vi* (*haben*) see through ● *vt* look through

durchseihen *vt sep* strain

durchsetzen *vt sep* force through; **sich d~** assert oneself; <*Mode:*> catch on

Durchsicht *f* check

durchsichtig *a* transparent

durchsickern *vi sep* (*sein*) seep through; <*Neuigkeit:*> leak out

durchstehen† *vt sep* (*fig*) come through

durchstreichen† *vt sep* cross out

durchsuch|en *vt insep* search. **D~ung** *f* **-, -en** search

durchwachsen *a* <*Speck*> streaky; (! *gemischt*) mixed

durchwählen *vi sep* (*haben*) (*Teleph*) dial direct

durchweg *adv* without exception

durchwühlen *vt insep* rummage through; ransack <*Haus*>

Durchzug *m* through draught

dürfen†

● *transitive & auxiliary verb*

····► (*Erlaubnis haben zu*) be allowed; may, can. **etw [tun] dürfen** be allowed to do sth. **darf ich das tun?** may *or* can I do that? **nein, das darfst du nicht** no you may not *or* cannot [do that]. **er sagte mir, ich dürfte sofort gehen** he told me I could go at once. **hier darf man nicht rauchen** smoking is prohibited here. **sie darf/durfte es nicht sehen** she must not/was not allowed to see it.

····► (*in Höflichkeitsformeln*) may. **darf ich rauchen?** may I smoke? **darf/dürfte ich um diesen Tanz bitten?** may/might I have the pleasure of this dance?

····► **dürfte** (*sollte*) should, ought. **jetzt dürften sie dort**

angekommen sein they should *or* ought to be there by now. **das dürfte nicht allzu schwer sein** that should not be too difficult. **ich hätte es nicht tun/sagen dürfen** I ought not to have done/ said it
● *intransitive verb*
····➤ (*irgendwohin gehen dürfen*) be allowed to go; may go; can go. **darf ich nach Hause?** may *or* can I go home? **sie durfte nicht ins Theater** she was not allowed to go the theatre

dürftig *a* poor; <*Mahlzeit*> scanty
dürr *a* dry; <*Boden*> arid; (*mager*) skinny. **D~e** *f* **-, -n** drought
Durst *m* **-[e]s** thirst; **D~ haben** be thirsty. **d~ig** *a* thirsty
Dusche *f* **-, -n** shower. **d~n** *vi/r* (*haben*) **[sich] d~n** have a shower
Düse *f* **-, -n** nozzle. **D~nflugzeug** *nt* jet
Dutzend *nt* **-s, -e** dozen. **d~weise** *adv* by the dozen
duzen *vt* **jdn d~** call s.o. 'du'
DVD *f* **-, -s** DVD
Dynam|ik *f* **-** dynamics *sg*; (*fig*) dynamism. **d~isch** *a* dynamic; <*Rente*> index-linked
Dynamit *nt* **-es** dynamite
Dynamo *m* **-s, -s** dynamo
Dynastie *f* **-, -n** dynasty
D-Zug /ˈde:-/ *m* express [train]

Ee

Ebbe *f* **-, -n** low tide
eben *a* level; (*glatt*) smooth; **zu e~er Erde** on the ground floor ● *adv* just; (*genau*) exactly; **e~ noch** only just; (*gerade vorhin*) just now; **das ist es e~!** that's just it! **E~bild** *nt* image
Ebene *f* **-, -n** (*Geog*) plain; (*Geom*) plane; (*fig: Niveau*) level
eben|falls *adv* also; **danke, e~falls** thank you, [the] same to you. **E~holz** *nt* ebony. **e~so** *adv* just the same; (*ebenso sehr*) just as much; **e~so gut** just as good; *adv* just as well; **e~so sehr** just as much; **e~so viel** just as much/many; **e~so wenig** just as little/few; (*noch*) no more
Eber *m* **-s,-** boar
ebnen *vt* level; (*fig*) smooth
Echo *nt* **-s, -s** echo
echt *a* genuine, real; authentic ● *adv* 🄵 really; typically. **E~heit** *f* **-** authenticity
Eck|ball *m* (*Sport*) corner. **E~e** *f* **-, -n** corner; **um die E~e bringen** 🄵 bump off. **e~ig** *a* angular; <*Klammern*> square; (*unbeholfen*) awkward. **E~zahn** *m* canine tooth
Ecu, ECU /eˈky:/ *m* **-[s], -[s]** ecu
edel *a* noble; (*wertvoll*) precious; (*fein*) fine. **e~mütig** *a* magnanimous. **E~stahl** *m* stainless steel. **E~stein** *m* precious stone
Efeu *m* **-s** ivy
Effekt *m* **-[e]s, -e** effect. **E~en** *pl* securities. **e~iv** *a* actual, *adv* -ly; (*wirksam*) effective
EG *f* **-** *abbr* (**Europäische Gemeinschaft**) EC
egal *a* **das ist mir e~** 🄵 it's all the same to me ● *adv* **e~ wie/ wo** no matter how/where
Ego|ismus *m* **-** selfishness. **E~ist(in)** *m* **-en, -en** (*f* **-, -nen**) egoist. **e~istisch** *a* selfish
eh *adv* (*Aust, fam*) anyway
ehe *conj* before; **ehe nicht** until

Ehe *f* **-, -n** marriage. **E~bett** *nt* double bed. **E~bruch** *m* adultery. **E~frau** *f* wife. **e~lich** *a* marital; <*Recht*> conjugal; <*Kind*> legitimate

ehemalig *a* former. **e~s** *adv* formerly

Ehe|mann *m* (*pl* **-männer**) husband. **E~paar** *nt* married couple

eher *adv* earlier, sooner; (*lieber, vielmehr*) rather; (*mehr*) more

Ehering *m* wedding ring

Ehr|e *f* **-, -n** honour. **e~en** *vt* honour. **e~enamtlich** *a* honorary ● *adv* in an honorary capacity. **E~engast** *m* guest of honour. **e~enhaft** *a* honourable. **E~ensache** *f* point of honour. **E~enwort** *nt* word of honour. **e~erbietig** *a* deferential. **E~furcht** *f* reverence; (*Scheu*) awe. **e~fürchtig** *a* reverent. **E~gefühl** *nt* sense of honour. **E~geiz** *m* ambition. **e~geizig** *a* ambitious. **e~lich** *a* honest; **e~lich gesagt** to be honest. **E~lichkeit** *f* - honesty. **e~los** *a* dishonourable. **e-würdig** *a* venerable; (*als Anrede*) Reverend

Ei *nt* **-[e]s, -er** egg

Eibe *f* **-, -n** yew

Eiche *f* **-, -n** oak. **E~l** *f* **-, -n** acorn

eichen *vt* standardize

Eichhörnchen *nt* **-s,-** squirrel

Eid *m* **-[e]s, -e** oath

Eidechse *f* **-, -n** lizard

eidlich *a* sworn ● *adv* on oath

Eidotter *m & nt* egg yolk

Eier|becher *m* egg-cup. **E~kuchen** *m* pancake; (*Omelett*) omelette. **E~schale** *f* eggshell. **E~schnee** *m* beaten egg-white. **E~stock** *m* ovary

Eifer *m* **-s** eagerness. **E~sucht** *f* jealousy. **e~süchtig** *a* jealous

eifrig *a* eager

Eigelb *nt* **-[e]s, -e** [egg] yolk

eigen *a* own; (*typisch*) characteristic (*dat* of); (*seltsam*) odd; (*genau*) particular. **E~art** *f* peculiarity. **e~artig** *a* peculiar. **e~händig** *a* personal; <*Unterschrift*> own. **E~heit** *f* **-, -en** peculiarity. **E~name** *m* proper name. **e~nützig** *a* selfish. **e~s** *adv* specially. **E~schaft** *f* **-, -en** quality; (*Phys*) property; (*Merkmal*) characteristic; (*Funktion*) capacity. **E~schaftswort** *nt* (*pl* **-wörter**) adjective. **E~sinn** *m* obstinacy. **e~sinnig** *a* obstinate

eigentlich *a* actual, real; (*wahr*) true ● *adv* actually, really; (*streng genommen*) strictly speaking

Eigen|tor *nt* own goal. **E~tum** *nt* **-s** property. **E~tümer(in)** *m* **-s,-** (*f* **-, -nen**) owner. **E~tumswohnung** *f* freehold flat. **e~willig** *a* self-willed; <*Stil*> highly individual

eignen (sich) *vr* be suitable

Eil|brief *m* express letter. **E~e** *f* - hurry; **E~e haben** be in a hurry; <*Sache:*> be urgent. **e~en** *vi* (*sein*) hurry ● (*haben*) (*drängen*) be urgent. **e~ig** *a* hurried; (*dringend*) urgent; **es e~ig haben** be in a hurry. **E~zug** *m* semi-fast train

Eimer *m* **-s,-** bucket; (*Abfall-*) bin

ein

● *indefinite article*

····➤ a, (*vor Vokal*) an. **ein Kleid/Apfel/Hotel/Mensch** a dress/an apple/a[n] hotel/a human being. **so ein** such a. **was für ein ...** (*Frage*) what kind of a ...? (*Ausruf*) what a ...!

● *adjective*

····➤ (*Ziffer*) one. **eine Mark** one mark. **wir haben nur eine**

Stunde we only have an/(*betont*) one hour. **eines Tages/Abends** one day/evening
····▸ (*derselbe*) the same. **einer Meinung sein** be of the same opinion. **mit jdm in einem Zimmer schlafen** sleep in the same room as s.o.

einander *pron* one another
Einäscherung *f* **-, -en** cremation
einatmen *vt/i sep* (*haben*) inhale, breathe in
Einbahnstraße *f* one-way street
einbalsamieren *vt sep* embalm
Einband *m* binding
Einbau *m* installation; (*Montage*) fitting. **e~en** *vt sep* install; (*montieren*) fit. **E~küche** *f* fitted kitchen
einbegriffen *pred a* included
Einberufung *f* call-up
Einbettzimmer *nt* single room
einbeulen *vt sep* dent
einbeziehen† *vt sep* **[mit] e~** include; (*berücksichtigen*) take into account
einbiegen† *vi sep* (*sein*) turn
einbild|en *vt sep* **sich** (*dat*) **etw e~en** imagine sth; **sich** (*dat*) **viel e~en** be conceited. **E~ung** *f* imagination; (*Dünkel*) conceit. **E~ungskraft** *f* imagination
einblenden *vt sep* fade in
Einblick *m* insight
einbrech|en† *vi sep* (*haben/sein*) break in; **bei uns ist eingebrochen worden** we have been burgled. **E~er** *m* burglar
einbringen† *vt sep* get in; bring in <*Geld*>
Einbruch *m* burglary; **bei E~ der Nacht** at nightfall
einbürger|n *vt sep* naturalize. **E~ung** *f* **-** naturalization
einchecken /-tʃɛkən/ *vt/i sep* (*haben*) check in
eindecken (sich) *vr sep* stock up
eindeutig *a* unambiguous; (*deutlich*) clear
eindicken *vt sep* (*Culin*) thicken
eindringen† *vi sep* (*sein*) **e~en in** (+ *acc*) penetrate into; (*mit Gewalt*) force one's/<*Wasser:*> its way into; (*Mil*) invade
Eindruck *m* impression
eindrücken *vt sep* crush
eindrucksvoll *a* impressive
ein|e(r,s) *pron* one; (*jemand*) someone; (*man*) one, you
einebnen *vt sep* level
eineiig *a* <*Zwillinge*> identical
eineinhalb *inv a* one and a half; **e~ Stunden** an hour and a half
Einelternfamilie *f* one-parent family
einengen *vt sep* restrict
Einer *m* **-s,-** (*Math*) unit. **e~** *pron s.* **eine(r,s)**. **e~lei** *inv a* ● *attrib a* one kind of; (*eintönig, einheitlich*) the same ● *pred a* [!] immaterial; **es ist mir e~lei** it's all the same to me. **e~seits** *adv* on the one hand
einfach *a* simple; <*Essen*> plain; <*Faden, Fahrt*> single; **e~er Soldat** private. **E~heit** *f* **-** simplicity
einfädeln *vt sep* thread; (*fig; arrangieren*) arrange
einfahr|en† *v sep* ● *vi* (*sein*) arrive; <*Zug:*> pull in ● *vt* (*Auto*) run in. **E~t** *f* arrival; (*Eingang*) entrance, way in; (*Auffahrt*) drive; (*Autobahn-*) access road; **keine E~t** no entry
Einfall *m* idea; (*Mil*) invasion. **e~en**† *vi sep* (*sein*) collapse; (*eindringen*) invade; **jdm e~en** occur to s.o.; **was fällt ihm ein!** what does he think he is doing!
Einfalt *f* **-** naïvety
einfarbig *a* of one colour; <*Stoff, Kleid*> plain

einfass|en *vt sep* edge; set <*Edelstein*>. **E~ung** *f* border, edging

einfetten *vt sep* grease

Einfluss *m* influence. **e~reich** *a* influential

einförmig *a* monotonous. **E~keit** *f* - monotony

einfrieren† *vt/i sep* (*sein*) freeze

einfügen *vt sep* insert; (*einschieben*) interpolate; **sich e~** fit in

einfühlsam *a* sensitive

Einfuhr *f* -, **-en** import

einführ|en *vt sep* introduce; (*einstecken*) insert; (*einweisen*) initiate; (*Comm*) import. **e~end** *a* introductory. **E~ung** *f* introduction; (*Einweisung*) initiation

Eingabe *f* petition; (*Computer*) input

Eingang *m* entrance, way in; (*Ankunft*) arrival

eingebaut *a* built-in; <*Schrank*> fitted

eingeben† *vt sep* hand in; (*Computer*) feed in

eingebildet *a* imaginary; (*überheblich*) conceited

Eingeborene(r) *m/f* native

eingehen† *v sep* ● *vi* (*sein*) come in; (*ankommen*) arrive; (*einlaufen*) shrink; (*sterben*) die; <*Zeitung, Firma:*> fold; **auf etw** (*acc*) **e~** go into sth; (*annehmen*) agree to sth ● *vt* enter into; contract <*Ehe*>; make <*Wette*>; take <*Risiko*>

eingemacht *a* (*Culin*) bottled

eingenommen *pred a* (*fig*) taken (**von** with); prejudiced (**gegen** against)

eingeschneit *a* snowbound

eingeschrieben *a* registered

Einge|ständnis *nt* admission. **e~stehen**† *vt sep* admit

eingetragen *a* registered

Eingeweide *pl* bowels, entrails

eingewöhnen (sich) *vr sep* settle in

eingießen† *vt sep* pour in; (*einschenken*) pour

eingleisig *a* single-track

eingliedern|n *vt sep* integrate. **E~ung** *f* integration

eingravieren *vt sep* engrave

eingreifen† *vi sep* (*haben*) intervene. **E~** *nt* **-s** intervention

Eingriff *m* intervention; (*Med*) operation

einhaken *vt/r sep* **jdn e~** *od* **sich bei jdm e~** take s.o.'s arm

einhalten† *v sep* ● *vt* keep; (*befolgen*) observe ● *vi* (*haben*) stop

einhändigen *vt sep* hand in

einhängen *vt sep* hang; put down <*Hörer*>

einheimisch *a* local; (*eines Landes*) native; (*Comm*) home-produced. **E~e(r)** *m/f* local native

Einheit *f* -, **-en** unity; (*Maß-, Mil*) unit. **e~lich** *a* uniform. **E~spreis** *m* standard price; (*Fahrpreis*) flat fare

einholen *vt sep* catch up with; (*aufholen*) make up for; (*erbitten*) seek; (*einkaufen*) buy

einhüllen *vt sep* wrap

einhundert *inv a* one hundred

einig *a* united; [**sich** (*dat*)] **e~ sein** be in agreement

einig|e(r,s) *pron* some; (*ziemlich viel*) quite a lot of; (*substantivisch*) **e~e** *pl* some; (*mehrere*) several; (*ziemlich viele*) quite a lot; **e~es** *sg* some things; **vor e~er Zeit** some time ago

einigen *vt* unite; unify <*Land*>; **sich e~** come to an agreement

einigermaßen *adv* to some extent; (*ziemlich*) fairly; (*ziemlich gut*) fairly well

Einigkeit *f* - unity; (*Übereinstimmung*) agreement

einjährig *a* one-year-old; **e~e Pflanze** annual

einkalkulieren *vt sep* take into account

einkassieren *vt sep* collect

Einkauf *m* purchase; (*Einkaufen*) shopping; **Einkäufe machen** do some shopping. **e~en** *vt sep* buy; **e~en gehen** go shopping. **E~swagen** *m* shopping trolley

einklammern *vt sep* bracket

Einklang *m* harmony; **in E~ stehen** be in accord (**mit** with)

einkleben *vt sep* stick in

einkleiden *vt sep* fit out

einklemmen *vt sep* clamp

einkochen *v sep* ● *vi* (*sein*) boil down ● *vt* preserve, bottle

Einkommen *nt* **-s** income. **E~[s]steuer** *f* income tax

Einkünfte *pl* income *sg*; (*Einnahmen*) revenue *sg*

einlad|en† *vt sep* load; (*auffordern*) invite; (*bezahlen für*) treat. **E~ung** *f* invitation

Einlage *f* enclosure; (*Schuh-*) arch support; (*Programm-*) interlude; (*Comm*) investment; (*Bank-*) deposit; **Suppe mit E~** soup with noodles/dumplings

Ein|lass *m* **-es** admittance. **e~lassen**† *vt sep* let in; run <*Bad, Wasser*>; **sich auf etw** (*acc*) **e~lassen** get involved in sth

einleben (sich) *vr sep* settle in

Einlege|arbeit *f* inlaid work. **e~n** *vt sep* put in; lay in <*Vorrat*>; lodge <*Protest*>; (*einfügen*) insert; (*Auto*) engage <*Gang*>; (*Culin*) pickle; (*marinieren*) marinade; **eine Pause e~n** have a break. **E~sohle** *f* insole

einleit|en *vt sep* initiate; (*eröffnen*) begin. **E~ung** *f* introduction

einleuchten *vi sep* (*haben*) be clear (*dat* to). **e~d** *a* convincing

einliefer|n *vt sep* take (**ins Krankenhaus** to hospital). **E~ung** *f* admission

einlösen *vt sep* cash <*Scheck*>; redeem <*Pfand*>; (*fig*) keep

einmachen *vt sep* preserve

einmal *adv* once; (*eines Tages*) one *or* some day; **noch/schon e~** again/before; **noch e~ so teuer** twice as expensive; **auf e~** at the same time; (*plötzlich*) suddenly; **nicht e~** not even. **E~eins** *nt* - [multiplication] tables *pl*. **e~ig** *a* (*einzigartig*) unique; (**!** *großartig*) fantastic

einmarschieren *vi sep* (*sein*) march in

einmisch|en (sich) *vr sep* interfere. **E~ung** *f* interference

Einnahme *f* **-, -n** taking; (*Mil*) capture; **E~n** *pl* income *sg*; (*Einkünfte*) revenue *sg*; (*Comm*) receipts; (*eines Ladens*) takings

einnehmen† *vt sep* take; have <*Mahlzeit*>; (*Mil*) capture; take up <*Platz*>

einordnen *vt sep* put in its proper place; (*klassifizieren*) classify; **sich e~** fit in; (*Auto*) get in lane

einpacken *vt sep* pack

einparken *vt sep* park

einpflanzen *vt sep* plant; implant <*Organ*>

einplanen *vt sep* allow for

einprägen *vt sep* impress (**jdm** [up]on s.o.); **sich** (*dat*) **etw e~en** memorize sth

einrahmen *vt sep* frame

einrasten *vi sep* (*sein*) engage

einräumen *vt sep* put away; (*zugeben*) admit; (*zugestehen*) grant

einrechnen *vt sep* include

einreden *v sep* ● *vt* **jdm/sich** (*dat*) **etw e~** persuade s.o./oneself of sth.

einreiben† *vt sep* rub (**mit** with)

einreichen *vt sep* submit; **die Scheidung e~** file for divorce

Einreih|er *m* **-s,-** single-breasted suit. **e~ig** *a* single-breasted

Einreise *f* entry. **e~n** *vi sep* (*sein*) enter (**nach Irland** Ireland)

einrenken *vt sep* (*Med*) set

einricht|en *vt sep* fit out; (*möblieren*) furnish; (*anordnen*) arrange; (*Med*) set <*Bruch*>; (*eröffnen*) set up; **sich e~en** furnish one's home; (*sich einschränken*) economize; (*sich vorbereiten*) prepare (**auf** + *acc* for). **E~ung** *f* furnishing; (*Möbel*) furnishings *pl*; (*Techn*) equipment; (*Vorrichtung*) device; (*Eröffnung*) setting up; (*Institution*) institution; (*Gewohnheit*) practice

einrosten *vi sep* (*sein*) rust; (*fig*) get rusty

eins *inv a & pron* one; **noch e~** one other thing; **mir ist alles e~** [!] it's all the same to me. **E~** *f* **-, -en** one; (*Sch*) ≈ A

einsam *a* lonely; (*allein*) solitary; (*abgelegen*) isolated. **E~keit** *f* **-** loneliness; solitude; isolation

einsammeln *vt sep* collect

Einsatz *m* use; (*Mil*) mission; (*Wett-*) stake; (*E~teil*) insert; **im E~** in action

einschalt|en *vt sep* switch on; (*einschieben*) interpolate; (*fig: beteiligen*) call in; **sich e~en** (*fig*) intervene. **E~quote** *f* (*TV*) viewing figures *pl*; ≈ ratings *pl*

einschätzen *vt sep* assess; (*bewerten*) rate

einschenken *vt sep* pour

einscheren *vi sep* (*sein*) pull in

einschicken *vt sep* send in

einschieben† *vt sep* push in; (*einfügen*) insert

einschiff|en (sich) *vr sep* embark. **E~ung** *f* **-** embarkation

einschlafen† *vi sep* (*sein*) go to sleep; (*aufhören*) peter out

einschläfern *vt sep* lull to sleep; (*betäuben*) put out; (*töten*) put to sleep. **e~d** *a* soporific

Einschlag *m* impact. **e~en**† *v sep* ● *vt* knock in; (*zerschlagen*) smash; (*drehen*) turn; take <*Weg*>; take up <*Laufbahn*> ● *vi* (*haben*) hit/<*Blitz:*> strike (**in etw** *acc* sth); (*Erfolg haben*) be a hit

einschleusen *vt sep* infiltrate

einschließ|en† *vt sep* lock in; (*umgeben*) enclose; (*einkreisen*) surround; (*einbeziehen*) include; **sich e~en** lock oneself in; **Bedienung eingeschlossen** service included. **e~lich** *adv* inclusive ● *prep* (+ *gen*) including

einschneiden† *vt/i sep* (*haben*) **[in] etw** *acc* **e~** cut into sth. **e~d** *a* (*fig*) drastic

Einschnitt *m* cut; (*Med*) incision; (*Lücke*) gap; (*fig*) decisive event

einschränk|en *vt sep* restrict; (*reduzieren*) cut back; **sich e~en** economize. **E~ung** *f* **-, -en** restriction; (*Reduzierung*) reduction; (*Vorbehalt*) reservation

Einschreib|[e]brief *m* registered letter. **e~en**† *vt sep* enter; register <*Brief*>; **sich e~en** put one's name down; (*sich anmelden*) enrol. **E~en** *nt* registered letter/packet; **als** *od* **per E~en** by registered post

einschüchtern *vt sep* intimidate

Einsegnung *f* **-, -en** confirmation

einsehen† *vt sep* inspect; (*lesen*) consult; (*begreifen*) see

einseitig *a* one-sided; (*Pol*) unilateral ● *adv* on one side;

(*fig*) one-sidedly; (*Pol*) unilaterally
einsenden† *vt sep* send in
einsetzen *v sep* ● *vt* put in; (*einfügen*) insert; (*verwenden*) use; put on <*Zug*>; call out <*Truppen*>; (*Mil*) deploy; (*ernennen*) appoint; (*wetten*) stake; (*riskieren*) risk ● *vi* (*haben*) start; <*Winter, Regen:*> set in
Einsicht *f* insight; (*Verständnis*) understanding; (*Vernunft*) reason. **e~ig** *a* understanding
Einsiedler *m* hermit
einsinken† *vi sep* (*sein*) sink in
einspannen *vt sep* harness; **jdn e~** [!] rope s.o. in
einsparen *vt sep* save
einsperren *vt sep* shut/(*im Gefängnis*) lock up
einsprachig *a* monolingual
einspritzen *vt sep* inject
Einspruch *m* objection; **E~ erheben** object; (*Jur*) appeal
einspurig *a* single-track; (*Auto*) single-lane
einst *adv* once; (*Zukunft*) one day
Einstand *m* (*Tennis*) deuce
einstecken *vt sep* put in; post <*Brief*>; (*Electr*) plug in; ([!] *behalten*) pocket; ([!] *hinnehmen*) take; suffer <*Niederlage*>; **etw e~** put sth in one's pocket
einsteigen† *vi sep* (*sein*) get in; (*in Bus/Zug*) get on
einstell|en *vt sep* put in; (*anstellen*) employ; (*aufhören*) stop; (*regulieren*) adjust, set; (*Optik*) focus; tune <*Motor, Zündung*>; tune to <*Sender*>; **sich e~en** turn up; <*Schwierigkeiten:*> arise; **sich e~en auf** (+ *acc*) adjust to; (*sich vorbereiten*) prepare for. **E~ung** *f* employment; (*Regulierung*) adjustment; (*TV, Auto*) tuning; (*Haltung*) attitude
einstig *a* former
einstimmig *a* unanimous. **E~keit** *f* - unanimity
einstöckig *a* single-storey
einstudieren *vt sep* rehearse
einstufen *vt sep* classify
Ein|sturz *m* collapse. **e~stürzen** *vi sep* (*sein*) collapse
einstweilen *adv* for the time being; (*inzwischen*) meanwhile
eintasten *vt sep* key in
eintauchen *vt/i sep* (*sein*) dip in
eintauschen *vt sep* exchange
eintausend *inv a* one thousand
einteil|en *vt sep* divide (**in** + *acc* into); (*Biol*) classify; **sich** (*dat*) **seine Zeit gut e~en** organize one's time well. **e~ig** *a* one piece. **E~ung** *f* division
eintönig *a* monotonous. **E~keit** *f* - monotony
Eintopf *m*, **E~gericht** *nt* stew
Eintracht *f* - harmony
Eintrag *m* **-[e]s,¨e** entry. **e~en**† *vt sep* enter; (*Admin*) register; **sich e~en** put one's name down
einträglich *a* profitable
Eintragung *f* **-, -en** registration
eintreffen† *vi sep* (*sein*) arrive; (*fig*) come true
eintreiben† *vt sep* drive in; (*einziehen*) collect
eintreten† *v sep* ● *vi* (*sein*) enter; (*geschehen*) occur; **in einen Klub e~** join a club; **e~ für** (*fig*) stand up for ● *vt* kick in
Eintritt *m* entrance; (*zu Veranstaltung*) admission; (*Beitritt*) joining; (*Beginn*) beginning. **E~skarte** *f* [admission] ticket
einüben *vt sep* practise
einundachtzig *inv a* eighty-one
Einvernehmen *nt* **-s** understanding; (*Übereinstimmung*) agreement
einverstanden *a* **e~ sein** agree
Einverständnis *nt* agreement; (*Zustimmung*) consent

Einwand *m* **-[e]s,⸚e** objection
Einwander|er *m* immigrant. **e~n** *vi sep* (*sein*) immigrate. **E~ung** *f* immigration
einwandfrei *a* perfect
einwärts *adv* inwards
einwechseln *vt sep* change
einwecken *vt sep* preserve, bottle
Einweg- *pref* non-returnable
einweichen *vt sep* soak
einweih|en *vt sep* inaugurate; (*Relig*) consecrate; (*einführen*) initiate; **in ein Geheimnis e~en** let into a secret. **E~ung** *f* **-, -en** inauguration; consecration; initiation
einweisen† *vt sep* direct; (*einführen*) initiate; **ins Krankenhaus e~** send to hospital
einwerfen† *vt sep* insert; post <*Brief*>; (*Sport*) throw in
einwickeln *vt sep* wrap [up]
einwillig|en *vi sep* (*haben*) consent, agree (**in** + *acc* to). **E~ung** *f* **-** consent
Einwohner|(in) *m* **-s,-** (*f* **-, -nen**) inhabitant. **E~zahl** *f* population
Einwurf *m* interjection; (*Einwand*) objection; (*Sport*) throw-in; (*Münz-*) slot
Einzahl *f* (*Gram*) singular
einzahl|en *vt sep* pay in. **E~ung** *f* payment; (*Einlage*) deposit
einzäunen *vt sep* fence in
Einzel *nt* **-s,-** (*Tennis*) singles *pl*. **E~bett** *nt* single bed. **E~gänger** *m* **-s,-** loner. **E~haft** *f* solitary confinement. **E~handel** *m* retail trade. **E~händler** *m* retailer. **E~haus** *nt* detached house. **E~heit** *f* **-, -en** detail. **E~karte** *f* single ticket. **E~kind** *nt* only child
einzeln *a* single; (*individuell*) individual; (*gesondert*) separate; odd <*Handschuh, Socken*>; **e~e Fälle** some cases. **E~e(r,s)** *pron* **der/die E~e** the individual; **E~e** *pl* some; **im E~en** in detail
Einzel|teil *nt* [component] part. **E~zimmer** *nt* single room
einziehen† *v sep* ● *vt* pull in; draw in <*Atem, Krallen*>; (*Zool, Techn*) retract; indent <*Zeile*>; (*aus dem Verkehr ziehen*) withdraw; (*beschlagnahmen*) confiscate; (*eintreiben*) collect; make <*Erkundigungen*>; (*Mil*) call up ● *vi* (*sein*) enter; (*umziehen*) move in; (*eindringen*) penetrate
einzig *a* only; (*einmalig*) unique; **eine e~e Frage** a a single question ● *adv* only; **e~ und allein** solely. **E~e(r,s)** *pron* **der/die/das E~e** the only one; **ein/kein E~er** a/not a single one; **das E~e, was mich stört** the only thing that bothers me
Eis *nt* **-es** ice; (*Speise-*) ice-cream; **Eis am Stiel** ice lolly; **Eis laufen** skate. **E~bahn** *f* ice rink. **E~bär** *m* polar bear. **E~becher** *m* ice-cream sundae. **E~berg** *m* iceberg. **E~diele** *f* ice-cream parlour
Eisen *nt* **-s,-** iron. **E~bahn** *f* railway
eisern *a* iron; (*fest*) resolute; **e~er Vorhang** (*Theat*) safety curtain; (*Pol*) Iron Curtain
Eis|fach *nt* freezer compartment. **e~gekühlt** *a* chilled. **e~ig** *a* icy. **E~kaffee** *m* iced coffee. **E~lauf** *m* skating. **E~läufer(in)** *m(f)* skater. **E~pickel** *m* ice-axe. **E~scholle** *f* ice-floe. **E~vogel** *m* kingfisher. **E~würfel** *m* ice-cube. **E~zapfen** *m* icicle. **E~zeit** *f* ice age

eitel *a* vain; (*rein*) pure. **E~keit** *f* - vanity
Eiter *m* **-s** pus. **e~n** *vi* (*haben*) discharge pus
Eiweiß *nt* **-es, -e** egg-white
Ekel *m* **-s** disgust; (*Widerwille*) revulsion. **e~haft** *a* nauseating; (*widerlich*) repulsive. **e~n** *vt*/*i* (*haben*) **mich** *od* **mir e~t [es] davor** it makes me feel sick ● *vr* **sich e~n vor** (+ *dat*) find repulsive
eklig *a* disgusting, repulsive
Ekzem *nt* **-s, -e** eczema
elastisch *a* elastic; (*federnd*) springy; (*fig*) flexible
Elch *m* **-[e]s, -e** elk
Elefant *m* **-en, -en** elephant
elegan|t *a* elegant. **E~z** *f* - elegance
Elektri|ker *m* **-s,-** electrician. **e~sch** *a* electric
Elektrizität *f* - electricity. **E~swerk** *nt* power station
Elektr|oartikel *mpl* electrical appliances. **E~ode** *f* **-, -n** electrode. **E~onik** *f* - electronics *sg*. **e~onisch** *a* electronic
Elend *nt* **-s** misery; (*Armut*) poverty. **e~** *a* miserable; (*krank*) poorly; (*gemein*) contemptible. **E~sviertel** *nt* slum
elf *inv a*, **E~** *f* **-, -en** eleven
Elfe *f* **-, -n** fairy
Elfenbein *nt* ivory
Elfmeter *m* (*Fußball*) penalty
elfte(r,s) *a* eleventh
Ell[en]bogen *m* elbow
Ellip|se *f* **-, -n** ellipse. **e~tisch** *a* elliptical
Elsass *nt* - Alsace
elsässisch *a* Alsatian
Elster *f* **-, -n** magpie
elter|lich *a* parental. **E~n** *pl* parents. **e~nlos** *a* orphaned. **E~nteil** *m* parent
Email /e'maj/ *nt* **-s, -s**, **E~le** /e'maljə/ *f* **-, -n** enamel
E-Mail /'i:me:l/ *f* **-, -s** e-mail; e-mail message
Emanzi|pation /-'tsio:n/ *f* - emancipation. **e~piert** *a* emancipated
Embargo *nt* **-s, -s** embargo
Embryo *m* **-s, -s** embryo
Emigr|ant(in) *m* **-en, -en** (*f* **-, -nen**) emigrant. **E~ation** /-'tsio:n/ *f* - emigration. **e~ieren** *vi* (*sein*) emigrate
Empfang *m* **-[e]s,¨e** reception; (*Erhalt*) receipt; **in E~ nehmen** receive; (*annehmen*) accept. **e~en**† *vt* receive; (*Biol*) conceive
Empfäng|er *m* **-s,-** recipient; (*Post-*) addressee; (*Zahlungs-*) payee; (*Radio, TV*) receiver. **E~nis** *f* - (*Biol*) conception
Empfängnisverhütung *f* contraception. **E~smittel** *nt* contraceptive
Empfangs|bestätigung *f* receipt. **E~dame** *f* receptionist. **E~halle** *f* [hotel] foyer
empfehl|en† *vt* recommend. **E~ung** *f* **-, -en** recommendation; (*Gruß*) regards *pl*
empfind|en† *vt* feel. **e~lich** *a* sensitive (**gegen** to); (*zart*) delicate. **E~lichkeit** *f* - sensitivity; delicacy; tenderness; touchiness. **E~ung** *f* **-, -en** sensation; (*Regung*) feeling
empor *adv* (*liter*) up[wards]
empören *vt* incense; **sich e~** be indignant; (*sich auflehnen*) rebel
Emporkömmling *m* **-s, -e** upstart
empör|t *a* indignant. **E~ung** *f* - indignation; (*Auflehnung*) rebellion
Ende *nt* **-s, -n** end; (*eines Films, Romans*) ending; (**[!]** *Stück*) bit; **zu E~ sein** be finished; **etw zu E~ schreiben** finish writing sth; **am E~** at the end; (*schließlich*) in the end; (**[!]** *vielleicht*) perhaps;

(**!** *erschöpft*) at the end of one's tether

endlen *vi* (*haben*) end. **e~gültig** *a* final; (*bestimmt*) definite

Endivie /-iə/ *f* **-, -n** endive

endllich *adv* at last, finally; (*schließlich*) in the end. **e~los** *a* endless. **E~station** *f* terminus. **E~ung** *f* **-, -en** (*Gram*) ending

Energie *f* **-** energy

energisch *a* resolute; (*nachdrücklich*) vigorous

eng *a* narrow; (*beengt*) cramped; (*anliegend*) tight; (*nah*) close; **e~ anliegend** tight-fitting

Engagement /ãgaʒəˈmã:/ *nt* **-s, -s** (*Theat*) engagement; (*fig*) commitment

Engel *m* **-s,-** angel

England *nt* **-s** England

Engländer *m* **-s,-** Englishman; (*Techn*) monkey-wrench; **die E~** the English *pl*. **E~in** *f* **-, -nen** Englishwoman

englisch *a* English. **E~** *nt* **-[s]** (*Lang*) English; **auf E~** in English

Engpass *m* (*fig*) bottle-neck

en gros /ãˈgro:/ *adv* wholesale

Enkel *m* **-s,-** grandson; **E~** *pl* grandchildren. **E~in** *f* **-, -nen** granddaughter. **E~kind** *nt* grandchild. **E~sohn** *m* grandson. **E~tochter** *f* granddaughter

Ensemble /ãˈsã:bəl/ *nt* **-s, -s** ensemble; (*Theat*) company

entartlen *vi* (*sein*) degenerate. **e~et** *a* degenerate

entbehren *vt* do without; (*vermissen*) miss

entbindlen† *vt* release (**von** from); (*Med*) deliver (**von** of) ● *vi* (*haben*) give birth. **E~ung** *f* delivery. **E~ungsstation** *f* maternity ward

entdecklen *vt* discover. **E~er** *m* **-s,-** discoverer; (*Forscher*) explorer. **E~ung** *f* **-, -en** discovery

Ente *f* **-, -n** duck

entehren *vt* dishonour

enteignen *vt* dispossess; expropriate <*Eigentum*>

enterben *vt* disinherit

Enterich *m* **-s, -e** drake

entfallen† *vi* (*sein*) not apply; **auf jdn e~** be s.o.'s share

entfernlen *vt* remove; **sich e~en** leave. **e~t** *a* distant; (*schwach*) vague; **2 Kilometer e~t** 2 kilometres away; **e~t verwandt** distantly related. **E~ung** *f* **-, -en** removal; (*Abstand*) distance; (*Reichweite*) range

entfliehen† *vi* (*sein*) escape

entfremden *vt* alienate

entfrosten *vt* defrost

entführlen *vt* abduct, kidnap; hijack <*Flugzeug*>. **E~er** *m* abductor, kidnapper; hijacker. **E~ung** *f* abduction, kidnapping; hijacking

entgegen *adv* towards ● *prep* (+ *dat*) contrary to. **e~gehen**† *vi sep* (*sein*) (+ *dat*) go to meet; (*fig*) be heading for. **e~gesetzt** *a* opposite; (*gegensätzlich*) opposing. **e~kommen**† *vi sep* (*sein*) (+ *dat*) come to meet; (*zukommen auf*) come towards; (*fig*) oblige. **E~kommen** *nt* **-s** helpfulness; (*Zugeständnis*) concession. **e~kommend** *a* approaching; <*Verkehr*> oncoming; (*fig*) obliging. **e~nehmen**† *vt sep* accept. **e~wirken** *vi sep* (*haben*) (+ *dat*) counteract; (*fig*) oppose

entgegnlen *vt* reply (**auf** + *acc* to). **E~ung** *f* **-, -en** reply

entgehen† *vi sep* (*sein*) (+ *dat*) escape; **jdm e~** (*unbemerkt bleiben*) escape s.o.'s notice; **sich** (*dat*) **etw e~ lassen** miss sth

Entgelt *nt* **-[e]s** payment; **gegen E~** for money
entgleis|en *vi* (*sein*) be derailed; (*fig*) make a gaffe. **E~ung** *f* **-, -en** derailment; (*fig*) gaffe
entgräten *vt* fillet, bone
Enthaarungsmittel *nt* depilatory
enthalt|en† *vt* contain; **in etw** (*dat*) **e~en sein** be contained/ (*eingeschlossen*) included in sth; **sich der Stimme e~en** (*Pol*) abstain. **e~sam** *a* abstemious. **E~ung** *f* (*Pol*) abstention
enthaupten *vt* behead
entheben† *vt* **jdn seines Amtes e~** relieve s.o. of his post
Enthüllung *f* **-, -en** revelation
Enthusias|mus *m* **-** enthusiast. **E~t** *m* **-en, -en** enthusiast
entkernen *vt* stone; core <*Apfel*>
entkleiden *vt* undress; **sich e~en** undress
entkommen† *vi* (*sein*) escape
entkorken *vt* uncork
entladen† *vt* unload; (*Electr*) discharge; **sich e~** discharge; <*Gewitter:*> break; <*Zorn:*> explode
entlang *adv & prep* (+ *preceding acc or following dat*) along; **die Straße e~** along the road; **an etw** (*dat*) **e~** along sth. **e~fahren**† *vi sep* (*sein*) drive along. **e~gehen**† *vi sep* (*sein*) walk along
entlarven *vt* unmask
entlass|en† *vt* dismiss; (*aus Krankenhaus*) discharge; (*aus der Haft*) release. **E~ung** *f* **-, -en** dismissal; discharge; release
entlast|en *vt* relieve the strain on; ease <*Gewissen, Verkehr*>; relieve (**von** of); (*Jur*) exonerate. **E~ung** *f* **-** relief; exoneration
entlaufen† *vi* (*sein*) run away
entleeren *vt* empty
entlegen *a* remote
entlohnen *vt* pay
entlüft|en *vt* ventilate. **E~er** *m* **-s,-** extractor fan. **E~ung** *f* ventilation
entmündigen *vt* declare incapable of managing one's own affairs
entmutigen *vt* discourage
entnehmen† *vt* take (*dat* from); (*schließen*) gather (*dat* from)
entpuppen (sich) *vr* (*fig*) turn out (**als etw** to be sth)
entrahmt *a* skimmed
entrichten *vt* pay
entrinnen† *vi* (*sein*) escape
entrüst|en *vt* fill with indignation; **sich e~en** be indignant (**über** + *acc* at). **e~et** *a* indignant. **E~ung** *f* **-** indignation
entsaft|en *vt* extract the juice from. **E~er** *m* **-s,-** juice extractor
entsagen *vi* (*haben*) (+ *dat*) renounce
entschädig|en *vt* compensate. **E~ung** *f* **-, -en** compensation
entschärfen *vt* defuse
entscheid|en† *vt/i* (*haben*) decide; **sich e~en** decide; <*Sache:*> be decided. **e~end** *a* decisive; (*kritisch*) crucial. **E~ung** *f* decision
entschließen† **(sich)** *vr* decide, make up one's mind; **sich anders e~** change one's mind
entschlossen *a* determined; (*energisch*) resolute; **kurz e~** without hesitation. **E~heit** *f* **-** determination
Entschluss *m* decision
entschlüsseln *vt* decode
entschuld|bar *a* excusable. **e~igen** *vt* excuse; **sich e~igen** apologize (**bei** to); **e~igen Sie [bitte]!** sorry! (*bei Frage*) excuse me. **E~igung** *f* **-, -en** apology;

(*Ausrede*) excuse; **um E~igung bitten** apologize

entsetz|en *vt* horrify. **E~en** *nt* **-s** horror. **e~lich** *a* horrible; (*schrecklich*) terrible

Entsorgung *f* **-** waste disposal

entspann|en *vt* relax; **sich e~en** relax; <*Lage:*> ease. **E~ung** *f* **-** relaxation; easing; (*Pol*) détente

entsprechen† *vi* (*haben*) (+ *dat*) correspond to; (*übereinstimmen*) agree with. **e~d** *a* corresponding; (*angemessen*) appropriate; (*zuständig*) relevant ● *adv* correspondingly; appropriately; (*demgemäß*) accordingly ● *prep* (+ *dat*) in accordance with

entspringen† *vi* (*sein*) <*Fluss:*> rise; (*fig*) arise, spring (*dat* from)

entstammen *vi* (*sein*) come/ (*abstammen*) be descended (*dat* from)

entsteh|en† *vi* (*sein*) come into being; (*sich bilden*) form; (*sich entwickeln*) develop; <*Brand:*> start; (*stammen*) originate. **E~ung** *f* **-** origin; formation; development

entstell|en *vt* disfigure; (*verzerren*) distort. **E~ung** *f* disfigurement; distortion

entstört *a* (*Electr*) suppressed

enttäusch|en *vt* disappoint. **E~ung** *f* disappointment

entwaffnen *vt* disarm

entwässer|n *vt* drain. **E~ung** *f* **-** drainage

entweder *conj & adv* either

entwerfen† *vt* design; (*aufsetzen*) draft; (*skizzieren*) sketch

entwert|en *vt* devalue; (*ungültig machen*) cancel. **E~er** *m* **-s,-** ticket-cancelling machine. **E~ung** *f* devaluation; cancelling

entwick|eln *vt* develop; **sich e~eln** develop. **E~lung** *f* **-, -en** development; (*Biol*) evolution. **E~lungsland** *nt* developing country

entwöhnen *vt* wean (*gen* from); cure <*Süchtige*>

entwürdigend *a* degrading

Entwurf *m* design; (*Konzept*) draft; (*Skizze*) sketch

entwurzeln *vt* uproot

entzie|hen† *vt* take away (*dat* from); **jdm den Führerschein e~hen** disqualify s.o. from driving; **sich e~hen** (+ *dat*) withdraw from. **E~hungskur** *f* treatment for drug/alcohol addiction

entziffern *vt* decipher

Entzug *m* withdrawal; (*Vorenthaltung*) deprivation

entzünd|en *vt* ignite; (*anstecken*) light; (*fig: erregen*) inflame; **sich e~en** ignite; (*Med*) become inflamed. **e~et** *a* (*Med*) inflamed. **e~lich** *a* inflammable. **E~ung** *f* (*Med*) inflammation

entzwei *a* broken

Enzian *m* **-s, -e** gentian

Enzyklo|pädie *f* **-, -en** encyclopaedia. **e~pädisch** *a* encyclopaedic

Enzym *nt* **-s, -e** enzyme

Epidemie *f* **-, -n** epidemic

Epi|lepsie *f* **-** epilepsy. **E~leptiker(in)** *m* **-s,-** (*f* **-, -nen**) epileptic. **e~leptisch** *a* epileptic

Epilog *m* **-s, -e** epilogue

Episode *f* **-, -n** episode

Epoche *f* **-, -n** epoch

Epos *nt* **-/Epen** epic

er *pron* he; (*Ding, Tier*) it

erachten *vt* consider (**für nötig** necessary). **E~** *nt* **-s meines E~s** in my opinion

erbarmen (sich) *vr* have pity/ <*Gott:*> mercy (*gen* on). **E~** *nt* **-s** pity; mercy

erbärmlich *a* wretched
erbauen *vt* build; (*fig*) edify; **nicht erbaut von** [!] not pleased about
Erbe¹ *m* **-n, -n** heir
Erbe² *nt* **-s** inheritance; (*fig*) heritage. **e~n** *vt* inherit
erbeuten *vt* get; (*Mil*) capture
Erbfolge *f* (*Jur*) succession
erbieten† (sich) *vr* offer (**zu** to)
Erbin *f* **-, -nen** heiress
erbitten† *vt* ask for
erbittert *a* bitter; (*heftig*) fierce
erblassen *vi* (*sein*) turn pale
erblich *a* hereditary
erblicken *vt* catch sight of
erblinden *vi* (*sein*) go blind
erbrechen† *vt* vomit ● *vi/r* **[sich] e~** vomit. **E~** *nt* **-s** vomiting
Erbschaft *f* **-, -en** inheritance
Erbse *f* **-, -n** pea
Erb|stück *nt* heirloom. **E~teil** *nt* inheritance
Erd|apfel *m* (*Aust*) potato. **E~beben** *nt* **-s,-** earthquake. **E~beere** *f* strawberry
Erde *f* **-, -n** earth; (*Erdboden*) ground; (*Fußboden*) floor. **e~n** *vt* (*Electr*) earth
erdenklich *a* imaginable
Erd|gas *nt* natural gas. **E~geschoss** *nt* ground floor. **E~kugel** *f* globe. **E~kunde** *f* geography. **E~nuss** *f* peanut. **E~öl** *nt* [mineral] oil
erdrosseln *vt* strangle
erdrücken *vt* crush to death
Erd|rutsch *m* landslide. **E~teil** *m* continent
erdulden *vt* endure
ereignen (sich) *vr* happen
Ereignis *nt* **-ses, -se** event. **e~los** *a* uneventful. **e~reich** *a* eventful
Eremit *m* **-en, -en** hermit
erfahr|en† *vt* learn, hear; (*erleben*) experience ● *a* experienced. **E~ung** *f* **-, -en** experience; **in E~ung bringen** find out
erfassen *vt* seize; (*begreifen*) grasp; (*einbeziehen*) include; (*aufzeichnen*) record
erfind|en† *vt* invent. **E~er** *m* **-s,-** inventor. **e~erisch** *a* inventive. **E~ung** *f* **-, -en** invention
Erfolg *m* **-[e]s, -e** success; (*Folge*) result; **E~ haben** be successful. **e~en** *vi* (*sein*) take place; (*geschehen*) happen. **e~los** *a* unsuccessful. **e~reich** *a* successful
erforder|lich *a* required, necessary. **e~n** *vt* require, demand
erforsch|en *vt* explore; (*untersuchen*) investigate. **E~ung** *f* exploration; investigation
erfreu|en *vt* please. **e~lich** *a* pleasing. **e~licherweise** *adv* happily. **e~t** *a* pleased
erfrier|en† *vi* (*sein*) freeze to death; <*Glied:*> become frostbitten; <*Pflanze:*> be killed by the frost. **E~ung** *f* **-, -en** frostbite
erfrisch|en *vt* refresh. **E~ung** *f* **-, -en** refreshment
erfüll|en *vt* fill; (*nachkommen*) fulfil; serve <*Zweck*>; discharge <*Pflicht:*> **sich e~en** come true. **E~ung** *f* fulfilment
erfunden *a* invented
ergänz|en *vt* complement; (*hinzufügen*) add. **E~ung** *f* **-, -en** complement; supplement; (*Zusatz*) addition
ergeben† *vt* produce; (*zeigen*) show, establish; **sich e~en** result; <*Schwierigkeit:*> arise; (*kapitulieren*) surrender; (*sich fügen*) submit ● *a* devoted; (*resigniert*) resigned

Ergebnis *nt* **-ses, -se** result. **e～los** *a* fruitless
ergiebig *a* productive; (*fig*) rich
ergreifen† *vt* seize; take <*Maßnahme, Gelegenheit*>; take up <*Beruf*>; (*rühren*) move; **die Flucht e～** flee. **e～d** *a* moving
ergriffen *a* deeply moved. **E～heit** *f* **-** emotion
ergründen *vt* (*fig*) get to the bottom of
erhaben *a* raised; (*fig*) sublime
Erhalt *m* **-[e]s** receipt. **e～en**† *vt* receive, get; (*gewinnen*) obtain; (*bewahren*) preserve, keep; (*instand halten*) maintain; (*unterhalten*) support; **am Leben e～en** keep alive ● *a* **gut/schlecht e～en** in good/bad condition; **e～en bleiben** survive
erhältlich *a* obtainable
Erhaltung *f* **-** preservation; maintenance
erhängen (sich) *vr* hang oneself
erheb|en† *vt* raise; levy <*Steuer*>; charge <*Gebühr*>; **Anspruch e～en** lay claim (**auf** + *acc* to); **Protest e～en** protest; **sich e～en** rise; <*Frage*:> arise. **e～lich** *a* considerable. **E～ung** *f* **-, -en** elevation; (*Anhöhe*) rise; (*Aufstand*) uprising; (*Ermittlung*) survey
erheiter|n *vt* amuse. **E～ung** *f* **-** amusement
erhitzen *vt* heat
erhöh|en *vt* raise; (*fig*) increase; **sich e～en** rise, increase. **E～ung** *f* **-, -en** increase
erhol|en (sich) *vr* recover (**von** from); (*nach Krankheit*) convalesce; (*sich ausruhen*) have a rest. **e～sam** *a* restful. **E～ung** *f* **-** recovery; (*Ruhe*) rest
erinner|n *vt* remind (**an** + *acc* of); **sich e～n** remember (**an jdn/etw** s.o./sth). **E～ung** *f* **-, -en** memory; (*Andenken*) souvenir
erkält|en (sich) *vr* catch a cold; **e～et sein** have a cold. **E～ung** *f* **-, -en** cold
erkenn|bar *a* recognizable; (*sichtbar*) visible. **e～en**† *vt* recognize; (*wahrnehmen*) distinguish. **E～tnis** *f* **-, -se** recognition; realization; (*Wissen*) knowledge; **die neuesten E～tnisse** the latest findings
Erker *m* **-s,-** bay
erklär|en *vt* declare; (*erläutern*) explain; **sich bereit e～en** agree (**zu** to). **e～end** *a* explanatory. **e～lich** *a* explicable; (*verständlich*) understandable. **e～licherweise** *adv* understandably. **E～ung** *f* **-, -en** declaration; explanation; **öffentliche E～ung** public statement
erkrank|en *vi* (*sein*) fall ill; be taken ill (**an** + *dat* with). **E～ung** *f* **-, -en** illness
erkundig|en (sich) *vr* enquire (**nach jdm/etw** after s.o./about sth). **E～ung** *f* **-, -en** enquiry
erlangen *vt* attain, get
Erlass *m* **-es,¨-e** (*Admin*) decree; (*Befreiung*) exemption; (*Straf-*) remission
erlassen† *vt* (*Admin*) issue; **jdm etw e～** exempt s.o. from sth; let s.o. off <*Strafe*>
erlauben *vt* allow, permit; **ich kann es mir nicht e～** I can't afford it
Erlaubnis *f* **-** permission. **E～schein** *m* permit
erläutern *vt* explain
Erle *f* **-, -n** alder
erleb|en *vt* experience; (*mit-*) see; have <*Überraschung*>. **E～nis** *nt* **-ses, -se** experience
erledigen *vt* do; (*sich befassen mit*) deal with; (*beenden*) finish; (*entscheiden*) settle; (*töten*) kill
erleichter|n *vt* lighten; (*vereinfachen*) make easier;

(*befreien*) relieve; (*lindern*) ease. **e~t** *a* relieved. **E~ung** *f* - relief

erleiden† *vt* suffer

erleuchten *vt* illuminate; **hell erleuchtet** brightly lit

erlogen *a* untrue, false

Erlös *m* **-es** proceeds *pl*

erlöschen† *vi* (*sein*) go out; (*vergehen*) die; (*aussterben*) die out; (*ungültig werden*) expire; **erloschener Vulkan** extinct volcano

erlös|en *vt* save; (*befreien*) release (**von** from); (*Relig*) redeem. **e~t** *a* relieved. **E~ung** *f* release; (*Erleichterung*) relief; (*Relig*) redemption

ermächtig|en *vt* authorize. **E~ung** *f* **-, -en** authorization

Ermahnung *f* exhortation; admonition

ermäßig|en *vt* reduce. **E~ung** *f* **-, -en** reduction

ermessen† *vt* judge; (*begreifen*) appreciate. **E~** *nt* **-s** discretion; (*Urteil*) judgement; **nach eigenem E~** at one's own discretion

ermitt|eln *vt* establish; (*herausfinden*) find out ● *vi* (*haben*) investigate (**gegen jdn** s.o.). **E~lungen** *fpl* investigations. **E~lungsverfahren** *nt* (*Jur*) preliminary inquiry

ermöglichen *vt* make possible

ermord|en *vt* murder. **E~ung** *f* **-, -en** murder

ermüd|en *vt* tire ● *vi* (*sein*) get tired. **E~ung** *f* - tiredness

ermutigen *vt* encourage. **e~d** *a* encouraging

ernähr|en *vt* feed; (*unterhalten*) support, keep; **sich e~en von** live/<*Tier*:> feed on. **E~er** *m* **-s,-** breadwinner. **E~ung** *f* - nourishment; nutrition; (*Kost*) diet

ernenn|en† *vt* appoint. **E~ung** *f* **-, -en** appointment

erneu|ern *vt* renew; (*auswechseln*) replace; change <*Verband*>; (*renovieren*) renovate. **E~erung** *f* - renewal; replacement; renovation. **e~t** *a* renewed; (*neu*) new ● *adv* again

ernst *a* serious; **e~ nehmen** take seriously. **E~** *m* **-es** seriousness; **im E~** seriously; **mit einer Drohung E~ machen** carry out a threat; **ist das dein E~?** are you serious? **e~haft** *a* serious. **e~lich** *a* serious

Ernte *f* **-, -n** harvest; (*Ertrag*) crop. **E~dankfest** *nt* harvest festival. **e~n** *vt* harvest; (*fig*) reap, win

ernüchtern *vt* sober up; (*fig*) bring down to earth. **e~d** *a* (*fig*) sobering

Erober|er *m* **-s,-** conqueror. **e~n** *vt* conquer. **E~ung** *f* **-, -en** conquest

eröffn|en *vt* open; **jdm etw e~en** announce sth to s.o. **E~ung** *f* opening; (*Mitteilung*) announcement

erörter|n *vt* discuss. **E~ung** *f* **-, -en** discussion

Erot|ik *f* - eroticism. **e~isch** *a* erotic

Erpel *m* **-s,-** drake

erpicht *a* **e~auf** (+ *acc*) keen on

erpress|en *vt* extort; blackmail <*Person*>. **E~er** *m* **-s,-** blackmailer. **E~ung** *f* - extortion; blackmail

erprob|en *vt* test. **e~t** *a* proven

erraten† *vt* guess

erreg|bar *a* excitable. **e~en** *vt* excite; (*hervorrufen*) arouse; **sich e~en** get worked up. **e~end** *a* exciting. **E~er** *m* **-s,-** (*Med*) germ. **e~t** *a* agitated; (*hitzig*) heated. **E~ung** *f* - excitement

erreich|bar *a* within reach; <*Ziel*> attainable; <*Person*>

available. **e~en** *vt* reach; catch <*Zug*>; live to <*Alter*>; (*durchsetzen*) achieve
errichten *vt* erect
erringen† *vt* gain, win
erröten *vi* (*sein*) blush
Errungenschaft *f* **-, -en** achievement; (**!** *Anschaffung*) acquisition
Ersatz *m* **-es** replacement, substitute; (*Entschädigung*) compensation. **E~reifen** *m* spare tyre. **E~teil** *nt* spare part
erschaffen† *vt* create
erschein|en† *vi* (*sein*) appear; <*Buch:*> be published. **E~ung** *f* **-, -en** appearance; (*Person*) figure; (*Phänomen*) phenomenon; (*Symptom*) symptom; (*Geist*) apparition
erschieß|en† *vt* shoot [dead]. **E~ungskommando** *nt* firing squad
erschlaffen *vi* (*sein*) go limp
erschlagen† *vt* beat to death; (*tödlich treffen*) strike dead; **vom Blitz e~ werden** be killed by lightning
erschließen† *vt* develop
erschöpf|en *vt* exhaust. **e~t** *a* exhausted. **E~ung** *f* **-** exhaustion
erschrecken† *vi* (*sein*) get a fright ● *vt* (*reg*) startle; (*beunruhigen*) alarm; **du hast mich erschreckt** you gave me a fright
erschrocken *a* frightened; (*erschreckt*) startled
erschütter|n *vt* shake; (*ergreifen*) upset deeply. **E~ung** *f* **-, -en** shock
erschwinglich *a* affordable
ersehen† *vt* (*fig*) see (**aus** from)
ersetzen *vt* replace; make good <*Schaden*>; refund <*Kosten*>; **jdm etw e~** compensate s.o. for sth
ersichtlich *a* obvious, apparent
erspar|en *vt* save. **E~nis** *f* **-, -se** saving; **E~nisse** savings
erst *adv* (*zuerst*) first; (*noch nicht mehr als*) only; (*nicht vor*) not until; **e~ dann** only then; **eben e~** [only] just
erstarren *vi* (*sein*) solidify; (*gefrieren*) freeze; (*steif werden*) go stiff; (*vor Schreck*) be paralysed
erstatten *vt* (*zurück-*) refund; **Bericht e~** report (**jdm** to s.o.)
Erstaufführung *f* first performance, première
erstaun|en *vt* amaze, astonish. **E~en** *nt* amazement, astonishment. **e~lich** *a* amazing
Erst|ausgabe *f* first edition. **e~e(r,s)** *a* first; (*beste*) best; **e~e Hilfe** first aid. **E~e(r)** *m/f* first; (*Beste*) best; **fürs E~e** for the time being; **als E~es** first of all; **er kam als E~er** he arrived first
erstechen† *vt* stab to death
ersteigern *vt* buy at an auction
erst|ens *adv* firstly, in the first place. **e~ere(r,s)** *a* the former; **der/die/das E~ere** the former
ersticken *vt* suffocate; smother <*Flammen*> ● *vi* (*sein*) suffocate. **E~** *nt* **-s** suffocation; **zum E~** stifling
erstklassig *a* first-class
ersuchen *vt* ask, request. **E~** *nt* **-s** request
ertappen *vt* **!** catch
erteilen *vt* give (**jdm** s.o.)
ertönen *vi* (*sein*) sound; (*erschallen*) ring out
Ertrag *m* **-[e]s,¨e** yield. **e~en**† *vt* bear
erträglich *a* bearable; (*leidlich*) tolerable
ertränken *vt* drown
ertrinken† *vi* (*sein*) drown

erübrigen (sich) *vr* be unnecessary
erwachsen *a* grown-up. **E∼e(r)** *m/f* adult, grown-up
erwäg|en† *vt* consider. **E∼ung** *f* **-, -en** consideration; **in E∼ung ziehen** consider
erwähn|en *vt* mention. **E∼ung** *f* **-, -en** mention
erwärmen *vt* warm; **sich e∼** warm up; (*fig*) warm (**für** to)
erwart|en *vt* expect; (*warten auf*) wait for. **E∼ung** *f* **-, -en** expectation
erweisen† *vt* prove; (*bezeigen*) do <*Gefallen, Dienst, Ehre*>; **sich e∼ als** prove to be
erweitern *vt* widen; dilate <*Pupille*>; (*fig*) extend, expand
Erwerb *m* **-[e]s** acquisition; (*Kauf*) purchase; (*Brot-*) livelihood; (*Verdienst*) earnings *pl*. **e∼en**† *vt* acquire; (*kaufen*) purchase. **e∼slos** *a* unemployed. **e∼stätig** *a* employed
erwider|n *vt* reply; return <*Besuch, Gruß*>. **E∼ung** *f* **-, -en** reply
erwirken *vt* obtain
erwürgen *vt* strangle
Erz *nt* **-es, -e** ore
erzähl|en *vt* tell (**jdm** s.o.) ● *vi* (*haben*) talk (**von** about). **E∼er** *m* **-s,-** narrator. **E∼ung** *f* **-, -en** story, tale
Erzbischof *m* archbishop
erzeug|en *vt* produce; (*Electr*) generate. **E∼er** *m* **-s,-** producer. **E∼nis** *nt* **-ses, -se** product; **landwirtschaftliche E∼nisse** farm produce *sg*
erzieh|en† *vt* bring up; (*Sch*) educate. **E∼er** *m* **-s,-** [private] tutor. **E∼erin** *f* **-, -nen** governess. **E∼ung** *f* **-** upbringing; education
erzielen *vt* achieve; score <*Tor*>
erzogen *a* **gut/schlecht e∼** well/badly brought up

es
● *pronoun*
····➤ (*Sache*) it; (*weibliche Person*) she/her; (*männliche Person*) he/him. **ich bin es** it's me. **wir sind traurig, ihr seid es auch** we are sad, and so are you. **er ist es, der ...** he is the one who .... **es sind Studenten** they are students
····➤ (*impers*) it. **es hat geklopft** there was a knock. **es klingelt** someone is ringing. **es wird schöner** the weather is improving. **es geht ihm gut/schlecht** he is well/unwell. **es lässt sich aushalten** it is bearable. **es gibt** there is *or* (*pl*) are
····➤ (*als formales Objekt*) **er hat es gut** he has it made; he's well off. **er meinte es gut** he meant well. **ich hoffe/glaube es** I hope/think so

Esche *f* **-, -n** ash
Esel *m* **-s,-** donkey; (🅸 *Person*) ass
Eskimo *m* **-[s], -[s]** Eskimo
Eskort|e *f* **-, -n** (*Mil*) escort. **e∼ieren** *vt* escort
essbar *a* edible
essen† *vt/i* (*haben*) eat; **zu Mittag/Abend e∼** have lunch/supper; **e∼ gehen** eat out. **E∼** *nt* **-s,-** food; (*Mahl*) meal; (*festlich*) dinner
Esser(in) *m* **-s,-** (*f* **-, -nen**) eater
Essig *m* **-s** vinegar. **E∼gurke** *f* [pickled] gherkin
Ess|löffel *m* ≈ dessertspoon. **E∼stäbchen** *ntpl* chopsticks. **E∼tisch** *m* dining-table. **E∼waren** *fpl* food *sg*; (*Vorräte*) provisions. **E∼zimmer** *nt* dining-room
Estland *nt* **-s** Estonia

etablieren (sich) *vr* establish oneself/<*Geschäft*:> itself
Etage /e'ta:ʒə/ *f* **-, -n** storey. **E~nbett** *nt* bunk-beds *pl.* **E~nwohnung** *f* flat
Etappe *f* **-, -n** stage
Etat /e'ta:/ *m* **-s, -s** budget
Eth|ik *f* **-** ethic; (*Sittenlehre*) ethics *sg.* **e~isch** *a* ethical
ethnisch *a* ethnic; **e~e Säuberung** ethnic cleansing
Etikett *nt* **-[e]s, -e[n]** label; (*Preis-*) tag. **e~ieren** *vt* label
Etui /e'tvi:/ *nt* **-s, -s** case
etwa *adv* (*ungefähr*) about; (*zum Beispiel*) for instance; (*womöglich*) perhaps; **nicht e~, dass** ... not that ...; **denkt nicht e~** ... don't imagine ...
etwas *pron* something; (*fragend/verneint*) anything; (*ein bisschen*) some, a little; **sonst noch e~?** anything else? **so e~ Ärgerliches!** what a nuisance! ● *adv* a bit
Etymologie *f* **-** etymology
EU *f* **-** *abbr* (**Europäische Union**) EU
euch *pron* (*acc of* **ihr** *pl*) you; (*dat*) [to] you; (*refl*) yourselves; (*einander*) each other
euer *poss pron pl* your. **e~e, e~t-** *s.* **eure, euret-**
Eule *f* **-, -n** owl
Euphorie *f* **-** euphoria
eur|e *poss pron pl* your. **e~e(r,s)** *poss pron* yours. **e~etwegen** *adv* for your sake; (*wegen euch*) because of you, on your account. **e~etwillen** *adv* **um e~etwillen** for your sake. **e~ige** *poss pron* **der/die/das e~ige** yours
Euro *m* **-[s], -s** euro. **E~-** *pref* Euro-
Europa *nt* **-s** Europe. **E~-** *pref* European
Europä|er(in) *m* **-s,-** (*f* **-, -nen**) European. **e~isch** *a* European
Euter *nt* **-s,-** udder
evakuier|en *vt* evacuate. **E~ung** *f* **-** evacuation
evan|gelisch *a* Protestant. **E~gelium** *nt* **-s, -ien** gospel
eventuell *a* possible ● *adv* possibly; (*vielleicht*) perhaps
Evolution /-'tsio:n/ *f* **-** evolution
ewig *a* eternal; (*endlos*) never-ending; **e~ dauern** ▮ take ages. **E~keit** *f* **-** eternity
Examen *nt* **-s,-** & **-mina** (*Sch*) examination
Exemplar *nt* **-s, -e** specimen; (*Buch*) copy. **e~isch** *a* exemplary
exerzieren *vt/i* (*haben*) (*Mil*) drill; (*üben*) practise
exhumieren *vt* exhume
Exil *nt* **-s** exile
Existenz *f* **-, -en** existence; (*Lebensgrundlage*) livelihood
existieren *vi* (*haben*) exist
exklusiv *a* exclusive. **e~e** *prep* (+ *gen*) excluding
exkommunizieren *vt* excommunicate
Exkremente *npl* excrement *sg*
Expedition /-'tsio:n/ *f* **-, -en** expedition
Experiment *nt* **-[e]s, -e** experiment. **e~ieren** *vi* (*haben*) experiment
Experte *m* **-n, -n** expert
explo|dieren *vi* (*sein*) explode. **E~sion** *f* **-, -en** explosion
Expor|t *m* **-[e]s, -e** export. **E~teur** /-'tø:ɐ/ *m* **-s, -e** exporter. **e~tieren** *vt* export
extra *adv* separately; (*zusätzlich*) extra; (*eigens*) specially; (▮ *absichtlich*) on purpose
extravagant *a* flamboyant; (*übertrieben*) extravagant
extravertiert *a* extrovert

extrem *a* extreme. **E~ist** *m* **-en, -en** extremist

Exzellenz *f* **-** (*title*) Excellency

Exzentr|iker *m* **-s,-** eccentric. **e~isch** *a* eccentric

Ff

Fabel *f* **-, -n** fable. **f~haft** *a* [!] fantastic

Fabrik *f* **-, -en** factory. **F~ant** *m* **-en, -en** manufacturer. **F~at** *nt* **-[e]s, -e** product; (*Marke*) make. **F~ation** /-'tsio:n/ *f* **-** manufacture

Fach *nt* **-[e]s,¨er** compartment; (*Schub-*) drawer; (*Gebiet*) field; (*Sch*) subject. **F~arbeiter** *m* skilled worker. **F~arzt** *m*, **F~ärztin** *f* specialist. **F~ausdruck** *m* technical term

Fächer *m* **-s,-** fan

Fach|gebiet *nt* field. **f~kundig** *a* expert. **f~lich** *a* technical; (*beruflich*) professional. **F~mann** *m* (*pl* **-leute**) expert. **f~männisch** *a* expert. **F~schule** *f* technical college. **F~werkhaus** *nt* half-timbered house. **F~wort** *nt* (*pl* **-wörter**) technical term

Fackel *f* **-, -n** torch

fade *a* insipid; (*langweilig*) dull

Faden *m* **-s,¨** thread; (*Bohnen-*) string; (*Naut*) fathom

Fagott *nt* **-[e]s, -e** bassoon

fähig *a* capable (**zu**/*gen* of); (*tüchtig*) able, competent. **F~keit** *f* **-, -en** ability; competence

fahl *a* pale

fahnd|en *vi* (*haben*) search (**nach** for). **F~ung** *f* **-, -en** search

Fahne *f* **-, -n** flag; (*Druck-*) galley [proof]; **eine F~ haben** [!] reek of alcohol. **F~nflucht** *f* desertion

Fahr|ausweis *m* ticket. **F~bahn** *f* carriageway; (*Straße*) road. **f~bar** *a* mobile

Fähre *f* **-, -n** ferry

fahr|en† *vi* (*sein*) go, travel; <*Fahrer:*> drive; <*Radfahrer:*> ride; (*verkehren*) run, (*ab-*) leave; <*Schiff:*> sail; **mit dem Auto**/**Zug f~en** go by car/train; **was ist in ihn gefahren?** [!] what has got into him? ● *vt* drive; ride <*Fahrrad*>; take <*Kurve*>. **f~end** *a* moving; (*f~bar*) mobile; (*nicht sesshaft*) travelling. **F~er** *m* **-s,-** driver. **F~erflucht** *f* failure to stop after an accident. **F~erhaus** *nt* driver's cab. **F~erin** *f* **-, -nen** woman driver. **F~gast** *m* passenger. **F~geld** *nt* fare. **F~gestell** *nt* chassis; (*Aviat*) undercarriage. **F~karte** *f* ticket. **F~kartenschalter** *m* ticket office. **f~lässig** *a* negligent. **F~lässigkeit** *f* **-** negligence. **F~lehrer** *m* driving instructor. **F~plan** *m* timetable. **f~planmäßig** *a* scheduled ● *adv* according to/(*pünktlich*) on schedule. **F~preis** *m* fare. **F~prüfung** *f* driving test. **F~rad** *nt* bicycle. **F~schein** *m* ticket. **F~schule** *f* driving school. **F~schüler(in)** *m(f)* learner driver. **F~stuhl** *m* lift

Fahrt *f* **-, -en** journey; (*Auto*) drive; (*Ausflug*) trip; (*Tempo*) speed

Fährte *f* **-, -n** track; (*Witterung*) scent

Fahr|tkosten *pl* travelling expenses. **F~werk** *nt* undercarriage. **F~zeug** *nt* **-[e]s, -e** vehicle; (*Wasser-*) craft, vessel

fair /fɛ:ɐ̯/ *a* fair

Fakultät *f* **-, -en** faculty
Falke *m* **-n, -n** falcon
Fall *m* **-[e]s,¨e** fall; (*Jur, Med, Gram*) case; **im F~[e]** in case (*gen* of); **auf jeden F~** in any case; (*bestimmt*) definitely; **für alle F¨~e** just in case; **auf keinen F~** on no account
Falle *f* **-, -n** trap
fallen† *vi* (*sein*) fall; (*sinken*) go down; **[im Krieg] f~** be killed in the war; **f~ lassen** drop <*etw, fig: Plan, jdn*>; make <*Bemerkung*>
fällen *vt* fell; (*fig*) pass <*Urteil*>
fällig *a* due; <*Wechsel*> mature; **längst f~** long overdue. **F~keit** *f* **-** (*Comm*) maturity
falls *conj* in case; (*wenn*) if
Fallschirm *m* parachute. **F~jäger** *m* paratrooper. **F~springer** *m* parachutist
Falltür *f* trapdoor
falsch *a* wrong; (*nicht echt, unaufrichtig*) false; (*gefälscht*) forged; <*Geld*> counterfeit; <*Schmuck*> fake ● *adv* wrongly; falsely; <*singen*> out of tune; **f~ gehen** <*Uhr:*> be wrong
fälschen *vt* forge, fake
Falschgeld *nt* counterfeit money
fälschlich *a* wrong; (*irrtümlich*) mistaken
Falsch|meldung *f* false report; (*absichtlich*) hoax report. **F~münzer** *m* **-s,-** counterfeiter
Fälschung *f* **-, -en** forgery, fake
Falte *f* **-, -n** fold; (*Rock-*) pleat; (*Knitter-*) crease; (*im Gesicht*) line; wrinkle
falten *vt* fold
Falter *m* **-s,-** butterfly; moth
faltig *a* creased; <*Gesicht*> lined; wrinkled
familiär *a* family ...; (*vertraut, zudringlich*) familiar; (*zwanglos*) informal
Familie /-iə/ *f* **-, -n** family. **F~nforschung** *f* genealogy. **F~nname** *m* surname. **F~nplanung** *f* family planning. **F~nstand** *m* marital status
Fan /fɛn/ *m* **-s, -s** fan
Fana|tiker *m* **-s,-** fanatic. **f~tisch** *a* fanatical
Fanfare *f* **-, -n** trumpet; (*Signal*) fanfare
Fang *m* **-[e]s,¨e** capture; (*Beute*) catch; **F¨~e** (*Krallen*) talons; (*Zähne*) fangs. **F~arm** *m* tentacle. **f~en**† *vt* catch; (*ein-*) capture; **gefangen nehmen** take prisoner. **F~en** *nt* **-s F~en spielen** play tag. **F~frage** *f* catch question
Fantasie *f* **-, -n** = **Phantasie**
Farb|aufnahme *f* colour photograph. **F~band** *nt* (*pl* **-bänder**) typewriter ribbon. **F~e** *f* **-, -n** colour; (*Maler-*) paint; (*zum Färben*) dye; (*Karten*) suit. **f~echt** *a* colour-fast
färben *vt* colour; dye <*Textilien, Haare*> ● *vi* (*haben*) not be colour-fast
farb|enblind *a* colour-blind. **f~enfroh** *a* colourful. **F~film** *m* colour film. **f~ig** *a* coloured ● *adv* in colour. **F~ige(r)** *m/f* coloured man/woman. **F~kasten** *m* box of paints. **f~los** *a* colourless. **F~stift** *m* crayon. **F~stoff** *m* dye; (*Lebensmittel-*) colouring. **F~ton** *m* shade
Färbung *f* **-, -en** colouring
Farn *m* **-[e]s, -e** fern
Färse *f* **-, -n** heifer
Fasan *m* **-[e]s, -e[n]** pheasant
Faschierte(s) *nt* (*Aust*) mince
Fasching *m* **-s** (*SGer*) carnival
Faschis|mus *m* **-** fascism. **F~t** *m* **-en, -en** fascist. **f~tisch** *a* fascist
Faser *f* **-, -n** fibre

Fass *nt* **-es,¨er** barrel, cask; **Bier vom F~** draught beer

Fassade *f* **-, -n** façade

fassbar *a* comprehensible; (*greifbar*) tangible

fassen *vt* take [hold of], grasp; (*ergreifen*) seize; (*fangen*) catch; (*ein-*) set; (*enthalten*) hold; (*fig: begreifen*) take in, grasp; conceive <*Plan*>; make <*Entschluss*>; **sich f~** compose oneself; **sich kurz f~** be brief; **nicht zu f~** (*fig*) unbelievable ● *vi* (*haben*) **f~ an** (+ *acc*) touch

Fassung *f* **-, -en** mount; (*Edelstein-*) setting; (*Electr*) socket; (*Version*) version; (*Beherrschung*) composure; **aus der F~ bringen** disconcert. **f~slos** *a* shaken; (*erstaunt*) flabbergasted. **F~svermögen** *nt* capacity

fast *adv* almost, nearly; **f~ nie** hardly ever

fast|en *vi* (*haben*) fast. **F~enzeit** *f* Lent. **F~nacht** *f* Shrovetide; (*Karneval*) carnival. **F~nachtsdienstag** *m* Shrove Tuesday

fatal *a* fatal; (*peinlich*) embarrassing

Fata Morgana *f* **- -/- -nen** mirage

fauchen *vi* (*haben*) spit, hiss ● *vt* snarl

faul *a* lazy; (*verdorben*) rotten, bad; <*Ausrede*> lame

faul|en *vi* (*sein*) rot; <*Zahn:*> decay; (*verwesen*) putrefy. **f~enzen** *vi* (*haben*) be lazy. **F~enzer** *m* **-s,-** lazy-bones *sg*. **F~heit** *f* **-** laziness

Fäulnis *f* **-** decay

Fauna *f* **-** fauna

Faust *f* **-,Fäuste** fist; **auf eigene F~** (*fig*) off one's own bat. **F~handschuh** *m* mitten. **F~schlag** *m* punch

Fauxpas /fo'pa/ *m* **-,-** /-**[s]**, **-s**/ gaffe

Favorit(in) /favo'ri:t(ɪn)/ *m* **-en, -en** (*f* **-, -nen**) (*Sport*) favourite

Fax *nt* **-, -[e]** fax. **f~en** *vt* fax

Faxen *fpl* ! antics; **F~ machen** fool about

Faxgerät *nt* fax machine

Februar *m* **-s, -e** February

fecht|en† *vi* (*haben*) fence. **F~er** *m* **-s,-** fencer

Feder *f* **-, -n** feather; (*Schreib-*) pen; (*Spitze*) nib; (*Techn*) spring. **F~ball** *m* shuttlecock; (*Spiel*) badminton. **F~busch** *m* plume. **f~leicht** *a* as light as a feather. **f~n** *vi* (*haben*) be springy; (*nachgeben*) give; (*hoch-*) bounce. **f~nd** *a* springy; (*elastisch*) elastic. **F~ung** *f* **-** (*Techn*) springs *pl*; (*Auto*) suspension

Fee *f* **-, -n** fairy

Fegefeuer *nt* purgatory

fegen *vt* sweep

Fehde *f* **-, -n** feud

fehl *a* **f~ am Platze** out of place. **F~betrag** *m* deficit. **f~en** *vi* (*haben*) be missing/(*Sch*) absent; (*mangeln*) be lacking; **mir f~t die Zeit** I haven't got the time; **was f~t ihm?** what's the matter with him? **das hat uns noch gefehlt!** that's all we need! **f~end** *a* missing; (*Sch*) absent

Fehler *m* **-s,-** mistake, error; (*Sport & fig*) fault; (*Makel*) flaw. **f~frei** *a* faultless. **f~haft** *a* faulty. **f~los** *a* flawless

Fehl|geburt *f* miscarriage. **F~griff** *m* mistake. **F~kalkulation** *f* miscalculation. **F~schlag** *m* failure. **f~schlagen**† *vi sep* (*sein*) fail. **F~start** *m* (*Sport*) false start. **F~zündung** *f* (*Auto*) misfire

Feier *f* **-, -n** celebration; (*Zeremonie*) ceremony; (*Party*) party. **F~abend** *m* end of the working day; **F~abend machen** stop work. **f~lich** *a* solemn; (*fömlich*) formal. **f~n** *vt* celebrate; hold <*Fest*> ● *vi* (*haben*) celebrate. **F~tag** *m* [public] holiday; (*kirchlicher*) feast-day; **erster/zweiter F~tag** Christmas Day / Boxing Day. **f~tags** *adv* on public holidays

feige *a* cowardly; **f~ sein** be a coward ● *adv* in a cowardly way

Feige *f* **-, -n** fig

Feig|heit *f* **-** cowardice. **F~ling** *m* **-s, -e** coward

Feile *f* **-, -n** file. **f~n** *vt/i* (*haben*) file

feilschen *vi* (*haben*) haggle

fein *a* fine; (*zart*) delicate; <*Strümpfe*> sheer; <*Unterschied*> subtle; (*scharf*) keen; (*vornehm*) refined; (*prima*) great; **sich f~ machen** dress up. **F~arbeit** *f* precision work

Feind(in) *m* **-es, -e** (*f* **-, -nen**) enemy. **f~lich** *a* enemy; (*f~selig*) hostile. **F~schaft** *f* **-, -en** enmity

fein|fühlig *a* sensitive. **F~gefühl** *nt* sensitivity; (*Takt*) delicacy. **F~heit** *f* **-, -en** fineness; delicacy; subtlety; refinement; **F~heiten** subtleties. **F~kostgeschäft** *nt* delicatessen [shop]

feist *a* fat

Feld *nt* **-[e]s, -er** field; (*Fläche*) ground; (*Sport*) pitch; (*Schach-*) square; (*auf Formular*) box. **F~bett** *nt* camp-bed. **F~forschung** *f* fieldwork. **F~herr** *m* commander. **F~stecher** *m* **-s,-** field-glasses *pl*. **F~webel** *m* **-s,-** (*Mil*) sergeant. **F~zug** *m* campaign

Felge *f* **-, -n** [wheel] rim

Fell *nt* **-[e]s, -e** (*Zool*) coat; (*Pelz*) fur; (*abgezogen*) skin, pelt

Fels *m* **-en, -en** rock. **F~block** *m* boulder. **F~en** *m* **-s,-** rock

Femininum *nt* **-s, -na** (*Gram*) feminine

Femin|st|(in) *m* **-en, -en** (*f* **-, -nen**) feminist. **f~isch** *a* feminist

Fenchel *m* **-s** fennel

Fenster *nt* **-s,-** window. **F~brett** *nt* window-sill. **F~scheibe** *f* [window-]pane

Ferien /'fe:riən/ *pl* holidays; (*Univ*) vacation *sg*; **F~ haben** be on holiday. **F~ort** *m* holiday resort

Ferkel *nt* **-s,-** piglet

fern *a* distant; **der F~e Osten** the Far East; **sich f~ halten** keep away ● *adv* far away; **von f~** from a distance ● *prep* (+ *dat*) far [away] from. **F~bedienung** *f* remote control. **F~e** *f* **-** distance; **in weiter F~e** far away; (*zeitlich*) in the distant future. **f~er** *a* further ● *adv* (*außerdem*) furthermore; (*in Zukunft*) in future. **f~gelenkt** *a* remote-controlled; <*Rakete*> guided. **F~gespräch** *nt* long-distance call. **F~glas** *nt* binoculars *pl*. **F~kurs[us]** *m* correspondence course. **F~licht** *nt* (*Auto*) full beam. **F~meldewesen** *nt* telecommunications *pl*. **F~rohr** *nt* telescope. **F~schreiben** *nt* telex

Fernseh|apparat *m* television set. **f~en†** *vi sep* (*haben*) watch television. **F~en** *nt* **-s** television. **F~er** *m* **-s,-** [television] viewer; (*Gerät*) television set

Fernsprech|amt *nt* telephone exchange. **F~er** *m* telephone

Fernsteuerung *f* remote control

Ferse *f* **-, -n** heel

fertig *a* finished; (*bereit*) ready; (*Comm*) ready-made; <*Gericht*> ready-to-serve; **f~ werden mit** finish; (*bewältigen*) cope with; **f~**

sein have finished; (*fig*) be through (**mit jdm** with s.o.); ([!] *erschöpft*) be all in/(*seelisch*) shattered; **etw f~ bringen** manage to do sth; (*beenden*) finish sth; **etw/jdn f~ machen** finish sth; (*bereitmachen*) get sth/s.o. ready; ([!] *erschöpfen*) wear s.o. out; (*seelisch*) shatter s.o.; **sich f~ machen** get ready; **etw f~ stellen** complete sth ● *adv* **f~ essen/lesen** finish eating/reading. **F~bau** *m* (*pl* **-bauten**) prefabricated building. **f~en** *vt* make. **F~gericht** *nt* ready-to-serve meal. **F~haus** *nt* prefabricated house. **F~keit** *f* **-, -en** skill. **F~stellung** *f* completion. **F~ung** *f* **-** manufacture

fẹsch *a* [!] attractive

Fẹssel *f* **-, -n** ankle

fẹsseln *vt* tie up; tie (**an** + *acc* to); (*fig*) fascinate

fẹst *a* firm; (*nicht flüssig*) solid; (*erstarrt*) set; (*haltbar*) strong; (*nicht locker*) tight; (*feststehend*) fixed; (*ständig*) steady; <*Anstellung*> permanent; <*Schlaf*> sound; <*Blick, Stimme*> steady; **f~ werden** harden; <*Gelee:*> set; **f~e Nahrung** solids *pl* ● *adv* firmly; tightly; steadily; soundly; (*kräftig, tüchtig*) hard; **f~ schlafen** be fast asleep; **f~ angestellt** permanent

Fẹst *nt* **-[e]s, -e** celebration; (*Party*) party; (*Relig*) festival; **frohes F~!** happy Christmas!

fẹst|binden† *vt sep* tie (**an** + *dat* to). **f~bleiben**† *vi sep* (*sein*) (*fig*) remain firm. **f~halten**† *v sep* ● *vt* hold on to; (*aufzeichnen*) record; **sich f~halten** hold on ● *vi* (*haben*) **f~halten an** (+ *dat*) (*fig*) stick to; cling to <*Tradition*>. **f~igen** *vt* strengthen. **F~iger** *m* **-s,-** styling lotion/(*Schaum-*) mousse. **F~igkeit** *f* **-** firmness; solidity; strength; steadiness. **F~land** *nt* mainland; (*Kontinent*) continent. **f~legen** *vt sep* (*fig*) fix, settle; lay down <*Regeln*>; tie up <*Geld*>; **sich f~legen** commit oneself

fẹstlich *a* festive. **F~keiten** *fpl* festivities

fẹst|liegen† *vi sep* (*haben*) be fixed, settled. **f~machen** *v sep* ● *vt* fasten/(*binden*) tie (**an** + *dat* to); (*f~legen*) fix, settle ● *vi* (*haben*) (*Naut*) moor. **F~mahl** *nt* feast. **F~nahme** *f* **-, -n** arrest. **f~nehmen**† *vt sep* arrest. **f~setzen** *vt sep* fix, settle; (*inhaftieren*) gaol; **sich f~setzen** collect. **f~sitzen**† *vi sep* (*haben*) be firm/<*Schraube:*> tight; (*haften*) stick; (*nicht weiterkommen*) be stuck. **F~spiele** *npl* festival *sg*. **f~stehen**† *vi sep* (*haben*) be certain. **f~stellen** *vt sep* fix; (*ermitteln*) establish; (*bemerken*) notice; (*sagen*) state. **F~tag** *m* special day

Fẹstung *f* **-, -en** fortress

Fẹstzug *m* [grand] procession

Fete /'fe:tə, 'fɛ:tə/ *f* **-, -n** party

fẹtt *a* fat; fatty; (*fettig*) greasy; (*üppig*) rich; <*Druck*> bold. **F~** *nt* **-[e]s, -e** fat; (*flüssig*) grease. **f~arm** *a* low-fat. **f~en** *vt* grease ● *vi* (*haben*) be greasy. **F~fleck** *m* grease mark. **f~ig** *a* greasy

Fẹtzen *m* **-s,-** scrap; (*Stoff*) rag

feucht *a* damp, moist; <*Luft*> humid. **F~igkeit** *f* **-** dampness; (*Nässe*) moisture; (*Luft-*) humidity. **F~igkeitscreme** *f* moisturizer

Feuer *nt* **-s,-** fire; (*für Zigarette*) light; (*Begeisterung*) passion; **F~ machen** light a fire. **F~alarm** *m* fire alarm. **f~gefährlich** *a* [in]flammable. **F~leiter** *f* fire-escape. **F∼löscher** *m* **-s,-** fire extinguisher. **F∼melder** *m* **-s,-** fire alarm. **f∼n** *vi* (*haben*) fire (**auf** + *acc* on). **F∼probe** *f* (*fig*) test. **f∼rot** *a* crimson. **F∼stein** *m* flint. **F∼stelle** *f* hearth. **F∼treppe** *f* fire-escape. **F∼wache** *f* fire station. **F∼waffe** *f* firearm. **F∼wehr** *f* **-, -en** fire brigade. **F∼wehrauto** *nt* fire-engine. **F∼wehrmann** *m* (*pl* **-männer** & **-leute**) fireman. **F∼werk** *nt* firework display, fireworks *pl*. **F∼zeug** *nt* lighter

feurig *a* fiery; (*fig*) passionate

Fiaker *m* **-s,-** (*Aust*) horse-drawn cab

Fichte *f* **-, -n** spruce

Fieber *nt* **-s** [raised] temperature; **F∼ haben** have a temperature. **f∼n** *vi* (*haben*) be feverish. **F∼thermometer** *nt* thermometer

fiebrig *a* feverish

Figur *f* **-, -en** figure; (*Roman-, Film-*) character; (*Schach-*) piece

Filet /fiˈle:/ *nt* **-s, -s** fillet

Filiale *f* **-, -n** (*Comm*) branch

Filigran *nt* **-s** filigree

Film *m* **-[e]s, -e** film; (*Kino-*) film; (*Schicht*) coating. **f∼en** *vt/i* (*haben*) film. **F∼kamera** *f* cine/(*für Kinofilm*) film camera

Filt|er *m* & (*Techn*) *nt* **-s,-** filter; (*Zigaretten-*) filter-tip. **f∼ern** *vt* filter. **F∼erzigarette** *f* filter-tipped cigarette. **f∼rieren** *vt* filter

Filz *m* **-es** felt. **F∼stift** *m* felt-tipped pen

Fimmel *m* **-s,-** 🅘 obsession

Finale *nt* **-s,-** (*Mus*) finale; (*Sport*) final

Finanz *f* **-, -en** finance. **F∼amt** *nt* tax office. **f∼iell** *a* financial. **f∼ieren** *vt* finance. **F∼minister** *m* minister of finance

find|en† *vt* find; (*meinen*) think; **den Tod f∼en** meet one's death; **wie f∼est du das?** what do you think of that? **es wird sich f∼en** it'll turn up; (*fig*) it'll be all right ● *vi* (*haben*) find one's way. **F∼er** *m* **-s,-** finder. **F∼erlohn** *m* reward. **f∼ig** *a* resourceful

Finesse *f* **-, -n** (*Kniff*) trick; **F∼n** (*Techn*) refinements

Finger *m* **-s,-** finger; **die F∼ lassen von** 🅘 leave alone. **F∼abdruck** *m* finger-mark; (*Admin*) fingerprint. **F∼hut** *m* thimble. **F∼nagel** *m* fingernail. **F∼spitze** *f* fingertip. **F∼zeig** *m* **-[e]s, -e** hint

Fink *m* **-en, -en** finch

Finn|e *m* **-n, -n, F∼in** *f* **-, -nen** Finn. **f∼isch** *a* Finnish. **F∼land** *nt* **-s** Finland

finster *a* dark; (*düster*) gloomy; (*unheildrohend*) sinister. **F∼nis** *f* **-** darkness; (*Astr*) eclipse

Firma *f* **-, -men** firm, company

Firmen|wagen *m* company car. **F∼zeichen** *nt* trade mark, logo

Firmung *f* **-, -en** (*Relig*) confirmation

Firnis *m* **-ses, -se** varnish. **f∼sen** *vt* varnish

First *m* **-[e]s, -e** [roof] ridge

Fisch *m* **-[e]s, -e** fish; **F∼e** (*Astr*) Pisces. **F∼dampfer** *m* trawler. **f∼en** *vt/i* (*haben*) fish. **F∼er** *m* **-s,-** fisherman. **F∼erei** *f* **-** fishing. **F∼händler** *m* fishmonger. **F∼reiher** *m* heron

Fiskus *m* **- der F∼** the Treasury

fit *a* fit. **F∼ness** *f* **-** fitness

fix *a* 🅘 quick; (*geistig*) bright; **f∼e Idee** obsession; **fix und fertig** all finished; (*bereit*) all ready; (🅘 *erschöpft*) shattered. **F∼er** *m* **-s,-** ☒ junkie

fixieren *vt* stare at; (*Phot*) fix

Fjord *m* **-[e]s, -e** fiord

flach *a* flat; (*eben*) level; (*niedrig*) low; (*nicht tief*) shallow

Fläche *f* **-, -n** area; (*Ober-*) surface; (*Seite*) face. **F~nmaß** *nt* square measure

Flachs *m* **-es** flax. **f~blond** *a* flaxen-haired; <*Haar*> flaxen

flackern *vi* (*haben*) flicker

Flagge *f* **-, -n** flag

Flair /flɛːɐ̯/ *nt* **-s** air, aura

Flak *f* **-, -[s]** anti-aircraft artillery/(*Geschütz*) gun

flämisch *a* Flemish

Flamme *f* **-, -n** flame; (*Koch-*) burner

Flanell *m* **-s** (*Tex*) flannel

Flank|e *f* **-, -n** flank. **f~ieren** *vt* flank

Flasche *f* **-, -n** bottle. **F~nbier** *nt* bottled beer. **F~nöffner** *m* bottle-opener

flatter|haft *a* fickle. **f~n** *vi* (*sein/haben*) flutter; <*Segel:*> flap

flau *a* (*schwach*) faint; (*Comm*) slack

Flaum *m* **-[e]s** down. **f~ig** *a* downy; **f~ig rühren** (*Aust Culin*) cream

flauschig *a* fleecy; <*Spielzeug*> fluffy

Flausen *fpl* [!] silly ideas

Flaute *f* **-, -n** (*Naut*) calm; (*Comm*) slack period; (*Schwäche*) low

fläzen (sich) *vr* [!] sprawl

Flechte *f* **-, -n** (*Med*) eczema; (*Bot*) lichen; (*Zopf*) plait. **f~n**† *vt* plait; weave <*Korb*>

Fleck *m* **-[e]s, -e[n]** spot; (*größer*) patch; (*Schmutz-*) stain, mark; **blauer F~** bruise. **f~en** *vi* (*haben*) stain. **f~enlos** *a* spotless. **F~entferner** *m* **-s,-** stain remover. **f~ig** *a* stained

Fledermaus *f* bat

Flegel *m* **-s,-** lout. **f~haft** *a* loutish

flehen *vi* (*haben*) beg (**um** for)

Fleisch *nt* **-[e]s** flesh; (*Culin*) meat; (*Frucht-*) pulp; **F~fressend** carnivorous. **F~er** *m* **-s,-** butcher. **F~fresser** *m* **-s,-** carnivore. **f~ig** *a* fleshy. **f~lich** *a* carnal. **F~wolf** *m* mincer

Fleiß *m* **-es** diligence; **mit F~** diligently; (*absichtlich*) on purpose. **f~ig** *a* diligent; (*arbeitsam*) industrious

fletschen *vt* **die Zähne f~** <*Tier:*> bare its teeth

flex|ibel *a* flexible; <*Einband*> limp. **F~ibilität** *f* **-** flexibility

flicken *vt* mend; (*mit Flicken*) patch. **F~** *m* **-s,-** patch

Flieder *m* **-s** lilac

Fliege *f* **-, -n** fly; (*Schleife*) bow-tie. **f~n**† *vi* (*sein*) fly; (*geworfen werden*) be thrown; ([!] *fallen*) fall; ([!] *entlassen werden*) be fired/(*von der Schule*) expelled; **in die Luft f~n** blow up ● *vt* fly. **f~nd** *a* flying. **F~r** *m* **-s,-** airman; (*Pilot*); pilot; ([!] *Flugzeug*) plane. **F~rangriff** *m* air raid

flieh|en† *vi* (*sein*) flee (**vor** + *dat* from); (*entweichen*) escape ● *vt* shun. **f~end** *a* fleeing; <*Kinn, Stirn*> receding

Fliese *f* **-, -n** tile

Fließ|band *nt* assembly line. **f~en**† *vi* (*sein*) flow; (*aus Wasserhahn*) run. **f~end** *a* flowing; <*Wasser*> running; <*Verkehr*> moving; (*geläufig*) fluent

flimmern *vi* (*haben*) shimmer; (*TV*) flicker

flink *a* nimble; (*schnell*) quick

Flinte *f* **-, -n** shotgun

Flirt /flœɐ̯t/ *m* **-s, -s** flirtation. **f~en** *vi* (*haben*) flirt

Flitter *m* **-s** sequins *pl*. **F~wochen** *fpl* honeymoon *sg*

flitzen *vi* (*sein*) [!] dash

Flock|e *f* **-, -n** flake; (*Wolle*) tuft. **f~ig** *a* fluffy

Floh *m* **-[e]s,¨e** flea

Flora *f* - flora
Florett *nt* **-[e]s, -e** foil
florieren *vi* (*haben*) flourish
Floskel *f* **-, -n** [empty] phrase
Floß *nt* **-es,¨-e** raft
Flosse *f* **-, -n** fin; (*Seehund-, Gummi-*) flipper; (☒ *Hand*) paw
Flöt|e *f* **-, -n** flute; (*Block-*) recorder. **f~en** *vi* (*haben*) play the flute/recorder; (! *pfeifen*) whistle ● *vt* play on the flute/ recorder. **F~ist(in)** *m* **-en, -en** (*f* **-, -nen**) flautist
flott *a* quick; (*lebhaft*) lively; (*schick*) smart
Flotte *f* **-, -n** fleet
flottmachen *vt sep* **wieder f~** (*Naut*) refloat; get going again <*Auto*>; put back on its feet <*Unternehmen*>
Flöz *nt* **-es, -e** [coal] seam
Fluch *m* **-[e]s,¨-e** curse. **f~en** *vi* (*haben*) curse, swear
Flucht *f* - flight; (*Entweichen*) escape; **die F~ ergreifen** take flight. **f~artig** *a* hasty
flücht|en *vi* (*sein*) flee (**vor** + *dat* from); (*entweichen*) escape ● *vr* **sich f~en** take refuge. **f~ig** *a* fugitive; (*kurz*) brief; <*Blick*> fleeting; <*Bekanntschaft*> passing; (*oberflächlich*) cursory; (*nicht sorgfältig*) careless. **f~ig kennen** know slightly. **F~igkeitsfehler** *m* slip. **F~ling** *m* **-s, -e** fugitive; (*Pol*) refugee
Fluchwort *nt* (*pl* **-wörter**) swear-word
Flug *m* **-[e]s,¨-e** flight. **F~abwehr** *f* anti-aircraft defence
Flügel *m* **-s,-** wing; (*Fenster-*) casement; (*Mus*) grand piano
Fluggast *m* [air] passenger
flügge *a* fully-fledged
Flug|gesellschaft *f* airline. **F~hafen** *m* airport. **F~lotse** *m* air-traffic controller. **F~platz** *m* airport; (*klein*) airfield. **F~preis** *m* air fare. **F~schein** *m* air ticket. **F~schneise** *f* flight path. **F~schreiber** *m* **-s,-** flight recorder. **F~schrift** *f* pamphlet. **F~steig** *m* **-[e]s, -e** gate. **F~zeug** *nt* **-[e]s, -e** aircraft, plane
Flunder *f* **-, -n** flounder
flunkern *vi* (*haben*) ! tell fibs
Flur *m* **-[e]s, -e** [entrance] hall; (*Gang*) corridor
Fluss *m* **-es,¨-e** river; (*Fließen*) flow; **im F~** (*fig*) in a state of flux. **f~abwärts** *adv* downstream. **f~aufwärts** *adv* upstream
flüssig *a* liquid; <*Lava*> molten; (*fließend*) fluent; <*Verkehr*> freely moving. **F~keit** *f* **-, -en** liquid; (*Anat*) fluid
Flusspferd *nt* hippopotamus
flüstern *vt/i* (*haben*) whisper
Flut *f* **-, -en** high tide; (*fig*) flood
Föderation /-ˈtsi̯o:n/ *f* **-, -en** federation
Fohlen *nt* **-s,-** foal
Föhn *m* **-s** föhn [wind]; (*Haartrockner*) hair-drier. **f~en** *vt* [blow-]dry
Folg|e *f* **-, -n** consequence; (*Reihe*) succession; (*Fortsetzung*) instalment; (*Teil*) part. **f~en** *vi* (*sein*) follow (**jdm/etw** s.o./sth); (*zuhören*) listen (*dat* to); **wie f~t** as follows ● (*haben*) (*gehorchen*) obey (**jdm** s.o.). **f~end** *a* following; **F~endes** the following
folger|n *vt* conclude (**aus** from). **F~ung** *f* **-, -en** conclusion
folg|lich *adv* consequently. **f~sam** *a* obedient
Folie /ˈfo:li̯ə/ *f* **-, -n** foil; (*Plastik-*) film
Folklore *f* - folklore
Folter *f* **-, -n** torture. **f~n** *vt* torture

Fön (P) *m* **-s, -e** hair-drier
Fonds /fõ:/ *m* **-,-** /-**[s], -s**/ fund
fönen* *vt s.* **föhnen**
Förder|band *nt* (*pl* **-bänder**) conveyor belt. **f~lich** *a* beneficial
fordern *vt* demand; (*beanspruchen*) claim; (*zum Kampf*) challenge
fördern *vt* promote; (*unterstützen*) encourage; (*finanziell*) sponsor; (*gewinnen*) extract
Forderung *f* **-, -en** demand; (*Anspruch*) claim
Förderung *f* **-** promotion; encouragement; (*Techn*) production
Forelle *f* **-, -n** trout
Form *f* **-, -en** form; (*Gestalt*) shape; (*Culin, Techn*) mould; (*Back-*) tin; **[gut] in F~** in good form
Formalität *f* **-, -en** formality
Format *nt* **-[e]s, -e** format; (*Größe*) size; (*fig: Bedeutung*) stature
formatieren *vt* format
Formel *f* **-, -n** formula
formen *vt* shape, mould; (*bilden*) form; **sich f~** take shape
förmlich *a* formal
form|los *a* shapeless; (*zwanglos*) informal. **F~sache** *f* formality
Formular *nt* **-s, -e** [printed] form
formulier|en *vt* formulate, word. **F~ung** *f* **-, -en** wording
forsch|en *vi* (*haben*) search (**nach** for). **f~end** *a* searching. **F~er** *m* **-s,-** research scientist; (*Reisender*) explorer. **F~ung** *f* **-, -en** research
Forst *m* **-[e]s, -e** forest
Förster *m* **-s,-** forester
Forstwirtschaft *f* forestry
Fort *nt* **-s, -s** (*Mil*) fort
fort *adv* away; **f~ sein** be away; (*gegangen/verschwunden*) have gone; **und so f~** and so on; **in einem f~** continuously. **F~bewegung** *f* locomotion. **F~bildung** *f* further education/training. **f~bleiben†** *vi sep* (*sein*) stay away. **f~bringen†** *vt sep* take away. **f~fahren†** *vi sep* (*sein*) go away ● (*haben/sein*) continue (**zu** to). **f~fallen†** *vi sep* (*sein*) be dropped/(*ausgelassen*) omitted; (*entfallen*) no longer apply; (*aufhören*) cease. **f~führen** *vt sep* continue. **f~gehen†** *vi sep* (*sein*) leave, go away; (*ausgehen*) go out; (*andauern*) go on. **f~geschritten** *a* advanced; (*spät*) late. **F~geschrittene(r)** *m/f* advanced student. **f~lassen†** *vt sep* let go; (*auslassen*) omit. **f~laufen†** *vi sep* (*sein*) run away; (*sich f~setzen*) continue. **f~laufend** *a* consecutive. **f~pflanzen (sich)** *vr sep* reproduce; <*Ton, Licht:*> travel. **F~pflanzung** *f* **-** reproduction. **F~pflanzungsorgan** *nt* reproductive organ. **f~schicken** *vt sep* send away; (*abschicken*) send off. **f~schreiten†** *vi sep* (*sein*) continue; (*Fortschritte machen*) progress, advance. **f~schreitend** *a* progressive; <*Alter*> advancing. **F~schritt** *m* progress; **F~schritte machen** make progress. **f~schrittlich** *a* progressive. **f~setzen** *vt sep* continue; **sich f~setzen** continue. **F~setzung** *f* **-, -en** continuation; (*Folge*) instalment; **F~setzung folgt** to be continued. **F~setzungsroman** *m* serialized novel, serial. **f~während** *a* constant. **f~ziehen†** *v sep* ● *vt* pull away ● *vi* (*sein*) move away
Fossil *nt* **-, -ien** /-iən/ fossil

Foto *nt* **-s, -s** photo. **F~apparat** *m* camera. **f~gen** *a* photogenic

Fotograf|(in) *m* **-en, -en** (*f* **-, -nen**) photographer. **F~ie** *f* **-, -n** photography; (*Bild*) photograph. **f~ieren** *vt* take a photo[graph] of ● *vi* (*haben*) take photographs. **f~isch** *a* photographic

Fotokopie *f* photocopy. **f~ren** *vt* photocopy. **F~rgerät** *nt* photocopier

Fötus *m* **-, -ten** foetus

Foul /faul/ *nt* **-s, -s** (*Sport*) foul. **f~en** *vt* foul

Fracht *f* **-, -en** freight. **F~er** *m* **-s,-** freighter. **F~gut** *nt* freight. **F~schiff** *nt* cargo boat

Frack *m* **-[e]s,¨e & -s** tailcoat

Frage *f* **-, -n** question; **nicht in F~ kommen** *s.* **infrage. F~bogen** *m* questionnaire. **f~n** *vt* (*haben*) ask; **sich f~n** wonder (**ob** whether). **f~nd** *a* questioning. **F~zeichen** *nt* question mark

frag|lich *a* doubtful; <*Person, Sache*> in question. **f~los** *adv* undoubtedly

Fragment *nt* **-[e]s, -e** fragment

fragwürdig *a* questionable; (*verdächtig*) dubious

Fraktion /-ˈtsi̯oːn/ *f* **-, -en** parliamentary party

Franken[1] *m* **-s,-** (*Swiss*) franc

Franken[2] *nt* **-s** Franconia

frankieren *vt* stamp, frank

Frankreich *nt* **-s** France

Fransen *fpl* fringe *sg*

Franz|ose *m* **-n, -n** Frenchman; **die F~osen** the French *pl*. **F~ösin** *f* **-, -nen** Frenchwoman. **f~ösisch** *a* French. **F~ösisch** *nt* **-[s]** (*Lang*) French

Fraß *m* **-es** feed; (*pej: Essen*) muck

Fratze *f* **-, -n** grotesque face; (*Grimasse*) grimace

Frau *f* **-, -en** woman; (*Ehe-*) wife; **F~Thomas** Mrs Thomas; **Unsere Liebe F~** (*Relig*) Our Lady

Frauen|arzt *m*, **F~ärztin** *f* gynaecologist. **F~rechtlerin** *f* **-, -nen** feminist

Fräulein *nt* **-s,-** single woman; (*jung*) young lady; (*Anrede*) Miss

frech *a* cheeky; (*unverschämt*) impudent. **F~heit** *f* **-, -en** cheekiness; impudence; (*Äußerung*) impertinence

frei *a* free; (*freischaffend*) freelance; <*Künstler*> independent; (*nicht besetzt*) vacant; (*offen*) open; (*bloß*) bare; **f~er Tag** day off; **sich** (*dat*) **f~ nehmen** take time off; **f~ machen** (*räumen*) clear; vacate <*Platz*>; (*befreien*) liberate; **f~ lassen** leave free; **ist dieser Platz f~?** is this seat taken? **'Zimmer f~'** 'vacancies' ● *adv* freely; (*ohne Notizen*) without notes; (*umsonst*) free

Frei|bad *nt* open-air swimming pool. **f~beruflich** *a & adv* freelance. **F~e** *nt* **im F~en** in the open air, out of doors. **F~gabe** *f* release. **f~geben**† *v sep* ● *vt* release; (*eröffnen*) open; **jdm einen Tag f~geben** give s.o. a day off ● *vi* (*haben*) **jdm f~geben** give s.o. time off. **f~gebig** *a* generous. **F~gebigkeit** *f* **-** generosity. **f~haben**† *v sep* ● *vt* **eine Stunde f~haben** have an hour off; (*Sch*) have a free period ● *vi* (*haben*) be off work/(*Sch*) school; (*beurlaubt sein*) have time off. **f~händig** *adv* without holding on

Freiheit *f* **-, -en** freedom, liberty. **F~sstrafe** *f* prison sentence

Frei|herr *m* baron. **F~körperkultur** *f* naturism. **F~lassung** *f* **-** release. **F~lauf** *m* free-wheel. **f~legen** *vt sep*

expose. **f~lich** *adv* admittedly; (*natürlich*) of course. **F~lichttheater** *nt* open-air theatre. **f~machen** *vt sep* (*frankieren*) frank; (*entkleiden*) bare; **einen Tag f~machen** take a day off. **F~maurer** *m* Freemason. **f~schaffend** *a* freelance. **f~schwimmen**† **(sich)** *v sep* pass one's swimming test. **f~sprechen**† *vt sep* acquit. **F~spruch** *m* acquittal. **f~stehen**† *vi sep* (*haben*) stand empty; **es steht ihm f~** (*fig*) he is free (**zu** to). **f~stellen** *vt sep* exempt (**von** from); **jdm etw f~stellen** leave sth up to s.o. **F~stil** *m* freestyle. **F~stoß** *m* free kick

Freitag *m* Friday. **f~s** *adv* on Fridays

Frei|tod *m* suicide. **F~umschlag** *m* stamped envelope. **f~weg** *adv* freely; (*offen*) openly. **f~willig** *a* voluntary. **F~willige(r)** *m/f* volunteer. **F~zeichen** *nt* ringing tone; (*Rufzeichen*) dialling tone. **F~zeit** *f* free *or* spare time; (*Muße*) leisure. **F~zeit-** *pref* leisure ... **F~zeitbekleidung** *f* casual wear. **f~zügig** *a* unrestricted; (*großzügig*) liberal

fremd *a* foreign; (*unbekannt*) strange; (*nicht das eigene*) other people's; **ein f~er Mann** a stranger; **f~e Leute** strangers; **unter f~em Namen** under an assumed name; **ich bin hier f~** I'm a stranger here. **F~e** *f* - **in der F~e** away from home; (*im Ausland*) in a foreign country. **F~e(r)** *m/f* stranger; (*Ausländer*) foreigner; (*Tourist*) tourist. **F~enführer** *m* [tourist] guide. **F~enverkehr** *m* tourism. **F~enzimmer** *nt* room [to let]; (*Gäste-*) guest room. **f~gehen**† *vi sep* (*sein*) 🄸 be unfaithful. **F~sprache** *f* foreign language. **F~wort** *nt* (*pl* **-wörter**) foreign word

Freske *f* **-, -n, Fresko** *nt* **-s, -ken** fresco

Fresse *f* **-, -n** ☒ (*Mund*) gob; (*Gesicht*) mug. **f~n**† *vt/i* (*haben*) eat. **F~n** *nt* **-s** feed; (☒ *Essen*) grub

Fressnapf *m* feeding bowl

Freud|e *f* **-, -n** pleasure; (*innere*) joy; **mit F~en** with pleasure; **jdm eine F~e machen** please s.o. **f~ig** *a* joyful

freuen *vt* please; **sich f~** be pleased (**über** + *acc* about); **sich f~ auf** (+ *acc*) look forward to; **es freut mich** I'm glad (**dass** that)

Freund *m* **-es, -e** friend; (*Verehrer*) boyfriend. **F~in** *f* **-, -nen** friend; (*Liebste*) girlfriend. **f~lich** *a* kind; (*umgänglich*) friendly; (*angenehm*) pleasant. **f~licherweise** *adv* kindly. **F~lichkeit** *f* **-, -en** kindness; friendliness; pleasantness

Freund|schaft *f* **-, -en** friendship; **F~schaft schließen** become friends. **f~lich** *a* friendly

Frieden *m* **-s** peace; **F~ schließen** make peace; **im F~** in peace-time; **lass mich in F~!** leave me alone! **F~svertrag** *m* peace treaty

Fried|hof *m* cemetery. **f~lich** *a* peaceful

frieren† *vi* (*haben*) <*Person*:> be cold; *impers* **es friert/hat gefroren** it is freezing/there has been a frost; **frierst du?** are you cold? ● (*sein*) (*gefrieren*) freeze

Fries *m* **-es, -e** frieze

frisch *a* fresh; (*sauber*) clean; (*leuchtend*) bright; (*munter*) lively; (*rüstig*) fit; **sich f~ machen** freshen up ● *adv* freshly, newly; **ein Bett f~**

beziehen put clean sheets on a bed; **f~ gestrichen!** wet paint! **F~e** *f* - freshness; brightness; liveliness; fitness. **F~haltepackung** *f* vacuum pack

Fri|seur /fri'zø:ɐ/ *m* **-s, -e** hairdresser; (*Herren-*) barber. **F~seursalon** *m* hairdressing salon. **F~seuse** /-'zø:zə/ *f* **-, -n** hairdresser

frisier|en *vt* **jdn/sich f~en** do s.o.'s/one's hair; **die Bilanz/einen Motor f~en** [!] fiddle the accounts/soup up an engine

Frisör *m* **-s, -e** = **Friseur**

Frist *f* **-, -en** period; (*Termin*) deadline; (*Aufschub*) time; **drei Tage F~** three days' grace. **f~los** *a* instant

Frisur *f* **-, -en** hairstyle

frittieren *vt* deep-fry

frivol /fri'vo:l/ *a* frivolous

froh *a* happy; (*freudig*) joyful; (*erleichtert*) glad

fröhlich *a* cheerful; (*vergnügt*) merry. **F~keit** *f* - cheerfulness; merriment

fromm *a* devout; (*gutartig*) docile

Frömmigkeit *f* - devoutness

Fronleichnam *m* Corpus Christi

Front *f* **-, -en** front. **f~al** *a* frontal; <*Zusammenstoß*> head-on ● *adv* from the front; <*zusammenstoßen*> head-on. **F~alzusammenstoß** *m* head-on collision

Frosch *m* **-[e]s,¨e** frog. **F~laich** *m* frog-spawn. **F~mann** *m* (*pl* **-männer**) frogman

Frost *m* **-[e]s,¨e** frost. **F~beule** *f* chilblain

frösteln *vi* (*haben*) shiver

frost|ig *a* frosty. **F~schutzmittel** *nt* antifreeze

Frottee *nt* & *m* **-s** towelling

frottier|en *vt* rub down. **F~[hand]tuch** *nt* terry towel

Frucht *f* **-,¨e** fruit; **F~ tragen** bear fruit. **f~bar** *a* fertile; (*fig*) fruitful. **F~barkeit** *f* - fertility

früh *a* early ● *adv* early; (*morgens*) in the morning; **heute f~** this morning; **von f~ an** *od* **auf** from an early age. **F~aufsteher** *m* **-s,-** early riser. **F~e** *f* - **in aller F~e** bright and early; **in der F~e** (*SGer*) in the morning. **f~er** *adv* earlier; (*eher*) sooner; (*ehemals*) formerly; (*vor langer Zeit*) in the old days; **f~er oder später** sooner or later; **ich wohnte f~er in X** I used to live in X. **f~ere(r,s)** *a* earlier; (*ehemalig*) former; (*vorige*) previous; **in f~eren Zeiten** in former times. **f~estens** *adv* at the earliest. **F~geburt** *f* premature birth/(*Kind*) baby. **F~jahr** *nt* spring. **F~ling** *m* **-s, -e** spring. **f~morgens** *adv* early in the morning. **f~reif** *a* precocious

Frühstück *nt* breakfast. **f~en** *vi* (*haben*) have breakfast

frühzeitig *a* & *adv* early; (*vorzeitig*) premature

Frustr|ation /-'tsio:n/ *f* **-, -en** frustration. **f~ieren** *vt* frustrate

Fuchs *m* **-es,¨e** fox; (*Pferd*) chestnut. **f~en** *vt* [!] annoy

Füchsin *f* **-, -nen** vixen

Fuge[1] *f* **-, -n** joint

Fuge[2] *f* **-, -n** (*Mus*) fugue

füg|en *vt* fit (**in** + *acc* into); (*an-*) join (**an** + *acc* on to); (*dazu-*) add (**zu** to); **sich f~en** fit (**in** + *acc* into); adjoin/(*folgen*) follow (**an** **etw** *acc* sth); (*fig: gehorchen*) submit (*dat* to). **f~sam** *a* obedient. **F~ung** *f* **-, -en eine F~ung des Schicksals** a stroke of fate

fühl|bar *a* noticeable. **f~en** *vt/i* (*haben*) feel; **sich f~en** feel (**krank/einsam** ill/lonely); ([!]

stolz sein) fancy oneself. **F~er** *m* **-s,-** feeler. **F~ung** *f* **-** contact

Fuhre *f* **-, -n** load

führ|en *vt* lead; guide <*Tourist*>; (*geleiten*) take; (*leiten*) run; (*befehligen*) command; (*verkaufen*) stock; bear <*Namen*>; keep <*Liste, Bücher*>; **bei** *od* **mit sich f~en** carry ● *vi* (*haben*) lead; (*verlaufen*) go, run; **zu etw f~en** lead to sth. **f~end** *a* leading. **F~er** *m* **-s,-** leader; (*Fremden-*) guide; (*Buch*) guide[book]. **F~erhaus** *nt* driver's cab. **F~erschein** *m* driving licence; **den F~erschein machen** take one's driving test. **F~erscheinentzug** *m* disqualification from driving. **F~ung** *f* **-, -en** leadership; (*Leitung*) management; (*Mil*) command; (*Betragen*) conduct; (*Besichtigung*) guided tour; (*Vorsprung*) lead; **in F~ung gehen** go into the lead

Fuhr|unternehmer *m* haulage contractor. **F~werk** *nt* cart

Fülle *f* **-, -n** abundance, wealth (**an** + *dat* of); (*Körper-*) plumpness. **f~n** *vt* fill; (*Culin*) stuff

Füllen *nt* **-s,-** foal

Füll|er *m* **-s,-** [!], **F~federhalter** *m* fountain pen. **F~ung** *f* **-, -en** filling; (*Braten-*) stuffing

fummeln *vi* (*haben*) fumble (**an** + *dat* with)

Fund *m* **-[e]s, -e** find

Fundament *nt* **-[e]s, -e** foundations *pl*. **f~al** *a* fundamental

Fundbüro *nt* lost-property office

fünf *inv a*, **F~** *f* **-, -en** five; (*Sch*) ≈ fail mark. **F~linge** *mpl* quintuplets. **f~te(r,s)** *a* fifth. **f~zehn** *inv a* fifteen. **f~zehnte(r,s)** *a* fifteenth. **f~zig** *inv a* fifty. **f~zigste(r,s)** *a* fiftieth

fungieren *vi* (*haben*) act (**als** as)

Funk *m* **-s** radio. **F~e** *m* **-n, -n** spark. **f~eln** *vi* (*haben*) sparkle; <*Stern:*> twinkle. **F~en** *m* **-s,-** spark. **f~en** *vt* radio. **F~sprechgerät** *nt* walkie-talkie. **F~spruch** *m* radio message. **F~streife** *f* [police] radio patrol

Funktion /-ˈtsi̯o:n/ *f* **-, -en** function; (*Stellung*) position; (*Funktionieren*) working; **außer F~** out of action. **F~är** *m* **-s, -e** official. **f~ieren** *vi* (*haben*) work

für *prep* (+ *acc*) for; **Schritt für Schritt** step by step; **was für [ein]** what [a]! (*fragend*) what sort of [a]? **Für** *nt* **das Für und Wider** the pros and cons *pl*

Furche *f* **-, -n** furrow

Furcht *f* **-** fear (**vor** + *dat* of); **F~erregend** terrifying. **f~bar** *a* terrible

fürcht|en *vt/i* (*haben*) fear; **sich f~en** be afraid (**vor** + *dat* of). **f~erlich** *a* dreadful

füreinander *adv* for each other

Furnier *nt* **-s, -e** veneer. **f~t** *a* veneered

Fürsorg|e *f* care; (*Admin*) welfare; ([!] *Geld*) ≈ social security. **F~er(in)** *m* **-s,-** (*f* **-, -nen**) social worker. **f~lich** *a* solicitous

Fürst *m* **-en, -en** prince. **F~entum** *nt* **-s,⸚er** principality. **F~in** *f* **-, -nen** princess

Furt *f* **-, -en** ford

Furunkel *m* **-s,-** (*Med*) boil

Fürwort *nt* (*pl* **-wörter**) pronoun

Furz *m* **-es, -e** (*vulg*) fart

Fusion *f* **-, -en** fusion; (*Comm*) merger

Fuß *m* **-es,⸚e** foot; (*Aust: Bein*) leg; (*Lampen-*) base; (*von Weinglas*) stem; **zu Fuß** on foot; **zu Fuß**

gehen walk; **auf freiem Fuß** free.
F~abdruck *m* footprint.
F~abtreter *m* **-s,-** doormat.
F~ball *m* football.
F~ballspieler *m* footballer.
F~balltoto *nt* football pools *pl.*
F~bank *f* footstool. **F~boden** *m* floor

Fussel *f* **-, -n** & *m* **-s, -[n]** piece of fluff; **F~n** fluff *sg.* **f~n** *vi* (*haben*) shed fluff

fußen *vi* (*haben*) be based (**auf** + *dat* on)

Fußgänger|(in) *m* **-s,-** (*f* **-, -nen**) pedestrian. **F~brücke** *f* footbridge. **F~zone** *f* pedestrian precinct

Fuß|geher *m* **-s,-** (*Aust*) = **F~gänger.** **F~gelenk** *nt* ankle. **F~hebel** *m* pedal.
F~nagel *m* toenail. **F~note** *f* footnote. **F~pflege** *f* chiropody.
F~rücken *m* instep. **F~sohle** *f* sole of the foot. **F~tritt** *m* kick. **F~weg** *m* footpath; **eine Stunde F~weg** an hour's walk

futsch *pred a* 🅸 gone

Futter[1] *nt* **-s** feed; (*Trocken-*) fodder

Futter[2] *nt* **-s,-** (*Kleider-*) lining

Futteral *nt* **-s, -e** case

füttern[1] *vt* feed

füttern[2] *vt* line

Futur *nt* **-s** (*Gram*) future

Gg

Gabe *f* **-, -n** gift; (*Dosis*) dose

Gabel *f* **-, -n** fork. **g~n (sich)** *vr* fork. **G~stapler** *m* **-s,-** fork-lift truck. **G~ung** *f* **-, -en** fork

gackern *vi* (*haben*) cackle

gaffen *vi* (*haben*) gape, stare

Gage /ˈɡaːʒə/ *f* **-, -n** (*Theat*) fee

gähnen *vi* (*haben*) yawn

Gala *f* **-** ceremonial dress. **G~vorstellung** *f* gala performance

Galerie *f* **-, -n** gallery

Galgen *m* **-s,-** gallows *sg.* **G~frist** *f* 🅸 reprieve

Galionsfigur *f* figurehead

Galle *f* **-** bile; (*G~nblase*) gall-bladder. **G~nblase** *f* gall-bladder. **G~nstein** *m* gallstone

Galopp *m* **-s** gallop; **im G~** at a gallop. **g~ieren** *vi* (*sein*) gallop

gamm|eln *vi* (*haben*) 🅸 loaf around. **G~ler(in)** *m* **-s,-** (*f* **-, -nen**) drop-out

Gams *f* **-, -en** (*Aust*) chamois

Gämse *f* **-, -n** chamois

Gang *m* **-[e]s,¨e** walk; (*G~art*) gait; (*Boten-*) errand; (*Funktionieren*) running; (*Verlauf, Culin*) course; (*Durch-*) passage; (*Korridor*) corridor; (*zwischen Sitzreihen*) aisle, gangway; (*Anat*) duct; (*Auto*) gear; **in G~ bringen** get going; **im G~e sein** be in progress; **Essen mit vier G¨en** four-course meal

gängig *a* common; (*Comm*) popular

Gangschaltung *f* gear change

Gangster /ˈɡɛŋstɐ/ *m* **-s,-** gangster

Ganove *m* **-n, -n** 🅸 crook

Gans *f* **-,¨e** goose

Gänse|blümchen *nt* **-s,-** daisy. **G~füßchen** *ntpl* inverted commas. **G~haut** *f* goose-pimples *pl.* **G~rich** *m* **-s, -e** gander

ganz *a* whole, entire; (*vollständig*) complete; (🅸 *heil*) undamaged, intact; **die g~e Zeit** all the time, the whole time; **eine**

g~e Weile/Menge quite a while/lot; *inv* **g~ Deutschland** the whole of Germany; **wieder g~ machen** [!] mend; **im Großen und G~en** on the whole ● *adv* quite; (*völlig*) completely, entirely; (*sehr*) very; **nicht g~** not quite; **g~ allein** all on one's own; **g~ und gar** completely, totally; **g~ und gar nicht** not at all. **G~e(s)** *nt* whole. **g~jährig** *adv* all the year round. **g~tägig** *a & adv* full-time; <*geöffnet*> all day. **g~tags** *adv* all day; <*arbeiten*> full-time

gar¹ *a* done, cooked

gar² *adv* **gar nicht/nichts/niemand** not/nothing/no one at all

Garage /ga'ra:ʒə/ *f* **-, -n** garage

Garantie *f* **-, -n** guarantee. **g~ren** *vt/i* (*haben*) **[für] etw g~ren** guarantee sth. **G~schein** *m* guarantee

Garderobe *f* **-, -n** (*Kleider*) wardrobe; (*Ablage*) cloakroom; (*Künstler-*) dressing-room. **G~nfrau** *f* cloakroom attendant

Gardine *f* **-, -n** curtain

garen *vt/i* (*haben*) cook

gären† *vi* (*haben*) ferment; (*fig*) seethe

Garn *nt* **-[e]s, -e** yarn; (*Näh-*) cotton

Garnele *f* **-, -n** shrimp; prawn

garnieren *vt* decorate; (*Culin*) garnish

Garnison *f* **-, -en** garrison

Garnitur *f* **-, -en** set; (*Möbel-*) suite

Garten *m* **-s,¨** garden. **G~arbeit** *f* gardening. **G~bau** *m* horticulture. **G~haus** *nt*, **G~laube** *f* summerhouse. **G~schere** *f* secateurs *pl*

Gärtner|(in) *m* **-s,-** (*f* **-, -nen**) gardener. **G~ei** *f* **-, -en** nursery

Gärung *f* **-** fermentation

Gas *nt* **-es, -e** gas; **Gas geben** [!] accelerate. **G~maske** *f* gas mask. **G~pedal** *nt* (*Auto*) accelerator

Gasse *f* **-, -n** alley; (*Aust*) street

Gast *m* **-[e]s,¨e** guest; (*Hotel-*) visitor; (*im Lokal*) patron; **zum Mittag G¨~e haben** have people to lunch; **bei jdm zu G~ sein** be staying with s.o. **G~arbeiter** *m* foreign worker. **G~bett** *nt* spare bed

Gäste|bett *nt* spare bed. **G~buch** *nt* visitors' book. **G~zimmer** *nt* [hotel] room; (*privat*) spare room

gast|freundlich *a* hospitable. **G~freundschaft** *f* hospitality. **G~geber** *m* **-s,-** host. **G~geberin** *f* **-, -nen** hostess. **G~haus** *nt*, **G~hof** *m* inn, hotel

gastlich *a* hospitable

Gastronomie *f* **-** gastronomy

Gast|spiel *nt* guest performance. **G~spielreise** *f* (*Theat*) tour. **G~stätte** *f* restaurant. **G~wirt** *m* landlord. **G~wirtin** *f* landlady. **G~wirtschaft** *f* restaurant

Gas|werk *nt* gasworks *sg*. **G~zähler** *m* gas-meter

Gatte *m* **-n, -n** husband

Gattin *f* **-, -nen** wife

Gattung *f* **-, -en** kind; (*Biol*) genus; (*Kunst*) genre

Gaudi *f* **-** (*Aust, fam*) fun

Gaumen *m* **-s,-** palate

Gauner *m* **-s,-** crook, swindler. **G~ei** *f* **-, -en** swindle

Gaze /'ga:zə/ *f* **-** gauze

Gazelle *f* **-, -n** gazelle

Gebäck *nt* **-s** [cakes and] pastries *pl*; (*Kekse*) biscuits *pl*

Gebälk *nt* **-s** timbers *pl*

geballt *a* <*Faust*> clenched

Gebärde *f* **-, -n** gesture

gebär|en† *vt* give birth to, bear; **geboren werden** be born. **G~mutter** *f* womb, uterus
Gebäude *nt* **-s,-** building
Gebeine *ntpl* [mortal] remains
Gebell *nt* **-s** barking
geben† *vt* give; (*tun, bringen*) put; (*Karten*) deal; (*aufführen*) perform; (*unterrichten*) teach; **etw verloren g~** give sth up as lost; **viel/wenig g~ auf** (+ *acc*) set great/little store by; **sich g~** (*nachlassen*) wear off; (*besser werden*) get better; (*sich verhalten*) behave ● *impers* **es gibt** there is/are; **was gibt es Neues/zum Mittag/im Kino?** what's the news/for lunch/on at the cinema? **es wird Regen g~** it's going to rain ● *vi* (*haben*) (*Karten*) deal
Gebet *nt* **-[e]s, -e** prayer
Gebiet *nt* **-[e]s, -e** area; (*Hoheits-*) territory; (*Sach-*) field
gebieten† *vt* command; (*erfordern*) demand ● *vi* (*haben*) rule
Gebilde *nt* **-s,-** structure
gebildet *a* educated; (*kultiviert*) cultured
Gebirg|e *nt* **-s,-** mountains *pl*. **g~ig** *a* mountainous
Gebiss *nt* **-es, -e** teeth *pl*; (*künstliches*) false teeth *pl*; dentures *pl*, (*des Zaumes*) bit
geblümt *a* floral, flowered
gebogen *a* curved
geboren *a* born; **g~er Deutscher** German by birth; **Frau X, g~e Y** Mrs X, née Y
Gebot *nt* **-[e]s, -e** rule
gebraten *a* fried
Gebrauch *m* use; (*Sprach-*) usage; **Gebräuche** customs; **in G~** in use; **G~ machen von** make use of. **g~en** *vt* use; **zu nichts zu g~en** useless
gebräuchlich *a* common; <*Wort*> in common use
Gebrauch|sanleitung, G~sanweisung *f* directions *pl* for use. **g~t** *a* used; (*Comm*) secondhand. **G~twagen** *m* used car
gebrechlich *a* frail, infirm
gebrochen *a* broken ● *adv* **g~ Englisch sprechen** speak broken English
Gebrüll *nt* **-s** roaring
Gebühr *f* **-, -en** charge, fee; **über G~** excessively. **g~end** *a* due; (*geziemend*) proper. **g~enfrei** *a* free ● *adv* free of charge. **g~enpflichtig** *a & adv* subject to a charge; **g~enpflichtige Straße** toll road
Geburt *f* **-, -en** birth; **von G~** by birth. **G~enkontrolle, G~enregelung** *f* birth-control. **G~enziffer** *f* birth-rate
gebürtig *a* native (**aus** of); **g~er Deutscher** German by birth
Geburts|datum *nt* date of birth. **G~helfer** *m* obstetrician. **G~hilfe** *f* obstetrics *sg*. **G~ort** *m* place of birth. **G~tag** *m* birthday. **G~urkunde** *f* birth certificate
Gebüsch *nt* **-[e]s, -e** bushes *pl*
Gedächtnis *nt* **-ses** memory; **aus dem G~** from memory
Gedanke *m* **-ns, -n** thought (**an** + *acc* of); (*Idee*) idea; **sich** (*dat*) **G~n machen** worry (**über** + *acc* about). **g~nlos** *a* thoughtless; (*zerstreut*) absent-minded. **G~nstrich** *m* dash
Gedärme *ntpl* intestines; (*Tier-*) entrails
Gedeck *nt* **-[e]s, -e** place setting; (*auf Speisekarte*) set meal
gedeihen† *vi* (*sein*) thrive, flourish
gedenken† *vi* (*haben*) propose (**etw zu tun** to do sth); **jds g~** remember s.o. **G~** *nt* **-s** memory

Gedenk|feier *f* commemoration. **G~gottesdienst** *m* memorial service
Gedicht *nt* **-[e]s, -e** poem
Gedräng|e *nt* **-s** crush, crowd. **g~t** *a* (*knapp*) concise ● *adv* **g~t voll** packed
Geduld *f* **-** patience; **G~ haben** be patient. **g~en (sich)** *vr* be patient. **g~ig** *a* patient. **G~[s]spiel** *nt* puzzle
gedunsen *a* bloated
geehrt *a* honoured; **Sehr g~er Herr X** Dear Mr X
geeignet *a* suitable; **im g~en Moment** at the right moment
Gefahr *f* **-, -en** danger; **in G~** in danger; **auf eigene G~** at one's own risk; **G~ laufen** run the risk (**etw zu tun** of doing sth)
gefähr|den *vt* endanger; (*fig*) jeopardize. **g~lich** *a* dangerous
gefahrlos *a* safe
Gefährt *nt* **-[e]s, -e** vehicle
Gefährte *m* **-n, -n, Gefährtin** *f* **-, -nen** companion
gefahrvoll *a* dangerous, perilous
Gefälle *nt* **-s,-** slope; (*Straßen-*) gradient
gefallen† *vi* (*haben*) **jdm g~** please s.o.; **er/es gefällt mir** I like him/it; **sich** (*dat*) **etw g~ lassen** put up with sth
Gefallen[1] *m* **-s,-** favour
Gefallen[2] *nt* **-s** pleasure (**an** + *dat* in); **dir zu G~** to please you
Gefallene|(r) *m* soldier killed in the war; **die G~n** the fallen
gefällig *a* pleasing; (*hübsch*) attractive; (*hilfsbereit*) obliging; **noch etwas g~?** will there be anything else? **G~keit** *f* **-, -en** favour; (*Freundlichkeit*) kindness
Gefangen|e(r) *m/f* prisoner. **G~nahme** *f* **-** capture. **g~nehmen*** *vt sep* **g~ nehmen**, *s.* **fangen. G~schaft** *f* **-** captivity
Gefängnis *nt* **-ses, -se** prison; (*Strafe*) imprisonment. **G~strafe** *f* imprisonment; (*Urteil*) prison sentence. **G~wärter** *m* [prison] warder
Gefäß *nt* **-es, -e** container; (*Blut-*) vessel
gefasst *a* composed; (*ruhig*) calm; **g~ sein auf** (+ *acc*) be prepared for
gefedert *a* sprung
gefeiert *a* celebrated
Gefieder *nt* **-s** plumage
gefleckt *a* spotted
Geflügel *nt* **-s** poultry. **G~klein** *nt* **-s** giblets *pl*. **g~t** *a* winged
Geflüster *nt* **-s** whispering
Gefolge *nt* **-s** retinue, entourage
gefragt *a* popular
Gefreite(r) *m* lance-corporal
gefrier|en† *vi* (*sein*) freeze. **G~fach** *nt* freezer compartment. **G~punkt** *m* freezing point. **G~schrank** *m* upright freezer. **G~truhe** *f* chest freezer
gefroren *a* frozen
gefügig *a* compliant; (*gehorsam*) obedient
Gefühl *nt* **-[e]s, -e** feeling; (*Empfindung*) sensation; (*G~sregung*) emotion; **im G~ haben** know instinctively. **g~los** *a* insensitive; (*herzlos*) unfeeling; (*taub*) numb. **g~smäßig** *a* emotional; (*instinktiv*) instinctive. **G~sregung** *f* emotion. **g~voll** *a* sensitive; (*sentimental*) sentimental
gefüllt *a* filled; (*voll*) full
gefürchtet *a* feared, dreaded
gefüttert *a* lined
gegeben *a* given; (*bestehend*) present; (*passend*) appropriate. **g~enfalls** *adv* if need be
gegen *prep* (+ *acc*) against; (*Sport*) versus; (*g~über*)

to[wards]; (*Vergleich*) compared with; (*Richtung, Zeit*) towards; (*ungefähr*) around; **ein Mittel g~** a remedy for ● *adv* **g~ 100 Leute** about 100 people. **G~angriff** *m* counter-attack

Gegend *f* **-, -en** area, region; (*Umgebung*) neighbourhood

gegeneinander *adv* against/ (*gegenüber*) towards one another

Gegen|fahrbahn *f* opposite carriageway. **G~gift** *nt* antidote. **G~maßnahme** *f* countermeasure. **G~satz** *m* contrast; (*Widerspruch*) contradiction; (*G~teil*) opposite; **im G~satz zu** unlike. **g~seitig** *a* mutual; **sich g~seitig hassen** hate one another. **G~stand** *m* object; (*Gram, Gesprächs-*) subject. **G~stück** *nt* counterpart; (*G~teil*) opposite. **G~teil** *nt* opposite, contrary; **im G~teil** on the contrary. **g~teilig** *a* opposite

gegenüber *prep* (+ *dat*) opposite; (*Vergleich*) compared with; **jdm g~ höflich sein** be polite to s.o. ● *adv* opposite. **G~** *nt* **-s** person opposite. **g~liegend** *a* opposite. **g~stehen**† *vi sep* (*haben*) (+ *dat*) face; **feindlich g~stehen** (+ *dat*) be hostile to. **g~stellen** *vt sep* confront; (*vergleichen*) compare

Gegen|verkehr *m* oncoming traffic. **G~vorschlag** *m* counter-proposal. **G~wart** *f* - present; (*Anwesenheit*) presence. **g~wärtig** *a* present ● *adv* at present. **G~wehr** *f* - resistance. **G~wert** *m* equivalent. **G~wind** *m* head wind. **g~zeichnen** *vt sep* countersign

geglückt *a* successful

Gegner|(in) *m* **-s,-** (*f* **-, -nen**) opponent. **g~isch** *a* opposing

Gehabe *nt* **-s** affected behaviour

Gehackte(s) *nt* mince

Gehalt *nt* **-[e]s,¨er** salary. **G~serhöhung** *f* rise

gehässig *a* spiteful

gehäuft *a* heaped

Gehäuse *nt* **-s,-** case; (*TV, Radio*) cabinet; (*Schnecken-*) shell

Gehege *nt* **-s,-** enclosure

geheim *a* secret; **g~ halten** keep secret; **im G~en** secretly. **G~dienst** *m* Secret Service. **G~nis** *nt* **-ses, -se** secret. **g~nisvoll** *a* mysterious

gehemmt *a* (*fig*) inhibited

gehen†

● *intransitive verb* (*sein*)

····➤ (*sich irgendwohin begeben*) go; (*zu Fuß*) walk. **tanzen/schwimmen/einkaufen gehen** go dancing/swimming/shopping. **schlafen gehen** go to bed. **zum Arzt gehen** go to the doctor's. **in die Schule gehen** go to school. **auf und ab gehen** walk up and down. **über die Straße gehen** cross the street

····➤ (*weggehen; fam: abfahren*) go; leave. **ich muss bald gehen** I must go soon. **Sie können gehen** you may go. **der Zug geht um zehn Uhr** [!] the train leaves *or* goes at ten o'clock

····➤ (*funktionieren*) work. **der Computer geht wieder/nicht mehr** the computer is working again/has stopped working. **meine Uhr geht falsch/richtig** my watch is wrong/right

····➤ (*möglich sein*) be possible. **ja, das geht** yes, I *or* we can manage that. **das geht nicht** that can't be done; ([!] *ist nicht akzeptabel*) it's not good enough, it's not on [!]. **es geht einfach nicht, dass du so spät nach Hause kommst** it simply won't do for you to come home so late

····➤ ([!] *gerade noch angehen*) **es geht [so]** it is all right. **Wie war**

die Party? — Es ging so How was the party? — Not bad *or* So-so
····➤ (*sich entwickeln*) do; go. **der Laden geht gut** the shop is doing well. **es geht alles nach Wunsch** everything is going to plan
····➤ (*impers*) **wie geht es Ihnen?** how are you? **es geht ihm gut/schlecht** (*gesundheitlich*) he is well/not well; (*geschäftlich*) he is doing well/badly; **ein gut g~des Geschäft** a thriving business
····➤ (*impers; sich um etw handeln*) **es geht um** it concerns. **worum geht es hier?** what is this all about? **es geht ihr nur ums Geld** she is only interested in money

Geheul *nt* **-s** howling
Gehilfe *m* **-n, -n, Gehilfin** *f* **-, -nen** trainee; (*Helfer*) assistant
Gehirn *nt* **-s** brain; (*Verstand*) brains *pl*. **G~erschütterung** *f* concussion. **G~hautentzündung** *f* meningitis. **G~wäsche** *f* brainwashing
gehoben *a* (*fig*) superior
Gehöft *nt* **-[e]s, -e** farm
Gehör *nt* **-s** hearing
gehorchen *vi* (*haben*) (+ *dat*) obey
gehören *vi* (*haben*) belong (*dat* to); **dazu gehört Mut** that takes courage; **es gehört sich nicht** it isn't done
gehörlos *a* deaf
Gehörn *nt* **-s, -e** horns *pl*; (*Geweih*) antlers *pl*
gehorsam *a* obedient. **G~** *m* **-s** obedience
Geh|steig *m* **-[e]s, -e** pavement. **G~weg** *m* = **Gehsteig;** (*Fußweg*) footpath
Geier *m* **-s,-** vulture
Geig|e *f* **-, -n** violin. **g~en** *vi* (*haben*) play the violin ● *vt* play on the violin. **G~er(in)** *m* **-s,-** (*f* **-, -nen**) violinist
geil *a* lecherous; randy; ([!] *toll*) great
Geisel *f* **-, -n** hostage
Geiß *f* **-, -en** (*SGer*) [nanny-]goat. **G~blatt** *nt* honeysuckle
Geist *m* **-[e]s, -er** mind; (*Witz*) wit; (*Gesinnung*) spirit; (*Gespenst*) ghost; **der Heilige G~** the Holy Ghost *or* Spirit
geistes|abwesend *a* absent-minded. **G~blitz** *m* brainwave. **g~gegenwärtig** *adv* with great presence of mind. **g~gestört** *a* [mentally] deranged. **g~krank** *a* mentally ill. **G~krankheit** *f* mental illness. **G~wissenschaften** *fpl* arts. **G~zustand** *m* mental state
geist|ig *a* mental; (*intellektuell*) intellectual. **g~lich** *a* spiritual; (*religiös*) religious; <*Musik*> sacred; <*Tracht*> clerical. **G~liche(r)** *m* clergyman. **G~lichkeit** *f* **-** clergy. **g~reich** *a* clever; (*witzig*) witty
Geiz *m* **-es** meanness. **g~en** *vi* (*haben*) be mean (**mit** with). **G~hals** *m* [!] miser. **g~ig** *a* mean, miserly. **G~kragen** *m* [!] miser
Gekicher *nt* **-s** giggling
geknickt *a* [!] dejected
gekonnt *a* accomplished ● *adv* expertly
gekränkt *a* offended, hurt
Gekritzel *nt* **-s** scribble
Gelächter *nt* **-s** laughter
geladen *a* loaded
gelähmt *a* paralysed
Geländer *nt* **-s,-** railings *pl*; (*Treppen-*) banisters *pl*
gelangen *vi* (*sein*) reach/(*fig*) attain (**zu etw/an etw** *acc* sth)
gelassen *a* composed; (*ruhig*) calm. **G~heit** *f* **-** equanimity; (*Fassung*) composure

Gelatine /ʒela-/ *f* - gelatine

geläufig *a* common, current; (*fließend*) fluent; **jdm g~ sein** be familiar to s.o.

gelaunt *a* **gut/schlecht g~ sein** be in a good/bad mood

gelb *a* yellow; (*bei Ampel*) amber; **das G~e vom Ei** the yolk of the egg. **G~** *nt* **-s,-** yellow. **g~lich** *a* yellowish. **G~sucht** *f* jaundice

Geld *nt* **-es, -er** money; **öffentliche G~er** public funds. **G~automat** *m* cashpoint machine. **G~beutel** *m*, **G~börse** *f* purse. **G~geber** *m* **-s,-** backer. **g~lich** *a* financial. **G~mittel** *ntpl* funds. **G~schein** *m* banknote. **G~schrank** *m* safe. **G~strafe** *f* fine. **G~stück** *nt* coin

Gelee /ʒe'le:/ *nt* **-s, -s** jelly

gelegen *a* situated; (*passend*) convenient

Gelegenheit *f* **-, -en** opportunity, chance; (*Anlass*) occasion; (*Comm*) bargain; **bei G~** some time. **G~sarbeit** *f* casual work. **G~skauf** *m* bargain

gelegentlich *a* occasional ● *adv* occasionally; (*bei Gelegenheit*) some time

Gelehrte(r) *m/f* scholar

Geleit *nt* **-[e]s** escort; **freies G~** safe conduct. **g~en** *vt* escort

Gelenk *nt* **-[e]s, -e** joint. **g~ig** *a* supple; (*Techn*) flexible

gelernt *a* skilled

Geliebte(r) *m/f* lover

gelingen† *vi* (*sein*) succeed, be successful. **G~** *nt* **-s** success

gellend *a* shrill

geloben *vt* promise [solemnly]; **das Gelobte Land** the Promised Land

Gelöbnis *nt* **-ses, -se** vow

gelöst *a* (*fig*) relaxed

gelten† *vi* (*haben*) be valid; <*Regel*:> apply; **g~ als** be regarded as; **etw nicht g~ lassen** not accept sth; **wenig/viel g~** be worth/(*fig*) count for little/a lot; **jdm g~** be meant for s.o.; **das gilt nicht** that doesn't count. **g~d** *a* valid; <*Preise*> current; <*Meinung*> prevailing; **g~d machen** assert <*Recht, Forderung*>; bring to bear <*Einfluss*>

Geltung *f* - validity; (*Ansehen*) prestige; **zur G~ bringen** set off

Gelübde *nt* **-s,-** vow

gelungen *a* successful

Gelüst *nt* **-[e]s, -e** desire

gemächlich *a* leisurely ● *adv* in a leisurely manner

Gemahl *m* **-s, -e** husband. **G~in** *f* **-, -nen** wife

Gemälde *nt* **-s,-** painting. **G~galerie** *f* picture gallery

gemäß *prep* (+ *dat*) in accordance with

gemäßigt *a* moderate; <*Klima*> temperate

gemein *a* common; (*unanständig*) vulgar; (*niederträchtig*) mean; **g~er Soldat** private

Gemeinde *f* **-, -n** [local] community; (*Admin*) borough; (*Pfarr-*) parish; (*bei Gottesdienst*) congregation. **G~rat** *m* local council/(*Person*) councillor. **G~wahlen** *fpl* local elections

gemein|gefährlich *a* dangerous. **G~heit** *f* **-, -en** commonness; vulgarity; meanness; (*Bemerkung, Handlung*) mean thing [to say/do]; **so eine G~heit!** how mean! **G~kosten** *pl* overheads. **g~nützig** *a* charitable. **g~sam** *a* common ● *adv* together

Gemeinschaft *f* **-, -en** community. **g~lich** *a* joint;

<*Besitz*> communal ● *adv* jointly; (*zusammen*) together. **G~sarbeit** *f* team-work

Gemenge *nt* **-s,-** mixture

Gemisch *nt* **-[e]s, -e** mixture. **g~t** *a* mixed

Gemme *f* **-, -n** engraved gem

Gemse* *f* **-, -n** *s.* **Gämse**

Gemurmel *nt* **-s** murmuring

Gemüse *nt* **-s,-** vegetable; (*coll*) vegetables *pl*. **G~händler** *m* greengrocer

gemustert *a* patterned

Gemüt *nt* **-[e]s, -er** nature, disposition; (*Gefühl*) feelings *pl*

gemütlich *a* cosy; (*gemächlich*) leisurely; (*zwanglos*) informal; <*Person*> genial; **es sich** (*dat*) **g~ machen** make oneself comfortable. **G~keit** *f* **-** cosiness

Gen *nt* **-s, -e** gene

genau *a* exact, precise; <*Waage, Messung*> accurate; (*sorgfältig*) meticulous; (*ausführlich*) detailed; **nichts G~es wissen** not know any details; **g~ genommen** strictly speaking; **g~!** exactly! **G~igkeit** *f* **-** exactitude; precision; accuracy; meticulousness

genauso *adv* just the same; (*g~sehr*) just as much; **g~ teuer** just as expensive; **g~ gut** just as good; *adv* just as well; **g~ sehr** just as much; **g~ viel** just as much/many; **g~ wenig** just as little/few; (*noch*) no more

Gendarm /ʒãˈdarm/ *m* **-en, -en** (*Aust*) policeman

Genealogie *f* **-** genealogy

genehmig|en *vt* grant; approve <*Plan*>. **G~ung** *f* **-, -en** permission; (*Schein*) permit

geneigt *a* sloping, inclined; (*fig*) well-disposed (*dat* towards)

General *m* **-s,¨-e** general. **G~direktor** *m* managing director. **G~probe** *f* dress rehearsal. **G~streik** *m* general strike

Generation /-ˈtsi̯o:n/ *f* **-, -en** generation

Generator *m* **-s, -en** /-ˈto:rən/ generator

generell *a* general

genes|en† *vi* (*sein*) recover. **G~ung** *f* **-** recovery; (*Erholung*) convalescence

Genetik *f* **-** genetics *sg*

genetisch *a* genetic

Genf *nt* **-s** Geneva. **G~er** *a* Geneva ...; **G~er See** Lake Geneva

genial *a* brilliant. **G~ität** *f* genius

Genick *nt* **-s, -e** [back of the] neck; **sich** (*dat*) **das G~ brechen** break one's neck

Genie /ʒeˈni:/ *nt* **-s, -s** genius

genieren /ʒeˈni:rən/ *vt* embarrass; **sich g~** feel *or* be embarrassed

genieß|bar *a* fit to eat/drink. **g~en**† *vt* enjoy; (*verzehren*) eat/drink

Genitiv *m* **-s, -e** genitive

genmanipuliert *a* genetically modified

Genom *nt* **-s, -e** genome

Genosse *m* **-n, -n** (*Pol*) comrade. **G~nschaft** *f* **-, -en** cooperative

Gentechnologie *f* genetic engineering

genug *inv a & adv* enough

Genüge *f* **zur G~** sufficiently. **g~n** *vi* (*haben*) be enough. **g~nd** *inv a* sufficient, enough; (*Sch*) fair ● *adv* sufficiently, enough

Genuss *m* **-es,¨-e** enjoyment; (*Vergnügen*) pleasure; (*Verzehr*) consumption

geöffnet *a* open

Geo|graphie, G~grafie *f* **-** geography. **g~graphisch, g~grafisch** *a* geographical.

G~logie *f* - geology. **g~logisch** *a* geological. **G~meter** *m* **-s,-** surveyor. **G~metrie** *f* - geometry. **g~metrisch** *a* geometric[al]

geordnet *a* well-ordered; (*stabil*) stable; **alphabetisch g~** in alphabetical order

Gepäck *nt* **-s** luggage, baggage. **G~ablage** *f* luggage-rack. **G~aufbewahrung** *f* left-luggage office. **G~schein** *m* left-luggage ticket; (*Aviat*) baggage check. **G~träger** *m* porter; (*Fahrrad-*) luggage carrier; (*Dach-*) roof-rack

Gepard *m* **-s, -e** cheetah

gepflegt *a* well-kept; <*Person*> well-groomed; <*Hotel*> first-class

gepunktet *a* spotted

gerade *a* straight; (*direkt*) direct; (*aufrecht*) upright; (*aufrichtig*) straightforward; <*Zahl*> even ● *adv* straight; directly; (*eben*) just; (*genau*) exactly; (*besonders*) especially; **g~ sitzen/stehen** sit/stand [up] straight; **g~ erst** only just. **G~** *f* **-, -n** straight line. **g~aus** *adv* straight ahead/on. **g~heraus** *adv* (*fig*) straight out. **g~so** *adv* just the same; **g~so gut** just as good; *adv* just as well. **g~stehen**† *vi sep* (*haben*) (*fig*) accept responsibility (**für** for). **g~zu** *adv* virtually; (*wirklich*) absolutely

Geranie /-iə/ *f* **-, -n** geranium

Gerät *nt* **-[e]s, -e** tool; (*Acker-*) implement; (*Küchen-*) utensil; (*Elektro-*) appliance; (*Radio-, Fernseh-*) set; (*Turn-*) piece of apparatus; (*coll*) equipment

geraten† *vi* (*sein*) get; **in Brand g~** catch fire; **in Wut g~** get angry; **gut g~** turn out well

Geratewohl *nt* **aufs G~** at random

geräuchert *a* smoked

geräumig *a* spacious, roomy

Geräusch *nt* **-[e]s, -e** noise. **g~los** *a* noiseless

gerben *vt* tan

gerecht *a* just; (*fair*) fair. **g~fertigt** *a* justified. **G~igkeit** *f* - justice; fairness

Gerede *nt* **-s** talk

geregelt *a* regular

gereizt *a* irritable

Geriatrie *f* - geriatrics *sg*

Gericht[1] *nt* **-[e]s, -e** (*Culin*) dish

Gericht[2] *nt* **-[e]s, -e** court [of law]; **vor G~** in court; **das Jüngste G~** the Last Judgement. **g~lich** *a* judicial; <*Verfahren*> legal ● *adv* **g~lich vorgehen** take legal action. **G~shof** *m* court of justice. **G~smedizin** *f* forensic medicine. **G~ssaal** *m* court-room. **G~svollzieher** *m* **-s,-** bailiff

gerieben *a* grated; ([!] *schlau*) crafty

gering *a* small; (*niedrig*) low; (*g~fügig*) slight. **g~fügig** *a* slight. **g~schätzig** *a* contemptuous; <*Bemerkung*> disparaging. **g~ste(r,s)** *a* least; **nicht im G~sten** not in the least

gerinnen† *vi* (*sein*) curdle; <*Blut:*> clot

Gerippe *nt* **-s,-** skeleton; (*fig*) framework

gerissen *a* [!] crafty

Germ *m* **-[e]s** & (*Aust*) *f* - yeast

German|e *m* **-n, -n** [ancient] German. **g~isch** *a* Germanic. **G~istik** *f* - German [language and literature]

gern[e] *adv* gladly; **g~ haben** like; (*lieben*) be fond of; **ich tanze g~** I like dancing; **willst du mit?—g~!** do you want to come?—I'd love to!

Gerste *f* - barley. **G~nkorn** *nt* (*Med*) stye

Geruch *m* **-[e]s,¨e** smell (**von/nach** of). **g~los** *a* odourless. **G~ssinn** *m* sense of smell

Gerücht *nt* **-[e]s, -e** rumour
gerührt *a* (*fig*) moved, touched
Gerümpel *nt* **-s** lumber, junk
Gerüst *nt* **-[e]s, -e** scaffolding; (*fig*) framework
gesammelt *a* collected; (*gefasst*) composed
gesamt *a* entire, whole. **G~ausgabe** *f* complete edition. **G~eindruck** *m* overall impression. **G~heit** *f* **-** whole. **G~schule** *f* comprehensive school. **G~summe** *f* total
Gesandte(r) *m/f* envoy
Gesang *m* **-[e]s,⸚e** singing; (*Lied*) song; (*Kirchen-*) hymn. **G~verein** *m* choral society
Gesäß *nt* **-es** buttocks *pl*
Geschäft *nt* **-[e]s, -e** business; (*Laden*) shop, store; (*Transaktion*) deal; **schmutzige G~e** shady dealings; **ein gutes G~machen** do very well (**mit** out of). **g~ig** *a* busy; <*Treiben*> bustling. **G~igkeit** *f* **-** activity. **g~lich** *a* business ... ● *adv* on business
Geschäfts|brief *m* business letter. **G~führer** *m* manager; (*Vereins-*) secretary. **G~mann** *m* (*pl* **-leute**) businessman. **G~stelle** *f* office; (*Zweigstelle*) branch. **g~tüchtig** *a* **g~tüchtig sein** be a good businessman/-woman. **G~zeiten** *fpl* hours of business
geschehen† *vi* (*sein*) happen (*dat* to); **das geschieht dir recht!** it serves you right! **gern g~!** you're welcome! **G~** *nt* **-s** events *pl*
gescheit *a* clever
Geschenk *nt* **-[e]s, -e** present, gift
Geschicht|e *f* **-, -n** history; (*Erzählung*) story; (**!** *Sache*) business. **g~lich** *a* historical
Geschick *nt* **-[e]s** fate; (*Talent*) skill. **G~lichkeit** *f* **-** skilfulness, skill. **g~t** *a* skilful; (*klug*) clever
geschieden *a* divorced
Geschirr *nt* **-s, -e** (*coll*) crockery; (*Porzellan*) china; (*Service*) service; (*Pferde-*) harness; **schmutziges G~** dirty dishes *pl*. **G~spülmaschine** *f* dishwasher. **G~tuch** *nt* tea-towel
Geschlecht *nt* **-[e]s, -er** sex; (*Gram*) gender; (*Generation*) generation. **g~lich** *a* sexual. **G~skrankheit** *f* venereal disease. **G~steile** *ntpl* genitals. **G~sverkehr** *m* sexual intercourse. **G~swort** *nt* (*pl* **-wörter**) article
geschliffen *a* (*fig*) polished
Geschmack *m* **-[e]s,⸚e** taste; (*Aroma*) flavour; (*G~ssinn*) sense of taste; **einen guten G~ haben** (*fig*) have good taste. **g~los** *a* tasteless; **g~los sein** (*fig*) be in bad taste. **g~voll** *a* (*fig*) tasteful
Geschoss *nt* **-es, -e** missile; (*Stockwerk*) storey, floor
Geschrei *nt* **-s** screaming; (*fig*) fuss
Geschütz *nt* **-es, -e** gun, cannon
geschützt *a* protected; <*Stelle*> sheltered
Geschwader *nt* **-s,-** squadron
Geschwätz *nt* **-es** talk
geschweige *conj* **g~ denn** let alone
Geschwindigkeit *f* **-, -en** speed; (*Phys*) velocity. **G~sbegrenzung, G~sbeschränkung** *f* speed limit
Geschwister *pl* brother[s] and sister[s]; siblings
geschwollen *a* swollen; (*fig*) pompous
Geschworene|(r) *m/f* juror; **die G~n** the jury *sg*

Geschwulst *f* -,⸚e swelling; (*Tumor*) tumour
geschwungen *a* curved
Geschwür *nt* **-s, -e** ulcer
gesellig *a* sociable; (*Zool*) gregarious; (*unterhaltsam*) convivial; **g~er Abend** social evening
Gesellschaft *f* **-, -en** company; (*Veranstaltung*) party; **die G~** society; **jdm G~ leisten** keep s.o. company. **g~lich** *a* social. **G~sspiel** *nt* party game
Gesetz *nt* **-es, -e** law. **G~entwurf** *m* bill. **g~gebend** *a* legislative. **G~gebung** *f* **-** legislation. **g~lich** *a* legal. **g~mäßig** *a* lawful; (*gesetzlich*) legal. **g~widrig** *a* illegal
gesichert *a* secure
Gesicht *nt* **-[e]s, -er** face; (*Aussehen*) appearance. **G~sfarbe** *f* complexion. **G~spunkt** *m* point of view. **G~szüge** *mpl* features
Gesindel *nt* **-s** riff-raff
Gesinnung *f* **-, -en** mind; (*Einstellung*) attitude
gesondert *a* separate
Gespann *nt* **-[e]s, -e** team; (*Wagen*) horse and cart/carriage
gespannt *a* taut; (*fig*) tense; <*Beziehungen*> strained; (*neugierig*) eager; (*erwartungsvoll*) expectant; **g~ sein, ob** wonder whether; **auf etw g~ sein** look forward eagerly to sth
Gespenst *nt* **-[e]s, -er** ghost. **g~isch** *a* ghostly; (*unheimlich*) eerie
Gespött *nt* **-[e]s** mockery; **zum G~ werden** become a laughing-stock
Gespräch *nt* **-[e]s-e** conversation; (*Telefon-*) call; **ins G~ kommen** get talking; **im G~ sein** be under discussion. **g~ig** *a* talkative, **G~sthema** *nt* topic of conversation
Gestalt *f* **-, -en** figure; (*Form*) shape, form; **G~ annehmen** (*fig*) take shape. **g~en** *vt* shape; (*organisieren*) arrange; (*schaffen*) create; (*entwerfen*) design; **sich g~en** turn out
Geständnis *nt* **-ses, -se** confession
Gestank *m* **-s** stench, [bad] smell
gestatten *vt* allow, permit; **nicht gestattet** prohibited; **g~ Sie?** may I?
Geste /'gɛ-, 'ge:stə/ *f* **-, -n** gesture
Gesteck *nt* **-[e]s, -e** flower arrangement
gestehen† *vt/i* (*haben*) confess; confess to <*Verbrechen*>
Gestein *nt* **-[e]s, -e** rock
Gestell *nt* **-[e]s, -e** stand; (*Flaschen-*) rack; (*Rahmen*) frame
gesteppt *a* quilted
gestern *adv* yesterday; **g~ Nacht** last night
gestrandet *a* stranded
gestreift *a* striped
gestrichelt *a* <*Linie*> dotted
gestrichen *a* **g~er Teelöffel** level teaspoon[ful]
gestrig /'gɛstrɪç/ *a* yesterday's; **am g~en Tag** yesterday
Gestrüpp *nt* **-s, -e** undergrowth
Gestüt *nt* **-[e]s, -e** stud [farm]
Gesuch *nt* **-[e]s, -e** request; (*Admin*) application. **g~t** *a* sought-after
gesund *a* healthy; **g~ sein** be in good health; <*Sport, Getränk*> be good for one; **wieder g~ werden** get well again
Gesundheit *f* **-** health; **G~!** (*bei Niesen*) bless you! **g~lich** *a* health ...; **g~licher Zustand** state of health ● *adv* **es geht ihm g~lich gut/schlecht** he is in good/poor health. **g~sschädlich** *a* harmful

getäfelt *a* panelled
Getöse *nt* **-s** racket, din
Getränk *nt* **-[e]s, -e** drink. **G~ekarte** *f* wine-list
getrauen *vt* **sich** (*dat*) **etw g~** dare [to] do sth; **sich g~** dare
Getreide *nt* **-s** (*coll*) grain
getrennt *a* separate; **g~ leben** live apart; **g~ schreiben** write as two words
getreu *a* faithful ● *prep* (+ *dat*) true to. **g~lich** *adv* faithfully
Getriebe *nt* **-s,-** bustle; (*Techn*) gear; (*Auto*) transmission; (*Gehäuse*) gearbox
getrost *adv* with confidence
Getto *nt* **-s, -s** ghetto
Getue *nt* **-s** [!] fuss
Getümmel *nt* **-s** tumult
geübt *a* skilled
Gewächs *nt* **-es, -e** plant
gewachsen *a* **jdm g~ sein** be a match for s.o.
Gewächshaus *nt* greenhouse
gewagt *a* daring
gewählt *a* refined
gewahr *a* **g~ werden** become aware (*acc/gen* of)
Gewähr *f* **-** guarantee
gewähr|en *vt* grant; (*geben*) offer. **g~leisten** *vt* guarantee
Gewahrsam *m* **-s** safekeeping; (*Haft*) custody
Gewalt *f* **-, -en** power; (*Kraft*) force; (*Brutalität*) violence; **mit G~** by force. **G~herrschaft** *f* tyranny. **g~ig** *a* powerful; ([!] *groß*) enormous; (*stark*) tremendous. **g~sam** *a* forcible; <*Tod*> violent. **g~tätig** *a* violent. **G~tätigkeit** *f* **-, -en** violence; (*Handlung*) act of violence
Gewand *nt* **-[e]s,¨-er** robe
gewandt *a* skilful. **G~heit** *f* **-** skill
Gewebe *nt* **-s,-** fabric; (*Anat*) tissue
Gewehr *nt* **-s, -e** rifle, gun
Geweih *nt* **-[e]s, -e** antlers *pl*
Gewerb|e *nt* **-s,-** trade. **g~lich** *a* commercial. **g~smäßig** *a* professional
Gewerkschaft *f* **-, -en** trade union. **G~ler(in)** *m* **-s,-** (*f* **-, -nen**) trade unionist
Gewicht *nt* **-[e]s, -e** weight; (*Bedeutung*) importance. **G~heben** *nt* **-s** weight-lifting
Gewinde *nt* **-s,-** [screw] thread
Gewinn *m* **-[e]s, -e** profit; (*fig*) gain, benefit; (*beim Spiel*) winnings *pl*; (*Preis*) prize; (*Los*) winning ticket. **G~beteiligung** *f* profit-sharing. **g~en**† *vt* win; (*erlangen*) gain; (*fördern*) extract ● *vi* (*haben*) win; **g~en an** (+ *dat*) gain in. **g~end** *a* engaging. **G~er(in)** *m* **-s,-** (*f* **-, -nen**) winner
Gewirr *nt* **-s, -e** tangle; (*Straßen-*) maze
gewiss *a* certain
Gewissen *nt* **-s,-** conscience. **g~haft** *a* conscientious. **g~los** *a* unscrupulous. **G~sbisse** *mpl* pangs of conscience
gewissermaßen *adv* to a certain extent; (*sozusagen*) as it were
Gewissheit *f* **-** certainty
Gewitt|er *nt* **-s,-** thunderstorm. **g~rig** *a* thundery
gewogen *a* (*fig*) well-disposed (*dat* towards)
gewöhnen *vt* **jdn/sich g~ an** (+ *acc*) get s.o. used to/get used to; **[an] jdn/etw gewöhnt sein** be used to s.o./sth
Gewohnheit *f* **-, -en** habit. **G~srecht** *nt* common law
gewöhnlich *a* ordinary; (*üblich*) usual; (*ordinär*) common
gewohnt *a* customary; (*vertraut*) familiar; (*üblich*) usual; **etw** (*acc*) **g~ sein** be used to sth
Gewölbe *nt* **-s,-** vault

Gewühl *nt* **-[e]s** crush

gewunden *a* winding

Gewürz *nt* **-es, -e** spice. **G~nelke** *f* clove

gezackt *a* serrated

gezähnt *a* serrated; <*Säge*> toothed

Gezeiten *fpl* tides

gezielt *a* specific; <*Frage*> pointed

geziert *a* affected

gezwungen *a* forced. **g~ermaßen** *adv* of necessity

Gicht *f* **-** gout

Giebel *m* **-s,-** gable

Gier *f* **-** greed (**nach** for). **g~ig** *a* greedy

gieß|en† *vt* pour; water <*Blumen, Garten*>; (*Techn*) cast ● *v impers* **es g~t** it is pouring [with rain]. **G~kanne** *f* watering-can

Gift *nt* **-[e]s, -e** poison; (*Schlangen-*) venom; (*Biol, Med*) toxin. **g~ig** *a* poisonous; <*Schlange*> venomous; (*Med, Chem*) toxic; (*fig*) spiteful. **G~müll** *m* toxic waste. **G~pilz** *m* toadstool

Gilde *f* **-, -n** guild

Gin /dʒɪn/ *m* **-s** gin

Ginster *m* **-s** (*Bot*) broom

Gipfel *m* **-s,-** summit, top; (*fig*) peak. **G~konferenz** *f* summit conference. **g~n** *vi* (*haben*) culminate (**in** + *dat* in)

Gips *m* **-es** plaster. **G~verband** *m* (*Med*) plaster cast

Giraffe *f* **-, -n** giraffe

Girlande *f* **-, -n** garland

Girokonto /ˈʒi:ro-/ *nt* current account

Gischt *m* **-[e]s** & *f* **-** spray

Gitar|re *f* **-, -n** guitar. **G~rist(in)** *m* **-en, -en** (*f* **-, -nen**) guitarist

Gitter *nt* **-s,-** bars *pl*; (*Rost*) gratting, grid; (*Geländer, Zaun*) railings *pl*; (*Fenster-*) grille; (*Draht-*) wire screen

Glanz *m* **-es** shine; (*von Farbe, Papier*) gloss; (*Seiden-*) sheen; (*Politur*) polish; (*fig*) brilliance; (*Pracht*) splendour

glänzen *vi* (*haben*) shine. **g~d** *a* shining, bright; <*Papier*> glossy; (*fig*) brilliant

glanz|los *a* dull. **G~stück** *nt* masterpiece

Glas *nt* **-es, ̈-er** glass; (*Brillen-*) lens; (*Fern-*) binoculars *pl*; (*Marmeladen-*) [glass] jar. **G~er** *m* **-s,-** glazier

glasieren *vt* glaze; ice <*Kuchen*>

glas|ig *a* glassy; (*durchsichtig*) transparent. **G~scheibe** *f* pane

Glasur *f* **-, -en** glaze; (*Culin*) icing

glatt *a* smooth; (*eben*) even; <*Haar*> straight; (*rutschig*) slippery; (*einfach*) straightforward; <*Absage*> flat; **g~ streichen** smooth out; **g~ rasiert** clean-shaven; **g~ gehen** go off smoothly; **das ist g~ gelogen** it's a downright lie

Glätte *f* **-** smoothness; (*Rutschigkeit*) slipperiness

Glatt|eis *nt* [black] ice. **g~weg** *adv* ☐ outright

Glatz|e *f* **-, -n** bald patch; (*Voll-*) bald head; **eine G~e bekommen** go bald. **g~köpfig** *a* bald

Glaube *m* **-ns** belief (**an** + *acc* in); (*Relig*) faith; **G~n schenken** (+ *dat*) believe. **g~n** *vt/i* (*haben*) believe (**an** + *acc* in); (*vermuten*) think; **jdm g~n** believe s.o; **nicht zu g~n** unbelievable, incredible. **G~nsbekenntnis** *nt* creed

gläubig *a* religious; (*vertrauend*) trusting. **G~e(r)** *m/f* (*Relig*) believer; **die G~en** the faithful. **G~er** *m* **-s,-** (*Comm*) creditor

glaub|lich *a* **kaum g~lich** scarcely believable. **g~würdig** *a* credible; <*Person*> reliable

gleich *a* same; (*identisch*) identical; (*g~wertig*) equal; **g~ bleibend** constant; **2 mal 5 [ist] g~ 10** two times 5 equals 10; **das ist mir g~** it's all the same to me; **ganz g~, wo/wer** no matter where/who ● *adv* equally; (*übereinstimmend*) identically, the same; (*sofort*) immediately; (*in Kürze*) in a minute; (*fast*) nearly; (*direkt*) right. **g~altrig** *a* [of] the same age. **g~bedeutend** *a* synonymous. **g~berechtigt** *a* equal. **G~berechtigung** *f* equality

gleichen† *vi* (*haben*) **jdm/etw g~** be like *or* resemble s.o./sth

gleich|ermaßen *adv* equally. **g~falls** *adv* also, likewise; **danke g~falls** thank you, the same to you. **G~gewicht** *nt* balance; (*Phys & fig*) equilibrium. **g~gültig** *a* indifferent; (*unwichtig*) unimportant. **G~gültigkeit** *f* indifference. **g~machen** *vt sep* make equal; **dem Erdboden g~machen** raze to the ground. **g~mäßig** *a* even, regular; (*beständig*) constant. **G~mäßigkeit** *f* - regularity

Gleichnis *nt* **-ses, -se** parable

Gleich|schritt *m* **im G~schritt** in step. **g~setzen** *vt sep* equate/(*g~stellen*) place on a par (*dat*/**mit** with). **g~stellen** *vt sep* place on a par (*dat* with). **G~strom** *m* direct current

Gleichung *f* **-, -en** equation

gleich|wertig *adv a* of equal value. **g~zeitig** *a* simultaneous

Gleis *nt* **-es, -e** track; (*Bahnsteig*) platform; **G~ 5** platform 5

gleiten† *vi* (*sein*) glide; (*rutschen*) slide. **g~d** *a* sliding; **g~de Arbeitszeit** flexitime

Gleitzeit *f* flexitime

Gletscher *m* **-s,-** glacier

Glied *nt* **-[e]s, -er** limb; (*Teil*) part; (*Ketten-*) link; (*Mitglied*) member; (*Mil*) rank. **g~ern** *vt* arrange; (*einteilen*) divide. **G~maßen** *fpl* limbs

glitschig *a* slippery

glitzern *vi* (*haben*) glitter

globalisier|en *vt* globalize. **G~ung** *f* **-, -en** globalization

Globus *m* **- & -busses, -ben & -busse** globe

Glocke *f* **-, -n** bell. **G~nturm** *m* bell-tower, belfry

glorreich *a* glorious

Glossar *nt* **-s, -e** glossary

Glosse *f* **-, -n** comment

glotzen *vi* (*haben*) stare

Glück *nt* **-[e]s** [good] luck; (*Zufriedenheit*) happiness; **G~ bringend** lucky; **G~/kein G~ haben** be lucky/unlucky; **zum G~** luckily, fortunately; **auf gut G~** on the off chance; (*wahllos*) at random. **g~en** *vi* (*sein*) succeed

glücklich *a* lucky, fortunate; (*zufrieden*) happy; (*sicher*) safe ● *adv* happily; safely. **g~erweise** *adv* luckily, fortunately

Glücksspiel *nt* game of chance; (*Spielen*) gambling

Glückwunsch *m* good wishes *pl*; (*Gratulation*) congratulations *pl*; **herzlichen G~!** congratulations! (*zum Geburtstag*) happy birthday! **G~karte** *f* greetings card

Glüh|birne *f* light-bulb. **g~en** *vi* (*haben*) glow. **g~end** *a* glowing; (*rot-*) red-hot; <*Hitze*> scorching; (*leidenschaftlich*) fervent. **G~faden** *m* filament. **G~wein** *m* mulled wine. **G~würmchen** *nt* **-s,-** glow-worm

Glukose *f* **-** glucose

Glut *f* **-** embers *pl*; (*Röte*) glow; (*Hitze*) heat; (*fig*) ardour

Glyzinie /-iə/ *f* **-, -n** wisteria

GmbH *abbr* (**Gesellschaft mit beschränkter Haftung**) ≈ plc
Gnade *f* - mercy; (*Gunst*) favour; (*Relig*) grace. **G~nfrist** *f* reprieve
gnädig *a* gracious; (*mild*) lenient; **g~e Frau** Madam
Gnom *m* **-en, -en** gnome
Gobelin /gobə'lɛ̃:/ *m* **-s, -s** tapestry
Gold *nt* **-[e]s** gold. **g~en** *a* gold ...; (*g~farben*) golden. **G~fisch** *m* goldfish. **g~ig** *a* sweet, lovely. **G~lack** *m* wallflower. **G~regen** *m* laburnum. **G~schmied** *m* goldsmith
Golf¹ *m* **-[e]s, -e** (*Geog*) gulf
Golf² *nt* **-s** golf. **G~platz** *m* golf-course. **G~schläger** *m* golf-club. **G~spieler(in)** *m(f)* golfer
Gondel *f* **-, -n** gondola; (*Kabine*) cabin
gönnen *vt* **jdm etw g~** not begrudge s.o. sth; **jdm etw nicht g~** begrudge s.o. sth
Gör *nt* **-s, -en, Göre** *f* **-, -n** 🄵 kid
Gorilla *m* **-s, -s** gorilla
Gosse *f* **-, -n** gutter
Got|ik *f* - Gothic. **g~isch** *a* Gothic
Gott *m* **-[e]s,¨-er** God; (*Myth*) god
Götterspeise *f* jelly
Gottes|dienst *m* service. **G~lästerung** *f* blasphemy
Gottheit *f* **-, -en** deity
Göttin *f* **-, -nen** goddess
göttlich *a* divine
gottlos *a* ungodly; (*atheistisch*) godless
Grab *nt* **-[e]s,¨-er** grave
graben† *vi* (*haben*) dig
Graben *m* **-s,¨** ditch; (*Mil*) trench
Grab|mal *nt* tomb. **G~stein** *m* gravestone, tombstone
Grad *m* **-[e]s, -e** degree
Graf *m* **-en, -en** count
Grafik *f* **-, -en** graphics *sg*; (*Kunst*) graphic arts *pl*; (*Druck*) print
Gräfin *f* **-, -nen** countess
grafisch *a* graphic; **g~e Darstellung** diagram
Grafschaft *f* **-, -en** county
Gram *m* **-s** grief
grämen (sich) *vr* grieve
Gramm *nt* **-s, -e** gram
Gram|matik *f* **-, -en** grammar. **g~matikalisch** *a* grammatical
Granat *m* **-[e]s, -e** (*Miner*) garnet. **G~e** *f* **-, -n** shell; (*Hand-*) grenade
Granit *m* **-s, -e** granite
Gras *nt* **-es,¨-er** grass. **g~en** *vi* (*haben*) graze. **G~hüpfer** *m* **-s,-** grasshopper
grässlich *a* dreadful
Grat *m* **-[e]s, -e** [mountain] ridge
Gräte *f* **-, -n** fishbone
Gratifikation /-'tsi̯o:n/ *f* **-, -en** bonus
gratis *adv* free [of charge]. **G~probe** *f* free sample
Gratu|lant(in) *m* **-en, -en** (*f* **-, -nen**) well-wisher. **G~lation** /-'tsi̯o:n/ *f* **-, -en** congratulations *pl*; (*Glückwünsche*) best wishes *pl*. **g~lieren** *vi* (*haben*) **jdm g~lieren** congratulate s.o. (**zu** on); (*zum Geburtstag*) wish s.o. happy birthday
grau *a*, **G~** *nt* **-s,-** grey
Gräuel *m* **-s,-** horror
grauen *v impers* **mir graut [es] davor** I dread it. **G~** *nt* **-s** dread. **g~haft** *a* gruesome; (*grässlich*) horrible
gräulich *a* horrible
grausam *a* cruel. **G~keit** *f* **-, -en** cruelty
graus|en *v impers* **mir graust davor** I dread it. **G~en** *nt* **-s** horror, dread. **g~ig** *a* gruesome
gravieren *vt* engrave. **g~d** *a* (*fig*) serious

graziös *a* graceful

greifen† *vt* take hold of; (*fangen*) catch ● *vi* (*haben*) reach (**nach** for); **um sich g~** (*fig*) spread

Greis *m* **-es, -e** old man. **G~in** *f* **-, -nen** old woman

grell *a* glaring; <*Farbe*> garish; (*schrill*) shrill

Gremium *nt* **-s, -ien** committee

Grenz|e *f* **-, -n** border; (*Staats-*) frontier; (*Grundstücks-*) boundary; (*fig*) limit. **g~en** *vi* (*haben*) border (**an** + *acc* on). **g~enlos** *a* boundless; (*maßlos*) infinite

Griech|e *m* **-n, -n** Greek. **G~enland** *nt* **-s** Greece. **G~in** *f* **-, -nen** Greek woman. **g~isch** *a* Greek. **G~isch** *nt* **-[s]** (*Lang*) Greek

Grieß *m* **-es** semolina

Griff *m* **-[e]s, -e** grasp, hold; (*Hand-*) movement of the hand; (*Tür-, Messer-*) handle; (*Schwert-*) hilt. **g~bereit** *a* handy

Grill *m* **-s, -s** grill; (*Garten-*) barbecue

Grille *f* **-, -n** (*Zool*) cricket

grill|en *vt* grill; (*im Freien*) barbecue ● *vi* (*haben*) have a barbecue. **G~fest** *nt* barbecue

Grimasse *f* **-, -n** grimace; **G~n schneiden** pull faces

grimmig *a* furious; <*Kälte*> bitter

grinsen *vi* (*haben*) grin

Grippe *f* **-, -n** influenza, [!] flu

grob *a* coarse; (*unsanft, ungefähr*) rough; (*unhöflich*) rude; (*schwer*) gross; <*Fehler*> bad; **g~ geschätzt** roughly. **G~ian** *m* **-s, -e** brute

Groll *m* **-[e]s** resentment. **g~en** *vi* (*haben*) be angry (*dat* with); <*Donner:*> rumble

Grönland *nt* **-s** Greenland

Gros *nt* **-ses,-** (*Maß*) gross

Groschen *m* **-s,-** (*Aust*) groschen; [!] ten-pfennig piece

groß *a* big; <*Anzahl, Summe*> large; (*bedeutend, stark*) great; (*g~artig*) grand; <*Buchstabe*> capital; **g~e Ferien** summer holidays; **der größte Teil** the majority *or* bulk; **g~ werden** <*Person:*> grow up; **g~ in etw** (*dat*) **sein** be good at sth; **G~ und Klein** young and old; **im G~en und Ganzen** on the whole ● *adv* <*feiern*> in style; ([!] *viel*) much

groß|artig *a* magnificent. **G~aufnahme** *f* close-up. **G~britannien** *nt* **-s** Great Britain. **G~buchstabe** *m* capital letter. **G~e(r)** *m/f* **unser G~er** our eldest; **die G~en** the grown-ups; (*fig*) the great *pl*

Größe *f* **-, -n** size; (*Ausmaß*) extent; (*Körper-*) height; (*Bedeutsamkeit*) greatness; (*Math*) quantity; (*Person*) great figure

Groß|eltern *pl* grandparents. **G~handel** *m* wholesale trade. **G~händler** *m* wholesaler. **G~macht** *f* superpower. **g~mütig** *a* magnanimous. **G~mutter** *f* grandmother. **G~schreibung** *f* capitalization. **g~spurig** *a* pompous; (*überheblich*) arrogant. **G~stadt** *f* [large] city. **g~städtisch** *a* city ... **G~teil** *m* large proportion; (*Hauptteil*) bulk

größtenteils *adv* for the most part

groß|tun† **(sich)** *vr sep* brag. **G~vater** *m* grandfather. **g~ziehen†** *vt sep* bring up; rear <*Tier*>. **g~zügig** *a* generous. **G~zügigkeit** *f* **-** generosity

Grotte *f* **-, -n** grotto

Grübchen *nt* **-s,-** dimple

Grube *f* **-, -n** pit

grübeln *vi* (*haben*) brood

Gruft *f* **-,¨e** [burial] vault

grün *a* green; **im G~en** out in the country; **die G~en** the Greens
Grund *m* **-[e]s,¨e** ground; (*Boden*) bottom; (*Hinter-*) background; (*Ursache*) reason; **aus diesem G~e** for this reason; **im G~e [genommen]** basically; **auf G~ laufen** (*Naut*) run aground; **zu G~e richten/gehen** *s.* **zugrunde.** **G~begriffe** *mpl* basics. **G~besitzer** *m* landowner
gründ|en *vt* found, set up; start <*Familie*>; (*fig*) base (**auf** + *acc* on); **sich g~en** be based (**auf** + *acc* on). **G~er(in)** *m* **-s,-** (*f* **-, -nen**) founder
Grund|farbe *f* primary colour. **G~form** *f* (*Gram*) infinitive. **G~gesetz** *nt* (*Pol*) constitution. **G~lage** *f* basis, foundation
gründlich *a* thorough. **G~keit** *f* - thoroughness
Gründonnerstag *m* Maundy Thursday
Grund|regel *f* basic rule. **G~riss** *m* ground-plan; (*fig*) outline. **G~satz** *m* principle. **g~sätzlich** *a* fundamental; (*im Allgemeinen*) in principle; (*prinzipiell*) on principle; **G~schule** *f* primary school. **G~stück** *nt* plot [of land]
Gründung *f* **-, -en** foundation
Grün|span *m* verdigris. **G~streifen** *m* grass verge; (*Mittel-*) central reservation
grunzen *vi* (*haben*) grunt
Gruppe *f* **-, -n** group; (*Reise-*) party
gruppieren *vt* group
Grusel|geschichte *f* horror story. **g~ig** *a* creepy
Gruß *m* **-es,¨e** greeting; (*Mil*) salute; **einen schönen G~ an X** give my regards to X; **viele/herzliche G¨~e** regards; **Mit freundlichen G¨~en** Yours sincerely/faithfully
grüßen *vt/i* (*haben*) say hallo (**jdn** to s.o.); (*Mil*) salute; **g~ Sie X von mir** give my regards to X; **grüß Gott!** (*SGer, Aust*) good morning/afternoon/evening!
gucken *vi* (*haben*) [!] look
Guerilla /ge'rɪlja/ *f* - guerrilla warfare. **G~kämpfer** *m* guerrilla
Gulasch *nt* & *m* **-[e]s** goulash
gültig *a* valid
Gummi *m* & *nt* **-s, -[s]** rubber; (*Harz*) gum. **G~band** *nt* (*pl* **-bänder**) elastic *or* rubber band
gummiert *a* gummed
Gummi|knüppel *m* truncheon. **G~stiefel** *m* gumboot, wellington. **G~zug** *m* elastic
Gunst *f* - favour
günstig *a* favourable; (*passend*) convenient
Gurgel *f* **-, -n** throat. **g~n** *vi* (*haben*) gargle
Gurke *f* **-, -n** cucumber; (*Essig-*) gherkin
Gurt *m* **-[e]s, -e** strap; (*Gürtel*) belt; (*Auto*) safety-belt. **G~band** *nt* (*pl* **-bänder**) waistband
Gürtel *m* **-s,-** belt. **G~linie** *f* waistline. **G~rose** *f* shingles *sg*
Guss *m* **-es,¨e** (*Techn*) casting; (*Strom*) stream; (*Regen-*) downpour; (*Torten-*) icing. **G~eisen** *nt* cast iron
gut *a* good; <*Gewissen*> clear; (*gütig*) kind (**zu** to); **jdm gut sein** be fond of s.o.; **im G~en** amicably; **schon gut** that's all right ● *adv* well; <*schmecken, riechen*> good; (*leicht*) easily; **gut zu sehen** clearly visible; **gut drei Stunden** a good three hours
Gut *nt* **-[e]s,¨er** possession, property; (*Land-*) estate; **Gut und Böse** good and evil; **Güter** (*Comm*) goods
Gutacht|en *nt* **-s,-** expert's report. **G~er** *m* **-s,-** expert

gutartig *a* good-natured; (*Med*) benign
Gute|(s) *nt* **etwas/nichts G~s** something/nothing good; **G~s tun** do good; **alles G~!** all the best!
Güte *f* **-, -n** goodness, kindness; (*Qualität*) quality
Güterzug *m* goods train
gut|gehen* *vi sep* (*sein*) **gut gehen**, *s.* **gehen**. **g~gehend*** *a* **gut gehend**, *s.* **gehen**. **g~gläubig** *a* trusting. **g~haben†** *vt sep* **fünfzig Mark g~haben** have fifty marks credit (**bei** with). **G~haben** *nt* **-s,-** [credit] balance; (*Kredit*) credit. **g~machen** *vt sep* make up for; make good <*Schaden*>. **g~mütig** *a* good-natured. **G~mütigkeit** *f* **-** good nature. **G~schein** *m* credit note; (*Bon*) voucher; (*Geschenk-*) gift token. **g~schreiben†** *vt sep* credit. **G~schrift** *f* credit
Guts|haus *nt* manor house
gut|tun* *vi sep* (*haben*) **gut tun**, *s.* **tun**. **g~willig** *a* willing
Gymnasium *nt* **-s, -ien** ≈ grammar school
Gymnastik *f* **-** [keep-fit] exercises *pl*; (*Turnen*) gymnastics *sg*
Gynäko|loge *m* **-n, -n** gynaecologist. **G~logie** *f* **-** gynaecology

Hh

H, h /haː/ *nt*, **-,-** (*Mus*) B, b

Haar *nt* **-[e]s, -e** hair; **sich** (*dat*) **die Haare** *od* **das H~ waschen** wash one's hair; **um ein H~** [!] very nearly. **H~bürste** *f* hairbrush. **h~en** *vi* (*haben*) shed hairs; <*Tier:*> moult ● *vr* **sich h~en** moult. **h~ig** *a* hairy; [!] tricky. **H~klemme** *f* hair-grip. **H~nadelkurve** *f* hairpin bend. **H~schnitt** *m* haircut. **H~spange** *f* slide. **H~waschmittel** *nt* shampoo
Habe *f* **-** possessions *pl*

haben†
● *transitive verb*
····➤ have; (*im Präsens*) have got [!]. **er hat kein Geld** he has no money *or* [!] he hasn't got any money. **ich habe/hatte die Grippe** I've got flu/I had flu. **was haben Sie da?** what have you got there? **wenn ich die Zeit hätte** if I had the time
····➤ (*empfinden*) **Angst/Hunger/Durst haben** be frightened/hungry/thirsty. **was hat er?** what's wrong with him?
····➤ (+ *Adj., es*) **es gut/schlecht haben** be well/badly off. **es schwer haben** be having a difficult time
····➤ (+ *zu*) (*müssen*) **du hast zu gehorchen** you must obey
● *auxiliary verb*
····➤ have. **ich habe/hatte ihn eben gesehen** I have *or* I've/I had *or* I'd just seen him. **er hat es gewusst** he knew it. **er hätte ihr geholfen** he would have helped her
● *reflexive verb*
····➤ ([!] *sich aufregen*) make a fuss. **hab dich nicht so!** don't make such a fuss!

Habgier *f* greed. **h~ig** *a* greedy
Habicht *m* **-[e]s, -e** hawk
Hachse *f* **-, -n** (*Culin*) knuckle

Hackbraten *m* meat loaf

Hacke¹ *f* **-, -n** hoe; (*Spitz-*) pick

Hacke² *f* **-, -n**, **Hacken** *m* **-s,-** heel

hack|en *vt* hoe; (*schlagen, zerkleinern*) chop; <*Vogel:*> peck. **H~fleisch** *nt* mince

Hafen *m* **-s,¨** harbour; (*See-*) port. **H~arbeiter** *m* docker. **H~stadt** *f* port

Hafer *m* **-s** oats *pl*. **H~flocken** *fpl* [rolled] oats

Haft *f* **-** (*Jur*) custody; (*H~strafe*) imprisonment. **h~bar** *a* (*Jur*) liable. **H~befehl** *m* warrant

haften *vi* (*haben*) cling; (*kleben*) stick; (*bürgen*) vouch/(*Jur*) be liable (**für** for)

Häftling *m* **-s, -e** detainee

Haftpflicht *f* (*Jur*) liability. **H~versicherung** *f* (*Auto*) third-party insurance

Haftung *f* **-** (*Jur*) liability

Hagebutte *f* **-, -n** rose-hip

Hagel *m* **-s** hail. **h~n** *vi* (*haben*) hail

hager *a* gaunt

Hahn *m* **-[e]s,¨e** cock; (*Techn*) tap

Hähnchen *nt* **-s,-** (*Culin*) chicken

Hai[fisch] *m* **-[e]s, -e** shark

Häkchen *nt* **-s,-** tick

häkel|n *vt/i* (*haben*) crochet. **H~nadel** *f* crochet-hook

Haken *m* **-s,-** hook; (*Häkchen*) tick; ([!] *Schwierigkeit*) snag. **h~** *vt* hook (**an** + *acc* to). **H~kreuz** *nt* swastika

halb *a* half; **auf h~em Weg** half-way ● *adv* half; **h~drei** half past two; **fünf [Minuten] vor/nach h~vier** twenty-five [minutes] past three/to four. **H~e(r,s)** *f/m/nt* half [a litre]

halber *prep* (+ *gen*) for the sake of; **Geschäfte h~** on business

Halbfinale *nt* semifinal

halbieren *vt* halve, divide in half; (*Geom*) bisect

Halb|insel *f* peninsula. **H~kreis** *m* semicircle. **H~kugel** *f* hemisphere. **h~laut** *a* low ● *adv* in an undertone. **h~mast** *adv* at half-mast. **H~mond** *m* half moon. **H~pension** *f* half-board. **h~rund** *a* semicircular. **H~schuh** *m* [flat] shoe. **h~tags** *adv* [for] half a day; **h~tags arbeiten** ≈ work part-time. **H~ton** *m* semitone. **h~wegs** *adv* half-way; (*ziemlich*) more or less. **h~wüchsig** *a* adolescent. **H~zeit** *f* (*Sport*) half-time; (*Spielzeit*) half

Halde *f* **-, -n** dump, tip

Hälfte *f* **-, -n** half; **zur H~** half

Halfter *f* **-, -n** & *nt* **-s,-** holster

Halle *f* **-, -n** hall; (*Hotel-*) lobby; (*Bahnhofs-*) station concourse

hallen *vi* (*haben*) resound; (*wider-*) echo

Hallen- *pref* indoor

hallo *int* hallo

Halluzination /-ˈtsi̯oːn/ *f* **-, -en** hallucination

Halm *m* **-[e]s, -e** stalk; (*Gras-*) blade

Hals *m* **-es,¨e** neck; (*Kehle*) throat; **aus vollem H~e** at the top of one's voice; <*lachen*> out loud. **H~band** *nt* (*pl* **-bänder**) collar. **H~schmerzen** *mpl* sore throat *sg*

halt *int* stop! (*Mil*) halt! [!] wait a minute!

Halt *m* **-[e]s, -e** hold; (*Stütze*) support; (*innerer*) stability; (*Anhalten*) stop; **H~ machen** stop. **h~bar** *a* durable; (*Tex*) hard-wearing; (*fig*) tenable; **h~bar bis** ... (*Comm*) use by ...

halten† *vt* hold; make <*Rede*>; give <*Vortrag*>; (*einhalten, bewahren*) keep; **[sich** (*dat*)**] etw h~** keep <*Hund*>; take <*Zeitung*>; **h~ für** regard as; **viel**

h~ von think highly of; **sich links h~** keep left; **sich h~ an** (+ *acc*) (*fig*) keep to ● *vi* (*haben*) hold; (*haltbar sein, bestehen bleiben*) keep; <*Freundschaft, Blumen*:> last; (*Halt machen*) stop; **auf sich** (*acc*) **h~** take pride in oneself; **zu jdm h~** be loyal to s.o.

Halte|stelle *f* stop. **H~verbot** *nt* waiting restriction; **'H~verbot'** 'no waiting'

Haltung *f* **-, -en** (*Körper-*) posture; (*Verhalten*) manner; (*Einstellung*) attitude; (*Fassung*) composure; (*Halten*) keeping

Hammel *m* **-s,-** ram; (*Culin*) mutton. **H~fleisch** *nt* mutton

Hammer *m* **-s,¨** hammer

hämmern *vt/i* (*haben*) hammer

Hamster *m* **-s,-** hamster. **h~n** *vt/i* ⓘ hoard

Hand *f* **-,¨e** hand; **jdm die H~ geben** shake hands with s.o.; **rechter/linker H~** on the right/left; **zweiter H~** second-hand; **unter der H~** unofficially; (*geheim*) secretly; **H~ und Fuß haben** (*fig*) be sound. **H~arbeit** *f* manual work; (*handwerklich*) handicraft; (*Nadelarbeit*) needlework; (*Gegenstand*) handmade article. **H~ball** *m* [German] handball. **H~bewegung** *f* gesture. **H~bremse** *f* handbrake. **H~buch** *nt* handbook, manual

Händedruck *m* handshake

Handel *m* **-s** trade, commerce; (*Unternehmen*) business; (*Geschäft*) deal; **H~ treiben** trade. **h~n** *vi* (*haben*) act; (*Handel treiben*) trade (**mit** in); **von etw** *od* **über etw** (*acc*) **h~n** deal with sth; **sich h~n um** be about, concern. **H~smarine** *f* merchant navy. **H~sschiff** *nt* merchant vessel. **H~sschule** *f* commercial college. **H~sware** *f* merchandise

Hand|feger *m* **-s,-** brush. **H~fläche** *f* palm. **H~gelenk** *nt* wrist. **H~gemenge** *nt* **-s,-** scuffle. **H~gepäck** *nt* hand-luggage. **h~geschrieben** *a* hand-written. **h~greiflich** *a* tangible; **h~greiflich werden** become violent. **H~griff** *m* handle

handhaben *vt insep* (*reg*) handle

Handikap /ˈhɛndikɛp/ *nt* **-s, -s** handicap

Handkuss *m* kiss on the hand

Händler *m* **-s,-** dealer, trader

handlich *a* handy

Handlung *f* **-, -en** act; (*Handeln*) action; (*Roman-*) plot; (*Geschäft*) shop. **H~sweise** *f* conduct

Hand|schellen *fpl* handcuffs. **H~schlag** *m* handshake. **H~schrift** *f* handwriting; (*Text*) manuscript. **H~schuh** *m* glove. **H~stand** *m* handstand. **H~tasche** *f* handbag. **H~tuch** *nt* towel

Handwerk *nt* craft, trade. **H~er** *m* **-s,-** craftsman; (*Arbeiter*) workman

Handy /ˈhɛndi/ *nt* **-s, -s** mobile phone

Hanf *m* **-[e]s** hemp

Hang *m* **-[e]s,¨e** slope; (*fig*) inclination

Hänge|brücke *f* suspension bridge. **H~matte** *f* hammock

hängen[1] *vt* (*reg*) hang

hängen[2]† *vi* (*haben*) hang; **h~ an** (+ *dat*) (*fig*) be attached to; **h~ lassen** leave

Hannover *nt* **-s** Hanover

hänseln *vt* tease

hantieren *vi* (*haben*) busy oneself

Happen *m* **-s,-** mouthful; **einen H~ essen** have a bite to eat

Harfe *f* **-, -n** harp

Harke *f* **-, -n** rake. **h~n** *vt/i* (*haben*) rake
harmlos *a* harmless; (*arglos*) innocent
Harmonie *f* **-, -n** harmony
Harmonika *f* **-, -s** accordion; (*Mund-*) mouth-organ
harmonisch *a* harmonious
Harn *m* **-[e]s** urine. **H~blase** *f* bladder
Harpune *f* **-, -n** harpoon
hart *a* hard; (*heftig*) violent; (*streng*) harsh
Härte *f* **-, -n** hardness; (*Strenge*) harshness; (*Not*) hardship. **h~n** *vt* harden
Hart|faserplatte *f* hardboard. **h~näckig** *a* stubborn; (*ausdauernd*) persistent. **H~näckigkeit** *f* **-** stubbornness; persistence
Harz *nt* **-es, -e** resin
Haschee *nt* **-s, -s** (*Culin*) hash
Haschisch *nt & m* **-[s]** hashish
Hase *m* **-n, -n** hare
Hasel *f* **-, -n** hazel. **H~maus** *f* dormouse. **H~nuss** *f* hazel-nut
Hass *m* **-es** hatred
hassen *vt* hate
hässlich *a* ugly; (*unfreundlich*) nasty. **H~keit** *f* **-** ugliness; nastiness
Hast *f* **-** haste. **h~ig** *a* hasty, hurried
hast, hat, hatte, hätte *s.* **haben**
Haube *f* **-, -n** cap; (*Trocken-*) drier; (*Kühler-*) bonnet
Hauch *m* **-[e]s** breath; (*Luft-*) breeze; (*Duft*) whiff; (*Spur*) tinge. **h~dünn** *a* very thin
Haue *f* **-, -n** pick; (🅸 *Prügel*) beating. **h~n**† *vt* beat; (*hämmern*) knock; (*meißeln*) hew; **sich h~n** fight; **übers Ohr h~n** 🅸 cheat ● *vi* (*haben*) bang (**auf** + *acc* on); **jdm ins Gesicht h~n** hit s.o. in the face
Haufen *m* **-s,-** heap, pile; (*Leute*) crowd
häufen *vt* heap *or* pile [up]; **sich h~** pile up; (*zunehmen*) increase
häufig *a* frequent
Haupt *nt* **-[e]s, Häupter** head. **H~bahnhof** *m* main station. **H~fach** *nt* main subject. **H~gericht** *nt* main course
Häuptling *m* **-s, -e** chief
Haupt|mahlzeit *f* main meal **H~mann** *m* (*pl* **-leute**) captain. **H~post** *f* main post office. **H~quartier** *nt* headquarters *pl*. **H~rolle** *f* lead; (*fig*) leading role. **H~sache** *f* main thing; **in der H~sache** in the main. **h~sächlich** *a* main. **H~satz** *m* main clause. **H~stadt** *f* capital. **H~verkehrsstraße** *f* main road. **H~verkehrszeit** *f* rush-hour. **H~wort** *nt* (*pl* **-wörter**) noun
Haus *nt* **-es, Häuser** house; (*Gebäude*) building; (*Schnecken-*) shell; **zu H~e** at home; **nach H~e** home. **H~arbeit** *f* housework; (*Sch*) homework. **H~arzt** *m* family doctor. **H~aufgaben** *fpl* homework *sg*. **H~besetzer** *m* **-s,-** squatter
hausen *vi* (*haben*) live; (*wüten*) wreak havoc
Haus|frau *f* housewife. **h~gemacht** *a* home-made. **H~halt** *m* **-[e]s, -e** household; (*Pol*) budget. **h~halten**† *vi sep* (*haben*) **h~halten mit** manage carefully; conserve <*Kraft*>. **H~hälterin** *f* **-, -nen** housekeeper. **H~haltsgeld** *nt* housekeeping [money]. **H~haltsplan** *m* budget. **H~herr** *m* head of the household; (*Gastgeber*) host
Hausierer *m* **-s,-** hawker
Hauslehrer *m* [private] tutor. **H~in** *f* governess

häuslich *a* domestic, <*Person*> domesticated
Haus|meister *m* caretaker. **H~ordnung** *f* house rules *pl*. **H~putz** *m* cleaning. **H~rat** *m* **-[e]s** household effects *pl*. **H~schlüssel** *m* front-door key. **H~schuh** *m* slipper. **H~suchung** *f* [police] search. **H~suchungsbefehl** *m* search-warrant. **H~tier** *nt* domestic animal; (*Hund, Katze*) pet. **H~tür** *f* front door. **H~wirt** *m* landlord. **H~wirtin** *f* landlady
Haut *f* **-,Häute** skin; (*Tier-*) hide. **H~arzt** *m* dermatologist
häuten *vt* skin; **sich h~** moult
haut|eng *a* skin-tight. **H~farbe** *f* colour; (*Teint*) complexion
Hebamme *f* **-, -n** midwife
Hebel *m* **-s,-** lever
heben† *vt* lift; (*hoch-, steigern*) raise; **sich h~** rise; <*Nebel:*> lift; (*sich verbessern*) improve
hebräisch *a* Hebrew
hecheln *vi* (*haben*) pant
Hecht *m* **-[e]s, -e** pike
Heck *nt* **-s, -s** (*Naut*) stern; (*Aviat*) tail; (*Auto*) rear
Hecke *f* **-, -n** hedge
Heck|fenster *nt* rear window. **H~tür** *f* hatchback
Heer *nt* **-[e]s, -e** army
Hefe *f* **-** yeast
Heft *nt* **-[e]s, -e** booklet; (*Sch*) exercise book; (*Zeitschrift*) issue. **h~en** *vt* (*nähen*) tack; (*stecken*) pin/(*klammern*) clip/(*mit Heftmaschine*) staple (**an** + *acc* to). **H~er** *m* **-s,-** file
heftig *a* fierce, violent; <*Regen*> heavy; <*Schmerz, Gefühl*> intense
Heft|klammer *f* staple; (*Büro-*) paper-clip. **H~maschine** *f* stapler. **H~zwecke** *f* **-, -n** drawing-pin

Heide[1] *m* **-n, -n** heathen
Heide[2] *f* **-, -n** heath; (*Bot*) heather. **H~kraut** *nt* heather
Heidelbeere *f* bilberry
Heidin *f* **-, -nen** heathen
heikel *a* difficult, tricky
heil *a* undamaged, intact; <*Person*> unhurt; **mit h~er Haut** [!] unscathed
Heil *nt* **-s** salvation
Heiland *m* **-s** (*Relig*) Saviour
Heil|anstalt *f* sanatorium; (*Nerven-*) mental hospital. **H~bad** *nt* spa. **h~bar** *a* curable
Heilbutt *m* **-[e]s, -e** halibut
heilen *vt* cure; heal <*Wunde*> ● *vi* (*sein*) heal
Heilgymnastik *f* physiotherapy
heilig *a* holy; (*geweiht*) sacred; **der H~e Abend** Christmas Eve; **die h~e Anna** Saint Anne; **h~ sprechen** canonize. **H~abend** *m* Christmas Eve. **H~e(r)** *m/f* saint. **H~enschein** *m* halo. **H~keit** *f* **-** sanctity, holiness. **H~tum** *nt* **-s,¨-er** shrine
heil|kräftig *a* medicinal. **H~kräuter** *ntpl* medicinal herbs. **H~mittel** *nt* remedy. **H~praktiker** *m* **-s,-** practitioner of alternative medicine. **H~sarmee** *f* Salvation Army. **H~ung** *f* **-** cure
Heim *nt* **-[e]s, -e** home; (*Studenten-*) hostel. **h~** *adv* home
Heimat *f* **-, -en** home; (*Land*) native land. **H~stadt** *f* home town
heim|begleiten *vt sep* see home. **H~computer** *m* home computer. **h~fahren**† *v sep* ● *vi* (*sein*) go/drive home ● *vt* take/drive home. **H~fahrt** *f* way home. **h~gehen**† *vi sep* (*sein*) go home
heimisch *a* native, indigenous; (*Pol*) domestic

Heim|kehr *f* - return [home]. **h~kehren** *vi sep (sein)* return home. **h~kommen**† *vi sep (sein)* come home

heimlich *a* secret; **etw h~ tun** do sth secretly. **H~keit** *f* **-, -en** secrecy; **H~keiten** secrets

Heim|reise *f* journey home. **H~spiel** *nt* home game. **h~suchen** *vt sep* afflict. **h~tückisch** *a* treacherous; <*Krankheit*> insidious. **h~wärts** *adv* home. **H~weg** *m* way home. **H~weh** *nt* **-s** homesickness; **H~weh haben** be homesick. **H~werker** *m* **-s,-** [home] handyman. **h~zahlen** *vt sep* **jdm etw h~zahlen** *(fig)* pay s.o. back for sth

Heirat *f* **-, -en** marriage. **h~en** *vt/i (haben)* marry. **H~santrag** *m* proposal; **jdm einen H~santrag machen** propose to s.o.

heiser *a* hoarse. **H~keit** *f* - hoarseness

heiß *a* hot; *(hitzig)* heated; *(leidenschaftlich)* fervent

heißen† *vi (haben)* be called; *(bedeuten)* mean; **ich heiße ...** my name is ...; **wie h~ Sie?** what is your name? **wie heißt ... auf Englisch?** what's the English for ...? ● *vt* call; **jdn etw tun h~** tell s.o. to do sth

heiter *a* cheerful; <*Wetter*> bright; *(amüsant)* amusing; **aus h~em Himmel** *(fig)* out of the blue

Heiz|anlage *f* heating; *(Auto)* heater. **H~decke** *f* electric blanket. **h~en** *vt* heat; light <*Ofen*> ● *vi (haben)* put the heating on; <*Ofen:*> give out heat. **H~gerät** *nt* heater. **H~kessel** *m* boiler. **H~körper** *m* radiator. **H~lüfter** *m* **-s,-** fan heater. **H~material** *nt* fuel. **H~ung** *f* **-, -en** heating; *(Heizkörper)* radiator

Hektar *nt & m* **-s,-** hectare

Held *m* **-en, -en** hero. **h~enhaft** *a* heroic. **H~entum** *nt* **-s** heroism. **H~in** *f* **-, -nen** heroine

helf|en† *vi (haben)* help (**jdm** s.o.); *(nützen)* be effective; **sich** *(dat)* **nicht zu h~en wissen** not know what to do; **es hilft nichts** it's no use. **H~er(in)** *m* **-s,-** (*f* **-, -nen**) helper, assistant

hell *a* light; *(Licht ausstrahlend, klug)* bright; <*Stimme*> clear; (🅸 *völlig*) utter; **h~es Bier** ≈ lager ● *adv* brightly

Hell|igkeit *f* - brightness. **H~seher(in)** *m* **-s,-** (*f* **-, -nen**) clairvoyant

Helm *m* **-[e]s, -e** helmet

Hemd *nt* **-[e]s, -en** vest; *(Ober-)* shirt

Hemisphäre *f* **-, -n** hemisphere

hemm|en *vt* check; *(verzögern)* impede; *(fig)* inhibit. **H~ung** *f* **-, -en** *(fig)* inhibition; *(Skrupel)* scruple; **H~ungen haben** be inhibited. **h~ungslos** *a* unrestrained

Hendl *nt* **-s, -[n]** *(Aust)* chicken

Hengst *m* **-[e]s, -e** stallion

Henkel *m* **-s,-** handle

Henne *f* **-, -n** hen

her *adv* here; *(zeitlich)* ago; **her mit ...!** give me ...! **von Norden/weit her** from the north/far away; **vom Thema her** as far as the subject is concerned; **her sein** come (**von** from); **es ist schon lange her** it was a long time ago

herab *adv* down [here]; **von oben h~** from above; *(fig)* condescending

herablassen† *vt sep* let down; **sich h~** condescend (**zu** to)

herab|sehen† *vi sep (haben)* look down (**auf** + *acc* on).

h~setzen *vt sep* reduce, cut; (*fig*) belittle

Heraldik *f* - heraldry

heran *adv* near; **[bis] h~ an** (+ *acc*) up to. **h~kommen**† *vi sep* (*sein*) approach; **h~kommen an** (+ *acc*) come up to; (*erreichen*) get at; (*fig*) measure up to. **h~machen (sich)** *vr sep* **sich h~machen an** (+ *acc*) approach; get down to <*Arbeit*>. **h~wachsen**† *vi sep* (*sein*) grow up. **h~ziehen**† *v sep* ● *vt* pull up (**an** + *acc* to); (*züchten*) raise; (*h~bilden*) train; (*hinzuziehen*) call in ● *vi* (*sein*) approach

herauf *adv* up [here]; **die Treppe h~** up the stairs. **h~setzen** *vt sep* raise, increase

heraus *adv* out (**aus** of); **h~ damit** *od* **mit der Sprache!** out with it! **h~bekommen**† *vt sep* get out; (*ausfindig machen*) find out; (*lösen*) solve; **Geld h~bekommen** get change. **h~finden**† *v sep* ● *vt* find out ● *vi* (*haben*) find one's way out. **h~fordern** *vt sep* provoke; challenge <*Person*>. **H~forderung** *f* provocation; challenge. **H~gabe** *f* handing over; (*Admin*) issue; (*Veröffentlichung*) publication. **h~geben**† *vt sep* hand over; (*Admin*) issue; (*veröffentlichen*) publish; edit <*Zeitschrift*>; **jdm Geld h~geben** give s.o. change ● *vi* (*haben*) give change (**auf** + *acc* for). **H~geber** *m* **-s,-** publisher; editor. **h~halten**† **(sich)** *vr sep* (*fig*) keep out (**aus** of). **h~kommen**† *vi sep* (*sein*) come out; (*aus Schwierigkeit, Takt*) get out; **auf eins** *od* **dasselbe h~kommen** [!] come to the same thing. **h~lassen**† *vt sep* let out. **h~nehmen**† *vt sep* take out; **sich zu viel h~nehmen** (*fig*) take liberties.

h~reden (sich) *vr sep* make excuses. **h~rücken** *v sep* ● *vt* move out; (*hergeben*) hand over ● *vi* (*sein*) **h~rücken mit** hand over; (*fig: sagen*) come out with. **h~schlagen**† *vt sep* knock out; (*fig*) gain. **h~stellen** *vt sep* put out; **sich h~stellen** turn out (**als** to be; **dass** that). **h~ziehen**† *vt sep* pull out

herb *a* sharp; <*Wein*> dry; (*fig*) harsh

herbei *adv* here. **h~führen** *vt sep* (*fig*) bring about. **h~schaffen** *vt sep* get. **h~sehnen** *vt sep* long for

Herberg|e *f* -, **-n** [youth] hostel; (*Unterkunft*) lodging. **H~svater** *m* warden

herbestellen *vt sep* summon

herbitten† *vt sep* ask to come

herbringen† *vt sep* bring [here]

Herbst *m* **-[e]s, -e** autumn. **h~lich** *a* autumnal

Herd *m* **-[e]s, -e** stove, cooker

Herde *f* -, **-n** herd; (*Schaf-*) flock

herein *adv* in [here]; **h~!** come in! **h~bitten**† *vt sep* ask in. **h~fallen**† *vi sep* (*sein*) [!] be taken in (**auf** + *acc* by). **h~kommen**† *vi sep* (*sein*) come in. **h~lassen**† *vt sep* let in. **h~legen** *vt sep* [!] take for a ride

Herfahrt *f* journey/drive here

herfallen† *vi sep* (*sein*) **~ über** (+ *acc*) attack; fall upon <*Essen*>

hergeben† *vt sep* hand over; (*fig*) give up

hergehen† *vi sep* (*sein*) **h~ vor** (+ *dat*) walk along in front of; **es ging lustig her** [!] there was a lot of merriment

herholen *vt sep* fetch; **weit hergeholt** (*fig*) far-fetched

Hering *m* **-s, -e** herring; (*Zeltpflock*) tent-peg

her|kommen† *vi sep* (*sein*) come here; **wo kommt das her?** where does it come from? **h~kömmlich** *a* traditional. **H~kunft** *f* - origin

herleiten *vt sep* derive

hermachen *vt sep* **viel/wenig h~** be impressive/unimpressive; (*wichtig nehmen*) make a lot of/ little fuss (**von** of); **sich h~ über** (+ *acc*) fall upon; tackle <*Arbeit*>

Hermelin¹ *nt* **-s, -e** (*Zool*) stoat

Hermelin² *m* **-s, -e** (*Pelz*) ermine

Hernie /'hɛrni̯ə/ *f* **-, -n** hernia

Heroin *nt* **-s** heroin

heroisch *a* heroic

Herr *m* **-n, -en** gentleman; (*Gebieter*) master (**über** + *acc* of); **[Gott,] der H~** the Lord [God]; **H~ Meier** Mr Meier; **Sehr geehrte H~en** Dear Sirs. **H~enhaus** *nt* manor [house]. **h~enlos** *a* ownerless; <*Tier*> stray

Herrgott *m* **der H~** the Lord

herrichten *vt sep* prepare; **wieder h~** renovate

Herrin *f* **-, -nen** mistress

herrlich *a* marvellous; (*großartig*) magnificent

Herrschaft *f* **-, -en** rule; (*Macht*) power; (*Kontrolle*) control; **meine H~en!** ladies and gentlemen!

herrsch|en *vi* (*haben*) rule; (*verbreitet sein*) prevail; **es h~te Stille** there was silence. **H~er(in)** *m* **-s,-** (*f* **-, -nen**) ruler

herrühren *vi sep* (*haben*) stem (**von** from)

herstammen *vi sep* (*haben*) come (**aus/von** from)

herstell|en *vt sep* establish; (*Comm*) manufacture, make. **H~er** *m* **-s,-** manufacturer, maker. **H~ung** *f* - establishment; manufacture

herüber *adv* over [here]

herum *adv* **im Kreis h~** [round] in a circle; **falsch h~** the wrong way round; **um ... h~** round ...; (*ungefähr*) [round] about ...; **h~sein** be over. **h~drehen** *vt sep* turn round/(*wenden*) over; turn <*Schlüssel*>. **h~gehen**† *vi sep* (*sein*) walk around; <*Zeit:*> pass; **h~gehen um** go round. **h~kommen**† *vi sep* (*sein*) get about; **h~kommen um** get round; come round <*Ecke*>; **um etw [nicht] h~kommen** (*fig*) [not] get out of sth. **h~sitzen**† *vi sep* (*haben*) sit around; **h~sitzen um** sit round. **h~sprechen**† **(sich)** *vr sep* <*Gerücht:*> get about. **h~treiben**† **(sich)** *vr sep* hang around. **h~ziehen**† *vi sep* (*sein*) move around; (*ziellos*) wander about

herunter *adv* down [here]; **die Treppe h~** down the stairs. **h~fallen**† *vi* fall off. **h~gekommen** *a* (*fig*) run-down; <*Gebäude*> dilapidated; <*Person*> down-at-heel. **h~kommen**† *vi sep* (*sein*) come down; (*fig*) go to rack and ruin; <*Firma, Person:*> go downhill; (*gesundheitlich*) get run down. **h~lassen**† *vt sep* let down, lower. **h~machen** *vt sep* **!** reprimand; (*herabsetzen*) run down. **h~spielen** *vt sep* (*fig*) play down

hervor *adv* out (**aus** of). **h~bringen**† *vt sep* produce; utter <*Wort*>. **h~gehen**† *vi sep* (*sein*) come/(*sich ergeben*) emerge/(*folgen*) follow (**aus** from). **h~heben**† *vt sep* (*fig*) stress, emphasize. **h~ragen** *vi sep* (*haben*) jut out; (*fig*) stand out. **h~ragend** *a* (*fig*) outstanding. **h~rufen**† *vt sep* (*fig*) cause. **h~stehen**† *vi sep* (*haben*) protrude. **h~treten**† *vi sep* (*sein*) protrude, bulge; (*fig*) stand out. **h~tun**† **(sich)** *vr sep* (*fig*) distinguish oneself; (*angeben*) show off

Herweg *m* way here

Herz *nt* **-ens, -en** heart; (*Kartenspiel*) hearts *pl*; **sich** (*dat*) **ein H~ fassen** pluck up courage. **H~anfall** *m* heart attack

herzhaft *a* hearty; (*würzig*) savoury

herziehen† *v sep* ● *vt* **hinter sich** (*dat*) **h~** pull along [behind one] ● *vi* (*sein*) **hinter jdm h~** follow along behind s.o.; **über jdn h~** 🄸 run s.o. down

herz|ig *a* sweet, adorable. **H~infarkt** *m* heart attack. **H~klopfen** *nt* **-s** palpitations *pl*

herzlich *a* cordial; (*warm*) warm; (*aufrichtig*) sincere; **h~en Dank!** many thanks! **h~e Grüße** kind regards

herzlos *a* heartless

Herzog *m* **-s,⸚e** duke. **H~in** *f* **-, -nen** duchess. **H~tum** *nt* **-s,⸚er** duchy

Herzschlag *m* heartbeat; (*Med*) heart failure

Hessen *nt* **-s** Hesse

heterosexuell *a* heterosexual

Hetze *f* **-** rush; (*Kampagne*) virulent campaign (**gegen** against). **h~n** *vt* chase; **sich h~n** hurry

Heu *nt* **-s** hay

Heuchelei *f* **-** hypocrisy

heuch|eln *vt* feign ● *vi* (*haben*) pretend. **H~ler(in)** *m* **-s,-** (*f* **-, -nen**) hypocrite. **h~lerisch** *a* hypocritical

heuer *adv* (*Aust*) this year

heulen *vi* (*haben*) howl; (🄸 *weinen*) cry

Heu|schnupfen *m* hay fever. **H~schober** *m* **-s,-** haystack. **H~schrecke** *f* **-, -n** grasshopper

heut|e *adv* today; (*heutzutage*) nowadays; **h~e früh** *od* **Morgen** this morning; **von h~e auf morgen** from one day to the next. **h~ig** *a* today's ...; (*gegenwärtig*) present; **der h~ige Tag** today. **h~zutage** *adv* nowadays

Hexe *f* **-, -n** witch. **h~n** *vi* (*haben*) work magic. **H~nschuss** *m* lumbago

Hieb *m* **-[e]s, -e** blow; (*Peitschen-*) lash; **H~e** hiding *sg*

hier *adv* here; **h~ sein/bleiben/lassen/behalten** be/stay/leave/keep here; **h~ und da** here and there; (*zeitlich*) now and again

hier|auf *adv* on this/these; (*antworten*) to this; (*zeitlich*) after this. **h~aus** *adv* out of *or* from this/these. **h~durch** *adv* through this/these; (*Ursache*) as a result of this. **h~her** *adv* here. **h~hin** *adv* here. **h~in** *adv* in this/these. **h~mit** *adv* with this/these; (*Comm*) herewith; (*Admin*) hereby. **h~nach** *adv* after this/these; (*demgemäß*) according to this/these. **h~über** *adv* over/(*höher*) above this/these; <*sprechen, streiten*> about this/these. **h~von** *adv* from this/these; (*h~über*) about this/these; (*Menge*) of this/these. **h~zu** *adv* to this/these; (*h~für*) for this/these. **h~zulande** *adv* here

hiesig *a* local. **H~e(r)** *m/f* local

Hilf|e *f* **-, -n** help, aid; **um H~e rufen** call for help. **h~los** *a* helpless. **H~losigkeit** *f* **-** helplessness. **h~reich** *a* helpful

Hilfs|arbeiter *m* unskilled labourer. **h~bedürftig** *a* needy; **h~bedürftig sein** be in need of help. **h~bereit** *a* helpful. **H~kraft** *f* helper. **H~mittel** *nt* aid. **H~verb** *nt* auxiliary verb

Himbeere *f* raspberry

Himmel *m* **-s,-** sky; (*Relig & fig*) heaven; (*Bett-*) canopy; **unter**

freiem H~ in the open air. **H~bett** *nt* four-poster [bed]. **H~fahrt** *f* Ascension

himmlisch *a* heavenly

hin *adv* there; **hin und her** to and fro; **hin und zurück** there and back; (*Rail*) return; **hin und wieder** now and again; **an** (+ *dat*) ... **hin** along; **auf** (+ *acc*) ... **hin** in reply to <*Brief, Anzeige*>; on <*jds Rat*>; **zu** *od* **nach ... hin** towards; **hin sein** [!] be gone; **es ist noch lange hin** it's a long time yet

hinauf *adv* up [there]. **h~gehen**† *vi sep* (*sein*) go up. **h~setzen** *vt sep* raise

hinaus *adv* out [there]; (*nach draußen*) outside; **zur Tür h~** out of the door; **auf Jahre h~** for years to come; **über etw** (*acc*) **h~** beyond sth; (*Menge*) [over and] above sth; **über etw** (*acc*) **h~ sein** (*fig*) be past sth. **h~gehen**† *vi sep* (*sein*) go out; <*Zimmer:*> face (**nach Norden** north); **h~gehen über** (+ *acc*) go beyond, exceed. **h~laufen**† *vi sep* (*sein*) run out; **h~laufen auf** (+ *acc*) (*fig*) amount to. **h~lehnen (sich)** *vr sep* lean out. **h~schieben**† *vt sep* push out; (*fig*) put off. **h~werfen**† *vt sep* throw out; ([!] *entlassen*) fire. **h~wollen**† *vi sep* (*haben*) want to go out; **h~wollen auf** (+ *acc*) (*fig*) aim at. **h~ziehen**† *v sep* ● *vt* pull out; (*in die Länge ziehen*) drag out; (*verzögern*) delay; **sich h~ziehen** drag on; be delayed ● *vi* (*sein*) move out. **h~zögern** *vt* delay; **sich h~zögern** be delayed

Hinblick *m* **im H~ auf** (+ *acc*) in view of; (*hinsichtlich*) regarding

hinder|lich *a* awkward; **jdm h~lich sein** hamper s.o. **h~n** *vt* hamper; (*verhindern*) prevent. **H~nis** *nt* **-ses, -se** obstacle. **H~nisrennen** *nt* steeplechase

Hindu *m* **-s, -s** Hindu. **H~ismus** *m* **-** Hinduism

hindurch *adv* through it/them

hinein *adv* in [there]; (*nach drinnen*) inside; **h~ in** (+ *acc*) into. **h~fallen**† *vi sep* (*sein*) fall in. **h~gehen**† *vi sep* (*sein*) go in; **h~gehen in** (+ *acc*) go into. **h~reden** *vi sep* (*haben*) **jdm h~reden** interrupt s.o.; (*sich einmischen*) interfere in s.o.'s affairs. **h~versetzen (sich)** *vr sep* **sich in jds Lage h~versetzen** put oneself in s.o.'s position. **h~ziehen**† *vt sep* pull in; **h~ziehen in** (+ *acc*) pull into; **in etw** (*acc*) **h~gezogen werden** (*fig*) become involved in sth

hin|fahren† *v sep* ● *vi* (*sein*) go/drive there ● *vt* take/drive there. **H~fahrt** *f* journey/drive there; (*Rail*) outward journey. **h~fallen**† *vi sep* (*sein*) fall. **h~fliegen**† *v sep* ● *vi* (*sein*) fly there; [!] fall ● *vt* fly there. **H~flug** *m* flight there; (*Admin*) outward flight

Hingeb|ung *f* **-** devotion. **h~ungsvoll** *a* devoted

hingehen† *vi sep* (*sein*) go/(*zu Fuß*) walk there; (*vergehen*) pass; **h~ zu** go up to; **wo gehst du hin**? where are you going?

hingerissen *a* rapt; **h~ sein** be carried away (**von** by)

hinhalten† *vt sep* hold out; (*warten lassen*) keep waiting

hinken *vi* (*haben/sein*) limp

hin|knien (sich) *vr sep* kneel down. **h~kommen**† *vi sep* (*sein*) get there; (*h~gehören*) belong, go; ([!] *auskommen*) manage (**mit** with); ([!] *stimmen*) be right. **h~laufen**† *vi sep* (*sein*) run/(*gehen*) walk there. **h~legen** *vt sep* lay *or* put down; **sich h~legen** lie down. **h~nehmen**† *vt sep* (*fig*) accept

hinreichen *v sep* ● *vt* hand (*dat* to) ● *vi* (*haben*) extend (**bis** to); (*ausreichen*) be adequate. **h~d** *a* adequate

Hinreise *f* journey there; (*Rail*) outward journey

hinreißen† *vt sep* (*fig*) carry away; **sich h~ lassen** get carried away. **h~d** *a* ravishing

hinricht|en *vt sep* execute. **H~ung** *f* execution

hinschreiben† *vt sep* write there; (*aufschreiben*) write down

hinsehen† *vi sep* (*haben*) look

hinsetzen *vt sep* put down; **sich h~** sit down

Hinsicht *f* - **in dieser H~** in this respect; **in finanzieller H~** financially. **h~lich** *prep* (+ *gen*) regarding

hinstellen *vt sep* put *or* set down; park <*Auto*>

hinstrecken *vt sep* hold out; **sich h~** extend

hinten *adv* at the back; **dort h~** back there; **nach/von h~** to the back/from behind. **h~herum** *adv* round the back; [!] by devious means

hinter *prep* (+ *dat/acc*) behind; (*nach*) after; **h~ jdm/etw herlaufen** run after s.o./sth; **h~ etw** (*dat*) **stecken** (*fig*) be behind sth; **h~ etw** (*acc*) **kommen** (*fig*) get to the bottom of sth; **etw h~ sich** (*acc*) **bringen** get sth over [and done] with

Hinterbliebene *pl* (*Admin*) surviving dependants; **die H~n** the bereaved family *sg*

hintere|(r,s) *a* back, rear; **h~s Ende** far end

hintereinander *adv* one behind/(*zeitlich*) after the other; **dreimal h~** three times in succession

Hintergedanke *m* ulterior motive

hintergehen† *vt* deceive

Hinter|grund *m* background. **H~halt** *m* **-[e]s, -e** ambush. **h~hältig** *a* underhand

hinterher *adv* behind, after; (*zeitlich*) afterwards

Hinter|hof *m* back yard. **H~kopf** *m* back of the head

hinterlassen† *vt* leave [behind]; (*Jur*) leave, bequeath (*dat* to). **H~schaft** *f* **-, -en** (*Jur*) estate

hinterlegen *vt* deposit

Hinter|leib *m* (*Zool*) abdomen. **H~list** *f* deceit. **h~listig** *a* deceitful. **H~n** *m* **-s,-** [!] bottom, backside. **H~rad** *nt* rear *or* back wheel. **h~rücks** *adv* from behind. **h~ste(r,s)** *a* last; **h~ste Reihe** back row. **H~teil** *nt* [!] behind. **H~treppe** *f* back stairs *pl*

hinterziehen† *vt* (*Admin*) evade

hinüber *adv* over *or* across [*there*]; **h~ sein** ([!] *unbrauchbar, tot*) have had it. **h~gehen**† *vi sep* (*sein*) go over *or* across; **h~gehen über** (+ *acc*) cross

hinunter *adv* down [there]. **h~gehen**† *vi sep* (*sein*) go down. **h~schlucken** *vt sep* swallow

Hinweg *m* way there

hinweg *adv* away, off; **h~ über** (+ *acc*) over; **über eine Zeit h~** over a period. **h~kommen**† *vt sep* (*sein*) **h~kommen über** (+ *acc*) (*fig*) get over. **h~sehen**† *vi sep* (*haben*) **h~sehen über** (+ *acc*) see over; (*fig*) overlook. **h~setzen** (sich) *vr sep* **sich h~setzen über** (+ *acc*) ignore

Hinweis *m* **-es, -e** reference; (*Andeutung*) hint; (*Anzeichen*) indication; **unter H~ auf** (+ *acc*) with reference to. **h~en**† *v sep* ● *vi* (*haben*) point (**auf** + *acc* to) ● *vt* **jdn auf etw** (*acc*) **h~en** point sth out to s.o.

hinwieder *adv* on the other hand

hin|zeigen *vi sep* (*haben*) point (**auf** + *acc* to). **h~ziehen**† *vt sep* pull; (*fig: in die Länge ziehen*) drag out; (*verzögern*) delay; **sich h~ziehen** drag on

hinzu *adv* in addition. **h~fügen** *vt sep* add. **h~kommen**† *vt sep* (*sein*) be added; (*ankommen*) arrive [on the scene]; join (**zu jdm** s.o.). **h~ziehen**† *vt sep* call in

Hiobsbotschaft *f* bad news *sg*

Hirn *nt* **-s** brain; (*Culin*) brains *pl*. **H~hautentzündung** *f* meningitis

Hirsch *m* **-[e]s, -e** deer; (*männlich*) stag; (*Culin*) venison

Hirse *f* **-** millet

Hirt *m* **-en, -en**, **Hirte** *m* **-n, -n** shepherd

hissen *vt* hoist

Histor|iker *m* **-s,-** historian. **h~isch** *a* historical; (*bedeutend*) historic

Hitz|e *f* **-** heat. **h~ig** *a* (*fig*) heated; <*Person*> hot-headed; (*jähzornig*) hot-tempered. **H~schlag** *m* heat-stroke

H-Milch /'ha:-/ *f* long-life milk

Hobby *nt* **-s, -s** hobby

Hobel *m* **-s,-** (*Techn*) plane; (*Culin*) slicer. **h~n** *vt/i* (*haben*) plane. **H~späne** *mpl* shavings

hoch *a* (*attrib* **hohe(r,s)**) high; <*Baum, Mast*> tall; <*Offizier*> high-ranking; <*Alter*> great; <*Summe*> large; <*Strafe*> heavy; **hohe Schuhe** ankle boots ● *adv* high; (*sehr*) highly; **h~ gewachsen** tall; **h~ begabt** highly gifted; **h~ gestellte Persönlichkeit** important person; **die Treppe h~** up the stairs; **sechs Mann h~** six of us/them. **H~** *nt* **-s, -s** cheer; (*Meteorol*) high

Hoch|achtung *f* high esteem. **H~achtungsvoll** *adv* Yours faithfully. **H~betrieb** *m* great activity; **in den Geschäften herrscht H~betrieb** the shops are terribly busy. **H~deutsch** *nt* High German. **H~druck** *m* high pressure. **H~ebene** *f* plateau. **h~fahren**† *vi sep* (*sein*) go up; (*auffahren*) start up; (*aufbrausen*) flare up. **h~gehen**† *vi sep* (*sein*) go up; (*explodieren*) blow up; (*aufbrausen*) flare up. **h~gestellt** *attrib a* <*Zahl*> superior; (*fig*) ***h~ gestellt**, *s.* **hoch**. **H~glanz** *m* high gloss. **h~gradig** *a* extreme. **h~hackig** *a* high-heeled. **h~halten**† *vt sep* hold up; (*fig*) uphold. **H~haus** *nt* high-rise building. **h~heben**† *vt sep* lift up; raise <*Hand*>. **h~kant** *adv* on end. **h~kommen**† *vi sep* (*sein*) come up; (*aufstehen*) get up; (*fig*) get on [in the world]. **H~konjunktur** *f* boom. **h~krempeln** *vt sep* roll up. **h~leben** *vi sep* (*haben*) **h~leben lassen** give three cheers for; **H~mut** *m* pride, arrogance. **h~näsig** *a* 🅃 snooty. **H~ofen** *m* blast-furnace. **h~ragen** *vi sep* rise [up]; <*Turm*:> soar. **H~ruf** *m* cheer. **H~saison** *f* high season. **h~schlagen**† *vt sep* turn up <*Kragen*>. **H~schule** *f* university; (*Musik-, Kunst-*) academy. **H~sommer** *m* midsummer. **H~spannung** *f* high/(*fig*) great tension. **h~spielen** *vt sep* (*fig*) magnify. **H~sprung** *m* high jump

höchst *adv* extremely, most

Hochstapler *m* **-s,-** confidence trickster

höchst|e(r,s) *a* highest; <*Baum, Turm*> tallest; (*oberste, größte*) top; **es ist h~e Zeit** it is high time. **h~ens** *adv* at most; (*es sei denn*) except perhaps. **H~geschwindigkeit** *f* top or maximum speed. **H~maß** *nt* maximum. **h~persönlich** *adv* in person. **H~preis** *m* top price. **H~temperatur** *f* maximum temperature

Hoch|verrat *m* high treason. **H~wasser** *nt* high tide; (*Überschwemmung*) floods *pl*. **H~würden** *m* **-s** Reverend; (*Anrede*) Father

Hochzeit *f* **-, -en** wedding. **H~skleid** *nt* wedding dress. **H~sreise** *f* honeymoon [trip]. **H~stag** *m* wedding day/ (*Jahrestag*) anniversary

Hocke *f* **- in der H~sitzen** squat. **h~n** *vi* (*haben*) squat ● *vr* **sich h~n** squat down

Hocker *m* **-s,-** stool

Höcker *m* **-s,-** bump; (*Kamel-*) hump

Hockey /hɔki/ *nt* **-s** hockey

Hode *f* **-, -n**, **Hoden** *m* **-s,-** testicle

Hof *m* **-[e]s,¨e** [court]yard; (*Bauern-*) farm; (*Königs-*) court; (*Schul-*) playground; (*Astr*) halo

hoffen *vt/i* (*haben*) hope (**auf** + *acc* for). **h~tlich** *adv* I hope, let us hope

Hoffnung *f* **-, -en** hope. **h~slos** *a* hopeless. **h~svoll** *a* hopeful

höflich *a* polite. **H~keit** *f* **-, -en** politeness, courtesy

hohe(r,s) *a s.* **hoch**

Höhe *f* **-, -n** height; (*Aviat, Geog*) altitude; (*Niveau*) level; (*einer Summe*) size; (*An-*) hill

Hoheit *f* **-, -en** (*Staats-*) sovereignty; (*Titel*) Highness. **H~sgebiet** *nt* [sovereign] territory. **H~szeichen** *nt* national emblem

Höhe|nlinie *f* contour line. **H~nsonne** *f* sun-lamp. **H~punkt** *m* (*fig*) climax, peak. **h~r** *a & adv* higher; **h~re Schule** secondary school

hohl *a* hollow; (*leer*) empty

Höhle *f* **-, -n** cave; (*Tier-*) den; (*Hohlraum*) cavity; (*Augen-*) socket

Hohl|maß *nt* measure of capacity. **H~raum** *m* cavity

Hohn *m* **-s** scorn, derision

höhnen *vt* deride

holen *vt* fetch, get; (*kaufen*) buy; (*nehmen*) take (**aus** from)

Holland *nt* **-s** Holland

Holländ|er *m* **-s,-** Dutchman; **die H~er** the Dutch *pl*. **H~erin** *f* **-, -nen** Dutchwoman. **h~isch** *a* Dutch

Höll|e *f* **-** hell. **h~isch** *a* infernal; (*schrecklich*) terrible

Holunder *m* **-s** (*Bot*) elder

Holz *nt* **-es,¨er** wood; (*Nutz-*) timber. **H~blasinstrument** *nt* woodwind instrument

hölzern *a* wooden

Holz|hammer *m* mallet. **h~ig** *a* woody. **H~kohle** *f* charcoal. **H~schnitt** *m* woodcut. **H~wolle** *f* wood shavings *pl*

Homöopathie *f* **-** homoeopathy

homosexuell *a* homosexual. **H~e(r)** *m/f* homosexual

Honig *m* **-s** honey. **H~wabe** *f* honeycomb

Hono|rar *nt* **-s, -e** fee. **h~rieren** *vt* remunerate; (*fig*) reward

Hopfen *m* **-s** hops *pl*; (*Bot*) hop

hopsen *vi* (*sein*) jump

horchen *vi* (*haben*) listen (**auf** + *acc* to); (*heimlich*) eavesdrop

hören *vt* hear; (*an-*) listen to ● *vi* (*haben*) hear; (*horchen*) listen; (*gehorchen*) obey; **h~ auf** (+ *acc*) listen to

Hör|er *m* **-s,-** listener; (*Teleph*) receiver. **H~funk** *m* radio. **H~gerät** *nt* hearing-aid

Horizon|t *m* **-[e]s** horizon. **h~tal** *a* horizontal
Hormon *nt* **-s, -e** hormone
Horn *nt* **-s,¨er** horn. **H~haut** *f* hard skin; (*Augen-*) cornea
Horn|isse *f* **-, -n** hornet
Horoskop *nt* **-[e]s, -e** horoscope
Horrorfilm *m* horror film
Hör|saal *m* (*Univ*) lecture hall. **H~spiel** *nt* radio play
Hort *m* **-[e]s, -e** (*Schatz*) hoard; (*fig*) refuge. **h~en** *vt* hoard
Hortensie /-iə/ *f* **-, -n** hydrangea
Hose *f* **-, -n**, **Hosen** *pl* trousers *pl*. **H~nrock** *m* culottes *pl*. **H~nschlitz** *m* fly, flies *pl*. **H~nträger** *mpl* braces
Hostess *f* **-, -tessen** hostess; (*Aviat*) air hostess
Hostie /ˈhɔstiə/ *f* **-, -n** (*Relig*) host
Hotel *nt* **-s, -s** hotel
hübsch *a* pretty; (*nett*) nice
Hubschrauber *m* **-s,-** helicopter
Huf *m* **-[e]s, -e** hoof. **H~eisen** *nt* horseshoe
Hüft|e *f* **-, -n** hip. **H~gürtel** *m* **-s,-** girdle
Hügel *m* **-s,-** hill. **h~ig** *a* hilly
Huhn *nt* **-s,¨er** chicken; (*Henne*) hen
Hühn|chen *nt* **-s,-** chicken. **H~erauge** *nt* corn. **H~erstall** *m* henhouse
Hülle *f* **-, -n** cover; (*Verpackung*) wrapping; (*Platten-*) sleeve. **h~n** *vt* wrap
Hülse *f* **-, -n** (*Bot*) pod; (*Etui*) case. **H~nfrüchte** *fpl* pulses
human *a* humane. **H~ität** *f* **-** humanity
Hummel *f* **-, -n** bumble-bee
Hummer *m* **-s,-** lobster
Humor *m* **-s** humour; **H~ haben** have a sense of humour. **h~voll** *a* humorous
humpeln *vi* (*sein/haben*) hobble
Humpen *m* **-s,-** tankard
Hund *m* **-[e]s, -e** dog; (*Jagd-*) hound. **H~ehütte** *f* kennel
hundert *inv a* one/a hundred. **H~** *nt* **-s, -e** hundred; **H~e** *od* **h~e von** hundreds of. **H~jahrfeier** *f* centenary. **h~prozentig** *a & adv* one hundred per cent. **h~ste(r,s)** *a* hundredth. **H~stel** *nt* **-s,-** hundredth
Hündin *f* **-, -nen** bitch
Hüne *m* **-n, -n** giant
Hunger *m* **-s** hunger; **H~ haben** be hungry. **h~n** *vi* (*haben*) starve. **H~snot** *f* famine
hungrig *a* hungry
Hupe *f* **-, -n** (*Auto*) horn. **h~n** *vi* (*haben*) sound one's horn
hüpfen *vi* (*sein*) skip; <*Frosch:*> hop; <*Grashüpfer:*> jump
Hürde *f* **-, -n** (*Sport & fig*) hurdle; (*Schaf-*) pen, fold
Hure *f* **-, -n** whore
hurra *int* hurray
husten *vi* (*haben*) cough. **H~** *m* **-s** cough. **H~saft** *m* cough mixture
Hut¹ *m* **-[e]s,¨e** hat; (*Pilz-*) cap
Hut² *f* **- auf der H~sein** be on one's guard (**vor** + *dat* against)
hüten *vt* watch over; tend <*Tiere*>; (*aufpassen*) look after; **das Bett h~ müssen** be confined to bed; **sich h~** be on one's guard (**vor** + *dat* against); **sich h~, etw zu tun** take care not to do sth
Hütte *f* **-, -n** hut; (*Hunde-*) kennel; (*Techn*) iron and steel works. **H~nkäse** *m* cottage cheese. **H~nkunde** *f* metallurgy
Hyäne *f* **-, -n** hyena
hydraulisch *a* hydraulic
Hygien|e /hyˈgieːnə/ *f* **-** hygiene. **h~isch** *a* hygienic
Hypno|se *f* **-** hypnosis. **h~tisch** *a* hypnotic. **H~tiseur** /-ˈzøːɐ̯/ *m*

-s, -e hypnotist. **h~tisieren** *vt* hypnotize
Hypochonder /hypo'xɔndɐ/ *m* -s,- hypochondriac
Hypothek *f* -, -en mortgage
Hypothese *f* -, -n hypothesis
Hys|terie *f* - hysteria. **h~terisch** *a* hysterical

Ii

ich *pron* I; **ich bins** it's me. **Ich** *nt* -[s], -[s] self; (*Psych*) ego
IC-Zug /i'tse:-/ *m* inter-city train
ideal *a* ideal. **I~** *nt* -s, -e ideal. **I~ismus** *m* - idealism. **I~ist(in)** *m* -en, -en (*f* -, -nen) idealist. **i~istisch** *a* idealistic
Idee *f* -, -n idea; **fixe I~** obsession
identifizieren *vt* identify
identisch *a* identical
Ideo|logie *f* -, -n ideology. **i~logisch** *a* ideological
idiomatisch *a* idiomatic
Idiot *m* -en, -en idiot. **i~isch** *a* idiotic
idyllisch /i'dʏlɪʃ/ *a* idyllic
Igel *m* -s,- hedgehog
ihm *pron* (*dat of* **er, es**) [to] him; (*Ding, Tier*) [to] it
ihn *pron* (*acc of* **er**) him; (*Ding, Tier*) it. **i~en** *pron* (*dat of* **sie** *pl*) [to] them. **I~en** *pron* (*dat of* **Sie**) [to] you
ihr *pron* (*2nd pers pl*) you ● (*dat of* **sie** *sg*) [to] her; (*Ding, Tier*) [to] it ● *poss pron* her; (*Ding, Tier*) its; (*pl*) their. **Ihr** *poss pron* your. **i~e(r,s)** *poss pron* hers; (*pl*) theirs. **I~e(r,s)** *poss pron* yours. **i~erseits** *adv* for her/(*pl*) their part. **I~erseits** *adv* on your part. **i~etwegen** *adv* for her/(*Ding, Tier*) its/(*pl*) their sake; (*wegen*) because of her/it/them, on her/its/their account. **I~etwegen** *adv* for your sake; (*wegen*) because of you, on your account. **i~ige** *poss pron* **der/die/das i~ige** hers; (*pl*) theirs. **I~ige** *poss pron* **der/die/das I~ige** yours. **i~s** *poss pron* hers; (*pl*) theirs. **I~s** *poss pron* yours
Ikone *f* -, -n icon
illegal *a* illegal
Illus|ion *f* -, -en illusion. **i~orisch** *a* illusory
Illustr|ation /-'tsio:n/ *f* -, -en illustration. **i~ieren** *vt* illustrate. **I~ierte** *f* -n, -[n] [illustrated] magazine
Iltis *m* -ses, -se polecat
im *prep* = **in dem**
Imbiss *m* snack. **I~stube** *f* snack-bar
Imit|ation /-'tsio:n/ *f* -, -en imitation. **i~ieren** *vt* imitate
Imker *m* -s,- bee-keeper
Immatrikul|ation /-'tsio:n/ *f* - (*Univ*) enrolment. **i~ieren** *vt* (*Univ*) enrol; **sich i~ieren** enrol
immer *adv* always; **für i~** for ever; (*endgültig*) for good; **i~ noch** still; **i~ mehr** more and more; **was i~** whatever. **i~hin** *adv* (*wenigstens*) at least; (*trotzdem*) all the same; (*schließlich*) after all. **i~zu** *adv* all the time
Immobilien /-iən/ *pl* real estate *sg*. **I~makler** *m* estate agent
immun *a* immune (**gegen** to)
Imperialismus *m* - imperialism
impf|en *vt* vaccinate, inoculate. **I~stoff** *m* vaccine. **I~ung** *f* -, -en vaccination, inoculation
imponieren *vi* (*haben*) impress (**jdm** s.o.)

Impor|t *m* **-[e]s, -e** import. **I~teur** /-'tøːɐ̯/ *m* **-s, -e** importer. **i~tieren** *vt* import

impoten|t *a* (*Med*) impotent. **I~z** *f* **-** (*Med*) impotence

imprägnieren *vt* waterproof

Impressionismus *m* **-** impressionism

improvisieren *vt/i* (*haben*) improvise

imstande *pred a* able (**zu** to); capable (**etw zu tun** of doing sth)

in *prep* (+ *dat*) in; (+ *acc*) into, in; (*bei Bus, Zug*) on; **in der Schule** at school; **in die Schule** to school ● *a* **in sein** be in

Inbegriff *m* embodiment

indem *conj* (*während*) while; (*dadurch*) by (+ -ing)

Inder(in) *m* **-s,-** (*f* **-, -nen**) Indian

indessen *conj* while ● *adv* (*unterdessen*) meanwhile

Indian|er(in) *m* **-s,-** (*f* **-, -nen**) (American) Indian. **i~isch** *a* Indian

Indien /'ɪndi̯ən/ *nt* **-s** India

indirekt *a* indirect

indisch *a* Indian

indiskret *a* indiscreet

indiskutabel *a* out of the question

Individu|alist *m* **-en, -en** individualist. **I~alität** *f* **-** individuality. **i~ell** *a* individual

Indizienbeweis /ɪn'diːt͡si̯ən-/ *m* circumstantial evidence

industr|ialisiert *a* industrialized. **I~ie** *f* **-, -n** industry. **i~iell** *a* industrial

ineinander *adv* in/into one another

Infanterie *f* **-** infantry

Infektion /-'t͡si̯oːn/ *f* **-, -en** infection. **I~skrankheit** *f* infectious disease

infizieren *vt* infect; **sich i~** become/ <*Person:*> be infected

Inflation /-'t͡si̯oːn/ *f* **-** inflation. **i~är** *a* inflationary

infolge *prep* (+ *gen*) as a result of. **i~dessen** *adv* consequently

Inform|atik *f* **-** information science. **I~ation** /-'t͡si̯oːn/ *f* **-, -en** information; **I~ationen** information *sg*. **i~ieren** *vt* inform; **sich i~ieren** find out (**über** + *acc* about)

infrage *adv* **etw i~ stellen** question sth; (*ungewiss machen*) make sth doubtful; **nicht i~ kommen** be out of the question

infrarot *a* infra-red

Ingenieur /ɪnʒe'ni̯øːɐ̯/ *m* **-s, -e** engineer

Ingwer *m* **-s** ginger

Inhaber(in) *m* **-s,-** (*f* **-, -nen**) holder; (*Besitzer*) proprietor; (*Scheck-*) bearer

inhaftieren *vt* take into custody

inhalieren *vt/i* (*haben*) inhale

Inhalt *m* **-[e]s, -e** contents *pl*; (*Bedeutung, Gehalt*) content; (*Geschichte*) story. **I~sangabe** *f* summary. **I~sverzeichnis** *nt* list/(*in Buch*) table of contents

Initiative /init͡si̯a'tiːvə/ *f* **-, -n** initiative

inklusive *prep* (+ *gen*) including ● *adv* inclusive

inkonsequent *a* inconsistent

inkorrekt *a* incorrect

Inkubationszeit /-'t͡si̯oːns-/ *f* (*Med*) incubation period

Inland *nt* **-[e]s** home country; (*Binnenland*) interior. **I~sgespräch** *nt* inland call

inmitten *prep* (+ *gen*) in the middle of; (*unter*) amongst

innen *adv* inside; **nach i~** inwards. **I~architekt(in)** *m(f)* interior designer. **I~minister** *m* Minister of the Interior; (*in UK*) Home Secretary. **I~politik** *f* domestic policy. **I~stadt** *f* town centre

inner|e(r,s) *a* inner; (*Med, Pol*) internal. **I~e(s)** *nt* interior; (*Mitte*) centre; (*fig: Seele*) inner being. **I~eien** *fpl* (*Culin*) offal *sg*. **i~halb** *prep* (+ *gen*) inside; (*zeitlich & fig*) within; (*während*) during ● *adv* **i~halb von** within. **i~lich** *a* internal

innig *a* sincere

innovativ *a* innovative

Innung *f* **-, -en** guild

ins *prep* = **in das**

Insasse *m* **-n, -n** inmate; (*im Auto*) occupant; (*Passagier*) passenger

insbesondere *adv* especially

Inschrift *f* inscription

Insekt *nt* **-[e]s, -en** insect. **I~envertilgungsmittel** *nt* insecticide

Insel *f* **-, -n** island

Inser|at *nt* **-[e]s, -e** [newspaper] advertisement. **i~ieren** *vt/i* (*haben*) advertise

insge|heim *adv* secretly. **i~samt** *adv* [all] in all

insofern, insoweit *adv* in this respect; **i~ als** in as much as

Insp|ektion /ɪnspɛkˈtsi̯oːn/ *f* **-, -en** inspection. **I~ektor** *m* **-en, -en** /-ˈtoːrən/ inspector

Install|ateur /ɪnstalaˈtøːɐ̯/ *m* **-s, -e** fitter; (*Klempner*) plumber. **i~ieren** *vt* install

instand *adv* **i~ halten** maintain; (*pflegen*) look after. **I~haltung** *f* **-** maintenance, upkeep

Instandsetzung *f* **-** repair

Instanz /-st-/ *f* **-, -en** authority

Instinkt /-st-/ *m* **-[e]s, -e** instinct. **i~iv** *a* instinctive

Institut /-st-/ *nt* **-[e]s, -e** institute

Instrument /-st-/ *nt* **-[e]s, -e** instrument. **I~almusik** *f* instrumental music

Insulin *nt* **-s** insulin

inszenier|en *vt* (*Theat*) produce. **I~ung** *f* **-, -en** production

Integr|ation /-ˈtsi̯oːn/ *f* **-** integration. **i~ieren** *vt* integrate; **sich i~ieren** integrate

Intellekt *m* **-[e]s** intellect. **i~uell** *a* intellectual

intelligen|t *a* intelligent. **I~z** *f* **-** intelligence

Intendant *m* **-en, -en** director

Intensivstation *f* intensive-care unit

interaktiv *a* interactive

inter|essant *a* interesting. **I~esse** *nt* **-s, -n** interest; **I~esse haben** be interested (**an** + *dat* in). **I~essengruppe** *f* pressure group. **I~essent** *m* **-en, -en** interested party; (*Käufer*) prospective buyer. **i~essieren** *vt* interest; **sich i~essieren** be interested (**für** in)

Inter|nat *nt* **-[e]s, -e** boarding school. **i~national** *a* international. **I~nist** *m* **-en, -en** specialist in internal diseases. **I~pretation** /-ˈtsi̯oːn/ *f* **-, -en** interpretation. **i~pretieren** *vt* interpret. **I~vall** *nt* **-s, -e** interval. **I~vention** /-ˈtsi̯oːn/ *f* **-, -en** intervention

Internet *nt* **-s, -s** Internet; **im I~** on the Internet

Interview /ˈɪntɐvjuː/ *nt* **-s, -s** interview. **i~en** /-ˈvjuːən/ *vt* interview

intim *a* intimate

intoleran|t *a* intolerant. **I~z** *f* **-** intolerance

intravenös *a* intravenous

Intrige *f* **-, -n** intrigue

introvertiert *a* introverted

Invalidenrente *f* disability pension

Invasion *f* **-, -en** invasion

Inven|tar *nt* **-s, -e** furnishings and fittings *pl*; (*Techn*) equipment; (*Bestand*) stock;

(*Liste*) inventory. **I∼tur** *f* **-, -en** stock-taking
investieren *vt* invest
inwie|fern *adv* in what way. **i∼weit** *adv* how far, to what extent
Inzest *m* **-[e]s** incest
inzwischen *adv* in the meantime
Irak (der) -[s] Iraq. **i∼isch** *a* Iraqi
Iran (der) -[s] Iran. **i∼isch** *a* Iranian
irdisch *a* earthly
Ire *m* **-n, -n** Irishman; **die I∼n** the Irish *pl*
irgend *adv* **wenn i∼ möglich** if at all possible. **i∼ein** *indef art* some/any; **i∼ein anderer** someone/anyone else. **i∼eine(r,s)** *pron* any one; (*jemand*) someone/anyone. **i∼etwas** *pron* something; anything. **i∼jemand** *pron* someone; anyone. **i∼wann** *pron* at some time [or other]/at any time. **i∼was** *pron* [!] something [or other]/anything. **i∼welche(r,s)** *pron* any. **i∼wer** *pron* someone/anyone. **i∼wie** *adv* somehow [or other]. **i∼wo** *adv* somewhere/anywhere
Irin *f* **-, -nen** Irishwoman
irisch *a* Irish
Irland *nt* **-s** Ireland
Ironie *f* **-** irony
ironisch *a* ironic
irre *a* mad, crazy; ([!] *gewaltig*) incredible. **I∼(r)** *m/f* lunatic. **i∼führen** *vt sep* (*fig*) mislead. **i∼machen** *vt sep* confuse. **i∼n** *vi/r* (*haben*) **[sich] i∼n** be mistaken ● *vi* (*sein*) wander. **I∼nanstalt** *f*, **I∼nhaus** *nt* lunatic asylum. **i∼werden**† *vi sep* (*sein*) get confused
Irrgarten *m* maze
irritieren *vt* irritate
Irr|sinn *m* madness, lunacy. **i∼sinnig** *a* mad; ([!] *gewaltig*) incredible. **I∼tum** *m* **-s,⸚er** mistake
Ischias *m* & *nt* **-** sciatica
Islam (der) -[s] Islam. **islamisch** *a* Islamic
Island *nt* **-s** Iceland
Isolier|band *nt* insulating tape. **i∼en** *vt* isolate; (*Phys, Electr*) insulate; (*gegen Schall*) soundproof. **I∼ung** *f* **-** isolation; insulation; soundproofing
Isra|el /ˈɪsrae:l/ *nt* **-s** Israel. **I∼eli** *m* **-[s], -s** & *f* **-, -[s]** Israeli. **i∼elisch** *a* Israeli
ist *s.* **sein; er ist** he is
Ital|ien /-iən/ *nt* **-s** Italy. **I∼iener(in)** *m* **-s,-** (*f* **-, -nen**) Italian. **i∼ienisch** *a* Italian. **I∼ienisch** *nt* **-[s]** (*Lang*) Italian

Jj

ja *adv*, **Ja** *nt* **-[s]** yes; **ich glaube ja** I think so; **ja nicht!** not on any account! **da seid ihr ja!** there you are!
Jacht *f* **-, -en** yacht
Jacke *f* **-, -n** jacket; (*Strick-*) cardigan
Jackett /ʒaˈkɛt/ *nt* **-s, -s** jacket
Jade *m* **-[s]** & *f* **-** jade
Jagd *f* **-, -en** hunt; (*Schießen*) shoot; (*Jagen*) hunting; shooting; (*fig*) pursuit (**nach** of); **auf die J∼ gehen** go hunting/shooting. **J∼gewehr** *nt* sporting gun. **J∼hund** *m* gun-dog; (*Hetzhund*) hound

jagen *vt* hunt; (*schießen*) shoot; (*verfolgen, wegjagen*) chase; (*treiben*) drive; **sich j~** chase each other; **in die Luft j~** blow up ● *vi* (*haben*) hunt, go hunting/shooting; (*fig*) chase (**nach** after) ● *vi* (*sein*) race, dash

Jäger *m* **-s,-** hunter

Jahr *nt* **-[e]s, -e** year. **j~elang** *adv* for years. **J~eszahl** *f* year. **J~eszeit** *f* season. **J~gang** *m* year; (*Wein*) vintage. **J~hundert** *nt* century

jährlich *a* annual, yearly

Jahr|markt *m* fair. **J~tausend** *nt* millennium. **J~zehnt** *nt* **-[e]s, -e** decade

Jähzorn *m* violent temper. **j~ig** *a* hot-tempered

Jalousie /ʒaluˈziː/ *f* **-, -n** venetian blind

Jammer *m* **-s** misery

jämmerlich *a* miserable; (*Mitleid erregend*) pitiful

jammern *vi* (*haben*) lament ● *vt* **jdn j~n** arouse s.o.'s pity

Jänner *m* **-s,-** (*Aust*) January

Januar *m* **-s, -e** January

Jap|an *nt* **-s** Japan. **J~aner(in)** *m* **-s,-** (*f* **-, -nen**) Japanese. **j~anisch** *a* Japanese. **J~anisch** *nt* **-[s]** (*Lang*) Japanese

jäten *vt/i* (*haben*) **weed**

jaulen *vi* (*haben*) yelp

Jause *f* **-, -n** (*Aust*) snack

jawohl *adv* yes

Jazz /jats, dʒɛs/ *m* **-** jazz

je *adv* (*jemals*) ever; (*jeweils*) each; (*pro*) per; **je nach** according to; **seit eh und je** always ● *conj* **je mehr, desto besser** the more the better ● *prep* (+ *acc*) per

Jeans /dʒiːns/ *pl* jeans

jed|e(r,s) *pron* every; (*j~er Einzelne*) each; (*j~er Beliebige*) any; (*substantivisch*) everyone; each one; anyone; **ohne j~en Grund** without any reason. **j~enfalls** *adv* in any case; (*wenigstens*) at least. **j~ermann** *pron* everyone. **j~erzeit** *adv* at any time. **j~esmal** *adv* every time

jedoch *adv & conj* however

jemals *adv* ever

jemand *pron* someone, somebody; (*fragend, verneint*) anyone, anybody

jen|e(r,s) *pron* that; (*pl*) those; (*substantivisch*) that one; (*pl*) those. **j~seits** *prep* (+ *gen*) [on] the other side of

jetzt *adv* now

jiddisch *a*, **J~** *nt* **-[s]** Yiddish

Job /dʒɔp/ *m* **-s, -s** job. **j~ben** *vi* (*haben*) [!] work

Joch *nt* **-[e]s, -e** yoke

Jockei, Jockey /ˈdʒɔki/ *m* **-s, -s** jockey

Jod *nt* **-[e]s** iodine

jodeln *vi* (*haben*) yodel

Joga *m & nt* **-[s]** yoga

joggen /ˈdʒɔgən/ *vi* (*haben/sein*) jog

Joghurt, Jogurt *m & nt* **-[s]** yoghurt

Johannisbeere *f* redcurrant

Joker *m* **-s,-** (*Karte*) joker

Jolle *f* **-, -n** dinghy

Jongleur /ʒõˈgløːɐ̯/ *m* **-s, -e** juggler

Jordanien /-i̯ən/ *nt* **-s** Jordan

Journalis|mus /ʒʊrnaˈlɪsmʊs/ *m* **-** journalism. **J~t(in)** *m* **-en, -en** (*f* **-, -nen**) journalist

Jubel *m* **-s** rejoicing, jubilation. **j~n** *vi* (*haben*) rejoice

Jubiläum *nt* **-s,-äen** jubilee; (*Jahrestag*) anniversary

jucken *vi* (*haben*) itch; **sich j~en** scratch; **es j~t mich** I have an itch

Jude *m* **-n, -n** Jew. **J~ntum** *nt* **-s** Judaism; (*Juden*) Jewry

Jüd|in *f* **-, -nen** Jewess. **j~isch** *a* Jewish

Judo *nt* **-[s]** judo

Jugend *f* **-** youth; (*junge Leute*) young people *pl.* **J~herberge** *f* youth hostel. **J~kriminalität** *f* juvenile delinquency. **j~lich** *a* youthful. **J~liche(r)** *m/f* young man/woman; **J~liche** *pl* young people. **J~stil** *m* art nouveau

Jugoslaw|ien /-i̯ən/ *nt* **-s** Yugoslavia. **j~isch** a Yugoslav

Juli *m* **-[s], -s** July

jung *a* young; <*Wein*> new ● *pron* **J~ und Alt** young and old. **J~e** *m* **-n, -n** boy. **J~e(s)** *nt* young animal/bird; (*Katzen-*) kitten; (*Bären-*) cub; (*Hunde-*) pup; **die J~en** the young *pl*

Jünger *m* **-s,-** disciple

Jung|frau *f* virgin; (*Astr*) Virgo. **J~geselle** *m* bachelor

Jüngling *m* **-s, -e** youth

jüngst|e(r,s) *a* youngest; (*neueste*) latest; **in j~er Zeit** recently

Juni *m* **-[s], -s** June

Jura *pl* law *sg*

Jurist|(in) *m* **-en, -en** (*f* **-, -nen**) lawyer. **j~isch** *a* legal

Jury /ʒy'ri:/ *f* **-, -s** jury; (*Sport*) judges *pl*

Justiz *f* **- die J~** justice

Juwel *nt* **-s, -en** & (*fig*) **-e** jewel. **J~ier** *m* **-es, -e** jeweller

Jux *m* **-es, -e** [!] joke; **aus Jux** for fun

Kk

Kabarett *nt* **-s, -s** & **-e** cabaret

Kabel *nt* **-s,-** cable. **K~fernsehen** *nt* cable television

Kabeljau *m* **-s, -e** & **-s** cod

Kabine *f* **-, -n** cabin; (*Umkleide-*) cubicle; (*Telefon-*) booth; (*einer K~nbahn*) car. **K~nbahn** *f* cable-car

Kabinett *nt* **-s, -e** (*Pol*) Cabinet

Kabriolett *nt* **-s, -s** convertible

Kachel *f* **-, -n** tile. **k~n** *vt* tile

Kadenz *f* **-, -en** (*Mus*) cadence

Käfer *m* **-s,-** beetle

Kaffee /'kafe:, ka'fe:/ *m* **-s, -s** coffee. **K~kanne** *f* coffee-pot. **K~maschine** *f* coffee-maker. **K~mühle** *f* coffee-grinder

Käfig *m* **-s, -e** cage

kahl *a* bare; (*haarlos*) bald; **k~geschoren** shaven

Kahn *m* **-s,¨-e** boat; (*Last-*) barge

Kai *m* **-s, -s** quay

Kaiser *m* **-s,-** emperor. **K~in** *f* **-, -nen** empress. **k~lich** *a* imperial. **K~reich** *nt* empire. **K~schnitt** *m* Caesarean [section]

Kajüte *f* **-, -n** (*Naut*) cabin

Kakao /ka'kau̯/ *m* **-s** cocoa

Kakerlak *m* **-s** & **-en, -en** cockroach

Kaktus *m* **-, -teen** /-'te:ən/ cactus

Kalb *nt* **-[e]s,¨-er** calf. **K~fleisch** *nt* veal

Kalender *m* **-s,-** calendar; (*Termin-*) diary

Kaliber *nt* **-s,-** calibre; (*Gewehr-*) bore

Kalium *nt* **-s** potassium

Kalk *m* **-[e]s, -e** lime; (*Kalzium*) calcium. **k~en** *vt* whitewash. **K~stein** *m* limestone

Kalkul|ation /-'tsio:n/ *f* **-, -en** calculation. **k~ieren** *vt/i* (*haben*) calculate

Kalorie *f* **-, -n** calorie

kalt *a* cold; **mir ist k~** I am cold

Kälte *f* **-** cold; (*Gefühls-*) coldness; **10 Grad K~** 10 degrees below zero

Kalzium *nt* **-s** calcium

Kamel *nt* **-s, -e** camel

Kamera *f* **-, -s** camera

Kamerad(in) *m* **-en, -en** (*f* **-, -nen**) companion; (*Freund*) mate; (*Mil, Pol*) comrade

Kameramann *m* (*pl* **-männer & -leute**) cameraman

Kamille *f* **-** camomile

Kamin *m* **-s, -e** fireplace; (*SGer: Schornstein*) chimney

Kamm *m* **-[e]s,⸚e** comb; (*Berg-*) ridge; (*Zool, Wellen-*) crest

kämmen *vt* comb; **jdn/sich k~** comb s.o.'s/one's hair

Kammer *f* **-, -n** small room; (*Techn, Biol, Pol*) chamber. **K~musik** *f* chamber music

Kammgarn *nt* (*Tex*) worsted

Kampagne /kam'panjə/ *f* **-, -n** (*Pol, Comm*) campaign

Kampf *m* **-es,⸚e** fight; (*Schlacht*) battle; (*Wett-*) contest; (*fig*) struggle

kämpf|en *vi* (*haben*) fight; **sich k~en durch** fight one's way through. **K~er(in)** *m* **-s,-** (*f* **-, -nen**) fighter

Kampfrichter *m* (*Sport*) judge

Kanada *nt* **-s** Canada

Kanad|ier(in) /-iɐ, -iərɪn/ *m* **-s,-** (*f* **-, -nen**) Canadian. **k~isch** *a* Canadian

Kanal *m* **-s,⸚e** canal; (*Abfluss-*) drain, sewer; (*Radio, TV*) channel; **der K~** the [English] Channel

Kanalisation /-'tsio:n/ *f* **-** sewerage system, drains *pl*

Kanarienvogel /-iən-/ *m* canary

Kanarisch *a* **K~e Inseln** Canaries

Kandidat(in) *m* **-en, -en** (*f* **-, -nen**) candidate

kandiert *a* candied

Känguru *nt* **-s, -s** kangaroo

Kaninchen *nt* **-s,-** rabbit

Kanister *m* **-s,-** canister; (*Benzin-*) can

Kännchen *nt* **-s,-** [small] jug; (*Kaffee-*) pot

Kanne *f* **-, -n** jug; (*Tee-*) pot; (*Öl-*) can; (*große Milch-*) churn

Kannibal|e *m* **-n, -n** cannibal. **K~ismus** *m* **-** cannibalism

Kanon *m* **-s, -s** canon; (*Lied*) round

Kanone *f* **-, -n** cannon, gun

kanonisieren *vt* canonize

Kantate *f* **-, -n** cantata

Kante *f* **-, -n** edge

Kanten *m* **-s,-** crust [of bread]

Kanter *m* **-s,-** canter

kantig *a* angular

Kantine *f* **-, -n** canteen

Kanton *m* **-s, -e** (*Swiss*) canton

Kanu *nt* **-s, -s** canoe

Kanzel *f* **-, -n** pulpit; (*Aviat*) cockpit

Kanzler *m* **-s,-** chancellor

Kap *nt* **-s, -s** (*Geog*) cape

Kapazität *f* **-, -en** capacity

Kapelle *f* **-, -n** chapel; (*Mus*) band

kapern *vt* (*Naut*) seize

kapieren *vt* [!] understand

Kapital *nt* **-s** capital. **K~ismus** *m* **-** capitalism. **K~ist** *m* **-en, -en** capitalist. **k~istisch** *a* capitalist

Kapitän *m* **-s, -e** captain

Kapitel *nt* **-s,-** chapter

Kaplan *m* **-s, -e** curate

Kappe *f* **-, -n** cap

Kapsel *f* **-, -n** capsule; (*Flaschen-*) top

kaputt *a* [!] broken; (*zerrissen*) torn; (*defekt*) out of order; (*ruiniert*) ruined; (*erschöpft*) worn out. **k~gehen**† *vi sep* (*sein*) [!] break; (*zerreißen*) tear; (*defekt werden*) pack up; <*Ehe, Freundschaft:*> break up. **k~lachen (sich)** *vr sep* [!] be in stitches. **k~machen** *vt sep* [!] break; (*zerreißen*) tear; (*defekt machen*) put out of order; (*erschöpfen*) wear out; **sich k~machen** wear oneself out

Kapuze *f* **-, -n** hood

Kapuzinerkresse *f* nasturtium

Karaffe *f* **-, -n** carafe; (*mit Stöpsel*) decanter

Karamell *m* **-s** caramel. **K~bonbon** *m & nt* ≈ toffee

Karat *nt* **-[e]s, -e** carat

Karawane *f* **-, -n** caravan

Kardinal *m* **-s,¨e** cardinal. **K~zahl** *f* cardinal number

Karfreitag *m* Good Friday

karg *a* meagre; (*frugal*) frugal; (*spärlich*) sparse; (*unfruchtbar*) barren; (*gering*) scant

Karibik *f* - Caribbean

kariert *a* check[ed]; <*Papier*> squared; **schottisch k~** tartan

Karik|atur *f* **-, -en** caricature; (*Journ*) cartoon. **k~ieren** *vt* caricature

Karneval *m* **-s, -e & -s** carnival

Kärnten *nt* **-s** Carinthia

Karo *nt* **-s, -s** (*Raute*) diamond; (*Viereck*) square; (*Muster*) check (*Kartenspiel*) diamonds *pl*

Karosserie *f* **-, -n** bodywork

Karotte *f* **-, -n** carrot

Karpfen *m* **-s,-** carp

Karren *m* **-s,-** cart; (*Hand-*) barrow. **k~** *vt* cart

Karriere /ka'rie:rə/ *f* **-, -n** career; **K~ machen** get to the top

Karte *f* **-, -n** card; (*Eintritts-, Fahr-*) ticket; (*Speise-*) menu; (*Land-*) map

Kartei *f* **-, -en** card index

Karten|spiel *nt* card-game; (*Spielkarten*) pack of cards. **K~vorverkauf** *m* advance booking

Kartoffel *f* **-, -n** potato. **K~brei** *m nt* mashed potatoes

Karton /kar'tɔŋ/ *m* **-s, -s** cardboard; (**Schachtel**) carton

Karussell *nt* **-s, -s & -e** roundabout

Käse *m* **-s,-** cheese

Kaserne *f* **-, -n** barracks *pl*

Kasino *nt* **-s, -s** casino

Kasperle *nt & m* **-s,-** Punch. **K~theater** *nt* Punch and Judy show/(*Bühne*) theatre

Kasse *f* **-, -n** till; (*Registrier-*) cash register; (*Zahlstelle*) cash desk; (*im Supermarkt*) check-out; (*Theater-*) box-office; (*Geld*) pool [of money], [!] kitty; (*Kranken-*) health insurance scheme; **knapp bei K~ sein** [!] be short of cash. **K~nwart** *m* **-[e]s, -e** treasurer. **K~nzettel** *m* receipt

Kasserolle *f* **-, -n** saucepan

Kassette *f* **-, -n** cassette; (*Film-, Farbband-*) cartridge. **K~nrekorder** /-rəkɔrdɐ/ *m* **-s,-** cassette recorder

kassier|en *vi* (*haben*) collect the money/(*im Bus*) the fares ● *vt* collect. **K~er(in)** *m* **-s,-** (*f* **-, -nen**) cashier

Kastanie /kas'ta:niə/ *f* **-, -n** [horse] chestnut, [!] conker

Kasten *m* **-s,¨** box; (*Brot-*) bin; (*Flaschen-*) crate; (*Brief-*) letter-box; (*Aust: Schrank*) cupboard

kastrieren *vt* castrate; neuter

Katalog *m* **-[e]s, -e** catalogue

Katalysator *m* **-s, -en** /-'to:rən/ catalyst; (*Auto*) catalytic converter

Katapult *nt* **-[e]s, -e** catapult
Katarrh, Katarr *m* **-s, -e** catarrh
Katastrophe *f* **-, -n** catastrophe
Katechismus *m* **-** catechism
Kategorie *f* **-, -n** category
Kater *m* **-s,-** tom-cat; ([!] *Katzenjammer*) hangover
Kathedrale *f* **-, -n** cathedral
Kath|olik(in) *m* **-en, -en** (*f* **-, -nen**) Catholic. **k∼olisch** *a* Catholic. **K∼olizismus** *m* **-** Catholicism
Kätzchen *nt* **-s,-** kitten; (*Bot*) catkin
Katze *f* **-, -n** cat. **K∼njammer** *m* [!] hangover. **K∼nsprung** *m* **ein K∼nsprung** [!] a stone's throw
Kauderwelsch *nt* **-[s]** gibberish
kauen *vt/i* (*haben*) chew; bite <*Nägel*>
Kauf *m* **-[e]s, Käufe** purchase; **guter K∼** bargain; **in K∼nehmen** (*fig*) put up with. **k∼en** *vt/i* (*haben*) buy; **k∼en bei** shop at
Käufer(in) *m* **-s,-** (*f* **-, -nen**) buyer; (*im Geschäft*) shopper
Kauf|haus *nt* department store. **K∼laden** *m* shop
käuflich *a* saleable; (*bestechlich*) corruptible; **k∼ erwerben** buy
Kauf|mann *m* (*pl* **-leute**) businessman; (*Händler*) dealer; (*dial*) grocer. **K∼preis** *m* purchase price
Kaugummi *m* chewing-gum
Kaulquappe *f* **-, -n** tadpole
kaum *adv* hardly
Kaution /-'tsio:n/ *f* **-, -en** surety; (*Jur*) bail; (*Miet-*) deposit
Kautschuk *m* **-s** rubber
Kauz *m* **-es, Käuze** owl
Kavalier *m* **-s, -e** gentleman
Kavallerie *f* **-** cavalry
Kaviar *m* **-s** caviare
keck *a* bold; cheeky
Kegel *m* **-s,-** skittle; (*Geom*) cone. **K∼bahn** *f* skittle-alley. **k∼n** *vi* (*haben*) play skittles
Kehl|e *f* **-, -n** throat; **aus voller K∼e** at the top of one's voice. **K∼kopf** *m* larynx. **K∼kopfentzündung** *f* laryngitis
Kehr|e *f* **-, -n** [hairpin] bend. **k∼en** *vi* (*haben*) (*fegen*) sweep ● *vt* sweep; (*wenden*) turn; **sich nicht k∼en an** (+ *acc*) not care about. **K∼icht** *m* **-[e]s** sweepings *pl*. **K∼reim** *m* refrain. **K∼seite** *f* (*fig*) drawback. **k∼tmachen** *vi sep* (*haben*) turn back; (*sich umdrehen*) turn round
Keil *m* **-[e]s, -e** wedge. **K∼riemen** *m* fan belt
Keim *m* **-[e]s, -e** (*Bot*) sprout; (*Med*) germ. **k∼en** *vi* (*haben*) germinate; (*austreiben*) sprout. **k∼frei** *a* sterile
kein *pron* no; not a; **k∼e fünf Minuten** less than five minutes. **k∼e(r,s)** *pron* no one, nobody; (*Ding*) none, not one. **k∼esfalls** *adv* on no account. **k∼eswegs** *adv* by no means. **k∼mal** *adv* not once. **k∼s** *pron* none, not one
Keks *m* **-[es], -[e]** biscuit
Kelch *m* **-[e]s, -e** goblet, cup; (*Relig*) chalice; (*Bot*) calyx
Kelle *f* **-, -n** ladle; (*Maurer*) trowel
Keller *m* **-s,-** cellar. **K∼ei** *f* **-, -en** winery. **K∼wohnung** *f* basement flat
Kellner *m* **-s,-** waiter. **K∼in** *f* **-, -nen** waitress
keltern *vt* press
keltisch *a* Celtic
Kenia *nt* **-s** Kenya
kenn|en† *vt* know; **k∼en lernen** get to know; (*treffen*) meet; **sich k∼en lernen** meet; (*näher*) get to know one another. **K∼er(in)** *m*

-s,- (*f* **-, -nen**) connoisseur; (*Experte*) expert. **k~tlich** *a* recognizable; **k~tlich machen** mark. **K~tnis** *f* **-, -se** knowledge; **zur K~tnis nehmen** take note of; **in K~tnis setzen** inform (**von** of). **K~wort** *nt* (*pl* **-wörter**) reference; (*geheimes*) password. **K~zeichen** *nt* distinguishing mark *or* feature; (*Merkmal*) characteristic, (*Markierung*) marking; (*Auto*) registration. **k~zeichnen** *vt* distinguish; (*markieren*) mark

kentern *vi* (*sein*) capsize

Keramik *f* **-, -en** pottery

Kerbe *f* **-, -n** notch

Kerker *m* **-s,-** dungeon; (*Gefängnis*) prison

Kerl *m* **-s, -e & -s** [!] fellow, bloke

Kern *m* **-s, -e** pip; (*Kirsch-*) stone; (*Nuss-*) kernel; (*Techn*) core; (*Atom-, Zell- & fig*) nucleus; (*Stadt-*) centre; (*einer Sache*) heart. **K~energie** *f* nuclear energy. **K~gehäuse** *nt* core. **k~los** *a* seedless. **K~physik** *f* nuclear physics *sg*

Kerze *f* **-, -n** candle. **K~nhalter** *m* **-s,-** candlestick

kess *a* pert

Kessel *m* **-s,-** kettle

Kette *f* **-, -n** chain; (*Hals-*) necklace. **k~n** *vt* chain (**an** + *acc* to). **K~nladen** *m* chain store

Ketze|r(in) *m* **-s,-** (*f* **-, -nen**) heretic. **K~rei** *f* **-** heresy

keuch|en *vi* (*haben*) pant. **K~husten** *m* whooping cough

Keule *f* **-, -n** club; (*Culin*) leg; (*Hühner-*) drumstick

keusch *a* chaste

Khaki *nt* **-** khaki

kichern *vi* (*haben*) giggle

Kiefer[1] *f* **-, -n** pine[-tree]

Kiefer[2] *m* **-s,-** jaw

Kiel *m* **-s, -e** (*Naut*) keel

Kiemen *fpl* gills

Kies *m* **-es** gravel. **K~el** *m* **-s,-**, **K~elstein** *m* pebble

Kilo *nt* **-s, -[s]** kilo. **K~gramm** *nt* kilogram. **K~hertz** *nt* kilohertz. **K~meter** *m* kilometre. **K~meterstand** *m* ≈ mileage. **K~watt** *nt* kilowatt

Kind *nt* **-es, -er** child; **von K~ auf** from childhood

Kinder|arzt *m*, **K~ärztin** *f* paediatrician. **K~bett** *nt* child's cot. **K~garten** *m* nursery school. **K~geld** *nt* child benefit. **K~lähmung** *f* polio. **k~leicht** *a* very easy. **k~los** *a* childless. **K~mädchen** *nt* nanny. **K~reim** *m* nursery rhyme. **K~spiel** *nt* children's game. **K~tagesstätte** *f* day nursery. **K~teller** *m* children's menu. **K~wagen** *m* pram. **K~zimmer** *nt* child's/children's room; (*für Baby*) nursery

Kind|heit *f* **-** childhood. **k~isch** *a* childish. **k~lich** *a* childlike

kinetisch *a* kinetic

Kinn *nt* **-[e]s, -e** chin. **K~lade** *f* jaw

Kino *nt* **-s, -s** cinema

Kiosk *m* **-[e]s, -e** kiosk

Kippe *f* **-, -n** (*Müll-*) dump; ([!] *Zigaretten-*) fag-end. **k~n** *vt* tilt; (*schütten*) tip (**in** + *acc* into) ● *vi* (*sein*) topple

Kirch|e *f* **-, -n** church. **K~enbank** *f* pew. **K~endiener** *m* verger. **K~enlied** *nt* hymn. **K~enschiff** *nt* nave. **K~hof** *m* churchyard. **k~lich** *a* church ... ● *adv* **k~lich getraut werden** be married in church. **K~turm** *m* church tower, steeple. **K~weih** *f* **-, -en** [village] fair

Kirmes *f* **-, -sen** = **Kirchweih**

Kirsche *f* **-, -n** cherry

Kissen *nt* **-s,-** cushion; (*Kopf-*) pillow

Kiste *f* **-, -n** crate; (*Zigarren-*) box

Kitsch *m* **-es** sentimental rubbish; (*Kunst*) kitsch
Kitt *m* **-s** [adhesive] cement; (*Fenster-*) putty
Kittel *m* **-s,-** overall, smock
Kitz *nt* **-es, -e** (*Zool*) kid
Kitz|el *m* **-s,-** tickle; (*Nerven-*) thrill. **k~eln** *vt/i* (*haben*) tickle. **k~lig** *a* ticklish
kläffen *vi* (*haben*) yap
Klage *f* **-, -n** lament; (*Beschwerde*) complaint; (*Jur*) action. **k~n** *vi* (*haben*) lament; (*sich beklagen*) complaint; (*Jur*) sue
Kläger(in) *m* **-s,-** (*f* **-, -nen**) (*Jur*) plaintiff
klamm *a* cold and damp; (*steif*) stiff. **K~** *f* **-, -en** (*Geog*) gorge
Klammer *f* **-, -n** (*Wäsche-*) peg; (*Büro-*) paper-clip; (*Heft-*) staple; (*Haar-*) grip; (*für Zähne*) brace; (*Techn*) clamp; (*Typ*) bracket. **k~n (sich)** *vr* cling (**an** + *acc* to)
Klang *m* **-[e]s,¨e** sound; (*K~farbe*) tone
Klapp|e *f* **-, -n** flap; ([!] *Mund*) trap. **k~en** *vt* fold; (*hoch-*) tip up ● *vi* (*haben*) [!] work out
Klapper *f* **-, -n** rattle. **k~n** *vi* (*haben*) rattle. **K~schlange** *f* rattlesnake
klapp|rig *a* rickety; (*schwach*) decrepit. **K~stuhl** *m* folding chair
Klaps *m* **-es, -e** smack
klar *a* clear; **sich** (*dat*) **k~ werden** make up one's mind; (*erkennen*) realize (**dass** that); **sich** (*dat*) **k~** *od* **im K~en sein** realize (**dass** that) ● *adv* clearly; ([!] *natürlich*) of course
klären *vt* clarify; **sich k~** clear; (*fig: sich lösen*) resolve itself
Klarheit *f* **-,-** clarity
Klarinette *f* **-, -n** clarinet
klar|machen *vt sep* make clear (*dat* to); **sich** (*dat*) **etw** **k~machen** understand sth. **k~stellen** *vt sep* clarify
Klärung *f* **-** clarification
Klasse *f* **-, -n** class; (*Sch*) class, form; (*Zimmer*) classroom. **k~** *inv a* [!] super. **K~narbeit** *f* [written] test. **K~nzimmer** *nt* classroom
Klass|ik *f* **-** classicism; (*Epoche*) classical period. **K~iker** *m* **-s,-** classical author/(*Mus*) composer. **k~isch** *a* classical; (*typisch*) classic
Klatsch *m* **-[e]s** gossip. **K~base** *f* [!] gossip. **k~en** *vt* slap; **Beifall k~en** applaud ● *vi* (*haben*) make a slapping sound; (*im Wasser*) splash; (*tratschen*) gossip; (*applaudieren*) clap. **k~nass** *a* [!] soaking wet
klauen *vt/i* (*haben*) [!] steal
Klausel *f* **-, -n** clause
Klaustrophobie *f* **-** claustrophobia
Klausur *f* **-, -en** (*Univ*) paper
Klavier *nt* **-s, -e** piano. **K~spieler(in)** *m(f)* pianist
kleb|en *vt* stick/(*mit Klebstoff*) glue (**an** + *acc* to) ● *vi* (*haben*) stick (**an** + *dat* to). **k~rig** *a* sticky. **K~stoff** *m* adhesive, glue. **K~streifen** *m* adhesive tape
Klecks *m* **-es, -e** stain; (*Tinten-*) blot; (*kleine Menge*) dab. **k~en** *vi* (*haben*) make a mess
Klee *m* **-s** clover
Kleid *nt* **-[e]s, -er** dress; **K~er** dresses; (*Kleidung*) clothes. **k~en** *vt* dress; (*gut stehen*) suit. **K~erbügel** *m* coat-hanger. **K~erbürste** *f* clothes-brush. **K~erhaken** *m* coat-hook. **K~erschrank** *m* wardrobe. **k~sam** *a* becoming. **K~ung** *f* **-** clothes *pl*, clothing. **K~ungsstück** *nt* garment
Kleie *f* **-** bran

klein *a* small, little; (*von kleinem Wuchs*) short; **k~ schneiden** cut up small. **von k~ auf** from childhood. **K~arbeit** *f* painstaking work. **K~e(r,s)** *m/f/nt* little one. **K~geld** *nt* [small] change. **K~handel** *m* retail trade. **K~heit** *f* - smallness; (*Wuchs*) short stature. **K~holz** *nt* firewood. **K~igkeit** *f* -, **-en** trifle; (*Mahl*) snack. **K~kind** *nt* infant. **k~laut** *a* subdued. **k~lich** *a* petty

klein|schreiben† *vt sep* write with a small [initial] letter. **K~stadt** *f* small town. **k~städtisch** *a* provincial

Kleister *m* **-s** paste. **k~n** *vt* paste

Klemme *f* -, **-n** [hair-]grip. **k~n** *vt* jam; **sich** (*dat*) **den Finger k~n** get one's finger caught ● *vi* (*haben*) jam, stick

Klempner *m* **-s,-** plumber

Klerus (der) - the clergy

Klette *f* -, **-n** burr

kletter|n *vi* (*sein*) climb. **K~pflanze** *f* climber

Klettverschluss *m* Velcro (P) fastening

klicken *vi* (*haben*) click

Klient(in)/ kli'ɛnt(ɪn)/ *m* **-en, -en** (*f* -, **-nen**) (*Jur*) client

Kliff *nt* **-[e]s, -e** cliff

Klima *nt* **-s** climate. **K~anlage** *f* air-conditioning

klimat|isch *a* climatic. **k~isiert** *a* air-conditioned

klimpern *vi* (*haben*) jingle; **k~ auf** (+ *dat*) tinkle on <*Klavier*>; strum <*Gitarre*>

Klinge *f* -, **-n** blade

Klingel *f* -, **-n** bell. **k~n** *vi* (*haben*) ring; **es k~t** there's a ring at the door

klingen† *vi* (*haben*) sound

Klinik *f* -, **-en** clinic

Klinke *f* -, **-n** [door] handle

Klippe *f* -, **-n** [submerged] rock

Klips *m* **-es, -e** clip; (*Ohr-*) clip-on ear-ring

klirren *vi* (*haben*) rattle <*Glas:*> chink

Klo *nt* **-s, -s** [I] loo

Klon *m* **-s, -e** clone. **k~en** *vt* clone

klopfen *vi* (*haben*) knock; (*leicht*) tap; <*Herz:*> pound; **es k~te** there was a knock at the door

Klops *m* **-es, -e** meatball

Klosett *nt* **-s, -s** lavatory

Kloß *m* **-es,¨-e** dumpling

Kloster *nt* **-s,¨** monastery; (*Nonnen-*) convent

klösterlich *a* monastic

Klotz *m* **-es,¨-e** block

Klub *m* **-s, -s** club

Kluft *f* -,**¨-e** cleft; (*fig: Gegensatz*) gulf

klug *a* intelligent; (*schlau*) clever. **K~heit** *f* - cleverness

Klump|en *m* **-s,-** lump

knabbern *vt/i* (*haben*) nibble

Knabe *m* **-n, -n** boy. **k~nhaft** *a* boyish

Knäckebrot *nt* crispbread

knack|en *vt/i* (*haben*) crack. **K~s** *m* **-es, -e** crack

Knall *m* **-[e]s, -e** bang. **K~bonbon** *m* cracker. **k~en** *vi* (*haben*) go bang; <*Peitsche:*> crack ● *vt* ([I] *werfen*) chuck; **jdm eine k~en** [I] clout s.o. **k~ig** *a* [I] gaudy

knapp *a* (*gering*) scant; (*kurz*) short; (*mangelnd*) scarce; (*gerade ausreichend*) bare; (*eng*) tight. **K~heit** *f* - scarcity

knarren *vi* (*haben*) creak

Knast *m* **-[e]s** [I] prison

knattern *vi* (*haben*) crackle; <*Gewehr:*> stutter

Knäuel *m & nt* **-s,-** ball

Knauf *m* **-[e]s, Knäufe** knob

knauserig *a* [I] stingy

knautschen *vt* [!] crumple ● *vi* (*haben*) crease
Knebel *m* **-s,-** gag. **k~n** *vt* gag
Knecht *m* **-[e]s, -e** farm-hand; (*fig*) slave
kneif|en† *vt* pinch ● *vi* (*haben*) pinch; ([!] *sich drücken*) chicken out. **K~zange** *f* pincers *pl*
Kneipe *f* **-, -n** [!] pub
knet|en *vt* knead; (*formen*) mould. **K~masse** *f* Plasticine (P)
Knick *m* **-[e]s, -e** bend; (*Kniff*) crease. **k~en** *vt* bend; (*kniffen*) fold; **geknickt sein** [!] be dejected
Knicks *m* **-es, -e** curtsy. **k~en** *vi* (*haben*) curtsy
Knie *nt* **-s,-** /ˈkniːə/ knee
knien /ˈkniːən/ *vi* (*haben*) kneel ● *vr* **sich k~** kneel [down]
Kniescheibe *f* kneecap
Kniff *m* **-[e]s, -e** pinch; (*Falte*) crease; ([!] *Trick*) trick. **k~en** *vt* fold
knipsen *vt* (*lochen*) punch; (*Phot*) photograph ● *vi* (*haben*) take a photograph/photographs
Knirps *m* **-es, -e** [!] little chap; (P) (*Schirm*) telescopic umbrella
knirschen *vi* (*haben*) grate; <*Schnee, Kies:*> crunch
knistern *vi* (*haben*) crackle; <*Papier:*> rustle
Knitter|falte *f* crease. **k~frei** *a* crease-resistant. **k~n** *vi* (*haben*) crease
knobeln *vi* (*haben*) toss (**um** for)
Knoblauch *m* **-s** garlic
Knöchel *m* **-s,-** ankle; (*Finger-*) knuckle
Knochen *m* **-s,-** bone. **K~mark** *nt* bone marrow
knochig *a* bony
Knödel *m* **-s,-** (*SGer*) dumpling
Knoll|e *f* **-, -n** tuber
Knopf *m* **-[e]s,¨-e** button; (*Griff*) knob
knöpfen *vt* button
Knopfloch *nt* buttonhole
Knorpel *m* **-s** gristle; (*Anat*) cartilage
Knospe *f* bud
Knoten *m* **-s,-** knot; (*Med*) lump; (*Haar-*) bun, chignon. **k~** *vt* knot. **K~punkt** *m* junction
knüll|en *vt* crumple ● *vi* (*haben*) crease. **K~er** *m* **-s,-** [!] sensation
knüpfen *vt* knot; (*verbinden*) attach (**an** + *acc* to)
Knüppel *m* **-s,-** club; (*Gummi-*) truncheon
knurren *vi* (*haben*) growl; <*Magen:*> rumble
knusprig *a* crunchy, crisp
knutschen *vi* (*haben*) [!] smooch
k.o. /kaˈʔoː/ *a* **k.o. schlagen** knock out; **k.o. sein** [!] be worn out
Koalition /koaliˈtsi̯oːn/ *f* **-, -en** coalition
Kobold *m* **-[e]s, -e** goblin, imp
Koch *m* **-[e]s,¨-e** cook; (*im Restaurant*) chef. **K~buch** *nt* cookery book. **k~en** *vt* cook; (*sieden*) boil; make <*Kaffee, Tee*>; **hart gekochtes Ei** hard-boiled egg ● *vi* (*haben*) cook; (*sieden*) boil; [!] seethe (**vor** + *dat* with). **K~en** *nt* **-s** cooking; (*Sieden*) boiling. **k~end** *a* boiling. **K~herd** *m* cooker, stove
Köchin *f* **-, -nen** [woman] cook
Koch|löffel *m* wooden spoon. **K~nische** *f* kitchenette. **K~platte** *f* hotplate. **K~topf** *m* saucepan
Köder *m* **-s,-** bait
Koffein /kɔfeˈiːn/ *nt* **-s** caffeine. **k~frei** *a* decaffeinated
Koffer *m* **-s,-** suitcase. **K~kuli** *m* luggage trolley. **K~raum** *m* (*Auto*) boot
Kognak /ˈkɔnjak/ *m* **-s, -s** brandy

Kohl *m* **-[e]s** cabbage
Kohle *f* **-, -n** coal. **K~[n]hydrat** *nt* **-[e]s, -e** carbohydrate. **K~nbergwerk** *nt* coal-mine, colliery. **K~ndioxid** *nt* carbon dioxide. **K~nsäure** *f* carbon dioxide. **K~nstoff** *m* carbon
Koje *f* **-, -n** (*Naut*) bunk
Kokain /koka'i:n/ *nt* **-s** cocaine
kokett *a* flirtatious. **k~ieren** *vi* (*haben*) flirt
Kokon /ko'kõ:/ *m* **-s, -s** cocoon
Kokosnuss (*f*) coconut
Koks *m* **-es** coke
Kolben *m* **-s,-** (*Gewehr-*) butt; (*Mais-*) cob; (*Techn*) piston; (*Chem*) flask
Kolibri *m* **-s, -s** humming-bird
Kolik *f* **-, -en** colic
Kollaborateur /-'tø:ɐ̯/ *m* **-s, -e** collaborator
Kolleg *nt* **-s, -s** & **-ien** /-i̯ən/ (*Univ*) course of lectures
Kolleg|e *m* **-n, -n, K~in** *f* **-, -nen** colleague. **K~ium** *nt* **-s, -ien** staff
Kollek|te *f* **-, -n** (*Relig*) collection. **K~tion** /-'ts̮i̯o:n/ *f* **-, -en** collection
Köln *nt* **-s** Cologne. **K~ischwasser, K~isch Wasser** *nt* eau-de-Cologne
Kolonie *f* **-, -n** colony
Kolonne *f* **-, -n** column; (*Mil*) convoy
Koloss *m* **-es, -e** giant
Koma *nt* **-s, -s** coma
Kombi *m* **-s, -s** = **K~wagen**. **K~nation** /-'ts̮i̯o:n/ *f* **-, -en** combination; (*Folgerung*) deduction; (*Kleidung*) co-ordinating outfit. **k~nieren** *vt* combine; (*fig*) reason; (*folgern*) deduce. **K~wagen** *m* estate car
Kombüse *f* **-, -n** (*Naut*) galley
Komet *m* **-en, -en** comet
Komfort /kɔm'fo:ɐ̯/ *m* **-s** comfort; (*Luxus*) luxury
Komik *f* **-** humour. **K~er** *m* **-s,-** comic, comedian
komisch *a* funny; <*Oper*> comic; (*sonderbar*) odd, funny. **k~erweise** *adv* funnily enough
Komitee *nt* **-s, -s** committee
Komma *nt* **-s, -s** & **-ta** comma; (*Dezimal-*) decimal point; **drei K~ fünf** three point five
Kommando *nt* **-s, -s** order; (*Befehlsgewalt*) command; (*Einheit*) detachment. **K~brücke** *f* bridge
kommen† *vi* (*sein*) come; (*eintreffen*) arrive; (*gelangen*) get (**nach** to); **k~ lassen** send for; **auf/hinter etw** (*acc*) **k~** think of/find out about sth; **um/zu etw k~** lose/acquire sth; **wieder zu sich k~** come round; **wie kommt das?** why is that? **k~d** *a* coming; **k~den Montag** next Monday
Kommen|tar *m* **-s, -e** commentary; (*Bemerkung*) comment. **k~tieren** *vt* comment on
kommerziell *a* commercial
Kommissar *m* **-s, -e** commissioner; (*Polizei-*) superintendent
Kommission *f* **-, -en** commission; (*Gremium*) committee
Kommode *f* **-, -n** chest of drawers
Kommunalwahlen *fpl* local elections
Kommunion *f* **-, -en** [Holy] Communion
Kommun|ismus *m* **-** Communism. **K~ist(in)** *m* **-en, -en** (*f* **-, -nen**) Communist. **k~istisch** *a* Communist
kommunizieren *vi* (*haben*) receive [Holy] Communion
Komödie /ko'mø:di̯ə/ *f* **-, -n** comedy

Kompagnon /ˈkɔmpanjõː/ *m* **-s, -s** (*Comm*) partner
Kompanie *f* **-, -n** (*Mil*) company
Komparse *m* **-n, -n** (*Theat*) extra
Kompass *m* **-es, -e** compass
komplett *a* complete
Komplex *m* **-es, -e** complex
Komplikation /-ˈtsi̯oːn/ *f* **-, -en** complication
Kompliment *nt* **-[e]s, -e** compliment
Komplize *m* **-n, -n** accomplice
komplizier|en *vt* complicate. **k~t** *a* complicated
Komplott *nt* **-[e]s, -e** plot
kompo|nieren *vt/i* (*haben*) compose. **K~nist** *m* **-en, -en** composer
Kompost *m* **-[e]s** compost
Kompott *nt* **-[e]s, -e** stewed fruit
Kompromiss *m* **-es, -e** compromise; **einen K~ schließen** compromise. **k~los** *a* uncompromising
Konden|sation /-ˈtsi̯oːn/ *f* **-** condensation. **k~sieren** *vt* condense
Kondensmilch *f* evaporated/ (*gesüßt*) condensed milk
Kondition /-ˈtsi̯oːn/ *f* **-** (*Sport*) fitness; **in K~** in form
Konditor *m* **-s, -en** /-ˈtoːrən/ confectioner. **K~ei** *f* **-, -en** patisserie
Kondo|lenzbrief *m* letter of condolence. **k~lieren** *vi* (*haben*) express one's condolences
Kondom *nt & m* **-s, -e** condom
Konfekt *nt* **-[e]s** confectionery; (*Pralinen*) chocolates *pl*
Konfektion /-ˈtsi̯oːn/ *f* **-** ready-to-wear clothes *pl*
Konferenz *f* **-, -en** conference; (*Besprechung*) meeting
Konfession *f* **-, -en** [religious] denomination. **k~ell** *a* denominational
Konfetti *nt* **-s** confetti
Konfirm|and(in) *m* **-en, -en** (*f* **-, -nen**) candidate for confirmation. **K~ation** /-ˈtsi̯oːn/ *f* **-, -en** (*Relig*) confirmation. **k~ieren** *vt* (*Relig*) confirm
Konfitüre *f* **-, -n** jam
Konflikt *m* **-[e]s, -e** conflict
Konföderation /-ˈtsi̯oːn/ *f* confederation
konfus *a* confused
Kongress *m* **-es, -e** congress
König *m* **-s, -e** king. **K~in** *f* **-, -nen** queen. **k~lich** *a* royal; (*hoheitsvoll*) regal; (*großzügig*) handsome. **K~reich** *nt* kingdom
Konjunktiv *m* **-s, -e** subjunctive
Konjunktur *f* **-** economic situation; (*Hoch-*) boom
konkret *a* concrete
Konkurren|t(in) *m* **-en, -en** (*f* **-, -nen**) competitor, rival. **K~z** *f* **-** competition; **jdm K~z machen** compete with s.o. **K~zkampf** *m* competition, rivalry
konkurrieren *vi* (*haben*) compete
Konkurs *m* **-es, -e** bankruptcy

können†
● *auxiliary verb*
····➤ (*vermögen*) be able to; (*Präsens*) can; (*Vergangenheit, Konditional*) could. **ich kann nicht schlafen** I cannot *or* can't sleep. **kann ich Ihnen helfen?** can I help you? **kann/könnte das explodieren?** can/could it explode? **es kann sein, dass er kommt** he may come

! Distinguish **konnte** and **könnte** (both can be 'could'): **er konnte sie nicht retten** he couldn't *or* was unable to rescue them. **er konnte sie noch retten** he was able to rescue them. **er könnte sie**

noch retten, wenn ... he could still rescue them if ...

····➤ (*dürfen*) can, may. **kann ich gehen?** can *or* may I go? **können wir mit[kommen]?** can *or* may we come too?

● *transitive verb*

····➤ (*beherrschen*) know <language>; be able to play <game>. **können Sie Deutsch?** do you know any German? **sie kann das [gut]** she can do that [well]. **ich kann nichts dafür** I can't help that, I'm not to blame

● *intransitive verb*

····➤ (*fähig sein*) **ich kann [heute] nicht** I can't [today]. **er kann nicht anders** there's nothing else he can do; (*es ist seine Art*) he can't help it. **er kann nicht mehr** [!] he can't go on; (*nicht mehr essen*) he can't eat any more

····➤ (*irgendwohin gehen können*) be able to go; can go. **ich kann nicht ins Kino** I can't go to the cinema. **er konnte endlich nach Florenz** at last he was able to go to Florence

konsequen|t *a* consistent; (*logisch*) logical. **K～z** *f* **-, -en** consequence

konservativ *a* conservative

Konserv|en *fpl* tinned or canned food *sg*. **K～endose** *f* tin, can. **K～ierungsmittel** *nt* preservative

Konsonant *m* **-en, -en** consonant

Konstitution /-'tsio:n/ *f* **-, -en** constitution. **k～ell** *a* constitutional

konstruieren *vt* construct; (*entwerfen*) design

Konstruk|tion /-'tsio:n/ *f* **-, -en** construction; (*Entwurf*) design. **k～tiv** *a* constructive

Konsul *m* **-s, -n** consul. **K～at** *nt* **-[e]-s, -e** consulate

Konsum *m* **-s** consumption. **K～güter** *npl* consumer goods

Kontakt *m* **-[e]s, -e** contact. **K～linsen** *fpl* contact lenses. **K～person** *f* contact

kontern *vt/i* (*haben*) counter

Kontinent /'kɔn-, kɔnti'nɛnt/ *m* **-[e]s, -e** continent

Konto *nt* **-s, -s** account. **K～auszug** *m* [bank] statement. **K～nummer** *f* account number. **K～stand** *m* [bank] balance

Kontrabass *m* double-bass

Kontroll|abschnitt *m* counterfoil. **K～e** *f* **-, -n** control; (*Prüfung*) check. **K～eur** /-'lø:ɐ̯/ *m* **-s, -e** [ticket] inspector. **k～ieren** *vt* check; inspect <*Fahrkarten*>; (*beherrschen*) control

Kontroverse *f* **-, -n** controversy

Kontur *f* **-, -en** contour

konventionell /-tsi̯o-/ *a* conventional

Konversationslexikon /-'tsi̯o:ns-/ *nt* encyclopaedia

konvert|ieren *vi* (*haben*) (*Relig*) convert. **K～it** *m* **-en, -en** convert

Konzentration /-'tsio:n/ *f* **-, -en** concentration. **K～slager** *nt* concentration camp

konzentrieren *vt* concentrate; **sich k～** concentrate (**auf** + *acc* on)

Konzept *nt* **-[e]s, -e** [rough] draft; **jdn aus dem K～bringen** put s.o. off his stroke

Konzern *m* **-s, -e** (*Comm*) group [of companies]

Konzert *nt* **-[e]s, -e** concert; (*Klavier-*) concerto

Konzession *f* **-, -en** licence; (*Zugeständnis*) concession

Kooperation /koˀɔpera'tsi̯o:n/ *f* cooperation

Koordin|ation /koˀɔrdina'tsi̯o:n/ *f* **-**

coordination. **k~ieren** *vt* coordinate

Kopf *m* **-[e]s,¨-e** head; **ein K~ Kohl/Salat** a cabbage/lettuce; **aus dem K~** from memory; (*auswendig*) by heart; **auf dem K~** (*verkehrt*) upside down; **K~ stehen** stand on one's head; **sich** (*dat*) **den K~ waschen** wash one's hair; **sich** (*dat*) **den K~ zerbrechen** rack one's brains. **K~ball** *m* header

köpfen *vt* behead; (*Fußball*) head

Kopf|ende *nt* head. **K~haut** *f* scalp. **K~hörer** *m* headphones *pl*. **K~kissen** *nt* pillow. **k~los** *a* panic-stricken. **K~rechnen** *nt* mental arithmetic. **K~salat** *m* lettuce. **K~schmerzen** *mpl* headache *sg*. **K~sprung** *m* header, dive. **K~stand** *m* headstand. **K~steinpflaster** *nt* cobble-stones *pl*. **K~tuch** *nt* headscarf. **k~über** *adv* head first; (*fig*) headlong. **K~wäsche** *f* shampoo. **K~weh** *nt* headache

Kopie *f* **-, -n** copy. **k~ren** *vt* copy

Koppel[1] *f* **-, -n** enclosure; (*Pferde-*) paddock

Koppel[2] *nt* **-s,-** (*Mil*) belt. **k~n** *vt* couple

Koralle *f* **-, -n** coral

Korb *m* **-[e]s,¨-e** basket; **jdm einen K~ geben** (*fig*) turn s.o. down. **K~ball** *m* [kind of] netball

Kord *m* **-s** (*Tex*) corduroy

Kordel *f* **-, -n** cord

Korinthe *f* **-, -n** currant

Kork *m* **-s,-** cork. **K~en** *m* **-s,-** cork. **K~enzieher** *m* **-s,-** corkscrew

Korn *nt* **-[e]s,¨-er** grain, (*Samen-*) seed; (*am Visier*) front sight

Körn|chen *nt* **-s,-** granule. **k~ig** *a* granular

Körper *m* **-s,-** body; (*Geom*) solid. **K~bau** *m* build, physique. **k~behindert** *a* physically disabled. **k~lich** *a* physical; <*Strafe*> corporal. **K~pflege** *f* personal hygiene. **K~schaft** *f* **-, -en** corporation, body

korrekt *a* correct. **K~or** *m* **-s, -en** /-ˈtoːrən/ proof-reader. **K~ur** *f* **-, -en** correction. **K~urabzug** *m* proof

Korrespon|dent(in) *m* **-en, -en** (*f* **-, -nen**) correspondent. **K~denz** *f* **-, -en** correspondence

Korridor *m* **-s, -e** corridor

korrigieren *vt* correct

Korrosion *f* **-** corrosion

korrup|t *a* corrupt. **K~tion** /-ˈtsi̯oːn/ *f* **-** corruption

Korsett *nt* **-[e]s, -e** corset

koscher *a* kosher

Kosename *m* pet name

Kosmet|ik *f* **-** beauty culture. **K~ika** *ntpl* cosmetics. **K~ikerin** *f* **-, -nen** beautician. **k~isch** *a* cosmetic; <*Chirurgie*> plastic

kosm|isch *a* cosmic. **K~onaut(in)** *m* **-en, -en** (*f* **-, -nen**) cosmonaut

Kosmos *m* **-** cosmos

Kost *f* **-** food; (*Ernährung*) diet; (*Verpflegung*) board

kostbar *a* precious. **K~keit** *f* **-, -en** treasure

kosten[1] *vt/i* (*haben*) **[von] etw k~** taste sth

kosten[2] *vt* cost; (*brauchen*) take; **wie viel kostet es?** how much is it? **K~** *pl* expense *sg*, cost *sg*; (*Jur*) costs; **auf meine K~** at my expense. **K~[vor]anschlag** *m* estimate. **k~los** *a* free ● *adv* free [of charge]

köstlich *a* delicious; (*entzückend*) delightful

Kostprobe *f* taste; (*fig*) sample

Kostüm *nt* **-s, -e** (*Theat*) costume; (*Verkleidung*) fancy dress; (*Schneider-*) suit. **k~iert** *a* **k~iert sein** be in fancy dress

Kot *m* **-[e]s** excrement

Kotelett /kɔt'lɛt/ *nt* **-s, -s** chop, cutlet. **K~en** *pl* sideburns

Köter *m* **-s,-** (*pej*) dog

Kotflügel *m* (*Auto*) wing

kotzen *vi* (*haben*) ☒ throw up

Krabbe *f* **-, -n** crab, shrimp

krabbeln *vi* (*sein*) crawl

Krach *m* **-[e]s,¨-e** din, racket; (*Knall*) crash; (! *Streit*) row; (! *Ruin*) crash. **k~en** *vi* (*haben*) crash; **es hat gekracht** there was a bang/(! *Unfall*) a crash ● (*sein*) break, crack; (*auftreffen*) crash (**gegen** into)

krächzen *vi* (*haben*) croak

Kraft *f* **-,¨-e** strength; (*Gewalt*) force; (*Arbeits-*) worker; **in/außer K~** in/no longer in force. **K~fahrer** *m* driver. **K~fahrzeug** *nt* motor vehicle. **K~fahrzeugbrief** *m* [vehicle] registration document

kräftig *a* strong; (*gut entwickelt*) sturdy; (*nahrhaft*) nutritious; (*heftig*) hard

kraft|los *a* weak. **K~probe** *f* trial of strength. **K~stoff** *m* (*Auto*) fuel. **K~wagen** *m* motor car. **K~werk** *nt* power station

Kragen *m* **-s,-** collar

Krähe *f* **-, -n** crow

krähen *vi* (*haben*) crow

Kralle *f* **-, -n** claw

Kram *m* **-s** ! things *pl*, ! stuff; (*Angelegenheiten*) business. **k~en** *vi* (*haben*) rummage about (**in** + *dat* in; **nach** for)

Krampf *m* **-[e]s,¨-e** cramp. **K~adern** *fpl* varicose veins. **k~haft** *a* convulsive; (*verbissen*) desperate

Kran *m* **-[e]s,¨-e** (*Techn*) crane

Kranich *m* **-s, -e** (*Zool*) crane

krank *a* sick; <*Knie, Herz*> bad; **k~ sein/werden** be/fall ill. **K~e(r)** *m/f* sick man/woman, invalid; **die K~en** the sick *pl*

kränken *vt* offend, hurt

Kranken|bett *nt* sick-bed. **K~geld** *nt* sickness benefit. **K~gymnast(in)** *m* **-en, -en** (*f* **-, -nen**) physiotherapist. **K~gymnastik** *f* physiotherapy. **K~haus** *nt* hospital. **K~kasse** *f* health insurance scheme/(*Amer*) office. **K~pflege** *f* nursing. **K~saal** *m* [hospital] ward. **K~schein** *m* certificate of entitlement to medical treatment. **K~schwester** *f* nurse. **K~versicherung** *f* health insurance. **K~wagen** *m* ambulance

Krankheit *f* **-, -en** illness, disease

kränklich *a* sickly

krank|melden *vt sep* **jdn k~melden** report s.o. sick; **sich k~melden** report sick

Kranz *m* **-es,¨-e** wreath

Krapfen *m* **-s,-** doughnut

Krater *m* **-s,-** crater

kratzen *vt/i* (*haben*) scratch. **K~er** *m* **-s,-** scratch

Kraul *nt* **-s** (*Sport*) crawl. **k~en¹** *vi* (*haben/sein*) (*Sport*) do the crawl

kraulen² *vt* tickle; **sich am Kopf k~** scratch one's head

kraus *a* wrinkled; <*Haar*> frizzy; (*verworren*) muddled. **K~e** *f* **-, -n** frill

kräuseln *vt* wrinkle; frizz <*Haar-*>; gather <*Stoff*>; **sich k~** wrinkle; (*sich kringeln*) curl; <*Haar:*> go frizzy

Kraut *nt* **-[e]s, Kräuter** herb; (*SGer*) cabbage; (*Sauer-*) sauerkraut

Krawall *m* **-s, -e** riot; (*Lärm*) row

Krawatte *f* **-, -n** [neck]tie

krea|tiv /krea'ti:f/ *a* creative. **K~tur** *f* **-, -en** creature

Krebs *m* **-es, -e** crayfish; (*Med*) cancer; (*Astr*) Cancer
Kredit *m* **-s, -e** credit; (*Darlehen*) loan; **auf K~** on credit. **K~karte** *f* credit card
Kreid|e *f* **-** chalk. **k~ig** *a* chalky
kreieren /kre'i:rən/ *vt* create
Kreis *m* **-es, -e** circle; (*Admin*) district
kreischen *vt/i* (*haben*) screech; (*schreien*) shriek
Kreisel *m* **-s,-** [spinning] top
kreis|en *vi* (*haben*) circle; revolve (**um** around). **k~förmig** *a* circular. **K~lauf** *m* cycle; (*Med*) circulation. **K~säge** *f* circular saw. **K~verkehr** *m* [traffic] roundabout
Krem *f* **-, -s** & *m* **-s, -e** cream
Krematorium *nt* **-s, -ien** crematorium
Krempe *f* **-, -n** [hat] brim
krempeln *vt* turn (**nach oben** up)
Krepp *m* **-s, -s** & **-e** crêpe
Kreppapier *nt* crêpe paper
Kresse *f* **-, -n** cress; (*Kapuziner-*) nasturtium
Kreta *nt* **-s** Crete
Kreuz *nt* **-es, -e** cross; (*Kreuzung*) intersection; (*Mus*) sharp; (*Kartenspiel*) clubs *pl*; (*Anat*) small of the back; **über K~** crosswise; **das K~ schlagen** cross oneself. **k~en** *vt* cross; **sich k~en** cross; <*Straßen:*> intersect; <*Meinungen:*> clash. ● *vi* (*haben/sein*) cruise. **K~fahrt** *f* (*Naut*) cruise. **K~gang** *m* cloister
kreuzig|en *vt* crucify. **K~ung** *f* **-, -en** crucifixion
Kreuz|otter *f* adder, common viper. **K~ung** *f* **-, -en** intersection; (*Straßen-*) crossroads *sg*. **K~verhör** *nt* cross-examination. **k~weise** *adv* crosswise. **K~worträtsel** *nt* crossword [puzzle]. **K~zug** *m* crusade
kribbel|ig *a* [!] edgy. **k~n** *vi* (*haben*) tingle; (*kitzeln*) tickle
kriech|en† *vi* (*sein*) crawl; (*fig*) grovel (**vor** + *dat* to). **K~spur** *f* (*Auto*) crawler lane. **K~tier** *nt* reptile
Krieg *m* **-[e]s, -e** war
kriegen *vt* [!] get; **ein Kind k~** have a baby
kriegs|beschädigt *a* war-disabled. **K~dienstverweigerer** *m* **-s,-** conscientious objector. **K~gefangene(r)** *m* prisoner of war. **K~gefangenschaft** *f* captivity. **K~gericht** *nt* court martial. **K~list** *f* stratagem. **K~rat** *m* council of war. **K~recht** *nt* martial law
Krimi *m* **-s, -s** [!] crime story/film. **K~nalität** *f* **-** crime; (*Vorkommen*) crime rate. **K~nalpolizei** *f* criminal investigation department. **K~nalroman** *m* crime novel. **k~nell** *a* criminal
Krippe *f* **-, -n** manger; (*Weihnachts-*) crib; (*Kinder-*) crèche. **K~nspiel** *nt* Nativity play
Krise *f* **-, -n** crisis
Kristall *nt* **-s** crystal; (*geschliffen*) cut glass
Kritik *f* **-, -en** criticism; (*Rezension*) review; **unter aller K~** [!] abysmal
Kriti|ker *m* **-s,-** critic; (*Rezensent*) reviewer. **k~sch** *a* critical. **k~sieren** *vt* criticize; review
kritzeln *vt/i* (*haben*) scribble
Krokodil *nt* **-s, -e** crocodile
Krokus *m* **-, -[se]** crocus
Krone *f* **-, -n** crown; (*Baum-*) top
krönen *vt* crown
Kronleuchter *m* chandelier
Krönung *f* **-, -en** coronation; (*fig: Höhepunkt*) crowning event

Kropf *m* **-[e]s,¨-e** (*Zool*) crop; (*Med*) goitre
Kröte *f* **-, -n** toad
Krücke *f* **-, -n** crutch
Krug *m* **-[e]s,¨-e** jug; (*Bier-*) tankard
Krümel *m* **-s,-** crumb. **k∼ig** *a* crumbly. **k∼n** *vt* crumble ● *vi* (*haben*) be crumbly
krumm *a* crooked; (*gebogen*) curved; (*verbogen*) bent
krümmen *vt* bend; crook <*Finger*>; **sich k∼** bend; (*sich winden*) writhe; (*vor Lachen*) double up
Krümmung *f* **-, -en** bend, curve
Krüppel *m* **-s,-** cripple
Kruste *f* **-, -n** crust; (*Schorf*) scab
Kruzifix *nt* **-es, -e** crucifix
Kub|a *nt* **-s** Cuba. **k∼anisch** *a* Cuban
Kübel *m* **-s,-** tub; (*Eimer*) bucket; (*Techn*) skip
Küche *f* **-, -n** kitchen; (*Kochkunst*) cooking; **kalte/warme K∼** cold/hot food
Kuchen *m* **-s,-** cake
Küchen|herd *m* cooker, stove. **K∼maschine** *f* food processor, mixer. **K∼schabe** *f* **-, -n** cockroach
Kuckuck *m* **-s, -e** cuckoo
Kufe *f* **-, -n** [sledge] runner
Kugel *f* **-, -n** ball; (*Geom*) sphere; (*Gewehr-*) bullet; (*Sport*) shot. **k∼förmig** *a* spherical. **K∼lager** *nt* ball-bearing. **k∼n** *vt/i* (*haben*) roll; **sich k∼n** (*vor Lachen*) fall about. **K∼schreiber** *m* **-s,-** ballpoint [pen]. **k∼sicher** *a* bullet-proof. **K∼stoßen** *nt* **-s** shot-putting
Kuh *f* **-,¨-e** cow
kühl *a* cool; (*kalt*) chilly. **K∼box** *f* **-, -en** cool-box. **K∼e** *f* **-** coolness; chilliness. **k∼en** *vt* cool; refrigerate <*Lebensmittel*>; chill <*Wein*>. **K∼er** *m* **-s,-** (*Auto*) radiator. **K∼erhaube** *f* bonnet. **K∼fach** *nt* frozen-food compartment. **K∼raum** *m* cold store. **K∼schrank** *m* refrigerator. **K∼truhe** *f* freezer. **K∼wasser** *nt* [radiator] water
kühn *a* bold
Kuhstall *m* cowshed
Küken *nt* **-s,-** chick; (*Enten-*) duckling
Kulissen *fpl* (*Theat*) scenery *sg;* (*seitlich*) wings; **hinter den K∼** (*fig*) behind the scenes
Kult *m* **-[e]s, -e** cult
kultivier|en *vt* cultivate. **k∼t** *a* cultured
Kultur *f* **-, -en** culture. **K∼beutel** *m* toiletbag. **k∼ell** *a* cultural. **K∼film** *m* documentary film
Kultusminister *m* Minister of Education and Arts
Kümmel *m* **-s** caraway; (*Getränk*) kümmel
Kummer *m* **-s** sorrow, grief; (*Sorge*) worry; (*Ärger*) trouble
kümmer|lich *a* puny; (*dürftig*) meagre; (*armselig*) wretched. **k∼n** *vt* concern; **sich k∼n um** look after; (*sich befassen*) concern oneself with; (*beachten*) take notice of
kummervoll *a* sorrowful
Kumpel *m* **-s,-** [!] mate
Kunde *m* **-n, -n** customer. **K∼ndienst** *m* [after-sales] service
Kundgebung *f* **-, -en** (*Pol*) rally
kündig|en *vt* cancel <*Vertrag*>; give notice of withdrawal for <*Geld*>; give notice to quit <*Wohnung*>; **seine Stellung k∼en** give [in one's] notice ● *vi* (*haben*) give [in one's] notice; **jdm k∼en** give s.o. notice. **K∼ung** *f* **-, -en** cancellation; notice [of withdrawal/dismissal/to quit]; (*Entlassung*) dismissal. **K∼ungsfrist** *f* period of notice

Kund|in *f* **-, -nen** [woman] customer. **K~schaft** *f* **-** clientele, customers *pl*

künftig *a* future ● *adv* in future

Kunst *f* **-,¨e** art; (*Können*) skill. **K~faser** *f* synthetic fibre. **K~galerie** *f* art gallery. **K~geschichte** *f* history of art. **K~gewerbe** *nt* arts and crafts *pl*. **K~griff** *m* trick

Künstler *m* **-s,-** artist; (*Könner*) master. **K~in** *f* **-, -nen** [woman] artist. **k~isch** *a* artistic

künstlich *a* artificial

Kunst|stoff *m* plastic. **K~stück** *nt* trick; (*große Leistung*) feat. **k~voll** *a* artistic; (*geschickt*) skilful

kunterbunt *a* multicoloured; (*gemischt*) mixed

Kupfer *nt* **-s** copper

Kupon /ku'põ:/ *m* **-s, -s** voucher; (*Zins-*) coupon; (*Stoff-*) length

Kuppe *f* **-, -n** [rounded] top

Kuppel *f* **-, -n** dome

kupp|eln *vt* couple (**an** + *acc* to) ● *vi* (*haben*) (*Auto*) operate the clutch. **K~lung** *f* **-, -en** coupling; (*Auto*) clutch

Kur *f* **-, -en** course of treatment, cure

Kür *f* **-, -en** (*Sport*) free exercise; (*Eislauf*) free programme

Kurbel *f* **-, -n** crank. **K~welle** *f* crankshaft

Kürbis *m* **-ses, -se** pumpkin

Kurier *m* **-s, -e** courier

kurieren *vt* cure

kurios *a* curious, odd. **K~ität** *f* **-, -en** oddness; (*Objekt*) curiosity

Kurort *m* health resort; (*Badeort*) spa

Kurs *m* **-es, -e** course; (*Aktien-*) price. **K~buch** *nt* timetable

kursieren *vi* (*haben*) circulate

kursiv *a* italic ● *adv* in italics. **K~schrift** *f* italics *pl*

Kursus *m* **-,Kurse** course

Kurswagen *m* through carriage

Kurtaxe *f* visitors' tax

Kurve *f* **-, -n** curve; (*Straßen-*) bend

kurz *a* short; (*knapp*) brief; (*rasch*) quick; (*schroff*) curt; **k~e Hosen** shorts; **vor k~em** a short time ago; **seit k~em** lately; **den Kürzeren ziehen** get the worst of it; **k~ vor** shortly before; **sich k~ fassen** be brief; **k~ und gut** in short; **zu k~ kommen** get less than one's fair share. **k~ärmelig** *a* short-sleeved. **k~atmig** *a* **k~atmig sein** be short of breath

Kürze *f* **-** shortness; (*Knappheit*) brevity; **in K~** shortly. **k~n** *vt* shorten; (*verringern*) cut

kurzfristig *a* short-term ● *adv* at short notice

kürzlich *adv* recently

Kurz|meldung *f* newsflash. **K~schluss** *m* short circuit. **K~schrift** *f* shorthand. **k~sichtig** *a* short-sighted. **K~sichtigkeit** *f* **-** short-sightedness. **K~streckenrakete** *f* short-range missile

Kürzung *f* **-, -en** shortening; (*Verringerung*) cut (*gen* in)

Kurz|waren *fpl* haberdashery *sg*. **K~welle** *f* short wave

kuscheln (sich) *vr* snuggle (**an** + *acc* up to)

Kusine *f* **-, -n** [female] cousin

Kuss *m* **-es,¨e** kiss

küssen *vt/i* (*haben*) kiss; **sich k~** kiss

Küste *f* **-, -n** coast

Küster *m* **-s,-** verger

Kutsch|e *f* **-, -n** [horse-drawn] carriage/(*geschlossen*) coach. **K~er** *m* **-s,-** coachman, driver

Kutte *f* **-, -n** (*Relig*) habit

Kutter *m* **-s,-** (*Naut*) cutter

Kuvert /ku'veːɐ̯/ *nt* **-s, -s** envelope

Ll

Labor *nt* **-s, -s** & **-e** laboratory. **L~ant(in)** *m* **-en, -en** (*f* **-, -nen**) laboratory assistant

Labyrinth *nt* **-[e]s, -e** maze, labyrinth

Lache *f* **-, -n** puddle; (*Blut-*) pool

lächeln *vi* (*haben*) smile. **L~** *nt* **-s** smile. **l~d** *a* smiling

lachen *vi* (*haben*) laugh. **L~** *nt* **-s** laugh; (*Gelächter*) laughter

lächerlich *a* ridiculous; **sich l~ machen** make a fool of oneself. **L~keit** *f* **-, -en** ridiculousness; (*Kleinigkeit*) triviality

Lachs *m* **-es, -e** salmon

Lack *m* **-[e]s, -e** varnish; (*Japan-*) lacquer; (*Auto*) paint. **l~en** *vt* varnish. **l~ieren** *vt* varnish; (*spritzen*) spray. **L~schuhe** *mpl* patent-leather shoes

laden† *vt* load; (*Electr*) charge; (*Jur: vor-*) summon

Laden *m* **-s,¨** shop; (*Fenster-*) shutter. **L~dieb** *m* shop-lifter. **L~schluss** *m* [shop] closing-time. **L~tisch** *m* counter

Laderaum *m* (*Naut*) hold

lädieren *vt* damage

Ladung *f* **-, -en** load; (*Naut, Aviat*) cargo; (*elektrische*) charge

Lage *f* **-, -n** position, situation; (*Schicht*) layer; **nicht in der L~ sein** not be in a position (**zu** to)

Lager *nt* **-s,-** camp; (*L~haus*) warehouse; (*Vorrat*) stock; (*Techn*) bearing; (*Erz-, Ruhe-*) bed; (*eines Tieres*) lair; **[nicht] auf L~** [not] in stock. **L~haus** *nt* warehouse. **l~n** *vt* store; (*legen*) lay; **sich l~n** settle. **L~raum** *m* store-room. **L~ung** *f* **-** storage

Lagune *f* **-, -n** lagoon

lahm *a* lame. **l~en** *vi* (*haben*) be lame

lähmen *vt* paralyse

Lähmung *f* **-, -en** paralysis

Laib *m* **-[e]s, -e** loaf

Laich *m* **-[e]s** (*Zool*) spawn

Laie *m* **-n, -n** layman; (*Theat*) amateur. **l~nhaft** *a* amateurish

Laken *nt* **-s,-** sheet

Lakritze *f* **-** liquorice

lallen *vt/i* (*haben*) mumble; <*Baby:*> babble

Lametta *nt* **-s** tinsel

Lamm *nt* **-[e]s,¨er** lamb

Lampe *f* **-, -n** lamp; (*Decken-, Wand-*) light; (*Glüh-*) bulb. **L~nfieber** *nt* stage fright

Lampion /lam'pi̯ɔŋ/ *m* **-s, -s** Chinese lantern

Land *nt* **-[e]s,¨er** country; (*Fest-*) land; (*Bundes-*) state, Land; (*Aust*) province; **auf dem L~e** in the country; **an L~ gehen** (*Naut*) go ashore. **L~arbeiter** *m* agricultural worker. **L~ebahn** *f* runway. **l~en** *vt/i* (*sein*) land; (🄸 *gelangen*) end up

Ländereien *pl* estates

Länderspiel *nt* international

Landesverrat *m* treason

Landkarte *f* map

ländlich *a* rural

Land|schaft *f* **-, -en** scenery; (*Geog, Kunst*) landscape; (*Gegend*) country[side]. **l~schaftlich** *a* scenic; (*regional*) regional. **L~streicher** *m* **-s,-** tramp. **L~tag** *m* state/(*Aust*) provincial parliament

Landung *f* **-, -en** landing

Lạnd|vermesser *m* **-s,-** surveyor. **L~weg** *m* country lane; **auf dem L~weg** overland. **L~wirt** *m* farmer. **L~wirtschaft** *f* agriculture; (*Hof*) farm. **l~wirtschaftlich** *a* agricultural

lạng¹ *adv & prep* (+ *preceding acc or preceding* **an** + *dat*) along; **den** *od* **am Fluss l~** along the river

lạng² *a* long; (*groß*) tall; **seit l~em** for a long time ● *adv* **eine Stunde l~** for an hour; **mein Leben l~** all my life. **l~ärmelig** *a* long-sleeved. **l~atmig** *a* long-winded. **l~e** *adv* a long time; <*schlafen*> late; **schon l~e** [for] a long time; (*zurückliegend*) a long time ago; **l~e nicht** not for a long time; (*bei weitem nicht*) nowhere near

Lạ̈nge *f* **-, -n** length; (*Geog*) longitude; **der L~nach** lengthways

Lạ̈ng|engrad *m* degree of longitude. **l~er** *a & adv* longer; (*längere Zeit*) [for] some time

Langeweile *f* **-** boredom; **L~ haben** be bored

lạng|fristig *a* long-term; <*Vorhersage*> long-range. **l~jährig** *a* long-standing; <*Erfahrung*> long

lạ̈nglich *a* oblong; **l~ rund** oval

lạ̈ngs *adv & prep* (+ *gen/dat*) along; (*der Länge nach*) lengthways

lạng|sam *a* slow. **L~samkeit** *f* **-** slowness

lạ̈ngst *adv* **[schon] l~** for a long time; (*zurückliegend*) a long time ago; **l~ nicht** nowhere near

Lạng|strecken- *pref* long-distance; (*Mil, Aviat*) long-range. **l~weilen** *vt* bore; **sich l~weilen** be bored. **l~weilig** *a* boring

Lạnze *f* **-, -n** lance

Lappalie /la'pa:li̯ə/ *f* **-, -n** trifle

Lạppen *m* **-s,-** cloth; (*Anat*) lobe

Lạ̈rche *f* **-, -n** larch

Lạ̈rm *m* **-s** noise. **l~end** *a* noisy

Larve /'larfə/ *f* **-, -n** larva; (*Maske*) mask

lạsch *a* listless; (*schlaff*) limp

Lạsche *f* **-, -n** tab, flap

Laser /'le:-, 'la:zɐ/ *m* **-s,-** laser

---

lạssen†

● *transitive verb*

····➤ (+ *inf; veranlassen*) **etw tun lassen** have *or* get sth done. **jdn etw tun lassen** make s.o. do sth.; get s.o. to do sth. **sich** *dat* **die Haare schneiden lassen** have *or* get one's hair cut. **jdn warten lassen** make *or* let s.o. wait; keep s.o. waiting. **jdn grüßen lassen** send one's regards to s.o. **jdn kommen/rufen lassen** send for s.o.

····➤ (+ *inf; erlauben*) let; allow; (*hineinlassen/herauslassen*) let *or* allow (**in** + *acc* into, **aus** + *dat* out of). **jdn etw tun lassen** let s.o. do sth; allow s.o. to do sth. **er ließ mich nicht ausreden** he didn't let me finish [what I was saying]

····➤ (*belassen, bleiben lassen*) leave. **jdn in Frieden lassen** leave s.o. in peace. **etw ungesagt lassen** leave sth unsaid

····➤ (*unterlassen*) stop. **das Rauchen lassen** stop smoking. **er kann es nicht lassen, sie zu quälen** he can't stop *or* he is forever tormenting her

····➤ (*überlassen*) **jdm etw lassen** let s.o. have sth

····➤ (*als Aufforderung*) **lass/lasst uns gehen/fahren!** let's go!

● *reflexive verb*

····➤ **das lässt sich machen** that can be done. **das lässt sich nicht beweisen** it can't be proved. **die Tür lässt sich leicht öffnen** the door opens easily

● *intransitive verb*
→ [!] **Lass mal. Ich mache das schon** Leave it. I'll do it

lässig *a* casual. **L~keit** *f* - casualness
Lasso *nt* **-s, -s** lasso
Last *f* **-, -en** load; (*Gewicht*) weight; (*fig*) burden; **L~en** charges; (*Steuern*) taxes. **L~auto** *nt* lorry. **l~en** *vi* (*haben*) weigh heavily/(*liegen*) rest (**auf** + *dat* on)
Laster¹ *m* **-s,-** [!] lorry
Laster² *nt* **-s,-** vice
läster|n *vt* blaspheme ● *vi* (*haben*) make disparaging remarks (**über** + *acc* about). **L~ung** *f* **-, -en** blasphemy
lästig *a* troublesome; **l~ sein/werden** be/become a nuisance
Last|kahn *m* barge. **L~[kraft]wagen** *m* lorry
Latein *nt* **-[s]** Latin. **L~amerika** *nt* Latin America. **l~isch** *a* Latin
Laterne *f* **-, -n** lantern; (*Straßen-*) street lamp. **L~npfahl** *m* lamp-post
latschen *vi* (*sein*) [!] traipse
Latte *f* **-, -n** slat; (*Tor-, Hochsprung-*) bar
Latz *m* **-es,¨-e** bib
Lätzchen *nt* **-s,-** [baby's] bib
Latzhose *f* dungarees *pl*
Laub *nt* **-[e]s** leaves *pl*; (*L~werk*) foliage. **L~baum** *m* deciduous tree
Laube *f* **-, -n** summer-house
Laub|säge *f* fretsaw. **L~wald** *m* deciduous forest
Lauch *m* **-[e]s** leeks *pl*
Lauer *f* **auf der L~ liegen** lie in wait. **l~n** *vi* (*haben*) lurk; **l~n auf** (+ *acc*) lie in wait for
Lauf *m* **-[e]s, Läufe** run; (*Laufen*) running; (*Verlauf*) course; (*Wett-*) race; (*Sport: Durchgang*) heat; (*Gewehr-*) barrel; **im L~[e]** (+ *gen*) in the course of. **L~bahn** *f* career. **l~en**† *vi* (*sein*) run; (*zu Fuß gehen*) walk; (*gelten*) be valid; **Ski/Schlittschuh l~en** ski/skate. **l~end** *a* running; (*gegenwärtig*) current; (*regelmäßig*) regular; **auf dem L~enden sein** be up to date ● *adv* continually
Läufer *m* **-s,-** (*Person, Teppich*) runner; (*Schach*) bishop
Lauf|gitter *nt* play-pen. **L~masche** *f* ladder. **L~zettel** *m* circular
Lauge *f* **-, -n** soapy water
Laun|e *f* **-, -n** mood; (*Einfall*) whim; **guter L~e sein, gute L~e haben** be in a good mood. **l~isch** *a* moody
Laus *f* **-,Läuse** louse; (*Blatt-*) greenfly
lauschen *vi* (*haben*) listen
laut *a* loud; (*geräuschvoll*) noisy; **l~ lesen** read aloud; **l~er stellen** turn up ● *prep* (+ *gen*/*dat*) according to. **L~** *m* **-es, -e** sound
Laute *f* **-, -n** (*Mus*) lute
lauten *vi* (*haben*) <*Text:*> run, read
läuten *vt*/*i* (*haben*) ring
lauter *a* pure; (*ehrlich*) honest; <*Wahrheit*> plain ● *a inv* sheer; (*nichts als*) nothing but
laut|hals *adv* at the top of one's voice; <*lachen*> out loud. **l~los** *a* silent, <*Stille*> hushed. **L~schrift** *f* phonetics *pl*. **L~sprecher** *m* loudspeaker. **L~stärke** *f* volume
lauwarm *a* lukewarm
Lava *f* **-, -ven** lava
Lavendel *m* **-s** lavender
lavieren *vi* (*haben*) manœuvre
Lawine *f* **-, -n** avalanche
Lazarett *nt* **-[e]s, -e** military hospital
leasen /ˈliːsən/ *vt* rent

Lebehoch *nt* cheer
leben *vt/i* (*haben*) live (**von** on); **leb wohl!** farewell! **L~** *nt* **-s,-** life; (*Treiben*) bustle; **am L~** alive. **l~d** *a* living
lebendig *a* live; (*lebhaft*) lively; (*anschaulich*) vivid; **l~ sein** be alive. **L~keit** *f* **-** liveliness; vividness
Lebens|abend *m* old age. **L~alter** *nt* age. **l~fähig** *a* viable. **L~gefahr** *f* mortal danger; **in L~gefahr** in mortal danger; <*Patient*> critically ill. **l~gefährlich** *a* extremely dangerous; <*Verletzung*> critical. **L~haltungskosten** *pl* cost of living *sg*. **l~länglich** *a* life ... ● *adv* for life. **L~lauf** *m* curriculum vitae. **L~mittel** *ntpl* food *sg*. **L~mittelgeschäft** *nt* food shop. **L~mittelhändler** *m* grocer. **L~retter** *m* rescuer; (*beim Schwimmen*) life-guard. **L~unterhalt** *m* livelihood; **seinen L~unterhalt verdienen** earn one's living. **L~versicherung** *f* life assurance. **L~wandel** *m* conduct. **l~wichtig** *a* vital. **L~zeit** *f* **auf L~zeit** for life
Leber *f* **-, -n** liver. **L~fleck** *m* mole
Lebe|wesen *nt* living being. **L~wohl** *nt* **-s, -s** & **-e** farewell
leb|haft *a* lively; <*Farbe*> vivid. **L~kuchen** *m* gingerbread. **l~los** *a* lifeless. **L~zeiten** *fpl* **zu jds L~zeiten** in s.o.'s lifetime
leck *a* leaking. **L~** *nt* **-s, -s** leak. **l~en**[1] *vi* (*haben*) leak
lecken[2] *vi* (*haben*) lick
lecker *a* tasty. **L~ bissen** *m* delicacy
Leder *nt* **-s,-** leather
ledig *a* single
leer *a* empty; (*unbesetzt*) vacant; **l~ laufen** (*Auto*) idle. **l~en** *vt* empty; **sich l~en** empty. **L~lauf** *m* (*Auto*) neutral. **L~ung** *f* **-, -en** (*Post*) collection
legal *a* legal. **l~isieren** *vt* legalize. **L~ität** *f* **-** legality
Legas|thenie *f* **-** dyslexia **L~theniker** *m* **-s,-** dyslexic
legen *vt* put; (*hin-, ver-*) lay; set <*Haare*>; **sich l~** lie down; (*nachlassen*) subside
Legende *f* **-, -n** legend
leger /le'ʒeːɐ/ *a* casual
Legierung *f* **-, -en** alloy
Legion *f* **-, -en** legion
Legislative *f* **-** legislature
legitim *a* legitimate. **L~ität** *f* **-** legitimacy
Lehm *m* **-s** clay
Lehn|e *f* **-, -n** (*Rücken-*) back; (*Arm-*) arm. **l~en** *vt* lean (**an** + *acc against*); **sich l~en** lean (**an** + *acc against*) ● *vi* (*haben*) be leaning (**an** + *acc against*)
Lehr|buch *nt* textbook. **L~e** *f* **-, -n** apprenticeship; (*Anschauung*) doctrine; (*Theorie*) theory; (*Wissenschaft*) science; (*Erfahrung*) lesson. **l~en** *vt/i* (*haben*) teach. **L~er** *m* **-s,-** teacher; (*Fahr-*) instructor. **L~erin** *f* **-, -nen** teacher. **L~erzimmer** *nt* staff-room. **L~fach** *nt* (*Sch*) subject. **L~gang** *m* course. **L~kraft** *f* teacher. **L~ling** *m* **-s, -e** apprentice; (*Auszubildender*) trainee. **L~plan** *m* syllabus. **l~reich** *a* instructive. **L~stelle** *f* apprenticeship. **L~stuhl** *m* (*Univ*) chair. **L~zeit** *f* apprenticeship
Leib *m* **-es, -er** body; (*Bauch*) belly. **L~eserziehung** *f* (*Sch*) physical education. **L~gericht** *nt* favourite dish. **l~lich** *a* physical; (*blutsverwandt*) real, natural. **L~wächter** *m* bodyguard

Leiche *f* **-, -n** [dead] body; corpse. **L~nbestatter** *m* **-s,-** undertaker. **L~nhalle** *f* mortuary. **L~nwagen** *m* hearse. **L~nzug** *m* funeral procession, cortège

Leichnam *m* **-s, -e** [dead] body

leicht *a* light; <*Stoff*> lightweight; (*gering*) slight; (*mühelos*) easy; **jdm l~ fallen** be easy for s.o.; **etw l~ machen** make sth easy (*dat* for); **es sich** (*dat*) **l~ machen** take the easy way out; **etw l~ nehmen** (*fig*) take sth lightly. **L~athletik** *f* [track and field] athletics *sg*. **L~gewicht** *nt* (*Boxen*) lightweight. **l~gläubig** *a* gullible. **l~hin** *adv* casually. **L~igkeit** *f* **-** lightness; (*Mühelosigkeit*) ease; (*L~sein*) easiness; **mit L~igkeit** with ease. **L~sinn** *m* carelessness; recklessness; (*Frivolität*) frivolity. **l~sinnig** *a* careless; (*unvorsichtig*) reckless

Leid *nt* **-[e]s** sorrow, grief; (*Böses*) harm; **es tut mir L~** I am sorry; **er tut mir L~** I feel sorry for him. **l~** *a* **jdn/etw l~ sein/werden** be/get tired of s.o./sth

Leide|form *f* passive. **l~n†** *vt/i* (*haben*) suffer (**an** + *dat* from); **jdn/etw nicht l~n können** dislike s.o./sth. **L~n** *nt* **-s,-** suffering; (*Med*) complaint; (*Krankheit*) disease. **l~nd** *a* suffering. **L~nschaft** *f* **-, -en** passion. **l~nschaftlich** *a* passionate

leider *adv* unfortunately; **l~er ja/nicht** I'm afraid so/not

Leier|kasten *m* barrel-organ. **l~n** *vt/i* (*haben*) wind; (*herunter-*) drone out

Leih|e *f* **-, -n** loan. **l~en†** *vt* lend; **sich** (*dat*) **etw l~en** borrow sth. **L~gabe** *f* loan. **L~gebühr** *f* rental; lending charge. **L~haus** *nt* pawnshop. **L~wagen** *m* hire-car. **l~weise** *adv* on loan

Leim *m* **-s** glue. **l~en** *vt* glue

Leine *f* **-, -n** rope; (*Wäsche-*) line; (*Hunde-*) lead, leash

Lein|en *nt* **-s** linen. **L~wand** *f* linen; (*Kunst*) canvas; (*Film-*) screen

leise *a* quiet; <*Stimme, Berührung*> soft; (*schwach*) faint; (*leicht*) light; **l~r stellen** turn down

Leiste *f* **-, -n** strip; (*Holz-*) batten; (*Anat*) groin

leist|en *vt* achieve, accomplish; **sich** (*dat*) **etw l~en** treat oneself to sth; ([!] *anstellen*) get up to sth; **ich kann es mir nicht l~en** I can't afford it. **L~ung** *f* **-, -en** achievement; (*Sport, Techn*) performance; (*Produktion*) output; (*Zahlung*) payment

Leit|artikel *m* leader, editorial. **l~en** *vt* run, manage; (*an-/hinführen*) lead; (*Mus, Techn, Phys*) conduct; (*lenken, schicken*) direct. **l~end** *a* leading; <*Posten*> executive

Leiter[1] *f* **-, -n** ladder

Leit|er[2] *m* **-s,-** director; (*Comm*) manager; (*Führer*) leader; (*Mus, Phys*) conductor. **L~erin** *f* **-, -nen** director; manageress; leader. **L~planke** *f* crash barrier. **L~spruch** *m* motto. **L~ung** *f* **-, -en** (*Führung*) direction; (*Comm*) management; (*Aufsicht*) control; (*Electr: Schnur*) lead, flex; (*Kabel*) cable; (*Telefon-*) line; (*Rohr-*) pipe; (*Haupt-*) main. **L~ungswasser** *nt* tap water

Lektion /-'tsio:n/ *f* **-, -en** lesson

Lekt|or *m* **-s, -en** /-'to:rən/, **L~orin** *f* **-, -nen** (*Univ*) assistant lecturer; (*Verlags-*) editor. **L~üre** *f* **-, -n** reading matter

Lende *f* **-, -n** loin

lenk|en *vt* guide; (*steuern*) steer; (*regeln*) control; **jds Aufmerksamkeit auf sich** (*acc*) **l~en** attract s.o.'s attention. **L~rad** *nt* steering-wheel. **L~stange** *f* handlebars *pl*. **L~ung** *f* - steering

Leopard *m* **-en, -en** leopard

Lepra *f* - leprosy

Lerche *f* **-, -n** lark

lernen *vt/i* (*haben*) learn; (*für die Schule*) study

Lesb|ierin /'lɛsbiərm/ *f* **-, -nen** lesbian. **l~isch** *a* lesbian

les|en† *vt/i* (*haben*) read; (*Univ*) lecture ● *vt* pick, gather. **L~en** *nt* **-s** reading. **L~er(in)** *m* **-s,-** (*f* **-, -nen**) reader. **l~erlich** *a* legible. **L~ezeichen** *nt* bookmark

lethargisch *a* lethargic

Lettland *nt* **-s** Latvia

letzt|e(r,s) *a* last; (*neueste*) latest; **in l~er Zeit** recently; **l~en Endes** in the end. **l~ens** *adv* recently; (*zuletzt*) lastly. **l~ere(r,s)** *a* the latter; **der/die/das L~ere** the latter

Leucht|e *f* **-, -n** light. **l~en** *vi* (*haben*) shine. **l~end** *a* shining. **L~er** *m* **-s,-** candlestick. **L~feuer** *nt* beacon. **L~rakete** *f* flare. **L~reklame** *f* neon sign. **L~röhre** *f* fluorescent tube. **L~turm** *m* lighthouse

leugnen *vt* deny

Leukämie *f* - leukaemia

Leumund *m* **-s** reputation

Leute *pl* people; (*Mil*) men; (*Arbeiter*) workers

Leutnant *m* **-s, -s** second lieutenant

Lexikon *nt* **-s, -ka** encyclopaedia; (*Wörterbuch*) dictionary

Libanon (der) -s Lebanon

Libelle *f* **-, -n** dragonfly

liberal *a* (*Pol*) Liberal

Libyen *nt* **-s** Libya

Licht *nt* **-[e]s, -er** light; (*Kerze*) candle; **L~ machen** turn on the light. **l~** *a* bright; (*Med*) lucid; (*spärlich*) sparse. **L~bild** *nt* [passport] photograph; (*Dia*) slide. **L~blick** *m* (*fig*) ray of hope. **l~en** *vt* thin out; **den Anker l~en** (*Naut*) weigh anchor; **sich l~en** become less dense; thin. **L~hupe** *f* headlight flasher; **die L~hupe betätigen** flash one's headlights. **L~maschine** *f* dynamo. **L~ung** *f* **-, -en** clearing

Lid *nt* **-[e]s, -er** [eye]lid. **L~schatten** *m* eye-shadow

lieb *a* dear; (*nett*) nice; (*artig*) good; **jdn l~ haben** be fond of s.o.; (*lieben*) love s.o.; **es wäre mir l~er** I should prefer it (**wenn** if)

Liebe *f* **-, -n** love. **l~n** *vt* love; (*mögen*) like; **sich l~n** love each other; (*körperlich*) make love. **l~nd** *a* loving. **l~nswert** *a* lovable. **l~nswürdig** *a* kind. **l~nswürdigerweise** *adv* very kindly

lieber *adv* rather; (*besser*) better; **l~ mögen** like better; **ich trinke l~ Tee** I prefer tea

Liebes|brief *m* love letter. **L~dienst** *m* favour. **L~kummer** *m* heartache. **L~paar** *nt* [pair of] lovers *pl*

lieb|evoll *a* loving, affectionate. **L~haber** *m* **-s,-** lover; (*Sammler*) collector. **L~haberei** *f* **-, -en** hobby. **L~kosung** *f* **-, -en** caress. **l~lich** *a* lovely; (*sanft*) gentle; (*süß*) sweet. **L~ling** *m* **-s, -e** darling; (*Bevorzugte*) favourite. **L~lings-** *pref* favourite. **l~los** *a* loveless; <*Eltern*> uncaring; (*unfreundlich*) unkind. **L~schaft** *f* **-, -en** [love] affair. **l~ste(r,s)** *a* dearest; (*bevorzugt*) favourite ● *adv* **am**

l~sten best [of all]; **jdn/etw am l~sten mögen** like s.o./sth best [of all]. **L~ste(r)** *m/f* beloved; (*Schatz*) sweetheart

Lied *nt* **-[e]s, -er** song

liederlich *a* slovenly; (*unordentlich*) untidy. **L~keit** *f* **-** slovenliness; untidiness

Lieferant *m* **-en, -en** supplier

liefer|bar *a* (*Comm*) available. **l~n** *vt* supply; (*zustellen*) deliver; (*hervorbringen*) yield. **L~ung** *f* **-, -en** delivery; (*Sendung*) consignment

Liege *f* **-, -n** couch. **l~n**† *vi* (*haben*) lie; (*gelegen sein*) be situated; **l~n bleiben** remain lying [there]; (*im Bett*) stay in bed; <*Ding:*> be left; <*Schnee:*> settle; <*Arbeit:*> remain undone; (*zurückgelassen werden*) be left behind; **l~n lassen** leave; (*zurücklassen*) leave behind; (*nicht fortführen*) leave undone; **l~n an** (+ *dat*) (*fig*) be due to; (*abhängen*) depend on; **jdm [nicht] l~n** [not] suit s.o.; **mir liegt viel daran** it is very important to me. **L~stuhl** *m* deck-chair. **L~stütz** *m* **-es, -e** press-up, (*Amer*) push-up. **L~wagen** *m* couchette car

Lift *m* **-[e]s, -e** & **-s** lift

Liga *f* **-, -gen** league

Likör *m* **-s, -e** liqueur

lila *inv a* mauve; (*dunkel*) purple

Lilie /'li:liə/ *f* **-, -n** lily

Liliputaner(in) *m* **-s,-** (*f* **-, -nen**) dwarf

Limo *f* **-, -[s]** [!], **L~nade** *f* **-, -n** fizzy drink; lemonade

Limousine /limu'zi:nə/ *f* **-, -n** saloon

lind *a* mild

Linde *f* **-, -n** lime tree

linder|n *vt* relieve, ease. **L~ung** *f* **-** relief

Lineal *nt* **-s, -e** ruler

Linie /-iə/ *f* **-, -n** line; (*Zweig*) branch; (*Bus-*) route; **L~ 4** number 4 [bus/tram]; **in erster L~** primarily. **L~nflug** *m* scheduled flight. **L~nrichter** *m* linesman

lin[i]iert *a* lined, ruled

Link|e *f* **-n, -n** left side; (*Hand*) left hand; (*Boxen*) left; **die L~e** (*Pol*) the left. **l~e(r,s)** *a* left; (*Pol*) leftwing; **l~e Masche** purl

links *adv* on the left; (*bei Stoff*) on the wrong side; (*verkehrt*) inside out; **l~ stricken** purl. **L~händer(in)** *m* **-s,-** (*f* **-, -nen**) lefthander. **l~händig** *a* & *adv* lefthanded

Linoleum /-leʊm/ *nt* **-s** lino, linoleum

Linse *f* **-, -n** lens; (*Bot*) lentil

Lippe *f* **-, -n** lip. **L~nstift** *m* lipstick

Liquid|ation /-'tsio:n/ *f* **-, -en** liquidation. **l~ieren** *vt* liquidate

lispeln *vt/i* (*haben*) lisp

List *f* **-, -en** trick, ruse

Liste *f* **-, -n** list

listig *a* cunning, crafty

Litanei *f* **-, -en** litany

Litauen *nt* **-s** Lithuania

Liter *m* & *nt* **-s,-** litre

Literatur *f* **-** literature

Liturgie *f* **-, -n** liturgy

Litze *f* **-, -n** braid

Lizenz *f* **-, -en** licence

Lob *nt* **-[e]s** praise

Lobby /'lɔbi/ *f* **-** (*Pol*) lobby

loben *vt* praise

löblich *a* praiseworthy

Lobrede *f* eulogy

Loch *nt* **-[e]s,¨er** hole. **l~en** *vt* punch a hole/holes in; punch <*Fahrkarte*>. **L~er** *m* **-s,-** punch

löcherig *a* full of holes

Locke *f* **-, -n** curl. **l~n**[1] *vt* curl; **sich l~n** curl

locken[2] *vt* lure, entice; (*reizen*) tempt. **l~d** *a* tempting

Lockenwickler *m* **-s,-** curler; (*Rolle*) roller

locker *a* loose; <*Seil*> slack; <*Erde*> light; (*zwanglos*) casual; (*zu frei*) lax. **l~n** *vt* loosen; slacken <*Seil*>; break up <*Boden*>; relax <*Griff*>; **sich l~n** become loose; <*Seil:*> slacken; (*sich entspannen*) relax

lockig *a* curly

Lockmittel *nt* bait

Loden *m* **-s** (*Tex*) loden

Löffel *m* **-s,-** spoon; (*L~ voll*) spoonful. **l~n** *vt* spoon up

Logarithmus *m* **-, -men** logarithm

Logbuch *nt* (*Naut*) log-book

Loge /'lo:ʒə/ *f* **-, -n** lodge; (*Theat*) box

Log|ik *f* **-** logic. **l~isch** *a* logical

Logo *nt* **-s, -s** logo

Lohn *m* **-[e]s,¨-e** wages *pl*, pay; (*fig*) reward. **L~empfänger** *m* wage-earner. **l~en** *vi/r* (*haben*) **[sich] l~en** be worth it *or* worth while ● *vt* be worth. **l~end** *a* worthwhile; (*befriedigend*) rewarding. **L~erhöhung** *f* [pay] rise. **L~steuer** *f* income tax

Lok *f* **-, -s** [!] = **Lokomotive**

Lokal *nt* **-s, -e** restaurant; (*Trink-*) bar

Lokomotiv|e *f* **-, -n** engine, locomotive. **L~führer** *m* engine driver

London *nt* **-s** London. **L~er** *a* London ... ● *m* **-s,-** Londoner

Lorbeer *m* **-s, -en** laurel. **L~blatt** *nt* (*Culin*) bay-leaf

Lore *f* **-, -n** (*Rail*) truck

Los *nt* **-es, -e** lot; (*Lotterie-*) ticket; (*Schicksal*) fate

los *pred a* **los sein** be loose; **jdn/etw los sein** be rid of s.o./sth; **was ist [mit ihm] los?** what's the matter [with him]? ● *adv* **los!** go on! **Achtung, fertig, los!** ready, steady, go!

lösbar *a* soluble

losbinden† *vt sep* untie

Lösch|blatt *nt* sheet of blotting-paper. **l~en** *vt* put out, extinguish; quench <*Durst*>; blot <*Tinte*>; (*tilgen*) cancel; (*streichen*) delete

Löschfahrzeug *nt* fire-engine

lose *a* loose

Lösegeld *nt* ransom

losen *vt* (*haben*) draw lots (**um** for)

lösen *vt* undo; (*lockern*) loosen; (*entfernen*) detach; (*klären*) solve; (*auflösen*) dissolve; cancel <*Vertrag*>; break off <*Beziehung*>; (*kaufen*) buy; **sich l~** come off; (*sich trennen*) detach oneself/itself; (*lose werden*) come undone; (*sich klären*) resolve itself; (*sich auflösen*) dissolve

los|fahren† *vi sep* (*sein*) start; <*Auto:*> drive off; **l~fahren auf** (+ *acc*) head for. **l~gehen**† *vi sep* (*sein*) set off; ([!] *anfangen*) start; <*Bombe:*> go off; **l~gehen auf** (+ *acc*) head for; (*fig: angreifen*) go for. **l~kommen**† *vi sep* (*sein*) get away (**von** from). **l~lassen**† *vt sep* let go of; (*freilassen*) release

löslich *a* soluble

los|lösen *vt sep* detach; **sich l~lösen** become detached; (*fig*) break away (**von** from). **l~machen** *vt sep* detach; untie. **l~reißen**† *vt sep* tear off; **sich l~reißen** break free; (*fig*) tear oneself away. **l~schicken** *vt sep* send off. **l~sprechen**† *vt sep* absolve (**von** from)

Losung *f* **-, -en** (*Pol*) slogan; (*Mil*) password

Lösung *f* **-, -en** solution. **L~smittel** *nt* solvent

loswerden† *vt sep* get rid of

Lot *nt* **-[e]s, -e** perpendicular; (*Blei-*) plumb[-bob]. **l~en** *vt* plumb

löt|en *vt* solder. **L~lampe** *f* blow-lamp

lotrecht *a* perpendicular

Lotse *m* **-n, -n** (*Naut*) pilot. **l~n** *vt* (*Naut*) pilot; (*fig*) guide

Lotterie *f* **-, -n** lottery

Lotto *nt* **-s, -s** lotto; (*Lotterie*) lottery

Löw|e *m* **-n, -n** lion; (*Astr*) Leo. **L~enzahn** *m* (*Bot*) dandelion. **L~in** *f* **-, -nen** lioness

loyal /loa'ja:l/ *a* loyal. **L~ität** *f* **-** loyalty

Luchs *m* **-es, -e** lynx

Lücke *f* **-, -n** gap. **l~nhaft** *a* incomplete; <*Wissen*> patchy. **l~nlos** *a* complete; <*Folge*> unbroken

Luder *nt* **-s,-** ☒ (*Frau*) bitch

Luft *f* **-,¨e** air; **tief L~ holen** take a deep breath; **in die L~ gehen** explode. **L~angriff** *m* air raid. **L~aufnahme** *f* aerial photograph. **L~ballon** *m* balloon. **L~blase** *f* air bubble. **L~druck** *m* atmospheric pressure

lüften *vt* air; raise <*Hut*>; reveal <*Geheimnis*>

Luft|fahrt *f* aviation. **L~fahrtgesellschaft** *f* airline. **L~gewehr** *nt* airgun. **l~ig** *a* airy; <*Kleid*> light. **L~kissenfahrzeug** *nt* hovercraft. **L~krieg** *m* aerial warfare. **l~leer** *a* **l~leerer Raum** vacuum. **L~linie** *f* **100 km L~linie** 100 km as the crow flies. **L~matratze** *f* air-bed, inflatable mattress. **L~pirat** *m* hijacker. **L~post** *f* airmail. **L~röhre** *f* windpipe. **L~schiff** *nt* airship. **L~schlange** *f* [paper] streamer. **L~schutzbunker** *m* air-raid shelter

Lüftung *f* **-** ventilation

Luft|veränderung *f* change of air. **L~waffe** *f* air force. **L~zug** *m* draught

Lüg|e *f* **-, -n** lie. **l~en**† *vt/i* (*haben*) lie. **L~ner(in)** *m* **-s,-** (*f* **-, -nen**) liar. **l~nerisch** *a* untrue; <*Person*> untruthful

Luke *f* **-, -n** hatch; (*Dach-*) skylight

Lümmel *m* **-s,-** lout

Lump *m* **-en, -en** scoundrel. **L~en** *m* **-s,-** rag; **in L~en** in rags. **L~enpack** *nt* riff-raff. **L~ensammler** *m* rag-and-bone man. **l~ig** *a* mean, shabby

Lunge *f* **-, -n** lungs *pl*; (*L~nflügel*) lung. **L~nentzündung** *f* pneumonia

Lupe *f* **-, -n** magnifying glass

Lurch *m* **-[e]s, -e** amphibian

Lust *f* **-,¨e** pleasure; (*Verlangen*) desire; (*sinnliche Begierde*) lust; **L~ haben** feel like (**auf etw** *acc* sth); **ich habe keine L~** I don't feel like it; (*will nicht*) I don't want to

lustig *a* jolly; (*komisch*) funny; **sich l~ machen über** (+ *acc*) make fun of

Lüstling *m* **-s, -e** lecher

lust|los *a* listless. **L~mörder** *m* sex killer. **L~spiel** *nt* comedy

lutsch|en *vt/i* (*haben*) suck. **L~er** *m* **-s,-** lollipop

Lüttich *nt* **-s** Liège

Luv *f & nt* **- nach Luv** (*Naut*) to windward

luxuriös *a* luxurious

Luxus *m* **-** luxury

Lymph|drüse /'lʏmf-/ *f*, **L~knoten** *m* lymph gland

lynchen /'lʏnçən/ *vt* lynch

Lyr|ik *f* **-** lyric poetry. **L~iker** *m* **-s,-** lyric poet. **l~isch** *a* lyrical

Mm

Mạchart *f* style

mạchen

● *transitive verb*

····➤ (*herstellen, zubereiten*) make <*money, beds, music, exception, etc*>. **aus Plastik/Holz gemacht** made of plastic/wood. **sich** (*dat*) **etw machen lassen** have sth made. **etw aus jdm machen** make s.o. into sth. **jdn zum Präsidenten machen** make s.o. president. **er machte sich** (*dat*) **viele Freunde/Feinde** he made a lot of friends/enemies. **jdm/sich** (*dat*) **[einen] Kaffee machen** make [some] coffee for s.o./oneself. **ein Foto machen** take a photo

····➤ (*verursachen*) make, cause <*difficulties*>; cause <*pain, anxiety*>. **jdm Arbeit machen** make [extra] work for s.o., cause s.o. extra work. **jdm Mut/Hoffnung machen** give s.o. courage/hope. **das macht Hunger/Durst** this makes you hungry/thirsty. **das macht das Wetter** that's [because of] the weather

····➤ (*ausführen, ordnen*) do <*job, repair* [!]*: room, washing, etc.*>; take <*walk, trip, exam, course*>. **sie machte mir die Haare** [!] she did my hair for me. **einen Besuch [bei jdm] machen** pay [s.o.] a visit

····➤ (*tun*) do <*nothing, everything*>. **was machst du [da]?** what are you doing? **so etwas macht man nicht** that [just] isn't done

····➤ **was macht ...?** (*wie ist es um ... bestellt?*) how is ...? **was macht die Gesundheit/Arbeit?** how are you keeping/how is the job [getting on]?

····➤ (*Math: ergeben*) be. **zwei mal zwei macht vier** two times two is four. **das macht 6 Mark [zusammen]** that's *or* that comes to six marks [altogether]

····➤ (*schaden*) **was macht das schon?** what does it matter? **[das] macht nichts!** [!] it doesn't matter

····➤ **machs gut!** [!] look after yourself!; (*auf Wiedersehen*) so long!

● *reflexive verb*

····➤ **sich machen** [!] do well

····➤ **sich an etw** (*acc*) **machen** get down to sth. **sie machte sich an die Arbeit** she got down to work

● *intransitive verb*

····➤ **das macht hungrig/durstig** it makes you hungry/thirsty. **das macht dick** it's fattening

Mạcht *f* **-,¨e** power. **M~haber** *m* **-s,-** ruler

mạ̈chtig *a* powerful ● *adv* [!] terribly

mạchtlos *a* powerless

Mädchen *nt* **-s,-** girl; (*Dienst-*) maid. **m~haft** *a* girlish. **M~name** *m* girl's name; (*vor der Ehe*) maiden name

Made *f* **-, -n** maggot

madig *a* maggoty

Madọnna *f* **-, -nen** madonna

Magazin *nt* **-s, -e** magazine; (*Lager*) warehouse; store-room

Magd *f* **-,¨e** maid

Magen *m* **-s,¨** stomach. **M~verstimmung** *f* stomach upset

mager *a* thin; <*Fleisch*> lean; <*Boden*> poor; (*dürftig*) meagre.

M∼keit *f* - thinness; leanness. **M∼sucht** *f* anorexia
Magie *f* - magic
Mag|ier /ˈmaːgiɐ/ *m* **-s,-** magician. **m∼isch** *a* magic
Magistrat *m* **-s, -e** city council
Magnet *m* **-en** & **-[e]s, -e** magnet. **m∼isch** *a* magnetic
Mahagoni *nt* **-s** mahogany
Mäh|drescher *m* **-s,-** combine harvester. **m∼en** *vt/i* (*haben*) mow
Mahl *nt* **-[e]s,¨er** & **-e** meal
mahlen† *vt* grind
Mahlzeit *f* meal; **M∼!** enjoy your meal!
Mähne *f* **-, -n** mane
mahn|en *vt/i* (*haben*) remind (**wegen** about); (*ermahnen*) admonish; (*auffordern*) urge (**zu** to). **M∼ung** *f* **-, -en** reminder; admonition
Mai *m* **-[e]s, -e** May; **der Erste Mai** May Day. **M∼glöckchen** *nt* **-s,-** lily of the valley
Mailand *nt* **-s** Milan
Mais *m* **-es** maize; (*Culin*) sweet corn
Majestät *f* **-, -en** majesty. **m∼isch** *a* majestic
Major *m* **-s, -e** major
Majoran *m* **-s** marjoram
makaber *a* macabre
Makel *m* **-s,-** blemish; (*Defekt*) flaw
Makkaroni *pl* macaroni *sg*
Makler *m* **-s,-** (*Comm*) broker
Makrele *f* **-, -n** mackerel
Makrone *f* **-, -n** macaroon
mal *adv* (*Math*) times; (*bei Maßen*) by; (🅵 *einmal*) once; (*eines Tages*) one day; **nicht mal** not even
Mal *nt* **-[e]s, -e** time; **zum ersten/letzten Mal** for the first/last time; **ein für alle Mal** once and for all; **jedes Mal** every time; **jedes Mal, wenn** whenever
Mal|buch *nt* colouring book. **m∼en** *vt/i* (*haben*) paint. **M∼er** *m* **-s,-** painter. **M∼erei** *f* **-, -en** painting. **M∼erin** *f* **-, -nen** painter. **m∼erisch** *a* picturesque
Mallorca /maˈlɔrka, -ˈjɔrka/ *nt* **-s** Majorca
malnehmen† *vt sep* multiply (**mit** by)
Malz *nt* **-es** malt
Mama /ˈmama, maˈmaː/ *f* **-s, -s** mummy
Mammut *nt* **-s, -e** & **-s** mammoth
mampfen *vt* 🅵 munch
man *pron* one, you; (*die Leute*) people, they; **man sagt** they say, it is said
manch|e(r,s) *pron* many a; **[so] m∼es Mal** many a time; **m∼e Leute** some people ● (*substantivisch*) **m∼er/m∼e** many a man/woman; **m∼e** *pl* some; (*Leute*) some people; (*viele*) many [people]; **m∼es** some things; (*vieles*) many things. **m∼erlei** *inv a* various ● *pron* various things
manchmal *adv* sometimes
Mandant(in) *m* **-en, -en** (*f* **-, -nen**) (*Jur*) client
Mandarine *f* **-, -n** mandarin
Mandat *nt* **-[e]s, -e** mandate; (*Jur*) brief; (*Pol*) seat
Mandel *f* **-, -n** almond; (*Anat*) tonsil. **M∼entzündung** *f* tonsillitis
Manege /maˈneːʒə/ *f* **-, -n** ring; (*Reit-*) arena
Mangel[1] *m* **-s,¨** lack; (*Knappheit*) shortage; (*Med*) deficiency; (*Fehler*) defect
Mangel[2] *f* **-, -n** mangle
mangel|haft *a* faulty, defective; (*Sch*) unsatisfactory. **m∼n**[1] *vi* (*haben*) **es m∼t an** (+ *dat*) there is a lack/(*Knappheit*) shortage of
mangeln[2] *vt* put through the mangle

Manie *f* **-, -n** mania
Manier *f* **-, -en** manner; **M~en** manners. **m~lich** *a* well-mannered ● *adv* properly
Manifest *nt* **-[e]s, -e** manifesto
Maniküre *f* **-, -n** manicure; (*Person*) manicurist. **m~n** *vt* manicure
Manko *nt* **-s, -s** disadvantage; (*Fehlbetrag*) deficit
Mann *m* **-[e]s,¨er** man; (*Ehe-*) husband
Männchen *nt* **-s,-** little man; (*Zool*) male
Mannequin /'manəkɛ̃/ *nt* **-s, -s** model
männlich *a* male; (*Gram & fig*) masculine; (*mannhaft*) manly; <*Frau*> mannish. **M~keit** *f* **-** masculinity; (*fig*) manhood
Mannschaft *f* **-, -en** team; (*Naut*) crew
Manöv|er *nt* **-s,-** manœuvre; (*Winkelzug*) trick. **m~rieren** *vt/i* (*haben*) manœuvre
Mansarde *f* **-, -n** attic room; (*Wohnung*) attic flat
Manschette *f* **-, -n** cuff. **M~nknopf** *m* cuff-link
Mantel *m* **-s,¨** coat; overcoat
Manuskript *nt* **-[e]s, -e** manuscript
Mappe *f* **-, -n** folder; (*Akten-*) briefcase; (*Schul-*) bag
Märchen *nt* **-s,-** fairy tale
Margarine *f* **-** margarine
Marienkäfer /ma'ri:ən-/ *m* lady-bird
Marihuana *nt* **-s** marijuana
Marine *f* marine; (*Kriegs-*) navy. **m~blau** *a* navy [blue]
marinieren *vt* marinade
Marionette *f* **-, -n** puppet, marionette
Mark[1] *f* **-,-** mark; **drei M~** three marks
Mark[2] *nt* **-[e]s** (*Knochen-*) marrow; (*Bot*) pith; (*Frucht-*) pulp
markant *a* striking
Marke *f* **-, -n** token; (*rund*) disc; (*Erkennungs-*) tag; (*Brief-*) stamp; (*Lebensmittel-*) coupon; (*Spiel-*) counter; (*Markierung*) mark; (*Fabrikat*) make; (*Tabak-*) brand. **M~nartikel** *m* branded article
markieren *vt* mark; (*[!] vortäuschen*) fake
Markise *f* **-, -n** awning
Markstück *nt* one-mark piece
Markt *m* **-[e]s,¨e** market; (*M~platz*) market-place. **M~forschung** *f* market research
Marmelade *f* **-, -n** jam; (*Orangen-*) marmalade
Marmor *m* **-s** marble
Marokko *nt* **-s** Morocco
Marone *f* **-, -n** [sweet] chestnut
Marsch *m* **-[e]s,¨e** march. **m~** *int* (*Mil*) march!
Marschall *m* **-s,¨e** marshal
marschieren *vi* (*sein*) march
Marter *f* **-, -n** torture. **m~n** *vt* torture
Märtyrer(in) *m* **-s,-** (*f* **-, -nen**) martyr
Marxismus *m* **-** Marxism
März *m* **-, -e** March
Marzipan *nt* **-s** marzipan
Masche *f* **-, -n** stitch; (*im Netz*) mesh; ([!] *Trick*) dodge. **M~ndraht** *m* wire netting
Maschin|e *f* **-, -n** machine; (*Flugzeug*) plane; (*Schreib-*) typewriter; **M~e schreiben** type. **m~egeschrieben** *a* typewritten, typed. **m~ell** *a* machine ... ● *adv* by machine. **M~enbau** *m* mechanical engineering. **M~engewehr** *nt* machine-gun. **M~ist** *m* **-en, -en** machinist; (*Naut*) engineer
Masern *pl* measles *sg*
Maserung *f* **-, -en** [wood] grain
Maske *f* **-, -n** mask; (*Theat*) make-up

maskieren *vt* mask; **sich m~** dress up (**als** as)
maskulin *a* masculine
Masochist *m* **-en, -en** masochist
Maß[1] *nt* **-es, -e** measure; (*Abmessung*) measurement; (*Grad*) degree; (*Mäßigung*) moderation; **in hohem Maße** to a high degree
Maß[2] *f* **-,-** (*SGer*) litre [of beer]
Massage /ma'sa:ʒə/ *f* **-, -n** massage
Massaker *nt* **-s,-** massacre
Maßband *nt* (*pl* **-bänder**) tape-measure
Masse *f* **-, -n** mass; (*Culin*) mixture; (*Menschen-*) crowd; **eine M~ Arbeit** [!] masses of work. **m~nhaft** *adv* in huge quantities. **M~nproduktion** *f* mass production. **m~nweise** *adv* in huge numbers
Masseu|r /ma'sø:ɐ/ *m* **-s, -e** masseur. **M~se** /-'sø:zə/ *f* **-, -n** masseuse
maß|gebend *a* authoritative; (*einflussreich*) influential. **m~geblich** *a* decisive. **m~geschneidert** *a* made-to-measure
massieren *vt* massage
massig *a* massive
mäßig *a* moderate; (*mittelmäßig*) indifferent. **m~en** *vt* moderate; **sich m~en** moderate; (*sich beherrschen*) restrain oneself. **M~ung** *f* **-** moderation
massiv *a* solid; (*stark*) heavy
Maß|krug *m* beer mug. **m~los** *a* excessive; (*grenzenlos*) boundless; (*äußerst*) extreme. **M~nahme** *f* **-, -n** measure
Maßstab *m* scale; (*Norm & fig*) standard. **m~sgerecht, m~sgetreu** *a* scale ... ● *adv* to scale
Mast[1] *m* **-[e]s, -en** pole; (*Überland-*) pylon; (*Naut*) mast
Mast[2] *f* **-** fattening
mästen *vt* fatten
masturbieren *vi* (*haben*) masturbate
Material *nt* **-s, -ien** /-iən/ material; (*coll*) materials *pl*. **M~ismus** *m* **-** materialism. **m~istisch** *a* materialistic
Mathe *f* **-** [!] maths *sg*
Mathe|matik *f* **-** mathematics *sg*. **M~matiker** *m* **-s,-** mathematician. **m~matisch** *a* mathematical
Matinee *f* **-, -n** (*Theat*) morning performance
Matratze *f* **-, -n** mattress
Matrose *m* **-n, -n** sailor
Matsch *m* **-[e]s** mud; (*Schnee-*) slush
matt *a* weak; (*gedämpft*) dim; (*glanzlos*) dull; <*Politur, Farbe*> matt. **M~** *nt* **-s** (*Schach*) mate
Matte *f* **-, -n** mat
Mattglas *nt* frosted glass
Matura *f* **-** (*Aust*) ≈ A levels *pl*
Mauer *f* **-, -n** wall. **M~werk** *nt* masonry
Maul *nt* **-[e]s, Mäuler** (*Zool*) mouth; **halts M~!** [!] shut up! **M~- und Klauenseuche** *f* foot-and-mouth disease. **M~korb** *m* muzzle. **M~tier** *nt* mule. **M~wurf** *m* mole
Maurer *m* **-s,-** bricklayer
Maus *f* **-,Mäuse** mouse
Maut *f* **-, -en** (*Aust*) toll. **M~straße** *f* toll road
maximal *a* maximum
Maximum *nt* **-s, -ma** maximum
Mayonnaise /majo'nɛ:zə/ *f* **-, -n** mayonnaise
Mechan|ik /me'ça:nɪk/ *f* **-** mechanics *sg*; (*Mechanismus*) mechanism. **M~iker** *m* **-s,-** mechanic. **m~isch** *a* mechanical. **m~isieren** *vt* mechanize. **M~ismus** *m* **-, -men** mechanism

meckern *vi* (*haben*) bleat; (**!** *nörgeln*) grumble
Medaill|e /meˈdaljə/ *f* **-, -n** medal. **M~on** /-ˈjõː/ *nt* **-s, -s** medallion; (*Schmuck*) locket
Medikament *nt* **-[e]s, -e** medicine
Medit|ation /-ˈtsioːn/ *f* **-, -en** meditation. **m~ieren** *vi* (*haben*) meditate
Medium *nt* **-s, -ien** medium; **die Medien** the media
Medizin *f* **-, -en** medicine. **M~er** *m* **-s,-** doctor; (*Student*) medical student. **m~isch** *a* medical; (*heilkräftig*) medicinal
Meer *nt* **-[e]s, -e** sea. **M~busen** *m* gulf. **M~enge** *f* strait. **M~esspiegel** *m* sea-level. **M~jungfrau** *f* mermaid. **M~rettich** *m* horseradish. **M~schweinchen** *nt* **-s,-** guinea-pig
Mehl *nt* **-[e]s** flour. **M~schwitze** *f* **-, -n** (*Culin*) roux
mehr *pron & adv* more; **nicht m~** no more; (*zeitlich*) no longer; **nichts m~** no more; (*nichtsweiter*) nothing else; **nie m~** never again. **m~eres** *pron* several things *pl*. **m~fach** *a* multiple; (*mehrmalig*) repeated ● *adv* several times. **M~fahrtenkarte** *f* book of tickets. **M~heit** *f* **-, -en** majority. **m~malig** *a* repeated. **m~mals** *adv* several times. **m~sprachig** *a* multilingual. **M~wertsteuer** *f* value-added tax, VAT. **M~zahl** *f* majority; (*Gram*) plural. **M~zweck-** *pref* multi-purpose
meiden† *vt* avoid, shun
Meile *f* **-, -n** mile. **m~nweit** *adv* [for] miles
mein *poss pron* my. **m~e(r,s)** *poss pron* mine; **die M~en** *od* **m~en** *pl* my family *sg*
Meineid *m* perjury
meinen *vt* mean; (*glauben*) think; (*sagen*) say
mein|erseits *adv* for my part. **m~etwegen** *adv* for my sake; (*wegen mir*) because of me; (**!** *von mir aus*) as far as I'm concerned
Meinung *f* **-, -en** opinion; **jdm die M~ sagen** give s.o. a piece of one's mind. **M~sumfrage** *f* opinion poll
Meise *f* **-, -n** (*Zool*) tit
Meißel *m* **-s,-** chisel. **m~n** *vt/i* (*haben*) chisel
meist *adv* mostly; (*gewöhnlich*) usually. **m~e** *a* **der/die/das m~e** most; **die m~en Leute** most people; **am m~en** [the] most ● *pron* **das m~e** most [of it]; **die m~en** most. **m~ens** *adv* mostly; (*gewöhnlich*) usually
Meister *m* **-s,-** master craftsman; (*Könner*) master; (*Sport*) champion. **m~n** *vt* master. **M~schaft** *f* **-, -en** mastery; (*Sport*) championship
meld|en *vt* report; (*anmelden*) register; (*ankündigen*) announce; **sich m~en** report (**bei** to); (*zum Militär*) enlist; (*freiwillig*) volunteer; (*Teleph*) answer; (*Sch*) put up one's hand; (*von sich hören lassen*) get in touch (**bei** with). **M~ung** *f* **-, -en** report; (*Anmeldung*) registration
melken† *vt* milk
Melodie *f* **-, -n** tune, melody
melodisch *a* melodic; melodious
Melone *f* **-, -n** melon
Memoiren /meˈmo̯aːrən/ *pl* memoirs
Menge *f* **-, -n** amount, quantity; (*Menschen-*) crowd; (*Math*) set; **eine M~ Geld** a lot of money. **m~n** *vt* mix
Mensa *f* **-, -sen** (*Univ*) refectory
Mensch *m* **-en, -en** human being; **der M~** man; **die M~en** people; **jeder/kein M~** everybody/

nobody. **M~enaffe** *m* ape. **m~enfeindlich** *a* antisocial. **M~enfresser** *m* **-s,-** cannibal; (*Zool*) man-eater. **m~enfreundlich** *a* philanthropic. **M~enleben** *nt* human life; (*Lebenszeit*) lifetime. **m~enleer** *a* deserted. **M~enmenge** *f* crowd. **M~enraub** *m* kidnapping. **M~enrechte** *ntpl* human rights. **m~enscheu** *a* unsociable. **m~enwürdig** *a* humane. **M~heit** *f* **-** **die M~heit** mankind, humanity. **m~lich** *a* human; (*human*) humane. **M~lichkeit** *f* **-** humanity

Menstru|ation /-'tsio:n/ *f* **-** menstruation. **m~ieren** *vi* (*haben*) menstruate

Mentalität *f* **-, -en** mentality

Menü *nt* **-s, -s** menu; (*festes M~*) set meal

Meridian *m* **-s, -e** meridian

merk|bar *a* noticeable. **M~blatt** *nt* [explanatory] leaflet. **m~en** *vt* notice; **sich** (*dat*) **etw m~en** remember sth. **M~mal** *nt* feature

merkwürdig *a* odd, strange

Messe[1] *f* **-, -n** (*Relig*) mass; (*Comm*) [trade] fair

Messe[2] *f* **-, -n** (*Mil*) mess

messen† *vt/i* (*haben*) measure; (*ansehen*) look at; **[bei jdm] Fieber m~** take s.o.'s temperature; **sich mit jdm m~ können** be a match for s.o.

Messer *nt* **-s,-** knife

Messias *m* **-** Messiah

Messing *nt* **-s** brass

Messung *f* **-, -en** measurement

Metabolismus *m* **-** metabolism

Metall *nt* **-s, -e** metal. **m~isch** *a* metallic

Metamorphose *f* **-, -n** metamorphosis

metaphorisch *a* metaphorical

Meteor *m* **-s, -e** meteor. **M~ologie** *f* **-** meteorology

Meter *m & nt* **-s,-** metre. **M~maß** *nt* tape-measure

Method|e *f* **-, -n** method. **m~isch** *a* methodical

Metropole *f* **-, -n** metropolis

Metzger *m* **-s,-** butcher. **M~ei** *f* **-, -en** butcher's shop

Meuterei *f* **-, -en** mutiny

meutern *vi* (*haben*) mutiny; ([!] *schimpfen*) grumble

Mexikan|er(in) *m* **-s,-** (*f* **-, -nen**) Mexican. **m~isch** *a* Mexican

Mexiko *nt* **-s** Mexico

miauen *vi* (*haben*) mew, miaow

mich *pron* (*acc of* **ich**) me; (*refl*) myself

Mieder *nt* **-s,-** bodice

Miene *f* **-, -n** expression

mies *a* [!] lousy

Miet|e *f* **-, -n** rent; (*Mietgebühr*) hire charge; **zur M~e wohnen** live in rented accommodation. **m~en** *vt* rent <*Haus, Zimmer*>; hire <*Auto, Boot*>. **M~er(in)** *m* **-s,-** (*f* **-, -nen**) tenant. **m~frei** *a & adv* rent-free. **M~shaus** *nt* block of rented flats. **M~vertrag** *m* lease. **M~wagen** *m* hire-car. **M~wohnung** *f* rented flat; (*zu vermieten*) flat to let

Migräne *f* **-, -n** migraine

Mikro|chip *m* microchip. **M~computer** *m* microcomputer. **M~film** *m* microfilm

Mikro|fon, M~phon *nt* **-s, -e** microphone. **M~skop** *nt* **-s, -e** microscope. **m~skopisch** *a* microscopic

Mikrowelle *f* microwave. **M~nherd** *m* microwave oven

Milbe *f* **-, -n** mite

Milch *f* **-** milk. **M~glas** *nt* opal glass. **m~ig** *a* milky. **M~mann**

m (*pl* **-männer**) milkman. **M~straße** *f* Milky Way

mild *a* mild; (*nachsichtig*) lenient. **M~e** *f* - mildness; leniency. **m~ern** *vt* make milder; (*mäßigen*) moderate; (*lindern*) ease; **sich m~ern** become milder; (*sich mäßigen*) moderate; <*Schmerz:*> ease; **m~ernde Umstände** mitigating circumstances

Milieu /mi'li̯ø:/ *nt* **-s, -s** [social] environment

Militär *nt* **-s** army; (*Soldaten*) troops *pl*; **beim M~** in the army. **m~isch** *a* military

Miliz *f* **-, -en** militia

Milliarde /mɪ'li̯ardə/ *f* **-, -n** thousand million, billion

Milli|gramm *nt* milligram. **M~meter** *m* & *nt* millimetre. **M~meterpapier** *nt* graph paper

Million /mɪ'li̯o:n/ *f* **-, -en** million. **M~är** *m* **-s, -e** millionaire

Milz *f* **-** (*Anat*) spleen. **M~brand** *m* anthrax

mimen *vt* (🄸 *vortäuschen*) act

Mimose *f* **-, -n** mimosa

Minderheit *f* **-, -en** minority

minderjährig *a* (*Jur*) under-age. **M~e(r)** *m*/*f* (*Jur*) minor

mindern *vt* diminish; decrease

minderwertig *a* inferior. **M~keit** *f* **-** inferiority. **M~keitskomplex** *m* inferiority complex

Mindest- *pref* minimum. **m~e** *a* & *pron* **der/die/das M~e** *od* **m~e** the least; **nicht im M~en** not in the least. **m~ens** *adv* at least. **M~lohn** *m* minimum wage. **M~maß** *nt* minimum

Mine *f* **-, -n** mine; (*Bleistift-*) lead; (*Kugelschreiber-*) refill. **M~nräumboot** *nt* minesweeper

Mineral *nt* **-s, -e** & **-ien** /-i̯ən/ mineral. **m~isch** *a* mineral. **M~wasser** *nt* mineral water

Miniatur *f* **-, -en** miniature

Minigolf *nt* miniature golf

minimal *a* minimal

Minimum *nt* **-s, -ma** minimum

Mini|ster *m*, **-s,-** minister. **m~steriell** *a* ministerial. **M~sterium** *nt* **-s, -ien** ministry

minus *conj, adv* & *prep* (+ *gen*) minus. **M~** *nt* **-** deficit; (*Nachteil*) disadvantage. **M~zeichen** *nt* minus [sign]

Minute *f* **-, -n** minute

mir *pron* (*dat of* **ich**) [to] me; (*refl*) myself

mischen *vt* mix; blend <*Tee, Kaffee*>; toss <*Salat*>; shuffle <*Karten*>; **sich m~en** mix; <*Person,*> mingle (**unter** + *acc* with); **sich m~en in** (+ *acc*) join in <*Gespräch*>; meddle in <*Angelegenheit*> ● *vi* (*haben*) shuffle the cards. **M~ling** *m* **-s, -e** half-caste. **M~ung** *f* **-, -en** mixture; blend

miserabel *a* abominable

missachten *vt* disregard

Miss|achtung *f* disregard. **M~bildung** *f* deformity

missbilligen *vt* disapprove of

Miss|billigung *f* disapproval. **M~brauch** *m* abuse

missbrauchen *vt* abuse; (*vergewaltigen*) rape

Misserfolg *m* failure

Misse|tat *f* misdeed. **M~täter** *m* 🄸 culprit

missfallen† *vi* (*haben*) displease (**jdm** s.o.)

Miss|fallen *nt* **-s** displeasure; (*Missbilligung*) disapproval. **M~geburt** *f* freak; (*fig*) monstrosity. **M~geschick** *nt* mishap; (*Unglück*) misfortune

miss|glücken *vi* (*sein*) fail. **m~gönnen** *vt* begrudge

misshandeln *vt* ill-treat
Misshandlung *f* ill-treatment
Mission *f* **-, -en** mission
Missionar(in) *m* **-s, -e** (*f* **-, -nen**) missionary
Missklang *m* discord
misslingen† *vi* (*sein*) fail; **es misslang ihr** she failed. **M~** *nt* **-s** failure
Missmut *m* ill humour. **m~ig** *a* morose
missraten† *vi* (*sein*) turn out badly
Miss|stand *m* abuse; (*Zustand*) undesirable state of affairs. **M~stimmung** *f* discord; (*Laune*) bad mood
misstrauen *vi* (*haben*) **jdm/etw m~** mistrust s.o./sth; (*Argwohn hegen*) distrust s.o./sth
Misstrau|en *nt* **-s** mistrust; (*Argwohn*) distrust. **M~ensvotum** *nt* vote of no confidence. **m~isch** *a* distrustful; (*argwöhnisch*) suspicious
Miss|verständnis *nt* misunderstanding. **m~verstehen**† *vt* misunderstand. **M~wirtschaft** *f* mismanagement
Mist *m* **-[e]s** manure; [!] rubbish
Mistel *f* **-, -n** mistletoe
Misthaufen *m* dungheap
mit *prep* (+ *dat*) with; <*sprechen*> to; (*mittels*) by; (*inklusive*) including; (*bei*) at; **mit Bleistift** in pencil; **mit lauter Stimme** in a loud voice; **mit drei Jahren** at the age of three ● *adv* (*auch*) as well; **mit anfassen** (*fig*) lend a hand
Mitarbeit *f* collaboration. **m~en** *vi sep* collaborate (**an** + *dat* on). **M~er(in)** *m(f)* collaborator; (*Kollege*) colleague; employee
Mitbestimmung *f* co-determination
mitbringen† *vt sep* bring [along]
miteinander *adv* with each other
Mitesser *m* (*Med*) blackhead
mitfahren† *vi sep* (*sein*) go/come along; **mit jdm m~** go with s.o.; (*mitgenommen werden*) be given a lift by s.o.
mitfühlen *vi sep* (*haben*) sympathize
mitgeben† *vt sep* **jdm etw m~** give s.o. sth to take with him
Mitgefühl *nt* sympathy
mitgehen† *vi sep* (*sein*) **mit jdm m~** go with s.o.
Mitgift *f* **-, -en** dowry
Mitglied *nt* member. **M~schaft** *f* **-** membership
mithilfe *prep* (+ *gen*) with the aid of
Mithilfe *f* assistance
mitkommen† *vi sep* (*sein*) come [along] too; (*fig: folgen können*) keep up; (*verstehen*) follow
Mitlaut *m* consonant
Mitleid *nt* pity, compassion; **M~ erregend** pitiful. **m~ig** *a* pitying; (*mitfühlend*) compassionate. **m~slos** *a* pitiless
mitmachen *v sep* ● *vt* take part in; (*erleben*) go through ● *vi* (*haben*) join in
Mitmensch *m* fellow man
mitnehmen† *vt sep* take along; (*mitfahren lassen*) give a lift to; (*fig: schädigen*) affect badly; (*erschöpfen*) exhaust; **'zum M~'** 'to take away'
mitreden *vi sep* (*haben*) join in [the conversation]; (*mit entscheiden*) have a say (**bei** in)
mitreißen† *vt sep* sweep along; (*fig: begeistern*) carry away; **m~d** rousing
mitsamt *prep* (+ *dat*) together with
mitschreiben† *vt sep* (*haben*) take down

Mitschuld *f* partial blame. **m~ig** *a* **m~ig sein** be partly to blame

Mitschüler(in) *m(f)* fellow pupil

mitspielen *vi sep (haben)* join in; *(Theat)* be in the cast; *(beitragen)* play a part

Mittag *m* midday, noon; *(Mahlzeit)* lunch; *(Pause)* lunch-break; **heute/gestern M~** at lunch-time today/yesterday; **[zu] M~ essen** have lunch. **M~essen** *nt* lunch. **m~s** *adv* at noon; *(als Mahlzeit)* for lunch; **um 12 Uhr m~s** at noon. **M~spause** *f* lunch-hour; *(Pause)* lunch-break. **M~sschlaf** *m* after-lunch nap

Mittäter|(in) *m(f)* accomplice. **M~schaft** *f* - complicity

Mitte *f* **-, -n** middle; *(Zentrum)* centre; **die goldene M~** the golden mean; **M~ Mai** in mid-May; **in unserer M~** in our midst

mitteil|en *vt sep* **jdm etw m~en** tell s.o. sth; *(amtlich)* inform s.o. of sth. **M~ung** *f* **-, -en** communication; *(Nachricht)* piece of news

Mittel *nt* **-s,-** means *sg*; *(Heil)* remedy; *(Medikament)* medicine; *(M~wert)* mean; *(Durchschnitt)* average; **M~** *pl (Geld-)* funds, resources. **m~** *pred a* medium; *(m~mäßig)* middling. **M~alter** *nt* Middle Ages *pl*. **m~alterlich** *a* medieval. **M~ding** *nt (fig)* cross. **m~europäisch** *a* Central European. **M~finger** *m* middle finger. **m~los** *a* destitute. **m~mäßig** *a* middling; **[nur] m~mäßig** mediocre. **M~meer** *nt* Mediterranean. **M~punkt** *m* centre; *(fig)* centre of attention

mittels *prep (+ gen)* by means of

Mittel|schule *f* = **Realschule**. **M~smann** *m (pl* **-männer)** intermediary, go-between. **M~stand** *m* middle class. **m~ste(r,s)** *a* middle. **M~streifen** *m (Auto)* central reservation. **M~stürmer** *m* centre-forward. **M~welle** *f* medium wave. **M~wort** *nt (pl* **-wörter)** participle

mitten *adv* **m~ in/auf** *(dat/acc)* in the middle of. **m~durch** *adv* [right] through the middle

Mitternacht *f* midnight

mittler|e(r,s) *a* middle; <*Größe, Qualität*> medium; *(durchschnittlich)* mean, average. **m~weile** *adv* meanwhile; *(seitdem)* by now

Mittwoch *m* **-s, -e** Wednesday. **m~s** *adv* on Wednesdays

mitunter *adv* now and again

mitwirk|en *vi sep (haben)* take part; *(helfen)* contribute. **M~ung** *f* participation

mix|en *vt* mix. **M~er** *m* **-s,-** *(Culin)* liquidizer, blender

Möbel *pl* furniture *sg*. **M~stück** *nt* piece of furniture. **M~wagen** *m* removal van

Mobiliar *nt* **-s** furniture

mobilisier|en *vt* mobilize. **M~ung** *f* - mobilization

Mobil|machung *f* - mobilization. **M~telefon** *nt* mobile phone

möblier|en *vt* furnish; **m~tes Zimmer** furnished room

mochte, möchte *s.* **mögen**

Mode *f* **-, -n** fashion; **M~ sein** be fashionable

Modell *nt* **-s, -e** model. **m~ieren** *vt* model

Modenschau *f* fashion show

Modera|tor *m* **-s, -en** /-'to:rən/, **M~torin** *f* **-, -nen** *(TV)* presenter

modern *a* modern; *(modisch)* fashionable. **m~isieren** *vt* modernize

Mode|schmuck *m* costume jewellery. **M~schöpfer** *m* fashion designer
modisch *a* fashionable
Modistin *f* **-, -nen** milliner
modrig *a* musty
modulieren *vt* modulate
Mofa *nt* **-s, -s** moped
mogeln *vi* (*haben*) [!] cheat

mögen†
● *transitive verb*
····➤ like. **sie mag ihn sehr [gern]** she likes him very much. **möchten Sie ein Glas Wein?** would you like a glass of wine? **lieber mögen** prefer. **ich möchte lieber Tee** I would prefer tea
● *auxiliary verb*
····➤ (*wollen*) want to. **sie mochte nicht länger bleiben** she didn't want to stay any longer. **ich möchte ihn [gerne] sprechen** I'd like to speak to him. **möchtest du nach Hause?** do you want to go home? *or* would you like to go home?
····➤ (*Vermutung, Möglichkeit*) may. **ich mag mich irren** I may be wrong. **wer/was mag das sein?** whoever/whatever can it be? **[das] mag sein** that may well be. **mag kommen, was da will** come what may

möglich *a* possible; **alle m~en** all sorts of; **über alles M~e sprechen** talk about all sorts of things. **m~erweise** *adv* possibly. **M~keit** *f* **-, -en** possibility. **M~keitsform** *f* subjunctive. **m~st** *adv* if possible; **m~st viel** as much as possible
Mohammedan|er(in) *m* **-s,-** (*f* **-, -nen**) Muslim. **m~isch** *a* Muslim
Mohn *m* **-s** poppy
Möhre, Mohrrübe *f* **-, -n** carrot
Mokka *m* **-s** mocha; (*Geschmack*) coffee
Molch *m* **-[e]s, -e** newt
Mole *f* **-, -n** (*Naut*) mole
Molekül *nt* **-s, -e** molecule
Molkerei *f* **-, -en** dairy
Moll *nt* **-** (*Mus*) minor
mollig *a* cosy; (*warm*) warm; (*rundlich*) plump
Moment *m* **-s, -e** moment; **M~ [mal]!** just a moment! **m~an** *a* momentary; (*gegenwärtig*) at the moment
Monarch *m* **-en, -en** monarch. **M~ie** *f* **-, -n** monarchy
Monat *m* **-s, -e** month. **m~elang** *adv* for months. **m~lich** *a & adv* monthly
Mönch *m* **-[e]s, -e** monk
Mond *m* **-[e]s, -e** moon
mondän *a* fashionable
Mond|finsternis *f* lunar eclipse. **m~hell** *a* moonlit. **M~sichel** *f* crescent moon. **M~schein** *m* moonlight
monieren *vt* criticize
Monitor *m* **-s, -en** /-'to:rən/ (*Techn*) monitor
Monogramm *nt* **-s, -e** monogram
Mono|log *m* **-s, -e** monologue. **M~pol** *nt* **-s, -e** monopoly. **m~ton** *a* monotonous
Monster *nt* **-s,-** monster
Monstrum *nt* **-s, -stren** monster
Monsun *m* **-s, -e** monsoon
Montag *m* Monday
Montage /mɔn'ta:ʒə/ *f* **-, -n** fitting; (*Zusammenbau*) assembly; (*Film-*) editing; (*Kunst*) montage
montags *adv* on Mondays
Montanindustrie *f* coal and steel industry
Monteur /mɔn'tø:ɐ̯/ *m* **-s, -e** fitter. **M~anzug** *m* overalls *pl*
montieren *vt* fit; (*zusammenbauen*) assemble

Monument *nt* **-[e]s, -e** monument. **m~al** *a* monumental

Moor *nt* **-[e]s, -e** bog; (*Heide-*) moor

Moos *nt* **es, -e** moss **m~ig** *a* mossy

Moped *nt* **-s, -s** moped

Mopp *m* **-s, -s** mop

Moral *f* **-** morals *pl*; (*Selbstvertrauen*) morale; (*Lehre*) moral. **m~isch** *a* moral

Mord *m* **-[e]s, -e** murder; (*Pol*) assassination. **M~anschlag** *m* murder/assassination attempt. **m~en** *vt/i* (*haben*) murder, kill

Mörder *m* **-s,-** murderer; (*Pol*) assassin. **M~in** *f* **-, -nen** murderess. **m~isch** *a* murderous; (🅘 *schlimm*) dreadful

morgen *adv* tomorrow; **m~ Abend** tomorrow evening

Morgen *m* **-s,-** morning; (*Maß*) ≈ acre; **am M~** in the morning; **heute/Montag M~** this/Monday morning. **M~dämmerung** *f* dawn. **M~rock** *m* dressing-gown. **M~rot** *nt* red sky in the morning. **m~s** *a* in the morning

morgig *a* tomorrow's; **der m~e Tag** tomorrow

Morphium *nt* **-s** morphine

morsch *a* rotten

Morsealphabet *nt* Morse code

Mörtel *m* **-s** mortar

Mosaik /moza'i:k/ *nt* **-s, -e[n]** mosaic

Moschee *f* **-, -n** mosque

Mosel *f* **-** Moselle

Moskau *nt* **-s** Moscow

Moskito *m* **-s, -s** mosquito

Moslem *m* **-s, -s** Muslim

Motiv *nt* **-s, -e** motive; (*Kunst*) motif

Motor /'mo:tɔr, mo'to:ɐ/ *m* **-s, -en** /-'to:rən/ engine; (*Elektro-*) motor. **M~boot** *nt* motor boat

motorisieren *vt* motorize

Motor|rad *nt* motor cycle. **M~roller** *m* motor scooter

Motte *f* **-, -n** moth. **M~nkugel** *f* mothball

Motto *nt* **-s, -s** motto

Möwe *f* **-, -n** gull

Mücke *f* **-, -n** gnat; (*kleine*) midge; (*Stech-*) mosquito

müd|e *a* tired; **es m~e sein** be tired (**etw zu tun** of doing sth). **M~igkeit** *f* **-** tiredness

muffig *a* musty; (🅘 *mürrisch*) grumpy

Mühe *f* **-, -n** effort; (*Aufwand*) trouble; **sich** (*dat*) **M~ geben** make an effort; (*sich bemühen*) try; **nicht der M~ wert** not worth while; **mit M~ und Not** with great difficulty; (*gerade noch*) only just. **m~los** *a* effortless

muhen *vi* (*haben*) moo

Mühl|e *f* **-, -n** mill; (*Kaffee-*) grinder. **M~stein** *m* millstone

Müh|sal *f* **-, -e** (*liter*) toil; (*Mühe*) trouble. **m~sam** *a* laborious; (*beschwerlich*) difficult

Mulde *f* **-, -n** hollow

Müll *m* **-s** refuse. **M~abfuhr** *f* refuse collection

Mullbinde *f* gauze bandage

Mülleimer *m* waste bin; (*Mülltonne*) dustbin

Müller *m* **-s,-** miller

Müll|halde *f* [rubbish] dump. **M~schlucker** *m* refuse chute. **M~tonne** *f* dustbin

multi|national *a* multinational. **M~plikation** /-'tsio:n/ *f* **-, -en** multiplication. **m~plizieren** *vt* multiply

Mumie /'mu:miə/ *f* **-, -n** mummy

Mumm *m* **-s** 🅘 energy

Mumps *m* **-** mumps

Mund *m* **-[e]s,⸚er** mouth; **ein M~ voll Suppe** a mouthful of soup; **halt den M~!** ☒ shut up!

M~art *f* dialect. **m~artlich** *a* dialect
Mündel *nt & m* **-s,-** (*Jur*) ward. **m~sicher** *a* gilt-edged
münden *vi* (*sein*) flow/<*Straße:*> lead (**in** + *acc* into)
Mundharmonika *f* mouth-organ
mündig *a* **m~ sein/werden** (*Jur*) be/come of age. **M~keit** *f* **-** (*Jur*) majority
mündlich *a* verbal; **m~e** Prüfung oral
Mündung *f* **-, -en** (*Fluss-*) mouth; (*Gewehr-*) muzzle
Mundwinkel *m* corner of the mouth
Munition /-'tsio:n/ *f* **-** ammunition
munkeln *vt/i* (*haben*) talk (**von** of); **es wird gemunkelt** rumour has it (**dass** that)
Münster *nt* **-s,-** cathedral
munter *a* lively; (*heiter*) merry; **m~ sein** (*wach*) be wide awake ; **gesund und m~** fit and well
Münz|e *f* **-, -n** coin; (*M~stätte*) mint. **M~fernsprecher** *m* payphone
mürbe *a* crumbly; <*Obst*> mellow; <*Fleisch*> tender. **M~teig** *m* short pastry
Murmel *f* **-, -n** marble
murmeln *vt/i* (*haben*) murmur; (*undeutlich*) mumble
Murmeltier *nt* marmot
murren *vt/i* (*haben*) grumble
mürrisch *a* surly
Mus *nt* **-es** purée
Muschel *f* **-, -n** mussel; [sea] shell
Museum /mu'ze:ʊm/ *nt* **-s, -seen** /-'ze:ən/ museum
Musik *f* **-** music. **m~alisch** *a* musical
Musiker(in) *m* **-s,-** (*f* **-, -nen**) musician
Musik|instrument *nt* musical instrument. **M~kapelle** *f* band. **M~pavillon** *m* bandstand
musisch *a* artistic
musizieren *vi* (*haben*) make music
Muskat *m* **-[e]s** nutmeg
Muskel *m* **-s, -n** muscle. **M~kater** *m* stiff and aching muscles *pl*
muskulös *a* muscular
muss *s.* **müssen**
Muße *f* **-** leisure

---

müssen†
● *auxiliary verb*
····➤ (*gezwungen/verpflichtet/notwendig sein*) have to; must. **er muss es tun** he must *or* has to do it; [!] he's got to do it. **ich musste schnell fahren** I had to drive fast. **das muss 1968 gewesen sein** it must have been in 1968. **er muss gleich hier sein** he must be here at any moment
····➤ (*in negativen Sätzen; ungezwungen*) **sie muss es nicht tun** she does not have to *or* [!] she hasn't got to do it. **es musste nicht so sein** it didn't have to be like that
····➤ **es müsste** (*sollte*) **doch möglich sein** it ought to *or* should be possible. **du müsstest es mal versuchen** you ought to *or* should try it
● *intransitive verb*
····➤ (*irgendwohin gehen müssen*) have to *or* must go. **ich muss nach Hause/zum Arzt** I have to *or* must go home/to the doctor. **ich musste mal [aufs Klo]** I had to go [to the loo]

---

müßig *a* idle
musste, müsste *s.* **müssen**
Muster *nt* **-s,-** pattern; (*Probe*) sample; (*Vorbild*) model. **M~beispiel** *nt* typical example;

(*Vorbild*) perfect example. **m~gültig, m~haft** *a* exemplary. **m~n** *vt* eye; (*inspizieren*) inspect. **M~ung** *f* **-, -en** inspection; (*Mil*) medical; (*Muster*) pattern

Mut *m* **-[e]s** courage; **jdm Mut machen** encourage s.o.; **zu M~e sein** = **zumute sein**, *s.* **zumute**

mut|ig *a* courageous. **m~los** *a* despondent

mutmaßen *vt* presume; (*Vermutungen anstellen*) speculate

Mutprobe *f* test of courage

Mutter¹ *f* **-,⸚** mother

Mutter² *f* **-, -n** (*Techn*) nut

Muttergottes *f* **-,-** madonna

Mutterland *nt* motherland

mütterlich *a* maternal; (*fürsorglich*) motherly. **m~erseits** *adv* on one's/the mother's side

Mutter|mal *nt* birthmark; (*dunkel*) mole. **M~schaft** *f* **-** motherhood. **m~seelenallein** *a & adv* all alone. **M~sprache** *f* mother tongue. **M~tag** *m* Mother's Day

Mütze *f* **-, -n** cap; **wollene M~** woolly hat

MwSt. *abbr* (**Mehrwertsteuer**) VAT

mysteriös *a* mysterious

Mystik /'mystik/ *f* **-** mysticism

myth|isch *a* mythical. **M~ologie** *f* **-** mythology

Nn

na *int* well; **na gut** all right then

Nabel *m* **-s,-** navel. **N~schnur** *f* umbilical cord

nach

- *preposition (+ dative)*

····➤ (*räumlich*) to. **nach London fahren** go to London. **der Zug nach München** the train to Munich; (*noch nicht abgefahren*) the train for Munich; the Munich train. **nach Hause gehen** go home. **nach Osten [zu]** eastwards; towards the east

····➤ (*zeitlich*) after; (*Uhrzeit*) past. **nach fünf Minuten/dem Frühstück** after five minutes/breakfast. **zehn [Minuten] nach zwei** ten [minutes] past two

····➤ (*[räumliche und zeitliche] Reihenfolge*) after. **nach Ihnen/dir!** after you!

····➤ (*mit bestimmten Verben*) for. **greifen/streben/schicken nach** grasp/strive/send for

····➤ (*gemäß*) according to. **nach der neuesten Mode gekleidet** dressed in [accordance with] the latest fashion. **dem Gesetz nach** in accordance with the law; by law. **nach meiner Ansicht** *od* **Meinung, meiner Ansicht** *od* **Meinung nach** in my view *or* opinion. **nach etwas schmecken/riechen** taste/smell of sth

- *adverb*

····➤ (*zeitlich*) **nach und nach** little by little; gradually. **nach wie vor** still

nachahm|en *vt sep* imitate. **N~ung** *f* **-, -en** imitation

Nachbar|(in) *m* **-n, -n** (*f* **-, -nen**) neighbour. **N~haus** *nt* house next door. **n~lich** *a* neighbourly; (*Nachbar-*) neighbouring. **N~schaft** *f* **-** neighbourhood

nachbestell|en *vt sep* reorder. **N~ung** *f* repeat order

nachbild|en *vt sep* copy, reproduce. **N~ung** *f* copy, reproduction

nachdatieren *vt sep* backdate

nachdem *conj* after; **je n~** it depends

nachdenk|en† *vi sep* (*haben*) think (**über** + *acc* about). **n~lich** *a* thoughtful

nachdrücklich *a* emphatic

nacheinander *adv* one after the other

Nachfahre *m* **-n, -n** descendant

Nachfolg|e *f* succession. **N~er(in)** *m* **-s,-** (*f* **-, -nen**) successor

nachforsch|en *vi sep* (*haben*) make enquiries. **N~ung** *f* enquiry

Nachfrage *f* (*Comm*) demand. **n~n** *vi sep* (*haben*) enquire

nachfüllen *vt sep* refill

nachgeben† *v sep* ● *vi* (*haben*) give way: (*sich fügen*) give in, yield ● *vt* **jdm Suppe n~** give s.o. more soup

Nachgebühr *f* surcharge

nachgehen† *vi sep* (*sein*) <*Uhr:*> be slow; **jdm/etw n~** follow s.o./sth; follow up <*Spur, Angelegenheit*>; pursue <*Angelegenheit*>

Nachgeschmack *m* after-taste

nachgiebig *a* indulgent; (*gefällig*) compliant. **N~keit** *f* **-** indulgence; compliance

nachgrübeln *vi sep* (*haben*) ponder (**über** + *acc* on)

nachhaltig *a* lasting

nachhelfen† *vi sep* (*haben*) help

nachher *adv* later; (*danach*) afterwards; **bis n~!** see you later!

Nachhilfeunterricht *m* coaching

Nachhinein *adv* **im N~** afterwards

nachhinken *vi sep* (*sein*) (*fig*) lag behind

nachholen *vt sep* (*später holen*) fetch later; (*mehr holen*) get more; (*später machen*) do later; (*aufholen*) catch up on

Nachkomme *m* **-n, -n** descendant. **n~n**† *vi sep* (*sein*) follow [later], come later; **etw** (*dat*) **n~n** (*fig*) comply with <*Bitte*>; carry out <*Pflicht*>. **N~nschaft** *f* **-** descendants *pl*, progeny

Nachkriegszeit *f* post-war period

Nachlass *m* **-es,¨e** discount; (*Jur*) [deceased's] estate

nachlassen† *v sep* ● *vi* (*haben*) decrease; <*Regen, Hitze:*> let up; <*Schmerz:*> ease; <*Sturm:*> abate; <*Augen, Leistungen:*> deteriorate ● *vt* **etw vom Preis n~** take sth off the price

nachlässig *a* careless; (*leger*) casual; (*unordentlich*) sloppy. **N~keit** *f* **-** carelessness; sloppiness

nachlesen† *vt sep* look up

nachlöse|n *vi sep* (*haben*) pay one's fare on the train/on arrival. **N~schalter** *m* excess-fare office

nachmachen *vt sep* (*später machen*) do later; (*imitieren*) imitate, copy; (*fälschen*) forge

Nachmittag *m* afternoon; **heute/gestern N~** this/ yesterday afternoon. **n~s** *adv* in the afternoon

Nachnahme *f* **etw per N~ schicken** send sth cash on delivery *or* COD
Nachname *m* surname
Nachporto *nt* excess postage
nachprüfen *vt sep* check, verify
Nachricht *f* **-, -en** [piece of] news *sg*; **N~en** news *sg*; **eine N~ hinterlassen** leave a message; **jdm N~ geben** inform s.o. **N~endienst** *m* (*Mil*) intelligence service
nachrücken *vi sep* (*sein*) move up
Nachruf *m* obituary
nachsagen *vt sep* repeat (**jdm** after s.o.); **jdm Schlechtes/Gutes n~** speak ill/well of s.o.
Nachsaison *f* late season
nachschicken *vt sep* (*später schicken*) send later; (*hinterher-*) send after (**jdm** s.o.); send on <*Post*> (**jdm** to s.o.)
nachschlagen† *v sep* ● *vt* look up ● *vi* (*haben*) **in einem Wörterbuch n~en** consult a dictionary; **jdm n~en** take after s.o.
Nachschrift *f* transcript; (*Nachsatz*) postscript
Nachschub *m* (*Mil*) supplies *pl*
nachsehen† *v sep* ● *vt* (*prüfen*) check; (*nachschlagen*) look up; (*hinwegsehen über*) overlook ● *vi* (*haben*) have a look; (*prüfen*) check; **im Wörterbuch n~** consult a dictionary
nachsenden† *vt sep* forward <*Post*> (**jdm** to s.o.); '**bitte n~**' 'please forward'
nachsichtig *a* forbearing; lenient; indulgent
Nachsilbe *f* suffix
nachsitzen† *vi sep* (*haben*) **n~ müssen** be kept in [after school]; **jdn n~ lassen** give s.o. detention. **N~** *nt* **-s** (*Sch*) detention
Nachspeise *f* dessert, sweet
nachsprechen† *vt sep* repeat (**jdm** after s.o.)
nachspülen *vt sep* rinse
nächst /-çst/ *prep* (+ *dat*) next to. **n~beste(r,s)** *a* first [available]; (*zweitbeste*) next best. **n~e(r,s)** *a* next; (*nächstgelegene*) nearest; <*Verwandte*> closest; **in n~er Nähe** close by; **am n~en sein** be nearest *or* closest ● *pron* **der/die/das N~e** the next; **der N~e bitte** next please; **als N~es** next; **fürs N~e** for the time being. **N~e(r)** *m* fellow man
nachstehend *a* following ● *adv* below
Nächst|enliebe *f* charity. **n~ens** *adv* shortly. **n~gelegen** *a* nearest
nachsuchen *vi sep* (*haben*) search; **n~ um** request
Nacht *f* **-,⸚e** night; **über/bei N~** overnight/at night; **morgen N~** tomorrow night; **heute N~** tonight; (*letzte Nacht*) last night; **gestern N~** last night; (*vorletzte Nacht*) the night before last. **N~dienst** *m* night duty
Nachteil *m* disadvantage; **zum N~** to the detriment (*gen* of)
Nacht|falter *m* moth. **N~hemd** *nt* night-dress; (*Männer-*) night-shirt
Nachtigall *f* **-, -en** nightingale
Nachtisch *m* dessert
Nachtklub *m* night-club
nächtlich *a* nocturnal, night ...
Nacht|lokal *nt* night-club. **N~mahl** *nt* (*Aust*) supper
Nachtrag *m* postscript; (*Ergänzung*) supplement. **n~en**† *vt sep* add; **jdm etw n~en** (*fig*) bear a grudge against s.o. for sth. **n~end** *a* vindictive; **n~end sein** bear grudges
nachträglich *a* subsequent, later; (*verspätet*) belated ● *adv*

later; (*nachher*) afterwards; (*verspätet*) belatedly

Nacht|ruhe *f* night's rest; **angenehme N~ruhe!** sleep well! **n~s** *adv* at night; **2 Uhr n~s** 2 o'clock in the morning. **N~schicht** *f* night-shift. **N~tisch** *m* bedside table. **N~tischlampe** *f* bedside lamp. **N~topf** *m* chamber-pot. **N~wächter** *m* night-watchman. **N~zeit** *f* night-time

Nachuntersuchung *f* check-up

Nachwahl *f* by-election

Nachweis *m* **-es, -e** proof. **n~bar** *a* demonstrable. **n~en†** *vt sep* prove; (*aufzeigen*) show; (*vermitteln*) give details of; **jdm nichts n~en können** have no proof against s.o.

Nachwelt *f* posterity

Nachwirkung *f* after-effect

Nachwuchs *m* new generation; (🅿 *Kinder*) offspring. **N~spieler** *m* young player

nachzahlen *vt/i sep* (*haben*) pay extra; (*später zahlen*) pay later; **Steuern n~** pay tax arrears

nachzählen *vt/i sep* (*haben*) count again; (*prüfen*) check

Nachzahlung *f* extra/later payment; (*Gehalts-*) back-payment

nachzeichnen *vt sep* copy

Nachzügler *m* **-s,-** latecomer; (*Zurückgebliebener*) straggler

Nacken *m* **-s,-** nape *or* back of the neck

nackt *a* naked; (*bloß, kahl*) bare; <*Wahrheit*> plain. **N~heit** *f* **-** nakedness, nudity. **N~kultur** *f* nudism. **N~schnecke** *f* slug

Nadel *f* **-, -n** needle; (*Häkel-*) hook; (*Schmuck-, Hut-*) pin. **N~arbeit** *f* needlework. **N~baum** *m* conifer. **N~stich** *m* stitch; (*fig*) pinprick. **N~wald** *m* coniferous forest

Nagel *m* **-s,⸚** nail. **N~haut** *f* cuticle. **N~lack** *m* nail varnish. **n~n** *vt* nail. **n~neu** *a* brand-new

nagen *vt/i* (*haben*) gnaw (**an** + *dat* at); **n~d** (*fig*) nagging

Nagetier *nt* rodent

nah *a, adv & prep* = **nahe**

Näharbeit *f* sewing

Nahaufnahme *f* close-up

nahe *a* nearby; (*zeitlich*) imminent; (*eng*) close; **der N~ Osten** the Middle East; **in n~r Zukunft** in the near future; **von n~m** [from] close to; **n~ sein** be close (*dat* to) ● *adv* near, close; <*verwandt*> closely; **n~ an** (+ *acc/dat*) near [to], close to; **n~ daran sein, etw zu tun** nearly do sth; **n~ liegen** be close; (*fig*) be highly likely; **n~ legen** (*fig*) recommend (**dat** to); **jdm n~ legen, etw zu tun** urge s.o. to do sth; **jdm n~ gehen** (*fig*) affect s.o. deeply; **jdm zu n~ treten** (*fig*) offend s.o. ● *prep* (+ *dat*) near [to], close to

Nähe *f* **-** nearness, proximity; **aus der N~** [from] close to; **in der N~** near *or* close by

nahe|gehen* *vi sep* (*sein*) **n~ gehen**, *s.* **nahe**. **n~legen*** *vt sep* **n~ legen**, *s.* **nahe**. **n~liegen*** *vi sep* (*haben*) **n~ liegen**, *s.* **nahe**

nähen *vt/i* (*haben*) sew; (*anfertigen*) make; (*Med*) stitch [up]

näher *a* closer; <*Weg*> shorter; <*Einzelheiten*> further ● *adv* closer; (*genauer*) more closely; **n~ kommen** come closer; (*fig*) get closer (**dat** to); **sich n~ erkundigen** make further enquiries; **n~ an** (+ *acc/dat*) nearer [to], closer to ● *prep* (+ *dat*) nearer [to], closer to. **N~e[s]** *nt* [further] details *pl*. **n~n (sich)** *vr* approach

nahezu *adv* almost
Nähgarn *nt* [sewing] cotton
Nahkampf *m* close combat
Näh|maschine *f* sewing machine. **N~nadel** *f* sewing-needle
nähren *vt* feed; (*fig*) nurture
nahrhaft *a* nutritious
Nährstoff *m* nutrient
Nahrung *f* - food, nourishment. **N~smittel** *nt* food
Nährwert *m* nutritional value
Naht *f* -,"e seam; (*Med*) suture. **n~los** *a* seamless
Nahverkehr *m* local service
Nähzeug *nt* sewing; (*Zubehör*) sewing kit
naiv /na'i:f/ *a* naïve. **N~ität** /-vi'tɛ:t/ *f* - naïvety
Name *m* **-ns, -n** name; **im N~n** (+ *gen*) in the name of; <*handeln*> on behalf of. **n~nlos** *a* nameless; (*unbekannt*) unknown, anonymous. **N~nstag** *m* name-day. **N~nsvetter** *m* namesake. **N~nszug** *m* signature. **n~ntlich** *adv* by name; (*besonders*) especially
namhaft *a* noted; (*ansehnlich*) considerable; **n~ machen** name
nämlich *adv* (*und zwar*) namely; (*denn*) because
nanu *int* hallo
Napf *m* **-[e]s,"e** bowl
Narbe *f* **-, -n** scar
Narkose *f* **-, -n** general anaesthetic. **N~arzt** *m* anaesthetist. **N~mittel** *nt* anaesthetic
Narr *m* **-en, -en** fool; **zum N~en halten** make a fool of. **n~en** *vt* fool
Närr|in *f* **-, -nen** fool. **n~isch** *a* foolish; (! *verrückt*) crazy (**auf** + *acc* about)
Narzisse *f* **-, -n** narcissus
naschen *vt/i* (*haben*) nibble (**an** + *dat* at)
Nase *f* **-, -n** nose
näseln *vi* (*haben*) speak through one's nose; **n~d** nasal
Nasen|bluten *nt* **-s** nosebleed. **N~loch** *nt* nostril
Nashorn *nt* rhinoceros
nass *a* wet
Nässe *f* - wet; wetness. **n~n** *vt* wet
Nation /na'tsio:n/ *f* **-, -en** nation. **n~al** *a* national. **N~alhymne** *f* national anthem. **N~alismus** *m* - nationalism. **N~alität** *f* **-, -en** nationality. **N~alspieler** *m* international
Natrium *nt* **-s** sodium
Natron *nt* **-s doppeltkohlensaures N~** bicarbonate of soda
Natter *f* **-, -n** snake; (*Gift-*) viper
Natur *f* **-, -en** nature; **von N~ aus** by nature. **n~alisieren** *vt* naturalize. **N~alisierung** *f* **-, -en** naturalization
Naturell *nt* **-s, -e** disposition
Natur|erscheinung *f* natural phenomenon. **N~forscher** *m* naturalist. **N~kunde** *f* natural history
natürlich *a* natural ● *adv* naturally; (*selbstverständlich*) of course. **N~keit** *f* - naturalness
natur|rein *a* pure. **N~schutz** *m* nature conservation; **unter N~schutz stehen** be protected. **N~schutzgebiet** *nt* nature reserve. **N~wissenschaft** *f* [natural] science. **N~wissenschaftler** *m* scientist
nautisch *a* nautical
Navigation /-'tsio:n/ *f* - navigation
Nazi *m* **-s, -s** Nazi
n.Chr. *abbr* (**nach Christus**) AD
Nebel *m* **-s,-** fog; (*leicht*) mist

neben *prep* (+ *dat/acc*) next to, beside; (+ *dat*) (*außer*) apart from. **n~an** *adv* next door
Neben|anschluss *m* (*Teleph*) extension. **N~ausgaben** *fpl* incidental expenses
nebenbei *adv* in addition; (*beiläufig*) casually
Neben|bemerkung *f* passing remark. **N~beruf** *m* second job
nebeneinander *adv* next to each other, side by side
Neben|eingang *m* side entrance. **N~fach** *nt* (*Univ*) subsidiary subject. **N~fluss** *m* tributary
nebenher *adv* in addition
nebenhin *adv* casually
Neben|höhle *f* sinus. **N~kosten** *pl* additional costs. **N~produkt** *nt* by-product. **N~rolle** *f* supporting role; (*Kleine*) minor role. **N~sache** *f* unimportant matter. **n~sächlich** *a* unimportant. **N~satz** *m* subordinate clause. **N~straße** *f* minor road; (*Seiten-*) side street. **N~wirkung** *f* side-effect. **N~zimmer** *nt* room next door
neblig *a* foggy; (*leicht*) misty
neck|en *vt* tease. **N~erei** *f* - teasing. **n~isch** *a* teasing
Neffe *m* **-n, -n** nephew
negativ *a* negative. **N~** *nt* **-s, -e** (*Phot*) negative
Neger *m* **-s,-** Negro
nehmen† *vt* take (*dat* from); **sich** (*dat*) **etw n~** take sth; help oneself to <*Essen*>
Neid *m* **-[e]s** envy, jealousy. **n~isch** *a* envious, jealous (**auf** + *acc* of); **auf jdn n~isch sein** envy s.o.
neig|en *vt* incline; (*zur Seite*) tilt; (*beugen*) bend; **sich n~en** incline; <*Boden:*> slope; <*Person:*> bend (**über** + *acc* over) ● *vi* (*haben*) **n~en zu** (*fig*) have a tendency towards; be prone to <*Krankheit*>; incline towards <*Ansicht*>; **dazu n~en, etw zu tun** tend to do sth. **N~ung** *f* **-, -en** inclination; (*Gefälle*) slope; (*fig*) tendency
nein *adv*, **N~** *nt* **-s** no
Nektar *m* **-s** nectar
Nelke *f* **-, -n** carnation; (*Culin*) clove
nenn|en† *vt* call; (*taufen*) name; (*angeben*) give; (*erwähnen*) mention; **sich n~en** call oneself. **n~enswert** *a* significant
Neon *nt* **-s** neon. **N~beleuchtung** *f* fluorescent lighting
Nerv *m* **-s, -en** /-fən/ nerve; **die N~en verlieren** lose control of oneself. **n~en** *vt* **jdn n~en** ☒ get on s.o.'s nerves. **N~enarzt** *m* neurologist. **n~enaufreibend** *a* nerve-racking. **N~enkitzel** *m* ! thrill. **N~ensystem** *nt* nervous system. **N~enzusammenbruch** *m* nervous breakdown
nervös *a* nervy, edgy; (*Med*) nervous; **n~ sein** be on edge
Nervosität *f* - nerviness, edginess
Nerz *m* **-es, -e** mink
Nessel *f* **-, -n** nettle
Nest *nt* **-[e]s, -er** nest; (! *Ort*) small place
nett *a* nice; (*freundlich*) kind
netto *adv* net
Netz *nt* **-es, -e** net; (*Einkaufs-*) string bag; (*Spinnen-*) web; (*auf Landkarte*) grid; (*System*) network; (*Electr*) mains *pl*. **N~haut** *f* retina. **N~karte** *f* area season ticket. **N~werk** *nt* network
neu *a* new; (*modern*) modern; **wie neu** as good as new; **das ist mir neu** it's news to me; **von n~em** all over again ● *adv* newly;

(*gerade erst*) only just; (*erneut*) again; **etw neu schreiben** rewrite sth; **neu vermähltes Paar** newly-weds *pl*. **N~auflage** *f* new edition; (*unverändert*) reprint. **N~bau** *m* (*pl* **-ten**) new house/building

Neu|e(r) *m/f* new person, newcomer; (*Schüler*) new boy/girl. **N~e(s)** *nt* **das N~e** the new; **etwas N~es** something new; (*Neuigkeit*) a piece of news; **was gibts N~es?** what's the news?

neuer|dings *adv* [just] recently. **N~ung** *f* **-, -en** innovation

neuest|e(r,s) *a* newest; (*letzte*) latest; **seit n~em** just recently. **N~e** *nt* **das N~e** the latest thing; (*Neuigkeit*) the latest news

neugeboren *a* newborn

Neugier, Neugierde *f* - curiosity; (*Wissbegierde*) inquisitiveness

neugierig *a* curious (**auf** + *acc* about); (*wissbegierig*) inquisitive

Neuheit *f* **-, -en** novelty; newness

Neuigkeit *f* **-, -en** piece of news; **N~en** news *sg*

Neujahr *nt* New Year's Day; **über N~** over the New Year

neulich *adv* the other day

Neumond *m* new moon

neun *inv a*, **N~** *f* **-, -en** nine. **n~te(r,s)** *a* ninth. **n~zehn** *inv a* nineteen. **n~zehnte(r,s)** *a* nineteenth. **n~zig** *inv a* ninety. **n~zigste(r,s)** *a* ninetieth

Neuralgie *f* **-, -n** neuralgia

neureich *a* nouveau riche

Neurologe *m* **-n, -n** neurologist

Neurose *f* **-, -n** neurosis

Neuschnee *m* fresh snow

Neuseeland *nt* **-s** New Zealand

neuste(r,s) *a* = **neueste(r,s)**

neutral *a* neutral. **N~ität** *f* - neutrality

Neutrum *nt* **-s, -tra** neuter noun

neu|vermählt* *a* **n~ vermählt**, *s.* **neu**. **N~zeit** *f* modern times *pl*

nicht *adv* not; **ich kann n~** I cannot *or* can't; **er ist n~ gekommen** he hasn't come; **bitte n~!** please don't! **n~ berühren!** do not touch! **du kennst ihn doch, n~?** you know him, don't you?

Nichte *f* **-, -n** niece

Nichtraucher *m* non-smoker

nichts *pron & a* nothing; **n~ mehr** no more; **n~ ahnend** unsuspecting; **n~ sagend** meaningless; (*uninteressant*) nondescript. **N~** *nt* - nothingness; (*fig: Leere*) void

Nichtschwimmer *m* non-swimmer

nichts|nutzig *a* good-for-nothing; (! *unartig*) naughty. **n~sagend*** *a* **n~ sagend**, *s.* **nichts**. **N~tun** *nt* **-s** idleness

Nickel *nt* **-s** nickel

nicken *vi* (*haben*) nod

Nickerchen *nt* **-s,-**, ! nap

nie *adv* never

nieder *a* low ● *adv* down. **n~brennen**† *vt/i sep* (*sein*) burn down. **N~deutsch** *nt* Low German. **N~gang** *m* (*fig*) decline. **n~gedrückt** *a* (*fig*) depressed. **n~geschlagen** *a* dejected, despondent. **N~kunft** *f* **-,¨e** confinement. **N~lage** *f* defeat

Niederlande (die) *pl* the Netherlands

Niederländ|er *m* **-s,-** Dutchman; **die N~er** the Dutch *pl*. **N~erin** *f* **-, -nen** Dutchwoman. **n~isch** *a* Dutch

nieder|lassen† *vt sep* let down; **sich n~lassen** settle; (*sich setzen*) sit down. **N~lassung** *f* **-, -en** settlement; (*Zweigstelle*) branch. **n~legen** *vt sep* put *or* lay down; resign <*Amt*>; **die**

Arbeit n~legen go on strike. **n~metzeln** *vt sep* massacre. **N~sachsen** *nt* Lower Saxony. **N~schlag** *m* precipitation; (*Regen*) rainfall; (*radioaktiver*) fallout. **n~schlagen**† *vt sep* knock down; lower <*Augen*>; (*unterdrücken*) crush. **n~schmettern** *vt sep* (*fig*) shatter. **n~setzen** *vt sep* put *or* set down; **sich n~setzen** sit down. **n~strecken** *vt sep* fell; (*durch Schuss*) gun down. **n~trächtig** *a* base, vile. **n~walzen** *vt sep* flatten

niedlich *a* pretty; sweet

niedrig *a* low; (*fig: gemein*) base ● *adv* low

niemals *adv* never

niemand *pron* nobody, no one

Niere *f* **-, -n** kidney; **künstliche N~** kidney machine

niesel|n *vi* (*haben*) drizzle. **N~regen** *m* drizzle

niesen *vi* (*haben*) sneeze. **N~** *nt* **-s** sneezing; (*Nieser*) sneeze

Niete¹ *f* **-, -n** rivet; (*an Jeans*) stud

Niete² *f* **-, -n** blank; [!] failure

nieten *vt* rivet

Nikotin *nt* **-s** nicotine

Nil *m* **-[s]** Nile. **N~pferd** *nt* hippopotamus

nimmer *adv* (*SGer*) not any more; **nie und n~** never

nirgend|s, n~wo *adv* nowhere

Nische *f* **-, -n** recess, niche

nisten *vi* (*haben*) nest

Nitrat *nt* **-[e]s, -e** nitrate

Niveau /ni'vo:/ *nt* **-s, -s** level; (*geistig, künstlerisch*) standard

nix *adv* [!] nothing

Nixe *f* **-, -n** mermaid

nobel *a* noble; ([!] *luxuriös*) luxurious; ([!] *großzügig*) generous

noch *adv* still; (*zusätzlich*) as well; (*mit Komparativ*) even; **n~ nicht** not yet; **gerade n~** only just; **n~ immer** *od* **immer n~** still; **n~ letzte Woche** only last week; **wer n~?** who else? **n~ etwas** something else; (*Frage*) anything else? **n~ einmal** again; **n~ ein Bier** another beer; **n~ größer** even bigger; **n~ so sehr** however much ● *conj* **weder ... n~** neither ... nor

nochmals *adv* again

Nomad|e *m* **-n, -n** nomad. **n~isch** *a* nomadic

nominier|en *vt* nominate. **N~ung** *f* **-, -en** nomination

Nonne *f* **-, -n** nun. **N~nkloster** *nt* convent

Nonstopflug *m* direct flight

Nord *m* **-[e]s** north. **N~amerika** *nt* North America

Norden *m* **-s** north

nordisch *a* Nordic

nördlich *a* northern; <*Richtung*> northerly ● *adv & prep* (+ *gen*) **n~ [von] der Stadt** [to the] north of the town

Nordosten *m* north-east

Nord|pol *m* North Pole. **N~see** *f* **-** North Sea. **N~westen** *m* north-west

Nörgelei *f* **-, -en** grumbling

nörgeln *vi* (*haben*) grumble

Norm *f* **-, -en** norm; (*Techn*) standard; (*Soll*) quota

normal *a* normal. **n~erweise** *adv* normally

normen *vt* standardize

Norwe|gen *nt* **-s** Norway. **N~ger(in)** *m* **-s,-** (*f* **-, -nen**) Norwegian. **n~gisch** *a* Norwegian

Nost|algie *f* **-** nostalgia. **n~algisch** *a* nostalgic

Not *f* **-,¨-e** need; (*Notwendigkeit*) necessity; (*Entbehrung*) hardship; (*seelisch*) trouble; **Not leiden** be in need, suffer hardship; **Not leidende**

Menschen needy people; **zur Not** if need be; (*äußerstenfalls*) at a pinch

Notar *m* **-s, -e** notary public

Not|arzt *m* emergency doctor. **N~ausgang** *m* emergency exit. **N~behelf** *m* **-[e]s, -e** makeshift. **N~bremse** *f* emergency brake. **N~dienst** *m* **N~dienst haben** be on call

Note *f* **-, -n** note; (*Zensur*) mark; **ganze/halbe N~** (*Mus*) semibreve/minim; **N~n lesen** read music; **persönliche N~** personal touch. **N~nblatt** *nt* sheet of music. **N~nschlüssel** *m* clef

Notfall *m* emergency; **für den N~** just in case. **n~s** *adv* if need be

notieren *vt* note down; (*Comm*) quote; **sich** (*dat*) **etw n~** make a note of sth

nötig *a* necessary; **n~ haben** need; **das N~ste** the essentials *pl* ● *adv* urgently. **n~enfalls** *adv* if need be. **N~ung** *f* **-** coercion

Notiz *f* **-, -en** note; (*Zeitungs-*) item; **[keine] N~ nehmen von** take [no] notice of. **N~buch** *nt* notebook. **N~kalender** *m* diary

Not|lage *f* plight. **n~landen** *vi* (*sein*) make a forced landing. **N~landung** *f* forced landing. **n~leidend*** *a* **Not leidend**, *s.* **Not**. **N~lösung** *f* stopgap

Not|ruf *m* emergency call; (*Naut, Aviat*) distress call; (*Nummer*) emergency services number. **N~signal** *nt* distress signal. **N~stand** *m* state of emergency. **N~unterkunft** *f* emergency accommodation. **N~wehr** *f* **-** (*Jur*) self-defence

notwendig *a* necessary; essential ● *adv* urgently. **N~keit** *f* **-, -en** necessity

Notzucht *f* **-** (*Jur*) rape

Nougat /'nu:gat/ *m & nt* **-s** nougat

Novelle *f* **-, -n** novella; (*Pol*) amendment

November *m* **-s,-** November

Novize *m* **-n, -n**, **Novizin** *f* **-, -nen** (*Relig*) novice

Nu *m* **im Nu** [!] in a flash

nüchtern *a* sober; (*sachlich*) matter-of-fact; (*schmucklos*) bare; (*ohne Würze*) bland; **auf n~en Magen** on an empty stomach

Nudel *f* **-, -n** piece of pasta; **N~n** pasta *sg*; (*Band-*) noodles. **N~holz** *nt* rolling-pin

Nudist *m* **-en, -en** nudist

nuklear *a* nuclear

null *inv a* zero, nought; (*Teleph*) O; (*Sport*) nil; (*Tennis*) love; **n~ Fehler** no mistakes; **n~ und nichtig** (*Jur*) null and void. **N~** *f* **-, -en** nought, zero; (*fig: Person*) nonentity. **N~punkt** *m* zero

numerieren* *vt s.* **nummerieren**

Nummer *f* **-, -n** number; (*Ausgabe*) issue; (*Darbietung*) item; (*Zirkus-*) act; (*Größe*) size. **n~ieren** *vt* number. **N~nschild** *nt* number plate

nun *adv* now; (*na*) well; (*halt*) just; **nun gut!** very well then!

nur *adv* only, just; **wo kann sie nur sein?** wherever can she be? **er soll es nur versuchen!** just let him try!

Nürnberg *nt* **-s** Nuremberg

nuscheln *vt/i* (*haben*) mumble

Nuss *f* **-,¨e** nut. **N~knacker** *m* **-s,-** nutcrackers *pl*

Nüstern *fpl* nostrils

Nut *f* **-, -en**, **Nute** *f* **-, -n** groove

Nutte *f* **-, -n** ☒ tart ☒

nutz|bar *a* usable; **n~bar machen** utilize; cultivate <*Boden*>. **n~bringend** *a* profitable

nutzen *vt* use, utilize; (*aus-*) take advantage of ● *vi* (*haben*) =

nützen. N~ *m* **-s** benefit; (*Comm*) profit; **N~ ziehen aus** benefit from; **von N~ sein** be useful

nützen *vi* (*haben*) be useful *or* of use (*dat* to); <*Mittel:*> be effective; **nichts n~** be useless *or* no use; **was nützt mir das?** what good is that to me? ● *vt* = **nutzen**

nützlich *a* useful. **N~keit** *f* - usefulness

nutz|los *a* useless; (*vergeblich*) vain. **N~losigkeit** *f* - uselessness. **N~ung** *f* - use, utilization

Nylon /'nailɔn/ *nt* **-s** nylon

Nymphe /'nʏmfə/ *f* **-, -n** nymph

Oo

o *int* **o ja/nein!** oh yes/no!

Oase *f* **-, -n** oasis

ob *conj* whether; **ob reich, ob arm** rich or poor; **und ob!** [!] you bet!

Obacht *f* **O~ geben** pay attention; **O~!** look out!

Obdach *nt* **-[e]s** shelter. **o~los** *a* homeless. **O~lose(r)** *m/f* homeless person; **die O~losen** the homeless *pl*

Obduktion /-'tsio:n/ *f* **-, -en** post-mortem

O-Beine *ntpl* [!] bow-legs, bandy legs

oben *adv* at the top; (*auf der Oberseite*) on top; (*eine Treppe hoch*) upstairs; (*im Text*) above; **da o~** up there; **o~ im Norden** up in the north; **siehe o~** see above; **o~ auf** (+ *acc/dat*) on top of; **nach o~** up[wards]; (*die Treppe hinauf*) upstairs; **von o~** from above/upstairs; **von o~ bis unten** from top to bottom/ <*Person*> to toe; **jdn von o~ bis unten mustern** look s.o. up and down; **o~ erwähnt** *od* **genannt** above-mentioned. **o~drein** *adv* on top of that

Ober *m* **-s,-** waiter

Ober|arm *m* upper arm. **O~arzt** *m* ≈ senior registrar. **O~deck** *nt* upper deck. **o~e(r,s)** *a* upper; (*höhere*) higher. **O~fläche** *f* surface. **o~flächlich** *a* superficial. **O~geschoss** *nt* upper storey. **o~halb** *adv & prep* (+ *gen*) above. **O~haupt** *nt* (*fig*) head. **O~haus** *nt* (*Pol*) upper house; (*in UK*) House of Lords. **O~hemd** *nt* [man's] shirt. **o~irdisch** *a* surface ... ● *adv* above ground. **O~kiefer** *m* upper jaw. **O~körper** *m* upper part of the body. **O~leutnant** *m* lieutenant. **O~lippe** *f* upper lip

Obers *nt* - (*Aust*) cream

Ober|schenkel *m* thigh. **O~schule** *f* grammar school. **O~seite** *f* upper/(*rechte Seite*) right side

Oberst *m* **-en & -s, -en** colonel

oberste(r,s) *a* top; (*höchste*) highest; <*Befehlshaber, Gerichtshof*> supreme; (*wichtigste*) first

Ober|stimme *f* treble. **O~teil** *nt* top. **O~weite** *f* chest/(*der Frau*) bust size

obgleich *conj* although

Obhut *f* - care

obig *a* above

Objekt *nt* **-[e]s, -e** object; (*Haus, Grundstück*) property

Objektiv *nt* **-s, -e** lens. **o~** *a* objective. **O~ität** *f* - objectivity

Oblate *f* **-, -n** (*Relig*) wafer

Obmann *m* (*pl* **-männer**) [jury] foreman; (*Sport*) referee
Oboe /o'bo:ə/ *f* **-, -n** oboe
Obrigkeit *f* **-** authorities *pl*
obschon *conj* although
Observatorium *nt* **-s, -ien** observatory
obskur *a* obscure; dubious
Obst *nt* **-es** (*coll*) fruit. **O~baum** *m* fruit-tree. **O~garten** *m* orchard. **O~händler** *m* fruiterer
obszön *a* obscene
O-Bus *m* trolley bus
obwohl *conj* although
Ochse *m* **-n, -n** ox
öde *a* desolate; (*unfruchtbar*) barren; (*langweilig*) dull. **Öde** *f* **-** desolation; barrenness; dullness
oder *conj* or; **du kennst ihn doch, o~?** you know him, don't you?
Ofen *m* **-s,¨** stove; (*Heiz-*) heater; (*Back-*) oven; (*Techn*) furnace
offen *a* open; <*Haar*> loose; <*Flamme*> naked; (*o~herzig*) frank; (*o~ gezeigt*) overt; (*unentschieden*) unsettled; **o~e Stelle** vacancy; **Wein o~ verkaufen** sell wine by the glass; **o~ bleiben** remain open; **o~ halten** hold open <*Tür*>; keep open <*Mund, Augen*>; **o~ lassen** leave open; leave vacant <*Stelle*>; **o~ stehen** be open; <*Rechnung:*> be outstanding; **jdm o~ stehen** (*fig*) be open to s.o.; *adv* **o~ gesagt** *od* **gestanden** to be honest. **o~bar** *a* obvious ● *adv* apparently. **o~baren** *vt* reveal. **O~barung** *f* **-, -en** revelation. **O~heit** *f* **-** frankness, openness. **o~sichtlich** *a* obvious
offenstehen* *vi sep* (*haben*) **offen stehen**, *s.* **offen**
öffentlich *a* public. **Ö~keit** *f* **-** public; **in aller Ö~keit** in public, publicly
Offerte *f* **-, -n** (*Comm*) offer
offiziell *a* official
Offizier *m* **-s, -e** (*Mil*) officer
öffn|en *vt/i* (*haben*) open; **sich ö~en** open. **Ö~er** *m* **-s,-** opener. **Ö~ung** *f* **-, -en** opening. **Ö~ungszeiten** *fpl* opening hours
oft *adv* often
öfter *adv* quite often. **ö~e(r,s)** *a* frequent; **des Ö~en** frequently. **ö~s** *adv* 🅸 quite often
oh *int* oh!
ohne *prep* (+ *acc*) without; **o~ mich!** count me out! **oben o~** topless ● *conj* **o~ zu überlegen** without thinking; **o~ dass ich es merkte** without my noticing it. **o~dies** *adv* anyway. **o~gleichen** *pred a* unparalleled. **o~hin** *adv* anyway
Ohn|macht *f* **-, -en** faint; (*fig*) powerlessness; **in O~macht fallen** faint. **o~mächtig** *a* unconscious; (*fig*) powerless; **o~mächtig werden** faint
Ohr *nt* **-[e]s, -en** ear
Öhr *nt* **-[e]s, -e** eye
Ohren|schmalz *nt* ear-wax. **O~schmerzen** *mpl* earache *sg*
Ohrfeige *f* slap in the face. **o~n** *vt* **jdn o~n** slap s.o.'s face
Ohr|läppchen *nt* **-s,-** ear-lobe. **O~ring** *m* ear-ring. **O~wurm** *m* earwig
oje *int* oh dear!
okay /o'ke:/ *a* & *adv* 🅸 OK
Öko|logie *f* **-** ecology. **ö~logisch** *a* ecological. **Ö~nomie** *f* **-** economy; (*Wissenschaft*) economics *sg*. **ö~nomisch** *a* economic; (*sparsam*) economical
Oktave *f* **-, -n** octave
Oktober *m* **-s,-** October
ökumenisch *a* ecumenical
Öl *nt* **-[e]s, -e** oil; **in Öl malen** paint in oils. **Ölbaum** *m* olivetree. **ölen** *vt* oil. **Ölfarbe** *f* oil-paint. **Ölfeld** *nt* oilfield.

Ölgemälde *nt* oil-painting. **ölig** *a* oily

Oliv|e *f* -, -n olive. **O~enöl** *nt* olive oil

Ölmessstab *m* dip-stick.

Ölsardinen *fpl* sardines in oil.

Ölstand *m* oil-level. **Öltanker** *m* oil-tanker. **Ölteppich** *m* oil-slick

Olympiade *f* -, -n Olympic Games *pl*, Olympics *pl*

Olymp|iasieger(in) /o'lympia-/ *m(f)* Olympic champion. **o~isch** *a* Olympic; **O~ische Spiele** Olympic Games

Ölzeug *nt* oilskins *pl*

Oma *f* -, -s [!] granny

Omnibus *m* bus; (*Reise-*) coach

onanieren *vi* (*haben*) masturbate

Onkel *m* -s,- uncle

Opa *m* -s, -s [!] grandad

Opal *m* -s, -e opal

Oper *f* -, -n opera

Operation /-'tsio:n/ *f* -, -en operation. **O~ssaal** *m* operating theatre

Operette *f* -, -n operetta

operieren *vt* operate on <*Patient, Herz*>; **sich o~ lassen** have an operation ● *vi* (*haben*) operate

Opernglas *nt* opera-glasses *pl*

Opfer *nt* -s,- sacrifice; (*eines Unglücks*) victim; **ein O~ bringen** make a sacrifice; **jdm/etw zum O~ fallen** fall victim to s.o./sth. **o~n** *vt* sacrifice

Opium *nt* -s opium

Opposition /-'tsio:n/ *f* - opposition. **O~spartei** *f* opposition party

Optik *f* - optics *sg*; ([!] *Objektiv*) lens. **O~er** *m* -s,- optician

optimal *a* optimum

Optimis|mus *m* - optimism. **O~t** *m* -en, -en optimist. **o~tisch** *a* optimistic

optisch *a* optical; <*Eindruck*> visual

Orakel *nt* -s,- oracle

Orange /o'rã:ʒə/ *f* -, -n orange. **o~** *inv a* orange. **O~ade** /orã'ʒa:də/ *f* -, -n orangeade. **O~nmarmelade** *f* [orange] marmalade

Oratorium *nt* -s, -ien oratorio

Orchester /ɔr'kɛstɐ/ *nt* -s,- orchestra

Orchidee /ɔrçi'de:ə/ *f* -, -n orchid

Orden *m* -s,- (*Ritter-, Kloster-*) order; (*Auszeichnung*) medal, decoration

ordentlich *a* neat, tidy; (*anständig*) respectable; (*ordnungsgemäß*, [!] *richtig*) proper; <*Mitglied, Versammlung*> ordinary; ([!] *gut*) decent; ([!] *gehörig*) good

Order *f* -, -s & -n order

ordinär *a* common

Ordination /-'tsio:n/ *f* -, -en (*Relig*) ordination; (*Aust*) surgery

ordn|en *vt* put in order; tidy; (*an-*) arrange. **O~er** *m* -s,- steward; (*Akten-*) file

Ordnung *f* - order; **O~ machen** tidy up; **in O~ bringen** put in order; (*aufräumen*) tidy; (*reparieren*) mend; (*fig*) put right; **in O~ sein** be in order; (*ordentlich sein*) be tidy; (*fig*) be all right; **[geht] in O~!** OK! **o~sgemäß** *a* proper. **O~sstrafe** *f* (*Jur*) fine. **o~swidrig** *a* improper

Ordonnanz, Ordonanz *f* -, -en (*Mil*) orderly

Organ *nt* -s, -e organ; voice

Organisation /-'tsio:n/ *f* -, -en organization

organisch *a* organic

organisieren *vt* organize; ([!] *beschaffen*) get [hold of]

Organismus *m* -, -men organism; (*System*) system

Organspenderkarte *f* donor card
Orgasmus *m* **-, -men** orgasm
Orgel *f* **-, -n** (*Mus*) organ. **O~pfeife** *f* organ-pipe
Orgie /ˈɔrgi̯ə/ *f* **-, -n** orgy
Orien|t /ˈo:ri̯ɛnt/ *m* **-s** Orient. **o~talisch** *a* Oriental
orientier|en /ori̯ɛnˈti:rən/ *vt* inform (**über** + *acc* about); **sich o~en** get one's bearings, orientate oneself; (*unterrichten*) inform oneself (**über** + *acc* about). **O~ung** *f* **-** orientation; **die O~ung verlieren** lose one's bearings
original *a* original. **O~** *nt* **-s, -e** original. **O~übertragung** *f* live transmission
originell *a* original; (*eigenartig*) unusual
Orkan *m* **-s, -e** hurricane
Ornament *nt* **-[e]s, -e** ornament
Ort *m* **-[e]s, -e** place; (*Ortschaft*) [small] town; **am Ort** locally; **am Ort des Verbrechens** at the scene of the crime
ortho|dox *a* orthodox. **O~graphie, O~grafie** *f* **-** spelling. **O~päde** *m* **-n, -n** orthopaedic specialist
örtlich *a* local
Ortschaft *f* **-, -en** [small] town; (*Dorf*) village; **geschlossene O~** (*Auto*) built-up area
Orts|gespräch *nt* (*Teleph*) local call. **O~verkehr** *m* local traffic. **O~zeit** *f* local time
Öse *f* **-, -n** eyelet; (*Schlinge*) loop; **Haken und Öse** hook and eye
Ost *m* **-[e]s** east
Osten *m* **-s** east; **nach O~** east
ostentativ *a* pointed
Osteopath *m* **-en, -en** osteopath
Oster|ei /ˈo:stɐʔai̯/ *nt* Easter egg. **O~fest** *nt* Easter. **O~glocke** *f* daffodil. **O~n** *nt* **-,-** Easter; **frohe O~n**! happy Easter!
Österreich *nt* **-s** Austria. **Ö~er** *m*, **-s,-**, **Ö~erin** *f* **-, -nen** Austrian. **ö~isch** *a* Austrian
östlich *a* eastern; <*Richtung*> easterly ● *adv & prep* (+ *gen*) **ö~ [von] der Stadt** [to the] east of the town
Ostsee *f* Baltic [Sea]
Otter[1] *m* **-s,-** otter
Otter[2] *f* **-, -n** adder
Ouverture /uvɛrˈty:rə/ *f* **-, -n** overture
oval *a* oval. **O~** *nt* **-s, -e** oval
Oxid, Oxyd *nt* **-[e]s, -e** oxide
Ozean *m* **-s, -e** ocean
Ozon *nt* **-s** ozone. **O~loch** *nt* hole in the ozone layer. **O~schicht** *f* ozone layer

Pp

paar *pron inv* **ein p~** a few; **ein p~ Mal** a few times; **alle p~ Tage** every few days. **P~** *nt* **-[e]s, -e** pair; (*Ehe-, Liebes-*) couple. **p~en** *vt* mate; (*verbinden*) combine; **sich p~en** mate. **P~ung** *f* **-, -en** mating. **p~weise** *adv* in pairs, in twos
Pacht *f* **-, -en** lease; (*P~summe*) rent. **p~en** *vt* lease
Pächter *m* **-s,-** lessee; (*eines Hofes*) tenant
Pachtvertrag *m* lease
Päckchen *nt* **-s,-** package, small packet
pack|en *vt/i* (*haben*) pack; (*ergreifen*) seize; (*fig: fesseln*) grip. **P~en** *m* **-s,-** bundle. **p~end** *a* (*fig*) gripping. **P~papier** *nt* [strong] wrapping

paper. **P~ung** *f* **-, -en** packet; (*Med*) pack
Pädagog|e *m* **-n, -n** educationalist; (*Lehrer*) teacher. **P~ik** *f* **-** educational science
Paddel *nt* **-s,-** paddle. **P~boot** *nt* canoe. **p~n** *vt/i* (*haben/sein*) paddle. **P~sport** *m* canoeing
Page /'pa:ʒə/ *m* **-n, -n** page
Paillette /pai̯'jɛtə/ *f* **-, -n** sequin
Paket *nt* **-[e]s, -e** packet; (*Post-*) parcel
Pakist|an *nt* **-s** Pakistan. **P~aner(in)** *m* **-s,-** (*f* **-, -nen**) Pakistani. **p~anisch** *a* Pakistani
Palast *m* **-[e]s,¨e** palace
Paläst|ina *nt* **-s** Palestine. **P~inenser(in)** *m* **-s,-** (*f* **-, -nen**) Palestinian. **p~inensisch** *a* Palestinian
Palette *f* **-, -n** palette
Palme *f* **-, -n** palm[-tree]
Pampelmuse *f* **-, -n** grapefruit
Panier|mehl *nt* (*Culin*) breadcrumbs *pl*. **p~t** *a* (*Culin*) breaded
Panik *f* **-** panic
Panne *f* **-, -n** breakdown; (*Reifen-*) flat tyre; (*Missgeschick*) mishap
Panther, Panter *m* **-s,-** panther
Pantine *f* **-, -n** [wooden] clog
Pantoffel *m* **-s, -n** slipper; mule
Pantomime¹ *f* **-, -n** mime
Pantomime² *m* **-n, -n** mime artist
Panzer *m* **-s,-** armour; (*Mil*) tank; (*Zool*) shell. **p~n** *vt* armourplate. **P~schrank** *m* safe
Papa /'papa, pa'pa:/ *m* **-s, -s** daddy
Papagei *m* **-s & -en, -en** parrot
Papier *nt* **-[e]s, -e** paper. **P~korb** *m* waste-paper basket. **P~schlange** *f* streamer. **P~waren** *fpl* stationery *sg*
Pappe *f* **-** cardboard
Pappel *f* **-, -n** poplar
pappig *a* 🅸 sticky
Papp|karton *m*, **P~schachtel** *f* cardboard box
Paprika *m* **-s, -[s]** [sweet] pepper; (*Gewürz*) paprika
Papst *m* **-[e]s,¨e** pope
päpstlich *a* papal
Parade *f* **-, -n** parade
Paradies *nt* **-es, -e** paradise
Paraffin *nt* **-s** paraffin
Paragraph, Paragraf *m* **-en, -en** section
parallel *a & adv* parallel. **P~e** *f* **-, -n** parallel
Paranuss *f* Brazil nut
Parasit *m* **-en, -en** parasite
parat *a* ready
Parcours /par'ku:ɐ̯/ *m* **-,-** /-[s], -s/ (*Sport*) course
Pardon /par'dõ:/ *int* sorry!
Parfüm *nt* **-s, -e & -s** perfume, scent. **p~iert** *a* perfumed, scented
parieren *vi* (*haben*) 🅸 obey
Park *m* **-s, -s** park. **p~en** *vt/i* (*haben*) park. **P~en** *nt* **-s** parking; '**P~en verboten**' 'no parking'
Parkett *nt* **-[e]s, -e** parquet floor; (*Theat*) stalls *pl*
Park|haus *nt* multi-storey car park. **P~kralle** *f* wheel clamp. **P~lücke** *f* parking space. **P~platz** *m* car park; parking space. **P~scheibe** *f* parking-disc. **P~schein** *m* car-park ticket. **P~uhr** *f* parking-meter. **P~verbot** *nt* parking ban; '**P~verbot**' 'no parking'
Parlament *nt* **-[e]s, -e** parliament. **p~arisch** *a* parliamentary
Parodie *f* **-, -n** parody
Parole *f* **-, -n** slogan; (*Mil*) password
Partei *f* **-, -en** (*Pol, Jur*) party; (*Miet-*) tenant; **für jdn P~**

ergreifen take s.o.'s part. **p~isch** *a* biased

Parterre /par'tɛr/ *nt* **-s, -s** ground floor; (*Theat*) rear stalls *pl*

Partie *f* **-, -n** part; (*Tennis, Schach*) game; (*Golf*) round; (*Comm*) batch; **eine gute P~ machen** marry well

Partikel *nt* **-s,-** particle

Partitur *f* **-, -en** (*Mus*) full score

Partizip *nt* **-s, -ien** /-i̯ən/ participle

Partner|(in) *m* **-s,-** (*f* **-, -nen**) partner. **P~schaft** *f* **-, -en** partnership. **P~stadt** *f* twin town

Party /'pa:ɐ̯ti/ *f* **-, -s** party

Parzelle *f* **-, -n** plot [of ground]

Pass *m* **-es, ¨e** passport; (*Geog, Sport*) pass

Passage /pa'sa:ʒə/ *f* **-, -n** passage; (*Einkaufs-*) shopping arcade

Passagier /pasa'ʒi:ɐ̯/ *m* **-s, -e** passenger

Passant(in) *m* **-en, -en** (*f* **-, -nen**) passer-by

Passe *f* **-, -n** yoke

passen *vi* (*haben*) fit; (*geeignet sein*) be right (**für** for); (*Sport*) pass the ball; (*aufgeben*) pass; **p~ zu** go [well] with; (*übereinstimmen*) match; **jdm p~** fit s.o.; (*gelegen sein*) suit s.o.; **[ich] passe** pass. **p~d** *a* suitable; (*angemessen*) appropriate; (*günstig*) convenient; (*übereinstimmend*) matching

passier|en *vt* pass; cross <*Grenze*>; (*Culin*) rub through a sieve ● *vi* (*sein*) happen (**jdm** to s.o.); **es ist ein Unglück p~t** there has been an accident. **P~schein** *m* pass

Passiv *nt* **-s, -e** (*Gram*) passive

Passstraße *f* pass

Paste *f* **-, -n** paste

Pastell *nt* **-[e]s, -e** pastel

Pastete *f* **-, -n** pie; (*Gänseleber-*) pâté

pasteurisieren /pastøri'zi:rən/ *vt* pasteurize

Pastor *m* **-s, -en** /-'to:rən/ pastor

Pate *m* **-n, -n** godfather; (*fig*) sponsor; **P~n** godparents. **P~nkind** *nt* godchild

Patent *nt* **-[e]s, -e** patent; (*Offiziers-*) commission. **p~** *a* [!] clever; <*Person*> resourceful. **p~ieren** *vt* patent

Pater *m* **-s,-** (*Relig*) Father

Patholog|e *m* **-n, -n** pathologist. **p~isch** *a* pathological

Patience /pa'si̯ã:s/ *f* **-, -n** patience

Patient(in) /pa'tsi̯ɛnt(ɪn)/ *m* **-en, -en** (*f* **-, -nen**) patient

Patin *f* **-, -nen** godmother

Patriot|(in) *m* **-en, -en** (*f* **-, -nen**) patriot. **p~isch** *a* patriotic. **P~ismus** *m* **-** patriotism

Patrone *f* **-, -n** cartridge

Patrouille /pa'trʊljə/ *f* **-, -n** patrol

Patsch|e *f* **in der P~e sitzen** [!] be in a jam. **p~nass** *a* [!] soaking wet

Patt *nt* **-s** stalemate

Patz|er *m* **-s,-** [!] slip. **p~ig** *a* [!] insolent

Pauk|e *f* **-, -n** kettledrum; **auf die P~e hauen** [!] have a good time; (*prahlen*) boast. **p~en** *vt/i* (*haben*) [!] swot

pauschal *a* all-inclusive; (*einheitlich*) flat-rate; (*fig*) sweeping <*Urteil*>; **p~e Summe** lump sum. **P~e** *f* **-, -n** lump sum. **P~reise** *f* package tour. **P~summe** *f* lump sum

Pause[1] *f* **-, -n** break; (*beim Sprechen*) pause; (*Theat*) interval; (*im Kino*) intermission; (*Mus*) rest; **P~ machen** have a break

Pause² *f* **-, -n** tracing. **p~n** *vt* trace
pausenlos *a* incessant
pausieren *vi* (*haben*) have a break; (*ausruhen*) rest
Pauspapier *nt* tracing-paper
Pavian *m* **-s, -e** baboon
Pavillon /ˈpavɪljõ/ *m* **-s, -s** pavilion
Pazifi|k *m* **-s** Pacific [Ocean]. **p~sch** *a* Pacific
Pazifist *m* **-en, -en** pacifist
Pech *nt* **-s** pitch; (*Unglück*) bad luck; **P~ haben** be unlucky
Pedal *nt* **-s, -e** pedal
Pedant *m* **-en, -en** pedant
Pediküre *f* **-, -n** pedicure
Pegel *m* **-s,-** level; (*Gerät*) water-level indicator. **P~stand** *m* [water] level
peilen *vt* take a bearing on
peinigen *vt* torment
peinlich *a* embarrassing, awkward; (*genau*) scrupulous; **es war mir sehr p~** I was very embarrassed
Peitsche *f* **-, -n** whip. **p~n** *vt* whip; (*fig*) lash ● *vi* (*sein*) lash (**an** + *acc* against). **P~nhieb** *m* lash
Pelikan *m* **-s, -e** pelican
Pell|e *f* **-, -n** skin. **p~en** *vt* peel; shell <*Ei*>; **sich p~en** peel
Pelz *m* **-es, -e** fur
Pendel *nt* **-s,-** pendulum. **p~n** *vi* (*haben*) swing ● *vi* (*sein*) commute. **P~verkehr** *m* shuttle-service; (*für Pendler*) commuter traffic
Pendler *m* **-s,-** commuter
penetrant *a* penetrating; (*fig*) obtrusive
Penis *m* **-, -se** penis
Penne *f* **-, -n** 🅇 school
Pension /pãˈzio:n/ *f* **-, -en** pension; (*Hotel*) guest-house; **bei voller/halber P~** with full/half board. **P~är(in)** *m* **-s, -e** (*f* **-, -nen**) pensioner. **P~at** *nt* **-[e]s, -e** boarding-school. **p~ieren** *vt* retire. **P~ierung** *f* - retirement
Pensum *nt* **-s** [allotted] work
Peperoni *f* **-,-** chilli
per *prep* (+ *acc*) by
Perfekt *nt* **-s** (*Gram*) perfect
Perfektion /-ˈtsio:n/ *f* - perfection
perforiert *a* perforated
Pergament *nt* **-[e]s, -e** parchment. **P~papier** *nt* grease-proof paper
Period|e *f* **-, -n** period. **p~isch** *a* periodic
Perl|e *f* **-, -n** pearl; (*Glas-, Holz-*) bead; (*Sekt-*) bubble. **P~mutt** *nt* **-s** mother-of-pearl
Pers|ien /-iən/ *nt* **-s** Persia. **p~isch** *a* Persian
Person *f* **-, -en** person; (*Theat*) character; **für vier P~en** for four people
Personal *nt* **-s** personnel, staff. **P~ausweis** *m* identity card. **P~chef** *m* personnel manager. **P~ien** /-iən/ *pl* personal particulars. **P~mangel** *m* staff shortage
persönlich *a* personal ● *adv* personally, in person. **P~keit** *f* **-, -en** personality
Perücke *f* **-, -n** wig
pervers *a* [sexually] perverted. **P~ion** *f* **-, -en** perversion
Pessimis|mus *m* - pessimism. **P~t** *m* **-en, -en** pessimist. **p~tisch** *a* pessimistic
Pest *f* - plague
Petersilie /-iə/ *f* - parsley
Petroleum /-leʊm/ *nt* **-s** paraffin
Petze *f* **-, -n** 🅇 sneak. **p~n** *vi* (*haben*) 🅇 sneak
Pfad *m* **-[e]s, -e** path. **P~finder** *m* **-s,-** [Boy] Scout. **P~finderin** *f* **-, -nen** [Girl] Guide
Pfahl *m* **-[e]s, ¨e** stake, post
Pfalz (die) - the Palatinate

Pfand *nt* **-[e]s,¨-er** pledge; (*beim Spiel*) forfeit; (*Flaschen-*) deposit
pfänd|en *vt* (*Jur*) seize.
P~erspiel *nt* game of forfeits
Pfandleiher *m* **-s,-** pawnbroker
Pfändung *f* **-, -en** (*Jur*) seizure
Pfann|e *f* **-, -n** [frying-]pan.
P~kuchen *m* pancake
Pfarr|er *m* **-s,-** vicar, parson; (*katholischer*) priest. **P~haus** *nt* vicarage
Pfau *m* **-s, -en** peacock
Pfeffer *m* **-s** pepper. **P~kuchen** *m* gingerbread. **P~minze** *f* **-** (*Bot*) peppermint. **p~n** *vt* pepper; (! *schmeißen*) chuck.
P~streuer *m* **-s,-** pepperpot
Pfeif|e *f* **-, -n** whistle; (*Tabak-, Orgel-*) pipe. **p~en**† *vt/i* (*haben*) whistle; (*als Signal*) blow the whistle
Pfeil *m* **-[e]s, -e** arrow
Pfeiler *m* **-s,-** pillar; (*Brücken-*) pier
Pfennig *m* **-s, -e** pfennig
Pferch *m* **-[e]s, -e** [sheep] pen
Pferd *nt* **-es, -e** horse; **zu P~e** on horseback. **P~erennen** *nt* horse-race; (*als Sport*) [horse-] racing. **P~eschwanz** *m* horse's tail; (*Frisur*) pony-tail.
P~estall *m* stable.
P~estärke *f* horsepower
Pfiff *m* **-[e]s, -e** whistle
Pfifferling *m* **-s, -e** chanterelle
pfiffig *a* smart
Pfingst|en *nt* **-s** Whitsun.
P~rose *f* peony
Pfirsich *m* **-s, -e** peach
Pflanz|e *f* **-, -n** plant. **p~en** *vt* plant. **P~enfett** *nt* vegetable fat. **p~lich** *a* vegetable
Pflaster *nt* **-s,-** pavement; (*Heft-*) plaster. **p~n** *vt* pave
Pflaume *f* **-, -n** plum
Pflege *f* **-** care; (*Kranken-*) nursing; **in P~ nehmen** look after; (*Admin*) foster <*Kind*>.
p~bedürftig *a* in need of care.
P~eltern *pl* foster-parents.
P~kind *nt* foster-child.
p~leicht *a* easy-care. **p~n** *vt* look after, care for; nurse <*Kranke*>; cultivate <*Künste, Freundschaft*>. **P~r(in)** *m* **-s,-** (*f* **-, -nen**) nurse; (*Tier-*) keeper
Pflicht *f* **-, -en** duty; (*Sport*) compulsory exercise/routine.
p~bewusst *a* conscientious.
P~gefühl *nt* sense of duty
pflücken *vt* pick
Pflug *m* **-[e]s,¨-e** plough
pflügen *vt/i* (*haben*) plough
Pforte *f* **-, -n** gate
Pförtner *m* **-s,-** porter
Pfosten *m* **-s,-** post
Pfote *f* **-, -n** paw
Pfropfen *m* **-s,-** stopper; (*Korken*) cork. **p~** *vt* graft (**auf** + *acc* on [to]); (! *pressen*) cram (**in** + *acc* into)
pfui *int* ugh
Pfund *nt* **-[e]s, -e & -** pound
Pfusch|arbeit *f* ! shoddy work.
p~en *vi* (*haben*) ! botch one's work. **P~erei** *f* **-, -en** ! botch-up
Pfütze *f* **-, -n** puddle
Phantasie *f* **-, -n** imagination; **P~n** fantasies; (*Fieber-*) hallucinations. **p~los** *a* unimaginative. **p~ren** *vi* (*haben*) fantasize; (*im Fieber*) be delirious. **p~voll** *a* imaginative
phantastisch *a* fantastic
pharma|zeutisch *a* pharmaceutical. **P~zie** *f* **-** pharmacy
Phase *f* **-, -n** phase
Philologie *f* **-** [study of] language and literature
Philosoph *m* **-en, -en** philosopher. **P~ie** *f* **-, -n** philosophy
philosophisch *a* philosophical
Phobie *f* **-, -n** phobia

Phonet|ik *f* - phonetics *sg*. **p~isch** *a* phonetic
Phosphor *m* **-s** phosphorus
Photo *nt*, **Photo-** = **Foto, Foto-**
Phrase *f* **-, -n** empty phrase
Physik *f* - physics *sg*. **p~alisch** *a* physical
Physiker(in) *m* **-s,-** (*f* **-, -nen**) physicist
Physiologie *f* - physiology
physisch *a* physical
Pianist(in) *m* **-en, -en** (*f* **-, -nen**) pianist
Pickel *m* **-s,-** pimple, spot; (*Spitzhacke*) pick. **p~ig** *a* spotty
Picknick *nt* **-s, -s** picnic
piep[s]|en *vi* (*haben*) <*Vogel:*> cheep; <*Maus:*> squeak; (*Techn*) bleep. **P~er** *m* **-s,-** bleeper
Pier *m* **-s, -e** [harbour] pier
Pietät /pie'tɛ:t/ *f* - reverence. **p~los** *a* irreverent
Pigment *nt* **-[e]s, -e** pigment. **P~ierung** *f* - pigmentation
Pik *nt* **-s, -s** (*Karten*) spades *pl*
pikant *a* piquant; (*gewagt*) racy
piken *vt* [!] prick
pikiert *a* offended, hurt
Pilger|(in) *m* **-s,-** (*f* **-, -nen**) pilgrim. **P~fahrt** *f* pilgrimage. **p~n** *vi* (*sein*) make a pilgrimage
Pille *f* **-, -n** pill
Pilot *m* **-en, -en** pilot
Pilz *m* **-es, -e** fungus; (*essbarer*) mushroom
pingelig *a* [!] fussy
Pinguin *m* **-s, -e** penguin
Pinie /-i̯ə/ *f* **-, -n** stone-pine
pinkeln *vi* (*haben*) [!] pee
Pinsel *m* **-s,-** [paint]brush
Pinzette *f* **-, -n** tweezers *pl*
Pionier *m* **-s, -e** (*Mil*) sapper; (*fig*) pioneer
Pirat *m* **-en, -en** pirate
Piste *f* **-, -n** (*Ski-*) run, piste; (*Renn-*) track; (*Aviat*) runway
Pistole *f* **-, -n** pistol
pitschnass *a* [!] soaking wet
pittoresk *a* picturesque
Pizza *f* **-, -s** pizza
Pkw /'pe:kave:/ *m* **-s, -s** car
plädieren *vi* (*haben*) plead (**für** for); **auf Freispruch p~** (*Jur*) ask for an acquittal
Plädoyer /plɛdoa'je:/ *nt* **-s, -s** (*Jur*) closing speech; (*fig*) plea
Plage *f* **-, -n** [hard] labour; (*Mühe*) trouble; (*Belästigung*) nuisance. **p~n** *vt* torment, plague; (*bedrängen*) pester; **sich p~n** struggle
Plakat *nt* **-[e]s, -e** poster
Plakette *f* **-, -n** badge
Plan *m* **-[e]s,¨e** plan
Plane *f* **-, -n** tarpaulin; (*Boden-*) groundsheet
planen *vt/i* (*haben*) plan
Planet *m* **-en, -en** planet
planier|en *vt* level. **P~raupe** *f* bulldozer
Planke *f* **-, -n** plank
plan|los *a* unsystematic. **p~mäßig** *a* systematic; <*Ankunft*> scheduled
Plansch|becken *nt* paddling pool. **p~en** *vi* (*haben*) splash about
Plantage /plan'ta:ʒə/ *f* **-, -n** plantation
Planung *f* - planning
plappern *vi* (*haben*) chatter ● *vt* talk <*Unsinn*>
plärren *vi* (*haben*) bawl
Plasma *nt* **-s** plasma
Plastik[1] *f* **-, -en** sculpture
Plast|ik[2] *nt* **-s** plastic. **p~isch** *a* three-dimensional; (*formbar*) plastic; (*anschaulich*) graphic
Plateau /pla'to:/ *nt* **-s, -s** plateau
Platin *nt* **-s** platinum
platonisch *a* platonic
plätschern *vi* (*haben*) splash; <*Bach:*> babble ● *vi* (*sein*) <*Bach:*> babble along
platt *a & adv* flat. **P~** *nt* **-[s]** (*Lang*) Low German

Plättbrett *nt* ironing-board
Platte *f* **-, -n** slab; (*Druck-*) plate; (*Metall-, Glas-*) sheet; (*Fliese*) tile; (*Koch-*) hotplate; (*Tisch-*) top; (*Schall-*) record, disc; (*zum Servieren*) [flat] dish, platter; **kalte P~** assorted cold meats and cheeses *pl*
Plätt|eisen *nt* iron. **p~en** *vt/i* (*haben*) iron
Plattenspieler *m* record-player
Platt|form *f* **-, -en** platform. **P~füße** *mpl* flat feet
Platz *m* **-es,¨-e** place; (*von Häusern umgeben*) square; (*Sitz-*) seat; (*Sport-*) ground; (*Fußball-*) pitch; (*Tennis-*) court; (*Golf-*) course; (*freier Raum*) room, space; **P~ nehmen** take a seat; **P~ machen** make room; **vom P~ stellen** (*Sport*) send off. **P~anweiserin** *f* **-, -nen** usherette
Plätzchen *nt* **-s,-** spot; (*Culin*) biscuit
platzen *vi* (*sein*) burst; (*auf-*) split; (🄵 *scheitern*) fall through; <*Verlobung:*> be off
Platz|karte *f* seat reservation ticket. **P~mangel** *m* lack of space. **P~patrone** *f* blank. **P~verweis** *m* (*Sport*) sending off. **P~wunde** *f* laceration
Plauderei *f* **-, -en** chat
plaudern *vi* (*haben*) chat
plausibel *a* plausible
pleite *a* 🄵 **p~ sein** be broke; <*Firma:*> be bankrupt. **P~** *f* **-, -n** 🄵 bankruptcy; (*Misserfolg*) flop; **P~ gehen** *od* **machen** go bankrupt
plissiert *a* [finely] pleated
Plomb|e *f* **-, -n** seal; (*Zahn-*) filling. **p~ieren** *vt* seal; fill <*Zahn*>
plötzlich *a* sudden
plump *a* plump; clumsy
plumpsen *vi* (*sein*) 🄵 fall
plündern *vt/i* (*haben*) loot
Plunderstück *nt* Danish pastry
Plural *m* **-s, -e** plural
plus *adv, conj & prep* (+ *dat*) plus. **P~** *nt* **-** surplus; (*Gewinn*) profit (*Vorteil*) advantage, plus. **P~punkt** *m* (*Sport*) point; (*fig*) plus
Po *m* **-s, -s** 🄵 bottom
Pöbel *m* **-s** mob, rabble. **p~haft** *a* loutish
pochen *vi* (*haben*) knock, <*Herz:*> pound; **p~ auf** (+ *acc*) (*fig*) insist on
pochieren /pɔˈʃiːrən/ *vt* poach
Pocken *pl* smallpox *sg*
Podest *nt* **-[e]s, -e** rostrum
Podium *nt* **-s, -ien** /-iən/ platform; (*Podest*) rostrum
Poesie /poeˈziː/ *f* **-** poetry
poetisch *a* poetic
Pointe /ˈpo̯ɛ̃ːtə/ *f* **-, -n** point (*of a joke*)
Pokal *m* **-s, -e** goblet; (*Sport*) cup
pökeln *vt* (*Culin*) salt
Poker *nt* **-s** poker
Pol *m* **-s, -e** pole. **p~ar** *a* polar. **P~arstern** *m* pole-star
Pole *m*, **-n, -n** Pole. **P~n** *nt* **-s** Poland
Police /poˈliːsə/ *f* **-, -n** policy
Polier *m* **-s, -e** foreman
polieren *vt* polish
Polin *f* **-, -nen** Pole
Politesse *f* **-, -n** [woman] traffic warden
Politik *f* **-** politics *sg*; (*Vorgehen, Maßnahme*) policy
Polit|iker(in) *m* **-s,-** (*f*, **-, -nen**) politician. **p~isch** *a* political
Politur *f* **-, -en** polish
Polizei *f* **-** police *pl*. **p~lich** *a* police ... ● *adv* by the police; <*sich anmelden*> with the police. **P~streife** *f* police patrol. **P~stunde** *f* closing time. **P~wache** *f* police station
Polizist *m* **-en, -en** policeman. **P~in** *f* **-, -nen** policewoman

Pollen *m* **-s** pollen
polnisch *a* Polish
Polster *nt* **-s,-** pad; (*Kissen*) cushion; (*Möbel-*) upholstery. **p~n** *vt* pad; upholster <*Möbel*>. **P~ung** *f* **-** padding; upholstery
Polter|abend *m* wedding-eve party. **p~n** *vi* (*haben*) thump, bang
Polyäthylen *nt* **-s** polythene
Polyester *m* **-s** polyester
Polyp *m* **-en, -en** polyp; **P~en** adenoids *pl*
Pommes frites /pɔm'fri:t/ *pl* chips; (*dünner*) French fries
Pomp *m* **-s** pomp
Pompon /põ'põ:/ *m* **-s, -s** pompon
pompös *a* ostentatious
Pony[1] *nt* **-s, -s** pony
Pony[2] *m* **-s, -s** fringe
Pop *m* **-[s]** pop
Popo *m* **-s, -s** [!] bottom
populär *a* popular
Pore *f* **-, -n** pore
Porno|graphie, Pornografie *f* **-** pornography. **p~graphisch, p~grafisch** *a* pornographic
Porree *m* **-s** leeks *pl*
Portal *nt* **-s, -e** portal
Portemonnaie /pɔrtmɔ'ne:/ *nt* **-s, -s** purse
Portier /pɔr'tie:/ *m* **-s, -s** doorman, porter
Portion /-'tsio:n/ *f* **-, -en** helping, portion
Portmonee *nt* **-s, -s** = **Portemonnaie**
Porto *nt* **-s** postage. **p~frei** *adv* post free, post paid
Porträ|t /pɔr'trɛ:/ *nt* **-s, -s** portrait. **p~tieren** *vt* paint a portrait of
Portugal *nt* **-s** Portugal
Portugies|e *m* **-n, -n, P~in** *f* **-, -nen** Portuguese. **p~isch** *a* Portuguese
Portwein *m* port
Porzellan *nt* **-s** china, porcelain
Posaune *f* **-, -n** trombone
Position /-'tsio:n/ *f* **-, -en** position
positiv *a* positive. **P~** *nt* **-s, -e** (*Phot*) positive
Post *f* **-** post office; (*Briefe*) mail, post; **mit der P~** by post
postalisch *a* postal
Post|amt *nt* post office. **P~anweisung** *f* postal money order. **P~bote** *m* postman
Posten *m* **-s,-** post; (*Wache*) sentry; (*Waren-*) batch; (*Rechnungs-*) item, entry
Poster *nt* & *m* **-s,-** poster
Postfach *nt* post-office *or* PO box
Post|karte *f* postcard. **p~lagernd** *adv* poste restante. **P~leitzahl** *f* postcode. **P~scheckkonto** *nt* ≈ National Girobank account. **P~stempel** *m* postmark
postum *a* posthumous
post|wendend *adv* by return of post. **P~wertzeichen** *nt* [postage] stamp
Potenz *f* **-, -en** potency; (*Math & fig*) power
Pracht *f* **-** magnificence, splendour
prächtig *a* magnificent; splendid
prachtvoll *a* magnificent
Prädikat *nt* **-[e]s, -e** rating; (*Comm*) grade; (*Gram*) predicate
prägen *vt* stamp (**auf** + *acc* on); emboss <*Leder*>; mint <*Münze*>; coin <*Wort*>; (*fig*) shape
prägnant *a* succinct
prähistorisch *a* prehistoric
prahl|en *vi* (*haben*) boast, brag (**mit** about)
Prakti|k *f* **-, -en** practice. **P~kant(in)** *m* **-en, -en** (*f* **-, -nen**) trainee
Prakti|kum *nt* **-s, -ka** practical training. **p~sch** *a* practical; (*nützlich*) handy; (*tatsächlich*)

virtual; **p~scher Arzt** general practitioner ● *adv* practically; virtually; (*in der Praxis*) in practice. **p~zieren** *vt/i* (*haben*) practise; (*anwenden*) put into practice; ([!] *bekommen*) get

Praline *f* **-, -n** chocolate

prall *a* bulging; (*dick*) plump; <*Sonne*> blazing ● *adv* **p~ gefüllt** full to bursting. **p~en** *vi* (*sein*) **p~ auf** (+ *acc*)/**gegen** collide with, hit; <*Sonne:*> blaze down on

Prämie /-iə/ *f* **-, -n** premium; (*Preis*) award

präm[i]ieren *vt* award a prize to

Pranger *m* **-s,-** pillory

Pranke *f* **-, -n** paw

Präparat *nt* **-[e]s, -e** preparation

Präsens *nt* **-** (*Gram*) present

präsentieren *vt* present

Präsenz *f* **-** presence

Präservativ *nt* **-s, -e** condom

Präsident|(in) *m* **-en, -en** (*f* **-, -nen**) president. **P~schaft** *f* **-** presidency

Präsidium *nt* **-s** presidency; (*Gremium*) executive committee; (*Polizei-*) headquarters *pl*

prasseln *vi* (*haben*) <*Regen:*> beat down; <*Feuer:*> crackle

Präteritum *nt* **-s** imperfect

Praxis *f* **-, -xen** practice; (*Erfahrung*) practical experience; (*Arzt-*) surgery; **in der P~** in practice

Präzedenzfall *m* precedent

präzis[e] *a* precise

predig|en *vt/i* (*haben*) preach. **P~t** *f* **-, -en** sermon

Preis *m* **-es, -e** price; (*Belohnung*) prize. **P~ausschreiben** *nt* competition

Preiselbeere *f* (*Bot*) cowberry; (*Culin*) ≈ cranberry

preisen† *vt* praise

preisgeben† *vt sep* abandon (*dat* to); reveal <*Geheimnis*>

preis|gekrönt *a* award-winning. **p~günstig** *a* reasonably priced ● *adv* at a reasonable price. **P~lage** *f* price range. **p~lich** *a* price ... ● *adv* in price. **P~richter** *m* judge. **P~schild** *nt* price-tag. **P~träger(in)** *m(f)* prize-winner. **p~wert** *a* reasonable

Prell|bock *m* buffers *pl*. **p~en** *vt* bounce; (*verletzen*) bruise; ([!] *betrügen*) cheat. **P~ung** *f* **-, -en** bruise

Premiere /prəˈmi̯eːrə/ *f* **-, -n** première

Premierminister(in) /prəˈmi̯eː-/ *m(f)* Prime Minister

Presse *f* **-, -n** press. **p~n** *vt* press

Pressluftbohrer *m* pneumatic drill

Preuß|en *nt* **-s** Prussia. **p~isch** *a* Prussian

prickeln *vi* (*haben*) tingle

Priester *m* **-s,-** priest

prima *inv* a first-class, first-rate; ([!] *toll*) fantastic

primär *a* primary

Primel *f* **-, -n** primula

primitiv *a* primitive

Prinz *m* **-en, -en** prince. **P~essin** *f* **-, -nen** princess

Prinzip *nt* **-s, -ien** /-i̯ən/ principle. **p~iell** *a* <*Frage*> of principle ● *adv* on principle

Prise *f* **-, -n P~ Salz** pinch of salt

Prisma *nt* **-s, -men** prism

privat *a* private, personal. **P~adresse** *f* home address. **p~isieren** *vt* privatize

Privileg *nt* **-[e]s, -ien** /-i̯ən/ privilege. **p~iert** *a* privileged

pro *prep* (+ *dat*) per. **Pro** *nt* **- das Pro und Kontra** the pros and cons *pl*

Probe *f* **-, -n** test, trial; (*Menge, Muster*) sample; (*Theat*) rehearsal; **auf die P~ stellen** put

to the test; **ein Auto P~ fahren** test-drive a car. **p~n** *vt/i* (*haben*) (*Theat*) rehearse. **p~weise** *adv* on a trial basis. **P~zeit** *f* probationary period
probieren *vt/i* (*haben*) try; (*kosten*) taste; (*proben*) rehearse
Problem *nt* **-s, -e** problem. **p~atisch** *a* problematic
problemlos *a* problem-free ● *adv* without any problems
Produkt *nt* **-[e]s, -e** product
Produk|tion /-'tsio:n/ *f* **-, -en** production. **p~tiv** *a* productive
Produ|zent *m* **-en, -en** producer. **p~zieren** *vt* produce
Professor *m* **-s, -en** /-'so:rən/ professor
Profi *m* **-s, -s** (*Sport*) professional
Profil *nt* **-s, -e** profile; (*Reifen-*) tread; (*fig*) image
Profit *m* **-[e]s, -e** profit. **p~ieren** *vi* (*haben*) profit (**von** from)
Prognose *f* **-, -n** forecast; (*Med*) prognosis
Programm *nt* **-s, -e** programme; (*Computer-*) program; (*TV*) channel; (*Comm: Sortiment*) range. **p~ieren** *vt/i* (*haben*) (*Computer*) program. **P~ierer(in)** *m* **-s,-** (*f* **-, -nen**) [computer] programmer
Projekt *nt* **-[e]s, -e** project
Projektor *m* **-s, -en** /-'to:rən/ projector
Prolet *m* **-en, -en** boor. **P~ariat** *nt* **-[e]s** proletariat
Prolog *m* **-s, -e** prologue
Promenade *f* **-, -n** promenade
Promille *pl* ! alcohol level *sg* in the blood; **zu viel P~ haben** ! be over the limit
Prominenz *f* **-** prominent figures *pl*
Promiskuität *f* **-** promiscuity
promovieren *vi* (*haben*) obtain one's doctorate
prompt *a* prompt
Pronomen *nt* **-s,-** pronoun
Propaganda *f* **-** propaganda; (*Reklame*) publicity
Propeller *m* **-s,-** propeller
Prophet *m* **-en, -en** prophet
prophezei|en *vt* prophesy. **P~ung** *f* **-, -en** prophecy
Proportion /-'tsio:n/ *f* **-, -en** proportion
Prosa *f* **-** prose
prosit *int* cheers!
Prospekt *m* **-[e]s, -e** brochure; (*Comm*) prospectus
prost *int* cheers!
Prostitu|ierte *f* **-n, -n** prostitute. **P~tion** /-'tsio:n/ *f* **-** prostitution
Protest *m* **-[e]s, -e** protest
Protestant|(in) *m* **-en, -en** (*f* **-, -nen**) (*Relig*) Protestant. **p~isch** *a* (*Relig*) Protestant
protestieren *vi* (*haben*) protest
Prothese *f* **-, -n** artificial limb; (*Zahn-*) denture
Protokoll *nt* **-s, -e** record; (*Sitzungs-*) minutes *pl*; (*diplomatisches*) protocol
protz|en *vi* (*haben*) show off (**mit etw** sth). **p~ig** *a* ostentatious
Proviant *m* **-s** provisions *pl*
Provinz *f* **-, -en** province
Provision *f* **-, -en** (*Comm*) commission
provisorisch *a* provisional, temporary
Provokation /-'tsio:n/ *f* **-, -en** provocation
provozieren *vt* provoke
Prozedur *f* **-, -en** [lengthy] business
Prozent *nt* **-[e]s, -e** & **-** per cent; **5 P~** 5 per cent. **P~satz** *m* percentage. **p~ual** *a* percentage ...
Prozess *m* **-es, -e** process; (*Jur*) lawsuit; (*Kriminal-*) trial
Prozession *f* **-, -en** procession
prüde *a* prudish

prüf|en *vt* test/(*über-*) check (**auf** + *acc* for); audit <*Bücher*>; (*Sch*) examine; **p~ender Blick** searching look. **P~er** *m* **-s,-** inspector; (*Buch-*) auditor; (*Sch*) examiner. **P~ling** *m* **-s, -e** examination candidate. **P~ung** *f* **-, -en** examination; (*Test*) test; (*Bücher-*) audit; (*fig*) trial

Prügel *m* **-s,-** cudgel; **P~** *pl* hiding *sg*, beating *sg*. **P~ei** *f* **-, -en** brawl, fight. **p~n** *vt* beat, thrash

Prunk *m* **-[e]s** magnificence, splendour

Psalm *m* **-s, -en** psalm

pst *int* shush!

Psychi|ater *m* **-s,-** psychiatrist. **P~atrie** *f* **-** psychiatry. **p~atrisch** *a* psychiatric

psychisch *a* psychological

Psycho|analyse *f* psychoanalysis. **P~loge** *m* **-n, -n** psychologist. **P~logie** *f* **-** psychology. **p~logisch** *a* psychological

Pubertät *f* **-** puberty

Publi|kum *nt* **-s** public; (*Zuhörer*) audience; (*Zuschauer*) spectators *pl*. **p~zieren** *vt* publish

Pudding *m* **-s, -s** blancmange; (*im Wasserbad gekocht*) pudding

Pudel *m* **-s,-** poodle

Puder *m* & [!] *nt* **-s,-** powder. **P~dose** *f* [powder] compact. **p~n** *vt* powder. **P~zucker** *m* icing sugar

Puff *m* & *nt* **-s, -s** [x] brothel

Puffer *m* **-s,-** (*Rail*) buffer; (*Culin*) pancake. **P~zone** *f* buffer zone

Pull|i *m* **-s, -s** jumper. **P~over** *m* **-s,-** jumper; (*Herren-*) pullover

Puls *m* **-es** pulse. **P~ader** *f* artery

Pult *nt* **-[e]s, -e** desk

Pulver *nt* **-s,-** powder. **p~ig** *a* powdery

Pulverkaffee *m* instant coffee

pummelig *a* [!] chubby

Pumpe *f* **-, -n** pump. **p~n** *vt/i* (*haben*) pump; ([!] *leihen*) lend; **[sich** (*dat*)**] etw p~n** ([!] *borgen*) borrow sth

Pumps /pœmps/ *pl* court shoes

Punkt *m* **-[e]s, -e** dot; (*Tex*) spot; (*Geom, Sport & fig*) point; (*Gram*) full stop, period; **P~ sechs Uhr** at six o'clock sharp

pünktlich *a* punctual. **P~keit** *f* **-** punctuality

Pupille *f* **-, -n** (*Anat*) pupil

Puppe *f* **-, -n** doll; (*Marionette*) puppet; (*Schaufenster-, Schneider-*) dummy; (*Zool*) chrysalis

pur *a* pure; ([!] *bloß*) sheer

Püree *nt* **-s, -s** purée; (*Kartoffel-*) mashed potatoes *pl*

purpurrot *a* crimson

Purzel|baum *m* [!] somersault. **p~n** *vi* (*sein*) [!] tumble

Puste *f* **-** [!] breath. **p~n** *vt/i* (*haben*) [!] blow

Pute *f* **-, -n** turkey

Putsch *m* **-[e]s, -e** coup

Putz *m* **-es** plaster; (*Staat*) finery. **p~en** *vt* clean; (*Aust*) dry-clean; (*zieren*) adorn; **sich p~en** dress up; **sich** (*dat*) **die Zähne/Nase p~en** clean one's teeth/blow one's nose. **P~frau** *f* cleaner, charwoman. **p~ig** *a* [!] amusing, cute; (*seltsam*) odd

Puzzlespiel /ˈpʊzl-/ *nt* jigsaw

Pyramide *f* **-, -n** pyramid

Qq

Quacksalber *m* **-s,-** quack
Quadrat *nt* **-[e]s, -e** square. **q~isch** *a* square
quaken *vi* (*haben*) quack; <*Frosch:*> croak
Quäker(in) *m* **-s,-** (*f* **-, -nen**) Quaker
Qual *f* **-, -en** torment; (*Schmerz*) agony
quälen *vt* torment; (*foltern*) torture; (*bedrängen*) pester; **sich q~** torment oneself; (*leiden*) suffer; (*sich mühen*) struggle
Quälerei *f* **-, -en** torture
Qualifi|kation /-ˈts̮io:n/ *f* **-, -en** qualification. **q~zieren** *vt* qualify. **q~ziert** *a* qualified; (*fähig*) competent; <*Arbeit*> skilled
Qualität *f* **-, -en** quality
Qualle *f* **-, -n** jellyfish
Qualm *m* **-s** [thick] smoke
qualvoll *a* agonizing
Quantum *nt* **-s, -ten** quantity; (*Anteil*) share, quota
Quarantäne *f* **-** quarantine
Quark *m* **-s** quark, ≈ curd cheese
Quartal *nt* **-s, -e** quarter
Quartett *nt* **-[e]s, -e** quartet
Quartier *nt* **-s, -e** accommodation; (*Mil*) quarters *pl*
Quarz *m* **-es** quartz
quasseln *vi* (*haben*) ! jabber
Quaste *f* **-, -n** tassel
Quatsch *m* **-[e]s** ! nonsense, rubbish; **Q~ machen** (*Unfug machen*) fool around; (*etw falsch machen*) do a silly thing. **q~en** ! *vi* (*haben*) talk; <*Wasser, Schlamm:*> squelch ● *vt* talk
Quecksilber *nt* mercury
Quelle *f* **-, -n** spring; (*Fluss- & fig*) source
quengeln *vi* ! whine
quer *adv* across, crosswise; (*schräg*) diagonally; **q~ gestreift** horizontally striped
Quere *f* **- der Q~ nach** across, crosswise; **jdm in die Q~ kommen** get in s.o.'s way
Quer|latte *f* crossbar. **Q~schiff** *nt* transept. **Q~schnitt** *m* cross-section. **q~schnittsgelähmt** *a* paraplegic. **Q~straße** *f* side-street. **Q~verweis** *m* cross-reference
quetschen *vt* squash; (*drücken*) squeeze; (*zerdrücken*) crush; (*Culin*) mash; **sich q~ in** (+ *acc*) squeeze into
Queue /kø:/ *nt* **-s, -s** cue
quieken *vi* (*haben*) squeal; <*Maus:*> squeak
quietschen *vi* (*haben*) squeal; <*Tür, Dielen:*> creak
Quintett *nt* **-[e]s, -e** quintet
quirlen *vt* mix
Quitte *f* **-, -n** quince
quittieren *vt* receipt <*Rechnung*>; sign for <*Geldsumme, Sendung*>; **den Dienst q~** resign
Quittung *f* **-, -en** receipt
Quiz /kvɪs/ *nt* **-, -** quiz
Quote *f* **-, -n** proportion

Rr

Rabatt *m* **-[e]s, -e** discount

Rabatte *f* **-, -n** (*Hort*) border
Rabattmarke *f* trading stamp
Rabbiner *m* **-s,-** rabbi
Rabe *m* **-n, -n** raven
Rache *f* **-** revenge, vengeance
Rachen *m* **-s,-** pharynx
rächen *vt* avenge; **sich r~** take revenge (**an** + *dat* on); <*Fehler:*> cost s.o. dear
Rad *nt* **-[e]s,¨er** wheel; (*Fahr-*) bicycle, [!] bike; **Rad fahren** cycle
Radar *m & nt* **-s** radar
Radau *m* **-s** [!] din, racket
radeln *vi* (*sein*) [!] cycle
Rädelsführer *m* ringleader
radfahr|en* *vi sep* (*sein*) **Rad fahren**, *s.* **Rad. R~er(in)** *m(f)* **-s,-** (*f* **-, -nen**) cyclist
radier|en *vt/i* (*haben*) rub out; (*Kunst*) etch. **R~gummi** *m* eraser, rubber. **R~ung** *f* **-, -en** etching
Radieschen /-'di:sçən/ *nt* **-s,-** radish
radikal *a* radical, drastic
Radio *nt* **-s, -s** radio
radioaktiv *a* radioactive. **R~ität** *f* **-** radioactivity
Radius *m* **-, -ien** /-i̯ən/ radius
Rad|kappe *f* hub-cap. **R~ler** *m* **-s,-** cyclist; (*Getränk*) shandy
raffen *vt* grab; (*kräuseln*) gather; (*kürzen*) condense
Raffin|ade *f* **-** refined sugar. **R~erie** *f* **-, -n** refinery. **R~esse** *f* **-, -n** refinement; (*Schlauheit*) cunning. **r~iert** *a* ingenious; (*durchtrieben*) crafty
ragen *vi* (*haben*) rise [up]
Rahm *m* **-s** (*SGer*) cream
rahmen *vt* frame. **R~** *m* **-s,-** frame; (*fig*) framework; (*Grenze*) limits *pl*; (*einer Feier*) setting
Rakete *f* **-, -n** rocket; (*Mil*) missile
Rallye /'rali/ *nt* **-s, -s** rally
rammen *vt* ram
Rampe *f* **-, -n** ramp; (*Theat*) front of the stage
Ramsch *m* **-[e]s** junk
ran *adv* = **heran**
Rand *m* **-[e]s,¨er** edge; (*Teller-, Gläser-, Brillen-*) rim; (*Zier-*) border, edging; (*Brief-*) margin; (*Stadt-*) outskirts *pl*; (*Ring*) ring
randalieren *vi* (*haben*) rampage
Randstreifen *m* (*Auto*) hard shoulder
Rang *m* **-[e]s,¨e** rank; (*Theat*) tier; **erster/zweiter R~** (*Theat*) dress/upper circle; **ersten R~es** first-class
rangieren /raŋ'ʒi:rən/ *vt* shunt ● *vi* (*haben*) rank (**vor** + *dat* before)
Rangordnung *f* order of importance; (*Hierarchie*) hierarchy
Ranke *f* **-, -n** tendril; (*Trieb*) shoot
ranken (sich) *vr* (*Bot*) trail; (*in die Höhe*) climb
Ranzen *m* **-s,-** (*Sch*) satchel
ranzig *a* rancid
Rappe *m* **-n, -n** black horse
Raps *m* **-es** (*Bot*) rape
rar *a* rare; **er macht sich rar** [!] we don't see much of him. **R~ität** *f* **-, -en** rarity
rasant *a* fast; (*schnittig, schick*) stylish
rasch *a* quick
rascheln *vi* (*haben*) rustle
Rasen *m* **-s,-** lawn
rasen *vi* (*sein*) tear [along]; <*Puls:*> race; <*Zeit:*> fly; **gegen eine Mauer r~** career into a wall ● *vi* (*haben*) rave; <*Sturm:*> rage. **r~d** *a* furious; (*tobend*) raving; <*Sturm, Durst*> raging; <*Schmerz*> excruciating; <*Beifall*> tumultuous
Rasenmäher *m* **-s,-** lawnmower
Rasier|apparat *m* razor. **r~en** *vt* shave; **sich r~en** shave.

R~klinge *f* razor blade. **R~wasser** *nt* aftershave [lotion]

Raspel *f* **-, -n** rasp; (*Culin*) grater. **r~n** *vt* grate

Rasse *f* **-, -n** race. **R~hund** *m* pedigree dog

Rassel *f* **-, -n** rattle. **r~n** *vi* (*haben*) rattle; <*Schlüssel:*> jangle; <*Kette:*> clank

Rassendiskriminierung *f* racial discrimination

Rassepferd *nt* thoroughbred.

rassisch *a* racial

Rassis|mus *m* **-** racism. **r~tisch** *a* racist

Rast *f* **-, -en** rest. **R~platz** *m* picnic area. **R~stätte** *f* motorway restaurant [and services]

Rasur *f* **-, -en** shave

Rat *m* **-[e]s** [piece of] advice; **sich** (*dat*) **keinen Rat wissen** not know what to do; **zu Rat[e] ziehen** = **zurate ziehen**, *s.* **zurate**

Rate *f* **-, -n** instalment

raten† *vt* guess; (*empfehlen*) advise ● *vi* (*haben*) guess; **jdm r~** advise s.o.

Ratenzahlung *f* payment by instalments

Rat|geber *m* **-s,-** adviser; (*Buch*) guide. **R~haus** *nt* town hall

ratifizier|en *vt* ratify. **R~ung** *f* **-, -en** ratification

Ration /ra'tsi̯o:n/ *f* **-, -en** ration. **r~ell** *a* efficient. **r~ieren** *vt* ration

rat|los *a* helpless; **r~los sein** not know what to do. **r~sam** *pred a* advisable; prudent. **R~schlag** *m* piece of advice; **R~schläge** advice *sg*

Rätsel *nt* **-s,-** riddle; (*Kreuzwort-*) puzzle; (*Geheimnis*) mystery. **r~haft** *a* puzzling, mysterious. **r~n** *vi* (*haben*) puzzle

Ratte *f* **-, -n** rat

rau *a* rough; (*unfreundlich*) gruff; <*Klima*> harsh, raw; (*heiser*) husky; <*Hals*> sore

Raub *m* **-[e]s** robbery; (*Menschen-*) abduction; (*Beute*) loot, booty. **r~en** *vt* steal; abduct <*Menschen*>

Räuber *m* **-s,-** robber

Raub|mord *m* robbery with murder. **R~tier** *nt* predator. **R~vogel** *m* bird of prey

Rauch *m* **-[e]s** smoke. **r~en** *vt/i* (*haben*) smoke. **R~en** *nt* **-s** smoking; '**R~en verboten**' 'no smoking'. **R~er** *m* **-s**, -smoker

Räucher|lachs *m* smoked salmon. **r~n** *vt* (*Culin*) smoke

rauf *adv* = **herauf, hinauf**

rauf|en *vt* pull ● *vr/i* (*haben*) **[sich] r~en** fight. **R~erei** *f* **-, -en** fight

rauh* *a s.* **rau**

Raum *m* **-[e]s, Räume** room; (*Gebiet*) area; (*Welt-*) space

räumen *vt* clear; vacate <*Wohnung*>; evacuate <*Gebäude, Gebiet, (Mil) Stellung*>; (*bringen*) put (**in**/**auf** + *acc* into/on); (*holen*) get (**aus** out of)

Raum|fahrer *m* astronaut. **R~fahrt** *f* space travel. **R~inhalt** *m* volume

räumlich *a* spatial

Raum|pflegerin *f* cleaner. **R~schiff** *nt* spaceship

Räumung *f* **-** clearing; vacating; evacuation. **R~sverkauf** *m* clearance/closing-down sale

Raupe *f* **-, -n** caterpillar

raus *adv* = **heraus, hinaus**

Rausch *m* **-[e]s, Räusche** intoxication; (*fig*) exhilaration; **einen R~haben** be drunk

rauschen *vi* (*haben*) <*Wasser, Wind:*> rush; <*Bäume Blätter:*> rustle ● *vi* (*sein*) rush [along]

Rauschgift *nt* [narcotic] drug; (*coll*) drugs *pl*. **R∼süchtige(r)** *m/f* drug addict

räuspern (sich) *vr* clear one's throat

rausschmeißen† *vt sep* [!] throw out; (*entlassen*) sack

Raute *f* **-, -n** diamond

Razzia *f* **-, -ien** /-i̯ən/ [police] raid

Reagenzglas *nt* test-tube

reagieren *vi* (*haben*) react (**auf** + *acc* to)

Reaktion /-'tsi̯o:n/ *f* **-, -en** reaction. **r∼är** *a* reactionary

Reaktor *m* **-s, -en** /-'to:rən/ reactor

realisieren *vt* realize

Realis|mus *m* - realism. **R∼t** *m* **-en, -en** realist. **r∼tisch** *a* realistic

Realität *f* **-, -en** reality

Realschule *f* ≈ secondary modern school

Rebe *f* **-, -n** vine

Rebell *m* **-en, -en** rebel. **r∼ieren** *vi* (*haben*) rebel. **R∼ion** *f* **-, -en** rebellion

rebellisch *a* rebellious

Rebhuhn *nt* partridge

Rebstock *m* vine

Rechen *m* **-s-** rake

Rechen|aufgabe *f* arithmetical problem; (*Sch*) sum. **R∼maschine** *f* calculator

recherchieren /reʃɛr'ʃi:rən/ *vt/i* (*haben*) investigate; (*Journ*) research

rechnen *vi* (*haben*) do arithmetic; (*schätzen*) reckon; (*zählen*) count (**zu** among; **auf** + *acc* on); **r∼ mit** reckon with; (*erwarten*) expect ● *vt* calculate, work out; (*fig*) count (**zu** among). **R∼** *nt* **-s** arithmetic

Rechner *m* **-s,-** calculator; (*Computer*) computer

Rechnung *f* **-, -en** bill; (*Comm*) invoice; (*Berechnung*) calculation; **R∼ führen über** (+ *acc*) keep account of. **R∼sjahr** *nt* financial year. **R∼sprüfer** *m* auditor

Recht *nt* **-[e]s, -e** law; (*Berechtigung*) right (**auf** + *acc* to); **im R∼ sein** be in the right; **R∼ haben/behalten** be right; **R∼ bekommen** be proved right; **jdm R∼ geben** agree with s.o.; **mit** *od* **zu R∼** rightly

recht *a* right; (*wirklich*) real; **ich habe keine r∼e Lust** I don't really feel like it; **es jdm r∼ machen** please s.o.; **jdm r∼ sein** be all right with s.o. **r∼ vielen Dank** many thanks

Recht|e *f* **-n, -[n]** right side; (*Hand*) right hand; (*Boxen*) right; **die R∼e** (*Pol*) the right; **zu meiner R∼en** on my right. **r∼e(r,s)** *a* right; (*Pol*) right-wing; **r∼e Masche** plain stitch. **R∼e(r)** *m/f* **der/die R∼e** the right man/woman; **R∼e(s)** *nt* **das R∼e** the right thing; **etwas R∼es lernen** learn something useful; **nach dem R∼en sehen** see that everything is all right

Rechteck *nt* **-[e]s, -e** rectangle. **r∼ig** *a* rectangular

rechtfertigen *vt* justify; **sich r∼en** justify oneself

recht|haberisch *a* opinionated. **r∼lich** *a* legal. **r∼mäßig** *a* legitimate

rechts *adv* on the right; (*bei Stoff*) on the right side; **von/nach r∼** from/to the right; **zwei r∼, zwei links stricken** knit two, purl two. **R∼anwalt** *m*, **R∼anwältin** *f* lawyer

Rechtschreib|programm *nt* spell checker. **R∼ung** *f* - spelling

Rechts|händer(in) *m* **-s,-** (*f* **-, -nen**) right-hander. **r∼händig**

a & adv right-handed. **r~kräftig** *a* legal. **R~streit** *m* law suit. **R~verkehr** *m* driving on the right. **r~widrig** *a* illegal. **R~wissenschaft** *f* jurisprudence

rechtzeitig *a & adv* in time

Reck *nt* **-[e]s, -e** horizontal bar

recken *vt* stretch

Redakteur /redak'tø:ɐ/ *m* **-s, -e** editor; (*Radio, TV*) producer

Redaktion /-'tsi̯o:n/ *f* **-, -en** editing; (*Radio, TV*) production; (*Abteilung*) editorial/production department

Rede *f* **-, -n** speech; **zur R~ stellen** demand an explanation from; **nicht der R~ wert** not worth mentioning

reden *vi* (*haben*) talk (**von** about; **mit** to); (*eine Rede halten*) speak ● *vt* talk; speak <*Wahrheit*>. **R~sart** *f* saying

Redewendung *f* idiom

redigieren *vt* edit

Redner *m* **-s,-** speaker

reduzieren *vt* reduce

Reeder *m* **-s,-** shipowner. **R~ei** *f* **-, -en** shipping company

Refer|at *nt* **-[e]s, -e** report; (*Abhandlung*) paper; (*Abteilung*) section. **R~ent(in)** *m* **-en, -en** (*f* **-, -nen**) speaker; (*Sachbearbeiter*) expert. **R~enz** *f* **-, -en** reference

Reflex *m* **-es, -e** reflex; (*Widerschein*) reflection. **R~ion** *f* **-, -en** reflection. **r~iv** *a* reflexive

Reform *f* **-, -en** reform. **R~ation** /-'tsi̯o:n/ *f* **-** (*Relig*) Reformation

Reform|haus *nt* health-food shop. **r~ieren** *vt* reform

Refrain /rə'frɛ̃:/ *m* **-s, -s** refrain

Regal *nt* **-s, -e** [set of] shelves *pl*

Regatta *f* **-, -ten** regatta

rege *a* active; (*lebhaft*) lively; (*geistig*) alert; <*Handel*> brisk

Regel *f* **-, -n** rule; (*Monats-*) period. **r~mäßig** *a* regular. **r~n** *vt* regulate; direct <*Verkehr*>; (*erledigen*) settle. **r~recht** *a* real, proper ● *adv* really. **R~ung** *f* **-, -en** regulation; settlement

regen *vt* move; **sich r~** move; (*wach werden*) stir

Regen *m* **-s,-** rain. **R~bogen** *m* rainbow. **R~bogenhaut** *f* iris

Regener|ation /-'tsi̯o:n/ *f* **-** regeneration. **r~ieren** *vt* regenerate

Regen|mantel *m* raincoat. **R~schirm** *m* umbrella. **R~tag** *m* rainy day. **R~wetter** *nt* wet weather. **R~wurm** *m* earthworm

Regie /re'ʒi:/ *f* **-** direction; **R~ führen** direct

regier|en *vt/i* (*haben*) govern, rule; <*Monarch:*> reign [over]; (*Gram*) take. **R~ung** *f* **-, -en** government; (*Herrschaft*) rule; (*eines Monarchen*) reign

Regiment *nt* **-[e]s, -er** regiment

Region *f* **-, -en** region. **r~al** *a* regional

Regisseur /reʒɪ'sø:ɐ/ *m* **-s, -e** director

Register *nt* **-s,-** register; (*Inhaltsverzeichnis*) index; (*Orgel-*) stop

Regler *m* **-s,-** regulator

reglos *a & adv* motionless

regn|en *vi* (*haben*) rain; **es r~et** it is raining. **r~erisch** *a* rainy

regul|är *a* normal; (*rechtmäßig*) legitimate. **r~ieren** *vt* regulate

Regung *f* **-, -en** movement; (*Gefühls-*) emotion. **r~slos** *a & adv* motionless

Reh *nt* **-[e]s, -e** roe-deer; (*Culin*) venison

Rehbock *m* roebuck

reib|en† *vt* rub; (*Culin*) grate ● *vi* (*haben*) rub. **R~ung** *f* **-**

friction. **r~ungslos** *a* (*fig*) smooth
reich *a* rich (**an** + *dat* in)
Reich *nt* **-[e]s, -e** empire; (*König-*) kingdom; (*Bereich*) realm
Reiche(r) *m/f* rich man/woman; **die R~en** the rich *pl*
reichen *vt* hand; (*anbieten*) offer ● *vi* (*haben*) be enough; (*in der Länge*) be long enough; **r~ bis zu** reach [up to]; (*sich erstrecken*) extend to; **mit dem Geld r~** have enough money
reich|haltig *a* extensive, large <*Mahlzeit*> substantial. **r~lich** *a* ample: <*Vorrat*> abundant. **R~tum** *m* **-s, -tümer** wealth (**an** + *dat* of); **R~tümer** riches. **R~weite** *f* reach; (*Techn, Mil*) range
Reif *m* **-[e]s** [hoar-]frost
reif *a* ripe; (*fig*) mature; **r~ für** ready for. **r~en** *vi* (*sein*) ripen; <*Wein, Käse & fig*> mature
Reifen *m* **-s,-** hoop; (*Arm-*) bangle; (*Auto-*) tyre. **R~druck** *m* tyre pressure. **R~panne** *f* puncture, flat tyre
reiflich *a* careful
Reihe *f* **-, -n** row; (*Anzahl & Math*) series; **der R~ nach** in turn; **wer ist an der R~?** whose turn is it? **r~n (sich)** *vr* **sich r~n an** (+ *acc*) follow. **R~nfolge** *f* order. **R~nhaus** *nt* terraced house
Reiher *m* **-s,-** heron
Reim *m* **-[e]s, -e** rhyme. **r~en** *vt* rhyme; **sich r~en** rhyme
rein[1] *a* pure; (*sauber*) clean; <*Unsinn, Dummheit*> sheer; **ins R~e schreiben** make a fair copy of
rein[2] *adv* = **herein, hinein**
Reineclaude /rɛ:nə'klo:də/ *f* **-, -n** greengage
Reinfall *m* [!] let-down; (*Misserfolg*) flop
Rein|gewinn *m* net profit. **R~heit** *f* **-** purity
reinig|en *vt* clean; (*chemisch*) dry-clean. **R~ung** *f* **-, -en** cleaning; (*chemische*) dry-cleaning; (*Geschäft*) dry cleaner's
reinlegen *vt sep* put in; [!] dupe; (*betrügen*) take for a ride
reinlich *a* clean. **R~keit** *f* **-** cleanliness
Reis *m* **-es** rice
Reise *f* **-, -n** journey; (*See-*) voyage; (*Urlaubs-, Geschäfts-*) trip. **R~andenken** *nt* souvenir. **R~büro** *nt* travel agency. **R~bus** *m* coach. **R~führer** *m* tourist guide; (*Buch*) guide. **R~gesellschaft** *f* tourist group. **R~leiter(in)** *m(f)* courier. **r~n** *vi* (*sein*) travel. **R~nde(r)** *m/f* traveller. **R~pass** *m* passport. **R~scheck** *m* traveller's cheque. **R~veranstalter** *m* **-s,-** tour operator. **R~ziel** *nt* destination
Reisig *nt* **-s** brushwood
Reißaus *m* **R~ nehmen** [!] run away
Reißbrett *nt* drawing-board
reißen† *vt* tear; (*weg-*) snatch; (*töten*) kill; **Witze r~** crack jokes; **an sich** (*acc*) **r~** snatch; seize <*Macht*>; **sich r~ um** [!] fight for ● *vi* (*sein*) tear; <*Seil, Faden:*> break ● *vi* (*haben*) **r~ an** (+ *dat*) pull at
Reißer *m* **-s,-** [!] thriller; (*Erfolg*) big hit
Reiß|nagel *m* = **R~zwecke. R~verschluss** *m* zip [fastener]. **R~wolf** *m* shredder. **R~zwecke** *f* **-, -n** drawing-pin
reit|en† *vt/i* (*sein*) ride. **R~er(in)** *m* **-s,-** (*f* **-, -nen**) rider. **R~hose** *f* riding breeches *pl*. **R~pferd** *nt* saddle-horse. **R~weg** *m* bridle-path

Reiz *m* **-es, -e** stimulus; (*Anziehungskraft*) attraction, appeal; (*Charme*) charm. **r~bar** *a* irritable. **R~barkeit** *f* - irritability. **r~en** *vt* provoke; (*Med*) irritate; (*interessieren, locken*) appeal to, attract; arouse <*Neugier*>; (*beim Kartenspiel*) bid. **R~ung** *f* -, **-en** (*Med*) irritation. **r~voll** *a* attractive

rekeln (sich) *vr* stretch

Reklamation /-'tsi̯o:n/ *f* -, **-en** (*Comm*) complaint

Reklam|e *f* -, **-n** advertising, publicity; (*Anzeige*) advertisement; (*TV, Radio*) commercial; **R~e machen** advertise (**für etw** sth). **r~ieren** *vt* complain about; (*fordern*) claim ● *vi* (*haben*) complain

Rekord *m* **-[e]s, -e** record

Rekrut *m* **-en, -en** recruit

Rek|tor *m* **-s, -en** /-'to:rən/ (*Sch*) head[master]; (*Univ*) vice-chancellor. **R~torin** *f* -, **-nen** head, headmistress; vice-chancellor

Relais /rə'lɛ:/ *nt* **-,-** /-s, -s/ (*Electr*) relay

relativ *a* relative

Religi|on *f* -, **-en** religion; (*Sch*) religious education. **r~ös** *a* religious

Reling *f* -, **-s** (*Naut*) rail

Reliquie /re'li:kvi̯ə/ *f* -, **-n** relic

rempeln *vt* jostle; (*stoßen*) push

Reneklode *f* -, **-n** greengage

Renn|bahn *f* race-track; (*Pferde-*) racecourse. **R~boot** *nt* speedboat. **r~en**† *vt/i* (*sein*) run; **um die Wette r~en** have a race. **R~en** *nt* **-s,-** race. **R~pferd** *nt* racehorse. **R~sport** *m* racing. **R~wagen** *m* racing car

renommiert *a* renowned; <*Hotel, Firma*> of repute

renovier|en *vt* renovate; redecorate <*Zimmer*>. **R~ung** *f* - renovation; redecoration

rentabel *a* profitable

Rente *f* -, **-n** pension; **in R~ gehen** [!] retire. **R~nversicherung** *f* pension scheme

Rentier *nt* reindeer

rentieren (sich) *vr* be profitable; (*sich lohnen*) be worth while

Rentner(in) *m* **-s,-** (*f* **-, -nen**) [old-age] pensioner

Reparatur *f* -, **-en** repair. **R~werkstatt** *f* repair workshop; (*Auto*) garage

reparieren *vt* repair, mend

Reportage /-'ta:ʒə/ *f* -, **-n** report

Reporter(in) *m* **-s,-** (*f* **-, -nen**) reporter

repräsentativ *a* representative (**für** of); (*eindrucksvoll*) imposing

Reprodu|ktion /-'tsi̯o:n/ *f* -, **-en** reproduction. **r~zieren** *vt* reproduce

Reptil *nt* **-s, -ien** /-i̯ən/ reptile

Republik *f* -, **-en** republic. **r~anisch** *a* republican

Requisiten *pl* (*Theat*) properties, [!] props

Reservat *nt* **-[e]s, -e** reservation

Reserve *f* -, **-n** reserve; (*Mil, Sport*) reserves *pl*. **R~rad** *nt* spare wheel

reservier|en *vt* reserve; **r~en lassen** book. **r~t** *a* reserved. **R~ung** *f* -, **-en** reservation

Reservoir /rezɛr'vo̯a:ɐ̯/ *nt* **-s, -s** reservoir

Residenz *f* -, **-en** residence

Resign|ation /-'tsi̯o:n/ *f* - resignation. **r~ieren** *vi* (*haben*) (*fig*) give up. **r~iert** *a* resigned

resolut *a* resolute

Resonanz *f* -, **-en** resonanance

Respekt /-sp-, -ʃp-/ *m* **-[e]s** respect (**vor** + *dat* for). **r~ieren** *vt* respect

respektlos *a* disrespectful

Ressort /rɛ'so:ɐ̯/ *nt* **-s, -s** department

Rest *m* **-[e]s, -e** remainder, rest; **R~e** remains; (*Essens-*) leftovers

Restaurant /rɛsto'rã:/ *nt* **-s, -s** restaurant

Restaur|ation /rɛstaura'tsi̯o:n/ *f* **-** restoration. **r~ieren** *vt* restore

Rest|betrag *m* balance. **r~lich** *a* remaining

Resultat *nt* **-[e]s, -e** result

rett|en *vt* save (**vor** + *dat* from); (*aus Gefahr befreien*) rescue; **sich r~en** save oneself; (*flüchten*) escape. **R~er** *m* **-s,-** rescuer; (*fig*) saviour

Rettich *m* **-s, -e** white radish

Rettung *f* **-, -en** rescue; (*fig*) salvation; **jds letzte R~** s.o.'s last hope. **R~sboot** *nt* lifeboat. **R~sdienst** *m* rescue service. **R~sgürtel** *m* lifebelt. **r~slos** *adv* hopelessly. **R~sring** *m* lifebelt. **R~swagen** *m* ambulance

retuschieren *vt* (*Phot*) retouch

Reue *f* **-** remorse; (*Relig*) repentance

Revanch|e /re'vã:ʃə/ *f* **-, -n** revenge; **R~e fordern** (*Sport*) ask for a return match. **r~ieren (sich)** *vr* take revenge; (*sich erkenntlich zeigen*) reciprocate (**mit** with)

Revers /re've:ɐ̯/ *nt* **-,-** /-[s], -s/ lapel

Revier *nt* **-s, -e** district; (*Zool & fig*) territory; (*Polizei-*) [police] station

Revision *f* **-, -en** revision; (*Prüfung*) check; (*Jur*) appeal

Revolution /-'tsi̯o:n/ *f* **-, -en** revolution. **r~är** *a* revolutionary. **r~ieren** *vt* revolutionize

Revolver *m* **-s,-** revolver

rezen|sieren *vt* review. **R~sion** *f* **-, -en** review

Rezept *nt* **-[e]s, -e** prescription; (*Culin*) recipe

Rezession *f* **-, -en** recession

R-Gespräch *nt* reverse-charge call

Rhabarber *m* **-s** rhubarb

Rhein *m* **-s** Rhine. **R~land** *nt* **-s** Rhineland. **R~wein** *m* hock

Rhetorik *f* **-** rhetoric

Rheum|a *nt* **-s** rheumatism. **r~atisch** *a* rheumatic. **R~atismus** *m* **-** rheumatism

Rhinozeros *nt* **-[ses], -se** rhinoceros

rhyth|misch /'rʏt-/ *a* rhythmic[al]. **R~mus** *m* **-, -men** rhythm

richten *vt* direct (**auf** + *acc* at); address <*Frage*> (**an** + *acc* to); aim <*Waffe*> (**auf** + *acc* at); (*einstellen*) set; (*vorbereiten*) prepare; (*reparieren*) mend; **in die Höhe r~** raise [up]; **sich r~** be directed (**auf** + *acc* at; **gegen** against); <*Blick:*> turn (**auf** + *acc* on); **sich r~ nach** comply with <*Vorschrift*>; fit in with <*jds Plänen*>; (*abhängen*) depend on ● *vi* (*haben*) **r~ über** (+ *acc*) judge

Richter *m* **-s,-** judge

richtig *a* right, correct; (*wirklich, echt*) real; **das R~e** the right thing ● *adv* correctly; really; **r~stellen** put right <*Uhr*>; (*fig*) correct <*Irrtum*>; **die Uhr geht r~** the clock is right

Richtlinien *fpl* guidelines

Richtung *f* **-, -en** direction

riechen† *vt/i* (*haben*) smell (**nach** of; **an etw** *dat* sth)

Riegel *m* **-s,-** bolt; (*Seife*) bar

Riemen *m* **-s,-** strap; (*Ruder*) oar

Riese *m* **-n, -n** giant

rieseln *vi* (*sein*) trickle; <*Schnee:*> fall lightly

riesengroß *a* huge, enormous

riesig *a* huge; (*gewaltig*) enormous ● *adv* [!] terribly
Riff *nt* **-[e]s, -e** reef
Rille *f* **-, -n** groove
Rind *nt* **-es, -er** ox; (*Kuh*) cow; (*Stier*) bull; (*R~fleisch*) beef; **R~er** cattle *pl*
Rinde *f* **-, -n** bark; (*Käse-*) rind; (*Brot-*) crust
Rinder|braten *m* roast beef. **R~wahnsinn** *m* [!] mad cow disease
Rindfleisch *nt* beef
Ring *m* **-[e]s, -e** ring
ringeln (sich) *vr* curl
ring|en† *vi* (*haben*) wrestle; (*fig*) struggle (**um/nach** for) ● *vt* wring <*Hände*>. **R~er** *m* **-s,-** wrestler. **R~kampf** *m* wrestling match; (*als Sport*) wrestling
rings|herum, r~um *adv* all around
Rinn|e *f* **-, -n** channel; (*Dach-*) gutter. **r~en†** *vi* (*sein*) run; <*Sand:*> trickle. **R~stein** *m* gutter
Rippe *f* **-, -n** rib. **R~nfellentzündung** *f* pleurisy
Risiko *nt* **-s, -s** & **-ken** risk
risk|ant *a* risky. **r~ieren** *vt* risk
Riss *m* **-es, -e** tear; (*Mauer-*) crack; (*fig*) rift
rissig *a* cracked; <*Haut*> chapped
Rist *m* **-[e]s, -e** instep
Ritt *m* **-[e]s, -e** ride
Ritter *m* **-s,-** knight
Ritual *nt* **-s, -e** ritual
Ritz *m* **-es, -e** scratch. **R~e** *f* **-, -n** crack; (*Fels-*) cleft; (*zwischen Betten, Vorhängen*) gap. **r~en** *vt* scratch
Rival|e *m* **-n, -n, R~in** *f* **-, -nen** rival. **R~ität** *f* **-, -en** rivalry
Robbe *f* **-, -n** seal
Robe *f* **-, -n** gown; (*Talar*) robe
Roboter *m* **-s,-** robot
robust *a* robust
röcheln *vi* (*haben*) breathe stertorously
Rochen *m* **-s,-** (*Zool*) ray
Rock[1] *m* **-[e]s,⸚e** skirt; (*Jacke*) jacket
Rock[2] *m* **-[s]** (*Mus*) rock
rodel|n *vi* (*sein/haben*) toboggan. **R~schlitten** *m* toboggan
roden *vt* clear <*Land*>; grub up <*Stumpf*>
Rogen *m* **-s,-** [hard] roe
Roggen *m* **-s** rye
roh *a* rough; (*ungekocht*) raw; <*Holz*> bare; (*brutal*) brutal. **R~bau** *m* **-[e]s, -ten** shell. **R~kost** *f* raw [vegetarian] food. **R~ling** *m* **-s, -e** brute. **R~öl** *nt* crude oil
Rohr *nt* **-[e]s, -e** pipe; (*Geschütz-*) barrel; (*Bot*) reed; (*Zucker-, Bambus-*) cane
Röhre *f* **-, -n** tube; (*Radio-*) valve; (*Back-*) oven
Rohstoff *m* raw material
Rokoko *nt* **-s** rococo
Roll|bahn *f* taxiway; (*Start-/Landebahn*) runway. **R~balken** *m* scroll bar
Rolle *f* **-, -n** roll; (*Garn-*) reel; (*Draht-*) coil; (*Techn*) roller; (*Seil-*) pulley; (*Lauf-*) castor; (*Theat*) part, role; **das spielt keine R~** (*fig*) that doesn't matter. **r~n** *vt* roll; (*auf-*) roll up; (*Computer*) scroll; **sich r~n** roll ● *vi* (*sein*) roll; <*Flugzeug:*> taxi. **R~r** *m* **-s,-** scooter. **R~rblades (P)** /-ble:ds/ *mpl* Rollerblades
Roll|feld *nt* airfield. **R~kragen** *m* polo-neck. **R~mops** *m* rollmop[s] *sg*
Rollo *nt* **-s, -s** [roller] blind
Roll|schuh *m* roller-skate; **R~schuh laufen** roller-skate. **R~stuhl** *m* wheelchair. **R~treppe** *f* escalator
Rom *nt* **-s** Rome

Roman *m* **-s, -e** novel. **r~isch** *a* Romanesque; <*Sprache*> Romance

Romant|ik *f* **-** romanticism. **r~isch** *a* romantic

Röm|er(in) *m* **-s,-** (*f* **-, -nen**) Roman. **r~isch** *a* Roman

Rommé, Rommee /'rɔme:/ *nt* **-s** rummy

röntgen *vt* X-ray. **R~aufnahme** *f*, **R~bild** *nt* X-ray. **R~strahlen** *mpl* X-rays

rosa *inv a*, **R~** *nt* **-[s],-** pink

Rose *f* **-, -n** rose. **R~nkohl** *m* [Brussels] sprouts *pl*. **R~nkranz** *m* (*Relig*) rosary

Rosine *f* **-, -n** raisin

Rosmarin *m* **-s** rosemary

Ross *nt* **-es,¨er** horse

Rost[1] *m* **-[e]s, -e** grating; (*Kamin-*) grate; (*Brat-*) grill

Rost[2] *m* **-[e]s** rust. **r~en** *vi* (*haben*) rust

rösten *vt* roast; toast <*Brot*>

rostfrei *a* stainless

rostig *a* rusty

rot *a*, **Rot** *nt* **-s,-** red; **rot werden** turn red; (*erröten*) go red, blush

Röte *f* **-** redness; (*Scham-*) blush

Röteln *pl* German measles *sg*

röten *vt* redden; **sich r~** turn red

rothaarig *a* red-haired

rotieren *vi* (*haben*) rotate

Rot|kehlchen *nt* **-s,-** robin. **R~kohl** *m* red cabbage

rötlich *a* reddish

Rotwein *m* red wine

Rou|lade /ru'la:də/ *f* **-, -n** beef olive. **R~leau** /-'lo:/ *nt* **-s, -s** [roller] blind

Routin|e /ru'ti:nə/ *f* **-, -n** routine; (*Erfahrung*) experience. **r~emäßig** *a* routine ... ● *adv* routinely. **r~iert** *a* experienced

Rowdy /'raudi/ *m* **-s, -s** hooligan

Rübe *f* **-, -n** beet; **rote R~** beetroot

Rubin *m* **-s, -e** ruby

Rubrik *f* **-, -en** column

Ruck *m* **-[e]s, -e** jerk

ruckartig *a* jerky

rück|bezüglich *a* (*Gram*) reflexive. **R~blende** *f* flashback. **R~blick** *m* (*fig*) review (**auf** + *acc* of). **r~blickend** *adv* in retrospect. **r~datieren** *vt* (*inf & pp only*) backdate

Rücken *m* **-s,-** back; (*Buch-*) spine; (*Berg-*) ridge. **R~lehne** *f* back. **R~mark** *nt* spinal cord. **R~schwimmen** *nt* backstroke. **R~wind** *m* following wind; (*Aviat*) tail wind

rückerstatten *vt* (*inf & pp only*) refund

Rückfahr|karte *f* return ticket. **R~t** *f* return journey

Rück|fall *m* relapse. **R~flug** *m* return flight. **R~frage** *f* [further] query. **r~fragen** *vi* (*haben*) (*inf & pp only*) check (**bei** with). **R~gabe** *f* return. **r~gängig** *a* **r~gängig machen** cancel; break off <*Verlobung*>. **R~grat** *nt* **-[e]s, -e** spine, backbone. **R~hand** *f* backhand. **R~kehr** return. **R~lagen** *fpl* reserves. **R~licht** *nt* rear-light. **R~reise** *f* return journey

Rucksack *m* rucksack

Rück|schau *f* review. **R~schlag** *m* (*Sport*) return; (*fig*) set-back. **r~schrittlich** *a* retrograde. **R~seite** *f* back; (*einer Münze*) reverse

Rücksicht *f* **-, -en** consideration. **R~nahme** *f* **-** consideration. **r~slos** *a* inconsiderate; (*schonungslos*) ruthless. **r~svoll** *a* considerate

Rück|sitz *m* back seat; (*Sozius*) pillion. **R~spiegel** *m* rear-view mirror. **R~spiel** *nt* return match. **R~stand** *m* (*Chem*) residue; (*Arbeits-*) backlog; **im R~stand sein** be behind.

r~ständig *a* (*fig*) backward. **R~stau** *m* (*Auto*) tailback. **R~strahler** *m* **-s,-** reflector. **R~tritt** *m* resignation; (*Fahrrad*) back pedalling

rückwärt|ig *a* back ..., rear ... **r~s** *adv* backwards. **R~sgang** *m* reverse [gear]

Rückweg *m* way back

rück|wirkend *a* retrospective. **R~wirkung** *f* retrospective force; **mit R~wirkung vom** backdated to. **R~zahlung** *f* repayment

Rüde *m* **-n, -n** [male] dog

Rudel *nt* **-s,-** herd; (*Wolfs-*) pack; (*Löwen-*) pride

Ruder *nt* **-s,-** oar; (*Steuer-*) rudder; **am R~** (*Naut & fig*) at the helm. **R~boot** *nt* rowing boat. **r~n** *vt/i* (*haben/sein*) row

Ruf *m* **-[e]s, -e** call; (*laut*) shout; (*Telefon*) telephone number; (*Ansehen*) reputation. **r~en**† *vt/i* (*haben*) call (**nach** for); **r~en lassen** send for

Ruf|name *m* forename by which one is known. **R~nummer** *f* telephone number. **R~zeichen** *nt* dialling tone

Rüge *f* **-, -n** reprimand. **r~n** *vt* reprimand; (*kritisieren*) criticize

Ruhe *f* **-** rest; (*Stille*) quiet; (*Frieden*) peace; (*innere*) calm; (*Gelassenheit*) composure; **R~ [da]!** quiet! **r~los** *a* restless. **r~n** *vi* (*haben*) rest (**auf** + *dat* on); <*Arbeit, Verkehr*:> have stopped. **R~pause** *f* rest, break. **R~stand** *m* retirement; **im R~stand** retired. **R~störung** *f* disturbance of the peace. **R~tag** *m* day of rest; **'Montag R~tag'** 'closed on Mondays'

ruhig *a* quiet; (*erholsam*) restful; (*friedlich*) peaceful; (*unbewegt, gelassen*) calm; **man kann r~ darüber sprechen** there's no harm in talking about it

Ruhm *m* **-[e]s** fame; (*Ehre*) glory

rühmen *vt* praise

ruhmreich *a* glorious

Ruhr *f* **-** (*Med*) dysentery

Rühr|ei *nt* scrambled eggs *pl*. **r~en** *vt* move; (*Culin*) stir; **sich r~en** move ● *vi* (*haben*) stir; **r~en an** (+ *acc*) touch; (*fig*) touch on. **r~end** *a* touching

Rührung *f* **-** emotion

Ruin *m* **-s** ruin. **R~e** *f* **-, -n** ruin; ruins *pl* (*gen* of). **r~ieren** *vt* ruin

rülpsen *vi* (*haben*) [!] belch

Rum *m* **-s** rum

Rumän|ien /-iən/ *nt* **-s** Romania. **r~isch** *a* Romanian

Rummel *m* **-s** [!] hustle and bustle; (*Jahrmarkt*) funfair

Rumpelkammer *f* junk-room

Rumpf *m* **-[e]s,¨-e** body, trunk; (*Schiffs-*) hull; (*Aviat*) fuselage

rund *a* round ● *adv* approximately; **r~ um** [a]round. **R~blick** *m* panoramic view. **R~brief** *m* circular [letter]

Runde *f* **-, -n** round; (*Kreis*) circle; (*eines Polizisten*) beat; (*beim Rennen*) lap; **eine R~ Bier** a round of beer

Rund|fahrt *f* tour. **R~frage** *f* poll

Rundfunk *m* radio; **im R~** on the radio. **R~gerät** *nt* radio [set]

Rund|gang *m* round; (*Spaziergang*) walk (**durch** round). **r~heraus** *adv* straight out. **r~herum** *adv* all around. **r~lich** *a* rounded; (*mollig*) plump. **R~reise** *f* [circular] tour. **R~schreiben** *nt* circular. **r~um** *adv* all round. **R~ung** *f* **-, -en** curve

Runzel *f* **-, -n** wrinkle

runzlig *a* wrinkled

Rüpel *m* **-s,-** [!] lout

rupfen *vt* pull out; pluck <*Geflügel*>
Rüsche *f* **-, -n** frill
Ruß *m* **-es** soot
Russe *m* **-n, -n** Russian
Rüssel *m* **-s,-** (*Zool*) trunk
Russ|in *f* **-, -nen** Russian. **r~isch** *a* Russian. **R~isch** *nt* **-[s]** (*Lang*) Russian
Russland *nt* **-s** Russia
rüsten *vi* (*haben*) prepare (**zu/für** for) ● *vr* **sich r~** get ready
rüstig *a* sprightly
rustikal *a* rustic
Rüstung *f* **-, -en** armament; (*Harnisch*) armour. **R~skontrolle** *f* arms control
Rute *f* **-, -n** twig; (*Angel-, Wünschel-*) rod; (*zur Züchtigung*) birch; (*Schwanz*) tail
Rutsch *m* **-[e]s, -e** slide. **R~bahn** *f* slide. **R~e** *f* **-, -n** chute. **r~en** *vt* slide; (*rücken*) move ● *vi* (*sein*) slide; (*aus-, ab-*) slip; (*Auto*) skid. **r~ig** *a* slippery
rütteln *vt* shake ● *vi* (*haben*) **r~ an** (+ *dat*) rattle

Ss

Saal *m* **-[e]s,Säle** hall; (*Theat*) auditorium; (*Kranken-*) ward
Saat *f* **-, -en** seed; (*Säen*) sowing; (*Gesätes*) crop
sabbern *vi* (*haben*) [!] slobber; <*Baby:*> dribble; (*reden*) jabber
Säbel *m* **-s,-** sabre
Sabo|tage /zabo'ta:ʒə/ *f* **-** sabotage. **S~teur** /-'tø:ɐ̯/ *m* **-s, -e** saboteur. **s~tieren** *vt* sabotage
Sach|bearbeiter *m* expert. **S~buch** *nt* non-fiction book
Sache *f* **-, -n** matter, business; (*Ding*) thing; (*fig*) cause
Sach|gebiet *nt* (*fig*) area, field. **s~kundig** *a* expert. **s~lich** *a* factual; (*nüchtern*) matter-of-fact
sächlich *a* (*Gram*) neuter
Sachse *m* **-n, -n** Saxon. **S~n** *nt* **-s** Saxony
sächsisch *a* Saxon
Sach|verhalt *m* **-[e]s** facts *pl*. **S~verständige(r)** *m/f* expert
Sack *m* **-[e]s,¨e** sack. **S~gasse** *f* cul-de-sac; (*fig*) impasse. **S~leinen** *nt* sacking
Sadis|mus *m* **-** sadism. **S~t** *m* **-en, -en** sadist
säen *vt/i* (*haben*) sow
Safe /ze:f/ *m* **-s, -s** safe
Saft *m* **-[e]s,¨e** juice; (*Bot*) sap. **s~ig** *a* juicy
Sage *f* **-, -n** legend
Säge *f* **-, -n** saw. **S~mehl** *nt* sawdust
sagen *vt* say; (*mitteilen*) tell; (*bedeuten*) mean
sägen *vt/i* (*haben*) saw
sagenhaft *a* legendary
Säge|späne *mpl* wood shavings. **S~werk** *nt* sawmill
Sahn|e *f* **-** cream. **S~ebonbon** *m & nt* ≈ toffee. **s~ig** *a* creamy
Saison /zɛ'zõ:/ *f* **-, -s** season
Saite *f* **-, -n** (*Mus, Sport*) string. **S~ninstrument** *nt* stringed instrument
Sakko *m & nt* **-s, -s** sports jacket
Sakrament *nt* **-[e]s, -e** sacrament
Sakristei *f* **-, -en** vestry
Salat *m* **-[e]s, -e** salad. **S~soße** *f* salad-dressing
Salbe *f* **-, -n** ointment
Salbei *m* **-s** & *f* **-** sage
salben *vt* anoint

Saldo *m* **-s, -dos** & **-den** balance
Salon /za'lõ:/ *m* **-s, -s** salon
salopp *a* casual; <*Benehmen*> informal
Salto *m* **-s, -s** somersault
Salut *m* **-[e]s, -e** salute. **s~ieren** *vi* (*haben*) salute
Salve *f* **-, -n** volley; (*Geschütz-*) salvo; (*von Gelächter*) burst
Salz *nt* **-es, -e** salt. **s~en**† *vt* salt. **S~fass** *nt* salt-cellar. **s~ig** *a* salty. **S~kartoffeln** *fpl* boiled potatoes. **S~säure** *f* hydrochloric acid
Samen *m* **-s,-** seed; (*Anat*) semen, sperm
Sammel|becken *nt* reservoir. **s~n** *vt/i* (*haben*) collect; (*suchen, versammeln*) gather; **sich s~n** collect; (*sich versammeln*) gather; (*sich fassen*) collect oneself. **S~name** *m* collective noun
Samm|ler(in) *m* **-s,-** (*f* **-, -nen**) collector. **S~lung** *f* **-, -en** collection; (*innere*) composure
Samstag *m* **-s, -e** Saturday. **s~s** *adv* on Saturdays
samt *prep* (+ *dat*) together with
Samt *m* **-[e]s** velvet
sämtlich *indef pron inv* all. **s~e(r,s)** *indef pron* all the; **s~e Werke** complete works
Sanatorium *nt* **-s, -ien** sanatorium
Sand *m* **-[e]s** sand
Sandale *f* **-, -n** sandal
Sand|bank *f* sandbank. **S~kasten** *m* sand-pit. **S~papier** *nt* sandpaper
sanft *a* gentle
Sänger(in) *m* **-s,-** (*f* **-, -nen**) singer
sanieren *vt* clean up; redevelop <*Gebiet*>; (*modernisieren*) modernize; make profitable <*Industrie, Firma*>; **sich s~** become profitable
sanitär *a* sanitary
Sanität|er *m* **-s,-** first-aid man; (*Fahrer*) ambulance man; (*Mil*) medical orderly. **S~swagen** *m* ambulance
Sanktion /zaŋk'tsio:n/ *f* **-, -en** sanction. **s~ieren** *vt* sanction
Saphir *m* **-s, -e** sapphire
Sardelle *f* **-, -n** anchovy
Sardine *f* **-, -n** sardine
Sarg *m* **-[e]s,⸚e** coffin
Sarkasmus *m* **-** sarcasm
Satan *m* **-s** Satan; (🄸 *Teufel*) devil
Satellit *m* **-en, -en** satellite. **S~enfernsehen** *nt* satellite television. **S~enschüssel** *f* satellite dish
Satin /za'tɛŋ/ *m* **-s** satin
Satire *f* **-, -n** satire
satt *a* full; <*Farbe*> rich; **s~ sein** have had enough [to eat]; **etw s~ haben** 🄸 be fed up with sth
Sattel *m* **-s,⸚** saddle. **s~n** *vt* saddle. **S~zug** *m* articulated lorry
sättigen *vt* satisfy; (*Chem & fig*) saturate ● *vi* (*haben*) be filling
Satz *m* **-es,⸚e** sentence; (*Teil-*) clause; (*These*) proposition; (*Math*) theorem; (*Mus*) movement; (*Tennis, Zusammengehöriges*) set; (*Boden-*) sediment; (*Kaffee-*) grounds *pl*; (*Steuer-, Zins-*) rate; (*Druck-*) setting; (*Schrift-*) type; (*Sprung*) leap, bound. **S~aussage** *f* predicate. **S~gegenstand** *m* subject. **S~zeichen** *nt* punctuation mark
Sau *f* **-,Säue** sow
sauber *a* clean; (*ordentlich*) neat; (*anständig*) decent; **s~ machen** clean. **S~keit** *f* **-** cleanliness; neatness
säuberlich *a* neat
Sauce /'zo:sə/ *f* **-, -n** sauce; (*Braten-*) gravy

Saudi-Arabien /-iən/ *nt* **-s** Saudi Arabia
sauer *a* sour; (*Chem*) acid; (*eingelegt*) pickled; (*schwer*) hard; **saurer Regen** acid rain. **S~kraut** *nt* sauerkraut
säuerlich *a* slightly sour
Sauerstoff *m* oxygen
saufen† *vt/i* (*haben*) drink; ☒ booze
Säufer *m* **-s,-** ☒ boozer
saugen† *vt/i* (*haben*) suck; (*staub-*) vacuum, hoover; **sich voll Wasser s~** soak up water
säugen *vt* suckle
Säugetier *nt* mammal
saugfähig *a* absorbent
Säugling *m* **-s, -e** infant
Säule *f* **-, -n** column
Saum *m* **-[e]s,Säume** hem; (*Rand*) edge
säumen *vt* hem; (*fig*) line
Sauna *f* **-, -nas** & **-nen** sauna
Säure *f* **-, -n** acidity; (*Chem*) acid
sausen *vi* (*haben*) rush; <*Ohren:*> buzz ● *vi* (*sein*) rush [along]
Saxophon, Saxofon *nt* **-s, -e** saxophone
S-Bahn *f* city and suburban railway
Scanner *m* **-s,-** scanner
sch *int* shush! (*fort*) shoo!
Schabe *f* **-, -n** cockroach
schaben *vt/i* (*haben*) scrape
schäbig *a* shabby
Schablone *f* **-, -n** stencil; (*Muster*) pattern; (*fig*) stereotype
Schach *nt* **-s** chess; **S~!** check! **S~brett** *nt* chessboard. **S~figur** *f* chess-man
schachmatt *a* **s~ setzen** checkmate; **s~!** checkmate!
Schachspiel *nt* game of chess
Schacht *m* **-[e]s,¨e** shaft
Schachtel *f* **-, -n** box; (*Zigaretten-*) packet
Schachzug *m* move
schade *a* **s~ sein** be a pity *or* shame; **zu s~ für** too good for; **[wie] s~!** what a pity *or* shame!
Schädel *m* **-s**, skull. **S~bruch** *m* fractured skull
schaden *vi* (*haben*) (+ *dat*) damage; (*nachteilig sein*) hurt. **S~** *m* **-s,¨** damage; (*Defekt*) defect; (*Nachteil*) disadvantage. **S~ersatz** *m* damages *pl*. **S~freude** *f* malicious glee
schädig|en *vt* damage, harm. **S~ung** *f* **-, -en** damage
schädlich *a* harmful
Schädling *m* **-s, -e** pest. **S~sbekämpfungsmittel** *nt* pesticide
Schaf *nt* **-[e]s, -e** sheep. **S~bock** *m* ram
Schäfer *m* **-s,-** shepherd. **S~hund** *m* sheepdog; **Deutscher S~hund** alsatian
schaffen[1]† *vt* create; (*herstellen*) establish; make <*Platz*>
schaffen[2] *v* (*reg*) ● *vt* manage [to do]; pass <*Prüfung*>; catch <*Zug*>; (*bringen*) take
Schaffner *m* **-s,-** conductor; (*Zug-*) ticket-inspector
Schaffung *f* **-** creation
Schaft *m* **-[e]s,¨e** shaft; (*Gewehr-*) stock; (*Stiefel-*) leg
Schal *m* **-s, -s** scarf
Schale *f* **-, -n** skin; (*abgeschält*) peel; (*Eier-, Nuss-, Muschel-*) shell; (*Schüssel*) dish
schälen *vt* peel; **sich s~** peel
Schall *m* **-[e]s** sound. **S~dämpfer** *m* silencer. **s~dicht** *a* soundproof. **s~en** *vi* (*haben*) ring out; (*nachhallen*) resound. **S~mauer** *f* sound barrier. **S~platte** *f* record, disc
schalt|en *vt* switch ● *vi* (*haben*) switch/<*Ampel:*> turn (**auf** + *acc* to); (*Auto*) change gear; ([!] *begreifen*) catch on. **S~er** *m* **-s,-** switch; (*Post-, Bank-*) counter; (*Fahrkarten-*) ticket window.

S~hebel *m* switch; (*Auto*) gear lever. **S~jahr** *nt* leap year. **S~ung** *f* **-, -en** circuit; (*Auto*) gear change
Scham *f* **-** shame; (*Anat*) private parts *pl*
schämen (sich) *vr* be ashamed
scham|haft *a* modest. **s~los** *a* shameless
Shampon *nt* **-s** shampoo. **s~ieren** *vt* shampoo
Schande *f* **-** disgrace, shame
schändlich *a* disgraceful
Schanktisch *m* bar
Schanze *f* **-, -n** [ski-]jump
Schar *f* **-, -en** crowd; (*Vogel-*) flock
Scharade *f* **-, -n** charade
scharen *vt* **um sich s~** gather round one; **sich s~ um** flock round. **s~weise** *adv* in droves
scharf *a* sharp; (*stark*) strong; (*stark gewürzt*) hot; <*Geruch*> pungent; <*Wind, Augen, Verstand*> keen; (*streng*) harsh; <*Galopp*> hard; <*Munition*> live; <*Hund*> fierce; **s~ einstellen** (*Phot*) focus; **s~ sein** (*Phot*) be in focus; **s~ sein auf** (+ *acc*) [!] be keen on
Schärfe *f* sharpness; strength; hotness; pungency; keenness; harshness. **s~n** *vt* sharpen
Scharf|richter *m* executioner. **S~schütze** *m* marksman. **S~sinn** *m* astutenes
Scharlach *m* **-s** scarlet fever
Scharlatan *m* **-s, -e** charlatan
Scharnier *nt* **-s, -e** hinge
Schärpe *f* **-, -n** sash
scharren *vi* (*haben*) scrape; <*Huhn*> scratch ● *vt* scrape
Schaschlik *m* & *nt* **-s, -s** kebab
Schatten *m* **-s,-** shadow; (*schattige Stelle*) shade. **S~riss** *m* silhouette. **S~seite** *f* shady side; (*fig*) disadvantage
schattier|en *vt* shade. **S~ung** *f* **-, -en** shading
schattig *a* shady
Schatz *m* **-es,⸚e** treasure; (*Freund, Freundin*) sweetheart
schätzen *vt* estimate; (*taxieren*) value; (*achten*) esteem; (*würdigen*) appreciate
Schätzung *f* **-, -en** estimate; (*Taxierung*) valuation
Schau *f* **-, -en** show. **S~ bild** *nt* diagram
Schauder *m* **-s** shiver; (*vor Abscheu*) shudder. **s~ haft** *a* dreadful. **s~n** *vi* (*haben*) shiver; (*vor Abscheu*) shudder
schauen *vi* (*haben*) (*SGer, Aust*) look; **s~, dass** make sure that
Schauer *m* **-s,-** shower; (*Schauder*) shiver. **S~geschichte** *f* horror story. **s~lich** *a* ghastly
Schaufel *f* **-, -n** shovel; (*Kehr-*) dustpan. **s~n** *vt* shovel; (*graben*) dig
Schaufenster *nt* shop-window. **S~puppe** *f* dummy
Schaukel *f* **-, -n** swing. **s~n** *vt* rock ● *vi* (*haben*) rock; (*auf einer Schaukel*) swing; (*schwanken*) sway. **S~pferd** *nt* rocking-horse. **S~stuhl** *m* rocking-chair
Schaum *m* **-[e]s** foam; (*Seifen-*) lather; (*auf Bier*) froth; (*als Frisier-, Rasiermittel*) mousse
schäumen *vi* (*haben*) foam, froth; <*Seife:*> lather
Schaum|gummi *m* foam rubber. **s~ig** *a* frothy; **s~ig rühren** (*Culin*) cream. **S~stoff** *m* [synthetic] foam. **S~wein** *m* sparkling wine
Schauplatz *m* scene
schaurig *a* dreadful; (*unheimlich*) eerie
Schauspiel *nt* play; (*Anblick*) spectacle. **S~er** *m* actor. **S~erin** *f* actress

Scheck *m* **-s, -s** cheque. **S~buch, S~heft** *nt* cheque-book. **S~karte** *f* cheque card
Scheibe *f* **-, -n** disc; (*Schieß-*) target; (*Glas-*) pane; (*Brot-, Wurst-*) slice. **S~nwischer** *m* **-s,-** windscreen-wiper
Scheich *m* **-s, -e** & **-s** sheikh
Scheide *f* **-, -n** sheath; (*Anat*) vagina
scheid|en† *vt* separate; (*unterscheiden*) distinguish; dissolve <*Ehe*>; **sich s~en lassen** get divorced ● *vi* (*sein*) leave; (*voneinander*) part. **S~ung** *f* **-, -en** divorce
Schein *m* **-[e]s, -e** light; (*Anschein*) appearance; (*Bescheinigung*) certificate; (*Geld-*) note. **s~bar** *a* apparent. **s~en**† *vi* (*haben*) shine; (*den Anschein haben*) seem, appear
scheinheilig *a* hypocritical
Scheinwerfer *m* **-s,-** floodlight; (*Such-*) searchlight; (*Auto*) headlight; (*Theat*) spotlight
Scheiße *f* **-** (*vulg*) shit. **s~n**† *vi* (*haben*) (*vulg*) shit
Scheit *nt* **-[e]s, -e** log
Scheitel *m* **-s,-** parting
scheitern *vi* (*sein*) fail
Schelle *f* **-, -n** bell. **s~n** *vi* (*haben*) ring
Schellfisch *m* haddock
Schelm *m* **-s, -e** rogue
Schelte *f* **-** scolding
Schema *nt* **-s, -mata** model, pattern; (*Skizze*) diagram
Schemel *m* **-s,-** stool
Schenke *f* **-, -n** tavern
Schenkel *m* **-s,-** thigh
schenken *vt* give [as a present]; **jdm Vertrauen s~** trust s.o.
Scherbe *f* **-, -n** [broken] piece
Schere *f* **-, -n** scissors *pl*; (*Techn*) shears *pl*; (*Hummer-*) claw. **s~n**[1]† *vt* shear; crop <*Haar*>
scheren[2] *vt* (*reg*) [!] bother; **sich nicht s~ um** not care about
Scherenschnitt *m* silhouette
Scherereien *fpl* [!] trouble *sg*
Scherz *m* **-es, -e** joke; **im/zum S~** as a joke. **s~en** *vi* (*haben*) joke
scheu *a* shy; <*Tier*> timid; **s~ werden** <*Pferd:*> shy
scheuchen *vt* shoo
scheuen *vt* be afraid of; (*meiden*) shun; **keine Mühe/Kosten s~** spare no effort/expense; **sich s~** be afraid (**vor** + *dat* of); shrink (**etw zu tun** from doing sth)
scheuern *vt* scrub; (*reiben*) rub; **[wund] s~n** chafe ● *vi* (*haben*) rub, chafe
Scheuklappen *fpl* blinkers
Scheune *f* **-, -n** barn
Scheusal *nt* **-s, -e** monster
scheußlich *a* horrible
Schi *m* **-s, -er** ski; **S~ fahren** *od* **laufen** ski
Schicht *f* **-, -en** layer; (*Geol*) stratum; (*Gesellschafts-*) class; (*Arbeits-*) shift. **S~arbeit** *f* shift work. **s~en** *vt* stack [up]
schick *a* stylish; <*Frau*> chic. **S~** *m* **-[e]s** style
schicken *vt/i* (*haben*) send; **s~ nach** send for
Schicksal *nt* **-s, -e** fate. **S~sschlag** *m* misfortune
Schieb|edach *nt* (*Auto*) sun-roof. **s~en**† *vt* push; (*gleitend*) slide; ([!] *handeln mit*) traffic in; **etw s~en auf** (+ *acc*) (*fig*) put sth down to; shift <*Schuld*> on to ● *vi* (*haben*) push. **S~etür** *f* sliding door. **S~ung** *f* **-, -en** [!] illicit deal; (*Betrug*) rigging, fixing
Schieds|gericht *nt* panel of judges; (*Jur*) arbitration tribunal. **S~richter** *m* referee; (*Tennis*) umpire; (*Jur*) arbitrator

schief *a* crooked; (*unsymmetrisch*) lopsided; (*geneigt*) slanting, sloping; (*nicht senkrecht*) leaning; <*Winkel*> oblique; (*fig*) false; suspicious ● *adv* not straight; **s~ gehen** [!] go wrong

Schiefer *m* **-s** slate

schielen *vi* (*haben*) squint

Schienbein *nt* shin

Schiene *f* **-, -n** rail; (*Gleit-*) runner; (*Med*) splint. **s~n** *vt* (*Med*) put in a splint

Schieß|bude *f* shooting-gallery. **s~en†** *vt* shoot; fire <*Kugel*>; score <*Tor*> ● *vi* (*haben*) shoot, fire (**auf** + *acc* at). **S~scheibe** *f* target. **S~stand** *m* shooting-range

Schifahr|en *nt* skiing. **S~er(in)** *m(f)* skier

Schiff *nt* **-[e]s, -e** ship; (*Kirchen-*) nave; (*Seiten-*) aisle

Schiffahrt* *f s.* **Schifffahrt**

schiff|bar *a* navigable. **S~bruch** *m* shipwreck. **s~brüchig** *a* shipwrecked. **S~fahrt** *f* shipping

Schikan|e *f* **-, -n** harassment; **mit allen S~en** [!] with every refinement. **s~ieren** *vt* harass

Schi|laufen *nt* **-s** skiing. **S~läufer(in)** *m(f)* **-s,- (*f* -, -nen)** skier

Schild¹ *m* **-[e]s, -e** shield

Schild² *nt* **-[e]s, -er** sign; (*Nummern-*) plate; (*Mützen-*) badge; (*Etikett*) label

Schilddrüse *f* thyroid [gland]

schilder|n *vt* describe. **S~ung** *f* **-, -en** description

Schild|kröte *f* tortoise; (*See-*) turtle. **S~patt** *nt* **-[e]s** tortoiseshell

Schilf *nt* **-[e]s** reeds *pl*

schillern *vi* (*haben*) shimmer

Schimmel *m* **-s,-** mould; (*Pferd*) white horse. **s~n** *vi* (*haben/sein*) go mouldy

schimmern *vi* (*haben*) gleam

Schimpanse *m* **-n, -n** chimpanzee

schimpf|en *vi* (*haben*) grumble (**mit** at; **über** + *acc* about); scold (**mit jdm** s.o.) ● *vt* call. **S~wort** *nt* (*pl* **-wörter**) swear-word

Schinken *m* **-s,-** ham. **S~speck** *m* bacon

Schippe *f* **-, -n** shovel. **s~n** *vt* shovel

Schirm *m* **-[e]s, -e** umbrella; (*Sonnen-*) sunshade; (*Lampen-*) shade; (*Augen-*) visor; (*Mützen-*) peak; (*Ofen-, Bild-*) screen; (*fig: Schutz*) shield. **S~herrschaft** *f* patronage. **S~mütze** *f* peaked cap

schizophren *a* schizophrenic. **S~ie** *f* **-** schizophrenia

Schlacht *f* **-, -en** battle

schlachten *vt* slaughter, kill

Schlacht|feld *nt* battlefield. **S~hof** *m* abattoir

Schlacke *f* **-, -n** slag

Schlaf *m* **-[e]s** sleep; **im S~** in one's sleep. **S~anzug** *m* pyjamas *pl*

Schläfe *f* **-, -n** (*Anat*) temple

schlafen† *vi* (*haben*) sleep; **s~ gehen** go to bed; **er schläft noch** he is still asleep

schlaff *a* limp; <*Seil*> slack; <*Muskel*> flabby

Schlaf|lied *nt* lullaby. **s~los** *a* sleepless. **S~losigkeit** *f* **-** insomnia. **S~mittel** *nt* sleeping drug

schläfrig *a* sleepy

Schlaf|saal *m* dormitory. **S~sack** *m* sleeping-bag. **S~tablette** *f* sleeping-pill. **S~wagen** *m* sleeping-car, sleeper. **s~wandeln** *vi* (*haben/sein*) sleep-walk. **S~zimmer** *nt* bedroom

Schlag *m* **-[e]s,⸚e** blow; (*Faust-*) punch; (*Herz-, Puls-, Trommel-*) beat; (*einer Uhr*) chime; (*Glocken-, Gong- & Med*) stroke; (*elektrischer*) shock; (*Art*) type; **S⸚e bekommen** get a beating; **S~ auf S~** in rapid succession. **S~ader** *f* artery. **S~anfall** *m* stroke. **S~baum** *m* barrier

schlagen† *vt* hit, strike; (*fällen*) fell; knock <*Loch, Nagel*> (**in** + *acc* into); (*prügeln, besiegen*) beat; (*Culin*) whisk <*Eiweiß*>; whip <*Sahne*>; (*legen*) throw; (*wickeln*) wrap; **sich s~** fight ● *vi* (*haben*) beat; <*Tür:*> bang; <*Uhr:*> strike; (*melodisch*) chime; **mit den Flügeln s~** flap its wings ● *vi* (*sein*) **in etw** (*acc*) **s~** <*Blitz, Kugel:*> strike sth; **nach jdm s~** (*fig*) take after s.o.

Schlager *m* **-s,-** popular song; (*Erfolg*) hit

Schläger *m* **-s,-** racket; (*Tischtennis-*) bat; (*Golf-*) club; (*Hockey-*) stick. **S~ei** *f* **-, -en** fight, brawl

schlag|fertig *a* quick-witted. **S~loch** *nt* pot-hole. **S~sahne** *f* whipped cream; (*ungeschlagen*) whipping cream. **S~seite** *f* (*Naut*) list. **S~stock** *m* truncheon. **S~wort** *nt* (*pl* **-worte**) slogan. **S~zeile** *f* headline. **S~zeug** *nt* (*Mus*) percussion. **S~zeuger** *m* **-s,-** percussionist; (*in Band*) drummer

Schlamm *m* **-[e]s** mud. **s~ig** *a* muddy

Schlamp|e *f* **-, -n** [!] slut. **s~en** *vi* (*haben*) [!] be sloppy (**bei** in). **s~ig** *a* slovenly; <*Arbeit*> sloppy

Schlange *f* **-, -n** snake; (*Menschen-, Auto-*) queue; **S~ stehen** queue

schlängeln (sich) *vr* wind; <*Person:*> weave (**durch** through)

schlank *a* slim. **S~heitskur** *f* slimming diet

schlapp *a* tired; (*schlaff*) limp

schlau *a* clever; (*gerissen*) crafty; **ich werde nicht s~ daraus** I can't make head or tail of it

Schlauch *m* **-[e]s,Schläuche** tube; (*Wasser-*) hose[pipe]. **S~boot** *nt* rubber dinghy

Schlaufe *f* **-, -n** loop

schlecht *a* bad; (*böse*) wicked; (*unzulänglich*) poor; **s~ werden** go bad; <*Wetter:*> turn bad; **mir ist s~** I feel sick; **s~ machen** [!] run down. **s~gehen*** *vi sep* (*sein*) **s~ gehen**, *s.* **gehen**

schlecken *vt/i* (*haben*) lick (**an etw** *dat* sth); (*auf-*) lap up

Schlegel *m* **-s,-** (*SGer: Keule*) leg; (*Hühner-*) drumstick

schleichen† *vi* (*sein*) creep; (*langsam gehen/fahren*) crawl ● *vr* **sich s~** creep. **s~d** *a* creeping

Schleier *m* **-s,-** veil; (*fig*) haze

Schleife *f* **-, -n** bow; (*Fliege*) bowtie; (*Biegung*) loop

schleifen[1] *v* (*reg*) ● *vt* drag ● *vi* (*haben*) trail, drag

schleifen[2]† *vt* grind; (*schärfen*) sharpen; cut <*Edelstein, Glas*>

Schleim *m* **-[e]s** slime; (*Anat*) mucus; (*Med*) phlegm. **s~ig** *a* slimy

schlendern *vi* (*sein*) stroll

schlenkern *vt/i* (*haben*) swing; **s~ mit** swing; dangle <*Beine*>

Schlepp|dampfer *m* tug. **S~e** *f* **-, -n** train. **s~en** *vt* drag; (*tragen*) carry; (*ziehen*) tow; **sich s~en** drag oneself; (*sich hinziehen*) drag on; **sich s~en mit** carry. **S~er** *m* **-s,-** tug; (*Traktor*) tractor. **S~kahn** *m* barge. **S~lift** *m* T-bar lift. **S~tau** *nt* tow-rope; **ins S~tau nehmen** take in tow

Schleuder *f* **-, -n** catapult; (*Wäsche-*) spin-drier. **s~n** *vt*

hurl; spin <*Wäsche*> ● *vi* (*sein*) skid; **ins S~n geraten** skid. **S~sitz** *m* ejector seat

Schleuse *f* **-, -n** lock; (*Sperre*) sluice[-gate]. **s~n** *vt* steer

Schlịche *pl* tricks

schlịcht *a* plain; simple

Schlichtung *f* **-** settlement; (*Jur*) arbitration

Schließe *f* **-, -n** clasp; buckle

schließen† *vt* close (*ab-*) lock; fasten <*Kleid, Verschluss*>; (*stilllegen*) close down; (*beenden, folgern*) conclude; enter into <*Vertrag*>; **sich s~** close; **etw s~ an** (+ *acc*) connect sth to; **sich s~ an** (+ *acc*) follow ● *vi* (*haben*) close, (*den Betrieb einstellen*) close down; (*den Schlüssel drehen*) turn the key; (*enden, folgern*) conclude

Schließ|fach *nt* locker. **s~lich** *adv* finally, in the end; (*immerhin*) after all. **S~ung** *f* **-, -en** closure

Schlịff *m* **-[e]s** cut; (*Schleifen*) cutting; (*fig*) polish

schlịmm *a* bad

Schlịnge *f* **-, -n** loop; (*Henkers-*) noose; (*Med*) sling; (*Falle*) snare

Schlịngel *m* **-s,-** [!] rascal

schlịngen† *vt* wind, wrap; tie <*Knoten*> ● *vi* (*haben*) bolt one's food

Schlịps *m* **-es, -e** tie

Schlịtten *m* **-s,-** sledge; (*Rodel-*) toboggan; (*Pferde-*) sleigh; **S~ fahren** toboggan

schlịttern *vi* (*haben/ sein*) slide

Schlịttschuh *m* skate; **S~ laufen** skate. **S~läufer(in)** *m(f)* **-s,-** (*f* **-, -nen**) skater

Schlịtz *m* **-es, -e** slit; (*für Münze*) slot; (*Jacken-*) vent; (*Hosen-*) flies *pl*. **s~en** *vt* slit

Schlọss *nt* **-es,⸚er** lock; (*Vorhänge-*) padlock; (*Verschluss*) clasp; (*Gebäude*) castle; palace

Schlọsser *m* **-s,-** locksmith; (*Auto-*) mechanic

Schlụcht *f* **-, -en** ravine, gorge

schlụchzen *vi* (*haben*) sob

Schlụck *m* **-[e]s, -e** mouthful; (*klein*) sip

Schlụckauf *m* **-s** hiccups *pl*

schlụcken *vt/i* (*haben*) swallow

Schlụmmer *m* **-s** slumber

Schlụnd *m* **-[e]s** [back of the] throat; (*fig*) mouth

schlụ̈pf|en *vi* (*sein*) slip; **[aus dem Ei] s~en** hatch. **S~er** *m* **-s,-** knickers *pl*. **s~rig** *a* slippery

schlụ̈rfen *vt/i* (*haben*) slurp

Schlụss *m* **-es,⸚e** end; (*S~folgerung*) conclusion; **zum S~** finally; **S~ machen** stop (**mit etw** sth); finish (**mit jdm** with s.o.)

Schlụ̈ssel *m* **-s,-** key; (*Schrauben-*) spanner; (*Geheim-*) code; (*Mus*) clef. **S~bein** *nt* collar-bone. **S~bund** *m & nt* bunch of keys. **S~loch** *nt* keyhole

Schlụssfolgerung *f* conclusion

schlụ̈ssig *a* conclusive

Schlụss|licht *nt* rear-light. **S~verkauf** *m* sale

schmạ̈chtig *a* slight

schmạckhaft *a* tasty

schmal *a* narrow; (*dünn*) thin; (*schlank*) slender; (*karg*) meagre

schmälern *vt* diminish; (*herabsetzen*) belittle

Schmạlz[1] *nt* **-es** lard; (*Ohren-*) wax

Schmạlz[2] *m* **-es** [!] schmaltz

Schmarotzer *m* **-s,-** parasite; (*Person*) sponger

schmạtzen *vi* (*haben*) eat noisily

schmausen *vi* (*haben*) feast

schmẹcken *vi* (*haben*) taste (**nach** of); **[gut] s~** taste good ● *vt* taste

Schmeichelei *f* **-, -en** flattery; (*Kompliment*) compliment
schmeichel|haft *a* complimentary, flattering. **s~n** *vi* (*haben*) (+ *dat*) flatter
schmeißen† *vt/i* (*haben*) **s~ [mit]** 🄵 chuck
Schmeißfliege *f* bluebottle
schmelz|en† *vt/i* (*sein*) melt; smelt <*Erze*>. **S~wasser** *nt* melted snow and ice
Schmerbauch *m* 🄵 paunch
Schmerz *m* **-es, -en** pain; (*Kummer*) grief; **S~en haben** be in pain. **s~en** *vt* hurt; (*fig*) grieve ● *vi* (*haben*) hurt, be painful. **S~ensgeld** *nt* compensation for pain and suffering. **s~haft** *a* painful. **s~los** *a* painless **s~stillend** *a* pain-killing; **s~stillendes Mittel** analgesic, pain-killer. **S~tablette** *f* pain-killer
Schmetterball *m* (*Tennis*) smash
Schmetterling *m* **-s, -e** butterfly
schmettern *vt* hurl; (*Tennis*) smash; (*singen*) sing ● *vi* (*haben*) sound
Schmied *m* **-[e]s, -e** blacksmith
Schmiede *f* **-, -n** forge. **S~eisen** *nt* wrought iron. **s~n** *vt* forge
Schmier|e *f* **-, -n** grease; (*Schmutz*) mess. **s~en** *vt* lubricate; (*streichen*) spread; (*schlecht schreiben*) scrawl ● *vi* (*haben*) smudge; (*schreiben*) scrawl. **S~geld** *nt* 🄵 bribe. **s~ig** *a* greasy; (*schmutzig*) grubby. **S~mittel** *nt* lubricant
Schminke *f* **-, -n** make-up. **s~n** *vt* make up; **sich s~n** put on make-up; **sich** (*dat*) **die Lippen s~n** put on lipstick
schmirgel|n *vt* sand down. **S~papier** *nt* emery-paper
schmollen *vi* (*haben*) sulk
schmor|en *vt/i* (*haben*) braise. **S~topf** *m* casserole
Schmuck *m* **-[e]s** jewellery; (*Verzierung*) ornament, decoration
schmücken *vt* decorate, adorn
schmuck|los *a* plain. **S~stück** *nt* piece of jewellery
Schmuggel *m* **-s** smuggling. **s~n** *vt* smuggle. **S~ware** *f* contraband
Schmuggler *m* **-s,-** smuggler
schmunzeln *vi* (*haben*) smile
schmusen *vi* (*haben*) cuddle
Schmutz *m* **-es** dirt. **s~en** *vi* (*haben*) get dirty. **s~ig** *a* dirty
Schnabel *m* **-s,⸚** beak, bill; (*eines Kruges*) lip; (*Tülle*) spout
Schnalle *f* **-, -n** buckle. **s~n** *vt* strap; (*zu-*) buckle
schnalzen *vi* (*haben*) **mit der Zunge s~** click one's tongue
schnapp|en *vi* (*haben*) **s~en nach** snap at; gasp for <*Luft*> ● *vt* snatch, grab; (🄵 *festnehmen*) nab. **S~schloss** *nt* spring lock. **S~schuss** *m* snapshot
Schnaps *m* **-es,⸚e** schnapps
schnarchen *vi* (*haben*) snore
schnaufen *vi* (*haben*) puff, pant
Schnauze *f* **-, -n** muzzle; (*eines Kruges*) lip; (*Tülle*) spout
schnäuzen (sich) *vr* blow one's nose
Schnecke *f* **-, -n** snail; (*Nackt-*) slug; (*Spirale*) scroll. **S~nhaus** *nt* snail-shell
Schnee *m* **-s** snow; (*Eier-*) beaten egg-white. **S~besen** *m* whisk. **S~brille** *f* snow-goggles *pl*. **S~fall** *m* snowfall. **S~flocke** *f* snowflake. **S~glöckchen** *nt* **-s,-** snowdrop. **S~kette** *f* snow chain. **S~mann** *m* (*pl* **-männer**) snowman. **S~pflug** *m* snowplough. **S~schläger** *m* whisk. **S~sturm** *m* snowstorm,

blizzard. **S~wehe** *f* **-, -n** snowdrift

Schneide *f* **-, -n** [cutting] edge; (*Klinge*) blade

schneiden† *vt* cut; (*in Scheiben*) slice; (*kreuzen*) cross; (*nicht beachten*) cut dead; **Gesichter s~** pull faces; **sich s~** cut oneself; (*über-*) intersect

Schneider *m* **-s,-** tailor. **S~in** *f* **-, -nen** dressmaker. **s~n** *vt* make <*Anzug, Kostüm*>

Schneidezahn *m* incisor

schneien *vi* (*haben*) snow; **es schneit** it is snowing

Schneise *f* **-, -n** path

schnell *a* quick; <*Auto, Tempo*> fast ● *adv* quickly; (*in s~em Tempo*) fast; (*bald*) soon; **mach s~!** hurry up! **S~igkeit** *f* **-** rapidity; (*Tempo*) speed. **S~kochtopf** *m* pressure-cooker. **s~stens** *adv* as quickly as possible. **S~zug** *m* express [train]

schnetzeln *vt* cut into thin strips

Schnipsel *m & nt* **-s,-** scrap

Schnitt *m* **-[e]s, -e** cut; (*Film-*) cutting; (*S~muster*) [paper] pattern; **im S~** (*durchschnittlich*) on average

Schnitte *f* **-, -n** slice [of bread]

schnittig *a* stylish; (*stromlinienförmig*) streamlined

Schnitt|lauch *m* chives *pl*. **S~muster** *nt* [paper] pattern. **S~punkt** *m* [point of] intersection. **S~wunde** *f* cut

Schnitzel *nt* **-s,-** scrap; (*Culin*) escalope. **s~n** *vt* shred

schnitzen *vt/i* (*haben*) carve

schnodderig *a* [!] brash

Schnorchel *m* **-s,-** snorkel

Schnörkel *m* **-s,-** flourish; (*Kunst*) scroll. **s~ig** *a* ornate

schnüffeln *vi* (*haben*) sniff (**an etw** *dat* sth); ([!] *spionieren*) snoop [around]

Schnuller *m* **-s,-** [baby's] dummy

Schnupf|en *m* **-s,-** [head] cold. **S~tabak** *m* snuff

schnuppern *vt/i* (*haben*) sniff (**an etw** *dat* sth)

Schnur *f* **-,⸚e** string; (*Kordel*) cord; (*Electr*) flex

schnüren *vt* tie; lace [up] <*Schuhe*>

Schnurr|bart *m* moustache. **s~en** *vi* (*haben*) hum; <*Katze:*> purr

Schnürsenkel *m* [shoe-]lace

Schock *m* **-[e]s, -s** shock. **s~en** *vt* [!] shock. **s~ieren** *vt* shock

Schöffe *m* **-n, -n** lay judge

Schokolade *f* **-** chocolate

Scholle *f* **-, -n** clod [of earth]; (*Eis-*) [ice-]floe; (*Fisch*) plaice

schon *adv* already; (*allein*) just; (*sogar*) even; (*ohnehin*) anyway; **s~ einmal** before; (*jemals*) ever; **s~ immer/oft/wieder** always/often/again; **s~ deshalb** for that reason alone; **das ist s~ möglich** that's quite possible; **ja s~, aber** well yes, but

schön *a* beautiful; <*Wetter*> fine; (*angenehm, nett*) nice; (*gut*) good; ([!] *beträchtlich*) pretty; **s~en Dank!** thank you very much!

schonen *vt* spare; (*gut behandeln*) look after. **s~d** *a* gentle

Schönheit *f* **-, -en** beauty. **S~sfehler** *m* blemish. **S~skonkurrenz** *f* beauty contest

Schonung *f* **-, -en** gentle care; (*nach Krankheit*) rest; (*Baum-*) plantation. **s~slos** *a* ruthless

Schonzeit *f* close season

schöpf|en *vt* scoop [up]; ladle <*Suppe*>; **Mut s~en** take heart. **s~erisch** *a* creative. **S~kelle**

f, **S~löffel** *m* ladle. **S~ung** *f* **-, -en** creation
Schoppen *m* **-s,-** (*SGer*) ≈ pint
Schorf *m* **-[e]s** scab
Schornstein *m* chimney. **S~feger** *m* **-s,-** chimney-sweep
Schoß *m* **-es,¨-e** lap; (*Frack-*) tail
Schössling *m* **-s, -e** (*Bot*) shoot
Schote *f* **-, -n** pod; (*Erbse*) pea
Schotte *m* **-n, -n** Scot, Scotsman
Schotter *m* **-s** gravel
schott|isch *a* Scottish, Scots. **S~land** *nt* **-s** Scotland
schraffieren *vt* hatch
schräg *a* diagonal; (*geneigt*) sloping; **s~ halten** tilt. **S~strich** *m* oblique stroke
Schramme *f* **-, -n** scratch
Schrank *m* **-[e]s,¨-e** cupboard; (*Kleider-*) wardrobe; (*Akten-, Glas-*) cabinet
Schranke *f* **-, -n** barrier
Schraube *f* **-, -n** screw; (*Schiffs-*) propeller. **s~n** *vt* screw; (*ab-*) unscrew; (*drehen*) turn. **S~nschlüssel** *m* spanner. **S~nzieher** *m* **-s,-** screwdriver
Schraubstock *m* vice
Schreck *m* **-[e]s, -e** fright. **S~en** *m* **-s,-** fright; (*Entsetzen*) horror
Schreck|gespenst *nt* spectre. **s~haft** *a* easily frightened; (*nervös*) jumpy. **s~lich** *a* terrible. **S~schuss** *m* warning shot
Schrei *m* **-[e]s, -e** cry, shout; (*gellend*) scream; **der letzte S~** [!] the latest thing
schreib|en† *vt/i* (*haben*) write; (*auf der Maschine*) type; **richtig/falsch s~en** spell right/wrong; **sich s~en** <*Wort:*> be spelt; (*korrespondieren*) correspond. **S~en** *nt* **-s,-** writing; (*Brief*) letter. **S~fehler** *m* spelling mistake. **S~heft** *nt* exercise book. **S~kraft** *f* clerical assistant; (*für Maschineschreiben*) typist. **S~maschine** *f* typewriter. **S~tisch** *m* desk. **S~ung** *f* **-, -en** spelling. **S~waren** *fpl* stationery *sg*.
schreien† *vt/i* (*haben*) cry; (*gellend*) scream; (*rufen, laut sprechen*) shout
Schreiner *m* **-s,-** joiner
schreiten† *vi* (*sein*) walk
Schrift *f* **-, -en** writing; (*Druck-*) type; (*Abhandlung*) paper; **die Heilige S~** the Scriptures *pl*. **S~führer** *m* secretary. **s~lich** *a* written ● *adv* in writing. **S~sprache** *f* written language. **S~steller(in)** *m* **-s,-** (*f* **-, -nen**) writer. **S~stück** *nt* document. **S~zeichen** *nt* character
schrill *a* shrill
Schritt *m* **-[e]s, -e** step; (*Entfernung*) pace; (*Gangart*) walk; (*der Hose*) crotch. **S~macher** *m* **-s,-** pace-maker. **s~weise** *adv* step by step
schroff *a* precipitous; (*abweisend*) brusque; (*unvermittelt*) abrupt; <*Gegensatz*> stark
Schrot *m* & *nt* **-[e]s** coarse meal; (*Blei-*) small shot. **S~flinte** *f* shotgun
Schrott *m* **-[e]s** scrap[-metal]; **zu S~ fahren** [!] write off. **S~platz** *m* scrap-yard
schrubben *vt/i* (*haben*) scrub
Schrull|e *f* **-, -n** whim; **alte S~e** [!] old crone. **s~ig** *a* cranky
schrumpfen *vi* (*sein*) shrink
schrump[e]lig *a* wrinkled
Schub *m* **-[e]s,¨-e** (*Phys*) thrust; (*S~fach*) drawer; (*Menge*) batch. **S~fach** *nt* drawer. **S~karre** *f*, **S~karren** *m* wheelbarrow. **S~lade** *f* drawer
Schubs *m* **-es, -e** push, shove **s~en** *vt* push, shove
schüchtern *a* shy. **S~heit** *f* **-** shyness

Schuft *m* **-[e]s, -e** (*pej*) swine
Schuh *m* **-[e]s, -e** shoe. **S~anzieher** *m* **-s,-** shoehorn. **S~band** *nt* (*pl* **-bänder**) shoelace. **S~creme** *f* shoe-polish. **S~löffel** *m* shoehorn. **S~macher** *m* **-s,-** shoemaker; (*zum Flicken*) [shoe]mender
Schul|abgänger *m* **-s,-** schoolleaver. **S~arbeiten, S~aufgaben** *fpl* homework *sg*.
Schuld *f* **-, -en** guilt; (*Verantwortung*) blame; (*Geld-*) debt; **S~en machen** get into debt; **S~ haben** be to blame (**an** + *dat* for); **jdm S~ geben** blame s.o. ● **s~ sein** be to blame (**an** + *dat* for). **s~en** *vt* owe
schuldig *a* guilty (*gen* of); (*gebührend*) due; **jdm etw s~ sein** owe s.o. sth. **S~keit** *f* **-** duty
schuld|los *a* innocent. **S~ner** *m* **-s,-** debtor
Schule *f* **-, -n** school; **in der/die S~** at/to school. **s~n** *vt* train
Schüler(in) *m* **-s,-** (*f* **-, -nen**) pupil
schul|frei *a* **s~freier Tag** day without school; **wir haben morgen s~frei** there's no school tomorrow. **S~hof** *m* [school] playground. **S~jahr** *nt* school year; (*Klasse*) form. **S~kind** *nt* schoolchild. **S~stunde** *f* lesson
Schulter *f* **-, -n** shoulder. **S~blatt** *nt* shoulder-blade
Schulung *f* **-** training
schummeln *vi* (*haben*) [!] cheat
Schund *m* **-[e]s** trash
Schuppe *f* **-, -n** scale; **S~n** *pl* dandruff *sg*. **s~n (sich)** *vr* flake [off]
Schuppen *m* **-s,-** shed
schürf|en *vt* mine; **sich** (*dat*) **das Knie s~en** graze one's knee ● *vi* (*haben*) **s~en nach** prospect for. **S~wunde** *f* abrasion, graze
Schürhaken *m* poker
Schurke *m* **-n, -n** villain
Schürze *f* **-, -n** apron
Schuss *m* **-es,⸚e** shot; (*kleine Menge*) dash
Schüssel *f* **-, -n** bowl; (*TV*) dish
Schuss|fahrt *f* (*Ski*) schuss. **S~waffe** *f* firearm
Schuster *m* **-s,-** = **Schuhmacher**
Schutt *m* **-[e]s** rubble. **S~abladeplatz** *m* rubbish dump
Schüttel|frost *m* shivering fit. **s~n** *vt* shake; **sich s~n** shake oneself/itself; (*vor Ekel*) shudder; **jdm die Hand s~n** shake s.o.'s hand
schütten *vt* pour; (*kippen*) tip; (*ver-*) spill ● *vi* (*haben*) **es schüttet** it is pouring [with rain]
Schutz *m* **-es** protection; (*Zuflucht*) shelter; (*Techn*) guard; **S~ suchen** take refuge. **S~anzug** *m* protective suit. **S~blech** *nt* mudguard. **S~brille** *f* goggles *pl*
Schütze *m* **-n, -n** marksman; (*Tor-*) scorer; (*Astr*) Sagittarius
schützen *vt* protect/(*Zuflucht gewähren*) shelter (**vor** + *dat* from) ● *vi* (*haben*) give protection/shelter (**vor** + *dat* from)
Schutz|engel *m* guardian angel. **S~heilige(r)** *m/f* patron saint
Schützling *m* **-s, -e** charge
schutz|los *a* defenceless, helpless. **S~mann** *m* (*pl* **-männer** & **-leute**) policeman. **S~umschlag** *m* dust-jacket
Schwaben *nt* **-s** Swabia
schwäbisch *a* Swabian
schwach *a* weak; (*nicht gut; gering*) poor; (*leicht*) faint
Schwäche *f* **-, -n** weakness. **s~n** *vt* weaken
schwäch|lich *a* delicate. **S~ling** *m* **-s, -e** weakling

Schwachsinn *m* mental deficiency. **s~ig** *a* mentally deficient; [!] idiotic

Schwager *m* **-s,¨** brother-in-law

Schwägerin *f* **-, -nen** sister-in-law

Schwalbe *f* **-, -n** swallow

Schwall *m* **-[e]s** torrent

Schwamm *m* **-[e]s,¨e** sponge; (*SGer: Pilz*) fungus; (*essbar*) mushroom. **s~ig** *a* spongy

Schwan *m* **-[e]s,¨e** swan

schwanger *a* pregnant

Schwangerschaft *f* **-, -en** pregnancy

Schwank *m* **-[e]s,¨e** (*Theat*) farce

schwank|en *vi* (*haben*) sway; <*Boot:*> rock; (*sich ändern*) fluctuate; (*unentschieden sein*) be undecided ● (*sein*) stagger. **S~ung** *f* **-, -en** fluctuation

Schwanz *m* **-es,¨e** tail

schwänzen *vt* [!] skip; **die Schule s~** play truant

Schwarm *m* **-[e]s,¨e** swarm; (*Fisch-*) shoal; ([!] *Liebe*) idol

schwärmen *vi* (*haben*) swarm; **s~ für** [!] adore; (*verliebt sein*) have a crush on

Schwarte *f* **-, -n** (*Speck-*) rind

schwarz *a* black; ([!] *illegal*) illegal; **s~er Markt** black market; **s~ gekleidet** dressed in black; **s~ auf weiß** in black and white; **s~ sehen** (*fig*) be pessimistic; **ins S~e treffen** score a bull's-eye. **S~** *nt* **-[e]s,-** black. **S~arbeit** *f* moonlighting. **s~arbeiten** *vi sep* (*haben*) moonlight. **S~e(r)** *m/f* black

Schwärze *f* **-** blackness. **s~n** *vt* blacken

Schwarz|fahrer *m* fare-dodger. **S~handel** *m* black market (**mit** in). **S~händler** *m* black marketeer. **S~markt** *m* black market. **S~wald** *m* Black Forest. **s~weiß** *a* black and white

schwatzen, (*SGer*) **schwätzen** *vi* (*haben*) chat; (*klatschen*) gossip; (*Sch*) talk [in class] ● *vt* talk

Schwebe *f* **- in der S~** (*fig*) undecided. **S~bahn** *f* cable railway. **s~n** *vi* (*haben*) float; (*fig*) be undecided; <*Verfahren:*> be pending; **in Gefahr s~n** be in danger ● (*sein*) float

Schwed|e *m* **-n, -n** Swede. **S~en** *nt* **-s** Sweden. **S~in** *f* **-, -nen** Swede. **s~isch** *a* Swedish

Schwefel *m* **-s** sulphur

schweigen† *vi* (*haben*) be silent; **ganz zu s~ von** let alone. **S~** *nt* **-s** silence; **zum S~ bringen** silence

schweigsam *a* silent; (*wortkarg*) taciturn

Schwein *nt* **-[e]s, -e** pig; (*Culin*) pork; [x] *Schuft*) swine; **S~ haben** [!] be lucky. **S~ebraten** *m* roast pork. **S~efleisch** *nt* pork. **S~erei** *f* **-, -en** [x] [dirty] mess; (*Gemeinheit*) dirty trick. **S~estall** *m* pigsty. **S~sleder** *nt* pigskin

Schweiß *m* **-es** sweat

schweißen *vt* weld

Schweiz (die) - Switzerland. **S~er** *a & m* **-s,-, S~erin** *f* **-, -nen** Swiss. **s~erisch** *a* Swiss

Schwelle *f* **-, -n** threshold; (*Eisenbahn-*) sleeper

schwell|en† *vi* (*sein*) swell. **S~ung** *f* **-, -en** swelling

schwer *a* heavy; (*schwierig*) difficult; (*mühsam*) hard; (*ernst*) serious; (*schlimm*) bad; **3 Pfund s~ sein** weigh 3 pounds ● *adv* heavily; with difficulty; (*mühsam*) hard; (*schlimm, sehr*) badly, seriously; **s~ krank/verletzt** seriously ill/injured; **s~ hören** be hard of hearing; **etw s~ nehmen** take sth seriously;

jdm s~ fallen be hard for s.o.; **es jdm s~ machen** make it *or* things difficult for s.o.; **sich s~ tun** have difficulty (**mit** with); **s~ zu sagen** difficult *or* hard to say

Schwere *f* - heaviness; (*Gewicht*) weight; (*Schwierigkeit*) difficulty; (*Ernst*) gravity. **S~losigkeit** *f* - weightlessness

schwer|fällig *a* ponderous, clumsy. **S~gewicht** *nt* heavyweight. **s~hörig** *a* **s~hörig sein** be hard of hearing. **S~kraft** *f* (*Phys*) gravity. **s~mütig** *a* melancholic. **S~punkt** *m* centre of gravity; (*fig*) emphasis

Schwert *nt* **-[e]s, -er** sword. **S~lilie** *f* iris

Schwer|verbrecher *m* serious offender. **s~wiegend** *a* weighty

Schwester *f* **-, -n** sister; (*Kranken-*) nurse. **s~lich** *a* sisterly

Schwieger|eltern *pl* parents-in-law. **S~mutter** *f* mother-in-law. **S~sohn** *m* son-in-law. **S~tochter** *f* daughter-in-law. **S~vater** *m* father-in-law

schwierig *a* difficult. **S~keit** *f* **-, -en** difficulty

Schwimm|bad *nt* swimming-baths *pl*. **S~becken** *nt* swimming-pool. **s~en**† *vt/i* (*sein/haben*) swim; (*auf dem Wasser treiben*) float. **S~weste** *f* life-jacket

Schwindel *m* **-s** dizziness, vertigo; ([!] *Betrug*) fraud; (*Lüge*) lie. **S~anfall** *m* dizzy spell. **s~frei** *a* **s~frei sein** have a good head for heights. **s~n** *vi* (*haben*) lie

Schwindl|er *m* **-s,-** liar; (*Betrüger*) fraud, con-man. **s~ig** *a* dizzy; **mir ist** *od* **wird s~ig** I feel dizzy

schwing|en† *vi* (*haben*) swing; (*Phys*) oscillate; (*vibrieren*) vibrate ● *vt* swing; wave <*Fahne*>; (*drohend*) brandish. **S~ung** *f* **-, -en** oscillation; vibration

Schwips *m* **-es, -e einen S~ haben** [!] be tipsy

schwitzen *vi* (*haben*) sweat; **ich schwitze** I am hot

schwören† *vt/i* (*haben*) swear (**auf** + *acc* by)

schwul *a* ([!] *homosexuell*) gay

schwül *a* close. **S~e** *f* - closeness

Schwung *m* **-[e]s,⸚e** swing; (*Bogen*) sweep; (*Schnelligkeit*) momentum; (*Kraft*) vigour. **s~los** *a* dull. **s~voll** *a* vigorous; <*Bogen, Linie*> sweeping; (*mitreißend*) spirited

Schwur *m* **-[e]s,⸚e** vow; (*Eid*) oath. **S~gericht** *nt* jury [court]

sechs *inv a*, **S~** *f* **-, -en** six; (*Sch*) ≈ fail mark. **s~eckig** *a* hexagonal. **s~te(r,s)** *a* sixth

sech|zehn *inv a* sixteen. **s~zehnte(r,s)** *a* sixteenth. **s~zig** *inv a* sixty. **s~zigste(r,s)** *a* sixtieth

See[1] *m* **-s, -n** /ˈzeːən/ lake

See[2] *f* - sea; **an die/der See** to/at the seaside; **auf See** at sea. **S~fahrt** *f* [sea] voyage; (*Schifffahrt*) navigation. **S~gang** *m* **schwerer S~gang** rough sea. **S~hund** *m* seal. **s~krank** *a* seasick

Seele *f* **-, -n** soul

seelisch *a* psychological; (*geistig*) mental

See|macht *f* maritime power. **S~mann** *m* (*pl* **-leute**) seaman, sailor. **S~not** *f* **in S~not** in distress. **S~räuber** *m* pirate. **S~reise** *f* [sea] voyage. **S~rose** *f* water-lily. **S~sack** *m* kitbag. **S~stern** *m* starfish. **S~tang** *m* seaweed.

s~tüchtig *a* seaworthy. **S~zunge** *f* sole

Segel *nt* **-s,-** sail. **S~boot** *nt* sailing-boat. **S~flugzeug** *nt* glider. **s~n** *vt/i* (*sein/haben*) sail. **S~schiff** *nt* sailing-ship. **S~sport** *m* sailing. **S~tuch** *nt* canvas

Segen *m* **-s** blessing

Segler *m* **-s,-** yachtsman

segnen *vt* bless

sehen† *vt* see; watch <*Fernsehsendung*>; **jdn/etw wieder s~** see s.o./sth again; **sich s~ lassen** show oneself ● *vi* (*haben*) see; (*blicken*) look (**auf** + *acc* at); (*ragen*) show (**aus** above); **gut/schlecht s~** have good/bad eyesight; **vom S~ kennen** know by sight; **s~ nach** keep an eye on; (*betreuen*) look after; (*suchen*) look for. **s~swert, s~swürdig** *a* worth seeing. **S~swürdigkeit** *f* **-, -en** sight

Sehne *f* **-, -n** tendon; (*eines Bogens*) string

sehnen (sich) *vr* long (**nach** for)

Sehn|sucht *f* **-** longing (**nach** for). **s~süchtig** *a* longing; <*Wunsch*> dearest

sehr *adv* very; (*mit Verb*) very much; **so s~, dass** so much that

seicht *a* shallow

seid *s.* **sein**[1]

Seide *f* **-, -n** silk

Seidel *nt* **-s,-** beer-mug

seiden *a* silk ... **S~papier** *nt* tissue paper. **S~raupe** *f* silk-worm

seidig *a* silky

Seife *f* **-, -n** soap. **S~npulver** *nt* soap powder. **S~nschaum** *m* lather

Seil *nt* **-[e]s, -e** rope; (*Draht-*) cable. **S~bahn** *f* cable railway. **s~springen**† *vi* (*sein*) (*inf & pp only*) skip. **S~tänzer(in)** *m(f)* tightrope walker

sein†[1]

● *intransitive verb* (*sein*)

····➤ be. **ich bin glücklich** I am happy. **er ist Lehrer/Schwede** he is a teacher/Swedish. **bist du es?** is that you? **sei still!** be quiet! **sie waren in Paris** they were in Paris. **morgen bin ich zu Hause** I shall be at home tomorrow. **er ist aus Berlin** he is *or* comes from Berlin

····➤ (*impers + dat*) **mir ist kalt/besser** I am cold/better. **ihr ist schlecht** she feels sick

····➤ (*existieren*) be. **es ist/sind ...** there is/are .... **es ist keine Hoffnung mehr** there is no more hope. **es sind vier davon** there are four of them. **es war einmal ein Prinz** once upon a time there was a prince

● *auxiliary verb*

····➤ (*zur Perfektumschreibung*) have. **er ist gestorben** he has died. **sie sind angekommen** they have arrived. **sie war dort gewesen** she had been there. **ich wäre gefallen** I would have fallen

····➤ (*zur Bildung des Passivs*) be. **wir sind gerettet worden/wir waren gerettet** we were saved

····➤ (+ *zu* + *Infinitiv*) be to be. **es war niemand zu sehen** there was no one to be seen. **das war zu erwarten** that was to be expected. **er ist zu bemitleiden** he is to be pitied. **die Richtlinien sind strengstens zu beachten** the guidelines are to be strictly followed

sein[2] *poss pron* his; (*Ding, Tier*) its; (*nach man*) one's; **sein Glück versuchen** try one's luck. **s~e(r,s)** *poss pron* his; (*nach man*) one's own; **das S~e tun** do one's share. **s~erseits** *adv* for his part. **s~erzeit** *adv* in those days. **s~etwegen** *adv* for his sake; (*wegen ihm*) because of him, on his account. **s~ige** *poss pron* **der/die/das s~ige** his

seins *poss pron* his; (*nach man*) one's own

seit *conj & prep* (+ *dat*) since; **s~ einiger** Zeit for some time [past]; **ich wohne s~ zehn Jahren hier** I've lived here for ten years. **s~dem** *conj* since ● *adv* since then

Seite *f* -, **-n** side; (*Buch-*) page; **zur S~ treten** step aside; **auf der einen/anderen S~** (*fig*) on the one/other hand

seitens *prep* (+ *gen*) on the part of

Seiten|schiff *nt* [side] aisle. **S~sprung** *m* infidelity. **S~stechen** *nt* **-s** (*Med*) stitch. **S~straße** *f* side-street. **S~streifen** *m* verge; (*Autobahn-*) hard shoulder

seither *adv* since then

seit|lich *a* side ... ● *adv* at/on the side; **s~lich von** to one side of ● *prep* (+ *gen*) to one side of. **s~wärts** *adv* on/to one side; (*zur Seite*) sideways

Sekret|är *m* **-s, -e** secretary; (*Schrank*) bureau. **S~ariat** *nt* **-[e]s, -e** secretary's office. **S~ärin** *f* -, **-nen** secretary

Sekt *m* **-[e]s** [German] sparkling wine

Sekte *f* -, **-n** sect

Sektor *m* **-s, -en** /-'to:rən/ sector

Sekunde *f* -, **-n** second

selber *pron* [!] = **selbst**

selbst *pron* oneself; **ich/du/er/sie s~** I myself /you yourself/ he himself/she herself; **wir/ihr/sie s~** we ourselves/you yourselves/they themselves; **ich schneide mein Haar s~** I cut my own hair; **von s~** of one's own accord; (*automatisch*) automatically; **s~ gemacht** home-made ● *adv* even

selbständig *a* = **selbstständig**. **S~keit** *f* - = **Selbstständigkeit**

Selbst|bedienung *f* self-service. **S~befriedigung** *f* masturbation. **s~bewusst** *a* self-confident. **S~bewusstsein** *nt* self-confidence. **S~bildnis** *nt* self-portrait. **S~erhaltung** *f* self-preservation. **s~gemacht*** *a* **s~ gemacht**, *s.* **selbst**. **s~haftend** *a* self-adhesive. **S~hilfe** *f* self-help. **s~klebend** *a* self-adhesive. **S~kostenpreis** *m* cost price. **S~laut** *m* vowel. **s~los** *a* selfless. **S~mord** *m* suicide. **S~mörder(in)** *m(f)* suicide. **s~mörderisch** *a* suicidal. **S~porträt** *nt* self-portrait. **s~sicher** *a* self-assured. **s~ständig** *a* independent; self-employed <*Handwerker*>; **sich s~ständig machen** set up on one's own. **S~ständigkeit** *f* - independence. **s~süchtig** *a* selfish. **S~tanken** *nt* self-service (*for petrol*). **s~tätig** *a* automatic. **S~versorgung** *f* self-catering. **s~verständlich** *a* natural; **etw für s~verständlich halten** take sth for granted; **das ist s~verständlich** that goes without saying; **s~verständlich!** of course! **S~verteidigung** *f* self-defence. **S~vertrauen** *nt* self-confidence. **S~verwaltung** *f* self-government

selig *a* blissfully happy; (*Relig*) blessed; (*verstorben*) late. **S~keit** *f* - bliss

Sellerie *m* **-s, -s** & *f* **-,-** celeriac; (*Stangen-*) celery

selten *a* rare ● *adv* rarely, seldom; (*besonders*) exceptionally. **S~heit** *f* **-, -en** rarity

seltsam *a* odd, strange. **s~erweise** *adv* oddly

Semester *nt* **-s,-** (*Univ*) semester

Semikolon *nt* **-s, -s** semicolon

Seminar *nt* **-s, -e** seminar; (*Institut*) department; (*Priester-*) seminary

Semmel *f* **-, -n** [bread] roll.. **S~brösel** *pl* breadcrumbs

Senat *m* **-[e]s, -e** senate. **S~or** *m* **-s, -en** /-'to:rən/ senator

senden[1]† *vt* send

sende|n[2] *vt* (*reg*) broadcast; (*über Funk*) transmit, send. **S~r** *m* **-s,-** [broadcasting] station; (*Anlage*) transmitter. **S~reihe** *f* series

Sendung *f* **-, -en** consignment, shipment; (*TV*) programme

Senf *m* **-s** mustard

senil *a* senile. **S~ität** *f* **-** senility

Senior *m* **-s, -en** /-'o:rən/ senior; **S~en** senior citizens. **S~enheim** *nt* old people's home

senken *vt* lower; bring down <*Fieber, Preise*>; bow <*Kopf*>; **sich s~** come down, fall; (*absinken*) subside

senkrecht *a* vertical. **S~e** *f* **-n, -n** perpendicular

Sensation /-'tsio:n/ *f* **-, -en** sensation. **s~ell** *a* sensational

Sense *f* **-, -n** scythe

sensibel *a* sensitive

sentimental *a* sentimental

September *m* **-s,-** September

Serie /'ze:riə/ *f* **-, -n** series; (*Briefmarken*) set; (*Comm*) range. **S~nnummer** *f* serial number

seriös *a* respectable; (*zuverlässig*) reliable

Serpentine *f* **-, -n** winding road; (*Kehre*) hairpin bend

Serum *nt* **-s,Sera** serum

Service[1] /zɛr'vi:s/ *nt* **-[s],-** /-'vi:s[əs], -'vi:sə/ service, set

Service[2] /'zø:ɐvɪs/ *m & nt* **-s** /-vɪs[əs]/ (*Comm, Tennis*) service

servier|en *vt/i* (*haben*) serve. **S~erin** *f* **-, -nen** waitress

Serviette *f* **-, -n** napkin, serviette

Servus *int* (*Aust*) cheerio; (*Begrüßung*) hallo

Sessel *m* **-s,-** armchair. **S~bahn** *f*, **S~lift** *m* chair-lift

sesshaft *a* settled

Set /zɛt/ *nt & m* **-[s], -s** set; (*Deckchen*) place-mat

setz|en *vt* put; (*abstellen*) set down; (*hin-*) sit down <*Kind*>; move <*Spielstein*>; (*pflanzen*) plant; (*schreiben, wetten*) put; **sich s~en** sit down; (*sinken*) settle ● *vi* (*sein*) leap ● *vi* (*haben*) **s~en auf** (+ *acc*) back

Seuche *f* **-, -n** epidemic

seufz|en *vi* (*haben*) sigh. **S~er** *m* **-s,-** sigh

Sex /zɛks/ *m* **-[es]** sex

Sexu|alität *f* **-** sexuality. **s~ell** *a* sexual

sezieren *vt* dissect

Shampoo /ʃam'pu:/, **Shampoon** /ʃam'po:n/ *nt* **-s** shampoo

siamesisch *a* Siamese

sich *refl pron* oneself; (*mit er/sie/es*) himself/herself/itself; (*mit sie pl*) themselves; (*mit Sie*) yourself; (*pl*) yourselves; (*einander*) each other; **s~ kennen** know oneself/ (*einander*) each other; **s~ waschen** have a wash; **s~** (*dat*) **die Haare kämmen** comb one's hair; **s~ wundern** be surprised; **s~ gut verkaufen** sell well; **von s~ aus** of one's own accord

Sichel *f* **-, -n** sickle

sicher *a* safe; (*gesichert*) secure; (*gewiss*) certain; (*zuverlässig*) reliable; sure <*Urteil*>; steady <*Hand*>; (*selbstbewusst*) self-confident; **bist du s~?** are you sure? ● *adv* safely; securely; certainly; reliably; self-confidently; (*wahrscheinlich*) most probably; **s~!** certainly! **s~gehen**† *vi sep* (*sein*) (*fig*) be sure

Sicherheit *f* - safety; (*Pol, Psych, Comm*) security; (*Gewissheit*) certainty; (*Zuverlässigkeit*) reliability; (*des Urteils*) surety; (*Selbstbewusstsein*) self-confidence. **S~sgurt** *m* safety-belt; (*Auto*) seat-belt. **S~snadel** *f* safety-pin

sicherlich *adv* certainly; (*wahrscheinlich*) most probably

sicher|n *vt* secure; (*garantieren*) safeguard; (*schützen*) protect; put the safety-catch on <*Pistole*>. **S~ung** *f* -, **-en** safeguard, protection; (*Gewehr-*) safety-catch; (*Electr*) fuse

Sicht *f* - view; (*S~weite*) visibility; **auf lange S~** in the long term. **s~bar** *a* visible. **S~vermerk** *m* visa. **S~weite** *f* visibility; **außer S~weite** out of sight

sie *pron* (*nom*) (*sg*) she; (*Ding, Tier*) it; (*pl*) they; (*acc*) (*sg*) her; (*Ding, Tier*) it; (*pl*) them

Sie *pron* you; **gehen/warten Sie!** go/wait!

Sieb *nt* **-[e]s, -e** sieve; (*Tee-*) strainer. **s~en¹** *vt* sieve, sift

sieben² *inv a*, **S~** *f* -, **-en** seven. **S~sachen** *fpl* [!] belongings. **s~te(r,s)** *a* seventh

sieb|te(r,s) *a* seventh. **s~zehn** *inv a* seventeen. **s~zehnte(r,s)** *a* seventeenth. **s~zig** *inv a* seventy. **s~zigste(r,s)** *a* seventieth

siede|n† *vt/i* (*haben*) boil. **S~punkt** *m* boiling point

Siedlung *f* -, **-en** [housing] estate; (*Niederlassung*) settlement

Sieg *m* **-[e]s, -e** victory

Siegel *nt* **-s,-** seal. **S~ring** *m* signet-ring

sieg|en *vi* (*haben*) win. **S~er(in)** *m* **-s,-** (*f* -, **-nen**) winner. **s~reich** *a* victorious

siezen *vt* **jdn s~** call s.o. 'Sie'

Signal *nt* **-s, -e** signal

Silbe *f* -, **-n** syllable

Silber *nt* **-s** silver. **s~n** *a* silver

Silhouette /zi'luɛtə/ *f* -, **-n** silhouette

Silizium *nt* **-s** silicon

Silo *m & nt* **-s, -s** silo

Silvester *nt* **-s** New Year's Eve

Sims *m & nt* **-es, -e** ledge

simultan *a* simultaneous

sind *s.* **sein¹**

Sinfonie *f* -, **-n** symphony

singen† *vt/i* (*haben*) sing

Singvogel *m* songbird

sinken† *vi* (*sein*) sink; (*nieder-*) drop; (*niedriger werden*) go down, fall; **den Mut s~ lassen** lose heart

Sinn *m* **-[e]s, -e** sense; (*Denken*) mind; (*Zweck*) point; **in gewissem S~e** in a sense; **es hat keinen S~** it is pointless. **S~bild** *nt* symbol

sinnlich *a* sensory; (*sexuell*) sensual; <*Genüsse*> sensuous. **S~keit** *f* - sensuality; sensuousness

sinn|los *a* senseless; (*zwecklos*) pointless. **s~voll** *a* meaningful; (*vernünftig*) sensible

Sintflut *f* flood

Siphon /'ziːfõ/ *m* **-s, -s** siphon

Sippe *f* -, **-n** clan

Sirene *f* -, **-n** siren

Sirup *m* **-s, -e** syrup; treacle

Sitte *f* -, **-n** custom; **S~n** manners

sittlich *a* moral. **S~keit** *f* - morality. **S~keitsverbrecher** *m* sex offender

sittsam *a* well-behaved; (*züchtig*) demure

Situ|ation /-ˈtsi̯o:n/ *f* **-, -en** situation. **s~iert** *a* **gut/schlecht s~iert** well/badly off

Sitz *m* **-es, -e** seat; (*Passform*) fit

sitzen† *vi* (*haben*) sit; (*sich befinden*) be; (*passen*) fit; (🄸 *treffen*) hit home; **[im Gefängnis] s~** 🄸 be in jail; **s~ bleiben** remain seated; 🄸 (*Sch*) stay *or* be kept down; (*nicht heiraten*) be left on the shelf; **s~ bleiben auf** (+ *dat*) be left with

Sitz|gelegenheit *f* seat. **S~platz** *m* seat. **S~ung** *f* **-, -en** session

Sizilien /-i̯ən/ *nt* **-s** Sicily

Skala *f* **-, -len** scale; (*Reihe*) range

Skalpell *nt* **-s, -e** scalpel

skalpieren *vt* scalp

Skandal *m* **-s, -e** scandal. **s~ös** *a* scandalous

Skandinav|ien /-i̯ən/ *nt* **-s** Scandinavia. **s~isch** *a* Scandinavian

Skat *m* **-s** skat

Skateboard /ˈske:tbo:ɐ̯t/ *nt* **-s, -s** skateboard

Skelett *nt* **-[e]s, -e** skeleton

Skep|sis *f* **-** scepticism. **s~tisch** *a* sceptical

Ski /ʃi:/ *m* **-s, -er** ski; **Ski fahren** *od* **laufen** ski. **S~fahrer(in), S~läufer(in)** *m(f)* **-s,-** (*f* **-, -nen**) skier. **S~sport** *m* skiing

Skizz|e *f* **-, -n** sketch. **s~ieren** *vt* sketch

Sklav|e *m* **-n, -n** slave. **S~erei** *f* **-** slavery. **S~in** *f* **-, -nen** slave

Skorpion *m* **-s, -e** scorpion; (*Astr*) Scorpio

Skrupel *m* **-s,-** scruple. **s~los** *a* unscrupulous

Skulptur *f* **-, -en** sculpture

Slalom *m* **-s, -s** slalom

Slaw|e *m* **-n, -n, S~in** *f* **-, -nen** Slav. **s~isch** *a* Slav; (*Lang*) Slavonic

Slip *m* **-s, -s** briefs *pl*

Smaragd *m* **-[e]s, -e** emerald

Smoking *m* **-s, -s** dinner jacket

Snob *m* **-s, -s** snob. **S~ismus** *m* **-** snobbery **s~istisch** *a* snobbish

so *adv* so; (*so sehr*) so much; (*auf diese Weise*) like this/that; (*solch*) such; (🄸 *sowieso*) anyway; (🄸 *umsonst*) free; (🄸 *ungefähr*) about; **so viel** so much; **so gut/bald wie** as good/soon as; **so ein Zufall!** what a coincidence! **mir ist so, als ob** I feel as if; **so oder so** in any case; **so um zehn Mark** 🄸 about ten marks; **so?** really? ● *conj* (*also*) so; (*dann*) then; **so dass** = **sodass**

sobald *conj* as soon as

Söckchen *nt* **-s,-** [ankle] sock

Socke *f* **-, -n** sock

Sockel *m* **-s,-** plinth, pedestal

Socken *m* **-s,-** sock

sodass *conj* so that

Sodawasser *nt* soda water

Sodbrennen *nt* **-s** heartburn

soeben *adv* just [now]

Sofa *nt* **-s, -s** settee, sofa

sofern *adv* provided [that]

sofort *adv* at once, immediately; (*auf der Stelle*) instantly

Software /ˈzɔftvɛ:ɐ̯/ *f* **-** software

sogar *adv* even

sogenannt *a* so-called

sogleich *adv* at once

Sohle *f* **-, -n** sole; (*Tal-*) bottom

Sohn *m* **-[e]s,¨e** son

Sojabohne *f* soya bean

solange *conj* as long as

solch *inv pron* such; **s~ ein(e)** such a; **s~ einer/eine/eins** one/(*Person*) someone like that. **s~e(r,s)** *pron* such ● (*substantivisch*) **ein s~er/eine s~e/ein s~es** one/(*Person*) someone like that; **s~e** *pl* those; (*Leute*) people like that

Soldat *m* **-en, -en** soldier

Söldner *m* **-s,-** mercenary

Solidarität *f* - solidarity
solide *a* solid; (*haltbar*) sturdy; (*sicher*) sound; (*anständig*) respectable
Solist(in) *m* **-en, -en** (*f* **-, -nen**) soloist
Soll *nt* **-s** (*Comm*) debit; (*Produktions-*) quota

sollen†
● *auxiliary verb*
····➤ (*Verpflichtung*) be [supposed *or* meant] to. **er soll morgen zum Arzt gehen** he is [supposed] to go to the doctor tomorrow. **die beiden Flächen sollen gleich groß sein** the two surfaces are meant to be *or* should be the same size. **du solltest ihn anrufen** you were meant to phone him *or* should have phoned him
····➤ (*Befehl*) **du sollst sofort damit aufhören** you're to stop that at once. **er soll hereinkommen** he is to come in; (*sagen Sie es ihm*) tell him to come in
····➤ **sollte** (*subjunctive*) should; ought to. **wir sollten früher aufstehen** we ought to *or* should get up earlier. **das hätte er nicht tun/sagen sollen** he shouldn't have done/said that
····➤ (*Zukunft, Geplantes*) be to. **ich soll die Abteilung übernehmen** I am to take over the department. **du sollst dein Geld zurückbekommen** you are to *or* shall get your money back. **es soll nicht wieder vorkommen** it won't happen again. **sie sollten ihr Reiseziel nie erreichen** they were never to reach their destination
····➤ (*Ratlosigkeit*) be to; shall. **was soll man nur machen?** what is one to do?; what shall I/we do? **ich weiß nicht, was ich machen soll** I don't know what I should do *or* what to do
····➤ (*nach Bericht*) be supposed to. **er soll sehr reich sein** he is supposed *or* is said to be very rich. **sie soll geheiratet haben** they say *or* I gather she has got married
····➤ (*Absicht*) be meant *or* supposed to. **was soll dieses Bild darstellen?** what is this picture supposed to represent? **das sollte ein Witz sein** that was meant *or* supposed to be a joke
····➤ (*in Bedingungssätzen*) should. **sollte er anrufen, falls** *od* **wenn er anrufen sollte** should he *or* if he should telephone
● *intransitive verb*
····➤ (*irgendwohin gehen sollen*) be [supposed] to go. **er soll morgen zum Arzt/nach Berlin** he is [supposed] to go to the doctor/to Berlin tomorrow. **ich sollte ins Theater** I was supposed to go to the theatre
····➤ (*sonstige Wendungen*) **soll er doch!** let him! **was soll das?** what's that in aid of? [!]

Solo *nt* **-s, -los** & **-li** solo
somit *adv* therefore, so
Sommer *m* **-s,-** summer. **s~lich** *a* summery; (*Sommer-*) summer ... ● *adv* **s~lich warm** as warm as summer. **S~sprossen** *fpl* freckles
Sonate *f* **-, -n** sonata
Sonde *f* **-, -n** probe
Sonder|angebot *nt* special offer. **s~bar** *a* odd. **S~fahrt** *f* special excursion. **S~fall** *m* special case. **s~gleichen** *adv* **eine Gemeinheit s~gleichen** unparalleled meanness. **S~ling** *m* **-s, -e** crank. **S~marke** *f* special stamp
sondern *conj* but; **nicht nur ... s~ auch** not only ... but also

Sonder|preis *m* special price. **S~schule** *f* special school

Sonett *nt* **-[e]s, -e** sonnet

Sonnabend *m* **-s, -e** Saturday. **s~s** *adv* on Saturdays

Sonne *f* **-, -n** sun. **s~n (sich)** *vr* sun oneself

Sonnen|aufgang *m* sunrise. **s~baden** *vi* (*haben*) sunbathe. **S~bank** *f* sunbed. **S~blume** *f* sunflower. **S~brand** *m* sunburn. **S~brille** *f* sunglasses *pl*. **S~energie** *f* solar energy. **S~finsternis** *f* solar eclipse. **S~milch** *f* suntan lotion. **S~öl** *nt* suntan oil. **S~schein** *m* sunshine. **S~schirm** *m* sunshade. **S~stich** *m* sunstroke. **S~uhr** *f* sundial. **S~untergang** *m* sunset. **S~wende** *f* solstice

sonnig *a* sunny

Sonntag *m* **-s, -e** Sunday. **s~s** *adv* on Sundays

sonst *adv* (*gewöhnlich*) usually; (*im Übrigen*) apart from that; (*andernfalls*) otherwise, or [else]; **wer/was/wie/wo s~?** who/what/how/where else? **s~ niemand** no one else; **s~ noch etwas?** anything else? **s~ noch Fragen?** any more questions? **s~ jemand** *od* **wer** someone/(*fragend, verneint*) anyone else; (*irgendjemand*) [just] anyone; **s~ wo** somewhere/(*fragend, verneint*) anywhere else; (*irgendwo*) [just] anywhere. **s~ig** *a* other

sooft *conj* whenever

Sopran *m* **-s, -e** soprano

Sorge *f* **-, -n** worry (**um** about); (*Fürsorge*) care; **sich** (*dat*) **S~n machen** worry. **s~n** *vi* (*haben*) **s~n für** look after, care for; (*vorsorgen*) provide for; (*sich kümmern*) see to; **dafür s~n, dass** see *or* make sure that ● *vr* **sich s~n** worry. **s~nfrei** *a* carefree. **s~nvoll** *a* worried. **S~recht** *nt* (*Jur*) custody

Sorg|falt *f* **-** care. **s~fältig** *a* careful

Sorte *f* **-, -n** kind, sort; (*Comm*) brand

sort|ieren *vt* sort [out]; (*Comm*) grade. **S~iment** *nt* **-[e]s, -e** range

sosehr *conj* however much

Soße *f* **-, -n** sauce; (*Braten-*) gravy; (*Salat-*) dressing

Souvenir /zuvəˈniːɐ̯/ *nt* **-s, -s** souvenir

souverän /zuvəˈrɛːn/ *a* sovereign

soviel *conj* however much; **s~ ich weiß** as far as I know ● *adv* ***so viel**, *s.* **viel**

soweit *conj* as far as; (*insoweit*) [in] so far as ● *adv* ***so weit**, *s.* **weit**

sowenig *conj* however little ● *adv* ***so wenig**, *s.* **wenig**

sowie *conj* as well as; (*sobald*) as soon as

sowieso *adv* anyway, in any case

sowjet|isch *a* Soviet. **S~union** *f* **-** Soviet Union

sowohl *adv* **s~ ... als** *od* **wie auch ...** ... as well as ...

sozial *a* social; <*Einstellung, Beruf*> caring. **S~arbeit** *f* social work. **S~demokrat** *m* social democrat. **S~hilfe** *f* social security

Sozialis|mus *m* **-** socialism. **S~t** *m* **-en, -en** socialist

Sozial|versicherung *f* National Insurance. **S~wohnung** *f* ≈ council flat

Soziologie *f* **-** sociology

Sozius *m* **-, -se** (*Comm*) partner; (*Beifahrersitz*) pillion

Spachtel *m* **-s,- &** *f* **-, -n** spatula

Spagat *m* **-[e]s, -e** (*Aust*) string; **S~ machen** do the splits *pl*

Spaghetti, Spagetti *pl* spaghetti *sg*
Spalier *nt* **-s, -e** trellis
Spalt|e *f* **-, -n** crack; (*Gletscher-*) crevasse; (*Druck-*) column; (*Orangen-*) segment. **s~en**† *vt* split. **S~ung** *f* **-, -en** splitting; (*Kluft*) split; (*Phys*) fission
Span *m* **-[e]s,¨e** [wood] chip
Spange *f* **-, -n** clasp; (*Haar-*) slide; (*Zahn-*) brace
Span|ien /-iən/ *nt* **-s** Spain. **S~ier** *m* **-s,-**, **S~ierin** *f* **-, -nen** Spaniard. **s~isch** *a* Spanish. **S~isch** *nt* **-[s]** (*Lang*) Spanish
Spann *m* **-[e]s** instep
Spanne *f* **-, -n** span; (*Zeit-*) space; (*Comm*) margin
spann|en *vt* stretch; put up <*Leine*>; (*straffen*) tighten; (*an-*) harness (**an** + *acc* to); **sich s~en** tighten ● *vi* (*haben*) be too tight. **s~end** *a* exciting. **S~ung** *f* **-, -en** tension; (*Erwartung*) suspense; (*Electr*) voltage
Spar|buch *nt* savings book. **S~büchse** *f* money-box. **s~en** *vt/i* (*haben*) save; (*sparsam sein*) economize (**mit/an** + *dat* on). **S~er** *m* **-s,-** saver
Spargel *m* **-s,-** asparagus
Spar|kasse *f* savings bank. **S~konto** *nt* deposit account
sparsam *a* economical; <*Person*> thrifty. **S~keit** *f* **-** economy; thrift
Sparschwein *nt* piggy bank
Sparte *f* **-, -n** branch; (*Zeitungs-*) section; (*Rubrik*) column
Spaß *m* **-es,¨e** fun; (*Scherz*) joke; **im/aus/zum S~** for fun; **S~ machen** be fun; <*Person:*> be joking; **viel S~!** have a good time! **s~en** *vi* (*haben*) joke. **S~vogel** *m* joker
Spastiker *m* **-s,-** spastic
spät *a* & *adv* late; **wie s~ ist es?** what time is it? **zu s~ kommen** be late
Spaten *m* **-s,-** spade
später *a* later; (*zukünftig*) future ● *adv* later
spätestens *adv* at the latest
Spatz *m* **-en, -en** sparrow
Spätzle *pl* (*Culin*) noodles
spazieren *vi* (*sein*) stroll; **s~gehen** go for a walk
Spazier|gang *m* walk; **einen S~gang machen** go for a walk. **S~gänger(in)** *m* **-s,-** (*f* **-, -nen**) walker. **S~stock** *m* walking-stick
Specht *m* **-[e]s, -e** woodpecker
Speck *m* **-s** bacon. **s~ig** *a* greasy
Spedi|teur /ʃpedi'tøːɐ̯/ *m* **-s, -e** haulage/(*für Umzüge*) removals contractor. **S~tion** /-'tsi̯oːn/ *f* **-, -en** carriage, haulage; (*Firma*) haulage/(*für Umzüge*) removals firm
Speer *m* **-[e]s, -e** spear; (*Sport*) javelin
Speiche *f* **-, -n** spoke
Speichel *m* **-s** saliva
Speicher *m* **-s,-** warehouse; (*dial: Dachboden*) attic; (*Computer*) memory. **s~n** *vt* store
Speise *f* **-, -n** food; (*Gericht*) dish; (*Pudding*) blancmange. **S~eis** *nt* ice-cream. **S~kammer** *f* larder. **S~karte** *f* menu. **s~n** *vi* (*haben*) eat ● *vt* feed. **S~röhre** *f* oesophagus. **S~saal** *m* dining-room. **S~wagen** *m* dining-car
Spektrum *nt* **-s, -tra** spectrum
Spekul|ant *m* **-en, -en** speculator. **s~ieren** *vi* (*haben*) speculate; **s~ieren auf** (+ *acc*) ! hope to get
Spelze *f* **-, -n** husk
spendabel *a* generous
Spende *f* **-, -n** donation. **s~n** *vt* donate; give <*Blut, Schatten*>;

Beifall s~n applaud. **S~r** *m* **-s,-** donor; (*Behälter*) dispenser

spendieren *vt* pay for

Sperling *m* **-s, -e** sparrow

Sperre *f* **-, -n** barrier; (*Verbot*) ban; (*Comm*) embargo. **s~n** *vt* close; (*ver-*) block; (*verbieten*) ban; cut off <*Strom, Telefon*>; stop <*Scheck, Kredit*>; **s~n in** (+ *acc*) put in <*Gefängnis, Käfig*>

Sperr|holz *nt* plywood. **S~müll** *m* bulky refuse. **S~stunde** *f* closing time

Spesen *pl* expenses

spezial|isieren (sich) *vr* specialize (**auf** + *acc* in). **S~ist** *m* **-en, -en** specialist. **S~ität** *f* **-, -en** speciality

spicken *vt* (*Culin*) lard; **gespickt mit** (*fig*) full of ● *vi* (*haben*) [!] crib (**bei** from)

Spiegel *m* **-s,-** mirror; (*Wasser-, Alkohol-*) level. **S~bild** *nt* reflection. **S~ei** *nt* fried egg. **s~n** *vt* reflect; **sich s~n** be reflected ● *vi* (*haben*) reflect [the light]; (*glänzen*) gleam. **S~ung** *f* **-, -en** reflection

Spiel *nt* **-[e]s, -e** game; (*Spielen*) playing; (*Glücks-*) gambling; (*Schau-*) play; (*Satz*) set; **auf dem S~ stehen** be at stake; **aufs S~ setzen** risk. **S~automat** *m* fruit machine. **S~bank** *f* casino. **S~dose** *f* musical box. **s~en** *vt/i* (*haben*) play; (*im Glücksspiel*) gamble; (*vortäuschen*) act; <*Roman:*> be set (**in** + *dat* in); **s~en mit** (*fig*) toy with

Spieler(in) *m* **-s,-** (*f* **-, -nen**) player; (*Glücks-*) gambler

Spiel|feld *nt* field, pitch. **S~marke** *f* chip. **S~plan** *m* programme. **S~platz** *m* playground. **S~raum** *m* (*fig*) scope; (*Techn*) clearance. **S~regeln** *fpl* rules [of the game]. **S~sachen** *fpl* toys. **S~verderber** *m* **-s,-** spoilsport. **S~waren** *fpl* toys. **S~warengeschäft** *nt* toyshop. **S~zeug** *nt* toy; (*S~sachen*) toys *pl*

Spieß *m* **-es, -e** spear; (*Brat-*) spit; skewer; (*Fleisch-*) kebab. **S~er** *m* **-s,-** [petit] bourgeois. **s~ig** *a* bourgeois

Spike[s]reifen /ˈʃpaik[s]-/ *m* studded tyre

Spinat *m* **-s** spinach

Spindel *f* **-, -n** spindle

Spinne *f* **-, -n** spider

spinn|en† *vt/i* (*haben*) spin; **er spinnt** [!] he's crazy. **S~[en]gewebe** *nt*, **S~webe** *f* **-, -n** cobweb

Spion *m* **-s, -e** spy

Spionage /ʃpioˈnaːʒə/ *f* **-** espionage, spying. **S~abwehr** *f* counter-espionage

spionieren *vi* (*haben*) spy

Spionin *f* **-, -nen** [woman] spy

Spiral|e *f* **-, -n** spiral. **s~ig** *a* spiral

Spirituosen *pl* spirits

Spiritus *m* **-** alcohol; (*Brenn-*) methylated spirits *pl*. **S~kocher** *m* spirit stove

spitz *a* pointed; (*scharf*) sharp; (*schrill*) shrill; <*Winkel*> acute. **S~bube** *m* scoundrel

Spitze *f* **-, -n** point; (*oberer Teil*) top; (*vorderer Teil*) front; (*Pfeil-, Finger-, Nasen-*) tip; (*Schuh-, Strumpf-*) toe; (*Zigarren-, Zigaretten-*) holder; (*Höchstleistung*) maximum; (*Tex*) lace; ([!] *Anspielung*) dig; **an der S~ liegen** be in the lead

Spitzel *m* **-s,-** informer

spitzen *vt* sharpen; purse <*Lippen*>; prick up <*Ohren*>. **S~geschwindigkeit** *f* top speed

Spitzname *m* nickname

Spleen /ʃpli:n/ *m* **-s, -e** obsession

Splitter *m* **-s,-** splinter. **s~n** *vi* (*sein*) shatter

sponsern *vt* sponsor

Spore *f* **-, -n** (*Biol*) spore

Sporn *m* **-[e]s, Sporen** spur

Sport *m* **-[e]s** sport; (*Hobby*) hobby. **S~art** *f* sport. **S~ler** *m* **-s,-** sportsman. **S~lerin** *f* **-, -nen** sportswoman. **s~lich** *a* sports ...; (*fair*) sporting; (*schlank*) sporty. **S~platz** *m* sports ground. **S~verein** *m* sports club. **S~wagen** *m* sports car; (*Kinder-*) push-chair, (*Amer*) stroller

Spott *m* **-[e]s** mockery

spotten *vi* (*haben*) mock; **s~ über** (+ *acc*) make fun of; (*höhnend*) ridicule

spöttisch *a* mocking

Sprach|e *f* **-, -n** language; (*Sprechfähigkeit*) speech; **zur S~e bringen** bring up. **S~fehler** *m* speech defect. **S~labor** *nt* language laboratory. **s~lich** *a* linguistic. **s~los** *a* speechless

Spray /ʃpre:/ *nt & m* **-s, -s** spray. **S~dose** *f* aerosol [can]

Sprechanlage *f* intercom

sprechen† *vi* (*haben*) speak/(*sich unterhalten*) talk (**über** + *acc*/**von** about/of); **Deutsch s~** speak German ● *vt* speak; (*sagen*) say; pronounce <*Urteil*>; **schuldig s~** find guilty; **Herr X ist nicht zu s~** Mr X is not available

Sprecher(in) *m* **-s,-** (*f* **-, -nen**) speaker; (*Radio, TV*) announcer; (*Wortführer*) spokesman, *f* spokeswoman

Sprechstunde *f* consulting hours *pl*; (*Med*) surgery. **S~nhilfe** *f* (*Med*) receptionist

Sprechzimmer *nt* consulting room

spreizen *vt* spread

spreng|en *vt* blow up; blast <*Felsen*>; (*fig*) burst; (*begießen*) water; (*mit Sprenger*) sprinkle; dampen <*Wäsche*>. **S~er** *m* **-s,-** sprinkler. **S~kopf** *m* warhead. **S~körper** *m* explosive device. **S~stoff** *m* explosive

Spreu *f* - chaff

Sprich|wort *nt* (*pl* **-wörter**) proverb. **s~wörtlich** *a* proverbial

Springbrunnen *m* fountain

spring|en† *vi* (*sein*) jump; (*Schwimmsport*) dive; <*Ball:*> bounce; (*spritzen*) spurt; (*zer-*) break; (*rissig werden*) crack; (*SGer: laufen*) run. **S~er** *m* **-s,-** jumper; (*Kunst-*) diver; (*Schach*) knight. **S~reiten** *nt* show-jumping

Sprint *m* **-s, -s** sprint

Spritz|e *f* **-, -n** syringe; (*Injektion*) injection; (*Feuer-*) hose. **s~en** *vt* spray; (*be-, ver-*) splash; (*Culin*) pipe; (*Med*) inject ● *vi* (*haben*) splash; <*Fett:*> spit ● *vi* (*sein*) splash; (*hervor-*) spurt. **S~er** *m* **-s,-** splash; (*Schuss*) dash

spröde *a* brittle; (*trocken*) dry

Sprosse *f* **-, -n** rung

Sprotte *f* **-, -n** sprat

Spruch *m* **-[e]s,¨-e** saying; (*Denk-*) motto; (*Zitat*) quotation. **S~band** *nt* (*pl* **-bänder**) banner

Sprudel *m* **-s,-** sparkling mineral water. **s~n** *vi* (*haben/sein*) bubble

Sprüh|dose *f* aerosol [can]. **s~en** *vt* spray ● *vi* (*sein*) <*Funken:*> fly; (*fig*) sparkle

Sprung *m* **-[e]s,¨-e** jump, leap; (*Schwimmsport*) dive; (**!** *Katzen-*) stone's throw; (*Riss*) crack. **S~brett** *nt* springboard. **S~schanze** *f* ski-jump. **S~seil** *nt* skipping-rope

Spucke *f* - spit. **s~n** *vt/i* (*haben*) spit; (*sich übergeben*) be sick

Spuk *m* **-[e]s, -e** [ghostly] apparition. **s~en** *vi* (*haben*) <*Geist:*> walk; **in diesem Haus s~t es** this house is haunted

Spülbecken *nt* sink

Spule *f* **-, -n** spool

Spüle *f* **-, -n** sink

spulen *vt* spool

spül|en *vt* rinse; (*schwemmen*) wash; **Geschirr s~en** wash up ● *vi* (*haben*) flush [the toilet]. **S~kasten** *m* cistern. **S~mittel** *nt* washing-up liquid

Spur *f* **-, -en** track; (*Fahr-*) lane; (*Fährte*) trail; (*Anzeichen*) trace; (*Hinweis*) lead

spürbar *a* noticeable

spür|en *vt* feel; (*seelisch*) sense. **S~hund** *m* tracker dog

spurlos *adv* without trace

spurten *vi* (*sein*) put on a spurt

sputen (sich) *vr* hurry

Staat *m* **-[e]s, -en** state; (*Land*) country; (*Putz*) finery. **s~lich** *a* state ... ● *adv* by the state

Staatsangehörig|e(r) *m|f* national. **S~keit** *f* **-** nationality

Staats|anwalt *m* state prosecutor. **S~beamte(r)** *m* civil servant. **S~besuch** *m* state visit. **S~bürger(in)** *m(f)* national. **S~mann** *m* (*pl* **-männer**) statesman. **S~streich** *m* coup

Stab *m* **-[e]s,¨e** rod; (*Gitter-*) bar (*Sport*) baton; (*Mil*) staff

Stäbchen *ntpl* chopsticks

Stabhochsprung *m* pole-vault

stabil *a* stable; (*gesund*) robust; (*solide*) sturdy

Stachel *m* **-s,-** spine; (*Gift-*) sting; (*Spitze*) spike. **S~beere** *f* goose-berry. **S~draht** *m* barbed wire. **S~schwein** *nt* porcupine

Stadion *nt* **-s, -ien** stadium

Stadium *nt* **-s, -ien** stage

Stadt *f* **-,¨e** town; (*Groß-*) city

städtisch *a* urban; (*kommunal*) municipal

Stadt|mitte *f* town centre. **S~plan** *m* street map. **S~teil** *m* district

Staffel *f* **-, -n** team; (*S~lauf*) relay; (*Mil*) squadron

Staffelei *f* **-, -en** easel

Staffel|lauf *m* relay race. **s~n** *vt* stagger; (*abstufen*) grade

Stahl *m* **-s** steel. **S~beton** *m* reinforced concrete

Stall *m* **-[e]s,¨e** stable; (*Kuh-*) shed; (*Schweine-*) sty; (*Hühner-*) coop; (*Kaninchen-*) hutch

Stamm *m* **-[e]s¨e** trunk; (*Sippe*) tribe; (*Wort-*) stem. **S~baum** *m* family tree; (*eines Tieres*) pedigree

stammeln *vt/i* (*haben*) stammer

stammen *vi* (*haben*) come/ (*zeitlich*) date (**von/aus** from)

stämmig *a* sturdy

Stamm|kundschaft *f* regulars *pl*. **S~lokal** *nt* favourite pub

stampfen *vi* (*haben*) stamp; <*Maschine:*> pound ● *vi* (*sein*) tramp ● *vt* pound; mash <*Kartoffeln*>

Stand *m* **-[e]s,¨e** standing position; (*Zustand*) state; (*Spiel-*) score; (*Höhe*) level; (*gesellschaftlich*) class; (*Verkaufs-*) stall; (*Messe-*) stand; (*Taxi-*) rank; **auf den neuesten S~ bringen** update

Standard *m* **-s, -s** standard

Standbild *nt* statue

Ständer *m* **-s,-** stand; (*Geschirr-*) rack; (*Kerzen-*) holder

Standes|amt *nt* registry office. **S~beamte(r)** *m* registrar

standhaft *a* steadfast

ständig *a* constant; (*fest*) permanent

Stand|licht *nt* sidelights *pl*. **S~ort** *m* position; (*Firmen-*) location; (*Mil*) garrison.

S~punkt *m* point of view. **S~uhr** *f* grandfather clock

Stange *f* **-, -n** bar; (*Holz-*) pole; (*Gardinen-*) rail; (*Hühner-*) perch; (*Zimt-*) stick; **von der S~** [!] off the peg

Stängel *m* **-s,-** stalk, stem

Stangenbohne *f* runner bean

Stanniol *nt* **-s** tin foil. **S~papier** *nt* silver paper

stanzen *vt* stamp; punch <*Loch*>

Stapel *m* **-s,-** stack, pile. **S~lauf** *m* launch[ing]. **s~n** *vt* stack *or* pile up

Star[1] *m* **-[e]s, -e** starling

Star[2] *m* **-[e]s** (*Med*) **[grauer] S~** cataract; **grüner S~** glaucoma

Star[3] *m* **-s, -s** (*Theat, Sport*) star

stark *a* strong; <*Motor*> powerful; <*Verkehr, Regen*> heavy; <*Hitze, Kälte*> severe; (*groß*) big; (*schlimm*) bad; (*dick*) thick; (*korpulent*) stout ● *adv* (*sehr*) very much

Stärk|e *f* **-, -n** strength; power; thickness; stoutness; (*Größe*) size; (*Mais-, Wäsche-*) starch. **S~emehl** *nt* cornflour. **s~en** *vt* strengthen; starch <*Wäsche*>; **sich s~en** fortify oneself. **S~ung** *f* **-, -en** strengthening; (*Erfrischung*) refreshment

starr *a* rigid; (*steif*) stiff

starren *vi* (*haben*) stare

Starrsinn *m* obstinacy. **s~ig** *a* obstinate

Start *m* **-s, -s** start; (*Aviat*) take-off. **S~bahn** *f* runway. **s~en** *vi* (*sein*) start; (*Aviat*) take off ● *vt* start; (*fig*) launch

Station /-ˈtsi̯oːn/ *f* **-, -en** station; (*Haltestelle*) stop; (*Abschnitt*) stage; (*Med*) ward; **S~ machen** break one's journey. **s~är** *adv* as an inpatient. **s~ieren** *vt* station

statisch *a* static

Statist(in) *m* **-en, -en** (*f* **-, -nen**) (*Theat*) extra

Statisti|k *f* **-, -en** statistics *sg*; (*Aufstellung*) statistics *pl*. **s~sch** *a* statistical

Stativ *nt* **-s, -e** (*Phot*) tripod

statt *prep* (+ *gen*) instead of; **an seiner s~** in his place; **an Kindes s~ annehmen** adopt ● *conj* **s~ etw zu tun** instead of doing sth. **s~dessen** *adv* instead

statt|finden† *vi sep* (*haben*) take place. **s~haft** *a* permitted

Statue /ˈʃtaːtu̯ə/ *f* **-, -n** statue

Statur *f* **-** build, stature

Status *m* **-** status. **S~symbol** *nt* status symbol

Statut *nt* **-[e]s, -en** statute

Stau *m* **-[e]s, -s** congestion; (*Auto*) [traffic] jam; (*Rück-*) tailback

Staub *m* **-[e]s** dust; **S~ wischen** dust; **S~ saugen** vacuum, hoover

Staubecken *nt* reservoir

staub|ig *a* dusty. **s~saugen** *vt/i* (*haben*) vacuum, hoover. **S~sauger** *m* **-s,-** vacuum cleaner, Hoover (P)

Staudamm *m* dam

stauen *vt* dam up; **sich s~** accumulate; <*Autos:*> form a tailback

staunen *vi* (*haben*) be amazed *or* astonished

Stau|see *m* reservoir. **S~ung** *f* **-, -en** congestion; (*Auto*) [traffic] jam

Steak /ʃteːk, steːk/ *nt* **-s, -s** steak

stechen† *vt* stick (**in** + *acc* in); (*verletzen*) prick; (*mit Messer*) stab; <*Insekt:*> sting; <*Mücke:*> bite ● *vi* (*haben*) prick; <*Insekt:*> sting; <*Mücke:*> bite; (*mit Stechuhr*) clock in/out; **in See s~** put to sea

Stech|ginster *m* gorse. **S~kahn** *m* punt. **S~palme** *f* holly. **S~uhr** *f* time clock

Steck|brief *m* 'wanted' poster. **S~dose** *f* socket. **s~en** *vt* put; (*mit Nadel, Reißzwecke*) pin; (*pflanzen*) plant ● *vi* (*haben*) be; (*fest-*) be stuck; **s~ bleiben** get stuck; **den Schlüssel s~ lassen** leave the key in the lock
Steckenpferd *nt* hobby-horse
Steck|er *m* **-s,-** (*Electr*) plug. **S~nadel** *f* pin
Steg *m* **-[e]s, -e** foot-bridge; (*Boots-*) landing stage; (*Brillen-*) bridge
stehen† *vi* (*haben*) stand; (*sich befinden*) be; (*still-*) be stationary; <*Maschine, Uhr:*> have stopped; **s~ bleiben** remain standing; <*Gebäude:*> be left standing; (*anhalten*) stop; <*Motor:*> stall; <*Zeit:*> stand still; **vor dem Ruin s~** face ruin; **zu jdm/etw s~** (*fig*) stand by s.o./sth; **jdm [gut] s~** suit s.o.; **sich gut s~** be on good terms; **es steht 3 zu 1** the score is 3–1. **s~d** *a* standing; (*sich nicht bewegend*) stationary; <*Gewässer*> stagnant
Stehlampe *f* standard lamp
stehlen† *vt/i* (*haben*) steal; **sich s~** steal, creep
Steh|platz *m* standing place. **S~vermögen** *nt* stamina, staying-power
steif *a* stiff
Steig|bügel *m* stirrup. **S~eisen** *nt* crampon
steigen† *vi* (*sein*) climb; (*hochgehen*) rise, go up; <*Schulden, Spannung:*> mount; **s~ auf** (+ *acc*) climb on [to] <*Stuhl*>; climb <*Berg, Leiter*>; get on <*Pferd, Fahrrad*>; **s~ in** (+ *acc*) climb into; get in <*Auto*>; get on <*Bus, Zug*>; **s~ aus** climb out of; get out of <*Bett, Auto*>; get off <*Bus, Zug*>; **s~de Preise** rising prices
steiger|n *vt* increase; **sich s~n** increase; (*sich verbessern*) improve. **S~ung** *f* **-, -en** increase; improvement; (*Gram*) comparison
steil *a* steep. **S~küste** *f* cliffs *pl*
Stein *m* **-[e]s, -e** stone; (*Ziegel-*) brick; (*Spiel-*) piece. **S~bock** *m* ibex; (*Astr*) Capricorn. **S~bruch** *m* quarry. **S~garten** *m* rockery. **S~gut** *nt* earthenware. **s~ig** *a* stony. **s~igen** *vt* stone. **S~kohle** *f* [hard] coal. **S~schlag** *m* rock fall
Stelle *f* **-, -n** place; (*Fleck*) spot; (*Abschnitt*) passage; (*Stellung*) job, post; (*Behörde*) authority; **auf der S~** immediately
stellen *vt* put; (*aufrecht*) stand; set <*Wecker, Aufgabe*>; ask <*Frage*>; make <*Antrag, Forderung, Diagnose*>; **zur Verfügung s~** provide; **lauter/leiser s~** turn up/down; **kalt/warm s~** chill/keep hot; **sich s~** [go and] stand; give oneself up (**der Polizei** to the police); **sich tot s~** pretend to be dead; **gut gestellt sein** be well off
Stellen|anzeige *f* job advertisement. **S~vermittlung** *f* employment agency. **s~weise** *adv* in places
Stellung *f* **-, -en** position; (*Arbeit*) job; **S~ nehmen** make a statement (**zu** on). **S~suche** *f* job-hunting
Stellvertreter *m* deputy
Stelzen *fpl* stilts. **s~** *vi* (*sein*) stalk
stemmen *vt* press; lift <*Gewicht*>
Stempel *m* **-s,-** stamp; (*Post-*) post-mark; (*Präge-*) die; (*Feingehalts-*) hallmark. **s~n** *vt* stamp; hallmark <*Silber*>; cancel <*Marke*>
Stengel* *m* **-s,-** *s.* **Stängel**
Steno *f* **-** [!] shorthand

Steno|gramm *nt* **-[e]s, -e** shorthand text. **S~grafie** *f* **-** shorthand. **s~grafieren** *vt* take down in shorthand ● *vi* (*haben*) do shorthand

Steppdecke *f* quilt

Steppe *f* **-, -n** steppe

Stepptanz *m* tap-dance

sterben† *vi* (*sein*) die (**an** + *dat* of); **im S~ liegen** be dying

sterblich *a* mortal. **S~keit** *f* **-** mortality

stereo *adv* in stereo. **S~anlage** *f* stereo [system]

steril *a* sterile. **s~isieren** *vt* sterilize. **S~ität** *f* **-** sterility

Stern *m* **-[e]s, -e** star. **S~bild** *nt* constellation. **S~chen** *nt* **-s,-** asterisk. **S~kunde** *f* astronomy. **S~schnuppe** *f* **-, -n** shooting star. **S~warte** *f* **-, -n** observatory

stets *adv* always

Steuer[1] *nt* **-s,-** steering-wheel; (*Naut*) helm; **am S~** at the wheel

Steuer[2] *f* **-, -n** tax

Steuer|bord *nt* **-[e]s** starboard [side]. **S~erklärung** *f* tax return. **s~frei** *a* & *adv* tax-free. **S~mann** *m* (*pl* **-leute**) helmsman; (*beim Rudern*) cox. **s~n** *vt* steer; (*Aviat*) pilot; (*Techn*) control ● *vi* (*haben*) be at the wheel/(*Naut*) helm. **s~pflichtig** *a* taxable. **S~rad** *nt* steering-wheel. **S~ruder** *nt* helm. **S~ung** *f* **-** steering; (*Techn*) controls *pl*. **S~zahler** *m* **-s,-** taxpayer

Stewardess /'stju:ɐdɛs/ *f* **-, -en** air hostess, stewardess

Stich *m* **-[e]s, -e** prick; (*Messer-*) stab; (*S~wunde*) stab wound; (*Bienen-*) sting; (*Mücken-*) bite; (*Schmerz*) stabbing pain; (*Näh-*) stitch; (*Kupfer-*) engraving; (*Kartenspiel*) trick

stick|en *vt/i* (*haben*) embroider. **S~erei** *f* **-** embroidery

Stickstoff *m* nitrogen

Stiefel *m* **-s,-** boot

Stief|kind *nt* stepchild. **S~mutter** *f* stepmother. **S~mütterchen** *nt* **-s,-** pansy. **S~sohn** *m* stepson. **S~tochter** *f* stepdaughter. **S~vater** *m* stepfather

Stiege *f* **-, -n** stairs *pl*

Stiel *m* **-[e]s, -e** handle; (*Blumen-, Gläser-*) stem; (*Blatt-*) stalk

Stier *m* **-[e]s, -e** bull; (*Astr*) Taurus

Stierkampf *m* bullfight

Stift[1] *m* **-[e]s, -e** pin; (*Nagel*) tack; (*Blei-*) pencil; (*Farb-*) crayon

Stift[2] *nt* **-[e]s, -e** [endowed] foundation. **s~en** *vt* endow; (*spenden*) donate; create <*Unheil, Verwirrung*>; bring about <*Frieden*>. **S~ung** *f* **-, -en** foundation; (*Spende*) donation

Stil *m* **-[e]s, -e** style

still *a* quiet; (*reglos, ohne Kohlensäure*) still; (*heimlich*) secret; **der S~e Ozean** the Pacific; **im S~en** secretly. **S~e** *f* **-** quiet; (*Schweigen*) silence

Stilleben* *nt s.* **Stillleben**

stillen *vt* satisfy; quench <*Durst*>; stop <*Schmerzen, Blutung*>; breast-feed <*Kind*>

still|halten† *vi sep* (*haben*) keep still. **S~leben** *nt* still life. **s~legen** *vt sep* close down. **S~schweigen** *nt* silence. **S~stand** *m* standstill; **zum S~stand bringen/kommen** stop. **s~stehen**† *vi sep* (*haben*) stand still; (*anhalten*) stop; <*Verkehr:*> be at a standstill

Stimm|bänder *ntpl* vocal cords. **s~berechtigt** *a* entitled to vote. **S~bruch** *m* **er ist im S~bruch** his voice is breaking

Stimme *f* **-, -n** voice; (*Wahl-*) vote

stimmen *vi* (*haben*) be right; (*wählen*) vote ● *vt* tune

Stimmung *f* **-, -en** mood; (*Atmosphäre*) atmosphere

Stimmzettel *m* ballot-paper

stink|en† *vi* (*haben*) smell/(*stark*) stink (**nach** of). **S~tier** *nt* skunk

Stipendium *nt* **-s, -ien** scholarship; (*Beihilfe*) grant

Stirn *f* **-, -en** forehead

stochern *vi* (*haben*) **s~ in** (+ *dat*) poke <*Feuer*>; pick at <*Essen*>

Stock[1] *m* **-[e]s,⸚e** stick; (*Ski-*) pole; (*Bienen-*) hive; (*Rosen-*) bush; (*Reb-*) vine

Stock[2] *m* **-[e]s,-** storey, floor. **S~bett** *nt* bunk-beds *pl.*

stock|en *vi* (*haben*) stop; <*Verkehr:*> come to a standstill; <*Person:*> falter. **S~ung** *f* **-, -en** hold-up

Stockwerk *nt* storey, floor

Stoff *m* **-[e]s, -e** substance; (*Tex*) fabric, material; (*Thema*) subject [matter]; (*Gesprächs-*) topic. **S~wechsel** *m* metabolism

stöhnen *vi* (*haben*) groan, moan

Stola *f* **-, -len** stole

Stollen *m* **-s,-** gallery; (*Kuchen*) stollen

stolpern *vi* (*sein*) stumble; **s~ über** (+ *acc*) trip over

stolz *a* proud (**auf** + *acc* of). **S~** *m* **-es** pride

stopfen *vt* stuff; (*stecken*) put; (*ausbessern*) darn ● *vi* (*haben*) be constipating

Stopp *m* **-s, -s** stop. **s~** *int* stop!

stoppelig *a* stubbly

stopp|en *vt* stop; (*Sport*) time ● *vi* (*haben*) stop. **S~uhr** *f* stop-watch

Stöpsel *m* **-s,-** plug; (*Flaschen-*) stopper

Storch *m* **-[e]s,⸚e** stork

Store /ʃtoːɐ̯/ *m* **-s, -s** net curtain

stören *vt* disturb; disrupt <*Rede*>; jam <*Sender*>; (*missfallen*) bother ● *vi* (*haben*) be a nuisance

stornieren *vt* cancel

störrisch *a* stubborn

Störung *f* **-, -en** disturbance; disruption; (*Med*) trouble; (*Radio*) interference; **technische S~** technical fault

Stoß *m* **-es,⸚e** push, knock; (*mit Ellbogen*) dig; (*Hörner-*) butt; (*mit Waffe*) thrust; (*Schwimm-*) stroke; (*Ruck*) jolt; (*Erd-*) shock; (*Stapel*) stack, pile. **S~dämpfer** *m* **-s,-** shock absorber

stoßen† *vt* push, knock; (*mit Füßen*) kick; (*mit Kopf*) butt; (*an-*) poke, nudge; (*treiben*) thrust; **sich s~** knock oneself; **sich** (*dat*) **den Kopf s~** hit one's head ● *vi* (*haben*) push; **s~ an** (+ *acc*) knock against; (*angrenzen*) adjoin ● *vi* (*sein*) **s~ gegen** knock against; bump into <*Tür*>; **s~ auf** (+ *acc*) bump into; (*entdecken*) come across; strike <*Öl*>

Stoß|stange *f* bumper. **S~verkehr** *m* rush-hour traffic. **S~zahn** *m* tusk. **S~zeit** *f* rush-hour

stottern *vt/i* (*haben*) stutter, stammer

Str. *abbr* (**Straße**) St

Strafanstalt *f* prison

Strafe *f* **-, -n** punishment; (*Jur & fig*) penalty; (*Geld-*) fine; (*Freiheits-*) sentence. **s~n** *vt* punish

straff *a* tight, taut. **s~en** *vt* tighten

Strafgesetz *nt* criminal law

sträf|lich *a* criminal. **S~ling** *m* **-s, -e** prisoner

Straf|mandat *nt* (*Auto*) [parking/speeding] ticket. **S~porto** *nt* excess postage. **S~raum** *m* penalty area. **S~stoß** *m* penalty. **S~tat** *f* crime

Strahl *m* **-[e]s, -en** ray; (*einer Taschenlampe*) beam; (*Wasser-*) jet. **s~en** *vi* (*haben*) shine; (*funkeln*) sparkle; (*lächeln*) beam. **S~enbehandlung** *f* radiotherapy. **S~ung** *f* - radiation

Strähne *f* **-, -n** strand

stramm *a* tight

Strampel|höschen /-sç-/ *nt* **-s,-** rompers *pl*. **s~n** *vi* (*haben*) <*Baby*:> kick

Strand *m* **-[e]s,¨e** beach. **s~en** *vi* (*sein*) run aground

Strang *m* **-[e]s,¨e** rope

Strapaz|e *f* **-, -n** strain. **s~ieren** *vt* be hard on; tax <*Nerven*>

Strass *m* **- & -es** paste

Straße *f* **-, -n** road; (*in der Stadt auch*) street; (*Meeres-*) strait. **S~nbahn** *f* tram. **S~nkarte** *f* road-map. **S~nsperre** *f* road-block

Strat|egie *f* **-, -n** strategy. **s~egisch** *a* strategic

Strauch *m* **-[e]s, Sträucher** bush

Strauß¹ *m* **-es, Sträuße** bunch [of flowers]; (*Bukett*) bouquet

Strauß² *m* **-es, -e** ostrich

streben *vi* (*haben*) strive (**nach** for) ● *vi* (*sein*) head (**nach/zu** for)

Streber *m* **-s,-** pushy person

Strecke *f* **-, -n** stretch, section; (*Entfernung*) distance; (*Rail*) line; (*Route*) route

strecken *vt* stretch; (*aus-*) stretch out; (*gerade machen*) straighten; (*Culin*) thin down; **den Kopf aus dem Fenster s~** put one's head out of the window

Streich *m* **-[e]s, -e** prank, trick

streicheln *vt* stroke

streichen† *vt* spread; (*weg-*) smooth; (*an-*) paint; (*aus-*) delete; (*kürzen*) cut ● *vi* (*haben*) **s~ über** (+ *acc*) stroke

Streich|holz *nt* match. **S~instrument** *nt* stringed instrument. **S~käse** *m* cheese spread. **S~orchester** *nt* string orchestra. **S~ung** *f* **-, -en** deletion; (*Kürzung*) cut

Streife *f* **-, -n** patrol

streifen *vt* brush against; (*berühren*) touch; (*verletzen*) graze; (*fig*) touch on <*Thema*>

Streifen *m* **-s,-** stripe; (*Licht-*) streak; (*auf der Fahrbahn*) line; (*schmales Stück*) strip

Streifenwagen *m* patrol car

Streik *m* **-s, -s** strike; **in den S~ treten** go on strike. **S~brecher** *m* strike-breaker, (*pej*) scab. **s~en** *vi* (*haben*) strike; 🄸 refuse; (*versagen*) pack up

Streit *m* **-[e]s, -e** quarrel; (*Auseinandersetzung*) dispute. **s~en†** *vr/i* (*haben*) **[sich] s~en** quarrel. **S~igkeiten** *fpl* quarrels. **S~kräfte** *fpl* armed forces

streng *a* strict; <*Blick, Ton*> stern; (*rau, nüchtern*) severe; <*Geschmack*> sharp; **s~ genommen** strictly speaking. **S~e** *f* - strictness; sternness; severity

Stress *m* **-es, -e** stress

streuen *vt* spread; (*ver-*) scatter; sprinkle <*Zucker, Salz*>; **die Straßen s~** grit the roads

streunen *vi* (*sein*) roam

Strich *m* **-[e]s, -e** line; (*Feder-, Pinsel-*) stroke; (*Morse-, Gedanken-*) dash. **S~kode** *m* bar code. **S~punkt** *m* semicolon

Strick *m* **-[e]s, -e** cord; (*Seil*) rope

strick|en *vt/i* (*haben*) knit. **S~jacke** *f* cardigan. **S~leiter** *f* rope-ladder. **S~nadel** *f* knitting-needle. **S~waren** *fpl* knitwear *sg*. **S~zeug** *nt* knitting

striegeln *vt* groom

strittig *a* contentious

Stroh *nt* **-[e]s** straw. **S~blumen** *fpl* everlasting flowers. **S~dach** *nt* thatched roof. **S~halm** *m* straw

Strolch *m* **-[e]s, -e** [!] rascal

Strom *m* **-[e]s,¨-e** river; (*Menschen-, Auto-, Blut-*) stream; (*Tränen-*) flood; (*Schwall*) torrent; (*Electr*) current, power; **gegen den S~** (*fig*) against the tide. **s~abwärts** *adv* downstream. **s~aufwärts** *adv* upstream

strömen *vi* (*sein*) flow; <*Menschen, Blut:*> stream, pour

Strom|kreis *m* circuit. **s~linienförmig** *a* streamlined. **S~sperre** *f* power cut

Strömung *f* **-, -en** current

Strophe *f* **-, -n** verse

Strudel *m* **-s,-** whirlpool; (*SGer Culin*) strudel

Strumpf *m* **-[e]s,¨-e** stocking; (*Knie-*) sock. **S~band** *nt* (*pl* **-bänder**) suspender. **S~hose** *f* tights *pl*

Strunk *m* **-[e]s,¨-e** stalk

struppig *a* shaggy

Stube *f* **-, -n** room. **s~nrein** *a* house-trained

Stuck *m* **-s** stucco

Stück *nt* **-[e]s, -e** piece; (*Zucker-*) lump; (*Seife*) tablet; (*Theater-*) play; (*Gegenstand*) item; (*Exemplar*) specimen; **ein S~** (*Entfernung*) some way. **S~chen** *nt* **-s,-** [little] bit. **s~weise** *adv* bit by bit; (*einzeln*) singly

Student|(in) *m* **-en, -en** (*f* **-, -nen**) student. **s~isch** *a* student ...

Studie /-iə/ *f* **-, -n** study

studieren *vt/i* (*haben*) study

Studio *nt* **-s, -s** studio

Studium *nt* **-s, -ien** studies *pl*

Stufe *f* **-, -n** step; (*Treppen-*) stair; (*Raketen-*) stage; (*Niveau*) level. **s~n** *vt* terrace; (*staffeln*) grade

Stuhl *m* **-[e]s,¨-e** chair; (*Med*) stools *pl*. **S~gang** *m* bowel movement

stülpen *vt* put (**über** + *acc* over)

stumm *a* dumb; (*schweigsam*) silent

Stummel *m* **-s,-** stump; (*Zigaretten-*) butt; (*Bleistift-*) stub

Stümper *m* **-s,-** bungler

stumpf *a* blunt; <*Winkel*> obtuse; (*glanzlos*) dull; (*fig*) apathetic. **S~** *m* **-[e]s,¨-e** stump

Stumpfsinn *m* apathy; tedium

Stunde *f* **-, -n** hour; (*Sch*) lesson

stunden *vt* **jdm eine Schuld s~** give s.o. time to pay a debt

Stunden|kilometer *mpl* kilometres per hour. **s~lang** *adv* for hours. **S~lohn** *m* hourly rate. **S~plan** *m* timetable. **s~weise** *adv* by the hour

stündlich *a & adv* hourly

stur *a* pigheaded

Sturm *m* **-[e]s,¨-e** gale; storm; (*Mil*) assault

stürm|en *vi* (*haben*) <*Wind:*> blow hard ● *vi* (*sein*) rush ● *vt* storm; (*bedrängen*) besiege. **S~er** *m* **-s,-** forward. **s~isch** *a* stormy; <*Überfahrt*> rough

Sturz *m* **-es,¨-e** [heavy] fall; (*Preis-*) sharp drop; (*Pol*) overthrow

stürzen *vi* (*sein*) fall [heavily]; (*in die Tiefe*) plunge; <*Preise:*> drop sharply; <*Regierung:*> fall; (*eilen*) rush ● *vt* throw; (*umkippen*) turn upside down; turn out <*Speise, Kuchen*>; (*Pol*) overthrow, topple; **sich s~** throw oneself (**aus/in** + *acc* out of/into)

Sturzhelm *m* crash-helmet

Stute *f* **-, -n** mare

Stütze *f* **-, -n** support

stützen *vt* support; (*auf-*) rest; **sich s~ auf** (+ *acc*) lean on
stutzig *a* puzzled; (*misstrauisch*) suspicious
Stützpunkt *m* (*Mil*) base
Substantiv *nt* **-s, -e** noun
Substanz *f* **-, -en** substance
Subvention /-'tsio:n/ *f* **-, -en** subsidy. **s~ieren** *vt* subsidize
Such|e *f* - search; **auf der S~e nach** looking for. **s~en** *vt* look for; (*intensiv*) search for; seek <*Hilfe, Rat*>; **'Zimmer gesucht'** 'room wanted' ● *vi* (*haben*) look, search (**nach** for). **S~er** *m* **-s,-** (*Phot*) viewfinder. **S~maschine** *f* search engine
Sucht *f* **-,¨e** addiction; (*fig*) mania
süchtig *a* addicted. **S~e(r)** *m/f* addict
Süd *m* **-[e]s** south. **S~afrika** *nt* South Africa. **S~amerika** *nt* South America. **s~deutsch** *a* South German
Süden *m* **-s** south; **nach S~** south
Süd|frucht *f* tropical fruit. **s~lich** *a* southern; <*Richtung*> southerly ● *adv & prep* (+ *gen*) **s~lich der Stadt** south of the town. **S~pol** *m* South Pole. **s~wärts** *adv* southwards
Sühne *f* **-, -n** atonement; (*Strafe*) penalty. **s~n** *vt* atone for
Sultanine *f* **-, -n** sultana
Sülze *f* **-, -n** [meat] jelly
Summe *f* **-, -n** sum
summen *vi* (*haben*) hum; <*Biene:*> buzz ● *vt* hum
summieren (sich) *vr* add up
Sumpf *m* **-[e]s,¨e** marsh, swamp
Sünd|e *f* **-, -n** sin. **S~enbock** *m* scapegoat. **S~er(in)** *m* **-s,-** (*f* **-, -nen**) sinner. **s~igen** *vi* (*haben*) sin
super *inv a* [!] great. **S~markt** *m* supermarket
Suppe *f* **-, -n** soup. **S~nlöffel** *m* soup-spoon. **S~nteller** *m* soup-plate. **S~nwürfel** *m* stock cube
Surf|brett /'sø:ɐf-/ *nt* surfboard. **s~en** *vi* (*haben*) surf. **S~en** *nt* **-s** surfing
surren *vi* (*haben*) whirr
süß *a* sweet. **S~e** *f* - sweetness. **s~en** *vt* sweeten. **S~igkeit** *f* **-, -en** sweet. **s~lich** *a* sweetish; (*fig*) sugary. **S~speise** *f* sweet. **S~stoff** *m* sweetener. **S~waren** *fpl* confectionery *sg*, sweets *pl*. **S~wasser-** *pref* freshwater ...
Sylvester *nt* **-s** = **Silvester**
Symbol *nt* **-s, -e** symbol. **S~ik** *f* - symbolism. **s~isch** *a* symbolic
Sym|metrie *f* - symmetry. **s~metrisch** *a* symmetrical
Sympathie *f* **-, -n** sympathy
sympathisch *a* agreeable; <*Person*> likeable
Symptom *nt* **-s, -e** symptom. **s~atisch** *a* symptomatic
Synagoge *f* **-, -n** synagogue
synchronisieren /zynkroni'zi:rən/ *vt* synchronize; dub <*Film*>
Syndikat *nt* **-[e]s, -e** syndicate
Syndrom *nt* **-s, -e** syndrome
synonym *a* synonymous. **S~** *nt* **-s, -e** synonym
Synthese *f* **-, -n** synthesis
Syrien /-iən/ *nt* **-s** Syria
System *nt* **-s, -e** system. **s~atisch** *a* systematic
Szene *f* **-, -n** scene

Tt

Tabak *m* **-s, -e** tobacco
Tabelle *f* **-, -n** table; (*Sport*) league table
Tablett *nt* **-[e]s, -s** tray
Tablette *f* **-, -n** tablet
tabu *a* taboo. **T~** *nt* **-s, -s** taboo
Tacho *m* **-s, -s**, **Tachometer** *m* & *nt* speedometer
Tadel *m* **-s,-** reprimand; (*Kritik*) censure; (*Sch*) black mark. **t~los** *a* impeccable. **t~n** *vt* reprimand; censure
Tafel *f* **-, -n** (*Tisch, Tabelle*) table; (*Platte*) slab; (*Anschlag-, Hinweis-*) board; (*Gedenk-*) plaque; (*Schiefer-*) slate; (*Wand-*) blackboard; (*Bild-*) plate; (*Schokolade*) bar
Täfelung *f* **-** panelling
Tag *m* **-[e]s, -e** day; **unter T~e** underground; **es wird Tag** it is getting light; **guten Tag!** good morning/afternoon!
Tage|buch *nt* diary. **t~lang** *adv* for days
Tages|anbruch *m* daybreak. **T~ausflug** *m* day trip. **T~decke** *f* bedspread. **T~karte** *f* day ticket; (*Speise-*) menu of the day. **T~licht** *nt* daylight. **T~mutter** *f* childminder. **T~ordnung** *f* agenda. **T~rückfahrkarte** *f* day return [ticket]. **T~zeit** *f* time of the day. **T~zeitung** *f* daily [news]paper
täglich *a* & *adv* daily; **zweimal t~** twice a day
tags *adv* by day; **t~ zuvor/darauf** the day before/after
tagsüber *adv* during the day
tag|täglich *a* daily ● *adv* every single day. **T~ung** *f* **-, -en** meeting; conference
Taill|e /'taljə/ *f* **-, -n** waist. **t~iert** /ta'ji:ɐt/ *a* fitted
Takt *m* **-[e]s, -e** tact; (*Mus*) bar; (*Tempo*) time; (*Rhythmus*) rhythm; **im T~** in time
Taktik *f* **-** tactics *pl.*
takt|los *a* tactless. **T~losigkeit** *f* **-** tactlessness. **T~stock** *m* baton. **t~voll** *a* tactful
Tal *nt* **-[e]s, -e** valley
Talar *m* **-s, -e** robe; (*Univ*) gown
Talent *nt* **-[e]s, -e** talent. **t~iert** *a* talented
Talg *m* **-s** tallow; (*Culin*) suet
Talsperre *f* dam
Tampon /tam'põ:/ *m* **-s, -s** tampon
Tank *m* **-s, -s** tank. **t~en** *vt* fill up with <*Benzin*> ● *vi* (*haben*) fill up with petrol; (*Aviat*) refuel. **T~er** *m* **-s,-** tanker. **T~stelle** *f* petrol station. **T~wart** *m* **-[e]s, -e** petrol-pump attendant
Tanne *f* **-, -n** fir [tree]. **T~nbaum** *m* fir tree; (*Weihnachtsbaum*) Christmas tree. **T~nzapfen** *m* fir cone
Tante *f* **-, -n** aunt
Tantiemen /tan'ti̯e:mən/ *pl* royalties
Tanz *m* **-es,¨e** dance. **t~en** *vt/i* (*haben*) dance
Tänzer(in) *m* **-s,-** (*f* **-, -nen**) dancer
Tapete *f* **-, -n** wallpaper
tapezieren *vt* paper
tapfer *a* brave. **T~keit** *f* **-** bravery
Tarif *m* **-s, -e** rate; (*Verzeichnis*) tariff
tarn|en *vt* disguise; (*Mil*) camouflage. **T~ung** *f* **-** disguise; camouflage
Tasche *f* **-, -n** bag; (*Hosen-, Mantel-*) pocket. **T~nbuch** *nt*

paperback. **T~ndieb** *m* pickpocket. **T~ngeld** *nt* pocket-money. **T~nlampe** *f* torch. **T~nmesser** *nt* penknife. **T~ntuch** *nt* handkerchief

Tasse *f* **-, -n** cup

Tastatur *f* **-, -en** keyboard

Tast|e *f* **-, -n** key; (*Druck-*) push-button. **t~en** *vi* (*haben*) feel, grope (**nach** for) ● *vt* key in <*Daten*>; **sich t~en** feel one's way (zu to)

Tat *f* **-, -en** action; (*Helden-*) deed; (*Straf-*) crime; **auf frischer Tat ertappt** caught in the act

Täter(in) *m* **-s,-** (*f* **-, -nen**) culprit; (*Jur*) offender

tätig *a* active; **t~ sein** work. **T~keit** *f* **-, -en** activity; (*Arbeit*) work, job

Tat|kraft *f* energy. **T~ort** *m* scene of the crime

tätowier|en *vt* tattoo. **T~ung** *f* **-, -en** tattooing; (*Bild*) tattoo

Tatsache *f* fact. **T~nbericht** *m* documentary

tatsächlich *a* actual

Tatze *f* **-, -n** paw

Tau[1] *m* **-[e]s** dew

Tau[2] *nt* **-[e]s, -e** rope

taub *a* deaf; (*gefühllos*) numb

Taube *f* **-, -n** pigeon; dove. **T~nschlag** *m* pigeon-loft

Taub|heit *f* **-** deafness. **t~stumm** *a* deaf and dumb

tauch|en *vt* dip, plunge; (*unter-*) duck ● *vi* (*haben/sein*) dive/(*ein-*) plunge (**in** + *acc* into); (*auf-*) appear (**aus** out of). **T~er** *m* **-s,-** diver. **T~eranzug** *m* diving-suit

tauen *vi* (*sein*) melt, thaw ● *impers* **es taut** it is thawing

Tauf|becken *nt* font. **T~e** *f* **-, -n** christening, baptism. **t~en** *vt* christen, baptize. **T~pate** *m* godfather

taugen *vi* (*haben*) **etwas/nichts t~** be good/no good

tauglich *a* suitable; (*Mil*) fit

Tausch *m* **-[e]s, -e** exchange, [!] swap. **t~en** *vt* exchange/ (*handeln*) barter (*gegen* for) ● *vi* (*haben*) swap (**mit etw** sth; **mit jdm** with s.o.)

täuschen *vt* deceive, fool; betray <*Vertrauen*>; **sich t~** delude oneself; (*sich irren*) be mistaken ● *vi* (*haben*) be deceptive. **t~d** *a* deceptive; <*Ähnlichkeit*> striking

Täuschung *f* **-, -en** deception; (*Irrtum*) mistake; (*Illusion*) delusion

tausend *inv a* one/a thousand. **T~** *nt* **-s, -e** thousand. **T~füßler** *m* **-s,-** centipede. **t~ste(r, s)** *a* thousandth. **T~stel** *nt* **-s,-** thousandth

Tau|tropfen *m* dewdrop. **T~wetter** *nt* thaw

Taxe *f* **-, -n** charge; (*Kur-*) tax; (*Taxi*) taxi

Taxi *nt* **-s, -s** taxi, cab. **T~fahrer** *m* taxi driver. **T~stand** *m* taxi rank

Teakholz /ˈti:k-/ *nt* teak

Team /ti:m/ *nt* **-s, -s** team

Techni|k *f* **-, -en** technology; (*Methode*) technique. **T~ker** *m* **-s,-** technician. **t~sch** *a* technical; (*technologisch*) technological; **T~sche Hochschule** Technical University

Techno|logie *f* **-, -n** technology. **t~logisch** *a* technological

Teddybär *m* teddy bear

Tee *m* **-s, -s** tea. **T~beutel** *m* tea-bag. **T~kanne** *f* teapot. **T~löffel** *m* teaspoon

Teer *m* **-s** tar. **t~en** *vt* tar

Tee|sieb *nt* tea-strainer. **T~wagen** *m* [tea] trolley

Teich *m* **-[e]s, -e** pond

Teig *m* **-[e]s, -e** pastry; (*Knet-*) dough; (*Rühr-*) mixture; (*Pfannkuchen-*) batter. **T~rolle** *f* rolling-pin. **T~waren** *fpl* pasta *sg*

Teil *m* **-[e]s, -e** part; (*Bestand-*) component; (*Jur*) party; **zum T~** partly; **zum großen/größten T~** for the most part ● *m & nt* **-[e]s** (*Anteil*) share; **ich für mein[en] T~** for my part ● *nt* **-[e]s, -e** part; (*Ersatz-*) spare part; (*Anbau-*) unit

teil|bar *a* divisible. **T~chen** *nt* **-s,-** particle. **t~en** *vt* divide; (*auf-*) share out; (*gemeinsam haben*) share; (*Pol*) partition <*Land*>; **sich** (*dat*) **etw t~en** share sth; **sich t~en** divide; (*sich gabeln*) fork; <*Meinungen:*> differ ● *vi* (*haben*) share

Teilhaber *m* **-s,-** (*Comm*) partner

Teilnahme *f* **-** participation; (*innere*) interest; (*Mitgefühl*) sympathy

teilnehm|en† *vi sep* (*haben*) **t~en an** (+ *dat*) take part in; (*mitfühlen*) share [in]. **T~er(in)** *m* **-s,-** (*f* **-, -nen**) participant; (*an Wettbewerb*) competitor

teil|s *adv* partly. **T~ung** *f* **-, -en** division; (*Pol*) partition. **t~weise** *a* partial ● *adv* partially, partly. **T~zahlung** *f* part-payment; (*Rate*) instalment. **T~zeitbeschäftigung** *f* part-time job

Teint /tɛ̃:/ *m* **-s, -s** complexion

Telearbeit *f* teleworking

Telefax *nt* fax

Telefon *nt* **-s, -e** [tele]phone. **T~anruf** *m*, **T~at** *nt* **-[e]s, -e** [tele]phone call. **T~buch** *nt* [tele]phone book. **t~ieren** *vi* (*haben*) [tele]phone

telefon|isch *a* [tele]phone ... ● *adv* by [tele]phone. **T~ist(in)** *m* **-en, -en** (*f* **-, -nen**) telephonist. **T~karte** *f* phone card. **T~nummer** *f* [tele]phone number. **T~zelle** *f* [tele]phone box

Telegraf *m* **-en, -en** telegraph. **T~enmast** *m* telegraph pole. **t~ieren** *vi* (*haben*) send a telegram. **t~isch** *a* telegraphic ● *adv* by telegram

Telegramm *nt* **-s, -e** telegram

Teleobjektiv *nt* telephoto lens

Telepathie *f* **-** telepathy

Teleskop *nt* **-s, -e** telescope

Telex *nt* **-, -[e]** telex. **t~en** *vt* telex

Teller *m* **-s,-** plate

Tempel *m* **-s,-** temple

Temperament *nt* **-s, -e** temperament; (*Lebhaftigkeit*) vivacity

Temperatur *f* **-, -en** temperature

Tempo *nt* **-s, -s** speed; **T~ [T~]!** hurry up!

Tendenz *f* **-, -en** trend; (*Neigung*) tendency

Tennis *nt* **-** tennis. **T~platz** *m* tennis-court. **T~schläger** *m* tennis-racket

Teppich *m* **-s,e** carpet. **T~boden** *m* fitted carpet

Termin *m* **-s, -e** date; (*Arzt-*) appointment. **T~kalender** *m* [appointments] diary

Terpentin *nt* **-s** turpentine

Terrasse *f* **-, -n** terrace

Terrier /ˈtɛri̯ɐ/ *m* **-s,-** terrier

Terrine *f* **-, -n** tureen

Territorium *nt* **-s, -ien** territory

Terror *m* **-s** terror. **t~isieren** *vt* terrorize. **T~ismus** *m* **-** terrorism. **T~ist** *m* **-en, -en** terrorist

Tesafilm (P) *m* ≈ Sellotape (P)

Test *m* **-[e]s, -s & -e** test

Testament *nt* **-[e]s, -e** will; **Altes/Neues T~** Old/New Testament. **T~svollstrecker** *m* **-s,-** executor

testen *vt* test

Tetanus *m* - tetanus
teuer *a* expensive; (*lieb*) dear; **wie t~?** how much?
Teufel *m* **-s,-** devil. **T~skreis** *m* vicious circle
teuflisch *a* fiendish
Text *m* **-[e]s, -e** text; (*Passage*) passage; (*Bild-*) caption; (*Lied-*) lyrics *pl*. **T~er** *m* **-s,-** copywriter; (*Schlager-*) lyricist
Textilien /-iən/ *pl* textiles; (*Textilwaren*) textile goods
Text|nachricht *f* text message. **T~verarbeitungssystem** *nt* word processor
Theater *nt* **-s,-** theatre; ([!] *Getue*) fuss. **T~kasse** *f* box-office. **T~stück** *nt* play
Theke *f* **-, -n** bar; (*Ladentisch*) counter
Thema *nt* **-s, -men** subject
Themse *f* - Thames
Theolo|ge *m* **-n, -n** theologian. **T~gie** *f* - theology
theor|etisch *a* theoretical. **T~ie** *f* **-, -n** theory
Therapeut(in) *m* **-en, -en** (*f* **-, -nen**) therapist
Therapie *f* **-, -n** therapy
Thermalbad *nt* thermal bath
Thermometer *nt* **-s,-** thermometer
Thermosflasche (P) *f* Thermos flask (P)
Thermostat *m* **-[e]s, -e** thermostat
These *f* **-, -n** thesis
Thrombose *f* **-, -n** thrombosis
Thron *m* **-[e]s, -e** throne. **t~en** *vi* (*haben*) sit [in state]. **T~folge** *f* succession. **T~folger** *m* **-s,-** heir to the throne
Thunfisch *m* tuna
Thymian *m* **-s** thyme
ticken *vi* (*haben*) tick
tief *a* deep; (*t~ liegend, niedrig*) low; (*t~gründig*) profound; **t~er Teller** soup-plate ● *adv* deep; low; (*sehr*) deeply, profoundly; <*schlafen*> soundly. **T~** *nt* **-s, -s** (*Meteorol*) depression. **T~bau** *m* civil engineering. **T~e** *f* **-, -n** depth. **T~garage** *f* underground car park. **t~gekühlt** *a* [deep-]frozen
Tiefkühl|fach *nt* freezer compartment. **T~kost** *f* frozen food. **T~truhe** *f* deep-freeze
Tiefsttemperatur *f* minimum temperature
Tier *nt* **-[e]s, -e** animal. **T~arzt** *m*, **T~ärztin** *f* vet, veterinary surgeon. **T~garten** *m* zoo. **T~kreis** *m* zodiac. **T~kunde** *f* zoology. **T~quälerei** *f* cruelty to animals
Tiger *m* **-s,-** tiger
tilgen *vt* pay off <*Schuld*>; (*streichen*) delete; (*fig: auslöschen*) wipe out
Tinte *f* **-, -n** ink. **T~nfisch** *m* squid
Tipp *m* **-s, -s** [!] tip
tipp|en *vt* [!] type ● *vi* (*haben*) (*berühren*) touch (**auf/an etw** *acc* sth); ([!] *Maschine schreiben*) type; **t~en auf** (+ *acc*) ([!] *wetten*) bet on. **T~schein** *m* pools/lottery coupon
tipptopp *a* [!] immaculate
Tirol *nt* **-s** [the] Tyrol
Tisch *m* **-[e]s, -e** table; (*Schreib-*) desk; **nach T~** after the meal. **T~decke** *f* table-cloth. **T~gebet** *nt* grace. **T~ler** *m* **-s,-** joiner; (*Möbel-*) cabinet-maker. **T~rede** *f* after-dinner speech. **T~tennis** *nt* table tennis
Titel *m* **-s,-** title
Toast /to:st/ *m* **-[e]s, -e** toast; (*Scheibe*) piece of toast. **T~er** *m* **-s,-** toaster
toben *vi* (*haben*) rave; <*Sturm:*> rage; <*Kinder:*> play boisterously

Tochter *f* -,¨ daughter. **T~gesellschaft** *f* subsidiary

Tod *m* **-es** death

Todes|angst *f* mortal fear. **T~anzeige** *f* death announcement; (*Zeitungs-*) obituary. **T~fall** *m* death. **T~opfer** *nt* fatality, casualty. **T~strafe** *f* death penalty. **T~urteil** *nt* death sentence

todkrank *a* dangerously ill

tödlich *a* fatal; <*Gefahr*> mortal

Toilette /toa'lɛtə/ *f* **-, -n** toilet. **T~npapier** *nt* toilet paper

toler|ant *a* tolerant. **T~anz** *f* **-** tolerance. **t~ieren** *vt* tolerate

toll *a* crazy, mad; ([!] *prima*) fantastic; (*schlimm*) awful ● *adv* (*sehr*) very; (*schlimm*) badly. **t~kühn** *a* foolhardy. **T~wut** *f* rabies. **t~wütig** *a* rabid

Tölpel *m* **-s,-** fool

Tomate *f* **-, -n** tomato. **T~nmark** *nt* tomato purée

Tombola *f* **-, -s** raffle

Ton[1] *m* **-[e]s** clay

Ton[2] *m* **-[e]s,¨e** tone; (*Klang*) sound; (*Note*) note; (*Betonung*) stress; (*Farb-*) shade; **der gute Ton** (*fig*) good form. **T~abnehmer** *m* **-s,-** pick-up. **t~angebend** *a* (*fig*) leading. **T~art** *f* tone [of voice]; (*Mus*) key. **T~band** *nt* (*pl* **-bänder**) tape. **T~bandgerät** *nt* tape recorder

tönen *vi* (*haben*) sound ● *vt* tint

Tonleiter *f* scale

Tonne *f* **-, -n** barrel, cask: (*Müll-*) bin; (*Maß*) tonne, metric ton

Topf *m* **-[e]s,¨e** pot; (*Koch-*) pan

Topfen *m* **-s** (Aust) ≈ curd cheese

Töpferei *f* **-, -en** pottery

Topf|lappen *m* oven-cloth. **T~pflanze** *f* potted plant

Tor *nt* **-[e]s, -e** gate; (*Einfahrt*) gateway; (*Sport*) goal

Torf *m* **-s** peat

torkeln *vi* (*sein/habe*) stagger

Tornister *m* **-s,-** knapsack; (*Sch*) satchel

Torpedo *m* **-s, -s** torpedo

Torpfosten *m* goal-post

Torte *f* **-, -n** gateau; (*Obst-*) flan

Tortur *f* **-, -en** torture

Torwart *m* **-s, -e** goalkeeper

tot *a* dead; **tot geboren** stillborn; **sich tot stellen** pretend to be dead

total *a* total. **T~schaden** *m* ≈ write-off

Tote|(r) *m/f* dead man/woman; (*Todesopfer*) fatality; **die T~n** the dead *pl*

töten *vt* kill

Toten|gräber *m* **-s,-** grave-digger. **T~kopf** *m* skull. **T~schein** *m* death certificate

totfahren† *vt sep* run over and kill

Toto *nt & m* **-s** football pools *pl*. **T~schein** *m* pools coupon

tot|schießen† *vt sep* shoot dead. **T~schlag** *m* (*Jur*) manslaughter. **t~schlagen**† *vt sep* kill

Tötung *f* **-, -en** killing; **fahrlässige T~** (*Jur*) manslaughter

Toup|et /tu'pe:/ *nt* **-s, -s** toupee. **t~ieren** *vt* back-comb

Tour /tu:ɐ/ *f* **-, -en** tour; (*Ausflug*) trip; (*Auto-*) drive; (*Rad-*) ride; (*Strecke*) distance; (*Techn*) revolution; ([!] *Weise*) way

Touris|mus /tu'rɪsmʊs/ *m* **-** tourism. **T~t** *m* **-en, -en** tourist

Tournee /tʊr'ne:/ *f* **-, -n** tour

Trab *m* **-[e]s** trot

Trabant *m* **-en, -en** satellite

traben *vi* (*haben/sein*) trot

Tracht *f* **-, -en** [national] costume

Tradition /-'tsio:n/ *f* **-, -en** tradition. **t~ell** *a* traditional

Trag|bahre *f* stretcher. **t~bar** *a* portable; <*Kleidung*> wearable
träge *a* sluggish; (*faul*) lazy; (*Phys*) inert
tragen† *vt* carry; (*an-*/ *aufhaben*) wear; (*fig*) bear ● *vi* (*haben*) carry; **gut t~** <*Baum:*> produce a good crop
Träger *m* **-s,-** porter; (*Inhaber*) bearer; (*eines Ordens*) holder; (*Bau-*) beam; (*Stahl-*) girder; (*Achsel-*) [shoulder] strap. **T~kleid** *nt* pinafore dress
Trag|etasche *f* carrier bag. **T~flächenboot, T~flügelboot** *nt* hydrofoil
Trägheit *f* - sluggishness; (*Faulheit*) laziness; (*Phys*) inertia
Trag|ik *f* - tragedy. **t~isch** *a* tragic
Tragödie /-i̯ə/ *f* **-, -n** tragedy
Train|er /ˈtrɛːnɐ/ *m* **-s,-** trainer; (*Tennis-*) coach. **t~ieren** *vt/i* (*haben*) train
Training /ˈtrɛːnɪŋ/ *nt* **-s** training. **T~sanzug** *m* tracksuit. **T~sschuhe** *mpl* trainers
Traktor *m* **-s, -en** /-ˈtoːrən/ tractor
trampeln *vi* (*haben*) stamp one's feet ● *vi* (*sein*) trample (**auf** + *acc* on) ● *vt* trample
trampen /ˈtrɛmpən/ *vi* (*sein*) [!] hitch-hike
Tranchiermesser /trãˈʃiːɐ̯-/ *nt* carving-knife
Träne *f* **-, -n** tear. **t~n** *vi* (*haben*) water. **T~ngas** *nt* tear-gas
Tränke *f* **-, -n** watering-place; (*Trog*) drinking-trough. **t~n** *vt* water <*Pferd*>; (*nässen*) soak (**mit** with)
Trans|formator *m* **-s, -en** /-ˈtoːrən/ transformer. **T~fusion** *f* **-, -en** [blood] transfusion
Transit /tranˈziːt/ *m* **-s** transit
Transparent *nt* **-[e]s, -e** banner; (*Bild*) transparency
transpirieren *vi* (*haben*) perspire
Transport *m* **-[e]s, -e** transport; (*Güter-*) consignment. **t~ieren** *vt* transport
Trapez *nt* **-es, -e** trapeze
Tratte *f* **-, -n** (*Comm*) draft
Traube *f* **-, -n** bunch of grapes; (*Beere*) grape; (*fig*) cluster. **T~nzucker** *m* glucose
trauen *vi* (*haben*) (+ *dat*) trust ● *vt* marry; **sich t~** dare (**etw zu tun** [to] do sth); venture (**in** + *acc*/**aus** into/out of)
Trauer *f* - mourning; (*Schmerz*) grief (**um** for); **T~ tragen** be [dressed] in mourning. **T~fall** *m* bereavement. **T~feier** *f* funeral service. **t~n** *vi* (*haben*) grieve; **t~n um** mourn [for]. **T~spiel** *nt* tragedy
Traum *m* **-[e]s, Träume** dream
Trauma *nt* **-s, -men** trauma
träumen *vt/i* (*haben*) dream
traumhaft *a* dreamlike; (*schön*) fabulous
traurig *a* sad; (*erbärmlich*) sorry. **T~keit** *f* - sadness
Trau|ring *m* wedding-ring. **T~schein** *m* marriage certificate. **T~ung** *f* **-, -en** wedding [ceremony]
Treff *nt* **-s, -s** (*Karten*) spades *pl*
treff|en† *vt* hit; <*Blitz:*> strike; (*fig: verletzen*) hurt; (*zusammenkommen mit*) meet; take <*Maßnahme*>; **sich t~en** meet (**mit jdm** s.o.); **sich gut t~en** be convenient ● *vi* (*haben*) hit the target; **t~en auf** (+ *acc*) meet; (*fig*) meet with. **T~en** *nt* **-s,-** meeting. **T~er** *m* **-s,-** hit; (*Los*) winner. **T~punkt** *m* meeting-place
treiben† *vt* drive; (*sich befassen mit*) do; carry on <*Gewerbe*>; indulge in <*Luxus*>; get up to <*Unfug*>; **Handel t~** trade ● *vi* (*sein*) drift; (*schwimmen*) float

● *vi* (*haben*) (*Bot*) sprout. **T~** *nt* **-s** activity

Treib|haus *nt* hothouse. **T~hauseffekt** *m* greenhouse effect. **T~holz** *nt* driftwood. **T~riemen** *m* transmission belt. **T~sand** *m* quicksand. **T~stoff** *m* fuel

trenn|bar *a* separable. **t~en** *vt* separate/(*abmachen*) detach (**von** from); divide, split <*Wort*>; **sich t~en** separate; (*auseinander gehen*) part; **sich t~en von** leave; (*fortgeben*) part with. **T~ung** *f* **-, -en** separation; (*Silben-*) division. **T~ungsstrich** *m* hyphen. **T~wand** *f* partition

trepp|ab *adv* downstairs. **t~auf** *adv* upstairs

Treppe *f* **-, -n** stairs *pl*; (*Außen-*) steps *pl*. **T~ngeländer** *nt* banisters *pl*

Tresor *m* **-s, -e** safe

Tresse *f* **-, -n** braid

Treteimer *m* pedal bin

treten† *vi* (*sein/haben*) step; (*versehentlich*) tread; (*ausschlagen*) kick (**nach** at); **in Verbindung t~** get in touch ● *vt* tread; (*mit Füßen*) kick

treu *a* faithful; (*fest*) loyal. **T~e** *f* **-** faithfulness; loyalty; (*eheliche*) fidelity. **T~ekarte** *f* loyalty card. **T~händer** *m* **-s,-** trustee. **t~los** *a* disloyal; (*untreu*) unfaithful

Tribüne *f* **-, -n** platform; (*Zuschauer-*) stand

Trichter *m* **-s,-** funnel; (*Bomben-*) crater

Trick *m* **-s, -s** trick. **T~film** *m* cartoon. **t~reich** *a* clever

Trieb *m* **-[e]s, -e** drive, urge; (*Instinkt*) instinct; (*Bot*) shoot. **T~verbrecher** *m* sex offender. **T~werk** *nt* (*Aviat*) engine; (*Uhr-*) mechanism

triefen† *vi* (*haben*) drip; (*nass sein*) be dripping (**von/vor** + *dat* with)

Trigonometrie *f* **-** trigonometry

Trikot[1] /tri'ko:/ *m* **-s** (*Tex*) jersey

Trikot[2] *nt* **-s, -s** (*Sport*) jersey; (*Fußball-*) shirt

Trimester *nt* **-s,-** term

Trimm-dich *nt* **-s** keep-fit

trimmen *vt* trim; tune <*Motor*>; **sich t~** keep fit

trink|en† *vt/i* (*haben*) drink. **T~er(in)** *m* **-s,-** (*f* **-, -nen**) alcoholic. **T~geld** *nt* tip. **T~spruch** *m* toast

trist *a* dreary

Tritt *m* **-[e]s, -e** step; (*Fuß-*) kick. **T~brett** *nt* step

Triumph *m* **-s, -e** triumph. **t~ieren** *vi* (*haben*) rejoice

trocken *a* dry. **T~haube** *f* drier. **T~heit** *f* **-, -en** dryness; (*Dürre*) drought. **t~legen** *vt sep* change <*Baby*>; drain <*Sumpf*>. **T~milch** *f* powdered milk

trockn|en *vt/i* (*sein*) dry. **T~er** *m* **-s,-** drier

Trödel *m* **-s** [!] junk. **t~n** *vi* (*haben*) dawdle

Trödler *m* **-s,-** [!] slowcoach; (*Händler*) junk-dealer

Trog *m* **-[e]s,¨e** trough

Trommel *f* **-, -n** drum. **T~fell** *nt* ear-drum. **t~n** *vi* (*haben*) drum

Trommler *m* **-s,-** drummer

Trompete *f* **-, -n** trumpet. **T~r** *m* **-s,-** trumpeter

Tropen *pl* tropics

Tropf *m* **-[e]s, -e** (*Med*) drip

tröpfeln *vt/i* (*sein/haben*) drip

tropfen *vt/i* (*sein/haben*) drip. **T~** *m* **-s,-** drop; (*fallend*) drip. **t~weise** *adv* drop by drop

Trophäe /tro'fɛ:ə/ *f* **-, -n** trophy

tropisch *a* tropical

Trost *m* **-[e]s** consolation, comfort

tröst|en *vt* console, comfort; **sich t~en** console oneself. **t~lich** *a* comforting

trost|los *a* desolate; (*elend*) wretched; (*reizlos*) dreary. **T~preis** *m* consolation prize

Trott *m* **-s** amble; (*fig*) routine

Trottel *m* **-s,-** [!] idiot

Trottoir /trɔ'to̯a:ɐ̯/ *nt* **-s, -s** pavement

trotz *prep* (+ *gen*) despite, in spite of. **T~** *m* **-es** defiance. **t~dem** *adv* nevertheless. **t~ig** *a* defiant; stubborn

trübe *a* dull; <*Licht*> dim; <*Flüssigkeit*> cloudy; (*fig*) gloomy

Trubel *m* **-s** bustle

trüben *vt* dull; make cloudy <*Flüssigkeit*>; (*fig*) spoil; strain <*Verhältnis*> **sich t~** <*Flüssigkeit:*> become cloudy; <*Himmel:*> cloud over; <*Augen:*> dim

Trüb|sal *f* **-** misery. **T~sinn** *m* melancholy. **t~sinnig** *a* melancholy

trügen† *vt* deceive ● *vi* (*haben*) be deceptive

Trugschluss *m* fallacy

Truhe *f* **-, -n** chest

Trümmer *pl* rubble *sg*; (*T~teile*) wreckage *sg*, (*fig*) ruins

Trumpf *m* **-[e]s,¨e** trump [card]. **t~en** *vi* (*haben*) play trumps

Trunk *m* **-[e]s** drink. **T~enheit** *f* **-** drunkenness; **T~enheit am Steuer** drink-driving

Trupp *m* **-s, -s** group; (*Mil*) squad. **T~e** *f* **-, -n** (*Mil*) unit; (*Theat*) troupe; **T~en** troops

Truthahn *m* turkey

Tschech|e *m* **-n, -n, T~in** *f* **-, -nen** Czech. **t~isch** *a* Czech. **T~oslowakei (die) -** Czechoslovakia

tschüs, tschüss *int* bye, cheerio

Tuba *f* **-, -ben** (*Mus*) tuba

Tube *f* **-, -n** tube

Tuberkulose *f* **-** tuberculosis

Tuch *nt* **-[e]s,¨er** cloth; (*Hals-, Kopf-*) scarf; (*Schulter-*) shawl

tüchtig *a* competent; (*reichlich, beträchtlich*) good; (*groß*) big ● *adv* competently; (*ausreichend*) well

Tück|e *f* **-, -n** malice. **t~isch** *a* malicious; (*gefährlich*) treacherous

Tugend *f* **-, -en** virtue. **t~haft** *a* virtuous

Tülle *f* **-, -n** spout

Tulpe *f* **-, -n** tulip

Tümmler *m* **-s,-** porpoise

Tumor *m* **-s, -en** /-'mo:rən/ tumour

Tümpel *m* **-[e]s,-** pond

Tumult *m* **-[e]s, -e** commotion; (*Aufruhr*) riot

tun† *vt* do; take <*Schritt, Blick*>; work <*Wunder*>; (*bringen*) put (**in** + *acc* into); **sich tun** happen; **jdm etwas tun** hurt s.o.; **das tut nichts** it doesn't matter ● *vi* (*haben*) act (**als ob** as if); **er tut nur so** he's just pretending; **jdm/etw gut tun** do s.o./sth. good; **zu tun haben** have things/work to do; **[es] zu tun haben mit** have to deal with. **Tun** *nt* **-s** actions *pl*

Tünche *f* **-, -n** whitewash; (*fig*) veneer. **t~n** *vt* whitewash

Tunesien /-i̯ən/ *nt* **-s** Tunisia

Tunfisch *m* = **Thunfisch**

Tunnel *m* **-s,-** tunnel

tupf|en *vt* dab ● *vi* (*haben*) **t~en an/auf** (+ *acc*) touch. **T~en** *m* **-s,-** spot. **T~er** *m* **-s,-** spot; (*Med*) swab

Tür *f* **-, -en** door

Turban *m* **-s, -e** turban

Turbine *f* **-, -n** turbine

Türk|e *m* **-n, -n** Turk. **T~ei (die)** **-** Turkey. **T~in** *f* **-, -nen** Turk

türkis *inv a* turquoise

türkisch *a* Turkish

Turm *m* **-[e]s,¨-e** tower; (*Schach*) rook, castle **Türm|chen** *nt* **-s,-** turret. **t~en** *vt* pile [up]; **sich t~en** pile up

Turmspitze *f* spire

turn|en *vi* (*haben*) do gymnastics. **T~en** *nt* **-s** gymnastics *sg*; (*Sch*) physical education, [!] gym. **T~er(in)** *m* **-s,-** (*f* **-, -nen**) gymnast. **T~halle** *f* gymnasium

Turnier *nt* **-s, -e** tournament; (*Reit-*) show

Turnschuhe *mpl* gym shoes; trainers

Türschwelle *f* doorstep, threshold

Tusche *f* **-, -n** [drawing] ink

tuscheln *vt/i* (*haben*) whisper

Tüte *f* **-, -n** bag; (*Comm*) packet; (*Eis-*) cornet; **in die T~ blasen** [!] be breathalysed

TÜV *m* **-** ≈ MOT [test]

Typ *m* **-s, -en** type; ([!] *Kerl*) bloke. **T~e** *f* **-, -n** type

Typhus *m* **-** typhoid

typisch *a* typical (**für** of)

Typus *m* **-, Typen** type

Tyrann *m* **-en, -en** tyrant. **T~ei** *f* **-** tyranny. **t~isch** *a* tyrannical. **t~isieren** *vt* tyrannize

Uu

U-Bahn *f* underground

übel *a* bad; (*hässlich*) nasty; **mir ist ü~** I feel sick; **jdm etw ü~ nehmen** hold sth against s.o. **Ü~keit** *f* **-** nausea

üben *vt/i* (*haben*) practise

über *prep* (+ *dat/acc*) over; (*höher als*) above; (*betreffend*) about; <*Buch, Vortrag*> on; <*Scheck, Rechnung*> for; (*quer ü~*) across; **ü~ Köln fahren** go via Cologne; **ü~ Ostern** over Easter; **die Woche ü~** during the week; **Fehler ü~ Fehler** mistake after mistake ● *adv* **ü~ und ü~** all over; **jdm ü~ sein** be better/ (*stärker*) stronger than s.o. ● *a* [!] **ü~ sein** be left over; **etw ü~ sein** be fed up with sth

überall *adv* everywhere

überanstrengen *vt insep* overtax; strain <*Augen*>

überarbeiten *vt insep* revise; **sich ü~en** overwork

überbieten† *vt insep* outbid; (*übertreffen*) surpass

Überblick *m* overall view; (*Abriss*) summary

überblicken *vt insep* overlook; (*abschätzen*) assess

überbringen† *vt insep* deliver

überbrücken *vt insep* (*fig*) bridge

überdies *adv* moreover

überdimensional *a* oversized

Überdosis *f* overdose

überdrüssig *a* **ü~ sein/werden** be/grow tired (*gen* of)

übereignen *vt insep* transfer

übereilt *a* over-hasty

übereinander *adv* one on top of/above the other; <*sprechen*> about each other

überein|kommen† *vi sep* (*sein*) agree. **Ü~kunft** *f* **-** agreement. **ü~stimmen** *vi sep* (*haben*) agree; <*Zahlen:*> tally; <*Ansichten:*> coincide; <*Farben:*> match. **Ü~stimmung** *f* agreement

überfahren† *vt insep* run over

Überfahrt *f* crossing

Überfall *m* attack; (*Bank-*) raid

überfallen† *vt insep* attack; raid <*Bank*>; (*bestürmen*) bombard (**mit** with)

Überfluss *m* abundance; (*Wohlstand*) affluence

überflüssig *a* superfluous

überfordern *vt insep* overtax

überführ|en *vt insep* transfer; (*Jur*) convict (*gen* of). **Ü~ung** *f* transfer; (*Straße*) flyover; (*Fußgänger-*) foot-bridge

überfüllt *a* overcrowded

Übergabe *f* handing over; transfer

Übergang *m* crossing; (*Wechsel*) transition

übergeben† *vt insep* hand over; (*übereignen*) transfer; **sich ü~** be sick

übergehen† *vt insep* (*fig*) pass over; (*nicht beachten*) ignore; (*auslassen*) leave out

Übergewicht *nt* excess weight; (*fig*) predominance; **Ü~ haben** be overweight

über|greifen† *vi sep* (*haben*) spread (**auf** + *acc* to). **Ü~griff** *m* infringement

über|groß *a* outsize; (*übertrieben*) exaggerated. **Ü~größe** *f* outsize

überhand *adv* **ü~ nehmen** increase alarmingly

überhäufen *vt insep* inundate (**mit** with)

überhaupt *adv* (*im Allgemeinen*) altogether; (*eigentlich*) anyway; (*überdies*) besides; **ü~ nicht/nichts** not/nothing at all

überheblich *a* arrogant. **Ü~keit** *f* - arrogance

überhol|en *vt insep* overtake; (*reparieren*) overhaul. **ü~t** *a* out-dated. **Ü~ung** *f* -, **-en** overhaul. **Ü~verbot** *nt* '**Ü~verbot**' 'no overtaking'

überhören *vt insep* fail to hear; (*nicht beachten*) ignore

überirdisch *a* supernatural

überkochen *vi sep* (*sein*) boil over

überlassen† *vt insep* **jdm etw ü~** leave sth to s.o.; (*geben*) let s.o. have sth; **sich** (*dat*) **selbst ü~ sein** be left to one's own devices

Überlauf *m* overflow

überlaufen† *vi sep* (*sein*) overflow; (*Mil, Pol*) defect

Überläufer *m* defector

überleben *vt/i insep* (*haben*) survive. **Ü~de(r)** *m/f* survivor

überlegen¹ *vt sep* put over

überlegen² *v insep* ● *vt* [**sich** *dat*] **ü~** think over, consider; **es sich** (*dat*) **anders ü~** change one's mind ● *vi* (*haben*) think, reflect

überlegen³ *a* superior. **Ü~heit** *f* - superiority

Überlegung *f* -, **-en** reflection

überliefer|n *vt insep* hand down. **Ü~ung** *f* tradition

überlisten *vt insep* outwit

Übermacht *f* superiority

übermäßig *a* excessive

Übermensch *m* superman. **ü~lich** *a* superhuman

übermitteln *vt insep* convey; (*senden*) transmit

übermorgen *adv* the day after tomorrow

übermüdet *a* overtired

Über|mut *m* high spirits *pl*. **ü~mütig** *a* high-spirited

übernächst|e(r,s) *a* next ... but one; **ü~es Jahr** the year after next

übernacht|en *vi insep* (*haben*) stay overnight. **Ü~ung** *f* -, **-en** overnight stay; **Ü~ung und Frühstück** bed and breakfast

Übernahme *f* - taking over; (*Comm*) take-over

übernatürlich *a* supernatural

übernehmen† *vt insep* take over; (*annehmen*) take on; **sich ü~** overdo things; (*finanziell*) over-reach oneself
überqueren *vt insep* cross
überrasch|en *vt insep* surprise. **ü~end** *a* surprising; (*unerwartet*) unexpected. **Ü~ung** *f* **-, -en** surprise
überreden *vt insep* persuade
Überreste *mpl* remains
Überschall- *pref* supersonic
überschätzen *vt insep* overestimate
Überschlag *m* rough estimate; (*Sport*) somersault
überschlagen[1]† *vt sep* cross <*Beine*>
überschlagen[2]† *vt insep* estimate roughly; (*auslassen*) skip; **sich ü~** somersault; <*Ereignisse:*> happen fast. ● *a* tepid
überschneiden† **(sich)** *vr insep* intersect, cross; (*zusammenfallen*) overlap
überschreiten† *vt insep* cross; (*fig*) exceed
Überschrift *f* heading; (*Zeitungs-*) headline
Über|schuss *m* surplus. **ü~schüssig** *a* surplus
überschwemm|en *vt insep* flood; (*fig*) inundate. **Ü~ung** *f* **-, -en** flood
Übersee in/nach Ü~ overseas; **aus/von Ü~** from overseas. **Ü~dampfer** *m* ocean liner. **ü~isch** *a* overseas
übersehen† *vt insep* look out over; (*abschätzen*) assess; (*nicht sehen*) overlook, miss; (*ignorieren*) ignore
übersenden† *vt insep* send
übersetzen[1] *vi sep* (*haben/sein*) cross [over]
übersetz|en[2] *vt insep* translate. **Ü~er(in)** *m* **-s,-** (*f* **-, -nen**) translator. **Ü~ung** *f* **-, -en** translation
Übersicht *f* overall view; (*Abriss*) summary; (*Tabelle*) table. **ü~lich** *a* clear
Übersiedlung *f* move
überspielen *vt insep* (*fig*) cover up; **auf Band ü~** tape
überstehen† *vt insep* come through; get over <*Krankheit*>; (*überleben*) survive
übersteigen† *vt insep* climb [over]; (*fig*) exceed
überstimmen *vt insep* outvote
Überstunden *fpl* overtime *sg*; **Ü~ machen** work overtime
überstürz|en *vt insep* rush; **sich ü~en** <*Ereignisse:*> happen fast. **ü~t** *a* hasty
übertrag|bar *a* transferable; (*Med*) infectious. **ü~en**† *vt insep* transfer; (*übergeben*) assign (*dat* to); (*Techn, Med*) transmit; (*Radio, TV*) broadcast; (*übersetzen*) translate; (*anwenden*) apply (**auf** + *acc* to) ● *a* transferred, figurative. **Ü~ung** *f* **-, -en** transfer; transmission; broadcast; translation, application
übertreffen† *vt insep* surpass; (*übersteigen*) exceed; **sich selbst ü~** excel oneself
übertreib|en† *vt insep* exaggerate; (*zu weit treiben*) overdo. **Ü~ung** *f* **-, -en** exaggeration
übertreten[1]† *vi sep* (*sein*) step over the line; (*Pol*) go over/ (*Relig*) convert (**zu** to)
übertret|en[2]† *vt insep* infringe; break <*Gesetz*>. **Ü~ung** *f* **-, -en** infringement; breach
übertrieben *a* exaggerated
übervölkert *a* overpopulated
überwachen *vt insep* supervise; (*kontrollieren*) monitor; (*bespitzeln*) keep under surveillance

überwältigen *vt insep* overpower; (*fig*) overwhelm
überweis|en† *vt insep* transfer; refer <*Patienten*>. **Ü~ung** *f* transfer; (*ärztliche*) referral
überwiegen† *v insep* ● *vi* (*haben*) predominate, ● *vt* outweigh
überwind|en† *vt insep* overcome; **sich ü~en** force oneself. **Ü~ung** *f* effort
Über|zahl *f* majority. **ü~zählig** *a* spare
überzeug|en *vt insep* convince; **sich [selbst] ü~en** satisfy oneself. **ü~end** *a* convincing. **Ü~ung** *f* **-, -en** conviction
überziehen[1]† *vt sep* put on
überziehen[2]† *vt insep* cover; overdraw <*Konto*>
Überzug *m* cover; (*Schicht*) coating
üblich *a* usual; (*gebräuchlich*) customary
U-Boot *nt* submarine
übrig *a* remaining; (*andere*) other; **alles Ü~e** [all] the rest; **im Ü~en** besides; (*ansonsten*) apart from that; **ü~ sein** *od* **bleiben** be left [over]; **etw ü~ lassen** leave sth [over]; **uns blieb nichts anderes ü~** we had no choice
Übung *f* **-, -en** exercise; (*Üben*) practice; **außer** *od* **aus der Ü~** out of practice
Ufer *nt* **-s,-** shore; (*Fluss-*) bank
Uhr *f* **-, -en** clock; (*Armband-*) watch; (*Zähler*) meter; **um ein U~** at one o'clock; **wie viel U~ ist es?** what's the time? **U~macher** *m* **-s,-** watch and clockmaker. **U~werk** *nt* clock/watch mechanism. **U~zeiger** *m* [clock-/watch-]hand. **U~zeit** *f* time
Uhu *m* **-s, -s** eagle owl
UKW *abbr* (*Ultrakurzwelle*) VHF
ulkig *a* funny; (*seltsam*) odd
Ulme *f* **-, -n** elm
Ultimatum *nt* **-s, -ten** ultimatum
Ultra|kurzwelle *f* very high frequency. **U~leichtflugzeug** *nt* microlight [aircraft]
Ultraschall *m* ultrasound
ultraviolett *a* ultraviolet
um *prep* (+ *acc*) [a]round; (*Uhrzeit*) at; <*bitten*> for; <*streiten*> over; <*sich sorgen*> about; <*betrügen*> out of; (*bei Angabe einer Differenz*) by; **um [... herum]** around, [round] about; **Tag um Tag** day after day; **um seinetwillen** for his sake ● *adv* (*ungefähr*) around, about; **um sein** [!] be over; <*Zeit*> be up ● *conj* **um zu** to; (*Absicht*) [in order] to; **zu müde, um zu ...** too tired to ...
umarm|en *vt insep* embrace, hug. **U~ung** *f* **-, -en** embrace, hug
Umbau *m* rebuilding; conversion (**zu** into). **u~en** *vt sep* rebuild; convert (**zu** into)
Umbildung *f* reorganization; (*Pol*) reshuffle
umbinden† *vt sep* put on
umblättern *v sep* ● *vt* turn [over] ● *vi* (*haben*) turn the page
umbringen† *vt sep* kill; **sich u~** kill oneself
umbuchen *v sep* ● *vt* change; (*Comm*) transfer ● *vi* (*haben*) change one's booking
umdrehen *v sep* ● *vt* turn round/(*wenden*) over; turn <*Schlüssel*>; (*umkrempeln*) turn inside out; **sich u~** turn round; (*im Liegen*) turn over ● *vi* (*haben/sein*) turn back
Umdrehung *f* turn; (*Motor-*) revolution
umeinander *adv* around each other; **sich u~ sorgen** worry about each other
umfahren[1]† *vt sep* run over
umfahren[2]† *vt insep* go round; bypass <*Ort*>

umfallen† *vi sep (sein)* fall over; *<Person:>* fall down

Umfang *m* girth; *(Geom)* circumference; *(Größe)* size. **u~reich** *a* extensive; *(dick)* big

umfassen *vt insep* consist of, comprise; *(umgeben)* surround. **u~d** *a* comprehensive

Umfrage *f* survey, poll

umfüllen *vt sep* transfer

umfunktionieren *vt sep* convert

Umgang *m* [social] contact; *(Umgehen)* dealing (**mit** with). **U~ssprache** *f* colloquial language

umgeb|en† *vt/i insep (haben)* surround ● *a* **u~en von** surrounded by. **U~ung** *f* **-, -en** surroundings *pl*

umgehen† *vt insep* avoid; *(nicht beachten)* evade; *<Straße:>* bypass

umgehend *a* immediate

Umgehungsstraße *f* bypass

umgekehrt *a* inverse; *<Reihenfolge>* reverse; **es war u~** it was the other way round

umgraben† *vt sep* dig [over]

Umhang *m* cloak

umhauen† *vt sep* knock down; *(fällen)* chop down

umhören (sich) *vr sep* ask around

Umkehr *f* **-** turning back. **u~en** *v sep* ● *vi (sein)* turn back ● *vt* turn round; turn inside out *<Tasche>*; *(fig)* reverse

umkippen *v sep* ● *vt* tip over; *(versehentlich)* knock over ● *vi (sein)* fall over; *<Boot:>* capsize

Umkleide|kabine *f* changing-cubicle. **u~n (sich)** *vr sep* change. **U~raum** *m* changing-room

umknicken *v sep* ● *vt* bend; *(falten)* fold ● *vi (sein)* bend; *(mit dem Fuß)* go over on one's ankle

umkommen† *vi sep (sein)* perish

Umkreis *m* surroundings *pl*; **im U~ von** within a radius of

umkreisen *vt insep* circle; *(Astr)* revolve around; *<Satellit:>* orbit

umkrempeln *vt sep* turn up; *(von innen nach außen)* turn inside out; *(ändern)* change radically

Umlauf *m* circulation; *(Astr)* revolution. **U~bahn** *f* orbit

Umlaut *m* umlaut

umlegen *vt sep* lay *or* put down; flatten *<Getreide>*; turn down *<Kragen>*; put on *<Schal>*; throw *<Hebel>*; *(verlegen)* transfer; (**!** *töten)* kill

umleit|en *vt sep* divert. **U~ung** *f* diversion

umliegend *a* surrounding

umpflanzen *vt sep* transplant

umranden *vt insep* edge

umräumen *vt sep* rearrange

umrechn|en *vt sep* convert. **U~ung** *f* conversion

umreißen† *vt insep* outline

Umriss *m* outline

umrühren *vt/i sep (haben)* stir

ums *pron* = **um das**

Umsatz *m (Comm)* turnover

umschalten *vt/i sep (haben)* switch over; **auf Rot u~** *<Ampel:>* change to red

Umschau *f* **U~ halten nach** look out for

Umschlag *m* cover; *(Schutz-)* jacket; *(Brief-)* envelope; *(Med)* compress; *(Hosen-)* turn-up. **u~en**† *v sep* ● *vt* turn up; turn over *<Seite>*; *(fällen)* chop down ● *vi (sein)* topple over; *<Wetter:>* change; *<Wind:>* veer

umschließen† *vt insep* enclose

umschreiben *vt insep* define; *(anders ausdrücken)* paraphrase

umschulen *vt sep* retrain; *(Sch)* transfer to another school

Umschwung *m* (*fig*) change; (*Pol*) U-turn
umsehen† **(sich)** *vr sep* look round; (*zurück*) look back; **sich u~ nach** look for
umsein* *vi sep* (*sein*) **um sein**, *s.* **um**
umseitig *a & adv* overleaf
umsetzen *vt sep* move; (*umpflanzen*) transplant; (*Comm*) sell
umsied|eln *v sep* ● *vt* resettle ● *vi* (*sein*) move. **U~lung** *f* resettlement
umso *conj* ~ **besser/mehr** all the better/more; **je mehr, ~ besser** the more the better
umsonst *adv* in vain; (*grundlos*) without reason; (*gratis*) free
Umstand *m* circumstance; (*Tatsache*) fact; (*Aufwand*) fuss; (*Mühe*) trouble; **unter U~en** possibly; **jdm U~e machen** put s.o. to trouble; **in andern U~en** pregnant
umständlich *a* laborious; (*kompliziert*) involved
Umstands|kleid *nt* maternity dress. **U~wort** *nt* (*pl* **-wörter**) adverb
Umstehende *pl* bystanders
umsteigen† *vi sep* (*sein*) change
umstellen[1] *vt insep* surround
umstell|en[2] *vt sep* rearrange; transpose <*Wörter*>; (*anders einstellen*) reset; (*Techn*) convert; (*ändern*) change; **sich u~en** adjust. **U~ung** *f* rearrangement; transposition; resetting; conversion; change; adjustment
umstritten *a* controversial; (*ungeklärt*) disputed
umstülpen *vt sep* turn upside down; (*von innen nach außen*) turn inside out
Um|sturz *m* coup. **u~stürzen** *v sep* ● *vt* overturn; (*Pol*) overthrow ● *vi* (*sein*) fall over
umtaufen *vt sep* rename
Umtausch *m* exchange. **u~en** *vt sep* change; exchange (**gegen** for)
umwechseln *vt sep* change
Umweg *m* detour; **auf U~en** (*fig*) in a roundabout way
Umwelt *f* environment. **u~freundlich** *a* environmentally friendly. **U~schutz** *m* protection of the environment
umwerfen† *vt sep* knock over; (*fig*) upset <*Plan*>
umziehen† *v sep* ● *vi* (*sein*) move ● *vt* change; **sich u~** change
umzingeln *vt insep* surround
Umzug *m* move; (*Prozession*) procession
unabänderlich *a* irrevocable; <*Tatsache*> unalterable
unabhängig *a* independent; **u~ davon, ob** irrespective of whether. **U~keit** *f* - independence
unablässig *a* incessant
unabsehbar *a* incalculable
unabsichtlich *a* unintentional
unachtsam *a* careless
unangebracht *a* inappropriate
unangenehm *a* unpleasant; (*peinlich*) embarrassing
Unannehmlichkeiten *fpl* trouble *sg*
unansehnlich *a* shabby
unanständig *a* indecent
unappetitlich *a* unappetizing
Unart *f* -, **-en** bad habit. **u~ig** *a* naughty
unauffällig *a* inconspicuous; unobtrusive
unaufgefordert *adv* without being asked
unauf|haltsam *a* inexorable. **u~hörlich** *a* incessant
unaufmerksam *a* inattentive
unaufrichtig *a* insincere
unausbleiblich *a* inevitable

unausstehlich *a* insufferable
unbarmherzig *a* merciless
unbeabsichtigt *a* unintentional
unbedenklich *a* harmless ● *adv* without hesitation
unbedeutend *a* insignificant; (*geringfügig*) slight
unbedingt *a* absolute; **nicht u~** not necessarily
unbefriedig|end *a* unsatisfactory. **u~t** *a* dissatisfied
unbefugt *a* unauthorized ● *adv* without authorization
unbegreiflich *a* incomprehensible
unbegrenzt *a* unlimited ● *adv* indefinitely
unbegründet *a* unfounded
Unbehagen *nt* unease; (*körperlich*) discomfort
unbekannt *a* unknown; (*nicht vertraut*) unfamiliar. **U~e(r)** *m/f* stranger
unbekümmert *a* unconcerned; (*unbeschwert*) carefree
unbeliebt *a* unpopular. **U~heit** *f* - unpopularity
unbemannt *a* unmanned
unbemerkt *a & adv* unnoticed
unbenutzt *a* unused
unbequem *a* uncomfortable; (*lästig*) awkward
unberechenbar *a* unpredictable
unberechtigt *a* unjustified; (*unbefugt*) unauthorized
unberührt *a* untouched; (*fig*) virgin; <*Landschaft*> unspoilt
unbescheiden *a* presumptuous
unbeschrankt *a* unguarded
unbeschränkt *a* unlimited ● *adv* without limit
unbeschwert *a* carefree
unbesiegt *a* undefeated
unbespielt *a* blank
unbeständig *a* inconsistent; <*Wetter*> unsettled
unbestechlich *a* incorruptible
unbestimmt *a* indefinite; <*Alter*> indeterminate; (*ungewiss*) uncertain; (*unklar*) vague
unbestritten *a* undisputed ● *adv* indisputably
unbeteiligt *a* indifferent; **u~ an** (+ *dat*) not involved in
unbetont *a* unstressed
unbewacht *a* unguarded
unbewaffnet *a* unarmed
unbeweglich *a & adv* motionless, still
unbewohnt *a* uninhabited
unbewusst *a* unconscious
unbezahlbar *a* priceless
unbrauchbar *a* useless
und *conj* and; **und so weiter** and so on; **nach und nach** bit by bit
Undank *m* ingratitude. **u~bar** *a* ungrateful; (*nicht lohnend*) thankless. **U~barkeit** *f* ingratitude
undeutlich *a* indistinct; vague
undicht *a* leaking; **u~e Stelle** leak
Unding *nt* absurdity
undiplomatisch *a* undiplomatic
unduldsam *a* intolerant
undurch|dringlich *a* impenetrable; <*Miene*> inscrutable. **u~führbar** *a* impracticable
undurch|lässig *a* impermeable. **u~sichtig** *a* opaque; (*fig*) doubtful
uneben *a* uneven. **U~heit** *f* **-, -en** unevenness; (*Buckel*) bump
unecht *a* false; **u~er Schmuck** imitation jewellery
unehelich *a* illegitimate
uneinig *a* (*fig*) divided; [**sich** (*dat*)] **u~ sein** disagree
uneins *a* **u~ sein** be at odds
unempfindlich *a* insensitive (**gegen** to); (*widerstandsfähig*) tough; (*Med*) immune

unendlich *a* infinite; (*endlos*) endless. **U~keit** *f* - infinity
unentbehrlich *a* indispensable
unentgeltlich *a* free, <*Arbeit*> unpaid ● *adv* free of charge
unentschieden *a* undecided; (*Sport*) drawn; **u~ spielen** draw. **U~** *nt* **-s,-** draw
unentschlossen *a* indecisive; (*unentschieden*) undecided
unentwegt *a* persistent; (*unaufhörlich*) incessant
unerfahren *a* inexperienced. **U~heit** *f* - inexperience
unerfreulich *a* unpleasant
unerhört *a* enormous; (*empörend*) outrageous
unerklärlich *a* inexplicable
unerlässlich *a* essential
unerlaubt *a* unauthorized ● *adv* without permission
unerschwinglich *a* prohibitive
unersetzlich *a* irreplaceable; <*Verlust*> irreparable
unerträglich *a* unbearable
unerwartet *a* unexpected
unerwünscht *a* unwanted; <*Besuch*> unwelcome
unfähig *a* incompetent; **u~, etw zu tun** incapable of doing sth; (*nicht in der Lage*) unable to do sth. **U~keit** *f* incompetence; inability (**zu** to)
unfair *a* unfair
Unfall *m* accident. **U~flucht** *f* failure to stop after an accident. **U~station** *f* casualty department
unfassbar *a* incomprehensible
Unfehlbarkeit *f* - infallibility
unfolgsam *a* disobedient
unförmig *a* shapeless
unfreiwillig *a* involuntary; (*unbeabsichtigt*) unintentional
unfreundlich *a* unfriendly; (*unangenehm*) unpleasant. **U~keit** *f* unfriendliness; unpleasantness
Unfriede[n] *m* discord
unfruchtbar *a* infertile; (*fig*) unproductive. **U~keit** *f* infertility
Unfug *m* **-s** mischief; (*Unsinn*) nonsense
Ungar|(in) *m* **-n, -n** (*f* **-, -nen**) Hungarian. **u~isch** *a* Hungarian. **U~n** *nt* **-s** Hungary
ungeachtet *prep* (+ *gen*) in spite of; **dessen u~** notwithstanding [this].
ungebraucht *a* unused
ungedeckt *a* uncovered; (*Sport*) unmarked; <*Tisch*> unlaid
Ungeduld *f* impatience. **u~ig** *a* impatient
ungeeignet *a* unsuitable
ungefähr *a* approximate, rough
ungefährlich *a* harmless
ungeheuer *a* enormous. **U~** *nt* **-s,-** monster
ungehorsam *a* disobedient. **U~** *m* disobedience
ungeklärt *a* unsolved; <*Frage*> unsettled; <*Ursache*> unknown
ungelegen *a* inconvenient
ungelernt *a* unskilled
ungemütlich *a* uncomfortable; (*unangenehm*) unpleasant
ungenau *a* inaccurate; vague. **U~igkeit** *f* **-, -en** inaccuracy
ungeniert /ˈʊnʒeniːɐ̯t/ *a* uninhibited ● *adv* openly
ungenießbar *a* inedible; <*Getränk*> undrinkable
ungenügend *a* inadequate; (*Sch*) unsatisfactory
ungepflegt *a* neglected; <*Person*> unkempt
ungerade *a* <*Zahl*> odd
ungerecht *a* unjust. **U~igkeit** *f* **-, -en** injustice
ungern *adv* reluctantly
ungesalzen *a* unsalted
Ungeschick|lichkeit *f* clumsiness. **u~t** *a* clumsy

ungeschminkt *a* without make-up; <*Wahrheit*> unvarnished
ungesetzlich *a* illegal
ungestört *a* undisturbed
ungesund *a* unhealthy
ungesüßt *a* unsweetened
ungetrübt *a* perfect
Ungetüm *nt* **-s, -e** monster
ungewiss *a* uncertain; **im U~en sein/lassen** be/leave in the dark. **U~heit** *f* uncertainty
ungewöhnlich *a* unusual
ungewohnt *a* unaccustomed; (*nicht vertraut*) unfamiliar
Ungeziefer *nt* **-s** vermin
ungezogen *a* naughty
ungezwungen *a* informal; (*natürlich*) natural
ungläubig *a* incredulous
unglaublich *a* incredible, unbelievable
ungleich *a* unequal; (*verschieden*) different. **U~heit** *f* - inequality. **u~mäßig** *a* uneven
Unglück *nt* **-s, -e** misfortune; (*Pech*) bad luck; (*Missgeschick*) mishap; (*Unfall*) accident. **u~lich** *a* unhappy; (*ungünstig*) unfortunate. **u~licherweise** *adv* unfortunately
ungültig *a* invalid; (*Jur*) void
ungünstig *a* unfavourable; (*unpassend*) inconvenient
Unheil *nt* **-s** disaster; **U~ anrichten** cause havoc
unheilbar *a* incurable
unheimlich *a* eerie; (*gruselig*) creepy; (🄸 *groß*) terrific ● *adv* eerily; (🄸 *sehr*) terribly
unhöflich *a* rude. **U~keit** *f* rudeness
unhygienisch *a* unhygienic
Uni *f* **-, -s** 🄸 university
uni /y'ni:/ *inv a* plain
Uniform *f* **-, -en** uniform
uninteressant *a* uninteresting
Union *f* **-, -en** union
universell *a* universal
Universität *f* **-, -en** university
Universum *nt* **-s** universe
unkenntlich *a* unrecognizable
unklar *a* unclear; (*ungewiss*) uncertain; (*vage*) vague; **im U~en sein** be in the dark
unkompliziert *a* uncomplicated
Unkosten *pl* expenses
Unkraut *nt* weed; (*coll*) weeds *pl*; **U~ jäten** weed. **U~vertilgungsmittel** *nt* weed-killer
unlängst *adv* recently
unlauter *a* dishonest; (*unfair*) unfair
unleserlich *a* illegible
unleugbar *a* undeniable
unlogisch *a* illogical
Unmenge *f* enormous amount/ (*Anzahl*) number
Unmensch *m* 🄸 brute. **u~lich** *a* inhuman
unmerklich *a* imperceptible
unmittelbar *a* immediate; (*direkt*) direct
unmöbliert *a* unfurnished
unmodern *a* old-fashioned
unmöglich *a* impossible. **U~keit** *f* - impossibility
Unmoral *f* immorality. **u~isch** *a* immoral
unmündig *a* under-age
Unmut *m* displeasure
unnatürlich *a* unnatural
unnormal *a* abnormal
unnötig *a* unnecessary
unordentlich *a* untidy; (*nachlässig*) sloppy. **U~nung** *f* disorder; (*Durcheinander*) muddle
unorthodox *a* unorthodox ● *adv* in an unorthodox manner
unparteiisch *a* impartial
unpassend *a* inappropriate; <*Moment*> inopportune
unpersönlich *a* impersonal

unpraktisch *a* impractical

unpünktlich *a* unpunctual ● *adv* late

unrealistisch *a* unrealistic

unrecht *a* wrong ● *n* **jdm u~ tun** do s.o. an injustice. **U~** *nt* wrong; **zu U~** wrongly; **U~ haben** be wrong; **jdm U~ geben** disagree with s.o. **u~mäßig** *a* unlawful

unregelmäßig *a* irregular

unreif *a* unripe; (*fig*) immature

unrein *a* impure; <*Luft*> polluted; <*Haut*> bad; **ins U~e schreiben** make a rough draft of

unrentabel *a* unprofitable

Unruh|e *f* **-, -n** restlessness; (*Erregung*) agitation; (*Besorgnis*) anxiety; **U~en** (*Pol*) unrest *sg.* **u~ig** *a* restless; (*laut*) noisy; (*besorgt*) anxious

uns *pron* (*acc*/*dat of* **wir**) us; (*refl*) ourselves; (*einander*) each other

unsauber *a* dirty; (*nachlässig*) sloppy

unschädlich *a* harmless

unscharf *a* blurred

unschätzbar *a* inestimable

unscheinbar *a* inconspicuous

unschlagbar *a* unbeatable

unschlüssig *a* undecided

Unschuld *f* **-** innocence; (*Jungfräulichkeit*) virginity. **u~ig** *a* innocent

unselbstständig, unselbständig *a* dependent ● *adv* **u~ denken** not think for oneself

unser *poss pron* our. **u~e(r,s)** *poss pron* ours. **u~erseits** *adv* for our part. **u~twegen** *adv* for our sake; (*wegen uns*) because of us, on our account

unsicher *a* unsafe; (*ungewiss*) uncertain; (*nicht zuverlässig*) unreliable; <*Schritte, Hand*> unsteady; <*Person*> insecure ● *adv* unsteadily. **U~heit** *f* uncertainty; unreliability; insecurity

unsichtbar *a* invisible

Unsinn *m* nonsense. **u~ig** *a* nonsensical, absurd

Unsitt|e *f* bad habit. **u~lich** *a* indecent

unsportlich *a* not sporty; (*unfair*) unsporting

uns|re(r,s) *poss pron* = **unsere(r,s). u~rige** *poss pron* **der/die/das u~rige** ours

unsterblich *a* immortal. **U~keit** *f* immortality

Unsumme *f* vast sum

unsympathisch *a* unpleasant; **er ist mir u~** I don't like him

untätig *a* idle

untauglich *a* unsuitable; (*Mil*) unfit

unten *adv* at the bottom; (*auf der Unterseite*) underneath; (*eine Treppe tiefer*) downstairs; (*im Text*) below; **hier/da u~** down here/there; **nach u~** down[wards]; (*die Treppe hinunter*) downstairs; **siehe u~** see below

unter *prep* (+ *dat*/*acc*) under; (*niedriger als*) below; (*inmitten, zwischen*) among; **u~ anderem** among other things; **u~ der Woche** during the week; **u~ sich** by themselves

Unter|arm *m* forearm. **U~bewusstsein** *nt* subconscious

unterbieten† *vt insep* undercut; beat <*Rekord*>

unterbinden† *vt insep* stop

unterbrech|en† *vt insep* interrupt; break <*Reise*>. **U~ung** *f* **-, -en** interruption, break

unterbringen† *vt sep* put; (*beherbergen*) put up

unterdessen *adv* in the meantime

unterdrück|en *vt insep* suppress; oppress <*Volk*>. **U~ung** *f* - suppression; oppression
untere(r,s) *a* lower
untereinander *adv* one below the other; (*miteinander*) among ourselves/yourselves/themselves
unterernähr|t *a* undernourished. **U~ung** *f* malnutrition
Unterführung *f* underpass; (*Fußgänger-*) subway
Untergang *m* (*Astr*) setting; (*Naut*) sinking; (*der Welt*) end
Untergebene(r) *m/f* subordinate
untergehen† *vi sep* (*sein*) (*Astr*) set; (*versinken*) go under; <*Schiff:*> go down, sink; (*zugrunde gehen*) disappear; <*Welt:*> come to an end
Untergeschoss *nt* basement
Untergrund *m* foundation; (*Hintergrund*) background. **U~bahn** *f* underground [railway]
unterhaken *vt sep* **jdn u~** take s.o.'s arm; **untergehakt** arm in arm
unterhalb *adv & prep* (+ *gen*) below
Unterhalt *m* maintenance
unterhalt|en† *vt insep* maintain; (*ernähren*) support; (*betreiben*) run; (*erheitern*) entertain; **sich u~en** talk; (*sich vergnügen*) enjoy oneself. **U~ung** *f* -, -**en** maintenance; (*Gespräch*) conversation; (*Zeitvertreib*) entertainment
Unter|haus *nt* (*Pol*) lower house; (*in UK*) House of Commons. **U~hemd** *nt* vest. **U~hose** *f* underpants *pl*. **u~irdisch** *a & adv* underground
Unterkiefer *m* lower jaw
unterkommen† *vi sep* (*sein*) find accommodation; (*eine Stellung finden*) get a job
Unterkunft *f* -, **-künfte** accommodation
Unterlage *f* pad; **U~n** papers
Unterlass *m* **ohne U~** incessantly
Unterlassung *f* -, **-en** omission
unterlegen *a* inferior; (*Sport*) losing; **zahlenmäßig u~** outnumbered (*dat* by). **U~e(r)** *m/f* loser
Unterleib *m* abdomen
unterliegen† *vi insep* (*sein*) lose (*dat* to); (*unterworfen sein*) be subject (*dat* to)
Unterlippe *f* lower lip
Untermiete *f* **zur U~ wohnen** be a lodger. **U~r(in)** *m(f)* lodger
unternehm|en† *vt insep* undertake; take <*Schritte*>; **etw/nichts u~en** do sth/nothing. **U~en** *nt* **-s,-** undertaking, enterprise; (*Betrieb*) concern. **U~er** *m* **-s,-** employer; (*Bau-*) contractor; (*Industrieller*) industrialist. **u~ungslustig** *a* enterprising
Unteroffizier *m* non-commissioned officer
unterordnen *vt sep* subordinate
Unterredung *f* -, **-en** talk
Unterricht *m* **-[e]s** teaching; (*Privat-*) tuition; (*U~sstunden*) lessons *pl*
unterrichten *vt/i insep* (*haben*) teach; (*informieren*) inform; **sich u~** inform oneself
Unterrock *m* slip
untersagen *vt insep* forbid
Untersatz *m* mat; (*mit Füßen*) stand; (*Gläser-*) coaster
unterscheid|en† *vt/i insep* (*haben*) distinguish; (*auseinander halten*) tell apart; **sich u~en** differ. **U~ung** *f* -, **-en** distinction
Unterschied *m* **-[e]s, -e** difference; (*Unterscheidung*) distinction; **im U~ zu ihm** unlike

him. **u~lich** *a* different; (*wechselnd*) varying

unterschlag|en† *vt insep* embezzle; (*verheimlichen*) suppress. **U~ung** *f* **-, -en** embezzlement; suppression

Unterschlupf *m* **-[e]s** shelter; (*Versteck*) hiding-place

unterschreiben† *vt/i insep* (*haben*) sign

Unter|schrift *f* signature; (*Bild-*) caption. **U~seeboot** *nt* submarine

Unterstand *m* shelter

unterste(r,s) *a* lowest, bottom

unterstehen† *v insep* ● *vi* (*haben*) be answerable (*dat* to); (*unterliegen*) be subject (*dat* to)

unterstellen[1] *vt sep* put underneath; (*abstellen*) store; **sich u~** shelter

unterstellen[2] *vt insep* place under the control (*dat* of); (*annehmen*) assume; (*fälschlich zuschreiben*) impute (*dat* to)

unterstreichen† *vt insep* underline

unterstütz|en *vt insep* support; (*helfen*) aid. **U~ung** *f* **-, -en** support; (*finanziell*) aid; (*regelmäßiger Betrag*) allowance; (*Arbeitslosen-*) benefit

untersuch|en *vt insep* examine; (*Jur*) investigate; (*prüfen*) test; (*überprüfen*) check; (*durchsuchen*) search. **U~ung** *f* **-, -en** examination; investigation; test; check; search. **U~ungshaft** *f* detention on remand

Untertan *m* **-s & -en, -en** subject

Untertasse *f* saucer

Unterteil *nt* bottom (part)

Untertitel *m* subtitle

untervermieten *vt/i insep* (*haben*) sublet

Unterwäsche *f* underwear

unterwegs *adv* on the way; (*außer Haus*) out; (*verreist*) away

Unterwelt *f* underworld

unterzeichnen *vt insep* sign

unterziehen† *vt insep* **etw einer Untersuchung/Überprüfung u~** examine/ check sth; **sich einer Operation/Prüfung u~** have an operation/take a test

Untier *nt* monster

untragbar *a* intolerable

untrennbar *a* inseparable

untreu *a* disloyal; (*in der Ehe*) unfaithful. **U~e** *f* disloyalty; infidelity

untröstlich *a* inconsolable

unübersehbar *a* obvious; (*groß*) immense

ununterbrochen *a* incessant

unveränderlich *a* invariable; (*gleichbleibend*) unchanging

unverändert *a* unchanged

unverantwortlich *a* irresponsible

unverbesserlich *a* incorrigible

unverbindlich *a* non-committal; (*Comm*) not binding ● *adv* without obligation

unverdaulich *a* indigestible

unver|gesslich *a* unforgettable. **u~gleichlich** *a* incomparable

unver|heiratet *a* unmarried. **u~käuflich** *a* not for sale; <*Muster*> free

unverkennbar *a* unmistakable

unverletzt *a* unhurt

unvermeidlich *a* inevitable

unver|mindert *a & adv* undiminished. **u~mutet** *a* unexpected

Unver|nunft *f* folly. **u~nünftig** *a* foolish

unverschämt *a* insolent; (**!** *ungeheuer*) outrageous. **U~heit** *f* **-, -en** insolence

unver|sehens *adv* suddenly. **u~sehrt** *a* unhurt; (*unbeschädigt*) intact

unverständlich *a* incomprehensible; (*undeutlich*) indistinct
unverträglich *a* incompatible; <*Person*> quarrelsome; (*unbekömmlich*) indigestible
unver|wundbar *a* invulnerable. **u~wüstlich** *a* indestructible; <*Person, Humor*> irrepressible; <*Gesundheit*> robust. **u~zeihlich** *a* unforgivable
unverzüglich *a* immediate
unvollendet *a* unfinished
unvollkommen *a* imperfect; (*unvollständig*) incomplete
unvollständig *a* incomplete
unvor|bereitet *a* unprepared. **u~hergesehen** *a* unforeseen
unvorsichtig *a* careless
unvorstellbar *a* unimaginable
unvorteilhaft *a* unfavourable; (*nicht hübsch*) unattractive
unwahr *a* untrue. **U~heit** *f* **-, -en** untruth. **u~scheinlich** *a* unlikely; (*unglaublich*) improbable; ([!] *groß*) incredible
unweit *adv & prep* (+ *gen*) not far
unwesentlich *a* unimportant
Unwetter *nt* **-s,-** storm
unwichtig *a* unimportant
unwider|legbar *a* irrefutable. **u~stehlich** *a* irresistible
Unwill|e *m* displeasure. **u~ig** *a* angry; (*widerwillig*) reluctant
unwirklich *a* unreal
unwirksam *a* ineffective
unwirtschaftlich *a* uneconomic
unwissen|d *a* ignorant. **U~heit** *f* **-** ignorance
unwohl *a* unwell; (*unbehaglich*) uneasy
unwürdig *a* unworthy (*gen* of)
Unzahl *f* vast number. **unzählig** *a* innumerable, countless
unzerbrechlich *a* unbreakable
unzerstörbar *a* indestructible
unzertrennlich *a* inseparable
Unzucht *f* sexual offence; **gewerbsmäßige U~** prostitution
unzüchtig *a* indecent; <*Schriften*> obscene
unzufrieden *a* dissatisfied; (*innerlich*) discontented. **U~heit** *f* dissatisfaction
unzulässig *a* inadmissible
unzurechnungsfähig *a* insane. **U~keit** *f* insanity
unzusammenhängend *a* incoherent
unzutreffend *a* inapplicable; (*falsch*) incorrect
unzuverlässig *a* unreliable
unzweifelhaft *a* undoubted
üppig *a* luxuriant; (*überreichlich*) lavish
uralt *a* ancient
Uran *nt* **-s** uranium
Uraufführung *f* first performance
Urenkel *m* great-grandson; (*pl*) great-grandchildren
Urgroß|mutter *f* great-grandmother. **U~vater** *m* great-grandfather
Urheber *m* **-s,-** originator; (*Verfasser*) author. **U~recht** *nt* copyright
Urin *m* **-s, -e** urine
Urkunde *f* **-, -n** certificate; (*Dokument*) document
Urlaub *m* **-s** holiday; (*Mil, Admin*) leave; **auf U~** on holiday/leave; **U~ haben** be on holiday/leave. **U~er(in)** *m* **-s,-** (*f* **-, -nen**) holiday-maker. **U~sort** *m* holiday resort
Urne *f* **-, -n** urn; (*Wahl-*) ballot-box
Ursache *f* cause; (*Grund*) reason; **keine U~!** don't mention it!
Ursprung *m* origin
ursprünglich *a* original; (*anfänglich*) initial; (*natürlich*) natural

Urteil *nt* **-s, -e** judgement; (*Meinung*) opinion; (*U~sspruch*) verdict; (*Strafe*) sentence. **u~en** *vi* (*haben*) judge

Urwald *m* primeval forest; (*tropischer*) jungle

Urzeit *f* primeval times *pl*

USA *pl* USA *sg*

usw. *abbr* (**und so weiter**) etc.

utopisch *a* Utopian

Vv

Vakuum /'va:kuʊm/ *nt* **-s** vacuum. **v~verpackt** *a* vacuum-packed

Vanille /va'nɪljə/ *f* **-** vanilla

variieren *vt/i* (*haben*) vary

Vase /'va:zə/ *f* **-, -n** vase

Vater *m* **-s,¨** father. **V~land** *nt* fatherland

väterlich *a* paternal; (*fürsorglich*) fatherly. **v~erseits** *adv* on one's/the father's side

Vater|schaft *f* **-** fatherhood; (*Jur*) paternity. **V~unser** *nt* **-s,-** Lord's Prayer

v. Chr. *abbr* (**vor Christus**) BC

Vegetar|ier(in) /vege'ta:riɐ, -iərɪn/ *m(f)* **-s,-** (*f* **-, -nen**) vegetarian. **v~isch** *a* vegetarian

Veilchen *nt* **-s, -n** violet

Vene /'ve:nə/ *f* **-, -n** vein

Venedig /ve'ne:dɪç/ *nt* **-s** Venice

Ventil /vɛn'ti:l/ *nt* **-s, -e** valve. **V~ator** *m* **-s, -en** /-'to:rən/ fan

verabred|en *vt* arrange; **sich [mit jdm] v~en** arrange to meet [s.o.]. **V~ung** *f* **-, -en** arrangement; (*Treffen*) appointment

verabschieden *vt* say goodbye to; (*aus dem Dienst*) retire; pass <*Gesetz*>; **sich v~** say goodbye

verachten *vt* despise

Verachtung *f* **-** contempt

verallgemeinern *vt/i* (*haben*) generalize

veränder|lich *a* changeable; (*Math*) variable. **v~n** *vt* change; **sich v~n** change; (*beruflich*) change one's job. **V~ung** *f* change

verängstigt *a* frightened, scared

verankern *vt* anchor

veranlag|t *a* **künstlerisch/ musikalisch v~t sein** have an artistic/a musical bent; **praktisch v~t** practically minded. **V~ung** *f* **-, -en** disposition; (*Neigung*) tendency; (*künstlerisch*) bent

veranlassen *vt* (*reg*) arrange for; (*einleiten*) institute; **jdn v~** prompt s.o. (**zu** to)

veranschlagen *vt* (*reg*) estimate

veranstalt|en *vt* organize; hold, give <*Party*>; make <*Lärm*>. **V~er** *m* **-s,-** organizer. **V~ung** *f* **-, -en** event

verantwort|lich *a* responsible; **v~lich machen** hold responsible. **V~ung** *f* **-** responsibility. **v~ungsbewusst** *a* responsible. **v~ungslos** *a* irresponsible. **v~ungsvoll** *a* responsible

verarbeiten *vt* use; (*Techn*) process; (*verdauen & fig*) digest

verärgern *vt* annoy

verausgaben (sich) *vr* spend all one's money

veräußern *vt* sell

Verb /vɛrp/ *nt* **-s, -en** verb

Verband *m* **-[e]s,¨e** association; (*Mil*) unit; (*Med*) bandage; (*Wund-*) dressing. **V~szeug** *nt* first-aid kit

verbann|en *vt* exile; (*fig*) banish. **V~ung** *f* - exile
verbergen† *vt* hide; **sich v~** hide
verbesser|n *vt* improve; (*berichtigen*) correct. **V~ung** *f* **-, -en** improvement; correction
verbeug|en (sich) *vr* bow. **V~ung** *f* bow
verbeulen *vt* dent
verbiegen† *vt* bend
verbieten† *vt* forbid; (*Admin*) prohibit, ban
verbillig|en *vt* reduce [in price]. **v~t** *a* reduced
verbinden† *vt* connect (**mit** to); (*zusammenfügen*) join; (*verknüpfen*) combine; (*in Verbindung bringen*) associate; (*Med*) bandage; dress <*Wunde*>; **jdm verbunden sein** (*fig*) be obliged to s.o.
verbindlich *a* friendly; (*bindend*) binding
Verbindung *f* connection; (*Verknüpfung*) combination; (*Kontakt*) contact; (*Vereinigung*) association; **chemiche V~** chemical compound; **in V~ stehen/sich in V~ setzen** be/get in touch
verbissen *a* grim
verbitter|n *vt* make bitter. **v~t** *a* bitter. **V~ung** *f* - bitterness
verblassen *vi* (*sein*) fade
Verbleib *m* **-s** whereabouts *pl*
verbleit *a* <*Benzin*> leaded
verblüff|en *vt* amaze, astound. **V~ung** *f* - amazement
verblühen *vi* (*sein*) wither, fade
verbluten *vi* (*sein*) bleed to death
verborgen *vt* lend
Verbot *nt* **-[e]s, -e** ban. **v~en** *a* forbidden; (*Admin*) prohibited
Verbrauch *m* **-[e]s** consumption. **v~en** *vt* use; consume <*Lebensmittel*>; (*erschöpfen*) use up. **V~er** *m* **-s,-** consumer
Verbrechen *nt* **-s,-** crime
Verbrecher *m* **-s,-** criminal
verbreit|en *vt* spread. **v~et** *a* widespread. **V~ung** *f* - spread; (*Verbreiten*) spreading
verbrenn|en† *vt/i* (*sein*) burn; cremate <*Leiche*>. **V~ung** *f* **-, -en** burning; cremation; (*Wunde*) burn
verbringen† *vt* spend
verbrühen *vt* scald
verbuchen *vt* enter
verbünd|en (sich) *vr* form an alliance. **V~ete(r)** *m/f* ally
verbürgen *vt* guarantee; **sich v~ für** vouch for
Verdacht *m* **-[e]s** suspicion; **in** *or* **im V~ haben** suspect
verdächtig *a* suspicious. **v~en** *vt* suspect (*gen* of). **V~te(r)** *m/f* suspect
verdamm|en *vt* condemn; (*Relig*) damn. **v~t** *a & adv* ⊠ damned; **v~t!** damn!
verdampfen *vt/i* (*sein*) evaporate
verdanken *vt* owe (*dat* to)
verdau|en *vt* digest. **v~lich** *a* digestible. **V~ung** *f* - digestion
Verdeck *nt* **-[e]s, -e** hood; (*Oberdeck*) top deck
verderb|en† *vi* (*sein*) spoil; <*Lebensmittel:*> go bad ● *vt* spoil; **ich habe mir den Magen verdorben** I have an upset stomach. **V~en** *nt* **-s** ruin. **v~lich** *a* perishable; (*schädlich*) pernicious
verdien|en *vt/i* (*haben*) earn; (*fig*) deserve. **V~er** *m* **-s,-** wage-earner
Verdienst[1] *m* **-[e]s** earnings *pl*
Verdienst[2] *nt* **-[e]s, -e** merit
verdient *a* well-deserved
verdoppeln *vt* double
verdorben *a* spoilt, ruined; <*Magen*> upset; (*moralisch*) corrupt; (*verkommen*) depraved

verdreh|en *vt* twist; roll <*Augen*>; (*fig*) distort. **v~t** *a* [!] crazy

verdreifachen *vt* treble, triple

verdrücken *vt* crumple; ([!] *essen*) polish off; **sich v~** [!] slip away

Verdruss *m* **-es** annoyance

verdünnen *vt* dilute; **sich v~** taper off

verdunst|en *vi* (*sein*) evaporate. **V~ung** *f* **-** evaporation

verdursten *vi* (*sein*) die of thirst

veredeln *vt* refine; (*Hort*) graft

verehr|en *vt* revere; (*Relig*) worship; (*bewundern*) admire; (*schenken*) give. **V~er(in)** *m* **-s,-** (*f* **-, -nen**) admirer. **V~ung** *f* **-** veneration; worship; admiration

vereidigen *vt* swear in

Verein *m* **-s, -e** society; (*Sport-*) club

vereinbar *a* compatible. **v~en** *vt* arrange. **V~ung** *f* **-, -en** agreement

vereinfachen *vt* simplify

vereinheitlichen *vt* standardize

vereinig|en *vt* unite; merge <*Firmen*>; **wieder v~en** reunite; reunify <*Land*>; **sich v~en** unite; **V~te Staaten [von Amerika]** United States *sg* [of America]. **V~ung** *f* **-, -en** union; (*Organisation*) organization

vereinzelt *a* isolated ● *adv* occasionally

vereist *a* frozen; <*Straße*> icy

vereitert *a* septic

verenden *vi* (*sein*) die

verengen *vt* restrict; **sich v~** narrow; <*Pupille:*> contract

vererb|en *vt* leave (*dat* to); (*Biol* & *fig*) pass on (*dat* to). **V~ung** *f* **-** heredity

verfahren† *vi* (*sein*) proceed; **v~ mit** deal with ● *vr* **sich v~** lose one's way ● *a* muddled. **V~** *nt* **-s,-** procedure; (*Techn*) process; (*Jur*) proceedings *pl*

Verfall *m* decay; (*eines Gebäudes*) dilapidation; (*körperlich* & *fig*) decline; (*Ablauf*) expiry. **v~en**† *vi* (*sein*) decay; <*Person, Sitten:*> decline; (*ablaufen*) expire; **v~en in** (+ *acc*) lapse into; **v~en auf** (+ *acc*) hit on <*Idee*>

verfärben (sich) *vr* change colour; <*Stoff:*> discolour

verfass|en *vt* write; (*Jur*) draw up; (*entwerfen*) draft. **V~er** *m* **-s,-** author. **V~ung** *f* (*Pol*) constitution; (*Zustand*) state

verfaulen *vi* (*sein*) rot, decay

verfechten† *vt* advocate

verfehlen *vt* miss

verfeinde|n (sich) *vr* become enemies; **v~t sein** be enemies

verfeinern *vt* refine; (*verbessern*) improve

verfilmen *vt* film

verfluch|en *vt* curse. **v~t** *a* & *adv* [!] damned; **v~t!** damn!

verfolg|en *vt* pursue; (*folgen*) follow; (*bedrängen*) pester; (*Pol*) persecute; **strafrechtlich v~en** prosecute. **V~er** *m* **-s,-** pursuer. **V~ung** *f* **-** pursuit; persecution

verfrüht *a* premature

verfügbar *a* available

verfüg|en *vt* order; (*Jur*) decree ● *vi* (*haben*) **v~en über** (+ *acc*) have at one's disposal. **V~ung** *f*-**, -en** order; (*Jur*) decree; **jdm zur V~ung stehen** be at s.o.'s disposal

verführ|en *vt* seduce; tempt. **V~ung** *f* seduction; temptation

vergangen *a* past; (*letzte*) last. **V~heit** *f* **-** past; (*Gram*) past tense

vergänglich *a* transitory

vergas|en *vt* gas. **V~er** *m* **-s,-** carburettor

vergeb|en† *vt* award (**an** + *dat* to); (*weggeben*) give away;

(*verzeihen*) forgive. **v~lich** *a* futile, vain ● *adv* in vain. **V~ung** *f* - forgiveness

vergehen† *vi* (*sein*) pass; **sich v~** violate (**gegen etw** sth). **V~** *nt* **-s,-** offence

vergelt|en† *vt* repay. **V~ung** *f* - retaliation; (*Rache*) revenge

vergessen† *vt* forget; (*liegen lassen*) leave behind

vergesslich *a* forgetful. **V~keit** *f* - forgetfulness

vergeuden *vt* waste, squander

vergewaltig|en *vt* rape. **V~ung** *f* **-, -en** rape

vergießen† *vt* spill; shed <*Tränen, Blut*>

vergift|en *vt* poison. **V~ung** *f* **-, -en** poisoning

Vergissmeinnicht *nt* **-[e]s, -[e]** forget-me-not

vergittert *a* barred

verglasen *vt* glaze

Vergleich *m* **-[e]s, -e** comparison; (*Jur*) settlement. **v~bar** *a* comparable. **v~en**† *vt* compare (**mit** with/to)

vergnüg|en (sich) *vr* enjoy oneself. **V~en** *nt* **-s,-** pleasure; (*Spaß*) fun; **viel V~en!** have a good time! **v~t** *a* cheerful; (*zufrieden*) happy. **V~ungen** *fpl* entertainments

vergolden *vt* gild; (*plattieren*) gold-plate

vergraben† *vt* bury

vergriffen *a* out of print

vergrößer|n *vt* enlarge; <*Linse:*> magnify; (*vermehren*) increase; (*erweitern*) extend; expand <*Geschäft*>; **sich v~n** grow bigger; <*Firma:*> expand; (*zunehmen*) increase. **V~ung** *f* **-, -en** magnification; increase; expansion; (*Phot*) enlargement. **V~ungsglas** *nt* magnifying glass

vergüt|en *vt* pay for; **jdm etw v~en** reimburse s.o. for sth.

V~ung *f* **-, -en** remuneration; (*Erstattung*) reimbursement

verhaft|en *vt* arrest. **V~ung** *f* **-, -en** arrest

verhalten† **(sich)** *vr* behave; (*handeln*) act; (*beschaffen sein*) be. **V~** *nt* **-s** behaviour, conduct

Verhältnis *nt* **-ses, -se** relationship; (*Liebes-*) affair; (*Math*) ratio; **V~se** circumstances; conditions. **v~mäßig** *adv* comparatively, relatively

verhand|eln *vt* discuss; (*Jur*) try ● *vi* (*haben*) negotiate. **V~lung** *f* (*Jur*) trial; **V~lungen** negotiations

Verhängnis *nt* **-ses** fate, doom

verhärten *vt*/*i* (*sein*) harden

verhasst *a* hated

verhätscheln *vt* spoil

verhauen† *vt* [!] beat; make a mess of <*Prüfung*>

verheilen *vi* (*sein*) heal

verheimlichen *vt* keep secret

verheirat|en (sich) *vr* get married (**mit** to); **sich wieder v~en** remarry. **v~et** *a* married

verhelfen† *vi* (*haben*) **jdm zu etw v~** help s.o. get sth

verherrlichen *vt* glorify

verhexen *vt* bewitch

verhinder|n *vt* prevent; **v~t sein** be unable to come

Verhör *nt* **-s, -e** interrogation; **ins V~ nehmen** interrogate. **v~en** *vt* interrogate; **sich v~en** mishear

verhungern *vi* (*sein*) starve

verhüt|en *vt* prevent. **V~ung** *f* - prevention. **V~ungsmittel** *nt* contraceptive

verirren (sich) *vr* get lost

verjagen *vt* chase away

verjüngen *vt* rejuvenate

verkalkt *a* [!] senile

verkalkulieren (sich) *vr* miscalculate

Verkauf *m* sale; **zum V~** for sale. **v~en** *vt* sell; **zu v~en** for sale

Verkäufer(in) *m(f)* seller; (*im Geschäft*) shop assistant

Verkehr *m* **-s** traffic; (*Kontakt*) contact; (*Geschlechts-*) intercourse; **aus dem V~ ziehen** take out of circulation. **v~en** *vi* (*haben*) operate; <*Bus, Zug:*> run; (*Umgang haben*) associate, mix (**mit** with); (*Gast sein*) visit (**bei jdm** s.o.)

Verkehrs|ampel *f* traffic lights *pl*. **V~unfall** *m* road accident. **V~verein** *m* tourist office. **V~zeichen** *nt* traffic sign

verkehrt *a* wrong; **v~ herum** *adv* the wrong way round; (*links*) inside out

verklagen *vt* sue (**auf** + *acc* for)

verkleid|en *vt* disguise; (*Techn*) line; **sich v~en** disguise oneself; (*für Kostümfest*) dress up. **V~ung** *f* **-, -en** disguise; (*Kostüm*) fancy dress; (*Techn*) lining

verkleiner|n *vt* reduce [in size]. **V~ung** *f* **-** reduction

verknittern *vt/i* (*sein*) crumple

verknüpfen *vt* knot together

verkommen† *vi* (*sein*) be neglected; (*sittlich*) go to the bad; (*verfallen*) decay; <*Haus:*> fall into disrepair; <*Gegend:*> become run-down; <*Lebensmittel:*> go bad ● *a* neglected; (*sittlich*) depraved; <*Haus*> dilapidated; <*Gegend*> run-down

verkörpern *vt* embody, personify

verkraften *vt* cope with

verkrampft *a* (*fig*) tense

verkriechen† **(sich)** *vr* hide

verkrümmt *a* crooked, bent

verkrüppelt *a* crippled; <*Glied*> deformed

verkühl|en (sich) *vr* catch a chill. **V~ung** *f* **-, -en** chill

verkümmern *vi* (*sein*) waste/ <*Pflanze:*> wither away

verkünden *vt* announce; pronounce <*Urteil*>

verkürzen *vt* shorten; (*verringern*) reduce; (*abbrechen*) cut short; while away <*Zeit*>

Verlag *m* **-[e]s, -e** publishing firm

verlangen *vt* ask for; (*fordern*) demand; (*berechnen*) charge. **V~** *nt* **-s** desire; (*Bitte*) request

verlänger|n *vt* extend; lengthen <*Kleid*>; (*zeitlich*) prolong; renew <*Pass, Vertrag*>; (*Culin*) thin down. **V~ung** *f* **-, -en** extension; renewal. **V~ungsschnur** *f* extension cable

verlassen† *vt* leave; (*im Stich lassen*) desert; **sich v~ auf** (+ *acc*) rely *or* depend on ● *a* deserted. **V~heit** *f* **-** desolation

verlässlich *a* reliable

Verlauf *m* course; **im V~** (+ *gen*) in the course of. **v~en**† *vi* (*sein*) run; (*ablaufen*) go; **gut v~en** go [off] well ● *vr* **sich v~en** lose one's way

verlegen *vt* move; (*verschieben*) postpone; (*vor-*) bring forward; (*verlieren*) mislay; (*versperren*) block; (*legen*) lay <*Teppich, Rohre*>; (*veröffentlichen*) publish; **sich v~ auf** (+ *acc*) take up <*Beruf*>; resort to <*Bitten*> ● *a* embarrassed. **V~heit** *f* **-** embarrassment

Verleger *m* **-s,-** publisher

verleihen† *vt* lend; (*gegen Gebühr*) hire out; (*überreichen*) award, confer; (*fig*) give

verlernen *vt* forget

verletz|en *vt* injure; (*kränken*) hurt; (*verstoßen gegen*) infringe; violate <*Grenze*>. **v~end** *a* hurtful, wounding. **V~te(r)** *m/f* injured person; (*bei Unfall*) casualty. **V~ung** *f* **-, -en** (*Verstoß*) infringement; violation

verleugnen *vt* deny; disown <*Freund*>
verleumd|en *vt* slander; (*schriftlich*) libel. **v~erisch** *a* slanderous; libellous. **V~ung** *f* **-, -en** slander; (*schriftlich*) libel
verlieben (sich) *vr* fall in love (**in** + *acc* with); **verliebt sein** be in love (**in** + *acc* with)
verlier|en† *vt* lose; shed <*Laub*> ● *vi* (*haben*) lose (**an etw** *dat* sth). **V~er** *m* **-s,-** loser
verlob|en (sich) *vr* get engaged (**mit** to); **v~t sein** be engaged. **V~te** *f* fiancée. **V~te(r)** *m* fiancé. **V~ung** *f* **-, -en** engagement
verlock|en *vt* tempt. **V~ung** *f* **-, -en** temptation
verloren *a* lost; **v~ gehen** get lost
verlos|en *vt* raffle. **V~ung** *f* **-, -en** raffle; (*Ziehung*) draw
Verlust *m* **-[e]s, -e** loss
vermachen *vt* leave, bequeath
Vermächtnis *nt* **-ses, -se** legacy
vermähl|en (sich) *vr* marry. **V~ung** *f* **-, -en** marriage
vermehren *vt* increase; propagate <*Pflanzen*>; **sich v~** increase; (*sich fortpflanzen*) breed
vermeiden† *vt* avoid
Vermerk *m* **-[e]s, -e** note. **v~en** note [down]
vermessen† *vt* measure; survey <*Gelände*> ● *a* presumptuous
vermiet|en *vt* let, rent [out]; hire out <*Boot, Auto*>; **zu v~en** to let; <*Boot:*> for hire. **V~er** *m* landlord. **V~erin** *f* landlady
vermindern *vt* reduce
vermischen *vt* mix
vermissen *vt* miss
vermisst *a* missing
vermitteln *vi* (*haben*) mediate ● *vt* arrange; (*beschaffen*) find; place <*Arbeitskräfte*>
Vermittl|er *m* **-s,-** agent; (*Schlichter*) mediator. **V~ung** *f* **-, -en** arrangement; (*Agentur*) agency; (*Teleph*) exchange; (*Schlichtung*) mediation
Vermögen *nt* **-s,-** fortune. **v~d** *a* wealthy
vermut|en *vt* suspect; (*glauben*) presume. **v~lich** *a* probable ● *adv* presumably. **V~ung** *f* **-, -en** supposition; (*Verdacht*) suspicion
vernachlässigen *vt* neglect
vernehm|en† *vt* hear; (*verhören*) question; (*Jur*) examine. **V~ung** *f* **-, -en** questioning
verneigen (sich) *vr* bow
vernein|en *vt* answer in the negative; (*ablehnen*) reject. **v~end** *a* negative. **V~ung** *f* **-, -en** negative answer
vernicht|en *vt* destroy; (*ausrotten*) exterminate. **V~ung** *f* **-** destruction; extermination
Vernunft *f* **-** reason
vernünftig *a* reasonable, sensible
veröffentlich|en *vt* publish. **V~ung** *f* **-, -en** publication
verordn|en *vt* prescribe (*dat* for). **V~ung** *f* **-, -en** prescription; (*Verfügung*) decree
verpachten *vt* lease [out]
verpack|en *vt* pack; (*einwickeln*) wrap. **V~ung** *f* packaging; wrapping
verpassen *vt* miss; (**!** *geben*) give
verpfänden *vt* pawn
verpflanzen *vt* transplant
verpfleg|en *vt* feed: **sich selbst v~en** cater for oneself. **V~ung** *f* **-** board; (*Essen*) food; **Unterkunft und V~ung** board and lodging
verpflicht|en *vt* oblige; (*einstellen*) engage; (*Sport*) sign; **sich v~en** undertake/ (*versprechen*) promise (**zu** to); (*vertraglich*) sign a contract.

V~ung *f* **-, -en** obligation, commitment

verprügeln *vt* beat up, thrash

Verputz *m* **-es** plaster. **v~en** *vt* plaster

Verrat *m* **-[e]s** betrayal, treachery. **v~en**† *vt* betray; give away <*Geheimnis*>

Verräter *m* **-s,-** traitor

verrech|nen *vt* settle; clear <*Scheck*>; **sich v~nen** make a mistake; (*fig*) miscalculate. **V~nungsscheck** *m* crossed cheque

verreisen *vi* (*sein*) go away; **verreist sein** be away

verrenken *vt* dislocate

verrichten *vt* perform, do

verriegeln *vt* bolt

verringer|n *vt* reduce; **sich v~n** decrease. **V~ung** *f* **-** reduction; decrease

verrost|en *vi* (*sein*) rust. **v~et** *a* rusty

verrückt *a* crazy, mad. **V~e(r)** *m/f* lunatic. **V~heit** *f* **-, -en** madness; (*Torheit*) folly

verrühren *vt* mix

verrunzelt *a* wrinkled

verrutschen *vt* (*sein*) slip

Vers /fɛrs/ *m* **-es, -e** verse

versag|en *vi* (*haben*) fail ● *vt* **sich etw v~en** deny oneself sth. **V~en** *nt* **-s,-** failure. **V~er** *m* **-s,-** failure

versalzen† *vt* put too much salt in/on; (*fig*) spoil

versamm|eln *vt* assemble. **V~lung** *f* assembly, meeting

Versand *m* **-[e]s** dispatch. **V~haus** *nt* mail-order firm

versäumen *vt* miss; lose <*Zeit*>; (*unterlassen*) neglect; **[es] v~, etw zu tun** fail to do sth

verschärfen *vt* intensify; tighten <*Kontrolle*>; increase <*Tempo*>; aggravate <*Lage*>; **sich v~** intensify; increase; <*Lage:*> worsen

verschätzen (sich) *vr* **sich v~ in** (+ *dat*) misjudge

verschenken *vt* give away

verscheuchen *vt* shoo/(*jagen*) chase away

verschicken *vt* send; (*Comm*) dispatch

verschieb|en† *vt* move; (*aufschieben*) put off, postpone; **sich v~en** move, shift; (*verrutschen*) slip; (*zeitlich*) be postponed. **V~ung** *f* shift; postponement

verschieden *a* different; **v~e** *pl* different; (*mehrere*) various; **V~es** some things; (*dieses und jenes*) various things; **das ist v~** it varies ● *adv* differently; **v~ groß** of different sizes. **v~artig** *a* diverse

verschimmel|n *vi* (*sein*) go mouldy. **v~t** *a* mouldy

verschlafen† *vi* (*haben*) oversleep ● *vt* sleep through <*Tag*>; **sich v~** oversleep ● *a* sleepy

verschlagen† *vt* lose <*Seite*>; **jdm die Sprache/den Atem v~** leave s.o. speechless/take s.o.'s breath away ● *a* sly

verschlechter|n *vt* make worse; **sich v~n** get worse, deteriorate. **V~ung** *f* **-, -en** deterioration

Verschleiß *m* **-es** wear and tear

verschleppen *vt* carry off; (*entführen*) abduct; spread <*Seuche*>; neglect <*Krankheit*>; (*hinausziehen*) delay

verschleudern *vt* sell at a loss

verschließen† *vt* close; (*abschließen*) lock; (*einschließen*) lock up

verschlimmer|n *vt* make worse; aggravate <*Lage*>; **sich v~n** get worse, deteriorate. **V~ung** *f* **-, -en** deterioration

verschlossen *a* reserved. **V~heit** *f* - reserve
verschlucken *vt* swallow; **sich v~** choke (**an** + *dat* on)
Verschluss *m* **-es,¨-e** fastener, clasp; (*Koffer-*) catch; (*Flaschen-*) top; (*luftdicht*) seal; (*Phot*) shutter
verschlüsselt *a* coded
verschmelzen† *vt/i* (*sein*) fuse
verschmerzen *vt* get over
verschmutz|en *vt* soil; pollute <*Luft*> ● *vi* (*sein*) get dirty. **V~ung** *f* - pollution
verschneit *a* snow-covered
verschnörkelt *a* ornate
verschnüren *vt* tie up
verschollen *a* missing
verschonen *vt* spare
verschossen *a* faded
verschränken *vt* cross
verschreiben† *vt* prescribe; **sich v~** make a slip of the pen
verschulden *vt* be to blame for. **V~** *nt* **-s** fault
verschuldet *a* **v~ sein** be in debt
verschütten *vt* spill; (*begraben*) bury
verschweigen† *vt* conceal, hide
verschwend|en *vt* waste. **V~ung** *f* - extravagance; (*Vergeudung*) waste
verschwiegen *a* discreet
verschwinden† *vi* (*sein*) disappear; **[mal] v~** [!] spend a penny
verschwommen *a* blurred
verschwör|en† **(sich)** *vr* conspire. **V~ung** *f* **-, -en** conspiracy
versehen† *vt* perform; hold <*Posten*>; keep <*Haushalt*>; **v~ mit** provide with; **sich v~** make a mistake. **V~** *nt* **-s,-** oversight; (*Fehler*) slip; **aus V~** by mistake. **v~tlich** *adv* by mistake
Versehrte(r) *m* disabled person
versengen *vt* singe; (*stärker*) scorch
versenken *vt* sink
versessen *a* keen (**auf** + *acc* on)
versetz|en *vt* move; transfer <*Person*>; (*Sch*) move up; (*verpfänden*) pawn; (*verkaufen*) sell; (*vermischen*) blend; **jdn v~en** ([!] *warten lassen*) stand s.o. up; **jdm in Angst/Erstaunen v~en** frighten/astonish s.o.; **sich in jds Lage v~en** put oneself in s.o.'s place. **V~ung** *f* **-, -en** move; transfer; (*Sch*) move to a higher class
verseuchen *vt* contaminate
versicher|n *vt* insure; (*bekräftigen*) affirm; **jdm v~n** assure s.o (**dass** that). **V~ung** *f*-, **-en** insurance; assurance
versiegeln *vt* seal
versiert /vɛr'ʒiːɐt/ *a* experienced
versilbert *a* silver-plated
Versmaß /'fɛrs-/ *nt* metre
versöhn|en *vt* reconcile; **sich v~en** become reconciled. **V~ung** *f* **-, -en** reconciliation
versorg|en *vt* provide, supply (**mit** with); provide for <*Familie*>; (*betreuen*) look after. **V~ung** *f* - provision, supply; (*Betreuung*) care
verspät|en (sich) *vr* be late. **v~et** *a* late; <*Zug*> delayed; <*Dank*> belated. **V~ung** *f* - lateness; **V~ung haben** be late
versperren *vt* block; bar <*Weg*>
verspiel|en *vt* gamble away. **v~t** *a* playful
verspotten *vt* mock, ridicule
versprech|en† *vt* promise; **sich v~en** make a slip of the tongue; **sich** (*dat*) **viel v~en von** have high hopes of; **ein viel v~ender Anfang** a promising start. **V~en** *nt* **-s,-** promise. **V~ungen** *fpl* promises
verstaatlich|en *vt* nationalize. **V~ung** *f* - nationalization

Verstand *m* **-[e]s** mind; (*Vernunft*) reason; **den V~ verlieren** go out of one's mind

verständig *a* sensible; (*klug*) intelligent. **v~en** *vt* notify, inform; **sich v~en** communicate; (*sich verständlich machen*) make oneself understood. **V~ung** *f* - notification; communication; (*Einigung*) agreement

verständlich *a* comprehensible; (*deutlich*) clear; (*begreiflich*) understandable; **sich v~ machen** make oneself understood. **v~erweise** *adv* understandably

Verständnis *nt* **-ses** understanding

verstärk|en *vt* strengthen, reinforce; (*steigern*) intensify, increase; amplify <*Ton*>. **V~er** *m* **-s,-** amplifier. **V~ung** *f* reinforcement; increase; amplification; (*Truppen*) reinforcements *pl*

verstaubt *a* dusty

verstauchen *vt* sprain

Versteck *nt* **-[e]s, -e** hiding-place; **V~ spielen** play hide-and-seek. **v~en** *vt* hide; **sich v~en** hide

verstehen† *vt* understand; (*können*) know; **falsch v~** misunderstand; **sich v~** understand one another; (*auskommen*) get on

versteiger|n *vt* auction. **V~ung** *f* auction

versteinert *a* fossilized

verstell|en *vt* adjust; (*versperren*) block; (*verändern*) disguise; **sich v~en** pretend. **V~ung** *f* - pretence

versteuern *vt* pay tax on

verstimm|t *a* disgruntled; <*Magen*> upset; (*Mus*) out of tune. **V~ung** *f* - ill humour; (*Magen-*) upset

verstockt *a* stubborn

verstopf|en *vt* plug; (*versperren*) block; **v~t** blocked; <*Person*> constipated. **V~ung** *f* **-, -en** blockage; (*Med*) constipation

verstorben *a* late, deceased. **V~e(r)** *m/f* deceased

verstört *a* bewildered

Verstoß *m* infringement. **v~en†** *vt* disown ● *vi* (*haben*) **v~en gegen** contravene, infringe

verstreuen *vt* scatter

verstümmeln *vt* mutilate; garble <*Text*>

Versuch *m* **-[e]s, -e** attempt; (*Experiment*) experiment. **v~en** *vt/i* (*haben*) try; **v~t sein** be tempted (**zu** to). **V~ung** *f* **-, -en** temptation

vertagen *vt* adjourn; (*aufschieben*) postpone; **sich v~** adjourn

vertauschen *vt* exchange; (*verwechseln*) mix up

verteidig|en *vt* defend. **V~er** *m* **-s,-** defender; (*Jur*) defence counsel. **V~ung** *f* **-, -en** defence

verteil|en *vt* distribute; (*zuteilen*) allocate; (*ausgeben*) hand out; (*verstreichen*) spread. **V~ung** *f* - distribution; allocation

vertief|en *vt* deepen; **v~t sein in** (+ *acc*) be engrossed in. **V~ung** *f* **-, -en** hollow, depression

vertikal /vɛrti'ka:l/ *a* vertical

vertilgen *vt* exterminate; kill [off] <*Unkraut*>

vertippen (sich) *vr* make a typing mistake

vertonen *vt* set to music

Vertrag *m* **-[e]s,¨e** contract; (*Pol*) treaty

vertragen† *vt* tolerate, stand; take <*Kritik, Spaß*>; **sich v~** get on

vertraglich *a* contractual

verträglich *a* good-natured; (*bekömmlich*) digestible

vertrauen *vi* (*haben*) trust (**jdm/etw** s.o./sth; **auf** + *acc* in). **V~** *nt* **-s** trust, confidence (**zu** in); **im V~** in confidence. **v~swürdig** *a* trustworthy

vertraulich *a* confidential; (*intim*) familiar

vertraut *a* intimate; (*bekannt*) familiar. **V~heit** *f* **-** intimacy; familiarity

vertreib|en† *vt* drive away; drive out <*Feind*>; (*Comm*) sell; **sich** (*dat*) **die Zeit v~en** pass the time. **V~ung** *f* **-, -en** expulsion

vertret|en† *vt* represent; (*einspringen für*) stand in *or* deputize for; (*verfechten*) support; hold <*Meinung*>; **sich** (*dat*) **den Fuß v~en** twist one's ankle. **V~er** *m* **-s,-** representative; deputy; (*Arzt-*) locum; (*Verfechter*) supporter. **V~ung** *f* **-, -en** representation; (*Person*) deputy; (*eines Arztes*) locum; (*Handels-*) agency

Vertrieb *m* **-[e]s** (*Comm*) sale

vertrocknen *vi* (*sein*) dry up

verüben *vt* commit

verunglücken *vi* (*sein*) be involved in an accident; (**Ⓘ** *missglücken*) go wrong; **tödlich v~** be killed in an accident

verunreinigen *vt* pollute; (*verseuchen*) contaminate

verursachen *vt* cause

verurteil|en *vt* condemn; (*Jur*) convict (**wegen** of); sentence (**zum Tode** to death). **V~ung** *f* **-** condemnation; (*Jur*) conviction

vervielfachen *vt* multiply

vervielfältigen *vt* duplicate

vervollständigen *vt* complete

verwählen (sich) *vr* misdial

verwahren *vt* keep; (*verstauen*) put away

verwahrlost *a* neglected; <*Haus*> dilapidated

Verwahrung *f* **-** keeping; **in V~ nehmen** take into safe keeping

verwaist *a* orphaned

verwalt|en *vt* administer; (*leiten*) manage; govern <*Land*>. **V~er** *m* **-s,-** administrator; manager. **V~ung** *f* **-, -en** administration; management; government

verwand|eln *vt* transform, change (**in** + *acc* into) **sich v~eln** change, turn (**in** + *acc* into). **V~lung** *f* transformation

verwandt *a* related (**mit** to). **V~e(r)** *m/f* relative. **V~schaft** *f* **-** relationship; (*Menschen*) relatives *pl*

verwarn|en *vt* warn, caution. **V~ung** *f* warning, caution

verwechs|eln *vt* mix up, confuse; (*halten für*) mistake (**mit** for). **V~lung** *f* **-, -en** mix-up

verweiger|n *vt/i* (*haben*) refuse (**jdm etw** s.o sth). **V~ung** *f* refusal

Verweis *m* **-es, -e** reference (**auf** + *acc* to); (*Tadel*) reprimand; **v~en**† *vt* refer (**auf/an** + *acc* to); (*tadeln*) reprimand; **von der Schule v~en** expel

verwelken *vi* (*sein*) wilt

verwend|en† *vt* use; spend <*Zeit, Mühe*>. **V~ung** *f* use

verwerten *vt* utilize, use

verwesen *vi* (*sein*) decompose

verwick|eln *vt* involve (**in** + *acc* in); **sich v~eln** get tangled up. **v~elt** *a* complicated

verwildert *a* wild; <*Garten*> overgrown; <*Aussehen*> unkempt

verwinden† *vt* (*fig*) get over

verwirklichen *vt* realize

verwirr|en *vt* tangle up; (*fig*) confuse; **sich v~en** get tangled; (*fig*) become confused. **v~t** *a* confused. **V~ung** *f* **-** confusion

verwischen *vt* smudge

verwittert *a* weathered

verwitwet *a* widowed

verwöhn|en *vt* spoil. **v~t** *a* spoilt

verworren *a* confused

verwund|bar *a* vulnerable. **v~en** *vt* wound

verwunder|lich *a* surprising. **v~n** *vt* surprise; **sich v~n** be surprised. **V~ung** *f* - surprise

Verwund|ete(r) *m* wounded soldier; **die V~eten** the wounded *pl*. **V~ung** *f* -, **-en** wound

verwüst|en *vt* devastate, ravage. **V~ung** *f* -, **-en** devastation

verzählen (sich) *vr* miscount

verzaubern *vt* bewitch; (*fig*) enchant; **v~ in** (+ *acc*) turn into

Verzehr *m* **-s** consumption. **v~en** *vt* eat

verzeih|en† *vt* forgive; **v~en Sie!** excuse me! **V~ung** *f* - forgiveness; **um V~ung bitten** apologize; **V~ung!** sorry! (*bei Frage*) excuse me!

Verzicht *m* **-[e]s** renunciation (**auf** + *acc* of). **v~en** *vi* (*haben*) do without; **v~en auf** (+ *acc*) give up; renounce <*Recht, Erbe*>

verziehen† *vt* pull out of shape; (*verwöhnen*) spoil; **sich v~** lose shape; <*Holz:*> warp; <*Gesicht:*> twist; (*verschwinden*) disappear; <*Nebel:*> disperse; <*Gewitter:*> pass ● *vi* (*sein*) move [away]

verzier|en *vt* decorate. **V~ung** *f* -, **-en** decoration

verzinsen *vt* pay interest on

verzöger|n *vt* delay; (*verlangsamen*) slow down. **V~ung** *f* -, **-en** delay

verzollen *vt* pay duty on; **haben Sie etwas zu v~?** have you anything to declare?

verzweif|eln *vi* (*sein*) despair. **v~elt** *a* desperate. **V~lung** *f* - despair; (*Ratlosigkeit*) desperation

verzweigen (sich) *vr* branch [out]

Veto /'ve:to/ *nt* **-s, -s** veto

Vetter *m* **-s, -n** cousin

vgl. *abbr* (**vergleiche**) cf.

Viadukt /vi̯a'dʊkt/ *nt* **-[e]s, -e** viaduct

Video /'vi:deo/ *nt* **-s, -s** video. **V~kassette** *f* video cassette. **V~recorder** /-rəkɔrdɐ/ *m* **-s,-** video recorder

Vieh *nt* **-[e]s** livestock; (*Rinder*) cattle *pl*; ([!] *Tier*) creature

viel *pron* a great deal/[!] a lot of; (*pl*) many, [!] a lot of; (*substantivisch*) **v~[es]** much, [!] a lot; **nicht/so/wie/zu v~** not/so/how/too much/ (*pl*) many; **v~e** *pl* many; **das v~e Geld** all that money ● *adv* much, [!] a lot; **v~ mehr/weniger** much more/less; **v~ zu groß/klein** much *or* far too big/small; **so v~ wie möglich** as much as possible; **so/zu v~ arbeiten** work so/too much

viel|deutig *a* ambiguous. **v~fach** *a* multiple ● *adv* many times; ([!] *oft*) frequently. **V~falt** *f* - diversity, [great] variety

vielleicht *adv* perhaps, maybe; ([!] *wirklich*) really

vielmals *adv* very much

vielmehr *adv* rather; (*im Gegenteil*) on the contrary

vielseitig *a* varied; <*Person*> versatile. **V~keit** *f* - versatility

vielversprechend* *a* **viel versprechend**, *s.* **versprechen**

vier *inv a*, **V~** *f* -, **-en** four; (*Sch*) ≈ fair. **V~eck** *nt* **-[e]s, -e** oblong, rectangle; (*Quadrat*) square. **v~eckig** *a* oblong, rectangular; square. **V~linge** *mpl* quadruplets

viertel /'fɪrtəl/ *inv a* quarter; **um v~ neun** at [a] quarter past eight; **um drei v~ neun** at [a] quarter to nine. **V~** *nt* **-s,-** quarter; (*Wein*) quarter litre; **V~ vor/nach sechs** [a] quarter to/past six. **V~finale** *nt* quarter-

final. **V~jahr** *nt* three months *pl*; (*Comm*) quarter. **v~jährlich** *a & adv* quarterly. **V~stunde** *f* quarter of an hour
vier|zehn /'fɪr-/ *inv a* fourteen. **v~zehnte(r,s)** *a* fourteenth. **v~zig** *inv a* forty. **v~zigste(r,s)** *a* fortieth
Villa /'vɪla/ *f* **-, -len** villa
violett /vio'lɛt/ *a* violet
Vio|line /vio'li:nə/ *f* **-, -n** violin. **V~linschlüssel** *m* treble clef
Virus /'vi:rʊs/ *nt* **-, -ren** virus
Visier /vi'zi:ɐ/ *nt* **-s, -e** visor
Visite /vi'zi:tə/ *f* **-, -n** round; **V~ machen** do one's round
Visum /'vi:zʊm/ *nt* **-s, -sa** visa
Vitamin /vita'mi:n/ *nt* **-s, -e** vitamin
Vitrine /vi'tri:nə/ *f* **-, -n** display cabinet/(*im Museum*) case
Vizepräsident /'fi:tsə-/ *m* vice president
Vogel *m* **-s,¨** bird; **einen V~ haben** ! have a screw loose. **V~scheuche** *f* **-, -n** scarecrow
Vokabeln /vo'ka:bəln/ *fpl* vocabulary *sg*
Vokal /vo'ka:l/ *m* **-s, -e** vowel
Volant /vo'lã:/ *m* **-s, -s** flounce
Volk *nt* **-[e]s,¨er** people *sg*; (*Bevölkerung*) people *pl*
Völker|kunde *f* ethnology. **V~mord** *m* genocide. **V~recht** *nt* international law
Volks|abstimmung *f* plebiscite. **V~fest** *nt* public festival. **V~hochschule** *f* adult education classes *pl*/(*Gebäude*) centre. **V~lied** *nt* folk-song. **V~tanz** *m* folk-dance. **v~tümlich** *a* popular. **V~wirt** *m* economist. **V~wirtschaft** *f* economics *sg*. **V~zählung** *f* [national] census
voll *a* full (**von** *od* **mit** of); <*Haar*> thick; <*Erfolg, Ernst*> complete; <*Wahrheit*> whole; **v~ machen** fill up; **v~ tanken** fill up with petrol ● *adv* (*ganz*) completely; <*arbeiten*> full-time; <*auszahlen*> in full; **v~ und ganz** completely
Vollblut *nt* thoroughbred
vollende|n *vt insep* complete. **v~t** *a* perfect
Vollendung *f* completion; (*Vollkommenheit*) perfection
voller *inv a* full of
Volleyball /'vɔli-/ *m* volleyball
vollführen *vt insep* perform
vollfüllen *vt sep* fill up
Vollgas *nt* **V~ geben** put one's foot down; **mit V~** flat out
völlig *a* complete
volljährig *a* **v~ sein** (*Jur*) be of age. **V~keit** *f* **-** (*Jur*) majority
Vollkaskoversicherung *f* fully comprehensive insurance
vollkommen *a* perfect; (*völlig*) complete
Voll|kornbrot *nt* wholemeal bread. **V~macht** *f* **-, -en** authority; (*Jur*) power of attorney. **V~mond** *m* full moon. **V~pension** *f* full board
vollständig *a* complete
vollstrecken *vt insep* execute; carry out <*Urteil*>
volltanken* *vi sep* (*haben*) **voll tanken**, *s.* **voll**
Volltreffer *m* direct hit
vollzählig *a* complete
vollziehen† *vt insep* carry out; perform <*Handlung*>; consummate <*Ehe*>; **sich v~** take place
Volt /vɔlt/ *nt* **-[s],-** volt
Volumen /vo'lu:mən/ *nt* **-s,-** volume
vom *prep* = **von dem**

von
● *preposition (+ dative)*

! Note that **von dem** can become **vom**

····➤ (*räumlich*) from; (*nach Richtungen*) of. **von hier an** from here on[ward]. **von Wien aus** [starting] from Vienna. **nördlich/südlich von Mannheim** [to the] north/south of Mannheim. **rechts/links von mir** to the right/left of me; on my right/left

····➤ (*zeitlich*) from. **von jetzt an** from now on. **von heute/morgen an** [as] from today/tomorrow; starting today/tomorrow

····➤ (*zur Angabe des Urhebers, der Ursache; nach Passiv*) by. **der Roman ist von Fontane** the novel is by Fontane. **sie hat ein Kind von ihm** she has a child by him. **er ist vom Blitz erschlagen worden** he was killed by lightning

····➤ (*anstelle eines Genitivs; Zugehörigkeit, Beschaffenheit, Menge etc.*) of. **ein Stück von dem Kuchen** a piece of the cake. **einer von euch** one of you. **eine Fahrt von drei Stunden** a drive of three hours; a three-hour drive. **das Brot von gestern** yesterday's bread. **ein Tal von erstaunlicher Schönheit** a valley of extraordinary beauty

····➤ (*beftreffend*) about. **handeln/wissen/erzählen** *od* **reden von ...** be/know/talk about .... **eine Geschichte von zwei Elefanten** a story about *or* of two elephants

voneinander *adv* from each other; <*abhängig*> on each other

vonseiten *prep* (+ *gen*) on the part of

vonstatten *adv* **v~ gehen** take place

vor *prep* (+ *dat*/*acc*) in front of; (*zeitlich, Reihenfolge*) before; (+ *dat*) (*bei Uhrzeit*) to; <*warnen, sich fürchten*> of; <*schützen, davonlaufen*> from; <*Respekt haben*> for; **vor Angst zittern** tremble with fear; **vor drei Tagen** three days ago; **vor allen Dingen** above all ● *adv* forward; **vor und zurück** backwards and forwards

Vorabend *m* eve

voran *adv* at the front; (*voraus*) ahead; (*vorwärts*) forward. **v~gehen**† *vi sep* (*sein*) lead the way; (*Fortschritte machen*) make progress. **v~kommen**† *vi sep* (*sein*) make progress; (*fig*) get on

Vor|anschlag *m* estimate. **V~anzeige** *f* advance notice. **V~arbeiter** *m* foreman

voraus *adv* ahead (*dat* of); (*vorn*) at the front; (*vorwärts*) forward ● **im Voraus** in advance. **v~bezahlen** *vt sep* pay in advance. **v~gehen**† *vi sep* (*sein*) go on ahead; **jdm/etw v~gehen** precede s.o./sth. **V~sage** *f* **-, -n** prediction. **v~sagen** *vt sep* predict

voraussetz|en *vt sep* take for granted; (*erfordern*) require; **vorausgesetzt, dass** provided that. **V~ung** *f* **-, -en** assumption; (*Erfordernis*) prerequisite

voraussichtlich *a* anticipated, expected ● *adv* probably

Vorbehalt *m* **-[e]s, -e** reservation

vorbei *adv* past (**an jdm/etw** s.o./sth); (*zu Ende*) over. **v~fahren**† *vi sep* (*sein*) drive/go past. **v~gehen**† *vi sep* (*sein*) go past; (*verfehlen*) miss; (*vergehen*) pass; ([!] *besuchen*) drop in (**bei** on)

vorbereit|en *vt sep* prepare; prepare for <*Reise*>; **sich v~en** prepare [oneself] (**auf** + *acc* for). **V~ung** *f* **-, -en** preparation

vorbestellen *vt sep* order/(*im Theater, Hotel*) book in advance

vorbestraft *a* **v~ sein** have a [criminal] record

vorbeug|en *v sep* ● *vt* bend forward; **sich v~en** bend *or* lean forward ● *vi* (*haben*) prevent (**etw** *dat* sth). **V~ung** *f* - prevention

Vorbild *nt* model. **v~lich** *a* exemplary, model

vorbringen† *vt sep* put forward; offer <*Entschuldigung*>

vordatieren *vt sep* post-date

Vorder|bein *nt* foreleg. **v~e(r,s)** *a* front. **V~grund** *m* foreground. **V~rad** *nt* front wheel. **V~seite** *f* front; (*einer Münze*) obverse. **v~ste(r,s)** *a* front, first. **V~teil** *nt* front

vor|drängeln (sich) *vr sep* [!] jump the queue. **v~drängen (sich)** *vr sep* push forward. **v~dringen**† *vi sep* (*sein*) advance

voreilig *a* rash

voreingenommen *a* biased, prejudiced. **V~heit** *f* - bias

vorenthalten† *vt sep* withhold

vorerst *adv* for the time being

Vorfahr *m* **-en, -en** ancestor

Vorfahrt *f* right of way; **'V~ beachten'** 'give way'. **V~sstraße** *f* ≈ major road

Vorfall *m* incident. **v~en**† *vi sep* (*sein*) happen

vorfinden† *vt sep* find

Vorfreude *f* [happy] anticipation

vorführ|en *vt sep* present, show; (*demonstrieren*) demonstrate; (*aufführen*) perform. **V~ung** *f* presentation; demonstration; performance

Vor|gabe *f* (*Sport*) handicap. **V~gang** *m* occurrence; (*Techn*) process. **V~gänger(in)** *m* **-s,-** (*f* **-, -nen**) predecessor

vorgehen† *vi sep* (*sein*) go forward; (*voraus-*) go on ahead; <*Uhr:*> be fast; (*verfahren*) act, proceed; (*geschehen*) happen, go on. **V~** *nt* **-s** action

vor|geschichtlich *a* prehistoric. **V~geschmack** *m* foretaste. **V~gesetzte(r)** *m/f* superior. **v~gestern** *adv* the day before yesterday; **v~gestern Abend** the evening before last

vorhaben† *vt sep* propose, intend (**zu** to); **etw v~** have sth planned. **V~** *nt* **-s,-** plan

Vorhand *f* (*Sport*) forehand

vorhanden *a* existing; **v~ sein** exist; be available

Vorhang *m* curtain

Vorhängeschloss *nt* padlock

vorher *adv* before[hand]

vorhergehend *a* previous

vorherrschend *a* predominant

Vorher|sage *f* **-, -n** prediction: (*Wetter-*) forecast. **v~sagen** *vt sep* predict; forecast <*Wetter*>. **v~sehen**† *vt sep* foresee

vorhin *adv* just now

vorige(r,s) *a* last, previous

Vor|kehrungen *fpl* precautions. **V~kenntnisse** *fpl* previous knowledge *sg*

vorkommen† *vi sep* (*sein*) happen; (*vorhanden sein*) occur; (*nach vorn kommen*) come forward; (*hervorkommen*) come out; (*zu sehen sein*) show; **jdm bekannt v~** seem familiar to s.o.

Vorkriegszeit *f* pre-war period

vorlad|en† *vt sep* (*Jur*) summons. **V~ung** *f* summons

Vorlage *f* model; (*Muster*) pattern; (*Gesetzes-*) bill

vorlassen† *vt sep* admit; **jdn v~** [!] let s.o. pass; (*den Vortritt lassen*) let s.o. go first

Vor|lauf *m* (*Sport*) heat. **V~läufer** *m* forerunner. **v~läufig** *a* provisional; (*zunächst*) for the time being. **v~laut** *a* forward. **V~leben** *nt* past

vorleg|en *vt sep* put on <*Kette*>; (*unterbreiten*) present; (*vorzeigen*) show. **V~er** *m* **-s,-** mat; (*Bett-*) rug

vorles|en† *vt sep* read [out]; **jdm v~en** read to s.o. **V~ung** *f* lecture

vorletzt|e(r,s) *a* last ... but one; **v~es Jahr** the year before last

Vorliebe *f* preference

vorliegen† *vt sep* (*haben*) be present/(*verfügbar*) available; (*bestehen*) exist, be

vorlügen† *vt sep* lie (*dat* to)

vormachen *vt sep* put up; put on <*Kette*>; push <*Riegel*>; (*zeigen*) demonstrate; **jdm etwas v~** ([!] *täuschen*) kid s.o.

Vormacht *f* supremacy

vormals *adv* formerly

vormerken *vt sep* make a note of; (*reservieren*) reserve

Vormittag *m* morning; **gestern/heute V~** yesterday/this morning. **v~s** *adv* in the morning

Vormund *m* **-[e]s, -munde** & **-münder** guardian

vorn *adv* at the front; **nach v~** to the front; **von v~** from the front/(*vom Anfang*) beginning; **von v~ anfangen** start afresh

Vorname *m* first name

vorne *adv* = **vorn**

vornehm *a* distinguished; smart

vornehmen† *vt sep* carry out; **sich** (*dat*) **v~, etw zu tun** plan to do sth

vornherein *adv* **von v~herein** from the start

Vor|ort *m* suburb. **V~rang** *m* priority, precedence (**vor** + *dat* over). **V~rat** *m* **-[e]s, ⸚e** supply, stock (**an** + *dat* of). **v~rätig** *a* available; **v~rätig haben** have in stock. **V~ratskammer** *f* larder. **V~recht** *nt* privilege. **V~richtung** *f* device. **V~runde** *f* qualifying round

vorsagen *vt/i sep* (*haben*) recite; **jdm v~** tell s.o. the answer

Vor|satz *m* resolution. **v~sätzlich** *a* deliberate; (*Jur*) premeditated

Vorschau *f* preview; (*Film-*) trailer

Vorschein *m* **zum V~kommen** appear

Vorschlag *m* suggestion, proposal. **v~en**† *vt sep* suggest, propose

vorschnell *a* rash

vorschreiben† *vt sep* lay down; dictate (*dat* to); **vorgeschriebene Dosis** prescribed dose

Vorschrift *f* regulation; (*Anweisung*) instruction; **jdm V~en machen** tell s.o. what to do. **v~smäßig** *a* correct

Vorschule *f* nursery school

Vorschuss *m* advance

vorseh|en† *v sep* ● *vt* intend (**für/als** for/as); (*planen*) plan; **sich v~en** be careful (**vor** + *dat* of) ● *vi* (*haben*) peep out. **V~ung** *f* **-** providence

Vorsicht *f* **-** care; (*bei Gefahr*) caution; **V~!** careful! (*auf Schild*) 'caution'. **v~ig** *a* careful; cautious. **V~smaßnahme** *f* precaution

Vorsilbe *f* prefix

Vorsitz *m* chairmanship; **den V~ führen** be in the chair. **V~ende(r)** *m/f* chairman

Vorsorge *f* **V~ treffen** take precautions; make provisions (**für** for). **v~n** *vi sep* (*haben*) provide (**für** for)

Vorspeise *f* starter

Vorspiel *nt* prelude. **v~en** *v sep* ● *vt* perform/ (*Mus*) play (*dat* for) ● *vi* (*haben*) audition

vorsprechen† *v sep* ● *vt* recite; (*zum Nachsagen*) say (*dat* to) ● *vi* (*haben*) (*Theat*) audition; **bei jdm v~** call on s.o.

Vor|sprung *m* projection; (*Fels-*) ledge; (*Vorteil*) lead (**vor** + *dat* over). **V~stadt** *f* suburb. **V~stand** *m* board [of directors]; (*Vereins-*) committee; (*Partei-*) executive

vorsteh|en† *vi sep* (*haben*) project, protrude; **einer Abteilung v~en** be in charge of a department. **V~er** *m* **-s,-** head

vorstell|en *vt sep* put forward <*Bein, Uhr*>; (*darstellen*) represent; (*bekannt machen*) introduce; **sich v~en** introduce oneself; (*als Bewerber*) go for an interview; **sich** (*dat*) **etw v~en** imagine sth. **V~ung** *f* introduction; (*bei Bewerbung*) interview; (*Aufführung*) performance; (*Idee*) idea; (*Phantasie*) imagination. **V~ungsgespräch** *nt* interview

Vorstoß *m* advance

Vorstrafe *f* previous conviction

Vortag *m* day before

vortäuschen *vt sep* feign, fake

Vorteil *m* advantage. **v~haft** *a* advantageous; flattering

Vortrag *m* **-[e]s,¨e** talk; (*wissenschaftlich*) lecture. **v~en**† *vt sep* perform; (*aufsagen*) recite; (*singen*) sing; (*darlegen*) present (*dat* to)

vortrefflich *a* excellent

Vortritt *m* precedence; **jdm den V~ lassen** let s.o. go first

vorüber *adv* **v~ sein** be over; **an etw** (*dat*) **v~** past sth. **v~gehend** *a* temporary

Vor|urteil *nt* prejudice. **V~verkauf** *m* advance booking

vorverlegen *vt sep* bring forward

Vor|wahl[nummer] *f* dialling code. **V~wand** *m* **-[e]s,¨e** pretext; (*Ausrede*) excuse

vorwärts *adv* forward[s]; **v~ kommen** make progress; (*fig*) get on *or* ahead

vorwegnehmen† *vt sep* anticipate

vorweisen† *vt sep* show

vorwiegend *adv* predominantly

Vorwort *nt* (*pl* **-worte**) preface

Vorwurf *m* reproach; **jdm Vorwürfe machen** reproach s.o. **v~svoll** *a* reproachful

Vorzeichen *nt* sign; (*fig*) omen

vorzeigen *vt sep* show

vorzeitig *a* premature

vorziehen† *vt sep* pull forward; draw <*Vorhang*>; (*lieber mögen*) prefer; favour

Vor|zimmer *nt* ante-room; (*Büro*) outer office. **V~zug** *m* preference; (*gute Eigenschaft*) merit, virtue; (*Vorteil*) advantage

vorzüglich *a* excellent

vulgär /vʊlˈgɛːɐ̯/ *a* vulgar ● *adv* in a vulgar way

Vulkan /vʊlˈkaːn/ *m* **-s, -e** volcano

Ww

Waage *f* **-, -n** scales *pl*; (*Astr*) Libra. **w~recht** *a* horizontal

Wabe *f* **-, -n** honeycomb

wach *a* awake; (*aufgeweckt*) alert; **w~ werden** wake up

Wach|e *f* **-, -n** guard; (*Posten*) sentry; (*Dienst*) guard duty; (*Naut*) watch; (*Polizei-*) station; **W~e halten** keep watch. **W~hund** *m* guard-dog

Wacholder *m* **-s** juniper

Wachposten *m* sentry
Wachs *nt* **-es** wax
wachsam *a* vigilant. **W~keit** *f* **-** vigilance
wachsen†[1] *vi* (*sein*) grow
wachs|en[2] *vt* (*reg*) wax. **W~figur** *f* waxwork
Wachstum *nt* **-s** growth
Wächter *m* **-s,-** guard; (*Park-*) keeper; (*Parkplatz-*) attendant
Wacht|meister *m* [police] constable. **W~posten** *m* sentry
wackel|ig *a* wobbly; <*Stuhl*> rickety; <*Person*> shaky. **W~kontakt** *m* loose connection. **w~n** *vi* (*haben*) wobble; (*zittern*) shake
Wade *f* **-, -n** (*Anat*) calf
Waffe *f* **-, -n** weapon; **W~n** arms
Waffel *f* **-, -n** waffle; (*Eis-*) wafer
Waffen|ruhe *f* cease-fire. **W~schein** *m* firearms licence. **W~stillstand** *m* armistice
Wagemut *m* daring
wagen *vt* risk; **es w~, etw zu tun** dare [to] do sth; **sich w~** (*gehen*) venture
Wagen *m* **-s,-** cart; (*Eisenbahn-*) carriage, coach; (*Güter-*) wagon; (*Kinder-*) pram; (*Auto*) car. **W~heber** *m* **-s,-** jack
Waggon /va'gõ:/ *m* **-s, -s** wagon
Wahl *f* **-, -en** choice; (*Pol, Admin*) election; (*geheime*) ballot; **zweite W~** (*Comm*) seconds *pl*
wähl|en *vt/i* (*haben*) choose; (*Pol, Admin*) elect; (*stimmen*) vote; (*Teleph*) dial. **W~er(in)** *m* **-s,-** (*f* **-, -nen**) voter. **w~erisch** *a* choosy, fussy
Wahl|fach *nt* optional subject. **w~frei** *a* optional. **W~kampf** *m* election campaign. **W~kreis** *m* constituency. **W~lokal** *nt* polling-station. **w~los** *a* indiscriminate. **W~spruch** *m* motto. **W~urne** *f* ballot-box
Wahn *m* **-[e]s** delusion; (*Manie*) mania
Wahnsinn *m* madness. **w~ig** *a* mad, insane; (🅵 *unsinnig*) crazy; (🅵 *groß*) terrible; **w~ig werden** go mad ● *adv* 🅵 terribly. **W~ige(r)** *m/f* maniac
wahr *a* true; (*echt*) real; **du kommst doch, nicht w~?** you are coming, aren't you?
während *prep* (+ *gen*) during ● *conj* while; (*wohingegen*) whereas
Wahrheit *f* **-, -en** truth. **w~sgemäß** *a* truthful
wahrnehm|en† *vt sep* notice; (*nutzen*) take advantage of; exploit <*Vorteil*>; look after <*Interessen*>. **W~ung** *f* **-, -en** perception
Wahrsagerin *f* **-, -nen** fortune-teller
wahrscheinlich *a* probable. **W~keit** *f* **-** probability
Währung *f* **-, -en** currency
Wahrzeichen *nt* symbol
Waise *f* **-, -n** orphan. **W~nhaus** *nt* orphanage. **W~nkind** *nt* orphan
Wal *m* **-[e]s, -e** whale
Wald *m* **-[e]s,¨-er** wood; (*groß*) forest. **w~ig** *a* wooded
Walis|er *m* **-s,-** Welshman. **w~isch** *a* Welsh
Wall *m* **-[e]s,¨-e** mound
Wallfahr|er(in) *m(f)* pilgrim. **W~t** *f* pilgrimage
Walnuss *f* walnut
Walze *f* **-, -n** roller. **w~n** *vt* roll
Walzer *m* **-s,-** waltz
Wand *f* **-,¨-e** wall; (*Trenn-*) partition; (*Seite*) side; (*Fels-*) face
Wandel *m* **-s** change
Wander|er *m* **-s,-, W~in** *f* **-, -nen** hiker, rambler. **w~n** *vi* (*sein*) hike, ramble; (*ziehen*) travel; (*gemächlich gehen*) wander; (*ziellos*) roam.

W~schaft *f* - travels *pl.* **W~ung** *f* -, **-en** hike, ramble. **W~weg** *m* footpath

Wandlung *f* -, **-en** change, transformation

Wand|malerei *f* mural. **W~tafel** *f* blackboard. **W~teppich** *m* tapestry

Wange *f* -, **-n** cheek

wann *adv* when

Wanne *f* -, **-n** tub

Wanze *f* -, **-n** bug

Wappen *nt* **-s,-** coat of arms. **W~kunde** *f* heraldry

war, wäre *s.* **sein**[1]

Ware *f* -, **-n** article; (*Comm*) commodity; (*coll*) merchandise; **W~n** goods. **W~nhaus** *nt* department store. **W~nprobe** *f* sample. **W~nzeichen** *nt* trademark

warm *a* warm; <*Mahlzeit*> hot; **w~ machen** heat ● *adv* warmly; **w~ essen** have a hot meal

Wärm|e *f* - warmth; (*Phys*) heat; **10 Grad W~e** 10 degrees above zero. **w~en** *vt* warm; heat <*Essen, Wasser*>. **W~flasche** *f* hot-water bottle

Warn|blinkanlage *f* hazard [warning] lights *pl.* **w~en** *vt/i* (*haben*) warn (**vor** + *dat* of). **W~ung** *f* -, **-en** warning

Warteliste *f* waiting list

warten *vi* (*haben*) wait (**auf** + *acc* for) ● *vt* service

Wärter(in) *m* **-s,-** (*f* -, **-nen**) keeper; (*Museums-*) attendant; (*Gefängnis-*) warder; (*Kranken-*) orderly

Warte|raum, W~saal *m* waiting-room. **W~zimmer** *nt* (*Med*) waiting-room

Wartung *f* - (*Techn*) service

warum *adv* why

Warze *f* -, **-n** wart

was *pron* what ● *rel pron* that; **alles, was ich brauche** all [that] I need ● *indef pron* (🅸 *etwas*) something; (*fragend, verneint*) anything; **so was Ärgerliches!** what a nuisance! ● *adv* 🅸 (*warum*) why; (*wie*) how

wasch|bar *a* washable. **W~becken** *nt* wash-basin

Wäsche *f* - washing; (*Unter-*) underwear

waschecht *a* colour-fast

Wäscheklammer *f* clothes-peg

waschen† *vt* wash; **sich w~** have a wash; **W~ und Legen** shampoo and set ● *vi* (*haben*) do the washing

Wäscherei *f* -, **-en** laundry

Wäsche|schleuder *f* spin-drier. **W~trockner** *m* tumble-drier

Wasch|küche *f* laundry-room. **W~lappen** *m* face-flannel. **W~maschine** *f* washing machine. **W~mittel** *nt* detergent. **W~pulver** *nt* washing-powder. **W~salon** *m* launderette. **W~zettel** *m* blurb

Wasser *nt* **-s** water. **W~ball** *m* beach-ball; (*Spiel*) water polo. **w~dicht** *a* watertight; <*Kleidung*> waterproof. **W~fall** *m* waterfall. **W~farbe** *f* water-colour. **W~hahn** *m* tap. **W~kraft** *f* water-power. **W~kraftwerk** *nt* hydroelectric power-station. **W~leitung** *f* water-main; **aus der W~leitung** from the tap. **W~mann** *m* (*Astr*) Aquarius

wässern *vt* soak; (*begießen*) water ● *vi* (*haben*) water

Wasser|ski *nt* **-s** water-skiing. **W~stoff** *m* hydrogen. **W~straße** *f* waterway. **W~waage** *f* spirit-level

wässrig *a* watery

watscheln *vi* (*sein*) waddle

Watt *nt* **-s,-** (*Phys*) watt

Watt|e *f* - cotton wool. **w~iert** *a* padded; (*gesteppt*) quilted

WC /ve'tse:/ *nt* **-s, -s** WC

web|en *vt/i* (*haben*) weave. **W~er** *m* **-s,-** weaver
Web|seite /'vɛp-/ *f* web page. **W~site** /-'sait/ *f* **-, -s** website
Webstuhl *m* loom
Wechsel *m* **-s,-** change; (*Tausch*) exchange; (*Comm*) bill of exchange. **W~geld** *nt* change. **w~haft** *a* changeable. **W~jahre** *npl* menopause *sg*. **W~kurs** *m* exchange rate. **w~n** *vt* change; (*tauschen*) exchange ● *vi* (*haben*) change; vary. **w~nd** *a* changing; varying. **W~strom** *m* alternating current. **W~stube** *f* bureau de change
weck|en *vt* wake [up]; (*fig*) awaken ● *vi* (*haben*) <*Wecker:*> go off. **W~er** *m* **-s,-** alarm [clock]
wedeln *vi* (*haben*) wave; **mit dem Schwanz w~** wag its tail
weder *conj* **w~ ... noch** neither ... nor
Weg *m* **-[e]s, -e** way; (*Fuß-*) path; (*Fahr-*) track; (*Gang*) errand; **sich auf den Weg machen** set off
weg *adv* away, off; (*verschwunden*) gone; **weg sein** be away; (*gegangen/verschwunden*) have gone; **Hände weg!** hands off!
wegen *prep* (+ *gen*) because of; (*um ... willen*) for the sake of; (*bezüglich*) about
weg|fahren† *vi sep* (*sein*) go away; (*abfahren*) leave. **W~fahrsperre** *f* immobilizer. **w~fallen†** *vi sep* (*sein*) be dropped/(*ausgelassen*) omitted; (*entfallen*) no longer apply. **w~geben†** *vt sep* give away. **w~gehen†** *vi sep* (*sein*) leave, go away; (*ausgehen*) go out. **w~kommen†** *vi sep* (*sein*) get away; (*verloren gehen*) disappear; **schlecht w~kommen** [!] get a raw deal. **w~lassen†** *vt sep* let go; (*auslassen*) omit. **w~laufen†** *vi sep* (*sein*) run away. **w~räumen** *vt sep* put away; (*entfernen*) clear away. **w~schicken** *vt sep* send away; (*abschicken*) send off. **w~tun†** *vt sep* put away; (*wegwerfen*) throw away
Wegweiser *m* **-s,-** signpost
weg|werfen† *vt sep* throw away. **w~ziehen†** *v sep* ● *vt* pull away ● *vi* (*sein*) move away
weh *a* sore; **weh tun** hurt; <*Kopf, Rücken:*> ache; **jdm weh tun** hurt s.o.
wehe *int* alas; **w~ [dir/euch]!** (*drohend*) don't you dare!
wehen *vi* (*haben*) blow; (*flattern*) flutter ● *vt* blow
Wehen *fpl* contractions
Wehr[1] *nt* **-[e]s, -e** weir
Wehr[2] *f* **sich zur W~ setzen** resist
Wehrdienst *m* military service. **W~verweigerer** *m* **-s,-** conscientious objector
wehren (sich) *vr* resist; (*gegen Anschuldigung*) protest; (*sich sträuben*) refuse
wehr|los *a* defenceless. **W~macht** *f* armed forces *pl*. **W~pflicht** *f* conscription
Weib *nt* **-[e]s, -er** woman; (*Ehe-*) wife. **W~chen** *nt* **-s,-** (*Zool*) female. **w~lich** *a* feminine; (*Biol*) female
weich *a* soft; (*gar*) done
Weiche *f* **-, -n** (*Rail*) points *pl*
Weich|heit *f* **-** softness. **w~lich** *a* soft; <*Charakter*> weak. **W~spüler** *m* **-s,-** (*Tex*) conditioner. **W~tier** *nt* mollusc
Weide[1] *f* **-, -n** (*Bot*) willow
Weide[2] *f* **-, -n** pasture. **w~n** *vt/i* (*haben*) graze
weiger|n (sich) *vr* refuse. **W~ung** *f* **-, -en** refusal

Weihe *f* **-, -n** consecration; (*Priester-*) ordination. **w~n** *vt* consecrate; (*zum Priester*) ordain

Weiher *m* **-s,-** pond

Weihnacht|en *nt* **-s** & *pl* Christmas. **w~lich** *a* Christmassy. **W~sbaum** *m* Christmas tree. **W~slied** *nt* Christmas carol. **W~smann** *m* (*pl* **-männer**) Father Christmas. **W~stag** *m* **erster/zweiter W~stag** Christmas Day/Boxing Day

Weih|rauch *m* incense. **W~wasser** *nt* holy water

weil *conj* because; (*da*) since

Weile *f* **-** while

Wein *m* **-[e]s, -e** wine; (*Bot*) vines *pl*; (*Trauben*) grapes *pl*. **W~bau** *m* wine-growing. **W~berg** *m* vineyard. **W~brand** *m* **-[e]s** brandy

weinen *vt/i* (*haben*) cry, weep

Wein|glas *nt* wineglass. **W~karte** *f* wine-list. **W~lese** *f* grape harvest. **W~liste** *f* wine-list. **W~probe** *f* wine-tasting. **W~rebe** *f*, **W~stock** *m* vine. **W~stube** *f* wine-bar. **W~traube** *f* bunch of grapes; (*W~beere*) grape

weise *a* wise

Weise *f* **-, -n** way; (*Melodie*) tune

Weisheit *f* **-, -en** wisdom. **W~szahn** *m* wisdom tooth

weiß *a*, **W~** *nt* **-,-** white

weissag|en *vt/i insep* (*haben*) prophesy. **W~ung** *f* **-, -en** prophecy

Weiß|brot *nt* white bread. **W~e(r)** *m/f* white man/woman. **w~en** *vt* whitewash. **W~wein** *m* white wine

Weisung *f* **-, -en** instruction; (*Befehl*) order

weit *a* wide; (*ausgedehnt*) extensive; (*lang*) long ● *adv* widely; <*offen, öffnen*> wide; (*lang*) far; **von w~em** from a distance; **bei w~em** by far; **w~ und breit** far and wide; **ist es noch w~?** is it much further? **so w~ wie möglich** as far as possible; **ich bin so w~** I'm ready; **w~ verbreitet** widespread; **w~ reichende Folgen** far-reaching consequences

Weite *f* **-, -n** expanse; (*Entfernung*) distance; (*Größe*) width. **w~n** *vt* widen; stretch <*Schuhe*>

weiter *a* further ● *adv* further; (*außerdem*) in addition; (*anschließend*) then; **etw w~ tun** go on doing sth; **w~ nichts/niemand** nothing/no one else; **und so w~** and so on

weiter|e(r,s) *a* further; **ohne w~es** just like that; (*leicht*) easily

weiter|erzählen *vt sep* go on with; (*w~sagen*) repeat. **w~fahren†** *vi sep* (*sein*) go on. **w~geben†** *vt sep* pass on. **w~hin** *adv* (*immer noch*) still; (*in Zukunft*) in future; (*außerdem*) furthermore; **etw w~hin tun** go on doing sth. **w~machen** *vi sep* (*haben*) carry on

weit|gehend *a* extensive ● *adv* to a large extent. **w~sichtig** *a* long-sighted; (*fig*) far-sighted. **W~sprung** *m* long jump. **w~verbreitet*** *a* **w~ verbreitet**, *s.* **weit**

Weizen *m* **-s** wheat

welch *inv pron* what; **w~ ein(e)** what a. **w~e(r,s)** *pron* which; **um w~e Zeit?** at what time? ● *rel pron* which; (*Person*) who ● *indef pron* some; (*fragend*) any; **was für w~e?** what sort of?

Wellblech *nt* corrugated iron

Well|e *f* **-, -n** wave; (*Techn*) shaft. **W~enlänge** *f* wavelength. **W~enlinie** *f* wavy line.

W∼enreiten *nt* surfing. **W∼ensittich** *m* **-s, -e** budgerigar. **w∼ig** *a* wavy

Wẹlt *f* **-, -en** world; **auf der W∼** in the world; **auf die** *od* **zur W∼ kommen** be born. **W∼all** *nt* universe. **w∼berühmt** *a* world-famous. **w∼fremd** *a* unworldly. **W∼kugel** *f* globe. **w∼lich** *a* worldly; (*nicht geistlich*) secular

Wẹltmeister|(in) *m(f)* world champion. **W∼schaft** *f* world championship

Wẹltraum *m* space. **W∼fahrer** *m* astronaut

Wẹltrekord *m* world record

wẹm *pron* (*dat of* **wer**) to whom

wẹn *pron* (*acc of* **wer**) whom

Wẹnde *f* **-, -n** change. **W∼kreis** *m* (*Geog*) tropic

Wẹndeltreppe *f* spiral staircase

wẹnden[1] *vt* (*reg*) turn ● *vi* (*haben*) turn [round]

wẹnden[2]† (*& reg*) *vt* turn; **sich w∼** turn; **sich an jdn w∼** turn/ (*schriftlich*) write to s.o.

Wẹnd|epunkt *m* (*fig*) turning-point. **W∼ung** *f* **-, -en** turn; (*Biegung*) bend; (*Veränderung*) change

wẹnig *pron* little; (*pl*) few; **so/zu w∼** so/too little/(*pl*) few; **w∼e** *pl* few ● *adv* little; (*kaum*) not much; **so w∼ wie möglich** as little as possible. **w∼er** *pron* less; (*pl*) fewer; **immer w∼er** less and less ● *adv & conj* less. **w∼ste(r,s)** *pron* least; **am w∼sten** least [of all]. **w∼stens** *adv* at least

wẹnn *conj* if; (*sobald*) when; **immer w∼** whenever; **w∼ nicht** *od* **außer w∼** unless; **w∼ auch** even though

wẹr *pron* who; (**!** *jemand*) someone; (*fragend*) anyone

Wẹrbe|agentur *f* advertising agency. **w∼n**† *vt* recruit; attract <*Kunden, Besucher*> ● *vi* (*haben*) **w∼n für** advertise; canvass for <*Partei*>. **W∼spot** /-sp-/ *m* **-s, -s** commercial

Wẹrbung *f* **-** advertising

---

werden†

● *intransitive verb* (*sein*)

····➤ (+ *adjective*) become; get; (*allmählich*) grow. **müde/alt/länger werden** become *or* get/ grow tired/old/longer. **taub/blind/wahnsinnig werden** go deaf/blind/mad. **blass werden** become *or* turn pale. **krank werden** become *or* fall ill. **es wird warm/dunkel** it is getting warm/dark. **mir wurde schlecht/schwindlig** I began to feel sick/dizzy

····➤ (+ *noun*) become. **Arzt/Lehrer/Mutter werden** become a doctor/teacher/mother. **er will Lehrer werden** he wants to be a teacher. **was ist aus ihm geworden?** what has become of him?

····➤ **werden zu** become; turn into. **das Erlebnis wurde zu einem Albtraum** the experience became *or* turned into a nightmare. **zu Eis werden** turn into ice

● *auxiliary verb*

····➤ (*Zukunft*) will; shall. **er wird bald hier sein** he will *or* he'll soon be here. **wir werden sehen** we shall see. **es wird bald regnen** it's going to rain soon

····➤ (*Konjunktiv*) **würde(n)** would. **ich würde es kaufen, wenn ...** I would buy it if .... **würden Sie so nett sein?** would you be so kind?

····➤ (*beim Passiv; pp* **worden**) be. **geliebt/geboren werden** be loved/born. **du wirst gerufen** you are being called. **er wurde gebeten** he was asked. **es wurde gemunkelt** it was rumoured. **mir wurde gesagt, dass ...** I was told that .... **das Haus ist gerade/ 1995 renoviert worden** the house has just been renovated/ was renovated in 1995

werfen† *vt* throw; cast <*Blick, Schatten*>; **sich w~** <*Holz:*> warp

Werft *f* **-, -en** shipyard

Werk *nt* **-[e]s, -e** work; (*Fabrik*) works *sg*, factory; (*Trieb-*) mechanism. **W~en** *nt* **-s** (*Sch*) handicraft. **W~statt** *f* **-,¨en** workshop; (*Auto-*) garage. **W~tag** *m* weekday. **w~tags** *adv* on weekdays. **w~tätig** *a* working

Werkzeug *nt* tool; (*coll*) tools *pl*. **W~leiste** *f* toolbar

Wermut *m* **-s** vermouth

wert *a* **viel w~** worth a lot; **nichts w~ sein** be worthless; **jds w~ sein** be worthy of s.o. **W~** *m* **-[e]s, -e** value; (*Nenn-*) denomination; **im W~ von** worth. **w~en** *vt* rate

Wert|gegenstand *m* object of value. **w~los** *a* worthless. **W~minderung** *f* depreciation. **W~papier** *nt* (*Comm*) security. **W~sachen** *fpl* valuables. **w~voll** *a* valuable

Wesen *nt* **-s,-** nature; (*Lebe-*) being; (*Mensch*) creature

wesentlich *a* essential; (*grundlegend*) fundamental ● *adv* considerably, much

weshalb *adv* why

Wespe *f* **-, -n** wasp

wessen *pron* (*gen of* **wer**) whose

westdeutsch *a* West German

Weste *f* **-, -n** waistcoat

Westen *m* **-s** west

Western *m* **-[s],-** western

Westfalen *nt* **-s** Westphalia

Westindien *nt* West Indies *pl*

west|lich *a* western; <*Richtung*> westerly ● *adv & prep* (+ *gen*) **w~lich [von] der Stadt** [to the] west of the town. **w~wärts** *adv* westwards

weswegen *adv* why

Wettbewerb *m* **-s, -e** competition

Wette *f* **-, -n** bet; **um die W~ laufen** race (**mit jdm** s.o.)

wetten *vt/i* (*haben*) bet (**auf** + *acc* on); **mit jdm w~** have a bet with s.o.

Wetter *nt* **-s,-** weather; (*Un-*) storm. **W~bericht** *m* weather report. **W~vorhersage** *f* weather forecast. **W~warte** *f* **-, -n** meteorological station

Wett|kampf *m* contest. **W~kämpfer(in)** *m(f)* competitor. **W~lauf** *m* race. **W~rennen** *nt* race. **W~streit** *m* contest

Whisky *m* **-s** whisky

wichtig *a* important; **w~ nehmen** take seriously. **W~keit** *f* **-** importance

Wicke *f* **-, -n** sweet pea

Wickel *m* **-s,-** compress

wickeln *vt* wind; (*ein-*) wrap; (*bandagieren*) bandage; **ein Kind frisch w~** change a baby

Widder *m* **-s,-** ram; (*Astr*) Aries

wider *prep* (+ *acc*) against; (*entgegen*) contrary to; **w~ Willen** against one's will

widerlegen *vt insep* refute

wider|lich *a* repulsive. **W~rede** *f* contradiction; **keine W~rede!** don't argue!

widerrufen† *vt/i insep* (*haben*) retract; revoke <*Befehl*>

Widersacher *m* **-s,-** adversary

widersetzen (sich) *vr insep* resist (**jdm/etw** s.o./sth)

widerspiegeln *vt sep* reflect

widersprechen† *vi insep* (*haben*) contradict (**jdm/etw** s.o./ sth)

Wider|spruch *m* contradiction; (*Protest*) protest.

w~sprüchlich *a* contradictory. **w~spruchslos** *adv* without protest

Widerstand *m* resistance; **W~ leisten** resist. **w~sfähig** *a* resistant; (*Bot*) hardy

widerstehen† *vi insep* (*haben*) resist (**jdm/etw** s.o/sth); (*anwidern*) be repugnant (**jdm** to *s.o.*)

Widerstreben *nt* **-s** reluctance

widerwärtig *a* disagreeable

Widerwill|e *m* aversion, repugnance. **w~ig** *a* reluctant

widm|en *vt* dedicate (*dat* to); (*verwenden*) devote (*dat* to); **sich w~en** (+ *dat*) devote oneself to. **W~ung** *f* **-, -en** dedication

wie *adv* how; **wie viel** how much/(*pl*) many; **um wie viel Uhr?** at what time? **wie viele?** how many? **wie ist Ihr Name?** what is your name? **wie ist das Wetter?** what is the weather like? ● *conj* as; (*gleich wie*) like; (*sowie*) as well as; (*als*) when, as; **so gut wie** as good as; **nichts wie** nothing but

wieder *adv* again; **jdn/etw w~ erkennen** recognize s.o./sth; **etw w~ verwenden/verwerten** reuse/recycle sth; **etw w~ gutmachen** make up for <*Schaden*>; redress <*Unrecht*>; (*bezahlen*) pay for sth

Wiederaufbau *m* reconstruction

wieder|bekommen† *vt sep* get back. **W~belebung** *f* **-** resuscitation. **w~bringen**† *vt sep* bring back. **w~erkennen*** *vt sep* **w~ erkennen**, *s.* **wieder**. **w~geben**† *vt sep* give back, return; (*darstellen*) portray; (*ausdrücken, übersetzen*) render; (*zitieren*) quote. **W~geburt** *f* reincarnation

Wiedergutmachung *f* **-** reparation; (*Entschädigung*) compensation

wiederherstellen *vt sep* re-establish; restore <*Gebäude*>; restore to health <*Kranke*>

wiederhol|en *vt insep* repeat; (*Sch*) revise; **sich w~en** recur; <*Person:*> repeat oneself. **w~t** *a* repeated. **W~ung** *f* **-, -en** repetition; (*Sch*) revision

Wieder|hören *nt* **auf W~hören!** goodbye! **W~käuer** *m* **-s,-** ruminant. **W~kehr** *f* **-** return; (*W~holung*) recurrence. **w~kommen**† *vi sep* (*sein*) come back

wiedersehen* *vt sep* **wieder sehen**, *s.* **sehen**. **W~** *nt* **-s,-** reunion; **auf W~!** goodbye!

wiedervereinig|en* *vt sep* **wieder vereinigen**, *s.* **vereinigen**. **W~ung** *f* reunification

wieder|verwenden* *vt sep* **w~ verwenden**, *s.* **wieder**. **w~verwerten*** *vt sep* **w~ verwerten**, *s.* **wieder**

Wiege *f* **-, -n** cradle

wiegen[1]† *vt/i* (*haben*) weigh

wiegen[2] *vt* (*reg*) rock. **W~lied** *nt* lullaby

wiehern *vi* (*haben*) neigh

Wien *nt* **-s** Vienna. **W~er** *a* Viennese ● *m* **-s,-** Viennese ● *f* **-,-** ≈ frankfurter. **w~erisch** *a* Viennese

Wiese *f* **-, -n** meadow

Wiesel *nt* **-s,-** weasel

wieso *adv* why

wieviel* *pron* **wie viel**, *s.* **wie**. **w~te(r,s)** *a* which; **der W~te ist heute?** what is the date today?

wieweit *adv* how far

wild *a* wild; <*Stamm*> savage; **w~er Streik** wildcat strike; **w~ wachsen** grow wild. **W~** *nt* **-[e]s** game; (*Rot-*) deer; (*Culin*) venison. **W~e(r)** *m/f* savage

Wilder|er *m* **-s,-** poacher. **w~n** *vt/i* (*haben*) poach

Wịld|heger, W~hüter *m* **-s,-** gamekeeper. **W~leder** *nt* suede. **W~nis** *f* **-** wilderness. **W~schwein** *nt* wild boar. **W~wẹstfilm** *m* western

Wịlle *m* **-ns** will. **W~nskraft** *f* will-power

wịllig *a* willing

willkọmmen *a* welcome; **w~ heißen** welcome. **W~** *nt* **-s** welcome

wịmmeln *vi* (*haben*) swarm

wịmmern *vi* (*haben*) whimper

Wịmpel *m* **-s,-** pennant

Wịmper *f* **-, -n** [eye]lash; **W~ntusche** *f* mascara

Wịnd *m* **-[e]s, -e** wind

Wịnde *f* **-, -n** (*Techn*) winch

Wịndel *f* **-, -n** nappy

wịnden† *vt* wind; make <*Kranz*>; **in die Höhe w~** winch up; **sich w~** wind (**um** round); (*sich krümmen*) writhe

Wịnd|hund *m* greyhound. **w~ig** *a* windy. **W~mühle** *f* windmill. **W~park** *m* wind farm. **W~pocken** *fpl* chickenpox *sg*. **W~schutzscheibe** *f* windscreen. **W~stille** *f* calm. **W~stoß** *m* gust of wind. **W~surfen** *nt* windsurfing

Wịndung *f* **-, -en** bend; (*Spirale*) spiral

Wịnkel *m* **-s,-** angle; (*Ecke*) corner. **W~messer** *m* **-s,-** protractor

wịnken *vi* (*haben*) wave

Wịnter *m* **-s,-** winter. **w~lich** *a* wintry; (*Winter-*) winter ... **W~schlaf** *m* hibernation; **W~sport** *m* winter sports *pl*

Wịnzer *m* **-s,-** winegrower

wịnzig *a* tiny, minute

Wịpfel *m* **-s,-** [tree-]top

Wịppe *f* **-, -n** see-saw

wịr *pron* we; **wir sind es** it's us

Wịrbel *m* **-s,-** eddy; (*Drehung*) whirl; (*Trommel-*) roll; (*Anat*) vertebra; (*Haar-*) crown; (*Aufsehen*) fuss. **w~n** *vt/i* (*sein/haben*) whirl. **W~säule** *f* spine. **W~sturm** *m* cyclone. **W~tier** *nt* vertebrate. **W~wind** *m* whirlwind

wịrd *s.* **werden**

wịrken *vi* (*haben*) have an effect (**auf** + *acc* on); (*zur Geltung kommen*) be effective; (*tätig sein*) work; (*scheinen*) seem ● *vt* (*Tex*) knit

wịrklich *a* real. **W~keit** *f* **-, -en** reality

wịrksam *a* effective

Wịrkung *f* **-, -en** effect. **w~slos** *a* ineffective. **w~svoll** *a* effective

wịrr *a* tangled; <*Haar*> tousled; (*verwirrt, verworren*) confused

Wịrt *m* **-[e]s, -e** landlord. **W~in** *f*-, **-nen** landlady

Wịrtschaft *f* **-, -en** economy; (*Gast-*) restaurant; (*Kneipe*) pub. **w~en** *vi* (*haben*) manage one's finances. **w~lich** *a* economic; (*sparsam*) economical. **W~sgeld** *nt* housekeeping [money]. **W~sprüfer** *m* auditor

Wịrtshaus *nt* inn; (*Kneipe*) pub

wịschen *vt/i* (*haben*) wipe; wash <*Fußboden*>

wịssen† *vt/i* (*haben*) know; **weißt du noch?** do you remember? **nichts w~ wollen von** not want anything to do with. **W~** *nt* **-s** knowledge; **meines W~s** to my knowledge

Wịssenschaft *f* **-, -en** science. **W~ler** *m* **-s,-** academic; (*Natur-*) scientist. **w~lich** *a* academic; scientific

wịssenswert *a* worth knowing

wịtter|n *vt* scent; (*ahnen*) sense. **W~ung** *f* **-** scent; (*Wetter*) weather

Wịtwe *f* **-, -n** widow. **W~r** *m* **-s,-** widower

Witz *m* **-es, -e** joke; (*Geist*) wit. **W~bold** *m* **-[e]s, -e** joker. **w~ig** *a* funny; witty

wo *adv* where; (*als*) when; (*irgendwo*) somewhere; **wo immer** wherever ● *conj* seeing that; (*obwohl*) although; (*wenn*) if

woanders *adv* somewhere else

wobei *adv* how; (*relativ*) during the course of which

Woche *f* **-, -n** week. **W~nende** *nt* weekend. **W~nkarte** *f* weekly ticket. **w~nlang** *adv* for weeks. **W~ntag** *m* day of the week; (*Werktag*) weekday. **w~tags** *adv* on weekdays

wöchentlich *a & adv* weekly

Wodka *m* **-s** vodka

wofür *adv* what ... for; (*relativ*) for which

Woge *f* **-, -n** wave

woher *adv* where from; **woher weißt du das?** how do you know that? **wohin** *adv* where [to]; **wohin gehst du?** where are you going?

wohl *adv* well; (*vermutlich*) probably; (*etwa*) about; (*zwar*) perhaps; **w~ kaum** hardly; **sich w~ fühlen** feel well/(*behaglich*) comfortable; **jdm w~ tun** do s.o. good. **W~** *nt* **-[e]s** welfare, well-being; **zum W~** (+ *gen*) for the good of; **zum W~!** cheers!

Wohl|befinden *nt* well-being. **W~behagen** *nt* feeling of well-being. **W~ergehen** *nt* **-s** welfare. **w~erzogen** *a* well brought-up

Wohlfahrt *f* **-** welfare. **W~sstaat** *m* Welfare State

wohl|habend *a* prosperous, well-to-do. **w~ig** *a* comfortable. **w~schmeckend** *a* tasty

Wohlstand *m* prosperity. **W~sgesellschaft** *f* affluent society

Wohltat *f* [act of] kindness; (*Annehmlichkeit*) treat; (*Genuss*) bliss

Wohltät|er *m* benefactor. **w~ig** *a* charitable

wohl|tuend *a* agreeable. **w~tun*** *vi sep* (*haben*) **w~ tun**, *s.* **wohl**

Wohlwollen *nt* **-s** goodwill; (*Gunst*) favour. **w~d** *a* benevolent

Wohn|block *m* block of flats. **w~en** *vi* (*haben*) live; (*vorübergehend*) stay. **W~gegend** *f* residential area. **w~haft** *a* resident. **W~haus** *nt* house. **W~heim** *nt* hostel; (*Alten-*) home. **w~lich** *a* comfortable. **W~mobil** *nt* **-s, -e** camper. **W~ort** *m* place of residence. **W~sitz** *m* place of residence

Wohnung *f* **-, -en** flat; (*Unterkunft*) accommodation. **W~snot** *f* housing shortage

Wohn|wagen *m* caravan. **W~zimmer** *nt* living-room

wölb|en *vt* curve; arch <*Rücken*>. **W~ung** *f* **-, -en** curve; (*Archit*) vault

Wolf *m* **-[e]s, ¨e** wolf; (*Fleisch-*) mincer; (*Reiß-*) shredder

Wolk|e *f* **-, -n** cloud. **W~enbruch** *m* cloudburst. **W~enkratzer** *m* skyscraper. **w~enlos** *a* cloudless. **w~ig** *a* cloudy

Woll|decke *f* blanket. **W~e** *f* **-, -n** wool

---

wollen†[1]

● *auxiliary verb*

····➤ (*den Wunsch haben*) want to. **ich will nach Hause gehen** I want to go home. **ich wollte Sie fragen, ob ...** I wanted to ask you if ...

····➤ (*im Begriff sein*) be about to. **wir wollten gerade gehen** we were just about to go
····➤ (*sich in der gewünschten Weise verhalten*) **will nicht** refuses to. **der Motor will nicht anspringen** the engine won't *or* refuses to start
● *intransitive verb*
····➤ want to. **ob du willst oder nicht** whether you want to or not. **ganz wie du willst** just as you like
····➤ ([!] *irgendwohin zu gehen wünschen*) **ich will nach Hause** I want to go home. **zu wem wollen Sie?** who[m] do you want to see?
····➤ ([!] *funktionieren*) **will nicht** won't go. **meine Beine wollen nicht mehr** my legs are giving up [!]
● *transitive verb*
····➤ want; (*beabsichtigen*) intend. **er will nicht, dass du ihm hilfst** he does not want you to help him. **das habe ich nicht gewollt** I never intended *or* meant that to happen

wollen² *a* woollen. **w~ig** *a* woolly. **W~sachen** *fpl* woollens

womit *adv* what ... with; (*relativ*) with which. **wonach** *adv* what ... after/<*suchen*> for/<*riechen*> of; (*relativ*) after/for/of which

woran *adv* what ... on/<*denken, sterben*> of; (*relativ*) on/of which; **woran hast du ihn erkannt?** how did you recognize him? **worauf** *adv* what ... on/<*warten*> for; (*relativ*) on/for which; (*woraufhin*) whereupon. **woraus** *adv* what ... from; (*relativ*) from which

Wort *nt* **-[e]s,¨er** & **-e** word; **jdm ins W~ fallen** interrupt s.o.

Wörterbuch *nt* dictionary

Wort|führer *m* spokesman. **w~getreu** *a* & *adv* word-for-word. **w~karg** *a* taciturn. **W~laut** *m* wording

wörtlich *a* literal; (*wortgetreu*) word-for-word

wort|los *a* silent ● *adv* without a word. **W~schatz** *m* vocabulary. **W~spiel** *nt* pun, play on words

worüber *adv* what ... over/<*lachen, sprechen*> about; (*relativ*) over/about which. **worum** *adv* what ... round/<*bitten, kämpfen*> for; (*relativ*) round/for which; **worum geht es?** what is it about? **wovon** *adv* what ... from/<*sprechen*> about; (*relativ*) from/about which. **wovor** *adv* what ... in front of; <*sich fürchten*> what ... of; (*relativ*) in front of which; of which. **wozu** *adv* what ... to/<*brauchen, benutzen*> for; (*relativ*) to/for which; **wozu?** what for?

Wrack *nt* **-s, -s** wreck

wringen† *vt* wring

Wucher|preis *m* extortionate price. **W~ung** *f* **-, -en** growth

Wuchs *m* **-es** growth; (*Gestalt*) stature

Wucht *f* **-** force

wühlen *vi* (*haben*) rummage; (*in der Erde*) burrow ● *vt* dig

Wulst *m* **-[e]s,¨e** bulge; (*Fett-*) roll

wund *a* sore; **w~ reiben** chafe; **sich w~ liegen** get bedsores. **W~brand** *m* gangrene

Wunde *f* **-, -n** wound

Wunder *nt* **-s,-** wonder, marvel; (*übernatürliches*) miracle; **kein W~!** no wonder! **w~bar** *a* miraculous; (*herrlich*) wonderful. **W~kind** *nt* infant prodigy. **w~n** *vt* surprise; **sich w~n** be surprised (**über** + *acc* at). **w~schön** *a* beautiful

Wundstarrkrampf *m* tetanus

Wunsch *m* **-[e]s,⸗e** wish; (*Verlangen*) desire; (*Bitte*) request
wünschen *vt* want; **sich** (*dat*) **etw w~** want sth; (*bitten um*) ask for sth; **jdm Glück/gute Nacht w~** wish s.o. luck/good night; **Sie w~?** can I help you? **w~swert** *a* desirable
Wunschkonzert *nt* musical request programme
wurde, würde *s.* **werden**
Würde *f* **-, -n** dignity; (*Ehrenrang*) honour. **w~los** *a* undignified. **W~nträger** *m* dignitary. **w~voll** *a* dignified ● *adv* with dignity
würdig *a* dignified; (*wert*) worthy
Wurf *m* **-[e]s,⸗e** throw; (*Junge*) litter
Würfel *m* **-s,-** cube; (*Spiel-*) dice; (*Zucker-*) lump. **w~n** *vi* (*haben*) throw the dice; **w~n um** play dice for ● *vt* throw; (*in Würfel schneiden*) dice. **W~zucker** *m* cube sugar
würgen *vt* choke ● *vi* (*haben*) retch; choke (**an** + *dat* on)
Wurm *m* **-[e]s,⸗er** worm; (*Made*) maggot. **w~en** *vi* (*haben*) **jdn w~en** 🅘 rankle [with s.o.]
Wurst *f* **-,⸗e** sausage; **das ist mir W~** 🅘 I couldn't care less
Würze *f* **-, -n** spice; (*Aroma*) aroma
Wurzel *f* **-, -n** root; **W~n schlagen** take root. **w~n** *vi* (*haben*) root
würz|en *vt* season. **w~ig** *a* tasty; (*aromatisch*) aromatic; (*pikant*) spicy
wüst *a* chaotic; (*wirr*) tangled; (*öde*) desolate; (*wild*) wild; (*schlimm*) terrible
Wüste *f* **-, -n** desert
Wut *f* **-** rage, fury. **W~anfall** *m* fit of rage
wüten *vi* (*haben*) rage. **w~d** *a* furious; **w~d machen** infuriate

Xx

x /ɪks/ *inv a* (*Math*) x; 🅘 umpteen. **X-Beine** *ntpl* knock-knees. **x-beinig, X-beinig** *a* knock-kneed. **x-beliebig** *a* 🅘 any. **x-mal** *adv* 🅘 umpteen times

Yy

Yoga /'jo:ga/ *m & nt* **-[s]** yoga

Zz

Zack|e *f* **-, -n** point; (*Berg-*) peak; (*Gabel-*) prong. **z~ig** *a* jagged; (*gezackt*) serrated
zaghaft *a* timid; (*zögernd*) tentative
zäh *a* tough; (*hartnäckig*) tenacious. **z~flüssig** *a* viscous; <*Verkehr*> slow-moving. **Z~igkeit** *f* **-** toughness; tenacity
Zahl *f* **-, -en** number; (*Ziffer, Betrag*) figure

zahlen *vt/i* (*haben*) pay; (*bezahlen*) pay for; **bitte z~!** the bill please!

zählen *vi* (*haben*) count; **z~ zu** (*fig*) be one/(*pl*) some of ● *vt* count; **z~ zu** add to; (*fig*) count among

zahlenmäßig *a* numerical

Zähler *m* **-s,-** meter

Zahl|grenze *f* fare-stage. **Z~karte** *f* paying-in slip. **z~los** *a* countless. **z~reich** *a* numerous; <*Anzahl, Gruppe*> large ● *adv* in large numbers. **Z~ung** *f* **-, -en** payment; **in Z~ung nehmen** take in part-exchange

Zählung *f* **-, -en** count

Zahlwort *nt* (*pl* **-wörter**) numeral

zahm *a* tame

zähmen *vt* tame; (*fig*) restrain

Zahn *m* **-[e]s,¨e** tooth; (*am Zahnrad*) cog. **Z~arzt** *m*, **Z~ärztin** *f* dentist. **Z~belag** *m* plaque. **Z~bürste** *f* toothbrush. **Z~fleisch** *nt* gums *pl*. **z~los** *a* toothless. **Z~pasta** *f* **-, -en** toothpaste. **Z~rad** *nt* cog-wheel. **Z~schmelz** *m* enamel. **Z~schmerzen** *mpl* toothache *sg*. **Z~spange** *f* brace. **Z~stein** *m* tartar. **Z~stocher** *m* **-s,-** toothpick

Zange *f* **-, -n** pliers *pl*; (*Kneif-*) pincers *pl*; (*Kohlen-, Zucker-*) tongs *pl*; (*Geburts-*) forceps *pl*

Zank *m* **-[e]s** squabble. **z~en** *vr* **sich z~en** squabble

Zäpfchen *nt* **-s,-** (*Anat*) uvula; (*Med*) suppository

zapfen *vt* tap, draw. **Z~streich** *m* (*Mil*) tattoo

Zapf|hahn *m* tap. **Z~säule** *f* petrol-pump

zappeln *vi* (*haben*) wriggle; <*Kind:*> fidget

zart *a* delicate; (*weich, zärtlich*) tender; (*sanft*) gentle. **Z~gefühl** *nt* tact

zärtlich *a* tender; (*liebevoll*) loving. **Z~keit** *f* **-, -en** tenderness; (*Liebkosung*) caress

Zauber *m* **-s** magic; (*Bann*) spell. **Z~er** *m* **-s,-** magician. **z~haft** *a* enchanting. **Z~künstler** *m* conjuror. **z~n** *vi* (*haben*) do magic; (*Zaubertricks ausführen*) do conjuring tricks ● *vt* produce as if by magic. **Z~stab** *m* magic wand. **Z~trick** *m* conjuring trick

Zaum *m* **-[e]s, Zäume** bridle

Zaun *m* **-[e]s, Zäune** fence

z.B. *abbr* (**zum Beispiel**) e.g.

Zebra *nt* **-s, -s** zebra. **Z~streifen** *m* zebra crossing

Zeche *f* **-, -n** bill; (*Bergwerk*) pit

zechen *vi* (*haben*) [!] drink

Zeder *f* **-, -n** cedar

Zeh *m* **-[e]s, -en** toe. **Z~e** *f* **-, -n** toe; (*Knoblauch-*) clove

zehn *inv a*, **Z~** *f* **-, -en** ten. **z~te(r,s)** *a* tenth. **Z~tel** *nt* **-s,-** tenth

Zeichen *nt* **-s,-** sign; (*Signal*) signal. **Z~setzung** *f* **-** punctuation. **Z~trickfilm** *m* cartoon

zeichn|en *vt/i* (*haben*) draw; (*kenn-*) mark; (*unter-*) sign. **Z~ung** *f* **-, -en** drawing

Zeige|finger *m* index finger. **z~n** *vt* show; **sich z~n** appear; (*sich herausstellen*) become clear ● *vi* (*haben*) point (**auf** + *acc* to). **Z~r** *m* **-s,-** pointer; (*Uhr-*) hand

Zeile *f* **-, -n** line; (*Reihe*) row

Zeit *f* **-, -en** time; **sich** (*dat*) **Z~ lassen** take one's time; **es hat Z~** theres's no hurry; **mit der Z~** in time; **in nächster Z~** in the near future; **zur Z~** (*rechtzeitig*) in time; *(*derzeit*) *s.* **zurzeit**; **eine Z~ lang** for a time *or* while

Zeit|alter *nt* age, era. **z~gemäß** *a* modern, up-to-date. **Z~genosse** *m*, **Z~genossin** *f* contemporary. **z~genössisch** *a* contemporary. **z~ig** *a & adv* early

zeitlich *a* <*Dauer*> in time; <*Folge*> chronological. ● *adv* **z~ begrenzt** for a limited time

zeit|los *a* timeless. **Z~lupe** *f* slow motion. **Z~punkt** *m* time. **z~raubend** *a* time-consuming. **Z~raum** *m* period. **Z~schrift** *f* magazine, periodical

Zeitung *f* **-, -en** newspaper. **Z~spapier** *nt* newspaper

Zeit|verschwendung *f* waste of time. **Z~vertreib** *m* pastime. **z~weise** *adv* at times. **Z~wort** *nt* (*pl* **-wörter**) verb. **Z~zünder** *m* time fuse

Zelle *f* **-, -n** cell; (*Telefon-*) box

Zelt *nt* **-[e]s, -e** tent; (*Fest-*) marquee. **z~en** *vi* (*haben*) camp. **Z~en** *nt* **-s** camping. **Z~plane** *f* tarpaulin. **Z~platz** *m* campsite

Zement *m* **-[e]s** cement

zen|sieren *vt* (*Sch*) mark; censor <*Presse, Film*>. **Z~sur** *f* **-, -en** (*Sch*) mark; (*Presse-*) censorship

Zentimeter *m & nt* centimetre. **Z~maß** *nt* tape-measure

Zentner *m* **-s,-** [metric] hundredweight (*50 kg*)

zentral *a* central. **Z~e** *f* **-, -n** central office; (*Partei-*) headquarters *pl*; (*Teleph*) exchange. **Z~heizung** *f* central heating

Zentrum *nt* **-s, -tren** centre

zerbrech|en† *vt/i* (*sein*) break. **z~lich** *a* fragile

zerdrücken *vt* crush

Zeremonie *f* **-, -n** ceremony

Zerfall *m* disintegration; (*Verfall*) decay. **z~en**† *vi* (*sein*) disintegrate; (*verfallen*) decay

zergehen† *vi* (*sein*) melt; (*sich auflösen*) dissolve

zerkleinern *vt* chop/(*schneiden*) cut up; (*mahlen*) grind

zerknüllen *vt* crumple [up]

zerkratzen *vt* scratch

zerlassen† *vt* melt

zerlegen *vt* take to pieces, dismantle; (*zerschneiden*) cut up; (*tranchieren*) carve

zerlumpt *a* ragged

zermalmen *vt* crush

zermürben *vt* (*fig*) wear down

zerplatzen *vi* (*sein*) burst

zerquetschen *vt* squash; crush

Zerrbild *nt* caricature

zerreißen† *vt* tear; (*in Stücke*) tear up; break <*Faden, Seil*> ● *vi* (*sein*) tear; break

zerren *vt* drag; pull <*Muskel*> ● *vi* (*haben*) pull (**an** + *dat* at)

zerrissen *a* torn

zerrütten *vt* ruin, wreck; shatter <*Nerven*>

zerschlagen† *vt* smash; smash up <*Möbel*>; **sich z~** (*fig*) fall through; <*Hoffnung:*> be dashed

zerschmettern *vt/i* (*sein*) smash

zerschneiden† *vt* cut; (*in Stücke*) cut up

zersplittern *vi* (*sein*) splinter; <*Glas:*> shatter ● *vt* shatter

zerspringen† *vi* (*sein*) shatter; (*bersten*) burst

Zerstäuber *m* **-s,-** atomizer

zerstör|en *vt* destroy; (*zunichte machen*) wreck. **Z~er** *m* **-s,-** destroyer. **Z~ung** *f* destruction

zerstreu|en *vt* scatter; disperse <*Menge*>; dispel <*Zweifel*>; **sich z~en** disperse; (*sich unterhalten*) amuse oneself. **z~t** *a* absent-minded

Zertifikat *nt* **-[e]s, -e** certificate

zertrümmern *vt* smash [up]; wreck <*Gebäude, Stadt*>

Zettel *m* **-s,-** piece of paper; (*Notiz*) note; (*Bekanntmachung*) notice

Zeug *nt* **-s** [!] stuff; (*Sachen*) things *pl*; (*Ausrüstung*) gear; **dummes Z~** nonsense

Zeuge *m* **-n, -n** witness. **z~n** *vi* (*haben*) testify; **z~n von** (*fig*) show ● *vt* father. **Z~naussage** *f* testimony. **Z~nstand** *m* witness box

Zeugin *f* **-, -nen** witness

Zeugnis *nt* **-ses, -se** certificate; (*Sch*) report; (*Referenz*) reference; (*fig: Beweis*) evidence

Zickzack *m* **-[e]s, -e** zigzag

Ziege *f* **-, -n** goat

Ziegel *m* **-s,-** brick; (*Dach-*) tile. **Z~stein** *m* brick

ziehen† *vt* pull; (*sanfter; zücken; zeichnen*) draw; (*heraus-*) pull out; extract <*Zahn*>; raise <*Hut*>; put on <*Bremse*>; move <*Schachfigur*>; (*dehnen*) stretch; make <*Grimasse, Scheitel*>; (*züchten*) breed; grow <*Rosen*>; **nach sich z~** (*fig*) entail ● *vr* **sich z~** (*sich erstrecken*) run; (*sich verziehen*) warp ● *vi* (*haben*) pull (**an** + *dat* on/at); <*Tee, Ofen:*> draw; (*Culin*) simmer; **es zieht** there is a draught; **solche Filme z~ nicht mehr** films like that are no longer popular ● *vi* (*sein*) (*um-*) move (**nach** to); <*Menge:*> march; <*Vögel:*> migrate; <*Wolken, Nebel:*> drift

Ziehharmonika *f* accordion

Ziehung *f* **-, -en** draw

Ziel *nt* **-[e]s, -e** destination; (*Sport*) finish; (*Z~scheibe & Mil*) target; (*Zweck*) aim, goal. **z~bewusst** *a* purposeful. **z~en** *vi* (*haben*) aim (**auf** + *acc* at). **z~los** *a* aimless. **Z~scheibe** *f* target

ziemlich *a* [!] fair ● *adv* rather, fairly

Zier|de *f* **-, -n** ornament. **z~en** *vt* adorn

zierlich *a* dainty

Ziffer *f* **-, -n** figure, digit; (*Zahlzeichen*) numeral. **Z~blatt** *nt* dial

Zigarette *f* **-, -n** cigarette

Zigarre *f* **-, -n** cigar

Zigeuner(in) *m* **-s,-** (*f* **-, -nen**) gypsy

Zimmer *nt* **-s,-** room. **Z~mädchen** *nt* chambermaid. **Z~mann** *m* (*pl* **-leute**) carpenter. **Z~nachweis** *m* accommodation bureau. **Z~pflanze** *f* house plant

Zimt *m* **-[e]s** cinnamon

Zink *nt* **-s** zinc

Zinn *m* **-s** tin; (*Gefäße*) pewter

Zins|en *mpl* interest *sg*; **Z~en tragen** earn interest. **Z~eszins** *m* **-es, -en** compound interest. **Z~fuß, Z~satz** *m* interest rate

Zipfel *m* **-s,-** corner; (*Spitze*) point

zirka *adv* about

Zirkel *m* **-s,-** [pair of] compasses *pl*; (*Gruppe*) circle

Zirkul|ation /-ˈtsio:n/ *f* **-** circulation. **z~ieren** *vi* (*sein*) circulate

Zirkus *m* **-, -se** circus

zirpen *vi* (*haben*) chirp

zischen *vi* (*haben*) hiss; <*Fett:*> sizzle ● *vt* hiss

Zit|at *nt* **-[e]s, -e** quotation. **z~ieren** *vt/i* (*haben*) quote

Zitr|onat *nt* **-[e]s** candied lemon-peel. **Z~one** *f* **-, -n** lemon

zittern *vi* (*haben*) tremble; (*vor Kälte*) shiver; (*beben*) shake

zittrig *a* shaky

Zitze *f* **-, -n** teat

zivil *a* civilian; <*Ehe, Recht*> civil. **Z~** *nt* **-s** civilian clothes *pl*. **Z~dienst** *m* community service

Zivili|sation /-'tsio:n/ *f* **-, -en** civilization. **z~sieren** *vt* civilize. **z~siert** *a* civilized
● *adv* in a civilized manner

Zivilist *m* **-en, -en** civilian

zögern *vi* (*haben*) hesitate. **Z~** *nt* **-s** hesitation. **z~d** *a* hesitant

Zoll[1] *m* **-[e]s,-** inch

Zoll[2] *m* **-[e]s,¨-e** [customs] duty; (*Behörde*) customs *pl*. **Z~abfertigung** *f* customs clearance. **Z~beamte(r)** *m* customs officer. **z~frei** *a & adv* duty-free. **Z~kontrolle** *f* customs check

Zone *f* **-, -n** zone

Zoo *m* **-s, -s** zoo

zoologisch *a* zoological

Zopf *m* **-[e]s,¨-e** plait

Zorn *m* **-[e]s** anger. **z~ig** *a* angry

---

zu

● *preposition (+ dative)*

> ! Note that **zu dem** can become **zum** and **zu der zur**

····➤ (*Richtung*) to; (*bei Beruf*) into. **wir gehen zur Schule** we are going to school. **ich muss zum Arzt** I must go to the doctor's. **zu ... hin** towards. **er geht zum Theater/Militär** he is going into the theatre/army

····➤ (*zusammen mit*) with. **zu dem Käse gab es Wein** there was wine with the cheese. **zu etw passen** go with sth

····➤ (*räumlich; zeitlich*) at. **zu Hause** at home. **zu ihren Füßen** at her feet. **zu Ostern** at Easter. **zur Zeit** (+ *gen*) at the time of

····➤ (*preislich*) at; for. **zum halben Preis** at half price. **das Stück zu zwei Mark** at *or* for two marks each. **eine Marke zu 60 Pfennig** a 60-pfennig stamp

····➤ (*Zweck, Anlass*) for. **zu diesem Zweck** for this purpose. **zum Spaß** for fun. **zum Lesen** for reading. **zum Geburtstag bekam ich ...** for my birthday I got .... **zum ersten Mal** for the first time

····➤ (*Art und Weise*) **zu meinem Erstaunen/Entsetzen** to my surprise/horror. **zu Fuß/Pferde** on foot/horseback. **zu Dutzenden** by the dozen. **wir waren zu dritt/viert** there were three/four of us

····➤ (*Zahlenverhältnis*) to. **es steht 5 zu 3** the score is 5–3

····➤ (*Ziel, Ergebnis*) into. **zu etw werden** turn into sth

····➤ (*gegenüber*) to; towards. **freundlich/hässlich zu jdm sein** be friendly/nasty to s.o.

····➤ (*über*) on; about. **sich zu etw äußern** to comment on sth

● *adverb*

····➤ (*allzu*) too. **zu groß/viel/weit** too big/much/far

····➤ (*Richtung*) towards. **nach dem Fluss zu** towards the river

····➤ (*geschlossen*) closed; (*an Schalter, Hahn*) off. **zu sein** be closed. **Augen zu!** close your eyes! **Tür zu!** shut the door!

● *conjunction*

····➤ to. **etwas zu essen** something to eat. **nicht zu glauben** unbelievable. **zu erörternde Probleme** problems to be discussed

---

zualler|erst *adv* first of all. **z~letzt** *adv* last of all

Zubehör *nt* **-s** accessories *pl*

zubereit|en *vt sep* prepare. **Z~ung** *f* **-** preparation; (*in Rezept*) method

zubinden† *vt sep* tie [up]

zubring|en† *vt sep* spend. **Z~er** *m* **-s,-** access road; (*Bus*) shuttle

Zucchini /tsu'ki:ni/ *pl* courgettes

Zucht *f* **-, -en** breeding; (*Pflanzen-*) cultivation; (*Art,*

Rasse) breed; (*von Pflanzen*) strain; (*Z~farm*) farm; (*Pferde-*) stud

züchtlen *vt* breed; cultivate, grow <*Rosen*>. **Z~er** *m* **-s,-** breeder; grower

Zuchthaus *nt* prison

Züchtung *f* **-, -en** breeding; (*Pflanzen-*) cultivation; (*Art, Rasse*) breed; (*von Pflanzen*) strain

zucken *vi* (*haben*) twitch; (*sich z~d bewegen*) jerk; <*Blitz:*> flash; <*Flamme:*> flicker ● *vt* **die Achseln z~** shrug one's shoulders

Zucker *m* **-s** sugar. **Z~dose** *f* sugar basin. **Z~guss** *m* icing. **z~krank** *a* diabetic. **Z~krankheit** *f* diabetes. **z~n** *vt* sugar. **Z~rohr** *nt* sugar cane. **Z~rübe** *f* sugar beet. **Z~watte** *f* candyfloss

zudecken *vt sep* cover up; (*im Bett*) tuck up; cover <*Topf*>

zudem *adv* moreover

zudrehen *vt sep* turn off

zueinander *adv* to one another; **z~ passen** go together; **z~ halten** (*fig*) stick together

zuerkennen† *vt sep* award (*dat* to)

zuerst *adv* first; (*anfangs*) at first

zufahrlen† *vi sep* (*sein*) **z~en auf** (+ *acc*) drive towards. **Z~t** *f* access; (*Einfahrt*) drive

Zufall *m* chance; (*Zusammentreffen*) coincidence; **durch Z~** by chance/ coincidence. **z~en**† *vi sep* (*sein*) close, shut; **jdm z~en** <*Aufgabe:*> fall/<*Erbe:*> go to s.o.

zufällig *a* chance, accidental ● *adv* by chance

Zuflucht *f* refuge; (*Schutz*) shelter

zufolge *prep* (+ *dat*) according to

zufrieden *a* contented; (*befriedigt*) satisfied; **sich z~ geben** be satisfied; **jdn z~ lassen** leave s.o. in peace; **jdn z~ stellen** satisfy s.o.; **z~ stellend** satisfactory. **Z~heit** *f* **-** contentment; satisfaction

zufrieren† *vi sep* (*sein*) freeze over

zufügen *vt sep* inflict (*dat* on); do <*Unrecht*> (*dat* to)

Zufuhr *f* **-** supply

Zug *m* **-[e]s,⸚e** train; (*Kolonne*) column; (*Um-*) procession; (*Mil*) platoon; (*Vogelschar*) flock; (*Ziehen, Zugkraft*) pull; (*Wandern, Ziehen*) migration; (*Schluck, Luft-*) draught; (*Atem-*) breath; (*beim Rauchen*) puff; (*Schach-*) move; (*beim Schwimmen, Rudern*) stroke; (*Gesichts-*) feature; (*Wesens-*) trait

Zugabe *f* (*Geschenk*) [free] gift; (*Mus*) encore

Zugang *m* access

zugänglich *a* accessible; <*Mensch:*> approachable

Zugbrücke *f* drawbridge

zugeben† *vt sep* add; (*gestehen*) admit; (*erlauben*) allow

zugehen† *vi sep* (*sein*) close; **jdm z~** be sent to s.o.; **z~ auf** (+ *acc*) go towards; **dem Ende z~** draw to a close; <*Vorräte:*> run low; **auf der Party ging es lebhaft zu** the party was pretty lively

Zugehörigkeit *f* **-** membership

Zügel *m* **-s,-** rein

zugelassen *a* registered

zügel|los *a* unrestrained. **z~n** *vt* rein in; (*fig*) curb

Zuge|ständnis *nt* concession. **z~stehen**† *vt sep* grant

zügig *a* quick

Zugkraft *f* pull; (*fig*) attraction

zugleich *adv* at the same time

Zugluft *f* draught

zugreifen† *vi sep* (*haben*) grab it/them; (*bei Tisch*) help oneself;

(*bei Angebot*) jump at it; (*helfen*) lend a hand
zugrunde *adv* **z~ richten** destroy; **z~ gehen** be destroyed; (*sterben*) die; **z~ liegen** form the basis (*dat* of)
zugunsten *prep* (+ *gen*) in favour of; <*Sammlung*> in aid of
zugute *adv* **jdm/etw z~ kommen** benefit s.o./sth
Zugvogel *m* migratory bird
zuhalten† *v sep* ● *vt* keep closed; (*bedecken*) cover; **sich** (*dat*) **die Nase z~** hold one's nose
Zuhälter *m* **-s,-** pimp
zuhause *adv* = **zu Hause**, *s.* **Haus**. **Z~** *nt* **-s,-** home
zuhör|en *vi sep* (*haben*) listen (*dat* to). **Z~er(in)** *m*(*f*) listener
zujubeln *vi sep* (*haben*) **jdm z~** cheer s.o.
zukleben *vt sep* seal
zuknöpfen *vt sep* button up
zukommen† *vi sep* (*sein*) **z~ auf** (+ *acc*) come towards; (*sich nähern*) approach; **z~ lassen** send (**jdm** s.o.); devote <*Pflege*> (*dat* to); **jdm z~** be s.o.'s right
Zukunft *f* - future. **zukünftig** *a* future ● *adv* in future
zulächeln *vi sep* (*haben*) smile (*dat* at)
zulangen *vi sep* (*haben*) help oneself
zulassen† *vt sep* allow, permit; (*teilnehmen lassen*) admit; (*Admin*) license, register; (*geschlossen lassen*) leave closed; leave unopened <*Brief*>
zulässig *a* permissible
Zulassung *f* **-, -en** admission; registration; (*Lizenz*) licence
zuleide *adv* **jdm etwas z~ tun** hurt s.o.
zuletzt *adv* last; (*schließlich*) in the end
zuliebe *adv* **jdm/etw z~** for the sake of s.o./sth
zum *prep* = **zu dem; zum Spaß** for fun; **etw zum Lesen** sth to read
zumachen *v sep* ● *vt* close, shut; do up <*Jacke*>; seal <*Umschlag*>; turn off <*Hahn*>; (*stilllegen*) close down ● *vi* (*haben*) close, shut; (*stillgelegt werden*) close down
zumal *adv* especially ● *conj* especially since
zumindest *adv* at least
zumutbar *a* reasonable
zumute *adv* **mir ist nicht danach z~** I don't feel like it
zumut|en *vt sep* **jdm etw z~en** ask *or* expect sth of s.o.; **sich** (*dat*) **zu viel z~en** overdo things. **Z~ung** *f* - imposition
zunächst *adv* first [of all]; (*anfangs*) at first; (*vorläufig*) for the moment ● *prep* (+ *dat*) nearest to
Zunahme *f* **-, -n** increase
Zuname *m* surname
zünd|en *vt/i* (*haben*) ignite. **Z~er** *m* **-s,-** detonator, fuse. **Z~holz** *nt* match. **Z~kerze** *f* sparking-plug. **Z~schlüssel** *m* ignition key. **Z~schnur** *f* fuse. **Z~ung** *f* **-, -en** ignition
zunehmen† *vi sep* (*haben*) increase (**an** + *dat* in); <*Mond*> wax; (*an Gewicht*) put on weight. **z~d** *a* increasing
Zuneigung *f* - affection
Zunft *f* **-,¨-e** guild
Zunge *f* **-, -n** tongue. **Z~nbrecher** *m* tongue-twister
zunutze *a* **sich** (*dat*) **etw z~ machen** make use of sth; (*ausnutzen*) take advantage of sth
zuoberst *adv* right at the top
zuordnen *vt sep* assign (*dat* to)
zupfen *vt/i* (*haben*) pluck (**an** + *dat* at); pull out <*Unkraut*>
zur *prep* = **zu der; zur Schule** to school; **zur Zeit** at present
zurate *adv* **z~ ziehen** consult

zurechnungsfähig *a* of sound mind

zurecht|finden† **(sich)** *vr sep* find one's way. **z~kommen**† *vi sep* (*sein*) cope (**mit** with); (*rechtzeitig kommen*) be in time. **z~legen** *vt sep* put out ready; **sich** (*dat*) **eine Ausrede z~legen** have an excuse all ready. **z~machen** *vt sep* get ready. **z~weisen**† *vt sep* reprimand. **Z~weisung** *f* reprimand

zureden *vi sep* (*haben*) **jdm z~** try to persuade s.o.

zurichten *vt sep* prepare; (*beschädigen*) damage; (*verletzen*) injure

zuriegeln *vt sep* bolt

zurück *adv* back; **Berlin, hin und z~** return to Berlin. **z~bekommen**† *vt sep* get back. **z~bleiben**† *vi sep* (*sein*) stay behind; (*nicht mithalten*) lag behind. **z~bringen**† *vt sep* bring back; (*wieder hinbringen*) take back. **z~erstatten** *vt sep* refund. **z~fahren**† *v sep* ● *vt* drive back ● *vi* (*sein*) return, go back; (*im Auto*) drive back; (*z~weichen*) recoil. **z~finden**† *vi sep* (*haben*) find one's way back. **z~führen** *v sep* ● *vt* take back; (*fig*) attribute (**auf** + *acc* to) ● *vi* (*haben*) lead back. **z~geben**† *vt sep* give back, return. **z~geblieben** *a* retarded. **z~gehen**† *vi sep* (*sein*) go back, return; (*abnehmen*) go down; **z~gehen auf** (+ *acc*) (*fig*) go back to

zurückgezogen *a* secluded. **Z~heit** *f* - seclusion

zurückhalt|en† *vt sep* hold back; (*abhalten*) stop; **sich z~en** restrain oneself. **z~end** *a* reserved. **Z~ung** *f* - reserve

zurück|kehren *vi sep* (*sein*) return. **z~kommen**† *vi sep* (*sein*) come back, return. **z~lassen**† *vt sep* leave behind; (*z~kehren lassen*) allow back. **z~legen** *vt sep* put back; (*reservieren*) keep; (*sparen*) put by; cover <*Strecke*>. **z~liegen**† *vi sep* (*haben*) be in the past; (*Sport*) be behind; **das liegt lange zurück** that was long ago. **z~melden (sich)** *vr sep* report back. **z~schicken** *vt sep* send back. **z~schlagen**† *v sep* ● *vi* (*haben*) hit back ● *vt* hit back; (*umschlagen*) turn back. **z~schrecken**† *vi sep* (*sein*) shrink back, recoil; (*fig*) shrink (**vor** + *dat* from). **z~stellen** *vt sep* put back; (*reservieren*) keep; (*fig*) put aside; (*aufschieben*) postpone. **z~stoßen**† *v sep* ● *vt* push back ● *vi* (*sein*) reverse, back. **z~treten**† *vi sep* (*sein*) step back; (*vom Amt*) resign; (*verzichten*) withdraw. **z~weisen**† *vt sep* turn away; (*fig*) reject. **z~zahlen** *vt sep* pay back. **z~ziehen**† *vt sep* draw back; (*fig*) withdraw; **sich z~ziehen** withdraw; (*vom Beruf*) retire

Zuruf *m* shout. **z~en**† *vt sep* shout (*dat* to)

zurzeit *adv* at present

Zusage *f* **-, -n** acceptance; (*Versprechen*) promise. **z~n** *v sep* ● *vt* promise ● *vi* (*haben*) accept

zusammen *adv* together; (*insgesamt*) altogether; **z~ sein** be together. **Z~arbeit** *f* cooperation. **z~arbeiten** *vi sep* (*haben*) cooperate. **z~bauen** *vt sep* assemble. **z~bleiben**† *vi sep* (*sein*) stay together. **z~brechen**† *vi sep* (*sein*) collapse. **Z~bruch** *m* collapse; (*Nerven- & fig*) breakdown. **z~fallen**† *vi sep* (*sein*) collapse; (*zeitlich*) coincide. **z~fassen** *vt sep* summarize, sum up.

Z~fassung *f* summary. **z~fügen** *vt sep* fit together. **z~gehören** *vi sep* (*haben*) belong together; (*z~passen*) go together. **z~gesetzt** *a* (*Gram*) compound. **z~halten**† *v sep* ● *vt* hold together; (*beisammenhalten*) keep together ● *vi* (*haben*) (*fig*) stick together. **Z~hang** *m* connection; (*Kontext*) context. **z~hanglos** *a* incoherent. **z~klappen** *v sep* ● *vt* fold up ● *vi* (*sein*) collapse. **z~kommen**† *vi sep* (*sein*) meet; (*sich sammeln*) accumulate. **Z~kunft** *f* **-,¨e** meeting. **z~laufen**† *vi sep* (*sein*) gather; <*Flüssigkeit:*> collect; <*Linien:*> converge. **z~leben** *vi sep* (*haben*) live together. **z~legen** *v sep* ● *vt* put together; (*z~falten*) fold up; (*vereinigen*) amalgamate; pool <*Geld*> ● *vi* (*haben*) club together. **z~nehmen**† *vt sep* gather up; summon up <*Mut*>; collect <*Gedanken*>; **sich z~nehmen** pull oneself together. **z~passen** *vi sep* (*haben*) go together, match. **Z~prall** *m* collision. **z~rechnen** *vt sep* add up. **z~schlagen**† *vt sep* smash up; (*prügeln*) beat up. **z~schließen**† **(sich)** *vr sep* join together; <*Firmen:*> merge. **Z~schluss** *m* union; (*Comm*) merger

Zusammensein *nt* **-s** get-together

zusammensetz|en *vt sep* put together; (*Techn*) assemble; **sich z~en** sit [down] together; (*bestehen*) be made up (**aus** from). **Z~ung** *f* **-, -en** composition; (*Techn*) assembly; (*Wort*) compound

zusammen|stellen *vt sep* put together; (*gestalten*) compile. **Z~stoß** *m* collision; (*fig*) clash. **z~treffen**† *vi sep* (*sein*) meet; (*zeitlich*) coincide. **z~zählen** *vt sep* add up. **z~ziehen**† *v sep* ● *vt* draw together; (*addieren*) add up; (*konzentrieren*) mass; **sich z~ziehen** contract; <*Gewitter:*> gather ● *vi* (*sein*) move in together; move in (**mit** with)

Zusatz *m* addition; (*Jur*) rider; (*Lebensmittel-*) additive. **zusätzlich** *a* additional ● *adv* in addition

zuschau|en *vi sep* (*haben*) watch. **Z~er(in)** *m* **-s,-** (*f* **-, -nen**) spectator; (*TV*) viewer

Zuschlag *m* surcharge; (*D-Zug-*) supplement. **z~pflichtig** *a* <*Zug*> for which a supplement is payable

zuschließen† *v sep* ● *vt* lock ● *vi* (*haben*) lock up

zuschneiden† *vt sep* cut out; cut to size <*Holz*>

zuschreiben† *vt sep* attribute (*dat* to); **jdm die Schuld z~** blame s.o.

Zuschrift *f* letter; (*auf Annonce*) reply

zuschulden *adv* **sich** (*dat*) **etwas z~ kommen lassen** do wrong

Zuschuss *m* contribution; (*staatlich*) subsidy

zusehends *adv* visibly

zusein* *vi sep* (*sein*) **zu sein**, *s.* **zu**

zusenden† *vt sep* send (*dat* to)

zusetzen *v sep* ● *vt* add; (*einbüßen*) lose

zusicher|n *vt sep* promise. **Z~ung** *f* promise.

zuspielen *vt sep* (*Sport*) pass

zuspitzen (sich) *vr sep* (*fig*) become critical

Zustand *m* condition, state

zustande *adv* **z~ bringen/kommen** bring/come about

zuständig *a* competent; (*verantwortlich*) responsible

zustehen† *vi sep* (*haben*) **jdm z~** be s.o.'s right; <*Urlaub:*> be due to s.o.

zusteigen† *vi sep* (*sein*) get on; **noch jemand zugestiegen?** tickets please; (*im Bus*) any more fares please?

zustell|en *vt sep* block; (*bringen*) deliver. **Z~ung** *f* delivery

zusteuern *v sep* ● *vi* (*sein*) head (**auf** + *acc* for) ● *vt* contribute

zustimm|en *vi sep* (*haben*) agree; (*billigen*) approve (*dat* of). **Z~ung** *f* consent; approval

zustoßen† *vi sep* (*sein*) happen (*dat* to)

Zustrom *m* influx

Zutat *f* (*Culin*) ingredient

zuteil|en *vt sep* allocate; assign <*Aufgabe*>. **Z~ung** *f* allocation

zutiefst *adv* deeply

zutragen† *vt sep* carry/(*fig*) report (*dat* to); **sich z~** happen

zutrau|en *vt sep* **jdm etw z~** believe s.o. capable of sth. **Z~en** *nt* **-s** confidence

zutreffen† *vi sep* (*haben*) be correct; **z~ auf** (+ *acc*) apply to

Zutritt *m* admittance

zuunterst *adv* right at the bottom

zuverlässig *a* reliable. **Z~keit** *f* **-** reliability

Zuversicht *f* **-** confidence. **z~lich** *a* confident

zuviel* *pron & adv* **zu viel**, *s.* **viel**

zuvor *adv* before; (*erst*) first

zuvorkommen† *vi sep* (*sein*) (+ *dat*) anticipate. **z~d** *a* obliging

Zuwachs *m* **-es** increase

zuwege *adv* **z~ bringen** achieve

zuweilen *adv* now and then

zuweisen† *vt sep* assign

Zuwendung *f* donation; (*Fürsorge*) care

zuwenig* *pron & adv* **zu wenig**, *s.* **wenig**

zuwerfen† *vt sep* slam <*Tür*>; **jdm etw z~** throw s.o. sth

zuwider *adv* **jdm z~ sein** be repugnant to s.o. ● *prep* (+ *dat*) contrary to

zuzahlen *vt sep* pay extra

zuziehen† *v sep* ● *vt* pull tight; draw <*Vorhänge*>; (*hinzu-*) call in; **sich** (*dat*) **etw z~** contract <*Krankheit*>; sustain <*Verletzung*>; incur <*Zorn*> ● *vi* (*sein*) move into the area

zuzüglich *prep* (+ *gen*) plus

Zwang *m* **-[e]s,¨e** compulsion; (*Gewalt*) force; (*Verpflichtung*) obligation

zwängen *vt* squeeze

zwanglos *a* informal. **Z~igkeit** *f* **-** informality

Zwangsjacke *f* straitjacket

zwanzig *inv a* twenty. **z~ste(r,s)** *a* twentieth

zwar *adv* admittedly

Zweck *m* **-[e]s, -e** purpose; (*Sinn*) point. **z~los** *a* pointless. **z~mäßig** *a* suitable; (*praktisch*) functional

zwei *inv a*, **Z~** *f* **-, -en** two; (*Sch*) ≈ B. **Z~bettzimmer** *nt* twin-bedded room

zweideutig *a* ambiguous

zwei|erlei *inv a* two kinds of ● *pron* two things. **z~fach** *a* double

Zweifel *m* **-s,-** doubt. **z~haft** *a* doubtful; (*fragwürdig*) dubious. **z~los** *adv* undoubtedly. **z~n** *vi* (*haben*) doubt (**an etw** *dat* sth)

Zweig *m* **-[e]s, -e** branch. **Z~stelle** *f* branch [office]

Zwei|kampf *m* duel. **z~mal** *adv* twice. **z~reihig** *a* <Anzug> double-breasted. **z~sprachig** *a* bilingual

zweit *adv* **zu z~** in twos; **wir waren zu z~** there were two of

us. **z~beste(r,s)** *a* second-best. **z~e(r,s)** *a* second
zweitens *adv* secondly
Zwerchfell *nt* diaphragm
Zwerg *m* **-[e]s, -e** dwarf
Zwickel *m* **-s,-** gusset
zwicken *vt/i* (*haben*) pinch
Zwieback *m* **-[e]s,¨-e** rusk
Zwiebel *f* **-, -n** onion; (*Blumen-*) bulb
Zwielicht *nt* half-light; (*Dämmerlicht*) twilight. **z~ig** *a* shady
Zwiespalt *m* conflict
Zwilling *m* **-s, -e** twin; **Z~e** (*Astr*) Gemini
zwingen† *vt* force; **sich z~** force oneself. **z~d** *a* compelling
Zwinger *m* **-s,-** run; (*Zucht-*) kennels *pl*
zwinkern *vi* (*haben*) blink; (*als Zeichen*) wink
Zwirn *m* **-[e]s** button thread
zwischen *prep* (+ *dat/acc*) between; (*unter*) among[st]. **Z~bemerkung** *f* interjection. **z~durch** *adv* in between; (*in der Z~zeit*) in the meantime. **Z~fall** *m* incident. **Z~landung** *f* stopover. **Z~raum** *m* gap, space. **Z~wand** *f* partition. **Z~zeit** *f* **in der Z~zeit** in the meantime
Zwist *m* **-[e]s, -e** discord; (*Streit*) feud
zwitschern *vi* (*haben*) chirp
zwo *inv a* two
zwölf *inv a* twelve. **z~te(r,s)** *a* twelfth
Zylind|er *m* **-s,-** cylinder; (*Hut*) top hat. **z~risch** *a* cylindrical
Zyn|iker *m* **-s,-** cynic. **z~isch** *a* cynical. **Z~ismus** *m* **-** cynicism
Zypern *nt* **-s** Cyprus
Zypresse *f* **-, -n** cypress
Zyste /ˈtsʏstə/ *f* **-, -n** cyst

Phrasefinder/Sprachführer

Key phrases	Nützliche Redewendungen
yes, please	ja bitte
no, thank you	nein danke
sorry!	Entschuldigung!
you're welcome	nichts zu danken
I don't understand	ich verstehe das nicht
Meeting people	**Wir lernen uns kennen**
hello/goodbye	hallo!/auf Wiedersehen!
how are you?	wie geht es Ihnen?/wie geht's?
fine, thank you	danke, gut
see you later!	bis nachher!
Asking questions	**Fragen**
do you speak English/German?	sprechen Sie/sprichst du Englisch/Deutsch?
what's your name?	wie heißen Sie?/wie heißt du?
where are you from?	woher kommen Sie?/woher kommst du?
how much is it?	wie viel kostet das?
how far is it?	wie weit ist es?
Statements about yourself	**Alles über mich**
my name is...	ich heiße...
I'm English	ich bin Engländer/Engländerin
I don't speak German/English very well	ich kann nicht gut Deutsch/Englisch sprechen
I'm here on holiday	ich bin auf Urlaub hier
I live near Manchester/Hamburg	ich wohne in der Nähe von Manchester/Hamburg
Emergencies	**Im Notfall**
can you help me, please?	können Sie mir bitte helfen?
I'm lost	ich habe mich verlaufen
call an ambulance	rufen Sie einen Krankenwagen
get the police/a doctor	holen Sie die Polizei/einen Arzt
watch out!	Vorsicht!

❶ Going Places

On the road	Auf der Straße
where's the nearest garage (for repairs)/petrol station (*Amer* filling station)?	wo ist die nächste Werkstatt/ Tankstelle?
what's the best way to get there?	wie komme ich am besten dorthin?
I've got a puncture	ich habe eine Reifenpanne
I'd like to hire a bike/car	ich möchte ein Rad/Auto mieten
where can I park around here?	wo kann man hier parken?
there's been an accident	es ist ein Unfall passiert
my car's broken down	mein Auto hat eine Panne
the car won't start	der Wagen springt nicht an

By rail	Mit der Bahn
where can I buy a ticket?	wo kann ich eine Fahrkarte kaufen?
what time is the next train to York/Berlin?	wann geht der nächste Zug nach York/Berlin?
do I have to change?	muss ich umsteigen?
can I take my bike on the train?	kann ich mein Rad im Zug mitnehmen?
which platform for the train to Bath/Cologne?	von welchem Bahnsteig fährt der Zug nach Bath/Köln ab?
the train is arriving on platform 2	der Zug fährt auf Gleis 2 ein
there's a train to London at 10 o'clock	es gibt einen Zug nach London um zehn Uhr
a single/return to Birmingham/ Frankfurt, please	einmal einfach/eine Rückfahrkarte nach Birmingham/ Frankfurt, bitte
I'd like a cheap day return/ an all-day ticket	ich möchte eine Tagesrückfahrkarte/Tageskarte
I'd like to reserve a seat	ich möchte einen Platz reservieren

At the airport	Am Flughafen
when's the next flight to Paris/Rome?	wann geht der nächste Flug nach Paris/Rom?
what time do I have to check in?	um wie viel Uhr muss ich einchecken?
where do I check in?	wo checkt man ein?
I'd like to confirm/cancel my flight	ich möchte meinen Flug bestätigen/stornieren
can I change my booking?	kann ich umbuchen?
I'd like a window seat/an aisle seat	ich möchte einen Fensterplatz/Platz am Gang

Asking how to get there	Nach dem Weg fragen
could you tell me the way to the castle?	können Sie mir bitte sagen, wie ich zum Schloss komme?
how long will it take me to walk there?	wie lange werde ich zu Fuß brauchen?
how far is it from here?	wie weit ist das von hier?
which bus do I take for the cathedral?	mit welchem Bus komme ich zum Dom?
where does this bus go?	wohin fährt dieser Bus?
where do I get the bus for...?	wo fährt der Bus nach... ab?
does this bus/train go to...?	fährt dieser Bus/Zug nach...?
which bus goes to...?	welcher Bus fährt nach...?
where do I get off?	wo muss ich aussteigen?
how much is the fare to the town centre (*Amer* center)?	was kostet es ins Stadtzentrum?
what time is the last bus?	wann fährt der letzte Bus?
how do I get to the airport?	wie komme ich zum Flughafen?
where's the nearest underground (*Amer* subway) station?	wo ist die nächste U-Bahn-Station?
is this the turning for...?	ist das die Abzweigung nach...?
take the first turning right	nehmen Sie die erste Straße rechts

❷ Keeping in touch

On the phone	Am Telefon
where can I buy a phone card?	wo kann man Telefonkarten kaufen?
may I use your phone?	darf ich Ihr Telefon benutzen?
do you have a mobile?	haben Sie ein Handy?
what is the code for Leipzig/Sheffield?	wie ist die Vorwahl von Leipzig/Sheffield?
I'd like to make a phone call	ich möchte gern telefonieren
I'd like to reverse the charges (*Amer* call collect)	ich möchte ein R-Gespräch anmelden
the line's engaged (*Amer* busy)	es ist besetzt
there's no answer	es meldet sich niemand
hello, this is Natalie	hallo, hier spricht Natalie
can I speak to Simon, please?	kann ich bitte Simon sprechen?
who's calling?	wer ist am Apparat?
sorry, I must have the wrong number	Entschuldigung, ich habe mich verwählt
just a moment, please	einen Augenblick bitte
please hold the line	bleiben sie bitte am Apparat
please tell him/her I called	richten Sie ihm/ihr bitte aus, dass ich angerufen habe
can I leave a message for Eva?	kann ich eine Nachricht für Eva hinterlassen?
I'll try again later	Ich versuche es später noch einmal
please tell her that Danielle called	sagen Sie ihr bitte, dass Danielle angerufen hat
can he/she ring me back?	kann er/sie mich zurückrufen?
my home number is...	meine Privatnummer ist...
my office number is...	meine Nummer im Büro ist...
my fax number is...	meine Faxnummer ist...
can I send a fax from here?	kann ich von hier faxen?
we were cut off	wir sind unterbrochen worden

Writing	Schreiben
can you give me your address?	können Sie mir Ihre/kannst du mir deine Adresse geben?
where is the nearest post office?	wo ist die nächste Post?
two one-mark stamps	zwei Briefmarken zu einer Mark
I'd like a stamp for a letter to Germany/Italy	ich hätte gern eine Briefmarke für einen Brief nach Deutschland/Italien
can I have stamps for two postcards to England/ the USA, please?	kann ich bitte Briefmarken für zwei Postkarten nach England/in die USA haben?
I'd like to send a parcel/ a telegram	ich möchte ein Paket abschicken/ein Telegramm aufgeben

On line	Online
are you on the Internet?	hast du Zugang zum Internet?
what's your e-mail address?	wie ist deine E-Mail-Adresse?
we could send it by e-mail	wir könnten es per E-Mail schicken
I'll e-mail it to you on Thursday	ich schicke es Ihnen am Donnerstag per E-Mail
I've looked for it on the Internet	ich habe es im Internet gesucht
he found the information surfing the net	er hat die Information beim Surfen im Internet gefunden

Meeting up	Verabredungen
what shall we do this evening?	was machen wir heute Abend?
where shall we meet?	wo treffen wir uns?
see you outside the cinema at 6 o'clock	ich treffe dich um sechs Uhr vor dem Kino
do you fancy joining in?	hast du Lust mitzumachen?
I can't today, I'm busy	ich kann heute nicht, ich habe keine Zeit

❸ Food and drink

Booking a restaurant	Vorbestellungen
can you recommend a good restaurant?	können Sie uns/mir ein gutes Restaurant empfehlen?
I'd like to reserve a table for four	ich möchte einen Tisch für vier Personen bestellen
a reservation for tomorrow evening at eight o'clock	eine Vorbestellung für morgen Abend um acht Uhr
I booked a table for two	ich habe einen Tisch für zwei Personen bestellt

Ordering	Wir möchten bestellen
could we see the menu/ wine list, please?	können wir bitte die Speisekarte/Weinkarte haben?
do you have a vegetarian/ children's menu?	haben Sie vegetarische Gerichte/Kinderportionen?
could we have some more bread/chips?	noch etwas Brot/noch Pommes frites, bitte
could I have the bill (*Amer* check), please?	die Rechnung bitte
we'd like something to drink first	wir hätten gern erst etwas zu trinken
a bottle/glass of mineral water, please	eine Flasche/ein Glas Mineral-wasser bitte
as a starter… to follow… and for dessert…	als Vorspeise… als Hauptge-richt… und zum Nachtisch…
a black/white coffee	einen Kaffee ohne Milch/ einen Kaffee mit Milch
we'd like to pay separately	wir möchten getrennt bezahlen

Reading a menu	Die Speisekarte
starters	Vorspeisen
soups/salads	Suppen/Salate
main dishes	Hauptgerichte

dish of the day	Tagesgericht
seafood	Meeresfrüchte
choice of vegetables	Gemüse nach Wahl
meat/game/poultry	Fleischgerichte/Wild/Geflügel
side dish	Beilage
desserts	Nachspeisen
drinks	Getränke

Any complaints?	**Beschwerden**
there's a mistake in the bill (*Amer* check)	die Rechnung stimmt nicht
the meat isn't cooked/is burnt	das Fleisch ist nicht durch/ist angebrannt
that's not what I ordered	das habe ich nicht bestellt
I asked for a small/large portion	ich habe eine kleine/große Portion bestellt
when can we order?	wann können wir bestellen?
we are still waiting for our drinks	wir warten immer noch auf unsere Getränke
my coffee is cold	mein Kaffee ist kalt
the wine is not chilled	der Wein ist nicht kalt genug

Food shopping	**Lebensmittel einkaufen**
where is the nearest supermarket?	wo ist der nächste Supermarkt?
is there a baker's/greengrocer near here?	gibt es eine Bäckerei/einen Gemüsehändler in der Nähe?
can I have a carrier bag, please?	kann ich bitte eine Tragetasche haben?
how much is it?	was kostet das?
I'll have that one/this jam	ich nehme den/die/das da/diese Marmelade
a loaf of bread, please	ein Brot bitte

❹ Places to stay

Camping	Camping
we're looking for a campsite	wir suchen einen Campingplatz
this is a list of local campsites	in diesem Campingführer stehen alle hiesigen Campingplätze
can we pitch our tent here?	können wir hier zelten?
can we park our caravan here?	können wir unseren Wohnwagen hier parken?
do you have space for a caravan/tent?	haben Sie Platz für einen Wohnwagen/ein Zelt?
are there shopping facilities?	gibt es Einkaufsmöglichkeiten?
how much is it per night?	was kostet es pro Nacht?
we go on a camping holiday every year	wir machen jedes Jahr Campingurlaub

At the hotel	Im Hotel
I'd like a double/single room with bath	ich möchte ein Doppelzimmer/ Einzelzimmer mit Bad
we have a reservation in the name of Milnes	wir haben auf den Namen Milnes reservieren lassen
I reserved two rooms	ich habe zwei Zimmer reservieren lassen
for three nights, from Friday to Sunday	für drei Nächte, von Freitag bis Sonntag
how much does the room cost?	was kostet das Zimmer?
I'd like to see the room first, please	ich möchte das Zimmer erst sehen, bitte
what time is breakfast?	wann gibt es Frühstück?
can I leave this in the safe?	kann ich das im Safe lassen?
bed and breakfast	Zimmer mit Frühstück
we'd like to stay another night	wir möchten noch eine Nacht bleiben
please call me at 7:30	bitte wecken Sie mich um 7:30

are there any messages for me?	hat jemand eine Nachricht für mich hinterlassen?

Hostels	Heime und Jugendherbergen
could you tell me where the youth hostel is?	können Sie mir sagen, wo die Jugendherberge ist?
what time does the hostel close?	um wie viel Uhr macht das Heim zu?
I spent the night in a youth hostel	ich habe in einer Jugendherberge übernachtet
the hostel we're staying in is great value	unser Wohnheim ist sehr preiswert
I'm staying in a youth hostel	ich wohne in einer Jugendherberge
I know a really good youth hostel in Dublin	ich kenne eine sehr gute Jugendherberge in Dublin
I'd like to go backpacking in Australia	ich würde gern in Australien mit dem Rucksack herum reisen

Rooms to let	Zimmer zu vermieten
I'm looking for a room with a reasonable rent	ich suche ein preiswertes Zimmer
I'd like to rent an apartment for three weeks	ich möchte eine Wohnung für drei Wochen mieten
where do I find out about rooms to let?	wo kann man sich nach Fremdenzimmern erkundigen?
what's the weekly rent for the flat?	was kostet die Wohnung pro Woche?
I'm staying with friends at the moment	ich wohne zur Zeit bei Freunden
I rent an apartment on the outskirts of town	ich habe eine Wohnung am Stadtrand gemietet
the room's fine—I'll take it	das Zimmer ist gut—ich nehme es

❺ Shopping and money

At the bank	In der Bank
I'd like to change some money	ich möchte gern Geld wechseln
I want to change 100 euros into pounds	ich möchte 100 Euro[s] in Pfund wechseln
do you take Eurocheques?	nehmen Sie Euroschecks?
what's the exchange rate today?	wie steht der Wechselkurs heute?
I prefer traveller's cheques (*Amer* traveler's checks) to cash	mir sind Reiseschecks lieber als Bargeld
I'd like to transfer some money from my account	ich möchte Geld von meinem Konto überweisen
I'll get some money from the cash machine	ich hole mir Geld vom Automaten
a £50 cheque (*Amer* check)	ein Scheck über 50 Pfund
can I cash this cheque (*Amer* check) here?	kann ich diesen Scheck hier einlösen?
can I get some cash with my credit card?	kann ich auf meine Kreditkarte Bargeld bekommen?

Finding the right shop	Das richtige Geschäft finden
where's the main shopping district?	wo ist das Haupteinkaufsviertel?
is the shopping centre (*Amer* mall) far from here?	ist das Einkaufszentrum weit von hier?
where's a good place to buy sunglasses/shoes?	wo kauft man am besten Schuhe/eine Sonnenbrille?
where can I buy batteries/postcards?	wo kann ich Batterien/Postkarten kaufen?
where's the nearest chemist (*Amer* drugstore)?	wo ist die nächste Drogerie?
what time do the shops open/close?	um wie viel Uhr machen die Läden auf/zu?
where did you get those?	wo hast du die her?
I'm looking for a present for my mother	ich suche ein Geschenk für meine Mutter

Are you being served?	Werden Sie schon bedient?
how much does that cost?	was kostet das?
can I try it on?	kann ich es anprobieren?
can you keep it for me?	können Sie es mir zurücklegen?
could you gift-wrap it for me, please?	können Sie es bitte in Geschenkpapier einwickeln?
please wrap it up well	verpacken Sie es bitte gut
can I pay by credit card/ cheque (*Amer* check)?	kann ich mit Kreditkarte/ Scheck zahlen?
do you have this in another colour?	haben Sie das in einer anderen Farbe?
I'm just looking	ich sehe mich nur um
a receipt, please	eine Quittung bitte
I need a bigger size	ich brauche die nächste Größe
I take a size…	ich habe Größe…
it doesn't suit me	das steht mir nicht

Changing things	Umtauschen
can I have a refund?	kann ich mein Geld zurückbekommen?
can you mend it for me?	können Sie es mir reparieren?
can I speak to the manager?	kann ich den Geschäftsführer/ die Geschäftsführerin sprechen?
it doesn't work	es funktioniert nicht
I'd like to change the dress	ich möchte das Kleid umtauschen
I bought this here yesterday	ich habe das gestern hier gekauft

❻ Sport and leisure

Keeping fit	Wir halten uns fit
where can we play football/squash?	wo kann man Fußball/Squash spielen?
is there a local sports centre (*Amer* center)?	gibt es hier ein Sportzentrum?
what's the charge per day?	was muss man pro Tag zahlen?
is there a reduction for children/a student discount?	gibt es eine Ermäßigung für Kinder/Studenten?
where can we go swimming/play tennis?	wo kann man schwimmen gehen/Tennis spielen?
do you have to be a member?	muss man Mitglied sein?
I play tennis on Mondays	ich spiele jeden Montag Tennis
I would like to go fishing/riding	ich würde gern angeln gehen/reiten
I want to do aerobics	ich will Aerobic machen
I love swimming/playing baseball	ich schwimme gern/spiele gern Baseball
we want to hire skis/snowboards	wir wollen Skier/Snowboards mieten

Watching sport	Zuschauen
is there a football match on Saturday?	gibt es am Samstag ein Fußballspiel?
who's playing?	wer spielt?
which teams are playing?	welche Mannschaften spielen?
where can I get tickets?	wo kann man Karten bekommen?
can you get me a ticket?	kannst du mir eine Karte besorgen?
I'd like to see a rugby/football match	ich würde gern ein Rugbyspiel/Fußballspiel sehen
my favourite (*Amer* favorite) team is Bayern	ich bin ein Bayern-Fan
let's watch the match on TV	sehen wir uns das Spiel im Fernsehen an

Going to the cinema/ theatre/club	Wir gehen ins Kino/Theater/ in einen Club
what's on at the cinema (*Amer* at the movies)?	was läuft im Kino?
what's on at the theatre?	was wird im Theater gespielt?
how long is the performance?	wie lange dauert die Vorstellung?
when does the box office open/close?	wann macht die Kasse auf/zu?
what time does the performance start?	um wie viel Uhr fängt die Aufführung an?
when does the film (*Amer* movie) finish?	wann ist der Film aus?
are there any tickets left?	gibt es noch Karten?
how much are the tickets?	was kosten die Karten?
where can I get a programme (*Amer* program)?	wo kann man ein Programm kaufen?
I want to book tickets for tonight	ich möchte für heute Abend Karten bestellen
I'd rather have seats in the stalls	Plätze im Parkett wären mir lieber
we'd like to go to a club	wir wollen in einen Club gehen
I go clubbing every weekend	ich gehe am Wochenende immer in Clubs

Hobbies	Hobbys
do you have any hobbies?	hast du irgendwelche Hobbys?
what do you do at the weekend?	was macht ihr am Wochenende?
I like yoga/listening to music	ich mache gern Yoga/höre gern Musik
I spend a lot of time surfing the Net	ich surfe viel im Internet
I read a lot	ich lese viel
I collect comics	ich sammle Comichefte

❼ Good timing

Telling the time	Uhrzeit
could you tell me the time?	können Sie mir sagen, wie spät es ist?
what time is it?	wie viel Uhr ist es?
it's 2 o'clock	es ist zwei Uhr
at about 8 o'clock	gegen acht Uhr
at 9 o'clock tomorrow	morgen um neun Uhr
from 10 o'clock onwards	ab zehn Uhr
the meeting starts at 8 p.m.	die Besprechung fängt um zwanzig Uhr an
at 5 o'clock in the morning/afternoon	um fünf Uhr morgens/um fünf Uhr nachmittags (um siebzehn Uhr)
at exactly 1 o'clock	um Punkt eins
it's five past.../quarter past...	es ist fünf nach.../Viertel nach...
it's half past one	es ist halb zwei
it's twenty-five to one	es ist fünf nach halb eins
it's quarter to/five to one	es ist Viertel vor/fünf vor eins
a quarter of an hour	eine Viertelstunde
three quarters of an hour	eine Dreiviertelstunde

Days and date	Wochentage und Datum
Sunday, Monday, Tuesday, Wednesday, Thursday, Friday, Saturday	Sonntag, Montag, Dienstag, Mittwoch, Donnerstag, Freitag, Samstag/Sonnabend
January, February, March, April, May, June, July, August, September, October, November, December	Januar, Februar, März, April, Mai, Juni, Juli, August, September, Oktober, November, Dezember
what's the date?	der Wievielte ist heute?
it's the second of June	heute ist der zweite Juni
we meet up every Monday	wir treffen uns jeden Montag

Der richtige Zeitpunkt ❼

she comes on Tuesdays	sie kommt immer dienstags
we're going away in August	wir verreisen im August
I forgot it was the first of April today	ich habe ganz vergessen, dass heute der erste April ist
on November 8th	am achten November
about the 8th of June	um den 8. Juni
put it in your diary	notiere es dir in deinem Terminkalender

Public holidays and special days	**Feste und Feiertage**
Bank holiday	gesetzlicher Feiertag
New Year's Day (Jan 1)	Neujahr
Epiphany (Jan 6)	Heilige Drei Könige
St Valentine's Day (Feb 14)	Valentinstag
Shrove Tuesday	Fastnachtsdienstag/ Faschingsdienstag
Ash Wednesday	Aschermittwoch
Mothering Sunday/Mother's Day	Muttertag
Palm Sunday	Palmsonntag
Maundy Thursday	Gründonnerstag
Good Friday	Karfreitag
Easter Day	Ostersonntag
Easter Monday	Ostermontag
May Day (May 1)	der Erste Mai
Father's Day	Vatertag
Day of German Unity (Oct 3)	Tag der Deutschen Einheit
First Sunday in Advent	erster Advent
St Nicholas' Day (Dec 6)	Nikolaus
Christmas Eve	Heiligabend
Christmas Day (Dec 25)	erster Weihnachtstag
Boxing Day (Dec 26)	zweiter Weihnachtstag
New Year's Eve (Dec 31)	Silvester

❽ Weights & measures/Maße u. Gewichte

Length/Längenmaße

inches/Zoll	0.39	3.9	7.8	11.7	15.6	19.7	39
cm/zentimeter	1	10	20	30	40	50	100

Distance/Entfernungen

miles/Meilen	0.62	6.2	12.4	18.6	24.9	31	62
km/Kilometer	1	10	20	30	40	50	100

Weight/Gewichte

pounds/Pfund	2.2	22	44	66	88	110	220
kg/Kilogramm	1	10	20	30	40	50	100

Capacity/Hohlmaße

gallons/Gallonen	0.22	2.2	4.4	6.6	8.8	11	22
litres/Liter	1	10	20	30	40	50	100

Temperature/Temperatur

°C	0	5	10	15	20	25	30	37	38	40
°F	32	41	50	59	68	77	86	98.4	100	104

Clothing and shoe sizes

Women's clothing sizes/Damengrößen

UK	8	10	12	14	16	18	
US	6	8	10	12	14	16	
Continent		36	38	40	42	44	46

Men's clothing sizes/Herrengrößen

UK/US	36	38	40	42	44	46
Continent	46	48	50	52	54	56

Men's and women's shoes/Schuhgrößen

UK women	4	5	6	7	7.5	8			
UK men				6	7	8	9	10	11
US	6.5	7.5	8.5	9.5	10.5	11.5	12.5	13.5	14.5
Continent	37	38	39	40	41	42	43	44	45

Aa

a /ə, *betont* eɪ/

vor einem Vokal **an**

• *indefinite article*
····➤ ein (*m*), eine (*f*), ein (*nt*). **a problem** ein Problem. **an apple** ein Apfel. **a cat** eine Katze. **have you got a pencil?** hast du einen Bleistift? **I gave it to a beggar** ich gab es einem Bettler

! There are some cases where **a** is not translated, such as when talking about people's professions or nationalities: **she is a lawyer** sie ist Rechsanwältin. **he's an Italian** er ist Italiener

····➤ (*with 'not'*) kein (*m*), keine (*f*), kein (*nt*), keine (*pl*). **that's not a problem/not a good idea** das ist kein Problem/keine gute Idee. **there was not a chance that ...** es bestand keine Möglichkeit, dass .... **she did not say a word** sie sagte kein Wort. **I didn't tell a soul** ich habe es keinem Menschen gesagt
····➤ (*per; each*) pro. **£300 a week** 300 Pfund pro Woche. **30 miles an hour** 30 Meilen pro Stunde. (*in prices*) **it costs 90p a pound** es kostet 90 Pence das Pfund.

aback /ə'bæk/ *adv* **be taken ~** verblüfft sein
abandon /ə'bændən/ *vt* verlassen; (*give up*) aufgeben
abate /ə'beɪt/ *vi* nachlassen
abattoir /'æbətwɑ:(r)/ *n* Schlachthof *m*
abb|ey /'æbɪ/ *n* Abtei *f*. **~ot** /-ət/ *n* Abt *m*
abbreviat|e /ə'bri:vɪeɪt/ *vt* abkürzen. **~ion** /-'eɪʃn/ *n* Abkürzung *f*
abdicat|e /'æbdɪkeɪt/ *vi* abdanken. **~ion** /-'keɪʃn/ *n* Abdankung *f*
abdom|en /'æbdəmən/ *n* Unterleib *m*. **~inal** /-'dɑmɪnl/ *a* Unterleibs-
abduct /əb'dʌkt/ *vt* entführen. **~ion** /-ʌkʃn/ *n* Entführung *f*
aberration /æbə'reɪʃn/ *n* Abweichung *f*; (*mental*) Verwirrung *f*
abeyance /ə'beɪəns/ *n* **in ~** [zeitweilig] außer Kraft
abhor /əb'hɔ:(r)/ *vt* (*pt/pp* **abhorred**) verabscheuen. **~rent** /-'hɒrənt/ *a* abscheulich
abid|e /ə'baɪd/ *vt* (*pt/pp* **abided**) (*tolerate*) aushalten; ausstehen <*person*>
ability /ə'bɪlətɪ/ *n* Fähigkeit *f*; (*talent*) Begabung *f*
abject /'æbdʒekt/ *a* erbärmlich; (*humble*) demütig
ablaze /ə'bleɪz/ *a* in Flammen
able /'eɪbl/ *a* (**-r, -st**) fähig; **be ~ to do sth** etw tun können. **~-'bodied** *a* körperlich gesund
ably /'eɪblɪ/ *adv* gekonnt
abnormal /æb'nɔ:ml/ *a* anormal; (*Med*) abnorm. **~ity** /-'mælətɪ/ *n* Abnormität *f*. **~ly** *adv* ungewöhnlich
aboard /ə'bɔ:d/ *adv & prep* an Bord (+ *gen*)
abol|ish /ə'bɒlɪʃ/ *vt* abschaffen. **~ition** /æbə'lɪʃn/ *n* Abschaffung *f*

abominable /ə'bɒmɪnəbl/ *a*, **-bly** *adv* abscheulich

aborigines /æbə'rɪdʒəni:z/ *npl* Ureinwohner *pl*

abort /ə'bɔ:t/ *vt* abtreiben. **~ion** /-ɔ:ʃn/ *n* Abtreibung *f*. **~ive** /-tɪv/ *a* <*attempt*> vergeblich

about /ə'baʊt/ *adv* umher, herum; (*approximately*) ungefähr; **be ~** (*in circulation*) umgehen; (*in existence*) vorhanden sein; **be ~ to do sth** im Begriff sein, etw zu tun; **there was no one ~** es war kein Mensch da; **run/play ~** herumlaufen/-spielen ● *prep* um (+ *acc*) [... herum]; (*concerning*) über (+ *acc*); **what is it ~?** worum geht es? <*book*:> wovon handelt es? **I know nothing ~ it** ich weiß nichts davon; **talk/know ~** reden/wissen von

about: ~-'face *n*, **~-'turn** *n* Kehrtwendung *f*

above /ə'bʌv/ *adv* oben ● *prep* über (+ *dat*/*acc*); **~ all** vor allem

above: ~-'board *a* legal. **~-mentioned** *a* oben erwähnt

abrasive /ə'breɪsɪv/ *a* Scheuer-; <*remark*> verletzend ● *n* Scheuermittel *nt*; (*Techn*) Schleifmittel *nt*

abreast /ə'brest/ *adv* nebeneinander; **keep ~ of** Schritt halten mit

abridge /ə'brɪdʒ/ *vt* kürzen

abroad /ə'brɔ:d/ *adv* im Ausland; **go ~** ins Ausland fahren

abrupt /ə'brʌpt/ *a*, **-ly** *adv* abrupt; (*sudden*) plötzlich; (*curt*) schroff

abscess /'æbsɪs/ *n* Abszess *m*

absence /'æbsəns/ *n* Abwesenheit *f*

absent /'æbsənt/ *a* abwesend; **be ~** fehlen

absentee /æbsən'ti:/ *n* Abwesende(r) *m*/*f*

absent-minded /æbsənt'maɪndɪd/ *a*, **-ly** *adv* geistesabwesend; (*forgetful*) zerstreut

absolute /'æbsəlu:t/ *a*, **-ly** *adv* absolut

absorb /əb'sɔ:b/ *vt* absorbieren, aufsaugen; **~ed in** vertieft in (+ *acc*). **~ent** /-ənt/ *a* saugfähig

absorption /əb'sɔ:pʃn/ *n* Absorption *f*

abstain /əb'steɪn/ *vi* sich enthalten (**from** *gen*)

abstemious /əb'sti:mɪəs/ *a* enthaltsam

abstention /əb'stenʃn/ *n* (*Pol*) [Stimm]enthaltung *f*

abstract /'æbstrækt/ *a* abstrakt ● *n* (*summary*) Abriss *m*

absurd /əb'sɜ:d/ *a*, **-ly** *adv* absurd. **~ity** *n* Absurdität *f*

abundan|ce /ə'bʌndəns/ *n* Fülle *f* (**of** an + *dat*). **~t** *a* reichlich

abuse¹ /ə'bju:z/ *vt* missbrauchen; (*insult*) beschimpfen

abus|e² /ə'bju:s/ *n* Missbrauch *m*; (*insults*) Beschimpfungen *pl*. **~ive** /-ɪʌ/ ausfallend

abysmal /ə'bɪʒml/ *a* **!** katastrophal

abyss /ə'bɪs/ *n* Abgrund *m*

academic /ækə'demɪk/ *a*, **-ally** *adv* akademisch

academy /ə'kædəmɪ/ *n* Akademie *f*

accelerat|e /ək'seləreɪt/ *vt*/*i* beschleunigen. **~ion** /-'reɪʃn/ *n* Beschleunigung *f*. **~or** *n* (*Auto*) Gaspedal *nt*

accent /'æksənt/ *n* Akzent *m*

accept /ək'sept/ *vt* annehmen; (*fig*) akzeptieren ● *vi* zusagen. **~able** /-əbl/ *a* annehmbar. **~ance** *n* Annahme *f*; (*of invitation*) Zusage *f*

access /'ækses/ *n* Zugang *m*. **~ible** /ək'sesəbl/ *a* zugänglich

accessor|y /ək'sesərɪ/ *n* (*Jur*) Mitschuldige(r) *m*/*f*; **~ies** *pl* (*fashion*) Accessoires *pl*; (*Techn*) Zubehör *nt*

accident /'æksɪdənt/ *n* Unfall *m*; (*chance*) Zufall *m*; **by ~** zufällig; (*unintentionally*) versehentlich. **~al** /-'dentl/ *a*, **-ly** *adv* zufällig; (*unintentional*) versehentlich

acclaim /ə'kleɪm/ *vt* feiern (**as** als)

acclimatize /ə'klaɪmətaɪz/ *vt* **become ~d** sich akklimatisieren

accommodat|e /ə'kɒmədeɪt/ *vt* unterbringen. **~ing** *a* entgegenkommend. **~ion** /-'deɪʃn/ *n* (*rooms*) Unterkunft *f*

accompan|iment /ə'kʌmpənɪmənt/ *n* Begleitung *f*. **~ist** *n* (*Mus*) Begleiter(in) *m(f)*

accompany /ə'kʌmpənɪ/ *vt* (*pt*/*pp* **-ied**) begleiten

accomplice /ə'kʌmplɪʃ/ *n* Komplize/-zin *m*/*f*

accomplish /ə'kʌmplɪʃ/ *vt* erfüllen <*task*>; (*achieve*) erreichen. **~ed** *a* fähig. **~ment** *n* Fertigkeit *f*; (*achievement*) Leistung *f*

accord /ə'kɔ:d/ *n* **of one's own ~** aus eigenem Antrieb. **~ance** *n* **in ~ance with** entsprechend (+ *dat*)

according /ə'kɔ:dɪŋ/ *adv* **~ to** nach (+ *dat*). **~ly** *adv* entsprechend

accordion /ə'kɔ:dɪən/ *n* Akkordeon *nt*

account /ə'kaʊnt/ *n* Konto *nt*; (*bill*) Rechnung *f*; (*description*) Darstellung *f*; (*report*) Bericht *m*; **~s** *pl* (*Comm*) Bücher *pl*; **on ~ of** wegen (+ *gen*); **on no ~** auf keinen Fall; **take into ~** in Betracht ziehen, berücksichtigen ● *vi* **~ for** Rechenschaft ablegen für; (*explain*) erklären

accountant /ə'kaʊntənt/ *n* Buchhalter(in) *m(f)*; (*chartered*) Wirtschaftsprüfer *m*

accumulat|e /ə'kju:mjʊleɪt/ *vt* ansammeln, anhäufen ● *vi* sich ansammeln, sich anhäufen. **~ion** /-'leɪʃn/ *n* Ansammlung *f*, Anhäufung *f*

accura|cy /'ækʊrəsɪ/ *n* Genauigkeit *f*. **~te** /-rət/ *a*, **-ly** *adv* genau

accusation /ækju:'zeɪʃn/ *n* Anklage *f*

accusative /ə'kju:zətɪv/ *a* & *n* **~ [case]** (*Gram*) Akkusativ *m*

accuse /ə'kju:z/ *vt* (*Jur*) anklagen (**of** *gen*); **~ s.o. of doing sth** jdn beschuldigen, etw getan zu haben

accustom /ə'kʌstəm/ *vt* gewöhnen (**to** an + *dat*); **grow** *or* **get ~ed to** sich gewöhnen an (+ *acc*). **~ed** *a* gewohnt

ace /eɪs/ *n* (*Cards, Sport*) Ass *nt*

ache /eɪk/ *n* Schmerzen *pl* ● *vi* weh tun, schmerzen

achieve /ə'tʃi:v/ *vt* leisten; (*gain*) erzielen; (*reach*) erreichen. **~ment** *n* (*feat*) Leistung *f*

acid /'æsɪd/ *a* sauer; (*fig*) beißend ● *n* Säure *f*. **~ity** /ə'sɪdətɪ/ *n* Säure *f*. **~' rain** *n* saurer Regen *m*

acknowledge /ək'nɒlɪdʒ/ *vt* anerkennen; (*admit*) zugeben; erwidern <*greeting*>; **~ receipt of** den Empfang bestätigen (+ *gen*). **~ment** *n* Anerkennung *f*; (*of letter*) Empfangsbestätigung *f*

acne /'æknɪ/ *n* Akne *f*

acorn /'eɪkɔ:n/ *n* Eichel *f*

acoustic /ə'ku:stɪk/ *a*, **-ally** *adv* akustisch. **~s** *npl* Akustik *f*

acquaint /ə'kweɪnt/ *vt* **be ~ed with** kennen; vertraut sein mit <*fact*>. **~ance** *n* (*person*) Bekannte(r) *m*/*f*; **make s.o.'s ~ance** jdn kennen lernen

acquire /ə'kwaɪə(r)/ *vt* erwerben

acquisit|ion /ækwɪ'zɪʃn/ *n* Erwerb *m*; (*thing*) Erwerbung *f*. **~ive** /æ'kwɪzətɪv/ *a* habgierig

acquit /ə'kwɪt/ *vt* (*pt/pp* **acquitted**) freisprechen

acre /'eɪkə(r)/ *n* ≈ Morgen *m*

acrimonious /ækrɪ'məʊnɪəs/ *a* bitter

acrobat /'ækrəbæt/ *n* Akrobat(in) *m(f)*. **~ic** /-'bætrɪk/ *a* akrobatisch

across /ə'krɒs/ *adv* hinüber/herüber; (*wide*) breit; (*not lengthwise*) quer; (*in crossword*) waagerecht; **come ~ sth** auf etw (*acc*) stoßen; **go ~** hinübergehen; **bring ~** herüberbringen ● *prep* über (+ *acc*); (*on the other side of*) auf der anderen Seite (+ *gen*)

act /ækt/ *n* Tat *f*; (*action*) Handlung *f*; (*law*) Gesetz *nt*; (*Theat*) Akt *m*; (*item*) Nummer *f* ● *vi* handeln; (*behave*) sich verhalten; (*Theat*) spielen; (*pretend*) sich verstellen; **~ as** fungieren als ● *vt* spielen <*role*>. **~ing** *a* (*deputy*) stellvertretend ● *n* (*Theat*) Schauspielerei *f*

action /'ækʃn/ *n* Handlung *f*; (*deed*) Tat *f*; (*Mil*) Einsatz *m*; (*Jur*) Klage *f*; (*effect*) Wirkung *f*; (*Techn*) Mechanismus *m*; **out of ~** <*machine:*> außer Betrieb; **take ~** handeln; **killed in ~** gefallen

activate /'æktɪveɪt/ *vt* betätigen

activ|e /'æktɪv/ *a*, **-ly** *adv* aktiv; **on ~e service** im Einsatz. **~ity** /-'tɪvətɪ/ *n* Aktivität *f*

act|or /'æktə(r)/ *n* Schauspieler *m*. **~ress** *n* Schauspielerin *f*

actual /'æktʃʊəl/ *a*, **-ly** *adv* eigentlich; (*real*) tatsächlich

acupuncture /'ækjʊ-/ *n* Akupunktur *f*

acute /ə'kju:t/ *a* scharf; <*angle*> spitz; <*illness*> akut. **~ly** *adv* sehr

ad /æd/ *n* 🅸 = **advertisement**

AD *abbr* (**Anno Domini**) n.Chr.

adamant /'ædəmənt/ *a* **be ~ that** darauf bestehen, dass

adapt /ə'dæpt/ *vt* anpassen; bearbeiten <*play*> ● *vi* sich anpassen. **~able** /-əbl/ *a* anpassungsfähig

adaptation /ædæp'teɪʃn/ *n* (*Theat*) Bearbeitung *f*

add /æd/ *vt* hinzufügen; (*Math*) addieren ● *vi* zusammenzählen, addieren; **~ to** hinzufügen zu; (*fig: increase*) steigern; (*compound*) verschlimmern. **~ up** *vt* zusammenzählen <*figures*> ● *vi* zusammenzählen, addieren

adder /'ædə(r)/ *n* Kreuzotter *f*

addict /'ædɪkt/ *n* Süchtige(r) *m/f*

addict|ed /ə'dɪktɪd/ *a* süchtig; **~ed to drugs** drogensüchtig. **~ion** /-ɪkʃn/ *n* Sucht *f*

addition /ə'dɪʃn/ *n* Hinzufügung *f*; (*Math*) Addition *f*; (*thing added*) Ergänzung *f*; **in ~** zusätzlich. **~al** *a*, **-ly** *adv* zusätzlich

additive /'ædɪtɪv/ *n* Zusatz *m*

address /ə'dres/ *n* Adresse *f*, Anschrift *f*; (*speech*) Ansprache *f* ● *vt* adressieren (**to** an + *acc*); (*speak to*) anreden <*person*>; sprechen vor (+ *dat*) <*meeting*>. **~ee** /ædre'si:/ *n* Empfänger *m*

adequate /'ædɪkwət/ *a*, **-ly** *adv* ausreichend

adhere /əd'hɪə(r)/ *vi* kleben/(*fig*) festhalten (**to** an + *dat*)

adhesive /əd'hi:sɪv/ *a* klebend ● *n* Klebstoff *m*

adjacent /ə'dʒeɪsnt/ *a* angrenzend

adjective /'ædʒɪktɪv/ *n* Adjektiv *nt*

adjoin /ə'dʒɔɪn/ *vt* angrenzen an (+ *acc*). **~ing** *a* angrenzend

adjourn /ə'dʒɜ:n/ *vt* vertagen (**until** auf + *acc*) ● *vi* sich vertagen. **~ment** *n* Vertagung *f*

adjudicate /ə'dʒu:dɪkeɪt/ *vi* (*in competition*) Preisrichter sein

adjust /ə'dʒʌst/ *vt* einstellen; (*alter*) verstellen ● *vi* sich anpassen (**to** *dat*). **~able** /-əbl/ *a* verstellbar. **~ment** *n* Einstellung *f*; Anpassung *f*

ad lib/æd'lɪb/ *adv* aus dem Stegreif ● *vi* (*pt/pp* **ad libbed**) [!] improvisieren

administer /əd'mɪnɪstə(r)/ *vt* verwalten; verabreichen <*medicine*>

administration /ədmɪnɪ'streɪʃn/ *n* Verwaltung *f*; (*Pol*) Regierung *f*

admirable /'ædmərəbl/ *a* bewundernswert

admiral /'ædmərəl/ *n* Admiral *m*

admiration /ædmə'reɪʃn/ *n* Bewunderung *f*

admire /əd'maɪə(r)/ *vt* bewundern. **~r** *n* Verehrer(in) *m(f)*

admission /əd'mɪʃn/ *n* Eingeständnis *nt*; (*entry*) Eintritt *m*

admit /əd'mɪt/ *vt* (*pt/pp* **admitted**) (*let in*) hereinlassen; (*acknowledge*) zugeben; **~ to sth** etw zugeben. **~tance** *n* Eintritt *m*. **~tedly** *adv* zugegebenermaßen

admonish /əd'mɒnɪʃ/ *vt* ermahnen

adolescen|ce /ædə'lesns/ *n* Jugend *f*, Pubertät *f*. **~t** *a* Jugend-; <*boy, girl*> halbwüchsig ● *n* Jugendliche(r) *m/f*

adopt /ə'dɒpt/ *vt* adoptieren; ergreifen <*measure*>; (*Pol*) annehmen <*candidate*>. **~ion** /-ɒpʃn/ *n* Adoption *f*

ador|able /ə'dɔ:rəbl/ *a* bezaubernd. **~ation** /ædə'reɪʃn/ *n* Anbetung *f*

adore /ə'dɔ:(r)/ *vt* (*worship*) anbeten; ([!] *like*) lieben

adorn /ə'dɔ:n/ *vt* schmücken. **~ment** *n* Schmuck *m*

Adriatic /eɪdrɪ'ætɪk/ *a* & *n* **~ [Sea]** Adria *f*

adrift /ə'drɪft/ *a* **be ~** treiben

adroit /ə'drɔɪt/ *a*, **-ly** *adv* gewandt, geschickt

adulation /ædjʊ'leɪʃn/ *n* Schwärmerei *f*

adult /'ædʌlt/ *n* Erwachsene(r) *m/f*

adulterate /ə'dʌltəreɪt/ *vt* verfälschen; panschen <*wine*>

adultery /ə'dʌltərɪ/ *n* Ehebruch *m*

advance /əd'vɑ:ns/ *n* Fortschritt *m*; (*Mil*) Vorrücken *nt*; (*payment*) Vorschuss *m*; **in ~** im Voraus ● *vi* vorankommen; (*Mil*) vorrücken; (*make progress*) Fortschritte machen ● *vt* fördern <*cause*>; vorbringen <*idea*>; vorschießen <*money*>. **~d** *a* fortgeschritten; (*progressive*) fortschrittlich. **~ment** *n* Förderung *f*; (*promotion*) Beförderung *f*

advantage /əd'vɑ:ntɪdʒ/ *n* Vorteil *m*; **take ~ of** ausnutzen. **~ous** /ædvən'teɪdʒəs/ *a* vorteilhaft

adventur|e /əd'ventʃə(r)/ *n* Abenteuer *nt*. **~er** *n* Abenteurer *m*. **~ous** /-rəs/ *a* abenteuerlich; <*person*> abenteuerlustig

adverb /'ædvɜ:b/ *n* Adverb *nt*

adverse /'ædvɜ:s/ *a* ungünstig

advert /'ædvɜ:t/ *n* [!] = **advertisement**

advertise /'ædvətaɪz/ *vt* Reklame machen für; (*by small ad*) inserieren ● *vi* Reklame machen; inserieren

advertisement /əd'vɜ:tɪsmənt/ *n* Anzeige *f*; (*publicity*) Reklame *f*; (*small ad*) Inserat *nt*

advertis|er /'ædvətaɪzə(r)/ *n* Inserent *m*. **~ing** *n* Werbung *f*

advice /əd'vaɪs/ *n* Rat *m*

advisable /əd'vaɪzəbl/ *a* ratsam

advis|e /əd'vaɪz/ *vt* raten (**s.o.** jdm); (*counsel*) beraten; (*inform*) benachrichtigen; **~e s.o. against sth** jdm von etw abraten ● *vi* raten. **~er** *n* Berater(in) *m(f)*. **~ory** /-ərɪ/ *a* beratend

advocate¹ /'ædvəkət/ *n* (*supporter*) Befürworter *m*

advocate² /'ædvəkeɪt/ *vt* befürworten

aerial /'eərɪəl/ *a* Luft- ● *n* Antenne *f*

aerobics /eə'rəʊbɪks/ *n* Aerobic *nt*

aero|drome /'eərədrəʊm/ *n* Flugplatz *m*. **~plane** *n* Flugzeug *nt*

aerosol /'eərəsɒl/ *n* Spraydose *f*

aesthetic /i:s'θetɪk/ *a* ästhetisch

affair /ə'feə(r)/ *n* Angelegenheit *f*, Sache *f*; (*scandal*) Affäre *f*; **[love-]~** [Liebes]verhältnis *nt*

affect /ə'fekt/ *vt* sich auswirken auf (+ *acc*); (*concern*) betreffen; (*move*) rühren; (*pretend*) vortäuschen. **~ation** /æfek'teɪʃn/ *n* Affektiertheit *f*. **~ed** *a* affektiert

affection /ə'fekʃn/ *n* Liebe *f*. **~ate** /-ət/ *a*, **-ly** *adv* liebevoll

affirm /ə'fɜ:m/ *vt* behaupten

affirmative /ə'fɜ:mətɪv/ *a* bejahend ● *n* Bejahung *f*

afflict /ə'flɪkt/ *vt* **be ~ed with** behaftet sein mit. **~ion** /-ɪkʃn/ *n* Leiden *nt*

affluen|ce /'æfluəns/ *n* Reichtum *m*. **~t** *a* wohlhabend. **~t society** *n* Wohlstandsgesellschaft *f*

afford /ə'fɔ:d/ *vt* **be able to ~ sth** sich (*dat*) etw leisten können. **~able** /-əbl/ *a* erschwinglich

affront /ə'frʌnt/ *n* Beleidigung *f* ● *vt* beleidigen

afloat /ə'fləʊt/ *a* **be ~** <*ship:*> flott sein; **keep ~** <*person:*> sich über Wasser halten

afraid /ə'freɪd/ *a* **be ~** Angst haben (**of** vor + *dat*); **I'm ~ not** leider nicht; **I'm ~ so** [ja] leider

Africa /'æfrɪkə/ *n* Afrika *nt*. **~n** *a* afrikanisch ● *n* Afrikaner(in) *m(f)*

after /'ɑ:ftə(r)/ *adv* danach ● *prep* nach (+ *dat*); **~ that** danach; **~ all** schließlich; **the day ~ tomorrow** übermorgen; **be ~** aus sein auf (+ *acc*) ● *conj* nachdem

after: ~-effect *n* Nachwirkung *f*. **~math** /-mɑ:θ/ *n* Auswirkungen *pl*. **~'noon** *n* Nachmittag *m*; **good ~noon!** guten Tag! **~-sales service** *n* Kundendienst *m*. **~shave** *n* Rasierwasser *nt*. **~thought** *n* nachträglicher Einfall *m*. **~wards** *adv* nachher

again /ə'gen/ *adv* wieder; (*once more*) noch einmal; **~ and ~** immer wieder

against /ə'genst/ *prep* gegen (+ *acc*)

age /eɪdʒ/ *n* Alter *nt*; (*era*) Zeitalter *nt*; **~s** 🅸 ewig; **under ~** minderjährig; **of ~** volljährig; **two years of ~** zwei Jahre alt ● *v* (*pres p* **ageing**) ● *vt* älter machen ● *vi* altern; (*mature*) reifen

aged¹ /eɪdʒd/ *a* **~ two** zwei Jahre alt

aged² /'eɪdʒɪd/ *a* betagt ● *n* **the ~** *pl* die Alten

ageless /'eɪdʒlɪʃ/ *a* ewig jung

agency /'eɪdʒənsɪ/ *n* Agentur *f*; (*office*) Büro *nt*

agenda /ə'dʒendə/ *n* Tagesordnung *f*

agent /'eɪdʒənt/ *n* Agent(in) *m(f)*; (*Comm*) Vertreter(in) *m(f)*; (*substance*) Mittel *nt*

aggravat|e /'ægrəveɪt/ *vt* verschlimmern; (🅸 *annoy*) ärgern. **~ion** /-'veɪʃn/ *n* 🅸 Ärger *m*

aggregate /'ægrɪgət/ *a* gesamt ● *n* Gesamtzahl *f*, (*sum*) Gesamtsumme *f*

aggress|ion /ə'greʃn/ *n* Aggression *f*. **~ive** /-sɪv/ *a*, **-ly** *adv* aggressiv. **~or** *n* Angreifer(in) *m(f)*

aggro /'ægrəʊ/ *n* [!] Ärger *m*

aghast /ə'gɑ:st/ *a* entsetzt

agil|e /'ædʒaɪl/ *a* flink, behände; <*mind*> wendig. **~ity** /ə'dʒɪlətɪ/ *n* Flinkheit *f*, Behändigkeit *f*

agitat|e /'ædʒɪteɪt/ *vt* bewegen; (*shake*) schütteln ● *vi* (*fig*) **~ for** agitieren für. **~ed** *a*, **-ly** *adv* erregt. **~ion** /-'teɪʃn/ *n* Erregung *f*; (*Pol*) Agitation *f*

ago /ə'gəʊ/ *adv* vor (+ *dat*); **a long time ~** vor langer Zeit; **how long ~ is it?** wie lange ist es her?

agony /'ægənɪ/ *n* Qual *f*; **be in ~** furchtbare Schmerzen haben

agree /ə'gri:/ *vt* vereinbaren; (*admit*) zugeben; **~ to do sth** sich bereit erklären, etw zu tun ● *vi* <*people, figures:*> übereinstimmen; (*reach agreement*) sich einigen; (*get on*) gut miteinander auskommen; (*consent*) einwilligen (**to** in + *acc*); **~ with s.o.** jdm zustimmen; <*food:*> jdm bekommen; **~ with sth** (*approve of*) mit etw einverstanden sein

agreeable /ə'gri:əbl/ *a* angenehm

agreed /ə'gri:d/ *a* vereinbart

agreement /ə'gri:mənt/ *n* Übereinstimmung *f*; (*consent*) Einwilligung *f*; (*contract*) Abkommen *nt*; **reach ~** sich einigen

agricultur|al /ægrɪ'kʌltʃərəl/ *a* landwirtschaftlich. **~e** /'ægrɪkʌltʃə(r)/ *n* Landwirtschaft *f*

aground /ə'graʊnd/ *a* gestrandet; **run ~** <*ship:*> stranden

ahead /ə'hed/ *adv* **straight ~** geradeaus; **be ~ of s.o./sth** vor jdm/etw sein; (*fig*) voraus sein; **go on ~** vorgehen; **get ~** vorankommen; **go ~!** [!] bitte! **look/plan ~** vorausblicken/-planen

aid /eɪd/ *n* Hilfe *f*; (*financial*) Unterstützung *f*; **in ~ of** zugunsten (+ *gen*) ● *vt* helfen (+ *dat*)

Aids /eɪdz/ *n* Aids *nt*

aim /eɪm/ *n* Ziel *nt*; **take ~** zielen ● *vt* richten (**at** auf + *acc*); ● *vi* zielen (**at** auf + *acc*); **~ to do sth** beabsichtigen, etw zu tun. **~less** *a*, **-ly** *adv* ziellos

air /eə(r)/ *n* Luft *f*; (*expression*) Miene *f*; (*appearance*) Anschein *m*; **be on the ~** <*programme:*> gesendet werden; <*person:*> auf Sendung sein; **by ~** auf dem Luftweg; (*airmail*) mit Luftpost ● *vt* lüften; vorbringen <*views*>

air: ~ bag *n* (*Auto*) Airbag *m*. **~-conditioned** *a* klimatisiert. **~-conditioning** *n* Klimaanlage *f*. **~craft** *n* Flugzeug *nt*. **~field** *n* Flugplatz *m*. **~ force** *n* Luftwaffe *f*. **~ freshener** *n* Raumspray *nt*. **~gun** *n* Luftgewehr *nt*. **~ hostess** *n* Stewardess *f*. **~ letter** *n* Aerogramm *nt*. **~line** *n* Fluggesellschaft *f*. **~mail** *n* Luftpost *f*. **~man** *n* Flieger *m*. **~plane** *n* (*Amer*) Flugzeug *nt*. **~port** *n* Flughafen *m*. **~-raid** *n* Luftangriff *m*. **~-raid shelter** *n* Luftschutzbunker *m*. **~ship** *n* Luftschiff *nt*. **~ ticket** *n* Flugschein *m*. **~tight** *a* luftdicht. **~-traffic controller** *n* Fluglotse *m*

airy /'eərɪ/ *a* (**-ier, -iest**) luftig; <*manner*> nonchalant

aisle /aɪl/ *n* Gang *m*

ajar /ə'dʒɑ:(r)/ *a* angelehnt

alarm /əlɑ:m/ *n* Alarm *m*; (*device*) Alarmanlage *f*; (*clock*) Wecker *m*; (*fear*) Unruhe *f* ● *vt* erschrecken

alas /ə'læs/ *int* ach!

album /'ælbəm/ *n* Album *nt*

alcohol /'ælkəhɒl/ *n* Alkohol *m*. **~ic** /-'hɒlɪk/ *a* alkoholisch ● *n* Alkoholiker(in) *m(f)*. **~ism** *n* Alkoholismus *m*

alert /ə'lɜ:t/ *a* aufmerksam ● *n* Alarm *m*

algebra /'ældʒɪbrə/ *n* Algebra *f*

Algeria /æl'dʒɪərɪə/ *n* Algerien *nt*

alias /'eɪlɪəs/ *n* Deckname *m* ● *adv* alias

alibi /'ælɪbaɪ/ *n* Alibi *nt*

alien /'eɪlɪən/ *a* fremd ● *n* Ausländer(in) *m(f)*

alienate /'eɪlɪəneɪt/ *vt* entfremden

alight¹ /ə'laɪt/ *vi* aussteigen (**from** aus)

alight² *a* **be ~** brennen; **set ~** anzünden

align /ə'laɪn/ *vt* ausrichten. **~ment** *n* Ausrichtung *f*

alike /ə'laɪk/ *a & adv* ähnlich; (*same*) gleich; **look ~** sich (*dat*) ähnlich sehen

alive /ə'laɪv/ *a* lebendig; **be ~** leben; **be ~ with** wimmeln von

---

all /ɔ:l/

● *adjective*

····➤ (*plural*) alle. **all [the] children** alle Kinder. **all our children** alle unsere Kinder. **all the books** alle Bücher. **all the others** alle anderen

····➤ (*singular = whole*) ganz. **all the wine** der ganze Wein. **all the town** die ganze Stadt. **all my money** mein ganzes Geld; all mein Geld. **all day** den ganzen Tag. **all Germany** ganz Deutschland

● *pronoun*

····➤ (*plural = all persons/things*) alle. **all are welcome** alle sind willkommen. **they all came** sie sind alle gekommen. **are we all here?** sind wir alle da? **the best pupils of all** die besten Schüler (von allen). **the most beautiful of all** der/die/das schönste von allen

····➤ (*singular = everything*) alles. **that is all** das ist alles. **all that I possess** alles, was ich besitze

····➤ **all of** ganz; (*with plural*) alle. **all of the money** das ganze Geld. **all of the paintings** alle Gemälde. **all of you/them** Sie/sie alle

····➤ (*in phrases*) **all in all** alles in allem. **in all** insgesamt. **most of all** am meisten. **once and for all** ein für alle Mal. **not at all** gar nicht

● *adverb*

····➤ (*completely*) ganz. **she was all alone** sie war ganz allein. **I was all dirty** ich war ganz schmutzig

····➤ (*in scores*) **four all** vier zu vier

····➤ **all right** (*things*) in Ordnung. **is everything all right?** ist alles in Ordnung? **is that all right for you?** passt das Ihnen? **I'm all right** mir geht es gut. **did you get home all right?** sind Sie gut nach Hause gekommen? **is it all right to go in?** kann ich reingehen? **yes, all right** ja, gut. **work out all right** gut gehen; klappen [!]

····➤ (*in phrases*) **all but** (*almost*) fast. **all at once** auf einmal. **all the better** umso besser. **all the same** (*nevertheless*) trotzdem

---

allege /ə'ledʒ/ *vt* behaupten

allegiance /ə'li:dʒəns/ *n* Treue *f*

allerg|ic /ə'lɜ:dʒɪk/ *a* allergisch (**to** gegen). **~y** /'ælədʒɪ/ *n* Allergie *f*

alleviate /ə'li:vɪeɪt/ *vt* lindern

alley /'ælɪ/ *n* Gasse *f*; (*for bowling*) Bahn *f*

alliance /ə'laɪəns/ *n* Verbindung *f*; (*Pol*) Bündnis *nt*

allied /'ælaɪd/ *a* alliiert

alligator /'ælɪgeɪtə(r)/ *n* Alligator *m*

allocat|e /'æləkeɪt/ *vt* zuteilen; (*share out*) verteilen. **~ion** /-'keɪʃn/ *n* Zuteilung *f*

allot /ə'lɒt/ *vt* (*pt/pp* **allotted**) zuteilen (**s.o.** jdm)

allow /ə'laʊ/ *vt* erlauben; (*give*) geben; (*grant*) gewähren; (*reckon*) rechnen; (*agree, admit*) zugeben; **~ for** berücksichtigen; **~ s.o. to do sth** jdm erlauben, etw zu tun; **be ~ed to do sth** etw tun dürfen

allowance /ə'laʊəns/ *n* [finanzielle] Unterstützung *f*; **make ~s for** berücksichtigen

alloy /'ælɔɪ/ *n* Legierung *f*

allude /ə'lu:d/ *vi* anspielen (**to** auf + *acc*)

allusion /ə'lu:ʒn/ *n* Anspielung *f*

ally¹ /'ælaɪ/ *n* Verbündete(r) *m/f*; **the Allies** *pl* die Alliierten

ally² /ə'laɪ/ *vt* (*pt/pp* **-ied**) verbinden; **~ oneself with** sich verbünden mit

almighty /ɔ:l'maɪtɪ/ *a* allmächtig; (🅸 *big*) Riesen- ● *n* **the A~** der Allmächtige

almond /'ɑ:mənd/ *n* (*Bot*) Mandel *f*

almost /'ɔ:lməʊst/ *adv* fast, beinahe

alone /ə'ləʊn/ *a & adv* allein; **leave me ~** lass mich in Ruhe; **leave that ~!** lass die Finger davon! **let ~** ganz zu schweigen von

along /ə'lɒŋ/ *prep* entlang (+ *acc*); **~ the river** den Fluss entlang ● *adv* **~ with** zusammen mit; **all ~** die ganze Zeit; **come ~** komm doch; **I'll bring it ~** ich bringe es mit

along'side *adv* daneben ● *prep* neben (+ *dat*)

aloud /ə'laʊd/ *adv* laut

alphabet /'ælfəbet/ *n* Alphabet *nt*. **~ical** /-'betɪkl/ *a*, **-ly** *adv* alphabetisch

alpine /'ælpaɪn/ *a* alpin; **A ~** Alpen-

Alps /ælps/ *npl* Alpen *pl*

already /ɔ:l'redɪ/ *adv* schon

Alsace /æl'sæs/ *n* Elsass *nt*

Alsatian /æl'seɪʃn/ *n* (*dog*) [deutscher] Schäferhund *m*

also /'ɔ:lsəʊ/ *adv* auch

altar /'ɔ:ltə(r)/ *n* Altar *m*

alter /'ɔ:ltə(r)/ *vt* ändern ● *vi* sich verändern. **~ation** /-'reɪʃn/ *n* Änderung *f*

alternate¹ /'ɔ:ltəneɪt/ *vi* [sich] abwechseln ● *vt* abwechseln

alternate² /ɔ:l'tɜ:nət/ *a*, **-ly** *adv* abwechselnd; **on ~ days** jeden zweiten Tag

alternative /ɔ:l'tɜ:nətɪv/ *a* andere(r,s); **~ medicine** Alternativmedizin *f* ● *n* Alternative *f*. **~ly** *adv* oder aber

although /ɔ:l'ðəʊ/ *conj* obgleich, obwohl

altitude /'æltɪtju:d/ *n* Höhe *f*

altogether /ɔ:ltə'geðə(r)/ *adv* insgesamt; (*on the whole*) alles in allem

aluminium /æljʊ'mɪnɪəm/ *n*, (*Amer*) **aluminum** /ə'lu:mɪnəm/ *n* Aluminium *nt*

always /'ɔ:lweɪz/ *adv* immer

am /æm/ *see* **be**

a.m. *abbr* (**ante meridiem**) vormittags

amass /ə'mæs/ *vt* anhäufen

amateur /'æmətə(r)/ *n* Amateur *m* ● *attrib* Amateur-; (*Theat*) Laien-. **~ish** *a* laienhaft

amaze /ə'meɪz/ *vt* erstaunen. **~d** *a* erstaunt. **~ment** *n* Erstaunen *nt*

amazing /ə'meɪzɪŋ/ *a*, **-ly** *adv* erstaunlich

ambassador /æm'bæsədə(r)/ *n* Botschafter *m*

amber /'æmbə(r)/ *n* Bernstein *m* ● *a* (*colour*) gelb

ambigu|ity/æmbɪ'gju:ətɪ/ *n* Zweideutigkeit *f*. **~ous** /-'bɪgjʊəs/ *a*, **-ly** *adv* zweideutig

ambiti|on /æm'bɪʃn/ *n* Ehrgeiz *m*; (*aim*) Ambition *f*. **~ous** /-ʃəs/ *a* ehrgeizig

amble /'æmbl/ *vi* schlendern

ambulance /'æmbjʊləns/ *n* Krankenwagen *m*. **~ man** *n* Sanitäter *m*

ambush /'æmbʊʃ/ *n* Hinterhalt *m* ● *vt* aus dem Hinterhalt überfallen

amen /ɑ:'men/ *int* amen

amend /ə'mend/ *vt* ändern. **~ment** *n* Änderung *f*

amenities /ə'mi:nətɪz/ *npl* Einrichtungen *pl*

America /ə'merɪkə/ *n* Amerika *nt*. **~n** *a* amerikanisch ● *n* Amerikaner(in) *m(f)*. **~nism** *n* Amerikanismus *m*

amiable /'eɪmɪəbl/ *a* nett

amicable /'æmɪkəbl/ *a*, **-bly** *adv* freundschaftlich; <*agreement*> gütlich

amid[st] /ə'mɪd[st]/ *prep* inmitten (+ *gen*)

ammonia /ə'məʊnɪə/ *n* Ammoniak *nt*

ammunition /æmjʊ'nɪʃn/ *n* Munition *f*

amnesty /'æmnəstɪ/ *n* Amnestie *f*

among[st] /ə'mʌŋ[st]/ *prep* unter (+ *dat*/*acc*); **~ yourselves** untereinander

amoral /eɪ'mɒrəl/ *a* amoralisch

amorous /'æmərəs/ *a* zärtlich

amount /ə'maʊnt/ *n* Menge *f*; (*sum of money*) Betrag *m*; (*total*) Gesamtsumme *f* ● *vi* **~ to** sich belaufen auf (+ *acc*); (*fig*) hinauslaufen auf (+ *acc*)

amphibi|an /æm'fɪbɪən/ *n* Amphibie *f*. **~ous** /-ɪəs/ *a* amphibisch

amphitheatre /'æmfɪ-/ *n* Amphitheater *nt*

ample /'æmpl/ *a* (**-r, -st**), **-ly** *adv* reichlich; (*large*) füllig

amplif|ier /'æmplɪfaɪə(r)/ *n* Verstärker *m*. **~y** /-faɪ/ *vt* (*pt*/*pp* **-ied**) weiter ausführen; verstärken <*sound*>

amputat|e /'æmpjʊteɪt/ *vt* amputieren. **~ion** /-'teɪʃn/ *n* Amputation *f*

amuse /ə'mju:z/ *vt* amüsieren, belustigen; (*entertain*) unterhalten. **~ment** *n* Belustigung *f*, Unterhaltung *f*

amusing /ə'mju:zɪŋ/ *a* amüsant

an /ən, *betont* æn/ *see* **a**

anaem|ia /ə'ni:mɪə/ *n* Blutarmut *f*, Anämie *f*. **~ic** *a* blutarm

anaesthetic /ænəs'θetɪk/ *n* Narkosemittel *nt*, Betäubungsmittel *nt*; **under [an] ~** in Narkose

anaesthetist /ə'ni:sθətɪst/ *n* Narkosearzt *m*

analogy /ə'nælədʒɪ/ *n* Analogie *f*

analyse /'ænəlaɪz/ *vt* analysieren

analysis /ə'næləsɪs/ *n* Analyse *f*

analyst /'ænəlɪst/ *n* Chemiker(in) *m(f)*; (*Psych*) Analytiker *m*

analytical /ænə'lɪtɪkl/ *a* analytisch

anarch|ist /'ænəkɪst/ *n* Anarchist *m*. **~y** *n* Anarchie *f*

anatom|ical /ænə'tɒmɪkl/ *a*, **-ly** *adv* anatomisch. **~y** /ə'nætəmɪ/ *n* Anatomie *f*

ancest|or /'ænsestə(r)/ *n* Vorfahr *m*. **~ry** *n* Abstammung *f*

anchor /'æŋkə(r)/ *n* Anker *m* ● *vi* ankern ● *vt* verankern

ancient /'eɪnʃənt/ *a* alt

and /ənd, *betont* ænd/ *conj* und; **~ so on** und so weiter; **six hundred ~ two** sechshundertzwei; **more ~ more** immer mehr; **nice ~ warm** schön warm

anecdote /ˈænɪkdəʊt/ *n* Anekdote *f*
angel /ˈeɪndʒl/ *n* Engel *m*. **~ic** /ænˈdʒelɪk/ *a* engelhaft
anger /ˈæŋgə(r)/ *n* Zorn *m* ● *vt* zornig machen
angle /ˈæŋgl/ *n* Winkel *m*; (*fig*) Standpunkt *m*; **at an ~** schräg
angler /ˈæŋglə(r)/ *n* Angler *m*
Anglican /ˈæŋglɪkən/ *a* anglikanisch ● *n* Anglikaner(in) *m(f)*
Anglo-Saxon /æŋgləʊˈsæksn/ *a* angelsächsich ● *n* Angelsächsisch *nt*
angry /ˈæŋgrɪ/ *a* (**-ier, -iest**), **-ily** *adv* zornig; **be ~ with** böse sein auf (+ *acc*)
anguish /ˈæŋgwɪʃ/ *n* Qual *f*
animal /ˈænɪml/ *n* Tier *nt* ● *a* tierisch
animat|e /ˈænɪmeɪt/ *vt* beleben. **~ed** *a* lebhaft
animosity /ænɪˈmɒsətɪ/ *n* Feindseligkeit *f*
ankle /ˈæŋkl/ *n* [Fuß]knöchel *m*
annex[e] /ˈæneks/ *n* Nebengebäude *nt*; (*extension*) Anbau *m*
annihilate /əˈnaɪəleɪt/ *vt* vernichten
anniversary /ænɪˈvɜːsərɪ/ *n* Jahrestag *m*
annotate /ˈænəteɪt/ *vt* kommentieren
announce /əˈnaʊns/ *vt* bekannt geben; (*over loudspeaker*) durchsagen; (*at reception*) ankündigen; (*Radio, TV*) ansagen; (*in newspaper*) anzeigen. **~ment** *n* Bekanntgabe *f*, Bekanntmachung *f*; Durchsage *f*; Ansage *f*; Anzeige *f*. **~r** *n* Ansager(in) *m(f)*
annoy /əˈnɔɪ/ *vt* ärgern; (*pester*) belästigen; **get ~ed** sich ärgern. **~ance** *n* Ärger *m*. **~ing** *a* ärgerlich
annual /ˈænjʊəl/ *a*, **-ly** *adv* jährlich ● *n* (*book*) Jahresalbum *nt*
anonymous /əˈnɒnɪməs/ *a*, **-ly** *adv* anonym
anorak /ˈænəræk/ *n* Anorak *m*
anorexi|a /ænəˈreksɪə/ *n* Magersucht *f*. **~c** *a* **be ~c** an Magersucht leiden
another /əˈnʌðə(r)/ *a & pron* ein anderer/eine andere/ein anderes; (*additional*) noch ein(e); **~ [one]** noch einer/eine/eins; **~ time** ein andermal; **one ~** einander
answer /ˈɑːnsə(r)/ *n* Antwort *f*; (*solution*) Lösung *f* ● *vt* antworten (**s.o.** jdm); beantworten <*question, letter*>; **~ the door/telephone** an die Tür/ans Telefon gehen ● *vi* antworten; (*Teleph*) sich melden; **~ back** eine freche Antwort geben. **~ing machine** *n* (*Teleph*) Anrufbeantworter *m*
ant /ænt/ *n* Ameise *f*
antagonis|m /ænˈtægənɪzm/ *n* Antagonismus *m*. **~tic** /-ˈnɪstɪk/ *a* feindselig
Antarctic /æntˈɑːktɪk/ *n* Antarktis *f*
antelope /ˈæntɪləʊp/ *n* Antilope *f*
antenatal /æntɪˈneɪtl/ *a* **~ care** Schwangerschaftsfürsorge *f*
antenna /ænˈtenə/ *n* Fühler *m*; (*Amer: aerial*) Antenne *f*
anthem /ˈænθəm/ *n* Hymne *f*
anthology /ænˈθɒlədʒɪ/ *n* Anthologie *f*
anthrax /ˈænθræks/ *n* Milzbrand *m*, Anthrax *m*
anthropology /ænθrəˈpɒlədʒɪ/ *n* Anthropologie *f*
antibiotic /æntɪbaɪˈɒtɪk/ *n* Antibiotikum *nt*
anticipat|e /ænˈtɪsɪpeɪt/ *vt* vorhersehen; (*forestall*) zuvorkommen (+ *dat*); (*expect*)

erwarten. **~ion** /-'peɪʃn/ *n* Erwartung *f*
anti'climax *n* Enttäuschung *f*
anti'clockwise *a & adv* gegen den Uhrzeigersinn
antics /'æntɪks/ *npl* Mätzchen *pl*
antidote /'æntɪdəʊt/ *n* Gegengift *nt*
'antifreeze *n* Frostschutzmittel *nt*
antipathy /æn'tɪpəθɪ/ *n* Abneigung *f*, Antipathie *f*
antiquated /'æntɪkweɪtɪd/ *a* veraltet
antique /æn'ti:k/ *a* antik ● *n* Antiquität *f*. **~ dealer** *n* Antiquitätenhändler *m*
antiquity /æn'tɪkwətɪ/ *n* Altertum *nt*
anti'septic *a* antiseptisch ● *n* Antiseptikum *nt*
anti'social *a* asozial; [!] ungesellig
antlers /'æntləz/ *npl* Geweih *nt*
anus /'eɪnəs/ *n* After *m*
anvil /'ænvɪl/ *n* Amboss *m*
anxiety /æŋ'zaɪətɪ/ *n* Sorge *f*
anxious /'æŋkʃəs/ *a*, **-ly** *adv* ängstlich; (*worried*) besorgt; **be ~ to do sth** etw gerne machen wollen
any /'enɪ/ *a* irgendein(e); *pl* irgendwelche; (*every*) jede(r,s); *pl* alle; (*after negative*) kein(e); *pl* keine; **~ colour/number you like** eine beliebige Farbe/Zahl; **have you ~ wine/apples?** haben Sie Wein/Äpfel? ● *pron* [irgend]einer/eine/eins; *pl* [irgend]welche; (*some*) welche(r,s); *pl* welche; (*all*) alle *pl*; (*negative*) keiner/keine/keins; *pl* keine; **I don't want ~ of it** ich will nichts davon; **there aren't ~** es gibt keine ● *adv* noch; **~ quicker/slower** noch schneller/langsamer; **is it ~ better?** geht es etwas besser? **would you like ~ more?** möchten Sie noch [etwas]? **I can't eat ~ more** ich kann nichts mehr essen
'anybody *pron* [irgend]jemand; (*after negative*) niemand; **~ can do that** das kann jeder
'anyhow *adv* jedenfalls; (*nevertheless*) trotzdem; (*badly*) irgendwie
'anyone *pron* = **anybody**
'anything *pron* [irgend]etwas; (*after negative*) nichts; (*everything*) alles
'anyway *adv* jedenfalls; (*in any case*) sowieso
'anywhere *adv* irgendwo; (*after negative*) nirgendwo; <*be, live*> überall; <*go*> überallhin
apart /ə'pɑ:t/ *adv* auseinander; **live ~** getrennt leben; **~ from** abgesehen von
apartment /ə'pɑ:tmənt/ *n* Zimmer *nt*; (*flat*) Wohnung *f*
ape /eɪp/ *n* [Menschen]affe *m* ● *vt* nachäffen
aperitif /ə'perəti:f/ *n* Aperitif *m*
apologetic /əpɒlə'dʒetɪk/ *a*, **-ally** *adv* entschuldigend; **be ~** sich entschuldigen
apologize /ə'pɒlədʒaɪz/ *vi* sich entschuldigen (**to** bei)
apology /ə'pɒlədʒɪ/ *n* Entschuldigung *f*
apostle /ə'pɒsl/ *n* Apostel *m*
apostrophe /ə'pɒstrəfɪ/ *n* Apostroph *m*
appal /ə'pɔ:l/ *vt* (*pt/pp* **appalled**) entsetzen. **~ling** *a* entsetzlich
apparatus /æpə'reɪtəs/ *n* Apparatur *f*; (*Sport*) Geräte *pl*; (*single piece*) Gerät *nt*
apparent /ə'pærənt/ *a* offenbar; (*seeming*) scheinbar. **~ly** *adv* offenbar, anscheinend
appeal /ə'pi:l/ *n* Appell *m*, Aufruf *m*; (*request*) Bitte *f*; (*attraction*) Reiz *m*; (*Jur*) Berufung *f* ● *vi* appellieren (**to** an + *acc*); (*ask*) bitten (**for** um);

(*be attractive*) zusagen (**to** *dat*); (*Jur*) Berufung einlegen. **~ing** *a* ansprechend

appear/ə'pɪə(r)/ *vi* erscheinen; (*seem*) scheinen; (*Theat*) auftreten. **~ance** *n* Erscheinen *nt*; (*look*) Aussehen *nt*; **to all ~ances** allem Anschein nach

appendicitis /əpendɪ'saɪtɪs/ *n* Blinddarmentzündung *f*

appendix /ə'pendɪks/ *n* (*pl* **-ices** /-ɪsi:z/) (*of book*) Anhang *m* ● (*pl* **-es**) (*Anat*) Blinddarm *m*

appetite /'æpɪtaɪt/ *n* Appetit *m*

appetizing /'æpɪtaɪzɪŋ/ *a* appetitlich

applau|d /ə'plɔ:d/ *vt/i* Beifall klatschen (+ *dat*). **~se** *n* Beifall *m*

apple /'æpl/ *n* Apfel *m*

appliance /ə'plaɪəns/ *n* Gerät *nt*

applicable /'æplɪkəbl/ *a* anwendbar (**to** auf + *acc*); (*on form*) **not ~** nicht zutreffend

applicant /'æplɪkənt/ *n* Bewerber(in) *m(f)*

application /æplɪ'keɪʃn/ *n* Anwendung *f*; (*request*) Antrag *m*; (*for job*) Bewerbung *f*; (*diligence*) Fleiß *m*

applied /ə'plaɪd/ *a* angewandt

apply /ə'plaɪ/ *vt* (*pt/pp* **-ied**) auftragen <*paint*>; anwenden <*force, rule*> ● *vi* zutreffen (**to** auf + *acc*); **~ for** beantragen; sich bewerben um <*job*>

appoint /ə'pɔɪnt/ *vt* ernennen; (*fix*) festlegen. **~ment** *n* Ernennung *f*; (*meeting*) Verabredung *f*; (*at doctor's, hairdresser's*) Termin *m*; (*job*) Posten *m*; **make an ~ment** sich anmelden

appreciable /ə'pri:ʃəbl/ *a* merklich; (*considerable*) beträchtlich

appreciat|e /ə'pri:ʃɪeɪt/ *vt* zu schätzen wissen; (*be grateful for*) dankbar sein für; (*enjoy*) schätzen; (*understand*) verstehen ● *vi* (*increase in value*) im Wert steigen. **~ion** /-'eɪʃn/ *n* (*gratitude*) Dankbarkeit *f*. **~ive** /-ətɪv/ *a* dankbar

apprehens|ion /æprɪ'henʃn/ *n* Festnahme *f*; (*fear*) Angst *f*. **~ive** /-sɪv/ *a* ängstlich

apprentice /ə'prentɪs/ *n* Lehrling *m*. **~ship** *n* Lehre *f*

approach /ə'prəʊtʃ/ *n* Näherkommen *nt*; (*of time*) Nahen *nt*; (*access*) Zugang *m*; (*road*) Zufahrt *f* ● *vi* sich nähern; <*time:*> nahen ● *vt* sich nähern (+ *dat*); (*with request*) herantreten an (+ *acc*); (*set about*) sich heranmachen an (+ *acc*). **~able** /-əbl/ *a* zugänglich

appropriate /ə'prəʊprɪət/ *a* angebracht, angemessen

approval /ə'pru:vl/ *n* Billigung *f*; **on ~** zur Ansicht

approv|e /ə'pru:v/ *vt* billigen ● *vi* **~e of sth/s.o.** mit etw/jdm einverstanden sein. **~ing** *a*, **-ly** *adv* anerkennend

approximate /ə'prɒksɪmət/ *a*, **-ly** *adv* ungefähr

approximation /əprɒksɪ'meɪʃn/ *n* Schätzung *f*

apricot /'eɪprɪkɒt/ *n* Aprikose *f*

April /'eɪprəl/ *n* April *m*; **make an ~ fool of** in den April schicken

apron /'eɪprən/ *n* Schürze *f*

apt /æpt/ *a*, **-ly** *adv* passend; **be ~ to do sth** dazu neigen, etw zu tun

aqualung /'ækwəlʌŋ/ *n* Tauchgerät *nt*

aquarium /ə'kweərɪəm/ *n* Aquarium *nt*

aquatic /ə'kwætɪk/ *a* Wasser-

Arab /'ærəb/ *a* arabisch ● *n* Araber(in) *m(f)*. **~ian** /ə'reɪbɪən/ *a* arabisch

Arabic /'ærəbɪk/ *a* arabisch

arbitrary /'ɑ:bɪtrərɪ/ *a*, **-ily** *adv* willkürlich

arbitrat|e /'ɑ:bɪtreɪt/ *vi* schlichten. **~ion** /-'treɪʃn/ *n* Schlichtung *f*

arc /ɑ:k/ *n* Bogen *m*

arcade /ɑ:'keɪd/ *n* Laubengang *m*; (*shops*) Einkaufspassage *f*

arch /ɑ:tʃ/ *n* Bogen *m*; (*of foot*) Gewölbe *nt* ● *vt* **~ its back** <*cat:*> einen Buckel machen

archaeological /ɑ:kɪə'lɒdʒɪkl/ *a* archäologisch

archaeolog|ist /ɑ:kɪ'ɒlədʒɪst/ *n* Archäologe *m*/-login *f*. **~y** *n* Archäologie *f*

archaic /ɑ:'keɪɪk/ *a* veraltet

arch'bishop /ɑ:tʃ-/ *n* Erzbischof *m*

archer /'ɑ:tʃə(r)/ *n* Bogenschütze *m*. **~y** *n* Bogenschießen *nt*

architect /'ɑ:kɪtekt/ *n* Architekt(in) *m(f)*. **~ural** /ɑ:kɪ'tektʃərəl/ *a*, **-ly** *adv* architektonisch

architecture /'ɑ:kɪtektʃə(r)/ *n* Architektur *f*

archives /'ɑ:kaɪvz/ *npl* Archiv *nt*

archway /'ɑ:tʃweɪ/ *n* Torbogen *m*

Arctic /'ɑ:ktɪk/ *a* arktisch ● *n* **the ~** die Arktis

ardent /'ɑ:dənt/ *a*, **-ly** *adv* leidenschaftlich

ardour /'ɑ:də(r)/ *n* Leidenschaft *f*

arduous /'ɑ:djʊəs/ *a* mühsam

are /ɑ:(r)/ *see* **be**

area /'eərɪə/ *n* (*surface*) Fläche *f*; (*Geom*) Flächeninhalt *m*; (*region*) Gegend *f*; (*fig*) Gebiet *nt*

arena /ə'ri:nə/ *n* Arena *f*

Argentina /ɑ:dʒən'ti:nə/ *n* Argentinien *nt*

Argentin|e /'ɑ:dʒəntaɪn/, **~ian** /-'tɪnɪən/ *a* argentinisch

argue /'ɑ:gju:/ *vi* streiten (**about** über + *acc*); <*two people:*> sich streiten; (*debate*) diskutieren; **don't ~!** keine Widerrede! ● *vt* (*debate*) diskutieren; (*reason*) **~ that** argumentieren, dass

argument /'ɑ:gjʊmənt/ *n* Streit *m*, Auseinandersetzung *f*; (*reasoning*) Argument *nt*; **have an ~** sich streiten. **~ative** /-'mentətɪv/ *a* streitlustig

aria /'ɑ:rɪə/ *n* Arie *f*

arise /ə'raɪz/ *vi* (*pt* **arose**, *pp* **arisen**) sich ergeben (**from** aus)

aristocracy /ærɪ'stɒkrəsɪ/ *n* Aristokratie *f*

aristocrat /'ærɪstəkræt/ *n* Aristokrat(in) *m(f)*. **~ic** /-'krætɪk/ *a* aristokratisch

arithmetic /ə'rɪθmətɪk/ *n* Rechnen *nt*

arm /ɑ:m/ *n* Arm *m*; (*of chair*) Armlehne *f*; **~s** *pl* (*weapons*) Waffen *pl*; (*Heraldry*) Wappen *nt* ● *vt* bewaffnen

armament /'ɑ:məmənt/ *n* Bewaffnung *f*; **~s** *pl* Waffen *pl*

'armchair *n* Sessel *m*

armed /ɑ:md/ *a* bewaffnet; **~ forces** Streitkräfte *pl*

armour /'ɑ:mə(r)/ *n* Rüstung *f*. **~ed** *a* Panzer-

'armpit *n* Achselhöhle *f*

army /'ɑ:mɪ/ *n* Heer *nt*; (*specific*) Armee *f*; **join the ~** zum Militär gehen

aroma /ə'rəʊmə/ *n* Aroma *nt*, Duft *m*. **~tic** /ærə'mætɪk/ *a* aromatisch

arose /ə'rəʊz/ *see* **arise**

around /ə'raʊnd/ *adv* **[all] ~** rings herum; **he's not ~** er ist nicht da; **travel ~** herumreisen ● *prep* um (+ *acc*) ... herum; (*approximately*) gegen

arouse /ə'raʊz/ *vt* aufwecken; (*excite*) erregen

arrange /ə'reɪndʒ/ *vt* arrangieren; anordnen <*furniture, books*>; (*settle*) abmachen. **~ment** *n*

Anordnung *f*; (*agreement*) Vereinbarung *f*; (*of flowers*) Gesteck *nt*; **make ~ments** Vorkehrungen treffen

arrest /ə'rest/ *n* Verhaftung *f*; **under ~** verhaftet ● *vt* verhaften

arrival /ə'raɪvl/ *n* Ankunft *f*; **new ~s** *pl* Neuankömmlinge *pl*

arrive /ə'raɪv/ *vi* ankommen; **~ at** (*fig*) gelangen zu

arrogan|ce /'ærəgəns/ *n* Arroganz *f*. **~t** *a*, **-ly** *adv* arrogant

arrow /'ærəʊ/ *n* Pfeil *m*

arse /ɑ:s/ *n* (*vulg*) Arsch *m*

arson /'ɑ:sn/ *n* Brandstiftung *f*. **~ist** /-sənɪst/ *n* Brandstifter *m*

art /ɑ:t/ *n* Kunst *f*; **work of ~** Kunstwerk *nt*; **~s and crafts** *pl* Kunstgewerbe *nt*; **A~s** *pl* (*Univ*) Geisteswissenschaften *pl*

artery /'ɑ:tərɪ/ *n* Schlagader *f*, Arterie *f*

'art gallery *n* Kunstgalerie *f*

arthritis /ɑ:'θraɪtɪs/ *n* Arthritis *f*

artichoke /'ɑ:tɪtʃəʊk/ *n* Artischocke *f*

article /'ɑ:tɪkl/ *n* Artikel *m*; (*object*) Gegenstand *m*; **~ of clothing** Kleidungsstück *nt*

artificial /ɑ:tɪ'fɪʃl/ *a*, **-ly** *adv* künstlich

artillery /ɑ:'tɪlərɪ/ *n* Artillerie *f*

artist /'ɑ:tɪst/ *n* Künstler(in) *m(f)*

artiste /ɑ:'ti:st/ *n* (*Theat*) Artist(in) *m(f)*

artistic /ɑ:'tɪstɪk/ *a*, **-ally** *adv* künstlerisch

as /æz/ *conj* (*because*) da; (*when*) als; (*while*) während ● *prep* als; **as a child/foreigner** als Kind/Ausländer ● *adv* **as well** auch; **as soon as** sobald; **as much as** so viel wie; **as quick as you** so schnell wie du; **as you know** wie Sie wissen; **as far as I'm concerned** was mich betrifft

asbestos /æz'bestɒs/ *n* Asbest *m*

ascend /ə'send/ *vi* [auf]steigen ● *vt* besteigen <*throne*>

ascent /ə'sent/ *n* Aufstieg *m*

ascertain /æsə'teɪn/ *vt* ermitteln

ash[1] /æʃ/ *n* (*tree*) Esche *f*

ash[2] *n* Asche *f*

ashamed /ə'ʃeɪmd/ *a* beschämt; **be ~** sich schämen (**of** über + *acc*)

ashore /ə'ʃɔ:(r)/ *adv* an Land

'ashtray *n* Aschenbecher *m*

Asia /'eɪʃə/ *n* Asien *nt*. **~n** *a* asiatisch ● *n* Asiat(in) *m(f)*. **~tic** /eɪʃɪ'ætɪk/ *a* asiatisch

aside /ə'saɪd/ *adv* beiseite

ask /ɑ:sk/ *vt/i* fragen; stellen <*question*>; (*invite*) einladen; **~ for** bitten um; verlangen <*s.o.*>; **~ after** sich erkundigen nach; **~ s.o. in** jdn hereinbitten; **~ s.o. to do sth** jdn bitten, etw zu tun

asleep /ə'sli:p/ *a* **be ~** schlafen; **fall ~** einschlafen

asparagus /ə'spærəgəs/ *n* Spargel *m*

aspect /'æspekt/ *n* Aspekt *m*

asphalt /'æsfælt/ *n* Asphalt *m*

aspire /ə'spaɪə(r)/ *vi* **~ to** streben nach

ass /æs/ *n* Esel *m*

assail /ə'seɪl/ *vt* bestürmen. **~ant** *n* Angreifer(in) *m(f)*

assassin /ə'sæsɪn/ *n* Mörder(in) *m(f)*. **~ate** *vt* ermorden. **~ation** /-'neɪʃn/ *n* [politischer] Mord *m*

assault /ə'sɔ:lt/ *n* (*Mil*) Angriff *m*; (*Jur*) Körperverletzung *f* ● *vt* [tätlich] angreifen

assemble /ə'sembl/ *vi* sich versammeln ● *vt* versammeln; (*Techn*) montieren

assembly /ə'semblɪ/ *n* Versammlung *f*; (*Sch*) Andacht *f*; (*Techn*) Montage *f*. **~ line** *n* Fließband *nt*

assent /ə'sent/ *n* Zustimmung *f*

assert /ə'sɜ:t/ *vt* behaupten; **~ oneself** sich durchsetzen. **~ion** /-ɜ:ʃn/ *n* Behauptung *f*

assess /ə'ses/ *vt* bewerten; (*fig & for tax purposes*) einschätzen: schätzen <*value*>. **~ment** *n* Einschätzung *f*; (*of tax*) Steuerbescheid *m*

asset /'æset/ *n* Vorteil *m*; **~s** *pl* (*money*) Vermögen *nt*; (*Comm*) Aktiva *pl*

assign /ə'saɪn/ *vt* zuweisen (**to** *dat*). **~ment** *n* (*task*) Aufgabe *f*

assist /ə'sɪst/ *vt/i* helfen (+ *dat*). **~ance** *n* Hilfe *f*. **~ant** *a* Hilfs- ● *n* Assistent(in) *m(f)*; (*in shop*) Verkäufer(in) *m(f)*

associat|e¹ /ə'səʊʃɪeɪt/ *vt* verbinden; (*Psych*) assoziieren ● *vi* **~ with** verkehren mit. **~ion** /-'eɪʃn/ *n* Verband *m*

associate² /ə'səʊʃɪət/ *a* assoziiert ● *n* Kollege *m*/-gin *f*

assort|ed /ə'sɔ:tɪd/ *a* gemischt. **~ment** *n* Mischung *f*

assum|e /ə'sju:m/ *vt* annehmen; übernehmen <*office*>; **~ing that** angenommen, dass

assumption /ə'sʌmpʃn/ *n* Annahme *f*; **on the ~** in der Annahme (**that** dass)

assurance /ə'ʃʊərəns/ *n* Versicherung *f*; (*confidence*) Selbstsicherheit *f*

assure /ə'ʃʊə(r)/ *vt* versichern (**s.o.** jdm); **I ~ you [of that]** das versichere ich Ihnen. **~d** *a* sicher

asterisk /'æstərɪsk/ *n* Sternchen *nt*

asthma /'æsmə/ *n* Asthma *nt*

astonish /ə'stɒnɪʃ/ *vt* erstaunen. **~ing** *a* erstaunlich. **~ment** *n* Erstaunen *nt*

astray /ə'streɪ/ *adv* **go ~** verloren gehen; <*person:*> sich verlaufen

astride /ə'straɪd/ *adv* rittlings ● *prep* rittlings auf (+ *dat/acc*)

astrolog|er /ə'strɒlədʒə(r)/ *n* Astrologe *m*/-gin *f*. **~y** *n* Astrologie *f*

astronaut /'æstrənɔ:t/ *n* Astronaut(in) *m(f)*

astronom|er /ə'strɒnəmə(r)/ *n* Astronom *m*. **~ical** /æstrə'nɒmɪkl/ *a* astronomisch. **~y** *n* Astronomie *f*

astute /ə'stju:t/ *a* scharfsinnig

asylum /ə'saɪləm/ *n* Asyl *nt*; **[lunatic] ~** Irrenanstalt *f*. **~-seeker** *n* Asylant *m*

---

at /æt, *unbetont* ət/

● *preposition*

····➤ (*expressing place*) an (+ *dat*). **at the station** am Bahnhof. **at the end** am Ende. **at the corner** an der Ecke. **at the same place** an der gleichen Stelle

····➤ (*at s.o.'s house or shop*) bei (+ *dat*). **at Lisa's** bei Lisa. **at my uncle's** bei meinem Onkel. **at the baker's/butcher's** beim Bäcker/Fleischer

····➤ (*inside a building*) in (+ *dat*). **at the theatre/supermarket** im Theater/Supermarkt. **we spent the night at a hotel** wir übernachteten in einem Hotel. **he is still at the office** er ist noch im Büro

····➤ (*expressing time*) (*with clock time*) um; (*with main festivals*) zu. **at six o'clock** um sechs Uhr. **at midnight** um Mitternacht. **at midday** um zwölf Uhr mittags. **at Christmas/Easter** zu Weihnachten/Ostern

····➤ (*expressing age*) mit. **at [the age of] forty** mit vierzig; im Alter von vierzig

····➤ (*expressing price*) zu. **at £2.50 [each]** zu *od* für [je] 2,50 Pfund

....➤ (*expressing speed*) mit. **at 30 m.p.h.** mit dreißig Meilen pro Stunde
....➤ (*in phrases*) **good/bad at languages** gut/schlecht in Sprachen. **two at a time** zwei auf einmal. **at that** (*at that point*) dabei; (*at that provocation*) daraufhin; (*moreover*) noch dazu

ate /et/ *see* **eat**
atheist /'eɪθɪɪst/ *n* Atheist(in) *m(f)*
athlet|e /'æθli:t/ *n* Athlet(in) *m(f)*. **~ic** /-'letɪk/ *a* sportlich. **~ics** /-'letɪks/ *n* Leichtathletik *f*
Atlantic /ət'læntɪk/ *a* & *n* **the ~ [Ocean]** der Atlantik
atlas /'ætləs/ *n* Atlas *m*
atmosphere /'ætməsfɪə(r)/ *n* Atmosphäre *f*
atom /'ætəm/ *n* Atom *nt*. **~ bomb** *n* Atombombe *f*
atomic /ə'tɒmɪk/ *a* Atom-
atrocious /ə'trəʊʃəs/ *a* abscheulich
atrocity /ə'trɒsətɪ/ *n* Gräueltat *f*
attach /ə'tætʃ/ *vt* befestigen (**to** an + *dat*); beimessen <*importance*> (**to** *dat*); **be ~ed to** (*fig*) hängen an (+ *dat*)
attack /ə'tæk/ *n* Angriff *m*; (*Med*) Anfall *m* ● *vt/i* angreifen. **~er** *n* Angreifer *m*
attain /ə'teɪn/ *vt* erreichen. **~able** /-əbl/ *a* erreichbar
attempt /ə'tempt/ *n* Versuch *m* ● *vt* versuchen
attend /ə'tend/ *vt* anwesend sein bei; (*go regularly to*) besuchen; (*take part in*) teilnehmen an (+ *dat*); (*accompany*) begleiten; <*doctor:*> behandeln ● *vi* anwesend sein; (*pay attention*) aufpassen; **~ to** sich kümmern um; (*in shop*) bedienen. **~ance** *n* Anwesenheit *f*; (*number*) Besucherzahl *f*. **~ant** *n* Wärter(in) *m(f)*; (*in car park*) Wächter *m*
attention /ə'tenʃn/ *n* Aufmerksamkeit *f*; **~!** (*Mil*) stillgestanden! **pay ~** aufpassen; **pay ~ to** beachten, achten auf (+ *acc*)
attentive /ə'tentɪv/ *a*, **-ly** *adv* aufmerksam
attic /'ætɪk/ *n* Dachboden *m*
attitude /'ætɪtju:d/ *n* Haltung *f*
attorney /ə'tɜ:nɪ/ *n* (*Amer: lawyer*) Rechtsanwalt *m*; **power of ~** Vollmacht *f*
attract /ə'trækt/ *vt* anziehen; erregen <*attention*>; **~ s.o.'s attention** jds Aufmerksamkeit auf sich (*acc*) lenken. **~ion** /-ækʃn/ *n* Anziehungskraft *f*; (*charm*) Reiz *m*; (*thing*) Attraktion *f*. **~ive** /-tɪv/ *a*, **-ly** *adv* attraktiv
attribute /ə'trɪbju:t/ *vt* zuschreiben (**to** *dat*)
aubergine /'əʊbəʒi:n/ *n* Aubergine *f*
auburn /'ɔ:bən/ *a* kastanienbraun
auction /'ɔ:kʃn/ *n* Auktion *f* Versteigerung *f* ● *vt* versteigern. **~eer** /-ʃə'nɪə(r)/ *n* Auktionator *m*
audaci|ous /ɔ:'deɪʃəs/ *a*, **-ly** *adv* verwegen. **~ty** /-'dæsətɪ/ *n* Verwegenheit *f*; (*impudence*) Dreistigkeit *f*
audible /'ɔ:dəbl/ *a*, **-bly** *adv* hörbar
audience /'ɔ:dɪəns/ *n* Publikum *nt*; (*Theat, TV*) Zuschauer *pl*; (*Radio*) Zuhörer *pl*; (*meeting*) Audienz *f*
audit /'ɔ:dɪt/ *n* Bücherrevision *f* ● *vt* (*Comm*) prüfen
audition /ɔ:'dɪʃn/ *n* (*Theat*) Vorsprechen *nt*; (*Mus*) Vorspielen *nt*; (*for singer*) Vorsingen *nt* ● *vi* vorsprechen; vorspielen; vorsingen

auditor /'ɔ:dɪtə(r)/ *n* Buchprüfer *m*

auditorium /ɔ:dɪ'tɔ:rɪəm/ *n* Zuschauerraum *m*

August /'ɔ:gəst/ *n* August *m*

aunt /ɑ:nt/ *n* Tante *f*

au pair /əʊ'peə(r)/ *n* ~ **[girl]** Au-pair-Mädchen *nt*

aura /'ɔ:rə/ *n* Fluidum *nt*

auspicious /ɔ:'spɪʃəs/ *a* günstig; <*occasion*> freudig

auster|e /ɒ'stɪə(r)/ *a* streng; (*simple*) nüchtern. **~ity** /-terətɪ/ *n* Strenge *f*; (*hardship*) Entbehrung *f*

Australia /ɒ'streɪlɪə/ *n* Australien *nt*. **~n** *a* australisch ● *n* Australier(in) *m(f)*

Austria /'ɒstrɪə/ *n* Österreich *nt* **~n** *a* österreichisch ● *n* Österreicher(in) *m(f)*

authentic /ɔ:'θentɪk/ *a* echt, authentisch. **~ate** *vt* beglaubigen. **~ity** /-'tɪsətɪ/ *n* Echtheit *f*

author /'ɔ:θə(r)/ *n* Schriftsteller *m*, Autor *m*; (*of document*) Verfasser *m*

authoritarian /ɔ:θɒrɪ'teərɪən/ *a* autoritär

authoritative /ɔ:'θɒrɪtətɪv/ *a* maßgebend

authority /ɔ:'θɒrətɪ/ *n* Autorität *f*; (*public*) Behörde *f*; **in ~** verantwortlich

authorization /ɔ:θəraɪ'zeɪʃn/ *n* Ermächtigung *f*

authorize /'ɔ:θəraɪz/ *vt* ermächtigen <*s.o.*>; genehmigen <*sth*>

autobi'ography /ɔ:tə-/ *n* Autobiographie *f*

autograph /'ɔ:tə-/ *n* Autogramm *nt*

automatic /ɔ:tə'mætɪk/ *a*, **-ally** *adv* automatisch

automation /ɔ:tə'meɪʃn/ *n* Automation *f*

automobile /'ɔ:təməbi:l/ *n* Auto *nt*

autonom|ous /ɔ:'tɒnəməs/ *a* autonom. **~y** *n* Autonomie *f*

autumn /'ɔ:təm/ *n* Herbst *m*. **~al** /-'tʌmnl/ *a* herbstlich

auxiliary /ɔ:g'zɪlɪərɪ/ *a* Hilfs- ● *n* Helfer(in) *m(f)*, Hilfskraft *f*

avail /ə'veɪl/ *n* **to no ~** vergeblich

available /ə'veɪləbl/ *a* verfügbar; (*obtainable*) erhältlich

avalanche /'ævəlɑ:nʃ/ *n* Lawine *f*

avenge /ə'vendʒ/ *vt* rächen

avenue /'ævənju:/ *n* Allee *f*

average /'ævərɪdʒ/ *a* Durchschnitts-, durchschnittlich ● *n* Durchschnitt *m*; **on ~** im Durchschnitt, durchschnittlich ● *vt* durchschnittlich schaffen

averse /ə'vɜ:s/ *a* **not be ~e to sth** etw (*dat*) nicht abgeneigt sein

avert /ə'vɜ:t/ *vt* abwenden

aviary /'eɪvɪərɪ/ *n* Vogelhaus *nt*

aviation /eɪvɪ'eɪʃn/ *n* Luftfahrt *f*

avocado /ævə'kɑ:dəʊ/ *n* Avocado *f*

avoid /ə'vɔɪd/ *vt* vermeiden; **~ s.o.** jdm aus dem Weg gehen. **~able** /-əbl/ *a* vermeidbar. **~ance** *n* Vermeidung *f*

await /ə'weɪt/ *vt* warten auf (+ *acc*)

awake /ə'weɪk/ *a* wach; **wide ~** hellwach ● *vi* (*pt* **awoke**, *pp* **awoken**) erwachen

awaken /ə'weɪkn/ *vt* wecken ● *vi* erwachen. **~ing** *n* Erwachen *nt*

award /ə'wɔ:d/ *n* Auszeichnung *f*; (*prize*) Preis *m* ● *vt* zuerkennen (**to s.o.** *dat*); verleihen <*prize*>

aware /ə'weə(r)/ *a* **become ~** gewahr werden (**of** *gen*); **be ~ that** wissen, dass. **~ness** *n* Bewusstsein *nt*

away /ə'weɪ/ *adv* weg, fort; (*absent*) abwesend; **four kilometres ~** vier Kilometer entfernt; **play ~** (*Sport*) auswärts spielen. **~ game** *n* Auswärtsspiel *nt*
awful /'ɔ:fl/ *a*, **-ly** *adv* furchtbar
awkward /'ɔ:kwəd/ *a* schwierig; (*clumsy*) ungeschickt; (*embarrassing*) peinlich; (*inconvenient*) ungünstig. **~ly** *adv* ungeschickt; (*embarrassedly*) verlegen
awning /'ɔ:nɪŋ/ *n* Markise *f*
awoke(n) /ə'wəʊk(n)/ *see* **awake**
axe /æks/ *n* Axt *f* ● *vt* (*pres p* **axing**) streichen
axle /'æksl/ *n* (*Techn*) Achse *f*

Bb

B /bi:/ *n* (*Mus*) H *nt*
baboon /bə'bu:n/ *n* Pavian *m*
baby /'beɪbɪ/ *n* Baby *nt*; (*Amer* [!]) Schätzchen *nt*
baby: ~ish *a* kindisch. **~-sit** *vi* babysitten. **~-sitter** *n* Babysitter *m*
bachelor /'bætʃələ(r)/ *n* Junggeselle *m*
back /bæk/ *n* Rücken *m*; (*reverse*) Rückseite *f*; (*of chair*) Rückenlehne *f*; (*Sport*) Verteidiger *m*; **at**/(*Auto*) **in the ~** hinten; **on the ~** auf der Rückseite; **~ to front** verkehrt ● *a* Hinter- ● *adv* zurück; **~ here/there** hier/da hinten; **~ at home** zu Hause; **go/pay ~** zurückgehen/-zahlen ● *vt* (*support*) unterstützen; (*with money*) finanzieren; (*Auto*) zurücksetzen; (*Betting*) [Geld] setzen auf (+ *acc*); (*cover the back of*) mit einer Verstärkung versehen ● *vi* (*Auto*) zurücksetzen. **~ down** *vi* klein beigeben. **~ in** *vi* rückwärts hineinfahren. **~ out** *vi* rückwärts hinaus-/herausfahren; (*fig*) aussteigen (**of** aus). **~ up** *vt* unterstützen; (*confirm*) bestätigen ● *vi* (*Auto*) zurücksetzen
back: ~ache *n* Rückenschmerzen *pl*. **~biting** *n* gehässiges Gerede *nt*. **~bone** *n* Rückgrat *nt*. **~date** *vt* rückdatieren; **~dated to** rückwirkend von. **~ 'door** *n* Hintertür *f*
backer /'bækə(r)/ *n* Geldgeber *m*
back: ~'fire *vi* (*Auto*) fehlzünden; (*fig*) fehlschlagen. **~ground** *n* Hintergrund *m*; **family ~ground** Familienverhältnisse *pl*. **~hand** *n* (*Sport*) Rückhand *f*. **~'handed** *a* <*compliment*> zweifelhaft
backing /'bækɪŋ/ *n* (*support*) Unterstützung *f*; (*material*) Verstärkung *f*
back: ~lash *n* (*fig*) Gegenschlag *m*. **~log** *n* Rückstand *m* (**of** an + *dat*). **~pack** *n* Rucksack *m*. **~ 'seat** *n* Rücksitz *m*. **~side** *n* [!] Hintern *m*. **~stroke** *n* Rückenschwimmen *nt*. **~-up** *n* Unterstützung *f*; (*Amer: traffic jam*) Stau *m*
backward /'bækwəd/ *a* zurückgeblieben; <*country*> rückständig ● *adv* rückwärts. **~s** rückwärts; **~s and forwards** hin und her
back 'yard *n* Hinterhof *m*; **not in my ~ yard** [!] nicht vor meiner Haustür
bacon /'beɪkn/ *n* [Schinken]speck *m*

bacteria /bæk'tɪərɪə/ *npl* Bakterien *pl*

bad /bæd/ *a* (**worse, worst**) schlecht; (*serious*) schwer, schlimm; (*naughty*) unartig; ~ **language** gemeine Ausdrucksweise *f*; **feel** ~ sich schlecht fühlen; (*feel guilty*) ein schlechtes Gewissen haben

badge /bædʒ/ *n* Abzeichen *nt*

badger /'bædʒə(r)/ *n* Dachs *m* ● *vt* plagen

badly /'bædlɪ/ *adv* schlecht; (*seriously*) schwer; ~ **off** schlecht gestellt; ~ **behaved** unerzogen; **want** ~ sich (*dat*) sehnsüchtig wünschen; **need** ~ dringend brauchen

bad-'mannered *a* mit schlechten Manieren

badminton /'bædmɪntən/ *n* Federball *m*

bad-'tempered *a* schlecht gelaunt

baffle /'bæfl/ *vt* verblüffen

bag /bæg/ *n* Tasche *f*; (*of paper*) Tüte *f*; (*pouch*) Beutel *m*; ~**s of** [!] jede Menge ● *vt* ([!] *reserve*) in Beschlag nehmen

baggage /'bægɪdʒ/ *n* [Reise]gepäck *nt*

baggy /'bægɪ/ *a* <*clothes*> ausgebeult

'**bagpipes** *npl* Dudelsack *m*

bail /beɪl/ *n* Kaution *f*; **on** ~ gegen Kaution ● *vt* ~ **s.o. out** jdn gegen Kaution freibekommen; (*fig*) jdm aus der Patsche helfen

bait /beɪt/ *n* Köder *m* ● *vt* mit einem Köder versehen; (*fig: torment*) reizen

bake /beɪk/ *vt*/*i* backen

baker /'beɪkə(r)/ *n* Bäcker *m*; ~**'s [shop]** Bäckerei *f*. ~**y** *n* Bäckerei *f*

baking /'beɪkɪŋ/ *n* Backen *nt*. ~**-powder** *n* Backpulver *nt*

balance /'bæləns/ *n* (*equilibrium*) Gleichgewicht *nt*, Balance *f*; (*scales*) Waage *f*; (*Comm*) Saldo *m*; (*outstanding sum*) Restbetrag *m*; **[bank]** ~ Kontostand *m*; **in the** ~ (*fig*) in der Schwebe ● *vt* balancieren; (*equalize*) ausgleichen; (*Comm*) abschließen <*books*> ● *vi* balancieren; (*fig & Comm*) sich ausgleichen. ~**d** *a* ausgewogen

balcony /'bælkənɪ/ *n* Balkon *m*

bald /bɔːld/ *a* (**-er, -est**) kahl; <*person*> kahlköpfig

bald|ly *adv* unverblümt. ~**ness** *n* Kahlköpfigkeit *f*

ball[1] /bɔːl/ *n* Ball *m*; (*Billiards, Croquet*) Kugel *f*; (*of yarn*) Knäuel *m & nt*; **on the** ~ [!] auf Draht

ball[2] *n* (*dance*) Ball *m*

ball-'bearing *n* Kugellager *nt*

ballerina /bælə'riːnə/ *n* Ballerina *f*

ballet /'bæleɪ/ *m* Ballett *nt*. ~ **dancer** *n* Balletttänzer(in) *m*(*f*)

balloon /bə'luːn/ *n* Luftballon *m*; (*Aviat*) Ballon *m*

ballot /'bælət/ *n* [geheime] Wahl *f*; (*on issue*) [geheime] Abstimmung *f*. ~**-box** *n* Wahlurne *f*. ~**-paper** *n* Stimmzettel *m*

ball: ~**point ['pen]** *n* Kugelschreiber *m*. ~**room** *n* Ballsaal *m*

balm /bɑːm/ *n* Balsam *m*

balmy /'bɑːmɪ/ *a* (**-ier, -iest**) *a* sanft

Baltic /'bɔːltɪk/ *a & n* **the** ~ **[Sea]** die Ostsee

bamboo /bæm'buː/ *n* Bambus *m*

ban /bæn/ *n* Verbot *nt* ● *vt* (*pt*/*pp* **banned**) verbieten

banal /bə'nɑːl/ *a* banal. ~**ity** /-'ælətɪ/ *n* Banalität *f*

banana /bə'nɑːnə/ *n* Banane *f*

band /bænd/ *n* Band *nt*; (*stripe*) Streifen *m*; (*group*) Schar *f*; (*Mus*) Kapelle *f*

bandage /ˈbændɪdʒ/ *n* Verband *m*; (*for support*) Bandage *f* ● *vt* verbinden; bandagieren <*limb*>

b. & b. *abbr of* **bed and breakfast**

bandit /ˈbændɪt/ *n* Bandit *m*

band: ~stand *n* Musikpavillon *m*. **~wagon** *n* **jump on the ~wagon** (*fig*) sich einer erfolgreichen Sache anschließen

bang /bæŋ/ *n* (*noise*) Knall *m*; (*blow*) Schlag *m* ● *adv* **go ~** knallen ● *int* bums! peng! ● *vt* knallen; (*shut noisily*) zuknallen; (*strike*) schlagen auf (+ *acc*); **~ one's head** sich (*dat*) den Kopf stoßen (**on** an + *acc*) ● *vi* schlagen; <*door*:> zuknallen

banger /ˈbæŋə(r)/ *n* (*firework*) Knallfrosch *m*; ([!] *sausage*) Wurst *f*; **old ~** ([!] *car*) Klapperkiste *f*

bangle /ˈbæŋgl/ *n* Armreifen *m*

banish /ˈbænɪʃ/ *vt* verbannen

banisters /ˈbænɪstəz/ *npl* [Treppen]geländer *nt*

banjo /ˈbændʒəʊ/ *n* Banjo *nt*

bank¹ /bæŋk/ *n* (*of river*) Ufer *nt*; (*slope*) Hang *m* ● *vi* (*Aviat*) in die Kurve gehen

bank² *n* Bank *f* ● **~ on** *vt* sich verlassen auf (+ *acc*)

ˈbank account *n* Bankkonto *nt*

banker /ˈbæŋkə(r)/ *n* Bankier *m*

bank: ~ ˈholiday *n* gesetzlicher Feiertag *m*. **~ing** *n* Bankwesen *nt*. **~note** *n* Banknote *f*

bankrupt /ˈbæŋkrʌpt/ *a* bankrott; **go ~** Bankrott machen ● *n* Bankrotteur *m* ● *vt* Bankrott machen. **~cy** *n* Bankrott *m*

banner /ˈbænə(r)/ *n* Banner *nt*; (*carried by demonstrators*) Transparent *nt*, Spruchband *nt*

banquet /ˈbæŋkwɪt/ *n* Bankett *nt*

baptism /ˈbæptɪzm/ *n* Taufe *f*

baptize /bæpˈtaɪz/ *vt* taufen

bar /bɑː(r)/ *n* Stange *f*; (*of cage*) [Gitter]stab *m*; (*of gold*) Barren *m*; (*of chocolate*) Tafel *f*; (*of soap*) Stück *nt*; (*long*) Riegel *m*; (*café*) Bar *f*; (*counter*) Theke *f*; (*Mus*) Takt *m*; (*fig: obstacle*) Hindernis *nt*; **parallel ~s** (*Sport*) Barren *m*; **behind ~s** [!] hinter Gittern ● *vt* (*pt/pp* **barred**) versperren <*way, door*>; ausschließen <*person*>

barbar|ic /bɑːˈbærɪk/ *a* barbarisch. **~ity** *n* Barbarei *f*. **~ous** /ˈbɑːbərəs/ *a* barbarisch

barbecue /ˈbɑːbɪkjuː/ *n* Grill *m*; (*party*) Grillfest *nt* ● *vt* [im Freien] grillen

barbed /ˈbɑːbd/ *a* **~ wire** Stacheldraht *m*

barber /ˈbɑːbə(r)/ *n* [Herren]friseur *m*

ˈbar code *n* Strichkode *m*

bare /beə(r)/ *a* (**-r, -st**) nackt, bloß; <*tree*> kahl; (*empty*) leer; (*mere*) bloß

bare: ~back *adv* ohne Sattel. **~faced** *a* schamlos. **~foot** *adv* barfuß. **~ˈheaded** *a* mit unbedecktem Kopf

barely /ˈbeəlɪ/ *adv* kaum

bargain /ˈbɑːgɪn/ *n* (*agreement*) Geschäft *nt*; (*good buy*) Gelegenheitskauf *m*; **into the ~** noch dazu; **make a ~** sich einigen ● *vi* handeln; (*haggle*) feilschen; **~ for** (*expect*) rechnen mit

barge /bɑːdʒ/ *n* Lastkahn *m*; (*towed*) Schleppkahn *m* ● *vi* **~ in** [!] hereinplatzen

baritone /ˈbærɪtəʊn/ *n* Bariton *m*

bark¹ /bɑːk/ *n* (*of tree*) Rinde *f*

bark² *n* Bellen *nt* ● *vi* bellen

barley /ˈbɑːlɪ/ *n* Gerste *f*

bar: ~maid *n* Schankmädchen *nt*. **~man** Barmann *m*

barmy /ˈbɑːmɪ/ *a* [!] verrückt
barn /bɑːn/ *n* Scheune *f*
barometer /bəˈrɒmɪtə(r)/ *n* Barometer *nt*
baron /ˈbærn/ *n* Baron *m*. **~ess** *n* Baronin *f*
barracks /ˈbærəks/ *npl* Kaserne *f*
barrage /ˈbærɑːʒ/ *n* (*in river*) Wehr *nt*; (*Mil*) Sperrfeuer *nt*; (*fig*) Hagel *m*
barrel /ˈbærl/ *n* Fass *nt*; (*of gun*) Lauf *m*; (*of cannon*) Rohr *nt*. **~-organ** *n* Drehorgel *f*
barren /ˈbærn/ *a* unfruchtbar; <*landscape*> öde
barricade /bærɪˈkeɪd/ *n* Barrikade *f* ● *vt* verbarrikadieren
barrier /ˈbærɪə(r)/ *n* Barriere *f*; (*across road*) Schranke *f*; (*Rail*) Sperre *f*; (*fig*) Hindernis *nt*
barrow /ˈbærəʊ/ *n* Karre *f*, Karren *m*
base /beɪs/ *n* Fuß *m*; (*fig*) Basis *f*; (*Mil*) Stützpunkt *m* ● *vt* stützen (**on** auf + *acc*); **be ~d on** basieren auf (+ *dat*)
base: ~ball *n* Baseball *m*. **~less** *a* unbegründet. **~ment** *n* Kellergeschoss *nt*
bash /bæʃ/ *n* Schlag *m*; **have a ~!** [!] probier es mal! ● *vt* hauen
basic /ˈbeɪsɪk/ *a* Grund-; (*fundamental*) grundlegend; (*essential*) wesentlich; (*unadorned*) einfach; **the ~s** das Wesentliche. **~ally** *adv* grundsätzlich
basin /ˈbeɪsn/ *n* Becken *nt*; (*for washing*) Waschbecken *nt*; (*for food*) Schüssel *f*
basis /ˈbeɪsɪs/ *n* (*pl* **-ses** /-siːz/) Basis *f*
bask /bɑːsk/ *vi* sich sonnen
basket /ˈbɑːskɪt/ *n* Korb *m*. **~ball** *n* Basketball *m*
Basle /bɑːl/ *n* Basel *nt*
bass /beɪs/ *a* Bass-; **~ voice** Bassstimme *f* ● *n* Bass *m*; (*person*) Bassist *m*
bassoon /bəˈsuːn/ *n* Fagott *nt*
bastard /ˈbɑːstəd/ *n* [✖] Schuft *m*
bat[1] /bæt/ *n* Schläger *m*; **off one's own ~** [!] auf eigene Faust ● *vt* (*pt/pp* **batted**) schlagen; **not ~ an eyelid** (*fig*) nicht mit der Wimper zucken
bat[2] *n* (*Zool*) Fledermaus *f*
batch /bætʃ/ *n* (*of people*) Gruppe *f*; (*of papers*) Stoß *m*; (*of goods*) Sendung *f*; (*of bread*) Schub *m*
bath /bɑːθ/ *n* (*pl* **-s** /bɑːðz/) Bad *nt*; (*tub*) Badewanne *f*; **~s** *pl* Badeanstalt *f*; **have a ~** baden
bathe /beɪð/ *n* Bad *nt* ● *vt/i* baden. **~r** *n* Badende(r) *m/f*
bathing /ˈbeɪðɪŋ/ *n* Baden *nt*. **~-cap** *n* Bademütze *f*. **~-costume** *n* Badeanzug *m*
bath: ~-mat *n* Bedematte *f*. **~room** *n* Badezimmer *nt*. **~-towel** *n* Badetuch *nt*
battalion /bəˈtælɪən/ *n* Bataillon *nt*
batter /ˈbætə(r)/ *n* (*Culin*) flüssiger Teig *m* ● *vt* schlagen. **~ed** *a* <*car*> verbeult; <*wife*> misshandelt
battery /ˈbætərɪ/ *n* Batterie *f*
battle /ˈbætl/ *n* Schlacht *f*; (*fig*) Kampf *m* ● *vi* (*fig*) kämpfen (**for** um)
battle: ~field *n* Schlachtfeld *nt*. **~ship** *n* Schlachtschiff *nt*
batty /ˈbætɪ/ *a* [!] verrückt
Bavaria /bəˈveərɪə/ *n* Bayern *nt*. **~n** *a* bayrisch ● *n* Bayer(in) *m(f)*
bawl /bɔːl/ *vt/i* brüllen
bay[1] /beɪ/ *n* (*Geog*) Bucht *f*; (*Archit*) Erker *m*
bay[2] *n* (*Bot*) [echter] Lorbeer *m*. **~-leaf** *n* Lorbeerblatt *nt*
bayonet /ˈbeɪənet/ *n* Bajonett *nt*

bay 'window *n* Erkerfenster *nt*
bazaar /bə'zɑ:(r)/ *n* Basar *m*
BC *abbr* (**before Christ**) v. Chr.

be /bi:/

(*pres* **am, are, is**, *pl* **are**; *pt* **was**, *pl* **were**; *pp* **been**)

● *intransitive verb*

....➤ (*expressing identity, nature, state, age etc.*) sein. **he is a teacher** er ist Lehrer. **she is French** sie ist Französin. **he is very nice** er ist sehr nett. **I am tall** ich bin groß. **you are thirty** du bist dreißig. **it was very cold** es war sehr kalt

....➤ (*expressing general position*) sein; (*lie*) liegen; (*stand*) stehen. **where is the bank?** wo ist die Bank? **the book is on the table** das Buch liegt auf dem Tisch. **the vase is on the shelf** die Vase steht auf dem Brett

....➤ (*feel*) **I am cold/hot** mir ist kalt/heiß. **I am ill** ich bin krank. **I am well** mir geht es gut. **how are you?** wie geht es Ihnen?

....➤ (*date*) **it is the 5th today** heute haben wir den Fünften

....➤ (*go, come, stay*) sein. **I have been to Vienna** ich bin in Wien gewesen. **have you ever been to London?** bist du schon einmal in London gewesen? **has the postman been?** war der Briefträger schon da? **I've been here for an hour** ich bin seit einer Stunde hier

....➤ (*origin*) **where are you from?** woher stammen *od* kommen Sie? **she is from Australia** sie stammt *od* ist aus Australien

....➤ (*cost*) kosten. **how much are the eggs?** was kosten die Eier?

....➤ (*in calculations*) **two threes are six** zweimal drei ist *od* sind sechs

....➤ (*exist*) **there is/are** es gibt (+ *acc*). **there's no fish left** es gibt keinen Fisch mehr

● *auxiliary verb*

....➤ (*forming continuous tenses: not translated*) **I'm working** ich arbeite. **I'm leaving tomorrow** ich reise morgen [ab]. **they were singing** sie sangen. **they will be coming on Tuesday** sie kommen am Dienstag

....➤ (*forming passive*) werden. **the child was found** das Kind wurde gefunden. **German is spoken here** hier wird Deutsch gesprochen; hier spricht man Deutsch

....➤ (*expressing arrangement, obligation, destiny*) sollen. **I am to go/inform you** ich soll gehen/ Sie unterrichten. **they were to fly today** sie sollten heute fliegen. **you are to do that immediately** das sollst du sofort machen. **you are not to ...** (*prohibition*) du darfst nicht .... **they were never to meet again** (*destiny*) sie sollten sich nie wieder treffen

....➤ (*in short answers*) **Are you disappointed? — Yes I am** Bist du enttäuscht? — Ja. (*negating previous statement*) **Aren't you coming? — Yes I am!** Kommst du nicht? — Doch!

....➤ (*in tag questions*) **isn't it? wasn't she? aren't they?** *etc.* nicht wahr. **it's a beautiful house, isn't it?** das Haus ist sehr schön, nicht wahr?

beach /bi:tʃ/ *n* Strand *m*
bead /bi:d/ *n* Perle *f*
beak /bi:k/ *n* Schnabel *m*
beam /bi:m/ *n* Balken *m*; (*of light*) Strahl *m* ● *vi* strahlen. **~ing** *a* [freude]strahlend
bean /bi:n/ *n* Bohne *f*
bear¹ /beə(r)/ *n* Bär *m*

bear² *vt/i* (*pt* **bore**, *pp* **borne**) tragen; (*endure*) ertragen; gebären <*child*>; **~ right** sich rechts halten. **~able** /-əbl/ *a* erträglich

beard /bɪəd/ *n* Bart *m*. **~ed** *a* bärtig

bearer /'beərə(r)/ *n* Träger *m*; (*of news, cheque*) Überbringer *m*; (*of passport*) Inhaber(in) *m(f)*

bearing /'beərɪŋ/ *n* Haltung *f*; (*Techn*) Lager *nt*; **get one's ~s** sich orientieren

beast /bi:st/ *n* Tier *nt*; ([!] *person*) Biest *nt*

beastly /'bi:stlɪ/ *a* (**-ier, -iest**) [!] scheußlich; <*person*> gemein

beat /bi:t/ *n* Schlag *m*; (*of policeman*) Runde *f*; (*rhythm*) Takt *m* ● *vt/i* (*pt* **beat**, *pp* **beaten**) schlagen; (*thrash*) verprügeln; klopfen <*carpet*>; (*hammer*) hämmern (**on** an + *acc*); **~ it!** [!] hau ab! **it ~s me** [!] das begreife ich nicht. **~ up** *vt* zusammenschlagen

beat|en /'bi:tn/ *a* **off the ~en track** abseits. **~ing** *n* Prügel *pl*

beauti|ful /'bju:tɪfl/ *a*, **-ly** *adv* schön. **~fy** /-faɪ/ *vt* (*pt/pp* **-ied**) verschönern

beauty /'bju:tɪ/ *n* Schönheit *f*. **~ parlour** *n* Kosmetiksalon *m*. **~ spot** *n* Schönheitsfleck *m*; (*place*) landschaftlich besonders reizvolles Fleckchen *nt*.

beaver /'bi:və(r)/ *n* Biber *m*

became /bɪ'keɪm/ *see* **become**

because /bɪ'kɒz/ *conj* weil ● *adv* **~ of** wegen (+ *gen*)

becom|e /bɪ'kʌm/ *vt/i* (*pt* **became**, *pp* **become**) werden. **~ing** *a* <*clothes*> kleidsam

bed /bed/ *n* Bett *nt*; (*layer*) Schicht *f*; (*of flowers*) Beet *nt*; **in ~** im Bett; **go to ~** ins *od* zu Bett gehen; **~ and breakfast** Zimmer mit Frühstück. **~clothes** *npl*, **~ding** *n* Bettzeug *nt*. **~room** *n* Schlafzimmer *nt*

'bedside *n* **at his ~** an seinem Bett. **~ 'lamp** *n* Nachttischlampe *f*. **~ 'table** *n* Nachttisch *m*

bed: ~'sitter *n*, **~'sitting-room** *n* Wohnschlafzimmer *nt*. **~spread** *n* Tagesdecke *f*. **~time** *n* **at ~time** vor dem Schlafengehen

bee /bi:/ *n* Biene *f*

beech /bi:tʃ/ *n* Buche *f*

beef /bi:f/ *n* Rindfleisch *nt*. **~burger** *n* Hamburger *m*

bee: ~hive *n* Bienenstock *m*. **~line** *n* **make a ~line for** [!] zusteuern auf (+ *acc*)

been /bi:n/ *see* **be**

beer /bɪə(r)/ *n* Bier *nt*

beet /bi:t/ *n* (*Amer: beetroot*) Rote Bete *f*; **[sugar] ~** Zuckerrübe *f*

beetle /'bi:tl/ *n* Käfer *m*

'beetroot *n* Rote Bete *f*

before /bɪ'fɔ:(r)/ *prep* vor (+ *dat/acc*); **the day ~ yesterday** vorgestern; **~ long** bald ● *adv* vorher; (*already*) schon; **never ~** noch nie; **~ that** davor ● *conj* (*time*) ehe, bevor. **~hand** *adv* vorher, im Voraus

beg /beg/ *v* (*pt/pp* **begged**) ● *vi* betteln ● *vt* (*entreat*) anflehen; (*ask*) bitten (**for** um)

began /bɪ'gæn/ *see* **begin**

beggar /'begə(r)/ *n* Bettler(in) *m(f)*; [!] Kerl *m*

begin /bɪ'gɪn/ *vt/i* (*pt* **began**, *pp* **begun**, *pres p* **beginning**) anfangen, beginnen; **to ~ with** anfangs. **~ner** *n* Anfänger(in) *m(f)*. **~ning** *n* Anfang *m*, Beginn *m*

begun /bɪ'gʌn/ *see* **begin**

behalf /bɪ'hɑ:f/ *n* **on ~ of** im Namen von; **on my ~** meinetwegen

behave /bɪˈheɪv/ *vi* sich verhalten; ~ **oneself** sich benehmen
behaviour /bɪˈheɪvjə(r)/ *n* Verhalten *nt*; **good/bad** ~ gutes/schlechtes Benehmen *nt*
behind /bɪˈhaɪnd/ *prep* hinter (+ *dat/acc*); **be** ~ **sth** hinter etw (*dat*) stecken ● *adv* hinten; (*late*) im Rückstand; **a long way** ~ weit zurück ● *n* [!] Hintern *m*. ~**hand** *adv* im Rückstand
beige /beɪʒ/ *a* beige
being /ˈbiːɪŋ/ *n* Dasein *nt*; **living** ~ Lebewesen *nt*; **come into** ~ entstehen
belated /bɪˈleɪtɪd/ *a*, **-ly** *adv* verspätet
belfry /ˈbelfrɪ/ *n* Glockenstube *f*; (*tower*) Glockenturm *m*
Belgian /ˈbeldʒən/ *a* belgisch ● *n* Belgier(in) *m(f)*
Belgium /ˈbeldʒəm/ *n* Belgien *nt*
belief /bɪˈliːf/ *n* Glaube *m*
believable /bɪˈliːvəbl/ *a* glaubhaft
believe /bɪˈliːv/ *vt/i* glauben (**s.o.** jdm; **in** an + *acc*). ~**r** *n* (*Relig*) Gläubige(r) *m/f*
belittle /bɪˈlɪtl/ *vt* herabsetzen
bell /bel/ *n* Glocke *f*; (*on door*) Klingel *f*
bellow /ˈbeləʊ/ *vt/i* brüllen
belly /ˈbelɪ/ *n* Bauch *m*
belong /bɪˈlɒŋ/ *vi* gehören (**to** *dat*); (*be member*) angehören (**to** *dat*). ~**ings** *npl* Sachen *pl*
beloved /bɪˈlʌvɪd/ *a* geliebt ● *n* Geliebte(r) *m/f*
below /bɪˈləʊ/ *prep* unter (+ *dat/acc*) ● *adv* unten; (*Naut*) unter Deck
belt /belt/ *n* Gürtel *m*; (*area*) Zone *f*; (*Techn*) [Treib]riemen *m* ● *vi* ([!] *rush*) rasen ● *vt* ([!] *hit*) hauen
bench /bentʃ/ *n* Bank *f*; (*work-*) Werkbank *f*
bend /bend/ *n* Biegung *f*; (*in road*) Kurve *f*; **round the** ~ [!] verrückt ● *v* (*pt/pp* **bent**) ● *vt* biegen; beugen <*arm, leg*> ● *vi* sich bücken; <*thing*:> sich biegen; <*road*:> eine Biegung machen. ~ **down** *vi* sich bücken. ~ **over** *vi* sich vornüberbeugen
beneath /bɪˈniːθ/ *prep* unter (+ *dat/acc*); ~ **him** (*fig*) unter seiner Würde ● *adv* darunter
benefactor /ˈbenɪfæktə(r)/ *n* Wohltäter(in) *m(f)*
beneficial /benɪˈfɪʃl/ *a* nützlich
benefit /ˈbenɪfɪt/ *n* Vorteil *m*; (*allowance*) Unterstützung *f*; (*insurance*) Leistung *f*; **sickness** ~ Krankengeld *nt* ● *v* (*pt/pp* **-fited**, *pres p* **-fiting**) ● *vt* nützen (+ *dat*) ● *vi* profitieren (**from** von)
benevolen|ce /bɪˈnevələns/ *n* Wohlwollen *nt*. ~**t** *a*, **-ly** *adv* wohlwollend
bent /bent/ *see* **bend** ● *a* <*person*> gebeugt; (*distorted*) verbogen; ([!] *dishonest*) korrupt; **be** ~ **on doing sth** darauf erpicht sein, etw zu tun ● *n* Hang *m*, Neigung *f* (**for** zu); **artistic** ~ künstlerische Ader *f*
bequeath /bɪˈkwiːð/ *vt* vermachen (**to** *dat*)
bereave|d /bɪˈriːvd/ *n* **the** ~**d** *pl* die Hinterbliebenen
beret /ˈbereɪ/ *n* Baskenmütze *f*
Berne /bɜːn/ *n* Bern *nt*
berry /ˈberɪ/ *n* Beere *f*
berth /bɜːθ/ *n* (*on ship*) [Schlaf]koje *f*; (*ship's anchorage*) Liegeplatz *m*; **give a wide** ~ **to** [!] einen großen Bogen machen um
beside /bɪˈsaɪd/ *prep* neben (+ *dat/acc*); ~ **oneself** außer sich (*dat*)
besides /bɪˈsaɪdz/ *prep* außer (+ *dat*) ● *adv* außerdem

besiege /bɪ'si:dʒ/ *vt* belagern

best /best/ *a & n* beste(r,s); **the ~** der/die/das Beste; **at ~** bestenfalls; **all the ~!** alles Gute! **do one's ~** sein Bestes tun; **the ~ part of a year** fast ein Jahr; **to the ~ of my knowledge** so viel ich weiß; **make the ~ of it** das Beste daraus machen ● *adv* am besten; **as ~ I could** so gut ich konnte. **~ 'man** *n* ≈ Trauzeuge *m*. **~'seller** *n* Bestseller *m*

bet /bet/ *n* Wette *f* ● *v* (*pt/pp* **bet** *or* **betted**) ● *vt* **~ s.o. £5** mit jdm um £5 wetten ● *vi* wetten; **~ on** [Geld] setzen auf (+ *acc*)

betray /bɪ'treɪ/ *vt* verraten. **~al** *n* Verrat *m*

better /'betə(r)/ *a* besser; **get ~** sich bessern; (*after illness*) sich erholen ● *adv* besser; **~ off** besser dran; **~ not** lieber nicht; **all the ~** umso besser; **the sooner the ~** je eher, desto besser; **think ~ of it** sich eines Besseren besinnen; **you'd ~ stay** du bleibst am besten hier ● *vt* verbessern; (*do better than*) übertreffen; **~ oneself** sich verbessern

between /bɪ'twi:n/ *prep* zwischen (+ *dat*/*acc*); **~ you and me** unter uns; **~ us** (*together*) zusammen ● *adv* **[in] ~** dazwischen

beware /bɪ'weə(r)/ *vi* sich in Acht nehmen (**of** vor + *dat*); **~ of the dog!** Vorsicht, bissiger Hund!

bewilder /bɪ'wɪldə(r)/ *vt* verwirren. **~ment** *n* Verwirrung *f*

bewitch /bɪ'wɪtʃ/ *vt* verzaubern; (*fig*) bezaubern

beyond /bɪ'jɒnd/ *prep* über (+ *acc*) ... hinaus; (*further*) weiter als; **~ reach** außer Reichweite; **~ doubt** ohne jeden Zweifel; **it's ~ me** [!] das geht über meinen Horizont ● *adv* darüber hinaus

bias /'baɪəs/ *n* Voreingenommenheit *f*; (*preference*) Vorliebe *f*; (*Jur*) Befangenheit *f* ● *vt* (*pt*/*pp* **biased**) (*influence*) beeinflussen. **~ed** *a* voreingenommen; (*Jur*) befangen

bib /bɪb/ *n* Lätzchen *nt*

Bible /'baɪbl/ *n* Bibel *f*

biblical /'bɪblɪkl/ *a* biblisch

bibliography /bɪblɪ'ɒgrəfɪ/ *n* Bibliographie *f*

bicycle /'baɪsɪkl/ *n* Fahrrad *nt* ● *vi* mit dem Rad fahren

bid /bɪd/ *n* Gebot *nt*; (*attempt*) Versuch *m* ● *vt*/*i* (*pt*/*pp* **bid**, *pres p* **bidding**) bieten (**for** auf + *acc*); (*Cards*) reizen

bidder /'bɪdə(r)/ *n* Bieter(in) *m(f)*

bide /baɪd/ *vt* **~ one's time** den richtigen Moment abwarten

big /bɪg/ *a* (**bigger, biggest**) groß ● *adv* **talk ~** [!] angeben

bigam|ist /'bɪgəmɪst/ *n* Bigamist *m*. **~y** *n* Bigamie *f*

big-'headed *a* [!] eingebildet

bigot /'bɪgət/ *n* Eiferer *m*. **~ed** *a* engstirnig

'bigwig *n* [!] hohes Tier *nt*

bike /baɪk/ *n* [!] [Fahr]rad *nt*

bikini /bɪ'ki:nɪ/ *n* Bikini *m*

bile /baɪl/ *n* Galle *f*

bilingual /baɪ'lɪŋgwəl/ *a* zweisprachig

bilious /'bɪljəs/ *a* (*Med*) **~ attack** verdorbener Magen *m*

bill[1] /bɪl/ *n* Rechnung *f*; (*poster*) Plakat *nt*; (*Pol*) Gesetzentwurf *m*; (*Amer: note*) Banknote *f*; **~ of exchange** Wechsel *m* ● *vt* eine Rechnung schicken (+ *dat*)

bill[2] *n* (*beak*) Schnabel *m*

'billfold *n* (*Amer*) Brieftasche *f*

billiards /'bɪljədz/ *n* Billard *nt*

billion /'bɪljən/ *n* (*thousand million*) Milliarde *f*; (*million million*) Billion *f*
bin /bɪn/ *n* Mülleimer *m*; (*for bread*) Kasten *m*
bind /baɪnd/ *vt* (*pt/pp* **bound**) binden (**to** an + *acc*); (*bandage*) verbinden; (*Jur*) verpflichten; (*cover the edge of*) einfassen. **~ing** *a* verbindlich ● *n* Einband *m*; (*braid*) Borte *f*; (*on ski*) Bindung *f*
binge /bɪndʒ/ *n* [!] **go on the ~** eine Sauftour machen
binoculars /bɪ'nɒkjʊləz/ *npl* **[pair of] ~** Fernglas *nt*
bio|'chemistry /baɪəʊ-/ *n* Biochemie *f*. **~degradable** /-dɪ'greɪdəbl/ *a* biologisch abbaubar
biograph|er /baɪ'ɒgrəfə(r)/ *n* Biograph(in) *m(f)*. **~y** *n* Biographie *f*
biological /baɪə'lɒdʒɪkl/ *a* biologisch
biolog|ist /baɪ'ɒlədʒɪst/ *n* Biologe *m*. **~y** *n* Biologie *f*
bio'terrorism /baɪəʊ-/ *n* Bioterrorismus *m*
birch /bɜːtʃ/ *n* Birke *f*; (*whip*) Rute *f*
bird /bɜːd/ *n* Vogel *m*; ([!] *girl*) Mädchen *nt*; **kill two ~s with one stone** zwei Fliegen mit einer Klappe schlagen
Biro (P) /'baɪrəʊ/ *n* Kugelschreiber *m*
birth /bɜːθ/ *n* Geburt *f*
birth: ~ certificate *n* Geburtsurkunde *f*. **~-control** *n* Geburtenregelung *f*. **~day** *n* Geburtstag *m*. **~-rate** *n* Geburtenziffer *f*
biscuit /'bɪskɪt/ *n* Keks *m*
bishop /'bɪʃəp/ *n* Bischof *m*
bit¹ /bɪt/ *n* Stückchen *nt*; (*for horse*) Gebiss *nt*; (*Techn*) Bohreinsatz *m*; **a ~** ein bisschen; **~ by ~** nach und nach; **a ~ of bread** ein bisschen Brot; **do one's ~** sein Teil tun
bit² *see* **bite**
bitch /bɪtʃ/ *n* Hündin *f*; [x] Luder *nt*. **~y** *a* gehässig
bit|e /baɪt/ *n* Biss *m*; **[insect] ~** Stich *m*; (*mouthful*) Bissen *m* ● *vt/i* (*pt* **bit**, *pp* **bitten**) beißen; <*insect:*> stechen; kauen <*one's nails*>. **~ing** *a* beißend
bitten /'bɪtn/ *see* **bite**
bitter /'bɪtə(r)/ *a*, **-ly** *adv* bitter; **~ly cold** bitterkalt ● *n* bitteres Bier *nt*. **~ness** *n* Bitterkeit *f*
bizarre /bɪ'zɑː(r)/ *a* bizarr
black /blæk/ *a* (**-er, -est**) schwarz; **be ~and blue** grün und blau sein ● *n* Schwarz *nt*; (*person*) Schwarze(r) *m/f* ● *vt* schwärzen; boykottieren <*goods*>
black: ~berry *n* Brombeere *f*. **~bird** *n* Amsel *f*. **~board** *n* (*Sch*) [Wand]tafel *f*. **~'currant** *n* schwarze Johannisbeere *f*
blacken *vt/i* schwärzen
black: ~ 'eye *n* blaues Auge *nt*. **B~ 'Forest** *n* Schwarzwald *m*. **~ 'ice** *n* Glatteis *nt*. **~list** *vt* auf die schwarze Liste setzen. **~mail** *n* Erpressung *f* ● *vt* erpressen. **~mailer** *n* Erpresser(in) *m(f)*. **~ 'market** *n* schwarzer Markt *m*. **~-out** *n* **have a ~-out** (*Med*) das Bewusstsein verlieren. **~ 'pudding** *n* Blutwurst *f*
bladder /'blædə(r)/ *n* (*Anat*) Blase *f*
blade /bleɪd/ *n* Klinge *f*; (*of grass*) Halm *m*
blame /bleɪm/ *n* Schuld *f* ● *vt* die Schuld geben (+ *dat*); **no one is to ~** keiner ist schuld daran. **~less** *a* schuldlos
bland /blænd/ *a* (**-er, -est**) mild
blank /blæŋk/ *a* leer; <*look*> ausdruckslos ● *n* Lücke *f*; (*cartridge*) Platzpatrone *f*. **~ 'cheque** *n* Blankoscheck *m*

blanket /ˈblæŋkɪt/ *n* Decke *f*; **wet ~** [!] Spielverderber(in) *m(f)*
blare /bleə(r)/ *vt/i* schmettern
blasé /ˈblɑːzeɪ/ *a* blasiert
blast /blɑːst/ *n* (*gust*) Luftstoß *m*; (*sound*) Schmettern *nt*; (*of horn*) Tuten *nt* ● *vt* sprengen ● *int* [✖] verdammt. **~ed** *a* [✖] verdammt
ˈblast-off *n* (*of missile*) Start *m*
blatant /ˈbleɪtənt/ *a* offensichtlich
blaze /bleɪz/ *n* Feuer *nt* ● *vi* brennen
blazer /ˈbleɪzə(r)/ *n* Blazer *m*
bleach /bliːtʃ/ *n* Bleichmittel *nt* ● *vt/i* bleichen
bleak /bliːk/ *a* (**-er, -est**) öde; (*fig*) trostlos
bleary-eyed /ˈblɪərɪ-/ *a* mit trüben/(*on waking up*) verschlafenen Augen
bleat /bliːt/ *vi* blöken
bleed /bliːd/ *v* (*pt/pp* **bled**) ● *vi* bluten ● *vt* entlüften <*radiator*>
bleep /bliːp/ *n* Piepton *m* ● *vi* piepsen ● *vt* mit dem Piepser rufen. **~er** *n* Piepser *m*
blemish /ˈblemɪʃ/ *n* Makel *m*
blend /blend/ *n* Mischung *f* ● *vt* mischen ● *vi* sich vermischen
bless /bles/ *vt* segnen. **~ed** /ˈblesɪd/ *a* heilig; [✖] verflixt. **~ing** *n* Segen *m*
blew /bluː/ *see* **blow²**
blight /blaɪt/ *n* (*Bot*) Brand *m*
blind /blaɪnd/ *a* blind; <*corner*> unübersichtlich; **~ man/woman** Blinde(r) *m/f* ● *n* **[roller] ~** Rouleau *nt* ● *vt* blenden
blind: ~ ˈalley *n* Sackgasse *f*. **~fold** *a & adv* mit verbundenen Augen ● *n* Augenbinde *f* ● *vt* die Augen verbinden (+ *dat*). **~ly** *adv* blindlings. **~ness** *n* Blindheit *f*
blink /blɪŋk/ *vi* blinzeln; <*light:*> blinken
bliss /blɪs/ *n* Glückseligkeit *f*. **~ful** *a* glücklich
blister /ˈblɪstə(r)/ *n* (*Med*) Blase *f*
blitz /blɪts/ *n* [!] Großaktion *f*
blizzard /ˈblɪzəd/ *n* Schneesturm *m*
bloated /ˈbləʊtɪd/ *a* aufgedunsen
blob /blɒb/ *n* Klecks *m*
block /blɒk/ *n* Block *m*; (*of wood*) Klotz *m*; (*of flats*) [Wohn]block *m* ● *vt* blockieren. **~ up** *vt* zustopfen
blockade /blɒˈkeɪd/ *n* Blockade *f* ● *vt* blockieren
blockage /ˈblɒkɪdʒ/ *n* Verstopfung *f*
block: ~head *n* [!] Dummkopf *m*. **~ ˈletters** *npl* Blockschrift *f*
bloke /bləʊk/ *n* [!] Kerl *m*
blonde /blɒnd/ *a* blond ● *n* Blondine *f*
blood /blʌd/ *n* Blut *nt*
blood: ~-curdling *a* markerschütternd. **~ donor** *n* Blutspender *m*. **~ group** *n* Blutgruppe *f*. **~hound** *n* Bluthund *m*. **~-poisoning** *n* Blutvergiftung *f*. **~ pressure** *n* Blutdruck *m*. **~shed** *n* Blutvergießen *nt*. **~shot** *a* blutunterlaufen. **~ sports** *npl* Jagdsport *m*. **~-stained** *a* blutbefleckt. **~ test** *n* Blutprobe *f*. **~thirsty** *a* blutdürstig. **~-vessel** *n* Blutgefäß *nt*
bloody /ˈblʌdɪ/ *a* (**-ier, -iest**) blutig; [✖] verdammt. **~-ˈminded** *a* [✖] stur
bloom /bluːm/ *n* Blüte *f* ● *vi* blühen
blossom /ˈblɒsəm/ *n* Blüte *f* ● *vi* blühen
blot /blɒt/ *n* [Tinten]klecks *m*; (*fig*) Fleck *m* ● **~ out** *vt* (*fig*) auslöschen
blotch /blɒtʃ/ *n* Fleck *m*. **~y** *a* fleckig

'**blotting-paper** *n* Löschpapier *nt*
blouse /blaʊz/ *n* Bluse *f*
blow[1] /bləʊ/ *n* Schlag *m*
blow[2] *v* (*pt* **blew**, *pp* **blown**) ● *vt* blasen; (*fam; squander*) verpulvern; ~ **one's nose** sich (*dat*) die Nase putzen ● *vi* blasen; <*fuse:*> durchbrennen. ~ **away** *vt* wegblasen ● *vi* wegfliegen. ~ **down** *vt* umwehen ● *vi* umfallen. ~ **out** *vt* (*extinguish*) ausblasen. ~ **over** *vi* umfallen; (*fig: die down*) vorübergehen. ~ **up** *vt* (*inflate*) aufblasen; (*enlarge*) vergrößern; (*shatter by explosion*) sprengen ● *vi* explodieren
'**blowlamp** *n* Lötlampe *f*
blown /bləʊn/ *see* **blow**[2]
'**blowtorch** *n* (*Amer*) Lötlampe *f*
blowy /'bləʊɪ/ *a* windig
blue /bluː/ *a* (**-r**, **-st**) blau; **feel** ~ deprimiert sein ● *n* Blau *nt*; **have the** ~**s** deprimiert sein; **out of the** ~ aus heiterem Himmel
blue: ~**bell** *n* Sternhyazinthe *f*. ~**berry** *n* Heidelbeere *f*. ~**bottle** *n* Schmeißfliege *f*. ~ **film** *n* Pornofilm *m*. ~**print** *n* (*fig*) Entwurf *m*
bluff /blʌf/ *n* Bluff *m* ● *vi* bluffen
blunder /'blʌndə(r)/ *n* Schnitzer *m* ● *vi* einen Schnitzer machen
blunt /blʌnt/ *a* stumpf; <*person*> geradeheraus. ~**ly** *adv* unverblümt, geradeheraus
blur /blɜː(r)/ *n* **it's all a** ~ alles ist verschwommen ● *vt* (*pt*/*pp* **blurred**) verschwommen machen; ~**red** verschwommen
blush /blʌʃ/ *n* Erröten *nt* ● *vi* erröten
bluster /'blʌstə(r)/ *n* Großtuerei *f*. ~**y** *a* windig
boar /bɔː(r)/ *n* Eber *m*
board /bɔːd/ *n* Brett *nt*; (*for notices*) schwarzes Brett *nt*; (*committee*) Ausschuss *m*; (*of directors*) Vorstand *m*; **on** ~ an Bord; **full** ~ Vollpension *f*; ~ **and lodging** Unterkunft und Verpflegung *pl* ● *vt* einsteigen in (+ *acc*); (*Naut, Aviat*) besteigen ● *vi* an Bord gehen. ~ **up** *vt* mit Brettern verschlagen
boarder /'bɔːdə(r)/ *n* Pensionsgast *m*; (*Sch*) Internatsschüler(in) *m*(*f*)
board: ~**-game** *n* Brettspiel *nt*. ~**ing-house** *n* Pension *f*. ~**ing-school** *n* Internat *nt*
boast /bəʊst/ *vt* sich rühmen (+ *gen*) ● *vi* prahlen (**about** mit). ~**ful** *a*, **-ly** *adv* prahlerisch
boat /bəʊt/ *n* Boot *nt*; (*ship*) Schiff *nt*
bob /bɒb/ *vi* (*pt*/*pp* **bobbed**) ~ **up and down** sich auf und ab bewegen
'**bob-sleigh** *n* Bob *m*
bodily /'bɒdɪlɪ/ *a* körperlich ● *adv* (*forcibly*) mit Gewalt
body /'bɒdɪ/ *n* Körper *m*; (*corpse*) Leiche *f*; (*corporation*) Körperschaft *f*. ~**guard** *n* Leibwächter *m*. ~**work** *n* (*Auto*) Karosserie *f*
bog /bɒg/ *n* Sumpf *m*
bogus /'bəʊgəs/ *a* falsch
boil[1] /bɔɪl/ *n* Furunkel *m*
boil[2] *n* **bring/come to the** ~ zum Kochen bringen/kommen ● *vt*/*i* kochen; ~**ed potatoes** Salzkartoffeln *pl*. ~ **down** *vi* (*fig*) hinauslaufen (**to** auf + *acc*). ~ **over** *vi* überkochen
boiler /'bɔɪlə(r)/ *n* Heizkessel *m*
'**boiling point** *n* Siedepunkt *m*
boisterous /'bɔɪstərəs/ *a* übermütig
bold /bəʊld/ *a* (**-er**, **-est**), **-ly** *adv* kühn; (*Typ*) fett. ~**ness** *n* Kühnheit *f*
bolster /'bəʊlstə(r)/ *n* Nackenrolle *f* ● *vt* ~ **up** Mut machen (+ *dat*)

bolt /bəʊlt/ *n* Riegel *m*; (*Techn*) Bolzen *m* ● *vt* schrauben (**to** an + *acc*); verriegeln <*door*>; hinunterschlingen <*food*> ● *vi* abhauen; <*horse:*> durchgehen

bomb /bɒm/ *n* Bombe *f* ● *vt* bombardieren

bombard /bɒm'bɑ:d/ *vt* beschießen; (*fig*) bombardieren

bombastic /bɒm'bæstɪk/ *a* bombastisch

bomber /'bɒmə(r)/ *n* (*Aviat*) Bomber *m*; (*person*) Bombenleger(in) *m(f)*

bond /bɒnd/ *n* (*fig*) Band *nt*; (*Comm*) Obligation *f*

bone /bəʊn/ *n* Knochen *m*; (*of fish*) Gräte *f* ● *vt* von den Knochen lösen <*meat*>; entgräten <*fish*>. **~-'dry** *a* knochentrocken

bonfire /'bɒn-/ *n* Gartenfeuer *nt*; (*celebratory*) Freudenfeuer *nt*

bonus /'bəʊnəs/ *n* Prämie *f*; (*gratuity*) Gratifikation *f*; (*fig*) Plus *nt*

bony /'bəʊnɪ/ *a* (**-ier, -iest**) knochig; <*fish*> grätig

boo /bu:/ *int* buh! ● *vt* ausbuhen ● *vi* buhen

boob /bu:b/ *n* ([!] *mistake*) Schnitzer *m*

book /bʊk/ *n* Buch *nt*; (*of tickets*) Heft *nt*; **keep the ~s** (*Comm*) die Bücher führen ● *vt/i* buchen; (*reserve*) [vor]bestellen; (*for offence*) aufschreiben

book: ~case *n* Bücherregal *nt*. **~-ends** *npl* Buchstützen *pl*. **~ing-office** *n* Fahrkartenschalter *m*. **~keeping** *n* Buchführung *f*. **~let** *n* Broschüre *f*. **~maker** *n* Buchmacher *m*. **~mark** *n* Lesezeichen *nt*. **~seller** *n* Buchhändler(in) *m(f)*. **~shop** *n* Buchhandlung *f*. **~stall** *n* Bücherstand *m*

boom /bu:m/ *n* (*Comm*) Hochkonjunktur *f*; (*upturn*) Aufschwung *m* ● *vi* dröhnen; (*fig*) blühen

boon /bu:n/ *n* Segen *m*

boost /bu:st/ *n* Auftrieb *m* ● *vt* Auftrieb geben (+ *dat*)

boot /bu:t/ *n* Stiefel *m*; (*Auto*) Kofferraum *m*

booth /bu:ð/ *n* Bude *f*; (*cubicle*) Kabine *f*

booty /'bu:tɪ/ *n* Beute *f*

booze /bu:z/ *n* [!] Alkohol *m* ● *vi* [!] saufen

border /'bɔ:də(r)/ *n* Rand *m*; (*frontier*) Grenze *f*; (*in garden*) Rabatte *f* ● *vi* **~ on** grenzen an (+ *acc*). **~line case** *n* Grenzfall *m*

bore[1] /bɔ:(r)/ *see* **bear[2]**

bor|e[2] *n* (*of gun*) Kaliber *nt*; (*person*) langweiliger Mensch *m*; (*thing*) langweilige Sache *f* ● *vt* langweilen; **be ~ed** sich langweilen. **~edom** *n* Langeweile *f*. **~ing** *a* langweilig

born /bɔ:n/ *pp* **be ~** geboren werden ● *a* geboren

borne /bɔ:n/ *see* **bear[2]**

borrow /'bɒrəʊ/ *vt* [sich (*dat*)] borgen *od* leihen (**from** von)

bosom /'bʊzm/ *n* Busen *m*

boss /bɒs/ *n* [!] Chef *m* ● *vt* herumkommandieren. **~y** *a* herrschsüchtig

botanical /bə'tænɪkl/ *a* botanisch

botan|ist /'bɒtənɪst/ *n* Botaniker(in) *m(f)*. **~y** *n* Botanik *f*

both /bəʊθ/ *a & pron* beide; **~[of] the children** beide Kinder; **~ of them** beide [von ihnen] ● *adv* **~ men and women** sowohl Männer als auch Frauen

bother /'bɒðə(r)/ *n* Mühe *f*; (*minor trouble*) Ärger *m* ● *int* [!] verflixt! ● *vt* belästigen; (*disturb*) stören ● *vi* sich kümmern (**about** um)

bottle /ˈbɒtl/ *n* Flasche *f* ● *vt* auf Flaschen abfüllen; (*preserve*) einmachen

bottle: ~-neck *n* (*fig*) Engpass *m*. **~-opener** *n* Flaschenöffner *m*

bottom /ˈbɒtəm/ *a* unterste(r,s) ● *n* (*of container*) Boden *m*; (*of river*) Grund *m*; (*of page, hill*) Fuß *m*; (*buttocks*) Hintern *m*; **at the ~** unten; **get to the ~ of sth** (*fig*) hinter etw (*acc*) kommen

bought /bɔ:t/ *see* **buy**

bounce /baʊns/ *vi* [auf]springen; <*cheque:*> [!] nicht gedeckt sein ● *vt* aufspringen lassen <*ball*>

bouncer /ˈbaʊnsə(r)/ *n* [!] Rausschmeißer *m*

bound¹ /baʊnd/ *n* Sprung *m* ● *vi* springen

bound² *see* **bind** ● *a* **~ for** <*ship*> mit Kurs auf (+ *acc*); **be ~ to do sth** etw bestimmt machen; (*obliged*) verpflichtet sein, etw zu machen

boundary /ˈbaʊndərɪ/ *n* Grenze *f*

bounds /baʊndz/ *npl* (*fig*) Grenzen *pl*; **out of ~** verboten

bouquet /bʊˈkeɪ/ *n* [Blumen]strauß *m*; (*of wine*) Bukett *nt*

bourgeois /ˈbʊəʒwɑ:/ *a* (*pej*) spießbürgerlich

bout /baʊt/ *n* (*Med*) Anfall *m*; (*Sport*) Kampf *m*

bow¹ /bəʊ/ *n* (*weapon & Mus*) Bogen *m*; (*knot*) Schleife *f*

bow² /baʊ/ *n* Verbeugung *f* ● *vi* sich verbeugen ● *vt* neigen <*head*>

bow³ /baʊ/ *n* (*Naut*) Bug *m*

bowel /ˈbaʊəl/ *n* Darm *m*. **~s** *pl* Eingeweide *pl*

bowl¹ /bəʊl/ *n* Schüssel *f*; (*shallow*) Schale *f*

bowl² *n* (*ball*) Kugel *f* ● *vt/i* werfen. **~ over** *vt* umwerfen

bowler /ˈbəʊlə(r)/ *n* (*Sport*) Werfer *m*

bowling /ˈbəʊlɪŋ/ *n* Kegeln *nt*. **~-alley** *n* Kegelbahn *f*

bowls /bəʊlz/ *n* Bowlsspiel *nt*

bow-ˈtie /bəʊ-/ *n* Fliege *f*

box¹ /bɒks/ *n* Schachtel *f*; (*wooden*) Kiste *f*; (*cardboard*) Karton *m*; (*Theat*) Loge *f*

box² *vt/i* (*Sport*) boxen

box|er /ˈbɒksə(r)/ *n* Boxer *m*. **~ing** *n* Boxen *nt*. **B~ing Day** *n* zweiter Weihnachtstag *m*

box: ~-office *n* (*Theat*) Kasse *f*. **~-room** *n* Abstellraum *m*

boy /bɔɪ/ *n* Junge *m*

boycott /ˈbɔɪkɒt/ *n* Boykott *m* ● *vt* boykottieren

boy: ~friend *n* Freund *m*. **~ish** *a* jungenhaft

bra /brɑ:/ *n* BH *m*

brace /breɪs/ *n* Strebe *f*, Stütze *f*; (*dental*) Zahnspange *f*; **~s** *npl* Hosenträger *mpl*

bracelet /ˈbreɪslɪt/ *n* Armband *nt*

bracing /ˈbreɪsɪŋ/ *a* stärkend

bracket /ˈbrækɪt/ *n* Konsole *f*; (*group*) Gruppe *f*; (*Typ*) **round/square ~s** runde/eckige Klammern ● *vt* einklammern

brag /bræg/ *vi* (*pt/pp* **bragged**) prahlen (**about** mit)

braille /breɪl/ *n* Blindenschrift *f*

brain /breɪn/ *n* Gehirn *nt*; **~s** (*fig*) Intelligenz *f*

brain: ~less *a* dumm. **~wash** *vt* einer Gehirnwäsche unterziehen. **~wave** *n* Geistesblitz *m*

brainy /ˈbreɪnɪ/ *a* (**-ier, -iest**) klug

brake /breɪk/ *n* Bremse *f* ● *vt/i* bremsen. **~-light** *n* Bremslicht *nt*

bramble /ˈbræmbl/ *n* Brombeerstrauch *m*

branch /brɑ:ntʃ/ *n* Ast *m*; (*fig*) Zweig *m*; (*Comm*) Zweigstelle *f*; (*shop*) Filiale *f* ● *vi* sich gabeln

brand /brænd/ *n* Marke *f* ● *vt* (*fig*) brandmarken als

brandish /ˈbrændɪʃ/ *vt* schwingen

brand-ˈnew *a* nagelneu

brandy /ˈbrændɪ/ *n* Weinbrand *m*

brash /bræʃ/ *a* nassforsch

brass /brɑːs/ *n* Messing *nt*; (*Mus*) Blech *nt*; **top ~** [!] hohe Tiere *pl*. **~ band** *n* Blaskapelle *f*

brassy /ˈbrɑːsɪ/ *a* (**-ier, -iest**) [!] ordinär

brat /bræt/ *n* (*pej*) Balg *nt*

bravado /brəˈvɑːdəʊ/ *n* Forschheit *f*

brave /breɪv/ *a* (**-r, -st**), **-ly** *adv* tapfer ● *vt* die Stirn bieten (+ *dat*). **~ry** /-ərɪ/ *n* Tapferkeit *f*

bravo /brɑːˈvəʊ/ *int* bravo!

brawl /brɔːl/ *n* Schlägerei *f*

brawn /brɔːn/ *n* (*Culin*) Sülze *f*

brawny /ˈbrɔːnɪ/ *a* muskulös

bray /breɪ/ *vi* iahen

brazen /ˈbreɪzn/ *a* unverschämt

Brazil /brəˈzɪl/ *n* Brasilien *nt*. **~ian** *a* brasilianisch. **~ nut** *n* Paranuss *f*

breach /briːtʃ/ *n* Bruch *m*; (*Mil & fig*) Bresche *f*; **~ of contract** Vertragsbruch *m*

bread /bred/ *n* Brot *nt*; **slice of ~ and butter** Butterbrot *nt*. **~crumbs** *npl* Brotkrümel *pl*; (*Culin*) Paniermehl *nt*

breadth /bredθ/ *n* Breite *f*

break /breɪk/ *n* Bruch *m*; (*interval*) Pause *f*; (*interruption*) Unterbrechung *f*; ([!] *chance*) Chance *f* ● *v* (*pt* **broke**, *pp* **broken**) ● *vt* brechen; (*smash*) zerbrechen; (*damage*) kaputtmachen [!]; (*interrupt*) unterbrechen; **~ one's arm** sich (*dat*) den Arm brechen ● *vi* brechen; <*day:*> anbrechen; <*storm:*> losbrechen; <*thing:*> kaputtgehen [!]; <*rope, thread:*> reißen; <*news:*> bekannt werden; **his voice is ~ing** er ist im Stimmbruch. **~ away** *vi* sich losreißen/(*fig*) sich absetzen (**from** von). **~ down** *vi* zusammenbrechen; (*Techn*) eine Panne haben; <*negotiations:*> scheitern ● *vt* aufbrechen <*door*>; aufgliedern <*figures*>. **~ in** *vi* einbrechen. **~ off** *vt/i* abbrechen; lösen <*engagement*>. **~ out** *vi* ausbrechen. **~ up** *vt* zerbrechen ● *vi* <*crowd:*> sich zerstreuen; <*marriage, couple:*> auseinander gehen; (*Sch*) Ferien bekommen

break|able /ˈbreɪkəbl/ *a* zerbrechlich. **~age** /-ɪdʒ/ *n* Bruch *m*. **~down** *n* (*Techn*) Panne *f*; (*Med*) Zusammenbruch *m*; (*of figures*) Aufgliederung *f*. **~er** *n* (*wave*) Brecher *m*

breakfast /ˈbrekfəst/ *n* Frühstück *nt*

break: ~through *n* Durchbruch *m*. **~water** *n* Buhne *f*

breast /brest/ *n* Brust *f*. **~bone** *n* Brustbein *nt*. **~-feed** *vt* stillen. **~-stroke** *n* Brustschwimmen *nt*

breath /breθ/ *n* Atem *m*; **out of ~** außer Atem; **under one's ~** vor sich (*acc*) hin

breathe /briːð/ *vt/i* atmen. **~ in** *vt/i* einatmen. **~ out** *vt/i* ausatmen

breathing *n* Atmen *nt*

breath: /ˈbreθ/ **~less** *a* atemlos. **~-taking** *a* atemberaubend

bred /bred/ *see* **breed**

breed /briːd/ *n* Rasse *f* ● *v* (*pt/pp* **bred**) ● *vt* züchten; (*give rise to*) erzeugen ● *vi* sich vermehren. **~er** *n* Züchter *m*. **~ing** *n* Zucht *f*; (*fig*) [gute] Lebensart *f*

breez|e /briːz/ *n* Lüftchen *nt*; (*Naut*) Brise *f*. **~y** *a* windig

brevity /ˈbrevətɪ/ *n* Kürze *f*

brew /bru:/ *n* Gebräu *nt* ● *vt* brauen; kochen <*tea*>. **~er** *n* Brauer *m*. **~ery** *n* Brauerei *f*

bribe /braɪb/ *n* (*money*) Bestechungsgeld *nt* ● *vt* bestechen. **~ry** /-ərɪ/ *n* Bestechung *f*

brick /brɪk/ *n* Ziegelstein *m*, Backstein *m*

'bricklayer *n* Maurer *m*

bridal /'braɪdl/ *a* Braut-

bride /braɪd/ *n* Braut *f*. **~groom** *n* Bräutigam *m*. **~smaid** *n* Brautjungfer *f*

bridge[1] /brɪdʒ/ *n* Brücke *f*; (*of nose*) Nasenrücken *m*; (*of spectacles*) Steg *m*

bridge[2] *n* (*Cards*) Bridge *nt*

bridle /'braɪdl/ *n* Zaum *m*

brief[1] /bri:f/ *a* (**-er, -est**) kurz; **be ~** <*person:*> sich kurz fassen

brief[2] *n* Instruktionen *pl*; (*Jur: case*) Mandat *nt*. **~case** *n* Aktentasche *f*

brief|ing /'bri:fɪŋ/ *n* Informationsgespräch *nt*. **~ly** *adv* kurz. **~ness** *n* Kürze *f*

briefs /bri:fs/ *npl* Slip *m*

brigade /brɪ'geɪd/ *n* Brigade *f*

bright /braɪt/ *a* (**-er, -est**), **-ly** *adv* hell; <*day*> heiter; **~ red** hellrot

bright|en /'braɪtn/ *v* **~en [up]** ● *vt* aufheitern ● *vi* sich aufheitern. **~ness** *n* Helligkeit *f*

brilliance /'brɪljəns/ *n* Glanz *m*; (*of person*) Genialität *f*

brilliant /'brɪljənt/ *a*, **-ly** *adv* glänzend; <*person*> genial

brim /brɪm/ *n* Rand *m*; (*of hat*) Krempe *f*

bring /brɪŋ/ *vt* (*pt/pp* **brought**) bringen; **~ them with you** bring sie mit; **I can't ~ myself to do it** ich bringe es nicht fertig. **~ about** *vt* verursachen. **~ along** *vt* mitbringen. **~ back** *vt* zurückbringen. **~ down** *vt* herunterbringen; senken <*price*>. **~ off** *vt* vollbringen. **~ on** *vt* (*cause*) verursachen. **~ out** *vt* herausbringen. **~ round** *vt* vorbeibringen; (*persuade*) überreden; wieder zum Bewusstsein bringen <*unconscious person*>. **~ up** *vt* heraufbringen; (*vomit*) erbrechen; aufziehen <*children*>; erwähnen <*question*>

brink /brɪŋk/ *n* Rand *m*

brisk /brɪsk/ *a* (**-er, -est,**) **-ly** *adv* lebhaft; (*quick*) schnell

bristle /'brɪsl/ *n* Borste *f*

Brit|ain /'brɪtn/ *n* Großbritannien *nt*. **~ish** *a* britisch; **the ~ish** die Briten *pl*. **~on** *n* Brite *m*/Britin *f*

Brittany /'brɪtənɪ/ *n* die Bretagne

brittle /'brɪtl/ *a* brüchig, spröde

broad /brɔ:d/ *a* (**-er, -est**) breit; <*hint*> deutlich; **in ~ daylight** am helllichten Tag. **~ beans** *npl* dicke Bohnen *pl*

'broadcast *n* Sendung *f* ● *vt/i* (*pt/pp* **-cast**) senden. **~er** *n* Rundfunk- und Fernsehpersönlichkeit *f*. **~ing** *n* Funk und Fernsehen *pl*

broaden /'brɔ:dn/ *vt* verbreitern; (*fig*) erweitern ● *vi* sich verbreitern

broadly /'brɔ:dlɪ/ *adv* breit; **~ speaking** allgemein gesagt

broad'minded *a* tolerant

broccoli /'brɒkəlɪ/ *n inv* Brokkoli *pl*

brochure /'brəʊʃə(r)/ *n* Broschüre *f*

broke /brəʊk/ *see* **break** ● *a* 🄸 pleite

broken /'brəʊkn/ *see* **break** ● *a* zerbrochen, 🄸 kaputt. **~-hearted** *a* untröstlich

broker /'brəʊkə(r)/ *n* Makler *m*

brolly /'brɒlɪ/ *n* 🄸 Schirm *m*

bronchitis /brɒŋ'kaɪtɪs/ *n* Bronchitis *f*

bronze /brɒnz/ *n* Bronze *f*

brooch /brəʊtʃ/ *n* Brosche *f*

brood /bru:d/ *vi* (*fig*) grübeln

broom /bru:m/ *n* Besen *m*; (*Bot*) Ginster *m*

broth /brɒθ/ *n* Brühe *f*

brothel /'brɒθl/ *n* Bordell *nt*

brother /'brʌðə(r)/ *n* Bruder *m*

brother: ~-in-law *n* (*pl* **-s-in-law**) Schwager *m*. **~ly** *a* brüderlich

brought /brɔ:t/ *see* **bring**

brow /braʊ/ *n* Augenbraue *f*; (*forehead*) Stirn *f*; (*of hill*) [Berg]kuppe *f*

brown /braʊn/ *a* (**-er, -est**) braun; ~ '**paper** Packpapier *nt* ● *n* Braun *nt* ● *vt* bräunen ● *vi* braun werden

browse /braʊz/ *vi* (*read*) schmökern; (*in shop*) sich umsehen. **~r** *n* (*Computing*) Browser *m*

bruise /bru:z/ *n* blauer Fleck *m* ● *vt* beschädigen <*fruit*>; ~ **one's arm** sich (*dat*) den Arm quetschen

brunette /bru:'net/ *n* Brünette *f*

brush /brʌʃ/ *n* Bürste *f*; (*with handle*) Handfeger *m*; (*for paint, pastry*) Pinsel *m*; (*bushes*) Unterholz *nt*; (*fig: conflict*) Zusammenstoß *m* ● *vt* bürsten; putzen <*teeth*>; ~ **against** streifen [gegen]; ~ **aside** (*fig*) abtun. ~ **off** *vt* abbürsten. ~ **up** *vt/i* (*fig*) ~ **up [on]** auffrischen

brusque /brʊsk/ *a*, **-ly** *adv* brüsk

Brussels /'brʌslz/ *n* Brüssel *nt*. ~ **sprouts** *npl* Rosenkohl *m*

brutal /'bru:tl/ *a*, **-ly** *adv* brutal. **~ity** /-'tælətɪ/ *n* Brutalität *f*

brute /bru:t/ *n* Unmensch *m*. ~ **force** *n* rohe Gewalt *f*

BSE *abbr* (**bovine spongiform encephalopathy**) BSE *f*

bubble /'bʌbl/ *n* [Luft]blase *f* ● *vi* sprudeln

buck¹ /bʌk/ *n* (*deer & Gym*) Bock *m*; (*rabbit*) Rammler *m* ● *vi* <*horse:*> bocken

buck² *n* (*Amer* [!]) Dollar *m*

buck³ *n* **pass the ~** die Verantwortung abschieben

bucket /'bʌkɪt/ *n* Eimer *m*

buckle /'bʌkl/ *n* Schnalle *f* ● *vt* zuschnallen ● *vi* sich verbiegen

bud /bʌd/ *n* Knospe *f*

buddy /'bʌdɪ/ *n* [!] Freund *m*

budge /bʌdʒ/ *vt* bewegen ● *vi* sich [von der Stelle] rühren

budget /'bʌdʒɪt/ *n* Budget *nt*; (*Pol*) Haushaltsplan *m*; (*money available*) Etat *m* ● *vi* (*pt/pp* **budgeted**) ~ **for sth** etw einkalkulieren

buff /bʌf/ *a* (*colour*) sandfarben ● *n* Sandfarbe *f*; [!] Fan *m* ● *vt* polieren

buffalo /'bʌfələʊ/ *n* (*inv or pl* **-es**) Büffel *m*

buffer /'bʌfə(r)/ *n* (*Rail*) Puffer *m*

buffet¹ /'bʊfeɪ/ *n* Büfett *nt*; (*on station*) Imbissstube *f*

buffet² /'bʌfɪt/ *vt* (*pt/pp* **buffeted**) hin und her werfen

bug /bʌg/ *n* Wanze *f*; ([!] *virus*) Bazillus *m*; ([!] *device*) Abhörgerät *nt*, [!] Wanze *f* ● *vt* (*pt/pp* **bugged**) [!] verwanzen <*room*>; abhören <*telephone*>; (*Amer: annoy*) ärgern

bugle /'bju:gl/ *n* Signalhorn

build /bɪld/ *n* (*of person*) Körperbau *m* ● *vt/i* (*pt/pp* **built**) bauen. ~ **on** *vt* anbauen (**to** an + *acc*). ~ **up** *vt* aufbauen ● *vi* zunehmen

builder /'bɪldə(r)/ *n* Bauunternehmer *m*

building /'bɪldɪŋ/ *n* Gebäude *nt*. ~ **site** *n* Baustelle *f*. ~ **society** *n* Bausparkasse *f*

built /bɪlt/ *see* **build.** ~**-in** *a* eingebaut. ~**-in 'cupboard** *n* Einbauschrank *m*. ~**-up area** *n* bebautes Gebiet *nt*; (*Auto*) geschlossene Ortschaft *f*

bulb /bʌlb/ *n* [Blumen]zwiebel *f*; (*Electr*) [Glüh]birne *f*

bulbous /'bʌlbəs/ *a* bauchig

Bulgaria /bʌl'geərɪə/ *n* Bulgarien *nt*

bulg|e /bʌldʒ/ *n* Ausbauchung *f* ● *vi* sich ausbauchen. ~**ing** *a* prall; <*eyes*> hervorquellend

bulk /bʌlk/ *n* Masse *f*; (*greater part*) Hauptteil *m*. ~**y** *a* sperrig; (*large*) massig

bull /bʊl/ *n* Bulle *m*, Stier *m*

'bulldog *n* Bulldogge *f*

bulldozer /'bʊldəʊzə(r)/ *n* Planierraupe *f*

bullet /'bʊlɪt/ *n* Kugel *f*

bulletin /'bʊlɪtɪn/ *n* Bulletin *nt*

'bullet-proof *a* kugelsicher

'bullfight *n* Stierkampf *m*. ~**er** *n* Stierkämpfer *m*

'bullfinch *n* Dompfaff *m*

bullock /'bʊlək/ *n* Ochse *m*

bull: ~**ring** *n* Stierkampfarena *f*. ~**'s-eye** *n* **score a** ~**'s-eye** ins Schwarze treffen

bully /'bʊlɪ/ *n* Tyrann *m* ● *vt* tyrannisieren

bum /bʌm/ *n* [x] Hintern *m*

bumble-bee /'bʌmbl-/ *n* Hummel *f*

bump /bʌmp/ *n* Bums *m*; (*swelling*) Beule *f*; (*in road*) holperige Stelle *f* ● *vt* stoßen; ~ **into** stoßen gegen; (*meet*) zufällig treffen. ~ **off** *vt* [!] um die Ecke bringen

bumper /'bʌmpə(r)/ *a* Rekord- ● *n* (*Auto*) Stoßstange *f*

bumpy /'bʌmpɪ/ *a* holperig

bun /bʌn/ *n* Milchbrötchen *nt*; (*hair*) [Haar]knoten *m*

bunch /bʌntʃ/ *n* (*of flowers*) Strauß *m*; (*of radishes, keys*) Bund *m*; (*of people*) Gruppe *f*; ~ **of grapes** [ganze] Weintraube *f*

bundle /'bʌndl/ *n* Bündel *nt* ● *vt* ~ **[up]** bündeln

bungalow /'bʌŋgələʊ/ *n* Bungalow *m*

bungle /'bʌŋgl/ *vt* verpfuschen

bunk /bʌŋk/ *n* [Schlaf]koje *f*. ~**-beds** *npl* Etagenbett *nt*

bunker /'bʌŋkə(r)/ *n* Bunker *m*

bunny /'bʌnɪ/ *n* [!] Kaninchen *nt*

buoy /bɔɪ/ *n* Boje *f*

buoyan|cy /'bɔɪənsɪ/ *n* Auftrieb *m*. ~**t** *a* **be** ~**t** schwimmen

burden /'bɜːdn/ *n* Last *f*

bureau /'bjʊərəʊ/ *n* (*pl* **-x** /-əʊz/ *or* **-s**) (*desk*) Sekretär *m*; (*office*) Büro *nt*

bureaucracy /bjʊə'rɒkrəsɪ/ *n* Bürokratie *f*

bureaucratic /bjʊərə'krætɪk/ *a* bürokratisch

burger /'bɜːgə(r)/ *n* Hamburger *m*

burglar /'bɜːglə(r)/ *n* Einbrecher *m*. ~ **alarm** *n* Alarmanlage *f*

burglary *n* Einbruch *m*

burgle /'bɜːgl/ *vt* einbrechen in (+ *acc*); **they have been** ~**d** bei ihnen ist eingebrochen worden

burial /'berɪəl/ *n* Begräbnis *nt*

burly /'bɜːlɪ/ *a* (**-ier, -iest**) stämmig

Burm|a /'bɜːmə/ *n* Birma *nt*. ~**ese** /-'miːz/ *a* birmanisch

burn /bɜːn/ *n* Verbrennung *f*; (*on skin*) Brandwunde *f*; (*on material*) Brandstelle *f* ● *v* (*pt/pp* **burnt** *or* **burned**) ● *vt* verbrennen ● *vi* brennen; <*food:*> anbrennen. ~ **down** *vt/i* niederbrennen

burnt /bɜːnt/ *see* **burn**

burp /bɜːp/ *vi* [!] aufstoßen

burrow /ˈbʌrəʊ/ *n* Bau *m* ● *vi* wühlen

burst /bɜːst/ *n* Bruch *m*; (*surge*) Ausbruch *m* ● *v* (*pt/pp* **burst**) ● *vt* platzen machen ● *vi* platzen; <*bud:*> aufgehen; ~ **into tears** in Tränen ausbrechen

bury /ˈberɪ/ *vt* (*pt/pp* **-ied**) begraben; (*hide*) vergraben

bus /bʌs/ *n* [Auto]bus *m*

bush /bʊʃ/ *n* Strauch *m*; (*land*) Busch *m*. **~y** *a* (**-ier, -iest**) buschig

busily /ˈbɪzɪlɪ/ *adv* eifrig

business /ˈbɪznɪs/ *n* Angelegenheit *f*; (*Comm*) Geschäft *nt*; **on** ~ geschäftlich; **he has no** ~ er hat kein Recht (**to** zu); **mind one's own** ~ sich um seine eigenen Angelegenheiten kümmern; **that's none of your** ~ das geht Sie nichts an. **~-like** *a* geschäftsmäßig. **~man** *n* Geschäftsmann *m*

ˈbus-stop *n* Bushaltestelle *f*

bust¹ /bʌst/ *n* Büste *f*

bust² *a* [!] kaputt; **go** ~ Pleite gehen ● *v* (*pt/pp* **busted** *or* **bust**) [!] ● *vt* kaputtmachen ● *vi* kaputtgehen

busy /ˈbɪzɪ/ *a* (**-ier, -iest**) beschäftigt; <*day*> voll; <*street*> belebt; (*with traffic*) stark befahren; (*Amer Teleph*) besetzt; **be** ~ zu tun haben ● *vt* ~ **oneself** sich beschäftigen (**with** mit)

but /bʌt, *unbetont* bət/ *conj* aber; (*after negative*) sondern ● *prep* außer (+ *dat*); ~ **for** (*without*) ohne (+ *acc*); **the last** ~ **one** der/die/das vorletzte; **the next** ~ **one** der/die/das übernächste ● *adv* nur

butcher /ˈbʊtʃə(r)/ *n* Fleischer *m*, Metzger *m*; **~'s [shop]** Fleischerei *f*, Metzgerei *f* ● *vt* [ab]schlachten

butler /ˈbʌtlə(r)/ *n* Butler *m*

butt /bʌt/ *n* (*of gun*) [Gewehr]kolben *m*; (*fig: target*) Zielscheibe *f*; (*of cigarette*) Stummel *m*; (*for water*) Regentonne *f* ● *vi* ~ **in** unterbrechen

butter /ˈbʌtə(r)/ *n* Butter *f* ● *vt* mit Butter bestreichen. ~ **up** *vt* [!] schmeicheln (+ *dat*)

butter: **~cup** *a* Butterblume *f*, Hahnenfuß *m*. **~fly** *n* Schmetterling *m*

buttocks /ˈbʌtəks/ *npl* Gesäß *nt*

button /ˈbʌtn/ *n* Knopf *m* ● *vt* ~ **[up]** zuknöpfen. **~hole** *n* Knopfloch *nt*

buy /baɪ/ *n* Kauf *m* ● *vt* (*pt/pp* **bought**) kaufen. **~er** *n* Käufer(in) *m(f)*

buzz /bʌz/ *n* Summen *nt* ● *vi* summen

buzzer /ˈbʌzə(r)/ *n* Summer *m*

by /baɪ/ *prep* (*close to*) bei (+ *dat*); (*next to*) neben (+ *dat/acc*); (*past*) an (+ *dat*) ... vorbei; (*to the extent of*) um (+ *acc*); (*at the latest*) bis; (*by means of*) durch; **by Mozart/Dickens** von Mozart/Dickens; ~ **oneself** allein; ~ **the sea** am Meer; ~ **car/bus** mit dem Auto/Bus; ~ **sea** mit dem Schiff; ~ **day/night** bei Tag/Nacht; ~ **the hour** pro Stunde; ~ **the metre** meterweise; **six metres** ~ **four** sechs mal vier Meter; **win** ~ **a length** mit einer Länge Vorsprung gewinnen; **miss the train** ~ **a minute** den Zug um eine Minute verpassen ● *adv* ~ **and large** im Großen und Ganzen; **put** ~ beiseite legen; **go/pass** ~ vorbeigehen

bye /baɪ/ *int* [!] tschüs

by: **~-election** *n* Nachwahl *f*. **~pass** *n* Umgehungsstraße *f*; (*Med*) Bypass *m* ● *vt* umfahren. **~-product** *n* Nebenprodukt *m*. **~stander** *n* Zuschauer(in) *m(f)*

Cc

cab /kæb/ *n* Taxi *nt*; (*of lorry, train*) Führerhaus *nt*
cabaret /ˈkæbəreɪ/ *n* Kabarett *nt*
cabbage /ˈkæbɪdʒ/ *n* Kohl *m*
cabin /ˈkæbɪn/ *n* Kabine *f*; (*hut*) Hütte *f*
cabinet /ˈkæbɪnɪt/ *n* Schrank *m*; **[display]** ~ Vitrine *f*; **C~** (*Pol*) Kabinett *nt*
cable /ˈkeɪbl/ *n* Kabel *nt*; (*rope*) Tau *nt*. ~ **ˈrailway** *n* Seilbahn *f*. ~ **ˈtelevision** *n* Kabelfernsehen *nt*
cackle /ˈkækl/ *vi* gackern
cactus /ˈkæktəs/ *n* (*pl* **-ti** /-taɪ/ *or* **-tuses**) Kaktus *m*
cadet /kəˈdet/ *n* Kadett *m*
cadge /kædʒ/ *vt/i* [!] schnorren
Caesarean /sɪˈzeərɪən/ *a* & *n* ~ **[section]** Kaiserschnitt *m*
café /ˈkæfeɪ/ *n* Café *nt*
cafeteria /kæfəˈtɪərɪə/ *n* Selbstbedienungsrestaurant *nt*
cage /keɪdʒ/ *n* Käfig *m*
cagey /ˈkeɪdʒɪ/ *a* [!] **be** ~ mit der Sprache nicht herauswollen
cake /keɪk/ *n* Kuchen *m*; (*of soap*) Stück *nt*. **~d** *a* verkrustet (**with** mit)
calamity /kəˈlæmətɪ/ *n* Katastrophe *f*
calculat|e /ˈkælkjʊleɪt/ *vt* berechnen; (*estimate*) kalkulieren. **~ing** *a* (*fig*) berechnend. **~ion** /-ˈleɪʃn/ *n* Rechnung *f*, Kalkulation *f*. **~or** *n* Rechner *m*
calendar /ˈkælɪndə(r)/ *n* Kalender *m*
calf[1] /kɑːf/ *n* (*pl* **calves**) Kalb *nt*
calf[2] *n* (*pl* **calves**) (*Anat*) Wade *f*
calibre /ˈkælɪbə(r)/ *n* Kaliber *nt*
call /kɔːl/ *n* Ruf *m*; (*Teleph*) Anruf *m*; (*visit*) Besuch *m* ● *vt* rufen; (*Teleph*) anrufen; (*wake*) wecken; ausrufen <*strike*>; (*name*) nennen; **be ~ed** heißen ● *vi* rufen; ~ **[in** *or* **round]** vorbeikommen. ~ **back** *vt* zurückrufen ● *vi* noch einmal vorbeikommen. ~ **for** *vt* rufen nach; (*demand*) verlangen; (*fetch*) abholen. ~ **off** *vt* zurückrufen <*dog*>; (*cancel*) absagen. ~ **on** *vt* bitten (**for** um); (*appeal to*) appellieren an (+ *acc*); (*visit*) besuchen. ~ **out** *vt* rufen; aufrufen <*names*> ● *vi* rufen. ~ **up** *vt* (*Mil*) einberufen; (*Teleph*) anrufen
call: ~-box *n* Telefonzelle *f*. **~er** *n* Besucher *m*; (*Teleph*) Anrufer *m*. **~ing** *n* Berufung *f*. **~-up** *n* (*Mil*) Einberufung *f*
calm /kɑːm/ *a* (**-er, -est**), **-ly** *adv* ruhig ● *n* Ruhe *f* ● *vt* ~ **[down]** beruhigen ● *vi* ~ **down** sich beruhigen. **~ness** *n* Ruhe *f*; (*of sea*) Stille *f*
calorie /ˈkælərɪ/ *n* Kalorie *f*
calves /kɑːvz/ *npl see* **calf**[1] & [2]
camcorder /ˈkæmkɔːdə(r)/ *n* Camcorder *m*
came /keɪm/ *see* **come**
camel /ˈkæml/ *n* Kamel *nt*
camera /ˈkæmərə/ *n* Kamera *f*
camouflage /ˈkæməflɑːʒ/ *n* Tarnung *f* ● *vt* tarnen
camp /kæmp/ *n* Lager *nt* ● *vi* campen; (*Mil*) kampieren
campaign /kæmˈpeɪn/ *n* Feldzug *m*; (*Comm, Pol*) Kampagne *f* ● *vi* (*Pol*) im Wahlkampf arbeiten
camp: ~-bed *n* Feldbett *nt*. **~er** *n* Camper *m*; (*Auto*) Wohnmobil *nt*. **~ing** *n* Camping *nt*. **~site** *n* Campingplatz *m*

can¹ /kæn/ *n* (*for petrol*) Kanister *m*; (*tin*) Dose *f*, Büchse *f*; **a ~ of beer** eine Dose Bier

can² /kæn, *unbetont* kən/

pres **can**, *pt* **could**

● *auxiliary verb*

····➤ (*be able to*) können. **I can't** *or* **cannot go** ich kann nicht gehen. **she couldn't** *or* **could not go** (*was unable to*) sie konnte nicht gehen; (*would not be able to*) sie könnte nicht gehen. **he could go if he had time** er könnte gehen, wenn er Zeit hätte. **if I could go** wenn ich gehen könnte. **that cannot be true** das kann nicht stimmen

····➤ (*know how to*) können. **can you swim?** können Sie schwimmen? **she can drive** sie kann Auto fahren

····➤ (*be allowed to*) dürfen. **you can't smoke here** hier dürfen Sie nicht rauchen. **can I go?** kann *od* darf ich gehen?

····➤ (*in requests*) können. **can I have a glass of water, please?** kann ich ein Glas Wasser haben, bitte? **could you ring me tomorrow?** könnten Sie mich morgen anrufen?

····➤ **could** (*expressing possibility*) könnte. **that could be so** das könnte *od* kann sein. **I could have killed him** ich hätte ihn umbringen können

Canad|a /ˈkænədə/ *n* Kanada *nt*. **~ian** /kəˈneɪdɪən/ *a* kanadisch ● *n* Kanadier(in) *m(f)*

canal /kəˈnæl/ *n* Kanal *m*

canary /kəˈneərɪ/ *n* Kanarienvogel *m*

cancel /ˈkænsl/ *vt/i* (*pt/pp* **cancelled**) absagen; abbestellen <*newspaper*>; (*Computing*) abbrechen; **be ~led** ausfallen. **~lation** /-əˈleɪʃn/ *n* Absage *f*

cancer /ˈkænsə(r)/ *n*, & (*Astr*) **C~** Krebs *m*. **~ous** /-rəs/ *a* krebsig

candid /ˈkændɪd/ *a*, **-ly** *adv* offen

candidate /ˈkændɪdət/ *n* Kandidat(in) *m(f)*

candle /ˈkændl/ *n* Kerze *f*. **~stick** *n* Kerzenständer *m*, Leuchter *m*

candy /ˈkændɪ/ *n* (*Amer*) Süßigkeiten *pl*; **[piece of] ~** Bonbon *m*

cane /keɪn/ *n* Rohr *nt*; (*stick*) Stock *m* ● *vt* mit dem Stock züchtigen

canine /ˈkeɪnaɪn/ *a* Hunde-. **~ tooth** *n* Eckzahn *m*

cannabis /ˈkænəbɪs/ *n* Haschisch *nt*

canned /kænd/ *a* Dosen-, Büchsen-

cannibal /ˈkænɪbl/ *n* Kannibale *m*. **~ism** /-bəlɪzm/ *n* Kannibalismus *m*

cannon /ˈkænən/ *n inv* Kanone *f*

cannot /ˈkænɒt/ *see* **can²**

canoe /kəˈnuː/ *n* Paddelboot *nt*; (*Sport*) Kanu *nt*

ˈcan-opener *n* Dosenöffner *m*

can't /kɑːnt/ = **cannot.** *See* **can²**

canteen /kænˈtiːn/ *n* Kantine *f*; **~ of cutlery** Besteckkasten *m*

canter /ˈkæntə(r)/ *n* Kanter *m* ● *vi* kantern

canvas /ˈkænvəs/ *n* Segeltuch *nt*; (*Art*) Leinwand *f*; (*painting*) Gemälde *nt*

canvass /ˈkænvəs/ *vi* um Stimmen werben

canyon /ˈkænjən/ *n* Cañon *m*

cap /kæp/ *n* Kappe *f*, Mütze *f*; (*nurse's*) Haube *f*; (*top, lid*) Verschluss *m*

capability /keɪpəˈbɪlətɪ/ *n* Fähigkeit *f*

capable /ˈkeɪpəbl/ *a*, **-bly** *adv* fähig; **be ~ of doing sth** fähig sein, etw zu tun

capacity /kə'pæsətɪ/ *n* Fassungsvermögen *nt*; (*ability*) Fähigkeit *f*; **in my ~ as** in meiner Eigenschaft als

cape[1] /keɪp/ *n* (*cloak*) Cape *nt*

cape[2] *n* (*Geog*) Kap *nt*

capital /'kæpɪtl/ *a* <*letter*> groß ● *n* (*town*) Hauptstadt *f*; (*money*) Kapital *nt*; (*letter*) Großbuchstabe *m*

capital|ism /'kæpɪtəlɪzm/ *n* Kapitalismus *m*. **~ist** /-ɪst/ *a* kapitalistisch ● *n* Kapitalist *m*. **~ 'letter** *n* Großbuchstabe *m*. **~ 'punishment** *n* Todesstrafe *f*

capsize /kæp'saɪz/ *vi* kentern ● *vt* zum Kentern bringen

captain /'kæptɪn/ *n* Kapitän *m*; (*Mil*) Hauptmann *m* ● *vt* anführen <*team*>

caption /'kæpʃn/ *n* Überschrift *f*; (*of illustration*) Bildtext *m*

captivate /'kæptɪveɪt/ *vt* bezaubern

captiv|e /'kæptɪv/ *a* **hold/take ~e** gefangen halten/nehmen ● *n* Gefangene(r) *m/f*. **~ity** /-'tɪvətɪ/ *n* Gefangenschaft *f*

capture /'kæptʃə(r)/ *n* Gefangennahme *f* ● *vt* gefangen nehmen; [ein]fangen <*animal*>; (*Mil*) einnehmen <*town*>

car /kɑ:(r)/ *n* Auto *nt*, Wagen *m*; **by ~** mit dem Auto *od* Wagen

caramel /'kærəmel/ *n* Karamell *m*

carat /'kærət/ *n* Karat *nt*

caravan /'kærəvæn/ *n* Wohnwagen *m*; (*procession*) Karawane *f*

carbon /'kɑ:bən/ *n* Kohlenstoff *m*; (*paper*) Kohlepapier *nt*; (*copy*) Durchschlag *m*

carbon: ~ copy *n* Durchschlag *m*. **~ paper** *n* Kohlepapier *nt*

carburettor /kɑ:bjʊ'retə(r)/ *n* Vergaser *m*

carcass /'kɑ:kəs/ *n* Kadaver *m*

card /kɑ:d/ *n* Karte *f*

'cardboard *n* Pappe *f*, Karton *m*. **~ 'box** *n* Pappschachtel *f*; (*large*) [Papp]karton *m*

'card-game *n* Kartenspiel *nt*

cardigan /'kɑ:dɪgən/ *n* Strickjacke *f*

cardinal /'kɑ:dɪnl/ *a* Kardinal- ● *n* (*Relig*) Kardinal *m*

card 'index *n* Kartei *f*

care /keə(r)/ *n* Sorgfalt *f*; (*caution*) Vorsicht *f*; (*protection*) Obhut *f*; (*looking after*) Pflege *f*; (*worry*) Sorge *f*; **~ of** (*on letter abbr* **c/o**) bei; **take ~** vorsichtig sein; **take into ~** in Pflege nehmen; **take ~ of** sich kümmern um ● *vi* **~ for** (*like*) mögen; (*look after*) betreuen; **I don't ~** das ist mir gleich

career /kə'rɪə(r)/ *n* Laufbahn *f*; (*profession*) Beruf *m* ● *vi* rasen

care: ~free *a* sorglos. **~ful** *a*, **-ly** *adv* sorgfältig; (*cautious*) vorsichtig. **~less** *a*, **-ly** *adv* nachlässig. **~lessness** *n* Nachlässigkeit *f*

'caretaker *n* Hausmeister *m*

'car ferry *n* Autofähre *f*

cargo /'kɑ:gəʊ/ *n* (*pl* **-es**) Ladung *f*

Caribbean /kærɪ'bi:ən/ *n* **the ~** die Karibik

caricature /'kærɪkətjʊə(r)/ *n* Karikatur *f* ● *vt* karikieren

caring /'keərɪŋ/ *a* <*parent*> liebevoll; <*profession, attitude*> sozial

carnation /kɑ:'neɪʃn/ *n* Nelke *f*

carnival /'kɑ:nɪvl/ *n* Karneval *m*

carol /'kærl/ *n* **[Christmas] ~** Weihnachtslied *nt*

carp[1] /kɑ:p/ *n inv* Karpfen *m*

carp[2] *vi* nörgeln

'car park *n* Parkplatz *m*; (*multi-storey*) Parkhaus *nt*; (*underground*) Tiefgarage *f*

carpent|er /ˈkɑːpɪntə(r)/ *n* Zimmermann *m*; (*joiner*) Tischler *m*. **~ry** *n* Tischlerei *f*
carpet /ˈkɑːpɪt/ *n* Teppich *m*
carriage /ˈkærɪdʒ/ *n* Kutsche *f*; (*Rail*) Wagen *m*; (*of goods*) Beförderung *f*; (*cost*) Frachtkosten *pl*; (*bearing*) Haltung *f*
carrier /ˈkærɪə(r)/ *n* Träger(in) *m(f)*; (*Comm*) Spediteur *m*; **~ [-bag]** Tragetasche *f*
carrot /ˈkærət/ *n* Möhre *f*, Karotte *f*
carry /ˈkærɪ/ *vt/i* (*pt/pp* **-ied**) tragen; **be carried away** [!] hingerissen sein. **~ off** *vt* wegtragen; gewinnen <*prize*>. **~ on** *vi* weitermachen; **~ on with** [!] eine Affäre haben mit ● *vt* führen; (*continue*) fortführen. **~ out** *vt* hinaus-/heraustragen; (*perform*) ausführen
cart /kɑːt/ *n* Karren *m*; **put the ~ before the horse** das Pferd beim Schwanz aufzäumen ● *vt* karren; ([!] *carry*) schleppen
carton /ˈkɑːtn/ *n* [Papp]karton *m*; (*for drink*) Tüte *f*; (*of cream, yoghurt*) Becher *m*
cartoon /kɑːˈtuːn/ *n* Karikatur *f*; (*joke*) Witzzeichnung *f*; (*strip*) Comic Strips *pl*; (*film*) Zeichentrickfilm *m*. **~ist** *n* Karikaturist *m*
cartridge /ˈkɑːtrɪdʒ/ *n* Patrone *f*; (*for film*) Kassette *f*
carve /kɑːv/ *vt* schnitzen; (*in stone*) hauen; (*Culin*) aufschneiden
carving /ˈkɑːvɪŋ/ *n* Schnitzerei *f*. **~-knife** *n* Tranchiermesser *nt*
ˈ**car wash** *n* Autowäsche *f*; (*place*) Autowaschanlage *f*
case¹ /keɪs/ *n* Fall *m*; **in any ~** auf jeden Fall; **just in ~** für alle Fälle; **in ~ he comes** falls er kommt
case² *n* Kasten *m*; (*crate*) Kiste *f*; (*for spectacles*) Etui *nt*; (*suitcase*) Koffer *m*; (*for display*) Vitrine *f*
cash /kæʃ/ *n* Bargeld *nt*; **pay [in] ~** [in] bar bezahlen; **~ on delivery** per Nachnahme ● *vt* einlösen <*cheque*>. **~ desk** *n* Kasse *f*
cashier /kæˈʃɪə(r)/ *n* Kassierer(in) *m(f)*
ˈ**cash: ~point [machine]** *n* Geldautomat *m*. **~ register** *n* Registrierkasse *f*
cassette /kəˈset/ *n* Kassette *f*. **~ recorder** *n* Kassettenrecorder *m*
cast /kɑːst/ *n* (*mould*) Form *f*; (*model*) Abguss *m*; (*Theat*) Besetzung *f*; **[plaster] ~** (*Med*) Gipsverband *m* ● *vt* (*pt/pp* **cast**) (*throw*) werfen; (*shed*) abwerfen; abgeben <*vote*>; gießen <*metal*>; (*Theat*) besetzen <*role*>. **~ off** *vi* (*Naut*) ablegen
castle /ˈkɑːsl/ *n* Schloss *nt*; (*fortified*) Burg *f*; (*Chess*) Turm *m*
ˈ**cast-offs** *npl* abgelegte Kleidung *f*
castor /ˈkɑːstə(r)/ *n* (*wheel*) [Lauf]rolle *f*
ˈ**castor sugar** *n* Streuzucker *m*
casual /ˈkæʒʊəl/ *a*, **-ly** *adv* (*chance*) zufällig; (*offhand*) lässig; (*informal*) zwanglos; (*not permanent*) Gelegenheits-; **~ wear** Freizeitbekleidung *f*
casualty /ˈkæʒʊəltɪ/ *n* [Todes]opfer *nt*; (*injured person*) Verletzte(r) *m/f*; **~ [department]** Unfallstation *f*
cat /kæt/ *n* Katze *f*
catalogue /ˈkætəlɒg/ *n* Katalog *m* ● *vt* katalogisieren
catapult /ˈkætəpʌlt/ *n* Katapult *nt* ● *vt* katapultieren
cataract /ˈkætərækt/ *n* (*Med*) grauer Star *m*
catarrh /kəˈtɑː(r)/ *n* Katarrh *m*

catastroph|e /kə'tæstrəfɪ/ *n* Katastrophe *f*. **~ic** /kætə'strɒfɪk/ *a* katastrophal

catch /kætʃ/ *n* (*of fish*) Fang *m*; (*fastener*) Verschluss *m*; (*on door*) Klinke *f*; (🅸 *snag*) Haken *m* 🅸 ● *v* (*pt/pp* **caught**) ● *vt* fangen; (*be in time for*) erreichen; (*travel by*) fahren mit; bekommen <*illness*>; **~ a cold** sich erkälten; **~ sight of** erblicken; **~ s.o. stealing** jdn beim Stehlen erwischen; **~ one's finger in the door** sich (*dat*) den Finger in der Tür [ein]klemmen ● *vi* (*burn*) anbrennen; (*get stuck*) klemmen. **~ on** *vi* 🅸 (*understand*) kapieren; (*become popular*) sich durchsetzen. **~ up** *vt* einholen ● *vi* aufholen; **~ up with** einholen <*s.o.*>; nachholen <*work*>

catching /'kætʃɪŋ/ *a* ansteckend

catch: ~-phrase *n*, **~word** *n* Schlagwort *nt*

catchy /'kætʃɪ/ *a* (**-ier, -iest**) einprägsam

categor|ical /kætɪ'gɒrɪkl/ *a*, **-ly** *adv* kategorisch. **~y** /'kætɪgərɪ/ *n* Kategorie *f*

cater /'keɪtə(r)/ *vi* **~ for** beköstigen; <*firm*:> das Essen liefern für <*party*>; (*fig*) eingestellt sein auf (+ *acc*). **~ing** *n* (*trade*) Gaststättengewerbe *nt*

caterpillar /'kætəpɪlə(r)/ *n* Raupe *f*

cathedral /kə'θi:drl/ *n* Dom *m*, Kathedrale *f*

Catholic /'kæθəlɪk/ *a* katholisch ● *n* Katholik(in) *m(f)*. **C ~ism** /kə'θɒlɪsɪzm/ *n* Katholizismus *m*

cattle /'kætl/ *npl* Vieh *nt*

catty /'kætɪ/ *a* (**-ier, -iest**) boshaft

caught /kɔ:t/ *see* **catch**

cauliflower /'kɒlɪ-/ *n* Blumenkohl *m*

cause /kɔ:z/ *n* Ursache *f*; (*reason*) Grund *m*; **good ~** gute Sache *f* ● *vt* verursachen; **~ s.o. to do sth** jdn veranlassen, etw zu tun

caution /'kɔ:ʃn/ *n* Vorsicht *f*; (*warning*) Verwarnung *f* ● *vt* (*Jur*) verwarnen

cautious /'kɔ:ʃəs/ *a*, **-ly** *adv* vorsichtig

cavalry /'kævəlrɪ/ *n* Kavallerie *f*

cave /keɪv/ *n* Höhle *f* ● *vi* **~ in** einstürzen

cavern /'kævən/ *n* Höhle *f*

caviare /'kævɪɑ:(r)/ *n* Kaviar *m*

cavity /'kævətɪ/ *n* Hohlraum *m*; (*in tooth*) Loch *nt*

CCTV *abbr* (**closed-circuit television**) CCTV *nt*; (*surveillance*) Videoüberwachung *f*

CD *abbr* (**compact disc**) CD *f*; **~-ROM** CD-ROM *f*

cease /si:s/ *vt/i* aufhören. **~-fire** *n* Waffenruhe *f*. **~less** *a*, **-ly** *adv* unaufhörlich

cedar /'si:də(r)/ *n* Zeder *f*

ceiling /'si:lɪŋ/ *n* [Zimmer]decke *f*; (*fig*) oberste Grenze *f*

celebrat|e /'selɪbreɪt/ *vt/i* feiern. **~ed** *a* berühmt (**for** wegen). **~ion** /-'breɪʃn/ *n* Feier *f*

celebrity /sɪ'lebrətɪ/ *n* Berühmtheit *f*

celery /'selərɪ/ *n* [Stangen]sellerie *m* & *f*

cell /sel/ *n* Zelle *f*

cellar /'selə(r)/ *n* Keller *m*

cellist /'tʃelɪst/ *n* Cellist(in) *m(f)*

cello /'tʃeləʊ/ *n* Cello *nt*

Celsius /'selsɪəs/ *a* Celsius

Celt /kelt/ *n* Kelte *m*/ Keltin *f*. **~ic** *a* keltisch

cement /sɪ'ment/ *n* Zement *m*; (*adhesive*) Kitt *m*

cemetery /'semətrɪ/ *n* Friedhof *m*

censor /'sensə(r)/ *n* Zensor *m* ● *vt* zensieren. **~ship** *n* Zensur *f*

census /'sensəs/ *n* Volkszählung *f*

cent /sent/ *n* Cent *m*

centenary /sen'ti:nərɪ/ *n*, (*Amer*) **centennial** /sen'tenɪəl/ *n* Hundertjahrfeier *f*

center /'sentə(r)/ *n* (*Amer*) = **centre**

centi|grade /'sentɪ-/ *a* Celsius. **~metre** *n* Zentimeter *m & nt*

central /'sentrəl/ *a*, **-ly** *adv* zentral. **~ 'heating** *n* Zentralheizung *f*. **~ize** *vt* zentralisieren

centre /'sentə(r)/ *n* Zentrum *nt*; (*middle*) Mitte *f* ● *v* (*pt/pp* **centred**) ● *vt* zentrieren. **~-'forward** *n* Mittelstürmer *m*

century /'sentʃərɪ/ *n* Jahrhundert *nt*

ceramic /sɪ'ræmɪk/ *a* Keramik-

cereal /'sɪərɪəl/ *n* Getreide *nt*; (*breakfast food*) Frühstücksflocken *pl*

ceremon|ial /serɪ'məʊnɪəl/ *a*, **-ly** *adv* zeremoniell, feierlich ● *n* Zeremoniell *nt*. **~ious** /-ɪəs/ *a*, **-ly** *adv* formell

ceremony /'serɪmənɪ/ *n* Zeremonie *f*, Feier *f*

certain /'sɜ:tn/ *a* sicher; (*not named*) gewiss; **for ~** mit Bestimmtheit; **make ~** (*check*) sich vergewissern (**that** dass); (*ensure*) dafür sorgen (**that** dass); **he is ~ to win** er wird ganz bestimmt siegen. **~ly** *adv* bestimmt, sicher; **~ly not!** auf keinen Fall! **~ty** *n* Sicherheit *f*, Gewissheit *f*; **it's a ~ty** es ist sicher

certificate /sə'tɪfɪkət/ *n* Bescheinigung *f*; (*Jur*) Urkunde *f*; (*Sch*) Zeugnis *nt*

certify /'sɜ:tɪfaɪ/ *vt* (*pt/pp* **-ied**) bescheinigen; (*declare insane*) für geisteskrank erklären

cf. *abbr* (*compare*) vgl.

chafe /tʃeɪf/ *vt* wund reiben

chaffinch /'tʃæfɪntʃ/ *n* Buchfink *m*

chain /tʃeɪn/ *n* Kette *f* ● *vt* ketten (**to** an + *acc*). **~ up** *vt* anketten

chain: ~ re'action *n* Kettenreaktion *f*. **~-smoker** *n* Kettenraucher *m*. **~ store** *n* Kettenladen *m*

chair /tʃeə(r)/ *n* Stuhl *m*; (*Univ*) Lehrstuhl *m*; (*Adm*) Vorsitzende(r) *m/f*. **~-lift** *n* Sessellift *m*. **~man** *n* Vorsitzende(r) *m/f*

chalet /'ʃæleɪ/ *n* Chalet *nt*

chalk /tʃɔ:k/ *n* Kreide *f*

challeng|e /'tʃælɪndʒ/ *n* Herausforderung *f*; (*Mil*) Anruf *m* ● *vt* herausfordern; (*Mil*) anrufen; (*fig*) anfechten <*statement*>. **~er** *n* Herausforderer *m*. **~ing** *a* herausfordernd; (*demanding*) anspruchsvoll

chamber /'tʃeɪmbə(r)/ *n* Kammer *f*; **C~ of Commerce** Handelskammer *f*. **~ music** *n* Kammermusik *f*

chamber music *n* Kammermusik *f*

chamois /'ʃæmɪ/ *n* **~[-leather]** Ledertuch *nt*

champagne /ʃæm'peɪn/ *n* Champagner *m*

champion /'tʃæmpɪən/ *n* (*Sport*) Meister(in) *m*(*f*); (*of cause*) Verfechter *m* ● *vt* sich einsetzen für. **~ship** *n* (*Sport*) Meisterschaft *f*

chance /tʃɑ:ns/ *n* Zufall *m*; (*prospect*) Chancen *pl*; (*likelihood*) Aussicht *f*; (*opportunity*) Gelegenheit *f*; **by ~** zufällig; **take a ~** ein Risiko eingehen; **give**

s.o. a ~ jdm eine Chance geben ● *attrib* zufällig ● *vt* **~ it** es riskieren

chancellor /ˈtʃɑːnsələ(r)/ *n* Kanzler *m*; (*Univ*) Rektor *m*

chancy /ˈtʃɑːnsɪ/ *a* riskant

change /tʃeɪndʒ/ *n* Veränderung *f*; (*alteration*) Änderung *f*; (*money*) Wechselgeld *nt*; **for a ~** zur Abwechslung ● *vt* wechseln; (*alter*) ändern; (*exchange*) umtauschen (**for** gegen); (*transform*) verwandeln; trocken legen <*baby*>; **~ one's clothes** sich umziehen; **~ trains** umsteigen ● *vi* sich verändern; (**~** *clothes*) sich umziehen; (**~** *trains*) umsteigen; **all ~!** alles aussteigen!

changeable /ˈtʃeɪndʒəbl/ *a* wechselhaft

ˈchanging-room *n* Umkleideraum *m*

channel /ˈtʃænl/ *n* Rinne *f*; (*Radio, TV*) Kanal *m*; (*fig*) Weg *m*; **the [English] C~** der Ärmelkanal; **the C~ Islands** die Kanalinseln

chant /tʃɑːnt/ *vt* singen; <*demonstrators:*> skandieren

chao|s /ˈkeɪɒs/ *n* Chaos *nt*. **~tic** /-ˈɒtɪk/ *a* chaotisch

chap /tʃæpl/ *n* [!] Kerl *m*

chapel /ˈtʃæpl/ *n* Kapelle *f*

chaplain /ˈtʃæplɪn/ *n* Geistliche(r) *m*

chapped /tʃæpt/ *a* <*skin*> aufgesprungen

chapter /ˈtʃæptə(r)/ *n* Kapitel *nt*

character /ˈkærɪktə(r)/ *n* Charakter *m*; (*in novel, play*) Gestalt *f*; (*Typ*) Schriftzeichen *nt*; **out of ~** uncharakteristisch; **quite a ~** [!] ein Original

characteristic /kærɪktəˈrɪstɪk/ *a*, **-ally** *adv* charakteristisch (**of** für) ● *n* Merkmal *nt*

characterize /ˈkærɪktəraɪz/ *vt* charakterisieren

charge /tʃɑːdʒ/ *n* (*price*) Gebühr *f*; (*Electr*) Ladung *f*; (*attack*) Angriff *m*; (*Jur*) Anklage *f*; **free of ~** kostenlos; **be in ~** verantwortlich sein (**of** für); **take ~** die Aufsicht übernehmen (**of** über + *acc*) ● *vt* berechnen <*fee*>; (*Electr*) laden; (*attack*) angreifen; (*Jur*) anklagen (**with** *gen*); **~ s.o. for sth** jdm etw berechnen

charitable /ˈtʃærɪtəbl/ *a* wohltätig; (*kind*) wohlwollend

charity /ˈtʃærətɪ/ *n* Nächstenliebe *f*; (*organization*) wohltätige Einrichtung *f*; **for ~** für Wohltätigkeitszwecke

charm /tʃɑːm/ *n* Reiz *m*; (*of person*) Charme *f*; (*object*) Amulett *nt* ● *vt* bezaubern. **~ing** *a*, **-ly** *adv* reizend; <*person, smile*> charmant

chart /tʃɑːt/ *n* Karte *f*; (*table*) Tabelle *f*

charter /ˈtʃɑːtə(r)/ *n* **~ [flight]** Charterflug *m* ● *vt* chartern; **~ed accountant** Wirtschaftsprüfer(in) *m(f)*

chase /tʃeɪs/ *n* Verfolgungsjagd *f* ● *vt* jagen, verfolgen. **~ away** *or* **off** *vt* wegjagen

chassis /ˈʃæsɪ/ *n* (*pl* **chassis** /-sɪz/) Chassis *nt*

chaste /tʃeɪst/ *a* keusch

chat /tʃæt/ *n* Plauderei *f*; **have a ~ with** plaudern mit ● *vi* (*pt/pp* **chatted**) plaudern. **~ show** *n* Talkshow *f*

chatter /ˈtʃætə(r)/ *n* Geschwätz *nt* ● *vi* schwatzen; <*child:*> plappern; <*teeth:*> klappern. **~box** *n* [!] Plappermaul *nt*

chatty /ˈtʃætɪ/ *a* (**-ier, -iest**) geschwätzig

chauffeur /ˈʃəʊfə(r)/ *n* Chauffeur *m*

cheap /tʃiːp/ *a* & *adv* (**-er, -est**), **-ly** *adv* billig. **~en** *vt* entwürdigen

cheat /tʃi:t/ *n* Betrüger(in) *m(f)*; (*at games*) Mogler *m* ● *vt* betrügen ● *vi* (*at games*) mogeln [!]

check¹ /tʃek/ *a* (*squared*) kariert ● *n* Karo *nt*

check² *n* Überprüfung *f*; (*inspection*) Kontrolle *f*; (*Chess*) Schach *nt*; (*Amer: bill*) Rechnung *f*; (*Amer: cheque*) Scheck *m*; (*Amer: tick*) Haken *m*; **keep a ~ on** kontrollieren ● *vt* [über]prüfen; (*inspect*) kontrollieren; (*restrain*) hemmen; (*stop*) aufhalten ● *vi* **[go and] ~** nachsehen. **~ in** *vi* sich anmelden; (*Aviat*) einchecken ● *vt* abfertigen; einchecken. **~ out** *vi* sich abmelden. **~ up** *vi* prüfen, kontrollieren; **~ up on** überprüfen

checked /tʃekt/ *a* kariert

check: ~-out *n* Kasse *f*. **~room** *n* (*Amer*) Garderobe *f*. **~-up** *n* (*Med*) [Kontroll]untersuchung *f*

cheek /tʃi:k/ *n* Backe *f*; (*impudence*) Frechheit *f*. **~y** *a*, **-ily** *adv* frech

cheer /tʃɪə(r)/ *n* Beifallsruf *m*; **three ~s** ein dreifaches Hoch (**for** auf + *acc*); **~s!** prost! (*goodbye*) tschüs! ● *vt* zujubeln (+ *dat*) ● *vi* jubeln. **~ up** *vt* aufmuntern; aufheitern ● *vi* munterer werden. **~ful** *a*, **-ly** *adv* fröhlich. **~fulness** *n* Fröhlichkeit *f*

cheerio /tʃɪərɪ'əʊ/ *int* [!] tschüs!

cheese /tʃi:z/ *n* Käse *m*. **~cake** *n* Käsekuchen *m*

chef /ʃef/ *n* Koch *m*

chemical /'kemɪkl/ *a*, **-ly** *adv* chemisch ● *n* Chemikalie *f*

chemist /'kemɪst/ *n* (*pharmacist*) Apotheker(in) *m(f)*; (*scientist*) Chemiker(in) *m(f)*; **~'s [shop]** Drogerie *f*; (*dispensing*) Apotheke *f*. **~ry** *n* Chemie *f*

cheque /tʃek/ *n* Scheck *m*. **~-book** *n* Scheckbuch *nt*. **~ card** *n* Scheckkarte *f*

cherish /'tʃerɪʃ/ *vt* lieben; (*fig*) hegen

cherry /'tʃerɪ/ *n* Kirsche *f* ● *attrib* Kirsch-

chess /tʃes/ *n* Schach *nt*

chess: ~board *n* Schachbrett *nt*. **~-man** *n* Schachfigur *f*

chest /tʃest/ *n* Brust *f*; (*box*) Truhe *f*

chestnut /'tʃesnʌt/ *n* Esskastanie *f*, Marone *f*; (*horse-*) [Ross]kastanie *f*

chest of 'drawers *n* Kommode *f*

chew /tʃu:/ *vt* kauen. **~ing-gum** *n* Kaugummi *m*

chick /tʃɪk/ *n* Küken *nt*

chicken /'tʃɪkɪn/ *n* Huhn *nt* ● *attrib* Hühner- ● *a* [!] feige

chief /tʃi:f/ *a* Haupt- ● *n* Chef *m*; (*of tribe*) Häuptling *m*. **~ly** *adv* hauptsächlich

child /tʃaɪld/ *n* (*pl* **~ren**) Kind *nt*

child: ~birth *n* Geburt *f*. **~hood** *n* Kindheit *f*. **~ish** *a* kindisch. **~less** *a* kinderlos. **~like** *a* kindlich. **~-minder** *n* Tagesmutter *f*

children /'tʃɪldrən/ *npl see* **child**

Chile /'tʃɪlɪ/ *n* Chile *nt*

chill /tʃɪl/ *n* Kälte *f*; (*illness*) Erkältung *f* ● *vt* kühlen

chilly /'tʃɪlɪ/ *a* kühl; **I felt ~** mich fröstelte [es]

chime /tʃaɪm/ *vi* läuten; <*clock:*> schlagen

chimney /'tʃɪmnɪ/ *n* Schornstein *m*. **~-pot** *n* Schornsteinaufsatz *m*. **~-sweep** *n* Schornsteinfeger *m*

chin /tʃɪn/ *n* Kinn *nt*

china /'tʃaɪnə/ *n* Porzellan *nt*

Chin|a *n* China *nt*. **~ese** /-'ni:z/ *a* chinesisch ● *n* (*Lang*)

Chinesisch *nt*; **the ~ese** *pl* die Chinesen

chink¹ /tʃɪŋk/ *n* (*slit*) Ritze *f*

chink² *n* Geklirr *nt* ● *vi* klirren; <*coins*:> klimpern

chip /tʃɪp/ *n* (*fragment*) Span *m*; (*in china, paintwork*) angeschlagene Stelle *f*; (*Computing, Gambling*) Chip *m*; **~s** *pl* (*Culin*) Pommes frites *pl*; (*Amer: crisps*) Chips *pl* ● *vt* (*pt*/*pp* **chipped**) (*damage*) anschlagen. **~ped** *a* angeschlagen

chirp /tʃɜ:p/ *vi* zwitschern; <*cricket*:> zirpen. **~y** *a* 🅇 munter

chit /tʃɪt/ *n* Zettel *m*

chocolate /ˈtʃɒkələt/ *n* Schokolade *f*; (*sweet*) Praline *f*

choice /tʃɔɪs/ *n* Wahl *f*; (*variety*) Auswahl *f* ● *a* auserlesen

choir /ˈkwaɪə(r)/ *n* Chor *m*. **~boy** *n* Chorknabe *m*

choke /tʃəʊk/ *n* (*Auto*) Choke *m* ● *vt* würgen; (*to death*) erwürgen ● *vi* sich verschlucken; **~ on** [fast] ersticken an (+ *dat*)

choose /tʃu:z/ *vt*/*i* (*pt* **chose**, *pp* **chosen**) wählen; (*select*) sich (*dat*) aussuchen; **~ to do/go** [freiwillig] tun/gehen; **as you ~** wie Sie wollen

choos[e]y /ˈtʃu:zɪ/ *a* 🅇 wählerisch

chop /tʃɒp/ *n* (*blow*) Hieb *m*; (*Culin*) Kotelett *nt* ● *vt* (*pt*/*pp* **chopped**) hacken. **~ down** *vt* abhacken; fällen <*tree*>. **~ off** *vt* abhacken

chop|per /ˈtʃɒpə(r)/ *n* Beil *nt*; 🅇 (*helicopter*) Hubschrauber *m*. **~py** *a* kabbelig

ˈchopsticks *npl* Essstäbchen *pl*

choral /ˈkɔ:rəl/ *a* Chor-

chord /kɔ:d/ *n* (*Mus*) Akkord *m*

chore /tʃɔ:(r)/ *n* lästige Pflicht *f*; **[household] ~s** Hausarbeit *f*

chorus /ˈkɔ:rəs/ *n* Chor *m*; (*of song*) Refrain *m*

chose, chosen /tʃəʊz, ˈtʃəʊzn/ *see* **choose**

Christ /kraɪst/ *n* Christus *m*

christen /ˈkrɪsn/ *vt* taufen

Christian /ˈkrɪstʃən/ *a* christlich ● *n* Christ(in) *m*(*f*). **~ity** /-strɪˈænətɪ/ *n* Christentum *nt*. **~ name** *n* Vorname *m*

Christmas /ˈkrɪsməs/ *n* Weihnachten *nt*. **~ card** *n* Weihnachtskarte *f*. **~ ˈDay** *n* erster Weihnachtstag *m*. **~ ˈEve** *n* Heiligabend *m*. **~ tree** *n* Weihnachtsbaum *m*

chrome /krəʊm/ *n*, **chromium** /ˈkrəʊmɪəm/ *n* Chrom *nt*

chronic /ˈkrɒnɪk/ *a* chronisch

chronicle /ˈkrɒnɪkl/ *n* Chronik *f*

chrysanthemum /krɪˈsænθəməm/ *n* Chrysantheme *f*

chubby /ˈtʃʌbɪ/ *a* (**-ier, -iest**) mollig

chuck /tʃʌk/ *vt* 🅇 schmeißen. **~ out** *vt* 🅇 rausschmeißen

chuckle /ˈtʃʌkl/ *vi* in sich (*acc*) hineinlachen

chum /tʃʌm/ *n* Freund(in) *m*(*f*)

chunk /tʃʌŋk/ *n* Stück *nt*

church /tʃɜ:tʃ/ *n* Kirche *f*. **~yard** *n* Friedhof *m*

churn /tʃɜ:n/ *vt* **~ out** am laufenden Band produzieren

cider /ˈsaɪdə(r)/ *n* ≈ Apfelwein *m*

cigar /sɪˈgɑ:(r)/ *n* Zigarre *f*

cigarette /sɪgəˈret/ *n* Zigarette *f*

cine-camera /ˈsɪnɪ-/ *n* Filmkamera *f*

cinema /ˈsɪnɪmə/ *n* Kino *nt*

cinnamon /ˈsɪnəmən/ *n* Zimt *m*

circle /ˈsɜ:kl/ *n* Kreis *m*; (*Theat*) Rang *m* ● *vt* umkreisen ● *vi* kreisen

circuit /ˈsɜ:kɪt/ *n* Runde *f*; (*racetrack*) Rennbahn *f*; (*Electr*)

Stromkreis *m*. **~ous** /sə'kju:ɪtəs/ *a* **~ route** Umweg *m*

circular /'sɜ:kjʊlə(r)/ *a* kreisförmig ● *n* Rundschreiben *nt*. **~ 'saw** *n* Kreissäge *f*. **~ 'tour** *n* Rundfahrt *f*

circulat|e /'sɜ:kjʊleɪt/ *vt* in Umlauf setzen ● *vi* zirkulieren. **~ion** /-'leɪʃn/ *n* Kreislauf *m*; (*of newspaper*) Auflage *f*

circumference /ʃə'kʌmfərəns/ *n* Umfang *m*

circumstance /'sɜ:kəmstəns/ *n* Umstand *m*; **~s** *pl* Umstände *pl*; (*financial*) Verhältnisse *pl*

circus /'sɜ:kəs/ *n* Zirkus *m*

cistern /'sɪstən/ *n* (*tank*) Wasserbehälter *m*; (*of WC*) Spülkasten *m*

cite /saɪt/ *vt* zitieren

citizen /'sɪtɪzn/ *n* Bürger(in) *m(f)*. **~ship** *n* Staatsangehörigkeit *f*

citrus /'sɪtrəs/ *n* **~ [fruit]** Zitrusfrucht *f*

city /'sɪtɪ/ *n* [Groß]stadt *f*

civic /'sɪvɪk/ *a* Bürger-

civil /'ʃɪvl/ *a* bürgerlich; <*aviation, defence*> zivil; (*polite*) höflich. **~ engi'neering** *n* Hoch- und Tiefbau *m*

civilian /sɪ'vɪljən/ *a* Zivil-; **in ~ clothes** in Zivil ● *n* Zivilist *m*

civiliz|ation /sɪvəlaɪ'zeɪʃn/ *n* Zivilisation *f*. **~e** /'sɪvəlaɪz/ *vt* zivilisieren

civil: ~'servant *n* Beamte(r) *m*/ Beamtin *f*. **C~ 'Service** *n* Staatsdienst *m*

claim /kleɪm/ *n* Anspruch *m*; (*application*) Antrag *m*; (*demand*) Forderung *f*; (*assertion*) Behauptung *f* ● *vt* beanspruchen; (*apply for*) beantragen; (*demand*) fordern; (*assert*) behaupten; (*collect*) abholen

clam /klæm/ *n* Klaffmuschel *f*

clamber /'klæmbə(r)/ *vi* klettern

clammy /'klæmɪ/ *a* **(-ier, -iest)** feucht

clamour /'klæmə(r)/ *n* Geschrei *nt* ● *vi* **~ for** schreien nach

clamp /klæmp/ *n* Klammer *f*; **[wheel] ~** Parkkralle *f* ● *vt* [ein]spannen ● *vi* 🅘 **~ down on** vorgehen gegen

clan /klæn/ *n* Clan *m*

clang /klæŋ/ *n* Schmettern *nt*. **~er** *n* 🅘 Schnitzer *m*

clank /klæŋk/ *vi* klirren

clap /klæp/ *n* **give s.o. a ~** jdm Beifall klatschen; **~ of thunder** Donnerschlag *m* ● *vt/i* (*pt/pp* **clapped**) Beifall klatschen (+ *dat*); **~ one's hands** [in die Hände] klatschen

clari|fication /klærɪfɪ'keɪʃn/ *n* Klärung *f*. **~fy** /'klærɪfaɪ/ *vt/i* (*pt/pp* **-ied**) klären

clarinet /klærɪ'net/ *n* Klarinette *f*

clarity /'klærətɪ/ *n* Klarheit *f*

clash /klæʃ/ *n* Geklirr *nt*; (*fig*) Konflikt *m* ● *vi* klirren; <*colours:*> sich beißen; <*events:*> ungünstig zusammenfallen

clasp /klɑ:sp/ *n* Verschluss *m* ● *vt* ergreifen; (*hold*) halten

class /klɑ:s/ *n* Klasse *f*; **travel first/second ~** erster/zweiter Klasse reisen ● *vt* einordnen

classic /'klæsɪk/ *a* klassisch ● *n* Klassiker *m*. **~al** *a* klassisch

classi|fication /klæsɪfɪ'keɪʃn/ *n* Klassifikation *f*. **~fy** /'klæsɪfaɪ/ *vt* (*pt/pp* **-ied**) klassifizieren

'classroom *n* Klassenzimmer *nt*

classy /'klɑ:sɪ/ *a* **(-ier, -iest)** 🅘 schick

clatter /'klætə(r)/ *n* Geklapper *nt* ● *vi* klappern

clause /klɔ:z/ *n* Klausel *f*; (*Gram*) Satzteil *m*

claw /klɔ:/ *n* Kralle *f*; (*of bird of prey & Techn*) Klaue *f*; (*of crab, lobster*) Schere *f* ● *vt* kratzen

clay /kleɪ/ *n* Lehm *m*; (*pottery*) Ton *m*

clean /kli:n/ *a* (**-er, -est**) sauber ● *adv* glatt ● *vt* sauber machen; putzen <*shoes, windows*>; **~ one's teeth** sich (*dat*) die Zähne putzen; **have sth ~ed** etw reinigen lassen. **~ up** *vt* sauber machen

cleaner /ˈkli:nə(r)/ *n* Putzfrau *f*; (*substance*) Reinigungsmittel *nt*; **[dry] ~'s** chemische Reinigung *f*

cleanliness /ˈklenlɪnɪs/ *n* Sauberkeit *f*

cleanse /klenz/ *vt* reinigen

clear /klɪə(r)/ *a* (**-er, -est**), **-ly** *adv* klar; (*obvious*) eindeutig; (*distinct*) deutlich; <*conscience*> rein; (*without obstacles*) frei; **make sth ~** etw klarmachen (**to** *dat*) ● *adv* **stand ~** zurücktreten; **keep ~ of** aus dem Wege gehen (+ *dat*) ● *vt* räumen; abräumen <*table*>; (*acquit*) freisprechen; (*authorize*) genehmigen; (*jump over*) überspringen; **~ one's throat** sich räuspern ● *vi* <*fog:*> sich auflösen. **~ away** *vt* wegräumen. **~ off** *vi* [!] abhauen. **~ out** *vt* ausräumen ● *vi* [!] abhauen. **~ up** *vt* (*tidy*) aufräumen; (*solve*) aufklären ● *vi* <*weather*>: sich aufklären

clearance /ˈklɪərəns/ *n* Räumung *f*; (*authorization*) Genehmigung *f*; (*customs*) [Zoll]abfertigung *f*; (*Techn*) Spielraum *m*. **~ sale** *n* Räumungsverkauf *m*

clench /klentʃ/ *vt* **~ one's fist** die Faust ballen; **~ one's teeth** die Zähne zusammenbeißen

clergy /ˈklɜ:dʒɪ/ *npl* Geistlichkeit *f*. **~man** *n* Geistliche(r) *m*

clerk /klɑ:k /klɜ:k/ *n* Büroangestellte(r) *m*/*f*; (*Amer: shop assistant*) Verkäufer(in) *m*(*f*)

clever /ˈklevə(r)/ *a* (**-er, -est**), **-ly** *adv* klug; (*skilful*) geschickt

cliché /ˈkli:ʃeɪ/ *n* Klischee *nt*

click /klɪk/ *vi* klicken

client /ˈklaɪənt/ *n* Kunde *m*/Kundin *f*; (*Jur*) Klient(in) *m*(*f*)

cliff /klɪf/ *n* Kliff *nt*

climate /ˈklaɪmət/ *n* Klima *nt*

climax /ˈklaɪmæks/ *n* Höhepunkt *m*

climb /klaɪm/ *n* Aufstieg *m* ● *vt* besteigen <*mountain*>; steigen auf (+ *acc*) <*ladder, tree*> ● *vi* klettern; (*rise*) steigen; <*road:*> ansteigen. **~ down** *vi* hinunter-/herunterklettern; (*from ladder, tree*) heruntersteigen; [!] nachgeben

climber /ˈklaɪmə(r)/ *n* Bergsteiger *m*; (*plant*) Kletterpflanze *f*

cling /klɪŋ/ *vi* (*pt*/*pp* **clung**) sich klammern (**to** an + *acc*); (*stick*) haften (**to** an + *dat*). **~ film** *n* Sichtfolie *f* mit Hafteffekt

clinic /ˈklɪnɪk/ *n* Klinik *f*. **~al** *a*, **-ly** *adv* klinisch

clink /klɪŋk/ *vi* klirren

clip[1] /klɪp/ *n* Klammer *f*; (*jewellery*) Klipp *m* ● *vt* (*pt*/*pp* **clipped**) anklammern (**to** an + *acc*)

clip[2] *n* (*extract*) Ausschnitt *m* ● *vt* schneiden; knipsen <*ticket*>. **~ping** *n* (*extract*) Ausschnitt *m*

cloak /kləʊk/ *n* Umhang *m*. **~room** *n* Garderobe *f*; (*toilet*) Toilette *f*

clobber /ˈklɒbə(r)/ *n* [!] Zeug *nt* ● *vt* ([!] *hit, defeat*) schlagen

clock /klɒk/ *n* Uhr *f*; ([!] *speedometer*) Tacho *m* ● *vi* **~ in/out** stechen

clock: ~wise *a* & *adv* im Uhrzeigersinn. **~work** *n* Uhrwerk *nt*; (*of toy*) Aufziehmechanismus *m*; **like ~work** [!] wie am Schnürchen

clod /klɒd/ *n* Klumpen *m*

clog /klɒg/ *vt/i* (*pt/pp* **clogged**) ~ **[up]** verstopfen

cloister /ˈklɔɪstə(r)/ *n* Kreuzgang *m*

clone /kləʊn/ *n* Klon *m* ● *vt* klonen

close¹ /kləʊs/ *a* (**-r, -st**) nah[e] (**to** *dat*); <*friend*> eng; <*weather*> schwül; **have a ~ shave** [!] mit knapper Not davonkommen ● *adv* nahe ● *n* (*street*) Sackgasse *f*

close² /kləʊz/ *n* Ende *nt*; **draw to a ~** sich dem Ende nähern ● *vt* zumachen, schließen; (*bring to an end*) beenden; sperren <*road*> ● *vi* sich schließen; <*shop*:> schließen, zumachen; (*end*) enden. **~ down** *vt* schließen; stilllegen <*factory*> ● *vi* schließen; <*factory*:> stillgelegt werden

closely /ˈkləʊslɪ/ *adv* eng, nah[e]; (*with attention*) genau

closet /ˈklɒzɪt/ *n* (*Amer*) Schrank *m*

close-up /ˈkləʊs-/ *n* Nahaufnahme *f*

closure /ˈkləʊʒə(r)/ *n* Schließung *f*; (*of factory*) Stilllegung *f*; (*of road*) Sperrung *f*

clot /klɒt/ *n* [Blut]gerinnsel *nt*; ([!] *idiot*) Trottel *m*

cloth /klɒθ/ *n* Tuch *nt*

clothe /kləʊð/ *vt* kleiden

clothes /kləʊðz/ *npl* Kleider *pl*. **~-line** *n* Wäscheleine *f*

clothing /ˈkləʊðɪŋ/ *n* Kleidung *f*

cloud /klaʊd/ *n* Wolke *f* ● *vi* ~ **over** sich bewölken

cloudy /ˈklaʊdɪ/ *a* (**-ier, -iest**) wolkig, bewölkt; <*liquid*> trübe

clout /klaʊt/ *n* [!] Schlag *m*; (*influence*) Einfluss *m*

clove /kləʊv/ *n* [Gewürz]nelke *f*; ~ **of garlic** Knoblauchzehe *f*

clover /ˈkləʊvə(r)/ *n* Klee *m*. **~ leaf** *n* Kleeblatt *nt*

clown /klaʊn/ *n* Clown *m* ● *vi* ~ **[about]** herumalbern

club /klʌb/ *n* Klub *m*; (*weapon*) Keule *f*; (*Sport*) Schläger *m*; **~s** *pl* (*Cards*) Kreuz *nt*, Treff *nt*

clue /kluː/ *n* Anhaltspunkt *m*; (*in crossword*) Frage *f*; **I haven't a ~** [!] ich habe keine Ahnung

clump /klʌmp/ *n* Gruppe *f*

clumsiness /ˈklʌmzɪnɪs/ *n* Ungeschicklichkeit *f*

clumsy /ˈklʌmzɪ/ *a* (**-ier, -iest**), **-ily** *adv* ungeschickt; (*unwieldy*) unförmig

clung /klʌŋ/ *see* **cling**

clutch /klʌtʃ/ *n* Griff *m*; (*Auto*) Kupplung *f*; **be in s.o.'s ~es** [!] in jds Klauen sein ● *vt* festhalten; (*grab*) ergreifen ● *vi* ~ **at** greifen nach

clutter /ˈklʌtə(r)/ *n* Kram *m* ● *vt* ~ **[up]** vollstopfen

c/o *abbr* (**care of**) bei

coach /kəʊtʃ/ *n* [Reise]bus *m*; (*Rail*) Wagen *m*; (*horse-drawn*) Kutsche *f*; (*Sport*) Trainer *m* ● *vt* Nachhilfestunden geben (+ *dat*); (*Sport*) trainieren

coal /kəʊl/ *n* Kohle *f*

coalition /kəʊəˈlɪʃn/ *n* Koalition *f*

ˈcoal-mine *n* Kohlenbergwerk *nt*

coarse /kɔːs/ *a* (**-r, -st**), **-ly** *adv* grob

coast /kəʊst/ *n* Küste *f* ● *vi* (*freewheel*) im Freilauf fahren; (*Auto*) im Leerlauf fahren. **~er** *n* (*mat*) Untersatz *m*

coast: ~guard *n* Küstenwache *f*. **~line** *n* Küste *f*

coat /kəʊt/ *n* Mantel *m*; (*of animal*) Fell *nt*; (*of paint*) Anstrich *m*; ~ **of arms** Wappen *nt* ● *vt* überziehen; (*with paint*) streichen. **~-hanger** *n* Kleiderbügel *m*. **~-hook** *n* Kleiderhaken *m*

coating /ˈkəʊtɪŋ/ *n* Überzug *m*, Schicht *f*; (*of paint*) Anstrich *m*

coax /kəʊks/ *vt* gut zureden (+ *dat*)

cobble¹ /'kɒbl/ *n* Kopfstein *m*; **~s** *pl* Kopfsteinpflaster *nt*

cobble² *vt* flicken. **~r** *n* Schuster *m*

cobweb /'kɒb-/ *n* Spinnengewebe *nt*

cock /kɒk/ *n* Hahn *m*; (*any male bird*) Männchen *nt* ● *vt* <*animal:*> **~ its ears** die Ohren spitzen; **~ the gun** den Hahn spannen

cockerel /'kɒkərəl/ *n* [junger] Hahn *m*

cockney /'kɒknɪ/ *n* (*dialect*) Cockney *nt*; (*person*) Cockney *m*

cock: ~pit *n* (*Aviat*) Cockpit *nt*. **~roach** /-rəʊtʃ/ *n* Küchenschabe *f*. **~tail** *n* Cocktail *m*. **~-up** *n* ☒ **make a ~-up** Mist bauen (**of** bei)

cocky /'kɒkɪ/ *a* (**-ier, -iest**) ! eingebildet

cocoa /'kəʊkəʊ/ *n* Kakao *m*

coconut /'kəʊkənʌt/ *n* Kokosnuß *f*

cod /kɒd/ *n inv* Kabeljau *m*

COD *abbr* (**cash on delivery**) per Nachnahme

coddle /'kɒdl/ *vt* verhätscheln

code /kəʊd/ *n* Kode *m*; (*Computing*) Code *m*; (*set of rules*) Kodex *m*. **~d** *a* verschlüsselt

coerc|e /kəʊ'ɜːs/ *vt* zwingen. **~ion** /-'ɜːʃn/ *n* Zwang *m*

coffee /'kɒfɪ/ *n* Kaffee *m*

coffee: ~-grinder *n* Kaffeemühle *f*. **~-pot** *n* Kaffeekanne *f*. **~-table** *n* Couchtisch *m*

coffin /'kɒfɪn/ *n* Sarg *m*

cogent /'kəʊdʒənt/ *a* überzeugend

coherent /kəʊ'hɪərənt/ *a* zusammenhängend; (*comprehensible*) verständlich

coil /kɔɪl/ *n* Rolle *f*; (*Electr*) Spule *f*; (*one ring*) Windung *f* ● *vt* **~ [up]** zusammenrollen

coin /kɔɪn/ *n* Münze *f* ● *vt* prägen

coincide /kəʊɪn'saɪd/ *vi* zusammenfallen; (*agree*) übereinstimmen

coinciden|ce /kəʊ'ɪnsɪdəns/ *n* Zufall *m*. **~tal** /-'dentl/ *a*, **-ly** *adv* zufällig

coke /kəʊk/ *n* Koks *m*

Coke (P) *n* (*drink*) Cola *f*

cold /kəʊld/ *a* (**-er, -est**) kalt; **I am** *or* **feel ~** mir ist kalt ● *n* Kälte *f*; (*Med*) Erkältung *f*

cold: ~-'blooded *a* kaltblütig. **~-'hearted** *a* kaltherzig. **~ly** *adv* (*fig*) kalt, kühl. **~ness** *n* Kälte *f*

collaborat|e /kə'læbəreɪt/ *vi* zusammenarbeiten (**with** mit); **~e on sth** mitarbeiten bei etw. **~ion** /-'reɪʃn/ *n* Zusammenarbeit *f*, Mitarbeit *f*; (*with enemy*) Kollaboration *f*. **~or** *n* Mitarbeiter(in) *m(f)*; Kollaborateur *m*

collaps|e /kə'læps/ *n* Zusammenbruch *m*; Einsturz *m* ● *vi* zusammenbrechen; <*roof, building*> einstürzen. **~ible** *a* zusammenklappbar

collar /'kɒlə(r)/ *n* Kragen *m*; (*for animal*) Halsband *nt*. **~-bone** *n* Schlüsselbein *nt*

colleague /'kɒliːg/ *n* Kollege *m*/Kollegin *f*

collect /kə'lekt/ *vt* sammeln; (*fetch*) abholen; einsammeln <*tickets*>; einziehen <*taxes*> ● *vi* sich [an]sammeln ● *adv* **call ~** (*Amer*) ein R-Gespräch führen

collection /kə'lekʃn/ *n* Sammlung *f*; (*in church*) Kollekte *f*; (*of post*) Leerung *f*; (*designer's*) Kollektion *f*

collector /kə'lektə(r)/ *n* Sammler(in) *m(f)*

college /ˈkɒlɪdʒ/ *n* College *nt*
collide /kəˈlaɪd/ *vi* zusammenstoßen
colliery /ˈkɒlɪərɪ/ *n* Kohlengrube *f*
collision /kəˈlɪʒn/ *n* Zusammenstoß *m*
colloquial /kəˈləʊkwɪəl/ *a*, **-ly** *adv* umgangssprachlich
Cologne /kəˈləʊn/ *n* Köln *nt*
colon /ˈkəʊlən/ *n* Doppelpunkt
colonel /ˈkɜːnl/ *n* Oberst *m*
colonial /kəˈləʊnɪəl/ *a* Kolonial-
colony /ˈkɒlənɪ/ *n* Kolonie *f*
colossal /kəˈlɒsl/ *a* riesig
colour /ˈkʌlə(r)/ *n* Farbe *f*; (*complexion*) Gesichtsfarbe *f*; (*race*) Hautfarbe *f*; **off ~** [!] nicht ganz auf der Höhe ● *vt* färben; **~ [in]** ausmalen
colour: ~-blind *a* farbenblind. **~ed** *a* farbig ● *n* (*person*) Farbige(r) *m/f*. **~-fast** *a* farbecht. **~ film** *n* Farbfilm *m*. **~ful** *a* farbenfroh. **~less** *a* farblos. **~ photo[graph]** *n* Farbaufnahme *f*. **~ television** *n* Farbfernsehen *nt*
column /ˈkɒləm/ *n* Säule *f*; (*of soldiers, figures*) Kolonne *f*; (*Typ*) Spalte *f*; (*Journ*) Kolumne *f*
comb /kəʊm/ *n* Kamm *m* ● *vt* kämmen; (*search*) absuchen; **~ one's hair** sich (*dat*) [die Haare] kämmen
combat /ˈkɒmbæt/ *n* Kampf *m*
combination /kɒmbɪˈneɪʃn/ *n* Kombination *f*
combine¹ /kəmˈbaɪn/ *vt* verbinden ● *vi* sich verbinden; <*people*:> sich zusammenschließen
combine² /ˈkɒmbaɪn/ *n* (*Comm*) Konzern *m*
combustion /kəmˈbʌstʃn/ *n* Verbrennung *f*
come /kʌm/ *vi* (*pt* **came**, *pp* **come**) kommen; (*reach*) reichen (**to** an + *acc*); **that ~s to £10** das macht £10; **~ into money** zu Geld kommen; **~ true** wahr werden; **~ in two sizes** in zwei Größen erhältlich sein; **the years to ~** die kommenden Jahre; **how ~?** [!] wie das? **~ about** *vi* geschehen. **~ across** *vi* herüberkommen; [!] klar werden ● *vt* stoßen auf (+ *acc*). **~ apart** *vi* sich auseinander nehmen lassen; (*accidentally*) auseinander gehen. **~ away** *vi* weggehen; <*thing*:> abgehen. **~ back** *vi* zurückkommen. **~ by** *vi* vorbeikommen ● *vt* (*obtain*) bekommen. **~ in** *vi* hereinkommen. **~ off** *vi* abgehen; (*take place*) stattfinden; (*succeed*) klappen [!]. **~ out** *vi* herauskommen; <*book*:> erscheinen; <*stain*:> herausgehen. **~ round** *vi* vorbeikommen; (*after fainting*) [wieder] zu sich kommen; (*change one's mind*) sich umstimmen lassen. **~ to** *vi* [wieder] zu sich kommen. **~ up** *vi* heraufkommen; <*plant*:> aufgehen; (*reach*) reichen (**to** bis); **~ up with** sich (*dat*) einfallen lassen
ˈcome-back *n* Comeback *nt*
comedian /kəˈmiːdɪən/ *n* Komiker *m*
ˈcome-down *n* Rückschritt *m*
comedy /ˈkɒmədɪ/ *n* Komödie *f*
comet /ˈkɒmɪt/ *n* Komet *m*
comfort /ˈkʌmfət/ *n* Bequemlichkeit *f*; (*consolation*) Trost *m* ● *vt* trösten
comfortable /ˈkʌmfətəbl/ *a*, **-bly** *adv* bequem
ˈcomfort station *n* (*Amer*) öffentliche Toilette *f*
comfy /ˈkʌmfɪ/ *a* [!] bequem
comic /ˈkɒmɪk/ *a* komisch ● *n* Komiker *m*; (*periodical*) Comic-Heft *nt*

coming /'kʌmɪŋ/ *a* kommend ● *n* Kommen *nt*

comma /'kɒmə/ *n* Komma *nt*

command /kə'mɑ:nd/ *n* Befehl *m*; (*Mil*) Kommando *nt*; (*mastery*) Beherrschung *f* ● *vt* befehlen (+ *dat*); kommandieren <*army*>

command|er /kə'mɑ:ndə(r)/ *n* Befehlshaber *m*. **~ing officer** *n* Befehlshaber *m*

commemorat|e /kə'memərert/ *vt* gedenken (+ *gen*). **~ion** /-'reɪʃn/ *n* Gedenken *nt*

commence /kə'mens/ *vt/i* anfangen, beginnen

commend /kə'mend/ *vt* loben; (*recommend*) empfehlen (**to** *dat*)

comment /'kɒment/ *n* Bemerkung *f*; **no ~!** kein Kommentar! ● *vi* sich äußern (**on** zu); **~ on** (*Journ*) kommentieren

commentary /'kɒməntrɪ/ *n* Kommentar *m*; **[running] ~** (*Radio, TV*) Reportage *f*

commentator /'kɒmənteɪtə(r)/ *n* Kommentator *m*; (*Sport*) Reporter *m*

commerce /'kɒmɜ:s/ *n* Handel *m*

commercial /kə'mɜ:ʃl/ *a*, **-ly** *adv* kommerziell ● *n* (*Radio, TV*) Werbespot *m*

commission /kə'mɪʃn/ *n* (*order for work*) Auftrag *m*; (*body of people*) Kommission *f*; (*payment*) Provision *f*; (*Mil*) [Offiziers]patent *nt*; **out of ~** außer Betrieb ● *vt* beauftragen <*s.o.*>; in Auftrag geben <*thing*>; (*Mil*) zum Offizier ernennen

commit /kə'mɪt/ *vt* (*pt/pp* **committed**) begehen; (*entrust*) anvertrauen (**to** *dat*); (*consign*) einweisen (**to** in + *acc*); **~ oneself** sich festlegen; (*involve oneself*) sich engagieren. **~ment** *n* Verpflichtung *f*; (*involvement*) Engagement *nt*. **~ted** *a* engagiert

committee /kə'mɪtɪ/ *n* Ausschuss *m*, Komitee *nt*

common /'kɒmən/ *a* (**-er, -est**) gemeinsam; (*frequent*) häufig; (*ordinary*) gewöhnlich; (*vulgar*) ordinär ● *n* Gemeindeland *nt*; **have in ~** gemeinsam haben; **House of C~s** Unterhaus *nt*

common: ~ly *adv* allgemein. **C~ 'Market** *n* Gemeinsamer Markt *m*. **~place** *a* häufig. **~-room** *n* Aufenthaltsraum *m*. **~ 'sense** *n* gesunder Menschenverstand *m*

commotion /kə'məʊʃn/ *n* Tumult *m*

communal /'kɒmjʊnl/ *a* gemeinschaftlich

communicate /kə'mju:nɪkeɪt/ *vt* mitteilen (**to** *dat*); übertragen <disease> ● *vi* sich verständigen

communication /kəmju:nɪ'keɪʃn/ *n* Verständigung *f*; (*contact*) Verbindung *f*; (*message*) Mitteilung *f*; **~s** *pl* (*technology*) Nachrichtenwesen *nt*

communicative /kə'mju:nɪkətɪv/ *a* mitteilsam

Communion /kə'mju:nɪən/ *n* **[Holy] ~** das [heilige] Abendmahl; (*Roman Catholic*) die [heilige] Kommunion

communis|m /'kɒmjʊnɪzm/ *n* Kommunismus *m*. **~t** /-ɪst/ *a* kommunistisch ● *n* Kommunist(in) *m(f)*

community /kə'mju:nətɪ/ *n* Gemeinschaft *f*; **local ~** Gemeinde *f*

commute /kə'mju:t/ *vi* pendeln. **~r** *n* Pendler(in) *m(f)*

compact /kəm'pækt/ *a* kompakt

companion /kəm'pænjən/ *n* Begleiter(in) *m(f)*. **~ship** *n* Gesellschaft *f*

company /ˈkʌmpənɪ/ *n* Gesellschaft *f*; (*firm*) Firma *f*; (*Mil*) Kompanie *f*; (🅸 *guests*) Besuch *m*. **~ car** *n* Firmenwagen *m*

comparable /ˈkɒmpərəbl/ *a* vergleichbar

comparative /kəmˈpærətɪv/ *a* vergleichend; (*relative*) relativ ● *n* (*Gram*) Komparativ *m*. **~ly** *adv* verhältnismäßig

compare /kəmˈpeə(r)/ *vt* vergleichen (**with/to** mit) ● *vi* sich vergleichen lassen

comparison /kəmˈpærɪsn/ *n* Vergleich *m*

compartment /kəmˈpɑ:tmənt/ *n* Fach *nt*; (*Rail*) Abteil *nt*

compass /ˈkʌmpəs/ *n* Kompass *m*

compassion /kəmˈpæʃn/ *n* Mitleid *nt*. **~ate** /-ʃənət/ *a* mitfühlend

compatible /kəmˈpætəbl/ *a* vereinbar; <*drugs*> verträglich; (*Techn*) kompatibel; **be ~** <*people:*> [gut] zueinander passen

compatriot /kəmˈpætrɪət/ *n* Landsmann *m* /-männin *f*

compel /kəmˈpel/ *vt* (*pt/pp* **compelled**) zwingen

compensat|e /ˈkɒmpənseɪt/ *vt* entschädigen. **~ion** /-ˈseɪʃn/ *n* Entschädigung *f*; (*fig*) Ausgleich *m*

compete /kəmˈpi:t/ *vi* konkurrieren; (*take part*) teilnehmen (**in** an + *dat*)

competen|ce /ˈkɒmpɪtəns/ *n* Fähigkeit *f*. **~t** *a* fähig

competition /kɒmpəˈtɪʃn/ *n* Konkurrenz *f*; (*contest*) Wettbewerb *m*; (*in newspaper*) Preisausschreiben *nt*

competitive /kəmˈpetətɪv/ *a* (*Comm*) konkurrenzfähig

competitor /kəmˈpetɪtə(r)/ *n* Teilnehmer *m*; (*Comm*) Konkurrent *m*

compile /kəmˈpaɪl/ *vt* zusammenstellen

complacen|cy /kəmˈpleɪsənsɪ/ *n* Selbstzufriedenheit *f*. **~t** *a*, **-ly** *adv* selbstzufrieden

complain /kəmˈpleɪn/ *vi* klagen (**about/of** über + *acc*); (*formally*) sich beschweren. **~t** *n* Klage *f*; (*formal*) Beschwerde *f*; (*Med*) Leiden *nt*

complement¹ /ˈkɒmplɪmənt/ *n* Ergänzung *f*; **full ~** volle Anzahl *f*

complement² /ˈkɒmplɪment/ *vt* ergänzen

complete /kəmˈpli:t/ *a* vollständig; (*finished*) fertig; (*utter*) völlig ● *vt* vervollständigen; (*finish*) abschließen; (*fill in*) ausfüllen. **~ly** *adv* völlig

completion /kəmˈpli:ʃn/ *n* Vervollständigung *f*; (*end*) Abschluss *m*

complex /ˈkɒmpleks/ *a* komplex ● *n* Komplex *m*

complexion /kəmˈplekʃn/ *n* Teint *m*; (*colour*) Gesichtsfarbe *f*

complexity /kəmˈpleksətɪ/ *n* Komplexität *f*

complicat|e /ˈkɒmplɪkeɪt/ *vt* komplizieren. **~ed** *a* kompliziert. **~ion** /-ˈkeɪʃn/ *n* Komplikation *f*

compliment /ˈkɒmplɪmənt/ *n* Kompliment *nt*; **~s** *pl* Grüße *pl* ● *vt* ein Kompliment machen (+ *dat*). **~ary** /-ˈmentərɪ/ *a* schmeichelhaft; (*given free*) Frei-

comply /kəmˈplaɪ/ *vi* (*pt/pp* **-ied**) **~ with** nachkommen (+ *dat*)

compose /kəmˈpəʊz/ *vt* verfassen; (*Mus*) komponieren; **be ~d of** sich zusammensetzen aus. **~r** *n* Komponist *m*

composition /kɒmpə'zɪʃn/ *n* Komposition *f*; (*essay*) Aufsatz *m*
compost /'kɒmpɒst/ *n* Kompost *m*
composure /kəm'pəʊʒə(r)/ *n* Fassung *f*
compound /'kɒmpaʊnd/ *a* zusammengesetzt; <*fracture*> kompliziert ● *n* (*Chem*) Verbindung *f*; (*Gram*) Kompositum *nt*
comprehen|d /kɒmprɪ'hend/ *vt* begreifen, verstehen. **~sible** *a*, **-bly** *adv* verständlich. **~sion** /-'henʃn/ *n* Verständnis *nt*
comprehensive /kɒmprɪ'hensɪv/ *a* & *n* umfassend; **~ [school]** Gesamtschule *f*. **~ insurance** *n* (*Auto*) Vollkaskoversicherung *f*
compress /kəm'pres/ *vt* zusammenpressen; **~ed air** Druckluft *f*
comprise /kəm'praɪz/ *vt* umfassen, bestehen aus
compromise /'kɒmprəmaɪz/ *n* Kompromiss *m* ● *vt* kompromittieren <*person*> ● *vi* einen Kompromiss schließen
compuls|ion /kəm'pʌlʃn/ *n* Zwang *m*. **~ive** /-sɪv/ *a* zwanghaft. **~ory** /-sərɪ/ *a* obligatorisch
comput|er /kəm'pju:tə(r)/ *n* Computer *m*. **~er game** *n* Computerspiel. **~erize** *vt* computerisieren <*data*>; auf Computer umstellen <*firm*>. **~-'literate** *a* mit Computern vertraut. **~ing** *n* Computertechnik *f*
comrade /'kɒmreɪd/ *n* Kamerad *m*; (*Pol*) Genosse *m*/Genossin *f*
con¹ /kɒn/ *see* **pro**
con² *n* 🄸 Schwindel *m* ● *vt* (*pt/pp* **conned**) 🄸 beschwindeln
concave /'kɒŋkeɪv/ *a* konkav
conceal /kən'si:l/ *vt* verstecken; (*keep secret*) verheimlichen
concede /kən'si:d/ *vt* zugeben; (*give up*) aufgeben
conceit /kən'si:t/ *n* Einbildung *f*. **~ed** *a* eingebildet
conceivable /kən'si:vəbl/ *a* denkbar
conceive /kən'si:v/ *vt* (*Biol*) empfangen; (*fig*) sich (*dat*) ausdenken ● *vi* schwanger werden
concentrat|e /'kɒnsəntreɪt/ *vt* konzentrieren ● *vi* sich konzentrieren. **~ion** /-'treɪʃn/ *n* Konzentration *f*
concern /kən'sɜ:n/ *n* Angelegenheit *f*; (*worry*) Sorge *f*; (*Comm*) Unternehmen *nt* ● *vt* (*be about, affect*) betreffen; (*worry*) kümmern; **be ~ed about** besorgt sein um; **~ oneself with** sich beschäftigen mit; **as far as I am ~ed** was mich angeht *od* betrifft. **~ing** *prep* bezüglich (+ *gen*)
concert /'kɒnsət/ *n* Konzert *nt*
concerto /kən'tʃeətəʊ/ *n* Konzert *nt*
concession /kən'seʃn/ *n* Zugeständnis *nt*; (*Comm*) Konzession *f*; (*reduction*) Ermäßigung *f*
concise /kən'saɪs/ *a*, **-ly** *adv* kurz
conclude /kən'klu:d/ *vt/i* schließen
conclusion /kən'klu:ʒn/ *n* Schluss *m*; **in ~** abschließend, zum Schluss
conclusive /kən'klu:sɪv/ *a* schlüssig
concoct /kən'kɒkt/ *vt* zusammenstellen; (*fig*) fabrizieren. **~ion** /-ɒkʃn/ *n* Zusammenstellung *f*; (*drink*) Gebräu *nt*
concrete /'kɒnkri:t/ *a* konkret ● *n* Beton *m* ● *vt* betonieren
concurrently /kən'kʌrəntlɪ/ *adv* gleichzeitig

concussion /kən'kʌʃn/ *n* Gehirnerschütterung *f*
condemn /kən'dem/ *vt* verurteilen; (*declare unfit*) für untauglich erklären. **~ation** /kɒndem'neɪʃn/ *n* Verurteilung *f*
condensation /kɒnden'seɪʃn/ *n* Kondensation *f*
condense /kən'dens/ *vt* zusammenfassen
condescend /kɒndɪ'send/ *vi* sich herablassen (**to** zu). **~ing** *a*, **-ly** *adv* herablassend
condition /kən'dɪʃn/ *n* Bedingung *f*; (*state*) Zustand *m*; **~s** *pl* Verhältnisse *pl*; **on ~ that** unter der Bedingung, dass ● *vt* (*Psych*) konditionieren. **~al** *a* bedingt ● *n* (*Gram*) Konditional *m*. **~er** *n* Pflegespülung *f*; (*for fabrics*) Weichspüler *m*
condolences /kən'dəʊlənsɪz/ *npl* Beileid *nt*
condom /'kɒndəm/ *n* Kondom *nt*
condominium /kɒndə'mɪnɪəm/ *n* (*Amer*) ≈ Eigentumswohnung *f*
conduct¹ /'kɒndʌkt/ *n* Verhalten *nt*; (*Sch*) Betragen *nt*
conduct² /kən'dʌkt/ *vt* führen; (*Phys*) leiten; (*Mus*) dirigieren. **~or** *n* Dirigent *m*; (*of bus*) Schaffner *m*; (*Phys*) Leiter *m*
cone *n* /kəʊn/ Kegel *m*; (*Bot*) Zapfen *m*; (*for ice-cream*) [Eis]tüte *f*; (*Auto*) Leitkegel *m*
confectioner /kən'fekʃənə(r)/ *n* Konditor *m*. **~y** *n* Süßwaren *pl*
conference /'kɒnfərəns/ *n* Konferenz *f*
confess /kən'fes/ *vt/i* gestehen; (*Relig*) beichten. **~ion** /-eʃn/ *n* Geständnis *nt*; (*Relig*) Beichte *f*
confetti /kən'fetɪ/ *n* Konfetti *nt*
confide /kən'faɪd/ *vt* anvertrauen ● *vi* **~ in s.o.** sich jdm anvertrauen
confidence /'kɒnfɪdəns/ *n* (*trust*) Vertrauen *nt*; (*self-assurance*) Selbstvertrauen *nt*; (*secret*) Geheimnis *nt*; **in ~** im Vertrauen. **~ trick** *n* Schwindel *m*
confident /'kɒnfɪdənt/ *a*, **-ly** *adv* zuversichtlich; (*self-assured*) selbstsicher
confidential /kɒnfɪ'denʃl/ *a*, **-ly** *adv* vertraulich
confine /kən'faɪn/ *vt* beschränken (**to** auf + *acc*). **~d** *a* (*narrow*) eng
confirm /kən'fɜ:m/ *vt* bestätigen; (*Relig*) konfirmieren; (*Roman Catholic*) firmen. **~ation** /kɒnfə-'meɪʃn/ *n* Bestätigung *f*; Konfirmation *f*; Firmung *f*
confiscat|e /'kɒnfɪskeɪt/ *vt* beschlagnahmen. **~ion** /-'keɪʃn/ *n* Beschlagnahme *f*
conflict¹ /'kɒnflɪkt/ *n* Konflikt *m*
conflict² /kən'flɪkt/ *vi* im Widerspruch stehen (**with** zu). **~ing** *a* widersprüchlich
conform /kən'fɔ:m/ *vi* <*person*:> sich anpassen; <*thing*:> entsprechen (**to** *dat*). **~ist** *n* Konformist *m*
confounded /kən'faʊndɪd/ *a* [!] verflixt
confront /kən'frʌnt/ *vt* konfrontieren. **~ation** /kɒnfrən'teɪʃn/ *n* Konfrontation *f*
confus|e /kən'fju:z/ *vt* verwirren; (*mistake for*) verwechseln (**with** mit). **~ing** *a* verwirrend. **~ion** /-ju:ʒn/ *n* Verwirrung *f*; (*muddle*) Durcheinander *nt*
congenial /kən'dʒi:nɪəl/ *a* angenehm
congest|ed /kən'dʒestɪd/ *a* verstopft; (*with people*) überfüllt. **~ion** /-estʃn/ *n* Verstopfung *f*; Überfüllung *f*
congratulat|e /kən'grætjʊleɪt/ *vt* gratulieren (+ *dat*) (**on** zu). **~ions** /-'leɪʃnz/ *npl* Glückwünsche *pl*; **~ions!** [ich] gratuliere!

congregation /kɒŋgrɪ'geɪʃn/ *n* (*Relig*) Gemeinde *f*
congress /'kɒŋgres/ *n* Kongress *m*. **~man** *n* Kongressabgeordnete(r) *m*
conical /'kɒnɪkl/ *a* kegelförmig
conifer /'kɒnɪfə(r)/ *n* Nadelbaum *m*
conjecture /kən'dʒektʃə(r)/ *n* Mutmaßung *f*
conjunction /kən'dʒʌŋkʃn/ *n* Konjunktion *f*; **in ~ with** zusammen mit
conjur|e /'kʌndʒə(r)/ *vi* zaubern ● *vt* **~e up** heraufbeschwören. **~or** *n* Zauberkünstler *m*
conk /kɒŋk/ *vi* **~ out** [!] <*machine:*> kaputtgehen
conker /'kɒŋkə(r)/ *n* [!] Kastanie *f*
'**con-man** *n* [!] Schwindler *m*
connect /kə'nekt/ *vt* verbinden (**to** mit); (*Electr*) anschließen (**to** an + *acc*); **be ~ed with** zu tun haben mit; (*be related to*) verwandt sein mit ● *vi* verbunden sein; <*train:*> Anschluss haben (**with** an + *acc*)
connection /kə'nekʃn/ *n* Verbindung *f*; (*Rail, Electr*) Anschluss *m*; **in ~ with** in Zusammenhang mit. **~s** *npl* Beziehungen *pl*
connoisseur /kɒnə'sɜ:(r)/ *n* Kenner *m*
conquer /'kɒŋkə(r)/ *vt* erobern; (*fig*) besiegen. **~or** *n* Eroberer *m*
conquest /'kɒŋkwest/ *n* Eroberung *f*
conscience /'kɒnʃəns/ *n* Gewissen *nt*
conscientious /kɒnʃɪ'enʃəs/ *a*, **-ly** *adv* gewissenhaft
conscious /'kɒnʃəs/ *a*, **-ly** *adv* bewusst; **[fully] ~** bei [vollem] Bewusstsein; **be/become ~ of sth** sich (*dat*) etw (*gen*) bewusst sein/werden. **~ness** *n* Bewusstsein *nt*
conscript /'kɒnskrɪpt/ *n* Einberufene(r) *m*
consecrat|e /'kɒnsɪkreɪt/ *vt* weihen; einweihen <*church*>. **~ion** /-'kreɪʃn/ *n* Weihe *f*; Einweihung *f*
consecutive /kən'sekjʊtɪv/ *a* aufeinanderfolgend. **-ly** *adv* fortlaufend
consent /kən'sent/ *n* Einwilligung *f*, Zustimmung *f* ● *vi* einwilligen (**to** in + *acc*), zustimmen (**to** *dat*)
consequen|ce /'kɒnsɪkwəns/ *n* Folge *f*. **~t** *a* daraus folgend. **~tly** *adv* folglich
conservation /kɒnsə'veɪʃn/ *n* Erhaltung *f*, Bewahrung *f*. **~ist** *n* Umweltschützer *m*
conservative /kən'sɜ:vətɪv/ *a* konservativ; <*estimate*> vorsichtig. **C~** (*Pol*) *a* konservativ ● *n* Konservative(r) *m*/*f*
conservatory /kən'sɜ:vətrɪ/ *n* Wintergarten *m*
conserve /kən'sɜ:v/ *vt* erhalten, bewahren; sparen <*energy*>
consider /kən'sɪdə(r)/ *vt* erwägen; (*think over*) sich (*dat*) überlegen; (*take into account*) berücksichtigen; (*regard as*) betrachten als; **~ doing sth** erwägen, etw zu tun. **~able** /-əbl/ *a*, **-bly** *adv* erheblich
consider|ate /kən'sɪdərət/ *a*, **-ly** *adv* rücksichtsvoll. **~ation** /-'reɪʃn/ *n* Erwägung *f*; (*thoughtfulness*) Rücksicht *f*; (*payment*) Entgelt *nt*; **take into ~ation** berücksichtigen. **~ing** *prep* wenn man bedenkt (**that** dass)
consist /kən'sɪst/ *vi* **~ of** bestehen aus
consisten|cy /kən'sɪstənsɪ/ *n* Konsequenz *f*; (*density*) Konsistenz *f*. **~t** *a* konsequent; (*unchanging*) gleichbleibend.

~tly *adv* konsequent; (*constantly*) ständig

consolation /kɒnsəˈleɪʃn/ *n* Trost *m*. **~ prize** *n* Trostpreis *m*

console /kənˈsəʊl/ *vt* trösten

consonant /ˈkɒnsənənt/ *n* Konsonant *m*

conspicuous /kənˈspɪkjʊəs/ *a* auffällig

conspiracy /kənˈspɪrəsɪ/ *n* Verschwörung *f*

constable /ˈkʌnstəbl/ *n* Polizist *m*

constant /ˈkɒnstənt/ *a*, **-ly** *adv* beständig; (*continuous*) ständig

constipat|ed /ˈkɒnstɪpeɪtɪd/ *a* verstopft. **~ion** /-ˈpeɪʃn/ *n* Verstopfung *f*

constituency /kənˈstɪtjʊənsɪ/ *n* Wahlkreis *m*

constitut|e /ˈkɒnstɪtjuːt/ *vt* bilden. **~ion** /-ˈtjuːʃn/ *n* (*Pol*) Verfassung *f*; (*of person*) Konstitution *f*

constraint /kənˈstreɪnt/ *n* Zwang *m*; (*restriction*) Beschränkung *f*; (*strained manner*) Gezwungenheit *f*

construct /kənˈstrʌkt/ *vt* bauen. **~ion** /-ʌkʃn/ *n* Bau *m*; (*Gram*) Konstruktion *f*; (*interpretation*) Deutung *f*; **under ~ion** im Bau

consul /ˈkɒnsl/ *n* Konsul *m*. **~ate** /ˈkɒnsjʊlət/ *n* Konsulat *nt*

consult /kənˈsʌlt/ *vt* [um Rat] fragen; konsultieren <*doctor*>; nachschlagen in (+ *dat*) <*book*>. **~ant** *n* Berater *m*; (*Med*) Chefarzt *m*. **~ation** /kɒnslˈteɪʃn/ *n* Beratung *f*; (*Med*) Konsultation *f*

consume /kɒnˈsjuːm/ *vt* verzehren; (*use*) verbrauchen. **~r** *n* Verbraucher *m*

consumption /kənˈsʌmpʃn/ *n* Konsum *m*; (*use*) Verbrauch *m*

contact /ˈkɒntækt/ *n* Kontakt *m*; (*person*) Kontaktperson *f* ● *vt* sich in Verbindung setzen mit. **~ ˈlenses** *npl* Kontaktlinsen *pl*

contagious /kənˈteɪdʒəs/ *a* direkt übertragbar

contain /kənˈteɪn/ *vt* enthalten; (*control*) beherrschen. **~er** *n* Behälter *m*; (*Comm*) Container *m*

contaminat|e /kənˈtæmɪneɪt/ *vt* verseuchen. **~ion** /-ˈneɪʃn/ *n* Verseuchung *f*

contemplat|e /ˈkɒntəmpleɪt/ *vt* betrachten; (*meditate*) nachdenken über (+ *acc*). **~ion** /-ˈpleɪʃn/ *n* Betrachtung *f*; Nachdenken *nt*

contemporary /kənˈtempərərɪ/ *a* zeitgenössisch ● *n* Zeitgenosse *m*/ -genossin *f*

contempt /kənˈtempt/ *n* Verachtung *f*; **beneath ~** verabscheuungswürdig. **~ible** /-əbl/ *a* verachtenswert. **~uous** /-tjʊəs/ *a*, **-ly** *adv* verächtlich

content[1] /ˈkɒntent/ *n* & **contents** *pl* Inhalt *m*

content[2] /kənˈtent/ *a* zufrieden ● *n* **to one's heart's ~** nach Herzenslust ● *vt* **~ oneself** sich begnügen (**with** mit). **~ed** *a*, **-ly** *adv* zufrieden

contentment /kənˈtentmənt/ *n* Zufriedenheit *f*

contest /ˈkɒntest/ *n* Kampf *m*; (*competition*) Wettbewerb *m*. **~ant** /kənˈtestənt/ *n* Teilnehmer *m*

context /ˈkɒntekst/ *n* Zusammenhang *m*

continent /ˈkɒntɪnənt/ *n* Kontinent *m*

continental /kɒntɪˈnentl/ *a* Kontinental-. **~ breakfast** *n* kleines Frühstück *nt*. **~ quilt** *n* Daunendecke *f*

continual /kənˈtɪnjʊəl/ *a*, **-ly** *adv* dauernd

continuation /kənˈtɪnjʊˈeɪʃn/ *n* Fortsetzung *f*

continue /kən'tɪnju:/ *vt* fortsetzen; **~ doing** *or* **to do sth** fortfahren, etw zu tun; **to be ~d** Fortsetzung folgt ● *vi* weitergehen; (*doing sth*) weitermachen; (*speaking*) fortfahren; <*weather:*> anhalten

continuity /kɒntɪ'nju:ətɪ/ *n* Kontinuität *f*

continuous /kən'tɪnjʊəs/ *a*, **-ly** *adv* anhaltend, ununterbrochen

contort /kən'tɔ:t/ *vt* verzerren. **~ion** /-ɔ:ʃn/ *n* Verzerrung *f*

contour /'kɒntʊə(r)/ *n* Kontur *f*; (*line*) Höhenlinie *f*

contracep|tion /kɒntrə'sepʃn/ *n* Empfängnisverhütung *f*. **~tive** /-tɪv/ *n* Empfängnisverhütungsmittel *nt*

contract[1] /'kɒntrækt/ *n* Vertrag *m*

contract[2] /kən'trækt/ *vi* sich zusammenziehen. **~or** *n* Unternehmer *m*

contradict /kɒntrə'dɪkt/ *vt* widersprechen (+ *dat*). **~ion** /-ɪkʃn/ *n* Widerspruch *m*. **~ory** /-ərɪ/ *a* widersprüchlich

contralto /kən'træltəʊ/ *n* Alt *m*; (*singer*) Altistin *f*

contraption /kən'træpʃn/ *n* [!] Apparat *m*

contrary /'kɒntrərɪ/ *a & adv* entgegengesetzt; **~ to** entgegen (+ *dat*) ● *n* Gegenteil *nt*; **on the ~** im Gegenteil

contrast[1] /'kɒntrɑ:st/ *n* Kontrast *m*

contrast[2] /kən'trɑ:st/ *vt* gegenüberstellen (**with** *dat*) ● *vi* einen Kontrast bilden (**with** zu). **~ing** *a* gegensätzlich; <*colour*> Kontrast-

contribut|e /kən'trɪbju:t/ *vt/i* beitragen; beisteuern <*money*>; (*donate*) spenden. **~ion** /kɒntrɪ'bju:ʃn/ *n* Beitrag *m*; (*donation*) Spende *f*. **~or** *n* Beitragende(r) *m/f*

contrivance /kən'traɪvəns/ *n* Vorrichtung *f*

control /kən'trəʊl/ *n* Kontrolle *f*; (*mastery*) Beherrschung *f*; (*Techn*) Regler *m*; **~s** *pl* (*of car, plane*) Steuerung *f*; **get out of ~** außer Kontrolle geraten ● *vt* (*pt/pp* **controlled**) kontrollieren; (*restrain*) unter Kontrolle halten; **~ oneself** sich beherrschen

controvers|ial /kɒntrə'vɜ:ʃl/ *a* umstritten. **~y** /'kɒntrəvɜ:ʃɪ/ *n* Kontroverse *f*

convalesce /kɒnvə'les/ *vi* sich erholen. **~nce** *n* Erholung *f*

convalescent home /kɒnvə'lesnt/ *n* Erholungsheim *nt*

convenience /kən'vi:nɪəns/ *n* Bequemlichkeit *f*; **[public] ~** öffentliche Toilette *f*; **with all modern ~s** mit allem Komfort

convenient /kən'vi:nɪənt/ *a*, **-ly** *adv* günstig; **be ~ for s.o.** jdm gelegen sein, jdm passen; **if it is ~ [for you]** wenn es Ihnen passt

convent /'kɒnvənt/ *n* [Nonnen]kloster *nt*

convention /kən'venʃn/ *n* (*custom*) Brauch *m*, Sitte *f*. **~al** *a*, **-ly** *adv* konventionell

converge /kən'vɜ:dʒ/ *vi* zusammenlaufen

conversation /kɒnvə'seɪʃn/ *n* Gespräch *nt*; (*Sch*) Konversation *f*

conversion /kən'vɜ:ʃn/ *n* Umbau *m*; (*Relig*) Bekehrung *f*; (*calculation*) Umrechnung *f*

convert[1] /'kɒnvɜ:t/ *n* Bekehrte(r) *m/f*, Konvertit *m*

convert[2] /kən'vɜ:t/ *vt* bekehren <*person*>; (*change*) umwandeln (**into** in + *acc*); umbauen <*building*>; (*calculate*) umrechnen; (*Techn*) umstellen. **~ible** /-əbl/ a verwandelbar ● *n* (*Auto*) Kabrio[lett] *nt*

convex /'kɒnveks/ *a* konvex

convey /kən'veɪ/ *vt* befördern; vermitteln <*idea, message*>. **~or belt** *n* Förderband *nt*

convict¹ /'kɒnvɪkt/ *n* Sträfling *m*

convict² /kən'vɪkt/ *vt* verurteilen (**of** wegen). **~ion** /-ɪkʃn/ *n* Verurteilung *f*; (*belief*) Überzeugung *f*; **previous ~ion** Vorstrafe *f*

convinc|e /kən'vɪns/ *vt* überzeugen. **~ing** *a*, **-ly** *adv* überzeugend

convoy /'kɒnvɔɪ/ *n* Konvoi *m*

convulse /kən'vʌls/ *vt* **be ~ed** sich krümmen (**with** vor + *dat*)

coo /kuː/ *vi* gurren

cook /kʊk/ *n* Koch *m*/ Köchin *f* ● *vt/i* kochen; **is it ~ed?** ist es gar? **~ the books** 🄸 die Bilanz frisieren. **~book** *n* (*Amer*) Kochbuch *nt*

cooker /'kʊkə(r)/ *n* [Koch]herd *m*; (*apple*) Kochapfel *m*. **~y** *n* Kochen *nt*. **~y book** *n* Kochbuch *nt*

cookie /'kʊkɪ/ *n* (*Amer*) Keks *m*

cool /kuːl/ *a* (**-er, -est**), **-ly** *adv* kühl ● *n* Kühle *f* ● *vt* kühlen ● *vi* abkühlen. **~-box** *n* Kühlbox *f*. **~ness** *n* Kühle *f*

coop /kuːp/ *vt* **~ up** einsperren

cooperat|e /kəʊ'ɒpəreɪt/ *vi* zusammenarbeiten. **~ion** /-'reɪʃn/ *n* Kooperation *f*

cooperative /kəʊ'ɒpərətɪv/ *a* hilfsbereit ● *n* Genossenschaft *f*

cop /kɒp/ *n* 🄸 Polizist *m*

cope /kəʊp/ *vi* 🄸 zurechtkommen; **~ with** fertig werden mit

copious /'kəʊpɪəs/ *a* reichlich

copper¹ /'kɒpə(r)/ *n* Kupfer *nt* ● *a* kupfern

copper² *n* 🄸 Polizist *m*

copper 'beech *n* Blutbuche *f*

coppice /'kɒpɪs/, **copse** /kɒps/ *ns* Gehölz *nt*

copy /'kɒpɪ/ *n* Kopie *f*; (*book*) Exemplar *nt* ● *vt* (*pt/pp* **-ied**) kopieren; (*imitate*) nachahmen; (*Sch*) abschreiben

copy: ~right *n* Copyright *nt*. **~-writer** *n* Texter *m*

coral /'kɒrl/ *n* Koralle *f*

cord /kɔːd/ *n* Schnur *f*; (*fabric*) Cordsamt *m*; **~s** *pl* Cordhose *f*

cordial /'kɔːdɪəl/ *a*, **-ly** *adv* herzlich ● *n* Fruchtsirup *m*

cordon /'kɔːdn/ *n* Kordon *m* ● *vt* **~ off** absperren

corduroy /'kɔːdərɔɪ/ *n* Cordsamt *m*

core /kɔː(r)/ *n* Kern *m*; (*of apple, pear*) Kerngehäuse *nt*

cork /kɔːk/ *n* Kork *m*; (*for bottle*) Korken *m*. **~screw** *n* Korkenzieher *m*

corn¹ /kɔːn/ *n* Korn *nt*; (*Amer: maize*) Mais *m*

corn² *n* (*Med*) Hühnerauge *nt*

corned beef /kɔːnd'biːf/ *n* Cornedbeef *nt*

corner /'kɔːnə(r)/ *n* Ecke *f*; (*bend*) Kurve *f*; (*football*) Eckball *m* ● *vt* (*fig*) in die Enge treiben; (*Comm*) monopolisieren <*market*>. **~-stone** *n* Eckstein *m*

cornet /'kɔːnɪt/ *n* (*Mus*) Kornett *nt*; (*for ice-cream*) [Eis]tüte *f*

corn: ~flour *n*, (*Amer*) **~starch** *n* Stärkemehl *nt*

corny /'kɔːnɪ/ *a* 🄸 abgedroschen

coronation /kɒrə'neɪʃn/ *n* Krönung *f*

coroner /'kɒrənə(r)/ *n* Beamte(r) *m*, der verdächtige Todesfälle untersucht

corporal /'kɔːpərəl/ *n* (*Mil*) Stabsunteroffizier *m*

corps /kɔː(r)/ *n* (*pl* **corps** /kɔːz/) Korps *nt*

corpse /kɔːps/ *n* Leiche *f*

correct /kə'rekt/ *a*, **-ly** *adv* richtig; (*proper*) korrekt ● *vt*

verbessern; (*Sch, Typ*) korrigieren. **~ion** /-ekʃn/ *n* Verbesserung *f*; (*Typ*) Korrektur *f*
correspond /kɒrɪ'spɒnd/ *vi* entsprechen (**to** *dat*); <*two things*:> sich entsprechen; (*write*) korrespondieren. **~ence** *n* Briefwechsel *m*; (*Comm*) Korrespondenz *f*. **~ent** *n* Korrespondent(in) *m(f)*. **~ing** *a*, **-ly** *adv* entsprechend
corridor /'kɒrɪdɔ:(r)/ *n* Gang *m*; (*Pol, Aviat*) Korridor *m*
corro|de /kə'rəʊd/ *vt* zerfressen ● *vi* rosten. **~sion** /-'rəʊʒn/ *n* Korrosion *f*
corrugated /'kɒrəgeɪtɪd/ *a* gewellt. **~ iron** *n* Wellblech *nt*
corrupt /kə'rʌpt/ *a* korrupt ● *vt* korrumpieren; (*spoil*) verderben. **~ion** /-ʌpʃn/ *n* Korruption *f*
corset /'kɔ:sɪt/ *n* & **-s** *pl* Korsett *nt*
Corsica /'kɔ:sɪkə/ *n* Korsika *nt*
cosh /kɒʃ/ *n* Totschläger *m*
cosmetic /kɒz'metɪk/ *a* kosmetisch ● *n* **~s** *pl* Kosmetika *pl*
cosset /'kɒsɪt/ *vt* verhätscheln
cost /kɒst/ *n* Kosten *pl*; **~s** *pl* (*Jur*) Kosten; **at all ~s** um jeden Preis ● *vt* (*pt/pp* **cost**) kosten; **it ~ me £20** es hat mich £20 gekostet ● *vt* (*pt/pp* **costed**) **~ [out]** die Kosten kalkulieren für
costly /'kɒstlɪ/ *a* (**-ier, -iest**) teuer
cost: ~ of 'living *n* Lebenshaltungskosten *pl*. **~ price** *n* Selbstkostenpreis *m*
costume /'kɒstju:m/ *n* Kostüm *nt*; (*national*) Tracht *f*. **~ jewellery** *n* Modeschmuck *m*
cosy /'kəʊzɪ/ *a* (**-ier, -iest**) gemütlich ● *n* (*tea-, egg-*) Wärmer *m*
cot /kɒt/ *n* Kinderbett *nt*; (*Amer: camp bed*) Feldbett *nt*
cottage /'kɒtɪdʒ/ *n* Häuschen *nt*. **~ 'cheese** *n* Hüttenkäse *m*
cotton /'kɒtn/ *n* Baumwolle *f*; (*thread*) Nähgarn *nt* ● *a* baumwollen ● *vi* **~ on** [!] kapieren
cotton 'wool *n* Watte *f*
couch /kaʊtʃ/ *n* Liege *f*
couchette /ku:'ʃet/ *n* (*Rail*) Liegeplatz *m*
cough /kɒf/ *n* Husten *m* ● *vi* husten. **~ up** *vt/i* husten; ([!] *pay*) blechen
'cough mixture *n* Hustensaft *m*
could /kʊd, *unbetont* kəd/ *see* **can**[2]
council /'kaʊnsl/ *n* Rat *m*; (*Admin*) Stadtverwaltung *f*; (*rural*) Gemeindeverwaltung *f*. **~ house** *n* ≈ Sozialwohnung *f*
councillor /'kaʊnsələ(r)/ *n* Ratsmitglied *nt*
'council tax *n* Gemeindesteuer *f*
count[1] /kaʊnt/ *n* Graf *m*
count[2] *n* Zählung *f*; **keep ~** zählen ● *vt/i* zählen. **~ on** *vt* rechnen auf (+ *acc*)
counter[1] /'kaʊntə(r)/ *n* (*in shop*) Ladentisch *m*; (*in bank*) Schalter *m*; (*in café*) Theke *f*; (*Games*) Spielmarke *f*
counter[2] *a* Gegen- ● *vt/i* kontern
counter'act *vt* entgegenwirken (+ *dat*)
'counterfeit /-fɪt/ *a* gefälscht
'counterfoil *n* Kontrollabschnitt *m*
'counterpart *n* Gegenstück *nt*
counter-pro'ductive *a* **be ~** das Gegenteil bewirken
'countersign *vt* gegenzeichnen
countess /'kaʊntɪs/ *n* Gräfin *f*
countless /'kaʊntlɪs/ *a* unzählig
country /'kʌntrɪ/ *n* Land *nt*; (*native land*) Heimat *f*; (*countryside*) Landschaft *f*; **in the ~** auf dem Lande. **~man** *n*

[fellow] ~man Landsmann *m*. **~side** *n* Landschaft *f*

county /ˈkaʊntɪ/ *n* Grafschaft *f*

coup /ku:/ *n* (*Pol*) Staatsstreich *m*

couple /ˈkʌpl/ *n* Paar *nt*; **a ~ of** (*two*) zwei ● *vt* verbinden

coupon /ˈku:pɒn/ *n* Kupon *m*; (*voucher*) Gutschein *m*; (*entry form*) Schein *m*

courage /ˈkʌrɪdʒ/ *n* Mut *m*. **~ous** /kəˈreɪdʒəs/ *a*, **-ly** *adv* mutig

courgettes /kʊəˈʒets/ *npl* Zucchini *pl*

courier /ˈkʊrɪə(r)/ *n* Bote *m*; (*diplomatic*) Kurier *m*; (*for tourists*) Reiseleiter(in) *m(f)*

course /kɔ:s/ *n* (*Naut, Sch*) Kurs *m*; (*Culin*) Gang *m*; (*for golf*) Platz *m*; **~ of treatment** (*Med*) Kur *f*; **of ~** natürlich, selbstverständlich; **in the ~ of** im Lauf[e] (+ *gen*)

court /kɔ:t/ *n* Hof *m*; (*Sport*) Platz *m*; (*Jur*) Gericht *nt*

courteous /ˈkɜ:tɪəs/ *a*, **-ly** *adv* höflich

courtesy /ˈkɜ:təsɪ/ *n* Höflichkeit *f*

court: ~ ˈmartial *n* (*pl* **~s martial**) Militärgericht *nt*. **~yard** *n* Hof *m*

cousin /ˈkʌzn/ *n* Vetter *m*, Cousin *m*; (*female*) Kusine *f*

cove /kəʊv/ *n* kleine Bucht *f*

cover /ˈkʌvə(r)/ *n* Decke *f*; (*of cushion*) Bezug *m*; (*of umbrella*) Hülle *f*; (*of typewriter*) Haube *f*; (*of book, lid*) Deckel *m*; (*of magazine*) Umschlag *m*; (*protection*) Deckung *f*, Schutz *m*; **take ~** Deckung nehmen; **under separate ~** mit getrennter Post ● *vt* bedecken; beziehen <*cushion*>; decken <*costs, needs*>; zurücklegen <*distance*>; (*Journ*) berichten über (+ *acc*); (*insure*) versichern. **~ up** *vt* zudecken; (*fig*) vertuschen

coverage /ˈkʌvərɪdʒ/ *n* (*Journ*) Berichterstattung *f* (**of** über + *acc*)

cover: ~ing *n* Decke *f*; (*for floor*) Belag *m*. **~-up** *n* Vertuschung *f*

cow /kaʊ/ *n* Kuh *f*

coward /ˈkaʊəd/ *n* Feigling *m*. **~ice** /-ɪs/ *n* Feigheit *f*. **~ly** *a* feige

ˈcowboy *n* Cowboy *m*; [!] unsolider Handwerker *m*

cower /ˈkaʊə(r)/ *vi* sich [ängstlich] ducken

ˈcowshed *n* Kuhstall *m*

cox /kɒks/ *n*, **coxswain** /ˈkɒksn/ *n* Steuermann *m*

coy /kɔɪ/ *a* (**-er, -est**) gespielt schüchtern

crab /kræb/ *n* Krabbe *f*

crack /kræk/ *n* Riss *m*; (*in china, glass*) Sprung *m*; (*noise*) Knall *m*; ([!] *joke*) Witz *m*; ([!] *attempt*) Versuch *m* ● *a* [!] erstklassig ● *vt* knacken <*nut, code*>; einen Sprung machen in (+ *acc*) <*china, glass*>; [!] reißen <*joke*>; [!] lösen <*problem*> ● *vi* <*china, glass:*> springen; <*whip:*> knallen. **~ down** *vi* [!] durchgreifen

cracked /krækt/ *a* gesprungen; <*rib*> angebrochen; ([!] *crazy*) verrückt

cracker /ˈkrækə(r)/ *n* (*biscuit*) Kräcker *m*; (*firework*) Knallkörper *m*; **[Christmas] ~** Knallbonbon *m*. **~s** *a* **be ~s** [!] einen Knacks haben

crackle /ˈkrækl/ *vi* knistern

cradle /ˈkreɪdl/ *n* Wiege *f*

craft *n* Handwerk *nt*; (*technique*) Fertigkeit *f*. **~sman** *n* Handwerker *m*

crafty /ˈkrɑ:ftɪ/ *a* (**-ier, -iest**), **-ily** *adv* gerissen

crag /kræg/ *n* Felszacken *m*

cram /kræm/ *v* (*pt*/*pp* **crammed**) ● *vt* hineinstopfen (**into** in + *acc*); vollstopfen (**with** mit) ● *vi* (*for exams*) pauken

cramp /kræmp/ *n* Krampf *m*. **~ed** *a* eng

cranberry /'krænbərɪ/ *n* (*Culin*) Preiselbeere *f*

crane /kreɪn/ *n* Kran *m*; (*bird*) Kranich *m*

crank /kræŋk/ *n* [!] Exzentriker *m*

'crankshaft *n* Kurbelwelle *f*

crash /kræʃ/ *n* (*noise*) Krach *m*; (*Auto*) Zusammenstoß *m*; (*Aviat*) Absturz *m* ● *vi* krachen (**into** gegen); <*cars*:> zusammenstoßen; <*plane*:> abstürzen ● *vt* einen Unfall haben mit <*car*>

crash: ~-helmet *n* Sturzhelm *m*. **~-landing** *n* Bruchlandung *f*

crate /kreɪt/ *n* Kiste *f*

crater /'kreɪtə(r)/ *n* Krater *m*

crawl /krɔ:l/ *n* (*Swimming*) Kraul *nt*; **do the ~** kraulen; **at a ~** im Kriechtempo ● *vi* kriechen; <*baby*:> krabbeln; **~ with** wimmeln von

crayon /'kreɪən/ *n* Wachsstift *m*; (*pencil*) Buntstift *m*

craze /kreɪz/ *n* Mode *f*

crazy /'kreɪzɪ/ *a* (**-ier, -iest**) verrückt; **be ~ about** verrückt sein nach

creak /kri:k/ *vi* knarren

cream /kri:m/ *n* Sahne *f*; (*Cosmetic, Med, Culin*) Creme *f* ● *a* (*colour*) cremefarben ● *vt* (*Culin*) cremig rühren. **~y** *a* sahnig; (*smooth*) cremig

crease /kri:s/ *n* Falte *f*; (*unwanted*) Knitterfalte *f* ● *vt* falten; (*accidentally*) zerknittern ● *vi* knittern

creat|e /kri:'eɪt/ *vt* schaffen. **~ion** /-'eɪʃn/ *n* Schöpfung *f*. **~ive** /-tɪv/ *a* schöpferisch. **~or** *n* Schöpfer *m*

creature /'kri:tʃə(r)/ *n* Geschöpf *nt*

crèche /kreʃ/ *n* Kinderkrippe *f*

credibility /kredə'bɪlətɪ/ *n* Glaubwürdigkeit *f*

credible /'kredəbl/ *a* glaubwürdig

credit /'kredɪt/ *n* Kredit *m*; (*honour*) Ehre *f* ● *vt* glauben; **~ s.o. with sth** (*Comm*) jdm etw gutschreiben; (*fig*) jdm etw zuschreiben. **~able** /-əbl/ *a* lobenswert

credit: ~ card *n* Kreditkarte *f*. **~or** *n* Gläubiger *m*

creep /kri:p/ *vi* (*pt*/*pp* **crept**) schleichen ● *n* [!] fieser Kerl *m*; **it gives me the ~s** es ist mir unheimlich. **~er** *n* Kletterpflanze *f*. **~y** *a* gruselig

cremat|e /krɪ'meɪt/ *vt* einäschern. **~ion** /-eɪʃn/ *n* Einäscherung *f*

crêpe /kreɪp/ *n* Krepp *m*. **~ paper** *n* Kreppapier *nt*

crept /krept/ *see* creep

crescent /'kresənt/ *n* Halbmond *m*

cress /kres/ *n* Kresse *f*

crest /krest/ *n* Kamm *m*; (*coat of arms*) Wappen *nt*

crew /kru:/ *n* Besatzung *f*; (*gang*) Bande *f*. **~ cut** *n* Bürstenschnitt *m*

crib[1] /krɪb/ *n* Krippe *f*

crib[2] *vt*/*i* (*pt*/*pp* **cribbed**) [!] abschreiben

cricket /'krɪkɪt/ *n* Kricket *nt*. **~er** *n* Kricketspieler *m*

crime /kraɪm/ *n* Verbrechen *nt*; (*rate*) Kriminalität *f*

criminal /'krɪmɪnl/ *a* kriminell, verbrecherisch; <*law, court*> Straf- ● *n* Verbrecher *m*

crimson /'krɪmzn/ *a* purpurrot

crinkle /'krɪŋkl/ *vt*/*i* knittern

cripple /ˈkrɪpl/ *n* Krüppel *m* ● *vt* zum Krüppel machen; (*fig*) lahmlegen. **~d** *a* verkrüppelt

crisis /ˈkraɪsɪs/ *n* (*pl* **-ses** /-si:z/) Krise *f*

crisp /ˈkrɪsp/ *a* (**-er, -est**) knusprig. **~bread** *n* Knäckebrot *nt*. **~s** *npl* Chips *pl*

criss-cross /ˈkrɪs-/ *a* schräg gekreuzt

criterion /kraɪˈtɪərɪən/ *n* (*pl* **-ria** /-rɪə/) Kriterium *nt*

critic /ˈkrɪtɪk/ *n* Kritiker *m*. **~al** *a* kritisch. **~ally** *adv* kritisch; **~ally ill** schwer krank

criticism /ˈkrɪtɪsɪzm/ *n* Kritik *f*

criticize /ˈkrɪtɪsaɪz/ *vt* kritisieren

croak /krəʊk/ *vi* krächzen; <*frog:*> quaken

crockery /ˈkrɒkərɪ/ *n* Geschirr *nt*

crocodile /ˈkrɒkədaɪl/ *n* Krokodil *nt*

crocus /ˈkrəʊkəs/ *n* (*pl* **-es**) Krokus *m*

crony /ˈkrəʊnɪ/ *n* Kumpel *m*

crook /krʊk/ *n* (*stick*) Stab *m*; ([!] *criminal*) Schwindler *m*, Gauner *m*

crooked /ˈkrʊkɪd/ *a* schief; (*bent*) krumm; ([!] *dishonest*) unehrlich

crop /krɒp/ *n* Feldfrucht *f*; (*harvest*) Ernte *f* ● *v* (*pt/pp* **cropped**) ● *vt* stutzen ● *vi* **~ up** [!] zur Sprache kommen; (*occur*) dazwischenkommen

croquet /ˈkrəʊkeɪ/ *n* Krocket *nt*

cross /krɒs/ *a*, **-ly** *adv* (*annoyed*) böse (**with** auf + *acc*); **talk at ~ purposes** aneinander vorbeireden ● *n* Kreuz *nt*; (*Bot, Zool*) Kreuzung *f* ● *vt* kreuzen <*cheque, animals*>; überqueren <*road*>; **~ oneself** sich bekreuzigen; **~ one's arms** die Arme verschränken; **~ one's legs** die Beine übereinander schlagen; **keep one's fingers ~ed for s.o.** jdm die Daumen drücken; **it ~ed my mind** es fiel mir ein ● *vi* (*go across*) hinübergehen/-fahren; <*lines:*> sich kreuzen. **~ out** *vt* durchstreichen

cross: ~-ˈcountry *n* (*Sport*) Crosslauf *m*. **~-ˈeyed** *a* schielend; **be ~-eyed** schielen. **~fire** *n* Kreuzfeuer *nt*. **~ing** *n* Übergang *m*; (*sea journey*) Überfahrt *f*. **~roads** *n* [Straßen]kreuzung *f*. **~-ˈsection** *n* Querschnitt *m*. **~wise** *adv* quer. **~word** *n* **~word [puzzle]** Kreuzworträtsel *nt*

crotchety /ˈkrɒtʃɪtɪ/ *a* griesgrämig

crouch /kraʊtʃ/ *vi* kauern

crow /krəʊ/ *n* Krähe *f*; **as the ~ flies** Luftlinie

crowd /kraʊd/ *n* [Menschen]menge *f* ● *vi* sich drängen. **~ed** /ˈkraʊdɪd/ *a* [gedrängt] voll

crown /kraʊn/ *n* Krone *f* ● *vt* krönen; überkronen <*tooth*>

crucial /ˈkru:ʃl/ *a* höchst wichtig; (*decisive*) entscheidend (**to** für)

crude /ˈkru:d/ *a* (**-r, -st**) primitiv; (*raw*) roh

cruel /ˈkru:əl/ *a* (**crueller, cruellest**), **-ly** *adv* grausam (**to** gegen). **~ty** *n* Grausamkeit *f*

cruis|e /kru:z/ *n* Kreuzfahrt *f* ● *vi* kreuzen; <*car:*> fahren. **~er** *n* (*Mil*) Kreuzer *m*; (*motor boat*) Kajütboot *nt*

crumb /krʌm/ *n* Krümel *m*

crumble /ˈkrʌmbl/ *vt/i* krümeln; (*collapse*) einstürzen

crumple /ˈkrʌmpl/ *vt* zerknittern ● *vi* knittern

crunch /krʌntʃ/ *n* [!] **when it comes to the ~** wenn es [wirklich] drauf ankommt ● *vt* mampfen ● *vi* knirschen

crusade /kruːˈseɪd/ *n* Kreuzzug *m*; (*fig*) Kampagne *f*. **~r** *n* Kreuzfahrer *m*; (*fig*) Kämpfer *m*
crush /krʌʃ/ *n* (*crowd*) Gedränge *nt* ● *vt* zerquetschen; zerknittern <*clothes*>; (*fig: subdue*) niederschlagen
crust /krʌst/ *n* Kruste *f*
crutch /krʌtʃ/ *n* Krücke *f*
cry /kraɪ/ *n* Ruf *m*; (*shout*) Schrei *m*; **a far ~ from** (*fig*) weit entfernt von ● *vi* (*pt/pp* **cried**) (*weep*) weinen; <*baby:*> schreien; (*call*) rufen
crypt /krɪpt/ *n* Krypta *f*. **~ic** *a* rätselhaft
crystal /ˈkrɪstl/ *n* Kristall *m*; (*glass*) Kristall *nt*
cub /kʌb/ *n* (*Zool*) Junge(s) *nt*
Cuba /ˈkjuːbə/ *n* Kuba *nt*
cubby-hole /ˈkʌbɪ-/ *n* Fach *nt*
cub|e /kjuːb/ *n* Würfel *m*. **~ic** *a* Kubik-
cubicle /ˈkjuːbɪkl/ *n* Kabine *f*
cuckoo /ˈkʊkuː/ *n* Kuckuck *m*. **~ clock** *n* Kuckucksuhr *f*
cucumber /ˈkjuːkʌmbə(r)/ *n* Gurke *f*
cuddl|e /ˈkʌdl/ *vt* herzen ● *vi* **~e up to** sich kuscheln an (+ *acc*). **~y** *a* kuschelig
cue[1] /kjuː/ *n* Stichwort *nt*
cue[2] *n* (*Billiards*) Queue *nt*
cuff /kʌf/ *n* Manschette *f*; (*Amer: turn-up*) [Hosen]aufschlag *m*; (*blow*) Klaps *m*; **off the ~** [!] aus dem Stegreif. **~-link** *n* Manschettenknopf *m*
cul-de-sac /ˈkʌldəsæk/ *n* Sackgasse *f*
culinary /ˈkʌlɪnərɪ/ *a* kulinarisch
culprit /ˈkʌlprɪt/ *n* Täter *m*
cult /kʌlt/ *n* Kult *m*
cultivate /ˈkʌltɪveɪt/ *vt* anbauen <*crop*>; bebauen <*land*>
cultural /ˈkʌltʃərəl/ *a* kulturell
culture /ˈkʌltʃə(r)/ *n* Kultur *f*. **~d** *a* kultiviert
cumbersome /ˈkʌmbəsəm/ *a* hinderlich; (*unwieldy*) unhandlich
cunning /ˈkʌnɪŋ/ *a* listig ● *n* List *f*
cup /kʌp/ *n* Tasse *f*; (*prize*) Pokal *m*
cupboard /ˈkʌbəd/ *n* Schrank *m*
Cup ˈFinal *n* Pokalendspiel *nt*
curable /ˈkjʊərəbl/ *a* heilbar
curate /ˈkjʊərət/ *n* Vikar *m*; (*Roman Catholic*) Kaplan *m*
curb /kɜːb/ *vt* zügeln
curdle /ˈkɜːdl/ *vi* gerinnen
cure /kjʊə(r)/ *n* [Heil]mittel *nt* ● *vt* heilen; (*salt*) pökeln; (*smoke*) räuchern; gerben <*skin*>
curiosity /kjʊərɪˈɒsətɪ/ *n* Neugier *f*; (*object*) Kuriosität *f*
curious /ˈkjʊərɪəs/ *a*, **-ly** *adv* neugierig; (*strange*) merkwürdig, seltsam
curl /kɜːl/ *n* Locke *f* ● *vt* locken ● *vi* sich locken
curly /ˈkɜːlɪ/ *a* (**-ier, -iest**) lockig
currant /ˈkʌrənt/ *n* (*dried*) Korinthe *f*
currency /ˈkʌrənsɪ/ *n* Geläufigkeit *f*; (*money*) Währung *f*; **foreign ~** Devisen *pl*
current /ˈkʌrənt/ *a* augenblicklich, gegenwärtig; (*in general use*) geläufig, gebräuchlich ● *n* Strömung *f*; (*Electr*) Strom *m*. **~ affairs** *or* **events** *npl* Aktuelle(s) *nt*. **~ly** *adv* zurzeit
curriculum /kəˈrɪkjʊləm/ *n* Lehrplan *m*. **~ vitae** /-ˈviːtaɪ/ *n* Lebenslauf *m*
curry /ˈkʌrɪ/ *n* Curry *nt* & *m*; (*meal*) Currygericht *nt*
curse /kɜːs/ *n* Fluch *m* ● *vt* verfluchen ● *vi* fluchen
cursor /ˈkɜːsə(r)/ *n* Cursor *m*
cursory /ˈkɜːsərɪ/ *a* flüchtig

curt /kɜ:t/ *a*, **-ly** *adv* barsch
curtain /ˈkɜ:tn/ *n* Vorhang *m*
curtsy /ˈkɜ:tsɪ/ *n* Knicks *m* ● *vi* (*pt/pp* **-ied**) knicksen
curve /kɜ:v/ *n* Kurve *f* ● *vi* einen Bogen machen; ~ **to the right/left** nach rechts/links biegen. ~**d** *a* gebogen
cushion /ˈkʊʃn/ *n* Kissen *nt* ● *vt* dämpfen; (*protect*) beschützen
cushy /ˈkʊʃɪ/ *a* (**-ier, -iest**) ⓘ bequem
custard /ˈkʌstəd/ *n* Vanillesoße *f*
custom /ˈkʌstəm/ *n* Brauch *m*; (*habit*) Gewohnheit *f*; (*Comm*) Kundschaft *f*. ~**ary** *a* üblich; (*habitual*) gewohnt. ~**er** *n* Kunde *m*/Kundin *f*
customs /ˈkʌstəmz/ *npl* Zoll *m*. ~ **officer** *n* Zollbeamte(r) *m*
cut /kʌt/ *n* Schnitt *m*; (*Med*) Schnittwunde *f*; (*reduction*) Kürzung *f*; (*in price*) Senkung *f*; ~ **[of meat]** [Fleisch]stück *nt* ● *vt/i* (*pt/pp* **cut**, *pres p* **cutting**) schneiden; (*mow*) mähen; abheben <*cards*>; (*reduce*) kürzen; senken <*price*>; ~ **one's finger** sich in den Finger schneiden; ~ **s.o.'s hair** jdm die Haare schneiden; ~ **short** abkürzen. ~ **back** *vt* zurückschneiden; (*fig*) einschränken, kürzen. ~ **down** *vt* fällen; (*fig*) einschränken. ~ **off** *vt* abschneiden; (*disconnect*) abstellen; **be** ~ **off** (*Teleph*) unterbrochen werden. ~ **out** *vt* ausschneiden; (*delete*) streichen; **be** ~ **out for** ⓘ geeignet sein zu. ~ **up** *vt* zerschneiden; (*slice*) aufschneiden
ˈ**cut-back** *n* Kürzung *f*
cute /kju:t/ *a* (**-r, -st**) ⓘ niedlich
cut ˈ**glass** *n* Kristall *nt*
cutlery /ˈkʌtlərɪ/ *n* Besteck *nt*
cutlet /ˈkʌtlɪt/ *n* Kotelett *nt*
ˈ**cut-price** *a* verbilligt
cutting /ˈkʌtɪŋ/ *a* <*remark*> bissig ● *n* (*from newspaper*) Ausschnitt *m*; (*of plant*) Ableger *m*
CV *abbr of* **curriculum vitae**
cyberspace /ˈsaɪbəspeɪs/ *n* Cyberspace *m*
cycl|e /ˈsaɪkl/ *n* Zyklus *m*; (*bicycle*) [Fahr]rad *nt* ● *vi* mit dem Rad fahren. ~**ing** *n* Radfahren *nt*. ~**ist** *n* Radfahrer(in) *m(f)*
cylind|er /ˈsɪlɪndə(r)/ *n* Zylinder *m*. ~**rical** /-ˈlɪndrɪkl/ *a* zylindrisch
cynic /ˈsɪnɪk/ *n* Zyniker *m*. ~**al** *a*, **-ly** *adv* zynisch. ~**ism** /-sɪzm/ *n* Zynismus *m*
Cyprus /ˈsaɪprəs/ *n* Zypern *nt*
Czech /tʃek/ *a* tschechisch; ~ **Republic** Tschechische Republik *f* ● *n* Tscheche *m*/ Tschechin *f*

Dd

dab /dæb/ *n* Tupfer *m*; (*of butter*) Klecks *m*
dabble /ˈdæbl/ *vi* ~ **in sth** (*fig*) sich nebenbei mit etw befassen
dachshund /ˈdækshʊnd/ *n* Dackel *m*
dad[dy] /ˈdæd[i]/ *n* ⓘ Vati *m*
daddy-ˈ**long-legs** *n* [Kohl]schnake *f*; (*Amer: spider*) Weberknecht *m*
daffodil /ˈdæfədɪl/ *n* Osterglocke *f*, gelbe Narzisse *f*
daft /dɑ:ft/ *a* (**-er, -est**) dumm
dagger /ˈdægə(r)/ *n* Dolch *m*
dahlia /ˈdeɪlɪə/ *n* Dahlie *f*

daily /ˈdeɪlɪ/ *a & adv* täglich
dainty /ˈdeɪntɪ/ *a* (**-ier, -iest**) zierlich
dairy /ˈdeərɪ/ *n* Molkerei *f*; (*shop*) Milchgeschäft *nt*. ~ **products** *pl* Milchprodukte *pl*
daisy /ˈdeɪzɪ/ *n* Gänseblümchen *nt*
dam /dæm/ *n* [Stau]damm *m* ● *vt* (*pt/pp* **dammed**) eindämmen
damage /ˈdæmɪdʒ/ *n* Schaden *m* (**to** an + *dat*); ~**s** *pl* (*Jur*) Schadenersatz *m* ● *vt* beschädigen; (*fig*) beeinträchtigen
damn /dæm/ *a, int & adv* ⊡ verdammt ● *n* **I don't care** *or* **give a** ~ ⊡ ich schere mich einen Dreck darum ● *vt* verdammen. ~**ation** /-ˈneɪʃn/ *n* Verdammnis *f*
damp /dæmp/ *a* (**-er, -est**) feucht ● *n* Feuchtigkeit *f*
damp|en *vt* anfeuchten; (*fig*) dämpfen. ~**ness** *n* Feuchtigkeit *f*
dance /dɑːns/ *n* Tanz *m*; (*function*) Tanzveranstaltung *f* ● *vt/i* tanzen. ~ **music** *n* Tanzmusik *f*
dancer /ˈdɑːnsə(r)/ *n* Tänzer(in) *m(f)*
dandelion /ˈdændɪlaɪən/ *n* Löwenzahn *m*
dandruff /ˈdændrʌf/ *n* Schuppen *pl*
Dane /deɪn/ *n* Däne *m*/Dänin *f*
danger /ˈdeɪndʒə(r)/ *n* Gefahr *f*; **in/out of** ~ in/außer Gefahr. ~**ous** /-rəs/ *a*, **-ly** *adv* gefährlich; ~**ously ill** schwer erkrankt
dangle /ˈdæŋgl/ *vi* baumeln ● *vt* baumeln lassen
Danish /ˈdeɪnɪʃ/ *a* dänisch. ~ ˈ**pastry** *n* Hefeteilchen *nt*
Danube /ˈdænjuːb/ *n* Donau *f*
dare /deə(r)/ *vt/i* (*challenge*) herausfordern (**to** zu); ~ **[to] do sth** [es] wagen, etw zu tun. ~**devil** *n* Draufgänger *m*
daring /ˈdeərɪŋ/ *a* verwegen ● *n* Verwegenheit *f*
dark /dɑːk/ *a* (**-er, -est**) dunkel; ~ **blue/brown** dunkelblau/-braun; ~ **horse** (*fig*) stilles Wasser *nt* ● *n* Dunkelheit *f*; **after** ~ nach Einbruch der Dunkelheit; **in the** ~ im Dunkeln
dark|en /ˈdɑːkn/ *vt* verdunkeln ● *vi* dunkler werden. ~**ness** *n* Dunkelheit *f*
ˈ**dark-room** *n* Dunkelkammer *f*
darling /ˈdɑːlɪŋ/ *a* allerliebst ● *n* Liebling *m*
darn /dɑːn/ *vt* stopfen
dart /dɑːt/ *n* Pfeil *m*; ~**s** *sg* (*game*) [Wurf]pfeil *m* ● *vi* flitzen
dash /dæʃ/ *n* (*Typ*) Gedankenstrich *m*; **a** ~ **of milk** ein Schuss Milch ● *vi* rennen ● *vt* schleudern. ~ **off** *vi* losstürzen ● *vt* (*write quickly*) hinwerfen
ˈ**dashboard** *n* Armaturenbrett *nt*
data /ˈdeɪtə/ *npl & sg* Daten *pl*. ~ **processing** *n* Datenverarbeitung *f*
date¹ /deɪt/ *n* (*fruit*) Dattel *f*
date² *n* Datum *nt*; ⊡ Verabredung *f*; **to** ~ bis heute; **out of** ~ überholt; (*expired*) ungültig; **be up to** ~ auf dem Laufenden sein ● *vt/i* datieren; (*Amer* ⊡: *go out with*) ausgehen mit
dated /ˈdeɪtɪd/ *a* altmodisch
dative /ˈdeɪtɪv/ *a & n* (*Gram*) ~ **[case]** Dativ *m*
daub /dɔːb/ *vt* beschmieren (**with** mit); schmieren <*paint*>
daughter /ˈdɔːtə(r)/ *n* Tochter *f*. ~**-in-law** *n* (*pl* ~**s-in-law**) Schwiegertochter *f*
dawdle /ˈdɔːdl/ *vi* trödeln
dawn /dɔːn/ *n* Morgendämmerung *f*; **at** ~ bei

Tagesanbruch ● *vi* anbrechen; **it ~ed on me** (*fig*) es ging mir auf

day /deɪ/ *n* Tag *m*; **~ by ~** Tag für Tag; **~ after ~** Tag um Tag; **these ~s** heutzutage; **in those ~s** zu der Zeit

day: ~-dream *n* Tagtraum *m* ● *vi* [mit offenen Augen] träumen. **~light** *n* Tageslicht *nt*. **~time** *n* **in the ~time** am Tage

daze /deɪz/ *n* **in a ~** wie benommen. **~d** *a* benommen

dazzle /'dæzl/ *vt* blenden

dead /ded/ *a* tot; <*flower*> verwelkt; (*numb*) taub; **~ body** Leiche *f*; **~ centre** genau in der Mitte ● *adv* **~ tired** todmüde; **~ slow** sehr langsam ● *n* **the ~** *pl* die Toten; **in the ~ of night** mitten in der Nacht

deaden /'dedn/ *vt* dämpfen <*sound*>; betäuben <*pain*>

dead: ~ 'end *n* Sackgasse *f*. **~ 'heat** *n* totes Rennen *nt*. **~line** *n* [letzter] Termin *m*

deadly /'dedlɪ/ *a* (**-ier, -iest**) tödlich; (🄸 *dreary*) sterbenslangweilig

deaf /def/ *a* (**-er, -est**) taub; **~ and dumb** taubstumm

deaf|en /'defn/ *vt* betäuben; (*permanently*) taub machen. **~ening** *a* ohrenbetäubend. **~ness** *n* Taubheit *f*

deal /di:l/ *n* (*transaction*) Geschäft *nt*; **whose ~?** (*Cards*) wer gibt? **a good** *or* **great ~** eine Menge; **get a raw ~** 🄸 schlecht wegkommen ● *v* (*pt/pp* **dealt** /delt/) ● *vt* (*Cards*) geben; **~ out** austeilen ● *vi* **~ in** handeln mit; **~ with** zu tun haben mit; (*handle*) sich befassen mit; (*cope with*) fertig werden mit; (*be about*) handeln von; **that's been dealt with** das ist schon erledigt

dealer /'di:lə(r)/ *n* Händler *m*

dean /di:n/ *n* Dekan *m*

dear /dɪə(r)/ *a* (**-er, -est**) lieb; (*expensive*) teuer; (*in letter*) liebe(r,s)/ (*formal*) sehr geehrte(r,s) ● *n* Liebe(r) *m/f* ● *int* **oh ~!** oje! **~ly** *adv* <*love*> sehr; <*pay*> teuer

death /deθ/ *n* Tod *m*; **three ~s** drei Todesfälle. **~ certificate** *n* Sterbeurkunde *f*

deathly *a* **~ silence** Totenstille *f* ● *adv* **~ pale** totenblass

death: ~ penalty *n* Todesstrafe *f*. **~-trap** *n* Todesfalle *f*

debatable /dɪ'beɪtəbl/ *a* strittig

debate /dɪ'beɪt/ *n* Debatte *f* ● *vt/i* debattieren

debauchery /dɪ'bɔ:tʃərɪ/ *n* Ausschweifung *f*

debit /'debɪt/ *n* **~ [side]** Soll *nt* ● *vt* (*pt/pp* **debited**) belasten; abbuchen <*sum*>

debris /'debri:/ *n* Trümmer *pl*

debt /det/ *n* Schuld *f*; **in ~** verschuldet. **~or** *n* Schuldner *m*

debut /'deɪbu:/ *n* Debüt *nt*

decade /'dekeɪd/ *n* Jahrzehnt *nt*

decaden|ce /'dekədəns/ *n* Dekadenz *f*. **~t** *a* dekadent

decaffeinated /dɪ'kæfɪneɪtɪd/ *a* koffeinfrei

decay /dɪ'keɪ/ *n* Verfall *m*; (*rot*) Verwesung *f*; (*of tooth*) Zahnfäule *f* ● *vi* verfallen; (*rot*) verwesen; <*tooth:*> schlecht werden

deceased /dɪ'si:sd/ *a* verstorben ● *n* **the ~d** der/die Verstorbene

deceit /dɪ'si:t/ *n* Täuschung *f*. **~ful** *a*, **-ly** *adv* unaufrichtig

deceive /dɪ'si:v/ *vt* täuschen; (*be unfaithful to*) betrügen

December /dɪ'sembə(r)/ *n* Dezember *m*

decency /'di:sənsɪ/ *n* Anstand *m*

decent /'di:sənt/ *a*, **-ly** *adv* anständig

decept|ion /dɪ'sepʃn/ *n* Täuschung *f*; (*fraud*) Betrug *m*. **~ive** /-tɪv/ *a*, **-ly** *adv* täuschend

decide /dɪ'saɪd/ *vt* entscheiden ● *vi* sich entscheiden (**on** für)

decided /dɪ'saɪdɪd/ *a*, **-ly** *adv* entschieden

decimal /'desɪml/ *a* Dezimal- ● *n* Dezimalzahl *f*. **~ 'point** *n* Komma *nt*

decipher /dɪ'saɪfə(r)/ *vt* entziffern

decision /dɪ'sɪʒn/ *n* Entscheidung *f*; (*firmness*) Entschlossenheit *f*

decisive /dɪ'saɪsɪv/ *a* ausschlaggebend; (*firm*) entschlossen

deck¹ /dek/ *vt* schmücken

deck² *n* (*Naut*) Deck *nt*; **on ~** an Deck; **~ of cards** (*Amer*) [Karten]spiel *nt*. **~-chair** *n* Liegestuhl *m*

declaration /deklə'reɪʃn/ *n* Erklärung *f*

declare /dɪ'kleə(r)/ *vt* erklären; angeben <*goods*>; **anything to ~?** etwas zu verzollen?

decline /dɪ'klaɪn/ *n* Rückgang *m*; (*in health*) Verfall *m* ● *vt* ablehnen; (*Gram*) deklinieren ● *vi* ablehnen; (*fall*) sinken; (*decrease*) nachlassen

decommission /di:kə'mɪʃn/ *vt* stilllegen; außer Dienst stellen <*Schiff*>

décor /'deɪkɔ:(r)/ *n* Ausstattung *f*

decorat|e /'dekəreɪt/ *vt* (*adorn*) schmücken; verzieren <*cake*>; (*paint*) streichen; (*wallpaper*) tapezieren; (*award medal to*) einen Orden verleihen (+ *dat*). **~ion** /-'reɪʃn/ *n* Verzierung *f*; (*medal*) Orden *m*; **~ions** *pl* Schmuck *m*. **~ive** /-rətɪv/ *a* dekorativ. **~or** *n* **painter and ~or** Maler und Tapezierer *m*

decoy /'di:kɔɪ/ *n* Lockvogel *m*

decrease¹ /'di:kri:s/ *n* Verringerung *f*; (*in number*) Rückgang *m*

decrease² /dɪ'kri:s/ *vt* verringern; herabsetzen <*price*> ● *vi* sich verringern; <*price:*> sinken

decrepit /dɪ'krepɪt/ *a* altersschwach

dedicat|e /'dedɪkeɪt/ *vt* widmen; (*Relig*) weihen. **~ed** *a* hingebungsvoll; <*person*> aufopfernd. **~ion** /-'keɪʃn/ *n* Hingabe *f*; (*in book*) Widmung *f*

deduce /dɪ'dju:s/ *vt* folgern (**from** aus)

deduct /dɪ'dʌkt/ *vt* abziehen

deduction /dɪ'dʌkʃn/ *n* Abzug *m*; (*conclusion*) Folgerung *f*

deed /di:d/ *n* Tat *f*; (*Jur*) Urkunde *f*

deep /di:p/ *a* (**-er, -est**), **-ly** *adv* tief; **go off the ~ end** [!] auf die Palme gehen ● *adv* tief

deepen /'di:pn/ *vt* vertiefen

deep-'freeze *n* Gefriertruhe *f*, (*upright*) Gefrierschrank *m*

deer /dɪə(r)/ *n inv* Hirsch *m*; (*roe*) Reh *nt*

deface /dɪ'feɪs/ *vt* beschädigen

default /dɪ'fɔ:lt/ *n* **win by ~** (*Sport*) kampflos gewinnen

defeat /dɪ'fi:t/ *n* Niederlage *f*; (*defeating*) Besiegung *f*; (*rejection*) Ablehnung *f* ● *vt* besiegen; ablehnen <*motion*>; (*frustrate*) vereiteln

defect /'di:fekt/ *n* Fehler *m*; (*Techn*) Defekt *m*. **~ive** /dɪ'fektɪv/ *a* fehlerhaft; (*Techn*) defekt

defence /dɪ'fens/ *n* Verteidigung *f*. **~less** *a* wehrlos

defend /dɪ'fend/ *vt* verteidigen; (*justify*) rechtfertigen. **~ant** *n* (*Jur*) Beklagte(r) *m/f*; (*in criminal court*) Angeklagte(r) *m/f*

defensive /dɪ'fensɪv/ *a* defensiv

defer /dɪ'fɜ:(r)/ *vt* (*pt*/*pp* **deferred**) (*postpone*) aufschieben

deferen|ce /'defərəns/ *n* Ehrerbietung *f*. **~tial** /-'renʃl/ *a*, **-ly** *adv* ehrerbietig

defian|ce /dɪ'faɪəns/ *n* Trotz *m*; **in ~ce of** zum Trotz (+ *dat*). **~t** *a*, **-ly** *adv* aufsässig

deficien|cy /dɪ'fɪʃənsɪ/ *n* Mangel *m*. **~t** *a* mangelhaft

deficit /'defɪsɪt/ *n* Defizit *nt*

define /dɪ'faɪn/ *vt* bestimmen; definieren <*word*>

definite /'defɪnɪt/ *a*, **-ly** *adv* bestimmt; (*certain*) sicher

definition /defɪ'nɪʃn/ *n* Definition *f*; (*Phot, TV*) Schärfe *f*

definitive /dɪ'fɪnətɪv/ *a* endgültig; (*authoritative*) maßgeblich

deflat|e /dɪ'fleɪt/ *vt* die Luft auslassen aus. **~ion** /-eɪʃn/ *n* (*Comm*) Deflation *f*

deflect /dɪ'flekt/ *vt* ablenken

deform|ed /dɪ'fɔ:md/ *a* missgebildet. **~ity** *n* Missbildung *f*

defraud /dɪ'frɔ:d/ *vt* betrügen (**of** um)

defray /dɪ'freɪ/ *vt* bestreiten

defrost /di:'frɒst/ *vt* entfrosten; abtauen <*fridge*>; auftauen <*food*>

deft /deft/ *a* (**-er, -est**), **-ly** *adv* geschickt. **~ness** *n* Geschicklichkeit *f*

defuse /di:'fju:z/ *vt* entschärfen

defy /dɪ'faɪ/ *vt* (*pt*/*pp* **-ied**) trotzen (+ *dat*); widerstehen (+ *dat*) <*attempt*>

degrading /dɪ'greɪdɪŋ/ *a* entwürdigend

degree /dɪ'gri:/ *n* Grad *m*; (*Univ*) akademischer Grad *m*; **20 ~s** 20 Grad

de-ice /di:'aɪs/ *vt* enteisen

deity /'di:ɪtɪ/ *n* Gottheit *f*

dejected /dɪ'dʒektɪd/ *a*, **-ly** *adv* niedergeschlagen

delay /dɪ'leɪ/ *n* Verzögerung *f*; (*of train, aircraft*) Verspätung *f*; **without ~** unverzüglich ● *vt* aufhalten; (*postpone*) aufschieben ● *vi* zögern

delegate[1] /'delɪgət/ *n* Delegierte(r) *m*/*f*

delegat|e[2] /'delɪgeɪt/ *vt* delegieren. **~ion** /-'geɪʃn/ *n* Delegation *f*

delet|e /dɪ'li:t/ *vt* streichen. **~ion** /-i:ʃn/ *n* Streichung *f*

deliberate /dɪ'lɪbərət/ *a*, **-ly** *adv* absichtlich; (*slow*) bedächtig

delicacy /'delɪkəsɪ/ *n* Feinheit *f*; Zartheit *f*; (*food*) Delikatesse *f*

delicate /'delɪkət/ *a* fein; <*fabric, health*> zart; <*situation*> heikel; <*mechanism*> empfindlich

delicatessen /delɪkə'tesn/ *n* Delikatessengeschäft *nt*

delicious /dɪ'lɪʃəs/ *a* köstlich

delight /dɪ'laɪt/ *n* Freude *f* ● *vt* entzücken ● *vi* **~ in** sich erfreuen an (+ *dat*). **~ed** *a* hocherfreut; **be ~ed** sich sehr freuen. **~ful** *a* reizend

delinquent /dɪ'lɪŋkwənt/ *a* straffällig ● *n* Straffällige(r) *m*/*f*

deli|rious /dɪ'lɪrɪəs/ *a* **be ~rious** im Delirium sein. **~rium** /-rɪəm/ *n* Delirium *nt*

deliver /dɪ'lɪvə(r)/ *vt* liefern; zustellen <*post, newspaper*>; halten <*speech*>; überbringen <*message*>; versetzen <*blow*>; (*set free*) befreien; **~ a baby** ein Kind zur Welt bringen. **~y** *n* Lieferung *f*; (*of post*) Zustellung *f*; (*Med*) Entbindung *f*; **cash on ~y** per Nachnahme

delta /'deltə/ *n* Delta *nt*

deluge /'delju:dʒ/ *n* Flut *f*; (*heavy rain*) schwerer Guss *m*

delusion /dɪ'lu:ʒn/ *n* Täuschung *f*

de luxe /də'lʌks/ *a* Luxus-

demand /dɪ'mɑ:nd/ *n* Forderung *f*; (*Comm*) Nachfrage *f*; **in ~** gefragt; **on ~** auf Verlangen ● *vt* verlangen, fordern (**of**/**from** von). **~ing** *a* anspruchsvoll

demented /dɪ'mentɪd/ *a* verrückt

demister /di:'mɪstə(r)/ *n* (*Auto*) Defroster *m*

demo /'deməʊ/ *n* (*pl* **~s**) [!] Demonstration *f*

democracy /dɪ'mɒkrəsɪ/ *n* Demokratie *f*

democrat /'deməkræt/ *n* Demokrat *m*. **~ic** /-'krætɪk/ *a*, **-ally** *adv* demokratisch

demo|lish /dɪ'mɒlɪʃ/ *vt* abbrechen; (*destroy*) zerstören. **~lition** /demə'lɪʃn/ *n* Abbruch *m*

demon /'di:mən/ *n* Dämon *m*

demonstrat|e /'demənstreɪt/ *vt* beweisen; vorführen <*appliance*> ● *vi* (*Pol*) demonstrieren. **~ion** /-'streɪʃn/ *n* Vorführung *f*; (*Pol*) Demonstration *f*

demonstrator /'demənstreɪtə(r)/ *n* Vorführer *m*; (*Pol*) Demonstrant *m*

demoralize /dɪ'mɒrəlaɪz/ *vt* demoralisieren

demote /dɪ'məʊt/ *vt* degradieren

demure /dɪ'mjʊə(r)/ *a*, **-ly** *adv* sittsam

den /den/ *n* Höhle *f*; (*room*) Bude *f*

denial /dɪ'naɪəl/ *n* Leugnen *nt*; **official ~** Dementi *nt*

denim /'denɪm/ *n* Jeansstoff *m*; **~s** *pl* Jeans *pl*

Denmark /'denmɑ:k/ *n* Dänemark *nt*

denounce /dɪ'naʊns/ *vt* denunzieren; (*condemn*) verurteilen

dens|e /dens/ *a* (**-r**, **-st**), **-ly** *adv* dicht; ([!] *stupid*) blöd[e]. **~ity** *n* Dichte *f*

dent /dent/ *n* Delle *f*, Beule *f* ● *vt* einbeulen; **~ed** /-ɪd/ verbeult

dental /'dentl/ *a* Zahn-; <*treatment*> zahnärztlich. **~ floss** /flɒs/ *n* Zahnseide *f*. **~ surgeon** *n* Zahnarzt *m*

dentist /'dentɪst/ *n* Zahnarzt *m*/-ärztin *f*. **~ry** *n* Zahnmedizin *f*

denture /'dentʃə(r)/ *n* Zahnprothese *f*; **~s** *pl* künstliches Gebiss *nt*

deny /dɪ'naɪ/ *vt* (*pt*/*pp* **-ied**) leugnen; (*officially*) dementieren; **~ s.o. sth** jdm etw verweigern

deodorant /di:'əʊdərənt/ *n* Deodorant *nt*

depart /dɪ'pɑ:t/ *vi* abfahren; (*Aviat*) abfliegen; (*go away*) weggehen/-fahren; (*deviate*) abweichen (**from** von)

department /dɪ'pɑ:tmənt/ *n* Abteilung *f*; (*Pol*) Ministerium *nt*. **~ store** *n* Kaufhaus *nt*

departure /dɪ'pɑ:tʃə(r)/ *n* Abfahrt *f*; (*Aviat*) Abflug *m*; (*from rule*) Abweichung *f*

depend /dɪ'pend/ *vi* abhängen (**on** von); (*rely*) sich verlassen (**on** auf + *acc*); **it all ~s** das kommt darauf an. **~able** /-əbl/ *a* zuverlässig. **~ant** *n* Abhängige(r) *m*/*f*. **~ence** *n* Abhängigkeit *f*. **~ent** *a* abhängig (**on** von)

depict /dɪ'pɪkt/ *vt* darstellen

deplor|able /dɪ'plɔ:rəbl/ *a* bedauerlich. **~e** *vt* bedauern

deploy /dɪ'plɔɪ/ *vt* (*Mil*) einsetzen

depopulate /di:'pɒpjʊleɪt/ *vt* entvölkern

deport /dɪ'pɔ:t/ *vt* deportieren, ausweisen. **~ation** /di:pɔ:'teɪʃn/ *n* Ausweisung *f*

depose /dɪ'pəʊz/ *vt* absetzen

deposit /dɪ'pɒzɪt/ *n* Anzahlung *f*; (*against damage*) Kaution *f*; (*on bottle*) Pfand *nt*; (*sediment*) Bodensatz *m*; (*Geol*) Ablagerung *f* ● *vt* (*pt*/*pp* **deposited**) legen; (*for* *safety*) deponieren; (*Geol*) ablagern. **~ account** *n* Sparkonto *nt*

depot /ˈdepəʊ/ *n* Depot *nt*; (*Amer: railway station*) Bahnhof *m*

deprave /dɪˈpreɪv/ *vt* verderben. **~d** *a* verkommen

depreciat|e /dɪˈpriːʃɪeɪt/ *vi* an Wert verlieren. **~ion** /-ˈeɪʃn/ *n* Wertminderung *f*; (*Comm*) Abschreibung *f*

depress /dɪˈpres/ *vt* deprimieren; (*press down*) herunterdrücken. **~ed** *a* deprimiert. **~ing** *a* deprimierend. **~ion** /-eʃn/ *n* Vertiefung *f*; (*Med*) Depression *f*; (*Meteorol*) Tief *nt*

deprivation /deprɪˈveɪʃn/ *n* Entbehrung *f*

deprive /dɪˈpraɪv/ *vt* **~ s.o. of sth** jdm etw entziehen. **~d** *a* benachteiligt

depth /depθ/ *n* Tiefe *f*; **in ~** gründlich; **in the ~s of winter** im tiefsten Winter

deputize /ˈdepjʊtaɪz/ *vi* **~ for** vertreten

deputy /ˈdepjʊtɪ/ *n* Stellvertreter *m* ● *attrib* stellvertretend

derail /dɪˈreɪl/ *vt* **be ~ed** entgleisen. **~ment** *n* Entgleisung *f*

derelict /ˈderəlɪkt/ *a* verfallen; (*abandoned*) verlassen

derisory /dɪˈraɪsərɪ/ *a* höhnisch; <*offer*> lächerlich

derivation /derɪˈveɪʃn/ *n* Ableitung *f*

derivative /dɪˈrɪvətɪv/ *a* abgeleitet ● *n* Ableitung *f*

derive /dɪˈraɪv/ *vt/i* (*obtain*) gewinnen (**from** aus); **be ~d from** <*word*:> hergeleitet sein aus

derogatory /dɪˈrɒgətrɪ/ *a* abfällig

derv /dɜːv/ *n* Diesel[kraftstoff] *m*

descend /dɪˈsend/ *vt/i* hinunter-/heruntergehen; <*vehicle, lift*:> hinunter-/herunterfahren; **be ~ed from** abstammen von. **~ant** *n* Nachkomme *m*

descent /dɪˈsent/ *n* Abstieg *m*; (*lineage*) Abstammung *f*

describe /dɪˈskraɪb/ *vt* beschreiben

descrip|tion /dɪˈskrɪpʃn/ *n* Beschreibung *f*; (*sort*) Art *f*. **~tive** /-tɪv/ *a* beschreibend; (*vivid*) anschaulich

desecrate /ˈdesɪkreɪt/ *vt* entweihen

desert¹ /ˈdezət/ *n* Wüste *f*. **~ island** verlassene Insel *f*

desert² /dɪˈzɜːt/ *vt* verlassen ● *vt* desertieren. **~ed** *a* verlassen. **~er** *n* (*Mil*) Deserteur *m*. **~ion** /-ɜːʃn/ *n* Fahnenflucht *f*

deserv|e /dɪˈzɜːv/ *vt* verdienen. **~edly** /-ɪdlɪ/ *adv* verdientermaßen. **~ing** *a* verdienstvoll

design /dɪˈzaɪn/ *n* Entwurf *m*; (*pattern*) Muster *nt*; (*construction*) Konstruktion *f*; (*aim*) Absicht *f* ● *vt* entwerfen; (*construct*) konstruieren; **be ~ed for** bestimmt sein für

designer /dɪˈzaɪnə(r)/ *n* Designer *m*; (*Techn*) Konstrukteur *m*; (*Theat*) Bühnenbildner *m*

desirable /dɪˈzaɪrəbl/ *a* wünschenswert; (*sexually*) begehrenswert

desire /dɪˈzaɪə(r)/ *n* Wunsch *m*; (*longing*) Verlangen *nt* (**for** nach); (*sexual*) Begierde *f* ● *vt* [sich (*dat*)] wünschen; (*sexually*) begehren

desk /desk/ *n* Schreibtisch *m*; (*Sch*) Pult *nt*

desolat|e /ˈdesələt/ *a* trostlos. **~ion** /-ˈleɪʃn/ *n* Trostlosigkeit *f*

despair /dɪ'speə(r)/ *n* Verzweiflung *f*; **in ~** verzweifelt ● *vi* verzweifeln

desperat|e /'despərət/ *a*, **-ly** *adv* verzweifelt; (*urgent*) dringend; **be ~e for** dringend brauchen. **~ion** /-'reɪʃn/ *n* Verzweiflung *f*

despicable /dɪ'spɪkəbl/ *a* verachtenswert

despise /dɪ'spaɪz/ *vt* verachten

despite /dɪ'spaɪt/ *prep* trotz (+ *gen*)

despondent /dɪ'spɒndənt/ *a* niedergeschlagen

dessert /dɪ'zɜ:t/ *n* Dessert *nt*, Nachtisch *m*. **~ spoon** *n* Dessertlöffel *m*

destination /destɪ'neɪʃn/ *n* [Reise]ziel *nt*; (*of goods*) Bestimmungsort *m*

destiny /'destɪnɪ/ *n* Schicksal *nt*

destitute /'destɪtju:t/ *a* völlig mittellos

destroy /dɪ'strɔɪ/ *vt* zerstören; (*totally*) vernichten. **~er** *n* (*Naut*) Zerstörer *m*

destruc|tion /dɪ'strʌkʃn/ *n* Zerstörung *f*, Vernichtung *f*. **-tive** /-tɪv/ *a* zerstörerisch; (*fig*) destruktiv

detach /dɪ'tætʃ/ *vt* abnehmen; (*tear off*) abtrennen. **~able** /-əbl/ *a* abnehmbar. **~ed** *a* **~ed house** Einzelhaus *nt*

detail /'di:teɪl/ *n* Einzelheit *f*, Detail *nt*; **in ~** ausführlich ● *vt* einzeln aufführen. **~ed** *a* ausführlich

detain /dɪ'teɪn/ *vt* aufhalten; <*police:*> in Haft behalten; (*take into custody*) in Haft nehmen

detect /dɪ'tekt/ *vt* entdecken; (*perceive*) wahrnehmen. **~ion** /-ekʃn/ *n* Entdeckung *f*

detective /dɪ'tektɪv/ *n* Detektiv *m*. **~ story** *n* Detektivroman *m*

detention /dɪ'tenʃn/ *n* Haft *f*; (*Sch*) Nachsitzen *nt*

deter /dɪ'tɜ:(r)/ *vt* (*pt/pp* **deterred**) abschrecken; (*prevent*) abhalten

detergent /dɪ'tɜ:dʒənt/ *n* Waschmittel *nt*

deteriorat|e /dɪ'tɪərɪəreɪt/ *vi* sich verschlechtern. **~ion** /'-reɪʃn/ *n* Verschlechterung *f*

determination /dɪtɜ:mɪ'neɪʃn/ *n* Entschlossenheit *f*

determine /dɪ'tɜ:mɪn/ *vt* bestimmen. **~d** *a* entschlossen

deterrent /dɪ'terənt/ *n* Abschreckungsmittel *nt*

detest /dɪ'test/ *vt* verabscheuen. **~able** /-əbl/ *a* abscheulich

detonate /'detəneɪt/ *vt* zünden

detour /'di:tʊə(r)/ *n* Umweg *m*

detract /dɪ'trækt/ *vi* **~ from** beeinträchtigen

detriment /'detrɪmənt/ *n* **to the ~ (of)** zum Schaden (+ *gen*). **~al** /-'mentl/ *a* schädlich (**to** *dat*)

deuce /dju:s/ *n* (*Tennis*) Einstand *m*

devaluation /di:væljʊ'eɪʃn/ *n* Abwertung *f*

de'value *vt* abwerten <*currency*>

devastat|e /'devəsteɪt/ *vt* verwüsten. **~ing** *a* verheerend. **~ion** /-'steɪʃn/ *n* Verwüstung *f*

develop /dɪ'veləp/ *vt* entwickeln; bekommen <*illness*>; erschließen <*area*> ● *vi* sich entwickeln (**into** zu). **~er** *n* **[property] ~er** Bodenspekulant *m*

development /dɪ'veləpmənt/ *n* Entwicklung *f*

deviat|e /'di:vɪeɪt/ *vi* abweichen. **~ion** /-'eɪʃn/ *n* Abweichung *f*

device /dɪ'vaɪs/ *n* Gerät *nt*; (*fig*) Mittel *nt*

devil /'devl/ *n* Teufel *m*. **~ish** *a* teuflisch

devious /'di:vɪəs/ *a* verschlagen

devise /dɪ'vaɪz/ *vt* sich (*dat*) ausdenken

devot|e /dɪ'vəʊt/ *vt* widmen (**to** *dat*). **~ed** *a*, **-ly** *adv* ergeben; <*care*> liebevoll; **be ~ed to s.o.** sehr an jdm hängen
devotion /dɪ'vəʊʃn/ *n* Hingabe *f*
devour /dɪ'vaʊə(r)/ *vt* verschlingen
devout /dɪ'vaʊt/ *a* fromm
dew /dju:/ *n* Tau *m*
dexterity /dek'sterətɪ/ *n* Geschicklichkeit *f*
diabet|es /daɪə'bi:ti:z/ *n* Zuckerkrankheit *f*. **~ic** /-'betɪk/ *n* Diabetiker(in) *m(f)*
diabolical /daɪə'bɒlɪkl/ *a* teuflisch
diagnose /daɪəg'nəʊz/ *vt* diagnostizieren
diagnosis /daɪəg'nəʊsɪs/ *n* (*pl* **-oses** /-si:z/) Diagnose *f*
diagonal /daɪ'ægənl/ *a*, **-ly** *adv* diagonal ● *n* Diagonale *f*
diagram /'daɪəgræm/ *n* Diagramm *nt*
dial /'daɪəl/ *n* (*of clock*) Zifferblatt *nt*; (*Techn*) Skala *f*; (*Teleph*) Wählscheibe *f* ● *vt/i* (*pt/pp* **dialled**) (*Teleph*) wählen; **~ direct** durchwählen
dialect /'daɪəlekt/ *n* Dialekt *m*
dialling: ~ code *n* Vorwahlnummer *f*. **~ tone** *n* Amtszeichen *nt*
dialogue /'daɪəlɒg/ *n* Dialog *m*
diameter /daɪ'æmɪtə(r)/ *n* Durchmesser *m*
diamond /'daɪəmənd/ *n* Diamant *m*; (*cut*) Brillant *m*; (*shape*) Raute *f*; **~s** *pl* (*Cards*) Karo *nt*
diaper /'daɪəpə(r)/ *n* (*Amer*) Windel *f*
diarrhoea /daɪə'ri:ə/ *n* Durchfall *m*
diary /'daɪərɪ/ *n* Tagebuch *nt*; (*for appointments*) [Termin]kalender *m*
dice /daɪs/ *n inv* Würfel *m*
dictat|e /dɪk'teɪt/ *vt/i* diktieren. **~ion** /-eɪʃn/ *n* Diktat *nt*
dictator /dɪk'teɪtə(r)/ *n* Diktator *m*. **~ial** /-tə'tɔ:rɪəl/ *a* diktatorisch. **~ship** *n* Diktatur *f*
dictionary /'dɪkʃənrɪ/ *n* Wörterbuch *nt*
did /dɪd/ *see* **do**
didn't /'dɪdnt/ = **did not**
die¹ /daɪ/ *n* (*Techn*) Prägestempel *m*; (*metal mould*) Gussform *f*
die² *vi* (*pres p* **dying**) sterben (**of** an + *dat*); <*plant, animal:*> eingehen; <*flower:*> verwelken; **be dying to do sth** [!] darauf brennen, etw zu tun; **be dying for sth** [!] sich nach etw sehnen. **~ down** *vi* nachlassen; <*fire:*> herunterbrennen. **~ out** *vi* aussterben
diesel /'di:zl/ *n* Diesel *m*. **~ engine** *n* Dieselmotor *m*
diet /'daɪət/ *n* Kost *f*; (*restricted*) Diät *f*; (*for slimming*) Schlankheitskur *f*; **be on a ~** Diät leben; eine Schlankheitskur machen ● *vi* diät leben; eine Schlankheitskur machen
differ /'dɪfə(r)/ *vi* sich unterscheiden; (*disagree*) verschiedener Meinung sein
differen|ce /'dɪfrəns/ *n* Unterschied *m*; (*disagreement*) Meinungsverschiedenheit *f*. **~t** *a* andere(r,s); (*various*) verschiedene; **be ~t** anders sein (**from** als)
differential /dɪfə'renʃl/ *a* Differenzial- ● *n* Unterschied *m*; (*Techn*) Differenzial *nt*
differentiate /dɪfə'renʃɪeɪt/ *vt/i* unterscheiden (**between** zwischen + *dat*)
differently /'dɪfrəntlɪ/ *adv* anders
difficult /'dɪfɪkəlt/ *a* schwierig, schwer. **~y** *n* Schwierigkeit *f*
diffiden|ce /'dɪfɪdəns/ *n* Zaghaftigkeit *f*. **~t** *a* zaghaft

dig /dɪg/ *n* (*poke*) Stoß *m*; (*remark*) spitze Bemerkung *f*; (*Archaeol*) Ausgrabung *f* ● *vt/i* (*pt/pp* **dug**, *pres p* **digging**) graben; umgraben <*garden*>. **~ out** *vt* ausgraben. **~ up** *vt* ausgraben; umgraben <*garden*>; aufreißen <*street*>

digest /dɪ'dʒest/ *vt* verdauen. **~ible** *a* verdaulich. **~ion** /-estʃn/ *n* Verdauung *f*

digit /'dɪdʒɪt/ *n* Ziffer *f*; (*finger*) Finger *m*; (*toe*) Zehe *f*

digital /'dɪdʒɪtl/ *a* Digital-; **~ camera** Digitalkamera *f*; **~ television** Digitalfernsehen *nt*

dignified /'dɪgnɪfaɪd/ *a* würdevoll

dignity /'dɪgnɪtɪ/ *n* Würde *f*

dilapidated /dɪ'læpɪdeɪtɪd/ *a* baufällig

dilatory /'dɪlətərɪ/ *a* langsam

dilemma /dɪ'lemə/ *n* Dilemma *nt*

dilettante /dɪlɪ'tæntɪ/ *n* Dilettant(in) *m(f)*

diligen|ce /'dɪlɪdʒəns/ *n* Fleiß *m*. **~t** *a*, **-ly** *adv* fleißig

dilute /daɪ'lu:t/ *vt* verdünnen

dim /dɪm/ *a* (**dimmer, dimmest**). **-ly** *adv* (*weak*) schwach; (*dark*) trüb[e]; (*indistinct*) undeutlich; (🄸 *stupid*) dumm, 🄸 doof ● *v* (*pt/pp* **dimmed**) ● *vt* dämpfen

dime /daɪm/ *n* (*Amer*) Zehncentstück *nt*

dimension /daɪ'menʃn/ *n* Dimension *f*; **~s** *pl* Maße *pl*

diminutive /dɪ'mɪnjʊtɪv/ *a* winzig ● *n* Verkleinerungsform *f*

dimple /'dɪmpl/ *n* Grübchen *nt*

din /dɪn/ *n* Krach *m*, Getöse *nt*

dine /daɪn/ *vi* speisen. **~r** *n* Speisende(r) *m/f*; (*Amer: restaurant*) Esslokal *nt*

dinghy /'dɪŋgɪ/ *n* Dinghi *nt*; (*inflatable*) Schlauchboot *nt*

dingy /'dɪndʒɪ/ *a* (**-ier, -iest**) trübe

dining /'daɪnɪŋ/: **~-car** *n* Speisewagen *m*. **~-room** *n* Esszimmer *nt*. **~-table** *n* Esstisch *m*

dinner /'dɪnə(r)/ *n* Abendessen *nt*; (*at midday*) Mittagessen *nt*; (*formal*) Essen *nt*. **~-jacket** *n* Smoking *m*

dinosaur /'daɪnəsɔ:(r)/ *n* Dinosaurier *m*

diocese /'daɪəsɪs/ *n* Diözese *f*

dip /dɪp/ *n* (*in ground*) Senke *f*; (*Culin*) Dip *m* ● *v* (*pt/pp* **dipped**) *vt* [ein]tauchen; **~ one's headlights** (*Auto*) [die Scheinwerfer] abblenden ● *vi* sich senken

diploma /dɪ'pləʊmə/ *n* Diplom *nt*

diplomacy /dɪ'pləʊməsɪ/ *n* Diplomatie *f*

diplomat /'dɪpləmæt/ *n* Diplomat *m*. **~ic** /-'mætɪk/ *a*, **-ally** *adv* diplomatisch

'dip-stick *n* (*Auto*) Ölmessstab *m*

dire /'daɪə(r)/ *a* (**-r, -st**) bitter; <*consequences*> furchtbar

direct /dɪ'rekt/ *a & adv* direkt ● *vt* (*aim*) richten (**at** auf / (*fig*) an + *acc*); (*control*) leiten; (*order*) anweisen; **~ a film/play** bei einem Film/Theaterstück Regie führen

direction /dɪ'rekʃn/ *n* Richtung *f*; (*control*) Leitung *f*; (*of play, film*) Regie *f*; **~s** *pl* Anweisungen *pl*; **~s for use** Gebrauchsanweisung *f*

directly /dɪ'rektlɪ/ *adv* direkt; (*at once*) sofort

director /dɪ'rektə(r)/ *n* (*Comm*) Direktor *m*; (*of play, film*) Regisseur *m*

directory /dɪ'rektərɪ/ *n* Verzeichnis *nt*; (*Teleph*) Telefonbuch *nt*

dirt /dɜ:t/ *n* Schmutz *m*; (*soil*) Erde *f*; **~ cheap** 🄸 spottbillig

dirty /'dɜ:tɪ/ *a* (**-ier, -iest**) schmutzig

dis|a'bility /dɪs-/ *n* Behinderung *f*. **~abled** /dɪ'seɪbld/ *a* [körper]behindert
disad'vantage *n* Nachteil *m*; **at a ~** im Nachteil. **~d** *a* benachteiligt
disa'gree *vi* nicht übereinstimmen (**with** mit); **I ~** ich bin anderer Meinung; **oysters ~ with me** Austern bekommen mir nicht
disa'greeable *a* unangenehm
disa'greement *n* Meinungsverschiedenheit *f*
disap'pear *vi* verschwinden. **~ance** *n* Verschwinden *nt*
disap'point *vt* enttäuschen. **~ment** *n* Enttäuschung *f*
disap'proval *n* Missbilligung *f*
disap'prove *vi* dagegen sein; **~ of** missbilligen
dis'arm *vt* entwaffnen ● *vi* (*Mil*) abrüsten. **~ament** *n* Abrüstung *f*. **~ing** *a* entwaffnend
disast|er /dɪ'zɑ:stə(r)/ *n* Katastrophe *f*; (*accident*) Unglück *nt*. **~rous** /-rəs/ *a* katastrophal
disbe'lief *n* Ungläubigkeit *f*; **in ~** ungläubig
disc /dɪsk/ *n* Scheibe *f*; (*record*) [Schall]platte *f*; (*CD*) CD *f*
discard /dɪ'skɑ:d/ *vt* ablegen; (*throw away*) wegwerfen
discerning /dɪ'sɜ:nɪŋ/ *a* anspruchsvoll
'discharge¹ *n* Ausstoßen *nt*; (*Naut, Electr*) Entladung *f*; (*dismissal*) Entlassung *f*; (*Jur*) Freispruch *m*; (*Med*) Ausfluss *m*
dis'charge² *vt* ausstoßen; (*Naut, Electr*) entladen; (*dismiss*) entlassen; (*Jur*) freisprechen <*accused*>
disciplinary /'dɪsɪplɪnərɪ/ *a* disziplinarisch
discipline /'dɪsɪplɪn/ *n* Disziplin *f* ● *vt* Disziplin beibringen (+ *dat*); (*punish*) bestrafen
'disc jockey *n* Diskjockey *m*
dis'claim *vt* abstreiten. **~er** *n* Verzichterklärung *f*
dis'clos|e *vt* enthüllen. **~ure** *n* Enthüllung *f*
disco /'dɪskəʊ/ *n* [!] Disko *f*
dis'colour *vt* verfärben ● *vi* sich verfärben
dis'comfort *n* Beschwerden *pl*; (*fig*) Unbehagen *nt*
discon'nect *vt* trennen; (*Electr*) ausschalten; (*cut supply*) abstellen
discon'tent *n* Unzufriedenheit *f*. **~ed** *a* unzufrieden
discon'tinue *vt* einstellen; (*Comm*) nicht mehr herstellen
'discord *n* Zwietracht *f*; (*Mus & fig*) Missklang *m*
discothèque /'dɪskətek/ *n* Diskothek *f*
'discount *n* Rabatt *m*
dis'courage *vt* entmutigen; (*dissuade*) abraten (+ *dat*)
dis'courteous *a*, **-ly** *adv* unhöflich
discover /dɪ'skʌvə(r)/ *vt* entdecken. **~y** *n* Entdeckung *f*
discreet /dɪ'skri:t/ *a*, **-ly** *adv* diskret
discretion /dɪ'skreʃn/ *n* Diskretion *f*; (*judgement*) Ermessen *nt*
discriminat|e /dɪ'skrɪmɪneɪt/ *vi* unterscheiden (**between** zwischen + *dat*); **~e against** diskriminieren. **~ing** *a* anspruchsvoll. **~ion** /-'neɪʃn/ *n* Diskriminierung *f*
discus /'dɪskəs/ *n* Diskus *m*
discuss /dɪ'skʌs/ *vt* besprechen; (*examine critically*) diskutieren. **~ion** /-ʌʃn/ *n* Besprechung *f*; Diskussion *f*
disdain /dɪs'deɪn/ *n* Verachtung *f*
disease /dɪ'zi:z/ *n* Krankheit *f*
disem'bark *vi* an Land gehen

disen'chant *vt* ernüchtern
disen'gage *vt* losmachen
disen'tangle *vt* entwirren
dis'figure *vt* entstellen
dis'grace *n* Schande *f*; **in ~** in Ungnade ● *vt* Schande machen (+ *dat*). **~ful** *a* schändlich
disgruntled /dɪs'grʌntld/ *a* verstimmt
disguise /dɪs'gaɪz/ *n* Verkleidung *f*; **in ~** verkleidet ● *vt* verkleiden; verstellen <*voice*>
disgust /dɪs'gʌst/ *n* Ekel *m*; **in ~** empört ● *vt* anekeln; (*appal*) empören. **~ing** *a* eklig; (*appalling*) abscheulich
dish /dɪʃ/ *n* Schüssel *f*; (*shallow*) Schale *f*; (*small*) Schälchen *nt*; (*food*) Gericht *nt*. **~ out** *vt* austeilen. **~ up** *vt* auftragen
'dishcloth *n* Spültuch *nt*
dis'hearten *vt* entmutigen
dis'honest *a* **-ly** *adv* unehrlich. **~y** *n* Unehrlichkeit *f*
dis'honour *n* Schande *f*. **~able** *a*, **-bly** *adv* unehrenhaft
'dishwasher *n* Geschirrspülmaschine *f*
disil'lusion *vt* ernüchtern. **~ment** *n* Ernüchterung *f*
disin'fect *vt* desinfizieren. **~ant** *n* Desinfektionsmittel *nt*
disin'herit *vt* enterben
dis'integrate *vi* zerfallen
dis'jointed *a* unzusammenhängend
disk /dɪsk/ *n* = **disc**
dis'like *n* Abneigung *f* ● *vt* nicht mögen
dislocate /'dɪsləkeɪt/ *vt* ausrenken
dis'lodge *vt* entfernen
dis'loyal *a*, **-ly** *adv* illoyal. **~ty** *n* Illoyalität *f*
dismal /'dɪzməl/ *a* trüb[e]; <*person*> trübselig
dismantle /dɪs'mæntl/ *vt* auseinander nehmen; (*take down*) abbauen
dis'may *n* Bestürzung *f*. **~ed** *a* bestürzt
dis'miss *vt* entlassen; (*reject*) zurückweisen. **~al** *n* Entlassung *f*; Zurückweisung *f*
diso'bedien|ce *n* Ungehorsam *m*. **~t** *a* ungehorsam
diso'bey *vt/i* nicht gehorchen (+ *dat*); nicht befolgen <*rule*>
dis'order *n* Unordnung *f*; (*Med*) Störung *f*. **~ly** *a* unordentlich
dis'organized *a* unorganisiert
dis'own *vt* verleugnen
disparaging /dɪ'spærɪdʒɪŋ/ *a*, **-ly** *adv* abschätzig
dispassionate /dɪ'spæʃənət/ *a*, **-ly** *adv* gelassen; (*impartial*) unparteiisch
dispatch /dɪ'spætʃ/ *n* (*Comm*) Versand *m*; (*Mil*) Nachricht *f*; (*report*) Bericht *m* ● *vt* [ab]senden; (*kill*) töten
dispel /dɪ'spel/ *vt* (*pt/pp* **dispelled**) vertreiben
dispensary /dɪ'spensərɪ/ *n* Apotheke *f*
dispense /dɪ'spens/ *vt* austeilen; **~ with** verzichten auf (+ *acc*). **~r** *n* (*device*) Automat *m*
disperse /dɪ'spɜːs/ *vt* zerstreuen ● *vi* sich zerstreuen
dispirited /dɪ'spɪrɪtɪd/ *a* entmutigt
display /dɪ'spleɪ/ *n* Ausstellung *f*; (*Comm*) Auslage *f*; (*performance*) Vorführung *f* ● *vt* zeigen; ausstellen <*goods*>
dis'please *vt* missfallen (+ *dat*)
dis'pleasure *n* Missfallen *nt*
disposable /dɪ'spəʊzəbl/ *a* Wegwerf-; <*income*> verfügbar
disposal /dɪ'spəʊzl/ *n* Beseitigung *f*; **be at s.o.'s ~** jdm zur Verfügung stehen

dispose /dɪ'spəʊz/ *vi* ~ **of** beseitigen; (*deal with*) erledigen

disposition /dɪspə'zɪʃn/ *n* Veranlagung *f*; (*nature*) Wesensart *f*

disproportionate /dɪsprə'pɔ:ʃənət/ *a*, **-ly** *adv* unverhältnismäßig

dis'prove *vt* widerlegen

dispute /dɪ'spju:t/ *n* Disput *m*; (*quarrel*) Streit *m* ● *vt* bestreiten

disqualifi'cation *n* Disqualifikation *f*

dis'qualify *vt* disqualifizieren; ~ **s.o. from driving** jdm den Führerschein entziehen

disre'gard *vt* nicht beachten

disre'pair *n* **fall into** ~ verfallen

dis'reputable *a* verrufen

disre'pute *n* Verruf *m*

disre'spect *n* Respektlosigkeit *f*. ~**ful** *a*, **-ly** *adv* respektlos

disrupt /dɪs'rʌpt/ *vt* stören. ~**ion** /-ʌpʃn/ *n* Störung *f*

dissatis'faction *n* Unzufriedenheit *f*

dis'satisfied *a* unzufrieden

dissect /dɪ'sekt/ *vt* zergliedern; (*Med*) sezieren. ~**ion** /-ekʃn/ *n* Zergliederung *f*; (*Med*) Sektion *f*

dissent /dɪ'sent/ *n* Nichtübereinstimmung *f* ● *vi* nicht übereinstimmen

dissident /'dɪsɪdənt/ *n* Dissident *m*

dis'similar *a* unähnlich (**to** *dat*)

dissociate /dɪ'səʊʃɪeɪt/ *vt* ~ **oneself** sich distanzieren (**from** von)

dissolute /'dɪsəlu:t/ *a* zügellos; <*life*> ausschweifend

dissolve /dɪ'zɒlv/ *vt* auflösen ● *vi* sich auflösen

dissuade /dɪ'sweɪd/ *vt* abbringen (**from** von)

distance /'dɪstəns/ *n* Entfernung *f*; **long/short** ~ lange/kurze Strecke *f*; **in the/from a** ~ in/aus der Ferne

distant /'dɪstənt/ *a* fern; (*aloof*) kühl; <*relative*> entfernt

dis'tasteful *a* unangenehm

distil /dɪ'stɪl/ *vt* (*pt/pp* **distilled**) brennen; (*Chem*) destillieren. ~**lery** /-ərɪ/ *n* Brennerei *f*

distinct /dɪ'stɪŋkt/ *a* deutlich; (*different*) verschieden. ~**ion** /-ɪŋkʃn/ *n* Unterschied *m*; (*Sch*) Auszeichnung *f*. ~**ive** /-tɪv/ *a* kennzeichnend; (*unmistakable*) unverwechselbar. ~**ly** *adv* deutlich

distinguish /dɪ'stɪŋgwɪʃ/ *vt/i* unterscheiden; (*make out*) erkennen; ~ **oneself** sich auszeichnen. ~**ed** *a* angesehen; <*appearance*> distinguiert

distort /dɪ'stɔ:t/ *vt* verzerren; (*fig*) verdrehen. ~**ion** /-ɔ:ʃn/ *n* Verzerrung *f*, (*fig*) Verdrehung *f*

distract /dɪ'strækt/ *vt* ablenken. ~**ion** /-ækʃn/ *n* Ablenkung *f*; (*despair*) Verzweiflung *f*

distraught /dɪ'strɔ:t/ *a* [völlig] aufgelöst

distress /dɪ'stres/ *n* Kummer *m*; (*pain*) Schmerz *m*; (*poverty, danger*) Not *f* ● *vt* Kummer/Schmerz bereiten (+ *dat*); (*sadden*) bekümmern; (*shock*) erschüttern. ~**ing** *a* schmerzlich; (*shocking*) erschütternd

distribut|e /dɪ'strɪbju:t/ *vt* verteilen; (*Comm*) vertreiben. ~**ion** /-'bju:ʃn/ *n* Verteilung *f*; Vertrieb *m*. ~**or** *n* Verteiler *m*

district /'dɪstrɪkt/ *n* Gegend *f*; (*Admin*) Bezirk *m*

dis'trust *n* Misstrauen *nt* ● *vt* misstrauen (+ *dat*). ~**ful** *a* misstrauisch

disturb /dɪ'stɜ:b/ *vt* stören; (*perturb*) beunruhigen; (*touch*) anrühren. ~**ance** *n* Unruhe *f*; (*interruption*) Störung *f*. ~**ed** *a* beunruhigt; **[mentally] ~ed** geistig gestört. **~ing** *a* beunruhigend

dis'used *a* stillgelegt; (*empty*) leer

ditch /dɪtʃ/ *n* Graben *m* ● *vt* ([!] *abandon*) fallen lassen <*plan*>

dither /'dɪðə(r)/ *vi* zaudern

ditto /'dɪtəʊ/ *n* dito; [!] ebenfalls

dive /daɪv/ *n* [Kopf]sprung *m*; (*Aviat*) Sturzflug *m*; ([!] *place*) Spelunke *f* ● *vi* einen Kopfsprung machen; (*when in water*) tauchen; (*Aviat*) einen Sturzflug machen; ([!] *rush*) stürzen

diver /'daɪvə(r)/ *n* Taucher *m*; (*Sport*) [Kunst]springer *m*

diverse /daɪ'vɜ:s/ *a* verschieden

diversify /daɪ'vɜ:sɪfaɪ/ *vt/i* (*pt/pp* **-ied**) variieren; (*Comm*) diversifizieren

diversion /daɪ'vɜ:ʃn/ *n* Umleitung *f*; (*distraction*) Ablenkung *f*

diversity /daɪ'vɜ:sətɪ/ *n* Vielfalt *f*

divert /daɪ'vɜ:t/ *vt* umleiten; ablenken <*attention*>; (*entertain*) unterhalten

divide /dɪ'vaɪd/ *vt* teilen; (*separate*) trennen; (*Math*) dividieren (**by** durch) ● *vi* sich teilen

dividend /'dɪvɪdend/ *n* Dividende *f*

divine /dɪ'vaɪn/ *a* göttlich

diving /'daɪvɪŋ/ *n* (*Sport*) Kunstspringen *nt*. **~-board** *n* Sprungbrett *nt*

divinity /dɪ'vɪnətɪ/ *n* Göttlichkeit *f*; (*subject*) Theologie *f*

division /dɪ'vɪʒn/ *n* Teilung *f*; (*separation*) Trennung *f*; (*Math, Mil*) Division *f*; (*Parl*) Hammelsprung *m*; (*line*) Trennlinie *f*; (*group*) Abteilung *f*

divorce /dɪ'vɔ:s/ *n* Scheidung *f* ● *vt* sich scheiden lassen von. **~d** *a* geschieden; **get ~d** sich scheiden lassen

DIY *abbr of* **do-it-yourself**

dizziness /'dɪzɪnɪs/ *n* Schwindel *m*

dizzy /'dɪzɪ/ *a* (**-ier, -iest**) schwindlig; **I feel ~** mir ist schwindlig

---

do /du:, *unbetont* də/

3 sg pres tense **does**; *pt* **did**; *pp* **done**

● *transitive verb*

····➤ (*perform*) machen <*homework, housework, exam, handstand etc*>; tun <*duty, favour, something, nothing*>; vorführen <*trick, dance*>; durchführen <*test*>. **what are you doing?** was tust *od* machst du? **what can I do for you?** was kann ich für Sie tun? **do something!** tu doch etwas! **have you nothing better to do?** hast du nichts Besseres zu tun? **do the washing-up /cleaning** abwaschen/sauber machen

····➤ (*as job*) **what does your father do?** was macht dein Vater?; was ist dein Vater von Beruf?

····➤ (*clean*) putzen; (*arrange*) [zurecht]machen <*hair*>

····➤ (*cook*) kochen; (*roast, fry*) braten. **well done** (*meat*) durch[gebraten]. **the potatoes aren't done yet** die Kartoffeln sind noch nicht richtig durch

····➤ (*solve*) lösen <*problem, riddle*>; machen <*puzzle*>

····➤ ([!] *swindle*) reinlegen. **do s.o. out of sth** jdn um etw bringen

● *intransitive verb*

····➤ (*with as or adverb*) es tun; es machen. **do as they do** mach es wie sie. **he can do as he likes** er kann tun *od* machen, was er will. **you did well** du hast es gut gemacht

····➤ (*get on*) vorankommen; (*in exams*) abschneiden. **do well/ badly at school** gut/schlecht in der Schule sein. **how are you doing?** wie geht's dir? **how do you do?** (*formal*) guten Tag!
····➤ **will do** (*serve purpose*) es tun; (*suffice*) [aus]reichen; (*be suitable*) gehen. **that won't do** das geht nicht. **that will do!** jetzt aber genug!
● *auxiliary verb*
····➤ (*in questions*) **do you know him?** kennst du ihn? **what does he want?** was will er?
····➤ (*in negation*) **I don't** *or* **do not wish to take part** ich will nicht teilnehmen. **don't be so noisy!** seid [doch] nicht so laut!
····➤ (*as verb substitute*) **you mustn't act as he does** du darfst nicht so wie er handeln. **come in, do!** komm doch herein!
····➤ (*in tag questions*) **don't you, doesn't he** *etc.* nicht wahr. **you went to Paris, didn't you?** du warst in Paris, nicht wahr?
····➤ (*in short questions*) **Does he live in London? — Yes, he does** Wohnt er in London? — Ja [, stimmt]
····➤ (*for special emphasis*) **I do love Greece** Griechenland gefällt mir wirklich gut
····➤ (*for inversion*) **little did he know that ...** er hatte keine Ahnung, dass ...
● *noun*
pl **do's** *or* **dos** /du:z/
····➤ (🅘 *celebration*) Feier *f*
● *phrasal verbs* ● **do away with** *vt* abschaffen. ● **do for** *vt* 🅘: **do for s.o.** jdn fertig machen 🅘; **be done for** erledigt sein. ● **do in** *vt* (🅧 *kill*) kaltmachen 🅧. ● **do up** *vt* (*fasten*) zumachen; binden <*shoe-lace, bow-tie*>; (*wrap*) einpacken; (*renovate*) renovieren. ● **do with** *vt*: **I could do with ...** ich brauche .... ● **do without** *vt*: **do without sth** auf etw (*acc*) verzichten; *vi* darauf verzichten

docile /ˈdəʊsaɪl/ *a* fügsam
dock¹ /dɒk/ *n* (*Jur*) Anklagebank *f*
dock² *n* Dock *nt* ● *vi* anlegen. **~er** *n* Hafenarbeiter *m*. **~yard** *n* Werft *f*
doctor /ˈdɒktə(r)/ *n* Arzt *m*/ Ärztin *f*; (*Univ*) Doktor *m* ● *vt* kastrieren; (*spay*) sterilisieren
doctrine /ˈdɒktrɪn/ *n* Lehre *f*
document /ˈdɒkjʊmənt/ *n* Dokument *nt*. **~ary** /-ˈmentərɪ/ *a* Dokumentar- ● *n* Dokumentarbericht *m*; (*film*) Dokumentarfilm *m*
dodge /dɒdʒ/ *n* 🅘 Trick *m*, Kniff *m* ● *vt/i* ausweichen (+ *dat*)
dodgy /ˈdɒdʒɪ/ *a* (**-ier, -iest**) 🅘 (*awkward*) knifflig; (*dubious*) zweifelhaft
doe /dəʊ/ *n* Ricke *f*; (*rabbit*) [Kaninchen]weibchen *nt*
does /dʌz/ *see* **do**
doesn't /ˈdʌznt/ = **does not**
dog /dɒg/ *n* Hund *m*
dog: ~-biscuit *n* Hundekuchen *m*. **~-collar** *n* Hundehalsband *nt*; (*Relig* 🅘) Kragen *m* eines Geistlichen. **~-eared** *a* **be ~-eared** Eselsohren haben
dogged /ˈdɒgɪd/ *a*, **-ly** *adv* beharrlich
dogma /ˈdɒgmə/ *n* Dogma *nt*. **~tic** /-ˈmætɪk/ *a* dogmatisch
do-it-yourself /du:ɪtjəˈself/ *n* Heimwerken *nt*. **~ shop** *n* Heimwerkerladen *m*
doldrums /ˈdɒldrəmz/ *npl* **be in the ~** niedergeschlagen sein; <*business*:> daniederliegen
dole /dəʊl/ *n* 🅘 Stempelgeld *nt*; **be on the ~** arbeitslos sein ● *vt* **~ out** austeilen
doll /dɒl/ *n* Puppe *f* ● *vt* 🅘 **~ oneself up** sich herausputzen

dollar /ˈdɒlə(r)/ *n* Dollar *m*
dolphin /ˈdɒlfɪn/ *n* Delphin *m*
domain /dəˈmeɪn/ *n* Gebiet *nt*
dome /dəʊm/ *n* Kuppel *m*
domestic /dəˈmestɪk/ *a* häuslich; (*Pol*) Innen-; (*Comm*) Binnen-. **~ animal** *n* Haustier *nt*. **~ flight** *n* Inlandflug *m*
dominant /ˈdɒmɪnənt/ *a* vorherrschend
dominat|e /ˈdɒmɪneɪt/ *vt* beherrschen ● *vi* dominieren. **~ion** /-ˈneɪʃn/ *n* Vorherrschaft *f*
domineering /dɒmɪˈnɪə(r)ɪŋ/ *a* herrschsüchtig
domino /ˈdɒmɪnəʊ/ *n* (*pl* **-es**) Dominostein *m*; **~es** *sg* (*game*) Domino *nt*
donat|e /dəʊˈneɪt/ *vt* spenden. **~ion** /-eɪʃn/ *n* Spende *f*
done /dʌn/ *see* **do**
donkey /ˈdɒŋkɪ/ *n* Esel *m*; **~'s years** [!] eine Ewigkeit. **~-work** *n* Routinearbeit *f*
donor /ˈdəʊnə(r)/ *n* Spender(in) *m(f)*
don't /dəʊnt/ = **do not**
doom /duːm/ *n* Schicksal *nt*; (*ruin*) Verhängnis *nt*
door /dɔː(r)/ *n* Tür *f*; **out of ~s** im Freien
door: ~man *n* Portier *m*. **~mat** *n* [Fuß]abtreter *m*. **~step** *n* Türschwelle *f*; **on the ~step** vor der Tür. **~way** *n* Türöffnung *f*
dope /dəʊp/ *n* [!] Drogen *pl*; ([!] *information*) Informationen *pl*; ([!] *idiot*) Trottel *m* ● *vt* betäuben; (*Sport*) dopen
dormant /ˈdɔːmənt/ *a* ruhend
dormitory /ˈdɔːmɪtərɪ/ *n* Schlafsaal *m*
dormouse /ˈdɔː-/ *n* Haselmaus *f*
dosage /ˈdəʊsɪdʒ/ *n* Dosierung *f*
dose /dəʊs/ *n* Dosis *f*
dot /dɒt/ *n* Punkt *m*; **on the ~** pünktlich. **~-com** *n* Dot-com-Firma *f*
dote /dəʊt/ *vi* **~ on** vernarrt sein in (+ *acc*)
dotted /ˈdɒtɪd/ *a* **~ line** punktierte Linie *f*; **be ~ with** bestreut sein mit
dotty /ˈdɒtɪ/ *a* (**-ier, -iest**) [!] verdreht
double /ˈdʌbl/ *a & adv* doppelt; <*bed, chin*> Doppel-; <*flower*> gefüllt ● *n* das Doppelte; (*person*) Doppelgänger *m*; **~s** *pl* (*Tennis*) Doppel *nt*; ● *vt* verdoppeln; (*fold*) falten ● *vi* sich verdoppeln. **~ up** *vi* sich krümmen (**with** vor + *dat*)
double: ~ˈbass *n* Kontrabass *m*. **~-breasted** *a* zweireihig. **~-click** *vt/i* doppelklicken (**on** auf + *acc*). **~ˈcross** *vt* ein Doppelspiel treiben mit. **~-ˈdecker** *n* Doppeldecker *m*. **~ˈglazing** *n* Doppelverglasung *f*. **~ ˈroom** *n* Doppelzimmer *nt*
doubly /ˈdʌblɪ/ *adv* doppelt
doubt /daʊt/ *n* Zweifel *m* ● *vt* bezweifeln. **~ful** *a*, **-ly** *adv* zweifelhaft; (*disbelieving*) skeptisch. **~less** *adv* zweifellos
dough /dəʊ/ *n* [fester] Teig *m*; ([!] *money*) Pinke *f*. **~nut** *n* Berliner [Pfannkuchen] *m*
dove /dʌv/ *n* Taube *f*
dowdy /ˈdaʊdɪ/ *a* (**-ier, -iest**) unschick
down¹ /daʊn/ *n* (*feathers*) Daunen *pl*
down² *adv* unten; (*with movement*) nach unten; **go ~** hinuntergehen; **come ~** herunterkommen; **~ there** da unten; **£50 ~** £50 Anzahlung; **~!** (*to dog*) Platz! **~ with ...!** nieder mit ...! ● *prep* **~ the road/stairs** die Straße/Treppe hinunter; **~ the river** den Fluss abwärts ● *vt* [!] (*drink*) runterkippen; **~ tools** die Arbeit niederlegen
down: ~cast *a* niedergeschlagen. **~fall** *n* Sturz

m; (*ruin*) Ruin *m*. **~'hearted** *a* entmutigt. **~'hill** *adv* bergab. **~payment** *n* Anzahlung *f*. **~pour** *n* Platzregen *m*. **~right** *a & adv* ausgesprochen. **~size** *vt* verschlanken ● *vi* abspecken. **~'stairs** *adv* unten; <*go*> nach unten ● *a* /'--/ im Erdgeschoss. **~'stream** *adv* stromabwärts. **~-to-'earth** *a* sachlich. **~town** *adv* (*Amer*) im Stadtzentrum. **~ward** *a* nach unten; <*slope*> abfallend ● *adv* **~[s]** abwärts, nach unten

doze /dəʊz/ *n* Nickerchen *nt* ● *vi* dösen. **~ off** *vi* einnicken

dozen /'dʌzn/ *n* Dutzend *nt*

Dr *abbr of* **doctor**

draft¹ /drɑ:ft/ *n* Entwurf *m*; (*Comm*) Tratte *f*; (*Amer Mil*) Einberufung *f* ● *vt* entwerfen; (*Amer Mil*) einberufen

draft² *n* (*Amer*) = **draught**

drag /dræg/ *n* **in ~** 🅸 <*man*> als Frau gekleidet ● *vt* (*pt/pp* **dragged**) schleppen; absuchen <*river*>. **~ on** *vi* sich in die Länge ziehen

dragon /'drægən/ *n* Drache *m*. **~-fly** *n* Libelle *f*

drain /dreɪn/ *n* Abfluss *m*; (*underground*) Kanal *m*; **the ~s** die Kanalisation ● *vt* entwässern <*land*>; ablassen <*liquid*>; das Wasser ablassen aus <*tank*>; abgießen <*vegetables*>; austrinken <*glass*> ● *vi* **~ [away]** ablaufen

drain|age /'dreɪnɪdʒ/ *n* Kanalisation *f*; (*of land*) Dränage *f*. **~ing board** *n* Abtropfbrett *nt*. **~-pipe** *n* Abflussrohr *nt*

drake /dreɪk/ *n* Enterich *m*

drama /'drɑ:mə/ *n* Drama *nt*

dramatic /drə'mætɪk/ *a*, **-ally** *adv* dramatisch

dramat|ist /'dræmətɪst/ *n* Dramatiker *m*. **~ize** *vt* für die Bühne bearbeiten; (*fig*) dramatisieren

drank /dræŋk/ *see* **drink**

drape /dreɪp/ *n* (*Amer*) Vorhang *m* ● *vt* drapieren

drastic /'dræstɪk/ *a*, **-ally** *adv* drastisch

draught /drɑ:ft/ *n* [Luft]zug *m*; **~s** *sg* (*game*) Damespiel *nt*; **there is a ~** es zieht

draught beer *n* Bier *nt* vom Fass

draughty /'drɑ:ftɪ/ *a* zugig

draw /drɔ:/ *n* Attraktion *f*; (*Sport*) Unentschieden *nt*; (*in lottery*) Ziehung *f* ● *v* (*pt* **drew**, *pp* **drawn**) ● *vt* ziehen; (*attract*) anziehen; zeichnen <*picture*>; abheben <*money*>; **~ the curtains** die Vorhänge zuziehen/(*back*) aufziehen ● *vi* (*Sport*) unentschieden spielen. **~ back** *vt* zurückziehen ● *vi* (*recoil*) zurückweichen. **~ in** *vt* einziehen ● *vi* einfahren. **~ out** *vt* herausziehen; abheben <*money*> ● *vi* ausfahren. **~ up** *vt* aufsetzen <*document*>; herrücken <*chair*> ● *vi* [an]halten

draw: ~back *n* Nachteil *m*. **~bridge** *n* Zugbrücke *f*

drawer /drɔ:(r)/ *n* Schublade *f*

drawing /'drɔ:ɪŋ/ *n* Zeichnung *f*

drawing: ~-board *n* Reißbrett *nt*. **~-pin** *n* Reißzwecke *f*. **~-room** *n* Wohnzimmer *nt*

drawl /drɔ:l/ *n* schleppende Aussprache *f*

drawn /drɔ:n/ *see* **draw**

dread /dred/ *n* Furcht *f* (**of** vor + *dat*) ● *vt* fürchten. **~ful** *a*, **-fully** *adv* fürchterlich

dream /dri:m/ *n* Traum *m* ● *vt/i* (*pt/pp* **dreamt** /dremt/ *or* **dreamed**) träumen (**about/of** von)

dreary /'drɪərɪ/ *a* (**-ier, -iest**) trüb[e]; (*boring*) langweilig

dregs /dregz/ *npl* Bodensatz *m*

drench /drentʃ/ *vt* durchnässen

dress /dres/ *n* Kleid *nt*; (*clothing*) Kleidung *f* ● *vt* anziehen; (*Med*) verbinden; ~ **oneself, get ~ed** sich anziehen ● *vi* sich anziehen. ~ **up** *vi* sich schön anziehen; (*in disguise*) sich verkleiden (**as** als)

dress: ~ circle *n* (*Theat*) erster Rang *m*. **~er** *n* (*furniture*) Anrichte *f*; (*Amer: dressing-table*) Frisiertisch *m*

dressing *n* (*Culin*) Soße *f*; (*Med*) Verband *m*

dressing: ~-gown *n* Morgenmantel *m*. **~-room** *n* Ankleidezimmer *nt*; (*Theat*) [Künstler]garderobe *f*. **~-table** *n* Frisiertisch *m*

dress: ~maker *n* Schneiderin *f*. **~ rehearsal** *n* Generalprobe *f*

drew /dru:/ *see* **draw**

dried /draɪd/ *a* getrocknet; ~ **fruit** Dörrobst *nt*

drier /'draɪə(r)/ *n* Trockner *m*

drift /drɪft/ *n* Abtrift *f*; (*of snow*) Schneewehe *f*; (*meaning*) Sinn *m* ● *vi* treiben; (*off course*) abtreiben; <*snow*:> Wehen bilden; (*fig*) <*person*:> sich treiben lassen

drill /drɪl/ *n* Bohrer *m*; (*Mil*) Drill *m* ● *vt/i* bohren (**for** nach); (*Mil*) drillen

drily /'draɪlɪ/ *adv* trocken

drink /drɪŋk/ *n* Getränk *nt*; (*alcoholic*) Drink *m*; (*alcohol*) Alkohol *m* ● *vt/i* (*pt* **drank**, *pp* **drunk**) trinken. ~ **up** *vt/i* austrinken

drink|able /'drɪŋkəbl/ *a* trinkbar. **~er** *n* Trinker *m*

'drinking-water *n* Trinkwasser *nt*

drip /drɪp/ *n* Tropfen *nt*; (*drop*) Tropfen *m*; (*Med*) Tropf *m*; ([!] *person*) Niete *f* ● *vi* (*pt/pp* **dripped**) tropfen

drive /draɪv/ *n* [Auto]fahrt *f*; (*entrance*) Einfahrt *f*; (*energy*) Elan *m*; (*Psych*) Trieb *m*; (*Pol*) Aktion *f*; (*Sport*) Treibschlag *m*; (*Techn*) Antrieb *m* ● *v* (*pt* **drove**, *pp* **driven**) ● *vt* treiben; fahren <*car*>; (*Sport: hit*) schlagen; (*Techn*) antreiben; ~ **s.o. mad** [!] jdn verrückt machen; **what are you driving at?** [!] worauf willst du hinaus? ● *vi* fahren. ~ **away** *vt* vertreiben ● *vi* abfahren. ~ **off** *vt* vertreiben ● *vi* abfahren. ~ **on** *vi* weiterfahren. ~ **up** *vi* vorfahren

drivel /'drɪvl/ *n* [!] Quatsch *m*

driven /'drɪvn/ *see* **drive**

driver /'draɪvə(r)/ *n* Fahrer(in) *m(f)*; (*of train*) Lokführer *m*

driving: ~ lesson *n* Fahrstunde *f*. ~ **licence** *n* Führerschein *m*. ~ **school** *n* Fahrschule *f*. ~ **test** Fahrprüfung *f*

drizzle /'drɪzl/ *n* Nieselregen *m* ● *vi* nieseln

drone /drəʊn/ *n* (*sound*) Brummen *nt*

droop /dru:p/ *vi* herabhängen

drop /drɒp/ *n* Tropfen *m*; (*fall*) Fall *m*; (*in price, temperature*) Rückgang *m* ● *v* (*pt/pp* **dropped**) ● *vt* fallen lassen; abwerfen <*bomb*>; (*omit*) auslassen; (*give up*) aufgeben ● *vi* fallen; (*fall lower*) sinken; <*wind*:> nachlassen. ~ **in** *vi* vorbeikommen. ~ **off** *vt* absetzen <*person*> ● *vi* abfallen; (*fall asleep*) einschlafen. ~ **out** *vi* herausfallen; (*give up*) aufgeben

drought /draʊt/ *n* Dürre *f*

drove /drəʊv/ *see* **drive**

drown /draʊn/ *vi* ertrinken ● *vt* ertränken; übertönen <*noise*>; **be ~ed** ertrinken

drowsy /'draʊzɪ/ *a* schläfrig

drudgery /'drʌdʒərɪ/ *n* Plackerei *f*

drug /drʌg/ *n* Droge *f* ● *vt* (*pt/pp* **drugged**) betäuben

drug: ~ addict *n* Drogenabhängige(r) *m/f.* **~store** *n* (*Amer*) Drogerie *f*; (*dispensing*) Apotheke *f*

drum /drʌm/ *n* Trommel *f*; (*for oil*) Tonne *f* ● *v* (*pt/pp* **drummed**) ● *vi* trommeln ● *vt* **~sth into s.o.** [!] jdm etw einbläuen. **~mer** *n* Trommler *m*; (*in pop-group*) Schlagzeuger *m*. **~stick** *n* Trommelschlegel *m*; (*Culin*) Keule *f*

drunk /drʌŋk/ *see* **drink** ● *a* betrunken; **get ~** sich betrinken ● *n* Betrunkene(r) *m*

drunk|ard /'drʌŋkəd/ *n* Trinker *m*. **~en** *a* betrunken

dry /draɪ/ *a* (**drier, driest**) trocken ● *vt/i* trocknen. **~ up** *vt/i* austrocknen

dry: ~-'clean *vt* chemisch reinigen. **~-'cleaner's** *n* (*shop*) chemische Reinigung *f*. **~ness** *n* Trockenheit *f*

dual /'dju:əl/ *a* doppelt

dual 'carriageway *n* ≈ Schnellstraße *f*

dubious /'dju:bɪəs/ *a* zweifelhaft

duchess /'dʌtʃɪs/ *n* Herzogin *f*

duck /dʌk/ *n* Ente *f* ● *vt* (*in water*) untertauchen ● *vi* sich ducken

duct /dʌkt/ *n* Rohr *nt*; (*Anat*) Gang *m*

dud /dʌd/ *a* [!] nutzlos; <*coin*> falsch; <*cheque*> ungedeckt; (*forged*) gefälscht

due /dju:/ *a* angemessen; **be ~** fällig sein; <*baby:*> erwartet werden; <*train:*> planmäßig ankommen; **~ to** (*owing to*) wegen (+ *gen*); **be ~ to** zurückzuführen sein auf (+ *acc*) ● *adv* **~ west** genau westlich

duel /'dju:əl/ *n* Duell *nt*

duet /dju:'et/ *n* Duo *nt*; (*vocal*) Duett *nt*

dug /dʌg/ *see* **dig**

duke /dju:k/ *n* Herzog *m*

dull /dʌl/ *a* (**-er, -est**) (*overcast, not bright*) trüb[e]; (*not shiny*) matt; <*sound*> dumpf; (*boring*) langweilig; (*stupid*) schwerfällig

duly /'dju:lɪ/ *adv* ordnungsgemäß

dumb /dʌm/ *a* (**-er, -est**) stumm. **~ down** *vt/i* verflachen

dummy /'dʌmɪ/ *n* (*tailor's*) [Schneider]puppe *f*; (*for baby*) Schnuller *m*; (*Comm*) Attrappe *f*

dump /dʌmp/ *n* Abfallhaufen *m*; (*for refuse*) Müllhalde *f*, Deponie *f*; ([!] *town*) Kaff *nt*; **be down in the ~s** [!] deprimiert sein ● *vt* abladen

dumpling /'dʌmplɪŋ/ *n* Kloß *m*

dunce /dʌns/ *n* Dummkopf *m*

dune /dju:n/ *n* Düne *f*

dung /dʌŋ/ *n* Mist *m*

dungarees /dʌŋgə'ri:z/ *npl* Latzhose *f*

dungeon /'dʌndʒən/ *n* Verlies *nt*

dunk /dʌŋk/ *vt* eintunken

duo /'dju:əʊ/ *n* Paar *nt*; (*Mus*) Duo *nt*

dupe /dju:p/ *n* Betrogene(r) *m/f* ● *vt* betrügen

duplicate¹ /'dju:plɪkət/ *n* Doppel *nt*; **in ~** in doppelter Ausfertigung *f*

duplicate² /'dju:plɪkeɪt/ *vt* kopieren; (*do twice*) zweimal machen

durable /'djʊərəbl/ *a* haltbar

duration /djʊə'reɪʃn/ *n* Dauer *f*

during /'djʊərɪŋ/ *prep* während (+ *gen*)

dusk /dʌsk/ *n* [Abend]dämmerung *f*

dust /dʌst/ *n* Staub *m* ● *vt* abstauben; (*sprinkle*) bestäuben (**with** mit) ● *vi* Staub wischen

dust: ~bin *n* Mülltonne *f*. **~-cart** *n* Müllwagen *m*. **~er** *n* Staubtuch *nt*. **~-jacket** *n* Schutzumschlag *m*. **~man** *n* Müllmann *m*. **~pan** *n* Kehrschaufel *f*

dusty /'dʌstɪ/ *a* (**-ier, -iest**) staubig

Dutch /dʌtʃ/ *a* holländisch ● *n* (*Lang*) Holländisch *nt*; **the ~** *pl* die Holländer. **~man** *n* Holländer *m*

dutiful /'dju:tɪfl/ *a*, **-ly** *adv* pflichtbewusst

duty /'dju:tɪ/ *n* Pflicht *f*; (*task*) Aufgabe *f*; (*tax*) Zoll *m*; **be on ~** Dienst haben. **~-free** *a* zollfrei

duvet /'du:veɪ/ *n* Steppdecke *f*

DVD *abbr* (**digital video disc**) DVD *f*

dwarf /dwɔ:f/ *n* (*pl* **-s** *or* **dwarves**) Zwerg *m*

dwell /dwel/ *vi* (*pt*/*pp* **dwelt**); **~ on** (*fig*) verweilen bei. **~ing** *n* Wohnung *f*

dwindle /'dwɪndl/ *vi* abnehmen, schwinden

dye /daɪ/ *n* Farbstoff *m* ● *vt* (*pres p* **dyeing**) färben

dying /'daɪɪŋ/ *see* **die**²

dynamic /daɪ'næmɪk/ *a* dynamisch

dynamite /'daɪnəmaɪt/ *n* Dynamit *nt*

dyslex|ia /dɪs'leksɪə/ *n* Legasthenie *f*. **~ic** *a* legasthenisch; **be ~ic** Legastheniker sein

Ee

each /i:tʃ/ *a & pron* jede(r,s); (*per*) je; **~ other** einander; **£1 ~** £1 pro Person; (*for thing*) pro Stück

eager /'i:gə(r)/ *a*, **-ly** *adv* eifrig; **be ~ to do sth** etw gerne machen wollen. **~ness** *n* Eifer *m*

eagle /'i:gl/ *n* Adler *m*

ear *n* Ohr *nt*. **~ache** *n* Ohrenschmerzen *pl*. **~-drum** *n* Trommelfell *nt*

earl /ɜ:l/ *n* Graf *m*

early /'ɜ:lɪ/ *a & adv* (**-ier, -iest**) früh; <*reply*> baldig; **be ~** früh dran sein

earn /ɜ:n/ *vt* verdienen

earnest /'ɜ:nɪst/ *a*, **-ly** *adv* ernsthaft ● *n* **in ~** im Ernst

earnings /'ɜ:nɪŋz/ *npl* Verdienst *m*

ear: ~phones *npl* Kopfhörer *pl*. **~-ring** *n* Ohrring *m*; (*clip-on*) Ohrklips *m*. **~shot** *n* **within/out of ~shot** in/außer Hörweite

earth /ɜ:θ/ *n* Erde *f*; (*of fox*) Bau *m* ● *vt* (*Electr*) erden

earthenware /'ɜ:θn-/ *n* Tonwaren *pl*

earthly /'ɜ:θlɪ/ *a* irdisch; **be no ~ use** [!] völlig nutzlos sein

'earthquake *n* Erdbeben *nt*

earthy /'ɜ:θɪ/ *a* erdig; (*coarse*) derb

ease /i:z/ *n* Leichtigkeit *f* ● *vt* erleichtern; lindern <*pain*> ● *vi* <*pain:*> nachlassen; <*situation:*> sich entspannen

easily /'i:zɪlɪ/ *adv* leicht, mit Leichtigkeit

east /i:st/ *n* Osten *m*; **to the ~ of** östlich von ● *a* Ost-, ost- ● *adv* nach Osten

Easter /'i:stə(r)/ *n* Ostern *nt* ● *attrib* Oster-. **~ egg** *n* Osterei *nt*

east|erly /'i:stəlɪ/ *a* östlich. **~ern** *a* östlich. **~ward[s]** /-wəd[z]/ *adv* nach Osten

easy /'i:zɪ/ *a* (**-ier, -iest**) leicht; **take it ~** [!] sich schonen; **go ~ with** [!] sparsam umgehen mit

easy: ~ chair *n* Sessel *m*. **~'going** *a* gelassen

eat /iːt/ *vt/i* (*pt* **ate**, *pp* **eaten**) essen; <*animal:*> fressen. **~ up** *vt* aufessen

eatable /ˈiːtəbl/ *a* genießbar

eau-de-Cologne /əʊdəkəˈləʊn/ *n* Kölnisch Wasser *nt*

eaves /iːvz/ *npl* Dachüberhang *m*. **~drop** *vi* (*pt/pp* **~ dropped**) [heimlich] lauschen

ebb /eb/ *n* (*tide*) Ebbe *f* ● *vi* zurückgehen; (*fig*) verebben

ebony /ˈebənɪ/ *n* Ebenholz *nt*

EC *abbr* (**European Community**) EG *f*

eccentric /ɪkˈsentrɪk/ *a* exzentrisch ● *n* Exzentriker *m*

ecclesiastical /ɪkliːzɪˈæstɪkl/ *a* kirchlich

echo /ˈekəʊ/ *n* (*pl* **-es**) Echo *nt*, Widerhall *m* ● *v* (*pt/pp* **echoed**, *pres p* **echoing**) ● *vi* widerhallen (**with** von)

eclipse /ɪˈklɪps/ *n* (*Astr*) Finsternis *f*

ecolog|ical /iːkəˈlɒdʒɪkl/ *a* ökologisch. **~y** /iːˈkɒlədʒɪ/ *n* Ökologie *f*

e-commerce /iːˈkɒmɜːs/ *n* E-Commerce *m*

economic /iːkəˈnɒmɪk/ *a* wirtschaftlich. **~al** *a* sparsam. **~ally** *adv* wirtschaftlich; (*thriftily*) sparsam. **~s** *n* Volkswirtschaft *f*

economist /ɪˈkɒnəmɪst/ *n* Volkswirt *m*; (*Univ*) Wirtschaftswissenschaftler *m*

economize /ɪˈkɒnəmaɪz/ *vi* sparen (**on** an + *dat*)

economy /ɪˈkɒnəmɪ/ *n* Wirtschaft *f*; (*thrift*) Sparsamkeit *f*

ecstasy /ˈekstəsɪ/ *n* Ekstase *f*

ecstatic /ɪkˈstætɪk/ *a*, **-ally** *adv* ekstatisch

eczema /ˈeksɪmə/ *n* Ekzem *nt*

eddy /ˈedɪ/ *n* Wirbel *m*

edge /edʒ/ *n* Rand *m*; (*of table, lawn*) Kante *f*; (*of knife*) Schneide *f*; **on ~** [!] nervös ● *vt* einfassen. **~ forward** *vi* sich nach vorn schieben

edgy /ˈedʒɪ/ *a* [!] nervös

edible /ˈedɪbl/ *a* essbar

edifice /ˈedɪfɪs/ *n* [großes] Gebäude *nt*

edit /ˈedɪt/ *vt* (*pt/pp* **edited**) redigieren; herausgeben <*anthology, dictionary*>; schneiden <*film, tape*>

edition /ɪˈdɪʃn/ *n* Ausgabe *f*; (*impression*) Auflage *f*

editor /ˈedɪtə(r)/ *n* Redakteur *m*; (*of anthology, dictionary*) Herausgeber *m*; (*of newspaper*) Chefredakteur *m*; (*of film*) Cutter(in) *m*(*f*)

editorial /edɪˈtɔːrɪəl/ *a* redaktionell, Redaktions- ● *n* (*Journ*) Leitartikel *m*

educate /ˈedjʊkeɪt/ *vt* erziehen. **~d** *a* gebildet

education /edjʊˈkeɪʃn/ *n* Erziehung *f*; (*culture*) Bildung *f*. **~al** *a* pädagogisch; <*visit*> kulturell

eel /iːl/ *n* Aal *m*

eerie /ˈɪərɪ/ *a* (**-ier, -iest**) unheimlich

effect /ɪˈfekt/ *n* Wirkung *f*, Effekt *m*; **take ~** in Kraft treten

effective /ɪˈfektɪv/ *a*, **-ly** *adv* wirksam, effektiv; (*striking*) wirkungsvoll, effektvoll; (*actual*) tatsächlich. **~ness** *n* Wirksamkeit *f*

effeminate /ɪˈfemɪnət/ *a* unmännlich

effervescent /efəˈvesnt/ *a* sprudelnd

efficiency /ɪˈfɪʃənsɪ/ *n* Tüchtigkeit *f*; (*of machine, organization*) Leistungsfähigkeit *f*

efficient /ɪˈfɪʃənt/ *a* tüchtig; <*machine, organization*>

leistungsfähig; <*method*> rationell. **~ly** *adv* gut; <*function*> rationell

effort /ˈefət/ *n* Anstrengung *f*; **make an ~** sich (*dat*) Mühe geben. **~less** *a*, **-ly** *adv* mühelos

e.g. *abbr* z.B.

egalitarian /ɪgælɪˈteərɪən/ *a* egalitär

egg *n* Ei *nt*. **~-cup** *n* Eierbecher *m*. **~shell** *n* Eierschale *f*

ego /ˈiːgəʊ/ *n* Ich *nt*. **~ism** *n* Egoismus *m*. **~ist** *n* Egoist *m*. **~tism** *n* Ichbezogenheit *f*. **~tist** *n* ichbezogener Mensch *m*

Egypt /ˈiːdʒɪpt/ *n* Ägypten *nt*. **~ian** /ɪˈdʒɪpʃn/ *a* ägyptisch ● *n* Ägypter(in) *m(f)*

eiderdown /ˈaɪdə-/ *n* (*quilt*) Daunendecke *f*

eigh|t /eɪt/ *a* acht ● *n* Acht *f*; (*boat*) Achter *m*. **~ˈteen** *a* achtzehn. **~ˈteenth** *a* achtzehnte(r,s)

eighth /eɪtθ/ *a* achte(r,s) ● *n* Achtel *nt*

eightieth /ˈeɪtɪɪθ/ *a* achtzigste(r,s)

eighty /ˈeɪtɪ/ *a* achtzig

either /ˈaɪðə(r)/ *a* & *pron* **~ [of them]** einer von [den] beiden; (*both*) beide; **on ~ side** auf beiden Seiten ● *adv* **I don't ~** ich auch nicht ● *conj* **~ ... or** entweder ... oder

eject /ɪˈdʒekt/ *vt* hinauswerfen

elaborate /ɪˈlæbərət/ *a*, **-ly** *adv* kunstvoll; (*fig*) kompliziert

elapse /ɪˈlæps/ *vi* vergehen

elastic /ɪˈlæstɪk/ *a* elastisch. **~ ˈband** *n* Gummiband *nt*

elasticity /ɪlæsˈtɪsətɪ/ *n* Elastizität *f*

elated /ɪˈleɪtɪd/ *a* überglücklich

elbow /ˈelbəʊ/ *n* Ellbogen *m*

elder¹ /ˈeldə(r)/ *n* Holunder *m*

eld|er² *a* ältere(r,s) ● *n* **the ~er** der/die Ältere. **~erly** *a* alt. **~est** *a* älteste(r,s) ● *n* **the ~est** der/die Älteste

elect /ɪˈlekt/ *vt* wählen. **~ion** /-ekʃn/ *n* Wahl *f*

elector /ɪˈlektə(r)/ *n* Wähler(in) *m(f)*. **~ate** /-rət/ *n* Wählerschaft *f*

electric /ɪˈlektrɪk/ *a*, **-ally** *adv* elektrisch

electrical /ɪˈlektrɪkl/ *a* elektrisch; **~ engineering** Elektrotechnik *f*

electric: ~ ˈblanket *n* Heizdecke *f*. **~ ˈfire** *n* elektrischer Heizofen *m*

electrician /ɪlekˈtrɪʃn/ *n* Elektriker *m*

electricity /ɪlekˈtrɪsətɪ/ *n* Elektrizität *f*; (*supply*) Strom *m*

electrify /ɪˈlektrɪfaɪ/ *vt* (*pt/pp* **-ied**) elektrifizieren. **~ing** *a* (*fig*) elektrisierend

electrocute /ɪˈlektrəkjuːt/ *vt* durch einen elektrischen Schlag töten

electrode /ɪˈlektrəʊd/ *n* Elektrode *f*

electronic /ɪlekˈtrɒnɪk/ *a* elektronisch. **~s** *n* Elektronik *f*

elegance /ˈelɪgəns/ *n* Eleganz *f*

elegant /ˈelɪgənt/ *a*, **-ly** *adv* elegant

elegy /ˈelɪdʒɪ/ *n* Elegie *f*

element /ˈelɪmənt/ *n* Element *nt*. **~ary** /-ˈmentərɪ/ *a* elementar

elephant /ˈelɪfənt/ *n* Elefant *m*

elevat|e /ˈelɪveɪt/ *vt* heben; (*fig*) erheben. **~ion** /-ˈveɪʃn/ *n* Erhebung *f*

elevator /ˈelɪveɪtə(r)/ *n* (*Amer*) Aufzug *m*, Fahrstuhl *m*

eleven /ɪˈlevn/ *a* elf ● *n* Elf *f*. **~th** *a* elfte(r,s); **at the ~th hour** [!] in letzter Minute

eligible /ˈelɪdʒəbl/ *a* berechtigt

eliminate /ɪ'lɪmɪneɪt/ *vt* ausschalten

élite /eɪ'li:t/ *n* Elite *f*

elm /elm/ *n* Ulme *f*

elocution /elə'kju:ʃn/ *n* Sprecherziehung *f*

elope /ɪ'əʊp/ *vi* durchbrennen [!]

eloquen|ce /'eləkwəns/ *n* Beredsamkeit *f*. **~t** *a*, **~ly** *adv* beredt

else /els/ *adv* sonst; **nothing ~** sonst nichts; **or ~** oder; (*otherwise*) sonst; **someone/ somewhere ~** jemand/irgendwo anders; **anyone ~** jeder andere; (*as question*) sonst noch jemand? **anything ~** alles andere; (*as question*) sonst noch etwas? **~where** *adv* woanders

elucidate /ɪ'lu:sɪdeɪt/ *vt* erläutern

elusive /ɪ'lu:sɪv/ *a* **be ~** schwer zu fassen sein

emaciated /ɪ'meɪsɪeɪtɪd/ *a* abgezehrt

e-mail /'i:meɪl/ *n* E-Mail *f* ● *vt* per E-Mail übermitteln *<Ergebnisse, Datei usw.>*; **~ s.o.** jdm eine E-Mail schicken. **~ address** *n* E-Mail-Adresse *f*. **~ message** *n* E-Mail *f*

emancipat|ed /ɪ'mænsɪpeɪtɪd/ *a* emanzipiert. **~ion** /-'peɪʃn/ *n* Emanzipation *f*; (*of slaves*) Freilassung *f*

embankment /ɪm'bæŋkmənt/ *n* Böschung *f*; (*of railway*) Bahndamm *m*

embark /ɪm'bɑ:k/ *vi* sich einschiffen. **~ation** /embɑ:'keɪʃn/ *n* Einschiffung *f*

embarrass /ɪm'bærəs/ *vt* in Verlegenheit bringen. **~ed** *a* verlegen. **~ing** *a* peinlich. **~ment** *n* Verlegenheit *f*

embassy /'embəsɪ/ *n* Botschaft *f*

embellish /ɪm'belɪʃ/ *vt* verzieren; (*fig*) ausschmücken

embezzle /ɪm'bezl/ *vt* unterschlagen. **~ment** *n* Unterschlagung *f*

emblem /'embləm/ *n* Emblem *nt*

embodiment /ɪm'bɒdɪmənt/ *n* Verkörperung *f*

embody /ɪm'bɒdɪ/ *vt* (*pt/pp* **-ied**) verkörpern; (*include*) enthalten

embrace /ɪm'breɪs/ *n* Umarmung *f* ● *vt* umarmen; (*fig*) umfassen ● *vi* sich umarmen

embroider /ɪm'brɔɪdə(r)/ *vt* besticken; sticken *<design>* ● *vi* sticken. **~y** *n* Stickerei *f*

embryo /'embrɪəʊ/ *n* Embryo *m*

emerald /'emərəld/ *n* Smaragd *m*

emer|ge /ɪ'mɜ:dʒ/ *vi* auftauchen (**from** aus); (*become known*) sich herausstellen; (*come into being*) entstehen. **~gence** /-əns/ *n* Auftauchen *nt*; Entstehung *f*

emergency /ɪ'mɜ:dʒənsɪ/ *n* Notfall *m*. **~ exit** *n* Notausgang *m*

emigrant /'emɪgrənt/ *n* Auswanderer *m*

emigrat|e /'emɪgreɪt/ *vi* auswandern. **~ion** /-'greɪʃn/ *n* Auswanderung *f*

eminent /'emɪnənt/ *a*, **-ly** *adv* eminent

emission /ɪ'mɪʃn/ *n* Ausstrahlung *f*; (*of pollutant*) Emission *f*

emit /ɪ'mɪt/ *vt* (*pt/pp* **emitted**) ausstrahlen *<light, heat>*; ausstoßen *<smoke, fumes, cry>*

emotion /ɪ'məʊʃn/ *n* Gefühl *nt*. **~al** *a* emotional; **become ~al** sich erregen

empathy /'empəθɪ/ *n* Einfühlungsvermögen *nt*

emperor /'empərə(r)/ *n* Kaiser *m*

emphasis /'emfəsɪs/ *n* Betonung *f*

emphasize /'emfəsaɪz/ *vt* betonen
emphatic /ɪm'fætɪk/ *a*, **-ally** *adv* nachdrücklich
empire /'empaɪə(r)/ *n* Reich *nt*
employ /ɪm'plɔɪ/ *vt* beschäftigen; (*appoint*) einstellen; (*fig*) anwenden. **~ee** /emplɔɪ'iː/ *n* Beschäftigte(r) *m/f*; (*in contrast to employer*) Arbeitnehmer *m*. **~er** *n* Arbeitgeber *m*. **~ment** *n* Beschäftigung *f*; (*work*) Arbeit *f*. **~ment agency** *n* Stellenvermittlung *f*
empress /'emprɪs/ *n* Kaiserin *f*
emptiness /'emptɪnɪs/ *n* Leere *f*
empty /'emptɪ/ *a* leer ● *vt* leeren; ausleeren <*container*> ● *vi* sich leeren
emulsion /ɪ'mʌlʃn/ *n* Emulsion *f*
enable /ɪ'neɪbl/ *vt* **~ s.o. to** es jdm möglich machen, zu
enact /ɪ'nækt/ *vt* (*Theat*) aufführen
enamel /ɪ'næml/ *n* Email *nt*; (*on teeth*) Zahnschmelz *m*; (*paint*) Lack *m*
enchant /ɪn'tʃɑːnt/ *vt* bezaubern. **~ing** *a* bezaubernd. **~ment** *n* Zauber *m*
encircle /ɪn'sɜːkl/ *vt* einkreisen
enclos|e /ɪn'kləʊz/ *vt* einschließen; (*in letter*) beilegen (**with** *dat*). **~ure** /-ʒə(r)/ *n* (*at zoo*) Gehege *nt*; (*in letter*) Anlage *f*
encore /'ɒŋkɔː(r)/ *n* Zugabe *f* ● *int* bravo!
encounter /ɪn'kaʊntə(r)/ *n* Begegnung *f* ● *vt* begegnen (+ *dat*); (*fig*) stoßen auf (+ *acc*)
encourag|e /ɪn'kʌrɪdʒ/ *vt* ermutigen; (*promote*) fördern. **~ement** *n* Ermutigung *f*. **~ing** *a* ermutigend
encroach /ɪn'krəʊtʃ/ *vi* **~ on** eindringen in (+ *acc*) <*land*>
encyclopaed|ia /ɪnsaɪklə'piːdɪə/ *n* Enzyklopädie *f*, Lexikon *nt*. **~ic** *a* enzyklopädisch
end /end/ *n* Ende *nt*; (*purpose*) Zweck *m*; **in the ~** schließlich; **at the ~ of May** Ende Mai; **on ~** hochkant; **for days on ~** tagelang; **make ~s meet** [!] [gerade] auskommen; **no ~ of** [!] unheimlich viel(e) ● *vt* beenden ● *vi* enden; **~ up in** ([!] *arrive at*) landen in (+ *dat*)
endanger /ɪn'deɪndʒə(r)/ *vt* gefährden
endeavour /ɪn'devə(r)/ *n* Bemühung *f* ● *vi* sich bemühen (**to** zu)
ending /'endɪŋ/ *n* Schluss *m*, Ende *nt*; (*Gram*) Endung *f*
endless /'endlɪs/ *a*, **-ly** *adv* endlos
endorse /en'dɔːs/ *vt* (*Comm*) indossieren; (*confirm*) bestätigen. **~ment** *n* (*Comm*) Indossament *nt*; (*fig*) Bestätigung *f*; (*on driving licence*) Strafvermerk *m*
endow /ɪn'daʊ/ *vt* stiften; **be ~ed with** (*fig*) haben
endurance /ɪn'djʊərəns/ *n* Durchhaltevermögen *nt*; **beyond ~** unerträglich
endure /ɪn'djʊə(r)/ *vt* ertragen
enemy /'enəmɪ/ *n* Feind *m* ● *attrib* feindlich
energetic /enə'dʒetɪk/ *a* tatkräftig; **be ~** voller Energie sein
energy /'enədʒɪ/ *n* Energie *f*
enforce /ɪn'fɔːs/ *vt* durchsetzen. **~d** *a* unfreiwillig
engage /ɪn'geɪdʒ/ *vt* einstellen <*staff*>; (*Theat*) engagieren; (*Auto*) einlegen <*gear*> ● *vi* sich beteiligen (**in** an + *dat*); (*Techn*) ineinandergreifen. **~d** *a* besetzt; <*person*> beschäftigt; (*to be married*) verlobt; **get ~d** sich verloben (**to** mit). **~ment** *n* Verlobung *f*; (*appointment*) Verabredung *f*; (*Mil*) Gefecht *nt*

engaging /ɪn'geɪdʒɪŋ/ *a* einnehmend

engine /'endʒɪn/ *n* Motor *m*; (*Naut*) Maschine *f*; (*Rail*) Lokomotive *f*; (*of jet plane*) Triebwerk *nt*. **~-driver** *n* Lokomotivführer *m*

engineer /endʒɪ'nɪə(r)/ *n* Ingenieur *m*; (*service, installation*) Techniker *m*; (*Naut*) Maschinist *m*; (*Amer*) Lokomotivführer *m*. **~ing** *n* **[mechanical] ~ing** Maschinenbau *m*

England /'ɪŋglənd/ *n* England *nt*

English /'ɪŋglɪʃ/ *a* englisch; **the ~ Channel** der Ärmelkanal ● *n* (*Lang*) Englisch *nt*; **in ~** auf Englisch; **into ~** ins Englische; **the ~** *pl* die Engländer. **~man** *n* Engländer *m*. **~woman** *n* Engländerin *f*

engrav|e /ɪn'greɪv/ *vt* eingravieren. **~ing** *n* Stich *m*

enhance /ɪn'hɑ:ns/ *vt* verschönern; (*fig*) steigern

enigma /ɪ'nɪgmə/ *n* Rätsel *nt*. **~tic** /enɪg'mætɪk/ *a* rätselhaft

enjoy /ɪn'dʒɔɪ/ *vt* genießen; **~ oneself** sich amüsieren; **~ cooking** gern kochen; **I ~ed it** es hat mir gut gefallen/ <*food:*> geschmeckt. **~able** /-əbl/ *a* angenehm, nett. **~ment** *n* Vergnügen *nt*

enlarge /ɪn'lɑ:dʒ/ *vt* vergrößern. **~ment** *n* Vergrößerung *f*

enlist /ɪn'lɪst/ *vt* (*Mil*) einziehen; **~ s.o.'s help** jdn zur Hilfe heranziehen ● *vi* (*Mil*) sich melden

enliven /ɪn'laɪvn/ *vt* beleben

enmity /'enmətɪ/ *n* Feindschaft *f*

enormity /ɪ'nɔ:mətɪ/ *n* Ungeheuerlichkeit *f*

enormous /ɪ'nɔ:məs/ *a*, **-ly** *adv* riesig

enough /ɪ'nʌf/ *a, adv & n* genug; **be ~** reichen; **funnily ~** komischerweise

enquir|e /ɪn'kwaɪə(r)/ *vi* sich erkundigen (**about** nach). **~y** *n* Erkundigung *f*; (*investigation*) Untersuchung *f*

enrage /ɪn'reɪdʒ/ *vt* wütend machen

enrich /ɪn'rɪtʃ/ *vt* bereichern

enrol /ɪn'rəʊl/ *v* (*pt/pp* **-rolled**) ● *vt* einschreiben ● *vi* sich einschreiben

ensemble /ɒn'sɒmbl/ *n* (*clothing & Mus*) Ensemble *nt*

enslave /ɪn'sleɪv/ *vt* versklaven

ensue /ɪn'sju:/ *vi* folgen; (*result*) sich ergeben (**from** aus)

ensure /ɪn'ʃʊə(r)/ *vt* sicherstellen; **~ that** dafür sorgen, dass

entail /ɪn'teɪl/ *vt* erforderlich machen; **what does it ~?** was ist damit verbunden?

entangle /ɪn'tæŋgl/ *vt* **get ~d** sich verfangen (**in** in + *dat*)

enter /'entə(r)/ *vt* eintreten/ <*vehicle:*> einfahren in (+ *acc*); einreisen in (+ *acc*) <*country*>; (*register*) eintragen; sich anmelden zu <*competition*> ● *vi* eintreten; <*vehicle:*> einfahren; (*Theat*) auftreten; (*register as competitor*) sich anmelden; (*take part*) sich beteiligen (**in** an + *dat*)

enterpris|e /'entəpraɪz/ *n* Unternehmen *nt*; (*quality*) Unternehmungsgeist *m*. **~ing** *a* unternehmend

entertain /entə'teɪn/ *vt* unterhalten; (*invite*) einladen; (*to meal*) bewirten <*guest*> ● *vi* unterhalten; (*have guests*) Gäste haben. **~er** *n* Unterhalter *m*. **~ment** *n* Unterhaltung *f*

enthral /ɪn'θrɔ:l/ *vt* (*pt/pp* **enthralled**) **be ~led** gefesselt sein (**by** von)

enthuse /ɪn'θjuːz/ *vi* **~ over** schwärmen von
enthusias|m /ɪn'θjuːzɪæzm/ *n* Begeisterung *f*. **~t** *n* Enthusiast *m*. **~tic** /-'æstɪk/ *a*, **-ally** *adv* begeistert
entice /ɪn'taɪs/ *vt* locken. **~ment** *n* Anreiz *m*
entire /ɪn'taɪə(r)/ *a* ganz. **~ly** *adv* ganz, völlig. **~ty** /-rətɪ/ *n* **in its ~ty** in seiner Gesamtheit
entitle /ɪn'taɪtl/ *vt* berechtigen; **~d** ... mit dem Titel ...; **be ~d to sth** das Recht auf etw (*acc*) haben. **~ment** *n* Berechtigung *f*; (*claim*) Anspruch *m* (**to** auf + *acc*)
entrance /'entrəns/ *n* Eintritt *m*; (*Theat*) Auftritt *m*; (*way in*) Eingang *m*; (*for vehicle*) Einfahrt *f*. **~ fee** *n* Eintrittsgebühr *f*
entrant /'entrənt/ *n* Teilnehmer(in) *m(f)*
entreat /ɪn'triːt/ *vt* anflehen (**for** um)
entrust /ɪn'trʌst/ *vt* **~ s.o. with sth, ~ sth to s.o.** jdm etw anvertrauen
entry /'entrɪ/ *n* Eintritt *m*; (*into country*) Einreise *f*; (*on list*) Eintrag *m*; **no ~** Zutritt/ (*Auto*) Einfahrt verboten
envelop /ɪn'veləp/ *vt* (*pt/pp* **enveloped**) einhüllen
envelope /'envələʊp/ *n* [Brief]umschlag *m*
enviable /'envɪəbl/ *a* beneidenswert
envious /'envɪəs/ *a*, **-ly** *adv* neidisch (**of** auf + *acc*)
environment /ɪn'vaɪərənmənt/ *n* Umwelt *f*
environmental /ɪnvaɪərən'mentl/ *a* Umwelt-. **~ist** *n* Umweltschützer *m*. **~ly** *adv* **~ly friendly** umweltfreundlich
envisage /ɪn'vɪzɪdʒ/ *vt* sich (*dat*) vorstellen
envoy /'envɔɪ/ *n* Gesandte(r) *m*
envy /'envɪ/ *n* Neid *m* ● *vt* (*pt/pp* **-ied**) **~ s.o. sth** jdn um etw beneiden
epic /'epɪk/ *a* episch ● *n* Epos *nt*
epidemic /epɪ'demɪk/ *n* Epidemie *f*
epilep|sy /'epɪlepsɪ/ *n* Epilepsie *f*. **~tic** /-'leptɪk/ *a* epileptisch ● *n* Epileptiker(in) *m(f)*
epilogue /'epɪlɒg/ *n* Epilog *m*
episode /'epɪsəʊd/ *n* Episode *f*; (*instalment*) Folge *f*
epitome /ɪ'pɪtəmɪ/ *n* Inbegriff *m*
epoch /'iːpɒk/ *n* Epoche *f*. **~-making** *a* epochemachend
equal /'iːkwl/ *a* gleich (**to** *dat*); **be ~ to a task** einer Aufgabe gewachsen sein ● *n* Gleichgestellte(r) *m/f* ● *vt* (*pt/pp* **equalled**) gleichen (+ *dat*); (*fig*) gleichkommen (+ *dat*). **~ity** /ɪ'kwɒlətɪ/ *n* Gleichheit *f*
equalize /'iːkwəlaɪz/ *vt/i* ausgleichen
equally /'iːkwəlɪ/ *adv* gleich; <*divide*> gleichmäßig; (*just as*) genauso
equat|e /ɪ'kweɪt/ *vt* gleichsetzen (**with** mit). **~ion** /-eɪʒn/ *n* (*Math*) Gleichung *f*
equator /ɪ'kweɪtə(r)/ *n* Äquator *m*
equestrian /ɪ'kwestrɪən/ *a* Reit-
equilibrium /iːkwɪ'lɪbrɪəm/ *n* Gleichgewicht *nt*
equinox /'iːkwɪnɒks/ *n* Tagundnachtgleiche *f*
equip /ɪ'kwɪp/ *vt* (*pt/pp* **equipped**) ausrüsten; (*furnish*) ausstatten. **~ment** *n* Ausrüstung *f*; Ausstattung *f*
equity /'ekwətɪ/ *n* Gerechtigkeit *f*
equivalent /ɪ'kwɪvələnt/ *a* gleichwertig; (*corresponding*) entsprechend ● *n* Äquivalent *nt*; (*value*) Gegenwert *m*; (*counterpart*) Gegenstück *nt*

era /ˈɪərə/ *n* Ära *f*, Zeitalter *nt*
eradicate /ɪˈrædɪkeɪt/ *vt* ausrotten
erase /ɪˈreɪz/ *vt* ausradieren; (*from tape*) löschen
erect /ɪˈrekt/ *a* aufrecht ● *vt* errichten. **~ion** /-ekʃn/ *n* Errichtung *f*; (*building*) Bau *m*; (*Biol*) Erektion *f*
ero|de /ɪˈrəʊd/ *vt* <*water*:> auswaschen; <*acid*:> angreifen. **~sion** /-əʊʒn/ *n* Erosion *f*
erotic /ɪˈrɒtɪk/ *a* erotisch
errand /ˈerənd/ *n* Botengang *m*
erratic /ɪˈrætɪk/ *a* unregelmäßig; <*person*> unberechenbar
erroneous /ɪˈrəʊnɪəs/ *a* falsch; <*belief, assumption*> irrig
error /ˈerə(r)/ *n* Irrtum *m*; (*mistake*) Fehler *m*; **in ~** irrtümlicherweise
erupt /ɪˈrʌpt/ *vi* ausbrechen. **~ion** /-ʌpʃn/ *n* Ausbruch *m*
escalat|e /ˈeskəleɪt/ *vt/i* eskalieren. **~or** *n* Rolltreppe *f*
escape /ɪˈskeɪp/ *n* Flucht *f*; (*from prison*) Ausbruch *m*; **have a narrow ~** gerade noch davonkommen ● *vi* flüchten; <*prisoner*:> ausbrechen; entkommen (**from** aus; **from s.o.** jdm); <*gas*:> entweichen ● *vt* **the name ~s me** der Name entfällt mir
escapism /ɪˈskeɪpɪzm/ *n* Eskapismus *m*
escort¹ /ˈeskɔːt/ *n* (*of person*) Begleiter *m*; (*Mil*) Eskorte *f*
escort² /ɪˈskɔːt/ *vt* begleiten; (*Mil*) eskortieren
Eskimo /ˈeskɪməʊ/ *n* Eskimo *m*
esoteric /esəˈterɪk/ *a* esoterisch
especially /ɪˈspeʃəlɪ/ *adv* besonders
espionage /ˈespɪənɑːʒ/ *n* Spionage *f*
essay /ˈeseɪ/ *n* Aufsatz *m*
essence /ˈesns/ *n* Wesen *nt*; (*Chem, Culin*) Essenz *f*
essential /ɪˈsenʃl/ *a* wesentlich; (*indispensable*) unentbehrlich ● *n* **the ~s** das Wesentliche; (*items*) das Nötigste. **~ly** *adv* im Wesentlichen
establish /ɪˈstæblɪʃ/ *vt* gründen; (*form*) bilden; (*prove*) beweisen
estate /ɪˈsteɪt/ *n* Gut *nt*; (*possessions*) Besitz *m*; (*after death*) Nachlass *m*; (*housing*) [Wohn]siedlung *f*. **~ agent** *n* Immobilienmakler *m*. **~ car** *n* Kombi[wagen] *m*
esteem /ɪˈstiːm/ *n* Achtung *f* ● *vt* hochschätzen
estimate¹ /ˈestɪmət/ *n* Schätzung *f*; (*Comm*) [Kosten]voranschlag *m*; **at a rough ~** grob geschätzt
estimat|e² /ˈestɪmeɪt/ *vt* schätzen. **~ion** /-ˈmeɪʃn/ *n* Einschätzung *f*
estuary /ˈestjʊərɪ/ *n* Mündung *f*
etc. /etˈsetərə/ *abbr* (**et cetera**) und so weiter, usw.
eternal /ɪˈtɜːnl/ *a*, **-ly** *adv* ewig
eternity /ɪˈθɜːnətɪ/ *n* Ewigkeit *f*
ethic|al /ˈeθɪkl/ *a* ethisch; (*morally correct*) moralisch einwandfrei. **~s** *n* Ethik *f*
Ethiopia /iːθɪˈəʊpɪə/ *n* Äthiopien *nt*
ethnic /ˈeθnɪk/ *a* ethnisch. **~ cleansing** *n* ethnische Säuberung
etiquette /ˈetɪket/ *n* Etikette *f*
EU *abbr* (**European Union**) EU *f*
eulogy /ˈjuːlədʒɪ/ *n* Lobrede *f*
euphemis|m /ˈjuːfəmɪzm/ *n* Euphemismus *m*. **~tic** /-ˈmɪstɪk/ *a*, **-ally** *adv* verhüllend
euro /ˈjʊərəʊ/ *n* Euro *m*. **E~cheque** *n* Euroscheck *m*. **~land** *n* Euroland *vt*
Europe /ˈjʊərəp/ *n* Europa *nt*

European /jʊərəˈpi:ən/ *a* europäisch; **~ Union** Europäische Union *f* ● *n* Europäer(in) *m(f)*
eurosceptic /ˈjʊərəʊskeptɪk/ *n* Euroskeptiker(in) *m(f)*
evacuat|e /ɪˈvækjʊeɪt/ *vt* evakuieren; räumen <*building, area*>. **~ion** /-ˈeɪʃn/ *n* Evakuierung *f*; Räumung *f*
evade /ɪˈveɪd/ *vt* sich entziehen (+ *dat*); hinterziehen <*taxes*>
evaluate /ɪˈvæljʊeɪt/ *vt* einschätzen
evange|lical /i:vænˈdʒelɪkl/ *a* evangelisch. **~list** /ɪˈvændʒəlɪst/ *n* Evangelist *m*
evaporat|e /ɪˈvæpəreɪt/ *vi* verdunsten. **~ion** /-ˈreɪʃn/ *n* Verdampfung *f*
evasion /ɪˈveɪʒn/ *n* Ausweichen *nt*; **tax ~** Steuerhinterziehung *f*
evasive /ɪˈveɪsɪv/ *a*, **-ly** *adv* ausweichend; **be ~** ausweichen
even /ˈi:vn/ *a* (*level*) eben; (*same, equal*) gleich; (*regular*) gleichmäßig; <*number*> gerade; **get ~ with** [!] es jdm heimzahlen ● *adv* sogar, selbst; **~ so** trotzdem; **not ~** nicht einmal ● *vt* **~ the score** ausgleichen
evening /ˈi:vnɪŋ/ *n* Abend *m*; **this ~** heute Abend; **in the ~** abends, am Abend. **~ class** *n* Abendkurs *m*
evenly /ˈi:vnlɪ/ *adv* gleichmäßig
event /ɪˈvent/ *n* Ereignis *nt*; (*function*) Veranstaltung *f*; (*Sport*) Wettbewerb *m*. **~ful** *a* ereignisreich
eventual /ɪˈventjʊəl/ *a* **his ~ success** der Erfolg, der ihm schließlich zuteil wurde. **~ly** *adv* schließlich
ever /ˈevə(r)/ *adv* je[mals]; **not ~** nie; **for ~** für immer; **hardly ~** fast nie; **~ since** seitdem
ˈevergreen *n* immergrüner Strauch *m*/ (*tree*) Baum *m*
everˈlasting *a* ewig
every /ˈevrɪ/ *a* jede(r,s); **~ one** jede(r,s) Einzelne; **~ other day** jeden zweiten Tag
every: ~body *pron* jeder[mann]; alle *pl*. **~day** *a* alltäglich. **~ one** *pron* jeder[mann]; alle *pl*. **~thing** *pron* alles. **~where** *adv* überall
evict /ɪˈvɪkt/ *vt* [aus der Wohnung] hinausweisen. **~ion** /-ɪkʃn/ *n* Ausweisung *f*
eviden|ce /ˈevɪdəns/ *n* Beweise *pl*; (*Jur*) Beweismaterial *nt*; (*testimony*) Aussage *f*; **give ~ce** aussagen. **~t** *a*, **-ly** *adv* offensichtlich
evil /ˈi:vl/ *a* böse ● *n* Böse *nt*
evoke /ɪˈvəʊk/ *vt* heraufbeschwören
evolution /i:vəˈlu:ʃn/ *n* Evolution *f*
evolve /ɪˈvɒlv/ *vt* entwickeln ● *vi* sich entwickeln
ewe /ju:/ *n* Schaf *nt*
exact /ɪgˈzækt/ *a*, **-ly** *adv* genau; **not ~ly** nicht gerade. **~ness** *n* Genauigkeit *f*
exaggerat|e /ɪgˈzædʒəreɪt/ *vt/i* übertreiben. **~ion** /-ˈreɪʃn/ *n* Übertreibung *f*
exam /ɪgˈzæm/ *n* [!] Prüfung *f*
examination /ɪgzæmɪˈneɪʃn/ *n* Untersuchung *f*; (*Sch*) Prüfung *f*
examine /ɪgˈzæmɪn/ *vt* untersuchen; (*Sch*) prüfen
example /ɪgˈzɑ:mpl/ *n* Beispiel *nt* (**of** für); **for ~** zum Beispiel; **make an ~ of** ein Exempel statuieren an (+ *dat*)
exasperat|e /ɪgˈzæspəreɪt/ *vt* zur Verzweiflung treiben. **~ion** /-ˈreɪʃn/ *n* Verzweiflung *f*
excavat|e /ˈekskəveɪt/ *vt* ausschachten; (*Archaeol*) ausgraben. **~ion** /-ˈveɪʃn/ *n* Ausgrabung *f*
exceed /ɪkˈsi:d/ *vt* übersteigen. **~ingly** *adv* äußerst

excel /ɪk'sel/ *v* (*pt/pp* **excelled**) *vi* sich auszeichnen ● *vt* ~ **oneself** sich selbst übertreffen

excellen|ce /'eksələns/ *n* Vorzüglichkeit *f*. **~t** *a*, **-ly** *adv* ausgezeichnet, vorzüglich

except /ɪk'sept/ *prep* außer (+ *dat*); ~ **for** abgesehen von ● *vt* ausnehmen

exception /ɪk'sepʃn/ *n* Ausnahme *f*. **~al** *a*, **-ly** *adv* außergewöhnlich

excerpt /'eksɜ:pt/ *n* Auszug *m*

excess /ɪk'ses/ *n* Übermaß *nt* (**of** an + *dat*); (*surplus*) Überschuss *m*; **~es** *pl* Exzesse *pl*

excessive /ɪk'sesɪv/ *a*, **-ly** *adv* übermäßig

exchange /ɪks'tʃeɪndʒ/ *n* Austausch *m*; (*Teleph*) Fernsprechamt *nt*; (*Comm*) [Geld]wechsel *m*; **in** ~ dafür ● *vt* austauschen (**for** gegen); tauschen <*places*>. ~ **rate** *n* Wechselkurs *m*

excitable /ɪk'saɪtəbl/ *a* [leicht] erregbar

excit|e /ɪk'saɪt/ *vt* aufregen; (*cause*) erregen. **~ed** *a*, **-ly** *adv* aufgeregt; **get ~ed** sich aufregen. **~ement** *n* Aufregung *f*; Erregung *f*. **~ing** *a* aufregend; <*story*> spannend

exclaim /ɪk'skleɪm/ *vt/i* ausrufen

exclamation /eksklə'meɪʃn/ *n* Ausruf *m*. ~ **mark** *n*, (*Amer*) ~ **point** *n* Ausrufezeichen *nt*

exclu|de /ɪk'sklu:d/ *vt* ausschließen. **~ding** *prep* ausschließlich (+ *gen*). **~sion** /-ʒn/ *n* Ausschluss *m*

exclusive /ɪk'sklu:sɪv/ *a*, **-ly** *adv* ausschließlich; (*select*) exklusiv

excrement /'ekskrɪmənt/ *n* Kot *m*

excrete /ɪk'skri:t/ *vt* ausscheiden

excruciating /ɪk'skru:ʃɪeɪtɪŋ/ *a* grässlich

excursion /ɪk'skɜ:ʃn/ *n* Ausflug *m*

excusable /ɪk'skju:zəbl/ *a* entschuldbar

excuse¹ /ɪk'skju:s/ *n* Entschuldigung *f*; (*pretext*) Ausrede *f*

excuse² /ɪk'skju:z/ *vt* entschuldigen; ~ **me!** Entschuldigung!

ex-di'rectory *a* **be** ~ nicht im Telefonbuch stehen

execute /'eksɪkju:t/ *vt* ausführen; (*put to death*) hinrichten

execution /eksɪ'kju:ʃn/ *n* Ausführung *f*; Hinrichtung *f*

executive /ɪg'zekjʊtɪv/ *a* leitend ● *n* leitende(r) Angestellte(r) *m/f*; (*Pol*) Exekutive *f*

exemplary /ɪg'zemplərɪ/ *a* beispielhaft

exemplify /ɪg'zemplɪfaɪ/ *vt* (*pt/pp* **-ied**) veranschaulichen

exempt /ɪg'zempt/ *a* befreit ● *vt* befreien (**from** von). **~ion** /-empʃn/ *n* Befreiung *f*

exercise /'eksəsaɪz/ *n* Übung *f*; **physical** ~ körperliche Bewegung *f* ● *vt* (*use*) ausüben; bewegen <*horse*> ● *vi* sich bewegen. ~ **book** *n* [Schul]heft *nt*

exert /ɪg'zɜ:t/ *vt* ausüben; ~ **oneself** sich anstrengen. **~ion** /-ɜ:ʃn/ *n* Anstrengung *f*

exhale /eks'heɪl/ *vt/i* ausatmen

exhaust /ɪg'zɔ:st/ *n* (*Auto*) Auspuff *m*; (*fumes*) Abgase *pl* ● *vt* erschöpfen. **~ed** *a* erschöpft. **~ing** *a* anstrengend. **~ion** /-ɔ:stʃn/ *n* Erschöpfung *f*. **~ive** /-ɪv/ *a* (*fig*) erschöpfend

exhibit /ɪg'zɪbɪt/ *n* Ausstellungsstück *nt*; (*Jur*) Beweisstück *nt* ● *vt* ausstellen

exhibition /eksɪˈbɪʃn/ *n* Ausstellung *f*; (*Univ*) Stipendium *nt*. **~ist** *n* Exhibitionist(in) *m(f)*
exhibitor /ɪgˈzɪbɪtə(r)/ *n* Aussteller *m*
exhilarat|ing /ɪgˈzɪləreɪtɪŋ/ *a* berauschend. **~ion** /-ˈreɪʃn/ *n* Hochgefühl *nt*
exhume /ɪgˈzjuːm/ *vt* exhumieren
exile /ˈeksaɪl/ *n* Exil *nt*; (*person*) im Exil Lebende(r) *m/f* ● *vt* ins Exil schicken
exist /ɪgˈzɪst/ *vi* bestehen, existieren. **~ence** /-əns/ *n* Existenz *f*; **be in ~ence** existieren
exit /ˈeksɪt/ *n* Ausgang *m*; (*Auto*) Ausfahrt *f*; (*Theat*) Abgang *m*
exorbitant /ɪgˈzɔːbɪtənt/ *a* übermäßig hoch
exotic /ɪgˈzɒtɪk/ *a* exotisch
expand /ɪkˈspænd/ *vt* ausdehnen; (*explain better*) weiter ausführen ● *vi* sich ausdehnen; (*Comm*) expandieren
expans|e /ɪkˈspæns/ *n* Weite *f*. **~ion** /-ænʃn/ *n* Ausdehnung *f*; (*Techn, Pol, Comm*) Expansion *f*
expect /ɪkˈspekt/ *vt* erwarten; (*suppose*) annehmen; **I ~ so** wahrscheinlich
expectan|cy /ɪkˈspektənsɪ/ *n* Erwartung *f*. **~t** *a*, **-ly** *adv* erwartungsvoll; **~t mother** werdende Mutter *f*
expectation /ekspekˈteɪʃn/ *n* Erwartung *f*
expedient /ɪkˈspiːdɪənt/ *a* zweckdienlich
expedite /ˈekspɪdaɪt/ *vt* beschleunigen
expedition /ekspɪˈdɪʃn/ *n* Expedition *f*
expel /ɪkˈspel/ *vt* (*pt/pp* **expelled**) ausweisen (**from** aus); (*from school*) von der Schule verweisen
expenditure /ɪkˈspendɪtʃə(r)/ *n* Ausgaben *pl*
expense /ɪkˈspens/ *n* Kosten *pl*; **business ~s** *pl* Spesen *pl*; **at my ~** auf meine Kosten
expensive /ɪkˈspensɪv/ *a*, **-ly** *adv* teuer
experience /ɪkˈspɪərɪəns/ *n* Erfahrung *f*; (*event*) Erlebnis *nt* ● *vt* erleben. **~d** *a* erfahren
experiment /ɪkˈsperɪmənt/ *n* Versuch *m*, Experiment *nt* ● /-ment/ *vi* experimentieren. **~al** /-ˈmentl/ *a* experimentell
expert /ˈekspɜːt/ *a*, **-ly** *adv* fachmännisch ● *n* Fachmann *m*, Experte *m*
expertise /ekspɜːˈtiːz/ *n* Sachkenntnis *f*
expire /ɪkˈspaɪə(r)/ *vi* ablaufen
expiry /ɪkˈspaɪərɪ/ *n* Ablauf *m*
explain /ɪkˈspleɪn/ *vt* erklären
explana|tion /ekspləˈneɪʃn/ *n* Erklärung *f*. **~tory** /ɪkˈsplænətərɪ/ *a* erklärend
explicit /ɪkˈsplɪsɪt/ *a*, **-ly** *adv* deutlich
explode /ɪkˈspləʊd/ *vi* explodieren ● *vt* zur Explosion bringen
exploit¹ /ˈeksplɔɪt/ *n* [Helden]tat *f*
exploit² /ɪkˈsplɔɪt/ *vt* ausbeuten. **~ation** /eksplɔɪˈteɪʃn/ *n* Ausbeutung *f*
exploration /ekspləˈreɪʃn/ *n* Erforschung *f*
explore /ɪkˈsplɔː(r)/ *vt* erforschen. **~r** *n* Forschungsreisende(r) *m*
explos|ion /ɪkˈspləʊʒn/ *n* Explosion *f*. **~ive** /-sɪv/ *a* explosiv ● *n* Sprengstoff *m*
export¹ /ˈekspɔːt/ *n* Export *m*, Ausfuhr *f*
export² /ɪkˈspɔːt/ *vt* exportieren, ausführen. **~er** *n* Exporteur *m*

expos|e /ɪk'spəʊz/ *vt* freilegen; (*to danger*) aussetzen (**to** *dat*); (*reveal*) aufdecken; (*Phot*) belichten. **~ure** /-ʒə(r)/ *n* Aussetzung *f*; (*Med*) Unterkühlung *f*; (*Phot*) Belichtung *f*; **24 ~ures** 24 Aufnahmen

express /ɪk'spres/ *adv* <*send*> per Eilpost ● *n* (*train*) Schnellzug *m* ● *vt* ausdrücken; **~ oneself** sich ausdrücken. **~ion** /-ʃn/ *n* Ausdruck *m*. **~ive** /-ɪv/ *a* ausdrucksvoll. **~ly** *adv* ausdrücklich

expulsion /ɪk'spʌlʃn/ *n* Ausweisung *f*; (*Sch*) Verweisung *f* von der Schule

exquisite /ek'skwɪzɪt/ *a* erlesen

extend /ɪk'stend/ *vt* verlängern; (*stretch out*) ausstrecken; (*enlarge*) vergrößern ● *vi* sich ausdehnen; <*table:*> sich ausziehen lassen

extension /ɪk'stenʃn/ *n* Verlängerung *f*; (*to house*) Anbau *m*; (*Teleph*) Nebenanschluss *m*

extensive /ɪk'stensɪv/ *a* weit; (*fig*) umfassend. **~ly** *adv* viel

extent /ɪk'stent/ *n* Ausdehnung *f*; (*scope*) Ausmaß *nt*, Umfang *m*; **to a certain ~** in gewissem Maße

exterior /ɪk'stɪərɪə(r)/ *a* äußere(r,s) ● *n* **the ~** das Äußere

exterminat|e /ɪk'stɜ:mɪneɪt/ *vt* ausrotten. **~ion** /-'neɪʃn/ *n* Ausrottung *f*

external /ɪk'stɜ:nl/ *a* äußere(r,s); **for ~ use only** (*Med*) nur äußerlich. **~ly** *adv* äußerlich

extinct /ɪk'stɪŋkt/ *a* ausgestorben; <*volcano*> erloschen. **~ion** /-ɪŋkʃn/ *n* Aussterben *nt*

extinguish /ɪk'stɪŋgwɪʃ/ *vt* löschen. **~er** *n* Feuerlöscher *m*

extort /ɪk'stɔ:t/ *vt* erpressen. **~ion** /-ɔ:ʃn/ *n* Erpressung *f*

extortionate /ɪk'stɔ:ʃənət/ *a* übermäßig hoch

extra /'ekstrə/ *a* zusätzlich ● *adv* extra; (*especially*) besonders ● *n* (*Theat*) Statist(in) *m(f)*; **~s** *pl* Nebenkosten *pl*; (*Auto*) Extras *pl*

extract¹ /'ekstrækt/ *n* Auszug *m*

extract² /ɪk'strækt/ *vt* herausziehen; ziehen <*tooth*>

extraordinary /ɪk'strɔ:dɪnərɪ/ *a*, **-ily** *adv* außerordentlich; (*strange*) seltsam

extravagan|ce /ɪk'strævəgəns/ *n* Verschwendung *f*; **an ~ce** ein Luxus *m*. **~t** *a* verschwenderisch

extrem|e /ɪk'stri:m/ *a* äußerste(r,s); (*fig*) extrem ● *n* Extrem *nt*; **in the ~e** im höchsten Grade. **~ely** *adv* äußerst. **~ist** *n* Extremist *m*

extricate /'ekstrɪkeɪt/ *vt* befreien

extrovert /'ekstrəvɜ:t/ *n* extravertierter Mensch *m*

exuberant /ɪg'zju:bərənt/ *a* überglücklich

exude /ɪg'zju:d/ *vt* absondern; (*fig*) ausstrahlen

exult /ɪg'zʌlt/ *vi* frohlocken

eye /aɪ/ *n* Auge *nt*; (*of needle*) Öhr *nt*; (*for hook*) Öse *f*; **keep an ~ on** aufpassen auf (+ *acc*) ● *vt* (*pt/pp* **eyed**, *pres p* **ey[e]ing**) ansehen

eye: ~brow *n* Augenbraue *f*. **~lash** *n* Wimper *f*. **~lid** *n* Augenlid *nt*. **~-shadow** *n* Lidschatten *m*. **~sight** *n* Sehkraft *f*. **~sore** *n* [!] Schandfleck *m*. **~witness** *n* Augenzeuge *m*

Ff

fable /ˈfeɪbl/ *n* Fabel *f*

fabric /ˈfæbrɪk/ *n* Stoff *m*

fabrication /fæbrɪˈkeɪʃn/ *n* Erfindung *f*

fabulous /ˈfæbjʊləs/ *a* [!] phantastisch

façade /fəˈsɑːd/ *n* Fassade *f*

face /feɪs/ *n* Gesicht *nt*; (*surface*) Fläche *f*; (*of clock*) Zifferblatt *nt*; **pull ~s** Gesichter schneiden; **in the ~ of** angesichts (+ *gen*); **on the ~ of it** allem Anschein nach ● *vt/i* gegenüberstehen (+ *dat*); **~ north** <*house:*> nach Norden liegen; **~ the fact that** sich damit abfinden, dass

face: ~-flannel *n* Waschlappen *m*. **~less** *a* anonym. **~-lift** *n* Gesichtsstraffung *f*

facet /ˈfæsɪt/ *n* Facette *f*; (*fig*) Aspekt *m*

facetious /fəˈsiːʃəs/ *a*, **-ly** *adv* spöttisch

facial /ˈfeɪʃl/ *a* Gesichts-

facile /ˈfæsaɪl/ *a* oberflächlich

facilitate /fəˈsɪlɪteɪt/ *vt* erleichtern

facility /fəˈsɪlətɪ/ *n* Leichtigkeit *f*; (*skill*) Gewandtheit *f*; **~ies** *pl* Einrichtungen *pl*

facsimile /fækˈsɪməlɪ/ *n* Faksimile *nt*

fact /fækt/ *n* Tatsache *f*; **in ~** tatsächlich; (*actually*) eigentlich

faction /ˈfækʃn/ *n* Gruppe *f*

factor /ˈfæktə(r)/ *n* Faktor *m*

factory /ˈfæktərɪ/ *n* Fabrik *f*

factual /ˈfæktʃʊəl/ *a*, **-ly** *adv* sachlich

faculty /ˈfækəltɪ/ *n* Fähigkeit *f*; (*Univ*) Fakultät *f*

fad /fæd/ *n* Fimmel *m*

fade /feɪd/ *vi* verblassen; <*material:*> verbleichen; <*sound:*> abklingen; <*flower:*> verwelken.

fag /fæg/ *n* (*chore*) Plage *f*; ([!] *cigarette*) Zigarette *f*

fail /feɪl/ *n* **without ~** unbedingt ● *vi* <*attempt:*> scheitern; (*grow weak*) nachlassen; (*break down*) versagen; (*in exam*) durchfallen; **~ to do sth** etw nicht tun ● *vt* nicht bestehen <*exam*>; durchfallen lassen <*candidate*>; (*disappoint*) enttäuschen

failing /ˈfeɪlɪŋ/ *n* Fehler *m*

failure /ˈfeɪljə(r)/ *n* Misserfolg *m*; (*breakdown*) Versagen *nt*; (*person*) Versager *m*

faint /feɪnt/ *a* (**-er, -est**), **-ly** *adv* schwach; **I feel ~** mir ist schwach ● *n* Ohnmacht *f* ● *vi* ohnmächtig werden. **~ness** *n* Schwäche *f*

fair[1] /feə(r)/ *n* Jahrmarkt *m*; (*Comm*) Messe *f*

fair[2] *a* (**-er, -est**) <*hair*> blond; <*skin*> hell; <*weather*> heiter; (*just*) gerecht, fair; (*quite good*) ziemlich gut; (*Sch*) genügend; **a ~ amount** ziemlich viel ● *adv* **play ~** fair sein. **~ly** *adv* gerecht; (*rather*) ziemlich. **~ness** *n* Blondheit *f*; Helle *f*; Gerechtigkeit *f*; (*Sport*) Fairness *f*

fairy /ˈfeərɪ/ *n* Elfe *f*; **good/wicked ~** gute/böse Fee *f*. **~ story, ~ tale** *n* Märchen *nt*

faith /feɪθ/ *n* Glaube *m*; (*trust*) Vertrauen *nt* (**in** zu)

faithful /ˈfeɪθfl/ *a*, **-ly** *adv* treu; (*exact*) genau; **Yours ~ly** Hochachtungsvoll. **~ness** *n* Treue *f*; Genauigkeit *f*

fake /feɪk/ *a* falsch ● *n* Fälschung *f*; (*person*) Schwindler *m* ● *vt* fälschen; (*pretend*) vortäuschen

falcon /ˈfɔːlkən/ *n* Falke *m*

fall /fɔːl/ *n* Fall *m*; (*heavy*) Sturz *m*; (*in prices*) Fallen *nt*; (*Amer: autumn*) Herbst *m*; **have a ~** fallen ● *vi* (*pt* **fell**, *pp* **fallen**) fallen; (*heavily*) stürzen; <*night:*> anbrechen; **~in love** sich verlieben; **~ back on** zurückgreifen auf (+ *acc*); **~ for s.o.** [!] sich in jdn verlieben; **~ for sth** [!] auf etw (*acc*) hereinfallen. **~ about** *vi* (*with laughter*) sich [vor Lachen] kringeln. **~ down** *vi* umfallen; <*thing:*> herunterfallen; <*building:*> einstürzen. **~ in** *vi* hineinfallen; (*collapse*) einfallen; (*Mil*) antreten; **~ in with** sich anschließen (+ *dat*). **~ off** *vi* herunterfallen; (*diminish*) abnehmen. **~ out** *vi* herausfallen; <*hair:*> ausfallen; (*quarrel*) sich überwerfen. **~ over** *vi* hinfallen. **~ through** *vi* durchfallen; <*plan:*> ins Wasser fallen

fallacy /ˈfæləsɪ/ *n* Irrtum *m*

fallible /ˈfæləbl/ *a* fehlbar

ˈfall-out *n* [radioaktiver] Niederschlag *m*

false /fɔːls/ *a* falsch; (*artificial*) künstlich. **~hood** *n* Unwahrheit *f*. **~ly** *adv* falsch

false ˈteeth *npl* [künstliches] Gebiss *nt*

falsify /ˈfɔːlsɪfaɪ/ *vt* (*pt/pp* **-ied**) fälschen

falter /ˈfɔːltə(r)/ *vi* zögern

fame /feɪm/ *n* Ruhm *m*.

familiar /fəˈmɪljə(r)/ *a* vertraut; (*known*) bekannt; **too ~** familiär. **~ity** /-lɪˈærətɪ/ *n* Vertrautheit *f*. **~ize** *vt* vertraut machen (**with** mit)

family /ˈfæməlɪ/ *n* Familie *f*

family: ~ ˈdoctor *n* Hausarzt *m*. **~ ˈlife** *n* Familienleben *nt*. **~ ˈplanning** *n* Familienplanung *f*. **~ ˈtree** *n* Stammbaum *m*

famine /ˈfæmɪn/ *n* Hungersnot *f*

famished /ˈfæmɪʃt/ *a* sehr hungrig

famous /ˈfeɪməs/ *a* berühmt

fan¹ /fæn/ *n* Fächer *m*; (*Techn*) Ventilator *m*

fan² *n* (*admirer*) Fan *m*

fanatic /fəˈnætɪk/ *n* Fanatiker *m*. **~al** *a*, **-ly** *adv* fanatisch. **~ism** /-sɪzm/ *n* Fanatismus *m*

fanciful /ˈfænsɪfl/ *a* fantastisch; (*imaginative*) fantasiereich

fancy /ˈfænsɪ/ *n* Fantasie *f*; **I have taken a real ~ to him** er hat es mir angetan ● *a* ausgefallen ● *vt* (*believe*) meinen; (*imagine*) sich (*dat*) einbilden; ([!] *want*) Lust haben auf (+ *acc*); **~ that!** stell dir vor! (*really*) tatsächlich! **~ ˈdress** *n* Kostüm *nt*

fanfare /ˈfænfeə(r)/ *n* Fanfare *f*

fang /fæŋ/ *n* Fangzahn *m*

ˈfan heater *n* Heizlüfter *m*

fantas|ize /ˈfæntəsaɪz/ *vi* fantasieren. **~tic** /-ˈtæstɪk/ *a* fantastisch. **~y** *n* Fantasie *f*

far /fɑː(r)/ *adv* weit; (*much*) viel; **by ~** bei weitem; **~ away** weit weg; **as ~ as I know** soviel ich weiß; **as ~ as the church** bis zur Kirche ● *a* **at the ~ end** am anderen Ende; **the F~ East** der Ferne Osten

farc|e /fɑːs/ *n* Farce *f*. **~ical** *a* lächerlich

fare /feə(r)/ *n* Fahrpreis *m*; (*money*) Fahrgeld *nt*; (*food*) Kost *f*; **air ~** Flugpreis *m*

farewell /feəˈwel/ *int* (*liter*) lebe wohl! ● *n* Lebewohl *nt*

far-ˈfetched *a* weit hergeholt

farm /fɑːm/ *n* Bauernhof *m* ● *vi* Landwirtschaft betreiben ● *vt* bewirtschaften <*land*>. **~er** *n* Landwirt *m*

farm: ~house *n* Bauernhaus *nt.* **~ing** *n* Landwirtschaft *f.* **~yard** *n* Hof *m*

far: ~-'reaching *a* weit reichend. **~-'sighted** *a* (*fig*) umsichtig; (*Amer: long-sighted*) weitsichtig

farther /'fɑ:ðə(r)/ *adv* weiter; **~ off** weiter entfernt

fascinat|e /'fæsɪneɪt/ *vt* faszinieren. **~ing** *a* faszinierend. **~ion** /-'neɪʃn/ *n* Faszination *f*

fascis|m /'fæʃɪzm/ *n* Faschismus *m.* **~t** *n* Faschist *m* ● *a* faschistisch

fashion /'fæʃn/ *n* Mode *f*; (*manner*) Art *f.* **~able** /-əbl/ *a*, **-bly** *adv* modisch

fast /fɑ:st/ *a* & *adv* (**-er, -est**) schnell; (*firm*) fest; <*colour*> waschecht; **be ~** <*clock:*> vorgehen; **be ~ asleep** fest schlafen

fasten /'fɑ:sn/ *vt* zumachen; (*fix*) befestigen (**to an** + *dat*). **~er** *n*, **~ing** *n* Verschluss *m*

fastidious /fə'stɪdɪəs/ *a* wählerisch; (*particular*) penibel

fat /fæt/ *a* (**fatter, fattest**) dick; <*meat*> fett ● *n* Fett *nt*

fatal /'feɪtl/ *a* tödlich; <*error*> verhängnisvoll. **~ity** /fə'tælətɪ/ *n* Todesopfer *nt.* **~ly** /-təlɪ/ *adv* tödlich

fate /feɪt/ *n* Schicksal *nt.* **~ful** *a* verhängnisvoll

'fat-head *n* [!] Dummkopf *m*

father /'fɑ:ðə(r)/ *n* Vater *m*; **F ~ Christmas** der Weihnachtsmann ● *vt* zeugen

father: ~hood *n* Vaterschaft *f.* **~-in-law** *n* (*pl* **~s-in-law**) Schwiegervater *m.* **~ly** *a* väterlich

fathom /'fæðəm/ *n* (*Naut*) Faden *m* ● *vt* verstehen

fatigue /fə'ti:g/ *n* Ermüdung *f*

fatten /'fætn/ *vt* mästen <*animal*>

fatty /'fætɪ/ *a* fett; <*foods*> fetthaltig

fatuous /'fætjʊəs/ *a* albern

fault /fɔ:lt/ *n* Fehler *m*; (*Techn*) Defekt *m*; (*Geol*) Verwerfung *f*; **at ~** im Unrecht; **find ~ with** etwas auszusetzen haben an (+ *dat*); **it's your ~** du bist schuld. **~less** *a*, **-ly** *adv* fehlerfrei

faulty /'fɔ:ltɪ/ *a* fehlerhaft

favour /'feɪvə(r)/ *n* Gunst *f*; **I am in ~** ich bin dafür; **do s.o. a ~** jdm einen Gefallen tun ● *vt* begünstigen; (*prefer*) bevorzugen. **~able** /-əbl/ *a*, **-bly** *adv* günstig; <*reply*> positiv

favourit|e /'feɪvərɪt/ *a* Lieblings- ● *n* Liebling *m*; (*Sport*) Favorit(in) *m(f).* **~ism** *n* Bevorzugung *f*

fawn /fɔ:n/ *a* rehbraun ● *n* Hirschkalb *nt*

fax /fæks/ *n* Fax *nt* ● *vt* faxen (**s.o.** jdm). **~ machine** *n* Faxgerät *nt*

fear /fɪə(r)/ *n* Furcht *f*, Angst *f* (**of** vor + *dat*) ● *vt/i* fürchten

fear|ful /'fɪəfl/ *a* besorgt; (*awful*) furchtbar. **~less** *a*, **-ly** *adv* furchtlos

feas|ibility /fi:zə'bɪlətɪ/ *n* Durchführbarkeit *f.* **~ible** *a* durchführbar; (*possible*) möglich

feast /fi:st/ *n* Festmahl *nt*; (*Relig*) Fest *nt* ● *vi* **~ [on]** schmausen

feat /fi:t/ *n* Leistung *f*

feather /'feðə(r)/ *n* Feder *f*

feature /'fi:tʃə(r)/ *n* Gesichtszug *m*; (*quality*) Merkmal *nt*; (*Journ*) Feature *nt* ● *vt* darstellen

February /'februərɪ/ *n* Februar *m*

fed /fed/ *see* **feed** ● *a* **be ~ up** [!] die Nase voll haben (**with** von)

federal /'fedərəl/ *a* Bundes-

federation /fedə'reɪʃn/ *n* Föderation *f*

fee /fi:/ *n* Gebühr *f*; (*professional*) Honorar *nt*

feeble /ˈfi:bl/ *a* (**-r, -st**), **-bly** *adv* schwach

feed /fi:d/ *n* Futter *nt*; (*for baby*) Essen *nt* ● *v* (*pt/pp* **fed**) ● *vt* füttern; (*support*) ernähren; (*into machine*) eingeben; speisen *<computer>* ● *vi* sich ernähren (**on** von)

ˈ**feedback** *n* Feedback *nt*

feel /fi:l/ *v* (*pt/pp* **felt**) ● *vt* fühlen; (*experience*) empfinden; (*think*) meinen ● *vi* sich fühlen; ~ **soft/hard** sich weich/hart anfühlen; **I** ~ **hot/ill** mir ist heiß/schlecht; ~**ing** *n* Gefühl *nt*; **no hard** ~**ings** nichts für ungut

feet /fi:t/ *see* **foot**

feline /ˈfi:laɪn/ *a* Katzen-; (*catlike*) katzenartig

fell¹ /fel/ *vt* fällen

fell² *see* **fall**

fellow /ˈfeləʊ/ *n* ([I] *man*) Kerl *m*

fellow: ~-ˈ**countryman** *n* Landsmann *m*. ~ **men** *pl* Mitmenschen *pl*

felt¹ /felt/ *see* **feel**

felt² *n* Filz *m*. ~**[-tipped]** ˈ**pen** *n* Filzstift *m*

female /ˈfi:meɪl/ *a* weiblich ● *nt* Weibchen *nt*; (*pej: woman*) Weib *nt*

femin|ine /ˈfemɪnɪn/ *a* weiblich ● *n* (*Gram*) Femininum *nt*. ~**inity** /-ˈnɪnətɪ/ *n* Weiblichkeit *f*. ~**ist** *a* feministisch ● *n* Feminist(in) *m(f)*

fenc|e /fens/ *n* Zaun *m*; ([I] *person*) Hehler *m* ● *vi* (*Sport*) fechten ● *vt* ~**e in** einzäunen. ~**er** *n* Fechter *m*. ~**ing** *n* Zaun *m*; (*Sport*) Fechten *nt*

fender /ˈfendə(r)/ *n* Kaminvorsetzer *m*; (*Naut*) Fender *m*; (*Amer: wing*) Kotflügel *m*

ferment /fəˈment/ *vi* gären ● *vt* gären lassen

fern /fɜ:n/ *n* Farn *m*

feroc|ious /fəˈrəʊʃəs/ *a* wild. ~**ity** /-ˈrɒsətɪ/ *n* Wildheit *f*

ferry /ˈferɪ/ *n* Fähre *f*

fertil|e /ˈfɜ:taɪl/ *a* fruchtbar. ~**ity** /fɜ:ˈtɪlətɪ/ *n* Fruchtbarkeit *f*

fertilize /ˈfɜ:təlaɪz/ *vt* befruchten; düngen *<land>*. ~**r** *n* Dünger *m*

fervent /ˈfɜ:vənt/ *a* leidenschaftlich

fervour /ˈfɜ:və(r)/ *n* Leidenschaft *f*

festival /ˈfestɪvl/ *n* Fest *nt*; (*Mus, Theat*) Festspiele *pl*

festiv|e /ˈfestɪv/ *a* festlich. ~**ities** /feˈstɪvətɪz/ *npl* Feierlichkeiten *pl*

festoon /feˈstu:n/ *vt* behängen (**with** mit)

fetch /fetʃ/ *vt* holen; (*collect*) abholen; (*be sold for*) einbringen

fetching /ˈfetʃɪŋ/ *a* anziehend

fête /feɪt/ *n* Fest *nt* ● *vt* feiern

feud /fju:d/ *n* Fehde *f*

feudal /ˈfju:dl/ *a* Feudal-

fever /ˈfi:və(r)/ *n* Fieber *nt*. ~**ish** *a* fiebrig; (*fig*) fieberhaft

few /fju:/ *a* (**-er, -est**) wenige; **every** ~ **days** alle paar Tage ● *n* **a** ~ ein paar; **quite a** ~ ziemlich viele

fiancé /fɪˈɒnseɪ/ *n* Verlobte(r) *m*. **fiancée** *n* Verlobte *f*

fiasco /fɪˈæskəʊ/ *n* Fiasko *nt*

fib /fɪb/ *n* kleine Lüge

fibre /ˈfaɪbə(r)/ *n* Faser *f*

fiction /ˈfɪkʃn/ *n* Erfindung *f*; **[works of]** ~ Erzählungsliteratur *f*. ~**al** *a* erfunden

fictitious /fɪkˈtɪʃəs/ *a* [frei] erfunden

fiddle /ˈfɪdl/ *n* [I] Geige *f*; (*cheating*) Schwindel *m* ● *vi* herumspielen (**with** mit) ● *vt* [I] frisieren *<accounts>*

fiddly /ˈfɪdlɪ/ *a* knifflig

fidelity /fɪˈdelətɪ/ *n* Treue *f*

fidget /ˈfɪdʒɪt/ *vi* zappeln. **~y** *a* zappelig

field /fiːld/ *n* Feld *nt*; (*meadow*) Wiese *f*; (*subject*) Gebiet *nt*

field: ~ events *npl* Sprung- und Wurfdisziplinen *pl*. **F~ 'Marshal** *n* Feldmarschall *m*

fiendish /ˈfiːndɪʃ/ *a* teuflisch

fierce /fɪəs/ *a* (**-r, -st**), **-ly** *adv* wild; (*fig*) heftig. **~ness** *n* Wildheit *f*; (*fig*) Heftigkeit *f*

fiery /ˈfaɪərɪ/ *a* (**-ier, -iest**) feurig

fifteen /fɪfˈtiːn/ *a* fünfzehn ● *n* Fünfzehn *f*. **~th** *a* fünfzehnte(r,s)

fifth /fɪfθ/ *a* fünfte(r,s)

fiftieth /ˈfɪftɪɪθ/ *a* fünfzigste(r,s)

fifty /ˈfɪftɪ/ *a* fünfzig

fig /fɪg/ *n* Feige *f*

fight /faɪt/ *n* Kampf *m*; (*brawl*) Schlägerei *f*; (*between children, dogs*) Rauferei *f* ● *v* (*pt/pp* **fought**) ● *vt* kämpfen gegen; (*fig*) bekämpfen ● *vi* kämpfen; (*brawl*) sich schlagen; <*children, dogs:*> sich raufen. **~er** *n* Kämpfer *m*; (*Aviat*) Jagdflugzeug *nt*. **~ing** *n* Kampf *m*

figurative /ˈfɪgjərətɪv/ *a*, **-ly** *adv* bildlich, übertragen

figure /ˈfɪgə(r)/ *n* (*digit*) Ziffer *f*; (*number*) Zahl *f*; (*sum*) Summe *f*; (*carving, sculpture, woman's*) Figur *f*; (*form*) Gestalt *f*; (*illustration*) Abbildung *f*; **good at ~s** gut im Rechnen ● *vi* (*appear*) erscheinen ● *vt* (*Amer: think*) glauben

filch /fɪltʃ/ *vt* [!] klauen

file¹ /faɪl/ *n* Akte *f*; (*for documents*) [Akten]ordner *m* ● *vt* ablegen <*documents*>; (*Jur*) einreichen

file² *n* (*line*) Reihe *f*; **in single ~** im Gänsemarsch

file³ *n* (*Techn*) Feile *f* ● *vt* feilen

fill /fɪl/ *n* **eat one's ~** sich satt essen ● *vt* füllen; plombieren <*tooth*> ● *vi* sich füllen. **~ in** *vt* auffüllen; ausfüllen <*form*>. **~ out** *vt* ausfüllen <*form*>. **~ up** *vi* sich füllen ● *vt* vollfüllen; (*Auto*) volltanken; ausfüllen <*form*>

fillet /ˈfɪlɪt/ *n* Filet *nt* ● *vt* (*pt/pp* **filleted**) entgräten

filling /ˈfɪlɪŋ/ *n* Füllung *f*; (*of tooth*) Plombe *f*. **~ station** *n* Tankstelle *f*

filly /ˈfɪlɪ/ *n* junge Stute *f*

film /fɪlm/ *n* Film *m* ● *vt/i* filmen; verfilmen <*book*>. **~ star** *n* Filmstar *m*

filter /ˈfɪltə(r)/ *n* Filter *m* ● *vt* filtern

filth /fɪlθ/ *n* Dreck *m*. **~y** *a* (**-ier, -iest**) dreckig

fin /fɪn/ *n* Flosse *f*

final /ˈfaɪnl/ *a* letzte(r,s); (*conclusive*) endgültig ● *n* (*Sport*) Endspiel *nt*; **~s** *pl* (*Univ*) Abschlussprüfung *f*

finale /fɪˈnɑːlɪ/ *n* Finale *nt*

final|ist /ˈfaɪnəlɪst/ *n* Finalist(in) *m(f)*

final|ize /ˈfaɪnəlaɪz/ *vt* endgültig festlegen. **~ly** *adv* schließlich

finance /faɪˈnæns/ *n* Finanz *f* ● *vt* finanzieren

financial /faɪˈnænʃl/ *a*, **-ly** *adv* finanziell

find /faɪnd/ *n* Fund *m* ● *vt* (*pt/pp* **found**) finden; (*establish*) feststellen; **go and ~** holen; **try to ~** suchen. **~ out** *vt* herausfinden; (*learn*) erfahren ● *vi* (*enquire*) sich erkundigen

fine¹ /faɪn/ *n* Geldstrafe *f* ● *vt* zu einer Geldstrafe verurteilen

fine² *a* (**-r, -st,**) **-ly** *adv* fein; <*weather*> schön; **he's ~** es geht ihm gut ● *adv* gut; **cut it ~** [!] sich (*dat*) wenig Zeit lassen

finesse /fɪˈnes/ *n* Gewandtheit *f*

finger /ˈfɪŋgə(r)/ *n* Finger *m* ● *vt* anfassen

finger: **~nail** *n* Fingernagel *m.* **~print** *n* Fingerabdruck *m.* **~tip** *n* Fingerspitze *f*

finicky /'fɪnɪkɪ/ *a* knifflig; (*choosy*) wählerisch

finish /'fɪnɪʃ/ *n* Schluss *m*; (*Sport*) Finish *nt*; (*line*) Ziel *nt*; (*of product*) Ausführung *f* ● *vt* beenden; (*use up*) aufbrauchen; **~ one's drink** austrinken; **~ reading** zu Ende lesen ● *vi* fertig werden; <*performance:*> zu Ende sein; <*runner:*> durchs Ziel gehen

Finland /'fɪnlənd/ *n* Finnland *nt*

Finn /fɪn/ *n* Finne *m*/ Finnin *f*. **~ish** *a* finnisch

fir /fɜ:(r)/ *n* Tanne *f*

fire /'faɪə(r)/ *n* Feuer *nt*; (*forest, house*) Brand *m*; **be on ~** brennen; **catch ~** Feuer fangen; **set ~ to** anzünden; <*arsonist:*> in Brand stecken; **under ~** unter Beschuss ● *vt* brennen <*pottery*>; abfeuern <*shot*>; schießen mit <*gun*>; (Ⓘ *dismiss*) feuern ● *vi* schießen (**at** auf + *acc*); <*engine:*> anspringen

fire: **~ alarm** *n* Feuermelder *m.* **~ brigade** *n* Feuerwehr *f.* **~-engine** *n* Löschfahrzeug *nt.* **~ extinguisher** *n* Feuerlöscher *m.* **~man** *n* Feuerwehrmann *m.* **~place** *n* Kamin *m.* **~side** *n* **by** *or* **at the ~side** am Kamin. **~ station** *n* Feuerwache *f.* **~wood** *n* Brennholz *nt.* **~work** *n* Feuerwerkskörper *m*; **~works** *pl* (*display*) Feuerwerk *nt*

firm¹ /fɜ:m/ *n* Firma *f*

firm² *a* (**-er, -est**), **-ly** *adv* fest; (*resolute*) entschlossen; (*strict*) streng

first /fɜ:st/ *a* & *n* erste(r,s); **at ~** zuerst; **at ~ sight** auf den ersten Blick; **from the ~** von Anfang an ● *adv* zuerst; (*firstly*) erstens

first: **~ 'aid** *n* erste Hilfe. **~-'aid kit** *n* Verbandkasten *m.* **~-class** *a* erstklassig; (*Rail*) erster Klasse ● /-'-/ *adv* <*travel*> erster Klasse. **~ 'floor** *n* erster Stock; (*Amer: ground floor*) Erdgeschoss *nt.* **~ly** *adv* erstens. **~ name** *n* Vorname *m.* **~-rate** *a* erstklassig

fish /fɪʃ/ *n* Fisch *m* ● *vt/i* fischen; (*with rod*) angeln

fish: **~bone** *n* Gräte *f.* **~erman** *n* Fischer *m.* **~ 'finger** *n* Fischstäbchen *nt*

fishing /'fɪʃɪŋ/ *n* Fischerei *f.* **~ boat** *n* Fischerboot *nt.* **~-rod** *n* Angel[rute] *f*

fish: **~monger** /-mʌŋgə(r)/ *n* Fischhändler *m.* **~y** *a* Fisch-; (Ⓘ *suspicious*) verdächtig

fission /'fɪʃn/ *n* (*Phys*) Spaltung *f*

fist /fɪst/ *n* Faust *f*

fit¹ /fɪt/ *n* (*attack*) Anfall *m*

fit² *a* (**fitter, fittest**) (*suitable*) geeignet; (*healthy*) gesund; (*Sport*) fit; **~ to eat** essbar

fit³ *n* (*of clothes*) Sitz *m*; **be a good ~** gut passen ● *v* (*pt/pp* **fitted**) ● *vi* (*be the right size*) passen ● *vt* anbringen (**to** an + *dat*); (*install*) einbauen; **~ with** versehen mit. **~ in** *vi* hineinpassen; (*adapt*) sich einfügen (**with** in + *acc*) ● *vt* (*accommodate*) unterbringen

fit|ness *n* Eignung *f*; **[physical] ~ness** Gesundheit *f*; (*Sport*) Fitness *f.* **~ted** *a* eingebaut; <*garment*> tailliert

fitted: **~ 'carpet** *n* Teppichboden *m.* **~ 'kitchen** *n* Einbauküche *f.* **~ 'sheet** *n* Spannlaken *nt*

fitting /'fɪtɪŋ/ *a* passend ● *n* (*of clothes*) Anprobe *f*; (*of shoes*) Weite *f*; (*Techn*) Zubehörteil *nt*; **~s** *pl* Zubehör *nt*

five /faɪv/ *a* fünf ● *n* Fünf *f.* **~r** *n* Fünfpfundschein *m*

fix /fɪks/ *n* (☒ *drugs*) Fix *m*; **be in a ~** Ⓘ in der Klemme sitzen ● *vt* befestigen (**to** an + *dat*); (*arrange*) festlegen; (*repair*) reparieren; (*Phot*) fixieren; ~ **a meal** Essen machen

fixed /'fɪkst/ *a* fest

fixture /'fɪkstʃə(r)/ *n* (*Sport*) Veranstaltung *f*; ~**s and fittings** zu einer Wohnung gehörende Einrichtungen *pl*

fizz /fɪz/ *vi* sprudeln

fizzle /'fɪzl/ *vi* ~ **out** verpuffen

fizzy /'fɪzɪ/ *a* sprudelnd. ~ **drink** *n* Brause[limonade] *f*

flabbergasted /'flæbəgɑ:stɪd/ *a* **be** ~ platt sein [!]

flabby /'flæbɪ/ *a* schlaff

flag /flæg/ *n* Fahne *f*; (*Naut*) Flagge *f*

'flag-pole *n* Fahnenstange *f*

flagrant /'fleɪgrənt/ *a* flagrant

'flagstone *n* [Pflaster]platte *f*

flair /fleə(r)/ *n* Begabung *f*

flake /fleɪk/ *n* Flocke *f* ● *vi* ~ **[off]** abblättern

flamboyant /flæm'bɔɪənt/ *a* extravagant

flame /fleɪm/ *n* Flamme *f*

flan /flæn/ *n* **[fruit]** ~ Obsttorte *f*

flank /flæŋk/ *n* Flanke *f*

flannel /'flænl/ *n* Flanell *m*; (*for washing*) Waschlappen *m*

flap /flæp/ *n* Klappe *f*; **in a** ~ [!] aufgeregt ● *v* (*pt*/*pp* **flapped**) *vi* flattern; [!] sich aufregen ● *vt* ~ **its wings** mit den Flügeln schlagen

flare /fleə(r)/ *n* Leuchtsignal *nt*. ● *vi* ~ **up** auflodern; ([!] *get angry*) aufbrausen

flash /flæʃ/ *n* Blitz *m*; **in a** ~ [!] im Nu ● *vi* blitzen; (*repeatedly*) blinken; ~ **past** vorbeirasen

flash: ~**back** *n* Rückblende *f*. ~**er** *n* (*Auto*) Blinker *m*. ~**light** *n* (*Phot*) Blitzlicht *nt*; (*Amer: torch*) Taschenlampe *f*. ~**y** *a* auffällig

flask /flɑ:sk/ *n* Flasche *f*

flat /flæt/ *a* (**flatter, flattest**) flach; <*surface*> eben; <*refusal*> glatt; <*beer*> schal; <*battery*> verbraucht/ (*Auto*) leer; <*tyre*> platt; (*Mus*) **A** ~ As *nt*; **B** ~ B *nt* ● *n* Wohnung *f*; ([!] *puncture*) Reifenpanne *f*

flat: ~**ly** *adv* <*refuse*> glatt. ~ **rate** *n* Einheitspreis *m*

flatten /'flætn/ *vt* platt drücken

flatter /'flætə(r)/ *vt* schmeicheln (+ *dat*). ~**y** *n* Schmeichelei *f*

flat 'tyre *n* Reifenpanne *f*

flaunt /flɔ:nt/ *vt* prunken mit

flautist /'flɔ:tɪst/ *n* Flötist(in) *m*(*f*)

flavour /'fleɪvə(r)/ *n* Geschmack *m* ● *vt* abschmecken. ~**ing** *n* Aroma *nt*

flaw /flɔ:/ *n* Fehler *m*. ~**less** *a* tadellos; <*complexion*> makellos

flea /fli:/ *n* Floh *m*

fleck /flek/ *n* Tupfen *m*

fled /fled/ *see* **flee**

flee /fli:/ *v* (*pt*/*pp* **fled**) ● *vi* fliehen (**from** vor + *dat*) ● *vt* flüchten aus

fleece /fli:s/ *n* Vlies *nt* ● *vt* [!] schröpfen

fleet /fli:t/ *n* Flotte *f*; (*of cars*) Wagenpark *m*

fleeting /'fli:tɪŋ/ *a* flüchtig

Flemish /'flemɪʃ/ *a* flämisch

flesh /fleʃ/ *n* Fleisch *nt*

flew /flu:/ *see* **fly²**

flex¹ /fleks/ *vt* anspannen <*muscle*>

flex² *n* (*Electr*) Schnur *f*

flexib|ility /fleksə'bɪlətɪ/ *n* Biegsamkeit *f*; (*fig*) Flexibilität *f*. ~**le** *a* biegsam; (*fig*) flexibel

flick /flɪk/ *vt* schnippen

flicker /'flɪkə(r)/ *vi* flackern

flier /'flaɪə(r)/ *n* = **flyer**

flight¹ /flaɪt/ *n* (*fleeing*) Flucht *f*

flight² *n* (*flying*) Flug *m*; ~ **of stairs** Treppe *f*

'flight recorder *n* Flugschreiber *m*

flimsy /ˈflɪmzɪ/ *a* (**-ier, -iest**) dünn; <*excuse*> fadenscheinig
flinch /flɪntʃ/ *vi* zurückzucken
fling /flɪŋ/ *vt* (*pt/pp* **flung**) schleudern
flint /flɪnt/ *n* Feuerstein *m*
flip /flɪp/ *vt/i* schnippen; ~ **through** durchblättern
flippant /ˈflɪpənt/ *a*, **-ly** *adv* leichtfertig
flirt /flɜ:t/ *n* kokette Frau *f* ● *vi* flirten
flirtat|ion /flɜ:ˈteɪʃn/ *n* Flirt *m*. ~**ious** /-ʃəs/ *a* kokett
flit /flɪt/ *vi* (*pt/pp* **flitted**) flattern
float /fləʊt/ *n* Schwimmer *m*; (*in procession*) Festwagen *m*; (*money*) Wechselgeld *nt* ● *vi* <*thing:*> schwimmen; <*person:*> sich treiben lassen; (*in air*) schweben
flock /flɒk/ *n* Herde *f*; (*of birds*) Schwarm *m* ● *vi* strömen
flog /flɒg/ *vt* (*pt/pp* **flogged**) auspeitschen; (🅘 *sell*) verkloppen
flood /flʌd/ *n* Überschwemmung *f*; (*fig*) Flut *f* ● *vt* überschwemmen
ˈ**floodlight** *n* Flutlicht *nt* ● *vt* (*pt/pp* **floodlit**) anstrahlen
floor /flɔ:(r)/ *n* Fußboden *m*; (*storey*) Stock *m*
floor: ~ **board** *n* Dielenbrett *nt*. ~**-polish** *n* Bohnerwachs *nt*. ~ **show** *n* Kabarettvorstellung *f*
flop /flɒp/ *n* 🅘 (*failure*) Reinfall *m*; (*Theat*) Durchfall *m* ● *vi* (*pt/pp* **flopped**) 🅘 (*fail*) durchfallen
floppy /ˈflɒpɪ/ *a* schlapp. ~ ˈ**disc** *n* Diskette *f*
floral /ˈflɔ:rl/ *a* Blumen-
florid /ˈflɒrɪd/ *a* <*complexion*> gerötet; <*style*> blumig
florist /ˈflɒrɪst/ *n* Blumenhändler(in) *m(f)*
flounder /ˈflaʊndə(r)/ *vi* zappeln
flour /ˈflaʊə(r)/ *n* Mehl *nt*
flourish /ˈflʌrɪʃ/ *n* große Geste *f*; (*scroll*) Schnörkel *m* ● *vi* gedeihen; (*fig*) blühen ● *vt* schwenken
flout /flaʊt/ *vt* missachten
flow /fləʊ/ *n* Fluss *m*; (*of traffic, blood*) Strom *m* ● *vi* fließen
flower /ˈflaʊə(r)/ *n* Blume *f* ● *vi* blühen
flower: ~**-bed** *n* Blumenbeet *nt*. ~**pot** *n* Blumentopf *m*. ~**y** *a* blumig
flown /fləʊn/ *see* **fly**[2]
flu /flu:/ *n* 🅘 Grippe *f*
fluctuat|e /ˈflʌktjʊeɪt/ *vi* schwanken. ~**ion** /-ˈeɪʃn/ *n* Schwankung *f*
fluent /ˈflu:ənt/ *a*, **-ly** *adv* fließend
fluff /flʌf/ *n* Fusseln *pl*; (*down*) Flaum *m*. ~**y** *a* (**-ier, -iest**) flauschig
fluid /ˈflu:ɪd/ *a* flüssig, (*fig*) veränderlich ● *n* Flüssigkeit *f*
fluke /flu:k/ *n* [glücklicher] Zufall *m*
flung /flʌŋ/ *see* **fling**
fluorescent /flʊəˈresnt/ *a* fluoreszierend
fluoride /ˈflʊəraɪd/ *n* Fluor *nt*
flush /flʌʃ/ *n* (*blush*) Erröten *nt* ● *vi* rot werden ● *vt* spülen ● *a* in einer Ebene (**with** mit); (🅘 *affluent*) gut bei Kasse
flustered /ˈflʌstəd/ *a* nervös
flute /flu:t/ *n* Flöte *f*
flutter /ˈflʌtə(r)/ *n* Flattern *nt* ● *vi* flattern
fly[1] /flaɪ/ *n* (*pl* **flies**) Fliege *f*
fly[2] *v* (*pt* **flew**, *pp* **flown**) ● *vi* fliegen; <*flag:*> wehen; (*rush*) sausen ● *vt* fliegen; führen <*flag*>
fly[3] *n* & **flies** *pl* (*on trousers*) Hosenschlitz *m*
flyer /ˈflaɪə(r)/ *n* Flieger(in) *m(f)*; (*leaflet*) Flugblatt *nt*
foal /fəʊl/ *n* Fohlen *nt*

foam /fəʊm/ *n* Schaum *m*; (*synthetic*) Schaumstoff *m* ● *vi* schäumen

fob /fɒb/ *vt* (*pt/pp* **fobbed**) ~ **sth off** etw andrehen (**on s.o.** jdm); ~ **s.o. off** jdn abspeisen (**with** mit)

focal /ˈfəʊkl/ *n* Brenn-

focus /ˈfəʊkəs/ *n* Brennpunkt *m*; **in** ~ scharf eingestellt ● *v* (*pt/pp* **focused** *or* **focussed**) ● *vt* einstellen (**on auf** + *acc*) ● *vi* (*fig*) sich konzentrieren (**on** auf + *acc*)

fog /fɒg/ *n* Nebel *m*

foggy /ˈfɒgɪ/ *a* (**foggier, foggiest**) neblig

ˈ**fog-horn** *n* Nebelhorn *nt*

foible /ˈfɔɪbl/ *n* Eigenart *f*

foil¹ /fɔɪl/ *n* Folie *f*; (*Culin*) Alufolie *f*

foil² *vt* (*thwart*) vereiteln

foil³ *n* (*Fencing*) Florett *nt*

fold *n* Falte *f*; (*in paper*) Kniff *m* ● *vt* falten; ~ **one's arms** die Arme verschränken ● *vi* sich falten lassen; (*fail*) eingehen. ~ **up** *vt* zusammenfalten; zusammenklappen <*chair*> ● *vi* sich zusammenfalten/-klappen lassen; [!] <*business*:> eingehen

fold|er /ˈfəʊldə(r)/ *n* Mappe *f*. ~**ing** *a* Klapp-

foliage /ˈfəʊlɪɪdʒ/ *n* Blätter *pl*; (*of tree*) Laub *nt*

folk /fəʊk/ *npl* Leute *pl*

folk: ~**-dance** *n* Volkstanz *m*. ~**-song** *n* Volkslied *nt*

follow /ˈfɒləʊ/ *vt/i* folgen (+ *dat*); (*pursue*) verfolgen; (*in vehicle*) nachfahren (+ *dat*). ~ **up** *vt* nachgehen (+ *dat*)

follow|er /ˈfɒləʊə(r)/ *n* Anhänger(in) *m(f)*. ~**ing** *a* folgend ● *n* Folgende(s) *nt*; (*supporters*) Anhängerschaft *f* ● *prep* im Anschluss an (+ *acc*)

folly /ˈfɒlɪ/ *n* Torheit *f*

fond /fɒnd/ *a* (**-er, -est**), **-ly** *adv* liebevoll; **be** ~ **of** gern haben; gern essen <*food*>

fondle /ˈfɒndl/ *vt* liebkosen

fondness /ˈfɒndnɪs/ *n* Liebe *f* (**for** zu)

food /fu:d/ *n* Essen *nt*; (*for animals*) Futter *nt*; (*groceries*) Lebensmittel *pl*. ~ **poisoning** *n* Lebensmittelvergiftung *f*. ~ **processor** *n* Küchenmaschine *f*

fool¹ /fu:l/ *n* (*Culin*) Fruchtcreme *f*

fool² *n* Narr *m*; **make a** ~ **of oneself** sich lächerlich machen ● *vt* hereinlegen ● *vi* ~ **around** herumalbern

ˈ**fool|hardy** *a* tollkühn. ~**ish** *a*, **-ly** *adv* dumm. ~**ishness** *n* Dummheit *f*. ~**proof** *a* narrensicher

foot /fʊt/ *n* (*pl* **feet**) Fuß *m*; (*measure*) Fuß *m* (*30,48 cm*); (*of bed*) Fußende *nt*; **on** ~ zu Fuß; **on one's feet** auf den Beinen; **put one's** ~ **in it** [!] ins Fettnäpfchen treten; **7** ~ *or* **feet** 7 fuß

foot: ~**-and-ˈmouth [disease]** *n* Maul-und Klauenseuche *f*. ~**ball** *n* Fußball *m*. ~**baller** *n* Fußballspieler *m*. ~**ball pools** *npl* Fußballtoto *nt*. ~**-bridge** *n* Fußgängerbrücke *f*. ~**hills** *npl* Vorgebirge *nt*. ~**hold** *n* Halt *m*. ~**ing** *n* Halt *m*. ~**lights** *npl* Rampenlicht *nt*. ~**note** *n* Fußnote *f*. ~**path** *n* Fußweg *m*. ~**print** *n* Fußabdruck *m*. ~**step** *n* Schritt *m*; **follow in s.o.'s** ~**steps** (*fig*) in jds Fußstapfen treten. ~**wear** *n* Schuhwerk *nt*

for /fɔ:(r), *unstressed* fə(r)/
● *preposition*
····> (*on behalf of; in place of; in favour of*) für (+ *acc*). **I did it for you** ich habe es für dich

gemacht. **I work for him/for a bank** ich arbeite für ihn/für eine Bank. **be 'for doing sth** dafür sein, etw zu tun. **cheque/bill for £5** Scheck/Rechnung über 5 Pfund. **for nothing** umsonst. **what have you got for a cold?** was haben Sie gegen Erkältungen?

····➤ (*expressing reason*) wegen (+ *gen*); (*with emotion*) aus. **famous for these wines** berühmt wegen dieser Weine *od* für diese Weine. **he was sentenced to death for murder** er wurde wegen Mordes zum Tode verurteilt. **were it not for you/your help** ohne dich/deine Hilfe. **for fear/love of** aus Angst vor (+ *dat*)/aus Liebe zu (+ *dat*)

····➤ (*expressing purpose*) (*with action, meal*) zu (+ *dat*); (*with object*) für (+ *acc*). **it's for washing the car** es ist zum Autowaschen. **we met for a discussion** wir trafen uns zu einer Besprechung. **for pleasure** zum Vergnügen. **meat for lunch** Fleisch zum Mittagessen. **what is that for?** wofür *od* wozu ist das? **a dish for nuts** eine Schale für Nüsse

····➤ (*expressing direction*) nach (+ *dat*); (*less precise*) in Richtung. **the train for Oxford** der Zug nach Oxford. **they were heading** *or* **making for London** sie fuhren in Richtung London

····➤ (*expressing time*) (*completed process*) ... lang; (*continuing process*) seit (+ *dat*). **I lived here for two years** ich habe zwei Jahre [lang] hier gewohnt. **I have been living here for two years** ich wohne hier seit zwei Jahren. **we are staying for a week** wir werden eine Woche bleiben

····➤ (*expressing difficulty, impossibility, embarrassment etc.*) + *dat*. **it's impossible/inconvenient for her** es ist ihr unmöglich/ungelegen. **it was embarrassing for our teacher** unserem Lehrer war es peinlich

● *conjunction*

····➤ denn. **he's not coming for he has no money** er kommt nicht mit, denn er hat kein Geld

forbade /fə'bæd/ *see* **forbid**

forbid /fə'bɪd/ *vt* (*pt* **forbade**, *pp* **forbidden**) verbieten (**s.o.** jdm). **~ding** *a* bedrohlich; (*stern*) streng

force /fɔːs/ *n* Kraft *f*; (*of blow*) Wucht *f*; (*violence*) Gewalt *f*; **in ~** gültig; (*in large numbers*) in großer Zahl; **come into ~** in Kraft treten; **the ~s** *pl* die Streitkräfte *pl* ● *vt* zwingen; (*break open*) aufbrechen

forced /fɔːst/ *a* gezwungen; **~ landing** Notlandung *f*

force: ~-'feed *vt* (*pt*/*pp* **-fed**) zwangsernähren. **~ful** *a*, **-ly** *adv* energisch

forceps /'fɔːseps/ *n inv* Zange *f*

forcible /'fɔːsəbl/ *a* gewaltsam

ford /fɔːd/ *n* Furt *f* ● *vt* durchwaten; (*in vehicle*) durchfahren

fore /fɔː(r)/ *a* vordere(r,s)

fore: ~arm *n* Unterarm *m*. **~cast** *n* Voraussage *f*; (*for weather*) Vorhersage *f* ● *vt* (*pt*/*pp* **~cast**) voraussagen, vorhersagen. **~finger** *n* Zeigefinger *m*. **~gone** *a* **be a ~gone conclusion** von vornherein feststehen. **~ground** *n* Vordergrund *m*. **~head** /'fɒrɪd/ *n* Stirn *f*. **~hand** *n* Vorhand *f*

foreign /'fɒrən/ *a* ausländisch; <*country*> fremd; **he is ~** er ist Ausländer. **~ currency** *n* Devisen *pl*. **~er** *n* Ausländer(in) *m(f)*. ~ **language** *n* Fremdsprache *f*

Foreign: ~ **Office** *n* ≈ Außenministerium *nt*. ~ **'Secretary** *n* ≈ Außenminister *m*

fore: ~**leg** *n* Vorderbein *nt*. ~**man** *n* Vorarbeiter *m*. ~**most** *a* führend ● *adv* **first and** ~**most** zuallererst. ~**name** *n* Vorname *m*. ~**runner** *n* Vorläufer *m*

fore'see *vt* (*pt* **-saw**, *pp* **-seen**) voraussehen, vorhersehen. ~**able** /-əbl/ *a* **in the** ~**able future** in absehbarer Zeit

'foresight *n* Weitblick *m*

forest /'fɒrɪst/ *n* Wald *m*. ~**er** *n* Förster *m*

forestry /'fɒrɪstrɪ/ *n* Forstwirtschaft *f*

'foretaste *n* Vorgeschmack *m*

forever /fə'revə(r)/ *adv* für immer

fore'warn *vt* vorher warnen

foreword /'fɔ:wɜ:d/ *n* Vorwort *nt*

forfeit /'fɔ:fɪt/ *n* (*in game*) Pfand *nt* ● *vt* verwirken

forgave /fə'geɪv/ *see* **forgive**

forge /fɔ:dʒ/ *n* Schmiede *f* ● *vt* schmieden; (*counterfeit*) fälschen. ~**r** *n* Fälscher *m*. ~**ry** *n* Fälschung *f*

forget /fə'get/ *vt/i* (*pt* **-got**, *pp* **-gotten**) vergessen; verlernen <*language, skill*>. ~**ful** *a* vergesslich. ~**fulness** *n* Vergesslichkeit *f*. ~**-me-not** *n* Vergissmeinnicht *nt*

forgive /fə'gɪv/ *vt* (*pt* **-gave**, *pp* **-given**) ~ **s.o. for sth** jdm etw vergeben *od* verzeihen

forgot(ten) /fə'gɒt(n)/ *see* **forget**

fork /fɔ:k/ *n* Gabel *f*; (*in road*) Gabelung *f* ● *vi* <*road:*> sich gabeln; ~ **right** rechts abzweigen

fork-lift 'truck *n* Gabelstapler *m*

forlorn /fə'lɔ:n/ *a* verlassen; <*hope*> schwach

form /fɔ:m/ *n* Form *f*; (*document*) Formular *nt*; (*bench*) Bank *f*; (*Sch*) Klasse *f* ● *vt* formen (**into** zu); (*create*) bilden ● *vi* sich bilden; <*idea:*> Gestalt annehmen

formal /'fɔ:ml/ *a*, **-ly** *adv* formell, förmlich. ~**ity** /-'mælətɪ/ *n* Förmlichkeit *f*; (*requirement*) Formalität *f*

format /'fɔ:mæt/ *n* Format *nt* ● *vt* formatieren

formation /fɔ:'meɪʃn/ *n* Formation *f*

former /'fɔmə(r)/ *a* ehemalig; **the** ~ der/die/das Erstere. ~**ly** *adv* früher

formidable /'fɔmɪdəbl/ *a* gewaltig

formula /'fɔ:mjʊlə/ *n* (*pl* **-ae** /-li:/ *or* **-s**) Formel *f*

formulate /'fɔ:mjʊleɪt/ *vt* formulieren

forsake /fə'seɪk/ *vt* (*pt* **-sook** /-sʊk/, *pp* **-saken**) verlassen

fort /fɔ:t/ *n* (*Mil*) Fort *nt*

forth /fɔ:θ/ *adv* **back and** ~ hin und her; **and so** ~ und so weiter

forth: ~**'coming** *a* bevorstehend; (*[!] communicative*) mitteilsam. ~**right** *a* direkt

fortieth /'fɔ:tɪɪθ/ *a* vierzigste(r,s)

fortification /fɔ:tɪfɪ'keɪʃn/ *n* Befestigung *f*

fortify /'fɔ:tɪfaɪ/ *vt* (*pt/pp* **-ied**) befestigen; (*fig*) stärken

fortnight /'fɔ:t-/ *n* vierzehn Tage *pl*. ~**ly** *a* vierzehntäglich ● *adv* alle vierzehn Tage

fortress /'fɔ:trɪs/ *n* Festung *f*

fortunate /'fɔ:tʃʊnət/ *a* glücklich; **be** ~ Glück haben. ~**ly** *adv* glüklicherweise

fortune /'fɔ:tʃu:n/ *n* Glück *nt*; (*money*) Vermögen *nt*. ~**-teller** *n* Wahrsagerin *f*

forty /'fɔ:tɪ/ *a* vierzig

forward /'fɔ:wəd/ *adv* vorwärts; (*to the front*) nach vorn ● *a*

Vorwärts-; (*presumptuous*) anmaßend ● *n* (*Sport*) Stürmer *m* ● *vt* nachsenden <*letter*>. **~s** *adv* vorwärts

fossil /ˈfɒsl/ *n* Fossil *nt*

foster /ˈfɒstə(r)/ *vt* fördern; in Pflege nehmen <*child*>. **~-child** *n* Pflegekind *nt*. **~-mother** *n* Pflegemutter *f*

fought /fɔːt/ *see* **fight**

foul /faʊl/ *a* (**-er, -est**) widerlich; <*language*> unflätig; **~ play** (*Jur*) Mord *m* ● *n* (*Sport*) Foul *nt* ● *vt* verschmutzen; (*obstruct*) blockieren; (*Sport*) foulen

found¹ /faʊnd/ *see* **find**

found² *vt* gründen

foundation /faʊnˈdeɪʃn/ *n* (*basis*) Gundlage *f*; (*charitable*) Stiftung *f*; **~s** *pl* Fundament *nt*

founder /ˈfaʊndə(r)/ *n* Gründer(in) *m(f)*

foundry /ˈfaʊndrɪ/ *n* Gießerei *f*

fountain /ˈfaʊntɪn/ *n* Brunnen *m*

four /fɔː(r)/ *a* vier ● *n* Vier *f*

four: ~ˈteen *a* vierzehn ● *n* Vierzehn *f*. **~ˈteenth** *a* vierzehnte(r,s)

fourth /fɔːθ/ *a* vierte(r,s)

fowl /faʊl/ *n* Geflügel *nt*

fox /fɒks/ *n* Fuchs *m* ● *vt* (*puzzle*) verblüffen

foyer /ˈfɔɪeɪ/ *n* Foyer *nt*; (*in hotel*) Empfangshalle *f*

fraction /ˈfrækʃn/ *n* Bruchteil *m*; (*Math*) Bruch *m*

fracture /ˈfræktʃə(r)/ *n* Bruch *m* ● *vt/i* brechen

fragile /ˈfrædʒaɪl/ *a* zerbrechlich

fragment /ˈfrægmənt/ *n* Bruchstück *nt*, Fragment *nt*

fragran|ce /ˈfreɪgrəns/ *n* Duft *m*. **~t** *a* duftend

frail /freɪl/ *a* (**-er, -est**) gebrechlich

frame /freɪm/ *n* Rahmen *m*; (*of spectacles*) Gestell *nt*; (*Anat*) Körperbau *m* ● *vt* einrahmen; (*fig*) formulieren; ☒ ein Verbrechen anhängen (+ *dat*). **~work** *n* Gerüst *nt*; (*fig*) Gerippe *nt*

franc /fræŋk/ *n* (*French, Belgian*) Franc *m*; (*Swiss*) Franken *m*

France /frɑːns/ *n* Frankreich *nt*

franchise /ˈfræntʃaɪz/ *n* (*Pol*) Wahlrecht *nt*; (*Comm*) Franchise *nt*

frank /fræŋk/ *a*, **-ly** *adv* offen

frankfurter /ˈfræŋkfɜːtə(r)/ *n* Frankfurter *f*

frantic /ˈfræntɪk/ *a*, **-ally** *adv* verzweifelt; außer sich (*dat*) (**with** vor)

fraternal /frəˈtɜːnl/ *a* brüderlich

fraud /frɔːd/ *n* Betrug *m*; (*person*) Betrüger(in) *m(f)*

fray /freɪ/ *vi* ausfransen

freak /friːk/ *n* Missbildung *f*; (*person*) Missgeburt *f* ● *a* anormal

freckle /ˈfrekl/ *n* Sommersprosse *f*

free /friː/ *a* (**freer, freest**) frei; <*ticket, copy, time*> Frei-; (*lavish*) freigebig; **~ [of charge]** kostenlos; **set ~** freilassen; (*rescue*) befreien ● *vt* (*pt/pp* **freed**) freilassen; (*rescue*) befreien; (*disentangle*) freibekommen

free: ~dom *n* Freiheit *f*. **~hold** *n* [freier] Grundbesitz *m*. **~lance** *a* & *adv* freiberuflich. **~ly** *adv* frei; (*voluntarily*) freiwillig; (*generously*) großzügig. **F~mason** *n* Freimaurer *m*. **~-range** *a* **~-range eggs** Landeier *pl*. **~ ˈsample** *n* Gratisprobe *f*. **~style** *n* Freistil *m*. **~way** *n* (*Amer*) Autobahn *f*

freez|e /friːz/ *vt* (*pt* **froze**, *pp* **frozen**) einfrieren; stoppen <*wages*> ● *vi* **it's ~ing** es friert. **~er** *n* Gefriertruhe *f*; (*upright*) Gefrierschrank *m*. **~ing** *a* eiskalt ● *n* **below ~ing** unter Null

freight /freɪt/ *n* Fracht *f*. **~er** *n* Frachter *m*. **~ train** *n* Güterzug *m*

French /frentʃ/ *a* französisch ● *n* (*Lang*) Französisch *nt*; **the ~** *pl* die Franzosen

French: ~ 'beans *npl* grüne Bohnen *pl*. **~ 'bread** *n* Stangenbrot *nt*. **~' fries** *npl* Pommes frites *pl*. **~man** *n* Franzose *m*. **~ 'window** *n* Terrassentür *f*. **~woman** *n* Französin *f*

frenzy /'frenzɪ/ *n* Raserei *f*

frequency /'fri:kwənsɪ/ *n* Häufigkeit *f*; (*Phys*) Frequenz *f*

frequent¹ /'fri:kwənt/ *a*, **-ly** *adv* häufig

frequent² /frɪ'kwent/ *vt* regelmäßig besuchen

fresh /freʃ/ *a* (**-er, -est**), **-ly** *adv* frisch; (*new*) neu; (*cheeky*) frech

freshness /'freʃnɪs/ *n* Frische *f*

'freshwater *a* Süßwasser-

fret /fret/ *vi* (*pt/pp* **fretted**) sich grämen. **~ful** *a* weinerlich

'fretsaw *n* Laubsäge *f*

friction /'frɪkʃn/ *n* Reibung *f*; (*fig*) Reibereien *pl*

Friday /'fraɪdeɪ/ *n* Freitag *m*

fridge /frɪdʒ/ *n* Kühlschrank *m*

fried /fraɪd/ *see* **fry²** ● *a* gebraten; **~ egg** Spiegelei *nt*

friend /frend/ *n* Freund(in) *m(f)*. **~liness** *n* Freundlichkeit *f*. **~ly** *a* (**-ier, -iest**) freundlich; **~ly with** befreundet mit. **~ship** *n* Freundschaft *f*

fright /fraɪt/ *n* Schreck *m*

frighten /'fraɪtn/ *vt* Angst machen (+ *dat*); (*startle*) erschrecken; **be ~ed** Angst haben (**of** vor + *dat*). **~ing** *a* Angst erregend

frightful /'fraɪtfl/ *a*, **-ly** *adv* schrecklich

frigid /'frɪdʒɪd/ *a* frostig; (*Psych*) frigide. **~ity** /-'dʒɪdətɪ/ *n* Frostigkeit *f*; Frigidität *f*

frill /frɪl/ *n* Rüsche *f*; (*paper*) Manschette *f*. **~y** *a* rüschenbesetzt

fringe /frɪndʒ/ *n* Fransen *pl*; (*of hair*) Pony *m*; (*fig: edge*) Rand *m*

frisk /frɪsk/ *vi* herumspringen ● *vt* (*search*) durchsuchen

frisky /'frɪskɪ/ *a* (**-ier, -iest**) lebhaft

fritter /'frɪtə(r)/ *vt* **~ [away]** verplempern [!]

frivol|ity /frɪ'vɒlətɪ/ *n* Frivolität *f*. **~ous** /'frɪvələs/ *a*, **-ly** *adv* frivol, leichtfertig

fro /frəʊ/ *see* **to**

frock /frɒk/ *n* Kleid *nt*

frog /frɒg/ *n* Frosch *m*. **~man** *n* Froschmann *m*

frolic /'frɒlɪk/ *vi* (*pt/pp* **frolicked**) herumtollen

from /frɒm/ *prep* von (+ *dat*); (*out of*) aus (+ *dat*); (*according to*) nach (+ *dat*); **~ Monday** ab Montag; **~ that day** seit dem Tag

front /frʌnt/ *n* Vorderseite *f*; (*fig*) Fassade *f*; (*of garment*) Vorderteil *nt*; (*sea~*) Strandpromenade *f*; (*Mil, Pol, Meteorol*) Front *f*; **in ~ of** vor; **in** or **at the ~** vorne; **to the ~** nach vorne ● *a* vordere(r,s); *<page, row>* erste(r,s); *<tooth, wheel>* Vorder-

front: ~ 'door *n* Haustür *f*. **~ 'garden** *n* Vorgarten *m*

frontier /'frʌntɪə(r)/ *n* Grenze *f*

frost /frɒst/ *n* Frost *m*; (*hoar-~*) Raureif *m*; **ten degrees of ~** zehn Grad Kälte. **~bite** *n* Erfrierung *f*. **~bitten** *a* erfroren

frost|ed /'frɒstɪd/ *a* **~ed glass** Mattglas *nt*. **~ing** *n* (*Amer Culin*) Zuckerguss *m*. **~y** *a*, **-ily** *adv* frostig

froth /frɒθ/ *n* Schaum *m* ● *vi* schäumen. **~y** *a* schaumig

frown /fraʊn/ *n* Stirnrunzeln *nt* ● *vi* die Stirn runzeln
froze /frəʊz/ *see* **freeze**
frozen /'frəʊzn/ *see* **freeze** ● *a* gefroren; (*Culin*) tiefgekühlt; **I'm ~** [!] mir ist eiskalt. **~ food** *n* Tiefkühlkost *f*
frugal /'fru:gl/ *a*, **-ly** *adv* sparsam; <*meal*> frugal
fruit /fru:t/ *n* Frucht *f*; (*collectively*) Obst *nt*. **~ cake** *n* englischer [Tee]kuchen *m*
fruitful *a* fruchtbar
fruit: ~ juice *n* Obstsaft *m*. **~less** *a*, **-ly** *adv* fruchtlos. **~ 'salad** *n* Obstsalat *m*
fruity /'fru:tɪ/ *a* fruchtig
frustrat|e /frʌ'streɪt/ *vt* vereiteln; (*Psych*) frustrieren. **~ion** /-eɪʃn/ *n* Frustration *f*
fry /fraɪ/ *vt/i* (*pt/pp* **fried**) [in der Pfanne] braten. **~ing-pan** *n* Bratpfanne *f*
fuel /'fju:əl/ *n* Brennstoff *m*; (*for car*) Kraftstoff *m*; (*for aircraft*) Treibstoff *m*
fugitive /'fju:dʒətɪv/ *n* Flüchtling *m*
fulfil /fʊl'fɪl/ *vt* (*pt/pp* **-filled**) erfüllen. **~ment** *n* Erfüllung *f*
full /fʊl/ *a & adv* (**-er, -est**) voll; (*detailed*) ausführlich; <*skirt*> weit; **~ of** voll von (+ *dat*), voller (+ *gen*); **at ~ speed** in voller Fahrt ● *n* **in ~** vollständig
full: ~ 'moon *n* Vollmond *m*. **~-scale** *a* <*model*> in Originalgröße; <*rescue, alert*> großangelegt. **~ 'stop** *n* Punkt *m*. **~-time** *a* ganztägig ● *adv* ganztags
fully /'fʊlɪ/ *adv* völlig; (*in detail*) ausführlich
fumble /'fʌmbl/ *vi* herumfummeln (**with** an + *dat*)
fume /fju:m/ *vi* vor Wut schäumen
fumes /fju:mz/ *npl* Dämpfe *pl*; (*from car*) Abgase *pl*
fun /fʌn/ *n* Spaß *m*; **for ~** aus *od* zum Spaß; **make ~ of** sich lustig machen über (+ *acc*); **have ~!** viel Spaß!
function /'fʌŋkʃn/ *n* Funktion *f*; (*event*) Veranstaltung *f* ● *vi* funktionieren; (*serve*) dienen (**as** als). **~al** *a* zweckmäßig
fund /fʌnd/ *n* Fonds *m*; (*fig*) Vorrat *m*; **~s** *pl* Geldmittel *pl* ● *vt* finanzieren
fundamental /fʌndə'mentl/ *a* grundlegend; (*essential*) wesentlich
funeral /'fju:nərl/ *n* Beerdigung *f*; (*cremation*) Feuerbestattung *f*
funeral: ~ march *n* Trauermarsch *m*. **~ service** *n* Trauergottesdienst *m*
'funfair *n* Jahrmarkt *m*
fungus /'fʌŋgəs/ *n* (*pl* **-gi** /-gaɪ/) Pilz *m*
funnel /'fʌnl/ *n* Trichter *m*; (*on ship, train*) Schornstein *m*
funnily /'fʌnɪlɪ/ *adv* komisch; **~ enough** komischerweise
funny /'fʌnɪ/ *a* (**-ier, -iest**) komisch
fur /fɜ:(r)/ *n* Fell *nt*; (*for clothing*) Pelz *m*; (*in kettle*) Kesselstein *m*. **~ 'coat** *n* Pelzmantel *m*
furious /'fjʊərɪəs/ *a*, **-ly** *adv* wütend (**with auf** + *acc*)
furnace /'fɜ:nɪs/ *n* (*Techn*) Ofen *m*
furnish /'fɜ:nɪʃ/ *vt* einrichten; (*supply*) liefern. **~ed** *a* **~ed room** möbliertes Zimmer *nt*. **~ings** *npl* Einrichtungsgegenstände *pl*
furniture /'fɜ:nɪtʃə(r)/ *n* Möbel *pl*
further /'fɜ:ðə(r)/ *a* weitere(r,s); **at the ~ end** am anderen Ende; **until ~ notice**bis auf weiteres ● *adv* weiter; **~ off** weiter entfernt ● *vt*fördern
furthest /'fɜ:ðɪst/ *a* am weitesten entfernt ● *adv* am weitesten
fury /'fjʊərɪ/ *n* Wut *f*

fuse[1] /fju:z/ *n* (*of bomb*) Zünder *m*; (*cord*) Zündschnur *f*

fuse[2] *n* (*Electr*) Sicherung *f* ● *vt/i* verschmelzen; **the lights have ~d** die Sicherung [für das Licht] ist durchgebrannt. **~-box***n* Sicherungskasten *m*

fuselage /'fju:zəlɑ:ʒ/ *n* (*Aviat*) Rumpf *m*

fuss /fʌs/ *n* Getue *nt*; **make a ~ of** verwöhnen; (*caress*) liebkosen ● *vi* Umstände machen

fussy /'fʌsɪ/ *a* (**-ier, -iest**) wählerisch; (*particular*) penibel

futil|e /'fju:taɪl/ *a* zwecklos. **~ity** /-'tɪlətɪ/ *n* Zwecklosigkeit *f*

future /'fju:tʃə(r)/ *a* zukünftig ● *n* Zukunft *f*; (*Gram*) [erstes] Futur *nt*

futuristic /fju:tʃə'rɪstɪk/ *a* futuristisch

fuzzy /'fʌzɪ/ *a* (**-ier, -iest**) <*hair*> kraus; (*blurred*) verschwommen

Gg

gabble /'gæbl/ *vi* schnell reden

gable /'geɪbl/ *n* Giebel *m*

gadget /'gædʒɪt/ *n* [kleines] Gerät *nt*

Gaelic /'geɪlɪk/ *n* Gälisch *nt*

gag /gæg/ *n* Knebel *m*; (*joke*) Witz *m*; (*Theat*) Gag *m* ● *vt* (*pt/pp* **gagged**) knebeln

gaiety /'geɪətɪ/ *n* Fröhlichkeit *f*

gaily /'geɪlɪ/ *adv* fröhlich

gain /geɪn/ *n* Gewinn *m*; (*increase*) Zunahme *f* ● *vt* gewinnen; (*obtain*) erlangen; **~ weight** zunehmen ● *vi* <*clock:*> vorgehen

gait /geɪt/ *n* Gang *m*

gala /'gɑ:lə/ *n* Fest *nt* ● *attrib* Gala-

galaxy /'gæləksɪ/ *n* Galaxie *f*; **the G~** die Milchstraße

gale /geɪl/ *n* Sturm *m*

gallant /'gælənt/ *a*, **-ly** *adv* tapfer; (*chivalrous*) galant. **~ry** *n* Tapferkeit *f*

'gall-bladder *n* Gallenblase *f*

gallery /'gælərɪ/ *n* Galerie *f*

galley /'gælɪ/ *n* (*ship's kitchen*) Kombüse *f*; **~ [proof]** [Druck]fahne *f*

gallon /'gælən/ *n* Gallone *f* (= *4,5 l*; *Amer = 3,785 l*)

gallop /'gæləp/ *n* Galopp *m* ● *vi* galoppieren

gallows /'gæləʊz/ *n* Galgen *m*

galore /gə'lɔ:(r)/ *adv* in Hülle und Fülle

gamble /'gæmbl/ *n* (*risk*) Risiko *nt* ● *vi* [um Geld] spielen; **~ on** (*rely*) sich verlassen auf (+ *acc*). **~r** *n* Spieler(in) *m(f)*

game /geɪm/ *n* Spiel *nt*; (*animals, birds*) Wild *nt*; **~s** (*Sch*) Sport *m* ● *a* (*brave*) tapfer; (*willing*) bereit (**for** zu). **~keeper** *n* Wildhüter *m*

gammon /'gæmən/ *n* [geräucherter] Schinken *m*

gang /gæŋ/ *n* Bande *f*; (*of workmen*) Kolonne *f*

gangling /'gæŋglɪŋ/ *a* schlaksig

gangrene /'gæŋgri:n/ *n* Wundbrand *m*

gangster /'gæŋstə(r)/ *n* Gangster *m*

gangway /'gæŋweɪ/ *n* Gang *m*; (*Naut, Aviat*) Gangway *f*

gaol /dʒeɪl/ *n* Gefängnis *nt* ● *vt* ins Gefängnis sperren. **~er** *n* Gefängniswärter *m*

gap /gæp/ *n* Lücke *f*; (*interval*) Pause *f*; (*difference*) Unterschied *m*

gap|e /geɪp/ *vi* gaffen; **~e at** anstarren. **~ing** *a* klaffend

garage /ˈgærɑːʒ/ *n* Garage *f*; (*for repairs*) Werkstatt *f*; (*for petrol*) Tankstelle *f*

garbage /ˈgɑːbɪdʒ/ *n* Müll *m*. **~ can** *n* (*Amer*) Mülleimer *m*

garbled /ˈgɑːbld/ *a* verworren

garden /ˈgɑːdn/ *n* Garten *m*; **[public] ~s** *pl* [öffentliche] Anlagen *pl* ● *vi* im Garten arbeiten. **~er** *n* Gärtner(in) *m(f)*. **~ing** *n* Gartenarbeit *f*

gargle /ˈgɑːgl/ *n* (*liquid*) Gurgelwasser *nt* ● *vi* gurgeln

garish /ˈgeərɪʃ/ *a* grell

garland /ˈgɑːlənd/ *n* Girlande *f*

garlic /ˈgɑːlɪk/ *n* Knoblauch *m*

garment /ˈgɑːmənt/ *n* Kleidungsstück *nt*

garnet /ˈgɑːnɪt/ *n* Granat *m*

garnish /ˈgɑːnɪʃ/ *n* Garnierung *f* ● *vt* garnieren

garrison /ˈgærɪsn/ *n* Garnison *f*

garrulous /ˈgærʊləs/ *a* geschwätzig

garter /ˈgɑːtə(r)/ *n* Strumpfband *nt*; (*Amer*: *suspender*) Strumpfhalter *m*

gas /gæs/ *n* Gas *nt*; (*Amer* [!]: *petrol*) Benzin *nt* ● *v* (*pt/pp* **gassed**) ● *vt* vergasen ● *vi* [!] schwatzen. **~ cooker** *n* Gasherd *m*. **~ 'fire** *n* Gasofen *m*

gash /gæʃ/ *n* Schnitt *m*; (*wound*) klaffende Wunde *f*

gasket /ˈgæskɪt/ *n* (*Techn*) Dichtung *f*

gas: ~ mask *n* Gasmaske *f*. **~-meter** *n* Gaszähler *m*

gasoline /ˈgæsəliːn/ *n* (*Amer*) Benzin *nt*

gasp /gɑːsp/ *vi* keuchen; (*in surprise*) hörbar die Luft einziehen

'gas station *n* (*Amer*) Tankstelle *f*

gastric /ˈgæstrɪk/ *a* Magen-

gastronomy /gæˈstrɒnəmɪ/ *n* Gastronomie *f*

gate /geɪt/ *n* Tor *nt*; (*to field*) Gatter *nt*; (*barrier*) Schranke *f*; (*at airport*) Flugsteig *m*

gate: ~crasher *n* ungeladener Gast *m*. **~way** *n* Tor *nt*

gather /ˈgæðə(r)/ *vt* sammeln; (*pick*) pflücken; (*conclude*) folgern (**from** aus) ● *vi* sich versammeln; <*storm*:> sich zusammenziehen. **~ing** *n* **family ~ing** Familientreffen *nt*

gaudy /ˈgɔːdɪ/ *a* (**-ier, -iest**) knallig

gauge /geɪdʒ/ *n* Stärke *f*; (*Rail*) Spurweite *f*; (*device*) Messinstrument *nt*

gaunt /gɔːnt/ *a* hager

gauze /gɔːz/ *n* Gaze *f*

gave /geɪv/ *see* **give**

gawky /ˈgɔːkɪ/ *a* (**-ier, -iest**) schlaksig

gay /geɪ/ *a* (**-er, -est**) fröhlich; [!] homosexuell, [!] schwul

gaze /geɪz/ *n* [langer] Blick *m* ● *vi* sehen; **~ at** ansehen

GB *abbr of* **Great Britain**

gear /gɪə(r)/ *n* Ausrüstung *f*; (*Techn*) Getriebe *nt*; (*Auto*) Gang *m*; **change ~** schalten

gear: ~box *n* (*Auto*) Getriebe *nt*. **~-lever** *n*, (*Amer*) **~-shift** *n* Schalthebel *m*

geese /giːs/ *see* **goose**

gel /dʒel/ *n* Gel *nt*

gelatine /ˈdʒelətɪn/ *n* Gelatine *f*

gem /dʒem/ *n* Juwel *nt*

gender /ˈdʒendə(r)/ *n* (*Gram*) Geschlecht *nt*

gene /dʒiːn/ *n* Gen *nt*

genealogy /dʒiːnɪˈælədʒɪ/ *n* Genealogie *f*

general /ˈdʒenrəl/ *a* allgemein ● *n* General *m*; **in ~** im

Allgemeinen. ~ **e'lection** *n* allgemeine Wahlen *pl*

generaliz|ation /dʒenrəlaɪ'zeɪʃn/ *n* Verallgemeinerung *f*. **~e** /'dʒenrəlaɪz/ *vi* verallgemeinern

generally /'dʒenrəlɪ/ *adv* im Allgemeinen

general prac'titioner *n* praktischer Arzt *m*

generate /'dʒenəreɪt/ *vt* erzeugen

generation /dʒenə'reɪʃn/ *n* Generation *f*

generator /'dʒenəreɪtə(r)/ *n* Generator *m*

generosity /dʒenə'rɒsɪtɪ/ *n* Großzügigkeit *f*

generous /'dʒenərəs/ *a*, **-ly** *adv* großzügig

genetic /dʒə'netɪk/ *a*, **-ally** *adv* genetisch; **~ally modified** gentechnisch verändert; genmanipuliert. ~ **engineering** *n* Gentechnologie *f*

Geneva /dʒɪ'ni:və/ *n* Genf *nt*

genial /'dʒi:nɪəl/ *a*, **-ly** *adv* freundlich

genitals /'dʒenɪtlz/ *pl* [äußere] Geschlechtsteile *pl*

genitive /'dʒenɪtɪv/ *a* & *n* ~ **[case]** Genitiv *m*

genius /'dʒi:nɪəs/ *n* (*pl* **-uses**) Genie *nt*; (*quality*) Genialität *f*

genome /'dʒi:nəʊm/ *n* Genom *nt*

genre /'ʒɑ̃rə/ *n* Gattung *f*, Genre *nt*

gent /dʒent/ *n* [!] Herr *m*; **the ~s** *sg* die Herrentoilette *f*

genteel /dʒen'ti:l/ *a* vornehm

gentle /'dʒentl/ *a* (**-r, -st**) sanft

gentleman /'dʒentlmən/ *n* Herr *m*; (*well-mannered*) Gentleman *m*

gent|leness /'dʒentlnɪs/ *n* Sanftheit *f*. **~ly** *adv* sanft

genuine /'dʒenjʊɪn/ *a* echt; (*sincere*) aufrichtig. **~ly** *adv* (*honestly*) ehrlich

geograph|ical /dʒɪə'græfɪkl/ *a*, **-ly** *adv* geographisch. **~y** /dʒɪ'ɒgrəfɪ/ *n* Geographie *f*, Erdkunde *f*

geological /dʒɪə'lɒdʒɪkl/ *a*, **-ly** *adv* geologisch

geolog|ist /dʒɪ'ɒlədʒɪst/ *n* Geologe *m*/-gin *f*. **~y** *n* Geologie *f*

geometr|ic(al) /dʒɪə'metrɪk(l)/ *a* geometrisch. **~y** /dʒɪ'ɒmətrɪ/ *n* Geometrie *f*

geranium /dʒə'reɪnɪəm/ *n* Geranie *f*

geriatric /dʒerɪ'ætrɪk/ *a* geriatrisch ● *n* geriatrischer Patient *m*

germ /dʒɜ:m/ *n* Keim *m*; **~s** *pl* [!] Bazillen *pl*

German /'dʒɜ:mən/ *a* deutsch ● *n* (*person*) Deutsche(r) *m/f*; (*Lang*) Deutsch *nt*; **in ~** auf Deutsch; **into ~** ins Deutsche

Germanic /dʒə'mænɪk/ *a* germanisch

Germany /'dʒɜ:mənɪ/ *n* Deutschland *nt*

germinate /'dʒɜ:mɪneɪt/ *vi* keimen

gesticulate /dʒe'stɪkjʊleɪt/ *vi* gestikulieren

gesture /'dʒestʃə(r)/ *n* Geste *f*

get /get/ *v*

pt **got**, *pp* **got** (*Amer also* **gotten**), *pres p* **getting**

● *transitive verb*

····➤ (*obtain, receive*) bekommen, [!] kriegen; (*procure*) besorgen; (*buy*) kaufen; (*fetch*) holen. **get a job/taxi for s.o.** jdm einen Job verschaffen/ein Taxi besorgen. **I must get some bread** ich muss Brot holen. **get permission** die Erlaubnis erhalten. **I couldn't get her on the phone** ich konnte sie nicht telefonisch erreichen

····▸ (*prepare*) machen <*meal*>. **he got the breakfast** er machte das Frühstück

····▸ (*cause*) **get s.o. to do sth** jdn dazu bringen, etw zu tun. **get one's hair cut** sich (*dat*) die Haare schneiden lassen. **get one's hands dirty** sich (*dat*) die Hände schmutzig machen

····▸ **get the bus/train** (*travel by*) den Bus/Zug nehmen; (*be in time for, catch*) den Bus/Zug erreichen

····▸ **have got** ([!] *have*) haben. **I've got a cold** ich habe eine Erkältung

····▸ **have got to do sth** etw tun müssen. **I've got to hurry** ich muss mich beeilen

····▸ ([!] *understand*) kapieren [!]. **I don't get it** ich kapiere nicht

● *intransitive verb*

····▸ (*become*) werden. **get older** älter werden. **the weather got worse** das Wetter wurde schlechter. **get to** kommen zu/nach <*town*>; (*reach*) erreichen. **get dressed** sich anziehen. **get married** heiraten.

● *phrasal verbs* ● **get about** *vi* (*move*) sich bewegen; (*travel*) herumkommen; (*spread*) sich verbreiten. ● **get at** *vt* (*have access*) herankommen an (+ *acc*); ([!] *criticize*) anmachen [!]. (*mean*) **what are you getting at?** worauf willst du hinaus? ● **get away** *vi* (*leave*) wegkommen; (*escape*) entkommen. ● **get back** *vi* zurückkommen; *vt* (*recover*) zurückbekommen; **get one's own back** sich revanchieren. ● **get by** *vi* vorbeikommen; (*manage*) sein Auskommen haben. ● **get down** *vi* heruntersteigen; **get down to** sich [heran]machen an (+ *acc*); *vt* (*depress*) deprimieren. ● **get in** *vi* (*into bus*) einsteigen; *vt* (*fetch*) hereinholen. ● **get off** *vi* (*dismount*) absteigen; (*from bus*) aussteigen; (*leave*) wegkommen; (*Jur*) freigesprochen werden; *vt* (*remove*) abbekommen. ● **get on** *vi* (*mount*) aufsteigen; (*to bus*) einsteigen; (*be on good terms*) gut auskommen (**with** mit + *dat*); (*make progress*) Fortschritte machen; **how are you getting on?** wie geht's? ● **get out** *vi* herauskommen; (*of car*) aussteigen; **get out of** (*avoid doing*) sich drücken um; *vt* (*take out*) herausholen; herausbekommen <*cork, stain*>. ● **get over** *vi* hinübersteigen; *vt* (*fig*) hinwegkommen über (+ *acc*). ● **get round** *vi* herumkommen; **I never get round to it** ich komme nie dazu; *vt* herumkriegen; (*avoid*) umgehen. ● **get through** *vi* durchkommen. ● **get up** *vi* aufstehen

get: ~away *n* Flucht *f*. **~-up** *n* Aufmachung *f*

ghastly /ˈgɑːstlɪ/ *a* (**-ier, -iest**) grässlich; (*pale*) blass

gherkin /ˈgɜːkɪn/ *n* Essiggurke *f*

ghost /gəʊst/ *n* Geist *m*, Gespenst *nt*. **~ly** *a* geisterhaft

ghoulish /ˈguːlɪʃ/ *a* makaber

giant /ˈdʒaɪənt/ *n* Riese *m* ● *a* riesig

gibberish /ˈdʒɪbərɪʃ/ *n* Kauderwelsch *nt*

giblets /ˈdʒɪblɪts/ *npl* Geflügelklein *nt*

giddiness /ˈgɪdɪnɪs/ *n* Schwindel *m*

giddy /ˈgɪdɪ/ *a* (**-ier, -iest**) schwindlig

gift /gɪft/ *n* Geschenk *nt*; (*to charity*) Gabe *f*; (*talent*) Begabung *f*. **~ed** /-ɪd/ *a* begabt

gigantic /dʒaɪˈgæntɪk/ *a* riesig, riesengroß

giggle /'gɪgl/ *n* Kichern *nt* ● *vi* kichern
gild /gɪld/ *vt* vergolden
gilt /gɪlt/ *a* vergoldet ● *n* Vergoldung *f*. **~-edged** *a* (*Comm*) mündelsicher
gimmick /'gɪmɪk/ *n* Trick *m*
gin /dʒɪn/ *n* Gin *m*
ginger /'dʒɪndʒə(r)/ *a* rotblond; <*cat*> rot ● *n* Ingwer *m*. **~bread** *n* Pfefferkuchen *m*
gingerly /'dʒɪndʒəlɪ/ *adv* vorsichtig
gipsy /'dʒɪpsɪ/ *n* = **gypsy**
giraffe /dʒɪ'rɑ:f/ *n* Giraffe *f*
girder /'gɜ:də(r)/ *n* (*Techn*) Träger *m*
girl /gɜ:l/ *n* Mädchen *nt*; (*young woman*) junge Frau *f*. **~friend** *n* Freundin *f*. **~ish** *a*, **-ly** *adv* mädchenhaft
gist /dʒɪst/ *n* **the ~** das Wesentliche
give /gɪv/ *n* Elastizität *f* ● *v* (*pt* **gave**, *pp* **given**) ● *vt* geben/(*as present*) schenken (**to** *dat*); (*donate*) spenden; <*lecture*> halten; <*one's name*> angeben ● *vi* geben; (*yield*) nachgeben. **~ away** *vt* verschenken; (*betray*) verraten; (*distribute*) verteilen. **~ back** *vt* zurückgeben. **~ in** *vt* einreichen ● *vi* (*yield*) nachgeben. **~ off** *vt* abgeben. **~ up** *vt/i* aufgeben; **~ oneself up** sich stellen. **~ way** *vi* nachgeben; (*Auto*) die Vorfahrt beachten
glacier /'glæsɪə(r)/ *n* Gletscher *m*
glad /glæd/ *a* froh (**of** über + *acc*)
gladly /'glædlɪ/ *adv* gern[e]
glamorous /'glæmərəs/ *a* glanzvoll; <*film star*> glamourös
glamour /'glæmə(r)/ *n* [betörender] Glanz *m*
glance /glɑ:ns/ *n* [flüchtiger] Blick *m* ● *vi* **~ at** einen Blick werfen auf (+ *acc*). **~ up** *vi* aufblicken
gland /glænd/ *n* Drüse *f*
glare /gleə(r)/ *n* grelles Licht *nt*; (*look*) ärgerlicher Blick *m* ● *vi* **~ at** böse ansehen
glaring /'gleərɪŋ/ *a* grell; <*mistake*> krass
glass /glɑ:s/ *n* Glas *nt*; (*mirror*) Spiegel *m*; **~es** *pl* (*spectacles*) Brille *f*. **~y** *a* glasig
glaze /gleɪz/ *n* Glasur *f*
gleam /gli:m/ *n* Schein *m* ● *vi* glänzen
glib /glɪb/ *a*, **-ly** *adv* (*pej*) gewandt
glid|e /glaɪd/ *vi* gleiten; (*through the air*) schweben. **~er** *n* Segelflugzeug *nt*. **~ing** *n* Segelfliegen *nt*
glimmer /'glɪmə(r)/ *n* Glimmen *nt* ● *vi* glimmen
glimpse /glɪmps/ *vt* flüchtig sehen
glint /glɪnt/ *n* Blitzen *nt* ● *vi* blitzen
glisten /'glɪsn/ *vi* glitzern
glitter /'glɪtə(r)/ *vi* glitzern
global /'gləʊbl/ *a*, **-ly** *adv* global
globaliz|e /'gləʊbəlaɪz/ *vt* globalisieren. **~ation** /-'zeɪʃn/ *n* Globalisierung *f*
globe /gləʊb/ *n* Kugel *f*; (*map*) Globus *m*
gloom /glu:m/ *n* Düsterkeit *f*; (*fig*) Pessimismus *m*
gloomy /'glu:mɪ/ *a* (**-ier, -iest**), **-ily** *adv* düster; (*fig*) pessimistisch
glorify /'glɔ:rɪfaɪ/ *vt* (*pt/pp* **-ied**) verherrlichen
glorious /'glɔ:rɪəs/ *a* herrlich; <*deed, hero*> glorreich
glory /'glɔ:rɪ/ *n* Ruhm *m*; (*splendour*) Pracht *f* ● *vi* **~ in** genießen
gloss /glɒs/ *n* Glanz *m* ● *a* Glanz- ● *vi* **~ over** beschönigen

glossary /'glɒsərɪ/ *n* Glossar *nt*
glossy /'glɒsɪ/ *a* (**-ier, -iest**) glänzend
glove /glʌv/ *n* Handschuh *m*
glow /gləʊ/ *n* Glut *f*; (*of candle*) Schein *m* ● *vi* glühen; <*candle:*> scheinen. **~ing** *a* glühend; <*account*> begeistert
glucose /'glu:kəʊs/ *n* Traubenzucker *m*, Glukose *f*
glue /glu:/ *n* Klebstoff *m* ● *vt* (*pres p* **gluing**) kleben (**to** an + *acc*)
glum /glʌm/ *a* (**glummer, glummest**), **-ly** *adv* niedergeschlagen
glut /glʌt/ *n* Überfluss *m* (**of** an + *dat*)
glutton /'glʌtən/ *n* Vielfraß *m*
GM *abbr* (**genetically modified**); **~ crops/food** gentechnisch veränderte Feldfrüchte/ Nahrungsmittel
gnash /næʃ/ *vt* **~ one's teeth** mit den Zähnen knirschen
gnat /næt/ *n* Mücke *f*
gnaw /nɔ:/ *vt/i* nagen (**at** an + *dat*)

go /gəʊ/

3 sg pres tense **goes;** *pt* **went;** *pp* **gone**

● *intransitive verb*
····➤ gehen; (*in vehicle*) fahren. **go by air** fliegen. **where are you going?** wo gehst du hin? **I'm going to France** ich fahre nach Frankreich. **go to the doctor's/dentist's** zum Arzt/Zahnarzt gehen. **go to the theatre/cinema** ins Theater/Kino gehen. **I must go to Paris/to the doctor's** ich muss nach Paris/zum Arzt. **go shopping** einkaufen gehen. **go swimming** schwimmen gehen. **go to see s.o.** jdn besuchen [gehen]
····➤ (*leave*) weggehen; (*on journey*) abfahren. **I must go now** ich muss jetzt gehen. **we're going on Friday** wir fahren am Freitag
····➤ (*work, function*) <*engine, clock*> gehen
····➤ (*become*) werden. **go deaf** taub werden. **go mad** verrückt werden. **he went red** er wurde rot
····➤ (*pass*) <*time*> vergehen
····➤ (*disappear*) weggehen; <*coat, hat, stain*> verschwinden. **my headache/my coat/the stain has gone** mein Kopfweh/mein Mantel/der Fleck ist weg
····➤ (*turn out, progress*) gehen; verlaufen. **everything's going very well** alles geht *od* verläuft sehr gut. **how did the party go?** wie war die Party? **go smoothly/according to plan** reibungslos/planmäßig verlaufen
····➤ (*match*) zusammenpassen. **the two colours don't go [together]** die beiden Farben passen nicht zusammen
····➤ (*cease to function*) kaputtgehen; <*fuse*> durchbrennen. **his memory is going** sein Gedächtnis lässt nach

● *auxiliary verb*
····➤ **be going to** werden + *inf.* **it's going to rain** es wird regnen. **I'm not going to** ich werde es nicht tun

● *noun*
pl **goes**
····➤ (*turn*) **it's your go** du bist jetzt an der Reihe *od* dran
····➤ (*attempt*) Versuch. **have a go at doing sth** versuchen, etw zu tun. **have another go!** versuch's noch mal!
····➤ (*energy, drive*) Energie
····➤ (*in phrases*) **on the go** auf Trab. **make a go of sth** das Beste aus etw machen

● *phrasal verbs*
● **go across** *vi* hinübergehen/ -fahren; *vt* überqueren. ● **go**

after *vt* (*pursue*) jagen. ● **go away** *vi* weggehen/-fahren; (*on holiday or business*) verreisen. ● **go back** *vi* zurückgehen/-fahren. ● **go back on** *vt* nicht [ein]halten <*promise*>. ● **go by** *vi* vorbeigehen/-fahren; <*time*> vergehen. ● **go down** *vi* hinuntergehen/-fahren; <*sun, ship*> untergehen; <*prices*> fallen; <*temperature, swelling*> zurückgehen. ● **go for** *vt* holen; ([!] *attack*) losgehen auf (+ *acc*). ● **go in** *vi* hineingehen/-fahren; ● **go in for** *vt* teilnehmen an (+ *dat*) <*competition*>; (*take up*) sich verlegen auf (+ *acc*). ● **go off** *vi* weggehen/-fahren; <*alarm clock*> klingeln; <*alarm, gun, bomb*> losgehen; <*light*> ausgehen; (*go bad*) schlecht werden; **go off well** gut verlaufen; *vt*: **go off sth** von etw abkommen. ● **go on** *vi* weitergehen/-fahren; <*light*> angehen; (*continue*) weitermachen; (*talking*) fortfahren; (*happen*) vorgehen. ● **go on at** *vt* [!] herumnörgeln an (+ *dat*). ● **go out** *vi* (*from home*) ausgehen; (*leave*) hinausgehen/-fahren; <*fire, light*> ausgehen; **go out to work/for a meal** arbeiten/essen gehen; **go out with s.o.** ([!] *date s.o.*) mit jdm gehen [!]. ● **go over** *vi* hinübergehen/-fahren; *vt* (*rehearse*) durchgehen. ● **go round** *vi* herumgehen/-fahren; (*visit*) vorbeigehen; (*turn*) sich drehen; (*be enough*) reichen. ● **go through** *vi* durchgehen/-fahren; *vt* (*suffer*) durchmachen; (*rehearse*) durchgehen; <*bags*> durchsuchen. ● **go through with** *vt* zu Ende machen. ● **go under** *vi* untergehen/-fahren; (*fail*) scheitern. ● **go up** *vi* hinaufgehen/-fahren; <*lift*> hochfahren; <*prices*> steigen. ● **go without** *vt*: **go without sth** auf etw (*acc*) verzichten; *vi* darauf verzichten

'go-ahead *a* fortschrittlich; (*enterprising*) unternehmend ● *n* (*fig*) grünes Licht *nt*

goal /gəʊl/ *n* Ziel *nt*; (*sport*) Tor *nt*. **~keeper** *n* Torwart *m*. **~-post** *n* Torpfosten *m*

goat /gəʊt/ *n* Ziege *f*

gobble /'gɒbl/ *vt* hinunterschlingen

God, god /gɒd/ *n* Gott *m*

god: ~child *n* Patenkind *nt*. **~-daughter** *n* Patentochter *f*. **~dess** *n* Göttin *f*. **~father** *n* Pate *m*. **~mother** *n* Patin *f*. **~parents** *npl* Paten *pl*. **~send** *n* Segen *m*. **~son** *n* Patensohn *m*

goggles /'gɒglz/ *npl* Schutzbrille *f*

going /'gəʊɪŋ/ *a* <*price, rate*> gängig; <*concern*> gut gehend ● *n* **it is hard ~** es ist schwierig

gold /gəʊld/ *n* Gold *nt* ● *a* golden

golden /'gəʊldn/ *a* golden. **~ 'wedding** *n* goldene Hochzeit *f*

gold: ~fish *n inv* Goldfisch *m*. **~-mine** *n* Goldgrube *f*. **~-plated** *a* vergoldet. **~smith** *n* Goldschmied *m*

golf /gɒlf/ *n* Golf *nt*

golf: ~-club *n* Golfklub *m*; (*implement*) Golfschläger *m*. **~-course** *n* Golfplatz *m*. **~er** *m* Golfspieler(in) *m(f)*

gone /gɒn/ *see* **go**

good /gʊd/ *a* (**better, best**) gut; (*well-behaved*) brav, artig; **~ at** gut in (+ *dat*); **a ~ deal** ziemlich viel; **~ morning/evening** guten Morgen/Abend ● *n* **for ~** für immer; **do ~** Gutes tun; **do s.o. ~** jdm gut tun; **it's no ~** es ist nutzlos; (*hopeless*) da ist nichts zu machen

goodbye /gʊd'baɪ/ *int* auf Wiedersehen; (*Teleph, Radio*) auf Wiederhören

good: G~ 'Friday *n* Karfreitag *m*. **~-'looking** *a* gut aussehend. **~-'natured** *a* gutmütig

goodness /'gʊdnɪs/ *n* Güte *f*; **thank ~!** Gott sei Dank!

goods /gʊdz/ *npl* Waren *pl*. **~ train** *n* Güterzug *m*

good'will *n* Wohlwollen *nt*; (*Comm*) Goodwill *m*

gooey /'gu:ɪ/ *a* [!] klebrig

goose /gu:s/ *n* (*pl* **geese**) Gans *f*

gooseberry /'gʊzbərɪ/ *n* Stachelbeere *f*

goose: /gu:s/ ~-flesh *n*, **~-pimples** *npl* Gänsehaut *f*

gorge /gɔ:dʒ/ *n* (*Geog*) Schlucht *f* ● *vt* **~ oneself** sich vollessen

gorgeous /'gɔ:dʒəs/ *a* prachtvoll; [!] herrlich

gorilla /gə'rɪlə/ *n* Gorilla *m*

gormless /'gɔ:mlɪs/ *a* [!] doof

gorse /gɔ:s/ *n inv* Stechginster *m*

gory /'gɔ:rɪ/ *a* (**-ier, -iest**) blutig; <*story*> blutrünstig

gosh /gɒʃ/ *int* [!] Mensch!

gospel /'gɒspl/ *n* Evangelium *nt*

gossip /'gɒsɪp/ *n* Klatsch *m*; (*person*) Klatschbase *f* ● *vi* klatschen

got /gɒt/ *see* **get; have ~** haben; **have ~ to** müssen; **have ~ to do sth** etw tun müssen

Gothic /'gɒθɪk/ *a* gotisch

gotten /'gɒtn/ *see* **get**

goulash /'gu:læʃ/ *n* Gulasch *nt*

gourmet /'gʊəmeɪ/ *n* Feinschmecker *m*

govern /'gʌvn/ *vt/i* regieren; (*determine*) bestimmen

government /'gʌvnmənt/ *n* Regierung *f*

governor /'gʌvənə(r)/ *n* Gouverneur *m*; (*on board*) Vorstandsmitglied *nt*; (*of prison*) Direktor *m*; ([!] *boss*) Chef *m*

gown /gaʊn/ *n* [elegantes] Kleid *nt*; (*Univ, Jur*) Talar *m*

GP *abbr of* **general practitioner**

grab /græb/ *vt* (*pt/pp* **grabbed**) ergreifen; **~ [hold of]** packen

grace /greɪs/ *n* Anmut *f*; (*before meal*) Tischgebet *nt*; **three days' ~** drei Tage Frist. **~ful** *a*, **-ly** *adv* anmutig

gracious /'greɪʃəs/ *a* gnädig; (*elegant*) vornehm

grade /greɪd/ *n* Stufe *f*; (*Comm*) Güteklasse *f*; (*Sch*) Note *f*; (*Amer, Sch: class*) Klasse *f*; (*Amer*) = **gradient** ● *vt* einstufen; (*Comm*) sortieren. **~ crossing** *n* (*Amer*) Bahnübergang *m*

gradient /'greɪdɪənt/ *n* Steigung *f*; (*downward*) Gefälle *nt*

gradual /'grædʒʊəl/ *a*, **-ly** *adv* allmählich

graduate /'grædʒʊət/ *n* Akademiker(in) *m*(*f*)

graffiti /grə'fi:ti/ *npl* Graffiti *pl*

graft /grɑ:ft/ *n* (*Bot*) Pfropfreis *nt*; (*Med*) Transplantat *nt*; ([!] *hard work*) Plackerei *f*

grain /greɪn/ *n* (*sand, salt, rice*) Korn *nt*; (*cereals*) Getreide *nt*; (*in wood*) Maserung *f*

gram /græm/ *n* Gramm *nt*

grammar /'græmə(r)/ *n* Grammatik *f*. **~ school** *n* ≈ Gymnasium *nt*

grammatical /grə'mætɪkl/ *a*, **-ly** *adv* grammatisch

grand /grænd/ *a* (**-er, -est**) großartig

grandad /'grændæd/ *n* [!] Opa *m*

'grandchild *n* Enkelkind *nt*

'granddaughter *n* Enkelin *f*

grandeur /'grændʒə(r)/ *n* Pracht *f*

'grandfather *n* Großvater *m*. **~ clock** *n* Standuhr *f*

grandiose /'grændɪəʊs/ *a* grandios

grand: ~mother *n* Großmutter *f*. **~parents** *npl* Großeltern *pl*. **~ pi'ano** *n* Flügel *m*. **~son** *n* Enkel *m*. **~stand** *n* Tribüne *f*

granite /ˈgrænɪt/ *n* Granit *m*

granny /ˈgrænɪ/ *n* [!] Oma *f*

grant /grɑːnt/ *n* Subvention *f*; (*Univ*) Studienbeihilfe *f* ● *vt* gewähren; (*admit*) zugeben; **take sth for ~ed** etw als selbstverständlich hinnehmen

grape /greɪp/ *n* [Wein]traube *f*; **bunch of ~s** [ganze] Weintraube *f*

grapefruit /ˈgreɪp-/ *n invar* Grapefruit *f*

graph /grɑːf/ *n* grafische Darstellung *f*

graphic /ˈgræfɪk/ *a*, **-ally** *adv* grafisch; (*vivid*) anschaulich

ˈ**graph paper** *n* Millimeterpapier *nt*

grapple /ˈgræpl/ *vi* ringen

grasp /grɑːsp/ *n* Griff *m* ● *vt* ergreifen; (*understand*) begreifen. **~ing** *a* habgierig

grass /grɑːs/ *n* Gras *nt*; (*lawn*) Rasen *m*. **~hopper** *n* Heuschrecke *f*

grassy /ˈgrɑːsɪ/ *a* grasig

grate¹ /greɪt/ *n* Feuerrost *m*; (*hearth*) Kamin *m*

grate² *vt* (*Culin*) reiben

grateful /ˈgreɪtfl/ *a*, **-ly** *adv* dankbar (**to** *dat*)

grater /ˈgreɪtə(r)/ *n* Reibe *f*

gratify /ˈgrætɪfaɪ/ *vt* (*pt/pp* **-ied**) befriedigen. **~ing** *a* erfreulich

gratis /ˈgrɑːtɪs/ *adv* gratis

gratitude /ˈgrætɪtjuːd/ *n* Dankbarkeit *f*

gratuitous /grəˈtjuːɪtəs/ *a* (*uncalled for*) überflüssig

grave¹ /greɪv/ *a* (**-r, -st**), **-ly** *adv* ernst; **~ly ill** schwer krank

grave² *n* Grab *nt*. **~-digger** *n* Totengräber *m*

gravel /ˈgrævl/ *n* Kies *m*

grave: ~stone *n* Grabstein *m*. **~yard** *n* Friedhof *m*

gravity /ˈgrævətɪ/ *n* Ernst *m*; (*force*) Schwerkraft *f*

gravy /ˈgreɪvɪ/ *n* [Braten]soße *f*

gray /greɪ/ *a* (*Amer*) = **grey**

graze¹ /greɪz/ *vi* <*animal:*> weiden

graze² *n* Schürfwunde *f* ● *vt* <*car*> streifen; <*knee*> aufschürfen

grease /griːs/ *n* Fett *nt*; (*lubricant*) Schmierfett *nt* ● *vt* einfetten; (*lubricate*) schmieren

greasy /ˈgriːsɪ/ *a* (**-ier, -iest**) fettig

great /greɪt/ *a* (**-er, -est**) groß; ([!] *marvellous*) großartig

great: ~-ˈaunt *n* Großtante *f*. **G~ ˈBritain** *n* Großbritannien *nt*. **~-ˈgrandchildren** *npl* Urenkel *pl*. **~-ˈgrandfather** *n* Urgroßvater *m*. **~-ˈgrandmother** *n* Urgroßmutter *f*

great|ly /ˈgreɪtlɪ/ *adv* sehr. **~ness** *n* Größe *f*

great-ˈuncle *n* Großonkel *m*

Greece /griːs/ *n* Griechenland *nt*

greed /griːd/ *n* [Hab]gier *f*

greedy /ˈgriːdɪ/ *a* (**-ier, -iest**), **-ily** *adv* gierig

Greek /griːk/ *a* griechisch ● *n* Grieche *m*/Griechin *f*; (*Lang*) Griechisch *nt*

green /griːn/ *a* (**-er, -est**) grün; (*fig*) unerfahren ● *n* Grün *nt*; (*grass*) Wiese *f*; **~s** *pl* Kohl *m*; **the G~s** *pl* (*Pol*) die Grünen *pl*

greenery /ˈgriːnərɪ/ *n* Grün *nt*

green: ~fly *n* Blattlaus *f*. **~grocer** *n* Obst- und Gemüsehändler *m*. **~house** *n* Gewächshaus *nt*

Greenland /ˈgriːnlənd/ *n* Grönland *nt*

greet /griːt/ *vt* grüßen; (*welcome*) begrüßen. **~ing** *n* Gruß *m*; (*welcome*) Begrüßung *f*

grew /gruː/ *see* **grow**

grey /greɪ/ *a* (**-er, -est**) grau ● *n* Grau *nt* ● *vi* grau werden. **~hound** *n* Windhund *m*

grid /grɪd/ *n* Gitter *nt*

grief /gri:f/ *n* Trauer *f*

grievance /ˈgri:vəns/ *n* Beschwerde *f*

grieve /gri:v/ *vi* trauern (**for** um)

grill /grɪl/ *n* Gitter *nt*; (*Culin*) Grill *m*; **mixed ~** Gemischtes *nt* vom Grill ● *vt*/*i* grillen; (*interrogate*) [streng] verhören

grille /grɪl/ *n* Gitter *nt*

grim /grɪm/ *a* (**grimmer, grimmest**), **-ly** *adv* ernst; <*determination*> verbissen

grimace /grɪˈmeɪs/ *n* Grimasse *f* ● *vi* Grimassen schneiden

grime /graɪm/ *n* Schmutz *m*

grimy /ˈgraɪmɪ/ *a* (**-ier, -iest**) schmutzig

grin /grɪn/ *n* Grinsen *nt* ● *vi* (*pt*/*pp* **grinned**) grinsen

grind /graɪnd/ *n* (Ⓘ *hard work*) Plackerei *f* ● *vt* (*pt*/*pp* **ground**) mahlen; (*smooth, sharpen*) schleifen; (*Amer: mince*) durchdrehen

grip /grɪp/ *n* Griff *m*; (*bag*) Reisetasche *f* ● *vt* (*pt*/*pp* **gripped**) ergreifen; (*hold*) festhalten

gripping /ˈgrɪpɪŋ/ *a* fesselnd

grisly /ˈgrɪzlɪ/ *a* (**-ier, -iest**) grausig

gristle /ˈgrɪsl/ *n* Knorpel *m*

grit /grɪt/ *n* [grober] Sand *m*; (*for roads*) Streugut *nt*; (*courage*) Mut *m* ● *vt* (*pt*/*pp* **gritted**) streuen <*road*>

groan /grəʊn/ *n* Stöhnen *nt* ● *vi* stöhnen

grocer /ˈgrəʊsə(r)/ *n* Lebensmittelhändler *m*; **~'s [shop]** Lebensmittelgeschäft *nt*. **~ies** *npl* Lebensmittel *pl*

groin /grɔɪn/ *n* (*Anat*) Leiste *f*

groom /gru:m/ *n* Bräutigam *m*; (*for horse*) Pferdepfleger(in) *m*(*f*) ● *vt* striegeln <*horse*>

groove /gru:v/ *n* Rille *f*

grope /grəʊp/ *vi* tasten (**for** nach)

gross /grəʊs/ *a* (**-er, -est**) fett; (*coarse*) derb; (*glaring*) grob; (*Comm*) brutto; <*salary, weight*> Brutto-. **~ly** *adv* (*very*) sehr

grotesque /grəʊˈtesk/ *a*, **-ly** *adv* grotesk

ground[1] /graʊnd/ *see* **grind**

ground[2] *n* Boden *m*; (*terrain*) Gelände *nt*; (*reason*) Grund *m*; (*Amer, Electr*) Erde *f*; **~s** *pl* (*park*) Anlagen *pl*; (*of coffee*) Satz *m*

ground: ~ floor *n* Erdgeschoss *nt*. **~ing** *n* Grundlage *f*. **~less** *a* grundlos. **~sheet** *n* Bodenplane *f*. **~work** *n* Vorarbeiten *pl*

group /gru:p/ *n* Gruppe *f* ● *vt* gruppieren ● *vi* sich gruppieren

grouse *vi* Ⓘ meckern

grovel /ˈgrɒvl/ *vi* (*pt*/*pp* **grovelled**) kriechen

grow /grəʊ/ *v* (*pt* **grew**, *pp* **grown**) ● *vi* wachsen; (*become*) werden; (*increase*) zunehmen ● *vt* anbauen. **~ up** *vi* aufwachsen; <*town:*> entstehen

growl /graʊl/ *n* Knurren *nt* ● *vi* knurren

grown /grəʊn/ *see* **grow**. **~-up** *a* erwachsen ● *n* Erwachsene(r) *m*/*f*

growth /grəʊθ/ *n* Wachstum *nt*; (*increase*) Zunahme *f*; (*Med*) Gewächs *nt*

grub /grʌb/ *n* (*larva*) Made *f*; (*fam: food*) Essen *nt*

grubby /ˈgrʌbɪ/ *a* (**-ier, -iest**) schmuddelig

grudg|e /grʌdʒ/ *n* Groll *m* ● *vt* **~e s.o. sth** jdm etw missgönnen. **~ing** *a*, **-ly** *adv* widerwillig

gruelling /ˈgru:əlɪŋ/ *a* strapaziös

gruesome /ˈgruːsəm/ *a* grausig

gruff /grʌf/ *a*, **-ly** *adv* barsch

grumble /ˈgrʌmbl/ *vi* schimpfen (**at** mit)

grumpy /ˈgrʌmpɪ/ *a* (**-ier, -iest**) griesgrämig

grunt /grʌnt/ *n* Grunzen *nt* ● *vi* grunzen

guarantee /gærənˈtiː/ *n* Garantie *f*; (*document*) Garantieschein *m* ● *vt* garantieren; garantieren für *<quality, success>*

guard /gɑːd/ *n* Wache *f*; (*security*) Wächter *m*; (*on train*) ≈ Zugführer *m*; (*Techn*) Schutz *m*; **be on ~** Wache stehen; **on one's ~** auf der Hut ● *vt* bewachen; (*protect*) schützen ● *vi* **~ against** sich hüten vor (+ *dat*). **~-dog** *n* Wachhund *m*

guarded /ˈgɑːdɪd/ *a* vorsichtig

guardian /ˈgɑːdɪən/ *n* Vormund *m*

guess /ges/ *n* Vermutung *f* ● *vt* erraten ● *vi* raten; (*Amer: believe*) glauben. **~work** *n* Vermutung *f*

guest /gest/ *n* Gast *m*. **~-house** *n* Pension *f*

guidance /ˈgaɪdəns/ *n* Führung *f*, Leitung *f*; (*advice*) Beratung *f*

guide /gaɪd/ *n* Führer(in) *m(f)*; (*book*) Führer *m*; **[Girl] G~** Pfadfinderin *f* ● *vt* führen, leiten. **~book** *n* Führer *m*

guided /ˈgaɪdɪd/ *a* **~ tour** Führung *f*

guide: ~-dog *n* Blindenhund *m*. **~lines** *npl* Richtlinien *pl*

guilt /gɪlt/ *n* Schuld *f*. **~ily** *adv* schuldbewusst

guilty /ˈgɪltɪ/ *a* (**-ier, -iest**) *a* schuldig (**of** *gen*); *<look>* schuldbewusst; *<conscience>* schlecht

guinea-pig /ˈgɪnɪ-/ *n* Meerschweinchen *nt*; (*person*) Versuchskaninchen *nt*

guitar /gɪˈtɑː(r)/ *n* Gitarre *f*. **~ist** *n* Gitarrist(in) *m(f)*

gulf /gʌlf/ *n* (*Geog*) Golf *m*; (*fig*) Kluft *f*

gull /gʌl/ *n* Möwe *f*

gullible /ˈgʌlɪbl/ *a* leichtgläubig

gully /ˈgʌlɪ/ *n* Schlucht *f*; (*drain*) Rinne *f*

gulp /gʌlp/ *n* Schluck *m* ● *vi* schlucken ● *vt* **~ down** hinunterschlucken

gum[1] /gʌm/ *n* & **-s** *pl* (*Anat*) Zahnfleisch *nt*

gum[2] *n* Gummi[harz] *nt*; (*glue*) Klebstoff *m*; (*chewing gum*) Kaugummi *m*

gummed /gʌmd/ *see* **gum**[2] ● *a* *<label>* gummiert

gun /gʌn/ *n* Schusswaffe *f*; (*pistol*) Pistole *f*; (*rifle*) Gewehr *nt*; (*cannon*) Geschütz *nt*

gun: ~fire *n* Geschützfeuer *nt*. **~man** bewaffneter Bandit *m*

gunner /ˈgʌnə(r)/ *n* Artillerist *m*

gunpowder *n* Schießpulver *nt*

gurgle /ˈgɜːgl/ *vi* gluckern; (*of baby*) glucksen

gush /gʌʃ/ *vi* strömen; (*enthuse*) schwärmen (**over** von)

gust /gʌst/ *n* (*of wind*) Windstoß *m*; (*Naut*) Bö *f*

gusto /ˈgʌstəʊ/ *n* **with ~** mit Schwung

gusty /ˈgʌstɪ/ *a* böig

gut /gʌt/ *n* Darm *m*; **~s** *pl* Eingeweide *pl*; ([!] *courage*) Schneid *m* ● *vt* (*pt/pp* **gutted**) (*Culin*) ausnehmen; **~ted by fire** ausgebrannt

gutter /ˈgʌtə(r)/ *n* Rinnstein *m*; (*fig*) Gosse *f*; (*on roof*) Dachrinne *f*

guy /gaɪ/ *n* [!] Kerl *m*

guzzle /ˈgʌzl/ *vt/i* schlingen; (*drink*) schlürfen

gym /dʒɪm/ *n* [!] Turnhalle *f*; (*gymnastics*) Turnen *nt*

gymnasium /dʒɪm'neɪzɪəm/ *n* Turnhalle *f*

gymnast /'dʒɪmnæst/ *n* Turner(in) *m(f)*. **~ics** /-'næstɪks/ *n* Turnen *nt*

gym shoes *pl* Turnschuhe *pl*

gynaecolog|ist /gaɪnɪ'kɒlədʒɪst/ *n* Frauenarzt *m* /-ärztin *f*. **~y** *n* Gynäkologie *f*

gypsy /'dʒɪpsɪ/ *n* Zigeuner(in) *m(f)*

Hh

habit /'hæbɪt/ *n* Gewohnheit *f*; (*Relig: costume*) Ordenstracht *f*; **be in the ~** die Angewohnheit haben (**of** zu)

habitat /'hæbɪtæt/ *n* Habitat *nt*

habitation /hæbɪ'teɪʃn/ *n* **unfit for human ~** für Wohnzwecke ungeeignet

habitual /hə'bɪtjʊəl/ *a* gewohnt; (*inveterate*) gewohnheitsmäßig. **~ly** *adv* gewohnheitsmäßig; (*constantly*) ständig

hack¹ /hæk/ *n* (*writer*) Schreiberling *m*; (*hired horse*) Mietpferd *nt*

hack² *vt* hacken; **~ to pieces** zerhacken

hackneyed /'hæknɪd/ *a* abgedroschen

'hacksaw *n* Metallsäge *f*

had /hæd/ *see* **have**

haddock /'hædək/ *n inv* Schellfisch *m*

haggard /'hægəd/ *a* abgehärmt

haggle /'hægl/ *vi* feilschen (**over** um)

hail¹ /heɪl/ *vt* begrüßen; herbeirufen <*taxi*> ● *vi* **~ from** kommen aus

hail² *n* Hagel *m* ● *vi* hageln. **~stone** *n* Hagelkorn *nt*

hair /heə(r)/ *n* Haar *nt*; **wash one's ~** sich (*dat*) die Haare waschen

hair: ~brush *n* Haarbürste *f*. **~cut** *n* Haarschnitt *m*; **have a ~cut** sich (*dat*) die Haare schneiden lassen. **~-do** *n* [!] Frisur *f*. **~dresser** *n* Friseur *m*/Friseuse *f*. **~-drier** *n* Haartrockner *m*; (*hand-held*) Föhn *m*. **~pin** *n* Haarnadel *f*. **~pin 'bend** *n* Haarnadelkurve *f*. **~-raising** *a* haarsträubend. **~-style** *n* Frisur *f*

hairy /'heərɪ/ *a* (**-ier, -iest**) behaart; (*excessively*) haarig; (*fam; frightening*) brenzlig

hake /heɪk/ *n inv* Seehecht *m*

half /hɑ:f/ *n* (*pl* **halves**) Hälfte *f*; **cut in ~** halbieren; **one and a ~** eineinhalb, anderthalb; **~ a dozen** ein halbes Dutzend; **~ an hour** eine halbe Stunde ● *a* & *adv* halb; **~ past two** halb drei; **[at] ~ price** zum halben Preis

half: ~-'hearted *a* lustlos. **~-'term** *n* schulfreie Tage nach dem halben Trimester. **~-'timbered** *a* Fachwerk-. **~-'time** *n* (*Sport*) Halbzeit *f*. **~-'way** *a* **the ~-way mark/stage** die Hälfte ● *adv* auf halbem Weg

halibut /'hælɪbət/ *n inv* Heilbutt *m*

hall /hɔ:l/ *n* Halle *f*; (*room*) Saal *m*; (*Sch*) Aula *f*; (*entrance*) Flur *m*; (*mansion*) Gutshaus *nt*; **~ of residence** Studentenheim *nt*

'hallmark *n* [Feingehalts]stempel *m*; (*fig*) Kennzeichen *nt* (**of** für)

hallo /hə'ləʊ/ *int* [guten] Tag! [!] hallo!

hallucination /həlu:sɪ'neɪʃn/ *n* Halluzination *f*

halo /'heɪləʊ/ *n* (*pl* **-es**) Heiligenschein *m*; (*Astr*) Hof *m*

halt /hɔ:lt/ *n* Halt *m*; **come to a ~** stehen bleiben; <*traffic:*> zum Stillstand kommen ● *vi* Halt machen; **~!** halt! **~ing** *a*, *adv* **-ly** zögernd

halve /hɑ:v/ *vt* halbieren; (*reduce*) um die Hälfte reduzieren

ham /hæm/ *n* Schinken *m*

hamburger /'hæmbɜ:gə(r)/ *n* Hamburger *m*

hammer /'hæmə(r)/ *n* Hammer *m* ● *vt/i* hämmern (**at** an + *acc*)

hammock /'hæmək/ *n* Hängematte *f*

hamper *vt* behindern

hamster /'hæmstə(r)/ *n* Hamster *m*

hand /hænd/ *n* Hand *f*; (*of clock*) Zeiger *m*; (*writing*) Handscrift *f*; (*worker*) Arbeiter(in) *m*(*f*); (*Cards*) Blatt *nt*; **on the one/ other ~** einer-/andererseits; **out of ~** außer Kontrolle; (*summarily*) kurzerhand; **in ~** unter Kontrolle; (*available*) verfügbar; **give s.o. a ~** jdm behilflich sein ● *vt* reichen (**to** *dat*). **~ in** *vt* abgeben. **~ out** *vt* austeilen. **~ over** *vt* überreichen

hand: ~bag *n* Handtasche *f*. **~book** *n* Handbuch *nt*. **~brake** *n* Handbremse *f*. **~cuffs** *npl* Handschellen *pl*. **~ful** *n* Handvoll *f*; **be [quite] a ~ful** [!] nicht leicht zu haben sein

handicap /'hændɪkæp/ *n* Behinderung *f*; (*Sport & fig*) Handikap *nt*. **~ped** *a* **mentally/ physically ~ped** geistig/ körperlich behindert

handkerchief /'hæŋkətʃɪf/ *n* (*pl* **~s** & **-chieves**) Taschentuch *nt*

handle /'hændl/ *n* Griff *m*; (*of door*) Klinke *f*; (*of cup*) Henkel *m*; (*of broom*) Stiel *m* ● *vt* handhaben; (*treat*) umgehen mit; (*touch*) anfassen. **~bars** *npl* Lenkstange *f*

hand: ~made *a* handgemacht. **~shake** *n* Händerdruck *m*

handsome /'hænsəm/ *a* gut aussehend; (*generous*) großzügig; (*large*) beträchtlich

hand: ~writing *n* Handschrift *f*. **~'written** *a* handgeschrieben

handy /'hændɪ/ *a* (**-ier, -iest**) handlich; <*person*> geschickt; **have/keep ~** griffbereit haben/ halten

hang /hæŋ/ *vt/i* (*pt/pp* **hung**) hängen; **~ wallpaper** tapezieren ● *vt* (*pt/pp* **hanged**) hängen <*criminal*> ● *n* **get the ~ of it** [!] den Dreh herauskriegen. **~ about** *vi* sich herumdrücken. **~ on** *vi* sich festhalten (**to** an + *dat*); ([!] *wait*) warten. **~ out** *vi* heraushängen; ([!] *live*) wohnen ● *vt* draußen aufhängen <*washing*>. **~ up** *vt/i* aufhängen

hangar /'hæŋə(r)/ *n* Flugzeughalle *f*

hanger /'hæŋə(r)/ *n* [Kleider]bügel *m*

hang: ~-glider *n* Drachenflieger *m*. **~-gliding** *n* Drachenfliegen *nt*. **~man** *n* Henker *m*. **~over** *n* [!] Kater *m* [!]. **~-up** *n* [!] Komplex *m*

hanker /'hæŋkə(r)/ *vi* **~ after sth** sich (*dat*) etw wünschen

hanky /'hæŋkɪ/ *n* [!] Taschentuch *nt*

haphazard /hæp'hæzəd/ *a*, **-ly** *adv* planlos

happen /'hæpn/ *vi* geschehen, passieren; **I ~ed to be there** ich war zufällig da; **what has ~ed to him?** was ist mit ihm los? (*become of*) was ist aus ihm geworden? **~ing** *n* Ereignis *nt*

happi|ly /ˈhæpɪlɪ/ *adv* glücklich; (*fortunately*) glücklicherweise. **~ness** *n* Glück *nt*

happy /ˈhæpɪ/ *a* (**-ier, -iest**) glücklich. **~-go-ˈlucky** *a* sorglos

harass /ˈhærəs/ *vt* schikanieren. **~ed** *a* abgehetzt. **~ment** *n* Schikane *f*; (*sexual*) Belästigung *f*

harbour /ˈhɑːbə(r)/ *n* Hafen *m*

hard /hɑːd/ *a* (**-er, -est**) hart; (*difficult*) schwer; **~ of hearing** schwerhörig ● *adv* hart; <*work*> schwer; <*pull*> kräftig; <*rain, snow*> stark; **be ~ up** ! knapp bei Kasse sein; **be ~ done by** ! ungerecht behandelt werden

hard: ~back *n* gebundene Ausgabe *f*. **~board** *n* Hartfaserplatte *f*. **~-boiled** *a* hart gekocht

harden /ˈhɑːdn/ *vi* hart werden

hard-ˈhearted *a* hartherzig

hard|ly /ˈhɑːdlɪ/ *adv* kaum; **~ly ever** kaum [jemals]. **~ness** *n* Härte *f*. **~ship** *n* Not *f*

hard: ~ ˈshoulder *n* (*Auto*) Randstreifen *m*. **~ware** *n* Haushaltswaren *pl*; (*Computing*) Hardware *f*. **~-ˈwearing** *a* strapazierfähig. **~-ˈworking** *a* fleißig

hardy /ˈhɑːdɪ/ *a* (**-ier, -iest**) abgehärtet; <*plant*> winterhart

hare /heə(r)/ *n* Hase *m*

harm /hɑːm/ *n* Schaden *m*; **it won't do any ~** es kann nichts schaden ● *vt* **~ s.o.** jdm etwas antun. **~ful** *a* schädlich. **~less** *a* harmlos

harmonious /hɑːˈməʊnɪəs/ *a*, **-ly** *adv* harmonisch

harmon|ize /ˈhɑːmənaɪz/ *vi* (*fig*) harmonieren. **~y** *n* Harmonie *f*

harness /ˈhɑːnɪs/ *n* Geschirr *nt*; (*of parachute*) Gurtwerk *nt* ● *vt* anschirren <*horse*>; (*use*) nutzbar machen

harp /hɑːp/ *n* Harfe *f*. **~ist** *n* Harfenist(in) *m(f)*

harpsichord /ˈhɑːpsɪkɔːd/ *n* Cembalo *nt*

harrowing /ˈhærəʊɪŋ/ *a* grauenhaft

harsh /hɑːʃ/ *a* (**-er, -est**), **-ly** *adv* hart; <*voice*> rau; <*light*> grell. **~ness** *n* Härte *f*; Rauheit *f*

harvest /ˈhɑːvɪst/ *n* Ernte *f* ● *vt* ernten

has /hæz/ *see* **have**

hassle /ˈhæsl/ *n* ! Ärger *m* ● *vt* schikanieren

haste /heɪst/ *n* Eile *f*

hasten /ˈheɪsn/ *vi* sich beeilen (**to** zu); (*go quickly*) eilen ● *vt* beschleunigen

hasty /ˈheɪstɪ/ *a* (**-ier, -iest**), **-ily** *adv* hastig; <*decision*> voreilig

hat /hæt/ *n* Hut *m*; (*knitted*) Mütze *f*

hatch¹ /hætʃ/ *n* (*for food*) Durchreiche *f*; (*Naut*) Luke *f*

hatch² *vi* **~[out]** ausschlüpfen ● *vt* ausbrüten

ˈhatchback *n* (*Auto*) Modell *nt* mit Hecktür

hate /heɪt/ *n* Hass *m* ● *vt* hassen. **~ful** *a* abscheulich

hatred /ˈheɪtrɪd/ *n* Hass *m*

haughty /ˈhɔːtɪ/ *a* (**-ier, -iest**), **-ily** *adv* hochmütig

haul /hɔːl/ *n* (*loot*) Beute *f* ● *vt/i* ziehen (**on** an + *dat*)

haunt /hɔːnt/ *n* Lieblingsaufenthalt *m* ● *vt* umgehen in (+ *dat*); **this house is ~ed** in diesem Haus spukt es

have /hæv/

3 sg pres tense **has**; *pt and pp* **had**

● *transitive verb*

····➤ (*possess*) haben. **he has [got] a car** er hat ein Auto. **she has [got] a brother** sie hat einen

Bruder. **we have [got] five minutes** wir haben fünf Minuten

....➤ (*eat*) essen; (*drink*) trinken; (*smoke*) rauchen. **have a cup of tea** eine Tasse Tee trinken. **have a pizza** eine Pizza essen. **have a cigarette** eine Zigarette rauchen. **have breakfast/dinner/lunch** frühstücken/zu Abend essen/zu Mittag essen

....➤ (*take esp. in shop, restaurant*) nehmen. **I'll have the soup/the red dress** ich nehme die Suppe/das rote Kleid. **have a cigarette!** nehmen Sie eine Zigarette!

....➤ (*get, receive*) bekommen. **I had a letter from her** ich bekam einen Brief von ihr. **have a baby** ein Baby bekommen

....➤ (*suffer*) haben <*illness, pain, disappointment*>; erleiden <*shock*>

....➤ (*organize*) **have a party** eine Party veranstalten. **they had a meeting** sie hielten eine Versammlung ab

....➤ (*take part in*) **have a game of football** Fußball spielen. **have a swim** schwimmen

....➤ (*as guest*) **have s.o. to stay** jdn zu Besuch haben

....➤ **have had it** [!] <*thing*> ausgedient haben; <*person*> geliefert sein. **you've had it now** jetzt ist es aus

....➤ **have sth done** etw machen lassen. **we had the house painted** wir haben das Haus malen lassen. **have a dress made** sich (*dat*) ein Kleid machen lassen. **have a tooth out** sich (*dat*) einen Zahn ziehen lassen. **have one's hair cut** sich (*dat*) die Haare schneiden lassen

....➤ **have to do sth** etw tun müssen. **I have to go now** ich muss jetzt gehen

● *auxiliary verb*

....➤ (*forming perfect and past perfect tenses*) haben; (*with verbs of motion and some others*) sein. **I have seen him** ich habe ihn gesehen. **he has never been there** er ist nie da gewesen. **I had gone** ich war gegangen. **if I had known ...** wenn ich gewusst hätte ...

....➤ (*in tag questions*) nicht wahr. **you've met her, haven't you?** du kennst sie, nicht wahr?

....➤ (*in short answers*) **Have you seen the film? — Yes, I have** Hast du den Film gesehen? — Ja [, stimmt]

● **have on** *vt* (*be wearing*) anhaben; (*dupe*) anführen

havoc /ˈhævək/ *n* Verwüstung *f*

hawk /hɔːk/ *n* Falke *m*

hawthorn /ˈhɔː-/ *n* Hagedorn *m*

hay /heɪ/ *n* Heu *nt*. **~ fever** *n* Heuschnupfen *m*. **~stack** *n* Heuschober *m*

hazard /ˈhæzəd/ *n* Gefahr *f*; (*risk*) Risiko *nt* ● *vt* riskieren. **~ous** /-əs/ *a* gefährlich; (*risky*) riskant

haze /ˈheɪz/ *n* Dunst *m*

hazel /ˈheɪzl/ *n* Haselbusch *m*. **~-nut** *n* Haselnuss *f*

hazy /ˈheɪzɪ/ *a* (**-ier, -iest**) dunstig; (*fig*) unklar

he /hiː/ *pron* er

head /hed/ *n* Kopf *m*; (*chief*) Oberhaupt *nt*; (*of firm*) Chef(in) *m(f)*; (*of school*) Schulleiter(in) *m(f)*; (*on beer*) Schaumkrone *f*; (*of bed*) Kopfende *nt*; **~ first** kopfüber ● *vt* anführen; (*Sport*) köpfen <*ball*> ● *vi* **~ for** zusteuern auf (+ *acc*). **~ache** *n* Kopfschmerzen *pl*

head|er /ˈhedə(r)/ *n* Kopfball *m*; (*dive*) Kopfsprung *m*. **~ing** *n* Überschrift *f*

head: ~lamp, ~light *n* (*Auto*) Scheinwerfer *m*. **~line** *n*

Schlagzeile *f*. **~long** *adv* kopfüber. **~'master** *n* Schulleiter *m*. **~'mistress** *n* Schulleiterin *f*. **~-on** *a & adv* frontal. **~phones** *npl* Kopfhörer *m*. **~quarters** *npl* Hauptquartier *nt*; (*Pol*) Zentrale *f*. **~-rest** *n* Kopfstütze *f*. **~room** *n* lichte Höhe *f*. **~scarf** *n* Kopftuch *nt*. **~strong** *a* eigenwillig. **~way** *n* **make ~way** Fortschritte machen. **~word** *n* Stichwort *nt*

heady /'hedɪ/ *a* berauschend

heal /hi:l/ *vt/i* heilen

health /helθ/ *n* Gesundheit *f*

health: ~ farm *n* Schönheitsfarm *f*. **~ foods** *npl* Reformkost *f*. **~-food shop** *n* Reformhaus *nt*. **~ insurance** *n* Krankenversicherung *f*

healthy /'helθɪ/ *a* (**-ier, -iest**), **-ily** *adv* gesund

heap /hi:p/ *n* Haufen *m*; **~s** [!] jede Menge ● *vt* **~ [up]** häufen

hear /hɪə(r)/ *vt/i* (*pt/pp* **heard**) hören; **~,~!** hört, hört! **he would not ~ of it** er ließ es nicht zu

hearing /'hɪərɪŋ/ *n* Gehör *nt*; (*Jur*) Verhandlung *f*. **~-aid** *n* Hörgerät *nt*

hearse /hɜ:s/ *n* Leichenwagen *m*

heart /hɑ:t/ *n* Herz *nt*; (*courage*) Mut *m*; **~s** *pl* (*Cards*) Herz *nt*; **by ~** auswendig

heart: ~ache *n* Kummer *m*. **~attack** *n* Herzanfall *m*. **~beat** *n* Herzschlag *m*. **~-breaking** *a* herzzerreißend. **~-broken** *a* untröstlich. **~burn** *n* Sodbrennen *nt*. **~en** *vt* ermutigen. **~felt** *a* herzlich[st]

hearth /hɑ:θ/ *n* Herd *m*; (*fireplace*) Kamin *m*

heart|ily /'hɑ:tɪlɪ/ *adv* herzlich; <*eat*> viel. **~less** *a*, **-ly** *adv* herzlos. **~y** *a* herzlich; <*meal*> groß; <*person*> burschikos

heat /hi:t/ *n* Hitze *f*; (*Sport*) Vorlauf *m* ● *vt* heiß machen; heizen <*room*>. **~ed** *a* geheizt; <*swimming pool*> beheizt; <*discussion*> hitzig. **~er** *n* Heizgerät *nt*; (*Auto*) Heizanlage *f*

heath /hi:θ/ *n* Heide *f*

heathen /'hi:ðn/ *a* heidnisch ● *n* Heide *m*/Heidin *f*

heather /'heðə(r)/ *n* Heidekraut *nt*

heating /'hi:tɪŋ/ *n* Heizung *f*

heat wave *n* Hitzewelle *f*

heave /hi:v/ *vt/i* ziehen; (*lift*) heben; ([!] *throw*) schmeißen

heaven /'hevn/ *n* Himmel *m*. **~ly** *a* himmlisch

heavy /'hevɪ/ *a* (**-ier, -iest**), **-ily** *adv* schwer; <*traffic, rain*> stark. **~weight** *n* Schwergewicht *nt*

heckle /'hekl/ *vt* [durch Zwischenrufe] unterbrechen. **~r** *n* Zwischenrufer *m*

hectic /'hektɪk/ *a* hektisch

hedge /hedʒ/ *n* Hecke *f*. **~hog** *n* Igel *m*

heed /hi:d/ *vt* beachten

heel[1] /hi:l/ *n* Ferse *f*; (*of shoe*) Absatz *m*; **down at ~** heruntergekommen

heel[2] *vi* **~ over** (*Naut*) sich auf die Seite legen

hefty /'heftɪ/ *a* (**-ier, -iest**) kräftig; (*heavy*) schwer

height /haɪt/ *n* Höhe *f*; (*of person*) Größe *f*. **~en** *vt* (*fig*) steigern

heir /eə(r)/ *n* Erbe *m*. **~ess** *n* Erbin *f*. **~loom** *n* Erbstück *nt*

held /held/ *see* **hold**[2]

helicopter /'helɪkɒptə(r)/ *n* Hubschrauber *m*

hell /hel/ *n* Hölle *f*; **go to ~!** [✖] geh zum Teufel! ● *int* verdammt!

hello /hə'ləʊ/ *int* [guten] Tag! [!] hallo!

helm /helm/ *n* [Steuer]ruder *nt*

helmet /'helmɪt/ *n* Helm *m*

help /help/ *n* Hilfe *f*; (*employees*) Hilfskräfte *pl*; **that's no ~** das nützt nichts ● *vt/i* helfen (**s.o.** jdm); ~ **oneself to sth** sich (*dat*) etw nehmen; ~ **yourself** (*at table*) greif zu; **I could not ~ laughing** ich musste lachen; **it cannot be ~ed** es lässt sich nicht ändern; **I can't ~ it** ich kann nichts dafür

help|er /ˈhelpə(r)/ *n* Helfer(in) *m(f)*. **~ful** *a*, -ly *adv* hilfsbereit; <*advice*> nützlich. **~ing** *n* Portion *f*. **~less** *a*, **-ly** *adv* hilflos

hem /hem/ *n* Saum *m* ● *vt* (*pt/pp* **hemmed**) säumen; ~ **in** umzingeln

hemisphere /ˈhemɪ-/ *n* Hemisphäre *f*

ˈhem-line *n* Rocklänge *f*

hen /hen/ *n* Henne *f*; (*any female bird*) Weibchen *nt*

hence /hens/ *adv* daher; **five years ~** in fünf Jahren. **~ˈforth** *adv* von nun an

ˈhenpecked *a* ~ **husband** Pantoffelheld *m*

her /hɜ:(r)/ *a* ihr ● *pron* (*acc*) sie; (*dat*) ihr

herald /ˈherəld/ *vt* verkünden. **~ry** *n* Wappenkunde *f*

herb /hɜ:b/ *n* Kraut *nt*

herbaceous /hɜ:ˈbeɪʃəs/ *a* ~ **border** Staudenrabatte *f*

herd /hɜ:d/ *n* Herde *f*. ~ **together** *vt* zusammentreiben

here /hɪə(r)/ *adv* hier; (*to this place*) hierher; **in ~** hier drinnen; **come/bring ~** herkommen/herbringen

hereditary /həˈredɪtərɪ/ *a* erblich

here|sy /ˈherəsɪ/ *n* Ketzerei *f*. **~tic** *n* Ketzer(in) *m(f)*

hereˈwith *adv* (*Comm*) beiliegend

heritage /ˈherɪtɪdʒ/ *n* Erbe *nt*

hero /ˈhɪərəʊ/ *n* (*pl* **-es**) Held *m*

heroic /hɪˈrəʊɪk/ *a*, **-ally** *adv* heldenhaft

heroin /ˈherəʊɪn/ *n* Heroin *nt*

hero|ine /ˈherəʊɪn/ *n* Heldin *f*. **~ism** *n* Heldentum *nt*

heron /ˈhern/ *n* Reiher *m*

herring /ˈherɪŋ/ *n* Hering *m*

hers /hɜ:z/ *poss pron* ihre(r), ihrs; **a friend of ~** ein Freund von ihr; **that is ~** das gehört ihr

herˈself *pron* selbst; (*refl*) sich; **by ~** allein

hesitant /ˈhezɪtənt/ *a*, **-ly** *adv* zögernd

hesitat|e /ˈhezɪteɪt/ *vi* zögern. **~ion** /-ˈteɪʃn/ *n* Zögern *nt*; **without ~ion** ohne zu zögern

hexagonal /hekˈsægənl/ *a* sechseckig

heyday /ˈheɪ-/ *n* Glanzzeit *f*

hi /haɪ/ *int* he! (*hallo*) Tag!

hiatus /haɪˈeɪtəs/ *n* (*pl* **-tuses**) Lücke *f*

hibernat|e /ˈhaɪbəneɪt/ *vi* Winterschlaf halten. **~ion** /-ˈneɪʃn/ *n* Winterschlaf *m*

hiccup /ˈhɪkʌp/ *n* Hick *m*; ([!] *hitch*) Panne *f*; **have the ~s** den Schluckauf haben ● *vi* hick machen

hid /hɪd/, **hidden** *see* **hide**

hide *v* (*pt* **hid**, *pp* **hidden**) ● *vt* verstecken; (*keep secret*) verheimlichen ● *vi* sich verstecken

hideous /ˈhɪdɪəs/ *a*, **-ly** *adv* hässlich; (*horrible*) grässlich

ˈhide-out *n* Versteck *nt*

hiding[1] /ˈhaɪdɪŋ/ *n* [!] **give s.o. a ~** jdn verdreschen

hiding[2] *n* **go into ~** untertauchen

hierarchy /ˈhaɪərɑ:kɪ/ *n* Hierarchie *f*

high /haɪ/ *a* (**-er, -est**) hoch; *attrib* hohe(r,s); <*meat*> angegangen; <*wind*> stark; (*on drugs*) high; **it's ~ time** es ist höchste Zeit ● *adv* hoch; ~ **and**

low überall ● *n* Hoch *nt*; (*temperature*) Höchsttemperatur *f*

high: ~brow *a* intellektuell. **~chair** *n* Kinderhochstuhl *m*. **~-handed** *a* selbstherrlich. **~-'heeled** *a* hochhackig. **~ jump** *n* Hochsprung *m*

'highlight *n* (*fig*) Höhepunkt *m*; **~s** *pl* (*in hair*) helle Strähnen *pl* ● *vt* (*emphasize*) hervorheben

highly /'haɪlɪ/ *adv* hoch; **speak ~ of** loben; **think ~ of** sehr schätzen. **~-'strung** *a* nervös

Highness /'haɪnɪs/ *n* Hoheit *f*

high: ~ season *n* Hochsaison *f*. **~ street** *n* Hauptstraße *f*. **~ 'tide** *n* Hochwasser *nt*. **~way** *n* **public ~way** öffentliche Straße *f*

hijack /'haɪdʒæk/ *vt* entführen. **~er** *n* Entführer *m*

hike /haɪk/ *n* Wanderung *f* ● *vi* wandern. **~r** *n* Wanderer *m*

hilarious /hɪ'leərɪəs/ *a* sehr komisch

hill /hɪl/ *n* Berg *m*; (*mound*) Hügel *m*; (*slope*) Hang *m*

hill: ~side *n* Hang *m*. **~y** *a* hügelig

him /hɪm/ *pron* (*acc*) ihn; (*dat*) ihm. **~'self** *pron* selbst; (*refl*) sich; **by ~self** allein

hind /haɪnd/ *a* Hinter-

hind|er /'hɪndə(r)/ *vt* hindern. **~rance** /-rəns/ *n* Hindernis *nt*

hindsight /'haɪnd-/ *n* **with ~** rückblickend

Hindu /'hɪndu:/ *n* Hindu *m* ● *a* Hindu-. **~ism** *n* Hinduismus *m*

hinge /hɪndʒ/ *n* Scharnier *nt*; (*on door*) Angel *f*

hint /hɪnt/ *n* Wink *m*, Andeutung *f*; (*advice*) Hinweis *m*; (*trace*) Spur *f* ● *vi* **~ at** anspielen auf (+ *acc*)

hip /hɪp/ *n* Hüfte *f*

hip 'pocket *n* Gesäßtasche *f*

hippopotamus /hɪpə'pɒtəməs/ *n* (*pl* **-muses** *or* **-mi** /-maɪ/) Nilpferd *nt*

hire /'haɪə(r)/ *vt* mieten <*car*>; leihen <*suit*>; einstellen <*person*>; **~[out]** vermieten; verleihen

his /hɪz/ *a* sein ● *poss pron* seine(r), seins; **a friend of ~** ein Freund von ihm; **that is ~** das gehört ihm

hiss /hɪs/ *n* Zischen *nt* ● *vt/i* zischen

historian /hɪ'stɔ:rɪən/ *n* Historiker(in) *m(f)*

historic /hɪ'stɒrɪk/ *a* historisch. **~al** *a*, **-ly** *adv* geschichtlich, historisch

history /'hɪstərɪ/ *n* Geschichte *f*

hit /hɪt/ *n* (*blow*) Schlag *m*; (🄸 *success*) Erfolg *m*; **direct ~** Volltreffer *m* ● *vt/i* (*pt/pp* **hit**, *pres p* **hitting**) schlagen; (*knock against, collide with, affect*) treffen; **~ the target** das Ziel treffen; **~ on** (*fig*) kommen auf (+ *acc*); **~ it off** gut auskommen (**with** mit); **~ one's head on sth** sich (*dat*) den Kopf an etw (*dat*) stoßen

hitch /hɪtʃ/ *n* Problem *nt*; **technical ~** Panne *f* ● *vt* festmachen (**to** an + *dat*); **~ up** hochziehen. **~-hike** *vi* 🄸 trampen. **~-hiker** *n* Anhalter(in) *m(f)*

hive /haɪv/ *n* Bienenstock *m*

hoard /hɔ:d/ *n* Hort *m* ● *vt* horten, hamstern

hoarding /'hɔ:dɪŋ/ *n* Bauzaun *m*; (*with advertisements*) Reklamewand *f*

hoar-frost /'hɔ:-/ *n* Raureif *m*

hoarse /hɔ:s/ *a* (**-r, -st**), **-ly** *adv* heiser. **~ness** *n* Heiserkeit *f*

hoax /həʊks/ *n* übler Scherz *m*; (*false alarm*) blinder Alarm *m*

hobble /'hɒbl/ *vi* humpeln

hobby /ˈhɒbɪ/ *n* Hobby *nt*. **~-horse** *n* (*fig*) Lieblingsthema *nt*

hockey /ˈhɒkɪ/ *n* Hockey *nt*

hoe /həʊ/ *n* Hacke *f* ● *vt* (*pres p* **hoeing**) hacken

hog /hɒg/ *vt* (*pt*/*pp* **hogged**) [!] mit Beschlag belegen

hoist /hɔɪst/ *n* Lastenaufzug *m* ● *vt* hochziehen; hissen <*flag*>

hold¹ /həʊld/ *n* (*Naut*) Laderaum *m*

hold² *n* Halt *m*; (*Sport*) Griff *m*; (*fig: influence*) Einfluss *m*; **get ~ of** fassen; ([!] *contact*) erreichen ● *v* (*pt*/*pp* **held**) ● *vt* halten; <*container*:> fassen; (*believe*) meinen; (*possess*) haben; anhalten <*breath*> ● *vi* <*rope*:> halten; <*weather*:> sich halten. **~ back** *vt* zurückhalten ● *vi* zögern. **~ on** *vi* (*wait*) warten; (*on telephone*) am Apparat bleiben; **~ on to** (*keep*) behalten; (*cling to*) sich festhalten an (+ *dat*). **~ out** *vt* hinhalten ● *vi* (*resist*) aushalten. **~ up** *vt* hochhalten; (*delay*) aufhalten; (*rob*) überfallen

ˈhold|all *n* Reisetasche *f*. **~er** *n* Inhaber(in) *m*(*f*); (*container*) Halter *m*. **~-up** *n* Verzögerung *f*; (*attack*) Überfall *m*

hole /həʊl/ *n* Loch *nt*

holiday /ˈhɒlədeɪ/ *n* Urlaub *m*; (*Sch*) Ferien *pl*; (*public*) Feiertag *m*; (*day off*) freier Tag *m*; **go on ~** in Urlaub fahren

holiness /ˈhəʊlɪnɪs/ *n* Heiligkeit *f*

Holland /ˈhɒlənd/ *n* Holland *nt*

hollow /ˈhɒləʊ/ *a* hohl; <*promise*> leer ● *n* Vertiefung *f*; (*in ground*) Mulde *f*. **~ out** *vt* aushöhlen

holly /ˈhɒlɪ/ *n* Stechpalme *f*

holster /ˈhəʊlstə(r)/ *n* Pistolentasche *f*

holy /ˈhəʊlɪ/ *a* (**-ier, -est**) heilig. **H~ Ghost** *or* **Spirit** *n* Heiliger Geist *m*

homage /ˈhɒmɪdʒ/ *n* Huldigung *f*; **pay ~ to** huldigen (+ *dat*)

home /həʊm/ *n* Zuhause *nt* (*house*) Haus *nt*; (*institution*) Heim *nt*; (*native land*) Heimat *f* ● *adv* **at ~** zu Hause; **come/go ~** nach Hause kommen/gehen

home: ~ adˈdress *n* Heimatanschrift *f*. **~ game** *n* Heimspiel *nt*. **~ help** *n* Haushaltshilfe *f*. **~land** *n* Heimatland *nt*. **~less** *a* obdachlos

homely /ˈhəʊmlɪ/ *a* (**-ier, -iest**) *a* gemütlich; (*Amer: ugly*) unscheinbar

home: ~-ˈmade *a* selbst gemacht. **H~ Office** *n* Innenministerium *nt*. **~ page** *n* Homepage *f*. **H~ ˈSecretary** Innenminister *m*. **~sick** *a* **be ~sick** Heimweh haben (**for** nach). **~sickness** *n* Heimweh *nt*. **~ ˈtown** *n* Heimatstadt *f*. **~work** *n* (*Sch*) Hausaufgaben *pl*

homoˈsexual *a* homosexuell ● *n* Homosexuelle(r) *m*/*f*

honest /ˈɒnɪst/ *a*, **-ly** *adv* ehrlich. **~y** *n* Ehrlichkeit *f*

honey /ˈhʌnɪ/ *n* Honig *m*; ([!] *darling*) Schatz *m*

honey: ~comb *n* Honigwabe *f*. **~moon** *n* Flitterwochen *pl*; (*journey*) Hochzeitsreise *f*

honorary /ˈɒnərərɪ/ *a* ehrenamtlich; <*member, doctorate*> Ehren-

honour /ˈɒnə(r)/ *n* Ehre *f* ● *vt* ehren; honorieren <*cheque*>. **~able** /-əbl/ *a*, **-bly** *adv* ehrenhaft

hood /hʊd/ *n* Kapuze *f*; (*of car, pram*) [Klapp]verdeck *nt*; (*over cooker*) Abzugshaube *f*; (*Auto, Amer*) Kühlerhaube *f*

hoof /hu:f/ *n* (*pl* **~s** *or* **hooves**) Huf *m*

hook /hʊk/ *n* Haken *m* ● *vt* festhaken (**to** an + *acc*)

hook|ed /hʊkt/ *a* **~ed nose** Hakennase *f*; **~ed on** [!] abhängig von; (*keen on*) besessen von. **~er** *n* (*Amer* [x]) Nutte *f*

hookey /ˈhʊkɪ/ *n* **play ~** (*Amer* [!]) schwänzen

hooligan /ˈhu:lɪgən/ *n* Rowdy *m*. **~ism** *n* Rowdytum *nt*

hooray /hʊˈreɪ/ *int* & *n* = **hurrah**

hoot /hu:t/ *n* Ruf *m*; **~s of laughter** schallendes Gelächter *nt* ● *vi* <*owl:*> rufen; <*car:*> hupen; (*jeer*) johlen. **~er** *n* (*of factory*) Sirene *f*; (*Auto*) Hupe *f*

hoover /ˈhu:və(r)/ *n* **H~** (**P**) Staubsauger *m* ● *vt/i* [staub]saugen

hop[1] /hɒp/ *n*, & **~s** *pl* Hopfen *m*

hop[2] *vi* (*pt/pp* **hopped**) hüpfen; **~ it!** [!] hau ab!

hope /həʊp/ *n* Hoffnung *f*; (*prospect*) Aussicht *f* (**of** auf + *acc*) ● *vt/i* hoffen (**for** auf + acc); **I ~ so** hoffentlich

hope|ful /ˈhəʊpfl/ *a* hoffnungsvoll; **be ~ful that** hoffen, dass. **~fully** *adv* hoffnungsvoll; (*it is hoped*) hoffentlich. **~less** *a*, **-ly** *adv* hoffnungslos; (*useless*) nutzlos; (*incompetent*) untauglich

horde /hɔ:d/ *n* Horde *f*

horizon /həˈraɪzn/ *n* Horizont *m*

horizontal /hɒrɪˈzɒntl/ *a*, **-ly** *adv* horizontal. **~ ˈbar** *n* Reck *nt*

horn /hɔ:n/ *n* Horn *nt*; (*Auto*) Hupe *f*

hornet /ˈhɔ:nɪt/ *n* Hornisse *f*

horoscope /ˈhɒrəskəʊp/ *n* Horoskop *nt*

horrible /ˈhɒrɪbl/ *a*, **-bly** *adv* schrecklich

horrid /ˈhɒrɪd/ *a* grässlich

horrific /həˈrɪfɪk/ *a* entsetzlich

horrify /ˈhɒrɪfaɪ/ *vt* (*pt/pp* **-ied**) entsetzen

horror /ˈhɒrə(r)/ *n* Entsetzen *nt*

hors-d'œuvre /ɔ:ˈdɜ:vr/ *n* Vorspeise *f*

horse /hɔ:s/ *n* Pferd *nt*

horse: ~back *n* **on ~back** zu Pferde. **~man** *n* Reiter *m*. **~power** *n* Pferdestärke *f*. **~-racing** *n* Pferderennen *nt*. **~radish** *n* Meerrettich *m*. **~shoe** *n* Hufeisen *nt*

ˈhorticulture *n* Gartenbau *m*

hose /həʊz/ *n* (*pipe*) Schlauch *m* ● *vt* **~ down** abspritzen

hosiery /ˈhəʊzɪərɪ/ *n* Strumpfwaren *pl*

hospitable /hɒˈspɪtəbl/ *a*, **-bly** *adv* gastfreundlich

hospital /ˈhɒspɪtl/ *n* Krankenhaus *nt*

hospitality /hɒspɪˈtælətɪ/ *n* Gastfreundschaft *f*

host /həʊst/ *n* Gastgeber *m*

hostage /ˈhɒstɪdʒ/ *n* Geisel *f*

hostel /ˈhɒstl/ *n* [Wohn]heim *nt*

hostess /ˈhəʊstɪs/ *n* Gastgeberin *f*

hostile /ˈhɒstaɪl/ *a* feindlich; (*unfriendly*) feindselig

hostilit|y /hɒˈstɪlətɪ/ *n* Feindschaft *f*; **~ies** *pl* Feindseligkeiten *pl*

hot /hɒt/ *a* (**hotter, hottest**) heiß; <*meal*> warm; (*spicy*) scharf; **I am** *or* **feel ~** mir ist heiß

hotel /həʊˈtel/ *n* Hotel *nt*

hot: ~head *n* Hitzkopf *m*. **~house** *n* Treibhaus *nt*. **~ly** *adv* (*fig*) heiß, heftig. **~plate** *n* Tellerwärmer *m*; (*of cooker*) Kochplatte *f*. **~ tap** *n* Warmwasserhahn *m*. **~-tempered** *a* jähzornig. **~-ˈwater bottle** *n* Wärmflasche *f*

hound /haʊnd/ *n* Jagdhund *m* ● *vt* (*fig*) verfolgen

hour /'aʊə(r)/ *n* Stunde *f*. **~ly** *a & adv* stündlich

house¹ /haʊs/ *n* Haus *nt*; **at my ~** bei mir

house² /haʊz/ *vt* unterbringen

house: /haʊs/ **~breaking** *n* Einbruch *m*. **~hold** *n* Haushalt *m*. **~holder** *n* Hausinhaber(in) *m(f)*. **~keeper** *n* Haushälterin *f*. **~keeping** *n* Hauswirtschaft *f*; (*money*) Haushaltsgeld *nt*. **~plant** *n* Zimmerpflanze *f*. **~trained** *a* stubenrein. **~warming** *n* **have a ~-warming party** Einstand feiern. **~wife** *n* Hausfrau *f*. **~work** *n* Hausarbeit *f*

housing /'haʊzɪŋ/ *n* Wohnungen *pl*; (*Techn*) Gehäuse *nt*

hovel /'hɒvl/ *n* elende Hütte *f*

hover /'hɒvə(r)/ *vi* schweben. **~craft** *n* Luftkissenfahrzeug *nt*

how /haʊ/ *adv* wie; **~ do you do?** guten Tag!; **and ~!** und ob!

how'ever *adv* (*in question*) wie; (*nevertheless*) jedoch, aber; **~ small** wie klein es auch sein mag

howl /haʊl/ *n* Heulen *nt* ● *vi* heulen; <*baby*:> brüllen

hub /hʌb/ *n* Nabe *f*

huddle /'hʌdl/ *vi* **~ together** sich zusammendrängen

huff /hʌf/ *n* **in a ~** beleidigt

hug /hʌg/ *n* Umarmung *f* ● *vt* (*pt/pp* **hugged**) umarmen

huge /hju:dʒ/ *a*, **-ly** *adv* riesig

hull /hʌl/ *n* (*Naut*) Rumpf *m*

hullo /hə'ləʊ/ *int* = **hallo**

hum /hʌm/ *n* Summen *nt*; Brummen *nt* ● *vt/i* (*pt/pp* **hummed**) summen; <*motor*:> brummen

human /'hju:mən/ *a* menschlich ● *n* Mensch *m*. **~ 'being** *n* Mensch *m*

humane /hju:'meɪn/ *a*, **-ly** *adv* human

humanitarian /hju:mænɪ'teərɪən/ *a* humanitär

humanity /hju:'mænətɪ/ *n* Menschheit *f*

humble /'hʌmbl/ *a* (**-r, -st**), **-bly** *adv* demütig ● *vt* demütigen

'humdrum *a* eintönig

humid /'hju:mɪd/ *a* feucht. **~ity** /-'mɪdətɪ/ *n* Feuchtigkeit *f*

humiliat|e /hju:'mɪlɪeɪt/ *vt* demütigen. **~ion** /-'eɪʃn/ *n* Demütigung *f*

humility /hju:'mɪlətɪ/ *n* Demut *f*

humorous /'hju:mərəs/ *a*, **-ly** *adv* humorvoll; <*story*> humoristisch

humour /'hju:mə(r)/ *n* Humor *m*; (*mood*) Laune *f*; **have a sense of ~** Humor haben

hump /hʌmp/ *n* Buckel *m*; (*of camel*) Höcker *m* ● *vt* schleppen

hunch /hʌntʃ/ *n* (*idea*) Ahnung *f*

'hunchback *n* Bucklige(r) *m/f*

hundred /'hʌndrəd/ *a* **one/a ~** [ein]hundert ● *n* Hundert *nt*; (*written figure*) Hundert *f*. **~th** *a* hundertste(r,s) ● *n* Hundertstel *nt*. **~weight** *n* ≈ Zentner *m*

hung /hʌŋ/ *see* **hang**

Hungarian /hʌŋ'geərɪən/ *a* ungarisch ● *n* Ungar(in) *m(f)*

Hungary /'hʌŋgərɪ/ *n* Ungarn *nt*

hunger /'hʌŋgə(r)/ *n* Hunger *m*. **~-strike** *n* Hungerstreik *m*

hungry /'hʌŋgrɪ/ *a* (**-ier, -iest**), **-ily** *adv* hungrig; **be ~** Hunger haben

hunt /hʌnt/ *n* Jagd *f*; (*for criminal*) Fahndung *f* ● *vt/i* jagen; fahnden nach <*criminal*>; **~ for** suchen. **~er** *n* Jäger *m*; (*horse*) Jagdpferd *nt*. **~ing** *n* Jagd *f*

hurdle /'hɜ:dl/ *n* (*Sport & fig*) Hürde *f*

hurl /hɜ:l/ *vt* schleudern

hurrah /hʊ'rɑ:/, **hurray** /hʊ'reɪ/ *int* hurra! ● *n* Hurra *nt*

hurricane /ˈhʌrɪkən/ *n* Orkan *m*

hurried /ˈhʌrɪd/ *a*, **-ly** *adv* eilig; (*superficial*) flüchtig

hurry /ˈhʌrɪ/ *n* Eile *f*; **be in a ~** es eilig haben ● *vi* (*pt/pp* **-ied**) sich beeilen; (*go quickly*) eilen. **~ up** *vi* sich beeilen ● *vt* antreiben

hurt /hɜːt/ *n* Schmerz *m* ● *vt/i* (*pt/pp* **hurt**) weh tun (+ *dat*); (*injure*) verletzen; (*offend*) kränken

hurtle /ˈhɜːtl/ *vi* **~ along** rasen

husband /ˈhʌzbənd/ *n* [Ehe]mann *m*

hush /hʌʃ/ *n* Stille *f* ● *vt* **~ up** vertuschen. **~ed** *a* gedämpft

husky /ˈhʌskɪ/ *a* (**-ier, -iest**) heiser; (*burly*) stämmig

hustle /ˈhʌsl/ *vt* drängen ● *n* Gedränge *nt*

hut /hʌt/ *n* Hütte *f*

hutch /hʌtʃ/ *n* [Kaninchen]stall *m*

hybrid /ˈhaɪbrɪd/ *a* hybrid ● *n* Hybride *f*

hydraulic /haɪˈdrɔːlɪk/ *a*, **-ally** *adv* hydraulisch

hydroeˈlectric /haɪdrəʊ-/ *a* hydroelektrisch

hydrogen /ˈhaɪdrədʒən/ *n* Wasserstoff *m*

hygien|e /ˈhaɪdʒiːn/ *n* Hygiene *f*. **~ic** /haɪˈdʒiːnɪk/ *a*, **-ally** *adv* hygienisch

hymn /hɪm/ *n* Kirchenlied *nt*. **~-book** *n* Gesangbuch *nt*

hyphen /ˈhaɪfn/ *n* Bindestrich *m*. **~ate** *vt* mit Bindestrich schreiben

hypno|sis /hɪpˈnəʊsɪs/ *n* Hypnose *f*. **~tic** /-ˈnɒtɪk/ *a* hypnotisch

hypno|tism /ˈhɪpnətɪzm/ *n* Hypnotik *f*. **~tist** /-tɪst/ *n* Hypnotiseur *m*. **~tize** *vt* hypnotisieren

hypochondriac /haɪpəˈkɒndrɪæk/ *n* Hypochonder *m*

hypocrisy /hɪˈpɒkrəsɪ/ *n* Heuchelei *f*

hypocrite /ˈhɪpəkrɪt/ *n* Heuchler(in) *m(f)*

hypodermic /haɪpəˈdɜːmɪk/ *a* & *n* **~ [syringe]** Injektionsspritze *f*

hypothe|sis /haɪˈpɒθəsɪs/ *n* Hypothese *f*. **~tical** /-əˈθetɪkl/ *a*, **-ly** *adv* hypothetisch

hyster|ia /hɪˈstɪərɪə/ *n* Hysterie *f*. **~ical** /-ˈsterɪkl/ *a*, **-ly** *adv* hysterisch. **~ics** /hɪˈsterɪks/ *npl* hysterischer Anfall *m*

Ii

I /aɪ/ *pron* ich

ice /aɪs/ *n* Eis *nt* ● *vt* mit Zuckerguss überziehen <*cake*>

ice: ~berg /-bɜːg/ *n* Eisberg *m*. **~box** *n* (*Amer*) Kühlschrank *m*. **~-ˈcream** *n* [Speise]eis *nt*. **~-cube** *n* Eiswürfel *m*

Iceland /ˈaɪslənd/ *n* Island *nt*

ice: ~ˈ lolly *n* Eis *nt* am Stiel. **~ rink** *n* Eisbahn *f*

icicle /ˈaɪsɪkl/ *n* Eiszapfen *m*

icing /ˈaɪsɪŋ/ *n* Zuckerguss *m*. **~ sugar** *n* Puderzucker *m*

icon /ˈaɪkɒn/ *n* Ikone *f*

icy /ˈaɪsɪ/ *a* (**-ier, -iest**), **-ily** *adv* eisig; <*road*> vereist

idea /aɪˈdɪə/ *n* Idee *f*; (*conception*) Vorstellung *f*; **I have no ~!** ich habe keine Ahnung!

ideal /aɪˈdɪəl/ *a* ideal ● *n* Ideal *nt*. **~ism** *n* Idealismus *m*. **~ist**

n Idealist(in) *m(f)*. **~istic** /-'lɪstɪk/ *a* idealistisch. **~ize** *vt* idealisieren. **~ly** *adv* ideal; (*in ideal circumstances*) idealerweise

identical /aɪ'dentɪkl/ *a* identisch; <*twins*> eineiig

identi|fication /aɪdentɪfɪ'keɪʃn/ *n* Identifizierung *f*; (*proof of identity*) Ausweispapiere *pl*. **~fy** /aɪ'dentɪfaɪ/ *vt* (*pt/pp* **-ied**) identifizieren

identity /aɪ'dentətɪ/ *n* Identität *f*. **~ card** *n* [Personal]ausweis *m*

idiom /'ɪdɪəm/ *n* [feste] Redewendung *f*. **~atic** /-'mætɪk/ *a*, **-ally** *adv* idiomatisch

idiosyncrasy /ɪdɪə'sɪŋkrəsɪ/ *n* Eigenart *f*

idiot /'ɪdɪət/ *n* Idiot *m*. **~ic** /-'ɒtɪk/ *a* idiotisch

idle /'aɪdl/ *a* (**-r, -st**), **-ly** *adv* untätig; (*lazy*) faul; (*empty*) leer; <*machine*> nicht in Betrieb ● *vi* faulenzen; <*engine:*> leer laufen. **~ness** *n* Untätigkeit *f*; Faulheit *f*

idol /'aɪdl/ *n* Idol *nt*. **~ize** /'aɪdəlaɪz/ *vt* vergöttern

idyllic /ɪ'dɪlɪk/ *a* idyllisch

i.e. *abbr* (**id est**) d.h.

if /ɪf/ *conj* wenn; (*whether*) ob; **as if** als ob

ignition /ɪg'nɪʃn/ *n* (*Auto*) Zündung *f*. **~ key** *n* Zündschlüssel *m*

ignoramus /ɪgnə'reɪməs/ *n* Ignorant *m*

ignoran|ce /'ɪgnərəns/ *n* Unwissenheit *f*. **~t** *a* unwissend

ignore /ɪg'nɔ:(r)/ *vt* ignorieren

ill /ɪl/ *a* krank; (*bad*) schlecht; **feel ~ at ease** sich unbehaglich fühlen ● *adv* schlecht

illegal /ɪ'li:gl/ *a*, **-ly** *adv* illegal

illegible /ɪ'ledʒəbl/ *a*, **-bly** *adv* unleserlich

illegitimate /ɪlɪ'dʒɪtɪmət/ *a* unehelich; <*claim*> unberechtigt

illicit /ɪ'lɪsɪt/ *a*, **-ly** *adv* illegal

illiterate /ɪ'lɪtərət/ *a* **be ~te** nicht lesen und schreiben können

illness /'ɪlnɪs/ *n* Krankheit *f*

illogical /ɪ'lɒdʒɪkl/ *a*, **-ly** *adv* unlogisch

ill-treat /ɪl'tri:t/ *vt* misshandeln. **~ment** *n* Misshandlung *f*

illuminat|e /ɪ'lu:mɪneɪt/ *vt* beleuchten. **~ion** /-'neɪʃn/ *n* Beleuchtung *f*

illusion /ɪ'lu:ʒn/ *n* Illusion *f*; **be under the ~ that** sich (*dat*) einbilden, dass

illustrat|e /'ɪləstreɪt/ *vt* illustrieren. **~ion** /-'streɪʃn/ *n* Illustration *f*

illustrious /ɪ'lʌstrɪəs/ *a* berühmt

image /'ɪmɪdʒ/ *n* Bild *nt*; (*statue*) Standbild *nt*; (*exact likeness*) Ebenbild *nt*; **[public] ~** Image *nt*

imagin|able /ɪ'mædʒɪnəbl/ *a* vorstellbar. **~ary** /-ərɪ/ *a* eingebildet

imagination /ɪmædʒɪ'neɪʃn/ *n* Fantasie *f*; (*fancy*) Einbildung *f*. **~ive** /ɪ'mædʒɪnətɪv/ *a*, **-ly** *adv* fantasievoll; (*full of ideas*) einfallsreich

imagine /ɪ'mædʒɪn/ *vt* sich (*dat*) vorstellen; (*wrongly*) sich (*dat*) einbilden

im'balance *n* Unausgeglichenheit *f*

imbecile /'ɪmbəsi:l/ *n* Schwachsinnige(r) *m/f*; (*pej*) Idiot *m*

imitat|e /'ɪmɪteɪt/ *vt* nachahmen, imitieren. **~ion** /-'teɪʃn/ *n* Nachahmung *f*, Imitation *f*

immaculate /ɪ'mækjʊlət/ *a*, **-ly** *adv* tadellos; (*Relig*) unbefleckt

imma'ture *a* unreif

immediate /ɪ'mi:dɪət/ *a* sofortig; (*nearest*) nächste(r,s). **~ly** *adv* sofort; **~ly next to** unmittelbar neben ● *conj* sobald

immemorial /ɪmə'mɔːrɪəl/ *a* **from time ~** seit Urzeiten
immense /ɪ'mens/ *a*, **-ly** *adv* riesig; [!] enorm
immerse /ɪ'mɜːs/ *vt* untertauchen
immigrant /'ɪmɪgrənt/ *n* Einwanderer *m*
immigration /ɪmɪ'greɪʃn/ *n* Einwanderung *f*
imminent /'ɪmɪnənt/ *a* **be ~** unmittelbar bevorstehen
immobil|e /ɪ'məʊbaɪl/ *a* unbeweglich. **~ize** /-bəlaɪz/ *vt* (*fig*) lähmen; (*Med*) ruhig stellen. **~izer** *n* (*Auto*) Wegfahrsperre *f*
immodest /ɪ'mɒdɪst/ *a* unbescheiden
immoral /ɪ'mɒrəl/ *a*, **-ly** *adv* unmoralisch. **~ity** /ɪmə'rælətɪ/ *n* Unmoral *f*
immortal /ɪ'mɔːtl/ *a* unsterblich. **~ity** /-'tælətɪ/ *n* Unsterblichkeit *f*. **~ize** *vt* verewigen
immune /ɪ'mjuːn/ *a* immun (**to**/**from** gegen)
immunity /ɪ'mjuːnətɪ/ *n* Immunität *f*
imp /ɪmp/ *n* Kobold *m*
impact /'ɪmpækt/ *n* Aufprall *m*; (*collision*) Zusammenprall *m*; (*of bomb*) Einschlag *m*; (*fig*) Auswirkung *f*
impair /ɪm'peə(r)/ *vt* beeinträchtigen
impart /ɪm'pɑːt/ *vt* übermitteln (**to** *dat*); vermitteln <*knowledge*>
im'partial *a* unparteiisch
im'passable *a* unpassierbar
impassioned /ɪm'pæʃnd/ *a* leidenschaftlich
im'passive *a*, **-ly** *adv* unbeweglich
im'patien|ce *n* Ungeduld *f*. **~t** *a*, **-ly** *adv* ungeduldig
impeccable /ɪm'pekəbl/ *a*, **-bly** *adv* tadellos
impede /ɪm'piːd/ *vt* behindern
impediment /ɪm'pedɪmənt/ *n* Hindernis *nt*; (*in speech*) Sprachfehler *m*
impel /ɪm'pel/ *vt* (*pt/pp* **impelled**) treiben
impending /ɪm'pendɪŋ/ *a* bevorstehend
impenetrable /ɪm'penɪtrəbl/ *a* undurchdringlich
imperative /ɪm'perətɪv/ *a* **be ~** dringend notwendig sein ● *n* (*Gram*) Imperativ *m*
imper'ceptible *a* nicht wahrnehmbar
im'perfect *a* unvollkommen; (*faulty*) fehlerhaft ● *n* (*Gram*) Imperfekt *nt*. **~ion** /-'fekʃn/ *n* Unvollkommenheit *f*; (*fault*) Fehler *m*
imperial /ɪm'pɪərɪəl/ *a* kaiserlich. **~ism** *n* Imperialismus *m*
im'personal *a* unpersönlich
impersonat|e /ɪm'pɜːsəneɪt/ *vt* sich ausgeben als; (*Theat*) nachahmen, imitieren. **~or** *n* Imitator *m*
impertinen|ce /ɪm'pɜːtɪnəns/ *n* Frechheit *f*. **~t** *a* frech
imperturbable /ɪmpə'tɜːbəbl/ *a* unerschütterlich
impetuous /ɪm'petjʊəs/ *a*, **-ly** *adv* ungestüm
impetus /'ɪmpɪtəs/ *n* Schwung *m*
implacable /ɪm'plækəbl/ *a* unerbittlich
im'plant *vt* einpflanzen
implement[1] /'ɪmplɪmənt/ *n* Gerät *nt*
implement[2] /'ɪmplɪment/ *vt* ausführen
implication /ɪmplɪ'keɪʃn/ *n* Verwicklung *f*; **~s** *pl* Auswirkungen *pl*; **by ~** implizit
implicit /ɪm'plɪsɪt/ *a*, **-ly** *adv* unausgesprochen; (*absolute*) unbedingt

implore /ɪm'plɔ:(r)/ *vt* anflehen
imply /ɪm'plaɪ/ *vt* (*pt/pp* **-ied**) andeuten; **what are you ~ing?** was wollen Sie damit sagen?
impo'lite *a*, **-ly** *adv* unhöflich
import¹ /'ɪmpɔ:t/ *n* Import *m*, Einfuhr *f*
import² /ɪm'pɔ:t/ *vt* importieren, einführen
importan|ce /ɪm'pɔ:tns/ *n* Wichtigkeit *f*. **~t** *a* wichtig
importer /ɪm'pɔ:tə(r)/ *n* Importeur *m*
impos|e /ɪm'pəʊz/ *vt* auferlegen (**on** *dat*) ● *vi* sich aufdrängen (**on** *dat*). **~ing** *a* eindrucksvoll
impossi'bility *n* Unmöglichkeit *f*
im'possible *a*, **-bly** *adv* unmöglich
impostor /ɪm'pɒstə(r)/ *n* Betrüger(in) *m(f)*
impoten|ce /'ɪmpətəns/ *n* Machtlosigkeit *f*; (*Med*) Impotenz *f*. **~t** *a* machtlos; (*Med*) impotent
impoverished /ɪm'pɒvərɪʃt/ *a* verarmt
im'practicable *a* undurchführbar
im'practical *a* unpraktisch
impre'cise *a* ungenau
im'press *vt* beeindrucken; **~ sth [up]on s.o.** jdm etw einprägen
impression /ɪm'preʃn/ *n* Eindruck *m*; (*imitation*) Nachahmung *f*; (*edition*) Auflage *f*. **~ism** *n* Impressionismus *m*
impressive /ɪm'presɪv/ *a* eindrucksvoll
im'prison *vt* gefangen halten; (*put in prison*) ins Gefängnis sperren
im'probable *a* unwahrscheinlich
impromptu /ɪm'prɒmptju:/ *a* improvisiert ● *adv* aus dem Stegreif
im'proper *a*, **-ly** *adv* inkorrekt; (*indecent*) unanständig
impro'priety *n* Unkorrektheit *f*
improve /ɪm'pru:v/ *vt* verbessern; verschönern <*appearance*> ● *vi* sich bessern; **~ [up]on** übertreffen. **~ment** /-mənt/ *n* Verbesserung *f*; (*in health*) Besserung *f*
improvise /'ɪmprəvaɪz/ *vt/i* improvisieren
im'prudent *a* unklug
impuden|ce /'ɪmpjʊdəns/ *n* Frechheit *f*. **~t** *a*, **-ly** *adv* frech
impuls|e /'ɪmpʌls/ *n* Impuls *m*; **on [an] ~e** impulsiv. **~ive** /-'pʌlsɪv/ *a*, **-ly** *adv* impulsiv
im'pur|e *a* unrein. **~ity** *n* Unreinheit *f*
in /ɪn/ *prep* in (+ *dat*/(*into*) + *acc*); **sit in the garden** im Garten sitzen; **go in the garden** in den Garten gehen; **in May** im Mai; **in 1992** [im Jahre] 1992; **in this heat** bei dieser Hitze; **in the evening** am Abend; **in the sky** am Himmel; **in the world** auf der Welt; **in the street** auf der Straße; **deaf in one ear** auf einem Ohr taub; **in the army** beim Militär; **in English/German** auf Englisch/Deutsch; **in ink/pencil** mit Tinte/Bleistift; **in a soft/loud voice** mit leiser/lauter Stimme; **in doing this, he ...** indem er das tut/tat, ... er ● *adv* (*at home*) zu Hause; (*indoors*) drinnen; **he's not in yet** er ist noch nicht da; **all in** alles inbegriffen; (! *exhausted*) kaputt; **day in, day out** tagaus, tagein; **have it in for s.o.** ! es auf jdn abgesehen haben; **send/go in** hineinschicken/-gehen; **come/bring in** hereinkommen/-bringen ● *a* (! *in fashion*) in ● *n* **the ins and outs** alle Einzelheiten *pl*
ina'bility *n* Unfähigkeit *f*
inac'cessible *a* unzugänglich
in'accura|cy *n* Ungenauigkeit *f*. **~te** *a*, **-ly** *adv* ungenau

in'ac|tive *a* untätig. **~'tivity** *n* Untätigkeit *f*
in'adequate *a*, **-ly** *adv* unzulänglich
inad'missible *a* unzulässig
inadvertently /ɪnəd'vɜ:təntlɪ/ *adv* versehentlich
inad'visable *a* nicht ratsam
inane /ɪ'neɪn/ *a*, **-ly** *adv* albern
in'animate *a* unbelebt
in'applicable *a* nicht zutreffend
inap'propriate *a* unangebracht
inar'ticulate *a* undeutlich; **be ~** sich nicht gut ausdrücken können
inat'tentive *a* unaufmerksam
in'audible *a*, **-bly** *adv* unhörbar
inaugural /ɪ'nɔ:gjʊrl/ *a* Antritts-
inau'spicious *a* ungünstig
inborn /'ɪnbɔ:n/ *a* angeboren
inbred /ɪn'bred/ *a* angeboren
incalculable /ɪn'kælkjʊləbl/ *a* nicht berechenbar; (*fig*) unabsehbar
in'capable *a* unfähig; **be ~ of doing sth** nicht fähig sein, etw zu tun
incapacitate /ɪnkə'pæsɪteɪt/ *vt* unfähig machen
incarnation /ɪnkɑ:'neɪʃn/ *n* Inkarnation *f*
incendiary /ɪn'sendɪərɪ/ *a* & *n* **~ [bomb]** Brandbombe *f*
incense¹ /'ɪnsens/ *n* Weihrauch *m*
incense² /ɪn'sens/ *vt* wütend machen
incentive /ɪn'sentɪv/ *n* Anreiz *m*
incessant /ɪn'sesnt/ *a*, **-ly** *adv* unaufhörlich
incest /'ɪnsest/ *n* Inzest *m*, Blutschande *f*
inch /ɪntʃ/ *n* Zoll *m* ● *vi* **~ forward** sich ganz langsam vorwärts schieben
incident /'ɪnsɪdənt/ *n* Zwischenfall *m*
incidental /ɪnsɪ'dentl/ *a* nebensächlich; <*remark*> beiläufig; <*expenses*> Neben-. **~ly** *adv* übrigens
incinerate /ɪn'sɪnəreɪt/ *vt* verbrennen
incision /ɪn'sɪʒn/ *n* Einschnitt *m*
incisive /ɪn'saɪsɪv/ *a* scharfsinnig
incite /ɪn'saɪt/ *vt* aufhetzen. **~ment** *n* Aufhetzung *f*
in'clement *a* rau
inclination /ɪnklɪ'neɪʃn/ *n* Neigung *f*
incline /ɪn'klaɪn/ *vt* neigen; **be ~d to do sth** dazu neigen, etw zu tun ● *vi* sich neigen
inclu|de /ɪn'klu:d/ *vt* einschließen; (*contain*) enthalten; (*incorporate*) aufnehmen (**in** in + *acc*). **~ding** *prep* einschließlich (+ *gen*). **~sion** /-u:ʒn/ *n* Aufnahme *f*
inclusive /ɪn'klu:sɪv/ *a* Inklusiv-; **~ of** einschließlich (+ *gen*)
incognito /ɪnkɒg'ni:təʊ/ *adv* inkognito
inco'herent *a*, **-ly** *adv* zusammenhanglos; (*incomprehensible*) unverständlich
income /'ɪnkəm/ *n* Einkommen *nt*. **~ tax** *n* Einkommensteuer *f*
'incoming *a* ankommend; <*mail, call*> eingehend
in'comparable *a* unvergleichlich
incom'patible *a* unvereinbar; **be ~** <*people:*> nicht zueinander passen
in'competen|ce *n* Unfähigkeit *f*. **~t** *a* unfähig
incom'plete *a* unvollständig
incompre'hensible *a* unverständlich
incon'ceivable *a* undenkbar
incon'clusive *a* nicht schlüssig

incongruous /ɪnˈkɒŋgrʊəs/ *a* unpassend

inconˈsiderate *a* rücksichtslos

inconˈsistent *a*, **-ly** *adv* widersprüchlich; (*illogical*) inkonsequent; **be ~** <*things*:> nicht übereinstimmen

inconsolable /ɪnkənˈsəʊləbl/ *a* untröstlich

inconˈspicuous *a* unauffällig

incontinen|ce /ɪnˈkɒntɪnəns/ *n* Inkontinenz *f*. **~t** *a* inkontinent

inconˈvenien|ce *n* Unannehmlichkeit *f*; (*drawback*) Nachteil *m*. **~t** *a*, **-ly** *adv* ungünstig; **be ~t for s.o.** jdm nicht passen

incorporate /ɪnˈkɔːpəreɪt/ *vt* aufnehmen; (*contain*) enthalten

incorˈrect *a*, **-ly** *adv* inkorrekt

incorrigible /ɪnˈkɒrɪdʒəbl/ *a* unverbesserlich

incorruptible /ɪnkəˈrʌptəbl/ *a* unbestechlich

increase¹ /ˈɪnkriːs/ *n* Zunahme *f*; (*rise*) Erhöhung *f*; **be on the ~** zunehmen

increas|e² /ɪnˈkriːs/ *vt* vergrößern; (*raise*) erhöhen ● *vi* zunehmen; (*rise*) sich erhöhen. **~ing** *a*, **-ly** *adv* zunehmend

inˈcredible *a*, **-bly** *adv* unglaublich

incredulous /ɪnˈkredjʊləs/ *a* ungläubig

incriminate /ɪnˈkrɪmɪneɪt/ *vt* (*Jur*) belasten

incur /ɪnˈkɜː(r)/ *vt* (*pt/pp* **incurred**) sich (*dat*) zuziehen; machen <*debts*>

inˈcurable *a*, **-bly** *adv* unheilbar

indebted /ɪnˈdetɪd/ *a* verpflichtet (**to** *dat*)

inˈdecent *a*, **-ly** *adv* unanständig

indeˈcision *n* Unentschlossenheit *f*

indeˈcisive *a* ergebnislos; <*person*> unentschlossen

indeed /ɪnˈdiːd/ *adv* in der Tat, tatsächlich; **very much ~** sehr

indefatigable /ɪndɪˈfætɪgəbl/ *a* unermüdlich

inˈdefinite *a* unbestimmt. **~ly** *adv* unbegrenzt; <*postpone*> auf unbestimmte Zeit

indent /ɪnˈdent/ *vt* (*Typ*) einrücken. **~ation** /-ˈteɪʃn/ *n* Einrückung *f*; (*notch*) Kerbe *f*

indeˈpenden|ce *n* Unabhängigkeit *f*; (*self-reliance*) Selbstständigkeit *f*. **~t** *a*, **-ly** *adv* unabhängig; selbstständig

indescribable /ɪndɪˈskraɪbəbl/ *a*, **-bly** *adv* unbeschreiblich

indestructible /ɪndɪˈstrʌktəbl/ *a* unzerstörbar

indeterminate /ɪndɪˈtɜːmɪnət/ *a* unbestimmt

index /ˈɪndeks/ *n* Register *nt*

index: ~ card *n* Karteikarte *f*. **~ finger** *n* Zeigefinger *m*. **~-linked** *a* <*pension*> dynamisch

India /ˈɪndɪə/ *n* Indien *nt*. **~n** *a* indisch; (*American*) indianisch ● *n* Inder(in) *m*(*f*); (*American*) Indianer(in) *m*(*f*)

Indian ˈsummer *n* Nachsommer *m*

indicat|e /ˈɪndɪkeɪt/ *vt* zeigen; (*point at*) zeigen auf (+ *acc*); (*hint*) andeuten; (*register*) anzeigen ● *vi* <*car*:> blinken. **~ion** /-ˈkeɪʃn/ *n* Anzeichen *nt*

indicative /ɪnˈdɪkətɪv/ *n* (*Gram*) Indikativ *m*

indicator /ˈɪndɪkeɪtə(r)/ *n* (*Auto*) Blinker *m*

inˈdifferen|ce *n* Gleichgültigkeit *f*. **~t** *a*, **-ly** *adv* gleichgültig; (*not good*) mittelmäßig

indiˈgest|ible *a* unverdaulich; (*difficult to digest*) schwer verdaulich. **~ion** *n* Magenverstimmung *f*

indigna|nt /ɪnˈdɪgnənt/ *a*, **-ly** *adv* entrüstet, empört. **~tion**

/-ˈneɪʃn/ *n* Entrüstung *f*, Empörung *f*
inˈdignity *n* Demütigung *f*
indiˈrect *a*, **-ly** *adv* indirekt
indiˈscreet *a* indiskret
indisˈcretion *n* Indiskretion *f*
indiˈspensable *a* unentbehrlich
indisposed /ɪndɪˈspəʊzd/ *a* indisponiert
indisputable /ɪndɪˈspju:təbl/ *a*, **-bly** *adv* unbestreitbar
indiˈstinct *a*, **-ly** *adv* undeutlich
indistinguishable /ɪndɪˈstɪŋgwɪʃəbl/ *a* **be ~** nicht zu unterscheiden sein
individual /ɪndɪˈvɪdjʊəl/ *a*, **-ly** *adv* individuell; (*single*) einzeln ● *n* Individuum *nt*. **~ity** /-ˈælətɪ/ *n* Individualität *f*
indiˈvisible *a* unteilbar
indoctrinate /ɪnˈdɒktrɪneɪt/ *vt* indoktrinieren
indolen|ce /ˈɪndələns/ *n* Faulheit *f*. **~t** *a* faul
indomitable /ɪnˈdɒmɪtəbl/ *a* unbeugsam
indoor /ˈɪndɔ:(r)/ *a* Innen-; <*clothes*> Haus-; <*plant*> Zimmer-; (*Sport*) Hallen-. **~s** /-ˈdɔ:z/ *adv* im Haus, drinnen; **go ~s** ins Haus gehen
indulge /ɪnˈdʌldʒ/ *vt* frönen (+ *dat*); verwöhnen <*child*> ● *vi* **~ in** frönen (+ *dat*). **~nce** /-əns/ *n* Nachgiebigkeit *f*; (*leniency*) Nachsicht *f*. **~nt** *a* [zu] nachgiebig; nachsichtig
industrial /ɪnˈdʌstrɪəl/ *a* Industrie-. **~ist** *n* Industrielle(r) *m*
industr|ious /ɪnˈdʌstrɪəs/ *a*, **-ly** *adv* fleißig. **~y** /ˈɪndəstrɪ/ *n* Industrie *f*; (*zeal*) Fleiß *m*
inebriated /ɪˈni:brɪeɪtɪd/ *a* betrunken
inˈedible *a* nicht essbar
ineffective *a*, **-ly** *adv* unwirksam; <*person*> untauglich
ineffˈicient *a* unfähig; <*organization*> nicht leistungsfähig; <*method*> nicht rationell
inˈeligible *a* nicht berechtigt
inept /ɪˈnept/ *a* ungeschickt
ineˈquality *n* Ungleichheit *f*
inertia /ɪˈnɜ:ʃə/ *n* Trägheit *f*
inescapable /ɪnɪˈskeɪpəbl/ *a* unvermeidlich
inestimable /ɪnˈestɪməbl/ *a* unschätzbar
inevitab|le /ɪnˈevɪtəbl/ *a* unvermeidlich. **~ly** *adv* zwangsläufig
ineˈxact *a* ungenau
inexˈcusable *a* unverzeihlich
inexhaustible /ɪnɪgˈzɔ:stəbl/ *a* unerschöpflich
inexˈpensive *a*, **-ly** *adv* preiswert
inexˈperience *n* Unerfahrenheit *f*. **~d** *a* unerfahren
inexplicable /ɪnɪkˈsplɪkəbl/ *a* unerklärlich
inˈfallible *a* unfehlbar
infamous /ˈɪnfəməs/ *a* niederträchtig; (*notorious*) berüchtigt
infan|cy /ˈɪnfənsɪ/ *n* frühe Kindheit *f*; (*fig*) Anfangsstadium *nt*. **~t** *n* Kleinkind *nt*. **~tile** *a* kindisch
infantry /ˈɪnfəntrɪ/ *n* Infanterie *f*
infatuated /ɪnˈfætʃʊeɪtɪd/ *a* vernarrt (**with** in + *acc*)
infect /ɪnˈfekt/ *vt* anstecken, infizieren; **become ~ed** <*wound*:> sich infizieren. **~ion** /-ˈfekʃn/ *n* Infektion *f*. **~ious** /-ˈfekʃəs/ *a* ansteckend
inferior /ɪnˈfɪərɪə(r)/ *a* minderwertig; (*in rank*) untergeordnet ● *n* Untergebene(r) *m/f*
inferiority /ɪnfɪərɪˈɒrətɪ/ *n* Minderwertigkeit *f*. **~ complex** *n* Minderwertigkeitskomplex *m*

infern|al /ɪn'fɜ:nl/ *a* höllisch. **~o** *n* flammendes Inferno *nt*
in'fertile *a* unfruchtbar
infest /ɪn'fest/ *vt* **be ~ed with** befallen sein von; <*place*> verseucht sein mit
infi'delity *n* Untreue *f*
infighting /'ɪnfaɪtɪŋ/ *n* (*fig*) interne Machtkämpfe *pl*
infinite /'ɪnfɪnət/ *a*, **-ly** *adv* unendlich
infinitive /ɪn'fɪnətɪv/ *n* (*Gram*) Infinitiv *m*
infinity /ɪn'fɪnətɪ/ *n* Unendlichkeit *f*
inflame /ɪn'fleɪm/ *vt* entzünden. **~d** *a* entzündet
in'flammable *a* feuergefährlich
inflammation /ɪnflə'meɪʃn/ *n* Entzündung *f*
inflammatory /ɪn'flæmətrɪ/ *a* aufrührerisch
inflat|e /ɪn'fleɪt/ *vt* aufblasen; (*with pump*) aufpumpen. **~ion** /-eɪʃn/ *n* Inflation *f*. **~ionary** /-eɪʃənərɪ/ *a* inflationär
in'flexible *a* starr; <*person*> unbeugsam
inflict /ɪn'flɪkt/ *vt* zufügen (**on** *dat*); versetzen <*blow*> (**on** *dat*)
influen|ce /'ɪnflʊəns/ *n* Einfluss *m* ● *vt* beeinflussen. **~tial** /-'enʃl/ *a* einflussreich
influenza /ɪnflʊ'enzə/ *n* Grippe *f*
inform /ɪn'fɔ:m/ *vt* benachrichtigen; (*officially*) informieren; **~ s.o. of sth** jdm etw mitteilen; **keep s.o. ~ed** jdn auf dem Laufenden halten ● *vi* **~ against** denunzieren
in'formal *a*, **-ly** *adv* zwanglos; (*unofficial*) inoffiziell. **~'ity** *n* Zwanglosigkeit *f*
informant /ɪn'fɔ:mənt/ *n* Gewährsmann *m*
informat|ion /ɪnfə'meɪʃn/ *n* Auskunft *f*; **a piece of ~ion** eine Auskunft. **~ive** /ɪn'fɔ:mətɪv/ *a* aufschlussreich; (*instructive*) lehrreich
informer /ɪn'fɔ:mə(r)/ *n* Spitzel *m*; (*Pol*) Denunziant *m*
infra-'red /ɪnfrə-/ *a* infrarot
in'frequent *a*, **-ly** *adv* selten
infringe /ɪn'frɪndʒ/ *vt/i* **~ [on]** verstoßen gegen. **~ment** *n* Verstoß *m*
infuriat|e /ɪn'fjʊərɪeɪt/ *vt* wütend machen. **~ing** *a* ärgerlich
ingenious /ɪn'dʒi:nɪəs/ *a* erfinderisch; <*thing*> raffiniert
ingenuity /ɪndʒɪ'nju:ətɪ/ *n* Geschicklichkeit *f*
ingrained /ɪn'greɪnd/ *a* eingefleischt; **be ~** <*dirt:*> tief sitzen
ingratiate /ɪn'greɪʃɪeɪt/ *vt* **~ oneself** sich einschmeicheln (**with** bei)
in'gratitude *n* Undankbarkeit *f*
ingredient /ɪn'gri:dɪənt/ *n* (*Culin*) Zutat *f*
ingrowing /'ɪngrəʊɪŋ/ *a* <*nail*> eingewachsen
inhabit /ɪn'hæbɪt/ *vt* bewohnen. **~ant** *n* Einwohner(in) *m(f)*
inhale /ɪn'heɪl/ *vt/i* einatmen; (*Med & when smoking*) inhalieren
inherent /ɪn'hɪərənt/ *a* natürlich
inherit /ɪn'herɪt/ *vt* erben. **~ance** /-əns/ *n* Erbschaft *f*, Erbe *nt*
inhibit|ed /ɪn'hɪbɪtɪd/ *a* gehemmt. **~ion** /-'bɪʃn/ *n* Hemmung *f*
inho'spitable *a* ungastlich
in'human *a* unmenschlich
inimitable /ɪ'nɪmɪtəbl/ *a* unnachahmlich
initial /ɪ'nɪʃl/ *a* anfänglich, Anfangs- ● *n* Anfangsbuchstabe *m*; **my ~s** meine Initialen. **~ly** *adv* anfangs, am Anfang
initiat|e /ɪ'nɪʃɪeɪt/ *vt* einführen. **~ion** /-'eɪʃn/ *n* Einführung *f*

initiative /ɪ'nɪʃətɪv/ *n* Initiative *f*
inject /ɪn'dʒekt/ *vt* einspritzen, injizieren. **~ion** /-ekʃn/ *n* Spritze *f*, Injektion *f*
injur|e /'ɪndʒə(r)/ *vt* verletzen. **~y** *n* Verletzung *f*
in'justice *n* Ungerechtigkeit *f*; **do s.o. an ~** jdm unrecht tun
ink /ɪŋk/ *n* Tinte *f*
inlaid /ɪn'leɪd/ *a* eingelegt
inland /'ɪnlənd/ *a* Binnen- ● *adv* landeinwärts
in-laws /'ɪnlɔ:z/ *npl* [!] Schwiegereltern *pl*
inlay /'ɪnleɪ/ *n* Einlegearbeit *f*
inlet /'ɪnlet/ *n* schmale Bucht *f*; (*Techn*) Zuleitung *f*
inmate /'ɪnmeɪt/ *n* Insasse *m*
inn /ɪn/ *n* Gasthaus *nt*
innate /ɪ'neɪt/ *a* angeboren
inner /'ɪnə(r)/ *a* innere(r,s). **~most** *a* innerste(r,s)
innocen|ce /'ɪnəsəns/ *n* Unschuld *f*. **~t** *a* unschuldig. **~tly** *adv* in aller Unschuld
innocuous /ɪ'nɒkjʊəs/ *a* harmlos
innovat|ion /ɪnə'veɪʃn/ *n* Neuerung *f*. **~ive** /'ɪnəvətɪv/ *a* innovativ. **~or** /'ɪnəveɪtə(r)/ *n* Neuerer *m*
innumerable /ɪ'nju:mərəbl/ *a* unzählig
inoculat|e /ɪ'nɒkjʊleɪt/ *vt* impfen. **~ion** /-'leɪʃn/ *n* Impfung *f*
inof'fensive *a* harmlos
in'operable *a* nicht operierbar
in'opportune *a* unpassend
inor'ganic *a* anorganisch
'in-patient *n* [stationär behandelter] Krankenhauspatient *m*
input /'ɪnpʊt/ *n* Input *m* & *nt*
inquest /'ɪnkwest/ *n* gerichtliche Untersuchung *f* der Todesursache
inquir|e /ɪn'kwaɪə(r)/ *vi* sich erkundigen (**about** nach); **~e into** untersuchen ● *vt* sich erkundigen nach. **~y** *n* Erkundigung *f*; (*investigation*) Untersuchung *f*
inquisitive /ɪn'kwɪzətɪv/ *a*, **-ly** *adv* neugierig
in'sane *a* geisteskrank; (*fig*) wahnsinnig
in'sanitary *a* unhygienisch
in'sanity *n* Geisteskrankheit *f*
insatiable /ɪn'seɪʃəbl/ *a* unersättlich
inscription /ɪn'skrɪpʃn/ *n* Inschrift *f*
inscrutable /ɪn'skru:təbl/ *a* unergründlich; <*expression*> undurchdringlich
insect /'ɪnsekt/ *n* Insekt *nt*. **~icide** /-'sektɪsaɪd/ *n* Insektenvertilgungsmittel *nt*
inse'cur|e *a* nicht sicher; (*fig*) unsicher. **~ity** *n* Unsicherheit *f*
in'sensitive *a* gefühllos; **~ to** unempfindlich gegen
in'separable *a* untrennbar; (*people*) unzertrennlich
insert¹ /'ɪnsɜ:t/ *n* Einsatz *m*
insert² /ɪn'sɜ:t/ *vt* einfügen, einsetzen; einstecken <*key*>; einwerfen <*coin*>. **~ion** /-ɜ:ʃn/ *n* (*insert*) Einsatz *m*; (*in text*) Einfügung *f*
inside /ɪn'saɪd/ *n* Innenseite *f*; (*of house*) Innere(s) *nt* ● *attrib* Innen- ● *adv* innen; (*indoors*) drinnen; **go ~** hineingehen; **come ~** hereinkommen; **~ out** links [herum]; **know sth ~ out** etw in- und auswendig kennen ● *prep* **~ [of]** in (+ *dat*/ (*into*) + *acc*)
insight /'ɪnsaɪt/ *n* Einblick *m* (**into** in + *acc*); (*understanding*) Einsicht *f*
insig'nificant *a* unbedeutend
insin'cere *a* unaufrichtig

insinuat|e /ɪn'sɪnjʊeɪt/ *vt* andeuten. **~ion** /-'eɪʃn/ *n* Andeutung *f*
insipid /ɪn'sɪpɪd/ *a* fade
insist /ɪn'sɪst/ *vi* darauf bestehen; **~ on** bestehen auf (+ *dat*) ● *vt* **~ that** darauf bestehen, dass. **~ence** *n* Bestehen *nt*. **~ent** *a*, **-ly** *adv* beharrlich; **be ~ent** darauf bestehen
'insole *n* Einlegesohle *f*
insolen|ce /'ɪnsələns/ *n* Unverschämtheit *f*. **~t** *a*, **-ly** *adv* unverschämt
in'soluble *a* unlöslich; (*fig*) unlösbar
in'solvent *a* zahlungsunfähig
insomnia /ɪn'sɒmnɪə/ *n* Schlaflosigkeit *f*
inspect /ɪn'spekt/ *vt* inspizieren; (*test*) prüfen; kontrollieren <*ticket*>. **~ion** /-ekʃn/ *n* Inspektion *f*. **~or** *n* Inspektor *m*; (*of tickets*) Kontrolleur *m*
inspiration /ɪnspə'reɪʃn/ *n* Inspiration *f*
inspire /ɪn'spaɪə(r)/ *vt* inspirieren
insta'bility *n* Unbeständigkeit *f*; (*of person*) Labilität *f*
install /ɪn'stɔ:l/ *vt* installieren. **~ation** /-stə'leɪʃn/ *n* Installation *f*
instalment /ɪn'stɔ:lmənt/ *n* (*Comm*) Rate *f*; (*of serial*) Fortsetzung *f*; (*Radio, TV*) Folge *f*
instance /'ɪnstəns/ *n* Fall *m*; (*example*) Beispiel *nt*; **in the first ~** zunächst; **for ~** zum Beispiel
instant /'ɪnstənt/ *a* sofortig; (*Culin*) Instant- ● *n* Augenblick *m*, Moment *m*. **~aneous** /-'teɪmɪəs/ *a* unverzüglich, unmittelbar
instant 'coffee *n* Pulverkaffee *m*
instantly /'ɪnstəntlɪ/ *adv* sofort
instead /ɪn'sted/ *adv* statt dessen; **~ of** statt (+ *gen*), anstelle von; **~ of me** an meiner Stelle; **~ of going** anstatt zu gehen
'instep *n* Spann *m*, Rist *m*
instigat|e /'ɪnstɪgeɪt/ *vt* anstiften; einleiten <*proceedings*>. **~ion** /-'geɪʃn/ *n* Anstiftung *f*; **at his ~ion** auf seine Veranlassung
instil /ɪn'stɪl/ *vt* (*pt/pp* **instilled**) einprägen (**into s.o.** jdm)
instinct /'ɪnstɪŋkt/ *n* Instinkt *m*. **~ive** /ɪn'stɪŋktɪv/ *a*, **-ly** *adv* instinktiv
institut|e /'ɪnstɪtju:t/ *n* Institut *nt*. **~ion** /-'tju:ʃn/ *n* Institution *f*; (*home*) Anstalt *f*
instruct /ɪn'strʌkt/ *vt* unterrichten; (*order*) anweisen. **~ion** /-ʌkʃn/ *n* Unterricht *m*; Anweisung *f*; **~ions** *pl* **for use** Gebrauchsanweisung *f*. **~ive** /-ɪv/ *a* lehrreich. **~or** *n* Lehrer(in) *m(f)*; (*Mil*) Ausbilder *m*
instrument /'ɪnstrʊmənt/ *n* Instrument *nt*. **~al** /-'mentl/ *a* Instrumental-
insu'bordi|nate *a* ungehorsam. **~nation** /-'neɪʃn/ *n* Ungehorsam *m*; (*Mil*) Insubordination *f*
insuf'ficient *a*, **-ly** *adv* nicht genügend
insulat|e /'ɪnsjʊleɪt/ *vt* isolieren. **~ing tape** *n* Isolierband *nt*. **~ion** /-'leɪʃn/ *n* Isolierung *f*
insult¹ /'ɪnsʌlt/ *n* Beleidigung *f*
insult² /ɪn'sʌlt/ *vt* beleidigen
insur|ance /ɪn'ʃʊərəns/ *n* Versicherung *f*. **~e** *vt* versichern
intact /ɪn'tækt/ *a* unbeschädigt; (*complete*) vollständig
'intake *n* Aufnahme *f*
in'tangible *a* nicht greifbar
integral /'ɪntɪgrl/ *a* wesentlich

integrat|e /'ɪntɪgreɪt/ *vt* integrieren ● *vi* sich integrieren. **~ion** /-'greɪʃn/ *n* Integration *f*

integrity /ɪn'tegrətɪ/ *n* Integrität *f*

intellect /'ɪntəlekt/ *n* Intellekt *m*. **~ual** /-'lektjʊəl/ *a* intellektuell

intelligen|ce /ɪn'telɪdʒəns/ *n* Intelligenz *f*; (*Mil*) Nachrichtendienst *m*; (*information*) Meldungen *pl*. **~t** *a*, **-ly** *adv* intelligent

intelligible /ɪn'telɪdʒəbl/ *a* verständlich

intend /ɪn'tend/ *vt* beabsichtigen; **be ~ed for** bestimmt sein für

intense /ɪn'tens/ *a* intensiv; *<pain>* stark. **~ly** *adv* äußerst; *<study>* intensiv

intensify /ɪn'tensɪfaɪ/ *v* (*pt/pp* **-ied**) ● *vt* intensivieren ● *vi* zunehmen

intensity /ɪn'tensətɪ/ *n* Intensität *f*

intensive /ɪn'tensɪv/ *a*, **-ly** *adv* intensiv; **be in ~ care** auf der Intensivstation sein

intent /ɪn'tent/ *a*, **-ly** *adv* aufmerksam; **~ on** (*absorbed in*) vertieft in (+ *acc*) ● *n* Absicht *f*

intention /ɪn'tenʃn/ *n* Absicht *f*. **~al** *a*, **-ly** *adv* absichtlich

inter'acti|on *n* Wechselwirkung *f*. **~ve** *a* interaktiv

intercede /ɪntə'si:d/ *vi* Fürsprache einlegen (**on behalf of** für)

intercept /ɪntə'sept/ *vt* abfangen

'interchange *n* Austausch *m*; (*Auto*) Autobahnkreuz *nt*

intercom /'ɪntəkɒm/ *n* [Gegen]sprechanlage *f*

'intercourse *n* (*sexual*) Geschlechtsverkehr *m*

interest /'ɪntrəst/ *n* Interesse *nt*; (*Comm*) Zinsen *pl* ● *vt* interessieren; **be ~ed** sich interessieren (**in** für). **~ing** *a* interessant. **~ rate** *n* Zinssatz *m*

interfere /ɪntə'fɪə(r)/ *vi* sich einmischen. **~nce** /-əns/ *n* Einmischung *f*; (*Radio, TV*) Störung *f*

interim /'ɪntərɪm/ *a* Zwischen-; (*temporary*) vorläufig

interior /ɪn'tɪərɪə(r)/ *a* innere(r,s), Innen- ● *n* Innere(s) *nt*

interject /ɪntə'dʒekt/ *vt* einwerfen. **~ion** /-ekʃn/ *n* Interjektion *f*; (*remark*) Einwurf *m*

interlude /'ɪntəlu:d/ *n* Pause *f*; (*performance*) Zwischenspiel *nt*

inter'marry *vi* untereinander heiraten; *<different groups:>* Mischehen schließen

intermediary /ɪntə'mi:dɪərɪ/ *n* Vermittler(in) *m(f)*

intermediate /ɪntə'mi:dɪət/ *a* Zwischen-

interminable /ɪn'tɜ:mɪnəbl/ *a* endlos [lang]

intermittent /ɪntə'mɪtənt/ *a* in Abständen auftretend

internal /ɪn'tɜ:nl/ *a* innere(r,s); *<matter, dispute>* intern. **~ly** *adv* innerlich; *<deal with>* intern

inter'national *a*, **-ly** *adv* international ● *n* Länderspiel *nt*; (*player*) Nationalspieler(in) *m(f)*

'Internet *n* Internet *nt*; **on the ~** im Internet

internment /ɪn'tɜ:nmənt/ *n* Internierung *f*

'interplay *n* Wechselspiel *nt*

interpolate /ɪn'tɜ:pəleɪt/ *vt* einwerfen

interpret /ɪn'tɜ:prɪt/ *vt* interpretieren; auslegen *<text>*; deuten *<dream>*; (*translate*) dolmetschen ● *vi* dolmetschen. **~ation** /-'teɪʃn/ *n* Interpretation *f*. **~er** *n* Dolmetscher(in) *m(f)*

interrogat|e /ɪn'terəgeɪt/ *vt* verhören. **~ion** /-'geɪʃn/ *n* Verhör *nt*

interrogative /ɪntə'rɒgətɪv/ *a* & *n* ~ **[pronoun]** Interrogativpronomen *nt*

interrupt /ɪntə'rʌpt/ *vt/i* unterbrechen; **don't ~!** red nicht dazwischen! **~ion** /-ʌpʃn/ *n* Unterbrechung *f*

intersect /ɪntə'sekt/ *vi* sich kreuzen; (*Geom*) sich schneiden. **~ion** /-ekʃn/ *n* Kreuzung *f*

interspersed /ɪntə'spɜ:st/ *a* ~ **with** durchsetzt mit

inter'twine *vi* sich ineinanderschlingen

interval /'ɪntəvl/ *n* Abstand *m*; (*Theat*) Pause *f*; (*Mus*) Intervall *nt*; **at hourly ~s** alle Stunde; **bright ~s** *pl* Aufheiterungen *pl*

interven|e /ɪntə'vi:n/ *vi* eingreifen; (*occur*) dazwischenkommen. **~tion** /-'venʃn/ *n* Eingreifen *nt*; (*Mil, Pol*) Intervention *f*

interview /'ɪntəvju:/ *n* (*Journ*) Interview *nt*; (*for job*) Vorstellungsgespräch *nt* ● *vt* interviewen; ein Vorstellungsgespräch führen mit. **~er** *n* Interviewer(in) *m(f)*

intimacy /'ɪntɪməsɪ/ *n* Vertrautheit *f*; (*sexual*) Intimität *f*

intimate /'ɪntɪmət/ *a*, **-ly** *adv* vertraut; <*friend*> eng; (*sexually*) intim

intimidat|e /ɪn'tɪmɪdeɪt/ *vt* einschüchtern. **~ion** /-'deɪʃn/ *n* Einschüchterung *f*

into /'ɪntə, *vor einem Vokal* 'ɪntʊ/ *prep* in (+ *acc*); **be ~** [!] sich auskennen mit; **7 ~ 21** 21 [geteilt] durch 7

in'tolerable *a* unerträglich

in'toleran|ce *n* Intoleranz *f*. **~t** *a* intolerant

intonation /ɪntə'neɪʃn/ *n* Tonfall *m*

intoxicat|ed /ɪn'tɒksɪkeɪtɪd/ *a* betrunken; (*fig*) berauscht. **~ion** /-'keɪʃn/ *n* Rausch *m*

intransigent /ɪn'trænsɪdʒənt/ *a* unnachgiebig

in'transitive *a*, **-ly** *adv* intransitiv

intrepid /ɪn'trepɪd/ *a* kühn, unerschrocken

intricate /'ɪntrɪkət/ *a* kompliziert

intrigu|e /ɪn'tri:g/ *n* Intrige *f* ● *vt* faszinieren. **~ing** *a* faszinierend

intrinsic /ɪn'trɪnsɪk/ *a* ~ **value** Eigenwert *m*

introduce /ɪntrə'dju:s/ *vt* vorstellen; (*bring in, insert*) einführen

introduct|ion /ɪntrə'dʌkʃn/ *n* Einführung *f*; (*to person*) Vorstellung *f*; (*to book*) Einleitung *f*. **~ory** /-tərɪ/ *a* einleitend

introvert /'ɪntrəvɜ:t/ *n* introvertierter Mensch *m*

intru|de /ɪn'tru:d/ *vi* stören. **~der** *n* Eindringling *m*. **~sion** /-u:ʒn/ *n* Störung *f*

intuit|ion /ɪntju:'ɪʃn/ *n* Intuition *f*. **~ive** /-'tju:ɪtɪv/ *a*, **-ly** *adv* intuitiv

inundate /'ɪnəndeɪt/ *vt* überschwemmen

invade /ɪn'veɪd/ *vt* einfallen in (+ *acc*). **~r** *n* Angreifer *m*

invalid¹ /'ɪnvəlɪd/ *n* Kranke(r) *m/f*

invalid² /ɪn'vælɪd/ *a* ungültig

in'valuable *a* unschätzbar; <*person*> unersetzlich

in'variab|le *a* unveränderlich. **~ly** *adv* immer

invasion /ɪn'veɪʒn/ *n* Invasion *f*

invent /ɪn'vent/ *vt* erfinden. **~ion** /-enʃn/ *n* Erfindung *f*.

~ive /-tɪv/ *a* erfinderisch. **~or** *n* Erfinder *m*
inventory /ˈɪnvəntrɪ/ *n* Bestandsliste *f*
invert /ɪnˈvɜ:t/ *vt* umkehren. **~ed commas** *npl* Anführungszeichen *pl*
invest /ɪnˈvest/ *vt* investieren, anlegen; **~ in** ([!] *buy*) sich (*dat*) zulegen
investigat|e /ɪnˈvestɪgeɪt/ *vt* untersuchen. **~ion** /-ˈgeɪʃn/ *n* Untersuchung *f*
invest|ment /ɪnˈvestmənt/ *n* Anlage *f*; **be a good ~ment** (*fig*) sich bezahlt machen. **~or** *n* Kapitalanleger *m*
invidious /ɪnˈvɪdɪəs/ *a* unerfreulich; (*unfair*) ungerecht
invincible /ɪnˈvɪnsəbl/ *a* unbesiegbar
inviolable /ɪnˈvaɪələbl/ *a* unantastbar
inˈvisible *a* unsichtbar
invitation /ɪnvɪˈteɪʃn/ *n* Einladung *f*
invit|e /ɪnˈvaɪt/ *vt* einladen. **~ing** *a* einladend
invoice /ˈɪnvɔɪs/ *n* Rechnung *f* ● *vt* **~ s.o.** jdm eine Rechnung schicken
inˈvoluntary *a*, **-ily** *adv* unwillkürlich
involve /ɪnˈvɒlv/ *vt* beteiligen; (*affect*) betreffen; (*implicate*) verwickeln; (*entail*) mit sich bringen; (*mean*) bedeuten; **be ~d in** beteiligt sein an (+ *dat*); (*implicated*) verwickelt sein in (+ *acc*); **get ~d with s.o.** sich mit jdm einlassen. **~d** *a* kompliziert
inˈvulnerable *a* unverwundbar; <*position*> unangreifbar
inward /ˈɪnwəd/ *a* innere(r,s). **~s** *adv* nach innen
iodine /ˈaɪədi:n/ *n* Jod *nt*
IOU *abbr* Schuldschein *m*
Iran /ɪˈrɑ:n/ *n* der Iran
Iraq /ɪˈrɑ:k/ *n* der Irak
irascible /ɪˈræsəbl/ *a* aufbrausend
irate /aɪˈreɪt/ *a* wütend
Ireland /ˈaɪələnd/ *n* Irland *nt*
iris /ˈaɪərɪs/ *n* (*Anat*) Regenbogenhaut *f*, Iris *f*; (*Bot*) Schwertlilie *f*
Irish /ˈaɪərɪʃ/ *a* irisch ● *n* **the ~** *pl* die Iren. **~man** *n* Ire *m*. **~woman** *n* Irin *f*
iron /ˈaɪən/ *a* Eisen-; (*fig*) eisern ● *n* Eisen *nt*; (*appliance*) Bügeleisen *nt* ● *vt/i* bügeln
ironic[al] /aɪˈrɒnɪk[l]/ *a* ironisch
ironing /ˈaɪənɪŋ/ *n* Bügeln *nt*; (*articles*) Bügelwäsche *f*. **~-board** *n* Bügelbrett *nt*
ironmonger /ˈ-mʌŋgə(r)/ *n* **~'s [shop]** Haushaltswarengeschäft *nt*
irony /ˈaɪərənɪ/ *n* Ironie *f*
irrational /ɪˈræʃənl/ *a* irrational
irreconcilable /ɪˈrekənsaɪləbl/ *a* unversöhnlich
irrefutable /ɪrɪˈfju:təbl/ *a* unwiderlegbar
irregular /ɪˈregjʊlə(r)/ *a*, **-ly** *adv* unregelmäßig; (*against rules*) regelwidrig. **~ity** /-ˈlærətɪ/ *n* Unregelmäßigkeit *f*; Regelwidrigkeit *f*
irrelevant /ɪˈreləvənt/ *a* irrelevant
irreparable /ɪˈrepərəbl/ *a* nicht wieder gutzumachen
irreplaceable /ɪrɪˈpleɪsəbl/ *a* unersetzlich
irrepressible /ɪrɪˈpresəbl/ *a* unverwüstlich; **be ~** <*person:*> nicht unterzukriegen sein
irresistible /ɪrɪˈzɪstəbl/ *a* unwiderstehlich
irresolute /ɪˈrezəlu:t/ *a* unentschlossen
irrespective /ɪrɪˈspektɪv/ *a* **~ of** ungeachtet (+ *gen*)

irresponsible /ɪrɪ'spɒnsəbl/ *a*, **-bly** *adv* unverantwortlich; <*person*> verantwortungslos

irreverent /ɪ'revərənt/ *a*, **-ly** *adv* respektlos

irrevocable /ɪ'revəkəbl/ *a*, **-bly** *adv* unwiderruflich

irrigat|e /'ɪrɪgeɪt/ *vt* bewässern. **~ion** /-'geɪʃn/ *n* Bewässerung *f*

irritable /'ɪrɪtəbl/ *a* reizbar

irritant /'ɪrɪtənt/ *n* Reizstoff *m*

irritat|e /'ɪrɪteɪt/ *vt* irritieren; (*Med*) reizen. **~ion** /-'teɪʃn/ *n* Ärger *m*; (*Med*) Reizung *f*

is /ɪz/ *see* **be**

Islam /'ɪzlɑ:m/ *n* der Islam. **~ic** /-'læmɪk/ *a* islamisch

island /'aɪlənd/ *n* Insel *f*. **~er** *n* Inselbewohner(in) *m(f)*

isolat|e /'aɪsəleɪt/ *vt* isolieren. **~ed** *a* (*remote*) abgelegen; (*single*) einzeln. **~ion** /-'leɪʃn/ *n* Isoliertheit *f*; (*Med*) Isolierung *f*

Israel /'ɪzreɪl/ *n* Israel *nt*. **~i** /ɪz'reɪlɪ/ *a* israelisch ● *n* Israeli *m/f*

issue /'ɪʃu:/ *n* Frage *f*; (*outcome*) Ergebnis *nt*; (*of magazine, stamps*) Ausgabe *f*; (*offspring*) Nachkommen *pl* ● *vt* ausgeben; ausstellen <*passport*>; erteilen <*order*>; herausgeben <*book*>; **be ~d with sth** etw erhalten

---

it /ɪt/

● *pronoun*

····▸ (*as subject*) er (*m*), sie (*f*), es (*nt*); (*in impersonal sentence*) es. **where is the spoon? It's on the table** wo ist der Löffel? Er liegt auf dem Tisch. **it was very kind of you** es war sehr nett von Ihnen. **it's five o'clock** es ist fünf Uhr

····▸ (*as direct object*) ihn (*m*), sie (*f*), es (*nt*). **that's my pencil — give it to me** das ist mein Bleistift — gib ihn mir.

····▸ (*as dative object*) ihm (*m*), ihr (*f*), ihm (*nt*). **he found a track and followed it** er fand eine Spur und folgte ihr.

····▸ (*after prepositions*)

! Combinations such as *with it*, *from it*, *to it* are translated by the prepositions with the prefix **da-** (**damit**, **davon**, **dazu**). Prepositions beginning with a vowel insert an 'r' (**daran**, **darauf**, **darüber**). **I can't do anything with it** ich kann nichts damit anfangen. **don't lean on it!** lehn dich nicht daran!

····▸ (*the person in question*) es. **it's me** ich bins. **is it you, Dad?** bist du es, Vater? **who is it?** wer ist da?

Italian /ɪ'tæljən/ *a* italienisch ● *n* Italiener(in) *m(f)*; (*Lang*) Italienisch *nt*

italics /ɪ'tælɪks/ *npl* Kursivschrift *f*; **in ~s** kursiv

Italy /'ɪtəlɪ/ *n* Italien *nt*

itch /ɪtʃ/ *n* Juckreiz *m*; **I have an ~** es juckt mich ● *vi* jucken; **I'm ~ing** [!] es juckt mich (**to** zu). **~y** *a* **be ~y** jucken

item /'aɪtəm/ *n* Gegenstand *m*; (*Comm*) Artikel *m*; (*on agenda*) Punkt *m*; (*on invoice*) Posten *m*; (*act*) Nummer *f*

itinerary /aɪ'tɪnərərɪ/ *n* [Reise]route *f*

its /ɪts/ *poss pron* sein; (*f*) ihr

it's = it is, it has

itself /ɪt'self/ *pron* selbst; (*refl*) sich; **by ~** von selbst; (*alone*) allein

ivory /'aɪvərɪ/ *n* Elfenbein *nt* ● *attrib* Elfenbein-

ivy /'aɪvɪ/ *n* Efeu *m*

Jj

jab /dʒæb/ *n* Stoß *m*; (🄵 *injection*) Spritze *f* ● *vt* (*pt/pp* **jabbed**) stoßen
jabber /ˈdʒæbə(r)/ *vi* plappern
jack /dʒæk/ *n* (*Auto*) Wagenheber *m*; (*Cards*) Bube *m* ● *vt* ~ **up** (*Auto*) aufbocken
jacket /ˈdʒækɪt/ *n* Jacke *f*; (*of book*) Schutzumschlag *m*
ˈ**jackpot** *n* **hit the** ~ das große Los ziehen
jade /dʒeɪd/ *n* Jade *m*
jagged /ˈdʒægɪd/ *a* zackig
jail /dʒeɪl/ = **gaol**
jam[1] /dʒæm/ *n* Marmelade *f*
jam[2] *n* Gedränge *nt*; (*Auto*) Stau *m*; (*fam. difficulty*) Klemme *f* ● *v* (*pt/pp* **jammed**) ● *vt* klemmen (**in** in + *acc*); stören <*broadcast*> ● *vi* klemmen
Jamaica /dʒəˈmeɪkə/ *n* Jamaika *nt*
jangle /ˈdʒæŋgl/ *vi* klimpern ● *vt* klimpern mit
January /ˈdʒænjʊərɪ/ *n* Januar *m*
Japan /dʒəˈpæn/ *n* Japan *nt*. ~**ese** /dʒæpəˈniːz/ *a* japanisch ● *n* Japaner(in) *m(f)*; (*Lang*) Japanisch *nt*
jar /dʒɑː(r)/ *n* Glas *nt*; (*earthenware*) Topf *m*
jargon /ˈdʒɑːgən/ *n* Jargon *m*
jaunt /dʒɔːnt/ *n* Ausflug *m*
jaunty /ˈdʒɔːntɪ/ *a* (**-ier, -iest**) **-ily** *adv* keck
javelin /ˈdʒævlɪn/ *n* Speer *m*
jaw /dʒɔː/ *n* Kiefer *m*
jazz /dʒæz/ *n* Jazz *m*. ~**y** *a* knallig
jealous /ˈdʒeləs/ *a*, **-ly** *adv* eifersüchtig (**of** auf + *acc*). ~**y** *n* Eifersucht *f*
jeans /dʒiːnz/ *npl* Jeans *pl*
jeer /dʒɪə(r)/ *vi* johlen; ~ **at** verhöhnen
jelly /ˈdʒelɪ/ *n* Gelee *nt*; (*dessert*) Götterspeise *f*. ~**fish** *n* Qualle *f*
jeopar|dize /ˈdʒepədaɪz/ *vt* gefährden. ~**dy** /-dɪ/ *n* **in** ~**dy** gefährdet
jerk /dʒɜːk/ *n* Ruck *m* ● *vt* stoßen; (*pull*) reißen ● *vi* rucken; <*limb, muscle:*> zucken. ~**ily** *adv* ruckweise. ~**y** *a* ruckartig
jersey /ˈdʒɜːzɪ/ *n* Pullover *m*; (*Sport*) Trikot *nt*; (*fabric*) Jersey *m*
jest /dʒest/ *n* **in** ~ im Spaß
jet *n* (*of water*) [Wasser]strahl *m*; (*nozzle*) Düse *f*; (*plane*) Düsenflugzeug *nt*
jet: ~-ˈ**black** *a* pechschwarz. ~-**proˈpelled** *a* mit Düsenantrieb
jetty /ˈdʒetɪ/ *n* Landesteg *m*; (*breakwater*) Buhne *f*
Jew /dʒuː/ *n* Jude *m* /Jüdin *f*
jewel /ˈdʒuːəl/ *n* Edelstein *m*; (*fig*) Juwel *nt*. ~**ler** *n* Juwelier *m*; ~**ler's [shop]** Juweliergeschäft *nt*. ~**lery** *n* Schmuck *m*
Jew|ess /ˈdʒuːɪs/ *n* Jüdin *f*. ~**ish** *a* jüdisch
jib /dʒɪb/ *vi* (*pt/pp* **jibbed**) (*fig*) sich sträuben (**at** gegen)
jigsaw /ˈdʒɪgsɔː/ *n* ~ **[puzzle]** Puzzlespiel *nt*
jilt /dʒɪlt/ *vt* sitzen lassen
jingle /ˈdʒɪŋgl/ *n* (*rhyme*) Verschen *nt* ● *vi* klimpern
jinx /dʒɪŋks/ *n* 🄵 **it's got a** ~ **on it** es ist verhext
jittery /ˈdʒɪtərɪ/ *a* 🄵 nervös
job /dʒɒb/ *n* Aufgabe *f*; (*post*) Stelle *f*, 🄵 Job *m*; **be a** ~ 🄵 nicht leicht sein; **it's a good** ~

that es ist [nur] gut, dass. **~less** *a* arbeitslos

jockey /ˈdʒɒkɪ/ *n* Jockei *m*

jocular /ˈdʒɒkjʊlə(r)/ *a*, **-ly** *adv* spaßhaft

jog /ˈdʒɒg/ *n* Stoß *m* ● *v* (*pt/pp* **jogged**) ● *vt* anstoßen; **~ s.o.'s memory** jds Gedächtnis nachhelfen ● *vi* (*Sport*) joggen. **~ging** *n* Jogging *nt*

john /dʒɒn/ *n* (*Amer* 🅸) Klo *nt*

join /dʒɔɪn/ *n* Nahtstelle *f* ● *vt* verbinden (**to** mit); sich anschließen (+ *dat*) <*person*>; (*become member of*) beitreten (+ *dat*); eintreten in (+ *acc*) <*firm*> ● *vi* <*roads:*> sich treffen. **~ in** *vi* mitmachen. **~ up** *vi* (*Mil*) Soldat werden ● *vt* zusammenfügen

joint /dʒɔɪnt/ *a*, **-ly** *adv* gemeinsam ● *n* Gelenk *nt*; (*in wood, brickwork*) Fuge *f*; (*Culin*) Braten *m*; (🅸 *bar*) Lokal *nt*

jok|e /dʒəʊk/ *n* Scherz *m*; (*funny story*) Witz *m*; (*trick*) Streich *m* ● *vi* scherzen. **~er** *n* Witzbold *m*; (*Cards*) Joker *m*. **~ing** *n* **~ing apart** Spaß beiseite. **~ingly** *adv* im Spaß

jolly /ˈdʒɒlɪ/ *a* (**-ier, -iest**) lustig ● *adv* 🅸 sehr

jolt /dʒəʊlt/ *n* Ruck *m* ● *vt* einen Ruck versetzen (+ *dat*) ● *vi* holpern

Jordan /ˈdʒɔːdn/ *n* Jordanien *nt*

jostle /ˈdʒɒsl/ *vt* anrempeln

jot /dʒɒt/ *vt* (*pt/pp* **jotted**) **~ [down]** sich (*dat*) notieren

journal /ˈdʒɜːnl/ *n* Zeitschrift *f*; (*diary*) Tagebuch *nt*. **~ese** /-əˈliːz/ *n* Zeitungsjargon *m*. **~ism** *n* Journalismus *m*. **~ist** *n* Journalist(in) *m(f)*

journey /ˈdʒɜːnɪ/ *n* Reise *f*

jovial /ˈdʒəʊvɪəl/ *a* lustig

joy /dʒɔɪ/ *n* Freude *f*. **~ful** *a*, **-ly** *adv* freudig, froh. **~ride** *n* 🅸 Spritztour *f* [im gestohlenen Auto]

jubil|ant /ˈdʒuːbɪlənt/ *a* überglücklich. **~ation** /-ˈleɪʃn/ *n* Jubel *m*

jubilee /ˈdʒuːbɪliː/ *n* Jubiläum *nt*

judder /ˈdʒʌdə(r)/ *vi* rucken

judge /dʒʌdʒ/ *n* Richter *m*; (*of competition*) Preisrichter *m* ● *vt* beurteilen; (*estimate*) [ein]schätzen ● *vi* urteilen (**by** nach). **~ment** *n* Beurteilung *f*; (*Jur*) Urteil *nt*; (*fig*) Urteilsvermögen *nt*

judic|ial /dʒuːˈdɪʃl/ *a* gerichtlich. **~ious** /-ʃəs/ *a* klug

jug /dʒʌg/ *n* Kanne *f*; (*small*) Kännchen *nt*; (*for water, wine*) Krug *m*

juggle /ˈdʒʌgl/ *vi* jonglieren. **~r** *n* Jongleur *m*

juice /dʒuːs/ *n* Saft *m*

juicy /ˈdʒuːsɪ/ *a* (**-ier, -iest**) saftig; 🅸 <*story*> pikant

juke-box /ˈdʒuːk-/ *n* Musikbox *f*

July /dʒʊˈlaɪ/ *n* Juli *m*

jumble /ˈdʒʌmbl/ *n* Durcheinander *nt* ● *vt* **~ [up]** durcheinander bringen. **~ sale** *n* [Wohltätigkeits]basar *m*

jump /dʒʌmp/ *n* Sprung *m*; (*in prices*) Anstieg *m*; (*in horse racing*) Hindernis *nt* ● *vi* springen; (*start*) zusammenzucken; **make s.o. ~** jdn erschrecken; **~ at** (*fig*) sofort zugreifen bei <*offer*>; **~ to conclusions** voreilige Schlüsse ziehen ● *vt* überspringen. **~ up** *vi* aufspringen

jumper /ˈdʒʌmpə(r)/ *n* Pullover *m*, Pulli *m*

jumpy /ˈdʒʌmpɪ/ *a* nervös

junction /ˈdʒʌŋkʃn/ *n* Kreuzung *f*; (*Rail*) Knotenpunkt *m*

June /dʒuːn/ *n* Juni *m*

jungle /ˈdʒʌŋgl/ *n* Dschungel *m*

junior /ˈdʒu:nɪə(r)/ *a* jünger; (*in rank*) untergeordnet; (*Sport*) Junioren- ● *n* Junior *m*

junk /dʒʌŋk/ *n* Gerümpel *nt*, Trödel *m*

junkie /ˈdʒʌŋkɪ/ *n* ☒ Fixer *m*

ˈjunk-shop *n* Trödelladen *m*

jurisdiction /dʒʊərɪsˈdɪkʃn/ *n* Gerichtsbarkeit *f*

jury /ˈdʒʊərɪ/ *n* **the ~** die Geschworenen *pl*; (*for competition*) die Jury

just /dʒʌst/ *a* gerecht ● *adv* gerade; (*only*) nur; (*simply*) einfach; (*exactly*) genau; **~ as tall** ebenso groß; **I'm ~ going** ich gehe schon

justice /ˈdʒʌstɪs/ *n* Gerechtigkeit *f*; **do ~ to** gerecht werden (+ *dat*)

justifiab|le /ˈdʒʌstɪfaɪəbl/ *a* berechtigt. **~ly** *adv* berechtigterweise

justi|fication /dʒʌstɪfɪˈkeɪʃn/ *n* Rechtfertigung *f*. **~fy** /ˈdʒʌstɪfaɪ/ *vt* (*pt/pp* **-ied**) rechtfertigen

justly /ˈdʒʌstlɪ/ *adv* zu Recht

jut /dʒʌt/ *vi* (*pt/pp* **jutted**) **~ out** vorstehen

juvenile /ˈdʒu:vənaɪl/ *a* jugendlich; (*childish*) kindisch ● *n* Jugendliche(r) *m/f*. **~ delinquency** *n* Jugendkriminalität *f*

Kk

kangaroo /kæŋgəˈru:/ *n* Känguru *nt*

kebab /kɪˈbæb/ *n* Spießchen *nt*

keel /ki:l/ *n* Kiel *m* ● *vi* **~ over** umkippen; (*Naut*) kentern

keen /ki:n/ *a* (**-er, -est**) (*sharp*) scharf; (*intense*) groß; (*eager*) eifrig, begeistert; **~ on** [!] erpicht auf (+ *acc*); **~ on s.o.** von jdm sehr angetan; **be ~ to do sth** etw gerne machen wollen. **~ly** *adv* tief. **~ness** *n* Eifer *m*, Begeisterung *f*

keep /ki:p/ *n* (*maintenance*) Unterhalt *m*; (*of castle*) Bergfried *m*; **for ~s** für immer ● *v* (*pt/pp* **kept**) ● *vt* behalten; (*store*) aufbewahren; (*not throw away*) aufheben; (*support*) unterhalten; (*detain*) aufhalten; freihalten <*seat*>; halten <*promise, animals*>; führen, haben <*shop*>; einhalten <*law, rules*>; **~ s.o. waiting** jdn warten lassen; **~ sth to oneself** etw nicht weitersagen ● *vi* (*remain*) bleiben; <*food:*> sich halten; **~ left/right** sich links/rechts halten; **~ on doing sth** etw weitermachen; (*repeatedly*) etw dauernd machen; **~ in with** sich gut stellen mit. **~ up** *vi* Schritt halten ● *vt* (*continue*) weitermachen

keep|er /ˈki:pə(r)/ *n* Wärter(in) *m(f)*. **~ing** *n* **be in ~ing with** passen zu

kennel /ˈkenl/ *n* Hundehütte *f*; **~s** *pl* (*boarding*) Hundepension *f*, (*breeding*) Zwinger *m*

Kenya /ˈkenjə/ *n* Kenia *nt*

kept /kept/ *see* **keep**

kerb /kɜ:b/ *n* Bordstein *m*

kernel /ˈkɜ:nl/ *n* Kern *m*

ketchup /ˈketʃʌp/ *n* Ketschup *m*

kettle /ˈketl/ *n* [Wasser]kessel *m*; **put the ~ on** Wasser aufsetzen

key /ki:/ *n* Schlüssel *m*; (*Mus*) Tonart *f*; (*of piano, typewriter*) Taste *f* ● *vt* **~ in** eintasten

key: ~board *n* Tastatur *f*; (*Mus*) Klaviatur *f*. **~hole** *n* Schlüsselloch *nt*. **~-ring** *n* Schlüsselring *m*

khaki /'kɑ:kɪ/ *a* khakifarben ● *n* Khaki *nt*

kick /kɪk/ *n* [Fuß]tritt *m*; **for ~s** [!] zum Spaß ● *vt* treten; **~ the bucket** [!] abkratzen ● *vi* <*animal*> ausschlagen

kid /kɪd/ *n* ([!] *child*) Kind *nt* ● *vt* (*pt/pp* **kidded**) [!] **~ s.o.** jdm etwas vormachen

kidnap /'kɪdnæp/ *vt* (*pt/pp* **-napped**) entführen. **~per** *n* Entführer *m*. **~ping** *n* Entführung *f*

kidney /'kɪdnɪ/ *n* Niere *f*

kill /kɪl/ *vt* töten; [!] totschlagen <*time*>; **~ two birds with one stone** zwei Fliegen mit einer Klappe schlagen. **~er** *n* Mörder(in) *m(f)*. **~ing** *n* Tötung *f*; (*murder*) Mord *m*

'killjoy *n* Spielverderber *m*

kilo /'ki:ləʊ/ *n* Kilo *nt*

kilo: /'kɪlə/: **~gram** *n* Kilogramm *nt*. **~metre** *n* Kilometer *m*. **~watt** *n* Kilowatt *nt*

kilt /kɪlt/ *n* Schottenrock *m*

kind[1] /kaɪnd/ *n* Art *f*; (*brand, type*) Sorte *f*; **what ~ of car?** was für ein Auto? **~ of** [!] irgendwie

kind[2] *a* (**-er, -est**) nett; **~ to animals** gut zu Tieren

kind|ly /'kaɪndlɪ/ *a* (**-ier, -iest**) nett ● *adv* netterweise; (*if you please*) gefälligst. **~ness** *n* Güte *f*; (*favour*) Gefallen *m*

king /kɪŋ/ *n* König *m*; (*Draughts*) Dame *f*. **~dom** *n* Königreich *nt*; (*fig & Relig*) Reich *nt*

king: ~fisher *n* Eisvogel *m*. **~-sized** *a* extragroß

kink /kɪŋk/ *n* Knick *m*. **~y** *a* [!] pervers

kiosk /'ki:ɒsk/ *n* Kiosk *m*

kip /kɪp/ *n* **have a ~** [!] pennen ● *vi* (*pt/pp* **kipped**) [!] pennen

kipper /'kɪpə(r)/ *n* Räucherhering *m*

kiss /kɪs/ *n* Kuss *m* ● *vt/i* küssen

kit /kɪt/ *n* Ausrüstung *f*; (*tools*) Werkzeug *nt*; (*construction ~*) Bausatz *m* ● *vt* (*pt/pp* **kitted**) **~out** ausrüsten

kitchen /'kɪtʃɪn/ *n* Küche *f* ● *attrib* Küchen-. **~ette** /kɪtʃɪ'net/ *n* Kochnische *f*

kitchen: ~'garden *n* Gemüsegarten *m*. **~'sink** *n* Spülbecken *nt*

kite /kaɪt/ *n* Drachen *m*

kitten /'kɪtn/ *n* Kätzchen *nt*

kitty /'kɪtɪ/ *n* (*money*) [gemeinsame] Kasse *f*

knack /næk/ *n* Trick *m*, Dreh *m*

knead /ni:d/ *vt* kneten

knee /ni:/ *n* Knie *nt*. **~cap** *n* Kniescheibe *f*

kneel /ni:l/ *vi* (*pt/pp* **knelt**) knien; **~ [down]** sich [nieder]knien

knelt /nelt/ *see* **kneel**

knew /nju:/ *see* **know**

knickers /'nɪkəz/ *npl* Schlüpfer *m*

knife /naɪf/ *n* (*pl* **knives**) Messer *nt* ● *vt* einen Messerstich versetzen (+ *dat*)

knight /naɪt/ *n* Ritter *m*; (*Chess*) Springer *m* ● *vt* adeln

knit /nɪt/ *vt/i* (*pt/pp* **knitted**) stricken; **~ one's brow** die Stirn runzeln. **~ting** *n* Stricken *nt*; (*work*) Strickzeug *nt*. **~ting-needle** *n* Stricknadel *f*. **~wear** *n* Strickwaren *pl*

knives /naɪvz/ *npl see* **knife**

knob /nɒb/ *n* Knopf *m*; (*on door*) Knauf *m*; (*small lump*) Beule *f*. **~bly** *a* knorrig; (*bony*) knochig

knock /nɒk/ *n* Klopfen *nt*; (*blow*) Schlag *m*; **there was a ~** es klopfte ● *vt* anstoßen; ([!] *criticize*) heruntermachen; **~ a hole in sth** ein Loch in etw (*acc*) schlagen; **~ one's head** sich (*dat*) den Kopf stoßen (**on** an + *dat*) ● *vi* klopfen. **~ about** *vt* schlagen ● *vi* [!] herumkommen.

~ **down** *vt* herunterwerfen; (*with fist*) niederschlagen; (*in car*) anfahren; (*demolish*) abreißen; ([I] *reduce*) herabsetzen. ~ **off** *vt* herunterwerfen; ([I] *steal*) klauen; ([I] *complete quickly*) hinhauen ● *vi* ([I] *cease work*) Feierabend machen. ~ **out** *vt* ausschlagen; (*make unconscious*) bewusstlos schlagen; (*Boxing*) k.o. schlagen. ~ **over** *vt* umwerfen; (*in car*) anfahren

knock: ~**-down** *a* ~**-down prices** Schleuderpreise *pl*. ~**er** *n* Türklopfer *m*. ~**-out** *n* (*Boxing*) K.o. *m*

knot /nɒt/ *n* Knoten *m* ● *vt* (*pt*/*pp* **knotted**) knoten

know /nəʊ/ *vt*/*i* (*pt* **knew**, *pp* **known**) wissen; kennen <*person*>; können <*language*>; **get to** ~ kennen lernen ● *n* **in the** ~ [I] im Bild

know: ~**-all** *n* [I] Alleswisser *m*. ~**-how** *n* [I] [Sach]kenntnis *f*. ~**ing** *a* wissend. ~**ingly** *adv* wissend; (*intentionally*) wissentlich

knowledge /ˈnɒlɪdʒ/ *n* Kenntnis *f* (**of** von/*gen*); (*general*) Wissen *nt*; (*specialized*) Kenntnisse *pl*. ~**able** /-əbl/ *a* **be** ~**able** viel wissen

known /nəʊn/ *see* **know** ● *a* bekannt

knuckle /ˈnʌkl/ *n* [Finger]knöchel *m*; (*Culin*) Hachse *f*

kosher /ˈkəʊʃə(r)/ *a* koscher

kudos /ˈkjuːdɒs/ *n* [I] Prestige *nt*

Ll

lab /læb/ *n* [I] Labor *nt*

label /ˈleɪbl/ *n* Etikett *nt* ● *vt* (*pt*/*pp* **labelled**) etikettieren

laboratory /ləˈbɒrətrɪ/ *n* Labor *nt*

laborious /ləˈbɔːrɪəs/ *a*, **-ly** *adv* mühsam

labour /ˈleɪbə(r)/ *n* Arbeit *f*; (*workers*) Arbeitskräfte *pl*; (*Med*) Wehen *pl*; **L**~ (*Pol*) die Labourpartei ● *attrib* Labour- ● *vi* arbeiten ● *vt* (*fig*) sich lange auslassen über (+ *acc*). ~**er** *n* Arbeiter *m*

ˈlabour-saving *a* arbeitssparend

lace /leɪs/ *n* Spitze *f*; (*of shoe*) Schnürsenkel *m* ● *vt* schnüren

lack /læk/ *n* Mangel *m* (**of** an + *dat*) ● *vt* **I** ~ **the time** mir fehlt die Zeit ● *vi* **be** ~**ing** fehlen

laconic /ləˈkɒnɪk/ *a*, **-ally** *adv* lakonisch

lacquer /ˈlækə(r)/ *n* Lack *m*; (*for hair*) [Haar]spray *m*

lad /læd/ *n* Junge *m*

ladder /ˈlædə(r)/ *n* Leiter *f*; (*in fabric*) Laufmasche *f*

ladle /ˈleɪdl/ *n* [Schöpf]kelle *f* ● *vt* schöpfen

lady /ˈleɪdɪ/ *n* Dame *f*; (*title*) Lady *f*

lady: ~**bird** *n*, (*Amer*) ~**bug** *n* Marienkäfer *m*. ~**like** *a* damenhaft

lag¹ /læg/ *vi* (*pt*/*pp* **lagged**) ~ **behind** zurückbleiben; (*fig*) nachhinken

lag² *vt* (*pt*/*pp* **lagged**) umwickeln <*pipes*>

lager /ˈlɑːgə(r)/ *n* Lagerbier *nt*

laid /leɪd/ *see* **lay²**
lain /leɪn/ *see* **lie²**
lake /leɪk/ *n* See *m*
lamb /læm/ *n* Lamm *nt*
lame /leɪm/ *a* (**-r, -st**) lahm
lament /lə'ment/ *n* Klage *f*; (*song*) Klagelied *nt* ● *vt* beklagen ● *vi* klagen
laminated /'læmɪneɪtɪd/ *a* laminiert
lamp /læmp/ *n* Lampe *f*; (*in street*) Laterne *f*. **~ post** *n* Laternenpfahl *m*. **~shade** *n* Lampenschirm *m*
lance /lɑːns/ *vt* (*Med*) aufschneiden
land /lænd/ *n* Land *nt*; **plot of ~** Grundstück *nt* ● *vt*/*i* landen; **~ s.o. with sth** [!] jdm etw aufhalsen
landing /'lændɪŋ/ *n* Landung *f*; (*top of stairs*) Treppenflur *m*. **~ stage** *n* Landesteg *m*
land: ~lady *n* Wirtin *f*. **~lord** *n* Wirt *m*; (*of land*) Grundbesitzer *m*; (*of building*) Hausbesitzer *m*. **~mark** *n* Erkennungszeichen *nt*; (*fig*) Meilenstein *m*. **~owner** *n* Grundbesitzer *m*. **~scape** /-skeɪp/ *n* Landschaft *f*. **~slide** *n* Erdrutsch *m*
lane /leɪn/ *n* kleine Landstraße *f*; (*Auto*) Spur *f*; (*Sport*) Bahn *f*; **'get in ~'** (*Auto*) 'bitte einordnen'
language /'læŋgwɪdʒ/ *n* Sprache *f*; (*speech, style*) Ausdrucksweise *f*
languid /'læŋgwɪd/ *a*, **-ly** *adv* träge
languish /'læŋgwɪʃ/ *vi* schmachten
lanky /'læŋkɪ/ *a* (**-ier, -iest**) schlaksig
lantern /'læntən/ *n* Laterne *f*
lap¹ /læp/ *n* Schoß *m*
lap² *n* (*Sport*) Runde *f*; (*of journey*) Etappe *f* ● *vi* (*pt*/*pp* **lapped**) plätschern (**against** gegen)
lap³ *vt* (*pt*/*pp* **lapped**) **~ up** aufschlecken
lapel /lə'pel/ *n* Revers *nt*
lapse /læps/ *n* Fehler *m*; (*moral*) Fehltritt *m*; (*of time*) Zeitspanne *f* ● *vi* (*expire*) erlöschen; **~ into** verfallen in (+ *acc*)
lard /lɑːd/ *n* [Schweine]schmalz *nt*
larder /'lɑːdə(r)/ *n* Speisekammer *f*
large /lɑːdʒ/ *a* (**-r, -st**) & *adv* groß; **by and ~** im Großen und Ganzen; **at ~** auf freiem Fuß. **~ly** *adv* großenteils
lark¹ /lɑːk/ *n* (*bird*) Lerche *f*
lark² *n* (*joke*) Jux *m* ● *vi* **~ about** herumalbern
laryngitis /lærɪn'dʒaɪtɪs/ *n* Kehlkopfentzündung *f*
larynx /'lærɪŋks/ *n* Kehlkopf *m*
laser /'leɪzə(r)/ *n* Laser *m*
lash /læʃ/ *n* Peitschenhieb *m*; (*eyelash*) Wimper *f* ● *vt* peitschen; (*tie*) festbinden (**to** an + *acc*). **~ out** *vi* um sich schlagen; (*spend*) viel Geld ausgeben (**on** für)
lass /læs/ *n* Mädchen *nt*
lasso /lə'suː/ *n* Lasso *nt*
last /lɑːst/ *a* & *n* letzte(r,s); **~ night** heute *od* gestern Nacht; (*evening*) gestern Abend; **at ~** endlich; **for the ~ time** zum letzten Mal; **the ~ but one** der/die/das vorletzte ● *adv* zuletzt; (*last time*) das letzte Mal; **he/she went ~** er/sie ging als Letzter/Letzte ● *vi* dauern; <*weather:*> sich halten; <*relationship:*> halten. **~ing** *a* dauerhaft. **~ly** *adv* schließlich, zum Schluss
latch /lætʃ/ *n* [einfache] Klinke *f*
late /leɪt/ *a* & *adv* (**-r, -st**) spät; (*delayed*) verspätet; (*deceased*) verstorben; **the ~st news** die neuesten Nachrichten; **stay up ~** bis spät aufbleiben; **arrive ~** zu spät ankommen; **I am ~** ich

komme zu spät *od* habe mich verspätet; **the train is ~** der Zug hat Verspätung. **~comer** *n* Zuspätkommende(r) *m/f.* **~ly** *adv* in letzter Zeit. **~ness** *n* Zuspätkommen *nt*; (*delay*) Verspätung *f*

later /ˈleɪtə(r)/ *a & adv* später; **~ on** nachher

lateral /ˈlætərəl/ *a* seitlich

lather /ˈlɑːðə(r)/ *n* [Seifen]schaum *m*

Latin /ˈlætɪn/ *a* lateinisch ● *n* Latein *nt.* **~ A'merica** *n* Lateinamerika *nt*

latitude /ˈlætɪtjuːd/ *n* (*Geog*) Breite *f*; (*fig*) Freiheit *f*

latter /ˈlætə(r)/ *a & n* **the ~** der/die/das Letztere

Latvia /ˈlætvɪə/ *n* Lettland *nt*

laudable /ˈlɔːdəbl/ *a* lobenswert

laugh /lɑːf/ *n* Lachen *nt*; **with a ~** lachend ● *vi* lachen (**at/about** über + *acc*); **~ at s.o.** (*mock*) jdn auslachen. **~able** /-əbl/ *a* lachhaft, lächerlich

laughter /ˈlɑːftə(r)/ *n* Gelächter *nt*

launch¹ /lɔːntʃ/ *n* (*boat*) Barkasse *f*

launch² *n* Stapellauf *m*; (*of rocket*) Abschuss *m*; (*of product*) Lancierung *f* ● *vt* vom Stapel lassen <*ship*>; zu Wasser lassen <*lifeboat*>; abschießen <*rocket*>; starten <*attack*>; (*Comm*) lancieren <*product*>

laund(e)rette /lɔːndret/ *n* Münzwäscherei *f*

laundry /ˈlɔːndrɪ/ *n* Wäscherei *f*; (*clothes*) Wäsche *f*

laurel /ˈlɒrl/ *n* Lorbeer *m*

lava /ˈlɑːvə/ *n* Lava *f*

lavatory /ˈlævətrɪ/ *n* Toilette *f*

lavender /ˈlævəndə(r)/ *n* Lavendel *m*

lavish /ˈlævɪʃ/ *a*, **-ly** *adv* großzügig; (*wasteful*) verschwenderisch ● *vt* **~ sth on s.o.** jdn mit etw überschütten

law /lɔː/ *n* Gesetz *nt*; (*system*) Recht *nt*; **study ~** Jura studieren; **~ and order** Recht und Ordnung

law: ~-abiding *a* gesetzestreu. **~ court** *n* Gerichtshof *m.* **~ful** *a* rechtmäßig. **~less** *a* gesetzlos

lawn /lɔːn/ *n* Rasen *m.* **~mower** *n* Rasenmäher *m*

lawyer /ˈlɔːjə(r)/ *n* Rechtsanwalt *m* /-anwältin *f*

lax /læks/ *a* lax, locker

laxative /ˈlæksətɪv/ *n* Abführmittel *nt*

laxity /ˈlæksətɪ/ *n* Laxheit *f*

lay¹ /leɪ/ *see* **lie²**

lay² *vt* (*pt/pp* **laid**) legen; decken <*table*>; **~ a trap** eine Falle stellen. **~ down** *vt* hinlegen; festlegen <*rules, conditions*>. **~ off** *vt* entlassen <*workers*> ● *vi* (🄸 *stop*) aufhören. **~ out** *vt* hinlegen; aufbahren <*corpse*>; anlegen <*garden*>; (*Typ*) gestalten

lay-by *n* Parkbucht *f*

layer /ˈleɪə(r)/ *n* Schicht *f*

lay: ~man *n* Laie *m.* **~out** *n* Anordnung *f*; (*design*) Gestaltung *f*; (*Typ*) Layout *nt*

laze /leɪz/ *vi* **~[about]** faulenzen

laziness /ˈleɪzɪnɪs/ *n* Faulheit *f*

lazy /ˈleɪzɪ/ *a* (**-ier, -iest**) faul. **~bones** *n* Faulenzer *m*

lead¹ /led/ *n* Blei *nt*; (*of pencil*) [Bleistift]mine *f*

lead² /liːd/ *n* Führung *f*; (*leash*) Leine *f*; (*flex*) Schnur *f*; (*clue*) Hinweis *m*, Spur *f*; (*Theat*) Hauptrolle *f*; (*distance ahead*) Vorsprung *m*; **be in the ~** in Führung liegen ● *vt/i* (*pt/pp* **led**) führen; leiten <*team*>; (*induce*) bringen; (*at cards*) ausspielen; **~ the way** vorangehen; **~ up to sth** (*fig*) etw (*dat*) vorangehen

leader /'li:də(r)/ *n* Führer *m*; (*of expedition, group*) Leiter(in) *m(f)*; (*of orchestra*) Konzertmeister *m*; (*in newspaper*) Leitartikel *m*. **~ship** *n* Führung *f*, Leitung *f*

leading /'li:dɪŋ/ *a* führend; **~ lady** Hauptdarstellerin *f*

leaf /li:f/ *n* (*pl* **leaves**) Blatt *nt* ● *vi* **~ through sth** etw durchblättern. **~let** *n* Merkblatt *nt*; (*advertising*) Reklameblatt *nt*; (*political*) Flugblatt *nt*

league /li:g/ *n* Liga *f*

leak /li:k/ *n* (*hole*) undichte Stelle *f*; (*Naut*) Leck *nt*; (*of gas*) Gasausfluss *m* ● *vi* undicht sein; <*ship:*> leck sein, lecken; <*liquid:*> auslaufen; <*gas:*> ausströmen ● *vt* auslaufen lassen; **~ sth to s.o.** (*fig*) jdm etw zuspielen. **~y** *a* undicht; (*Naut*) leck

lean¹ /li:n/ *a* (**-er, -est**) mager

lean² *v* (*pt/pp* **leaned** *or* **leant** /lent/) ● *vt* lehnen (**against/on** an + *acc*) ● *vi* <*person*> sich lehnen (**against/on** an + *acc*); (*not be straight*) sich neigen; **be ~ing against** lehnen an (+ *dat*). **~ back** *vi* sich zurücklehnen. **~ forward** *vi* sich vorbeugen. **~ out** *vi* sich hinauslehnen. **~ over** *vi* sich vorbeugen

leaning /'li:nɪŋ/ *a* schief ● *n* Neigung *f*

leap /li:p/ *n* Sprung *m* ● *vi* (*pt/pp* **leapt** /lept/ *or* **leaped**) springen; **he leapt at it** [!] er griff sofort zu. **~ year** *n* Schaltjahr *nt*

learn /lɜ:n/ *vt/i* (*pt/pp* **learnt** *or* **learned**) lernen; (*hear*) erfahren; **~ to swim** schwimmen lernen

learn|ed /'lɜ:nɪd/ *a* gelehrt. **~er** *n* Anfänger *m*; **~er [driver]** Fahrschüler(in) *m(f)*. **~ing** *n* Gelehrsamkeit *f*

lease /li:s/ *n* Pacht *f*; (*contract*) Mietvertrag *m* ● *vt* pachten

leash /li:ʃ/ *n* Leine *f*

least /li:st/ *a* geringste(r,s) ● *n* **the ~** das wenigste; **at ~** wenigstens, mindestens; **not in the ~** nicht im Geringsten ● *adv* am wenigsten

leather /'leðə(r)/ *n* Leder *nt*

leave /li:v/ *n* Erlaubnis *f*; (*holiday*) Urlaub *m*; **on ~** auf Urlaub; **take one's ~** sich verabschieden ● *v* (*pt/pp* **left**) ● *vt* lassen; (*go out of, abandon*) verlassen; (*forget*) liegen lassen; (*bequeath*) vermachen (**to** *dat*); **~ it to me!** überlassen Sie es mir! **there is nothing left** es ist nichts mehr übrig ● *vi* [weg]gehen/-fahren; <*train, bus:*> abfahren. **~ behind** *vt* zurücklassen; (*forget*) liegen lassen. **~ out** *vt* liegen lassen; (*leave outside*) draußen lassen; (*omit*) auslassen

leaves /li:vz/ *see* **leaf**

Lebanon /'lebənən/ *n* Libanon *m*

lecherous /'letʃərəs/ *a* lüstern

lecture /'lektʃə(r)/ *n* Vortrag *m*; (*Univ*) Vorlesung *f*; (*reproof*) Strafpredigt *f* ● *vi* einen Vortrag/eine Vorlesung halten (**on** über + *acc*) ● *vt* **~ s.o.** jdm eine Strafpredigt halten. **~r** *n* Vortragende(r) *m/f*; (*Univ*) Dozent(in) *m(f)*

led /led/ *see* **lead²**

ledge /ledʒ/ *n* Leiste *f*; (*shelf, of window*) Sims *m*; (*in rock*) Vorsprung *m*

ledger /'ledʒə(r)/ *n* Hauptbuch *nt*

leech /li:tʃ/ *n* Blutegel *m*

leek /li:k/ *n* Stange *f* Porree; **~s** *pl* Porree *m*

left¹ /left/ *see* **leave**

left² *a* linke(r,s) ● *adv* links; <*go*> nach links ● *n* linke Seite *f*; **on the ~** links; **from/to the ~** von/nach links; **the ~** (*Pol*) die Linke

left: ~-'handed *a* linkshändig. **~-'luggage [office]** *n* Gepäckaufbewahrung *f*. **~overs**

npl Reste *pl*. **~-'wing** *a* (*Pol*) linke(r,s)
leg /leg/ *n* Bein *nt*; (*Culin*) Keule *f*; (*of journey*) Etappe *f*
legacy /'legəsɪ/ *n* Vermächtnis *nt*, Erbschaft *f*
legal /'li:gl/ *a*, **-ly** *adv* gesetzlich; <*matters*> rechtlich; <*department, position*> Rechts-; **be ~** [gesetzlich] erlaubt sein
legality /lɪ'gælətɪ/ *n* Legalität *f*
legend /'ledʒənd/ *n* Legende *f*. **~ary** *a* legendär
legible /'ledʒəbl/ *a*, **-bly** *adv* leserlich
legion /'li:dʒn/ *n* Legion *f*
legislat|e /'ledʒɪsleɪt/ *vi* Gesetze erlassen. **~ion** /-'leɪʃn/ *n* Gesetzgebung *f*; (*laws*) Gesetze *pl*
legislative /'ledʒɪslətɪv/ *a* gesetzgebend
legitimate /lɪ'dʒɪtɪmət/ *a* rechtmäßig; (*justifiable*) berechtigt
leisure /'leʒə(r)/ *n* Freizeit *f*; **at your ~** wenn Sie Zeit haben. **~ly** *a* gemächlich
lemon /'lemən/ *n* Zitrone *f*. **~ade** /-'neɪd/ *n* Zitronenlimonade *f*
lend /lend/ *vt* (*pt/pp* **lent**) leihen (**s.o. sth** jdm etw)
length /leŋθ/ *n* Länge *f*; (*piece*) Stück *nt*; (*of wallpaper*) Bahn *f*; (*of time*) Dauer *f*
length|en /'leŋθən/ *vt* länger machen ● *vi* länger werden. **~ways** *adv* der Länge nach
lengthy /'leŋθɪ/ *a* (**-ier, -iest**) langwierig
lenien|t /'li:nɪənt/ *a*, **-ly** *adv* nachsichtig
lens /lenz/ *n* Linse *f*; (*Phot*) Objektiv *nt*; (*of spectacles*) Glas *nt*
lent /lent/ *see* **lend**
Lent *n* Fastenzeit *f*
lentil /'lentl/ *n* (*Bot*) Linse *f*
leopard /'lepəd/ *n* Leopard *m*
leotard /'li:ətɑ:d/ *n* Trikot *nt*
lesbian /'lezbɪən/ *a* lesbisch ● *n* Lesbierin *f*
less /les/ *a, adv, n & prep* weniger; **~ and ~** immer weniger
lessen /'lesn/ *vt* verringern ● *vi* nachlassen; <*value:*> abnehmen
lesser /'lesə(r)/ *a* geringere(r,s)
lesson /'lesn/ *n* Stunde *f*; (*in textbook*) Lektion *f*; (*Relig*) Lesung *f*; **teach s.o. a ~** (*fig*) jdm eine Lehre erteilen
lest /lest/ *conj* (*liter*) damit ... nicht
let /let/ *vt* (*pt/pp* **let**, *pres p* **letting**) lassen; (*rent*) vermieten; **~ alone** (*not to mention*) geschweige denn; **~ us go** gehen wir; **~ me know** sagen Sie mir Bescheid; **~ oneself in for sth** [!] sich (*dat*) etw einbrocken. **~ down** *vt* hinunter-/herunterlassen; (*lengthen*) länger machen; **~ s.o. down** [!] jdn im Stich lassen; (*disappoint*) jdn enttäuschen. **~ in** *vt* hereinlassen. **~ off** *vt* abfeuern <*gun*>; hochgehen lassen <*firework, bomb*>; (*emit*) ausstoßen; (*excuse from*) befreien von; (*not punish*) frei ausgehen lassen. **~ out** *vt* hinaus-/herauslassen; (*make larger*) auslassen. **~ through** *vt* durchlassen. **~ up** *vi* [!] nachlassen
'let-down *n* Enttäuschung *f*, [!] Reinfall *m*
lethal /'li:θl/ *a* tödlich
letharg|ic /lɪ'θɑ:dʒɪk/ *a* lethargisch. **~y** /'leθədʒɪ/ *n* Lethargie *f*
letter /'letə(r)/ *n* Brief *m*; (*of alphabet*) Buchstabe *m*. **~-box** *n* Briefkasten *m*. **~-head** *n* Briefkopf *m*. **~ing** *n* Beschriftung *f*
lettuce /'letɪs/ *n* [Kopf]salat *m*

'let-up *n* [!] Nachlassen *nt*

level /'levl/ *a* eben; (*horizontal*) waagerecht; (*in height*) auf gleicher Höhe; <*spoonful*> gestrichen; **one's ~ best** sein Möglichstes ● *n* Höhe *f*; (*fig*) Ebene *f*, Niveau *nt*; (*stage*) Stufe *f*; **on the ~** [!] ehrlich ● *vt* (*pt/pp* **levelled**) einebnen

level 'crossing *n* Bahnübergang *m*

lever /'li:və(r)/ *n* Hebel *m* ● *vt* **~ up** mit einem Hebel anheben. **~age** /-rɪdʒ/ *n* Hebelkraft *f*

lewd /lju:d/ *a* (**-er, -est**) anstößig

liabilit|y /laɪə'bɪlətɪ/ *n* Haftung *f*; **~ies** *pl* Verbindlichkeiten *pl*

liable /'laɪəbl/ *a* haftbar; **be ~ to do sth** etw leicht tun können

liaise /lɪ'eɪz/ *vi* [!] Verbindungsperson sein

liaison /lɪ'eɪzɒn/ *n* Verbindung *f*; (*affair*) Verhältnis *nt*

liar /'laɪə(r)/ *n* Lügner(in) *m(f)*

libel /'laɪbl/ *n* Verleumdung *f* ● *vt* (*pt/pp* **libelled**) verleumden. **~lous** *a* verleumderisch

liberal /'lɪbərl/ *a*, **-ly** *adv* tolerant; (*generous*) großzügig. **L~** *a* (*Pol*) liberal ● *n* Liberale(r) *m/f*

liberat|e /'lɪbəreɪt/ *vt* befreien. **~ed** *a* <*woman*> emanzipiert. **~ion** /-'reɪʃn/ *n* Befreiung *f*. **~or** *n* Befreier *m*

liberty /'lɪbətɪ/ *n* Freiheit *f*; **take liberties** sich (*dat*) Freiheiten erlauben

librarian /laɪ'breərɪən/ *n* Bibliothekar(in) *m(f)*

library /'laɪbrərɪ/ *n* Bibliothek *f*

Libya /'lɪbɪə/ *n* Libyen *nt*

lice /laɪs/ *see* **louse**

licence /'laɪsns/ *n* Genehmigung *f*; (*Comm*) Lizenz *f*; (*for TV*) ≈ Fernsehgebühr *f*; (*for driving*) Führerschein *m*; (*for alcohol*) Schankkonzession *f*

license /'laɪsns/ *vt* eine Genehmigung/(*Comm*) Lizenz erteilen (+ *dat*); **be ~d** <*car:*> zugelassen sein; <*restaurant:*> Schankkonzession haben. **~ plate** *n* (*Amer*) Nummernschild *nt*

lick /lɪk/ *n* Lecken *nt*; **a ~ of paint** ein bisschen Farbe ● *vt* lecken; ([!] *defeat*) schlagen

lid /lɪd/ *n* Deckel *m*; (*of eye*) Lid *nt*

lie[1] /laɪ/ *n* Lüge *f*; **tell a ~** lügen ● *vi* (*pt/pp* **lied**, *pres p* **lying**) lügen; **~ to** belügen

lie[2] *vi* (*pt* **lay**, *pp* **lain**, *pres p* **lying**) liegen; **here ~s ...** hier ruht ... **~ down** *vi* sich hinlegen

'lie-in *n* **have a ~** [sich] ausschlafen

lieu /lju:/ *n* **in ~ of** statt (+ *gen*)

lieutenant /lef'tenənt/ *n* Oberleutnant *m*

life /laɪf/ *n* (*pl* **lives**) Leben *nt*; **lose one's ~** ums Leben kommen

life: ~-boat *n* Rettungsboot *nt*. **~-guard** *n* Lebensretter *m*. **~-jacket** *n* Schwimmweste *f*. **~less** *a* leblos. **~like** *a* naturgetreu. **~long** *a* lebenslang. **~ preserver** *n* (*Amer*) Rettungsring *m*. **~-size(d)** *a* ... in Lebensgröße. **~time** *n* Leben *nt*; **in s.o.'s ~time** zu jds Lebzeiten; **the chance of a ~time** eine einmalige Gelegenheit

lift /lɪft/ *n* Aufzug *m*, Lift *m*; **give s.o. a ~** jdn mitnehmen; **get a ~** mitgenommen werden ● *vt* heben; aufheben <*restrictions*> ● *vi* <*fog:*> sich lichten. **~ up** *vt* hochheben

light[1] /laɪt/ *a* (**-er, -est**) (*not dark*) hell; **~ blue** hellblau ● *n* Licht *nt*; (*lamp*) Lampe *f*; **have you [got] a ~?** haben Sie Feuer? ● *vt* (*pt/pp* **lit** *or* **lighted**) anzünden

<fire, cigarette>; (*illuminate*) beleuchten. ~ **up** *vi* *<face:>* sich erhellen

light² *a* (**-er, -est**) (*not heavy*) leicht; ~ **sentence** milde Strafe *f* ● *adv* **travel** ~ mit wenig Gepäck reisen

'light-bulb *n* Glühbirne *f*

lighten¹ /'laɪtn/ *vt* heller machen

lighten² *vt* leichter machen *<load>*

lighter /'laɪtə(r)/ *n* Feuerzeug *nt*

light: ~-'hearted *a* unbekümmert. **~house** *n* Leuchtturm *m*. **~ing** *n* Beleuchtung *f*. **~ly** *adv* leicht; **get off ~ly** glimpflich davonkommen

lightning /'laɪtnɪŋ/ *n* Blitz *m*

'lightweight *a* leicht ● *n* (*Boxing*) Leichtgewicht *nt*

like¹ /laɪk/ *a* ähnlich; (*same*) gleich ● *prep* wie; (*similar to*) ähnlich (+ *dat*); ~ **this** so; **what's he ~?** wie ist er denn? ● *conj* ([!] *as*) wie; (*Amer: as if*) als ob

like² *vt* mögen; **I should/would ~** ich möchte; **I ~ the car** das Auto gefällt mir; ~ **dancing/singing** gern tanzen/singen ● *n* **~s and dislikes** *pl* Vorlieben und Abneigungen *pl*

like|able /'laɪkəbl/ *a* sympathisch. **~lihood** /-lɪhʊd/ *n* Wahrscheinlichkeit *f*. **~ly** *a* (**-ier, -iest**) & *adv* wahrscheinlich; **not ~ly!** [!] auf gar keinen Fall!

'like-minded *a* gleich gesinnt

liken /'laɪkən/ *vt* vergleichen (**to** mit)

like|ness /'laɪknɪs/ *n* Ähnlichkeit *f*. **~wise** *adv* ebenso

liking /'laɪkɪŋ/ *n* Vorliebe *f*; **is it to your ~?** gefällt es Ihnen?

lilac /'laɪlək/ *n* Flieder *m*

lily /'lɪlɪ/ *n* Lilie *f*

limb /lɪm/ *n* Glied *nt*

lime /laɪm/ *n* (*fruit*) Limone *f*; (*tree*) Linde *f*. **~light** *n* **be in the ~light** im Rampenlicht stehen

limit /'lɪmɪt/ *n* Grenze *f*; (*limitation*) Beschränkung *f*; **that's the ~!** [!] das ist doch die Höhe! ● *vt* beschränken (**to** auf + *acc*). **~ation** /-'teɪʃn/ *n* Beschränkung *f*. **~ed** *a* beschränkt. **~ed company** Gesellschaft *f* mit beschränkter Haftung

limousine /'lɪməzi:n/ *n* Limousine *f*

limp¹ /lɪmp/ *n* Hinken *nt* ● *vi* hinken

limp² *a* (**-er -est**), **-ly** *adv* schlaff

limpid /'lɪmpɪd/ *a* klar

line¹ /laɪn/ *n* Linie *f*; (*length of rope, cord*) Leine *f*; (*Teleph*) Leitung *f*; (*of writing*) Zeile *f*; (*row*) Reihe *f*; (*wrinkle*) Falte *f*; (*of business*) Branche *f*; (*Amer: queue*) Schlange *f*; **in ~ with** gemäß (+ *dat*) ● *vt* säumen *<street>*

line² *vt* füttern *<garment>*; (*Techn*) auskleiden

lined¹ /laɪnd/ *a* (*wrinkled*) faltig; *<paper>* liniert

lined² *a* *<garment>* gefüttert

'line dancing *n* Linedance-Tanzen *nt*

linen /'lɪnɪn/ *n* Leinen *nt*; (*articles*) Wäsche *f*

liner /'laɪnə(r)/ *n* Passagierschiff *nt*

'linesman *n* (*Sport*) Linienrichter *m*

linger /'lɪŋgə(r)/ *vi* [zurück]bleiben

lingerie /'læʒərɪ/ *n* Damenunterwäsche *f*

linguist /'lɪŋgwɪst/ *n* Sprachkundige(r) *m/f*

linguistic /lɪŋ'gwɪstɪk/ *a*, **-ally** *adv* sprachlich

lining /'laɪnɪŋ/ *n* (*of garment*) Futter *nt*; (*Techn*) Auskleidung *f*

link /lɪŋk/ *n* (*of chain*) Glied *nt* (*fig*) Verbindung *f* ● *vt* verbinden; ~ **arms** sich unterhaken
links /lɪŋks/ *n or npl* Golfplatz *m*
lint /lɪnt/ *n* Verbandstoff *m*
lion /ˈlaɪən/ *n* Löwe *m*; **~'s share** (*fig*) Löwenanteil *m*. **~ess** *n* Löwin *f*
lip /lɪp/ *n* Lippe *f*; (*edge*) Rand *m*; (*of jug*) Schnabel *m*
lip: ~-reading *n* Lippenlesen *nt*. **~-service** *n* **pay ~-service** ein Lippenbekenntnis ablegen (**to** zu). **~stick** *n* Lippenstift *m*
liqueur /lɪˈkjʊə(r)/ *n* Likör *m*
liquid /ˈlɪkwɪd/ *n* Flüssigkeit *f* ● *a* flüssig
liquidation /lɪkwɪˈdeɪʃn/ *n* Liquidation *f*
liquidize /ˈlɪkwɪdaɪz/ *vt* [im Mixer] pürieren. **~r** *n* Mixer *m*
liquor /ˈlɪkə(r)/ *n* Alkohol *m*. **~ store** *n* (*Amer*) Spirituosengeschäft *nt*
lisp /lɪsp/ *n* Lispeln *nt* ● *vt*/*i* lispeln
list[1] /lɪst/ *n* Liste *f* ● *vt* aufführen
list[2] *vi* <*ship*:> Schlagseite haben
listen /ˈlɪsn/ *vi* zuhören (**to** *dat*); ~ **to the radio** Radio hören. **~er** *n* Zuhörer(in) *m*(*f*); (*Radio*) Hörer(in) *m*(*f*)
listless /ˈlɪstlɪs/ *a*, **-ly** *adv* lustlos
lit /lɪt/ *see* **light[1]**
literacy /ˈlɪtərəsɪ/ *n* Lese- und Schreibfertigkeit *f*
literal /ˈlɪtərl/ *a* wörtlich. **~ly** *adv* buchstäblich
literary /ˈlɪtərərɪ/ *a* literarisch
literate /ˈlɪtərət/ *a* **be ~** lesen und schreiben können
literature /ˈlɪtrətʃə(r)/ *n* Literatur *f*; [!] Informationsmaterial *nt*
lithe /laɪð/ *a* geschmeidig
Lithuania /lɪθjʊˈeɪnɪə/ *n* Litauen *nt*
litre /ˈliːtə(r)/ *n* Liter *m* & *nt*
litter /ˈlɪtə(r)/ *n* Abfall *m*; (*Zool*) Wurf *m*. **~-bin** *n* Abfalleimer *m*
little /ˈlɪtl/ *a* klein; (*not much*) wenig ● *adv* & *n* wenig; **a ~** ein bisschen/wenig; **~ by ~** nach und nach
live[1] /laɪv/ *a* lebendig; <*ammunition*> scharf; **~ broadcast** Live-Sendung *f*; **be ~** (*Electr*) unter Strom stehen
live[2] /lɪv/ *vi* leben; (*reside*) wohnen. **~ on** *vt* leben von; (*eat*) sich ernähren von ● *vi* weiterleben
liveli|hood /ˈlaɪvlɪhʊd/ *n* Lebensunterhalt *m*. **~ness** *n* Lebendigkeit *f*
lively /ˈlaɪvlɪ/ *a* (**-ier, -iest**) lebhaft, lebendig
liver /ˈlɪvə(r)/ *n* Leber *f*
lives /laɪvz/ *see* life
livid /ˈlɪvɪd/ *a* [!] wütend
living /ˈlɪvɪŋ/ *a* lebend ● *n* **earn one's ~** seinen Lebensunterhalt verdienen. **~-room** *n* Wohnzimmer *nt*
lizard /ˈlɪzəd/ *n* Eidechse *f*
load /ləʊd/ *n* Last *f*; (*quantity*) Ladung *f*; (*Electr*) Belastung *f*; **~s of** [!] jede Menge ● *vt* laden <*goods, gun*>; beladen <*vehicle*>; **~ a camera** einen Film in eine Kamera einlegen. **~ed** *a* beladen; ([!] *rich*) steinreich
loaf /ləʊf/ *n* (*pl* **loaves**) Brot *nt*
loan /ləʊn/ *n* Leihgabe *f*; (*money*) Darlehen *nt*; **on ~** geliehen ● *vt* leihen (*to dat*)
loath /ləʊθ/ *a* **be ~ to do sth** etw ungern tun
loath|e /ləʊð/ *vt* verabscheuen. **~ing** *n* Abscheu *m*
loaves /ləʊvz/ *see* **loaf**

lobby /ˈlɒbɪ/ *n* Foyer *nt*; (*anteroom*) Vorraum *m*; (*Pol*) Lobby *f*

lobster /ˈlɒbstə(r)/ *n* Hummer *m*

local /ˈləʊkl/ *a* hiesig; <*time, traffic*> Orts-; **~ anaesthetic** örtliche Betäubung; **I'm not ~** ich bin nicht von hier ● *n* Hiesige(r) *m*/*f*; ([!] *public house*) Stammkneipe *f*. **~ call** *n* (*Teleph*) Ortsgespräch *nt*

locality /ləʊˈkælətɪ/ *n* Gegend *f*

locally /ˈləʊkəlɪ/ *adv* am Ort

locat|e /ləʊˈkeɪt/ *vt* ausfindig machen; **be ~ed** sich befinden. **~ion** /-ˈkeɪʃn/ *n* Lage *f*; **filmed on ~ion** als Außenaufnahme gedreht

lock¹ /lɒk/ *n* (*hair*) Strähne *f*

lock² *n* (*on door*) Schloss *nt*; (*on canal*) Schleuse *f* ● *vt* abschließen ● *vi* sich abschließen lassen. **~ in** *vt* einschließen. **~ out** *vt* ausschließen. **~ up** *vt* abschließen; einsperren <*person*>

locker /ˈlɒkə(r)/ *n* Schließfach *nt*; (*Mil*) Spind *m*

lock: ~-out *n* Aussperrung *f*. **~smith** *n* Schlosser *m*

locomotive /ləʊkəˈməʊtɪv/ *n* Lokomotive *f*

locum /ˈləʊkəm/ *n* Vertreter(in) *m*(*f*)

locust /ˈləʊkəst/ *n* Heuschrecke *f*

lodge /lɒdʒ/ *n* (*porter's*) Pförtnerhaus *nt* ● *vt* (*submit*) einreichen; (*deposit*) deponieren ● *vi* zur Untermiete wohnen (**with** bei); (*become fixed*) stecken bleiben. **~r** *n* Untermieter(in) *m*(*f*)

lodging /ˈlɒdʒɪŋ/ *n* Unterkunft *f*; **~s** *pl* möbliertes Zimmer *nt*

loft /lɒft/ *n* Dachboden *m*

lofty /ˈlɒftɪ/ *a* (**-ier, -iest**) hoch

log /lɒg/ *n* Baumstamm *m*; (*for fire*) [Holz]scheit *nt*; **sleep like a ~** [!] wie ein Murmeltier schlafen ● *vi* **~ off** sich abmelden; **~ on** sich anmelden

loggerheads /ˈlɒgə-/ *npl* **be at ~** [!] sich in den Haaren liegen

logic /ˈlɒdʒɪk/ *n* Logik *f*. **~al** *a*, **-ly** *adv* logisch

logo /ˈləʊgəʊ/ *n* Symbol *nt*, Logo *nt*

loiter /ˈlɔɪtə(r)/ *vi* herumlungern

loll /lɒl/ *vi* sich lümmeln

loll|ipop /ˈlɒlɪpɒp/ *n* Lutscher *m*. **~y** *n* Lutscher *m*; ([!] *money*) Moneten *pl*

London /ˈlʌndən/ *n* London *nt* ● *attrib* Londoner. **~er** *n* Londoner(in) *m*(*f*)

lone /ləʊn/ *a* einzeln. **~liness** *n* Einsamkeit *f*

lonely /ˈləʊnlɪ/ *a* (**-ier, -iest**) einsam

lone|r /ˈləʊnə(r)/ *n* Einzelgänger *m*. **~some** *a* einsam

long¹ /lɒŋ/ *a* (**-er** /ˈlɒŋgə(r)/, **-est** /ˈlɒŋgɪst/) lang; <*journey*> weit; **a ~ time** lange; **a ~ way** weit; **in the ~ run** auf lange Sicht; (*in the end*) letzten Endes ● *adv* lange; **all day ~** den ganzen Tag; **not ~ ago** vor kurzem; **before ~** bald; **no ~er** nicht mehr; **as** *or* **so ~ as** solange; **so ~!** [!] tschüs!

long² *vi* **~ for** sich sehnen nach

long-ˈdistance *a* Fern-; (*Sport*) Langstrecken-

longing /ˈlɒŋɪŋ/ *a*, **-ly** *adv* sehnsüchtig ● *n* Sehnsucht *f*

longitude /ˈlɒŋgɪtjuːd/ *n* (*Geog*) Länge *f*

long: ~ jump *n* Weitsprung *m*. **~-lived** /-lɪvd/ *a* langlebig. **~-range** *a* (*Mil, Aviat*) Langstrecken-; <*forecast*> langfristig. **~-sighted** *a* weitsichtig. **~-sleeved** *a* langärmelig. **~-suffering** *a* langmütig. **~-term** *a* langfristig. **~ wave** *n* Langwelle. **~-winded** /-ˈwɪndɪd/ *a* langatmig

loo /lu:/ *n* [!] Klo *nt*

look /lʊk/ *n* Blick *m*; (*appearance*) Aussehen *nt*; **[good] ~s** *pl* [gutes] Aussehen *nt*; **have a ~ at** sich (*dat*) ansehen; **go and have a ~** sieh mal nach ● *vi* sehen; (*search*) nachsehen; (*seem*) aussehen; **don't ~** sieh nicht hin; **~ here!** hören Sie mal! **~ at** ansehen; **~ for** suchen; **~ forward to** sich freuen auf (+ *acc*); **~ in on** vorbeischauen bei; **~ into** (*examine*) nachgehen (+ *dat*); **~ like** aussehen wie; **~ on to** <*room:*> gehen auf (+ *acc*). **~ after** *vt* betreuen. **~ down** *vi* hinuntersehen; **~ down on s.o.** (*fig*) auf jdn herabsehen. **~ out** *vi* hinaus-/heraussehen; (*take care*) aufpassen; **~ out for** Ausschau halten nach; **~ out!** Vorsicht! **~ round** *vi* sich umsehen. **~ up** *vi* aufblicken; **~ up to s.o.** (*fig*) zu jdm aufsehen ● *vt* nachschlagen <*word*>

'look-out *n* Wache *f*; (*prospect*) Aussicht *f*; **be on the ~ for** Ausschau halten nach

loom¹ /lu:m/ *n* Webstuhl *m*

loom² *vi* auftauchen

loony /'lu:nɪ/ *a* [!] verrückt

loop /lu:p/ *n* Schlinge *f*; (*in road*) Schleife *f*. **~hole** *n* Hintertürchen *nt*; (*in the law*) Lücke *f*

loose /lu:s/ *a* (**-r, -st**), **-ly** *adv* lose; (*not tight enough*) locker; (*inexact*) frei; **be at a ~ end** nichts zu tun haben. **~ 'change** *n* Kleingeld *nt*

loosen /'lu:sn/ *vt* lockern

loot /lu:t/ *n* Beute *f* ● *vt/i* plündern. **~er** *n* Plünderer *m*

lop /lɒp/ *vt* (*pt/pp* **lopped**) stutzen

lop'sided *a* schief

lord /lɔ:d/ *n* Herr *m*; (*title*) Lord *m*; **House of L~ s** ≈ Oberhaus *nt*; **the L~'s Prayer** das Vaterunser

lorry /'lɒrɪ/ *n* Last[kraft]wagen *m*

lose /lu:z/ *v* (*pt/pp* **lost**) ● *vt* verlieren; (*miss*) verpassen ● *vi* verlieren; <*clock:*> nachgehen; **get lost** verloren gehen; <*person*> sich verlaufen. **~r** *n* Verlierer *m*

loss /lɒs/ *n* Verlust *m*; **be at a ~** nicht mehr weiter wissen

lost /lɒst/ *see* **lose**. **~ 'property office** *n* Fundbüro *nt*

lot¹ /lɒt/ Los *nt*; (*at auction*) Posten *m*; **draw ~s** losen (**for** um)

lot² *n* **the ~** alle; (*everything*) alles; **a ~ [of]** viel; (*many*) viele; **~s of** [!] eine Menge; **it has changed a ~** es hat sich sehr verändert

lotion /'ləʊʃn/ *n* Lotion *f*

lottery /'lɒtərɪ/ *n* Lotterie *f*. **~ ticket** *n* Los *nt*

loud /laʊd/ *a* (**-er, -est**), **-ly** *adv* laut; <*colours*> grell ● *adv* **[out]** **~** laut. **~'speaker** *n* Lautsprecher *m*

lounge /laʊndʒ/ *n* Wohnzimmer *nt*; (*in hotel*) Aufenthaltsraum *m*. ● *vi* sich lümmeln

louse /laʊs/ *n* (*pl* **lice**) Laus *f*

lousy /'laʊzɪ/ *a* (**-ier, -iest**) [!] lausig

lout /laʊt/ *n* Flegel *m*, Lümmel *m*

lovable /'lʌvəbl/ *a* liebenswert

love /lʌv/ *n* Liebe *f*; (*Tennis*) null; **in ~** verliebt ● *vt* lieben; **~ doing sth** etw sehr gerne machen. **~ affair** *n* Liebesverhältnis *nt*. **~ letter** *n* Liebesbrief *m*

lovely /'lʌvlɪ/ *a* (**-ier, -iest**) schön

lover /'lʌvə(r)/ *n* Liebhaber *m*

love: ~ song *n* Liebeslied *nt*. **~ story** *n* Liebesgeschichte *f*

loving /'lʌvɪŋ/ *a*, **-ly** *adv* liebevoll

low /ləʊ/ *a* (**-er, -est**) niedrig; <*cloud, note*> tief; <*voice*> leise; (*depressed*) niedergeschlagen ● *adv* niedrig; <*fly, sing*> tief; <*speak*> leise ● *n* (*Meteorol*) Tief *nt*; (*fig*) Tiefstand *m*

low: ~brow *a* geistig anspruchslos. **~-cut** *a* <*dress*> tief ausgeschnitten

lower /'ləʊə(r)/ *a & adv see* **low** ● *vt* niedriger machen; (*let down*) herunterlassen; (*reduce*) senken

low: ~-'fat *a* fettarm. **~lands** /-ləndz/ *npl* Tiefland *nt*. **~ 'tide** *n* Ebbe *f*

loyal /'lɔɪəl/ *a*, **-ly** *adv* treu. **~ty** *n* Treue *f*. **~ty card** *n* Treuekarte *f*

lozenge /'lɒzɪndʒ/ *n* Pastille *f*

Ltd *abbr* (**Limited**) GmbH

lubricant /'lu:brɪkənt/ *n* Schmiermittel *nt*

lubricat|e /'lu:brɪkeɪt/ *vt* schmieren. **~ion** /-'keɪʃn/ *n* Schmierung *f*

lucid /'lu:sɪd/ *a* klar. **~ity** /-'sɪdətɪ/ *n* Klarheit *f*

luck /lʌk/ *n* Glück *nt*; **bad ~** Pech *nt*; **good ~!** viel Glück! **~ily** *adv* glücklicherweise, zum Glück

lucky /'lʌkɪ/ *a* (**-ier, -iest**) glücklich; <*day, number*> Glücks-; **be ~** Glück haben; <*thing:*> Glück bringen

lucrative /'lu:krətɪv/ *a* einträglich

ludicrous /'lu:dɪkrəs/ *a* lächerlich

lug /lʌg/ *vt* (*pt/pp* **lugged**) 🄵 schleppen

luggage /'lʌgɪdʒ/ *n* Gepäck *nt*

luggage: ~-rack *in* Gepäckablage *f*. **~-van** *n* Gepäckwagen *m*

lukewarm /'lu:k-/ *a* lauwarm

lull /lʌl/ *n* Pause *f* ● *vt* **~ to sleep** einschläfern

lullaby /'lʌləbaɪ/ *n* Wiegenlied *nt*

lumber /'lʌmbə(r)/ *n* Gerümpel *nt*; (*Amer: timber*) Bauholz *nt* ● *vt* **~ s.o. with sth** jdm etw aufhalsen. **~jack** *n* (*Amer*) Holzfäller *m*

luminous /'lu:mɪnəs/ *a* leuchtend

lump /lʌmp/ *n* Klumpen *m*; (*of sugar*) Stück *nt*; (*swelling*) Beule *f*; (*in breast*) Knoten *m*; (*tumour*) Geschwulst *f*; **a ~ in one's throat** 🄵 ein Kloß im Hals

lump: ~ sugar *n* Würfelzucker *m*. **~ 'sum** *n* Pauschalsumme *f*

lumpy /'lʌmpɪ/ *a* (**-ier, -iest**) klumpig

lunacy /'lu:nəsɪ/ *n* Wahnsinn *m*

lunar /'lu:nə(r)/ *a* Mond-

lunatic /'lu:nətɪk/ *n* Wahnsinnige(r) *m/f*

lunch /lʌntʃ/ *n* Mittagessen *nt* ● *vi* zu Mittag essen

luncheon /'lʌntʃn/ *n* Mittagessen *nt*. **~ voucher** *n* Essensbon *m*

lunch: ~-hour *n* Mittagspause *f*. **~-time** *n* Mittagszeit *f*

lung /lʌŋ/ *n* Lungenflügel *m*; **~s** *pl* Lunge *f*

lunge /lʌndʒ/ *vi* sich stürzen (**at** auf + *acc*)

lurch[1] /lɜ:tʃ/ *n* **leave in the ~** 🄵 im Stich lassen

lurch[2] *vi* <*person:*> torkeln

lure /ljʊə(r)/ *vt* locken

lurid /'lʊərɪd/ *a* grell; (*sensational*) reißerisch

lurk /lɜ:k/ *vi* lauern

luscious /'lʌʃəs/ *a* lecker, köstlich

lush /lʌʃ/ *a* üppig

lust /lʌst/ *n* Begierde *f*. **~ful** *a* lüstern

lustre /'lʌstə(r)/ *n* Glanz *m*

lusty /'lʌstɪ/ *a* (**-ier, -iest**) kräftig

luxuriant /lʌg'ʒʊərɪənt/ *a* üppig

luxurious /lʌg'ʒʊərɪəs/ *a*, **-ly** *adv* luxuriös

luxury /'lʌkʃərɪ/ *n* Luxus *m* ● *attrib* Luxus-

lying /'laɪɪŋ/ *see* **lie**[1], **lie**[2]

lynch /lɪntʃ/ *vt* lynchen

lyric /'lɪrɪk/ *a* lyrisch. **~al** *a* lyrisch; (*enthusiastic*) schwärmerisch. **~ poetry** *n* Lyrik *f*. **~s** *npl* [Lied]text *m*

Mm

mac /mæk/ *n* [!] Regenmantel *m*

macabre /mə'kɑ:br/ *a* makaber

macaroni /mækə'rəʊnɪ/ *n* Makkaroni *pl*

machinations /mækɪ'neɪʃnz/ *pl* Machenschaften *pl*

machine /mə'ʃi:n/ *n* Maschine *f* ● *vt* (*sew*) mit der Maschine nähen; (*Techn*) maschinell bearbeiten. **~-gun** *n* Maschinengewehr *nt*

machinery /mə'ʃi:nərɪ/ *n* Maschinerie *f*

mackerel /'mækrl/ *n inv* Makrele *f*

mackintosh /'mækɪntoʃ/ *n* Regenmantel *m*

mad /mæd/ *a* (**madder, maddest**) verrückt; (*dog*) tollwütig; (*fam: angry*) böse (**at** auf + *acc*)

madam /'mædəm/ *n* gnädige Frau *f*

mad 'cow disease *n* [!] Rinderwahnsinn *m*

madden /'mædn/ *vt* (*make angry*) wütend machen

made /meɪd/ *see* **make**; **~ to measure** maßgeschneidert

mad|ly /'mædlɪ/ *adv* [!] wahnsinnig. **~man** *n* Irre(r) *m*. **~ness** *n* Wahnsinn *m*

madonna /mə'dɒnə/ *n* Madonna *f*

magazine /mægə'zi:n/ *n* Zeitschrift *f*; (*Mil, Phot*) Magazin *nt*

maggot /'mægət/ *n* Made *f*

magic /'mædʒɪk/ *n* Zauber *m*; (*tricks*) Zauberkunst *f* ● *a* magisch; <*word, wand*> Zauber-. **~al** *a* zauberhaft

magician /mə'dʒɪʃn/ *n* Zauberer *m*; (*entertainer*) Zauberkünstler *m*

magistrate /'mædʒɪstreɪt/ *n* ≈ Friedensrichter *m*

magnet /'mægnɪt/ *n* Magnet *m*. **~ic** /-'netik/ *a* magnetisch. **~ism** *n* Magnetismus *m*

magnification /mægnɪfɪ'keɪʃn/ *n* Vergrößerung *f*

magnificen|ce /mæg'nɪfɪsəns/ *n* Großartigkeit *f*. **~t** *a*, **-ly** *adv* großartig

magnify /'mægnɪfaɪ/ *vt* (*pt/pp* **-ied**) vergrößern; (*exaggerate*) übertreiben. **~ing glass** *n* Vergrößerungsglas *nt*

magnitude /'mægnɪtju:d/ *n* Größe *f*; (*importance*) Bedeutung *f*

magpie /'mægpaɪ/ *n* Elster *f*

mahogany /mə'hɒgənɪ/ *n* Mahagoni *nt*

maid /meɪd/ *n* Dienstmädchen *nt*; **old ~** (*pej*) alte Jungfer *f*

maiden /'meɪdn/ *a* <*speech, voyage*> Jungfern-. **~ name** *n* Mädchenname *m*

mail /meɪl/ *n* Post *f* ● *vt* mit der Post schicken

mail: ~-bag *n* Postsack *m*. **~box** *n* (*Amer*) Briefkasten *m*. **~ing list** *n* Postversandliste *f*. **~man**

n (*Amer*) Briefträger *m*. **~-order firm** *n* Versandhaus *nt*

maim /meɪm/ *vt* verstümmeln

main /meɪn/ *a* Haupt- ● *n* (*water, gas, electricity*) Hauptleitung *f*

main: ~land /-lənd/ *n* Festland *nt*. **~ly** *adv* hauptsächlich. **~stay** *n* (*fig*) Stütze *f*. **~ street** *n* Hauptstraße *f*

maintain /meɪn'teɪn/ *vt* aufrechterhalten; (*keep in repair*) instand halten; (*support*) unterhalten; (*claim*) behaupten

maintenance /'meɪntənəns/ *n* Aufrechterhaltung *f*; (*care*) Instandhaltung *f*; (*allowance*) Unterhalt *m*

maize /meɪz/ *n* Mais *m*

majestic /mə'dʒestɪk/ *a*, **-ally** *adv* majestätisch

majesty /'mædʒəstɪ/ *n* Majestät *f*

major /'meɪdʒə(r)/ *a* größer ● *n* (*Mil*) Major *m*; (*Mus*) Dur *nt* ● *vi* **~ in** als Hauptfach studieren

majority /mə'dʒɒrətɪ/ *n* Mehrheit *f*; **in the ~** in der Mehrzahl

major road *n* Hauptverkehrsstraße *f*

make /meɪk/ *n* (*brand*) Marke *f* ● *v* (*pt/pp* **made**) ● *vt* machen; (*force*) zwingen; (*earn*) verdienen; halten <*speech*>; treffen <*decision*>; erreichen <*destination*> ● *vi* **~ do** *vi* zurechtkommen (**with** mit). **~ for** *vi* zusteuern auf (+ *acc*). **~ off** *vi* sich davonmachen (**with** mit). **~ out** *vt* (*distinguish*) ausmachen; (*write out*) ausstellen; (*assert*) behaupten. **~ up** *vt* (*constitute*) bilden; (*invent*) erfinden; (*apply cosmetics to*) schminken; **~ up one's mind** sich entschließen ● *vi* sich versöhnen; **~ up for sth** etw wieder gutmachen; **~ up for lost time** verlorene Zeit aufholen

'make-believe *n* Phantasie *f*

maker /'meɪkə(r)/ *n* Hersteller *m*

make: ~ shift *a* behelfsmäßig ● *n* Notbehelf *m*. **~-up** *n* Make-up *nt*

maladjusted /mælə'dʒʌstɪd/ *a* verhaltensgestört

male /meɪl/ *a* männlich ● *n* Mann *m*; (*animal*) Männchen *nt*. **~ nurse** *n* Krankenpfleger *m*. **~ voice 'choir** *n* Männerchor *m*

malice /'mælɪs/ *n* Bosheit *f*

malicious /mə'lɪʃəs/ *a*, **-ly** *adv* böswillig

malign /mə'laɪn/ *vt* verleumden

malignant /mə'lɪgnənt/ *a* bösartig

mallet /'mælɪt/ *n* Holzhammer *m*

malnu'trition /mæl-/ *n* Unterernährung *f*

mal'practice *n* Berufsvergehen *nt*

malt /mɔːlt/ *n* Malz *nt*

mal'treat /mæl-/ *vt* misshandeln. **~ment** *n* Misshandlung *f*

mammal /'mæml/ *n* Säugetier *nt*

mammoth /'mæməθ/ *a* riesig

man /mæn/ *n* (*pl* **men**) Mann *m*; (*mankind*) der Mensch; (*chess*) Figur *f*; (*draughts*) Stein *m* ● *vt* (*pt/pp* **manned**) bemannen <*ship*>; bedienen <*pump*>; besetzen <*counter*>

manage /'mænɪdʒ/ *vt* leiten; verwalten <*estate*>; (*cope with*) fertig werden mit; **~ to do sth** es schaffen, etw zu tun ● *vi* zurechtkommen; **~ on** auskommen mit. **~able** /-əbl/ *a* <*tool*> handlich; <*person*> fügsam. **~ment** /-mənt/ *n* Leitung *f*; **the ~ment** die Geschäftsleitung *f*

manager /'mænɪdʒə(r)/ *n* Geschäftsführer *m*; (*of bank*) Direktor *m*; (*of estate*) Verwalter *m*; (*Sport*) [Chef]trainer *m*. **~ess** *n* Geschäftsführerin *f*.

~ial /-'dʒɪərɪəl/ *a* **~ial staff** Führungskräfte *pl*
managing /'mænɪdʒɪŋ/ *a* **~ director** Generaldirektor *m*
mandat|e /'mændeɪt/ *n* Mandat *nt*. **~ory** /-dətrɪ/ *a* obligatorisch
mane /meɪn/ *n* Mähne *f*
manful /'mænfl/ *a*, **-ly** *adv* mannhaft
man: ~'handle *vt* grob behandeln <*person*>. **~hole** *n* Kanalschacht *m*. **~hood** *n* Mannesalter *nt*; (*quality*) Männlichkeit *f*. **~-hour** *n* Arbeitsstunde *f*. **~-hunt** *n* Fahndung *f*
mania /'meɪnɪə/ *n* Manie *f*. **~c** /-ɪæk/ *n* Wahnsinnige(r) *m/f*
manicure /'mænɪkjʊə(r)/ *n* Maniküre *f* ● *vt* maniküren
manifest /'mænɪfest/ *a*, **-ly** *adv* offensichtlich
manifesto /mænɪ'festəʊ/ *n* Manifest *nt*
manifold /'mænɪfəʊld/ *a* mannigfaltig
manipulat|e /mə'nɪpjʊleɪt/ *vt* handhaben; (*pej*) manipulieren. **~ion** /-'leɪʃn/ *n* Manipulation *f*
man'kind *n* die Menschheit
manly /'mænlɪ/ *a* männlich
'man-made *a* künstlich. **~ fibre** *n* Kunstfaser *f*
manner /'mænə(r)/ *n* Weise *f*; (*kind, behaviour*) Art *f*; **[good/bad] ~s** [gute/schlechte] Manieren *pl*. **~ism** *n* Angewohnheit *f*
manœuvrable /mə'nu:vrəbl/ *a* manövrierfähig
manœuvre /mə'nu:və(r)/ *n* Manöver *nt* ● *vt/i* manövrieren
manor /'mænə(r)/ *n* Gutshof *m*; (*house*) Gutshaus *nt*
'manpower *n* Arbeitskräfte *pl*
mansion /'mænʃn/ *n* Villa *f*
'manslaughter *n* Totschlag *m*
mantelpiece /'mæntl-/ *n* Kaminsims *m & nt*
manual /'mænjʊəl/ *a* Hand- ● *n* Handbuch *nt*
manufacture /mænjʊ'fæktʃə(r)/ *vt* herstellen ● *n* Herstellung *f*. **~r** *n* Hersteller *m*
manure /mə'njʊə(r)/ *n* Mist *m*
manuscript /'mænjʊskrɪpt/ *n* Manuskript *nt*
many /'menɪ/ *a* viele ● *n* **a good/great ~** sehr viele
map /mæp/ *n* Landkarte *f*; (*of town*) Stadtplan *m*
maple /'meɪpl/ *n* Ahorn *m*
mar /mɑ:(r)/ *vt* (*pt/pp* **marred**) verderben
marathon /'mærəθən/ *n* Marathon *m*
marble /'mɑ:bl/ *n* Marmor *m*; (*for game*) Murmel *f*
March /mɑ:tʃ/ *n* März *m*
march *n* Marsch *m* ● *vi* marschieren ● *vt* marschieren lassen; **~ s.o. off** jdn abführen
mare /'meə(r)/ *n* Stute *f*
margarine /mɑ:dʒə'ri:n/ *n* Margarine *f*
margin /'mɑ:dʒɪn/ *n* Rand *m*; (*leeway*) Spielraum *m*; (*Comm*) Spanne *f*. **~al** *a*, **-ly** *adv* geringfügig
marigold /'mærɪgəʊld/ *n* Ringelblume *f*
marina /mə'ri:nə/ *n* Jachthafen *m*
marine /mə'ri:n/ *a* Meeres- ● *n* Marine *f*; (*sailor*) Marineinfanterist *m*
marital /'mærɪtl/ *a* ehelich. **~ status** *n* Familienstand *m*
maritime /'mærɪtaɪm/ *a* See-
mark¹ /mɑ:k/ *n* (*currency*) Mark *f*
mark² *n* Fleck *m*; (*sign*) Zeichen *nt*; (*trace*) Spur *f*; (*target*) Ziel *nt*; (*Sch*) Note *f* ● *vt* markieren; (*spoil*) beschädigen; (*characterize*) kennzeichnen; (*Sch*) korrigieren;

(*Sport*) decken; ~ **time** (*Mil*) auf der Stelle treten; (*fig*) abwarten. ~ **out** *vt* markieren

marked /mɑ:kt/ *a*, ~**ly** /-kɪdlɪ/ *adv* deutlich; (*pronounced*) ausgeprägt

market /'mɑ:kɪt/ *n* Markt *m* ● *vt* vertreiben; (*launch*) auf den Markt bringen. ~**ing** *n* Marketing *nt*. ~ **re'search** *n* Marktforschung *f*

marking /'mɑ:kɪŋ/ *n* Markierung *f*; (*on animal*) Zeichnung *f*

marksman /'mɑ:ksmən/ *n* Scharfschütze *m*

marmalade /'mɑ:məleɪd/ *n* Orangenmarmelade *f*

maroon /mə'ru:n/ *a* dunkelrot

marooned /mə'ru:nd/ *a* (*fig*) von der Außenwelt abgeschnitten

marquee /mɑ:'ki:/ *n* Festzelt *nt*

marquetry /'mɑ:kɪtrɪ/ *n* Einlegearbeit *f*

marriage /'mærɪdʒ/ *n* Ehe *f*; (*wedding*) Hochzeit *f*. ~**able** /-əbl/ *a* heiratsfähig

married /'mærɪd/ *see* **marry** ● *a* verheiratet. ~ **life** *n* Eheleben *nt*

marrow /'mærəʊ/ *n* (*Anat*) Mark *nt*; (*vegetable*) Kürbis *m*

marr|y /'mærɪ/ *vt/i* (*pt/pp* **married**) heiraten; (*unite*) trauen; **get** ~**ied** heiraten

marsh /mɑ:ʃ/ *n* Sumpf *m*

marshal /'mɑ:ʃl/ *n* Marschall *m*; (*steward*) Ordner *m*

marshy /'mɑ:ʃɪ/ *a* sumpfig

martial /'mɑ:ʃl/ *a* kriegerisch. ~ '**law** *n* Kriegsrecht *nt*

martyr /'mɑ:tə(r)/ *n* Märtyrer(in) *m(f)*. ~**dom** /-dəm/ *n* Martyrium *nt*

marvel /'mɑ:vl/ *n* Wunder *nt* ● *vi* (*pt/pp* **marvelled**) staunen (**at** über + *acc*). ~**lous** /-vələs/ a, **-ly** adv wunderbar

Marxis|m /'mɑ:ksɪzm/ *n* Marxismus *m*. ~**t** *a* marxistisch ● *n* Marxist(in) *m(f)*

marzipan /'mɑ:zɪpæn/ *n* Marzipan *nt*

mascot /'mæskət/ *n* Maskottchen *nt*

masculin|e /'mæskjʊlɪn/ *a* männlich ● *n* (*Gram*) Maskulinum *nt*. ~**ity** /-'lɪnətɪ/ *n* Männlichkeit *f*

mash /mæʃ/ *n* [!], ~**ed potatoes** *npl* Kartoffelpüree *nt*

mask /mɑ:sk/ *n* Maske *f* ● *vt* maskieren

masochis|m /'mæsəkɪzm/ *n* Masochismus *m*. ~**t** /-ɪst/ *n* Masochist *m*

mason /'meɪsn/ *n* Steinmetz *m*. ~**ry** *n* Mauerwerk *nt*

mass[1] /mæs/ *n* (*Relig*) Messe *f*

mass[2] *n* Masse *f* ● *vi* sich sammeln; (*Mil*) sich massieren

massacre /'mæsəkə(r)/ *n* Massaker *nt* ● *vt* niedermetzeln

massage /'mæsɑ:ʒ/ *n* Massage *f* ● *vt* massieren

masseu|r /mæ'sɜ:(r)/ *n* Masseur *m*. ~**se** /-'sɜ:z/ *n* Masseuse *f*

massive /'mæsɪv/ *a* massiv; (*huge*) riesig

mass: ~ '**media** *npl* Massenmedien *pl*. ~-**pro'duce** *vt* in Massenproduktion herstellen. ~ **pro'duction** *n* Massenproduktion *f*

mast /mɑ:st/ *n* Mast *m*

master /'mɑ:stə(r)/ *n* Herr *m*; (*teacher*) Lehrer *m*; (*craftsman, artist*) Meister *m*; (*of ship*) Kapitän *m* ● *vt* meistern; beherrschen <*language*>

master: ~**ly** *a* meisterhaft. ~**mind** *n* führender Kopf *m* ● *vt* der führende Kopf sein von. ~**piece** *n* Meisterwerk *nt*. ~**y** *n* (*of subject*) Beherrschung *f*

mat /mæt/ *n* Matte *f*; (*on table*) Untersatz *m*

match¹ /mætʃ/ *n* Wettkampf *m*; (*in ball games*) Spiel *nt*; (*Tennis*) Match *nt*; (*marriage*) Heirat *f*; **be a good ~** <*colours:*> gut zusammenpassen; **be no ~ for s.o.** jdm nicht gewachsen sein ● *vt* (*equal*) gleichkommen (+ *dat*); (*be like*) passen zu; (*find sth similar*) etwas Passendes finden zu ● *vi* zusammenpassen

match² *n* Streichholz *nt*. **~box** *n* Streichholzschachtel *f*

mate¹ /meɪt/ *n* Kumpel *m*; (*assistant*) Gehilfe *m*; (*Naut*) Maat *m*; (*Zool*) Männchen *nt*; (*female*) Weibchen *nt* ● *vi* sich paaren

mate² *n* (*Chess*) Matt *nt*

material /məˈtɪərɪəl/ *n* Material *nt*; (*fabric*) Stoff *m*; **raw ~s** Rohstoffe *pl* ● *a* materiell

material|ism /məˈtɪərɪəlɪzm/ *n* Materialismus *m*. **~istic** /-ˈlɪstɪk/ *a* materialistisch. **~ize** /-laɪz/ *vi* sich verwirklichen

maternal /məˈtɜːnl/ *a* mütterlich

maternity /məˈtɜːnətɪ/ *n* Mutterschaft *f*. **~ clothes** *npl* Umstandskleidung *f*. **~ ward** *n* Entbindungsstation *f*

mathematic|al /mæθəˈmætɪkl/ *a*, **-ly** *adv* mathematisch. **~ian** /-məˈtɪʃn/ *n* Mathematiker(in) *m*(*f*)

mathematics /mæθəˈmætɪks/ *n* Mathematik *f*

maths /mæθs/ *n* [!] Mathe *f*

matinée /ˈmætɪneɪ/ *n* (*Theat*) Nachmittagsvorstellung *f*

matrimony /ˈmætrɪmənɪ/ *n* Ehe *f*

matron /ˈmeɪtrən/ *n* (*of hospital*) Oberin *f*; (*of school*) Hausmutter *f*

matt /mæt/ *a* matt

matted /ˈmætɪd/ *a* verfilzt

matter /ˈmætə(r)/ *n* (*affair*) Sache *f*; (*Phys: substance*) Materie *f*; **money ~s** Geldangelegenheiten *pl*; **what is the ~?** was ist los? ● *vi* wichtig sein; **~ to s.o.** jdm etwas ausmachen; **it doesn't ~** es macht nichts. **~-of-fact** *a* sachlich

mattress /ˈmætrɪs/ *n* Matratze *f*

matur|e /məˈtjʊə(r)/ *a* reif; (*Comm*) fällig ● *vi* reifen; <*person:*> reifer werden; (*Comm*) fällig werden ● *vt* reifen lassen. **~ity** *n* Reife *f*; (*Comm*) Fälligkeit *f*

mauve /məʊv/ *a* lila

maximum /ˈmæksɪməm/ *a* maximal ● *n* (*pl* **-ima**) Maximum *nt*. **~ speed** *n* Höchstgeschwindigkeit *f*

---

may /meɪ/

pres **may**, *pt* **might**

● *auxiliary verb*

····➤ (*expressing possibility*) können. **she may come** es kann sein, dass sie kommt; es ist möglich, dass sie kommt. **she might come** (*more distant possibility*) sie könnte kommen. **it may/might rain** es könnte regnen. **I may be wrong** vielleicht irre ich mich. **he may have missed his train** vielleicht hat er seinen Zug verpasst

····➤ (*expressing permission*) dürfen. **may I come in?** darf ich reinkommen? **you may smoke** Sie dürfen rauchen

····➤ (*expressing wish*) **may the best man win!** auf dass der Beste gewinnt!

····➤ (*expressing concession*) **he may be slow but he's accurate** mag *od* kann sein, dass er langsam ist, aber dafür ist er auch genau

····➤ **may/might as well** ebenso gut können. **we may/might as well go** wir könnten eigentlich ebensogut [auch] gehen. **we**

might as well give up da können wir gleich aufgeben

May *n* Mai *m*

maybe /'meɪbi:/ *adv* vielleicht

'**May Day** *n* der Erste Mai

mayonnaise /meɪə'neɪz/ *n* Mayonnaise *f*

mayor /'meə(r)/ *n* Bürgermeister *m*. **~ess** *n* Bürgermeisterin *f*; (*wife of mayor*) Frau Bürgermeister *f*

maze /meɪz/ *n* Irrgarten *m*; (*fig*) Labyrinth *nt*

me /mi:/ *pron* (*acc*) mich; (*dat*) mir; **it's ~** [!] ich bin es

meadow /'medəʊ/ *n* Wiese *f*

meagre /'mi:gə(r)/ *a* dürftig

meal /mi:l/ *n* Mahlzeit *f*; (*food*) Essen *nt*; (*grain*) Schrot *m*

mean[1] /mi:n/ *a* (**-er, -est**) (*miserly*) geizig; (*unkind*) gemein; (*poor*) schäbig

mean[2] *a* mittlere(r,s) ● *n* (*average*) Durchschnitt *m*

mean[3] *vt* (*pt*/*pp* **meant**) heißen; (*signify*) bedeuten; (*intend*) beabsichtigen; **I ~ it** das ist mein Ernst; **~ well** es gut meinen; **be meant for** <*present*:> bestimmt sein für; <*remark*:> gerichtet sein an (+ *acc*)

meaning /'mi:nɪŋ/ *n* Bedeutung *f*. **~ful** *a* bedeutungsvoll. **~less** *a* bedeutungslos

means /mi:nz/ *n* Möglichkeit *f*, Mittel *nt*; **~ of transport** Verkehrsmittel *nt*; **by ~ of** durch; **by all ~!** aber natürlich! **by no ~** keineswegs ● *npl* (*resources*) [Geld]mittel *pl*

meant /ment/ *see* **mean**[3]

'**meantime** *n* **in the ~** in der Zwischenzeit ● *adv* inzwischen

'**meanwhile** *adv* inzwischen

measles /'mi:zlz/ *n* Masern *pl*

measure /'meʒə(r)/ *n* Maß *nt*; (*action*) Maßnahme *f* ● *vt*/*i* messen; **~ up to** (*fig*) herankommen an (+ *acc*). **~d** *a* gemessen. **~ment** /-mənt/ *n* Maß *nt*

meat /mi:t/ *n* Fleisch *nt*

mechan|ic /mɪ'kænɪk/ *n* Mechaniker *m*. **~ical** *a*, **-ly** *adv* mechanisch. **~ical engineering** Maschinenbau *m*

mechan|ism /'mekənɪzm/ *n* Mechanismus *m*. **~ize** *vt* mechanisieren

medal /'medl/ *n* Orden *m*; (*Sport*) Medaille *f*

medallist /'medəlɪst/ *n* Medaillengewinner(in) *m*(*f*)

meddle /'medl/ *vi* sich einmischen (**in** in + *acc*); (*tinker*) herumhantieren (**with** an + *acc*)

media /'mi:dɪə/ *see* **medium** ● *n pl* **the ~** die Medien *pl*

mediat|e /'mi:dɪeɪt/ *vi* vermitteln. **~or** *n* Vermittler(in) *m*(*f*)

medical /'medɪkl/ *a* medizinisch; <*treatment*> ärztlich ● *n* ärztliche Untersuchung *f*. **~ insurance** *n* Krankenversicherung *f*. **~ student** *n* Medizinstudent *m*

medicat|ed /'medɪkeɪtɪd/ *a* medizinisch. **~ion** /-'keɪʃn/ *n* (*drugs*) Medikamente *pl*

medicinal /mɪ'dɪsɪnl/ *a* medizinisch; <*plant*> heilkräftig

medicine /'medsən/ *n* Medizin *f*; (*preparation*) Medikament *nt*

medieval /medɪ'i:vl/ *a* mittelalterlich

mediocr|e /mi:dɪ'əʊkə(r)/ *a* mittelmäßig. **~ity** /-'ɒkrətɪ/ *n* Mittelmäßigkeit *f*

meditat|e /'medɪteɪt/ *vi* nachdenken (**on** über + *acc*). **~ion** /-'teɪʃn/ *n* Meditation *f*

Mediterranean /medɪtə'reɪnɪən/ *n* Mittelmeer *nt* ● *a* Mittelmeer-

medium /'mi:dɪəm/ *a* mittlere(r,s); <*steak*> medium; **of**

~ **size** von mittlerer Größe ● *n* (*pl* **media**) Medium *nt*; (*means*) Mittel *nt*
medium: ~**-sized** *a* mittelgroß. ~ **wave** *n* Mittelwelle *f*
medley /ˈmedlɪ/ *n* Gemisch *nt*; (*Mus*) Potpourri *nt*
meek /mi:k/ *a* (**-er, -est**), **-ly** *adv* sanftmütig; (*unprotesting*) widerspruchslos
meet /mi:t/ *v* (*pt/pp* **met**) ● *vt* treffen; (*by chance*) begegnen (+ *dat*); (*at station*) abholen; (*make the acquaintance of*) kennen lernen; stoßen auf (+ *acc*) <*problem*>; bezahlen <*bill*>; erfüllen <*requirements*> ● *vi* sich treffen; (*for the first time*) sich kennen lernen
meeting /ˈmi:tɪŋ/ *n* Treffen *nt*; (*by chance*) Begegnung *f*; (*discussion*) Besprechung *f*; (*of committee*) Sitzung *f*; (*large*) Versammlung *f*
megalomania /megələˈmeɪnɪə/ *n* Größenwahnsinn *m*
megaphone /ˈmegəfəʊn/ *n* Megaphon *nt*
melancholy /ˈmelənkəlɪ/ *a* melancholisch ● *n* Melancholie *f*
mellow /ˈmeləʊ/ *a* (**-er, -est**) <*fruit*> ausgereift; <*sound, person*> sanft ● *vi* reifer werden
melodious /mɪˈləʊdɪəs/ *a* melodiös
melodramatic /melədrəˈmætɪk/ *a*, **-ally** *adv* melodramatisch
melody /ˈmelədɪ/ *n* Melodie *f*
melon /ˈmelən/ *n* Melone *f*
melt /melt/ *vt/i* schmelzen
member /ˈmembə(r)/ *n* Mitglied *nt*; (*of family*) Angehörige(r) *m/f*; **M~ of Parliament** Abgeordnete(r) *m/f*. ~**ship** *n* Mitgliedschaft *f*; (*members*) Mitgliederzahl *f*
memento /mɪˈmentəʊ/ *n* Andenken *nt*
memo /ˈmeməʊ/ *n* Mitteilung *f*
memoirs /ˈmemwɑ:z/ *n pl* Memoiren *pl*
memorable /ˈmemərəbl/ *a* denkwürdig
memorial /mɪˈmɔ:rɪəl/ *n* Denkmal *nt*. ~ **service** *n* Gedenkfeier *f*
memorize /ˈmeməraɪz/ *vt* sich (*dat*) einprägen
memory /ˈmemərɪ/ *n* Gedächtnis *nt*; (*thing remembered*) Erinnerung *f*; (*of computer*) Speicher *m*; **from** ~ auswendig; **in** ~ **of** zur Erinnerung an (+ *acc*)
men /men/ *see* **man**
menac|e /ˈmenɪs/ *n* Drohung *f*; (*nuisance*) Plage *f* ● *vt* bedrohen. ~**ing** *a*, ~**ly** *adv* drohend
mend /mend/ *vt* reparieren; (*patch*) flicken; ausbessern <*clothes*>
ˈ**menfolk** *n pl* Männer *pl*
menial /ˈmi:nɪəl/ *a* niedrig
menopause /ˈmenə-/ *n* Wechseljahre *pl*
mental /ˈmentl/ *a*, **-ly** *adv* geistig; (🄸 *mad*) verrückt. ~ **aˈrithmetic** *n* Kopfrechnen *nt*. ~ ˈ**illness** *n* Geisteskrankheit *f*
mentality /menˈtælətɪ/ *n* Mentalität *f*
mention /ˈmenʃn/ *n* Erwähnung *f* ● *vt* erwähnen; **don't** ~ **it** keine Ursache; bitte
menu /ˈmenju:/ *n* Speisekarte *f*
merchandise /ˈmɜ:tʃəndaɪz/ *n* Ware *f*
merchant /ˈmɜ:tʃənt/ *n* Kaufmann *m*; (*dealer*) Händler *m*. ~ ˈ**navy** *n* Handelsmarine *f*
merci|ful /ˈmɜ:sɪfl/ *a* barmherzig. ~**fully** *adv* 🄸 glücklicherweise. ~**less** *a*, **-ly** *adv* erbarmungslos
mercury /ˈmɜ:kjʊrɪ/ *n* Quecksilber *nt*

mercy /ˈmɜːsɪ/ *n* Barmherzigkeit *f*, Gnade *f*; **be at s.o.'s ~** jdm ausgeliefert sein
mere /mɪə(r)/ *a*, **-ly** *adv* bloß
merest /ˈmɪərɪst/ *a* kleinste(r,s)
merge /mɜːdʒ/ *vi* zusammenlaufen; (*Comm*) fusionieren
merger /ˈmɜːdʒə(r)/ *n* Fusion *f*
meringue /məˈræŋ/ *n* Baiser *nt*
merit /ˈmerɪt/ *n* Verdienst *nt*; (*advantage*) Vorzug *m*; (*worth*) Wert *m* ● *vt* verdienen
merry /ˈmerɪ/ *a* (**-ier, -iest**) fröhlich
merry-go-round *n* Karussell *nt*
mesh /meʃ/ *n* Masche *f*
mesmerized /ˈmezməraɪzd/ *a* (*fig*) [wie] gebannt
mess /mes/ *n* Durcheinander *nt*; (*trouble*) Schwierigkeiten *pl*; (*something spilt*) Bescherung *f* [!]; (*Mil*) Messe *f*; **make a ~ of** (*botch*) verpfuschen ● *vt* **~ up** in Unordnung bringen; (*botch*) verpfuschen ● *vi* **~ about** herumalbern; (*tinker*) herumspielen (**with** mit)
message /ˈmesɪdʒ/ *n* Nachricht *f*; **give s.o. a ~** jdm etwas ausrichten
messenger /ˈmesɪndʒə(r)/ *n* Bote *m*
Messrs /ˈmesəz/ *n pl see* **Mr**; (*on letter*) **~ Smith** Firma Smith
messy /ˈmesɪ/ *a* (**-ier, -iest**) schmutzig; (*untidy*) unordentlich
met /met/ *see* **meet**
metal /ˈmetl/ *n* Metall *nt* ● *a* Metall-. **~lic** /mɪˈtælɪk/ *a* metallisch
metaphor /ˈmetəfə(r)/ *n* Metapher *f*. **~ical** /-ˈfɒrɪkl/ *a*, **-ly** *adv* metaphorisch
meteor /ˈmiːtɪə(r)/ *n* Meteor *m*. **~ic** /-ˈɒrɪk/ *a* kometenhaft
meteorological /miːtɪərəˈlɒdʒɪkl/ *a* Wetter-
meteorolog|ist /miːtɪəˈrɒlədʒɪst/ *n* Meteorologe *m*/ -gin *f*. **~y** *n* Meteorologie *f*
meter[1] /ˈmiːtə(r)/ *n* Zähler *m*
meter[2] *n* (*Amer*) = **metre**
method /ˈmeθəd/ *n* Methode *f*; (*Culin*) Zubereitung *f*
methodical /mɪˈθɒdɪkl/ *a*, **-ly** *adv* systematisch, methodisch
methylated /ˈmeθɪleɪtɪd/ *a* **~ spirit[s]** Brennspiritus *m*
meticulous /mɪˈtɪkjʊləs/ *a*, **-ly** *adv* sehr genau
metre /ˈmiːtə(r)/ *n* Meter *m* & *n*; (*rhythm*) Versmaß *nt*
metric /ˈmetrɪk/ *a* metrisch
metropolis /mɪˈtrɒpəlɪs/ *n* Metropole *f*
metropolitan /metrəˈpɒlɪtən/ *a* haupstädtisch; (*international*) weltstädtisch
mew /mjuː/ *n* Miau *nt* ● *vi* miauen
Mexican /ˈmeksɪkən/ *a* mexikanisch ● *n* Mexikaner(in) *m*(*f*). **'Mexico** *n* Mexiko *nt*
miaow /mɪˈaʊ/ *n* Miau *nt* ● *vi* miauen
mice /maɪs/ *see* **mouse**
micro: ~film *n* Mikrofilm *m*. **~light [aircraft]** *n* Ultraleichtflugzeug *nt*. **~phone** *n* Mikrofon *nt*. **~scope** /-skəʊp/ *n* Mikroskop *nt*. **~scopic** /-ˈskɒpɪk/ *a* mikroskopisch. **~wave [oven]** *n* Mikrowellenherd *m*
mid /mɪd/ *a* **~ May** Mitte Mai; **in ~ air** in der Luft
midday /mɪdˈdeɪ/ *n* Mittag *m*
middle /ˈmɪdl/ *a* mittlere(r,s); **the M~ Ages** das Mittelalter; **the ~ class[es]** der Mittelstand; **the M~ East** der Nahe Osten ● *n* Mitte *f*; **in the ~ of the night** mitten in der Nacht
middle: ~-aged *a* mittleren Alters. **~-class** *a* bürgerlich

midge /mɪdʒ/ *n* [kleine] Mücke *f*
midget /ˈmɪdʒɪt/ *n* Liliputaner(in) *m(f)*
Midlands /ˈmɪdləndz/ *npl* **the ~** Mittelengland *n*
ˈmidnight *n* Mitternacht *f*
midriff /ˈmɪdrɪf/ *n* 🄸 Taille *f*
midst /mɪdst/ *n* **in the ~ of** mitten in (+ *dat*); **in our ~** unter uns
mid: ~summer *n* Hochsommer *m*. **~way** *adv* auf halbem Wege. **~wife** *n* Hebamme *f*. **~ˈwinter** *n* Mitte *f* des Winters
might[1] /maɪt/ *v aux* **I ~** vielleicht; **it ~ be true** es könnte wahr sein; **he asked if he ~ go** er fragte, ob er gehen dürfte; **you ~ have drowned** du hättest ertrinken können
might[2] *n* Macht *f*
mighty /ˈmaɪtɪ/ *a* (**-ier, -iest**) mächtig
migraine /ˈmiːgreɪn/ *n* Migräne *f*
migrat|e /maɪˈgreɪt/ *vi* abwandern; <*birds*:> ziehen. **~ion** /-ˈgreɪʃn/ *n* Wanderung *f*; (*of birds*) Zug *m*
mike /maɪk/ *n* 🄸 Mikrofon *nt*
mild /maɪld/ *a* (**-er, -est**) mild
mild|ly /ˈmaɪldlɪ/ *adv* leicht; **to put it ~ly** gelinde gesagt. **~ness** *n* Milde *f*
mile /maɪl/ *n* Meile *f* (= *1,6 km*); **~s too big** 🄸 viel zu groß
mile|age /-ɪdʒ/ *n* Meilenzahl *f*; (*of car*) Meilenstand *m*
militant /ˈmɪlɪtənt/ *a* militant
military /ˈmɪlɪtrɪ/ *a* militärisch. **~ service** *n* Wehrdienst *m*
milk /mɪlk/ *n* Milch *f* ● *vt* melken
milk: ~man *n* Milchmann *m*. **~shake** *n* Milchmixgetränk *nt*. **~tooth** *n* Milchzahn *m*
milky /ˈmɪlkɪ/ *a* (**-ier, -iest**) milchig. **M~ Way** *n* (*Astr*) Milchstraße *f*
mill /mɪl/ *n* Mühle *f*; (*factory*) Fabrik *f*
millennium /mɪˈlenɪəm/ *n* Jahrtausend *nt*
milli|gram /ˈmɪlɪ-/ *n* Milligramm *nt*. **~metre** *n* Millimeter *m & nt*
million /ˈmɪljən/ *n* Million *f*; **a ~ pounds** eine Million Pfund. **~aire** /-ˈneə(r)/ *n* Millionär(in) *m(f)*
mime /maɪm/ *n* Pantomime *f* ● *vt* pantomimisch darstellen
mimic /ˈmɪmɪk/ *n* Imitator *m* ● *vt* (*pt/pp* **mimicked**) nachahmen
mince /mɪns/ *n* Hackfleisch *nt* ● *vt* (*Culin*) durchdrehen; **not ~ words** kein Blatt vor den Mund nehmen
mince: ~meat *n* Masse *f* aus Korinthen, Zitronat *usw*; **make ~ meat of** (*fig*) vernichtend schlagen. **~ˈ pie** *n* mit 'mincemeat' gefülltes Pastetchen *nt*
mincer /ˈmɪnsə(r)/ *n* Fleischwolf *m*
mind /maɪnd/ *n* Geist *m*; (*sanity*) Verstand *m*; **give s.o. a piece of one's ~** jdm gehörig die Meinung sagen; **make up one's ~** sich entschließen; **be out of one's ~** nicht bei Verstand sein; **have sth in ~** etw im Sinn haben; **bear sth in ~** an etw (*acc*) denken; **have a good ~ to** große Lust haben, zu; **I have changed my ~** ich habe es mir anders überlegt ● *vt* aufpassen auf (+ *acc*); **I don't ~ the noise** der Lärm stört mich nicht; **~ the step!** Achtung Stufe! ● *vi* (*care*) sich kümmern (**about** um); **I don't ~** mir macht es nichts aus; **never ~!** macht nichts! **do you ~ if?** haben Sie etwas dagegen, wenn? **~ out** *vi* aufpassen
ˈmindless *a* geistlos

mine¹ /maɪn/ *poss pron* meine(r), meins; **a friend of ~** ein Freund von mir; **that is ~** das gehört mir

mine² *n* Bergwerk *nt*; (*explosive*) Mine *f* ● *vt* abbauen; (*Mil*) verminen

miner /ˈmaɪnə(r)/ *n* Bergarbeiter *m*

mineral /ˈmɪnərl/ *n* Mineral *nt*. **~ water** *n* Mineralwasser *nt*

minesweeper /ˈmaɪn-/ *n* Minenräumboot *nt*

mingle /ˈmɪŋgl/ *vi* **~ with** sich mischen unter (+ *acc*)

miniature /ˈmɪnɪtʃə(r)/ *a* Klein- ● *n* Miniatur *f*

mini|bus /ˈmɪnɪ-/ *n* Kleinbus *m*. **~cab** *n* Kleintaxi *nt*

minim|al /ˈmɪnɪməl/ *a* minimal. **~um** *n* (*pl* **-ima**) Minimum *nt* ● *a* Mindest-

mining /ˈmaɪnɪŋ/ *n* Bergbau *m*

miniskirt /ˈmɪnɪ-/ *n* Minirock *m*

minister /ˈmɪnɪstə(r)/ *n* Minister *m*; (*Relig*) Pastor *m*. **~ial** /-ˈstɪərɪəl/ *a* ministeriell

ministry /ˈmɪnɪstrɪ/ *n* (*Pol*) Ministerium *nt*

mink /mɪŋk/ *n* Nerz *m*

minor /ˈmaɪnə(r)/ *a* kleiner; (*less important*) unbedeutend ● *n* Minderjährige(r) *m/f*; (*Mus*) Moll *nt*

minority /maɪˈnɒrətɪ/ *n* Minderheit *f*

minor road *n* Nebenstraße *f*

mint¹ /mɪnt/ *n* Münzstätte *f* ● *a* <*stamp*> postfrisch; **in ~ condition** wie neu ● *vt* prägen

mint² *n* (*herb*) Minze *f*; (*sweet*) Pfefferminzbonbon *m & nt*

minus /ˈmaɪnəs/ *prep* minus, weniger; (**[!]** *without*) ohne

minute¹ /ˈmɪnɪt/ *n* Minute *f*; **in a ~** (*shortly*) gleich; **~s** *pl* (*of meeting*) Protokoll *nt*

minute² /maɪˈnjuːt/ *a* winzig

mirac|le /ˈmɪrəkl/ *n* Wunder *nt*. **~ulous** /-ˈrækjʊləs/ *a* wunderbar

mirror /ˈmɪrə(r)/ *n* Spiegel *m* ● *vt* widerspiegeln

mirth /mɜːθ/ *n* Heiterkeit *f*

misadˈventure /mɪs-/ *n* Missgeschick *nt*

misappreˈhension *n* Missverständnis *nt*; **be under a ~** sich irren

misbeˈhav|e *vi* sich schlecht benehmen. **~iour** *n* schlechtes Benehmen *nt*

misˈcalcu|late *vt* falsch berechnen ● *vi* sich verrechnen. **~ˈlation** *n* Fehlkalkulation *f*

ˈmiscarriage *n* Fehlgeburt *f*

miscellaneous /mɪsəˈleɪnɪəs/ *a* vermischt

mischief /ˈmɪstʃɪf/ *n* Unfug *m*

mischievous /ˈmɪstʃɪvəs/ *a*, **-ly** *adv* schelmisch; (*malicious*) boshaft

misconˈception *n* falsche Vorstellung *f*

misˈconduct *n* unkorrektes Verhalten *nt*; (*adultery*) Ehebruch *m*

miser /ˈmaɪzə(r)/ *n* Geizhals *m*

miserable /ˈmɪzrəbl/ *a*, **-bly** *adv* unglücklich; (*wretched*) elend

miserly /ˈmaɪzəlɪ/ *adv* geizig

misery /ˈmɪzərɪ/ *n* Elend *nt*; (**[!]** *person*) Miesepeter *m*

misˈfire *vi* fehlzünden; (*go wrong*) fehlschlagen

ˈmisfit *n* Außenseiter(in) *m(f)*

misˈfortune *n* Unglück *nt*

misˈgivings *npl* Bedenken *pl*

misˈguided *a* töricht

mishap /ˈmɪshæp/ *n* Missgeschick *nt*

misinˈform *vt* falsch unterrichten

misinˈterpret *vt* missdeuten

misˈjudge *vt* falsch beurteilen

misˈlay *vt* (*pt/pp* **-laid**) verlegen

mis'lead *vt* (*pt*/*pp* **-led**) irreführen. **~ing** *a* irreführend

mis'manage *vt* schlecht verwalten. **~ment** *n* Misswirtschaft *f*

misnomer /mɪs'nəʊmə(r)/ *n* Fehlbezeichnung *f*

'misprint *n* Druckfehler *m*

mis'quote *vt* falsch zitieren

misrepre'sent *vt* falsch darstellen

miss /mɪs/ *n* Fehltreffer *m* ● *vt* verpassen; (*fail to hit or find*) verfehlen; (*fail to attend*) versäumen; (*fail to notice*) übersehen; (*feel the loss of*) vermissen ● *vi* (*fail to hit*) nicht treffen. **~ out** *vt* auslassen

Miss *n* (*pl* **-es**) Fräulein *nt*

missile /'mɪsaɪl/ *n* [Wurf]geschoss *nt*; (*Mil*) Rakete *f*

missing /'mɪsɪŋ/ *a* fehlend; (*lost*) verschwunden; (*Mil*) vermisst; **be ~** fehlen

mission /'mɪʃn/ *n* Auftrag *m*; (*Mil*) Einsatz *m*; (*Relig*) Mission *f*

missionary /'mɪʃənrɪ/ *n* Missionar(in) *m(f)*

mis'spell *vt* (*pt*/*pp* **-spelt** or **-spelled**) falsch schreiben

mist /mɪst/ *n* Dunst *m*; (*fog*) Nebel *m*; (*on window*) Beschlag *m* ● *vi* **~ up** beschlagen

mistake /mɪ'steɪk/ *n* Fehler *m*; **by ~** aus Versehen ● *vt* (*pt* **mistook**, *pp* **mistaken**); **~ for** verwechseln mit

mistaken /mɪ'steɪkən/ *a* falsch; **be ~** sich irren. **~ly** *adv* irrtümlicherweise

mistletoe /'mɪsltəʊ/ *n* Mistel *f*

mistress /'mɪstrɪs/ *n* Herrin *f*; (*teacher*) Lehrerin *f*; (*lover*) Geliebte *f*

mis'trust *n* Misstrauen *nt* ● *vt* misstrauen (+ *dat*)

misty /'mɪstɪ/ *a* (**-ier, -iest**) dunstig; (*foggy*) neblig; (*fig*) unklar

misunder'stand *vt* (*pt*/*pp* **-stood**) missverstehen. **~ing** *n* Missverständnis *nt*

misuse[1] /mɪs'ju:z/ *vt* missbrauchen

misuse[2] /mɪs'ju:s/ *n* Missbrauch *m*

mitigating /'mɪtɪgeɪtɪŋ/ *a* mildernd

mix /mɪks/ *n* Mischung *f* ● *vt* mischen ● *vi* sich mischen; **~ with** (*associate with*) verkehren mit. **~ up** *vt* mischen; (*muddle*) durcheinander bringen; (*mistake for*) verwechseln (**with** mit)

mixed /mɪkst/ *a* gemischt; **be ~ up** durcheinander sein

mixer /'mɪksə(r)/ *n* Mischmaschine *f*; (*Culin*) Küchenmaschine *f*

mixture /'mɪkstʃə(r)/ *n* Mischung *f*; (*medicine*) Mixtur *f*; (*Culin*) Teig *m*

'mix-up *n* Durcheinander *nt*; (*confusion*) Verwirrung *f*; (*mistake*) Verwechslung *f*

moan /məʊn/ *n* Stöhnen *nt* ● *vi* stöhnen; (*complain*) jammern

mob /mɒb/ *n* Horde *f*; (*rabble*) Pöbel *m*; (! *gang*) Bande *f* ● *vt* (*pt*/*pp* **mobbed**) herfallen über (+ *acc*); belagern <*celebrity*>

mobile /'məʊbaɪl/ *a* beweglich ● *n* Mobile *nt*; (*telephone*) Handy *nt*. **~ 'home** *n* Wohnwagen *m*. **~ 'phone** *n* Handy *nt*

mobility /mə'bɪlətɪ/ *n* Beweglichkeit *f*

mock /mɒk/ *a* Schein- ● *vt* verspotten. **~ery** *n* Spott *m*

'mock-up *n* Modell *nt*

mode /məʊd/ *n* [Art und] Weise *f*; (*fashion*) Mode *f*

model /'mɒdl/ *n* Modell *nt*; (*example*) Vorbild *nt*; **[fashion] ~** Mannequin *nt* ● *a* Modell-;

(*exemplary*) Muster- ● *v* (*pt*/*pp* **modelled**) ● *vt* formen, modellieren; vorführen <*clothes*> ● *vi* Mannequin sein; (*for artist*) Modell stehen

moderate[1] /ˈmɒdəreɪt/ *vt* mäßigen

moderate[2] /ˈmɒdərət/ *a* mäßig; <*opinion*> gemäßigt. **~ly** *adv* mäßig; (*fairly*) einigermaßen

moderation /mɒdəˈreɪʃn/ *n* Mäßigung *f*; **in ~** mit Maß[en]

modern /ˈmɒdn/ *a* modern. **~ize** *vt* modernisieren. **~ ˈlanguages** *npl* neuere Sprachen *pl*

modest /ˈmɒdɪst/ *a* bescheiden; (*decorous*) schamhaft. **~y** *n* Bescheidenheit *f*

modif|ication /mɒdɪfɪˈkeɪʃn/ *n* Abänderung *f*. **~y** /ˈmɒdɪfaɪ/ *vt* (*pt*/*pp* **-fied**) abändern

moist /mɔɪst/ *a* (**-er**, **-est**) feucht

moisten /ˈmɔɪsn/ *vt* befeuchten

moistur|e /ˈmɔɪstʃə(r)/ *n* Feuchtigkeit *f*. **~izer** *n* Feuchtigkeitscreme *f*

molar /ˈməʊlə(r)/ *n* Backenzahn *m*

mole[1] /məʊl/ *n* Leberfleck *m*

mole[2] *n* (*Zool*) Maulwurf *m*

molecule /ˈmɒlɪkjuːl/ *n* Molekül *nt*

molest /məˈlest/ *vt* belästigen

mollify /ˈmɒlɪfaɪ/ *vt* (*pt*/*pp* **-ied**) besänftigen

mollycoddle /ˈmɒlɪkɒdl/ *vt* verzärteln

molten /ˈməʊltən/ *a* geschmolzen

mom /mɒm/ *n* (*Amer fam*) Mutti *f*

moment /ˈməʊmənt/ *n* Moment *m*, Augenblick *m*; **at the ~** im Augenblick, augenblicklich. **~ary** *a* vorübergehend

momentous /məˈmentəs/ *a* bedeutsam

momentum /məˈmentəm/ *n* Schwung *m*

monarch /ˈmɒnək/ *n* Monarch(in) *m*(*f*). **~y** *n* Monarchie *f*

monastery /ˈmɒnəstrɪ/ *n* Kloster *nt*

Monday /ˈmʌndeɪ/ *n* Montag *m*

money /ˈmʌnɪ/ *n* Geld *nt*

money: ~-box *n* Sparbüchse *f*. **~-lender** *n* Geldverleiher *m*. **~ order** *n* Zahlungsanweisung *f*

mongrel /ˈmʌŋgrəl/ *n* Promenadenmischung *f*

monitor /ˈmɒnɪtə(r)/ *n* (*Techn*) Monitor *m* ● *vt* überwachen <*progress*>; abhören <*broadcast*>

monk /mʌŋk/ *n* Mönch *m*

monkey /ˈmʌŋkɪ/ *n* Affe *m*

mono /ˈmɒnəʊ/ *n* Mono *nt*

monogram /ˈmɒnəgræm/ *n* Monogramm *nt*

monologue /ˈmɒnəlɒg/ *n* Monolog *m*

monopol|ize /məˈnɒpəlaɪz/ *vt* monopolisieren. **~y** *n* Monopol *nt*

monosyllable /ˈmɒnəsɪləbl/ *n* einsilbiges Wort *nt*

monotone /ˈmɒnətəʊn/ *n* **in a ~** mit monotoner Stimme

monoton|ous /məˈnɒtənəs/ *a*, **-ly** *adv* eintönig, monoton; (*tedious*) langweillig. **~y** *n* Eintönigkeit *f*, Monotonie *f*

monster /ˈmɒnstə(r)/ *n* Ungeheuer *nt*; (*cruel person*) Unmensch *m*

monstrosity /mɒnˈstrɒsətɪ/ *n* Monstrosität *f*

monstrous /ˈmɒnstrəs/ *a* ungeheuer; (*outrageous*) ungeheuerlich

month /mʌnθ/ *n* Monat *m*. **~ly** *a* & *adv* monatlich ● *n* (*periodical*) Monatszeitschrift *f*

monument /ˈmɒnjʊmənt/ *n* Denkmal *nt*. **~al** /-ˈmentl/ *a* (*fig*) monumental

moo /mu:/ *n* Muh *nt* ● *vi* (*pt/pp* **mooed**) muhen

mood /mu:d/ *n* Laune *f*; **be in a good/bad ~** gute/schlechte Laune haben

moody /ˈmu:dɪ/ *a* (**-ier, -iest**) launisch

moon /mu:n/ *n* Mond *m*; **over the ~** [!] überglücklich

moon: ~light *n* Mondschein *m*. **~lighting** *n* [!] ≈ Schwarzarbeit *f*. **~lit** *a* mondhell

moor[1] /mʊə(r)/ *n* Moor *nt*

moor[2] *vt* (*Naut*) festmachen ● *vi* anlegen

mop /mɒp/ *n* Mopp *m*; **~ of hair** Wuschelkopf *m* ● *vt* (*pt/pp* **mopped**) wischen. **~ up** *vt* aufwischen

moped /ˈməʊped/ *n* Moped *nt*

moral /ˈmɒrl/ *a*, **-ly** *adv* moralisch, sittlich; (*virtuous*) tugendhaft ● *n* Moral *f*; **~s** *pl* Moral *f*

morale /məˈrɑ:l/ *n* Moral *f*

morality /məˈrælətɪ/ *n* Sittlichkeit *f*

morbid /ˈmɔ:bɪd/ *a* krankhaft; (*gloomy*) trübe

more /mɔ:(r)/ *a, adv & n* mehr; (*in addition*) noch; **a few ~** noch ein paar; **any ~** noch etwas; **once ~** noch einmal; **~ or less** mehr oder weniger; **some ~ tea?** noch etwas Tee? **~ interesting** interessanter; **~ [and ~] quickly** [immer] schneller

moreover /mɔ:ˈrəʊvə(r)/ *adv* außerdem

morgue /mɔ:g/ *n* Leichenschauhaus *nt*

morning /ˈmɔ:nɪŋ/ *n* Morgen *m*; **in the ~** morgens, am Morgen; (*tomorrow*) morgen früh

Morocco /məˈrɒkəʊ/ *n* Marokko *nt*

moron /ˈmɔ:rɒn/ *n* [!] Idiot *m*

morose /məˈrəʊs/ *a*, **-ly** *adv* mürrisch

morsel /ˈmɔ:sl/ *n* Happen *m*

mortal /ˈmɔ:tl/ *a* sterblich; (*fatal*) tödlich ● *n* Sterbliche(r) *m/f*. **~ity** /mɔ:ˈtælətɪ/ *n* Sterblichkeit *f*. **~ly** *adv* tödlich

mortar /ˈmɔ:tə(r)/ *n* Mörtel *m*

mortgage /ˈmɔ:gɪdʒ/ *n* Hypothek *f* ● *vt* hypothekarisch belasten

mortuary /ˈmɔ:tjʊərɪ/ *n* Leichenhalle *f*; (*public*) Leichenschauhaus *nt*; (*Amer: undertaker's*) Bestattungsinstitut *nt*

mosaic /məʊˈzeɪɪk/ *n* Mosaik *nt*

Moscow /ˈmɒskəʊ/ *n* Moskau *nt*

mosque /mɒsk/ *n* Moschee *f*

mosquito /mɒsˈki:təʊ/ *n* (*pl* **-es**) [Stech]mücke *f*, Schnake *f*; (*tropical*) Moskito *m*

moss /mɒs/ *n* Moos *nt*. **~y** *a* moosig

most /məʊst/ *a* der/die/das meiste; (*majority*) die meisten; **for the ~ part** zum größten Teil ● *adv* am meisten; (*very*) höchst; **the ~ interesting day** der interessanteste Tag; **~ unlikely** höchst unwahrscheinlich ● *n* das meiste; **~ of them** die meisten [von ihnen]; **at [the] ~** höchstens; **~ of the time** die meiste Zeit. **~ly** *adv* meist

MOT *n* ≈ TÜV *m*

motel /məʊˈtel/ *n* Motel *nt*

moth /mɒθ/ *n* Nachtfalter *m*; **[clothes-] ~** Motte *f*

ˈmothball *n* Mottenkugel *f*

mother /ˈmʌðə(r)/ *n* Mutter *f*

mother: ~hood *n* Mutterschaft *f*. **~-in-law** *n* (*pl* **~s-in-law**) Schwiegermutter *f*. **~land** *n* Mutterland *nt*. **~ly** *a* mütterlich. **~-of-pearl** *n* Perlmutter *f*. **~-to-be** *n* werdende Mutter *f*

mothproof /ˈmɒθ-/ *a* mottenfest

motif /məʊ'ti:f/ *n* Motiv *nt*
motion /'məʊʃn/ *n* Bewegung *f*; (*proposal*) Antrag *m*. **~less** *a*, **-ly** *adv* bewegungslos
motivat|e /'məʊtɪveɪt/ *vt* motivieren. **~ion** /-'veɪʃn/ *n* Motivation *f*
motive /'məʊtɪv/ *n* Motiv *nt*
motor /'məʊtə(r)/ *n* Motor *m*; (*car*) Auto *nt* ● *a* Motor-; (*Anat*) motorisch ● *vi* [mit dem Auto] fahren
motor: ~bike *n* [!] Motorrad *nt*. **~ boat** *n* Motorboot *nt*. **~ car** *n* Auto *nt*, Wagen *m*. **~cycle** *n* Motorrad *nt*. **~cyclist** *n* Motorradfahrer *m*. **~ing** *n* Autofahren *nt*. **~ist** *n* Autofahrer(in) *m(f)*. **~ vehicle** *n* Kraftfahrzeug *nt*. **~way** *n* Autobahn *f*
mottled /'mɒtld/ *a* gesprenkelt
motto /'mɒtəʊ/ *n* (*pl* **-es**) Motto *nt*
mould¹ /məʊld/ *n* (*fungus*) Schimmel *m*
mould² *n* Form *f* ● *vt* formen (**into** zu). **~ing** *n* (*Archit*) Fries *m*
mouldy /'məʊldɪ/ *a* schimmelig; ([!] *worthless*) schäbig
mound /maʊnd/ *n* Hügel *m*; (*of stones*) Haufen *m*
mount *n* (*animal*) Reittier *nt*; (*of jewel*) Fassung *f*; (*of photo, picture*) Passepartout *nt* ● *vt* (*get on*) steigen auf (+ *acc*); (*on pedestal*) montieren auf (+ *acc*); besteigen <*horse*>; fassen <*jewel*>; aufziehen <*photo, picture*> ● *vi* aufsteigen; <*tension:*> steigen. **~ up** *vi* sich häufen; (*add up*) sich anhäufen
mountain /'maʊntɪn/ *n* Berg *m*
mountaineer /maʊntɪ'nɪə(r)/ *n* Bergsteiger(in) *m(f)*. **~ing** *n* Bergsteigen *nt*
mountainous /'maʊntɪnəs/ *a* bergig, gebirgig
mourn /mɔ:n/ *vt* betrauern ● *vi* trauern (**for** um). **~er** *n* Trauernde(r) *m/f*. **~ful** *a*, **-ly** *adv* trauervoll. **~ing** *n* Trauer *f*
mouse /maʊs/ *n* (*pl* **mice**) Maus *f*. **~trap** *n* Mausefalle *f*
moustache /mə'stɑ:ʃ/ *n* Schnurrbart *m*
mouth¹ /maʊð/ *vt* **~ sth** etw lautlos mit den Lippen sagen
mouth² /maʊθ/ *n* Mund *m*; (*of animal*) Maul *nt*; (*of river*) Mündung *f*
mouth: ~ful *n* Mundvoll *m*; (*bite*) Bissen *m*. **~-organ** *n* Mundharmonika *f*. **~wash** *n* Mundwasser *nt*
movable /'mu:vəbl/ *a* beweglich
move /mu:v/ *n* Bewegung *f*; (*fig*) Schritt *m*; (*moving house*) Umzug *m*; (*in board game*) Zug *m*; **on the ~** unterwegs; **get a ~ on** [!] sich beeilen ● *vt* bewegen; (*emotionally*) rühren; (*move along*) rücken; (*in board game*) ziehen; (*take away*) wegnehmen; wegfahren <*car*>; (*rearrange*) umstellen; (*transfer*) versetzen <*person*>; verlegen <*office*>; (*propose*) beantragen; **~ house** umziehen ● *vi* sich bewegen; (*move house*) umziehen; **don't ~!** stillhalten! (*stop*) stillstehen! **~ along** *vt/i* weiterrücken. **~ away** *vt/i* wegrücken; (*move house*) wegziehen. **~ in** *vi* einziehen. **~ off** *vi* <*vehicle:*> losfahren. **~ out** *vi* ausziehen. **~ over** *vt/i* [zur Seite] rücken. **~ up** *vi* aufrücken
movement /'mu:vmənt/ *n* Bewegung *f*; (*Mus*) Satz *m*; (*of clock*) Uhrwerk *nt*
movie /'mu:vɪ/ *n* (*Amer*) Film *m*; **go to the ~s** ins Kino gehen
moving /'mu:vɪŋ/ *a* beweglich; (*touching*) rührend
mow /məʊ/ *vt* (*pt* **mowed**, *pp* **mown** *or* **mowed**) mähen

mower /ˈməʊə(r)/ *n* Rasenmäher *m*

MP *abbr see* **Member of Parliament**

Mr /ˈmɪstə(r)/ *n* (*pl* **Messrs**) Herr *m*

Mrs /ˈmɪsɪz/ *n* Frau *f*

Ms /mɪz/ *n* Frau *f*

much /mʌtʃ/ *a, adv & n* viel; **as ~ as** so viel wie; **~ loved** sehr geliebt

muck /mʌk/ *n* Mist *m*; (Ⓘ *filth*) Dreck *m*. **~ about** *vi* herumalbern; (*tinker*) herumspielen (**with** mit). **~ out** *vt* ausmisten. **~ up** *vt* Ⓘ vermasseln; (*make dirty*) schmutzig machen

mucky /ˈmʌkɪ/ *a* (**-ier, -iest**) dreckig

mud /mʌd/ *n* Schlamm *m*

muddle /ˈmʌdl/ *n* Durcheinander *nt*; (*confusion*) Verwirrung *f* ● *vt* **~ [up]** durcheinander bringen

muddy /ˈmʌdɪ/ *a* (**-ier, -iest**) schlammig; <*shoes*> schmutzig

ˈmudguard *n* Kotflügel *m*; (*on bicycle*) Schutzblech *nt*

muffle /ˈmʌfl/ *vt* dämpfen

muffler /ˈmʌflə(r)/ *n* Schal *m*; (*Amer, Auto*) Auspufftopf *m*

mug¹ /mʌg/ *n* Becher *m*; (*for beer*) Bierkrug *m*; (Ⓘ *face*) Visage *f*; (Ⓘ *simpleton*) Trottel *m*

mug² *vt* (*pt/pp* **mugged**) überfallen. **~ger** *n* Straßenräuber *m*. **~ging** *n* Straßenraub *m*

muggy /ˈmʌgɪ/ *a* (**-ier, -iest**) schwül

mule /mju:l/ *n* Maultier *nt*

mulled /mʌld/ *a* **~ wine** Glühwein *m*

multi /ˈmʌltɪ/: **~coloured** *a* vielfarbig, bunt. **~lingual** /-ˈlɪŋgwəl/ *a* mehrsprachig. **~ˈnational** *a* multinational

multiple /ˈmʌltɪpl/ *a* vielfach; (*with pl*) mehrere ● *n* Vielfache(s) *nt*

multiplication /mʌltɪplɪˈkeɪʃn/ *n* Multiplikation *f*

multiply /ˈmʌltɪplaɪ/ *v* (*pt/pp* **-ied**) ● *vt* multiplizieren (**by** mit) ● *vi* sich vermehren

multistorey *a* **~ car park** Parkhaus *nt*

mum /mʌm/ *n* Ⓘ Mutti *f*

mumble /ˈmʌmbl/ *vt/i* murmeln

mummy¹ /ˈmʌmɪ/ *n* Ⓘ Mutti *f*

mummy² *n* (*Archaeol*) Mumie *f*

mumps /mʌmps/ *n* Mumps *m*

munch /mʌntʃ/ *vt/i* mampfen

municipal /mju:ˈnɪsɪpl/ *a* städtisch

munitions /mju:ˈnɪʃnz/ *npl* Kriegsmaterial *nt*

mural /ˈmjʊərəl/ *n* Wandgemälde *nt*

murder /ˈmɜ:də(r)/ *n* Mord *m* ● *vt* ermorden. **~er** *n* Mörder *m*. **~ess** *n* Mörderin *f*. **~ous** /-rəs/ *a* mörderisch

murky /ˈmɜ:kɪ/ *a* (**-ier, -iest**) düster

murmur /ˈmɜ:mə(r)/ *n* Murmeln *nt* ● *vt/i* murmeln

muscle /ˈmʌsl/ *n* Muskel *m*

muscular /ˈmʌskjʊlə(r)/ *a* Muskel-; (*strong*) muskulös

museum /mju:ˈzɪəm/ *n* Museum *nt*

mushroom /ˈmʌʃrʊm/ *n* [essbarer] Pilz *m*, *esp* Champignon *m* ● *vi* (*fig*) wie Pilze aus dem Boden schießen

mushy /ˈmʌʃɪ/ *a* breiig

music /ˈmju:zɪk/ *n* Musik *f*; (*written*) Noten *pl*; **set to ~** vertonen

musical /ˈmju:zɪkl/ *a* musikalisch ● *n* Musical *nt*. **~ box** *n* Spieldose *f*. **~ instrument** *n* Musikinstrument *nt*

musician /mju:'zɪʃn/ *n* Musiker(in) *m(f)*

'**music-stand** *n* Notenständer *m*

Muslim /'mʊzlɪm/ *a* mohammedanisch ● *n* Mohammedaner(in) *m(f)*

must /mʌst/ *v aux* (*nur Präsens*) müssen; (*with negative*) dürfen ● *n* **a** ~ [!] ein Muss *nt*

mustard /'mʌstəd/ *n* Senf *m*

musty /'mʌstɪ/ *a* (**-ier, -iest**) muffig

mute /mju:t/ *a* stumm

mutilat|e /'mju:tɪleɪt/ *vt* verstümmeln. **~ion** /-'leɪʃn/ *n* Verstümmelung *f*

mutin|ous /'mju:tɪnəs/ *a* meuterisch. **~y** *n* Meuterei *f* ● *vi* (*pt/pp* **-ied**) meutern

mutter /'mʌtə(r)/ *n* Murmeln *nt* ● *vt/i* murmeln

mutton /'mʌtn/ *n* Hammelfleisch *nt*

mutual /'mju:tjʊəl/ *a* gegenseitig; ([!] *common*) gemeinsam. **~ly** *adv* gegenseitig

muzzle /'mʌzl/ *n* (*of animal*) Schnauze *f*; (*of firearm*) Mündung *f*; (*for dog*) Maulkorb *m*

my /maɪ/ *a* mein

myself /maɪ'self/ *pron* selbst; (*refl*) mich; **by ~** allein; **I thought to ~** ich habe mir gedacht

mysterious /mɪ'stɪərɪəs/ *a*, **-ly** *adv* geheimnisvoll; (*puzzling*) mysteriös, rätselhaft

mystery /'mɪstərɪ/ *n* Geheimnis *nt*; (*puzzle*) Rätsel *nt*; **~ [story]** Krimi *m*

mysti|c[al] /'mɪstɪk[l]/ *a* mystisch. **~cism** /-sɪzm/ *n* Mystik *f*

mystified /'mɪstɪfaɪd/ *a* **be ~** vor einem Rätsel stehen

mystique /mɪ'sti:k/ *n* geheimnisvoller Zauber *m*

myth /mɪθ/ *n* Mythos *m*; ([!] *untruth*) Märchen *nt*. **~ical** *a* mythisch; (*fig*) erfunden

mythology /mɪ'θɒlədʒɪ/ *n* Mythologie *f*

Nn

nab /næb/ *vt* (*pt/pp* **nabbed**) [!] erwischen

nag¹ /næg/ *n* (*horse*) Gaul *m*

nag² *vt/i* (*pp/pp* **nagged**) herumnörgeln (**s.o.** an jdm)

nail /neɪl/ *n* (*Anat, Techn*) Nagel *m*; **on the ~** [!] sofort ● *vt* nageln (**to** an + *acc*)

nail: ~-brush *n* Nagelbürste *f*. **~-file** *n* Nagelfeile *f*. **~ scissors** *npl* Nagelschere *f*. **~ varnish** *n* Nagellack *m*

naïve /naɪ'i:v/ *a*, **-ly** *adv* naiv. **~ty** /-ətɪ/ *n* Naivität *f*

naked /'neɪkɪd/ *a* nackt; *<flame>* offen; **with the ~ eye** mit bloßem Auge. **~ness** *n* Nacktheit *f*

name /neɪm/ *n* Name *m*; (*reputation*) Ruf *m*; **by ~** dem Namen nach; **by the ~ of** namens; **call s.o. ~s** [!] jdn beschimpfen ● *vt* nennen; (*give a name to*) einen Namen geben (+ *dat*); (*announce publicly*) den Namen bekannt geben von. **~less** *a* namenlos. **~ly** *adv* nämlich

name: ~-plate *n* Namensschild *nt*. **~sake** *n* Namensvetter *m*/ Namensschwester *f*

nanny /'nænɪ/ *n* Kindermädchen *nt*

nap /næp/ *n* Nickerchen *nt*

napkin /ˈnæpkɪn/ *n* Serviette *f*

nappy /ˈnæpɪ/ *n* Windel *f*

narcotic /nɑːˈkɒtɪk/ *n* (*drug*) Rauschgift *nt*

narrat|e /nəˈreɪt/ *vt* erzählen. **~ion** /-eɪʃn/ *n* Erzählung *f*

narrative /ˈnærətɪv/ *n* Erzählung *f*

narrator /nəˈreɪtə(r)/ *n* Erzähler(in) *m(f)*

narrow /ˈnærəʊ/ *a* (**-er, -est**) schmal; (*restricted*) eng; <*margin, majority*> knapp; **have a ~ escape** mit knapper Not davonkommen ● *vi* sich verengen. **~-ˈminded** *a* engstirnig

nasal /ˈneɪzl/ *a* nasal; (*Med & Anat*) Nasen-

nasty /ˈnɑːstɪ/ *a* (**-ier, -iest**) übel; (*unpleasant*) unangenehm; (*unkind*) boshaft; (*serious*) schlimm

nation /ˈneɪʃn/ *n* Nation *f*; (*people*) Volk *nt*

national /ˈnæʃənl/ *a* national; <*newspaper*> überregional; <*campaign*> landesweit ● *n* Staatsbürger(in) *m(f)*

national: ~ ˈanthem *n* Nationalhymne *f*. **N~ ˈHealth Service** *n* staatlicher Gesundheitsdienst *m*. **N~ Inˈsurance** *n* Sozialversicherung *f*

nationalism /ˈnæʃənəlɪzm/ *n* Nationalismus *m*

nationality /næʃəˈnælətɪ/ *n* Staatsangehörigkeit *f*

national|ization /næʃənəlaɪˈzeɪʃn/ *n* Verstaatlichung *f*. **~ize** /ˈnæʃənəlaɪz/ *vt* verstaatlichen

native /ˈneɪtɪv/ *a* einheimisch; (*innate*) angeboren ● *n* Eingeborene(r) *m/f*; (*local inhabitant*) Einheimische(r) *m/f*; **a ~ of Vienna** ein gebürtiger Wiener

native: ~ ˈland *n* Heimatland *nt*. **~ ˈlanguage** *n* Muttersprache *f*

natter /ˈnætə(r)/ *vi* [!] schwatzen

natural /ˈnætʃrəl/ *a*, **-ly** *adv* natürlich; **~[-coloured]** naturfarben

natural: ~ ˈgas *n* Erdgas *nt*. **~ ˈhistory** *n* Naturkunde *f*

naturalist /ˈnætʃrəlɪst/ *n* Naturforscher *m*

natural|ization /nætʃrəlaɪˈzeɪʃn/ *n* Einbürgerung *f*. **~ize** /ˈnætʃrəlaɪz/ *vt* einbürgern

nature /ˈneɪtʃə(r)/ *n* Natur *f*; (*kind*) Art *f*; **by ~** von Natur aus. **~ reserve** *n* Naturschutzgebiet *nt*

naughty /ˈnɔːtɪ/ *a* (**-ier, -iest**), **-ily** *adv* unartig; (*slightly indecent*) gewagt

nausea /ˈnɔːzɪə/ *n* Übelkeit *f*

nautical /ˈnɔːtɪkl/ *a* nautisch. **~ mile** *n* Seemeile *f*

naval /ˈneɪvl/ *a* Marine-

nave /neɪv/ *n* Kirchenschiff *nt*

navel /ˈneɪvl/ *n* Nabel *m*

navigable /ˈnævɪgəbl/ *a* schiffbar

navigat|e /ˈnævɪgeɪt/ *vi* navigieren ● *vt* befahren <*river*>. **~ion** /-ˈgeɪʃn/ *n* Navigation *f*

navy /ˈneɪvɪ/ *n* [Kriegs]marine *f* ● *a* **~ [blue]** marineblau

near /nɪə(r)/ *a* (**-er, -est**) nah[e]; **the ~est bank** die nächste Bank ● *adv* nahe; **draw ~** sich nähern ● *prep* nahe an (+ *dat/acc*); in der Nähe von

near: ~by *a* nahe gelegen, nahe liegend. **~ly** *adv* fast, beinahe; **not ~ly** bei weitem nicht. **~ness** *n* Nähe *f*. **~ side** *n* Beifahrerseite *f*. **~-sighted** *a* (*Amer*) kurzsichtig

neat /ni:t/ *a* (**-er, -est**), **-ly** *adv* adrett; (*tidy*) ordentlich; (*clever*) geschickt; (*undiluted*) pur. **~ness** *n* Ordentlichkeit *f*

necessarily /'nesəserəlɪ/ *adv* notwendigerweise; **not ~** nicht unbedingt

necessary /'nesəsərɪ/ *a* nötig, notwendig

necessit|ate /nɪ'sesɪteɪt/ *vt* notwendig machen. **~y** *n* Notwendigkeit *f*; **work from ~y** arbeiten, weil man es nötig hat

neck /nek/ *n* Hals *m*; **~ and ~** Kopf an Kopf

necklace /'neklɪs/ *n* Halskette *f*

neckline *n* Halsausschnitt *m*

née /neɪ/ *a* **~ X** geborene X

need /ni:d/ *n* Bedürfnis *nt*; (*misfortune*) Not *f*; **be in ~ of** brauchen; **in case of ~** notfalls; **if ~ be** wenn nötig; **there is a ~ for** es besteht ein Bedarf an (+ *dat*); **there is no ~ for that** das ist nicht nötig ● *vt* brauchen; **you ~ not go** du brauchst nicht zu gehen; **~ I come?** muss ich kommen? **I ~ to know** ich muss es wissen

needle /'ni:dl/ *n* Nadel *f*

needless /'ni:dlɪs/ *a*, **-ly** *adv* unnötig; **~ to say** selbstverständlich, natürlich

'needlework *n* Nadelarbeit *f*

needy /'ni:dɪ/ *a* (**-ier, -iest**) bedürftig

negation /nɪ'geɪʃn/ *n* Verneinung *f*

negative /'negətɪv/ *a* negativ ● *n* Verneinung *f*; (*photo*) Negativ *nt*

neglect /nɪ'glekt/ *n* Vernachlässigung *f* ● *vt* vernachlässigen; (*omit*) versäumen (**to** zu). **~ed** *a* verwahrlost. **~ful** *a* nachlässig

negligen|ce /'neglɪdʒəns/ *n* Nachlässigkeit *f*. **~t** *a*, **-ly** *adv* nachlässig

negligible /'neglɪdʒəbl/ *a* unbedeutend

negotiat|e /nɪ'gəʊʃɪeɪt/ *vt* aushandeln; (*Auto*) nehmen <*bend*> ● *vi* verhandeln. **~ion** /-'eɪʃn/ *n* Verhandlung *f*. **~or** *n* Unterhändler(in) *m(f)*

Negro /'ni:grəʊ/ *a* Neger- ● *n* (*pl* **-es**) Neger *m*

neigh /neɪ/ *vi* wiehern

neighbour /'neɪbə(r)/ *n* Nachbar(in) *m(f)*. **~hood** *n* Nachbarschaft *f*. **~ing** *a* Nachbar-. **~ly** *a* [gut]nachbarlich

neither /'naɪðə(r)/ *a & pron* keine(r, s) [von beiden] ● *adv* **~... nor** weder ... noch ● *conj* auch nicht

neon /'ni:ɒn/ *n* Neon *nt*

nephew /'nevju:/ *n* Neffe *m*

nepotism /'nepətɪzm/ *n* Vetternwirtschaft *f*

nerve /nɜ:v/ *n* Nerv *m*; ([!] *courage*) Mut *m*; ([!] *impudence*) Frechheit *f*. **~-racking** *a* nervenaufreibend

nervous /'nɜ:vəs/ *a*, **-ly** *adv* (*afraid*) ängstlich; (*highly strung*) nervös; (*Anat, Med*) Nerven-. **~ 'breakdown** *n* Nervenzusammenbruch *m*. **~ness** Ängstlichkeit *f*

nervy /'nɜ:vɪ/ *a* (**-ier, -iest**) nervös; (*Amer: impudent*) frech

nest /nest/ *n* Nest *nt* ● *vi* nisten

nestle /'nesl/ *vi* sich schmiegen (**against** an + *acc*)

net¹ /net/ *n* Netz *nt*; (*curtain*) Store *m*

net² *a* netto; <*salary, weight*> Netto-

'netball *n* ≈ Korbball *m*

Netherlands /'neðələndz/ *npl* **the ~** die Niederlande *pl*

nettle /'netl/ *n* Nessel *f*

'network *n* Netz *nt*

neurolog|ist /njʊəˈrɒlədʒɪst/ *n* Neurologe *m*/ -gin *f*. **~y** *n* Neurologie *f*

neur|osis /njʊəˈrəʊsɪs/ *n* (*pl* **-oses** /-siːz/) Neurose *f*. **~otic** /-ˈrɒtɪk/ *a* neurotisch

neuter /ˈnjuːtə(r)/ *a* (*Gram*) sächlich ● *n* (*Gram*) Neutrum *nt* ● *vt* kastrieren; (*spay*) sterilisieren

neutral /ˈnjuːtrl/ *a* neutral ● *n* **in ~** (*Auto*) im Leerlauf. **~ity** /-ˈtrælətɪ/ *n* Neutralität *f*

never /ˈnevə(r)/ *adv* nie, niemals; ([!] *not*) nicht; **~ mind** macht nichts; **well I ~!** ja so was! **~-ending** *a* endlos

nevertheless /nevəðəˈles/ *adv* dennoch, trotzdem

new /njuː/ *a* (**-er, -est**) neu

new: ~comer *n* Neuankömmling *m*. **~fangled** /-ˈfæŋgld/ *a* (*pej*) neumodisch. **~-laid** *a* frisch gelegt

ˈnewly *adv* frisch. **~-weds** *npl* Jungverheiratete *pl*

new: ~ ˈmoon *n* Neumond *m*. **~ness** *n* Neuheit *f*

news /njuːz/ *n* Nachricht *f*; (*Radio, TV*) Nachrichten *pl*; **piece of ~** Neuigkeit *f*

news: ~agent *n* Zeitungshändler *m*. **~ bulletin** *n* Nachrichtensendung *f*. **~letter** *n* Mitteilungsblatt *nt*. **~paper** *n* Zeitung *f*; (*material*) Zeitungspapier *nt*. **~reader** *n* Nachrichtensprecher(in) *m(f)*

New: ~ Year's ˈDay *n* Neujahr *nt*. **~ Year's ˈEve** *n* Silvester *nt*. **~ Zealand** /ˈziːlənd/ *n* Neuseeland *nt*

next /nekst/ *a* & *n* nächste(r, s); **who's ~?** wer kommt als Nächster dran? **the ~ best** das nächstbeste; **~ door** nebenan; **my ~ of kin** mein nächster Verwandter; **~ to nothing** fast gar nichts; **the week after ~** übernächste Woche ● *adv* als Nächstes; **~ to** neben

nib /nɪb/ *n* Feder *f*

nibble /ˈnɪbl/ *vt/i* knabbern (**at** an + *dat*)

nice /naɪs/ *a* (**-r, -st**) nett; <*day, weather*> schön; <*food*> gut; <*distinction*> fein. **~ly** *adv* nett; (*well*) gut

niche /niːʃ/ *n* Nische *f*; (*fig*) Platz *m*

nick /nɪk/ *n* Kerbe *f*; ([!] *prison*) Knast *m*; ([!] *police station*) Revier *nt*; **in good ~** [!] in gutem Zustand ● *vt* einkerben; (*steal*) klauen; ([!] *arrest*) schnappen

nickel /ˈnɪkl/ *n* Nickel *nt*; (*Amer*) Fünfcentstück *nt*

ˈnickname *n* Spitzname *m*

nicotine /ˈnɪkətiːn/ *n* Nikotin *nt*

niece /niːs/ *n* Nichte *f*

Nigeria /naɪˈdʒɪərɪə/ *n* Nigeria *nt*. **~n** *a* nigerianisch ● *n* Nigerianer(in) *m(f)*

night /naɪt/ *n* Nacht *f*; (*evening*) Abend *m*; **at ~** nachts

night: ~-club *n* Nachtklub *m*. **~-dress** *n* Nachthemd *nt*. **~fall** *n* **at ~fall** bei Einbruch der Dunkelheit. **~-gown** *n*, [!] **~ie** /ˈnaɪtɪ/ *n* Nachthemd *nt*

nightingale /ˈnaɪtɪŋgeɪl/ *n* Nachtigall *f*

night: ~-life *n* Nachtleben *nt*. **~ly** *a* nächtlich ● *adv* jede Nacht. **~mare** *n* Albtraum *m*. **~-time** *n* **at ~-time** bei Nacht

nil /nɪl/ *n* null

nimble /ˈnɪmbl/ *a* (**-r, -st**), **-bly** *adv* flink

nine /naɪn/ *a* neun ● *n* Neun *f*. **~ˈteen** *a* neunzehn. **~ˈteenth** *a* neunzehnte(r, s)

ninetieth /ˈnaɪntɪɪθ/ *a* neunzigste(r, s)

ninety /ˈnaɪntɪ/ *a* neunzig

ninth /naɪnθ/ *a* neunte(r, s)

nip /nɪp/ *vt* kneifen; (*bite*) beißen; ~ **in the bud** (*fig*) im Keim ersticken ● *vi* (🅸 *run*) laufen

nipple /ˈnɪpl/ *n* Brustwarze *f*; (*Amer: on bottle*) Sauger *m*

nitwit /ˈnɪtwɪt/ *n* 🅸 Dummkopf *m*

no /nəʊ/ *adv* nein ● *n* (*pl* **noes**) Nein *nt* ● *a* kein(e); (*pl*) keine; **in no time** [sehr] schnell; **no parking/smoking** Parken/Rauchen verboten; **no one** = **nobody**

nobility /nəʊˈbɪlətɪ/ *n* Adel *m*

noble /ˈnəʊbl/ *a* (**-r, -st**) edel; (*aristocratic*) adlig. **~man** *n* Adlige(r) *m*

nobody /ˈnəʊbədɪ/ *pron* niemand, keiner ● *n* **a** ~ ein Niemand *m*

nocturnal /nɒkˈtɜːnl/ *a* nächtlich; <*animal, bird*> Nacht-

nod /nɒd/ *n* Nicken *nt* ● *v* (*pt/pp* **nodded**) ● *vi* nicken ● *vt* ~ **one's head** mit dem Kopf nicken

noise /nɔɪz/ *n* Geräusch *nt*; (*loud*) Lärm *m*. **~less** *a*, **-ly** *adv* geräuschlos

noisy /ˈnɔɪzɪ/ *a* (**-ier, -iest**), **-ily** *adv* laut; <*eater*> geräuschvoll

nomad /ˈnəʊmæd/ *n* Nomade *m*. **~ic** /-ˈmædɪk/ *a* nomadisch; <*life, tribe*> Nomaden-

nominal /ˈnɒmɪnl/ *a*, **-ly** *adv* nominell

nominat|e /ˈnɒmɪneɪt/ *vt* nominieren, aufstellen; (*appoint*) ernennen. **~ion** /-ˈneɪʃn/ *n* Nominierung *f*; Ernennung *f*

nominative /ˈnɒmɪnətɪv/ *a* & *n* (*Gram*) **~[case]** Nominativ *m*

nonchalant /ˈnɒnʃələnt/ *a*, **-ly** *adv* nonchalant; <*gesture*> lässig

nondescript /ˈnɒndɪskrɪpt/ *a* unbestimmbar; <*person*> unscheinbar

none /nʌn/ *pron* keine(r)/keins; ~ **of it/this** nichts davon ● *adv* ~ **too** nicht gerade; ~ **too soon** [um] keine Minute zu früh; ~ **the less** dennoch

nonentity /nɒˈnentətɪ/ *n* Null *f*

non-exˈistent *a* nicht vorhanden

non-ˈfiction *n* Sachliteratur *f*

nonplussed /nɒnˈplʌst/ *a* verblüfft

nonsens|e /ˈnɒnsəns/ *n* Unsinn *m*. **~ical** /ˈ-sensɪkl/ *a* unsinnig

non-ˈsmoker *n* Nichtraucher *m*

non-ˈstop *adv* ununterbrochen; <*fly*> nonstop

non-ˈswimmer *n* Nichtschwimmer *m*

non-ˈviolent *a* gewaltlos

noodles /ˈnuːdlz/ *npl* Bandnudeln *pl*

noon /nuːn/ *n* Mittag *m*; **at** ~ um 12 Uhr mittags

noose /nuːs/ *n* Schlinge *f*

nor /nɔː(r)/ *adv* noch ● *conj* auch nicht

Nordic /ˈnɔːdɪk/ *a* nordisch

norm /nɔːm/ *n* Norm *f*

normal /ˈnɔːml/ *a* normal. **~ity** /-ˈmælətɪ/ *n* Normalität *f*. **~ly** *adv* normal; (*usually*) normalerweise

north /nɔːθ/ *n* Norden *m*; **to the** ~ **of** nördlich von ● *a* Nord-, nord- ● *adv* nach Norden

north: N~ America *n* Nordamerika *nt*. **~-east** *a* Nordost- ● *n* Nordosten *m*

norther|ly /ˈnɔːðəlɪ/ *a* nördlich. **~n** *a* nördlich. **N~n Ireland** *n* Nordirland *nt*

north: N~ ˈPole *n* Nordpol *m*. **N~ ˈSea** *n* Nordsee *f*. **~ward[s]** /-wəd[z]/ *adv* nach Norden. **~-west** *a* Nordwest- ● *n* Nordwesten *m*

Nor|way /ˈnɔːweɪ/ *n* Norwegen *nt*. **~wegian** /-ˈwiːdʒn/ *a* norwegisch ● *n* Norweger(in) *m(f)*

nose /nəʊz/ *n* Nase

'nosebleed *n* Nasenbluten *nt*

nostalg|ia /nɒ'stældʒɪə/ *n* Nostalgie *f*. **~ic** *a* nostalgisch

nostril /'nɒstrəl/ *n* Nasenloch *nt*

nosy /'nəʊzɪ/ *a* (**-ier, -iest**) [!] neugierig

not /nɒt/

● *adverb*

····➤ nicht. **I don't know** ich weiß nicht. **isn't she pretty?** ist sie nicht hübsch?

····➤ **not a** kein. **he is not a doctor** er ist kein Arzt. **she didn't wear a hat** sie trug keinen Hut. **there was not a person to be seen** es gab keinen Menschen zu sehen. **not a thing** gar nichts. **not a bit** kein bisschen

····➤ (*in elliptical phrases*) **I hope not** ich hoffe nicht. **of course not** natürlich nicht. **not at all** überhaupt nicht; (*in polite reply to thanks*) keine Ursache; gern geschehen. **certainly not!** auf keinen Fall! **not I** ich nicht

····➤ **not ... but ...** nicht ... sondern .... **it was not a small town but a big one** es war keine kleine Stadt, sondern eine große

notab|le /'nəʊtəbl/ *a* bedeutend; (*remarkable*) bemerkenswert. **~ly** *adv* insbesondere

notation /nəʊ'teɪʃn/ *n* Notation *f*; (*Mus*) Notenschrift *f*

notch /nɒtʃ/ *n* Kerbe *f*

note /nəʊt/ *n* (*written comment*) Notiz *f*, Anmerkung *f*; (*short letter*) Briefchen *nt*, Zettel *m*; (*bank* ~) Banknote *f*, Schein *m*; (*Mus*) Note *f*; (*sound*) Ton *m*; (*on piano*) Taste *f*; **half/whole** ~ (*Amer*) halbe/ganze Note *f*; **of** ~ von Bedeutung; **make a** ~ **of** notieren ● *vt* beachten; (*notice*) bemerken (**that** dass)

'notebook *n* Notizbuch *nt*

noted /'nəʊtɪd/ *a* bekannt (**for** für)

note: ~paper *n* Briefpapier *nt*. **~worthy** *a* beachtenswert

nothing /'nʌθɪŋ/ *n, pron & adv* nichts; **for** ~ umsonst; ~ **but** nichts als; ~ **much** nicht viel; ~ **interesting** nichts Interessantes

notice /'nəʊtɪs/ *n* (*on board*) Anschlag *m*, Bekanntmachung *f*; (*announcement*) Anzeige *f*; (*review*) Kritik *f*; (*termination of lease, employment*) Kündigung *f*; **give [in one's]** ~ kündigen; **give s.o.** ~ jdm kündigen; **take no** ~! ignoriere es! ● *vt* bemerken. **~able** /-əbl/, *a*, **-bly** *adv* merklich. **~-board** *n* Anschlagbrett *nt*

noti|fication /nəʊtɪfɪ'keɪʃn/ *n* Benachrichtigung *f*. **~fy** /'nəʊtɪfaɪ/ *vt* (*pt/pp* **-ied**) benachrichtigen

notion /'nəʊʃn/ *n* Idee *f*

notorious /nəʊ'tɔ:rɪəs/ *a* berüchtigt

notwith'standing *prep* trotz (+ *gen*) ● *adv* trotzdem, dennoch

nought /nɔ:t/ *n* Null *f*

noun /naʊn/ *n* Substantiv *nt*

nourish /'nʌrɪʃ/ *vt* nähren. **~ing** *a* nahrhaft. **~ment** *n* Nahrung *f*

novel /'nɒvl/ *a* neu[artig] ● *n* Roman *m*. **~ist** *n* Romanschriftsteller(in) *m*(*f*). **~ty** *n* Neuheit *f*

November /nəʊ'vembə(r)/ *n* November *m*

novice /'nɒvɪs/ *n* Neuling *m*; (*Relig*) Novize *m*/Novizin *f*

now /naʊ/ *adv & conj* jetzt; ~ **[that]** jetzt, wo; **just** ~ gerade, eben; **right** ~ sofort; ~ **and again** hin und wieder; **now, now!** na, na!

'nowadays *adv* heutzutage

nowhere /'nəʊ-/ *adv* nirgendwo, nirgends

nozzle /ˈnɒzl/ *n* Düse *f*
nuance /ˈnju:ɑ̃s/ *n* Nuance *f*
nuclear /ˈnju:klɪə(r)/ *a* Kern-. ~ **deˈterrent** *n* nukleares Abschreckungsmittel *nt*
nucleus /ˈnju:klɪəs/ *n* (*pl* **-lei** /-lɪaɪ/) Kern *m*
nude /nju:d/ *a* nackt ● *n* (*Art*) Akt *m*; **in the** ~ nackt
nudge /nʌdʒ/ *vt* stupsen
nud|ist /ˈnju:dɪst/ *n* Nudist *m*. ~**ity** *n* Nacktheit *f*
nuisance /ˈnju:sns/ *n* Ärgernis *nt*; (*pest*) Plage *f*; **be a** ~ ärgerlich sein
null /nʌl/ *a* ~ **and void** null und nichtig
numb /nʌm/ *a* gefühllos, taub ● *vt* betäuben
number /ˈnʌmbə(r)/ *n* Nummer *f*; (*amount*) Anzahl *f*; (*Math*) Zahl *f* ● *vt* nummerieren; (*include*) zählen (**among** zu). ~ **plate** *n* Nummernschild *nt*
numeral /ˈnju:mərl/ *n* Ziffer *f*
numerical /nju:ˈmerɪkl/ *a*, **-ly** *adv* numerisch; **in** ~ **order** zahlenmäßig geordnet
numerous /ˈnju:mərəs/ *a* zahlreich
nun /nʌn/ *n* Nonne *f*
nurse /nɜ:s/ *n* [Kranken]schwester *f*; (*male*) Krankenpfleger *m*; **children's** ~ Kindermädchen *nt* ● *vt* pflegen
nursery /ˈnɜ:sərɪ/ *n* Kinderzimmer *nt*; (*Hort*) Gärtnerei *f*; **[day]** ~ Kindertagesstätte *f*. ~ **rhyme** *n* Kinderreim *m*. ~ **school** *n* Kindergarten *m*
nursing /ˈnɜ:sɪŋ/ *n* Krankenpflege *f*. ~ **home** *n* Pflegeheim *nt*
nut /nʌt/ *n* Nuss *f*; (*Techn*) [Schrauben]mutter *f*; ([!] *head*) Birne *f* [!]; **be** ~**s** [!] spinnen [!]. ~**crackers** *npl* Nussknacker *m*. ~**meg** *n* Muskat *m*
nutrient /ˈnju:trɪənt/ *n* Nährstoff *m*
nutrit|ion /nju:ˈtrɪʃn/ *n* Ernährung *f*. ~**ious** /-ʃəs/ *a* nahrhaft
ˈnutshell *n* Nussschale *f*; **in a** ~ (*fig*) kurz gesagt
nylon /ˈnaɪlɒn/ *n* Nylon *nt*

Oo

O /əʊ/ *n* (*Teleph*) null
oak /əʊk/ *n* Eiche *f*
OAP *abbr* (**old-age pensioner**) Rentner(in) *m(f)*
oar /ɔ:(r)/ *n* Ruder *nt*. ~**sman** *n* Ruderer *m*
oasis /əʊˈeɪsɪs/ *n* (*pl* **oases** /-si:z/) Oase *f*
oath /əʊθ/ *n* Eid *m*; (*swear-word*) Fluch *m*
oatmeal /ˈəʊt-/ *n* Hafermehl *nt*
oats /əʊts/ *npl* Hafer *m*; (*Culin*) **[rolled]** ~ Haferflocken *pl*
obedien|ce /əˈbi:dɪəns/ *n* Gehorsam *m*. ~**t** *a*, **-ly** *adv* gehorsam
obey /əˈbeɪ/ *vt/i* gehorchen (+ *dat*); befolgen <*instructions, rules*>
obituary /əˈbɪtjʊərɪ/ *n* Nachruf *m*; (*notice*) Todesanzeige *f*
object¹ /ˈɒbdʒɪkt/ *n* Gegenstand *m*; (*aim*) Zweck *m*; (*intention*) Absicht *f*; (*Gram*) Objekt *nt*; **money is no** ~ Geld spielt keine Rolle
object² /əbˈdʒekt/ *vi* Einspruch erheben (**to** gegen); (*be against*) etwas dagegen haben

objection /əb'dʒekʃn/ *n* Einwand *m*; **have no ~** nichts dagegen haben. **~able** /-əbl/ *a* anstößig; <*person*> unangenehm

objectiv|e /əb'dʒektɪv/ *a*, **-ly** *adv* objektiv ● *n* Ziel *nt*. **~ity** /-'tɪvətɪ/ *n* Objektivität *f*

objector /əb'dʒektə(r)/ *n* Gegner *m*

obligation /ɒblɪ'geɪʃn/ *n* Pflicht *f*; **without ~** unverbindlich

obligatory /ə'blɪgətrɪ/ *a* obligatorisch; **be ~** Vorschrift sein

oblig|e /ə'blaɪdʒ/ *vt* verpflichten; (*compel*) zwingen; (*do a small service*) einen Gefallen tun (+ *dat*). **~ing** *a* entgegenkommend

oblique /ə'bli:k/ *a* schräg; <*angle*> schief; (*fig*) indirekt

obliterate /ə'blɪtəreɪt/ *vt* auslöschen

oblivion /ə'blɪvɪən/ *n* Vergessenheit *f*

oblivious /ə'blɪvɪəs/ *a* **be ~** sich (*dat*) nicht bewusst sein (**of** *gen*)

oblong /'ɒblɒŋ/ *a* rechteckig ● *n* Rechteck *nt*

obnoxious /əb'nɒkʃəs/ *a* widerlich

oboe /'əʊbəʊ/ *n* Oboe *f*

obscen|e /əb'si:n/ *a* obszön. **~ity** /-'senətɪ/ *n* Obszönität *f*

obscur|e /əb'skjʊə(r)/ *a* dunkel; (*unknown*) unbekannt ● *vt* verdecken; (*confuse*) verwischen. **~ity** *n* Dunkelheit *f*; Unbekanntheit *f*

observa|nce /əb'zɜ:vns/ *n* (*of custom*) Einhaltung *f*. **~nt** *a* aufmerksam. **~tion** /ɒbzə'veɪʃn/ *n* Beobachtung *f*; (*remark*) Bemerkung *f*

observatory /əb'zɜ:vətrɪ/ *n* Sternwarte *f*

observe /əb'zɜ:v/ *vt* beobachten; (*say, notice*) bemerken; (*keep, celebrate*) feiern; (*obey*) einhalten. **~r** *n* Beobachter *m*

obsess /əb'ses/ *vt* **be ~ed by** besessen sein von. **~ion** /-eʃn/ *n* Besessenheit *f*; (*persistent idea*) fixe Idee *f*. **~ive** /-ɪv/ *a*, **-ly** *adv* zwanghaft

obsolete /'ɒbsəli:t/ *a* veraltet

obstacle /'ɒbstəkl/ *n* Hindernis *nt*

obstina|cy /'ɒbstɪnəsɪ/ *n* Starrsinn *m*. **~te** /-nət/ *a*, **-ly** *adv* starrsinnig; <*refusal*> hartnäckig

obstruct /əb'strʌkt/ *vt* blockieren; (*hinder*) behindern. **~ion** /-ʌkʃn/ *n* Blockierung *f*; Behinderung *f*; (*obstacle*) Hindernis *nt*. **~ive** /-ɪv/ *a* **be ~ive** Schwierigkeiten bereiten

obtain /əb'teɪn/ *vt* erhalten. **~able** /-əbl/ *a* erhältlich

obtrusive /əb'tru:sɪv/ *a* aufdringlich; <*thing*> auffällig

obtuse /əb'tju:s/ *a* begriffsstutzig

obvious /'ɒbvɪəs/ *a*, **-ly** *adv* offensichtlich, offenbar

occasion /ə'keɪʒn/ *n* Gelegenheit *f*; (*time*) Mal *nt*; (*event*) Ereignis *nt*; (*cause*) Anlass *m*, Grund *m*; **on the ~ of** anlässlich (+ *gen*)

occasional /ə'keɪʒənl/ *a* gelegentlich. **~ly** *adv* gelegentlich, hin und wieder

occult /ɒ'kʌlt/ *a* okkult

occupant /'ɒkjʊpənt/ *n* Bewohner(in) *m(f)*; (*of vehicle*) Insasse *m*

occupation /ɒkjʊ'peɪʃn/ *n* Beschäftigung *f*; (*job*) Beruf *m*; (*Mil*) Besetzung *f*; (*period*) Besatzung *f*. **~al** *a* Berufs-. **~al therapy** *n* Beschäftigungstherapie *f*

occupier /'ɒkjʊpaɪə(r)/ *n* Bewohner(in) *m(f)*

occupy /'ɒkjʊpaɪ/ *vt* (*pt/pp* **occupied**) besetzen <*seat*, (*Mil*) *country*>; einnehmen <*space*>; in Anspruch nehmen <*time*>; (*live* *in*) bewohnen; (*fig*) bekleiden <*office*>; (*keep busy*) beschäftigen

occur /ə'kɜ:(r)/ *vi* (*pt/pp* **occurred**) geschehen; (*exist*) vorkommen, auftreten; **it ~ red to me that** es fiel mir ein, dass. **~rence** /ə'kʌrəns/ *n* Auftreten *nt*; (*event*) Ereignis *nt*

ocean /'əʊʃn/ *n* Ozean *m*

o'clock /ə'klɒk/ *adv* **[at] 7 ~** [um] 7 Uhr

octagonal /ɒk'tægənl/ *a* achteckig

October /ɒk'təʊbə(r)/ *n* Oktober *m*

octopus /'ɒktəpəs/ *n* (*pl* **-puses**) Tintenfisch *m*

odd /ɒd/ *a* (**-er, -est**) seltsam, merkwürdig; <*number*> ungerade; (*not of set*) einzeln; **forty ~** über vierzig; **~ jobs** Gelegenheitsarbeiten *pl*; **the ~ one out** die Ausnahme; **at ~ moments** zwischendurch

odd|ity /'ɒdɪtɪ/ *n* Kuriosität *f*. **~ly** *adv* merkwürdig; **~ly enough** merkwürdigerweise **~ment** *n* (*of fabric*) Rest *m*

odds /ɒdz/ *npl* (*chances*) Chancen *pl*; **at ~** uneinig; **~ and ends** Kleinkram *m*

ode /əʊd/ *n* Ode *f*

odious /'əʊdɪəs/ *a* widerlich

odour /'əʊdə(r)/ *n* Geruch *m*. **~less** *a* geruchlos

---

of /ɒv, *unbetont* əv/

● *preposition*

····➤ (*indicating belonging, origin*) von (+ *dat*); genitive. **the mother of twins** die Mutter von Zwillingen. **the mother of the twins** die Mutter der Zwillinge *or* von den Zwillingen. **the Queen of England** die Königin von England. **a friend of mine** ein Freund von mir. **a friend of the teacher's** ein Freund des Lehrers. **the brother of her father** der Bruder ihres Vaters. **the works of Shakespeare** Shakespeares Werke. **it was nice of him** es war nett von ihm

····➤ (*made of*) aus (+ *dat*). **a dress of cotton** ein Kleid aus Baumwolle

····➤ (*following number*) **five of us** fünf von uns. **the two of us** wir zwei. **there were four of us waiting** wir waren vier, die warteten

····➤ (*followed by number, description*) von (+ *dat*). **a girl of ten** ein Mädchen von zehn Jahren. **a distance of 50 miles** eine Entfernung von 50 Meilen. **a man of character** ein Mann von Charakter. **a woman of exceptional beauty** eine Frau von außerordentlicher Schönheit. **a person of strong views** ein Mensch mit festen Ansichten

! **of** is not translated after measures and in some other cases: **a pound of apples** ein Pfund Äpfel; **a cup of tea** eine Tasse Tee; **a glass of wine** ein Glas Wein; **the city of Chicago** die Stadt Chicago; **the fourth of January** der vierte Januar

---

off /ɒf/ *prep* von (+ *dat*); **~ the coast** vor der Küste; **get ~ the ladder/bus** von der Leiter/aus dem Bus steigen ● *adv* weg; <*button, lid, handle*> ab; <*light*> aus; <*brake*> los; <*machine*> abgeschaltet; <*tap*> zu; (*on appliance*) **'off'** 'aus'; **2 kilometres ~** 2 Kilometer entfernt; **a long way ~** weit weg; (*time*) noch lange hin; **~ and on** hin und wieder; **with his hat/coat ~** ohne Hut/Mantel; **20% ~** 20% Nachlass; **be ~** (*leave*) [weg]gehen; (*Sport*) starten; <*food:*> schlecht sein; **be well ~**

gut dran sein; (*financially*) wohlhabend sein; **have a day ~** einen freien Tag haben

offal /ˈɒfl/ *n* (*Culin*) Innereien *pl*

offence /əˈfens/ *n* (*illegal act*) Vergehen *nt*; **give/take ~** Anstoß erregen/nehmen (**at** an + *dat*)

offend /əˈfend/ *vt* beleidigen. **~er** *n* (*Jur*) Straftäter *m*

offensive /əˈfensɪv/ *a* anstößig; (*Mil, Sport*) offensiv ● *n* Offensive *f*

offer /ˈɒfə(r)/ *n* Angebot *nt*; **on (special) ~** im Sonderangebot ● *vt* anbieten (**to** *dat*); leisten <*resistance*>; **~ to do sth** sich anbieten, etw zu tun. **~ing** *n* Gabe *f*

offˈhand *a* brüsk; (*casual*) lässig

office /ˈɒfɪs/ *n* Büro *nt*; (*post*) Amt *nt*

officer /ˈɒfɪsə(r)/ *n* Offizier *m*; (*official*) Beamte(r) *m*/ Beamtin *f*; (*police*) Polizeibeamte(r) *m*/ -beamtin *f*

official /əˈfɪʃl/ *a* offiziell, amtlich ● *n* Beamte(r) *m*/ Beamtin *f*; (*Sport*) Funktionär *m*. **~ly** *adv* offiziell

officious /əˈfɪʃəs/ *a*, **-ly** *adv* übereifrig

ˈoff-licence *n* Wein und Spirituosenhandlung *f*

off-ˈload *vt* ausladen

ˈoff-putting *a* [!] abstoßend

offˈset *vt* (*pt/pp* **-set**, *pres p* **-setting**) ausgleichen

ˈoffshoot *n* Schössling *m*; (*fig*) Zweig *m*

ˈoffshore *a* Offshore-

offˈside *a* (*Sport*) abseits

ˈoffspring *n* Nachwuchs *m*

offˈstage *adv* hinter den Kulissen

off-ˈwhite *a* fast weiß

often /ˈɒfn/ *adv* oft; **every so ~** von Zeit zu Zeit

oh /əʊ/ *int* oh! ach! **oh dear**! o weh!

oil /ɔɪl/ *n* Öl *nt*; (*petroleum*) Erdöl *nt* ● *vt* ölen

oil: ~field *n* Ölfeld *nt*. **~-painting** *n* Ölgemälde *nt*. **~ refinery** *n* [Erd]ölraffinerie *f*. **~-tanker** *n* Öltanker *m*. **~ well** *n* Ölquelle *f*

oily /ˈɔɪlɪ/ *a* (**-ier, -iest**) ölig

ointment /ˈɔɪntmənt/ *n* Salbe *f*

OK /əʊˈkeɪ/ *a & int* [!] in Ordnung; okay ● *adv* (*well*) gut ● *vt* (*auch* **okay**) (*pt/pp* **okayed**) genehmigen

old /əʊld/ *a* (**-er, -est**) alt; (*former*) ehemalig

old: ~ ˈage *n* Alter *nt*. **~-age ˈpensioner** *n* Rentner(in) *m(f)*. **~ boy** *n* ehemaliger Schüler. **~-ˈfashioned** *a* altmodisch. **~ girl** *n* ehemalige Schülerin *f*

olive /ˈɒlɪv/ *n* Olive *f*; (*colour*) Oliv *nt* ● *a* olivgrün. **~ ˈoil** *n* Olivenöl *nt*

Olympic /əˈlɪmpɪk/ *a* olympisch ● *n* **the ~s** die Olympischen Spiele *pl*

omelette /ˈɒmlɪt/ *n* Omelett *nt*

ominous /ˈɒmɪnəs/ *a* bedrohlich

omission /əˈmɪʃn/ *n* Auslassung *f*; (*failure to do*) Unterlassung *f*

omit /əˈmɪt/ *vt* (*pt/pp* **omitted**) auslassen; **~ to do sth** es unterlassen, etw zu tun

omnipotent /ɒmˈnɪpətənt/ *a* allmächtig

on /ɒn/ *prep* auf (+ *dat*/(*on to*) + *acc*); (*on vertical surface*) an (+ *dat*/(*on to*) + *acc*); (*about*) über (+ *acc*); **on Monday** [am] Montag; **on Mondays** montags; **on the first of May** am ersten Mai; **on arriving** als ich ankam; **on one's finger** am Finger; **on the right/left** rechts/links; **on the Rhine** am Rhein; **on the radio/television** im Radio/Fernsehen; **on the bus/train** im Bus/Zug; **go on the**

bus/train mit dem Bus/Zug fahren; **on me** (*with me*) bei mir; **it's on me** [!] das spendiere ich ● *adv* (*further on*) weiter; (*switched on*) an; <*brake*> angezogen; <*machine*> angeschaltet; (*on appliance*) '**on**' 'ein'; **with/without his hat/coat on** mit/ohne Hut/Mantel; **be on** <*film*:> laufen; <*event*:> stattfinden; **be on at** [!] bedrängen (**zu** to); **it's not on** [!] das geht nicht; **on and on** immer weiter; **on and off** hin und wieder; **and so on** und so weiter

once /wʌns/ *adv* einmal; (*formerly*) früher; **at ~** sofort; (*at the same time*) gleichzeitig; **~ and for all** ein für alle Mal ● *conj* wenn; (*with past tense*) als

'oncoming *a* **~ traffic** Gegenverkehr *m*

one /wʌn/ *a* ein(e); (*only*) einzig; **not ~** kein(e); **~ day/evening** eines Tages/Abends ● *n* Eins *f* ● *pron* eine(r)/eins; (*impersonal*) man; **which ~** welche(r,s); **~ another** einander; **~ by ~** einzeln; **~ never knows** man kann nie wissen

one: ~-parent 'family *n* Einelternfamilie *f*. **~'self** *pron* selbst; (*refl*) sich; **by ~self** allein. **~-sided** *a* einseitig. **~-way** *a* <*street*> Einbahn-; <*ticket*> einfach

onion /'ʌnjən/ *n* Zwiebel *f*

on-'line *adv* online

'onlooker *n* Zuschauer(in) *m(f)*

only /'əʊnlɪ/ *a* einzige(r,s); **an ~ child** ein Einzelkind *nt* ● *adv & conj* nur; **~ just** gerade erst; (*barely*) gerade noch

'onset *n* Beginn *m*; (*of winter*) Einsetzen *nt*

onward[s] /'ɒnwəd[z]/ *adv* vorwärts; **from then ~** von der Zeit an

ooze /u:z/ *vi* sickern

opaque /əʊ'peɪk/ *a* undurchsichtig

open /'əʊpən/ *a*, **-ly** *adv* offen; **be ~** <*shop*:> geöffnet sein; **in the ~ air** im Freien ● *n* **in the ~** im Freien ● *vt* öffnen, aufmachen; (*start, set up*) eröffnen ● *vi* sich öffnen; <*flower*:> aufgehen; <*shop*:> öffnen, aufmachen; (*be started*) eröffnet werden. **~ up** *vt* öffnen, aufmachen

'open day *n* Tag *m* der offenen Tür

opener /'əʊpənə(r)/ *n* Öffner *m*

opening /'əʊpənɪŋ/ *n* Öffnung *f*; (*beginning*) Eröffnung *f*; (*job*) Einstiegsmöglichkeit *f*. **~ hours** *npl* Öffnungszeiten *pl*

open: ~-'minded *a* aufgeschlossen. **~ 'sandwich** *n* belegtes Brot *nt*

opera /'ɒpərə/ *n* Oper *f*. **~-house** *n* Opernhaus *nt*. **~-singer** *n* Opernsänger(in) *m(f)*

operate /'ɒpəreɪt/ *vt* bedienen <*machine, lift*>; betätigen <*lever, brake*>; (*fig: run*) betreiben ● *vi* (*Techn*) funktionieren; (*be in action*) in Betrieb sein; (*Mil & fig*) operieren; **~ [on]** (*Med*) operieren

operatic /ɒpə'rætɪk/ *a* Opern-

operation /ɒpə'reɪʃn/ *n* (*see* **operate**) Bedienung *f*; Betätigung *f*; Operation *f*; **in ~** (*Techn*) in Betrieb; **come into ~** (*fig*) in Kraft treten; **have an ~** (*Med*) operiert werden. **~al** *a* **be ~al** in Betrieb sein; <*law*:> in Kraft sein

operative /'ɒpərətɪv/ *a* wirksam

operator /'ɒpəreɪtə(r)/ *n* (*user*) Bedienungsperson *f*; (*Teleph*) Vermittlung *f*

operetta /ɒpə'retə/ *n* Operette *f*

opinion /ə'pɪnjən/ *n* Meinung *f*; **in my ~** meiner Meinung nach. **~ated** *a* rechthaberisch

opponent /ə'pəʊnənt/ *n* Gegner(in) *m(f)*

opportun|e /'ɒpətju:n/ *a* günstig. **~ist** /-'tju:nɪst/ *n* Opportunist *m*

opportunity /ɒpə'tju:nətɪ/ *n* Gelegenheit *f*

oppos|e /ə'pəʊz/ *vt* Widerstand leisten (+ *dat*); (*argue against*) sprechen gegen; **be ~ed to sth** gegen etw sein; **as ~ed to** im Gegensatz zu. **~ing** *a* gegnerisch

opposite /'ɒpəzɪt/ *a* entgegengesetzt; <*house, side*> gegenüberliegend; **~ number** (*fig*) Gegenstück *nt*; **the ~ sex** das andere Geschlecht ● *n* Gegenteil *nt* ● *adv* gegenüber ● *prep* gegenüber (+ *dat*)

opposition /ɒpə'zɪʃn/ *n* Widerstand *m*; (*Pol*) Opposition *f*

oppress /ə'pres/ *vt* unterdrücken. **~ion** /-eʃn/ *n* Unterdrücken *f*. **~ive** /-ɪv/ *a* tyrannisch; <*heat*> drückend

opt /ɒpt/ *vi* **~ for** sich entscheiden für

optical /'ɒptɪkl/ *a* optisch

optician /ɒp'tɪʃn/ *n* Optiker *m*

optimis|m /'ɒptɪmɪzm/ *n* Optimismus *m*. **~t** /-mɪst/ *n* Optimist *m*. **~tic** /-'mɪstɪk/ *a*, **-ally** *adv* optimistisch

optimum /'ɒptɪməm/ *a* optimal

option /'ɒpʃn/ *n* Wahl *f*; (*Comm*) Option *f*. **~al** *a* auf Wunsch erhältlich; <*subject*> wahlfrei

opu|lence /'ɒpjʊləns/ *n* Prunk *m*. **~lent** *a* prunkvoll

or /ɔ:(r)/ *conj* oder; (*after negative*) noch; **or [else]** sonst; **in a year or two** in ein bis zwei Jahren

oral /'ɔ:rl/ *a*, **-ly** *adv* mündlich; (*Med*) oral ● *n* Mündliche(s) *nt*

orange /'ɒrɪndʒ/ *n* Apfelsine *f*, Orange *f*; (*colour*) Orange *nt* ● *a* orangefarben

oratorio /ɒrə'tɔ:rɪəʊ/ *n* Oratorium *nt*

oratory /'ɒrətərɪ/ *n* Redekunst *f*

orbit /'ɔ:bɪt/ *n* Umlaufbahn *f* ● *vt* umkreisen

orchard /'ɔ:tʃəd/ *n* Obstgarten *m*

orches|tra /'ɔ:kɪstrə/ *n* Orchester *nt*. **~tral** /-'kestrəl/ *a* Orchester-. **~trate** *vt* orchestrieren

ordeal /ɔ:'di:l/ *n* (*fig*) Qual *f*

order /'ɔ:də(r)/ *n* Ordnung *f*; (*sequence*) Reihenfolge *f*; (*condition*) Zustand *m*; (*command*) Befehl *m*; (*in restaurant*) Bestellung *f*; (*Comm*) Auftrag *m*; (*Relig, medal*) Orden *m*; **out of ~** <*machine*> außer Betrieb; **in ~ that** damit; **in ~ to help** um zu helfen ● *vt* (*put in* **~**) ordnen; (*command*) befehlen (+ *dat*); (*Comm, in restaurant*) bestellen; (*prescribe*) verordnen

orderly /'ɔ:dəlɪ/ *a* ordentlich; (*not unruly*) friedlich ● *n* (*Mil, Med*) Sanitäter *m*

ordinary /'ɔ:dɪnərɪ/ *a* gewöhnlich, normal

ore /ɔ:(r)/ *n* Erz *nt*

organ /'ɔ:gən/ *n* (*Biol & fig*) Organ *nt*; (*Mus*) Orgel *f*

organic /ɔ:'gænɪk/ *a*, **-ally** *adv* organisch; (*without chemicals*) biodynamisch; <*crop*> biologisch angebaut; <*food*> Bio-. **~ farming** *n* biologischer Anbau *m*

organism /'ɔ:gənɪzm/ *n* Organismus *m*

organist /'ɔ:gənɪst/ *n* Organist *m*

organization /ɔ:gənaɪ'zeɪʃn/ *n* Organisation *f*

organize /'ɔ:gənaɪz/ *vt* organisieren; veranstalten <*event*>. **~r** *n* Organisator *m*; Veranstalter *m*

orgy /'ɔ:dʒɪ/ *n* Orgie *f*

Orient /'ɔ:rɪənt/ *n* Orient *m*. **o~al** /-'entl/ *a* orientalisch ● *n* Orientale *m*/Orientalin *f*

orientation /ˈɔːrɪənˈteɪʃn/ *n* Orientierung *f*
origin /ˈɒrɪdʒɪn/ *n* Ursprung *m*; (*of person, goods*) Herkunft *f*
original /əˈrɪdʒənl/ *a* ursprünglich; (*not copied*) original; (*new*) originell ● *n* Original *nt*. **~ity** /-ˈnælətɪ/ *n* Originalität *f*. **~ly** *adv* ursprünglich
originate /əˈrɪdʒɪneɪt/ *vi* entstehen
ornament /ˈɔːnəmənt/ *n* Ziergegenstand *m*; (*decoration*) Verzierung *f*. **~al** /-ˈmentl/ *a* dekorativ
ornate /ɔːˈneɪt/ *a* reich verziert
ornithology /ɔːnɪˈθɒlədʒɪ/ *n* Vogelkunde *f*
orphan /ˈɔːfn/ *n* Waisenkind *nt*, Waise *f*. **~age** /-ɪdʒ/ *n* Waisenhaus *nt*
orthodox /ˈɔːθədɒks/ *a* orthodox
ostensible /ɒˈstensəbl/ *a*, **-bly** *adv* angeblich
ostentat|ion /ɒstenˈteɪʃn/ *n* Protzerei *f* [!]. **~ious** /-ʃəs/ *a* protzig [!]
osteopath /ˈɒstɪəpæθ/ *n* Osteopath *m*
ostrich /ˈɒstrɪtʃ/ *n* Strauß *m*
other /ˈʌðə(r)/ *a, pron & n* andere(r,s); **the ~ [one]** der/die/das andere; **the ~ two** die zwei anderen; **no ~s** sonst keine; **any ~ questions?** sonst noch Fragen? **every ~ day** jeden zweiten Tag; **the ~ day** neulich; **the ~ evening** neulich abends; **someone/something or ~** irgendjemand/-etwas ● *adv* anders; **~ than him** außer ihm; **somehow/somewhere or ~** irgendwie/irgendwo
ˈotherwise *adv* sonst; (*differently*) anders
ought /ɔːt/ *v aux* **I/we ~ to stay** ich sollte/wir sollten eigentlich bleiben; **he ~ not to have done it** er hätte es nicht machen sollen
ounce /aʊns/ *n* Unze *f* (*28, 35 g*)
our /ˈaʊə(r)/ *a* unser
ours /ˈaʊəz/ *poss pron* unsere(r,s); **a friend of ~** ein Freund von uns; **that is ~** das gehört uns
ourselves /aʊəˈselvz/ *pron* selbst; (*refl*) uns; **by ~** allein
out /aʊt/ *adv* (*not at home*) weg; (*outside*) draußen; (*not alight*) aus; (*unconscious*) bewusstlos; **be ~** *<sun:>* scheinen; *<flower>* blühen; *<workers>* streiken; *<calculation:>* nicht stimmen; (*Sport*) aus sein; (*fig: not feasible*) nicht infrage kommen; **~ and about** unterwegs; **have it ~ with s.o.** [!] jdn zur Rede stellen; **get ~!** [!] raus! **~ with it!** [!] heraus damit! ● *prep* **~ of** aus (+ *dat*); **go ~ (of) the door** zur Tür hinausgehen; **be ~ of bed/ the room** nicht im Bett/im Zimmer sein; **~ of breath/danger** außer Atem/Gefahr; **~ of work** arbeitslos; **nine ~ of ten** neun von zehn; **be ~ of sugar** keinen Zucker mehr haben
ˈoutboard *a* **~ motor** Außenbordmotor *m*
ˈoutbreak *n* Ausbruch *m*
ˈoutbuilding *n* Nebengebäude *nt*
ˈoutburst *n* Ausbruch *m*
ˈoutcast *n* Ausgestoßene(r) *m/f*
ˈoutcome *n* Ergebnis *nt*
ˈoutcry *n* Aufschrei *m* [der Entrüstung]
outˈdated *a* überholt
outˈdo *vt* (*pt* **-did**, *pp* **-done**) übertreffen, übertrumpfen
ˈoutdoor *a* *<life, sports>* im Freien; **~ swimming pool** Freibad *nt*
outˈdoors *adv* draußen; **go ~** nach draußen gehen
ˈouter *a* äußere(r,s)

'outfit *n* Ausstattung *f*; (*clothes*) Ensemble *nt*; ([!] *organization*) Laden *m*
'outgoing *a* ausscheidend; <*mail*> ausgehend; (*sociable*) kontaktfreudig. **~s** *npl* Ausgaben *pl*
out'grow *vi* (*pt* **-grew**, *pp* **-grown**) herauswachsen aus
outing /'aʊtɪŋ/ *n* Ausflug *m*
'outlaw *n* Geächtete(r) *m/f* ● *vt* ächten
'outlay *n* Auslagen *pl*
'outlet *n* Abzug *m*; (*for water*) Abfluss *m*; (*fig*) Ventil *nt*; (*Comm*) Absatzmöglichkeit *f*
'outline *n* Umriss *m*; (*summary*) kurze Darstellung *f* ● *vt* umreißen
out'live *vt* überleben
'outlook *n* Aussicht *f*; (*future prospect*) Aussichten *pl*; (*attitude*) Einstellung *f*
out'moded *a* überholt
out'number *vt* zahlenmäßig überlegen sein (+ *dat*)
'out-patient *n* ambulanter Patient *m*
'outpost *n* Vorposten *m*
'output *n* Leistung *f*; Produktion *f*
'outrage *n* Gräueltat *f*; (*fig*) Skandal *m*; (*indignation*) Empörung *f*. **~ous** /-'reɪdʒəs/ *a* empörend
'outright[1] *a* völlig, total; <*refusal*> glatt
out'right[2] *adv* ganz; (*at once*) sofort; (*frankly*) offen
'outset *n* Anfang *m*
'outside[1] *a* äußere(r,s); **~ wall** Außenwand *f* ● *n* Außenseite *f*; **from the ~** von außen; **at the ~** höchstens
out'side[2] *adv* außen; (*out of doors*) draußen; **go ~** nach draußen gehen ● *prep* außerhalb (+ *gen*); (*in front of*) vor (+ *dat/acc*)
out'sider *n* Außenseiter *m*
'outsize *a* übergroß
'outskirts *npl* Rand *m*
out'spoken *a* offen; **be ~** kein Blatt vor den Mund nehmen
out'standing *a* hervorragend; (*conspicuous*) bemerkenswert; (*Comm*) ausstehend
'outstretched *a* ausgestreckt
out'vote *vt* überstimmen
'outward /-wəd/ *a* äußerlich; **~ journey** Hinreise *f* ● *adv* nach außen. **~ly** *adv* nach außen hin, äußerlich. **~s** *adv* nach außen
out'wit *vt* (*pt/pp* **-witted**) überlisten
oval /'əʊvl/ *a* oval ● *n* Oval *nt*
ovation /əʊ'veɪʃn/ *n* Ovation *f*
oven /'ʌvn/ *n* Backofen *m*
over /'əʊvə(r)/ *prep* über (+ *acc/dat*); **~ dinner** beim Essen; **~ the phone** am Telefon; **~ the page** auf der nächsten Seite ● *adv* (*remaining*) übrig; (*ended*) zu Ende; **~ again** noch einmal; **~ and ~** immer wieder; **~ here/there** hier/da drüben; **all ~** (*everywhere*) überall; **it's all ~** es ist vorbei; **I ache all ~** mir tut alles weh
overall[1] /'əʊvərɔːl/ *n* Kittel *m*; **~s** *pl* Overall *m*
overall[2] /əʊvər'ɔːl/ *a* gesamt; (*general*) allgemein ● *adv* insgesamt
over'balance *vi* das Gleichgewicht verlieren
over'bearing *a* herrisch
'overboard *adv* (*Naut*) über Bord
'overcast *a* bedeckt
over'charge *vt* **~ s.o.** jdm zu viel berechnen ● *vi* zu viel verlangen
'overcoat *n* Mantel *m*

over'come *vt* (*pt* **-came**, *pp* **-come**) überwinden; **be ~ by** überwältigt werden von
over'crowded *a* überfüllt
over'do *vt* (*pt* **-did**, *pp* **-done**) übertreiben; (*cook too long*) zu lange kochen; **~ it** ([!] *do too much*) sich übernehmen
'overdose *n* Überdosis *f*
'overdraft *n* [Konto]überziehung *f*; **have an ~** sein Konto überzogen haben
over'due *a* überfällig
over'estimate *vt* überschätzen
'overflow¹ *n* Überschuss *m*; (*outlet*) Überlauf *m*
over'flow² *vi* überlaufen
over'grown *a* <*garden*> überwachsen
'overhang¹ *n* Überhang *m*
over'hang² *vt/i* (*pt/pp* **-hung**) überhängen (über + *acc*)
'overhaul¹ *n* Überholung *f*
over'haul² *vt* (*Techn*) überholen
over'head¹ *adv* oben
'overhead² *a* Ober-; (*ceiling*) Decken-. **~s** *npl* allgemeine Unkosten *pl*
over'hear *vt* (*pt/pp* **-heard**) mit anhören <*conversation*>
over'heat *vi* zu heiß werden
over'joyed *a* überglücklich
'overland *a & adv* /--'-/ auf dem Landweg; **~ route** Landroute *f*
over'lap *vi* (*pt/pp* **-lapped**) sich überschneiden
over'leaf *adv* umseitig
over'load *vt* überladen
over'look *vt* überblicken; (*fail to see, ignore*) übersehen
over'night¹ *adv* über Nacht; **stay ~** übernachten
'overnight² *a* Nacht-; **~ stay** Übernachtung *f*
'overpass *n* Überführung *f*
over'pay *vt* (*pt/pp* **-paid**) überbezahlen
over'populated *a* übervölkert
over'power *vt* überwältigen. **~ing** *a* überwältigend
over'priced *a* zu teuer
over'rated *a* überbewertet
overre'act *vi* überreagieren. **~ion** *n* Überreaktion *f*
over'riding *a* Haupt-
over'rule *vt* ablehnen; **we were ~d** wir wurden überstimmt
over'run *vt* (*pt* **-ran**, *pp* **-run**, *pres p* **-running**) überrennen; überschreiten <*time*>; **be ~ with** überlaufen sein von
over'seas¹ *adv* in Übersee; **go ~** nach Übersee gehen
'overseas² *a* Übersee-
over'see *vt* (*pt* **-saw**, *pp* **-seen**) beaufsichtigen
over'shadow *vt* überschatten
over'shoot *vt* (*pt/pp* **-shot**) hinausschießen über (+ *acc*)
'oversight *n* Versehen *nt*
over'sleep *vi* (*pt/pp* **-slept**) [sich] verschlafen
over'step *vt* (*pt/pp* **-stepped**) überschreiten
overt /əʊ'vɜːt/ *a* offen
over'take *vt/i* (*pt* **-took**, *pp* **-taken**) überholen
over'throw *vt* (*pt* **-threw**, *pp* **-thrown**) (*Pol*) stürzen
'overtime *n* Überstunden *pl* ● *adv* **work ~** Überstunden machen
over'tired *a* übermüdet
overture /'əʊvətjʊə(r)/ *n* (*Mus*) Ouvertüre *f*; **~s** *pl* (*fig*) Annäherungsversuche *pl*
over'turn *vt* umstoßen ● *vi* umkippen
over'weight *a* übergewichtig; **be ~** Übergewicht haben
overwhelm /-'welm/ *vt* überwältigen. **~ing** *a* überwältigend
over'work *n* Überarbeitung *f* ● *vt* überfordern ● *vi* sich überarbeiten

over'wrought *a* überreizt
ow|e /əʊ/ *vt* schulden/ (*fig*) verdanken (**[to] s.o.** jdm); **~e s.o. sth** jdm etw schuldig sein. **'~ing to** *prep* wegen (+ *gen*)
owl /aʊl/ *n* Eule *f*
own¹ /əʊn/ *a & pron* eigen; **it's my ~** es gehört mir; **a car of my ~** mein eigenes Auto; **on one's ~** allein; **get one's ~ back** [!] sich revanchieren
own² *vt* besitzen; **I don't ~ it** es gehört mir nicht. **~ up** *vi* es zugeben
owner /'əʊnə(r)/ *n* Eigentümer(in) *m(f)*, Besitzer(in) *m(f)*; (*of shop*)Inhaber(in) *m(f)*. **~ship** *n* Besitz *m*
oxygen /'ɒksɪdʒən/ *n* Sauerstoff *m*
oyster /'ɔɪstə(r)/ *n* Auster *f*

Pp

pace /peɪs/ *n* Schritt *m*; (*speed*) Tempo *nt*; **keep ~ with** Schritt halten mit ● *vi* **~ up and down** auf und ab gehen. **~-maker** *n* (*Sport & Med*) Schrittmacher *m*
Pacific /pə'sɪfɪk/ *a & n* **the ~ [Ocean]** der Pazifik
pacifist /'pæsɪfɪst/ *n* Pazifist *m*
pacify /'pæsɪfaɪ/ *vt* (*pt/pp* **-ied**) beruhigen
pack /pæk/ *n* Packung *f*, (*Mil*) Tornister *m*; (*of cards*) [Karten]spiel *nt*; (*gang*) Bande *f*, (*of hounds*) Meute *f*, (*of wolves*) Rudel *nt*; **a ~ of lies** ein Haufen Lügen ● *vt/i* packen; einpacken <*article*>; **be ~ed** (*crowded*) [gedrängt] voll sein. **~ up** *vt* einpacken ● *vi* [!] <*machine:*> kaputtgehen
package /'pækɪdʒ/ *n* Paket *nt*. **~ holiday** *n* Pauschalreise *f*
packet /'pækɪt/ *n* Päckchen *nt*
packing /'pækɪŋ/ *n* Verpackung *f*
pact /pækt/ *n* Pakt *m*
pad /pæd/ *n* Polster *nt*; (*for writing*) [Schreib]block *m* ● *vt* (*pt/pp* **padded**) polstern
padding /'pædɪŋ/ *n* Polsterung *f*, (*in written work*) Füllwerk *nt*
paddle¹ /'pædl/ *n* Paddel *nt* ● *vt* (*row*) paddeln
paddle² *vi* waten
paddock /'pædək/ *n* Koppel *f*
padlock /'pædlɒk/ *n* Vorhängeschloss *nt* ● *vt* mit einem Vorhängeschloss verschließen
paediatrician /pi:dɪə'trɪʃn/ *n* Kinderarzt *m* /-ärztin *f*
pagan /'peɪgən/ *a* heidnisch ● *n* Heide *m*/Heidin *f*
page¹ /peɪdʒ/ *n* Seite *f*
page² *n* (*boy*) Page *m* ● *vt* ausrufen <*person*>
paid /'peɪd/ *see* **pay** ● *a* bezahlt; **put ~ to** [!] zunichte machen
pail /peɪl/ *n* Eimer *m*
pain /peɪn/ *n* Schmerz *m*; **be in ~** Schmerzen haben; **take ~s** sich (*dat*) Mühe geben; **~ in the neck** [!] Nervensäge *f*
pain: ~ful *a* schmerzhaft; (*fig*) schmerzlich. **~-killer** *n* schmerzstillendes Mittel *nt*. **~less** *a*, **-ly** *adv* schmerzlos
painstaking /'peɪnzteɪkɪŋ/ *a* sorgfältig
paint /peɪnt/ *n* Farbe *f* ● *vt/i* streichen; <*artist:*> malen. **~brush** *n* Pinsel *m*. **~er** *n* Maler *m*; (*decorator*) Anstreicher *m*. **~ing** *n* Malerei *f*, (*picture*) Gemälde *nt*

pair /peə(r)/ *n* Paar *nt*; ~ **of trousers** Hose *f* ● *vi* ~ **off** Paare bilden

pajamas /pə'dʒɑ:məz/ *n pl* (*Amer*) Schlafanzug *m*

Pakistan /pɑ:kɪ'stɑ:n/ *n* Pakistan *nt*. ~**i** *a* pakistanisch ● *n* Pakistaner(in) *m(f)*

pal /pæl/ *n* Freund(in) *m(f)*

palace /'pælɪs/ *n* Palast *m*

palatable /'pælətəbl/ *a* schmackhaft

palate /'pælət/ *n* Gaumen *m*

palatial /pə'leɪʃl/ *a* palastartig

pale *a* (**-r, -st**) blass ● *vi* blass werden. ~**ness** *n* Blässe *f*

Palestin|e /'pælɪstaɪn/ *n* Palästina *nt*. ~**ian** /pælə'stɪnɪən/ *a* palästinensisch ● *n* Palästinenser(in) *m(f)*

palette /'pælɪt/ *n* Palette *f*

palm /pɑ:m/ *n* Handfläche *f*; (*tree, symbol*) Palme *f* ● *vt* ~ **sth off on s.o.** jdm etw andrehen. **P**~ '**Sunday** *n* Palmsonntag *m*

palpable /'pælpəbl/ *a* tastbar; (*perceptible*) spürbar

palpitations /'pælpɪ'teɪʃnz/ *npl* Herzklopfen *nt*

paltry /'pɔ:ltrɪ/ *a* (**-ier, -iest**) armselig

pamper /'pæmpə(r)/ *vt* verwöhnen

pamphlet /'pæmflɪt/ *n* Broschüre *f*

pan /pæn/ *n* Pfanne *f*; (*saucepan*) Topf *m*; (*of scales*) Schale *f*

panacea /pænə'si:ə/ *n* Allheilmittel *nt*

'**pancake** *n* Pfannkuchen *m*

panda /'pændə/ *n* Panda *m*

pandemonium /pændɪ'məʊnɪəm/ *n* Höllenlärm *m*

pane /peɪn/ *n* [Glas]scheibe *f*

panel /'pænl/ *n* Tafel *f*, Platte *f*; ~ **of experts** Expertenrunde *f*; ~ **of judges** Jury *f*. ~**ling** *n* Täfelung *f*

pang /pæŋ/ *n* ~**s of hunger** Hungergefühl *nt*; ~**s of conscience** Gewissensbisse *pl*

panic /'pænɪk/ *n* Panik *f* ● *vi* (*pt/pp* **panicked**) in Panik geraten. ~**-stricken** *a* von Panik ergriffen

panoram|a /pænə'rɑ:mə/ *n* Panorama *nt*. ~**ic** /-'ræmɪk/ *a* Panorama-

pansy /'pænzɪ/ *n* Stiefmütterchen *nt*

pant /pænt/ *vi* keuchen; <*dog:*> hecheln

panther /'pænθə(r)/ *n* Panther *m*

panties /'pæntɪz/ *npl* [Damen]slip *m*

pantomime /'pæntəmaɪm/ *n* [zu Weihnachten aufgeführte] Märchenvorstellung *f*

pantry /pæntrɪ/ *n* Speisekammer *f*

pants /pænts/ *npl* Unterhose *f*; (*woman's*) Schlüpfer *m*; (*trousers*) Hose *f*

'**pantyhose** *n* (*Amer*) Strumpfhose *f*

paper /'peɪpə(r)/ *n* Papier *nt*; (*newspaper*) Zeitung *f*; (*exam* ~) Testbogen *m*; (*exam*) Klausur *f*; (*treatise*) Referat *nt*; ~**s** *pl* (*documents*) Unterlagen *pl*; (*for identification*) [Ausweis]papiere *pl* ● *vt* tapezieren

paper: ~**back** *n* Taschenbuch *nt*. ~**-clip** *n* Büroklammer *f*. ~**weight** *n* Briefbeschwerer *m*. ~**work** *n* Schreibarbeit *f*

par /pɑ:(r)/ *n* (*Golf*) Par *nt*; **on a** ~ gleichwertig (**with** *dat*)

parable /'pærəbl/ *n* Gleichnis *nt*

parachut|e /'pærəʃu:t/ *n* Fallschirm *m* ● *vi* [mit dem Fallschirm] abspringen. ~**ist** *n* Fallschirmspringer *m*

parade /pə'reɪd/ *n* Parade *f*; (*procession*) Festzug *m* ● *vt* (*show off*) zur Schau stellen

paradise /'pærədaɪs/ *n* Paradies *nt*

paradox /'pærədɒks/ *n* Paradox *nt*. **~ical** /-'dɒksɪkl/ paradox

paraffin /'pærəfɪn/ *n* Paraffin *nt*

paragraph /'pærəgrɑ:f/ *n* Absatz *m*

parallel /'pærəlel/ *a* & *adv* parallel ● *n* (*Geog*) Breitenkreis *m*; (*fig*) Parallele *f*

paralyse /'pærəlaɪz/ *vt* lähmen; (*fig*) lahm legen

paralysis /pə'ræləsɪs/ *n* (*pl* **-ses** /-si:z/) Lähmung *f*

paranoid /'pærənɔɪd/ *a* [krankhaft] misstrauisch

parapet /'pærəpɪt/ *n* Brüstung *f*

paraphernalia /pærəfə'neɪlɪə/ *n* Kram *m*

parasite /'pærəsaɪt/ *n* Parasit *m*, Schmarotzer *m*

paratrooper /'pærətru:pə(r)/ *n* Fallschirmjäger *m*

parcel /'pɑ:sl/ *n* Paket *nt*

parch /pɑ:tʃ/ *vt* austrocknen; **be ~ed** <*person:*> einen furchtbaren Durst haben

parchment /'pɑ:tʃmənt/ *n* Pergament *nt*

pardon /'pɑ:dn/ *n* Verzeihung *f*; (*Jur*) Begnadigung *f*; **~?** [!] bitte? **I beg your ~** wie bitte? (*sorry*) Verzeihung! ● *vt* verzeihen; (*Jur*) begnadigen

parent /'peərənt/ *n* Elternteil *m*; **~s** *pl* Eltern *pl*. **~al** /pə'rentl/ *a* elterlich

parenthesis /pə'renθəsɪs/ *n* (*pl* **-ses** /-si:z/) Klammer *f*

parish /'pærɪʃ/ *n* Gemeinde *f*. **~ioner** /pə'rɪʃənə(r)/ *n* Gemeindemitglied *nt*

park /pɑ:k/ *n* Park *m* ● *vt/i* parken

parking /'pɑ:kɪŋ/ *n* Parken *nt*; **'no ~'** 'Parken verboten'. **~-lot** *n* (*Amer*) Parkplatz *m*. **~-meter** *n* Parkuhr *f*. **~ space** *n* Parkplatz *m*

parliament /'pɑ:ləmənt/ *n* Parlament *nt*. **~ary** /-'mentərɪ/ *a* parlamentarisch

parochial /pə'rəʊkɪəl/ *a* Gemeinde-; (*fig*) beschränkt

parody /'pærədɪ/ *n* Parodie *f* ● *vt* (*pt/pp* **-ied**) parodieren

parole /pə'rəʊl/ *n* **on ~** auf Bewährung

parquet /'pɑ:keɪ/ *n* **~ floor** Parkett *nt*

parrot /'pærət/ *n* Papagei *m*

parsley /'pɑ:slɪ/ *n* Petersilie *f*

parsnip /'pɑ:snɪp/ *n* Pastinake *f*

parson /'pɑ:sn/ *n* Pfarrer *m*

part /pɑ:t/ *n* Teil *m*; (*Techn*) Teil *nt*; (*area*) Gegend *f*; (*Theat*) Rolle *f*; (*Mus*) Part *m*; **spare ~** Ersatzteil *nt*; **for my ~** meinerseits; **on the ~ of** vonseiten (+ *gen*); **take s.o.'s ~** für jdn Partei ergreifen; **take ~ in** teilnehmen an (+ *dat*) ● *adv* teils ● *vt* trennen; scheiteln <*hair*> ● *vi* <*people:*> sich trennen; **~ with** sich trennen von

partial /'pɑ:ʃl/ *a* Teil-; **be ~ to** mögen. **-ly** *adv* teilweise

particip|ant /pɑ:'tɪsɪpənt/ *n* Teilnehmer(in) *m(f)*. **~ate** /-peɪt/ *vi* teilnehmen (**in** an + *dat*). **~ation** /-'peɪʃn/ *n* Teilnahme *f*

particle /'pɑ:tɪkl/ *n* Körnchen *nt*; (*Phys*) Partikel *nt*; (*Gram*) Partikel *f*

particular /pə'tɪkjʊlə(r)/ *a* besondere(r,s); (*precise*) genau; (*fastidious*) penibel; **in ~** besonders. **~ly** *adv* besonders. **~s** *npl* nähere Angaben *pl*

parting /'pɑ:tɪŋ/ *n* Abschied *m*; (*in hair*) Scheitel *m*

partition /pɑːˈtɪʃn/ *n* Trennwand *f*; (*Pol*) Teilung *f* ● *vt* teilen

partly /ˈpɑːtlɪ/ *adv* teilweise

partner /ˈpɑːtnə(r)/ *n* Partner(in) *m(f)*; (*Comm*) Teilhaber *m*. **~ship** *n* Partnerschaft *f*; (*Comm*) Teilhaberschaft *f*

partridge /ˈpɑːtrɪdʒ/ *n* Rebhuhn *nt*

part-ˈtime *a & adv* Teilzeit-; **be** *or* **work ~** Teilzeitarbeit machen

party /ˈpɑːtɪ/ *n* Party *f*, Fest *nt*; (*group*) Gruppe *f*; (*Pol, Jur*) Partei *f*

pass /pɑːs/ *n* Ausweis *m*; (*Geog, Sport*) Pass *m*; (*Sch*) ≈ ausreichend; **get a ~** bestehen ● *vt* vorbeigehen/-fahren an (+ *dat*); (*overtake*) überholen; (*hand*) reichen; (*Sport*) abgeben, abspielen; (*approve*) annehmen; (*exceed*) übersteigen; bestehen <*exam*>; machen <*remark*>; fällen <*judgement*>; (*Jur*) verhängen <*sentence*>; **~ the time** sich (*dat*) die Zeit vertreiben; **~ one's hand over sth** mit der Hand über etw (*acc*) fahren ● *vi* vorbeigehen/-fahren; (*get by*) vorbeikommen; (*overtake*) überholen; <*time:*> vergehen; (*in exam*) bestehen; **~ away** *vi* sterben. **~ down** *vt* herunterreichen; (*fig*) weitergeben. **~ out** *vi* ohnmächtig werden. **~ round** *vt* herumreichen. **~ up** *vt* heraufreichen; (🄸 *miss*) vorübergehen lassen

passable /ˈpɑːsəbl/ *a* <*road*> befahrbar; (*satisfactory*) passabel

passage /ˈpæsɪdʒ/ *n* Durchgang *m*; (*corridor*) Gang *m*; (*voyage*) Überfahrt *f*; (*in book*) Passage *f*

passenger /ˈpæsɪndʒə(r)/ *n* Fahrgast *m*; (*Naut, Aviat*) Passagier *m*; (*in car*) Mitfahrer *m*. **~ seat** *n* Beifahrersitz *m*

passer-by /pɑːsəˈbaɪ/ *n* (*pl* **-s-by**) Passant(in) *m(f)*

passion /ˈpæʃn/ *n* Leidenschaft *f*. **~ate** /-ət/ *a*, **-ly** *adv* leidenschaftlich

passive /ˈpæsɪv/ *a* passiv ● *n* Passiv *nt*

pass: ~port *n* [Reise]pass *m*. **~word** *n* Kennwort *nt*; (*Mil*) Losung *f*

past /pɑːst/ *a* vergangene(r,s); (*former*) ehemalig; **that's all ~** das ist jetzt vorbei ● *n* Vergangenheit *f* ● *prep* an (+ *dat*) ... vorbei; (*after*) nach; **at ten ~ two** um zehn nach zwei ● *adv* vorbei; **go ~** vorbeigehen

pasta /ˈpæstə/ *n* Nudeln *pl*

paste /peɪst/ *n* Brei *m*; (*adhesive*) Kleister *m*; (*jewellery*) Strass *m* ● *vt* kleistern

pastel /ˈpæstl/ *n* Pastellfarbe *f*; (*drawing*) Pastell *nt* ● *attrib* Pastell-

pastime /ˈpɑːstaɪm/ *n* Zeitvertreib *m*

pastry /ˈpeɪstrɪ/ *n* Teig *m*; **cakes and ~ies** Kuchen und Gebäck

pasture /ˈpɑːstʃə(r)/ *n* Weide *f*

pasty /ˈpæstɪ/ *n* Pastete *f*

pat /pæt/ *n* Klaps *m*; (*of butter*) Stückchen *nt* ● *vt* (*pt/pp* **patted**) tätscheln; **~ s.o. on the back** jdm auf die Schulter klopfen

patch /pætʃ/ *n* Flicken *m*; (*spot*) Fleck *m*; **not a ~ on** 🄸 gar nicht zu vergleichen mit ● *vt* flicken. **~ up** *vt* [zusammen]flicken; beilegen <*quarrel*>

patchy /ˈpætʃɪ/ *a* ungleichmäßig

patent /ˈpeɪtnt/ *n* Patent *nt* ● *vt* patentieren. **~ leather** *n* Lackleder *nt*

paternal /pəˈtɜːnl/ *a* väterlich

path /pɑːθ/ *n* (*pl* **-s** /pɑːðz/) [Fuß]weg *m*, Pfad *m*; (*orbit, track*) Bahn *f*; (*fig*) Weg *m*

pathetic /pə'θetɪk/ *a* Mitleid erregend; <*attempt*> erbärmlich
patience /'peɪʃns/ *n* Geduld *f*; (*game*) Patience *f*
patient /'peɪʃnt/ *a*, **-ly** *adv* geduldig ● *n* Patient(in) *m(f)*
patio /'pætɪəʊ/ *n* Terrasse *f*
patriot /'pætrɪət/ *n* Patriot(in) *m(f)*. **~ic** /-'ɒtɪk/ *a* patriotisch. **~ism** *n* Patriotismus *m*
patrol /pə'trəʊl/ *n* Patrouille *f* ● *vt/i* patrouillieren [in (+ *dat*)]; <*police:*> auf Streife gehen/fahren [in (+ *dat*)]. **~ car** *n* Streifenwagen *m*
patron /'peɪtrən/ *n* Gönner *m*; (*of charity*) Schirmherr *m*; (*of the arts*) Mäzen *m*; (*customer*) Kunde *m*/Kundin *f*; (*Theat*) Besucher *m*. **~age** /'pætrənɪdʒ/ *n* Schirmherrschaft *f*
patroniz|e /'pætrənaɪz/ *vt* (*fig*) herablassend behandeln. **~ing** *a*, **-ly** *adv* gönnerhaft
patter *n* (*speech*) Gerede *nt*
pattern /'pætn/ *n* Muster *nt*
paunch /pɔ:ntʃ/ *n* [Schmer]bauch *m*
pause /pɔ:z/ *n* Pause *f* ● *vi* innehalten
pave /peɪv/ *vt* pflastern; **~ the way** den Weg bereiten (**for** *dat*). **~ment** *n* Bürgersteig *m*
paw /pɔ:/ *n* Pfote *f*; (*of large animal*) Pranke *f*, Tatze *f*
pawn¹ /pɔ:n/ *n* (*Chess*) Bauer *m*; (*fig*) Schachfigur *f*
pawn² *vt* verpfänden. **~ broker** *n* Pfandleiher *m*
pay /peɪ/ *n* Lohn *m*; (*salary*) Gehalt *nt*; **be in the ~ of** bezahlt werden von ● *v* (*pt/pp* **paid**) ● *vt* bezahlen; zahlen <*money*>; **~ s.o. a visit** jdm einen Besuch abstatten; **~ s.o. a compliment** jdm ein Kompliment machen ● *vi* zahlen; (*be profitable*) sich bezahlt machen; (*fig*) sich lohnen; **~ for sth** etw bezahlen. **~ back** *vt* zurückzahlen. **~ in** *vt* einzahlen. **~ off** *vt* abzahlen <*debt*> ● *vi* (*fig*) sich auszahlen
payable /'peɪəbl/ *a* zahlbar; **make ~ to** ausstellen auf (+ *acc*)
payment /'peɪmənt/ *n* Bezahlung *f*; (*amount*) Zahlung *f*
pea /pi:/ *n* Erbse *f*
peace /pi:s/ *n* Frieden *m*; **for my ~ of mind** zu meiner eigenen Beruhigung
peace|ful *a*, **-ly** *adv* friedlich. **~maker** *n* Friedensstifter *m*
peach /pi:tʃ/ *n* Pfirsich *m*
peacock /'pi:kɒk/ *n* Pfau *m*
peak /pi:k/ *n* Gipfel *m*; (*fig*) Höhepunkt *m*. **~ed 'cap** *n* Schirmmütze *f*. **~ hours** *npl* Hauptbelastungszeit *f*; (*for traffic*) Hauptverkehrszeit *f*
peal /pi:l/ *n* (*of bells*) Glockengeläut *nt*; **~s of laughter** schallendes Gelächter *nt*
'peanut *n* Erdnuss *f*
pear /peə(r)/ *n* Birne *f*
pearl /pɜ:l/ *n* Perle *f*
peasant /'peznt/ *n* Bauer *m*
peat /pi:t/ *n* Torf *m*
pebble /'pebl/ *n* Kieselstein *m*
peck /pek/ *n* Schnabelhieb *m*; (*kiss*) flüchtiger Kuss *m* ● *vt/i* picken/(*nip*) hacken (**at** nach)
peculiar /pɪ'kju:lɪə(r)/ *a* eigenartig, seltsam; **~ to** eigentümlich (+ *dat*). **~ity** /-'ærətɪ/ *n* Eigenart *f*
pedal /'pedl/ *n* Pedal *nt* ● *vt* fahren <*bicycle*> ● *vi* treten
pedantic /pɪ'dæntɪk/ *a*, **-ally** *adv* pedantisch
pedestal /'pedɪstl/ *n* Sockel *m*
pedestrian /pɪ'destrɪən/ *n* Fußgänger(in) *m(f)* ● *a* (*fig*) prosaisch. **~ 'crossing** *n* Fußgängerüberweg *m*. **~ 'precinct** *n* Fußgängerzone *f*

pedigree /ˈpedɪgriː/ *n* Stammbaum *m* ● *attrib* <*animal*> Rasse-
pedlar /ˈpedlə(r)/ *n* Hausierer *m*
peek /piːk/ *vi* [!] gucken
peel /piːl/ *n* Schale *f* ● *vt* schälen; ● *vi* <*skin:*> sich schälen; <*paint:*> abblättern. **~ings** *npl* Schalen *pl*
peep /piːp/ *n* kurzer Blick *m* ● *vi* gucken. **~-hole** *n* Guckloch *nt*
peer¹ /pɪə(r)/ *vi* **~ at** forschend ansehen
peer² *n* Peer *m*; **his ~s** *pl* seinesgleichen
peg /peg/ *n* (*hook*) Haken *m*; (*for tent*) Pflock *m*, Hering *m*; (*for clothes*) [Wäsche]klammer *f*; **off the ~** [!] von der Stange
pejorative /pɪˈdʒɒrətɪv/ *a*, **-ly** *adv* abwertend
pelican /ˈpelɪkən/ *n* Pelikan *m*
pellet /ˈpelɪt/ *n* Kügelchen *nt*
pelt¹ /pelt/ *n* (*skin*) Pelz *m*, Fell *nt*
pelt² *vt* bewerfen ● *vi* **~ [down]** <*rain:*> [hernieder]prasseln
pelvis /ˈpelvɪs/ *n* (*Anat*) Becken *nt*
pen¹ /pen/ *n* (*for animals*) Hürde *f*
pen² *n* Federhalter *m*; (*ballpoint*) Kugelschreiber *m*
penal /ˈpiːnl/ *a* Straf-. **~ize** *vt* bestrafen; (*fig*) benachteiligen
penalty /ˈpenltɪ/ *n* Strafe *f*; (*fine*) Geldstrafe *f*; (*Sport*) Strafstoß *m*; (*Football*) Elfmeter *m*
penance /ˈpenəns/ *n* Buße *f*
pence /pens/ *see* **penny**
pencil /ˈpensɪl/ *n* Bleistift *m* ● *vt* (*pt/pp* **pencilled**) mit Bleistift schreiben. **~-sharpener** *n* Bleistiftspitzer *m*
pendulum /ˈpendjʊləm/ *n* Pendel *nt*
penetrat|e /ˈpenɪtreɪt/ *vt* durchdringen; **~e into** eindringen in (+ *acc*). **~ing** *a* durchdringend. **~ion** /-ˈtreɪʃn/ *n* Durchdringen *nt*
ˈpenfriend *n* Brieffreund(in) *m(f)*
penguin /ˈpeŋgwɪn/ *n* Pinguin *m*
penicillin /penɪˈsɪlɪn/ *n* Penizillin *nt*
peninsula /pəˈnɪnsʊlə/ *n* Halbinsel *f*
penis /ˈpiːnɪs/ *n* Penis *m*
penitentiary /penɪˈtenʃərɪ/ *n* (*Amer*) Gefängnis *nt*
pen: ~knife *n* Taschenmesser *nt*. **~-name** *n* Pseudonym *nt*
penniless /ˈpenɪlɪs/ *a* mittellos
penny /ˈpenɪ/ *n* (*pl* **pence**; *single coins* **pennies**) Penny *m*; (*Amer*) Centstück *nt*; **the ~'s dropped** [!] der Groschen ist gefallen
pension /ˈpenʃn/ *n* Rente *f*; (*of civil servant*) Pension *f*. **~er** *n* Rentner(in) *m(f)*; Pensionär(in) *m(f)*
pensive /ˈpensɪv/ *a* nachdenklich
pent-up /ˈpentʌp/ *a* angestaut
penultimate /peˈnʌltɪmət/ *a* vorletzte(r,s)
people /ˈpiːpl/ *npl* Leute *pl*, Menschen *pl*; (*citizens*) Bevölkerung *f*; **the ~** das Volk; **English ~** die Engländer; **~ say** man sagt; **for four ~** für vier Personen ● *vt* bevölkern
pepper /ˈpepə(r)/ *n* Pfeffer *m*; (*vegetable*) Paprika *m*
pepper: ~mint *n* Pfefferminz *nt*; (*Bot*) Pfefferminze *f*. **~pot** *n* Pfefferstreuer *m*
per /pɜː(r)/ *prep* pro; **~ cent** Prozent *nt*
percentage /pəˈsentɪdʒ/ *n* Prozentsatz *m*; (*part*) Teil *m*
perceptible /pəˈseptəbl/ *a* wahrnehmbar
percept|ion /pəˈsepʃn/ *n* Wahrnehmung *f*. **~ive** /-tɪv/ *a* feinsinnig

perch¹ /pɜ:tʃ/ *n* Stange *f* ● *vi* <*bird:*> sich niederlassen

perch² *n inv* (*fish*) Barsch *m*

percussion /pəˈkʌʃn/ *n* Schlagzeug *nt*. **~ instrument** *n* Schlaginstrument *nt*

perennial /pəˈrenɪəl/ *a* <*problem*> immer wiederkehrend ● *n* (*Bot*) mehrjährige Pflanze *f*

perfect¹ /ˈpɜ:fɪkt/ *a* perfekt, vollkommen; ([!] *utter*) völlig ● *n* (*Gram*) Perfekt *nt*

perfect² /pəˈfekt/ *vt* vervollkommnen. **~ion** /-ekʃn/ *n* Vollkommenheit *f*; **to ~ion** perfekt

perfectly /ˈpɜ:fɪktlɪ/ *adv* perfekt; (*completely*) vollkommen, völlig

perforated /ˈpɜ:fəreɪtɪd/ *a* perforiert

perform /pəˈfɔ:m/ *vt* ausführen; erfüllen <*duty*>; (*Theat*) aufführen <*play*>; spielen <*role*> ● *vi* (*Theat*) auftreten; (*Techn*) laufen. **~ance** *n* Aufführung *f*; (*at theatre, cinema*) Vorstellung *f*; (*Techn, Sport*) Leistung *f*. **~er** *n* Künstler(in) *m(f)*

perfume /ˈpɜ:fju:m/ *n* Parfüm *nt*; (*smell*) Duft *m*

perhaps /pəˈhæps/ *adv* vielleicht

perilous /ˈperələs/ *a* gefährlich

perimeter /pəˈrɪmɪtə(r)/ *n* [äußere] Grenze *f*; (*Geom*) Umfang *m*

period /ˈpɪərɪəd/ *n* Periode *f*; (*Sch*) Stunde *f*; (*full stop*) Punkt *m* ● *attrib* <*costume*> zeitgenössisch; <*furniture*> antik. **~ic** /-ˈɒdɪk/ *a*, **-ally** *adv* periodisch. **~ical** /-ˈɒdɪkl/ *n* Zeitschrift *f*

peripher|al /pəˈrɪfərl/ *a* nebensächlich. **~y** *n* Peripherie *f*

perish /ˈperɪʃ/ *vi* <*rubber:*> verrotten; <*food:*> verderben; (*liter: die*) ums Leben kommen. **~able** /-əbl/ *a* leicht verderblich. **~ing** *a* ([!] *cold*) eiskalt

perjur|e /ˈpɜ:dʒə(r)/ *vt* **~e oneself** einen Meineid leisten. **~y** *n* Meineid *m*

perk¹ /pɜ:k/ *n* [!] [Sonder]vergünstigung *f*

perk² *vi* **~ up** munter werden

perm /pɜ:m/ *n* Dauerwelle *f* ● *vt* **~ s.o.'s hair** jdm eine Dauerwelle machen

permanent /ˈpɜ:mənənt/ *a* ständig; <*job, address*> fest. **~ly** *adv* ständig; <*work, live*> dauernd, permanent; <*employed*> fest

permissible /pəˈmɪsəbl/ *a* erlaubt

permission /pəˈmɪʃn/ *n* Erlaubnis *f*

permit¹ /pəˈmɪt/ *vt* (*pt/pp* **-mitted**) erlauben (**s.o.** jdm)

permit² /ˈpɜ:mɪt/ *n* Genehmigung *f*

perpendicular /pɜ:pənˈdɪkjʊlə(r)/ *a* senkrecht ● *n* Senkrechte *f*

perpetual /pəˈpetjʊəl/ *a*, **-ly** *adv* ständig, dauernd

perpetuate /pəˈpetjʊeɪt/ *vt* bewahren; verewigen <*error*>

perplex /pəˈpleks/ *vt* verblüffen. **~ed** *a* verblüfft

persecut|e /ˈpɜ:sɪkju:t/ *vt* verfolgen. **~ion** /-ˈkju:ʃn/ *n* Verfolgung *f*

perseverance /pɜ:sɪˈvɪərəns/ *n* Ausdauer *f*

persevere /pɜ:sɪˈvɪə(r)/ *vi* beharrlich weitermachen

Persia /ˈpɜ:ʃə/ *n* Persien *nt*

Persian /ˈpɜ:ʃn/ *a* persisch; <*cat, carpet*> Perser-

persist /pəˈsɪst/ *vi* beharrlich weitermachen; (*continue*) anhalten; <*view:*> weiter bestehen; **~ in doing sth** dabei bleiben, etw zu tun. **~ence** *n* Beharrlichkeit *f*. **~ent** *a*, **-ly** *adv* beharrlich; (*continuous*) anhaltend

person /ˈpɜːsn/ *n* Person *f*; **in ~** persönlich

personal /ˈpɜːsənl/ *a*, **-ly** *adv* persönlich. **~ 'hygiene** *n* Körperpflege *f*

personality /pɜːsəˈnælətɪ/ *n* Persönlichkeit *f*

personify /pəˈsɒnɪfaɪ/ *vt* (*pt/pp* **-ied**) personifizieren, verkörpern

personnel /pɜːsəˈnel/ *n* Personal *nt*

perspective /pəˈspektɪv/ *n* Perspektive *f*

persp|iration /pɜːspɪˈreɪʃn/ *n* Schweiß *m*. **~ire** /-ˈspaɪə(r)/ *vi* schwitzen

persua|de /pəˈsweɪd/ *vt* überreden; (*convince*) überzeugen. **~sion** /-eɪʒn/ *n* Überredung *f*; (*powers of ~sion*) Überredungskunst *f*

persuasive /pəˈsweɪsɪv/ *a*, **-ly** *adv* beredsam; (*convincing*) überzeugend

pertinent /ˈpɜːtɪnənt/ *a* relevant (**to** für)

perturb /pəˈtɜːb/ *vt* beunruhigen

peruse /pəˈruːz/ *vt* lesen

pervers|e /pəˈvɜːs/ *a* eigensinnig. **~ion** /-ɜːʃn/ *n* Perversion *f*

pervert¹ /pəˈvɜːt/ *vt* verdrehen; verführen <*person*>

pervert² /ˈpɜːvɜːt/ *n* Perverse(r) *m*

pessimis|m /ˈpesɪmɪzm/ *n* Pessimismus *m*. **~t** /-mɪst/ *n* Pessimist *m*. **~tic** /-ˈmɪstɪk/ *a*, **-ally** *adv* pessimistisch

pest /pest/ *n* Schädling *m*; (**[!]** *person*) Nervensäge *f*

pester /ˈpestə(r)/ *vt* belästigen

pesticide /ˈpestɪsaɪd/ *n* Schädlingsbekämpfungsmittel *nt*

pet /pet/ *n* Haustier *nt*; (*favourite*) Liebling *m* ● *vt* (*pt/pp* **petted**) liebkosen

petal /ˈpetl/ *n* Blütenblatt *nt*

peter /ˈpiːtə(r)/ *vi* **~ out** allmählich aufhören

petition /pəˈtɪʃn/ *n* Bittschrift *f*

pet 'name *n* Kosename *m*

petrified /ˈpetrɪfaɪd/ *a* vor Angst wie versteinert

petrol /ˈpetrl/ *n* Benzin *nt*

petroleum /pɪˈtrəʊlɪəm/ *n* Petroleum *nt*

petrol: ~-pump *n* Zapfsäule *f*. **~ station** *n* Tankstelle *f*. **~ tank** *n* Benzintank *m*

petticoat /ˈpetɪkəʊt/ *n* Unterrock *m*

petty /ˈpetɪ/ *a* (**-ier, -iest**) kleinlich. **~ 'cash** *n* Portokasse *f*

petulant /ˈpetjʊlənt/ *a* gekränkt

pew /pjuː/ *n* [Kirchen]bank *f*

pharmaceutical /fɑːməˈsjuːtɪkl/ *a* pharmazeutisch

pharmac|ist /ˈfɑːməsɪst/ *n* Apotheker(in) *m(f)*. **~y** *n* Pharmazie *f*; (*shop*) Apotheke *f*

phase /feɪz/ *n* Phase *f* ● *vt* **~ in/out** allmählich einführen/abbauen

Ph.D. (*abbr of* **Doctor of Philosophy**) Dr. phil.

pheasant /ˈfeznt/ *n* Fasan *m*

phenomen|al /fɪˈnɒmɪnl/ *a* phänomenal. **~on** *n* (*pl* **-na**) Phänomen *nt*

philharmonic /fɪlɑːˈmɒnɪk/ *n* (*orchestra*) Philharmoniker *pl*

Philippines /ˈfɪlɪpiːnz/ *npl* Philippinen *pl*

philistine /ˈfɪlɪstaɪn/ *n* Banause *m*

philosoph|er /fɪˈlɒsəfə(r)/ *n* Philosoph *m*. **~ical** /fɪləˈsɒfɪkl/ *a*, **-ly** *adv* philosophisch. **~y** *n* Philosophie *f*

phlegmatic /fleg'mætɪk/ *a* phlegmatisch

phobia /'fəʊbɪə/ *n* Phobie *f*

phone /fəʊn/ *n* Telefon *nt*; **be on the ~** Telefon haben; (*be phoning*) telefonieren ● *vt* anrufen ● *vi* telefonieren. **~ back** *vt/i* zurückrufen. **~ book** *n* Telefonbuch *nt*. **~ box** *n* Telefonzelle *f*. **~ card** *n* Telefonkarte *f*. **~-in** *n* (*Radio*) Hörersendung *f*. **~ number** *n* Telefonnummer *f*

phonetic /fə'netɪk/ *a* phonetisch. **~s** *n* Phonetik *f*

phoney /'fəʊnɪ/ *a* (**-ier, -iest**) falsch; (*forged*) gefälscht

photo /'fəʊtəʊ/ *n* Foto *nt*, Aufnahme *f*. **~copier** *n* Fotokopiergerät *nt*. **~copy** *n* Fotokopie *f* ● *vt* fotokopieren

photogenic /fəʊtəʊ'dʒenɪk/ *a* fotogen

photograph /'fəʊtəgrɑːf/ *n* Fotografie *f*, Aufnahme *f* ● *vt* fotografieren

photograph|er /fə'tɒgrəfə(r)/ *n* Fotograf(in) *m(f)*. **~ic** /fəʊtə'græfɪk/ *a*, **-ally** *adv* fotografisch. **~y** *n* Fotografie *f*

phrase /freɪz/ *n* Redensart *f* ● *vt* formulieren. **~-book** *n* Sprachführer *m*

physical /'fɪzɪkl/ *a*, **-ly** *adv* körperlich

physician /fɪ'zɪʃn/ *n* Arzt *m*/ Ärztin *f*

physic|ist /'fɪzɪsɪst/ *n* Physiker(in) *m(f)*. **~s** *n* Physik *f*

physio'therap|ist /fɪzɪəʊ-/ *n* Physiotherapeut(in) *m(f)*. **~y** *n* Physiotherapie *f*

physique /fɪ'ziːk/ *n* Körperbau *m*

pianist /'pɪənɪst/ *n* Klavierspieler(in) *m(f)*; (*professional*) Pianist(in) *m(f)*

piano /pɪ'ænəʊ/ *n* Klavier *nt*

pick[1] /pɪk/ *n* Spitzhacke *f*

pick[2] *n* Auslese *f*; **take one's ~** sich (*dat*) aussuchen ● *vt/i* (*pluck*) pflücken; (*select*) wählen, sich (*dat*) aussuchen; **~ and choose** wählerisch sein; **~ a quarrel** einen Streit anfangen; **~ holes in** [!] kritisieren; **~ at one's food** im Essen herumstochern. **~ on** *vt* wählen; ([!] *find fault with*) herumhacken auf (+ *dat*). **~ up** *vt* in die Hand nehmen; (*off the ground*) aufheben; hochnehmen <*baby*>; (*learn*) lernen; (*acquire*) erwerben; (*buy*) kaufen; (*Teleph*) abnehmen <*receiver*>; auffangen <*signal*>; (*collect*) abholen; aufnehmen <*passengers*>; <*police:*> aufgreifen <*criminal*>; sich holen <*illness*>; [!] aufgabeln <*girl*>; **~ oneself up** aufstehen ● *vi* (*improve*) sich bessern

'pickaxe *n* Spitzhacke *f*

picket /'pɪkɪt/ *n* Streikposten *m*

pickle /'pɪkl/ *n* (*Amer: gherkin*) Essiggurke *f*; **~s** *pl* [Mixed] Pickles *pl* ● *vt* einlegen

pick: ~pocket *n* Taschendieb *m*. **~-up** *n* (*truck*) Lieferwagen *m*

picnic /'pɪknɪk/ *n* Picknick *nt* ● *vi* (*pt/pp* **-nicked**) picknicken

picture /'pɪktʃə(r)/ *n* Bild *nt*; (*film*) Film *m*; **as pretty as a ~** bildhübsch; **put s.o. in the ~** (*fig*) jdn ins Bild setzen ● *vt* (*imagine*) sich (*dat*) vorstellen

picturesque /pɪktʃə'resk/ *a* malerisch

pie /paɪ/ *n* Pastete *f*; (*fruit*) Kuchen *m*

piece /piːs/ *n* Stück *nt*; (*of set*) Teil *nt*; (*in game*) Stein *m*; (*Journ*) Artikel *m*; **a ~ of bread/ paper** ein Stück Brot/Papier; **a ~ of news/advice** eine Nachricht/ ein Rat; **take to ~s** auseinander nehmen ● *vt* **~ together** zusammensetzen; (*fig*) zusammenstückeln. **~meal** *adv* stückweise

pier /pɪə(r)/ *n* Pier *m*; (*pillar*) Pfeiler *m*

pierc|e /pɪəs/ *vt* durchstechen. **~ing** *a* durchdringend

pig /pɪg/ *n* Schwein *nt*

pigeon /ˈpɪdʒɪn/ *n* Taube *f*. **~-hole** *n* Fach *nt*

piggy|back /ˈpɪgɪbæk/ *n* **give s.o. a ~back** jdn huckepack tragen. **~ bank** *n* Sparschwein *nt*

pig'headed *a* 🄵 starrköpfig

pigment /ˈpɪgmənt/ *n* Pigment *nt*

pig: ~skin *n* Schweinsleder *nt*. **~sty** *n* Schweinestall *m*. **~tail** *n* 🄵 Zopf *m*

pilchard /ˈpɪltʃəd/ *n* Sardine *f*

pile¹ /paɪl/ *n* (*of fabric*) Flor *m*

pile² *n* Haufen *m* ● *vt* **~ sth on to sth** etw auf etw (*acc*) häufen. **~ up** *vt* häufen ● *vi* sich häufen

piles /paɪlz/ *npl* Hämorrhoiden *pl*

'pile-up *n* Massenkarambolage *f*

pilgrim /ˈpɪlgrɪm/ *n* Pilger(in) *m(f)*. **~age** /-ɪdʒ/ *n* Pilgerfahrt *f*, Wallfahrt *f*

pill /pɪl/ *n* Pille *f*

pillar /ˈpɪlə(r)/ *n* Säule *f*. **~-box** *n* Briefkasten *m*

pillow /ˈpɪləʊ/ *n* Kopfkissen *nt*. **~case** *n* Kopfkissenbezug *m*

pilot /ˈpaɪlət/ *n* Pilot *m*; (*Naut*) Lotse *m* ● *vt* fliegen <*plane*>; lotsen <*ship*>. **~-light** *n* Zündflamme *f*

pimple /ˈpɪmpl/ *n* Pickel *m*

pin /pɪn/ *n* Stecknadel *f*; (*Techn*) Bolzen *m*, Stift *m*; (*Med*) Nagel *m*; **I have ~s and needles in my leg** 🄵 mein Bein ist eingeschlafen ● *vt* (*pt/pp* **pinned**) anstecken (**to/on** an + *acc*); (*sewing*) stecken; (*hold down*) festhalten

pinafore /ˈpɪnəfɔ:(r)/ *n* Schürze *f*. **~ dress** *n* Kleiderrock *m*

pincers /ˈpɪnsəz/ *npl* Kneifzange *f*; (*Zool*) Scheren *pl*

pinch /pɪntʃ/ *n* Kniff *m*; (*of salt*) Prise *f*; **at a ~** 🄵 zur Not ● *vt* kneifen, zwicken; (*fam; steal*) klauen; **~ one's finger** sich (*dat*) den Finger klemmen ● *vi* <*shoe:*> drücken

pine¹ /paɪn/ *n* (*tree*) Kiefer *f*

pine² *vi* **~ for** sich sehnen nach

pineapple /ˈpaɪn-/ *n* Ananas *f*

'ping-pong *n* Tischtennis *nt*

pink /pɪŋk/ *a* rosa

pinnacle /ˈpɪnəkl/ *n* Gipfel *m*; (*on roof*) Turmspitze *f*

pin: ~point *vt* genau festlegen. **~stripe** *n* Nadelstreifen *m*

pint /paɪnt/ *n* Pint *nt* (*0,57 l, Amer: 0,47 l*)

pioneer /paɪəˈnɪə(r)/ *n* Pionier *m* ● *vt* bahnbrechende Arbeit leisten für

pious /ˈpaɪəs/ *a*, **-ly** *adv* fromm

pip¹ /pɪp/ *n* (*seed*) Kern *m*

pip² *n* (*sound*) Tonsignal *nt*

pipe /paɪp/ *n* Pfeife *f*; (*for water, gas*) Rohr *nt* ● *vt* in Rohren leiten; (*Culin*) spritzen

pipe: ~-dream *n* Luftschloss *nt*. **~line** *n* Pipeline *f*; **in the ~line** 🄵 in Vorbereitung

piping /ˈpaɪpɪŋ/ *a* **~ hot** kochend heiß

pirate /ˈpaɪərət/ *n* Pirat *m*

piss /pɪs/ *vi* 🅇 pissen

pistol /ˈpɪstl/ *n* Pistole *f*

piston /ˈpɪstən/ *n* (*Techn*) Kolben *m*

pit /pɪt/ *n* Grube *f*; (*for orchestra*) Orchestergraben *m*; (*for audience*) Parkett *nt*; (*Motor racing*) Box *f*

pitch¹ /pɪtʃ/ *n* (*steepness*) Schräge *f*; (*of voice*) Stimmlage *f*; (*of sound*) [Ton]höhe *f*; (*Sport*) Feld *nt*; (*of street trader*)

Standplatz *m*; (*fig: degree*) Grad *m* ● *vt* werfen; aufschlagen <*tent*> ● *vi* fallen

pitch² *n* (*tar*) Pech *nt*. **~-'black** *a* pechschwarz. **~-'dark** *a* stockdunkel

piteous /'pɪtɪəs/ *a* erbärmlich

'pitfall *n* (*fig*) Falle *f*

pith /pɪθ/ *n* (*Bot*) Mark *nt*; (*of orange*) weiße Haut *f*

pithy /'pɪθɪ/ *a* (**-ier, -iest**) (*fig*) prägnant

piti|ful /'pɪtɪfl/ *a* bedauernswert. **~less** *a* mitleidslos

'pit stop *n* Boxenstopp *m*

pittance /'pɪtns/ *n* Hungerlohn *m*

pity /'pɪtɪ/ *n* Mitleid *nt*, Erbarmen *nt*; **[what a] ~!** [wie] schade! **take ~ on** sich erbarmen über (+ *acc*) ● *vt* bemitleiden

pivot /'pɪvət/ *n* Drehzapfen *m* ● *vi* sich drehen (**on** um)

pizza /'pi:tsə/ *n* Pizza *f*

placard /'plækɑ:d/ *n* Plakat *nt*

placate /plə'keɪt/ *vt* beschwichtigen

place /pleɪs/ *n* Platz *m*; (*spot*) Stelle *f*; (*town, village*) Ort *m*; (**[!]** *house*) Haus *nt*; **out of ~** fehl am Platze; **take ~** stattfinden ● *vt* setzen; (*upright*) stellen; (*flat*) legen; (*remember*) unterbringen **[!]**; **~ an order** eine Bestellung aufgeben; **be ~d** (*in race*) sich platzieren. **~-mat** *n* Set *nt*

placid /'plæsɪd/ *a* gelassen

plague /pleɪg/ *n* Pest *f* ● *vt* plagen

plaice /pleɪs/ *n inv* Scholle *f*

plain /pleɪn/ *a* (**-er, -est**) klar; (*simple*) einfach; (*not pretty*) nicht hübsch; (*not patterned*) einfarbig; <*chocolate*> zartbitter; **in ~ clothes** in Zivil ● *adv* (*simply*) einfach ● *n* Ebene *f*. **~ly** *adv* klar, deutlich; (*simply*) einfach; (*obviously*) offensichtlich

plait /plæt/ *n* Zopf *m* ● *vt* flechten

plan /plæn/ *n* Plan *m* ● *vt* (*pt/pp* **planned**) planen; (*intend*) vorhaben

plane¹ /pleɪn/ *n* (*tree*) Platane *f*

plane² *n* Flugzeug *nt*; (*Geom & fig*) Ebene *f*

plane³ *n* (*Techn*) Hobel *m* ● *vt* hobeln

planet /'plænɪt/ *n* Planet *m*

plank /plæŋk/ *n* Brett *nt*; (*thick*) Planke *f*

planning /'plænɪŋ/ *n* Planung *f*

plant /plɑ:nt/ *n* Pflanze *f*; (*Techn*) Anlage *f*; (*factory*) Werk *nt* ● *vt* pflanzen; (*place in position*) setzen; **~ oneself** sich hinstellen. **~ation** /plæn'teɪʃn/ *n* Plantage *f*

plaque /plɑ:k/ *n* [Gedenk]tafel *f*; (*on teeth*) Zahnbelag *m*

plaster /'plɑ:stə(r)/ *n* Verputz *m*; (*sticking ~*) Pflaster *nt*; **~ [of Paris]** Gips *m* ● *vt* verputzen <*wall*>; (*cover*) bedecken mit

plastic /'plæstɪk/ *n* Kunststoff *m*, Plastik *nt* ● *a* Kunststoff-, Plastik-; (*malleable*) formbar, plastisch

plastic 'surgery *n* plastische Chirurgie *f*

plate /pleɪt/ *n* Teller *m*; (*flat sheet*) Platte *f*; (*with name, number*) Schild *nt*; (*gold and silverware*) vergoldete/versilberte Ware *f*; (*in book*) Tafel *f* ● *vt* (*with gold*) vergolden; (*with silver*) versilbern

platform /'plætfɔ:m/ *n* Plattform *f*; (*stage*) Podium *nt*; (*Rail*) Bahnsteig *m*; **~ 5** Gleis 5

platinum /'plætɪnəm/ *n* Platin *nt*

platitude /'plætɪtju:d/ *n* Plattitüde *f*

plausible /'plɔ:zəbl/ *a* plausibel

play /pleɪ/ *n* Spiel *nt*; [Theater]stück *nt*; (*Radio*) Hörspiel *nt*; (*TV*) Fernsehspiel *nt*;

~ on words Wortspiel *nt* ● *vt/i* spielen; ausspielen <*card*>; **~ safe** sichergehen. **~ down** *vt* herunterspielen. **~ up** *vi* [!] Mätzchen machen

play: ~er *n* Spieler(in) *m(f)*. **~ful** *a*, **-ly** *adv* verspielt. **~ground** *n* Spielplatz *m*; (*Sch*) Schulhof *m*. **~group** *n* Kindergarten *m*

playing: ~-card *n* Spielkarte *f*. **~-field** *n* Sportplatz *m*

play: ~mate *n* Spielkamerad *m*. **~thing** *n* Spielzeug *nt*. **~wright** /-raɪt/ *n* Dramatiker *m*

plc *abbr* (**public limited company**) ≈ GmbH

plea /pliː/ *n* Bitte *f*; **make a ~ for** bitten um

plead /pliːd/ *vi* flehen (**for** um); **~ guilty** sich schuldig bekennen; **~ with s.o.** jdn anflehen

pleasant /ˈplezənt/ *a* angenehm; <*person*> nett. **~ly** *adv* angenehm; <*say, smile*> freundlich

pleas|e /pliːz/ *adv* bitte ● *vt* gefallen (+ *dat*); **~e s.o.** jdm eine Freude machen; **~e oneself** tun, was man will. **~ed** *a* erfreut; **be ~ed with/about sth** sich über etw (*acc*) freuen. **~ing** *a* erfreulich

pleasure /ˈpleʒə(r)/ *n* Vergnügen *nt*; (*joy*) Freude *f*; **with ~** gern[e]

pleat /pliːt/ *n* Falte *f* ● *vt* fälteln

pledge /pledʒ/ *n* Versprechen *nt* ● *vt* verpfänden; versprechen

plentiful /ˈplentɪfl/ *a* reichlich

plenty /ˈplentɪ/ *n* eine Menge; (*enough*) reichlich; **~ of money/people** viel Geld/viele Leute

pliable /ˈplaɪəbl/ *a* biegsam

pliers /ˈplaɪəz/ *npl* [Flach]zange *f*

plight /plaɪt/ *n* [Not]lage *f*

plinth /plɪnθ/ *n* Sockel *m*

plod /plɒd/ *vi* (*pt/pp* **plodded**) trotten; (*work*) sich abmühen

plonk /plɒŋk/ *n* [!] billiger Wein *m*

plot /plɒt/ *n* Komplott *nt*; (*of novel*) Handlung *f*; **~ of land** Stück *nt* Land ● *vt* einzeichnen ● *vi* ein Komplott schmieden

plough /plaʊ/ *n* Pflug *m* ● *vt/i* pflügen

ploy /plɔɪ/ *n* [!] Trick *m*

pluck /plʌk/ *n* Mut *m* ● *vt* zupfen; rupfen <*bird*>; pflücken <*flower*>; **~ up courage** Mut fassen

plucky /ˈplʌkɪ/ *a* (**-ier, -iest**) tapfer, mutig

plug /plʌg/ *n* Stöpsel *m*; (*wood*) Zapfen *m*; (*cotton wool*) Bausch *m*; (*Electr*) Stecker *m*; (*Auto*) Zündkerze *f*; ([!] *advertisement*) Schleichwerbung *f* ● *vt* zustopfen; ([!] *advertise*) Schleichwerbung machen für. **~ in** *vt* (*Electr*) einstecken

plum /plʌm/ *n* Pflaume *f*

plumage /ˈpluːmɪdʒ/ *n* Gefieder *nt*

plumb|er /ˈplʌmə(r)/ *n* Klempner *m*. **~ing** *n* Wasserleitungen *pl*

plume /pluːm/ *n* Feder *f*

plump /plʌmp/ *a* (**-er, -est**) mollig, rundlich ● *vt* **~ for** wählen

plunge /plʌndʒ/ *n* Sprung *m*; **take the ~** [!] den Schritt wagen ● *vt/i* tauchen

plural /ˈplʊərl/ *a* pluralisch ● *n* Mehrzahl *f*, Plural *m*

plus /plʌs/ *prep* plus (+ *dat*) ● *a* Plus- ● *n* Pluszeichen *nt*; (*advantage*) Plus *nt*

plush[y] /ˈplʌʃ[ɪ]/ *a* luxuriös

ply /plaɪ/ *vt* (*pt/pp* **plied**) ausüben <*trade*>; **~ s.o. with drink** jdm ein Glas nach dem anderen eingießen. **~wood** *n* Sperrholz *nt*

p.m. *adv* (*abbr of* **post meridiem**) nachmittags

pneumatic /nju:ˈmætɪk/ *a* pneumatisch. ~ **ˈdrill** *n* Presslufthammer *m*

pneumonia /nju:ˈməʊnɪə/ *n* Lungenentzündung *f*

poach /pəʊtʃ/ *vt* (*Culin*) pochieren; (*steal*) wildern. ~**er** *n* Wilddieb *m*

pocket /ˈpɒkɪt/ *n* Tasche *f*; **be out of** ~ [an einem Geschäft] verlieren ● *vt* einstecken. ~**-book** *n* Notizbuch *nt*; (*wallet*) Brieftasche *f*. ~**-money** *n* Taschengeld *nt*

pod /pɒd/ *n* Hülse *f*

poem /ˈpəʊɪm/ *n* Gedicht *nt*

poet /ˈpəʊɪt/ *n* Dichter(in) *m(f)*. ~**ic** /-ˈetɪk/ *a* dichterisch

poetry /ˈpəʊɪtrɪ/ *n* Dichtung *f*

poignant /ˈpɔɪnjənt/ *a* ergreifend

point /pɔɪnt/ *n* Punkt *m*; (*sharp end*) Spitze *f*; (*meaning*) Sinn *m*; (*purpose*) Zweck *m*; (*Electr*) Steckdose *f*; ~**s** *pl* (*Rail*) Weiche *f*; ~ **of view** Standpunkt *m*; **good/bad** ~**s** gute/schlechte Seiten; **what is the** ~**?** wozu? **the** ~ **is** es geht darum; **up to a** ~ bis zu einem gewissen Grade; **be on the** ~ **of doing sth** im Begriff sein, etw zu tun ● *vt* richten (**at** auf + *acc*); ausfugen <*brickwork*> ● *vi* deuten (**at/to** auf + *acc*); (*with finger*) mit dem Finger zeigen. ~ **out** *vt* zeigen auf (+ *acc*); ~ **sth out to s.o.** jdn auf etw (*acc*) hinweisen

point-ˈblank *a* aus nächster Entfernung; (*fig*) rundweg

point|ed /ˈpɔɪntɪd/ *a* spitz; <*question*> gezielt. ~**less** *a* zwecklos, sinnlos

poise /pɔɪz/ *n* Haltung *f*

poison /ˈpɔɪzn/ *n* Gift *nt* ● *vt* vergiften. ~**ous** *a* giftig

poke /pəʊk/ *n* Stoß *m* ● *vt* stoßen; schüren <*fire*>; (*put*) stecken

poker[1] /ˈpəʊkə(r)/ *n* Schüreisen *nt*

poker[2] *n* (*Cards*) Poker *nt*

poky /ˈpəʊkɪ/ *a* (**-ier, -iest**) eng

Poland /ˈpəʊlənd/ *n* Polen *nt*

polar /ˈpəʊlə(r)/ *a* Polar-. ~**ˈbear** *n* Eisbär *m*

Pole /pəʊl/ *n* Pole *m*/Polin *f*

pole[1] *n* Stange *f*

pole[2] *n* (*Geog, Electr*) Pol *m*

ˈpole-vault *n* Stabhochsprung *m*

police /pəˈli:s/ *npl* Polizei *f*

police: ~**man** *n* Polizist *m*. ~ **station** *n* Polizeiwache *f*. ~**woman** *n* Polizistin *f*

policy[1] /ˈpɒlɪsɪ/ *n* Politik *f*

policy[2] *n* (*insurance*) Police *f*

Polish /ˈpəʊlɪʃ/ *a* polnisch

polish /ˈpɒlɪʃ/ *n* (*shine*) Glanz *m*; (*for shoes*) [Schuh]creme *f*; (*for floor*) Bohnerwachs *m*; (*for furniture*) Politur *f*; (*for silver*) Putzmittel *nt*; (*for nails*) Lack *m*; (*fig*) Schliff *m* ● *vt* polieren; bohnern <*floor*>. ~ **off** *vt* [!] verputzen <*food*>; erledigen <*task*>

polite /pəˈlaɪt/ *a*, **-ly** *adv* höflich. ~**ness** *n* Höflichkeit *f*

politic|al /pəˈlɪtɪkl/ *a*, **-ly** *adv* politisch. ~**ian** /pɒlɪˈtɪʃn/ *n* Politiker(in) *m(f)*

politics /ˈpɒlətɪks/ *n* Politik *f*

poll /pəʊl/ *n* Abstimmung *f*; (*election*) Wahl *f*; **[opinion]** ~ [Meinungs]umfrage *f*

pollen /ˈpɒlən/ *n* Blütenstaub *m*, Pollen *m*

polling /ˈpəʊlɪŋ/: ~**-booth** *n* Wahlkabine *f*. ~**-station** *n* Wahllokal *nt*

pollut|e /pəˈlu:t/ *vt* verschmutzen. ~**ion** /-u:ʃn/ *n* Verschmutzung *f*

polo /ˈpəʊləʊ/ *n* Polo *nt*. ~**-neck** *n* Rollkragen *m*

polystyrene /pɒlɪ'staɪriːn/ *n* Polystyrol *nt*; (*for packing*) Styropor (P) *nt*

polythene /'pɒlɪθiːn/ *n* Polyäthylen *nt*. **~ bag** *n* Plastiktüte *f*

pomp /pɒmp/ *n* Pomp *m*

pompous /'pɒmpəs/ *a*, **-ly** *adv* großspurig

pond /pɒnd/ *n* Teich *m*

ponder /'pɒndə(r)/ *vi* nachdenken

ponderous /'pɒndərəs/ *a* schwerfällig

pony /'pəʊnɪ/ *n* Pony *nt*. **~-tail** *n* Pferdeschwanz *m*

poodle /'puːdl/ *n* Pudel *m*

pool /puːl/ *n* [Schwimm]becken *nt*; (*pond*) Teich *m*; (*of blood*) Lache *f*; (*common fund*) [gemeinsame] Kasse *f*; **~s** *pl* [Fußball]toto *nt* ● *vt* zusammenlegen

poor /pʊə(r)/ *a* (**-er, -est**) arm; (*not good*) schlecht; **in ~ health** nicht gesund. **~ly** *a* **be ~ly** krank sein ● *adv* ärmlich; (*badly*) schlecht

pop¹ /pɒp/ *n* Knall *m* ● *v* (*pt*/*pp* **popped**) ● *vt* ([!] *put*) stecken (**in** in + *acc*) ● *vi* knallen; (*burst*) platzen. **~ in** *vi* [!] reinschauen. **~ out** *vi* [!] kurz rausgehen

pop² *n* [!] Popmusik *f*, Pop *m* ● *attrib* Pop-

'popcorn *n* Puffmais *m*

pope /pəʊp/ *n* Papst *m*

poplar /'pɒplə(r)/ *n* Pappel *f*

poppy /'pɒpɪ/ *n* Mohn *m*

popular /'pɒpjʊlə(r)/ *a* beliebt, populär; <*belief*> volkstümlich. **~ity** /-'lærətɪ/ *n* Beliebtheit *f*, Popularität *f*

populat|e /'pɒpjʊleɪt/ *vt* bevölkern. **~ion** /-'leɪʃn/ *n* Bevölkerung *f*

porcelain /'pɔːsəlɪn/ *n* Porzellan *nt*

porch /pɔːtʃ/ *n* Vorbau *m*; (*Amer*) Veranda *f*

porcupine /'pɔːkjʊpaɪn/ *n* Stachelschwein *nt*

pore /pɔː(r)/ *n* Pore *f*

pork /pɔːk/ *n* Schweinefleisch *nt*

porn /pɔːn/ *n* [!] Porno *m*

pornograph|ic /pɔːnə'græfɪk/ *a* pornographisch. **~y** /-'nɒgrəfɪ/ *n* Pornographie *f*

porridge /'pɒrɪdʒ/ *n* Haferbrei *m*

port¹ /pɔːt/ *n* Hafen *m*; (*town*) Hafenstadt *f*

port² *n* (*Naut*) Backbord *nt*

port³ *n* (*wine*) Portwein *m*

portable /'pɔːtəbl/ *a* tragbar

porter /'pɔːtə(r)/ *n* Portier *m*; (*for luggage*) Gepäckträger *m*

'porthole *n* Bullauge *nt*

portion /'pɔːʃn/ *n* Portion *f*; (*part, share*) Teil *nt*

portrait /'pɔːtrɪt/ *n* Porträt *nt*

portray /pɔː'treɪ/ *vt* darstellen. **~al** *n* Darstellung *f*

Portug|al /'pɔːtjʊgl/ *n* Portugal *nt*. **~uese** /-'giːz/ *a* portugiesisch ● *n* Portugiese *m*/ -giesin *f*

pose /pəʊz/ *n* Pose *f* ● *vt* aufwerfen <*problem*>; stellen <*question*> ● *vi* posieren; (*for painter*) Modell stehen

posh /pɒʃ/ *a* [!] feudal

position /pə'zɪʃn/ *n* Platz *m*; (*posture*) Haltung *f*; (*job*) Stelle *f*; (*situation*) Lage *f*, Situation *f*; (*status*) Stellung *f* ● *vt* platzieren; **~ oneself** sich stellen

positive /'pɒzətɪv/ *a*, **-ly** *adv* positiv; (*definite*) eindeutig; (*real*) ausgesprochen ● *n* Positiv *nt*

possess /pə'zes/ *vt* besitzen. **~ion** /pə'zeʃn/ *n* Besitz *m*; **~ions** *pl* Sachen *pl*

possessive /pə'zesɪv/ *a* Possessiv-; **be ~ about s.o.** zu sehr an jdm hängen

possibility /pɒsə'bɪlətɪ/ *n* Möglichkeit *f*

possib|le /'pɒsəbl/ *a* möglich. **~ly** *adv* möglicherweise; **not ~ly** unmöglich

post¹ /pəʊst/ *n* (*pole*) Pfosten *m*

post² *n* (*place of duty*) Posten *m*; (*job*) Stelle *f*

post³ *n* (*mail*) Post *f*; **by ~** mit der Post ● *vt* aufgeben <*letter*>; (*send by ~*) mit der Post schicken; **keep s.o. ~ed** jdn auf dem Laufenden halten

postage /'pəʊstɪdʒ/ *n* Porto *nt*

postal /'pəʊstl/ *a* Post-. **~ order** *n* ≈ Geldanweisung *f*

post: ~-box *n* Briefkasten *m*. **~card** *n* Postkarte *f*; (*picture*) Ansichtskarte *f*. **~code** *n* Postleitzahl *f*. **~-'date** *vt* vordatieren

poster /'pəʊstə(r)/ *n* Plakat *nt*

posterity /pɒ'sterətɪ/ *n* Nachwelt *f*

posthumous /'pɒstjʊməs/ *a*, **-ly** *adv* postum

post: ~man *n* Briefträger *m*. **~mark** *n* Poststempel *m*

post-mortem /-'mɔːtəm/ *n* Obduktion *f*

'post office *n* Post *f*

postpone /pəʊst'pəʊn/ *vt* aufschieben; **~ until** verschieben auf (+ *acc*). **~ment** *n* Verschiebung *f*

postscript /'pəʊstskrɪpt/ *n* Nachschrift *f*

posture /'pɒstʃə(r)/ *n* Haltung *f*

pot /pɒt/ *n* Topf *m*; (*for tea, coffee*) Kanne *f*; **~s of money** [!] eine Menge Geld

potato /pə'teɪtəʊ/ *n* (*pl* **-es**) Kartoffel *f*

potent /'pəʊtənt/ *a* stark

potential /pə'tenʃl/ *a*, **-ly** *adv* potenziell ● *n* Potenzial *nt*

pot: ~-hole *n* Höhle *f*; (*in road*) Schlagloch *nt*. **~-shot** *n* **take a ~-shot at** schießen auf (+ *acc*)

potter /'pɒtə(r)/ *n* Töpfer(in) *m*(*f*). **~y** *n* Töpferei *f*; (*articles*) Töpferwaren *pl*

potty /'pɒtɪ/ *a* (**-ier, -iest**) [!] verrückt ● *n* Töpfchen *nt*

pouch /paʊtʃ/ *n* Beutel *m*

poultry /'pəʊltrɪ/ *n* Geflügel *nt*

pounce /paʊns/ *vi* zuschlagen; **~ on** sich stürzen auf (+ *acc*)

pound¹ /paʊnd/ *n* (*money & 0,454 kg*) Pfund *nt*

pound² *vi* <*heart:*> hämmern; (*run heavily*) stampfen

pour /pɔː(r)/ *vt* gießen; einschenken <*drink*> ● *vi* strömen; (*with rain*) gießen. **~ out** *vi* ausströmen ● *vt* ausschütten; einschenken <*drink*>

pout /paʊt/ *vi* einen Schmollmund machen

poverty /'pɒvətɪ/ *n* Armut *f*

powder /'paʊdə(r)/ *n* Pulver *nt*; (*cosmetic*) Puder *m* ● *vt* pudern

power /'paʊə(r)/ *n* Macht *f*; (*strength*) Kraft *f*; (*Electr*) Strom *m*; (*nuclear*) Energie *f*; (*Math*) Potenz *f*. **~ cut** *n* Stromsperre *f*. **~ed** *a* betrieben (**by** mit); **~ed by electricity** mit Elektroantrieb. **~ful** *a* mächtig; (*strong*) stark. **~less** *a* machtlos. **~-station** *n* Kraftwerk *nt*

practicable /'præktɪkəbl/ *a* durchführbar, praktikabel

practical /'præktɪkl/ *a*, **-ly** *adv* praktisch. **~ 'joke** *n* Streich *m*

practice /'præktɪs/ *n* Praxis *f*; (*custom*) Brauch *m*; (*habit*) Gewohnheit *f*; (*exercise*) Übung *f*; (*Sport*) Training *nt*; **in ~** (*in reality*) in der Praxis; **out of ~** außer Übung; **put into ~** ausführen

practise /'præktɪs/ *vt* üben; (*carry out*) praktizieren; ausüben

<*profession*> ● *vi* üben; <*doctor*:> praktizieren. **~d** *a* geübt

praise /preɪz/ *n* Lob *nt* ● *vt* loben. **~worthy** *a* lobenswert

pram /præm/ *n* Kinderwagen *m*

prank /præŋk/ *n* Streich *m*

prawn /prɔːn/ *n* Garnele *f*, Krabbe *f*

pray /preɪ/ *vi* beten. **~er** /preə(r)/ *n* Gebet *nt*

preach /priːtʃ/ *vt/i* predigen. **~er** *n* Prediger *m*

pre-arˈrange /priː-/ *vt* im Voraus arrangieren

precarious /prɪˈkeərɪəs/ *a*, **-ly** *adv* unsicher

precaution /prɪˈkɔːʃn/ *n* Vorsichtsmaßnahme *f*

precede /prɪˈsiːd/ *vt* vorangehen (+ *dat*)

preceden|ce /ˈpresɪdəns/ *n* Vorrang *m*. **~t** *n* Präzedenzfall *m*

preceding /prɪˈsiːdɪŋ/ *a* vorhergehend

precinct /ˈpriːsɪŋkt/ *n* Bereich *m*; (*traffic-free*) Fußgängerzone *f*; (*Amer: district*) Bezirk *m*

precious /ˈpreʃəs/ *a* kostbar; <*style*> preziös ● *adv* [!] **~ little** recht wenig

precipice /ˈpresɪpɪs/ *n* Steilabfall *m*

precipitation /prɪsɪpɪˈteɪʃn/ *n* (*Meteorol*) Niederschlag *m*

precis|e /prɪˈsaɪs/ *a*, **-ly** *adv* genau. **~ion** /-ˈsɪʒn/ *n* Genauigkeit *f*

precocious /prɪˈkəʊʃəs/ *a* frühreif

pre|conˈceived /priː-/ *a* vorgefasst. **~conˈception** *n* vorgefasste Meinung *f*

predator /ˈpredətə(r)/ *n* Raubtier *nt*

predecessor /ˈpriːdɪsesə(r)/ *n* Vorgänger(in) *m(f)*

predicat|e /ˈpredɪkət/ *n* (*Gram*) Prädikat *nt*. **~ive** /prɪˈdɪkətɪv/ *a*, **-ly** *adv* prädikativ

predict /prɪˈdɪkt/ *vt* voraussagen. **~able** /-əbl/ *a* voraussehbar; <*person*> berechenbar. **~ion** /-ˈdɪkʃn/ *n* Voraussage *f*

preˈdomin|ant /prɪ-/ *a* vorherrschend. **~antly** *adv* hauptsächlich, überwiegend. **~ate** *vi* vorherrschen

preen /priːn/ *vt* putzen

prefab /ˈpriːfæb/ *n* [!] [einfaches] Fertighaus *nt*. **~ˈricated** *a* vorgefertigt

preface /ˈprefɪs/ *n* Vorwort *nt*

prefect /ˈpriːfekt/ *n* Präfekt *m*

prefer /prɪˈfɜː(r)/ *vt* (*pt/pp* **preferred**) vorziehen; **I ~ to walk** ich gehe lieber zu Fuß; **I ~ wine** ich trinke lieber Wein

prefera|ble /ˈprefərəbl/ *a* **be ~ble** vorzuziehen sein (**to** *dat*). **~bly** *adv* vorzugsweise

preferen|ce /ˈprefərəns/ *n* Vorzug *m*. **~tial** /-ˈrenʃl/ *a* bevorzugt

pregnan|cy /ˈpregnənsɪ/ *n* Schwangerschaft *f*. **~t** *a* schwanger; <*animal*> trächtig

prehiˈstoric /priː-/ *a* prähistorisch

prejudice /ˈpredʒʊdɪs/ *n* Vorurteil *nt*; (*bias*) Voreingenommenheit *f* ● *vt* einnehmen (**against** gegen). **~d** *a* voreingenommen

preliminary /prɪˈlɪmɪnərɪ/ *a* Vor-

prelude /ˈpreljuːd/ *n* Vorspiel *nt*

premature /ˈprematjʊə(r)/ *a* vorzeitig; <*birth*> Früh-. **~ly** *adv* zu früh

preˈmeditated /priː-/ *a* vorsätzlich

premier /ˈpremɪə(r)/ *a* führend ● *n* (*Pol*) Premier[minister] *m*

premiere /'premɪeə(r)/ *n* Premiere *f*

premises /'premɪsɪz/ *npl* Räumlichkeiten *pl*; **on the ~** im Haus

premium /'pri:mɪəm/ *n* Prämie *f*; **be at a ~** hoch im Kurs stehen

premonition /premə'nɪʃn/ *n* Vorahnung *f*

preoccupied /prɪ'ɒkjʊpaɪd/ *a* [in Gedanken] beschäftigt

preparation /prepə'reɪʃn/ *n* Vorbereitung *f*; (*substance*) Präparat *nt*

preparatory /prɪ'pærətrɪ/ *a* Vor-

prepare /prɪ'peə(r)/ *vt* vorbereiten; anrichten <*meal*> ● *vi* sich vorbereiten (**for** auf + *acc*); **~d to** bereit zu

preposition /prepə'zɪʃn/ *n* Präposition *f*

preposterous /prɪ'pɒstərəs/ *a* absurd

prerequisite /pri:'rekwɪzɪt/ *n* Voraussetzung *f*

Presbyterian /prezbɪ'tɪərɪən/ *a* presbyterianisch ● *n* Presbyterianer(in) *m(f)*

prescribe /prɪ'skraɪb/ *vt* vorschreiben; (*Med*) verschreiben

prescription /prɪ'skrɪpʃn/ *n* (*Med*) Rezept *nt*

presence /'prezns/ *n* Anwesenheit *f*, Gegenwart *f*; **~ of mind** Geistesgegenwart *f*

present¹ /'preznt/ *a* gegenwärtig; **be ~** anwesend sein; (*occur*) vorkommen ● *n* Gegenwart *f*; (*Gram*) Präsens *nt*; **at ~** zurzeit; **for the ~** vorläufig

present² *n* (*gift*) Geschenk *nt*

present³ /prɪ'zent/ *vt* überreichen; (*show*) zeigen; vorlegen <*cheque*>; (*introduce*) vorstellen; **~ s.o. with sth** jdm etw überreichen. **~able** /-əbl/ *a* **be ~able** sich zeigen lassen können

presentation /prezn'teɪʃn/ *n* Überreichung *f*

presently /'prezntlɪ/ *adv* nachher; (*Amer: now*) zurzeit

preservation /prezə'veɪʃn/ *n* Erhaltung *f*

preservative /prɪ'zɜ:vətɪv/ *n* Konservierungsmittel *nt*

preserve /prɪ'zɜ:v/ *vt* erhalten; (*Culin*) konservieren; (*bottle*) einmachen ● *n* (*Hunting & fig*) Revier *nt*; (*jam*) Konfitüre *f*

preside /prɪ'zaɪd/ *vi* den Vorsitz haben (**over** bei)

presidency /'prezɪdənsɪ/ *n* Präsidentschaft *f*

president /'prezɪdənt/ *n* Präsident *m*; (*Amer: chairman*) Vorsitzende(r) *m/f*. **~ial** /-'denʃl/ *a* Präsidenten-; <*election*> Präsidentschafts-

press /pres/ *n* Presse *f* ● *vt/i* drücken; drücken auf (+ *acc*) <*button*>; pressen <*flower*>; (*iron*) bügeln; (*urge*) bedrängen; **~ for** drängen auf (+ *acc*); **be ~ed for time** in Zeitdruck sein. **~ on** *vi* weitergehen/-fahren; (*fig*) weitermachen

press: ~ cutting *n* Zeitungsausschnitt *m*. **~ing** *a* dringend

pressure /'preʃə(r)/ *n* Druck *m*. **~-cooker** *n* Schnellkochtopf *m*

pressurize /'preʃəraɪz/ *vt* Druck ausüben auf (+ *acc*). **~d** *a* Druck-

prestig|e /pre'sti:ʒ/ *n* Prestige *nt*. **~ious** /-'stɪdʒəs/ *a* Prestige-

presumably /prɪ'zju:məblɪ/ *adv* vermutlich

presume /prɪ'zju:m/ *vt* vermuten

presumpt|ion /prɪ'zʌmpʃn/ *n* Vermutung *f*; (*boldness*) Anmaßung *f*. **~uous** /-'zʌmptjʊəs/ *a*, **-ly** *adv* anmaßend

pretence /prɪ'tens/ *n* Verstellung *f*; (*pretext*) Vorwand *m*

pretend /prɪ'tend/ *vt* (*claim*) vorgeben; ~ **that** so tun, als ob; ~ **to be** sich ausgeben als

pretentious /prɪ'tenʃəs/ *a* protzig

pretext /'pri:tekst/ *n* Vorwand *m*

pretty /'prɪtɪ/ *a* (**-ier, -iest**), **~ily** *adv* hübsch ● *adv* ([!] *fairly*) ziemlich

prevail /prɪ'veɪl/ *vi* siegen; <*custom*:> vorherrschen; ~ **on s.o. to do sth** jdn dazu bringen, etw zu tun

prevalen|ce /'prevələns/ *n* Häufigkeit *f*. **~t** *a* vorherrschend

prevent /prɪ'vent/ *vt* verhindern, verhüten; ~ **s.o. [from] doing sth** jdn daran hindern, etw zu tun. **~ion** /-enʃn/ *n* Verhinderung *f*, Verhütung *f*. **~ive** /-ɪv/ *a* vorbeugend

preview /'pri:vju:/ *n* Voraufführung *f*

previous /'pri:vɪəs/ *a* vorhergehend; ~ **to** vor (+ *dat*). **~ly** *adv* vorher, früher

prey /preɪ/ *n* Beute *f*; **bird of** ~ Raubvogel *m*

price /praɪs/ *n* Preis *m* ● *vt* (*Comm*) auszeichnen. **~less** *a* unschätzbar; (*fig*) unbezahlbar

prick /prɪk/ *n* Stich *m* ● *vt/i* stechen

prickl|e /'prɪkl/ *n* Stachel *m*; (*thorn*) Dorn *m*. **~y** *a* stachelig; <*sensation*> stechend

pride /praɪd/ *n* Stolz *m*; (*arrogance*) Hochmut *m* ● *vt* ~ **oneself on** stolz sein auf (+ *acc*)

priest /pri:st/ *n* Priester *m*

prim /prɪm/ *a* (**primmer, primmest**) prüde

primarily /'praɪmərɪlɪ/ *adv* hauptsächlich, in erster Linie

primary /'praɪmərɪ/ *a* Haupt-. ~ **school** *n* Grundschule *f*

prime[1] /praɪm/ *a* Haupt-; (*first-rate*) erstklassig

prime[2] *vt* scharf machen <*bomb*>; grundieren <*surface*>

Prime Minister /praɪ'mɪnɪstə(r)/ *n* Premierminister(in) *m(f)*

primitive /'prɪmɪtɪv/ *a* primitiv

primrose /'prɪmrəʊz/ *n* gelbe Schlüsselblume *f*

prince /prɪns/ *n* Prinz *m*

princess /prɪn'ses/ *n* Prinzessin *f*

principal /'prɪnsəpl/ *a* Haupt- ● *n* (*Sch*) Rektor(in) *m(f)*

principally /'prɪnsəplɪ/ *adv* hauptsächlich

principle /'prɪnsəpl/ *n* Prinzip *nt*, Grundsatz *m*; **in/on** ~ im/aus Prinzip

print /prɪnt/ *n* Druck *m*; (*Phot*) Abzug *m*; **in** ~ gedruckt; (*available*) erhältlich; **out of** ~ vergriffen ● *vt* drucken; (*write in capitals*) in Druckschrift schreiben; (*Computing*) ausdrucken; (*Phot*) abziehen. **~ed matter** *n* Drucksache *f*

print|er /'prɪntə(r)/ *n* Drucker *m*. **~ing** *n* Druck *m*

'printout *n* (*Computing*) Ausdruck *m*

prior /'praɪə(r)/ *a* frühere(r,s); ~ **to** vor (+ *dat*)

priority /praɪ'ɒrətɪ/ *n* Priorität *f*, Vorrang *m*

prise /praɪz/ *vt* ~ **open/up** aufstemmen/hochstemmen

prison /'prɪzn/ *n* Gefängnis *nt*. **~er** *n* Gefangene(r) *m/f*

privacy /'prɪvəsɪ/ *n* Privatsphäre *f*; **have no** ~ nie für sich sein

private /'praɪvət/ *a*, **-ly** *adv* privat; (*confidential*) vertraulich; <*car, secretary, school*> Privat- ● *n* (*Mil*) [einfacher] Soldat *m*; **in** ~ privat; (*confidentially*) vertraulich

privation /praɪˈveɪʃn/ *n* Entbehrung *f*

privilege /ˈprɪvəlɪdʒ/ *n* Privileg *nt*. **~d** *a* privilegiert

prize /praɪz/ *n* Preis *m* ● *vt* schätzen

pro /prəʊ/ *n* 🅸 Profi *m*; **the ~s and cons** das Für und Wider

probability /prɒbəˈbɪlətɪ/ *n* Wahrscheinlichkeit *f*

probable /ˈprɒbəbl/ *a*, **-bly** *adv* wahrscheinlich

probation /prəˈbeɪʃn/ *n* (*Jur*) Bewährung *f*

probe /prəʊb/ *n* Sonde *f*; (*fig: investigation*) Untersuchung *f*

problem /ˈprɒbləm/ *n* Problem *nt*; (*Math*) Textaufgabe *f*. **~atic** /-ˈmætɪk/ *a* problematisch

procedure /prəˈsiːdʒə(r)/ *n* Verfahren *nt*

proceed /prəˈsiːd/ *vi* gehen; (*in vehicle*) fahren; (*continue*) weitergehen/-fahren; (*speaking*) fortfahren; (*act*) verfahren

proceedings /prəˈsiːdɪŋz/ *npl* Verfahren *nt*; (*Jur*) Prozess *m*

proceeds /ˈprəʊsiːdz/ *npl* Erlös *m*

process /ˈprəʊses/ *n* Prozess *m*; (*procedure*) Verfahren *nt*; **in the ~** dabei ● *vt* verarbeiten; (*Admin*) bearbeiten; (*Phot*) entwickeln

procession /prəˈseʃn/ *n* Umzug *m*, Prozession *f*

proclaim /prəˈkleɪm/ *vt* ausrufen

proclamation /prɒkləˈmeɪʃn/ *n* Proklamation *f*

procure /prəˈkjʊə(r)/ *vt* beschaffen

prod /prɒd/ *n* Stoß *m* ● *vt* stoßen

prodigy /ˈprɒdɪdʒɪ/ *n* **[infant] ~** Wunderkind *nt*

produce¹ /ˈprɒdjuːs/ *n* landwirtschaftliche Erzeugnisse *pl*

produce² /prəˈdjuːs/ *vt* erzeugen, produzieren; (*manufacture*) herstellen; (*bring out*) hervorholen; (*cause*) hervorrufen; inszenieren <*play*>; (*Radio, TV*) redigieren. **~r** *n* Erzeuger *m*, Produzent *m*; Hersteller *m*; (*Theat*) Regisseur *m*; (*Radio, TV*) Redakteur(in) *m(f)*

product /ˈprɒdʌkt/ *n* Erzeugnis *nt*, Produkt *nt*. **~ion** /prəˈdʌkʃn/ *n* Produktion *f*; (*Theat*) Inszenierung *f*

productiv|e /prəˈdʌktɪv/ *a* produktiv; <*land, talks*> fruchtbar. **~ity** /-ˈtɪvətɪ/ *n* Produktivität *f*

profession /prəˈfeʃn/ *n* Beruf *m*. **~al** *a*, **-ly** *adv* beruflich; (*not amateur*) Berufs-; (*expert*) fachmännisch; (*Sport*) professionell ● *n* Fachmann *m*; (*Sport*) Profi *m*

professor /prəˈfesə(r)/ *n* Professor *m*

proficien|cy /prəˈfɪʃnsɪ/ *n* Können *nt*. **~t** *a* **be ~t in** beherrschen

profile /ˈprəʊfaɪl/ *n* Profil *nt*; (*character study*) Porträt *nt*

profit /ˈprɒfɪt/ *n* Gewinn *m*, Profit *m* ● *vi* **~ from** profitieren von. **~able** /-əbl/ *a*, **-bly** *adv* gewinnbringend; (*fig*) nutzbringend

profound /prəˈfaʊnd/ *a*, **-ly** *adv* tief

program /ˈprəʊgræm/ (*Amer & Computing*) *n* Programm *nt* ● *vt* (*pt/pp* **programmed**) programmieren

programme /ˈprəʊgræm/ *n* Programm *nt*; (*Radio, TV*) Sendung *f*. **~r** *n* (*Computing*) Programmierer(in) *m(f)*

progress¹ /ˈprəʊgres/ *n* Vorankommen *nt*; (*fig*) Fortschritt *m*; **in ~** im Gange;

make ~ (*fig*) Fortschritte machen
progress² /prə'gres/ *vi* vorankommen; (*fig*) fortschreiten. **~ion** /-eʃn/ *n* Folge *f*; (*development*) Entwicklung *f*
progressive /prə'gresɪv/ *a* fortschrittlich. **~ly** *adv* zunehmend
prohibit /prə'hɪbɪt/ *vt* verbieten (**s.o.** jdm). **~ive** /-ɪv/ *a* unerschwinglich
project¹ /'prɒdʒekt/ *n* Projekt *nt*; (*Sch*) Arbeit *f*
project² /prə'dʒekt/ *vt* projizieren <*film*>; (*plan*) planen ● *vi* (*jut out*) vorstehen
projector /prə'dʒektə(r)/ *n* Projektor *m*
prolific /prə'lɪfɪk/ *a* fruchtbar; (*fig*) produktiv
prologue /'prəʊlɒg/ *n* Prolog *m*
prolong /prə'lɒŋ/ *vt* verlängern
promenade /prɒmə'nɑ:d/ *n* Promenade *f* ● *vi* spazieren gehen
prominent /'prɒmɪnənt/ *a* vorstehend; (*important*) prominent; (*conspicuous*) auffällig
promiscuous /prə'mɪskjʊəs/ *a* **be ~ous** häufig den Partner wechseln
promis|e /'prɒmɪs/ *n* Versprechen *nt* ● *vt/i* versprechen (**s.o.** jdm). **~ing** *a* viel versprechend
promot|e /prə'məʊt/ *vt* befördern; (*advance*) fördern; (*publicize*) Reklame machen für; **be ~ed** (*Sport*) aufsteigen. **~ion** /-əʊʃn/ *n* Beförderung *f*; (*Sport*) Aufstieg *m*; (*Comm*) Reklame *f*
prompt /prɒmpt/ *a* prompt, unverzüglich; (*punctual*) pünktlich ● *adv* pünktlich ● *vt/i* veranlassen (**to** zu); (*Theat*) soufflieren (+ *dat*). **~er** *n* Souffleur *m*/Souffleuse *f*. **~ly** *adv* prompt
prone /prəʊn/ *a* **be** *or* **lie ~** auf dem Bauch liegen; **be ~ to** neigen zu
pronoun /'prəʊnaʊn/ *n* Fürwort *nt*, Pronomen *nt*
pronounce /prə'naʊns/ *vt* aussprechen; (*declare*) erklären. **~d** *a* ausgeprägt; (*noticeable*) deutlich. **~ment** *n* Erklärung *f*
pronunciation /prənʌnsɪ'eɪʃn/ *n* Aussprache *f*
proof /pru:f/ *n* Beweis *m*; (*Typ*) Korrekturbogen *m*. **~-reader** *n* Korrektor *m*
prop¹ /prɒp/ *n* Stütze *f* ● *vt* (*pt/pp* **propped**) **~ against** lehnen an (+ *acc*). **~ up** *vt* stützen
prop² *n* (*Theat* [!]) Requisit *nt*
propaganda /prɒpə'gændə/ *n* Propaganda *f*
propel /prə'pel/ *vt* (*pt/pp* **propelled**) [an]treiben. **~ler** *n* Propeller *m*
proper /'prɒpə(r)/ *a*, **-ly** *adv* richtig; (*decent*) anständig
property /'prɒpətɪ/ *n* Eigentum *nt*; (*quality*) Eigenschaft *f*; (*Theat*) Requisit *nt*; (*land*) [Grund]besitz *m*; (*house*) Haus *nt*
prophecy /'prɒfəsɪ/ *n* Prophezeiung *f*
prophesy /'prɒfɪsaɪ/ *vt* (*pt/pp* **-ied**) prophezeien
prophet /'prɒfɪt/ *n* Prophet *m*. **~ic** /prə'fetɪk/ *a* prophetisch
proportion /prə'pɔ:ʃn/ *n* Verhältnis *nt*; (*share*) Teil *m*; **~s** *pl* Proportionen; (*dimensions*) Maße. **~al** *a*, **-ly** *adv* proportional
proposal /prə'pəʊzl/ *n* Vorschlag *m*; (*of marriage*) [Heirats]antrag *m*
propose /prə'pəʊz/ *vt* vorschlagen; (*intend*) vorhaben; einbringen <*motion*> ● *vi* einen Heiratsantrag machen

proposition /prɒpəˈzɪʃn/ *n* Vorschlag *m*
proprietor /prəˈpraɪətə(r)/ *n* Inhaber(in) *m(f)*
propriety /prəˈpraɪətɪ/ *n* Korrektheit *f*; (*decorum*) Anstand *m*
prose /prəʊz/ *n* Prosa *f*
prosecut|e /ˈprɒsɪkju:t/ *vt* strafrechtlich verfolgen. **~ion** /-ˈkju:ʃn/ *n* strafrechtliche Verfolgung *f*; **the ~ion** die Anklage. **~or** *n* **[Public] P~or** Staatsanwalt *m*
prospect /ˈprɒspekt/ *n* Aussicht *f*
prospect|ive /prəˈspektɪv/ *a* (*future*) zukünftig. **~or** *n* Prospektor *m*
prospectus /prəˈspektəs/ *n* Prospekt *m*
prosper /ˈprɒspə(r)/ *vi* gedeihen, florieren; <*person*> Erfolg haben. **~ity** /-ˈsperətɪ/ *n* Wohlstand *m*
prosperous /ˈprɒspərəs/ *a* wohlhabend
prostitut|e /ˈprɒstɪtju:t/ *n* Prostituierte *f*. **~ion** /-ˈtju:ʃn/ *n* Prostitution *f*
prostrate /ˈprɒstreɪt/ *a* ausgestreckt
protagonist /prəʊˈtægənɪst/ *n* Kämpfer *m*; (*fig*) Protagonist *m*
protect /prəˈtekt/ *vt* schützen (**from** vor + *dat*); beschützen <*person*>. **~ion** /-ekʃn/ *n* Schutz *m*. **~ive** /-ɪv/ *a* Schutz-; (*fig*) beschützend. **~or** *n* Beschützer *m*
protein /ˈprəʊti:n/ *n* Eiweiß *nt*
protest¹ /ˈprəʊtest/ *n* Protest *m*
protest² /prəˈtest/ *vi* protestieren
Protestant /ˈprɒtɪstənt/ *a* protestantisch ● *n* Protestant(in) *m(f)*
protester /prəˈtestə(r)/ *n* Protestierende(r) *m/f*
prototype /ˈprəʊtə-/ *n* Prototyp *m*
protrude /prəˈtru:d/ *vi* [her]vorstehen
proud /praʊd/ *a*, **-ly** *adv* stolz (**of** auf + *acc*)
prove /pru:v/ *vt* beweisen ● *vi* **~ to be** sich erweisen als
proverb /ˈprɒvɜ:b/ *n* Sprichwort *nt*
provide /prəˈvaɪd/ *vt* zur Verfügung stellen; spenden <*shade*>; **~ s.o. with sth** jdn mit etw versorgen *od* versehen ● *vi* **~ for** sorgen für
provided /prəˈvaɪdɪd/ *conj* **~ [that]** vorausgesetzt [dass]
providen|ce /ˈprɒvɪdəns/ *n* Vorsehung *f*. **~tial** /-ˈdenʃl/ *a* **be ~tial** ein Glück sein
provinc|e /ˈprɒvɪns/ *n* Provinz *f*; (*fig*) Bereich *m*. **~ial** /prəˈvɪnʃl/ *a* provinziell
provision /prəˈvɪʒn/ *n* Versorgung *f* (*of* mit); **~s** *pl* Lebensmittel *pl*. **~al** *a*, **-ly** *adv* vorläufig
provocat|ion /prɒvəˈkeɪʃn/ *n* Provokation *f*. **~ive** /prəˈvɒkətɪv/ *a*, **-ly** *adv* provozierend; (*sexually*) aufreizend
provoke /prəˈvəʊk/ *vt* provozieren; (*cause*) hervorrufen
prow /praʊ/ *n* Bug *m*
prowl /praʊl/ *vi* herumschleichen
proximity /prɒkˈsɪmətɪ/ *n* Nähe *f*
pruden|ce /ˈpru:dns/ *n* Umsicht *f*. **~t** *a*, **-ly** *adv* umsichtig; (*wise*) klug
prudish /ˈpru:dɪʃ/ *a* prüde
prune¹ /pru:n/ *n* Backpflaume *f*
prune² *vt* beschneiden
pry /praɪ/ *vi* (*pt/pp* **pried**) neugierig sein
psalm /sɑ:m/ *n* Psalm *m*

psychiatric /saɪkɪ'ætrɪk/ *a* psychiatrisch

psychiatr|ist /saɪ'kaɪətrɪst/ *n* Psychiater(*in*) *m*(*f*). **~y** *n* Psychiatrie *f*

psychic /'saɪkɪk/ *a* übersinnlich

psycho|a'nalysis /saɪkəʊ-/ *n* Psychoanalyse *f*. **~'analyst** *n* Psychoanalytiker(in) *m*(*f*)

psychological /saɪkə'lɒdʒɪkl/ *a*, **-ly** *adv* psychologisch; <*illness*> psychisch

psycholog|ist /saɪ'kɒlədʒɪst/ *n* Psychologe *m*/ -login *f*. **~y** *n* Psychologie *f*

P.T.O. *abbr* (**please turn over**) b.w.

pub /pʌb/ *n* [!] Kneipe *f*

puberty /'pju:bətɪ/ *n* Pubertät *f*

public /'pʌblɪk/ *a*, **-ly** *adv* öffentlich; **make ~** publik machen ● *n* **the ~** die Öffentlichkeit

publican /'pʌblɪkən/ *n* [Gast]wirt *m*

publication /pʌblɪ'keɪʃn/ *n* Veröffentlichung *f*

public: ~ 'holiday *n* gesetzlicher Feiertag *m*. **~ 'house** *n* [Gast]wirtschaft *f*

publicity /pʌb'lɪsətɪ/ *n* Publicity *f*; (*advertising*) Reklame *f*

publicize /'pʌblɪsaɪz/ *vt* Reklame machen für

public: ~ 'school *n* Privatschule *f*; (*Amer*) staatliche Schule *f*. **~-'spirited** *a* **be ~-spirited** Gemeinsinn haben

publish /'pʌblɪʃ/ *vt* veröffentlichen. **~er** *n* Verleger(in) *m*(*f*); (*firm*) Verlag *m*. **~ing** *n* Verlagswesen *nt*

pudding /'pʊdɪŋ/ *n* Pudding *m*; (*course*) Nachtisch *m*

puddle /'pʌdl/ *n* Pfütze *f*

puff /pʌf/ *n* (*of wind*) Hauch *m*; (*of smoke*) Wölkchen *nt* ● *vt* blasen, pusten; **~ out** ausstoßen. ● *vi* keuchen; **~ at** paffen an (+ *dat*) <*pipe*>. **~ed** *a* (*out of breath*) aus der Puste. **~ pastry** *n* Blätterteig *m*

pull /pʊl/ *n* Zug *m*; (*jerk*) Ruck *m*; ([!] *influence*) Einfluss *m* ● *vt* ziehen; ziehen an (+ *dat*) <*rope*>; **~ a muscle** sich (*dat*) einen Muskel zerren; **~ oneself together** sich zusammennehmen; **~ one's weight** tüchtig mitarbeiten; **~ s.o.'s leg** [!] jdn auf den Arm nehmen. **~ down** *vt* herunterziehen; (*demolish*) abreißen. **~ in** *vt* hereinziehen ● *vi* (*Auto*) einscheren. **~ off** *vt* abziehen; [!] schaffen. **~ out** *vt* herausziehen ● *vi* (*Auto*) ausscheren. **~ through** *vt* durchziehen ● *vi* (*recover*) durchkommen. **~ up** *vt* heraufziehen; ausziehen <*plant*> ● *vi* (*Auto*) anhalten

pullover /'pʊləʊvə(r)/ *n* Pullover *m*

pulp /pʌlp/ *n* Brei *m*; (*of fruit*) [Frucht]fleisch *nt*

pulpit /'pʊlpɪt/ *n* Kanzel *f*

pulse /pʌls/ *n* Puls *m*

pulses /'pʌlsɪz/ *npl* Hülsenfrüchte *pl*

pummel /'pʌml/ *vt* (*pt*/*pp* **pummelled**) mit den Fäusten bearbeiten

pump /pʌmp/ *n* Pumpe *f* ● *vt* pumpen; [!] aushorchen. **~ up** *vt* (*inflate*) aufpumpen

pumpkin /'pʌmpkɪn/ *n* Kürbis *m*

pun /pʌn/ *n* Wortspiel *nt*

punch¹ /pʌntʃ/ *n* Faustschlag *m*; (*device*) Locher *m* ● *vt* boxen; lochen <*ticket*>; stanzen <*hole*>

punch² *n* (*drink*) Bowle *f*

punctual /'pʌŋktjʊəl/ *a*, **-ly** *adv* pünktlich. **~ity** /-'ælətɪ/ *n* Pünktlichkeit *f*

punctuat|e /'pʌŋktjʊeɪt/ *vt* mit Satzzeichen versehen. **~ion** /-'eɪʃn/ *n* Interpunktion *f*

puncture /'pʌŋktʃə(r)/ *n* Loch *nt*; (*tyre*) Reifenpanne *f* ● *vt* durchstechen

punish /'pʌnɪʃ/ *vt* bestrafen. **~able** /-əbl/ *a* strafbar. **~ment** *n* Strafe *f*

punt /pʌnt/ *n* (*boat*) Stechkahn *m*

puny /'pju:nɪ/ *a* (**-ier, -iest**) mickerig

pup /pʌp/ *n* = **puppy**

pupil /'pju:pl/ *n* Schüler(in) *m(f)*; (*of eye*) Pupille *f*

puppet /'pʌpɪt/ *n* Puppe *f*; (*fig*) Marionette *f*

puppy /'pʌpɪ/ *n* junger Hund *m*

purchase /'pɜ:tʃəs/ *n* Kauf *m*; (*leverage*) Hebelkraft *f* ● *vt* kaufen. **~r** *n* Käufer *m*

pure /pjʊə(r)/ *a* (**-r, -st,**) **-ly** *adv* rein

purge /pɜ:dʒ/ *n* (*Pol*) Säuberungsaktion *f* ● *vt* reinigen

puri|fication /pjʊərɪfɪ'keɪʃn/ *n* Reinigung *f*. **~fy** /'pjʊərɪfaɪ/ *vt* (*pt/pp* **-ied**) reinigen

puritanical /pjʊərɪ'tænɪkl/ *a* puritanisch

purity /'pjʊərɪtɪ/ *n* Reinheit *f*

purple /'pɜ:pl/ *a* [dunkel]lila

purpose /'pɜ:pəs/ *n* Zweck *m*; (*intention*) Absicht *f*; (*determination*) Entschlossenheit *f*; **on ~** absichtlich. **~ful** *a*, **-ly** *adv* entschlossen. **~ly** *adv* absichtlich

purr /pɜ:(r)/ *vi* schnurren

purse /pɜ:s/ *n* Portemonnaie *nt*; (*Amer: handbag*) Handtasche *f*

pursue /pə'sju:/ *vt* verfolgen; (*fig*) nachgehen (+ *dat*). **~r** /-ə(r)/ *n* Verfolger *m*

pursuit /pə'sju:t/ *n* Verfolgung *f*; Jagd *f*; (*pastime*) Beschäftigung *f*

pus /pʌs/ *n* Eiter *m*

push /pʊʃ/ *n* Stoß *m*; **get the ~** [!] hinausfliegen ● *vt/i* schieben; (*press*) drücken; (*roughly*) stoßen. **~ off** *vt* hinunterstoßen ● *vi* ([!] *leave*) abhauen. **~ on** *vi* (*continue*) weitergehen/-fahren; (*with activity*) weitermachen. **~ up** *vt* hochschieben; hochtreiben <*price*>

push: ~-button *n* Druckknopf *m*. **~-chair** *n* [Kinder]sportwagen *m*

pushy /'pʊʃɪ/ *a* [!] aufdringlich

puss /pʊs/ *n*, **pussy** /'pʊsɪ/ *n* Mieze *f*

put /pʊt/ *vt* (*pt/pp* **put**, *pres p* **putting**) tun; (*place*) setzen; (*upright*) stellen; (*flat*) legen; (*express*) ausdrücken; (*say*) sagen; (*estimate*) schätzen (**at** auf + *acc*); **~ aside** *or* **by** beiseite legen ● *vi* **~ to sea** auslaufen ● *a* **stay ~** dableiben. **~ away** *vt* wegräumen. **~ back** *vt* wieder hinsetzen/-stellen/-legen; zurückstellen <*clock*>. **~ down** *vt* hinsetzen/-stellen/-legen; (*suppress*) niederschlagen; (*kill*) töten; (*write*) niederschreiben; (*attribute*) zuschreiben (**to** *dat*). **~ forward** *vt* vorbringen; vorstellen <*clock*>. **~ in** *vt* hineinsetzen/-stellen/-legen; (*insert*) einstecken; (*submit*) einreichen ● *vi* **~ in for** beantragen. **~ off** *vt* ausmachen <*light*>; (*postpone*) verschieben; **~ s.o. off** jdn abbestellen; (*disconcert*) jdn aus der Fassung bringen. **~ on** *vt* anziehen <*clothes, brake*>; sich (*dat*) aufsetzen <*hat*>; (*Culin*) aufsetzen; anmachen <*light*>; aufführen <*play*>; annehmen <*accent*>; **~ on weight** zunehmen. **~ out** *vt* hinaussetzen/-stellen/-legen; ausmachen <*fire, light*>; ausstrecken <*hand*>; (*disconcert*) aus der Fassung bringen; **~ s.o./oneself out** jdm/sich Umstände machen. **~ through** *vt* durchstecken; (*Teleph*) verbinden (**to** mit). **~ up** *vt* errichten <*building*>; aufschlagen <*tent*>; aufspannen <*umbrella*>; anschlagen <*notice*>; erhöhen <*price*>; unterbringen <*guest*> ● *vi* (*at hotel*) absteigen in (+ *dat*); **~ up with sth** sich (*dat*) etw bieten lassen

putrid /ˈpju:trɪd/ *a* faulig

putty /ˈpʌtɪ/ *n* Kitt *m*

puzzl|e /ˈpʌzl/ *n* Rätsel *nt*; (*jigsaw*) Puzzlespiel *nt* ● *vt* **it ~es me** es ist mir rätselhaft. **~ing** *a* rätselhaft

pyjamas /pəˈdʒɑ:məz/ *npl* Schlafanzug *m*

pylon /ˈpaɪlən/ *n* Mast *m*

pyramid /ˈpɪrəmɪd/ *n* Pyramide *f*

python /ˈpaɪθn/ *n* Pythonschlange *f*

Qq

quack /kwæk/ *n* Quaken *nt*; (*doctor*) Quacksalber *m* ● *vi* quaken

quadrangle /ˈkwɒdræŋgl/ *n* Viereck *nt*; (*court*) Hof *m*

quadruped /ˈkwɒdrʊped/ *n* Vierfüßer *m*

quadruple /ˈkwɒdrʊpl/ *a* vierfach ● *vt* vervierfachen ● *vi* sich vervierfachen

quaint /kweɪnt/ *a* (**-er, -est**) malerisch; (*odd*) putzig

quake /kweɪk/ *n* [!] Erdbeben *nt* ● *vi* beben; (*with fear*) zittern

qualif|ication /kwɒlɪfɪˈkeɪʃn/ *n* Qualifikation *f*; (*reservation*) Einschränkung *f*. **~ied** /-faɪd/ *a* qualifiziert; (*trained*) ausgebildet; (*limited*) bedingt

qualify /ˈkwɒlɪfaɪ/ *v* (*pt/pp* **-ied**) ● *vt* qualifizieren; (*entitle*) berechtigen; (*limit*) einschränken ● *vi* sich qualifizieren

quality /ˈkwɒlətɪ/ *n* Qualität *f*; (*characteristic*) Eigenschaft *f*

qualm /kwɑ:m/ *n* Bedenken *pl*

quantity /ˈkwɒntətɪ/ *n* Quantität *f*, Menge *f*; **in ~** in großen Mengen

quarantine /ˈkwɒrəntɪ:n/ *n* Quarantäne *f*

quarrel /ˈkwɒrl/ *n* Streit *m* ● *vi* (*pt/pp* **quarrelled**) sich streiten. **~some** *a* streitsüchtig

quarry[1] /ˈkwɒrɪ/ *n* (*prey*) Beute *f*

quarry[2] *n* Steinbruch *m*

quart /kwɔ:t/ *n* Quart *nt*

quarter /ˈkwɔ:tə(r)/ *n* Viertel *nt*; (*of year*) Vierteljahr *nt*; (*Amer*) 25-Cent-Stück *nt*; **~s** *pl* Quartier *nt*; **at [a] ~ to six** um Viertel vor sechs ● *vt* vierteln; (*Mil*) einquartieren (**on** bei). **~-ˈfinal** *n* Viertelfinale *nt*

quarterly /ˈkwɔ:təlɪ/ *a & adv* vierteljährlich

quartet /kwɔ:ˈtet/ *n* Quartett *nt*

quartz /kwɔ:ts/ *n* Quarz *m*

quay /ki:/ *n* Kai *m*

queasy /ˈkwi:zɪ/ *a* **I feel ~** mir ist übel

queen /kwi:n/ *n* Königin *f*; (*Cards, Chess*) Dame *f*

queer /kwɪə(r)/ *a* (**-er, -est**) eigenartig; (*dubious*) zweifelhaft; (*ill*) unwohl

quell /kwel/ *vt* unterdrücken

quench /kwentʃ/ *vt* löschen

query /ˈkwɪərɪ/ *n* Frage *f*; (*question mark*) Fragezeichen *nt* ● *vt* (*pt/pp* **-ied**) infrage stellen; reklamieren <*bill*>

quest /kwest/ *n* Suche *f* (**for** nach)

question /ˈkwestʃn/ *n* Frage *f*; (*for discussion*) Thema *nt*; **out of the ~** ausgeschlossen; **the**

person in ~ die fragliche Person ● *vt* infrage stellen; ~ **s.o.** jdn ausfragen; <*police:*> jdn verhören. ~**able** /-əbl/ *a* zweifelhaft. ~ **mark** *n* Fragezeichen *nt*
questionnaire /kwestʃə'neə(r)/ *n* Fragebogen *m*
queue /kju:/ *n* Schlange *f* ● *vi* ~ **[up]** Schlange stehen, sich anstellen (**for** nach)
quibble /'kwɪbl/ *vi* Haarspalterei treiben
quick /kwɪk/ *a* (**-er, -est**), **-ly** *adv* schnell; **be** ~! mach schnell! ● *adv* schnell. ~**en** *vt* beschleunigen ● *vi* sich beschleunigen
quick: ~**sand** *n* Treibsand *m*. ~**-tempered** *a* aufbrausend
quid /kwɪd/ *n inv* 🅸 Pfund *nt*
quiet /'kwaɪət/ *a* (**-er, -est**), **-ly** *adv* still; (*calm*) ruhig; (*soft*) leise; **keep** ~ **about** 🅸 nichts sagen von ● *n* Stille *f*, Ruhe *f*
quiet|en /'kwaɪətn/ *vt* beruhigen ● *vi* ~**en down** ruhig werden. ~**ness** *n* Stille *f*, Ruhe *f*
quilt /kwɪlt/ *n* Steppdecke *f*. ~**ed** *a* Stepp-
quintet /kwɪn'tet/ *n* Quintett *nt*
quirk /kwɜ:k/ *n* Eigenart *f*
quit /kwɪt/ *v* (*pt/pp* **quitted** or **quit**) ● *vt* verlassen; (*give up*) aufgeben; ~ **doing sth** aufhören, etw zu tun ● *vi* gehen
quite /kwaɪt/ *adv* ganz; (*really*) wirklich; ~ **[so]!** genau! ~ **a few** ziemlich viele
quits /kwɪts/ *a* quitt
quiver /'kwɪvə(r)/ *vi* zittern
quiz /kwɪz/ *n* Quiz *nt* ● *vt* (*pt/pp* **quizzed**) ausfragen. ~**zical** *a*, **-ly** *adv* fragend
quota /'kwəʊtə/ *n* Anteil *m*; (*Comm*) Kontingent *nt*
quotation /kwəʊ'teɪʃn/ *n* Zitat *nt*; (*price*) Kostenvoranschlag *m*; (*of shares*) Notierung *f*. ~ **marks** *npl* Anführungszeichen *pl*
quote /kwəʊt/ *n* 🅸 = **quotation; in** ~**s** in Anführungszeichen ● *vt/i* zitieren

Rr

rabbi /'ræbaɪ/ *n* Rabbiner *m*; (*title*) Rabbi *m*
rabbit /'ræbɪt/ *n* Kaninchen *nt*
rabid /'ræbɪd/ *a* fanatisch; <*animal*> tollwütig
rabies /'reɪbi:z/ *n* Tollwut *f*
race¹ /reɪs/ *n* Rasse *f*
race² *n* Rennen *nt*; (*fig*) Wettlauf *m* ● *vi* [am Rennen] teilnehmen; <*athlete, horse:*> laufen; (🅸 *rush*) rasen ● *vt* um die Wette laufen mit; an einem Rennen teilnehmen lassen <*horse*>
race: ~**course** *n* Rennbahn *f*. ~**horse** *n* Rennpferd *nt*. ~**track** *n* Rennbahn *f*
racial /'reɪʃl/ *a*, **-ly** *adv* rassisch; <*discrimination*> Rassen-
racing /'reɪsɪŋ/ *n* Rennsport *m*; (*horse-*) Pferderennen *nt*. ~ **car** *n* Rennwagen *m*. ~ **driver** *n* Rennfahrer *m*
racis|m /'reɪsɪzm/ *n* Rassismus *m*. ~**t** /-ɪst/ *a* rassistisch ● *n* Rassist *m*
rack¹ /ræk/ *n* Ständer *m*; (*for plates*) Gestell *nt* ● *vt* ~ **one's brains** sich (*dat*) den Kopf zerbrechen
rack² *n* **go to** ~ **and ruin** verfallen; (*fig*) herunterkommen

racket /ˈrækɪt/ *n* (*Sport*) Schläger *m*; (*din*) Krach *m*; (*swindle*) Schwindelgeschäft *nt*
racy /ˈreɪsɪ/ *a* (**-ier, -iest**) schwungvoll; (*risqué*) gewagt
radar /ˈreɪdɑ:(r)/ *n* Radar *m*
radian|ce /ˈreɪdɪəns/ *n* Strahlen *nt*. **~t** *a*, **-ly** *adv* strahlend
radiat|e /ˈreɪdɪeɪt/ *vt* ausstrahlen ● *vi* <*heat:*> ausgestrahlt werden; <*roads:*> strahlenförmig ausgehen. **~ion** /-ˈeɪʃn/ *n* Strahlung *f*
radiator /ˈreɪdɪeɪtə(r)/ *n* Heizkörper *m*; (*Auto*) Kühler *m*
radical /ˈrædɪkl/ *a*, **-ly** *adv* radikal ● *n* Radikale(r) *m/f*
radio /ˈreɪdɪəʊ/ *n* Radio *nt*; **by ~** über Funk ● *vt* funken <*message*>
radio|ˈactive *a* radioaktiv. **~acˈtivity** *n* Radioaktivität *f*
radish /ˈrædɪʃ/ *n* Radieschen *nt*
radius /ˈreɪdɪəs/ *n* (*pl* **-dii** /-dɪaɪ/) Radius *m*, Halbmesser *m*
raffle /ˈræfl/ *n* Tombola *f*
raft /rɑ:ft/ *n* Floß *nt*
rafter /ˈrɑ:ftə(r)/ *n* Dachsparren *m*
rag /ræg/ *n* Lumpen *m*; (*pej: newspaper*) Käseblatt *nt*
rage /reɪdʒ/ *n* Wut *f*; **all the ~** [!] der letzte Schrei ● *vi* rasen
ragged /ˈrægɪd/ *a* zerlumpt; <*edge*> ausgefranst
raid /reɪd/ *n* Überfall *m*; (*Mil*) Angriff *m*; (*police*) Razzia *f* ● *vt* überfallen; (*Mil*) angreifen; <*police*> eine Razzia durchführen in (+ *dat*); (*break in*) eindringen in (+ *acc*). **~er** *n* Eindringling *m*; (*of bank*) Bankräuber *m*
rail /reɪl/ *n* Schiene *f*; (*pole*) Stange *f*; (*hand~*) Handlauf *m*; (*Naut*) Reling *f*; **by ~** mit der Bahn
railings /ˈreɪlɪŋz/ *npl* Geländer *nt*
ˈrailroad *n* (*Amer*) = **railway**
ˈrailway *n* [Eisen]bahn *f*. **~ station** *n* Bahnhof *m*
rain /reɪn/ *n* Regen *m* ● *vi* regnen
rain: ~bow *n* Regenbogen *m*. **~coat** *n* Regenmantel *m*. **~fall** *n* Niederschlag *m*
rainy /ˈreɪnɪ/ *a* (**-ier, -iest**) regnerisch
raise /reɪz/ *n* (*Amer*) Lohnerhöhung *f* ● *vt* erheben; (*upright*) aufrichten; (*make higher*) erhöhen; (*lift*) [hoch]heben; aufziehen <*child, animal*>; aufwerfen <*question*>; aufbringen <*money*>
raisin /ˈreɪzn/ *n* Rosine *f*
rake /reɪk/ *n* Harke *f*, Rechen *m* ● *vt* harken, rechen
rally /ˈrælɪ/ *n* Versammlung *f*; (*Auto*) Rallye *f*; (*Tennis*) Ballwechsel *m* ● *vt* sammeln
ram /ræm/ *n* Schafbock *m* ● *vt* (*pt/pp* **rammed**) rammen
rambl|e /ˈræmbl/ *n* Wanderung *f* ● *vi* wandern; (*in speech*) irrereden. **~er** *n* Wanderer *m*; (*rose*) Kletterrose *f*. **~ing** *a* weitschweifig; <*club*> Wander-
ramp /ræmp/ *n* Rampe *f*; (*Aviat*) Gangway *f*
rampage[1] /ˈræmpeɪdʒ/ *n* **be/go on the ~** randalieren
rampage[2] /ræmˈpeɪdʒ/ *vi* randalieren
ramshackle /ˈræmʃækl/ *a* baufällig
ran /ræn/ *see* **run**
ranch /rɑ:ntʃ/ *n* Ranch *f*
random /ˈrændəm/ *a* willkürlich; **a ~ sample** eine Stichprobe ● *n* **at ~** aufs Geratewohl; <*choose*> willkürlich
rang /ræŋ/ *see* **ring**[2]
range /reɪndʒ/ *n* Serie *f*, Reihe *f*; (*Comm*) Auswahl *f*, Angebot *nt* (**of** an + *dat*); (*of mountains*)

Kette *f*; (*Mus*) Umfang *m*; (*distance*) Reichweite *f*; (*for shooting*) Schießplatz *m*; (*stove*) Kohlenherd *m* ● *vi* reichen; ~ **from ... to** gehen von ... bis. ~**r** *n* Aufseher *m*

rank /ræŋk/ *n* (*row*) Reihe *f*; (*Mil*) Rang *m*; (*social position*) Stand *m*; **the ~ and file** die breite Masse ● *vt/i* einstufen; ~ **among** zählen zu

ransack /'rænsæk/ *vt* durchwühlen; (*pillage*) plündern

ransom /'rænsəm/ *n* Lösegeld *nt*; **hold s.o. to ~** Lösegeld für jdn fordern

rape /reɪp/ *n* Vergewaltigung *f* ● *vt* vergewaltigen

rapid /'ræpɪd/ *a*, **-ly** *adv* schnell. ~**ity** /rə'pɪdətɪ/ *n* Schnelligkeit *f*

rapist /'reɪpɪst/ *n* Vergewaltiger *m*

raptur|e /'ræptʃə(r)/ *n* Entzücken *nt*. ~**ous** /-rəs/ *a*, **-ly** *adv* begeistert

rare¹ /reə(r)/ *a* (**-r**, **-st**), **-ly** *adv* selten

rare² *a* (*Culin*) englisch gebraten

rarefied /'reərɪfaɪd/ *a* dünn

rarity /'reərətɪ/ *n* Seltenheit *f*

rascal /'rɑːskl/ *n* Schlingel *m*

rash¹ /ræʃ/ *n* (*Med*) Ausschlag *m*

rash² *a* (**-er**, **-est**), **-ly** *adv* voreilig

rasher /'ræʃə(r)/ *n* Speckscheibe *f*

raspberry /'rɑːzbərɪ/ *n* Himbeere *f*

rat /ræt/ *n* Ratte *f*; (! *person*) Schuft *m*; **smell a ~** ! Lunte riechen

rate /reɪt/ *n* Rate *f*; (*speed*) Tempo *nt*; (*of payment*) Satz *m*; (*of exchange*) Kurs *m*; ~**s** *pl* (*taxes*) ≈ Grundsteuer *f*; **at any ~** auf jeden Fall; **at this ~** auf diese Weise ● *vt* einschätzen; ~ **among** zählen zu ● *vi* ~ **as** gelten als

rather /'rɑːðə(r)/ *adv* lieber; (*fairly*) ziemlich; ~**!** und ob!

rating /'reɪtɪŋ/ *n* Einschätzung *f*; (*class*) Klasse *f*; (*sailor*) [einfacher] Matrose *m*; ~**s** *pl* (*Radio, TV*) ≈ Einschaltquote *f*

ratio /'reɪʃɪəʊ/ *n* Verhältnis *nt*

ration /'ræʃn/ *n* Ration *f* ● *vt* rationieren

rational /'ræʃənl/ *a*, **-ly** *adv* rational. ~**ize** *vt/i* rationalisieren

rattle /'rætl/ *n* Rasseln *nt*; (*of windows*) Klappern *nt*; (*toy*) Klapper *f* ● *vi* rasseln; klappern ● *vt* rasseln mit

raucous /'rɔːkəs/ *a* rau

rave /reɪv/ *vi* toben; ~ **about** schwärmen von

raven /'reɪvn/ *n* Rabe *m*

ravenous /'rævənəs/ *a* heißhungrig

ravine /rə'viːn/ *n* Schlucht *f*

raving /'reɪvɪŋ/ *a* ~ **mad** ! total verrückt

ravishing /'rævɪʃɪŋ/ *a* hinreißend

raw /rɔː/ *a* (**-er**, **-est**) roh; (*not processed*) Roh-; <*skin*> wund; <*weather*> nasskalt; (*inexperienced*) unerfahren; **get a ~ deal** ! schlecht wegkommen. ~ **ma'terials** *npl* Rohstoffe *pl*

ray /reɪ/ *n* Strahl *m*

razor /'reɪzə(r)/ *n* Rasierapparat *m*. ~ **blade** *n* Rasierklinge *f*

re /riː/ *prep* betreffs (+ *gen*)

reach /riːtʃ/ *n* Reichweite *f*; (*of river*) Strecke *f*; **within/out of ~** in/außer Reichweite ● *vt* erreichen; (*arrive at*) ankommen in (+ *dat*); (~ *as far as*) reichen bis zu; kommen zu <*decision, conclusion*>; (*pass*) reichen ● *vi* reichen (**to** bis zu); ~ **for** greifen nach

re'act /rɪ-/*vi* reagieren (**to** auf + *acc*)

re'action /rɪ-/ *n* Reaktion *f*. **~ary** *a* reaktionär
reactor /rɪ'æktə(r)/ *n* Reaktor *m*
read /ri:d/ *vt/i* (*pt/pp* **read** /red/) lesen; (*aloud*) vorlesen (**to** *dat*); (*Univ*) studieren; ablesen <*meter*>. **~ out** *vt* vorlesen
readable /'ri:dəbl/ *a* lesbar
reader /'ri:də(r)/ *n* Leser(in) *m(f)*; (*book*) Lesebuch *nt*
readily /'redɪlɪ/ *adv* bereitwillig; (*easily*) leicht
reading /'ri:dɪŋ/ *n* Lesen *nt*; (*Pol, Relig*) Lesung *f*
rea'djust /ri:-/ *vt* neu einstellen ● *vi* sich umstellen (**to** auf + *acc*)
ready /'redɪ/ *a* (**-ier, -iest**) fertig; (*willing*) bereit; (*quick*) schnell; **get ~** sich fertig machen; (*prepare to*) sich bereitmachen
ready: ~-'made *a* fertig. **~-to-'wear** *a* Konfektions-
real /rɪəl/ *a* wirklich; (*genuine*) echt; (*actual*) eigentlich ● *adv* (*Amer* [!]) echt. **~ estate** *n* Immobilien *pl*
realis|m /'rɪəlɪzm/ *n* Realismus *m*. **~t** /-lɪst/ *n* Realist *m*. **~tic** /-'lɪstɪk/ *a*, **-ally** *adv* realistisch
reality /rɪ'ælətɪ/ *n* Wirklichkeit *f*
realization /rɪəlaɪ'zeɪʃn/ *n* Erkenntnis *f*
realize /'rɪəlaɪz/ *vt* einsehen; (*become aware*) gewahr werden; verwirklichen <*hopes, plans*>; einbringen <*price*>
really /'rɪəlɪ/ *adv* wirklich; (*actually*) eigentlich
realm /relm/ *n* Reich *nt*
realtor /'ri:əltə(r)/ *n* (*Amer*) Immobilienmakler *m*
reap /ri:p/ *vt* ernten
reap'pear /ri:-/ *vi* wiederkommen
rear¹ /rɪə(r)/ *a* Hinter-; (*Auto*) Heck- ● *n* **the ~** der hintere Teil; **from the ~** von hinten
rear² *vt* aufziehen ● *vi* **~ [up]** <*horse:*> sich aufbäumen
rear'range /ri:-/ *vt* umstellen
reason /'ri:zn/ *n* Grund *m*; (*good sense*) Vernunft *f*; (*ability to think*) Verstand *m*; **within ~** in vernünftigen Grenzen ● *vi* argumentieren; **~ with** vernünftig reden mit. **~able** /-əbl/ *a* vernünftig; (*not expensive*) preiswert. **~ably** /-əblɪ/ *adv* (*fairly*) ziemlich
reas'sur|ance /ri:-/ *n* Beruhigung *f*; Versicherung *f*. **~e** *vt* beruhigen; **~e s.o. of sth** jdm etw (*gen*) versichern
rebel¹ /'rebl/ *n* Rebell *m*
rebel² /rɪ'bel/ *vi* (*pt/pp* **rebelled**) rebellieren. **~lion** /-ɪən/ *n* Rebellion *f*. **~lious** /-ɪəs/ *a* rebellisch
re'bound¹ /rɪ-/ *vi* abprallen
'rebound² /ri:-/ *n* Rückprall *m*
re'build /ri:-/ *vt* (*pt/pp* **-built**) wieder aufbauen
rebuke /rɪ'bju:k/ *n* Tadel *m* ● *vt* tadeln
re'call /rɪ-/ *n* Erinnerung *f* ● *vt* zurückrufen; abberufen <*diplomat*>; (*remember*) sich erinnern an (+ *acc*)
recant /rɪ'kænt/ *vi* widerrufen
recap /'ri:kæp/ *vt/i* [!] = **recapitulate**
recapitulate /ri:kə'pɪtjʊleɪt/ *vt/i* zusammenfassen; rekapitulieren
re'capture /ri:-/ *vt* wieder gefangen nehmen <*person*>; wieder einfangen <*animal*>
reced|e /rɪ'si:d/ *vi* zurückgehen. **~ing** *a* <*forehead, chin*> fliehend
receipt /rɪ'si:t/ *n* Quittung *f*; (*receiving*) Empfang *m*; **~s** *pl* (*Comm*) Einnahmen *pl*
receive /rɪ'si:v/ *vt* erhalten, bekommen; empfangen <*guests*>. **~r** *n* (*Teleph*) Hörer *m*; (*of stolen goods*) Hehler *m*

recent /'ri:sənt/ *a* kürzlich erfolgte(r,s). **~ly** *adv* vor kurzem
receptacle /rɪ'septəkl/ *n* Behälter *m*
reception /rɪ'sepʃn/ *n* Empfang *m*; **~ [desk]** (*in hotel*) Rezeption *f*. **~ist** *n* Empfangsdame *f*
receptive /rɪ'septɪv/ *a* aufnahmefähig; **~ to** empfänglich für
recess /rɪ'ses/ *n* Nische *f*; (*holiday*) Ferien *pl*
recession /rɪ'seʃn/ *n* Rezession *f*
re'charge /ri:-/ *vt* [wieder] aufladen
recipe /'resəpɪ/ *n* Rezept *nt*
recipient /rɪ'sɪpɪənt/ *n* Empfänger *m*
recital /rɪ'saɪtl/ *n* (*of poetry, songs*) Vortrag *m*; (*of instrumental music*) Konzert *nt*
recite /rɪ'saɪt/ *vt* aufsagen; (*before audience*) vortragen
reckless /'reklɪs/ *a*, **-ly** *adv* leichtsinnig; (*careless*) rücksichtslos. **~ness** *n* Leichtsinn *m*; (*carelessness*) Rücksichtslosigkeit *f*
reckon /'rekən/ *vt* rechnen; (*consider*) glauben ● *vi* **~ on/with** rechnen mit
re'claim /rɪ-/ *vt* zurückfordern; zurückgewinnen <*land*>
reclin|e /rɪ'klaɪn/ *vi* liegen. **~ing seat** *n* Liegesitz *m*
recluse /rɪ'klu:s/ *n* Einsiedler(in) *m(f)*
recognition /rekəg'nɪʃn/ *n* Erkennen *nt*; (*acknowledgement*) Anerkennung *f*; **in ~** als Anerkennung (**of** *gen*)
recognize /'rekəgnaɪz/ *vt* erkennen; (*know again*) wieder erkennen; (*acknowledge*) anerkennen
re'coil /rɪ-/ *vi* zurückschnellen; (*in fear*) zurückschrecken
recollect /rekə'lekt/ *vt* sich erinnern an (+ *acc*). **~ion** /-ekʃn/ *n* Erinnerung *f*
recommend /rekə'mend/ *vt* empfehlen. **~ation** /-'deɪʃn/ *n* Empfehlung *f*
recon|cile /'rekənsaɪl/ *vt* versöhnen; **~cile oneself to** sich abfinden mit. **~ciliation** /-sɪlɪ'eɪʃn/ *n* Versöhnung *f*
reconnaissance /rɪ'kɒnɪsns/ *n* (*Mil*) Aufklärung *f*
reconnoitre /rekə'nɔɪtə(r)/ *vi* (*pres p* **-tring**) auf Erkundung ausgehen
recon'sider /ri:-/ *vt* sich (*dat*) noch einmal überlegen
recon'struct /ri:-/ *vt* wieder aufbauen; rekonstruieren <*crime*>
record¹ /rɪ'kɔ:d/ *vt* aufzeichnen; (*register*) registrieren; (*on tape*) aufnehmen
record² /'rekɔ:d/ *n* Aufzeichnung *f*; (*Jur*) Protokoll *nt*; (*Mus*) [Schall]platte *f*; (*Sport*) Rekord *m*; **~s** *pl* Unterlagen *pl*; **off the ~** inoffiziell; **have a [criminal] ~** vorbestraft sein
recorder /rɪ'kɔ:də(r)/ *n* (*Mus*) Blockflöte *f*
recording /rɪ'kɔ:dɪŋ/ *n* Aufnahme *f*
re-'count¹ /ri:-/ *vt* nachzählen
're-count² /ri:-/ *n* (*Pol*) Nachzählung *f*
recover /rɪ'kʌvə(r)/ *vt* zurückbekommen ● *vi* sich erholen. **~y** *n* Wiedererlangung *f*; (*of health*) Erholung *f*
recreation /rekrɪ'eɪʃn/ *n* Erholung *f*; (*hobby*) Hobby *nt*. **~al** *a* Freizeit-; **be ~al** erholsam sein
recruit /rɪ'kru:t/ *n* (*Mil*) Rekrut *m*; **new ~** (*member*) neues Mitglied *nt*; (*worker*) neuer Mitarbeiter *m* ● *vt* rekrutieren;

anwerben <*staff*>. **~ment** *n* Rekrutierung *f*; Anwerbung *f*
rectang|le /'rektæŋgl/ *n* Rechteck *nt*. **~ular** /-'tæŋgjʊlə(r)/ *a* rechteckig
rectify /'rektɪfaɪ/ *vt* (*pt*/*pp* **-ied**) berichtigen
rector /'rektə(r)/ *n* Pfarrer *m*; (*Univ*) Rektor *m*. **~y** *n* Pfarrhaus *nt*
recur /rɪ'kɜ:(r)/ *vi* (*pt*/*pp* **recurred**) sich wiederholen; <*illness:*> wiederkehren
recurren|ce /rɪ'kʌrəns/ *n* Wiederkehr *f*. **~t** *a* wiederkehrend
recycle /ri:'saɪkl/ *vt* wieder verwerten
red /red/ *a* (**redder, reddest**) rot ● *n* Rot *nt*
redd|en /'redn/ *vt* röten ● *vi* rot werden. **~ish** *a* rötlich
re'decorate /ri:-/ *vt* renovieren; (*paint*) neu streichen; (*wallpaper*) neu tapezieren
redeem /rɪ'di:m/ *vt* einlösen; (*Relig*) erlösen
redemption /rɪ'dempʃn/ *n* Erlösung *f*
red: **~-haired** *a* rothaarig. **~-'handed** *a* **catch s.o. ~-handed** jdn auf frischer Tat ertappen. **~ 'herring** *n* falsche Spur *f*. **~-hot** *a* glühend heiß. **~ 'light** *n* (*Auto*) rote Ampel *f*. **~ness** *n* Röte *f*
re'do /ri:-/ *vt* (*pt* **-did**, *pp* **-done**) noch einmal machen
re'double /ri:-/ *vt* verdoppeln
red 'tape *n* [!] Bürokratie *f*
reduc|e /rɪ'dju:s/ *vt* verringern, vermindern; (*in size*) verkleinern; ermäßigen <*costs*>; herabsetzen <*price, goods*>; (*Culin*) einkochen lassen. **~tion** /-'dʌkʃn/ *n* Verringerung *f*; (*in price*) Ermäßigung *f*; (*in size*) Verkleinerung *f*
redundan|cy /rɪ'dʌndənsɪ/ *n* Beschäftigungslosigkeit *f*. **~t** *a* überflüssig; **make ~t** entlassen; **be made ~t** beschäftigungslos werden
reed /ri:d/ *n* [Schilf]rohr *nt*; **~s** *pl* Schilf *nt*
reef /ri:f/ *n* Riff *nt*
reek /ri:k/ *vi* riechen (**of** nach)
reel /ri:l/ *n* Rolle *f*, Spule *f* ● *vi* (*stagger*) taumeln ● *vt* **~ off** (*fig*) herunterrasseln
refectory /rɪ'fektərɪ/ *n* Refektorium *nt*; (*Univ*) Mensa *f*
refer /rɪ'fɜ:(r)/ *v* (*pt*/*pp* **referred**) ● *vt* verweisen (**to** an + *acc*); übergeben, weiterleiten <*matter*> (**to** an + *acc*) ● *vi* **~ to** sich beziehen auf (+ *acc*); (*mention*) erwähnen; (*concern*) betreffen; (*consult*) sich wenden an (+ *acc*); nachschlagen in (+ *dat*) <*book*>; **are you ~ring to me?** meinen Sie mich?
referee /refə'ri:/ *n* Schiedsrichter *m*; (*Boxing*) Ringrichter *m*; (*for job*) Referenz *f* ● *vt*/*i* (*pt*/*pp* **refereed**) Schiedsrichter/Ringrichter sein (bei)
reference /'refərəns/ *n* Erwähnung *f*; (*in book*) Verweis *m*; (*for job*) Referenz *f*; **with ~ to** in Bezug auf (+ *acc*); **make [a] ~ to** erwähnen. **~ book** *n* Nachschlagewerk *nt*
referendum /refə'rendəm/ *n* Volksabstimmung *f*
re'fill¹ /ri:-/ *vt* nachfüllen
'refill² /ri:-/ *n* (*for pen*) Ersatzmine *f*
refine /rɪ'faɪn/ *vt* raffinieren. **~d** *a* fein, vornehm. **~ment** *n* Vornehmheit *f*; (*Techn*) Verfeinerung *f*. **~ry** /-ərɪ/ *n* Raffinerie *f*
reflect /rɪ'flekt/ *vt* reflektieren; <*mirror:*> [wider]spiegeln; **be ~ed in** sich spiegeln in (+ *dat*) ● *vi* nachdenken (**on** über + *acc*). **~ion** /-ekʃn/ *n* Reflexion *f*;

(*image*) Spiegelbild *nt*; **on ~ion** nach nochmaliger Überlegung. **~or** *n* Rückstrahler *m*

reflex /'ri:fleks/ *n* Reflex *m*

reflexive /rɪ'fleksɪv/ *a* reflexiv

reform /rɪ'fɔ:m/ *n* Reform *f* ● *vt* reformieren ● *vi* sich bessern

refrain¹ /rɪ'freɪn/ *n* Refrain *m*

refrain² *vi* **~ from doing sth** etw nicht tun

refresh /rɪ'freʃ/ *vt* erfrischen. **~ing** *a* erfrischend. **~ments** *npl* Erfrischungen *pl*

refrigerat|e /rɪ'frɪdʒəreɪt/ *vt* kühlen. **~or** *n* Kühlschrank *m*

re'fuel /ri:-/ *vt/i* (*pt/pp* **-fuelled**) auftanken

refuge /'refju:dʒ/ *n* Zuflucht *f*; **take ~** Zuflucht nehmen

refugee /refjʊ'dʒi:/ *n* Flüchtling *m*

'refund¹ /ri:-/ *n* **get a ~** sein Geld zurückbekommen

re'fund² /rɪ-/ *vt* zurückerstatten

refusal /rɪ'fju:zl/ *n* (*see* **refuse¹**) Ablehnung *f*; Weigerung *f*

refuse¹ /rɪ'fju:z/ *vt* ablehnen; (*not grant*) verweigern; **~ to do sth** sich weigern, etw zu tun ● *vi* ablehnen; sich weigern

refuse² /'refju:s/ *n* Müll *m*

refute /rɪ'fju:t/ *vt* widerlegen

re'gain /rɪ-/ *vt* wiedergewinnen

regal /'ri:gl/ *a*, **-ly** *adv* königlich

regard /rɪ'ga:d/ *n* (*heed*) Rücksicht *f*; (*respect*) Achtung *f*; **~s** *pl* Grüße *pl*; **with ~ to** in Bezug auf (+ *acc*) ● *vt* ansehen, betrachten (**as** als). **~ing** *prep* bezüglich (+ *gen*). **~less** *adv* ohne Rücksicht (**of** auf + *acc*)

regatta /rɪ'gætə/ *n* Regatta *f*

regime /reɪ'ʒi:m/ *n* Regime *nt*

regiment /'redʒɪmənt/ *n* Regiment *nt*. **~al** /-'mentl/ *a* Regiments-

region /'ri:dʒən/ *n* Region *f*; **in the ~ of** (*fig*) ungefähr. **~al** *a*, **-ly** *adv* regional

register /'redʒɪstə(r)/ *n* Register *nt*; (*Sch*) Anwesenheitsliste *f* ● *vt* registrieren; (*report*) anmelden; einschreiben <*letter*>; aufgeben <*luggage*> ● *vi* (*report*) sich anmelden

registrar /redʒɪ'stra:(r)/ *n* Standesbeamte(r) *m*

registration /redʒɪ'streɪʃn/ *n* Registrierung *f*; Anmeldung *f*. **~ number** *n* Autonummer *f*

registry office /'redʒɪstrɪ-/ *n* Standesamt *nt*

regret /rɪ'gret/ *n* Bedauern *nt* ● *vt* (*pt/pp* **regretted**) bedauern. **~fully** *adv* mit Bedauern

regrettab|le /rɪ'gretəbl/ *a* bedauerlich. **~ly** *adv* bedauerlicherweise

regular /'regjʊlə(r)/ *a*, **-ly** *adv* regelmäßig; (*usual*) üblich ● *n* (*in pub*) Stammgast *m*; (*in shop*) Stammkunde *m*. **~ity** /-'lærətɪ/ *n* Regelmäßigkeit *f*

regulat|e /'regjʊleɪt/ *vt* regulieren. **~ion** /-'leɪʃn/ *n* (*rule*) Vorschrift *f*

rehears|al /rɪ'hɜ:sl/ *n* (*Theat*) Probe *f*. **~e** *vt* proben

reign /reɪn/ *n* Herrschaft *f* ● *vi* herrschen, regieren

rein /reɪn/ *n* Zügel *m*

reindeer /'reɪndɪə(r)/ *n inv* Rentier *nt*

reinforce /ri:ɪn'fɔ:s/ *vt* verstärken. **~ment** *n* Verstärkung *f*; **send ~ments** Verstärkung schicken

reiterate /ri:'ɪtəreɪt/ *vt* wiederholen

reject /rɪ'dʒekt/ *vt* ablehnen. **~ion** /-ekʃn/ *n* Ablehnung *f*

rejects /'ri:dʒekts/ *npl* (*Comm*) Ausschussware *f*

rejoic|e /rɪ'dʒɔɪs/ *vi* (*liter*) sich freuen. **~ing** *n* Freude *f*

re'join /rɪ-/ *vt* sich wieder anschließen (+ *dat*); wieder beitreten (+ *dat*) <*club, party*>

rejuvenate /rɪ'dʒu:vəneɪt/ *vt* verjüngen

relapse /rɪ'læps/ *n* Rückfall *m* ● *vi* einen Rückfall erleiden

relate /rɪ'leɪt/ *vt* (*tell*) erzählen; (*connect*) verbinden

relation /rɪ'leɪʃn/ *n* Beziehung *f*; (*person*) Verwandte(r) *m/f*. **~ship** *n* Beziehung *f*; (*link*) Verbindung *f*; (*blood tie*) Verwandtschaft *f*; (*affair*) Verhältnis *nt*

relative /'relətɪv/ *n* Verwandte(r) *m/f* ● *a* relativ; (*Gram*) Relativ-. **~ly** *adv* relativ, verhältnismäßig

relax /rɪ'læks/ *vt* lockern, entspannen ● *vi* sich lockern, sich entspannen. **~ation** /-'seɪʃn/ *n* Entspannung *f*. **~ing** *a* entspannend

relay¹ /ri:'leɪ/ *vt* (*pt/pp* **-layed**) weitergeben; (*Radio, TV*) übertragen

relay² /'ri:leɪ/ *n*. **~ [race]** *n* Staffel *f*

release /rɪ'li:s/ *n* Freilassung *f*, Entlassung *f*; (*Techn*) Auslöser *m* ● *vt* freilassen; (*let go of*) loslassen; (*Techn*) auslösen; veröffentlichen <*information*>

relent /rɪ'lent/ *vi* nachgeben. **~less** *a*, **-ly** *adv* erbarmungslos; (*unceasing*) unaufhörlich

relevan|ce /'reləvəns/ *n* Relevanz *f*. **~t** *a* relevant (**to** für)

reliab|ility /rɪlaɪə'bɪlətɪ/ *n* Zuverlässigkeit *f*. **~le** /-'laɪəbl/ *a*, **-ly** *adv* zuverlässig

relian|ce /rɪ'laɪəns/ *n* Abhängigkeit *f* (**on** von). **~t** *a* angewiesen (**on** auf + *acc*)

relic /'relɪk/ *n* Überbleibsel *nt*; (*Relig*) Reliquie *f*

relief /rɪ'li:f/ *n* Erleichterung *f*; (*assistance*) Hilfe *f*; (*replacement*) Ablösung *f*; (*Art*) Relief *nt*

relieve /rɪ'li:v/ *vt* erleichtern; (*take over from*) ablösen; **~ of** entlasten von

religion /rɪ'lɪdʒən/ *n* Religion *f*

religious /rɪ'lɪdʒəs/ *a* religiös

relinquish /rɪ'lɪŋkwɪʃ/ *vt* loslassen; (*give up*) aufgeben

relish /'relɪʃ/ *n* Genuss *m*; (*Culin*) Würze *f* ● *vt* genießen

reluctan|ce /rɪ'lʌktəns/ *n* Widerstreben *nt*. **~t** *a* widerstrebend; **be ~t** zögern (**to** zu). **~tly** *adv* ungern, widerstrebend

rely /rɪ'laɪ/ *vi* (*pt/pp* **-ied**) **~ on** sich verlassen auf (+ *acc*); (*be dependent on*) angewiesen sein auf (+ *acc*)

remain /rɪ'meɪn/ *vi* bleiben; (*be left*) übrig bleiben. **~der** *n* Rest *m*. **~ing** *a* restlich. **~s** *npl* Reste *pl*; **[mortal] ~s** [sterbliche] Überreste *pl*

remand /rɪ'mɑ:nd/ *n* **on ~** in Untersuchungshaft ● *vt* **~ in custody** in Untersuchungshaft schicken

remark /rɪ'mɑ:k/ *n* Bemerkung *f* ● *vt* bemerken. **~able** /-əbl/ *a*, **-bly** *adv* bemerkenswert

remarry /ri:-/ *vi* wieder heiraten

remedy /'remədɪ/ *n* [Heil]mittel *nt* (**for** gegen); (*fig*) Abhilfe *f* ● *vt* (*pt/pp* **-ied**) abhelfen (+ *dat*); beheben <*fault*>

remember /rɪ'membə(r)/ *vt* sich erinnern an (+ *acc*); **~ to do sth** daran denken, etw zu tun ● *vi* sich erinnern

remind /rɪ'maɪnd/ *vt* erinnern (**of** an + *acc*). **~er** *n* Andenken *nt*; (*letter, warning*) Mahnung *f*

reminisce /remɪ'nɪs/ *vi* sich seinen Erinnerungen hingeben. **~nces** /-ənsɪs/ *npl*

Erinnerungen *pl.* **~nt** *a* **be ~nt of** erinnern an (+ *acc*)

remnant /'remnənt/ *n* Rest *m*

remorse /rɪ'mɔ:s/ *n* Reue *f*. **~ful** *a*, **-ly** *adv* reumütig. **~less** *a*, **-ly** *adv* unerbittlich

remote /rɪ'məʊt/ *a* fern; (*isolated*) abgelegen; (*slight*) gering. **~ con'trol** *n* Fernsteuerung *f*; (*for TV*) Fernbedienung *f*

remotely /rɪ'məʊtlɪ/ *adv* entfernt; **not ~** nicht im Entferntesten

re'movable /rɪ-/ *a* abnehmbar

removal /rɪ'mu:vl/ *n* Entfernung *f*; (*from house*) Umzug *m*. **~ van** *n* Möbelwagen *m*

remove /rɪ'mu:v/ *vt* entfernen; (*take off*) abnehmen; (*take out*) herausnehmen

render /'rendə(r)/ *vt* machen; erweisen <*service*>; (*translate*) wiedergeben; (*Mus*) vortragen

renegade /'renɪgeɪd/ *n* Abtrünnige(r) *m*/*f*

renew /rɪ'nju:/ *vt* erneuern; verlängern <*contract*>. **~al** *n* Erneuerung *f*; Verlängerung *f*

renounce /rɪ'naʊns/ *vt* verzichten auf (+ *acc*)

renovat|e /'renəveɪt/ *vt* renovieren. **~ion** /-'veɪʃn/ *n* Renovierung *f*

renown /rɪ'naʊn/ *n* Ruf *m*. **~ed** *a* berühmt

rent /rent/ *n* Miete *f* ● *vt* mieten; (*hire*) leihen; **~ [out]** vermieten; verleihen. **~al** *n* Mietgebühr *f*; Leihgebühr *f*

renunciation /rɪnʌnsɪ'eɪʃn/ *n* Verzicht *m*

re'open /ri:-/ *vt*/*i* wieder aufmachen

re'organize /ri:-/ *vt* reorganisieren

rep /rep/ *n* [!] Vertreter *m*

repair /rɪ'peə(r)/ *n* Reparatur *f*; **in good/bad ~** in gutem/schlechtem Zustand ● *vt* reparieren

repatriate /ri:'pætrɪeɪt/ *vt* repatriieren

re'pay /ri:-/ *vt* (*pt*/*pp* **-paid**) zurückzahlen; **~ s.o. for sth** jdm etw zurückzahlen. **~ment** *n* Rückzahlung *f*

repeal /rɪ'pi:l/ *n* Aufhebung *f* ● *vt* aufheben

repeat /rɪ'pi:t/ *n* Wiederholung *f* ● *vt*/*i* wiederholen; **~ after me** sprechen Sie mir nach. **~ed** *a*, **-ly** *adv* wiederholt

repel /rɪ'pel/ *vt* (*pt*/*pp* **repelled**) abwehren; (*fig*) abstoßen. **~lent** *a* abstoßend

repent /rɪ'pent/ *vi* Reue zeigen. **~ance** *n* Reue *f*. **~ant** *a* reuig

repercussions /ri:pə'kʌʃnz/ *npl* Auswirkungen *pl*

repertoire, /'repətwɑ:(r)/ **repertory** /'repətrɪ/ *n* Repertoire *nt*

repetit|ion /repɪ'tɪʃn/ *n* Wiederholung *f*. **~ive** /rɪ'petɪtɪv/ *a* eintönig

re'place /rɪ-/ *vt* zurücktun; (*take the place of*) ersetzen; (*exchange*) austauschen. **~ment** *n* Ersatz *m*

'replay /ri:-/ *n* (*Sport*) Wiederholungsspiel *nt*; **[action] ~** Wiederholung *f*

replenish /rɪ'plenɪʃ/ *vt* auffüllen <*stocks*>; (*refill*) nachfüllen

replica /'replɪkə/ *n* Nachbildung *f*

reply /rɪ'plaɪ/ *n* Antwort *f* (**to** auf + *acc*) ● *vt*/*i* (*pt*/*pp* **replied**) antworten

report /rɪ'pɔ:t/ *n* Bericht *m*; (*Sch*) Zeugnis *nt*; (*rumour*) Gerücht *nt*; (*of gun*) Knall *m* ● *vt* berichten; (*notify*) melden; **~ s.o. to the police** jdn anzeigen ● *vi* berichten (**on** über + *acc*);

(*present oneself*) sich melden (**to** bei). **~er** *n* Reporter(in) *m(f)*

reprehensible /reprɪˈhensəbl/ *a* tadelnswert

represent /reprɪˈzent/ *vt* darstellen; (*act for*) vertreten, repräsentieren. **~ation** /-ˈteɪʃn/ *n* Darstellung *f*

representative /reprɪˈzentətɪv/ *a* repräsentativ (**of** für) ● *n* Bevollmächtigte(r) *m/(f)*; (*Comm*) Vertreter(in) *m(f)*; (*Amer, Pol*) Abgeordnete(r) *m/f*

repress /rɪˈpres/ *vt* unterdrücken. **~ion** /-eʃn/ *n* Unterdrückung *f*. **~ive** /-ɪv/ *a* repressiv

reprieve /rɪˈpriːv/ *n* Begnadigung *f*; (*fig*) Gnadenfrist *f* ● *vt* begnadigen

reprimand /ˈreprɪmɑːnd/ *n* Tadel *m* ● *vt* tadeln

ˈreprint¹ /riː-/ *n* Nachdruck *m*

reˈprint² /riː-/ *vt* neu auflegen

reprisal /rɪˈpraɪzl/ *n* Vergeltungsmaßnahme *f*

reproach /rɪˈprəʊtʃ/ *n* Vorwurf *m* ● *vt* Vorwürfe *pl* machen (+ *dat*). **~ful** *a*, **-ly** *adv* vorwurfsvoll

reproˈduc|e /riː-/ *vt* wiedergeben, reproduzieren ● *vi* sich fortpflanzen. **~tion** /-ˈdʌkʃn/ *n* Reproduktion *f*; (*Biol*) Fortpflanzung *f*

reptile /ˈreptaɪl/ *n* Reptil *nt*

republic /rɪˈpʌblɪk/ *n* Republik *f*. **~an** *a* republikanisch ● *n* Republikaner(in) *m(f)*

repugnan|ce /rɪˈpʌgnəns/ *n* Widerwille *m*. **~t** *a* widerlich

repuls|ion /rɪˈpʌlʃn/ *n* Widerwille *m*. **~ive** /-ɪv/ *a* abstoßend, widerlich

reputable /ˈrepjʊtəbl/ *a* <*firm*> von gutem Ruf; (*respectable*) anständig

reputation /repjʊˈteɪʃn/ *n* Ruf *m*

request /rɪˈkwest/ *n* Bitte *f* ● *vt* bitten

require /rɪˈkwaɪə(r)/ *vt* (*need*) brauchen; (*demand*) erfordern; **be ~d to do sth** etw tun müssen. **~ment** *n* Bedürfnis *nt*; (*condition*) Erfordernis *nt*

reˈsale /riː-/ *n* Weiterverkauf *m*

rescue /ˈreskjuː/ *n* Rettung *f* ● *vt* retten. **~r** *n* Retter *m*

research /rɪˈsɜːtʃ/ *n* Forschung *f* ● *vt* erforschen; (*Journ*) recherchieren. **~er** *n* Forscher *m*; (*Journ*) Rechercheur *m*

resem|blance /rɪˈzembləns/ *n* Ähnlichkeit *f*. **~ble** /-bl/ *vt* ähneln (+ *dat*)

resent /rɪˈzent/ *vt* übel nehmen; einen Groll hegen gegen <*person*>. **~ful** *a*, **-ly** *adv* verbittert. **~ment** *n* Groll *m*

reservation /rezəˈveɪʃn/ *n* Reservierung *f*; (*doubt*) Vorbehalt *m*; (*enclosure*) Reservat *nt*

reserve /rɪˈzɜːv/ *n* Reserve *f*; (*for animals*) Reservat *nt*; (*Sport*) Reservespieler(in) *m(f)* ● *vt* reservieren; <*client:*> reservieren lassen; (*keep*) aufheben; sich (*dat*) vorbehalten <*right*>. **~d** *a* reserviert

reservoir /ˈrezəvwɑː(r)/ *n* Reservoir *nt*

reˈshuffle /riː-/ *n* (*Pol*) Umbildung *f* ● *vt* (*Pol*) umbilden

residence /ˈrezɪdəns/ *n* Wohnsitz *m*; (*official*) Residenz *f*; (*stay*) Aufenthalt *m*

resident /ˈrezɪdənt/ *a* ansässig (**in** in + *dat*); <*housekeeper, nurse*> im Haus wohnend ● *n* Bewohner(in) *m(f)*; (*of street*) Anwohner *m*. **~ial** /-ˈdenʃl/ *a* Wohn-

residue /ˈrezɪdjuː/ *n* Rest *m*; (*Chem*) Rückstand *m*

resign /rɪˈzaɪn/ *vt* **~ oneself to** sich abfinden mit ● *vi* kündigen; (*from public office*) zurücktreten.

~ation /rezɪg'neɪʃn/ *n* Resignation *f*; (*from job*) Kündigung *f*, Rücktritt *m*. **~ed** *a*, **-ly** *adv* resigniert
resilient /rɪ'zɪlɪənt/ *a* federnd; (*fig*) widerstandsfähig
resin /'rezɪn/ *n* Harz *nt*
resist /rɪ'zɪst/ *vt*/*i* sich widersetzen (+ *dat*), (*fig*) widerstehen (+ *dat*). **~ance** *n* Widerstand *m*. **~ant** *a* widerstandsfähig
resolut|e /'rezəlu:t/ *a*, **-ly** *adv* entschlossen. **~ion** /-'lu:ʃn/ *n* Entschlossenheit *f*; (*intention*) Vorsatz *m*; (*Pol*) Resolution *f*
resolve /rɪ'zɒlv/ *n* Entschlossenheit *f*; (*decision*) Beschluss *m* ● *vt* beschließen; (*solve*) lösen
resort /rɪ'zɔ:t/ *n* (*place*) Urlaubsort *m*; **as a last ~** wenn alles andere fehlschlägt ● *vi* **~ to** (*fig*) greifen zu
resound /rɪ'zaʊnd/ *vi* widerhallen
resource /rɪ'sɔ:s/ *n* **~s** *pl* Ressourcen *pl*. **~ful** *a* findig
respect /rɪ'spekt/ *n* Respekt *m*, Achtung *f* (**for** vor + *dat*); (*aspect*) Hinsicht *f*; **with ~ to** in Bezug auf (+ *acc*) ● *vt* respektieren, achten
respect|able /rɪ'spektəbl/ *a*, **-bly** *adv* ehrbar; (*decent*) anständig; (*considerable*) ansehnlich. **~ful** *a*, **-ly** *adv* respektvoll
respective /rɪ'spektɪv/ *a* jeweilig. **~ly** *adv* beziehungsweise
respiration /respə'reɪʃn/ *n* Atmung *f*
respite /'respaɪt/ *n* [Ruhe]pause *f*; (*delay*) Aufschub *m*
respond /rɪ'spɒnd/ *vi* antworten; (*react*) reagieren (**to** auf + *acc*)
response /rɪ'spɒns/ *n* Antwort *f*; Reaktion *f*
responsibility /rɪspɒnsɪ'bɪlətɪ/ *n* Verantwortung *f*; (*duty*) Verpflichtung *f*
responsib|le /rɪ'spɒnsəbl/ *a* verantwortlich; (*trustworthy*) verantwortungsvoll. **~ly** *adv* verantwortungsbewusst
rest¹ /rest/ *n* Ruhe *f*; (*holiday*) Erholung *f*; (*interval & Mus*) Pause *f*; **have a ~** eine Pause machen; (*rest*) sich ausruhen ● *vt* ausruhen; (*lean*) lehnen (**on** an/auf + *acc*) ● *vi* ruhen; (*have a rest*) sich ausruhen
rest² *n* **the ~** der Rest; (*people*) die Übrigen *pl* ● *vi* **it ~s with you** es ist an Ihnen (**to** zu)
restaurant /'rest(ə)rɒnt/ *n* Restaurant *nt*, Gaststätte *f*
restful /'restfl/ *a* erholsam
restive /'restɪv/ *a* unruhig
restless /'restlɪs/ *a*, **-ly** *adv* unruhig
restoration /restə'reɪʃn/ *n* (*of building*) Restaurierung *f*
restore /rɪ'stɔ:(r)/ *vt* wiederherstellen; restaurieren <*building*>
restrain /rɪ'streɪn/ *vt* zurückhalten; **~ oneself** sich beherrschen. **~ed** *a* zurückhaltend. **~t** *n* Zurückhaltung *f*
restrict /rɪ'strɪkt/ *vt* einschränken; **~ to** beschränken auf (+ *acc*). **~ion** /-ɪkʃn/ *n* Einschränkung *f*; Beschränkung *f*. **~ive** /-ɪv/ *a* einschränkend
'rest room *n* (*Amer*) Toilette *f*
result /rɪ'zʌlt/ *n* Ergebnis *nt*, Resultat *nt*; (*consequence*) Folge *f*; **as a ~** als Folge (**of** *gen*) ● *vi* sich ergeben (**from** aus); **~ in** enden in (+ *dat*); (*lead to*) führen zu
resume /rɪ'zju:m/ *vt* wieder aufnehmen ● *vi* wieder beginnen
résumé /'rezʊmeɪ/ *n* Zusammenfassung *f*

resumption /rɪˈzʌmpʃn/ *n* Wiederaufnahme *f*
resurrect /rezəˈrekt/ *vt* (*fig*) wieder beleben. **~ion** /-ekʃn/ *n* **the R ~ion** (*Relig*) die Auferstehung
resuscitat|e /rɪˈsʌsɪteɪt/ *vt* wieder beleben. **~ion** /-ˈteɪʃn/ *n* Wiederbelebung *f*
retail /ˈriːteɪl/ *n* Einzelhandel *m* ● *a* Einzelhandels- ● *adv* im Einzelhandel ● *vt* im Einzelhandel verkaufen ● *vi* **~ at** im Einzelhandel kosten. **~er** *n* Einzelhändler *m*
retain /rɪˈteɪn/ *vt* behalten
retaliat|e /rɪˈtælɪeɪt/ *vi* zurückschlagen. **~ion** /-ˈeɪʃn/ *n* Vergeltung *f*; **in ~ion** als Vergeltung
retarded /rɪˈtɑːdɪd/ *a* zurückgeblieben
reticen|ce /ˈretɪsns/ *n* Zurückhaltung *f*. **~t** *a* zurückhaltend
retina /ˈretɪnə/ *n* Netzhaut *f*
retinue /ˈretɪnjuː/ *n* Gefolge *nt*
retire /rɪˈtaɪə(r)/ *vi* in den Ruhestand treten; (*withdraw*) sich zurückziehen. **~d** *a* im Ruhestand. **~ment** *n* Ruhestand *m*
retiring /rɪˈtaɪərɪŋ/ *a* zurückhaltend
retort /rɪˈtɔːt/ *n* scharfe Erwiderung *f*; (*Chem*) Retorte *f* ● *vt* scharf erwidern
reˈtrace /rɪ-/ *vt* **~ one's steps** denselben Weg zurückgehen
reˈtrain /riː-/ *vt* umschulen ● *vi* umgeschult werden
retreat /rɪˈtriːt/ *n* Rückzug *m*; (*place*) Zufluchtsort *m* ● *vi* sich zurückziehen
reˈtrial /riː-/ *n* Wiederaufnahmeverfahren *nt*
retrieve /rɪˈtriːv/ *vt* zurückholen; (*from wreckage*) bergen; (*Computing*) wieder auffinden
retrograde /ˈretrəgreɪd/ *a* rückschrittlich
retrospect /ˈretrəspekt/ *n* **in ~** rückblickend. **~ive** /-ɪv/ *a*, **-ly** *adv* rückwirkend; (*looking back*) rückblickend
return /rɪˈtɜːn/ *n* Rückkehr *f*; (*giving back*) Rückgabe *f*; (*Comm*) Ertrag *m*; (*ticket*) Rückfahrkarte *f*; (*Aviat*) Rückflugschein *m*; **by ~ [of post]** postwendend; **in ~** dafür; **in ~ for** für; **many happy ~s!** herzlichen Glückwunsch zum Geburtstag! ● *vt* zurückgehen/-fahren; (*come back*) zurückkommen ● *vt* zurückgeben; (*put back*) zurückstellen/-legen; (*send back*) zurückschicken
return ticket *n* Rückfahrkarte *f*; (*Aviat*) Rückflugschein *m*
reunion /riːˈjuːnɪən/ *n* Wiedervereinigung *f*; (*social gathering*) Treffen *nt*
reunite /riːjuːˈnaɪt/ *vt* wieder vereinigen
reˈuse *vt* wieder verwenden
rev /rev/ *n* (*Auto* 🄸) Umdrehung *f* ● *vt/i* **~ [up]** den Motor auf Touren bringen
reveal /rɪˈviːl/ *vt* zum Vorschein bringen; (*fig*) enthüllen. **~ing** *a* (*fig*) aufschlussreich
revel /ˈrevl/ *vi* (*pt/pp* **revelled**) **~ in sth** etw genießen
revelation /revəˈleɪʃn/ *n* Offenbarung *f*, Enthüllung *f*
revenge /rɪˈvendʒ/ *n* Rache *f*; (*fig & Sport*) Revanche *f* ● *vt* rächen
revenue /ˈrevənjuː/ *n* [Staats]einnahmen *pl*
revere /rɪˈvɪə(r)/ *vt* verehren. **~nce** /ˈrevərəns/ *n* Ehrfurcht *f*
Reverend /ˈrevərənd/ *a* **the ~ X** Pfarrer X; (*Catholic*) Hochwürden X

reverent /ˈrevərənt/ *a*, **-ly** *adv* ehrfürchtig

reversal /rɪˈvɜːsl/ *n* Umkehrung *f*

reverse /rɪˈvɜːs/ *a* umgekehrt ● *n* Gegenteil *nt*; (*back*) Rückseite *f*; (*Auto*) Rückwärtsgang *m* ● *vt* umkehren; (*Auto*) zurücksetzen ● *vi* zurücksetzen

revert /rɪˈvɜːt/ *vi* **~ to** zurückfallen an (+ *acc*)

review /rɪˈvjuː/ *n* Rückblick *m* (**of** auf + *acc*); (*re-examination*) Überprüfung *f*; (*Mil*) Truppenschau *f*; (*of book, play*) Kritik *f*, Rezension *f* ● *vt* zurückblicken auf (+ *acc*); überprüfen <*situation*>; rezensieren <*book, play*>. **~er** *n* Kritiker *m*, Rezensent *m*

revis|e /rɪˈvaɪz/ *vt* revidieren; (*for exam*) wiederholen. **~ion** /-ˈvɪʒn/ *n* Revision *f*; (*for exam*) Wiederholung *f*

revival /rɪˈvaɪvl/ *n* Wiederbelebung *f*

revive /rɪˈvaɪv/ *vt* wieder beleben; (*fig*) wieder aufleben lassen ● *vi* wieder aufleben

revolt /rɪˈvəʊlt/ *n* Aufstand *m* ● *vi* rebellieren ● *vt* anwidern. **~ing** *a* widerlich, eklig

revolution /revəˈluːʃn/ *n* Revolution *f*; (*Auto*) Umdrehung *f*. **~ary** /-ərɪ/ *a* revolutionär. **~ize** *vt* revolutionieren

revolve /rɪˈvɒlv/ *vi* sich drehen; **~ around** kreisen um

revolv|er /rɪˈvɒlvə(r)/ *n* Revolver *m*. **~ing** *a* Dreh-

revue /rɪˈvjuː/ *n* Revue *f*; (*satirical*) Kabarett *nt*

revulsion /rɪˈvʌlʃn/ *n* Abscheu *m*

reward /rɪˈwɔːd/ *n* Belohnung *f* ● *vt* belohnen. **~ing** *a* lohnend

reˈwrite /riː-/ *vt* (*pt* **rewrote**, *pp* **rewritten**) noch einmal [neu] schreiben; (*alter*) umschreiben

rhetoric /ˈretərɪk/ *n* Rhetorik *f*. **~al** /rɪˈtɒrɪkl/ *a* rhetorisch

rheumatism /ˈruːmətɪzm/ *n* Rheumatismus *m*, Rheuma *nt*

Rhine /raɪn/ *n* Rhein *m*

rhinoceros /raɪˈnɒsərəs/ *n* Nashorn *nt*, Rhinozeros *nt*

rhubarb /ˈruːbɑːb/ *n* Rhabarber *m*

rhyme /raɪm/ *n* Reim *m* ● *vt* reimen ● *vi* sich reimen

rhythm /ˈriðm/ *n* Rhythmus *m*. **~ic[al]** *a*, **-ally** *adv* rhythmisch

rib /rɪb/ *n* Rippe *f*

ribbon /ˈrɪbən/ *n* Band *nt*; (*for typewriter*) Farbband *nt*

rice /raɪs/ *n* Reis *m*

rich /rɪtʃ/ *a* (**-er, -est**), **-ly** *adv* reich; <*food*> gehaltvoll; (*heavy*) schwer ● *n* **the ~** *pl* die Reichen; **~es** *pl* Reichtum *m*

ricochet /ˈrɪkəʃeɪ/ *vi* abprallen

rid /rɪd/ *vt* (*pt/pp* **rid**, *pres p* **ridding**) befreien (**of** von); **get ~ of** loswerden

riddance /ˈrɪdns/ *n* **good ~!** auf Nimmerwiedersehen!

ridden /ˈrɪdn/ *see* **ride**

riddle /ˈrɪdl/ *n* Rätsel *nt*

riddled /ˈrɪdld/ *a* **~ with** durchlöchert mit

ride /raɪd/ *n* Ritt *m*; (*in vehicle*) Fahrt *f*; **take s.o. for a ~** [!] jdn reinlegen ● *v* (*pt* **rode**, *pp* **ridden**) ● *vt* reiten <*horse*>; fahren mit <*bicycle*> ● *vi* reiten; (*in vehicle*) fahren. **~r** *n* Reiter(in) *m(f)*; (*on bicycle*) Fahrer(in) *m(f)*

ridge /rɪdʒ/ *n* Erhebung *f*; (*on roof*) First *m*; (*of mountain*) Grat *m*, Kamm *m*

ridicule /ˈrɪdɪkjuːl/ *n* Spott *m* ● *vt* verspotten, spotten über (+ *acc*)

ridiculous /rɪˈdɪkjʊləs/ *a*, **-ly** *adv* lächerlich
riding /ˈraɪdɪŋ/ *n* Reiten *nt* ● *attrib* Reit-
riff-raff /ˈrɪfræf/ *n* Gesindel *nt*
rifle /ˈraɪfl/ *n* Gewehr *nt* ● *vt* plündern; ~ **through** durchwühlen
rift /rɪft/ *n* Spalt *m*; (*fig*) Riss *m*
rig /rɪg/ *n* Ölbohrturm *m*; (*at sea*) Bohrinsel *f* ● *vt* (*pt/pp* **rigged**) ~ **out** ausrüsten; ~ **up** aufbauen
right /raɪt/ *a* richtig; (*not left*) rechte(r,s); **be** ~ <*person:*> Recht haben; <*clock:*> richtig gehen; **put** ~ wieder in Ordnung bringen; (*fig*) richtig stellen; **that's** ~! das stimmt! ● *adv* richtig; (*directly*) direkt; (*completely*) ganz; (*not left*) rechts; <*go*> nach rechts; ~ **away** sofort ● *n* Recht *nt*; (*not left*) rechte Seite *f*; **on the** ~ rechts; **from/to the** ~ von/nach rechts; **be in the** ~ Recht haben; **by** ~**s** eigentlich; **the R**~ (*Pol*) die Rechte. ~ **angle** *n* rechter Winkel *m*
rightful /ˈraɪtfl/ *a*, **-ly** *adv* rechtmäßig
right-ˈhanded *a* rechtshändig
rightly /ˈraɪtlɪ/ *adv* mit Recht
right-ˈwing *a* (*Pol*) rechte(r,s)
rigid /ˈrɪdʒɪd/ *a* starr; (*strict*) streng. ~**ity** /-ˈdʒɪdətɪ/ *n* Starrheit *f*; Strenge *f*
rigorous /ˈrɪgərəs/ *a*, **-ly** *adv* streng
rigour /ˈrɪgə(r)/ *n* Strenge *f*
rim /rɪm/ *n* Rand *m*; (*of wheel*) Felge *f*
rind /raɪnd/ *n* (*on fruit*) Schale *f*; (*on cheese*) Rinde *f*; (*on bacon*) Schwarte *f*
ring[1] /rɪŋ/ *n* Ring *m*; (*for circus*) Manege *f*; **stand in a** ~ im Kreis stehen ● *vt* umringen
ring[2] *n* Klingeln *nt*; **give s.o. a** ~ (*Teleph*) jdn anrufen ● *v* (*pt* **rang**, *pp* **rung**) ● *vt* läuten; ~ **[up]** (*Teleph*) anrufen ● *vi* <*bells:*> läuten; <*telephone:*> klingeln. ~ **back** *vt/i* (*Teleph*) zurückrufen
ring: ~**leader** *n* Rädelsführer *m*. ~ **road** *n* Umgehungsstraße *f*
rink /rɪŋk/ *n* Eisbahn *f*
rinse /rɪns/ *n* Spülung *f*; (*hair colour*) Tönung *f* ● *vt* spülen
riot /ˈraɪət/ *n* Aufruhr *m*; ~**s** *pl* Unruhen *pl*; **run** ~ randalieren ● *vi* randalieren. ~**er** *n* Randalierer *m*. ~**ous** /-əs/ *a* aufrührerisch; (*boisterous*) wild
rip /rɪp/ *n* Riss *m* ● *vt/i* (*pt/pp* **ripped**) zerreißen; ~ **open** aufreißen. ~ **off** *vt* 🅸 neppen
ripe /raɪp/ *a* (**-r, -st**) reif
ripen /ˈraɪpn/ *vi* reifen ● *vt* reifen lassen
ripeness /ˈraɪpnɪs/ *n* Reife *f*
ˈrip-off *n* 🅸 Nepp *m*
ripple /ˈrɪpl/ *n* kleine Welle *f*
rise /raɪz/ *n* Anstieg *m*; (*fig*) Aufstieg *m*; (*increase*) Zunahme *f*; (*in wages*) Lohnerhöhung *f*; (*in salary*) Gehaltserhöhung *f*; **give** ~ **to** Anlass geben zu ● *vi* (*pt* **rose**, *pp* **risen**) steigen; <*ground:*> ansteigen; <*sun, dough:*> aufgehen; <*river:*> entspringen; (*get up*) aufstehen; (*fig*) aufsteigen (**to** zu). ~**r** *n* **early** ~**r** Frühaufsteher *m*
rising /ˈraɪzɪŋ/ *a* steigend; <*sun*> aufgehend ● *n* (*revolt*) Aufstand *m*
risk /rɪsk/ *n* Risiko *nt*; **at one's own** ~ auf eigene Gefahr ● *vt* riskieren
risky /ˈrɪskɪ/ *a* (**-ier, -iest**) riskant
rite /raɪt/ *n* Ritus *m*
ritual /ˈrɪtjʊəl/ *a* rituell ● *n* Ritual *nt*
rival /ˈraɪvl/ *a* rivalisierend ● *n* Rivale *m*/Rivalin *f*. ~**ry** *n* Rivalität *f*; (*Comm*) Konkurrenzkampf *m*

river /ˈrɪvə(r)/ *n* Fluss *m*
rivet /ˈrɪvɪt/ *n* Niete *f* ● *vt* [ver]nieten; **~ed by** (*fig*) gefesselt von
road /rəʊd/ *n* Straße *f*; (*fig*) Weg *m*
road: ~-map *n* Straßenkarte *f*. **~ safety** *n* Verkehrssicherheit *f*. **~side** *n* Straßenrand *m*. **~way** *n* Fahrbahn *f*. **~-works** *npl* Straßenarbeiten *pl*. **~worthy** *a* verkehrssicher
roam /rəʊm/ *vi* wandern
roar /rɔː(r)/ *n* Gebrüll *nt*; **~s of laughter** schallendes Gelächter *nt* ● *vi* brüllen; (*with laughter*) schallend lachen. **~ing** *a* <*fire*> prasselnd; **do a ~ing trade** [!] ein Bombengeschäft machen
roast /rəʊst/ *a* gebraten, Brat-; **~ beef/pork** Rinder-/Schweinebraten *m* ● *n* Braten *m* ● *vt/i* braten; rösten <*coffee, chestnuts*>
rob /rɒb/ *vt* (*pt/pp* **robbed**) berauben (**of** *gen*); ausrauben <*bank*>. **~ber** *n* Räuber *m*. **~bery** *n* Raub *m*
robe /rəʊb/ *n* Robe *f*; (*Amer: bathrobe*) Bademantel *m*
robin /ˈrɒbɪn/ *n* Rotkehlchen *nt*
robot /ˈrəʊbɒt/ *n* Roboter *m*
robust /rəʊˈbʌst/ *a* robust
rock¹ /rɒk/ *n* Fels *m*; **on the ~s** <*ship*> aufgelaufen; <*marriage*> kaputt; <*drink*> mit Eis
rock² *vt/i* schaukeln
rock³ *n* (*Mus*) Rock *m*
rockery /ˈrɒkərɪ/ *n* Steingarten *m*
rocket /ˈrɒkɪt/ *n* Rakete *f*
rocking: ~-chair *n* Schaukelstuhl *m*. **~-horse** *n* Schaukelpferd *nt*
rocky /ˈrɒkɪ/ *a* (**-ier, -iest**) felsig; (*unsteady*) wackelig
rod /rɒd/ *n* Stab *m*; (*stick*) Rute *f*; (*for fishing*) Angel[rute] *f*
rode /rəʊd/ *see* **ride**
rodent /ˈrəʊdnt/ *n* Nagetier *nt*
rogue /rəʊg/ *n* Gauner *m*
role /rəʊl/ *n* Rolle *f*
roll /rəʊl/ *n* Rolle *f*; (*bread*) Brötchen *nt*; (*list*) Liste *f*; (*of drum*) Wirbel *m* ● *vi* rollen; **be ~ing in money** [!] Geld wie Heu haben ● *vt* rollen; walzen <*lawn*>; ausrollen <*pastry*>. **~ over** *vi* sich auf die andere Seite rollen. **~ up** *vt* aufrollen; hochkrempeln <*sleeves*> ● *vi* [!] auftauchen
roller /ˈrəʊlə(r)/ *n* Rolle *f*; (*lawn, road*) Walze *f*; (*hair*) Lockenwickler *m*. **R~blades (P)** *npl* Rollerblades (P) *mpl*. **~ blind** *n* Rollo *nt*. **~-coaster** *n* Berg-und-Talbahn *f*. **~-skate** *n* Rollschuh *m*
ˈrolling-pin *n* Teigrolle *f*
Roman /ˈrəʊmən/ *a* römisch ● *n* Römer(in) *m(f)*
romance /rəˈmæns/ *n* Romantik *f*; (*love-affair*) Romanze *f*; (*book*) Liebesgeschichte *f*
Romania /rəʊˈmeɪnɪə/ *n* Rumänien *nt*. **~n** *a* rumänisch ● *n* Rumäne *m*/-nin *f*
romantic /rəʊˈmæntɪk/ *a*, **-ally** *adv* romantisch. **~ism** /-tɪsɪzm/ *n* Romantik *f*
Rome /rəʊm/ *n* Rom *nt*
romp /rɒmp/ *vi* [herum]tollen
roof /ruːf/ *n* Dach *nt*; (*of mouth*) Gaumen *m* ● *vt* **~ [over]** überdachen. **~-top** *n* Dach *nt*
rook /rʊk/ *n* Saatkrähe *f*; (*Chess*) Turm *m*
room /ruːm/ *n* Zimmer *nt*; (*for functions*) Saal *m*; (*space*) Platz *m*. **~y** *a* geräumig
roost /ruːst/ *n* Hühnerstange *f*
root¹ /ruːt/ *n* Wurzel *f*; **take ~** anwachsen ● *vi* Wurzeln schlagen. **~ out** *vt* (*fig*) ausrotten

root² *vi* ~ **about** wühlen; ~ **for s.o.** [!] für jdn sein

rope /rəʊp/ *n* Seil *nt*; **know the ~s** [!] sich auskennen. ~ **in** *vt* [!] einspannen

rose¹ /rəʊz/ *n* Rose *f*; (*of watering-can*) Brause *f*

rose² *see* **rise**

rostrum /ˈrɒstrəm/ *n* Podium *nt*

rosy /ˈrəʊzɪ/ *a* (**-ier, -iest**) rosig

rot /rɒt/ *n* Fäulnis *f*; ([!] *nonsense*) Quatsch *m* ● *vi* (*pt/pp* **rotted**) [ver]faulen

rota /ˈrəʊtə/ *n* Dienstplan *m*

rotary /ˈrəʊtərɪ/ *a* Dreh-; (*Techn*) Rotations-

rotat|e /rəʊˈteɪt/ *vt* drehen ● *vi* sich drehen; (*Techn*) rotieren. **~ion** /-eɪʃn/ *n* Drehung *f*; **in ~ion** im Wechsel

rote /rəʊt/ *n* **by** ~ auswendig

rotten /ˈrɒtn/ *a* faul; [!] mies; <*person*> fies

rough /rʌf/ *a* (**-er, -est**) rau; (*uneven*) uneben; (*coarse, not gentle*) grob; (*brutal*) roh; (*turbulent*) stürmisch; (*approximate*) ungefähr ● *adv* **sleep** ~ im Freien übernachten ● *vt* ~ **it** primitiv leben. ~ **out** *vt* im Groben entwerfen

roughage /ˈrʌfɪdʒ/ *n* Ballaststoffe *pl*

rough ˈdraft *n* grober Entwurf *m*

rough|ly /ˈrʌflɪ/ *adv* (*see* **rough**) rau; grob; roh; ungefähr. **~ness** *n* Rauheit *f*

ˈrough paper *n* Konzeptpapier *nt*

round /raʊnd/ *a* (**-er, -est**) rund ● *n* Runde *f*; (*slice*) Scheibe *f*; **do one's ~s** seine Runde machen ● *prep* um (+ *acc*); ~ **the clock** rund um die Uhr ● *adv* **all** ~ ringsherum; **ask s.o.** ~ jdn einladen ● *vt* biegen um <*corner*>. ~ **off** *vt* abrunden. ~ **up** *vt* aufrunden; zusammentreiben <*animals*>; festnehmen <*criminals*>

roundabout /ˈraʊndəbaʊt/ *a* ~ **route** Umweg *m* ● *n* Karussell *nt*; (*for traffic*) Kreisverkehr *m*

round ˈtrip *n* Rundreise *f*

rous|e /raʊz/ *vt* wecken; (*fig*) erregen. **~ing** *a* mitreißend

route /ruːt/ *n* Route *f*; (*of bus*) Linie *f*

routine /ruːˈtiːn/ *a*, **-ly** *adv* routinemäßig ● *n* Routine *f*; (*Theat*) Nummer *f*

row¹ /rəʊ/ *n* (*line*) Reihe *f*

row² *vt/i* rudern

row³ /raʊ/ *n* [!] Krach *m* ● *vi* [!] sich streiten

rowdy /ˈraʊdɪ/ *a* (**-ier, -iest**) laut

rowing boat /ˈrəʊɪŋ-/ *n* Ruderboot *nt*

royal /rɔɪəl/ *a*, **-ly** *adv* königlich

royalt|y /ˈrɔɪəltɪ/ *n* Königtum *nt*; (*persons*) Mitglieder *pl* der königlichen Familie; **-ies** *pl* (*payments*) Tantiemen *pl*

RSI *abbr* (**repetitive strain injury**) chronisches Überlastungssyndrom *nt*

rub /rʌb/ *vt* (*pt/pp* **rubbed**) reiben; (*polish*) polieren; **don't ~ it in** [!] reib es mir nicht unter die Nase. ~ **off** *vt* abreiben ● *vi* abgehen. ~ **out** *vt* ausradieren

rubber /ˈrʌbə(r)/ *n* Gummi *m*; (*eraser*) Radiergummi *m*. ~ **band** *n* Gummiband *nt*

rubbish /ˈrʌbɪʃ/ *n* Abfall *m*, Müll *m*; ([!] *nonsense*) Quatsch *m*; ([!] *junk*) Plunder *m*. ~ **bin** *n* Abfalleimer *m*. ~ **dump** *n* Abfallhaufen *m*; (*official*) Müllhalde *f*

rubble /ˈrʌbl/ *n* Trümmer *pl*

ruby /ˈruːbɪ/ *n* Rubin *m*

rudder /ˈrʌdə(r)/ *n* [Steuer]ruder *nt*

rude /ruːd/ *a* (**-r, -st**), **-ly** *adv* unhöflich; (*improper*) unanständig. **~ness** *n* Unhöflichkeit *f*

rudimentary /ru:dɪˈmentərɪ/ *a* elementar; (*Biol*) rudimentär

ruffian /ˈrʌfɪən/ *n* Rüpel *m*

ruffle /ˈrʌfl/ *vt* zerzausen

rug /rʌg/ *n* Vorleger *m*, [kleiner] Teppich *m*; (*blanket*) Decke *f*

rugged /ˈrʌgɪd/ *a* <*coastline*> zerklüftet

ruin /ˈru:ɪn/ *n* Ruine *f*; (*fig*) Ruin *m* ● *vt* ruinieren

rule /ru:l/ *n* Regel *f*; (*control*) Herrschaft *f*; (*government*) Regierung *f*; (*for measuring*) Lineal *nt*; **as a ~** in der Regel ● *vt* regieren, herrschen über (+ *acc*); (*fig*) beherrschen; (*decide*) entscheiden; ziehen <*line*> ● *vi* regieren, herrschen. **~ out** *vt* ausschließen

ruled /ru:ld/ *a* <*paper*> liniert

ruler /ˈru:lə(r)/ *n* Herrscher(in) *m(f)*; (*measure*) Lineal *nt*

ruling /ˈru:lɪŋ/ *a* herrschend; <*factor*> entscheidend; (*Pol*) regierend ● *n* Entscheidung *f*

rum /rʌm/ *n* Rum *m*

rumble /ˈrʌmbl/ *n* Grollen *nt* ● *vi* grollen; <*stomach:*> knurren

rummage /ˈrʌmɪdʒ/ *vi* wühlen; **~ through** durchwühlen

rumour /ˈru:mə(r)/ *n* Gerücht *nt* ● *vt* **it is ~ed that** es geht das Gerücht, dass

rump /rʌmp/ *n* Hinterteil *nt*. **~ steak** *n* Rumpsteak *nt*

run /rʌn/ *n* Lauf *m*; (*journey*) Fahrt *f*; (*series*) Serie *f*, Reihe *f*; (*Theat*) Laufzeit *f*; (*Skiing*) Abfahrt *f*; (*enclosure*) Auslauf *m*; (*Amer: ladder*) Laufmasche *f*; **~ of bad luck** Pechsträhne *f*; **be on the ~** flüchtig sein; **in the long ~** auf lange Sicht ● *v* (*pt* **ran**, *pp* **run**, *pres p* **running**) ● *vi* laufen; (*flow*) fließen; <*eyes:*> tränen; <*bus:*> verkehren; <*butter, ink:*> zerfließen; <*colours:*> [ab]färben; (*in election*) kandidieren ● *vt* laufen lassen; einlaufen lassen <*bath*>; (*manage*) führen, leiten; (*drive*) fahren; eingehen <*risk*>; (*Journ*) bringen <*article*>; **~ one's hand over sth** mit der Hand über etw (*acc*) fahren. **~ away** *vi* weglaufen. **~ down** *vi* hinunter-/herunterlaufen; <*clockwork:*> ablaufen; <*stocks:*> sich verringern ● *vt* (*run over*) überfahren; (*reduce*) verringern; ([!] *criticize*) heruntermachen. **~ in** *vi* hinein-/hereinlaufen. **~ off** *vi* weglaufen ● *vt* abziehen <*copies*>. **~ out** *vi* hinaus-/herauslaufen; <*supplies, money:*> ausgehen; **I've ~ out of sugar** ich habe keinen Zucker mehr. **~ over** *vt* überfahren. **~ up** *vi* hinauf-/heraufläufen; (*towards*) hinlaufen ● *vt* machen <*debts*>; auflaufen lassen <*bill*>; (*sew*) schnell nähen

ˈrunaway *n* Ausreißer *m*

run-ˈdown *a* <*area*> verkommen

rung[1] /rʌŋ/ *n* (*of ladder*) Sprosse *f*

rung[2] *see* **ring**[2]

runner /ˈrʌnə(r)/ *n* Läufer *m*; (*Bot*) Ausläufer *m*; (*on sledge*) Kufe *f*. **~ bean** *n* Stangenbohne *f*. **~-up** *n* Zweite(r) *m/f*

running /ˈrʌnɪŋ/ *a* laufend; <*water*> fließend; **four times ~** viermal nacheinander ● *n* Laufen *nt*; (*management*) Führung *f*, Leitung *f*; **be/not be in the ~** eine/keine Chance haben

runny /ˈrʌnɪ/ *a* flüssig

run: ~-up *n* (*Sport*) Anlauf *m*; (*to election*) Zeit *f* vor der Wahl. **~way** *n* Start- und Landebahn *f*

rupture /ˈrʌptʃə(r)/ *n* Bruch *m* ● *vt/i* brechen

rural /ˈrʊərəl/ *a* ländlich

ruse /ru:z/ *n* List *f*

rush[1] /rʌʃ/ *n* (*Bot*) Binse *f*

rush² *n* Hetze *f*; **in a ~** in Eile ● *vi* sich hetzen; (*run*) rasen; <*water:*> rauschen ● *vt* hetzen, drängen. **~-hour** *n* Hauptverkehrszeit *f*, Stoßzeit *f*

Russia /ˈrʌʃə/ *n* Russland *nt*. **~n** *a* russisch ● *n* Russe *m*/ Russin *f*; (*Lang*) Russisch *nt*

rust /rʌst/ *n* Rost *m* ● *vi* rosten

rustle /ˈrʌsl/ *vi* rascheln ● *vt* rascheln mit; (*Amer*) stehlen <*cattle*>. **~ up** *vt* [!] improvisieren

ˈrustproof *a* rostfrei

rusty /ˈrʌstɪ/ *a* (**-ier, -iest**) rostig

rut /rʌt/ *n* Furche *f*

ruthless /ˈruːθlɪs/ *a*, **-ly** *adv* rücksichtslos. **~ness** *n* Rücksichtslosigkeit *f*

rye /raɪ/ *n* Roggen *m*

Ss

sabbath /ˈsæbəθ/ *n* Sabbat *m*

sabotage /ˈsæbətɑːʒ/ *n* Sabotage *f* ● *vt* sabotieren

sachet /ˈsæʃeɪ/ *n* Beutel *m*; (*scented*) Kissen *nt*

sack *n* Sack *m*; **get the ~** [!] rausgeschmissen werden ● *vt* [!] rausschmeißen

sacred /ˈseɪkrɪd/ *a* heilig

sacrifice /ˈsækrɪfaɪs/ *n* Opfer *nt* ● *vt* opfern

sacrilege /ˈsækrɪlɪdʒ/ *n* Sakrileg *nt*

sad /sæd/ *a* (**sadder, saddest**) traurig; <*loss, death*> schmerzlich. **~den** *vt* traurig machen

saddle /ˈsædl/ *n* Sattel *m* ● *vt* satteln; **~ s.o. with sth** [!] jdm etw aufhalsen

sadist /ˈseɪdɪst/ *n* Sadist *m*. **~ic** /səˈdɪstɪk/ *a*, **-ally** *adv* sadistisch

sad|ly /ˈsædlɪ/ *adv* traurig; (*unfortunately*) leider. **~ness** *n* Traurigkeit *f*

safe /seɪf/ *a* (**-r, -st**) sicher; <*journey*> gut; (*not dangerous*) ungefährlich; **~ and sound** gesund und wohlbehalten ● *n* Safe *m*. **~guard** *n* Schutz *m* ● *vt* schützen. **~ly** *adv* sicher; <*arrive*> gut

safety /ˈseɪftɪ/ *n* Sicherheit *f*. **~-belt** *n* Sicherheitsgurt *m*. **~-pin** *n* Sicherheitsnadel *f*. **~-valve** *n* [Sicherheits]ventil *nt*

sag /sæg/ *vi* (*pt*/*pp* **sagged**) durchhängen

saga /ˈsɑːgə/ *n* Saga *f*; (*fig*) Geschichte *f*

said /sed/ *see* **say**

sail /seɪl/ *n* Segel *nt*; (*trip*) Segelfahrt *f* ● *vi* segeln; (*on liner*) fahren; (*leave*) abfahren (**for** nach) ● *vt* segeln mit

sailing /ˈseɪlɪŋ/ *n* Segelsport *m*. **~-boat** *n* Segelboot *nt*. **~-ship** *n* Segelschiff *nt*

sailor /ˈseɪlə(r)/ *n* Seemann *m*; (*in navy*) Matrose *m*

saint /seɪnt/ *n* Heilige(r) *m*/*f*. **~ly** *a* heilig

sake /seɪk/ *n* **for the ~ of ...** um ... (*gen*) willen; **for my/your ~** um meinet-/deinetwillen

salad /ˈsæləd/ *n* Salat *m*. **~-dressing** *n* Salatsoße *f*

salary /ˈsælərɪ/ *n* Gehalt *nt*

sale /seɪl/ *n* Verkauf *m*; (*event*) Basar *m*; (*at reduced prices*) Schlussverkauf *m*; **for ~** zu verkaufen

sales|man *n* Verkäufer *m*. **~woman** *n* Verkäuferin *f*

saliva /səˈlaɪvə/ *n* Speichel *m*

salmon /ˈsæmən/ *n* Lachs *m*

saloon /sə'lu:n/ *n* Salon *m*; (*Auto*) Limousine *f*; (*Amer: bar*) Wirtschaft *f*

salt /sɔ:lt/ *n* Salz *nt* ● *a* salzig; <*water, meat*> Salz- ● *vt* salzen; (*cure*) pökeln; streuen <*road*>. **~-cellar** *n* Salzfass *nt*. **~ 'water** *n* Salzwasser *nt*. **~y** *a* salzig

salute /sə'lu:t/ *n* (*Mil*) Gruß *m* ● *vt/i* (*Mil*) grüßen

salvage /'sælvɪdʒ/ *n* (*Naut*) Bergung *f* ● *vt* bergen

salvation /sæl'veɪʃn/ *n* Rettung *f*; (*Relig*) Heil *nt*

same /seɪm/ *a & pron* **the ~** der/die/das gleiche; (*pl*) die gleichen; (*identical*) der-/die-/dasselbe; (*pl*) dieselben ● *adv* **the ~** gleich; **all the ~** trotzdem

sample /'sɑ:mpl/ *n* Probe *f*; (*Comm*) Muster *nt* ● *vt* probieren; kosten <*food*>

sanatorium /sænə'tɔ:rɪəm/ *n* Sanatorium *nt*

sanction /'sæŋkʃn/ *n* Sanktion *f* ● *vt* sanktionieren

sanctuary /'sæŋktjʊərɪ/ *n* (*Relig*) Heiligtum *nt*; (*refuge*) Zuflucht *f*; (*for wildlife*) Tierschutzgebiet *nt*

sand /sænd/ *n* Sand *m* ● *vt* **~ [down]** [ab]schmirgeln

sandal /'sændl/ *n* Sandale *f*

sand: ~bank *n* Sandbank *f*. **~paper** *n* Sandpapier *nt*. **~-pit** *n* Sandkasten *m*

sandwich /'sænwɪdʒ/ *n*; Sandwich *m* ● *vt* **~ed between** eingeklemmt zwischen

sandy /'sændɪ/ *a* (**-ier, -iest**) sandig; <*beach, soil*> Sand-; <*hair*> rotblond

sane /seɪn/ *a* (**-r, -st**) geistig normal; (*sensible*) vernünftig

sang /sæŋ/ *see* **sing**

sanitary /'sænɪtərɪ/ *a* hygienisch; <*system*> sanitär. **~ napkin** *n* (*Amer*), **~ towel** *n* [Damen]binde *f*

sanitation /sænɪ'teɪʃn/ *n* Kanalisation und Abfallbeseitigung *pl*

sanity /'sænətɪ/ *n* [gesunder] Verstand *m*

sank /sæŋk/ *see* **sink**

sap /sæp/ *n* (*Bot*) Saft *m* ● *vt* (*pt/pp* **sapped**) schwächen

sarcas|m /'sɑ:kæzm/ *n* Sarkasmus *m*. **~tic** /-'kæstɪk/ *a*, **-ally** *adv* sarkastisch

sardine /sɑ:'di:n/ *n* Sardine *f*

sash /sæʃ/ *n* Schärpe *f*

sat /sæt/ *see* **sit**

satchel /'sætʃl/ *n* Ranzen *m*

satellite /'sætəlaɪt/ *n* Satellit *m*. **~ television** *n* Satellitenfernsehen *nt*

satin /'sætɪn/ *n* Satin *m*

satire /'sætaɪə(r)/ *n* Satire *f*

satirical /sə'tɪrɪkl/ *a*, **-ly** *adv* satirisch

satir|ist /'sætərɪst/ *n* Satiriker(in) *m(f)*

satisfaction /sætɪs'fækʃn/ *n* Befriedigung *f*; **to my ~** zu meiner Zufriedenheit

satisfactory /sætɪs'fæktərɪ/ *a*, **-ily** *adv* zufrieden stellend

satisfy /'sætɪsfaɪ/ *vt* (*pp/pp* **-ied**) befriedigen; zufrieden stellen <*customer*>; (*convince*) überzeugen; **be ~ied** zufrieden sein. **~ing** *a* befriedigend; <*meal*> sättigend

saturate /'sætʃəreɪt/ *vt* durchtränken; (*Chem & fig*) sättigen

Saturday /'sætədeɪ/ *n* Samstag *m*

sauce /sɔ:s/ *n* Soße *f*; (🄸 *cheek*) Frechheit *f*. **~pan** *n* Kochtopf *m*

saucer /'sɔ:sə(r)/ *n* Untertasse *f*

saucy /'sɔ:ʃɪ/ *a* (**-ier, -iest**) frech

Saudi Arabia /saʊdɪə'reɪbɪə/ *n* Saudi-Arabien *n*

sauna /ˈsɔ:nə/ *n* Sauna *f*

saunter /ˈsɔ:ntə(r)/ *vi* schlendern

sausage /ˈsɒsɪdʒ/ *n* Wurst *f*

savage /ˈsævɪdʒ/ *a* wild; (*fierce*) scharf; (*brutal*) brutal ● *n* Wilde(r) *m/f*. **~ry** *n* Brutalität *f*

save /seɪv/ *n* (*Sport*) Abwehr *f* ● *vt* retten (**from** vor + *dat*); (*keep*) aufheben; (*not waste*) sparen; (*collect*) sammeln; (*avoid*) ersparen; (*Sport*) verhindern <*goal*> ● *vi* ~ **[up]** sparen

saver /ˈseɪvə(r)/ *n* Sparer *m*

saving /ˈseɪvɪŋ/ *n* (*see* **save**) Rettung *f*; Sparen *nt*; Ersparnis *f*; **~s** *pl* (*money*) Ersparnisse *pl*

savour /ˈseɪvə(r)/ *n* Geschmack *m* ● *vt* auskosten. **~y** *a* würzig

saw¹ /sɔ:/ *see* **see**

saw² *n* Säge *f* ● *vt/i* (*pt* **sawed**, *pp* **sawn** *or* **sawed**) sägen

saxophone /ˈsæksəfəʊn/ *n* Saxophon *nt*

say /seɪ/ *n* Mitspracherecht *nt*; **have one's ~** seine Meinung sagen ● *vt/i* (*pt/pp* **said**) sagen; sprechen <*prayer*>; **that is to ~** das heißt; **that goes without ~ing** das versteht sich von selbst. **~ing** *n* Redensart *f*

scab /skæb/ *n* Schorf *m*; (*pej*) Streikbrecher *m*

scaffolding /ˈskæfəldɪŋ/ *n* Gerüst *nt*

scald /skɔ:ld/ *vt* verbrühen

scale¹ /skeɪl/ *n* (*of fish*) Schuppe *f*

scale² *n* Skala *f*; (*Mus*) Tonleiter *f*; (*ratio*) Maßstab *m* ● *vt* (*climb*) erklettern. **~ down** *vt* verkleinern

scales /skeɪlz/ *npl* (*for weighing*) Waage *f*

scalp /skælp/ *n* Kopfhaut *f*

scamper /ˈskæmpə(r)/ *vi* huschen

scan /skæn/ *n* (*Med*) Szintigramm *nt* ● *v* (*pt/pp* **scanned**) ● *vt* absuchen; (*quickly*) flüchtig ansehen; (*Med*) szintigraphisch untersuchen

scandal /ˈskændl/ *n* Skandal *m*; (*gossip*) Skandalgeschichten *pl*. **~ize** /-dəlaɪz/ *vt* schockieren. **~ous** /-əs/ *a* skandalös

Scandinavia /skændɪˈneɪvɪə/ *n* Skandinavien *nt*. **~n** *a* skandinavisch ● *n* Skandinavier(in) *m(f)*

scanner /ˈskænə(r)/ *n* Scanner *m*

scanty /ˈskæntɪ/ *a* (**-ier, -iest**), **-ily** *adv* spärlich; <*clothing*> knapp

scapegoat /ˈskeɪp-/ *n* Sündenbock *m*

scar /skɑ:(r)/ *n* Narbe *f*

scarc|e /skeəs/ *a* (**-r, -st**) knapp; **make oneself ~e** 🅘 sich aus dem Staub machen. **~ely** *adv* kaum. **~ity** *n* Knappheit *f*

scare /skeə(r)/ *n* Schreck *m*; (*panic*) [allgemeine] Panik *f* ● *vt* Angst machen (+ *dat*); **be ~d** Angst haben (**of** vor + *dat*)

scarf /skɑ:f/ *n* (*pl* **scarves**) Schal *m*; (*square*) Tuch *nt*

scarlet /ˈskɑ:lət/ *a* scharlachrot

scary /ˈskeərɪ/ *a* unheimlich

scathing /ˈskeɪðɪŋ/ *a* bissig

scatter /ˈskætə(r)/ *vt* verstreuen; (*disperse*) zerstreuen ● *vi* sich zerstreuen. **~ed** *a* verstreut; <*showers*> vereinzelt

scatty /ˈskætɪ/ *a* (**-ier, -iest**) 🅘 verrückt

scene /si:n/ *n* Szene *f*; (*sight*) Anblick *m*; (*place of event*) Schauplatz *m*; **behind the ~s** hinter den Kulissen

scenery /ˈsi:nərɪ/ *n* Landschaft *f*; (*Theat*) Szenerie *f*

scenic /ˈsi:nɪk/ *a* landschaftlich schön

scent /sent/ *n* Duft *m*; (*trail*) Fährte *f*; (*perfume*) Parfüm *nt*. **~ed** *a* parfümiert

sceptic|al /ˈskeptɪkl/ *a*, **-ly** *adv* skeptisch. **~ism** /-tɪsɪzm/ *n* Skepsis *f*

schedule /ˈʃedjuːl/ *n* Programm *nt*; (*of work*) Zeitplan *m*; (*timetable*) Fahrplan *m*; **behind ~** im Rückstand; **according to ~** planmäßig ● *vt* planen

scheme /skiːm/ *n* Programm *nt*; (*plan*) Plan *m*; (*plot*) Komplott *nt* ● *vi* Ränke schmieden

schizophrenic /skɪtsəˈfrenɪk/ *a* schizophren

scholar /ˈskɒlə(r)/ *n* Gelehrte(r) *m/f*. **~ly** *a* gelehrt. **~ship** *n* Gelehrtheit *f*; (*grant*) Stipendium *nt*

school /skuːl/ *n* Schule *f*; (*Univ*) Fakultät *f* ● *vt* schulen

school: ~boy *n* Schüler *m*. **~girl** *n* Schülerin *f*. **~ing** *n* Schulbildung *f*. **~master** *n* Lehrer *m*. **~mistress** *n* Lehrerin *f*. **~-teacher** *n* Lehrer(in) *m(f)*

scien|ce /ˈsaɪəns/ *n* Wissenschaft *f*. **~tific** /-ˈtɪfɪk/ *a* wissenschaftlich. **~tist** *n* Wissenschaftler *m*

scissors /ˈsɪzəz/ *npl* Schere *f*; **a pair of ~** eine Schere

scoff[1] /skɒf/ *vi* **~ at** spotten über (+ *acc*)

scoff[2] *vt* [!] verschlingen

scold /skəʊld/ *vt* ausschimpfen

scoop /skuːp/ *n* Schaufel *f*; (*Culin*) Portionierer *m*; (*Journ*) Exklusivmeldung *f* ● *vt* **~ out** aushöhlen; (*remove*) auslöffeln

scooter /ˈskuːtə(r)/ *n* Roller *m*

scope /skəʊp/ *n* Bereich *m*; (*opportunity*) Möglichkeiten *pl*

scorch /skɔːtʃ/ *vt* versengen. **~ing** *a* glühend heiß

score /skɔː(r)/ *n* [Spiel]stand *m*; (*individual*) Punktzahl *f*; (*Mus*) Partitur *f*; (*Cinema*) Filmmusik *f*; **on that ~** was das betrifft ● *vt* erzielen; schießen <goal>; (*cut*) einritzen ● *vi* Punkte erzielen; (*Sport*) ein Tor schießen; (*keep score*) Punkte zählen. **~r** *n* Punktezähler *m*; (*of goals*) Torschütze *m*

scorn /skɔːn/ *n* Verachtung *f* ● *vt* verachten. **~ful** *a*, **-ly** *adv* verächtlich

Scot /skɒt/ *n* Schotte *m*/Schottin *f*

Scotch /skɒtʃ/ *a* schottisch ● *n* (*whisky*) Scotch *m*

Scot|land /ˈskɒtlənd/ *n* Schottland *nt*. **~s, ~tish** *a* schottisch

scoundrel /ˈskaʊndrl/ *n* Schurke *m*

scour /ˈskaʊə(r)/ *vt* (*search*) absuchen; (*clean*) scheuern

scout /skaʊt/ *n* (*Mil*) Kundschafter *m*; **[Boy] S~** Pfadfinder *m*

scowl /skaʊl/ *n* böser Gesichtsausdruck *m* ● *vi* ein böses Gesicht machen

scram /skræm/ *vi* [!] abhauen

scramble /ˈskræmbl/ *n* Gerangel *nt* ● *vi* klettern; **~ for** sich drängen nach. **~d ˈegg[s]** *n[pl]* Rührei *nt*

scrap[1] /skræp/ *n* ([!] *fight*) Rauferei *f* ● *vi* sich raufen

scrap[2] *n* Stückchen *nt*; (*metal*) Schrott *m*; **~s** *pl* Reste; **not a ~** kein bisschen ● *vt* (*pt/pp* **scrapped**) aufgeben

ˈscrapbook *n* Sammelalbum *nt*

scrape /skreɪp/ *vt* schaben; (*clean*) abkratzen; (*damage*) [ver]schrammen. **~ through** *vi* gerade noch durchkommen. **~ together** *vt* zusammenkriegen

scrappy /ˈskræpɪ/ *a* lückenhaft

ˈscrapyard *n* Schrottplatz *m*

scratch /skrætʃ/ *n* Kratzer *m*; **start from ~** von vorne anfangen; **not be up to ~** zu wünschen übrig lassen ● *vt/i* kratzen; (*damage*) zerkratzen

scrawl /skrɔ:l/ *n* Gekrakel *nt* ● *vt/i* krakeln

scream /skri:m/ *n* Schrei *m* ● *vt/i* schreien

screech /skri:tʃ/ *n* Kreischen *nt* ● *vt/i* kreischen

screen /skri:n/ *n* Schirm *m*; (*Cinema*) Leinwand *f*; (*TV*) Bildschirm *m* ● *vt* schützen; (*conceal*) verdecken; vorführen <*film*>; (*examine*) überprüfen; (*Med*) untersuchen

screw /skru:/ *n* Schraube *f* ● *vt* schrauben. **~ up** *vt* festschrauben; (*crumple*) zusammenknüllen; zusammenkneifen <*eyes*>; (☒ *bungle*) vermasseln

ˈ**screwdriver** *n* Schraubenzieher *m*

scribble /ˈskrɪbl/ *n* Gekritzel *nt* ● *vt/i* kritzeln

script /skrɪpt/ *n* Schrift *f*; (*of speech, play*) Text *m*; (*Radio, TV*) Skript *nt*; (*of film*) Drehbuch *nt*

scroll /skrəʊl/ *n* Rolle *f* ● *vt* **~ up/down** nach oben/unten rollen. **~ bar** *n* Rollbalken *m*

scrounge /skraʊndʒ/ *vt/i* schnorren. **~r** *n* Schnorrer *m*

scrub[1] /skrʌb/ *n* (*land*) Buschland *nt*, Gestrüpp *nt*

scrub[2] *vt/i* (*pt/pp* **scrubbed**) schrubben

scruff /skrʌf/ *n* **by the ~ of the neck** beim Genick

scruffy /ˈskrʌfɪ/ *a* (**-ier, -iest**) vergammelt

scrum /skrʌm/ *n* Gedränge *nt*

scruple /ˈskru:pl/ *n* Skrupel *m*

scrupulous /ˈskru:pjʊləs/ *a*, **-ly** *adv* gewissenhaft

scuffle /ˈskʌfl/ *n* Handgemenge *nt*

sculpt|or /ˈskʌlptə(r)/ *n* Bildhauer(in) *m(f)*. **~ure** /-tʃə(r)/ *n* Bildhauerei *f*; (*piece of work*) Skulptur *f*, Plastik *f*

scum /skʌm/ *n* Schmutzschicht *f*; (*people*) Abschaum *m*

scurry /ˈskʌrɪ/ *vi* (*pt/pp* **-ied**) huschen

scuttle[1] /ˈskʌtl/ *vt* versenken <*ship*>

scuttle[2] *vi* schnell krabbeln

sea /si:/ *n* Meer *nt*, See *f*; **at ~** auf See; **by ~** mit dem Schiff. **~food** *n* Meeresfrüchte *pl*. **~gull** *n* Möwe *f*

seal[1] /si:l/ *n* (*Zool*) Seehund *m*

seal[2] *n* Siegel *nt* ● *vt* versiegeln; (*fig*) besiegeln. **~ off** *vt* abriegeln

ˈ**sea-level** *n* Meeresspiegel *m*

seam /si:m/ *n* Naht *f*; (*of coal*) Flöz *nt*

ˈ**seaman** *n* Seemann *m*; (*sailor*) Matrose *m*

seance /ˈseɪɑ:ns/ *n* spiritistische Sitzung *f*

search /sɜ:tʃ/ *n* Suche *f*; (*official*) Durchsuchung *f* ● *vt* durchsuchen; absuchen <*area*> ● *vi* suchen (**for** nach). **~ engine** *n* Suchmaschine *f*. **~ing** *a* prüfend, forschend. **~light** *n* [Such]scheinwerfer *m*. **~-party** *n* Suchmannschaft *f*

sea: ~sick *a* seekrank. **~side** *n* **at/to the ~side** am/ans Meer

season /ˈsi:zn/ *n* Jahreszeit *f*; (*social, tourist, sporting*) Saison *f* ● *vt* (*flavour*) würzen. **~al** *a* Saison-. **~ing** *n* Gewürze *pl*

ˈ**season ticket** *n* Dauerkarte *f*

seat /si:t/ *n* Sitz *m*; (*place*) Sitzplatz *m*; (*bottom*) Hintern *m*; **take a ~** Platz nehmen ● *vt* setzen; (*have seats for*) Sitzplätze bieten (+ *dat*); **remain ~ed** sitzen bleiben. **~-belt** *n* Sicherheitsgurt *m*; **fasten one's ~-belt** sich anschnallen

sea: ~weed *n* [See]tang *m*. **~worthy** *a* seetüchtig

seclu|ded /sɪ'klu:dɪd/ *a* abgelegen. **~sion** /-ʒn/ *n* Zurückgezogenheit *f*

second /'sekənd/ *a* zweite(r,s); **on ~ thoughts** nach weiterer Überlegung ● *n* Sekunde *f*; (*Sport*) Sekundant *m*; **~s** *pl* (*goods*) Waren zweiter Wahl ● *adv* (*in race*) an zweiter Stelle ● *vt* unterstützen <*proposal*>

secondary /'sekəndrɪ/ *a* zweitrangig; (*Phys*) Sekundär-. **~ school** *n* höhere Schule *f*

second: ~-best *a* zweitbeste(r,s). **~ 'class** *adv* <*travel, send*> zweiter Klasse. **~-class** *a* zweitklassig

'second hand *n* (*on clock*) Sekundenzeiger *m*

second-'hand *a* gebraucht ● *adv* aus zweiter Hand

secondly /'sekəndlɪ/ *adv* zweitens

second-'rate *a* zweitklassig

secrecy /'si:krəsɪ/ *n* Heimlichkeit *f*

secret /'si:krɪt/ *a* geheim; <*agent, police*> Geheim-; <*drinker, lover*> heimlich ● *n* Geheimnis *nt*

secretarial /sekrə'teərɪəl/ *a* Sekretärinnen-; <*work, staff*> Sekretariats-

secretary /'sekrətərɪ/ *n* Sekretär(in) *m(f)*

secretive /'si:krətɪv/ *a* geheimtuerisch

secretly /'si:krɪtlɪ/ *adv* heimlich

sect /sekt/ *n* Sekte *f*

section /'sekʃn/ *n* Teil *m*; (*of text*) Abschnitt *m*; (*of firm*) Abteilung *f*; (*of organization*) Sektion *f*

sector /'sektə(r)/ *n* Sektor *m*

secular /'sekjʊlə(r)/ *a* weltlich

secure /sɪ'kjʊə(r)/ *a*, **-ly** *adv* sicher; (*firm*) fest; (*emotionally*) geborgen ● *vt* sichern; (*fasten*) festmachen; (*obtain*) sich (*dat*) sichern

securit|y /sɪ'kjʊərətɪ/ *n* Sicherheit *f*; (*emotional*) Geborgenheit *f*; **~ies** *pl* Wertpapiere *pl*

sedan /sɪ'dæn/ *n* (*Amer*) Limousine *f*

sedate /sɪ'deɪt/ *a*, **-ly** *adv* gesetzt

sedative /'sedətɪv/ *a* beruhigend ● *n* Beruhigungsmittel *nt*

sediment /'sedɪmənt/ *n* [Boden]satz *m*

seduce /sɪ'dju:s/ *vt* verführen

seduct|ion /sɪ'dʌkʃn/ *n* Verführung *f*. **~ive** /-tɪv/ *a*, **-ly** *adv* verführerisch

see /si:/ *v* (*pt* **saw**, *pp* **seen**) ● *vt* sehen; (*understand*) einsehen; (*imagine*) sich (*dat*) vorstellen; (*escort*) begleiten; **go and ~** nachsehen; (*visit*) besuchen; **~ you later!** bis nachher! **~ing that** da ● *vi* sehen; (*check*) nachsehen; **~ about** sich kümmern um. **~ off** *vt* verabschieden; (*chase away*) vertreiben. **~ through** *vt* (*fig*) durchschauen <*person*>

seed /si:d/ *n* Samen *m*; (*of grape*) Kern *m*; (*fig*) Saat *f*; (*Tennis*) gesetzter Spieler *m*; **go to ~** Samen bilden; (*fig*) herunterkommen. **~ed** *a* (*Tennis*) gesetzt

seedy /'si:dɪ/ *a* (**-ier, -iest**) schäbig; <*area*> heruntergekommen

seek /si:k/ *vt* (*pt/pp* **sought**) suchen

seem /si:m/ *vi* scheinen

seen /si:n/ *see* **see**

seep /si:p/ *vi* sickern

seethe /si:ð/ *vi* **~ with anger** vor Wut schäumen

'see-through *a* durchsichtig

segment /ˈsegmənt/ *n* Teil *m*; (*of worm*) Segment *nt*; (*of orange*) Spalte *f*

segregat|e /ˈsegrɪgeɪt/ *vt* trennen. **~ion** /-ˈgeɪʃn/ *n* Trennung *f*

seize /si:z/ *vt* ergreifen; (*Jur*) beschlagnahmen; **~ s.o. by the arm** jdn am Arm packen. **~ up** *vi* (*Techn*) sich festfressen

seldom /ˈseldəm/ *adv* selten

select /sɪˈlekt/ *a* ausgewählt; (*exclusive*) exklusiv ● *vt* auswählen; aufstellen <*team*>. **~ion** /-ekʃn/ *n* Auswahl *f*

self /self/ *n* (*pl* **selves**) Ich *nt*

self: ~-asˈsurance *n* Selbstsicherheit *f*. **~-asˈsured** *a* selbstsicher. **~-ˈcatering** *n* Selbstversorgung *f*. **~-ˈcentred** *a* egozentrisch. **~-ˈconfidence** *n* Selbstbewusstsein *nt*, Selbstvertrauen *nt*. **~-ˈconfident** *a* selbstbewusst. **~-ˈconscious** *a* befangen. **~-conˈtained** *a* <*flat*> abgeschlossen. **~-conˈtrol** *n* Selbstbeherrschung *f*. **~-deˈfence** *n* Selbstverteidigung *f*; (*Jur*) Notwehr *f*. **~-emˈployed** selbstständig. **~-eˈsteem** *n* Selbstachtung *f*. **~-ˈevident** *a* offensichtlich. **~-inˈdulgent** *a* maßlos. **~-ˈinterest** *n* Eigennutz *m*

self|ish /ˈselfɪʃ/ *a*, **-ly** *adv* egoistisch, selbstsüchtig. **~less** *a*, **-ly** *adv* selbstlos

self: ~-ˈpity *n* Selbstmitleid *nt*. **~-ˈportrait** *n* Selbstporträt *nt*. **~-reˈspect** *n* Selbstachtung *f*. **~-ˈrighteous** *a* selbstgerecht. **~-ˈsacrifice** *n* Selbstaufopferung *f*. **~-ˈsatisfied** *a* selbstgefällig. **~-ˈservice** *n* Selbstbedienung *f* ● *attrib* Selbstbedienungs-. **~-sufˈficient** *a* selbstständig

sell /sel/ *v* (*pt/pp* **sold**) ● *vt* verkaufen; **be sold out** ausverkauft sein ● *vi* sich verkaufen. **~ off** *vt* verkaufen

seller /ˈselə(r)/ *n* Verkäufer *m*

Sellotape (P) /ˈseləʊ-/, *n* ≈ Tesafilm (P) *m*

ˈsell-out *n* **be a ~** ausverkauft sein; ([!] *betrayal*) Verrat sein

selves /selvz/ *see* **self**

semester /sɪˈmestə(r)/ *n* (*Amer*) Semester *nt*

semi|breve /ˈsemɪbri:v/ *n* (*Mus*) ganze Note *f*. **~circle** *n* Halbkreis *m*. **~ˈcircular** *a* halbkreisförmig. **~ˈcolon** *n* Semikolon *nt*. **~-deˈtached** *a* & *n* **~-detached [house]** Doppelhaushälfte *f*. **~-ˈfinal** *n* Halbfinale *nt*

seminar /ˈsemɪnɑ:(r)/ *n* Seminar *nt*

senat|e /ˈsenət/ *n* Senat *m*. **~or** *n* Senator *m*

send /send/ *vt/i* (*pt/pp* **sent**) schicken; **~ for** kommen lassen <*person*>; sich (*dat*) schicken lassen <*thing*>. **~er** *n* Absender *m*. **~-off** *n* Verabschiedung *f*

senile /ˈsi:naɪl/ *a* senil

senior /ˈsi:nɪə(r)/ *a* älter; (*in rank*) höher ● *n* Ältere(r) *m/f*; (*in rank*) Vorgesetzte(r) *m/f*. **~ ˈcitizen** *n* Senior(in) *m(f)*

seniority /si:nɪˈɒrətɪ/ *n* höheres Alter *nt*; (*in rank*) höherer Rang *m*

sensation /senˈseɪʃn/ *n* Sensation *f*; (*feeling*) Gefühl *nt*. **~al** *a*, **-ly** *adv* sensationell

sense /sens/ *n* Sinn *m*; (*feeling*) Gefühl *nt*; (*common ~*) Verstand *m*; **make ~** Sinn ergeben ● *vt* spüren. **~less** *a*, **-ly** *adv* sinnlos; (*unconscious*) bewusstlos

sensible /ˈsensəbl/ *a*, **-bly** *adv* vernünftig; <*suitable*> zweckmäßig

sensitiv|e /ˈsensətɪv/ *a*, **-ly** *adv* empfindlich; (*understanding*) einfühlsam. **~ity** /-'tɪvətɪ/ *n* Empfindlichkeit *f*

sensual /'sensjʊəl/ *a* sinnlich. **-ity** /-'ælətɪ/ *n* Sinnlichkeit *f*

sensuous /'sensjʊəs/ *a* sinnlich

sent /sent/ *see* **send**

sentence /'sentəns/ *n* Satz *m*; (*Jur*) Urteil *nt*; (*punishment*) Strafe *f* ● *vt* verurteilen

sentiment /'sentɪmənt/ *n* Gefühl *nt*; (*opinion*) Meinung *f*; (*sentimentality*) Sentimentalität *f* **~al** /-'mentl/ *a* sentimental. **~ality** /-'tælətɪ/ *n* Sentimentalität *f*

sentry /'sentrɪ/ *n* Wache *f*

separable /'sepərəbl/ *a* trennbar

separate¹ /'sepərət/ *a*, **-ly** *adv* getrennt, separat

separat|e² /'sepəreɪt/ *vt* trennen ● *vi* sich trennen. **~ion** /-'reɪʃn/ *n* Trennung *f*

September /sep'tembə(r)/ *n* September *m*

septic /'septɪk/ *a* vereitert

sequel /'si:kwl/ *n* Folge *f*; (*fig*) Nachspiel *nt*

sequence /'si:kwəns/ *n* Reihenfolge *f*

serenade /serə'neɪd/ *n* Ständchen *nt* ● *vt* **~ s.o.** jdm ein Ständchen bringen

seren|e /sɪ'ri:n/ *a*, **-ly** *adv* gelassen. **~ity** /-'renətɪ/ *n* Gelassenheit *f*

sergeant /'sɑ:dʒənt/ *n* (*Mil*) Feldwebel *m*; (*in police*) Polizeimeister *m*

serial /'sɪərɪəl/ *n* Fortsetzungsgeschichte *f*; (*Radio, TV*) Serie *f*. **~ize** *vt* in Fortsetzungen veröffentlichen/ (*Radio, TV*) senden

series /'sɪəri:z/ *n inv* Serie *f*

serious /'sɪərɪəs/ *a*, **-ly** *adv* ernst; <*illness, error*> schwer. **~ness** *n* Ernst *m*

sermon /'sɜ:mən/ *n* Predigt *f*

servant /'sɜ:vənt/ *n* Diener(in) *m(f)*

serve /sɜ:v/ *n* (*Tennis*) Aufschlag *m* ● *vt* dienen (+ *dat*); bedienen <*customer, guest*>; servieren <*food*>; verbüßen <*sentence*>; **it ~s you right!** das geschieht dir recht! ● *vi* dienen; (*Tennis*) aufschlagen

service /'sɜ:vɪs/ *n* Dienst *m*; (*Relig*) Gottesdienst *m*; (*in shop, restaurant*) Bedienung *f*; (*transport*) Verbindung *f*; (*maintenance*) Wartung *f*; (*set of crockery*) Service *nt*; (*Tennis*) Aufschlag *m*; **~s** *pl* Dienstleistungen *pl*; (*on motorway*) Tankstelle und Raststätte *f*; **in the ~s** beim Militär; **out of/in ~** <*machine:*> außer/in Betrieb ● *vt* (*Techn*) warten

service: ~ area *n* Tankstelle und Raststätte *f*. **~ charge** *n* Bedienungszuschlag *m*. **~man** *n* Soldat *m*. **~ station** *n* Tankstelle *f*

serviette /sɜ:vɪ'et/ *n* Serviette *f*

servile /'sɜ:vaɪl/ *a* unterwürfig

session /'seʃn/ *n* Sitzung *f*

set /set/ *n* Satz *m*; (*of crockery*) Service *nt*; (*of cutlery*) Garnitur *f*; (*TV, Radio*) Apparat *m*; (*Math*) Menge *f*; (*Theat*) Bühnenbild *nt*; (*Cinema*) Szenenaufbau *m*; (*of people*) Kreis *m* ● *a* (*ready*) fertig, bereit; (*rigid*) fest; <*book*> vorgeschrieben; **be ~ on doing sth** entschlossen sein, etw zu tun ● *v* (*pt/pp* **set**, *pres p* **setting**) ● *vt* setzen; (*adjust*) einstellen; stellen <*task, alarm clock*>; festsetzen, festlegen <*date, limit*>; aufgeben <*homework*>; zusammenstellen <*questions*>; [ein]fassen <*gem*>; einrichten <*bone*>; legen <*hair*>; decken <*table*> ● *vi* <*sun:*> untergehen;

(*become hard*) fest werden. ~ **back** *vt* zurücksetzen; (*hold up*) aufhalten; ([!] *cost*) kosten. ~ **off** *vi* losgehen; (*in vehicle*) losfahren ● *vt* auslösen <*alarm*>; explodieren lassen <*bomb*>. ~ **out** *vi* losgehen; (*in vehicle*) losfahren ● *vt* auslegen; (*state*) darlegen. ~ **up** *vt* aufbauen; (*fig*) gründen

settee /se'ti:/ *n* Sofa *nt*, Couch *f*

setting /'setɪŋ/ *n* Rahmen *m*; (*surroundings*) Umgebung *f*

settle /'setl/ *vt* (*decide*) entscheiden; (*agree*) regeln; (*fix*) festsetzen; (*calm*) beruhigen; (*pay*) bezahlen ● *vi* sich niederlassen; <*snow, dust:*> liegen bleiben; (*subside*) sich senken; <*sediment:*> sich absetzen. ~ **down** *vi* sich beruhigen; (*permanently*) sesshaft werden. ~ **up** *vi* abrechnen

settlement /'setlmənt/ *n* (*see* **settle**) Entscheidung *f*; Regelung *f*; Bezahlung *f*; (*Jur*) Vergleich *m*; (*colony*) Siedlung *f*

settler /'setlə(r)/ *n* Siedler *m*

'set-up *n* System *nt*

seven /'sevn/ *a* sieben. ~**'teen** *a* siebzehn. ~**'teenth** *a* siebzehnte(r,s)

seventh /'sevnθ/ *a* siebte(r,s)

seventieth /'sevntɪɪθ/ *a* siebzigste(r,s)

seventy /'sevntɪ/ *a* siebzig

several /'sevrl/ *a & pron* mehrere, einige

sever|e /sɪ'vɪə(r)/ *a* (**-r, -st,**) **-ly** *adv* streng; <*pain*> stark; <*illness*> schwer. ~**ity** /-'verətɪ/ *n* Strenge *f*, Schwere *f*

sew /səʊ/ *vt/i* (*pt* **sewed**, *pp* **sewn** *or* **sewed**) nähen

sewage /'su:ɪdʒ/ *n* Abwasser *nt*

sewer /'su:ə(r)/ *n* Abwasserkanal *m*

sewing /'səʊɪŋ/ *n* Nähen *nt*; (*work*) Näharbeit *f*. ~ **machine** *n* Nähmaschine *f*

sewn /səʊn/ *see* **sew**

sex /seks/ *n* Geschlecht *nt*; (*sexuality, intercourse*) Sex *m*. ~**ist** *a* sexistisch

sexual /'seksjʊəl/ *a*, **-ly** *adv* sexuell. ~ **'intercourse** *n* Geschlechtsverkehr *m*

sexuality /seksjʊ'ælətɪ/ *n* Sexualität *f*

sexy /'seksɪ/ *a* (**-ier, -iest**) sexy

shabby /'ʃæbɪ/ *a* (**-ier, -iest**), **-ily** *adv* schäbig

shack /ʃæk/ *n* Hütte *f*

shade /ʃeɪd/ *n* Schatten *m*; (*of colour*) [Farb]ton *m*; (*for lamp*) [Lampen]schirm *m*; (*Amer: window-blind*) Jalousie *f* ● *vt* beschatten

shadow /'ʃædəʊ/ *n* Schatten *m* ● *vt* (*follow*) beschatten

shady /'ʃeɪdɪ/ *a* (**-ier, -iest**) schattig; ([!] *disreputable*) zwielichtig

shaft /ʃɑ:ft/ *n* Schaft *m*; (*Techn*) Welle *f*; (*of light*) Strahl *m*; (*of lift*) Schacht *m*

shaggy /'ʃægɪ/ *a* (**-ier, -iest**) zottig

shake /ʃeɪk/ *n* Schütteln *nt* ● *v* (*pt* **shook**, *pp* **shaken**) ● *vt* schütteln; (*shock*) erschüttern; ~ **hands with s.o.** jdm die Hand geben ● *vi* wackeln; (*tremble*) zittern. ~ **off** *vt* abschütteln

shaky /'ʃeɪkɪ/ *a* (**-ier, -iest**) wackelig; <*hand, voice*> zittrig

shall /ʃæl/ *v aux* **we ~ see** wir werden sehen; **what ~ I do?** was soll ich machen?

shallow /'ʃæləʊ/ *a* (**-er, -est**) seicht; <*dish*> flach; (*fig*) oberflächlich

sham /ʃæm/ *a* unecht ● *n* Heuchelei *f* ● *vt* (*pt/pp* **shammed**) vortäuschen

shambles /'ʃæmblz/ *n* Durcheinander *nt*
shame /ʃeɪm/ *n* Scham *f*; (*disgrace*) Schande *f*; **be a ~** schade sein; **what a ~!** wie schade!
shame|ful /'ʃeɪmfl/ *a*, **-ly** *adv* schändlich. **~less** *a*, **-ly** *adv* schamlos
shampoo /ʃæm'pu:/ *n* Shampoo *nt* ● *vt* schamponieren
shan't /ʃɑ:nt/ = **shall not**
shape /ʃeɪp/ *n* Form *f*; (*figure*) Gestalt *f* ● *vt* formen (**into** zu). **~less** *a* formlos; <*clothing*> unförmig
share /ʃeə(r)/ *n* [An]teil *m*; (*Comm*) Aktie *f* ● *vt/i* teilen. **~holder** *n* Aktionär(in) *m(f)*
shark /ʃɑ:k/ *n* Hai[fisch] *m*
sharp /ʃɑ:p/ *a* (**-er, -est**), **-ly** *adv* scharf; (*pointed*) spitz; (*severe*) heftig; (*sudden*) steil; (*alert*) clever; (*unscrupulous*) gerissen ● *adv* scharf; (*Mus*) zu hoch; **at six o'clock ~** Punkt sechs Uhr ● *n* (*Mus*) Kreuz *nt*. **~en** *vt* schärfen; [an]spitzen <*pencil*>
shatter /'ʃætə(r)/ *vt* zertrümmern; (*fig*) zerstören; **~ed** <*person:*> erschüttert; (🅘 *exhausted*) kaputt ● *vi* zersplittern
shave /ʃeɪv/ *n* Rasur *f*; **have a ~** sich rasieren ● *vt* rasieren ● *vi* sich rasieren. **~r** *n* Rasierapparat *m*
shawl /ʃɔ:l/ *n* Schultertuch *nt*
she /ʃi:/ *pron* sie
shears /ʃɪəz/ *npl* [große] Schere *f*
shed¹ /ʃed/ *n* Schuppen *m*
shed² *vt* (*pt/pp* **shed**, *pres p* **shedding**) verlieren; vergießen <*blood, tears*>; **~ light on** Licht bringen in (+ *acc*)
sheep /ʃi:p/ *n inv* Schaf *nt*. **~-dog** *n* Hütehund *m*
sheepish /'ʃi:pɪʃ/ *a*, **-ly** *adv* verlegen
sheer /ʃɪə(r)/ *a* rein; (*steep*) steil; (*transparent*) hauchdünn
sheet /ʃi:t/ *n* Laken *nt*, Betttuch *nt*; (*of paper*) Blatt *nt*; (*of glass, metal*) Platte *f*
shelf /ʃelf/ *n* (*pl* **shelves**) Brett *nt*, Bord *nt*; (*set of shelves*) Regal *nt*
shell /ʃel/ *n* Schale *f*; (*of snail*) Haus *nt*; (*of tortoise*) Panzer *m*; (*on beach*) Muschel *f*; (*Mil*) Granate *f* ● *vt* pellen; enthülsen <*peas*>; (*Mil*) [mit Granaten] beschießen. **~ out** *vi* 🅘 blechen
'**shellfish** *n inv* Schalentiere *pl*; (*Culin*) Meeresfrüchte *pl*
shelter /'ʃeltə(r)/ *n* Schutz *m*; (*air-raid ~*) Luftschutzraum *m* ● *vt* schützen (**from** vor + *dat*) ● *vi* sich unterstellen. **~ed** *a* geschützt; <*life*> behütet
shelve /ʃelv/ *vt* auf Eis legen; (*abandon*) aufgeben
shelving /'ʃelvɪŋ/ *n* (*shelves*) Regale *pl*
shepherd /'ʃepəd/ *n* Schäfer *m* ● *vt* führen
sherry /'ʃerɪ/ *n* Sherry *m*
shield /ʃi:ld/ *n* Schild *m*; (*for eyes*) Schirm *m*; (*Techn & fig*) Schutz *m* ● *vt* schützen (**from** vor + *dat*)
shift /ʃɪft/ *n* Verschiebung *f*; (*at work*) Schicht *f* ● *vt* rücken; (*take away*) wegnehmen; (*rearrange*) umstellen; schieben <*blame*> (**on to** auf + *acc*) ● *vi* sich verschieben; (🅘 *rush*) rasen
shifty /'ʃɪftɪ/ *a* (**-ier, -iest**) (*pej*) verschlagen
shimmer /'ʃɪmə(r)/ *n* Schimmer *m* ● *vi* schimmern
shin /ʃɪn/ *n* Schienbein *nt*
shine /ʃaɪn/ *n* Glanz *m* ● *v* (*pt/pp* **shone**) ● *vi* leuchten; (*reflect light*) glänzen; <*sun:*> scheinen ● *vt* **~ a light on** beleuchten

shingle /ˈʃɪŋgl/ *n* (*pebbles*) Kiesel *pl*

shiny /ˈʃaɪnɪ/ *a* (**-ier, -iest**) glänzend

ship /ʃɪp/ *n* Schiff *nt* ● *vt* (*pt/pp* **shipped**) verschiffen

ship: ~building *n* Schiffbau *m*. **~ment** *n* Sendung *f*. **~per** *n* Spediteur *m*. **~ping** *n* Versand *m*; (*traffic*) Schifffahrt *f*. **~shape** *a & adv* in Ordnung. **~wreck** *n* Schiffbruch *m*. **~wrecked** *a* schiffbrüchig. **~yard** *n* Werft *f*

shirt /ʃɜːt/ *n* [Ober]hemd *nt*; (*for woman*) Hemdbluse *f*

shit /ʃɪt/ *n* (*vulg*) Scheiße *f* ● *vi* (*pt/pp* **shit**) (*vulg*) scheißen

shiver /ˈʃɪvə(r)/ *n* Schauder *m* ● *vi* zittern

shoal /ʃəʊl/ *n* (*fish*) Schwarm *m*

shock /ʃɒk/ *n* Schock *m*; (*Electr*) Schlag *m*; (*impact*) Erschütterung *f* ● *vt* einen Schock versetzen (+ *dat*); (*scandalize*) schockieren. **~ing** *a* schockierend; ([!] *bad*) fürchterlich

shoddy /ˈʃɒdɪ/ *a* (**-ier, -iest**) minderwertig

shoe /ʃuː/ *n* Schuh *m*; (*of horse*) Hufeisen *nt* ● *vt* (*pt/pp* **shod**, *pres p* **shoeing**) beschlagen <*horse*>

shoe: ~horn *n* Schuhanzieher *m*. **~-lace** *n* Schnürsenkel *m*. **~-string** *n* **on a ~-string** [!] mit ganz wenig Geld

shone /ʃɒn/ *see* **shine**

shoo /ʃuː/ *vt* scheuchen ● *int* sch!

shook /ʃʊk/ *see* **shake**

shoot /ʃuːt/ *n* (*Bot*) Trieb *m*; (*hunt*) Jagd *f* ● *v* (*pt/pp* **shot**) ● *vt* schießen; (*kill*) erschießen; drehen <*film*> ● *vi* schießen. **~ down** *vt* abschießen. **~ out** *vi* (*rush*) herausschießen. **~ up** *vi* (*grow*) in die Höhe schießen/<*prices:*> schnellen

shop /ʃɒp/ *n* Laden *m*, Geschäft *nt*; (*workshop*) Werkstatt *f*; **talk ~** [!] fachsimpeln ● *vi* (*pt/pp* **shopped**, *pres p* **shopping**) einkaufen; **go ~ping** einkaufen gehen

shop: ~ assistant *n* Verkäufer(in) *m(f)*. **~keeper** *n* Ladenbesitzer(in) *m(f)*. **~-lifter** *n* Ladendieb *m*. **~-lifting** *n* Ladendiebstahl *m*

shopping /ˈʃɒpɪŋ/ *n* Einkaufen *nt*; (*articles*) Einkäufe *pl*; **do the ~** einkaufen. **~ bag** *n* Einkaufstasche *f*. **~ centre** *n* Einkaufszentrum *nt*. **~ trolley** *n* Einkaufswagen *m*

shop-ˈwindow *n* Schaufenster *nt*

shore /ʃɔː(r)/ *n* Strand *m*; (*of lake*) Ufer *nt*

short /ʃɔːt/ *a* (**-er, -est**) kurz; <*person*> klein; (*curt*) schroff; **a ~ time ago** vor kurzem; **be ~ of ...** zu wenig ... haben; **be in ~ supply** knapp sein ● *adv* kurz; (*abruptly*) plötzlich; (*curtly*) kurz angebunden; **in ~** kurzum; **~ of** (*except*) außer; **go ~** Mangel leiden

shortage /ˈʃɔːtɪdʒ/ *n* Mangel *m* (**of** an + *dat*); (*scarcity*) Knappheit *f*

short: ~bread *n* ≈ Mürbekekse *pl*. **~ ˈcircuit** *n* Kurzschluss *m*. **~coming** *n* Fehler *m*. **~ ˈcut** *n* Abkürzung *f*

shorten /ˈʃɔːtn/ *vt* [ab]kürzen; kürzer machen <*garment*>

short: ~hand *n* Kurzschrift *f*, Stenographie *f*. **~list** *n* engere Auswahl *f*

short|ly /ˈʃɔːtlɪ/ *adv* in Kürze; **~ly before/after** kurz vorher/danach. **~ness** *n* Kürze *f*; (*of person*) Kleinheit *f*

shorts /ʃɔːts/ *npl* Shorts *pl*

short: ~-ˈsighted *a* kurzsichtig. **~-sleeved** *a* kurzärmelig. **~ ˈstory** *n* Kurzgeschichte *f*.

~-'tempered *a* aufbrausend. **~-term** *a* kurzfristig. **~ wave** *n* Kurzwelle *f*

shot /ʃɒt/ *see* **shoot** ● *n* Schuss *m*; (*pellets*) Schrot *m*; (*person*) Schütze *m*; (*Phot*) Aufnahme *f*; (*injection*) Spritze *f*; (🅸 *attempt*) Versuch *m*; **like a ~** 🅸 sofort. **~gun** *n* Schrotflinte *f*. **~-put** *n* (*Sport*) Kugelstoßen *nt*

should /ʃʊd/ *v aux* **you ~ go** du solltest gehen; **I ~ have seen him** ich hätte ihn sehen sollen; **I ~ like** ich möchte; **this ~ be enough** das müsste eigentlich reichen; **if he ~ be there** falls er da sein sollte

shoulder /ˈʃəʊldə(r)/ *n* Schulter *f* ● *vt* schultern; (*fig*) auf sich (*acc*) nehmen. **~-blade** *n* Schulterblatt *nt*

shout /ʃaʊt/ *n* Schrei *m* ● *vt/i* schreien. **~ down** *vt* niederschreien

shouting /ˈʃaʊtɪŋ/ *n* Geschrei *nt*

shove /ʃʌv/ *n* Stoß *m* ● *vt* stoßen; (🅸 *put*) tun ● *vi* drängeln. **~ off** *vi* 🅸 abhauen

shovel /ˈʃʌvl/ *n* Schaufel *f* ● *vt* (*pt/pp* **shovelled**) schaufeln

show /ʃəʊ/ *n* (*display*) Pracht *f*; (*exhibition*) Ausstellung *f*, Schau *f*; (*performance*) Vorstellung *f*; (*Theat, TV*) Show *f*; **on ~** ausgestellt ● *v* (*pt* **showed**, *pp* **shown**) ● *vt* zeigen; (*put on display*) ausstellen; vorführen *<film>* ● *vi* sichtbar sein; *<film:>* gezeigt werden. **~ in** *vt* hereinführen. **~ off** *vi* 🅸 angeben ● *vt* vorführen; (*flaunt*) angeben mit. **~ up** *vi* [deutlich] zu sehen sein; (🅸 *arrive*) auftauchen ● *vt* deutlich zeigen; (🅸 *embarrass*) blamieren

shower /ˈʃaʊə(r)/ *n* Dusche *f*; (*of rain*) Schauer *m*; **have a ~** duschen ● *vt* **~ with** überschütten mit ● *vi* duschen

'show-jumping *n* Springreiten *nt*

shown /ʃəʊn/ *see* **show**

show: ~-off *n* Angeber(in) *m(f)*. **~room** *n* Ausstellungsraum *m*

showy /ˈʃəʊɪ/ *a* protzig

shrank /ʃræŋk/ *see* **shrink**

shred /ʃred/ *n* Fetzen *m*; (*fig*) Spur *f* ● *vt* (*pt/pp* **shredded**) zerkleinern; (*Culin*) schnitzeln. **~der** *n* Reißwolf *m*; (*Culin*) Schnitzelwerk *nt*

shrewd /ʃru:d/ *a* (**-er, -est**), **-ly** *adv* klug. **~ness** *n* Klugheit *f*

shriek /ʃri:k/ *n* Schrei *m* ● *vt/i* schreien

shrill /ʃrɪl/ *a*, **-y** *adv* schrill

shrimp /ʃrɪmp/ *n* Garnele *f*, Krabbe *f*

shrink /ʃrɪŋk/ *vi* (*pt* **shrank**, *pp* **shrunk**) schrumpfen; *<garment:>* einlaufen; (*draw back*) zurückschrecken (**from** vor + *dat*)

shrivel /ˈʃrɪvl/ *vi* (*pt/pp* **shrivelled**) verschrumpeln

Shrove /ʃrəʊv/ *n* **~' Tuesday** Fastnachtsdienstag *m*

shrub /ʃrʌb/ *n* Strauch *m*

shrug /ʃrʌg/ *n* Achselzucken *nt* ● *vt/i* (*pt/pp* **shrugged**) **~ [one's shoulders]** die Achseln zucken

shrunk /ʃrʌŋk/ *see* **shrink**

shudder /ˈʃʌdə(r)/ *n* Schauder *m* ● *vi* schaudern; (*tremble*) zittern

shuffle /ˈʃʌfl/ *vi* schlurfen ● *vt* mischen *<cards>*

shun /ʃʌn/ *vt* (*pt/pp* **shunned**) meiden

shunt /ʃʌnt/ *vt* rangieren

shut /ʃʌt/ *v* (*pt/pp* **shut**, *pres p* **shutting**) ● *vt* zumachen, schließen ● *vi* sich schließen; *<shop:>* schließen, zumachen. **~ down** *vt* schließen; stilllegen *<factory>* ● *vi* schließen. **~ up** *vt* abschließen; (*lock in*) einsperren ● *vi* [!] den Mund halten

shutter /ˈʃʌtə(r)/ *n* [Fenster]laden *m*; (*Phot*) Verschluss *m*

shuttle /ˈʃʌtl/ *n* (*Tex*) Schiffchen *nt*

shuttle service *n* Pendelverkehr *m*

shy /ʃaɪ/ *a* (**-er, -est**), **-ly** *adv* schüchtern; (*timid*) scheu. **~ness** *n* Schüchternheit *f*

siblings /ˈsɪblɪŋz/ *npl* Geschwister *pl*

Sicily /ˈsɪsɪlɪ/ *n* Sizilien *nt*

sick /sɪk/ *a* krank; <*humour*> makaber; **be ~** (*vomit*) sich übergeben; **be ~ of sth** [!] etw satt haben; **I feel ~** mir ist schlecht

sick|ly /ˈsɪklɪ/ *a* (**-ier, -iest**) kränklich. **~ness** *n* Krankheit *f*; (*vomiting*) Erbrechen *nt*

side /saɪd/ *n* Seite *f*; **on the ~** (*as sideline*) nebenbei; **~ by ~** nebeneinander; (*fig*) Seite an Seite; **take ~s** Partei ergreifen (**with** für) ● *attrib* Seiten- ● *vi* **~ with** Partei ergreifen für

side: ~board *n* Anrichte *f*. **~-effect** *n* Nebenwirkung *f*. **~lights** *npl* Standlicht *nt*. **~line** *n* Nebenbeschäftigung *f*. **~-show** *n* Nebenattraktion *f*. **~-step** *vt* ausweichen (+ *dat*). **~walk** *n* (*Amer*) Bürgersteig *m*. **~ways** *adv* seitwärts

siding /ˈsaɪdɪŋ/ *n* Abstellgleis *nt*

siege /siːdʒ/ *n* Belagerung *f*; (*by police*) Umstellung *f*

sieve /sɪv/ *n* Sieb *nt* ● *vt* sieben

sift /sɪft/ *vt* sieben; (*fig*) durchsehen

sigh /saɪ/ *n* Seufzer *m* ● *vi* seufzen

sight /saɪt/ *n* Sicht *f*; (*faculty*) Sehvermögen *nt*; (*spectacle*) Anblick *m*; (*on gun*) Visier *nt*; **~s** *pl* Sehenswürdigkeiten *pl*; **at first ~** auf den ersten Blick; **lose ~ of** aus dem Auge verlieren; **know by ~** vom Sehen kennen ● *vt* sichten

ˈsightseeing *n* **go ~** die Sehenswürdigkeiten besichtigen

sign /saɪn/ *n* Zeichen *nt*; (*notice*) Schild *nt* ● *vt/i* unterschreiben; <*author, artist:*> signieren. **~ on** *vi* (*as unemployed*) sich arbeitslos melden; (*Mil*) sich verpflichten

signal /ˈsɪgnl/ *n* Signal *nt* ● *vt/i* (*pt/pp* **signalled**) signalisieren; **~ to s.o.** jdm ein Signal geben

signature /ˈsɪgnətʃə(r)/ *n* Unterschrift *f*; (*of artist*) Signatur *f*

significan|ce /sɪgˈnɪfɪkəns/ *n* Bedeutung *f*. **~t** *a*, **-ly** *adv* (*important*) bedeutend

signify /ˈsɪgnɪfaɪ/ *vt* (*pt/pp* **-ied**) bedeuten

signpost /ˈsaɪn-/ *n* Wegweiser *m*

silence /ˈsaɪləns/ *n* Stille *f*; (*of person*) Schweigen *nt* ● *vt* zum Schweigen bringen. **~r** *n* (*on gun*) Schalldämpfer *m*; (*Auto*) Auspufftopf *m*

silent /ˈsaɪlənt/ *a*, **-ly** *adv* still; (*without speaking*) schweigend; **remain ~** schweigen

silhouette /sɪluːˈet/ *n* Silhouette *f*; (*picture*) Schattenriss *m* ● *vt* **be ~d** sich als Silhouette abheben

silicon /ˈsɪlɪkən/ *n* Silizium *nt*

silk /sɪlk/ *n* Seide *f* ● *attrib* Seiden-

silky /ˈsɪlkɪ/ *a* (**-ier, -iest**) seidig

sill /ʃɪl/ *n* Sims *m* & *nt*

silly /ˈʃɪlɪ/ *a* (**-ier, -iest**) dumm, albern

silver /ˈsɪlvə(r)/ *a* silbern; <*coin, paper*> Silber- ● *n* Silber *nt*

silver: ~-plated *a* versilbert. **~ware** *n* Silber *nt*

similar /ˈsɪmɪlə(r)/ *a*, **-ly** *adv* ähnlich. **~ity** /-ˈlærətɪ/ *n* Ähnlichkeit *f*

simmer /ˈsɪmə(r)/ *vi* leise kochen, ziehen ● *vt* ziehen lassen

simple /ˈsɪmpl/ *a* (**-r, -st**) einfach; <*person*> einfältig. **~-ˈminded** *a* einfältig

simplicity /sɪmˈplɪsətɪ/ *n* Einfachheit *f*

simpli|fication /sɪmplɪfɪˈkeɪʃn/ *n* Vereinfachung *f*. **~fy** /ˈsɪmplɪfaɪ/ *vt* (*pt/pp* **-ied**) vereinfachen

simply /ˈsɪmplɪ/ *adv* einfach

simulate /ˈsɪmjʊleɪt/ *vt* vortäuschen; (*Techn*) simulieren

simultaneous /sɪmlˈteɪnɪəs/ *a*, **-ly** *adv* gleichzeitig

sin /sɪn/ *n* Sünde *f* ● *vi* (*pt/pp* **sinned**) sündigen

---

since /sɪns/

● *preposition*

····➤ seit (+ *dat*). **he's been living here since 1991** er wohnt* seit 1991 hier. **I had been waiting since 8 o'clock** ich wartete* [schon] seit 8 Uhr. **since seeing you** seit ich dich gesehen habe. **how long is it since your interview?** wie lange ist es seit deinem Vorstellungsgespräch?

● *adverb*

····➤ seitdem. **I haven't spoken to her since** seitdem habe ich mit ihr nicht gesprochen. **the house has been empty ever since** das Haus steht seitdem leer. **he has since remarried** er hat danach wieder geheiratet. **long since** vor langer Zeit

● *conjunction*

····➤ seit. **since she has been living in Germany** seit sie in Deutschland wohnt*. **since they had been in London** seit sie in London waren*. **how long is it since he left?** wie lange ist es her, dass er weggezogen ist? **it's a year since he left** es ist ein Jahr her, dass er weggezogen ist

····➤ (*because*) da. **since she was ill, I had to do it** da sie krank war, musste ich es tun

! *Note the different tenses in German

---

sincere /sɪnˈsɪə(r)/ *a* aufrichtig; (*heartfelt*) herzlich. **~ly** *adv* aufrichtig; **Yours ~ly** Mit freundlichen Grüßen

sincerity /sɪnˈserətɪ/ *n* Aufrichtigkeit *f*

sinful /ˈsɪnfl/ *a* sündhaft

sing /sɪŋ/ *vt/i* (*pt* **sang**, *pp* **sung**) singen

singe /sɪndʒ/ *vt* (*pres p* **singeing**) versengen

singer /ˈsɪŋə(r)/ *n* Sänger(in) *m(f)*

single /ˈsɪŋgl/ *a* einzeln; (*one only*) einzig; (*unmarried*) ledig; <*ticket*> einfach; <*room, bed*> Einzel- ● *n* (*ticket*) einfache Fahrkarte *f*; (*record*) Single *f*; **~s** *pl* (*Tennis*) Einzel *nt* ● *vt* **~ out** auswählen

single: ~-handed *a & adv* allein. **~ ˈparent** *n* Alleinerziehende(r) *m/f*

singly /ˈsɪŋglɪ/ *adv* einzeln

singular /ˈsɪŋgjʊlə(r)/ *a* eigenartig; (*Gram*) im Singular ● *n* Singular *m*

sinister /ˈsɪnɪstə(r)/ *a* finster

sink /sɪŋk/ *n* Spülbecken *nt* ● *v* (*pt* **sank**, *pp* **sunk**) ● *vi* sinken ● *vt* versenken <*ship*>; senken <*shaft*>. **~ in** *vi* einsinken; (**!** *be understood*) kapiert werden

sinner /ˈsɪnə(r)/ *n* Sünder(in) *m(f)*

sip /sɪp/ *n* Schlückchen *nt* ● *vt* (*pt/pp* **sipped**) in kleinen Schlucken trinken

siphon /ˈsaɪfn/ *n* (*bottle*) Siphon *m*. **~ off** *vt* mit einem Saugheber ablassen

sir /sɜː(r)/ *n* mein Herr; **S~** (*title*) Sir; **Dear S~s** Sehr geehrte Herren

siren /ˈsaɪrən/ *n* Sirene *f*

sister /ˈsɪstə(r)/ *n* Schwester *f*; (*nurse*) Oberschwester *f*. **~-in-law** *n* Schwägerin *f*

sit /sɪt/ *v* (*pt/pp* **sat**, *pres p* **sitting**) ● *vi* sitzen; (*sit down*) sich setzen; <*committee:*> tagen ● *vt* setzen; machen <*exam*>. **~ back** *vi* sich zurücklehnen. **~ down** *vi* sich setzen. **~ up** *vi* [aufrecht] sitzen; (*rise*) sich aufsetzen; (*not slouch*) gerade sitzen

site /saɪt/ *n* Gelände *nt*; (*for camping*) Platz *m*; (*Archaeol*) Stätte *f*

sitting /ˈsɪtɪŋ/ *n* Sitzung *f*; (*for meals*) Schub *m*

situat|e /ˈsɪtjʊeɪt/ *vt* legen; **be ~ed** liegen. **~ion** /-ˈeɪʃn/ *n* Lage *f*; (*circumstances*) Situation *f*; (*job*) Stelle *f*

six /sɪks/ *a* sechs. **~teen** *a* sechzehn. **~teenth** *a* sechzehnte(r,s)

sixth /sɪksθ/ *a* sechste(r,s)

sixtieth /ˈsɪkstɪɪθ/ *a* sechzigste(r,s)

sixty /ˈsɪkstɪ/ *a* sechzig

size /saɪz/ *n* Größe *f*

sizzle /ˈsɪzl/ *vi* brutzeln

skate /skeɪt/ *n* Schlittschuh *m* ● *vi* Schlittschuh laufen. **~board** *n* Skateboard *nt* ● *vi* Skateboard fahren. **~boarding** *n* Skateboardfahren *nt*. **~r** *n* Eisläufer(in) *m(f)*

skating /ˈskeɪtɪŋ/ *n* Eislaufen *nt*. **~-rink** *n* Eisbahn *f*

skeleton /ˈskelɪtn/ *n* Skelett *nt*. **~ ˈkey** *n* Dietrich *m*

sketch /sketʃ/ *n* Skizze *f*; (*Theat*) Sketch *m* ● *vt* skizzieren

sketchy /ˈsketʃɪ/ *a* (**-ier, -iest**), **-ily** *adv* skizzenhaft

ski /skiː/ *n* Ski *m* ● *vi* (*pt/pp* **skied**, *pres p* **skiing**) Ski fahren *or* laufen

skid /skɪd/ *n* Schleudern *nt* ● *vi* (*pt/pp* **skidded**) schleudern

skier /ˈskiːə(r)/ *n* Skiläufer(in) *m(f)*

skiing /ˈskiːɪŋ/ *n* Skilaufen *nt*

skilful /ˈskɪlfl/ *a*, **-ly** *adv* geschickt

skill /skɪl/ *n* Geschick *nt*. **~ed** *a* geschickt; (*trained*) ausgebildet

skim /skɪm/ *vt* (*pt/pp* **skimmed**) entrahmen <*milk*>

skimp /skɪmp/ *vt* sparen an (+ *dat*)

skimpy /ˈskɪmpɪ/ *a* (**-ier, -iest**) knapp

skin /skɪn/ *n* Haut *f*; (*on fruit*) Schale *f* ● *vt* (*pt/pp* **skinned**) häuten; schälen <*fruit*>

skin: ~-deep *a* oberflächlich. **~-diving** *n* Sporttauchen *nt*

skinny /ˈskɪnɪ/ *a* (**-ier, -iest**) dünn

skip[1] /skɪp/ *n* Container *m*

skip[2] *n* Hüpfer *m* ● *v* (*pt/pp* **skipped**) *vi* hüpfen; (*with rope*) seilspringen ● *vt* überspringen

skipper /ˈskɪpə(r)/ *n* Kapitän *m*

ˈskipping-rope *n* Sprungseil *nt*

skirmish /ˈskɜːmɪʃ/ *n* Gefecht *nt*

skirt /skɜːt/ *n* Rock *m* ● *vt* herumgehen um

skittle /ˈskɪtl/ *n* Kegel *m*

skive /skaɪv/ *vi* [!] blaumachen

skull /skʌl/ *n* Schädel *m*

sky /skaɪ/ *n* Himmel *m*. **~light** *n* Dachluke *f*. **~scraper** *n* Wolkenkratzer *m*

slab /slæb/ *n* Platte *f*; (*slice*) Scheibe *f*; (*of chocolate*) Tafel *f*

slack /slæk/ *a* (**-er, -est**) schlaff, locker; <*person*> nachlässig; (*Comm*) flau ● *vi* bummeln

slacken /'slækn/ *vi* sich lockern; (*diminish*) nachlassen ● *vt* lockern; (*diminish*) verringern
slain /sleɪn/ *see* **slay**
slam /slæm/ *v* (*pt/pp* **slammed**) ● *vt* zuschlagen; (*put*) knallen [!]; ([!] *criticize*) verreißen ● *vi* zuschlagen
slander /'slɑ:ndə(r)/ *n* Verleumdung *f* ● *vt* verleumden
slang /slæŋ/ *n* Slang *m*. **~y** *a* salopp
slant /slɑ:nt/ *n* Schräge *f*; **on the ~** schräg ● *vt* abschrägen; (*fig*) färben <*report*> ● *vi* sich neigen
slap /slæp/ *n* Schlag *m* ● *vt* (*pt/pp* **slapped**) schlagen; (*put*) knallen [!] ● *adv* direkt
slapdash *a* [!] schludrig
slash /slæʃ/ *n* Schlitz *m* ● *vt* aufschlitzen; [drastisch] reduzieren <*prices*>
slat /slæt/ *n* Latte *f*
slate /sleɪt/ *n* Schiefer *m* ● *vt* [!] heruntermachen; verreißen <*performance*>
slaughter /'slɔ:tə(r)/ *n* Schlachten *nt*; (*massacre*) Gemetzel *nt* ● *vt* schlachten; abschlachten <*men*>
Slav /slɑ:v/ *a* slawisch ● *n* Slawe *m*/ Slawin *f*
slave /sleɪv/ *n* Sklave *m*/ Sklavin *f* ● *vi* **~ [away]** schuften
slavery /'sleɪvərɪ/ *n* Sklaverei *f*
slay /sleɪ/ *vt* (*pt* **slew**, *pp* **slain**) ermorden
sledge /sledʒ/ *n* Schlitten *m*
sleek /sli:k/ *a* (**-er, -est**) seidig; (*well-fed*) wohlgenährt
sleep /sli:p/ *n* Schlaf *m*; **go to ~** einschlafen; **put to ~** einschläfern ● *v* (*pt/pp* **slept**) ● *vi* schlafen ● *vt* (*accommodate*) Unterkunft bieten für. **~er** *n* Schläfer(in) *m(f)*; (*Rail*) Schlafwagen *m*; (*on track*) Schwelle *f*
sleeping: ~-bag *n* Schlafsack *m*. **~-pill** *n* Schlaftablette *f*
sleep: ~less *a* schlaflos. **~-walking** *n* Schlafwandeln *nt*
sleepy /'sli:pɪ/ *a* (**-ier, -iest**), **-ily** *adv* schläfrig
sleet /sli:t/ *n* Schneeregen *m*
sleeve /sli:v/ *n* Ärmel *m*; (*for record*) Hülle *f*. **~less** *a* ärmellos
sleigh /sleɪ/ *n* [Pferde]schlitten *m*
slender /'slendə(r)/ *a* schlank; (*fig*) gering
slept /slept/ *see* **sleep**
slew *see* **slay**
slice /slaɪs/ *n* Scheibe *f* ● *vt* in Scheiben schneiden
slick /slɪk/ *a* clever
slid|e /slaɪd/ *n* Rutschbahn *f*; (*for hair*) Spange *f*; (*Phot*) Dia *nt* ● *v* (*pt/pp* **slid**) ● *vi* rutschen ● *vt* schieben. **~ing** *a* gleitend; <*door, seat*> Schiebe-
slight /slaɪt/ *a* (**-er, -est**), **-ly** *adv* leicht; <*importance*> gering; <*acquaintance*> flüchtig; (*slender*) schlank; **not in the ~est** nicht im Geringsten; **~ly better** ein bisschen besser ● *vt* kränken, beleidigen ● *n* Beleidigung *f*
slim /slɪm/ *a* (**slimmer, slimmest**) schlank; <*volume*> schmal; (*fig*) gering ● *vi* eine Schlankheitskur machen
slim|e /slaɪm/ *n* Schleim *m*. **~y** *a* schleimig
sling /slɪŋ/ *n* (*Med*) Schlinge *f* ● *vt* (*pt/pp* **slung**) [!] schmeißen
slip /slɪp/ *n* (*mistake*) Fehler *m*, [!] Patzer *m*; (*petticoat*) Unterrock *m*; (*paper*) Zettel *m*; **give s.o. the ~** [!] jdm entwischen; **~ of the tongue** Versprecher *m* ● *v* (*pt/pp* **slipped**) ● *vi* rutschen; (*fall*) ausrutschen; (*go quickly*) schlüpfen ● *vt* schieben; **~ s.o.'s mind** jdm entfallen. **~ away** *vi*

sich fortschleichen. **~ up** *vi* [!] einen Schnitzer machen

slipper /ˈslɪpə(r)/ *n* Hausschuh *m*

slippery /ˈslɪpərɪ/ *a* glitschig; <*surface*> glatt

slipshod /ˈslɪpʃɒd/ *a* schludrig

ˈslip-up *n* [!] Schnitzer *m*

slit /slɪt/ *n* Schlitz *m* ● *vt* (*pt/pp* **slit**) aufschlitzen

slither /ˈslɪðə(r)/ *vi* rutschen

slog /slɒg/ *n* **[hard]** ~ Schinderei *f* ● *vi* (*pt/pp* **slogged**) schuften

slogan /ˈsləʊgən/ *n* Schlagwort *nt*; (*advertising*) Werbespruch *m*

slop|e /sləʊp/ *n* Hang *m*; (*inclination*) Neigung *f* ● *vi* sich neigen. **~ing** *a* schräg

sloppy /ˈslɒpɪ/ *a* (**-ier, -iest**) schludrig; (*sentimental*) sentimental

slosh /slɒʃ/ *vi* [!] schwappen

slot /slɒt/ *n* Schlitz *m*; (*TV*) Sendezeit *f* ● *v* (*pt/pp* **slotted**) ● *vt* einfügen ● *vi* sich einfügen (**in** in + *acc*)

ˈslot-machine *n* Münzautomat *m*; (*for gambling*) Spielautomat *m*

slouch /slaʊtʃ/ *vi* sich schlecht halten

slovenly /ˈslʌvnlɪ/ *a* schlampig

slow /sləʊ/ *a* (**-er, -est**), **-ly** *adv* langsam; **be ~** <*clock:*> nachgehen; **in ~ motion** in Zeitlupe ● *adv* langsam ● *vt* verlangsamen ● *vi* **~ down, ~ up** langsamer werden. **~ness** *n* Langsamkeit *f*

sludge /slʌdʒ/ *n* Schlamm *m*

slug /slʌg/ *n* Nacktschnecke *f*

sluggish /ˈslʌgɪʃ/ *a*, **-ly** *adv* träge

sluice /slu:s/ *n* Schleuse *f*

slum /slʌm/ *n* Elendsviertel *nt*

slumber /ˈslʌmbə(r)/ *n* Schlummer *m* ● *vi* schlummern

slump /slʌmp/ *n* Sturz *m* ● *vi* fallen; (*crumple*) zusammensacken; <*prices:*> stürzen; <*sales:*> zurückgehen

slung /slʌŋ/ *see* **sling**

slur /slɜ:(r)/ *vt* (*pt/pp* **slurred**) undeutlich sprechen

slurp /slɜ:p/ *vt/i* schlürfen

slush /slʌʃ/ *n* [Schnee]matsch *m*; (*fig*) Kitsch *m*

slut /slʌt/ *n* Schlampe *f* [!]

sly /slaɪ/ *a* (**-er, -est**), **-ly** *adv* verschlagen ● *n* **on the ~** heimlich

smack /smæk/ *n* Schlag *m*, Klaps *m* ● *vt* schlagen ● *adv* [!] direkt

small /smɔ:l/ *a* (**-er, -est**) klein ● *adv* **chop up ~** klein hacken ● *n* **~ of the back** Kreuz *nt*

small: ~ ads *npl* Kleinanzeigen *pl*. **~ ˈchange** *n* Kleingeld *nt*. **~pox** *n* Pocken *pl*. **~ talk** *n* leichte Konversation *f*

smart /smɑ:t/ *a* (**-er, -est**), **-ly** *adv* schick; (*clever*) schlau, clever; (*brisk*) flott; (*Amer* [!]: *cheeky*) frech ● *vi* brennen

smarten /ˈsmɑ:tn/ *vt* **~ oneself up** mehr auf sein Äußeres achten

smash /smæʃ/ *n* Krach *m*; (*collision*) Zusammenstoß *m*; (*Tennis*) Schmetterball *m* ● *vt* zerschlagen; (*strike*) schlagen; (*Tennis*) schmettern ● *vi* zerschmettern; (*crash*) krachen (**into** gegen). **~ing** *a* [!] toll

smear /smɪə(r)/ *n* verschmierter Fleck *m*; (*Med*) Abstrich *m*; (*fig*) Verleumdung *f* ● *vt* schmieren; (*coat*) beschmieren (**with** mit); (*fig*) verleumden ● *vi* schmieren

smell /smel/ *n* Geruch *m*; (*sense*) Geruchssinn *m* ● *v* (*pt/pp* **smelt** *or* **smelled**) ● *vt* riechen; (*sniff*) riechen an (+ *dat*) ● *vi* riechen (**of** nach)

smelly /ˈsmelɪ/ *a* (**-ier, -iest**) übel riechend

smelt /smelt/ *see* **smell**

smile /smaɪl/ *n* Lächeln *nt* ● *vi* lächeln; ~ **at** anlächeln

smirk /smɜ:k/ *vi* feixen

smith /smɪθ/ *n* Schmied *m*

smock /smɒk/ *n* Kittel *m*

smog /smɒg/ *n* Smog *m*

smoke /sməʊk/ *n* Rauch *m* ● *vt/i* rauchen; (*Culin*) räuchern. **~less** *a* rauchfrei; <*fuel*> rauchlos

smoker /'sməʊkə(r)/ *n* Raucher *m*; (*Rail*) Raucherabteil *nt*

smoking /'sməʊkɪŋ/ *n* Rauchen *nt*; **'no ~'** 'Rauchen verboten'

smoky /'sməʊkɪ/ *a* (**-ier, -iest**) verraucht; <*taste*> rauchig

smooth /smu:ð/ *a* (**-er, -est**), **-ly** *adv* glatt ● *vt* glätten. **~ out** *vt* glatt streichen

smother /'smʌðə(r)/ *vt* ersticken; (*cover*) bedecken; (*suppress*) unterdrücken

smoulder /'sməʊldə(r)/ *vi* schwelen

smudge /smʌdʒ/ *n* Fleck *m* ● *vt* verwischen ● *vi* schmieren

smug /smʌg/ *a* (**smugger, smuggest**), **-ly** *adv* selbstgefällig

smuggl|e /'smʌgl/ *vt* schmuggeln. **~er** *n* Schmuggler *m*. **~ing** *n* Schmuggel *m*

snack /snæk/ *n* Imbiss *m*. **~-bar** *n* Imbissstube *f*

snag /snæg/ *n* Schwierigkeit *f*, [!] Haken *m*

snail /sneɪl/ *n* Schnecke *f*; **at a ~'s pace** im Schneckentempo

snake /sneɪk/ *n* Schlange *f*

snap /snæp/ *n* Knacken *nt*; (*photo*) Schnappschuss *m* ● *attrib* <*decision*> plötzlich ● *v* (*pt/pp* **snapped**) ● *vi* [entzwei]brechen; ~ **at** (*bite*) schnappen nach; (*speak sharply*) [scharf] anfahren ● *vt* zerbrechen; (*say*) fauchen; (*Phot*) knipsen. ~ **up** *vt* wegschnappen

snappy /'snæpɪ/ *a* (**-ier, -iest**) (*smart*) flott; **make it ~!** ein bisschen schnell!

'snapshot *n* Schnappschuss *m*

snare /sneə(r)/ *n* Schlinge *f*

snarl /snɑ:l/ *vi* [mit gefletschten Zähnen] knurren

snatch /snætʃ/ *n* (*fragment*) Fetzen *pl* ● *vt* schnappen; (*steal*) klauen; entführen <*child*>; ~ **sth from s.o.** jdm etw entreißen

sneak /sni:k/ *n* [!] Petze *f* ● *vi* schleichen; ([!] *tell tales*) petzen ● *vt* (*take*) mitgehen lassen ● *vi* ~ **in/out** sich hinein-/hinausschleichen

sneakers /'sni:kəz/ *npl* (*Amer*) Turnschuhe *pl*

sneer /snɪə(r)/ *vi* höhnisch lächeln; (*mock*) spotten

sneeze /sni:z/ *n* Niesen *nt* ● *vi* niesen

snide /snaɪd/ *a* [!] abfällig

sniff /snɪf/ *vi* schnüffeln ● *vt* schnüffeln an (+ *dat*)

snigger /'snɪgə(r)/ *vi* [boshaft] kichern

snip /snɪp/ *n* Schnitt *m* ● *vt/i* ~ **[at]** schnippeln an (+ *dat*)

snippet /'snɪpɪt/ *n* Schnipsel *m*; (*of information*) Bruchstück *nt*

snivel /'snɪvl/ *vi* (*pt/pp* **snivelled**) flennen

snob /snɒb/ *n* Snob *m*. **~bery** *n* Snobismus *m*. **~bish** *a* snobistisch

snoop /snu:p/ *vi* [!] schnüffeln

snooty /'snu:tɪ/ *a* [!] hochnäsig

snooze /snu:z/ *n* Nickerchen *nt* ● *vi* dösen

snore /snɔ:(r)/ *vi* schnarchen

snorkel /'snɔ:kl/ *n* Schnorchel *m*

snort /snɔ:t/ *vi* schnauben

snout /snaʊt/ *n* Schnauze *f*

snow /snəʊ/ *n* Schnee *m* ● *vi* schneien; **~ed under with** (*fig*) überhäuft mit

snow: ~ball *n* Schneeball *m*. **~drift** *n* Schneewehe *f*. **~drop** *n* Schneeglöckchen *nt*. **~fall** *n* Schneefall *m*. **~flake** *n* Schneeflocke *f*. **~man** *n* Schneemann *m*. **~plough** *n* Schneepflug *m*

snub /snʌb/ *n* Abfuhr *f* ● *vt* (*pt*/*pp* **snubbed**) brüskieren

'snub-nosed *a* stupsnasig

snuffle /'snʌfl/ *vi* schnüffeln

snug /snʌg/ *a* (**snugger, snuggest**) behaglich, gemütlich

snuggle /'snʌgl/ *vi* sich kuscheln (**up to** an + *acc*)

so /səʊ/ *adv* so; **so am I** ich auch; **so I see** das sehe ich; **that is so** das stimmt; **so much the better** umso besser; **if so** wenn ja; **so as to** um zu; **so long**! [!] tschüs! ● *pron* **I hope so** hoffentlich; **I think so** ich glaube schon; **I'm afraid so** leider ja; **so saying/doing, he/she** ... indem er/sie das sagte/tat, ... ● *conj* (*therefore*) also; **so that** damit; **so what**! na und! **so you see** wie du siehst

soak /səʊk/ *vt* nass machen; (*steep*) einweichen; ([!] *fleece*) schröpfen ● *vi* weichen; <*liquid:*> sickern. **~ up** *vt* aufsaugen

soaking /'səʊkɪŋ/ *a* & *adv* **~ [wet]** patschnass [!]

soap /səʊp/ *n* Seife *f*. **~ opera** *n* Seifenoper *f*. **~ powder** *n* Seifenpulver *nt*

soapy /'səʊpɪ/ *a* (**-ier, -iest**) seifig

soar /sɔ:(r)/ *vi* aufsteigen; <*prices:*> in die Höhe schnellen

sob /sɒb/ *n* Schluchzer *m* ● *vi* (*pt*/*pp* **sobbed**) schluchzen

sober /'səʊbə(r)/ *a*, **-ly** *adv* nüchtern; (*serious*) ernst; <*colour*> gedeckt. **~ up** *vi* nüchtern werden

'so-called *a* sogenannt

soccer /'sɒkə(r)/ *n* [!] Fußball *m*

sociable /'səʊʃəbl/ *a* gesellig

social /'səʊʃl/ *a* gesellschaftlich; (*Admin, Pol, Zool*) sozial

socialis|m /'səʊʃəlɪzm/ *n* Sozialismus *m*. **~t** /-ɪst/ *a* sozialistisch ● *n* Sozialist *m*

socialize /'səʊʃəlaɪz/ *vi* [gesellschaftlich] verkehren

socially /'səʊʃəlɪ/ *adv* gesellschaftlich; **know ~** privat kennen

social: ~ se'curity *n* Sozialhilfe *f*. **~ worker** *n* Sozialarbeiter(in) *m(f)*

society /sə'saɪətɪ/ *n* Gesellschaft *f*; (*club*) Verein *m*

sociolog|ist /səʊsɪ'ɒlədʒɪst/ *n* Soziologe *m*. **~y** *n* Soziologie *f*

sock /sɒk/ *n* Socke *f*; (*knee-length*) Kniestrumpf *m*

socket /'sɒkɪt/ *n* (*of eye*) Augenhöhle *f*; (*of joint*) Gelenkpfanne *f*; (*wall plug*) Steckdose *f*

soda /'səʊdə/ *n* Soda *nt*; (*Amer*) Limonade *f*. **~ water** *n* Sodawasser *nt*

sodden /'sɒdn/ *a* durchnässt

sofa /'səʊfə/ *n* Sofa *nt*. **~ bed** *n* Schlafcouch *f*

soft /sɒft/ *a* (**-er, -est**), **-ly** *adv* weich; (*quiet*) leise; (*gentle*) sanft; ([!] *silly*) dumm. **~ drink** *n* alkoholfreies Getränk *nt*

soften /'sɒfn/ *vt* weich machen; (*fig*) mildern ● *vi* weich werden

soft: ~ toy *n* Stofftier *nt*. **~ware** *n* Software *f*

soggy /'sɒgɪ/ *a* (**-ier, -iest**) aufgeweicht

soil[1] /sɔɪl/ *n* Erde *f*, Boden *m*

soil[2] *vt* verschmutzen

solar /'səʊlə(r)/ *a* Sonnen-

sold /səʊld/ *see* **sell**

soldier /'səʊldʒə(r)/ *n* Soldat *m* ● *vi* **~ on** [unbeirrbar] weitermachen

sole[1] /səʊl/ *n* Sohle *f*

sole[2] *n* (*fish*) Seezunge *f*

sole³ *a* einzig. **~ly** *adv* einzig und allein
solemn /'sɒləm/ *a*, **-ly** *adv* feierlich; (*serious*) ernst
solicitor /sə'lɪsɪtə(r)/ *n* Rechtsanwalt *m*/-anwältin *f*
solid /'sɒlɪd/ *a* fest; (*sturdy*) stabil; (*not hollow, of same substance*) massiv; (*unanimous*) einstimmig; (*complete*) ganz
solidarity /sɒlɪ'dærətɪ/ *n* Solidarität *f*
solidify /sə'lɪdɪfaɪ/ *vi* (*pt/pp* **-ied**) fest werden
solitary /'sɒlɪtərɪ/ *a* einsam; (*sole*) einzig
solitude /'sɒlɪtju:d/ *n* Einsamkeit *f*
solo /'səʊləʊ/ *n* Solo *nt* ● *a* Solo-; <*flight*> Allein- ● *adv* solo. **~ist** *n* Solist(in) *m(f)*
solstice /'sɒlstɪs/ *n* Sonnenwende *f*
soluble /'sɒljʊbl/ *a* löslich
solution /sə'lu:ʃn/ *n* Lösung *f*
solvable /'sɒlvəbl/ *a* lösbar
solve /sɒlv/ *vt* lösen
solvent /'sɒlvənt/ *n* Lösungsmittel *nt*
sombre /'sɒmbə(r)/ *a* dunkel; <*mood*> düster
some /sʌm/ *a & pron* etwas; (*a little*) ein bisschen; (*with pl noun*) einige; (*a few*) ein paar; (*certain*) manche(r,s); (*one or the other*) [irgend]ein; **~ day** eines Tages; **I want ~** ich möchte etwas/ (*pl*) welche; **will you have ~ wine?** möchten Sie Wein? **do ~ shopping** einkaufen
some: ~body /-bədɪ/ *pron & n* jemand; (*emphatic*) irgendjemand. **~how** *adv* irgendwie. **~one** *pron & n* = **somebody**
somersault /'sʌməsɔ:lt/ *n* Purzelbaum *m* [!]; (*Sport*) Salto *m*; **turn a ~** einen Purzelbaum schlagen/einen Salto springen
'something *pron & adv* etwas; (*emphatic*) irgendetwas; **~ different** etwas anderes; **~ like this** so etwas [wie das]
some: ~time *adv* irgendwann ● *a* ehemalig. **~times** *adv* manchmal. **~what** *adv* ziemlich. **~where** *adv* irgendwo; <*go*> irgendwohin
son /sʌn/ *n* Sohn *m*
song /sɒŋ/ *n* Lied *nt*. **~bird** *n* Singvogel *m*
'son-in-law *n* (*pl* **~s-in-law**) Schwiegersohn *m*
soon /su:n/ *adv* (**-er, -est**) bald; (*quickly*) schnell; **too ~** zu früh; **as ~ as possible** so bald wie möglich; **~er or later** früher oder später; **no ~er had I arrived than ...** kaum war ich angekommen, da ...; **I would ~er stay** ich würde lieber bleiben
soot /sʊt/ *n* Ruß *m*
sooth|e /su:ð/ *vt* beruhigen; lindern <*pain*>. **~ing** *a*, **-ly** *adv* beruhigend; lindernd
sophisticated /sə'fɪstɪkeɪtɪd/ *a* weltgewandt; (*complex*) hoch entwickelt
sopping /'sɒpɪŋ/ *a & adv* **~ [wet]** durchnässt
soppy /'sɒpɪ/ *a* (**-ier, -iest**) [!] rührselig
soprano /sə'prɑ:nəʊ/ *n* Sopran *m*; (*woman*) Sopranistin *f*
sordid /'sɔ:dɪd/ *a* schmutzig
sore /sɔ:(r)/ *a* (**-r, -st**) wund; (*painful*) schmerzhaft; **have a ~ throat** Halsschmerzen haben ● *n* wunde Stelle *f*. **~ly** *adv* sehr
sorrow /'sɒrəʊ/ *n* Kummer *m*
sorry /'sɒrɪ/ *a* (**-ier, -iest**) (*sad*) traurig; (*wretched*) erbärmlich; **I am ~** es tut mir Leid; **she is** *or* **feels ~ for him** er tut ihr Leid; **I am ~ to say** leider; **~!** Entschuldigung!
sort /sɔ:t/ *n* Art *f*, (*brand*) Sorte *f*; **he's a good ~** [!] er ist in

Ordnung ● *vt* sortieren. ~ **out** *vt* sortieren; (*fig*) klären

sought /sɔ:t/ *see* **seek**

soul /səʊl/ *n* Seele *f*

sound[1] /saʊnd/ *a* (**-er, -est**) gesund; (*sensible*) vernünftig; (*secure*) solide; (*thorough*) gehörig ● *adv* **be ~ asleep** fest schlafen

sound[2] *n* (*strait*) Meerenge *f*

sound[3] *n* Laut *m*; (*noise*) Geräusch *nt*; (*Phys*) Schall *m*; (*Radio, TV*) Ton *m*; (*of bells, music*) Klang *m*; **I don't like the ~ of it** [!] das hört sich nicht gut an ● *vi* [er]tönen; (*seem*) sich anhören ● *vt* (*pronounce*) aussprechen; schlagen <*alarm*>; (*Med*) abhorchen <*chest*>

soundly /ˈsaʊndlɪ/ *adv* solide; <*sleep*> fest; <*defeat*> vernichtend

ˈsoundproof *a* schalldicht

soup /su:p/ *n* Suppe *f*

sour /ˈsaʊə(r)/ *a* (**-er, -est**) sauer; (*bad-tempered*) griesgrämig, verdrießlich

source /sɔ:s/ *n* Quelle *f*

south /saʊθ/ *n* Süden *m*; **to the ~ of** südlich von ● *a* Süd-, süd- ● *adv* nach Süden

south: S~ ˈAfrica *n* Südafrika *nt*. **S~ Aˈmerica** *n* Südamerika *nt*. **~-ˈeast** *n* Südosten *m*

southerly /ˈsʌðəlɪ/ *a* südlich

southern /ˈsʌðən/ *a* südlich

ˈsouthward[s] /-wəd[z]/ *adv* nach Süden

souvenir /su:vəˈnɪə(r)/ *n* Andenken *nt*, Souvenir *nt*

Soviet /ˈsəʊvɪət/ *a* <*History*> sowjetisch; **~ Union** Sowjetunion *f*

sow[1] /saʊ/ *n* Sau *f*

sow[2] /səʊ/ *vt* (*pt* **sowed**, *pp* **sown** *or* **sowed**) säen

soya /ˈsɔɪə/ *n* **~ bean** Sojabohne *f*

spa /spɑ:/ *n* Heilbad *nt*

space /speɪs/ *n* Raum *m*; (*gap*) Platz *m*; (*Astr*) Weltraum *m* ● *vt* **~ [out]** [in Abständen] verteilen

space: ~craft *n* Raumfahrzeug *nt*. **~ship** *n* Raumschiff *nt*

spacious /ˈspeɪʃəs/ *a* geräumig

spade /speɪd/ *n* Spaten *m*; (*for child*) Schaufel *f*; **~s** *pl* (*Cards*) Pik *nt*

Spain /speɪn/ *n* Spanien *nt*

span[1] /spæn/ *n* Spanne *f*; (*of arch*) Spannweite *f* ● *vt* (*pt/pp* **spanned**) überspannen; umspannen <*time*>

span[2] *see* **spick**

Span|iard /ˈspænjəd/ *n* Spanier(in) *m(f)*. **~ish** *a* spanisch ● *n* (*Lang*) Spanisch *nt*; **the ~ish** *pl* die Spanier

spank /spæŋk/ *vt* verhauen

spanner /ˈspænə(r)/ *n* Schraubenschlüssel *m*

spare /speə(r)/ *a* (*surplus*) übrig; (*additional*) zusätzlich; <*seat, time*> frei; <*room*> Gäste-; <*bed, cup*> Extra- ● *n* (*part*) Ersatzteil *nt* ● *vt* ersparen; (*not hurt*) verschonen; (*do without*) entbehren; (*afford to give*) erübrigen. **~ ˈwheel** *n* Reserverad *nt*

sparing /ˈspeərɪŋ/ *a*, **-ly** *adv* sparsam

spark /spɑ:k/ *n* Funke *nt*. **~[ing]-plug** *n* (*Auto*) Zündkerze *f*

sparkl|e /ˈspɑ:kl/ *n* Funkeln *nt* ● *vi* funkeln. **~ing** *a* funkelnd; <*wine*> Schaum-

sparrow /ˈspærəʊ/ *n* Spatz *m*

sparse /spɑ:s/ *a* spärlich. **~ly** *adv* spärlich; <*populated*> dünn

spasm /ˈspæzm/ *n* Anfall *m*; (*cramp*) Krampf *m*. **~odic** /-ˈmɒdɪk/ *a*, **-ally** *adv* sporadisch

spastic /ˈspæstɪk/ *a* spastisch [gelähmt] ● *n* Spastiker(in) *m(f)*

spat /spæt/ *see* **spit²**

spatter /'spætə(r)/ *vt* spritzen; ~ **with** bespritzen mit

spawn /spɔ:n/ *n* Laich *m* ● *vt* (*fig*) hervorbringen

speak /spi:k/ *v* (*pt* **spoke**, *pp* **spoken**) ● *vi* sprechen (**to** mit) ~**ing!** (*Teleph*) am Apparat! ● *vt* sprechen; sagen <*truth*>. ~ **up** *vi* lauter sprechen; ~ **up for oneself** seine Meinung äußern

speaker /spi:kə(r)/ *n* Sprecher(in) *m(f)*; (*in public*) Redner(in) *m(f)*; (*loudspeaker*) Lautsprecher *m*

spear /spɪə(r)/ *n* Speer *m* ● *vt* aufspießen

spec /spek/ *n* **on** ~ [!] auf gut Glück

special /'speʃl/ *a* besondere(r,s), speziell. ~**ist** *n* Spezialist *m*; (*Med*) Facharzt *m*/-ärztin *f*. ~**ity** /-ʃɪ'ælətɪ/ *n* Spezialität *f*

special|ize /'speʃəlaɪz/ *vi* sich spezialisieren (**in** auf + *acc*). ~**ly** *adv* speziell; (*particularly*) besonders

species /'spi:ʃi:z/ *n* Art *f*

specific /spə'sɪfɪk/ *a* bestimmt; (*precise*) genau; (*Phys*) spezifisch. ~**ally** *adv* ausdrücklich

specification /spesɪfɪ'keɪʃn/ *n* & ~**s** *pl* genaue Angaben *pl*

specify /'spesɪfaɪ/ *vt* (*pt*/*pp* **-ied**) [genau] angeben

specimen /spesɪmən/ *n* Exemplar *nt*; (*sample*) Probe *f*; (*of urine*) Urinprobe *f*

speck /spek/ *n* Fleck *m*

speckled /'spekld/ *a* gesprenkelt

spectacle /'spektəkl/ *n* (*show*) Schauspiel *nt*; (*sight*) Anblick *m*. ~**s** *npl* Brille *f*

spectacular /spek'tækjʊlə(r)/ *a* spektakulär

spectator /spek'teɪtə(r)/ *n* Zuschauer(in) *m(f)*

speculat|e /'spekjʊleɪt/ *vi* spekulieren. ~**ion** /-'leɪʃn/ *n* Spekulation *f*. ~**or** *n* Spekulant *m*

sped /sped/ *see* **speed**

speech /spi:tʃ/ *n* Sprache *f*; (*address*) Rede *f*. ~**less** *a* sprachlos

speed /spi:d/ *n* Geschwindigkeit *f*; (*rapidity*) Schnelligkeit *f* ● *vi* (*pt*/*pp* **sped**) schnell fahren ● (*pt*/*pp* **speeded**) (*go too fast*) zu schnell fahren. ~ **up** (*pt*/*pp* **speeded up**) ● *vt*/*i* beschleunigen

speed: ~**boat** *n* Rennboot *nt*. ~ **camera** *n* Geschwindigkeitsüberwachungskamera *f*. ~**ing** *n* Geschwindigkeitsüberschreitung *f*. ~ **limit** *n* Geschwindigkeitsbeschränkung *f*

speedometer /spi:'dɒmɪtə(r)/ *n* Tachometer *m*

speedy /'spi:dɪ/ *a* (**-ier, -iest**), **-ily** *adv* schnell

spell¹ /spel/ *n* Weile *f*; (*of weather*) Periode *f*

spell² *v* (*pt*/*pp* **spelled** or **spelt**) ● *vt* schreiben; (*aloud*) buchstabieren; (*fig: mean*) bedeuten ● *vi* richtig schreiben; (*aloud*) buchstabieren. ~ **out** *vt* buchstabieren; (*fig*) genau erklären

spell³ *n* Zauber *m*; (*words*) Zauberspruch *m*. ~**bound** *a* wie verzaubert

'spell checker *n* Rechtschreibprogramm *nt*

spelling /'spelɪŋ/ *n* (*of a word*) Schreibweise *f*; (*orthography*) Rechtschreibung *f*

spelt /spelt/ *see* **spell²**

spend /spend/ *vt*/*i* (*pt*/*pp* **spent**) ausgeben; verbringen <*time*>

spent /spent/ *see* **spend**

sperm /spɜ:m/ *n* Samen *m*

sphere /sfɪə(r)/ *n* Kugel *f*; (*fig*) Sphäre *f*

spice /spaɪs/ *n* Gewürz *nt*; (*fig*) Würze *f*

spicy /ˈspaɪsɪ/ *a* würzig, pikant

spider /ˈspaɪdə(r)/ *n* Spinne *f*

spik|e /spaɪk/ *n* Spitze *f*; (*Bot, Zool*) Stachel *m*; (*on shoe*) Spike *m*. **~y** *a* stachelig

spill /spɪl/ *v* (*pt/pp* **spilt** *or* **spilled**) ● *vt* verschütten ● *vi* überlaufen

spin /spɪn/ *v* (*pt/pp* **spun**, *pres p* **spinning**) ● *vt* drehen; spinnen <*wool*>; schleudern <*washing*> ● *vi* sich drehen

spinach /ˈspɪnɪdʒ/ *n* Spinat *m*

spindl|e /ˈspɪndl/ *n* Spindel *f*. **~y** *a* spindeldürr

spin-ˈdrier *n* Wäscheschleuder *f*

spine /spaɪn/ *n* Rückgrat *nt*; (*of book*) [Buch]rücken *m*; (*Bot, Zool*) Stachel *m*. **~less** *a* (*fig*) rückgratlos

ˈspin-off *n* Nebenprodukt *nt*

spinster /ˈspɪnstə(r)/ *n* ledige Frau *f*

spiral /ˈspaɪrl/ *a* spiralig ● *n* Spirale *f* ● *vi* (*pt/pp* **spiralled**) sich hochwinden. **~ ˈstaircase** *n* Wendeltreppe *f*

spire /ˈspaɪə(r)/ *n* Turmspitze *f*

spirit /ˈspɪrɪt/ *n* Geist *m*; (*courage*) Mut *m*; **~s** *pl* (*alcohol*) Spirituosen *pl*; **in low ~s** niedergedrückt. **~ away** *vt* verschwinden lassen

spirited /ˈspɪrɪtɪd/ *a* lebhaft; (*courageous*) beherzt

spiritual /ˈspɪrɪtjʊəl/ *a* geistig; (*Relig*) geistlich

spit¹ /spɪt/ *n* (*for roasting*) [Brat]spieß *m*

spit² *n* Spucke *f* ● *vt/i* (*pt/pp* **spat**, *pres p* **spitting**) spucken; <*cat:*> fauchen; <*fat:*> spritzen; **it's ~ting with rain** es tröpfelt

spite /spaɪt/ *n* Boshaftigkeit *f*; **in ~ of** trotz (+ *gen*) ● *vt* ärgern. **~ful** *a*, **-ly** *adv* gehässig

splash /splæʃ/ *n* Platschen *nt*; ([!] *drop*) Schuss *m*; **~ of colour** Farbfleck *m* ● *vt* spritzen; **~ s.o. with sth** jdn mit etw bespritzen ● *vi* spritzen. **~ about** *vi* planschen

splendid /ˈsplendɪd/ *a* herrlich, großartig

splendour /ˈsplendə(r)/ *n* Pracht *f*

splint /splɪnt/ *n* (*Med*) Schiene *f*

splinter /ˈsplɪntə(r)/ *n* Splitter *m* ● *vi* zersplittern

split /splɪt/ *n* Spaltung *f*; (*Pol*) Bruch *m*; (*tear*) Riss *m* ● *v* (*pt/pp* **split**, *pres p* **splitting**) ● *vt* spalten; (*share*) teilen; (*tear*) zerreißen ● *vi* sich spalten; (*tear*) zerreißen; **~ on s.o.** [!] jdn verpfeifen. **~ up** *vt* aufteilen ● *vi* <*couple:*> sich trennen

splutter /ˈsplʌtə(r)/ *vi* prusten

spoil /spɔɪl/ *n* **~s** *pl* Beute *f* ● *v* (*pt/pp* **spoilt** *or* **spoiled**) ● *vt* verderben; verwöhnen <*person*> ● *vi* verderben. **~sport** *n* Spielverderber *m*

spoke¹ /spəʊk/ *n* Speiche *f*

spoke², **spoken** /ˈspəʊkn/ *see* **speak**

ˈspokesman *n* Sprecher *m*

sponge /spʌndʒ/ *n* Schwamm *m* ● *vt* abwaschen ● *vi* **~ on** schmarotzen bei. **~-bag** *n* Waschbeutel *m*. **~-cake** *n* Biskuitkuchen *m*

sponsor /ˈspɒnsə(r)/ *n* Sponsor *m*; (*godparent*) Pate *m*/Patin *f* ● *vt* sponsern

spontaneous /spɒnˈteɪnɪəs/ *a*, **-ly** *adv* spontan

spoof /spuːf/ *n* [!] Parodie *f*

spooky /ˈspuːkɪ/ *a* (**-ier, -iest**) [!] gespenstisch

spool /spuːl/ *n* Spule *f*

spoon /spu:n/ *n* Löffel *m* ● *vt* löffeln. **~ful** *n* Löffel *m*
sporadic /spəˈrædɪk/ *a*, **-ally** *adv* sporadisch
sport /spɔ:t/ *n* Sport *m* ● *vt* [stolz] tragen. **~ing** *a* sportlich
sports: ~ car *n* Sportwagen *m*. **~ coat** *n*, **~ jacket** *n* Sakko *m*. **~man** *n* Sportler *m*. **~woman** *n* Sportlerin *f*
sporty /ˈspɔ:tɪ/ *a* (**-ier, -iest**) sportlich
spot /spɒt/ *n* Fleck *m*; (*place*) Stelle *f* (*dot*) Punkt *m*; (*drop*) Tropfen *m*; (*pimple*) Pickel *m*; **~s** *pl* (*rash*) Ausschlag *m*; **on the ~** auf der Stelle ● *vt* (*pt*/*pp* **spotted**) entdecken
spot: ~ 'check *n* Stichprobe *f*. **~less** *a* makellos; ([!] *very clean*) blitzsauber. **~light** *n* Scheinwerfer *m*; (*fig*) Rampenlicht *nt*
spotted /ˈspɒtɪd/ *a* gepunktet
spouse /spaʊz/ *n* Gatte *m*/Gattin *f*
spout /spaʊt/ *n* Schnabel *m*, Tülle *f* ● *vi* schießen (**from** aus)
sprain /spreɪn/ *n* Verstauchung *f* ● *vt* verstauchen
sprang /spræŋ/ *see* **spring²**
sprawl /sprɔ:l/ *vi* sich ausstrecken
spray¹ /spreɪ/ *n* (*of flowers*) Strauß *m*
spray² *n* Sprühnebel *m*; (*from sea*) Gischt *m*; (*device*) Spritze *f*; (*container*) Sprühdose *f*; (*preparation*) Spray *nt* ● *vt* spritzen; (*with aerosol*) sprühen
spread /spred/ *n* Verbreitung *f*; (*paste*) Aufstrich *m*; ([!] *feast*) Festessen *nt* ● *v* (*pt*/*pp* **spread**) ● *vt* ausbreiten; streichen <*butter, jam*>; bestreichen <*bread, surface*>; streuen <*sand, manure*>; verbreiten <*news, disease*>; verteilen <*payments*> ● *vi* sich ausbreiten. **~ out** *vt* ausbreiten; (*space out*) verteilen ● *vi* sich verteilen
spree /spri:/ *n* [!] **go on a shopping ~** groß einkaufen gehen
sprightly /ˈspraɪtlɪ/ *a* (**-ier, -iest**) rüstig
spring¹ /sprɪŋ/ *n* Frühling *m* ● *attrib* Frühlings-
spring² *n* (*jump*) Sprung *m*; (*water*) Quelle *f*; (*device*) Feder *f*; (*elasticity*) Elastizität *f* ● *v* (*pt* **sprang**, *pp* **sprung**) ● *vi* springen; (*arise*) entspringen (**from** *dat*) ● *vt* **~ sth on s.o.** jdn mit etw überfallen
spring: ~-'cleaning *n* Frühjahrsputz *m*. **~time** *n* Frühling *m*
sprinkl|e /ˈsprɪŋkl/ *vt* sprengen; (*scatter*) streuen; bestreuen <*surface*>. **~ing** *n* dünne Schicht *f*
sprint /sprɪnt/ *n* Sprint *m* ● *vi* rennen; (*Sport*) sprinten. **~er** *n* Kurzstreckenläufer(in) *m*(*f*)
sprout /spraʊt/ *n* Trieb *m*; **[Brussels] ~s** *pl* Rosenkohl *m* ● *vi* sprießen
sprung /sprʌŋ/ *see* **spring²**
spud /spʌd/ *n* [!] Kartoffel *f*
spun /spʌn/ *see* **spin**
spur /spɜ:(r)/ *n* Sporn *m*; (*stimulus*) Ansporn *m*; **on the ~ of the moment** ganz spontan ● *vt* (*pt*/*pp* **spurred**) **~ [on]** (*fig*) anspornen
spurn /spɜ:n/ *vt* verschmähen
spurt /spɜ:t/ *n* (*Sport*) Spurt *m*; **put on a ~** spurten ● *vi* spritzen
spy /spaɪ/ *n* Spion(in) *m*(*f*) ● *vi* spionieren; **~ on s.o.** jdm nachspionieren. ● *vt* ([!] *see*) sehen
spying /ˈspaɪɪŋ/ *n* Spionage *f*
squabble /ˈskwɒbl/ *n* Zank *m* ● *vi* sich zanken
squad /skwɒd/ *n* Gruppe *f*; (*Sport*) Mannschaft *f*

squadron /ˈskwɒdrən/ *n* (*Mil*) Geschwader *nt*

squalid /ˈskwɒlɪd/ *a*, **-ly** *adv* schmutzig

squall /skwɔːl/ *n* Bö *f* ● *vi* brüllen

squalor /ˈskwɒlə(r)/ *n* Schmutz *m*

squander /ˈskwɒndə(r)/ *vt* vergeuden

square /skweə(r)/ *a* quadratisch; <*metre, mile*> Quadrat-; <*meal*> anständig; **all ~** [I] quitt ● *n* Quadrat *nt*; (*area*) Platz *m*; (*on chessboard*) Feld *nt* ● *vt* (*settle*) klären; (*Math*) quadrieren

squash /skwɒʃ/ *n* Gedränge *nt*; (*drink*) Fruchtsaftgetränk *nt*; (*Sport*) Squash *nt* ● *vt* zerquetschen; (*suppress*) niederschlagen. **~y** *a* weich

squat /skwɒt/ *a* gedrungen ● *vi* (*pt/pp* **squatted**) hocken; **~ in a house** ein Haus besetzen. **~ter** *n* Hausbesetzer *m*

squawk /skwɔːk/ *vi* krächzen

squeak /skwiːk/ *n* Quieken *nt*; (*of hinge, brakes*) Quietschen *nt* ● *vi* quieken; quietschen

squeal /skwiːl/ *n* Kreischen *nt* ● *vi* kreischen

squeamish /ˈskwiːmɪʃ/ *a* empfindlich

squeeze /skwiːz/ *n* Druck *m*; (*crush*) Gedränge *nt* ● *vt* drücken; (*to get juice*) ausdrücken; (*force*) zwängen

squiggle /ˈskwɪgl/ *n* Schnörkel *m*

squint /skwɪnt/ *n* Schielen *nt* ● *vi* schielen

squirm /skwɜːm/ *vi* sich winden

squirrel /ˈskwɪrl/ *n* Eichhörnchen *nt*

squirt /skwɜːt/ *n* Spritzer *m* ● *vt/i* spritzen

St *abbr* (**Saint**) St.; (**Street**) Str.

stab /stæb/ *n* Stich *m*; ([I] *attempt*) Versuch *m* ● *vt* (*pt/pp* **stabbed**) stechen; (*to death*) erstechen

stability /stəˈbɪlətɪ/ *n* Stabilität *f*

stable[1] /ˈsteɪbl/ *a* (**-r**, **-st**) stabil

stable[2] *n* Stall *m*; (*establishment*) Reitstall *m*

stack /stæk/ *n* Stapel *m*; (*of chimney*) Schornstein *m* ● *vt* stapeln

stadium /ˈsteɪdɪəm/ *n* Stadion *nt*

staff /stɑːf/ *n* (*stick & Mil*) Stab *m* ● (*& pl*) (*employees*) Personal *nt*; (*Sch*) Lehrkräfte *pl* ● *vt* mit Personal besetzen. **~-room** *n* (*Sch*) Lehrerzimmer *nt*

stag /stæg/ *n* Hirsch *m*

stage /steɪdʒ/ *n* Bühne *f*; (*in journey*) Etappe *f*; (*in process*) Stadium *nt*; **by** *or* **in ~s** in Etappen ● *vt* aufführen; (*arrange*) veranstalten

stagger /ˈstægə(r)/ *vi* taumeln ● *vt* staffeln <*holidays*>; versetzt anordnen <*seats*>; **I was ~ed** es hat mir die Sprache verschlagen. **~ing** *a* unglaublich

stagnant /ˈstægnənt/ *a* stehend; (*fig*) stagnierend

stagnate /stægˈneɪt/ *vi* (*fig*) stagnieren

stain /steɪn/ *n* Fleck *m*; (*for wood*) Beize *f* ● *vt* färben; beizen <*wood*>; **~ed glass** farbiges Glas *nt*. **~less** *a* <*steel*> rostfrei

stair /steə(r)/ *n* Stufe *f*; **~s** *pl* Treppe *f*. **~case** *n* Treppe *f*

stake /steɪk/ *n* Pfahl *m*; (*wager*) Einsatz *m*; (*Comm*) Anteil *m*; **be at ~** auf dem Spiel stehen ● *vt* **~ a claim to sth** Anspruch auf etw (*acc*) erheben

stale /steɪl/ *a* (**-r**, **-st**) alt; <*air*> verbraucht. **~mate** *n* Patt *nt*

stalk /stɔːk/ *n* Stiel *m*, Stängel *m*

stall /stɔːl/ *n* Stand *m*; **~s** *pl* (*Theat*) Parkett *nt* ● *vi* <*engine*>

stehen bleiben; (*fig*) ausweichen ● *vt* abwürgen <*engine*>

stalwart /'stɔ:lwət/ *a* treu ● *n* treuer Anhänger *m*

stamina /'stæmɪnə/ *n* Ausdauer *f*

stammer /'stæmə(r)/ *n* Stottern *nt* ● *vt/i* stottern

stamp /stæmp/ *n* Stempel *m*; (*postage* ~) [Brief]marke *f* ● *vt* stempeln; (*impress*) prägen; (*put postage on*) frankieren ● *vi* stampfen. ~ **out** *vt* [aus]stanzen; (*fig*) ausmerzen

stampede /stæm'pi:d/ *n* wilde Flucht *f* ● *vi* in Panik fliehen

stance /stɑ:ns/ *n* Haltung *f*

stand /stænd/ *n* Stand *m*; (*rack*) Ständer *m*; (*pedestal*) Sockel *m*; (*Sport*) Tribüne *f*; (*fig*) Einstellung *f* ● *v* (*pt/pp* **stood**) ● *vi* stehen; (*rise*) aufstehen; (*be candidate*) kandidieren; (*stay valid*) gültig bleiben; ~ **still** stillstehen; ~ **firm** (*fig*) festbleiben; ~ **to reason** logisch sein; ~ **in for** vertreten; ~ **for** (*mean*) bedeuten ● *vt* stellen; (*withstand*) standhalten (+ *dat*); (*endure*) ertragen; vertragen <*climate*>; (*put up with*) aushalten; haben <*chance*>; ~ **s.o. a beer** jdm ein Bier spendieren; **I can't ~ her** [!] ich kann sie nicht ausstehen. ~ **by** *vi* daneben stehen; (*be ready*) sich bereithalten ● *vt* ~ **by s.o.** (*fig*) zu jdm stehen. ~ **down** *vi* (*retire*) zurücktreten. ~ **out** *vi* hervorstehen; (*fig*) herausragen. ~ **up** *vi* aufstehen; ~ **up for** eintreten für; ~ **up to** sich wehren gegen

standard /'stændəd/ *a* Normal- ● *n* Maßstab *m*; (*Techn*) Norm *f*; (*level*) Niveau *nt*; (*flag*) Standarte *f*; ~**s** *pl* (*morals*) Prinzipien *pl*. ~**ize** *vt* standardisieren; (*Techn*) normen

'**stand-in** *n* Ersatz *m*

standing /'stændɪŋ/ *a* (*erect*) stehend; (*permanent*) ständig ● *n* Rang *m*; (*duration*) Dauer *f*. ~-**room** *n* Stehplätze *pl*

stand: ~-**offish** /stænd'ɒfɪʃ/ *a* distanziert. ~**point** *n* Standpunkt *m*. ~**still** *n* Stillstand *m*; **come to a ~still** zum Stillstand kommen

stank /stæŋk/ *see* **stink**

staple[1] /'steɪpl/ *a* Grund-

staple[2] *n* Heftklammer *f* ● *vt* heften. ~**r** *n* Heftmaschine *f*

star /stɑ:(r)/ *n* Stern *m*; (*asterisk*) Sternchen *nt*; (*Theat, Sport*) Star *m* ● *vi* (*pt/pp* **starred**) die Hauptrolle spielen

starboard /'stɑ:bəd/ *n* Steuerbord *nt*

starch /stɑ:tʃ/ *n* Stärke *f* ● *vt* stärken. ~**y** *a* stärkehaltig; (*fig*) steif

stare /steə(r)/ *n* Starren *nt* ● *vt* starren; ~ **at** anstarren

stark /stɑ:k/ *a* (**-er, -est**) scharf; <*contrast*> krass

starling /'stɑ:lɪŋ/ *n* Star *m*

start /stɑ:t/ *n* Anfang *m*, Beginn *m*; (*departure*) Aufbruch *m*; (*Sport*) Start *m*; **from the ~** von Anfang an; **for a ~** erstens ● *vi* anfangen, beginnen; (*set out*) aufbrechen; <*engine:*> anspringen; (*Auto, Sport*) starten; (*jump*) aufschrecken; **to ~ with** zuerst ● *vt* anfangen, beginnen; (*cause*) verursachen; (*found*) gründen; starten <*car, race*>; in Umlauf setzen <*rumour*>. ~**er** *n* (*Culin*) Vorspeise *f*; (*Auto, Sport*) Starter *m*. ~**ing-point** *n* Ausgangspunkt *m*

startle /'stɑ:tl/ *vt* erschrecken

starvation /stɑ:'veɪʃn/ *n* Verhungern *nt*

starve /stɑ:v/ *vi* hungern; (*to death*) verhungern ● *vt* verhungern lassen

state /steɪt/ *n* Zustand *m*; (*Pol*) Staat *m*; ~ **of play** Spielstand *m*; **be in a** ~ <*person*:> aufgeregt sein ● *attrib* Staats-, staatlich ● *vt* erklären; (*specify*) angeben

stately /ˈsteɪtlɪ/ *a* (**-ier, -iest**) stattlich. ~ ˈ**home** *n* Schloss *nt*

statement /ˈsteɪtmənt/ *n* Erklärung *f*; (*Jur*) Aussage *f*; (*Banking*) Auszug *m*

ˈ**statesman** *n* Staatsmann *m*

static /ˈstætɪk/ *a* statisch; **remain** ~ unverändert bleiben

station /ˈsteɪʃn/ *n* Bahnhof *m*; (*police*) Wache *f*; (*radio*) Sender *m*; (*space, weather*) Station *f*; (*Mil*) Posten *m*; (*status*) Rang *m* ● *vt* stationieren; (*post*) postieren. ~**ary** /-ərɪ/ *a* stehend; **be** ~**ary** stehen

stationery /ˈsteɪʃənrɪ/ *n* Briefpapier *nt*; (*writing materials*) Schreibwaren *pl*

ˈ**station-wagon** *n* (*Amer*) Kombi[wagen] *n*

statistic /stəˈtɪstɪk/ *n* statistische Tatsache *f*. ~**al** *a*, **-ly** *adv* statistisch. ~**s** *n & pl* Statistik *f*

statue /ˈstætjuː/ *n* Statue *f*

stature /ˈstætʃə(r)/ *n* Statur *f*; (*fig*) Format *nt*

status /ˈsteɪtəs/ *n* Status *m*, Rang *m*

statut|e /ˈstætjuːt/ *n* Statut *nt*. ~**ory** *a* gesetzlich

staunch /stɔːntʃ/ *a* (**-er, -est**), **-ly** *adv* treu

stave /steɪv/ *vt* ~ **off** abwenden

stay /steɪ/ *n* Aufenthalt *m* ● *vi* bleiben; (*reside*) wohnen; ~ **the night** übernachten. ~ **behind** *vi* zurückbleiben. ~ **in** *vi* zu Hause bleiben; (*Sch*) nachsitzen. ~ **up** *vi* <*person*:>. aufbleiben

steadily /ˈstedɪlɪ/ *adv* fest; (*continually*) stetig

steady /ˈstedɪ/ *a* (**-ier, -iest**) fest; (*not wobbly*) stabil; <*hand*> ruhig; (*regular*) regelmäßig; (*dependable*) zuverlässig

steak /steɪk/ *n* Steak *nt*

steal /stiːl/ *vt/i* (*pt* **stole**, *pp* **stolen**) stehlen (**from** *dat*). ~ **in/out** *vi* sich hinein-/hinausstehlen

stealthy /stelθɪ/ *a* heimlich

steam /stiːm/ *n* Dampf *m* ● *vt* (*Culin*) dämpfen, dünsten ● *vi* dampfen. ~ **up** *vi* beschlagen

ˈ**steam engine** *n* Dampfmaschine *f*; (*Rail*) Dampflokomotive *f*

steamer /ˈstiːmə(r)/ *n* Dampfer *m*

steamy /ˈstiːmɪ/ *a* dampfig

steel /stiːl/ *n* Stahl *m*

steep /stiːp/ *a*, **-ly** *adv* steil; ([!] *exorbitant*) gesalzen

steeple /ˈstiːpl/ *n* Kirchturm *m*

steer /stɪə(r)/ *vt/i* (*Auto*) lenken; (*Naut*) steuern; ~ **clear of s.o./sth** jdm/ etw aus dem Weg gehen. ~**ing** *n* (*Auto*) Lenkung *f*. ~**ing-wheel** *n* Lenkrad *nt*

stem[1] /stem/ *n* Stiel *m*; (*of word*) Stamm *m*

stem[2] *vt* (*pt/pp* **stemmed**) eindämmen; stillen <*bleeding*>

stench /stentʃ/ *n* Gestank *m*

stencil /ˈstensl/ *n* Schablone *f*

step /step/ *n* Schritt *m*; (*stair*) Stufe *f*; ~**s** *pl* (*ladder*) Trittleiter *f*; **in** ~ im Schritt; ~ **by** ~ Schritt für Schritt; **take** ~**s** (*fig*) Schritte unternehmen ● *vi* (*pt/pp* **stepped**) treten; ~ **in** (*fig*) eingreifen. ~ **up** *vt* (*increase*) erhöhen, steigen; verstärken <*efforts*>

step: ~**brother** *n* Stiefbruder *m*. ~**child** *n* Stiefkind *nt*. ~**daughter** *n* Stieftochter *f*. ~**father** *n* Stiefvater *m*. ~**-ladder** *n* Trittleiter *f*. ~**mother** *n* Stiefmutter *f*. ~**sister** *n* Stiefschwester *f*. ~**son** *n* Stiefsohn *m*

stereo /'sterɪəʊ/ *n* Stereo *nt*; (*equipment*) Stereoanlage *f*. **~phonic** /-'fɒnɪk/ *a* stereophon

stereotype /'sterɪətaɪp/ *n* stereotype Figur *f*

steril|e /'steraɪl/ *a* steril. **~ize** /'sterɪlaɪz/ *vt* sterilisieren

sterling /'stɜ:lɪŋ/ *a* Sterling-; (*fig*) gediegen ● *n* Sterling *m*

stern[1] /stɜ:n/ *a* (**-er, -est**), **-ly** *adv* streng

stern[2] *n* (*of boat*) Heck *nt*

stew /stju:/ *n* Eintopf *m*; **in a ~** [!] aufgeregt ● *vt/i* schmoren; **~ed fruit** Kompott *nt*

steward /'stju:əd/ *n* Ordner *m*; (*on ship, aircraft*) Steward *m*. **~ess** *n* Stewardess *f*

stick[1] /stɪk/ *n* Stock *m*; (*of chalk*) Stück *nt*; (*of rhubarb*) Stange *f*; (*Sport*) Schläger *m*

stick[2] *v* (*pt/pp* **stuck**) ● *vt* stecken; (*stab*) stechen; (*glue*) kleben; ([!] *put*) tun; ([!] *endure*) aushalten ● *vi* stecken; (*adhere*) kleben, haften (**to** an + *dat*); (*jam*) klemmen; **~ at it** [!] dranbleiben; **~ up for** [!] eintreten für; **be stuck** nicht weiterkönnen; <*vehicle:*> festsitzen, festgefahren sein; <*drawer:*> klemmen; **be stuck with sth** [!] etw am Hals haben. **~ out** *vi* abstehen; (*project*) vorstehen ● *vt* hinausstrecken; herausstrecken <*tongue*>

sticker /'stɪkə(r)/ *n* Aufkleber *m*

'sticking plaster *n* Heftpflaster *nt*

sticky /'stɪkɪ/ *a* (**-ier, -iest**) klebrig; (*adhesive*) Klebe-

stiff /stɪf/ *a* (**-er, -est**), **-ly** *adv* steif; <*brush*> hart; <*dough*> fest; (*difficult*) schwierig; <*penalty*> schwer; **be bored ~** [!] sich zu Tode langweilen. **~en** *vt* steif machen ● *vi* steif werden. **~ness** *n* Steifheit *f*

stifl|e /'staɪfl/ *vt* ersticken; (*fig*) unterdrücken. **~ing** *a* **be ~ing** zum Ersticken sein

still /stɪl/ *a* still; <*drink*> ohne Kohlensäure; **keep ~** stillhalten; **stand ~** stillstehen ● *adv* noch; (*emphatic*) immer noch; (*nevertheless*) trotzdem; **~ not** immer noch nicht

'stillborn *a* tot geboren

still 'life *n* Stillleben *nt*

stilted /'stɪltɪd/ *a* gestelzt, geschraubt

stimulant /'stɪmjʊlənt/ *n* Anregungsmittel *nt*

stimulat|e /'stɪmjʊleɪt/ *vt* anregen. **~ion** /-'leɪʃn/ *n* Anregung *f*

stimulus /'stɪmjʊləs/ *n* (*pl* **-li** /-laɪ/) Reiz *m*

sting /stɪŋ/ *n* Stich *m*; (*from nettle, jellyfish*) Brennen *nt*; (*organ*) Stachel *m* ● *v* (*pt/pp* **stung**) ● *vt* stechen ● *vi* brennen; <*insect:*> stechen

stingy /'stɪndʒɪ/ *a* (**-ier, -iest**) geizig, [!] knauserig

stink /stɪŋk/ *n* Gestank *m* ● *vi* (*pt* **stank**, *pp* **stunk**) stinken (**of** nach)

stipulat|e /'stɪpjʊleɪt/ *vt* vorschreiben. **~ion** /-'leɪʃn/ *n* Bedingung *f*

stir /stɜ:(r)/ *n* (*commotion*) Aufregung *f* ● *v* (*pt/pp* **stirred**) *vt* rühren ● *vi* sich rühren

stirrup /'stɪrəp/ *n* Steigbügel *m*

stitch /stɪtʃ/ *n* Stich *m*; (*Knitting*) Masche *f*; (*pain*) Seitenstechen *nt*; **be in ~es** [!] sich kaputtlachen ● *vt* nähen

stock /stɒk/ *n* Vorrat *m* (**of** an + *dat*); (*in shop*) [Waren]bestand *m*; (*livestock*) Vieh *nt*; (*lineage*) Abstammung *f*; (*Finance*) Wertpapiere *pl*; (*Culin*) Brühe *f*; (*plant*) Levkoje *f*; **in/out of ~** vorrätig/nicht vorrätig; **take ~** (*fig*) Bilanz ziehen ● *a* Standard-

● *vt* <*shop*:> führen; auffüllen <*shelves*>. **~ up** *vi* sich eindecken (**with** mit)

stock: ~broker *n* Börsenmakler *m*. **S~ Exchange** *n* Börse *f*

stocking /ˈstɒkɪŋ/ *n* Strumpf *m*

stock: ~market *n* Börse *f*. **~-taking** *n* (*Comm*) Inventur *f*

stocky /ˈstɒkɪ/ *a* (**-ier, -iest**) untersetzt

stodgy /ˈstɒdʒɪ/ *a* pappig [und schwer verdaulich]

stoke /stəʊk/ *vt* heizen

stole /stəʊl/, **stolen** /ˈstəʊlən/ *see* **steal**

stomach /ˈstʌmək/ *n* Magen *m*. **~-ache** *n* Magenschmerzen *pl*

stone /stəʊn/ *n* Stein *m*; (*weight*) 6,35kg ● *a* steinern; <*wall, Age*> Stein- ● *vt* mit Steinen bewerfen; entsteinen <*fruit*>. **~-cold** *a* eiskalt. **~-ˈdeaf** *n* [!] stocktaub

stony /ˈstəʊnɪ/ *a* steinig

stood /stʊd/ *see* **stand**

stool /stuːl/ *n* Hocker *m*

stoop /stuːp/ *n* **walk with a ~** gebeugt gehen ● *vi* sich bücken

stop /stɒp/ *n* Halt *m*; (*break*) Pause *f*; (*for bus*) Haltestelle *f*; (*for train*) Station *f*; (*Gram*) Punkt *m*; (*on organ*) Register *nt*; **come to a ~** stehen bleiben; **put a ~ to sth** etw unterbinden ● *v* (*pt/pp* **stopped**) ● *vt* anhalten, stoppen; (*switch off*) abstellen; (*plug, block*) zustopfen; (*prevent*) verhindern; **~ s.o. doing sth** jdn daran hindern, etw zu tun; **~ doing sth** aufhören, etw zu tun; **~ that!** hör auf damit! ● *vi* anhalten; (*cease*) aufhören; <*clock*:> stehen bleiben ● *int* halt!

stop: ~gap *n* Notlösung *f*. **~over** *n* (*Aviat*) Zwischenlandung *f*

stoppage /ˈstɒpɪdʒ/ *n* Unterbrechung *f*; (*strike*) Streik *m*

stopper /ˈstɒpə(r)/ *n* Stöpsel *m*

stop-watch *n* Stoppuhr *f*

storage /ˈstɔːrɪdʒ/ *n* Aufbewahrung *f*; (*in warehouse*) Lagerung *f*; (*Computing*) Speicherung *f*

store /stɔː(r)/ *n* (*stock*) Vorrat *m*; (*shop*) Laden *m*; (*department ~*) Kaufhaus *nt*; (*depot*) Lager *nt*; **in ~** auf Lager; **be in ~ for s.o.** (*fig*) jdm bevorstehen ● *vt* aufbewahren; (*in warehouse*) lagern; (*Computing*) speichern. **~-room** *n* Lagerraum *m*

storey /ˈstɔːrɪ/ *n* Stockwerk *nt*

stork /stɔːk/ *n* Storch *m*

storm /stɔːm/ *n* Sturm *m*; (*with thunder*) Gewitter *nt* ● *vt/i* stürmen. **~y** *a* stürmisch

story /ˈstɔːrɪ/ *n* Geschichte *f*; (*in newspaper*) Artikel *m*; ([!] *lie*) Märchen *nt*

stout /staʊt/ *a* (**-er, -est**) beleibt; (*strong*) fest

stove /stəʊv/ *n* Ofen *m*; (*for cooking*) Herd *m*

stow /stəʊ/ *vt* verstauen. **~away** *n* blinder Passagier *m*

straggl|e /ˈstrægl/ *vi* hinterherhinken. **~er** *n* Nachzügler *m*. **~y** *a* strähnig

straight /streɪt/ *a* (**-er, -est**) gerade; (*direct*) direkt; (*clear*) klar; <*hair*> glatt; <*drink*>; pur; **be ~** (*tidy*) in Ordnung sein ● *adv* gerade; (*directly*) direkt, geradewegs; (*clearly*) klar; **~ away** sofort; **~ on** *or* **ahead** geradeaus; **~ out** (*fig*) geradeheraus; **sit/stand up ~** gerade sitzen/stehen

straighten /ˈstreɪtn/ *vt* gerade machen; (*put straight*) gerade richten ● *vi* gerade werden; **~ [up]** <*person*:> sich aufrichten. **~ out** *vt* gerade biegen

straightˈforward *a* offen; (*simple*) einfach

strain /'streɪn/ *n* Belastung *f*; **~s** *pl* (*of music*) Klänge *pl* ● *vt* belasten; (*overexert*) überanstrengen; (*injure*) zerren <*muscle*>; (*Culin*) durchseihen; abgießen <*vegetables*>. **~ed** *a* <*relations*> gespannt. **~er** *n* Sieb *nt*

strait /streɪt/ *n* Meerenge *f*; **in dire ~s** in großen Nöten

strand¹ /strænd/ *n* (*of thread*) Faden *m*; (*of hair*) Strähne *f*

strand² *vt* **be ~ed** festsitzen

strange /streɪndʒ/ *a* (**-r**, **-st**) fremd; (*odd*) seltsam, merkwürdig. **~ly** *adv* seltsam, merkwürdig; **~ enough** seltsamerweise. **~r** *n* Fremde(r) *m/f*

strangle /'stræŋgl/ *vt* erwürgen; (*fig*) unterdrücken

strap /stræp/ *n* Riemen *m*; (*for safety*) Gurt *m*; (*to grasp in vehicle*) Halteriemen *m*; (*of watch*) Armband *nt*; (*shoulder ~*) Träger *m* ● *vt* (*pt/pp* **strapped**) schnallen

strapping /'stræpɪŋ/ *a* stramm

strategic /strə'ti:dʒɪk/ *a*, **-ally** *adv* strategisch

strategy /'strætədʒɪ/ *n* Strategie *f*

straw /strɔ:/ *n* Stroh *nt*; (*single piece, drinking*) Strohhalm *m*; **that's the last ~** jetzt reichts aber

strawberry /'strɔ:bərɪ/ *n* Erdbeere *f*

stray /streɪ/ *a* streunend ● *n* streunendes Tier *nt* ● *vi* sich verirren; (*deviate*) abweichen

streak /stri:k/ *n* Streifen *m*; (*in hair*) Strähne *f*; (*fig: trait*) Zug *m*

stream /stri:m/ *n* Bach *m*; (*flow*) Strom *m*; (*current*) Strömung *f*; (*Sch*) Parallelzug *m* ● *vi* strömen

'streamline *vt* (*fig*) rationalisieren. **~d** *a* stromlinienförmig

street /stri:t/ *n* Straße *f*. **~car** *n* (*Amer*) Straßenbahn *f*. **~lamp** *n* Straßenlaterne *f*

strength /streŋθ/ *n* Stärke *f*; (*power*) Kraft *f*; **on the ~ of** auf Grund (+ *gen*). **~en** *vt* stärken; (*reinforce*) verstärken

strenuous /'strenjʊəs/ *a* anstrengend

stress /stres/ *n* (*emphasis*) Betonung *f*; (*strain*) Belastung *f*; (*mental*) Stress *m* ● *vt* betonen; (*put a strain on*) belasten. **~ful** *a* stressig [!]

stretch /stretʃ/ *n* (*of road*) Strecke *f*; (*elasticity*) Elastizität *f*; **at a ~** ohne Unterbrechung; **have a ~** sich strecken ● *vt* strecken; (*widen*) dehnen; (*spread*) ausbreiten; fordern <*person*>; **~ one's legs** sich (*dat*) die Beine vertreten ● *vt* sich erstrecken; (*become wider*) sich dehnen; <*person:*> sich strecken. **~er** *n* Tragbahre *f*

strict /strɪkt/ *a* (**-er, -est**), **-ly** *adv* streng; **~ly speaking** streng genommen

stride /straɪd/ *n* [großer] Schritt *m*; **take sth in one's ~** mit etw gut fertig werden ● *vi* (*pt* **strode**, *pp* **stridden**) [mit großen Schritten] gehen

strident /straɪdnt/ *a*, **-ly** *adv* schrill; <*colour*> grell

strife /straɪf/ *n* Streit *m*

strike /straɪk/ *n* Streik *m*; (*Mil*) Angriff *m*; **be on ~** streiken ● *v* (*pt/pp* **struck**) ● *vt* schlagen; (*knock against, collide with*) treffen; anzünden <*match*>; stoßen auf (+ *acc*) <*oil, gold*>; abbrechen <*camp*>; (*impress*) beeindrucken; (*occur to*) einfallen (+ *dat*); **~ s.o. a blow** jdm einen Schlag versetzen ● *vi* treffen; <*lightning:*> einschlagen; <*clock:*> schlagen; (*attack*) zuschlagen; <*workers:*> streiken

striker /'straɪkə(r)/ *n* Streikende(r) *m/f*

striking /'straɪkɪŋ/ *a* auffallend

string /strɪŋ/ *n* Schnur *f*; (*thin*) Bindfaden *m*; (*of musical instrument, racket*) Saite *f*; (*of bow*) Sehne *f*; (*of pearls*) Kette *f*; **the ~s** (*Mus*) die Streicher *pl*; **pull ~s** [!] seine Beziehungen spielen lassen ● *vt* (*pt/pp* **strung**) (*thread*) aufziehen <*beads*>

stringent /'strɪndʒnt/ *a* streng

strip /strɪp/ *n* Streifen *m* ● *v* (*pt/pp* **stripped**) ● *vt* ablösen; ausziehen <*person, clothes*>; abziehen <*bed*>; abbeizen <*wood, furniture*>; auseinander nehmen <*machine*>; (*deprive*) berauben (*of gen*); **~ sth off sth** etw von etw entfernen ● *vi* (*undress*) sich ausziehen

stripe /straɪp/ *n* Streifen *m*. **~d** *a* gestreift

stripper /'strɪpə(r)/ *n* Stripperin *f*; (*male*) Stripper *m*

strive /straɪv/ *vi* (*pt* **strove**, *pp* **striven**) sich bemühen (**to** zu); **~ for** streben nach

strode /strəʊd/ *see* **stride**

stroke¹ /strəʊk/ *n* Schlag *m*; (*of pen*) Strich *m*; (*Swimming*) Zug *m*; (*style*) Stil *m*; (*Med*) Schlaganfall *m*; **~ of luck** Glücksfall *m*

stroke² ● *vt* streicheln

stroll /strəʊl/ *n* Bummel *m* [!] ● *vi* bummeln [!]. **~er** *n* (*Amer: pushchair*) [Kinder]sportwagen *m*

strong /strɒŋ/ *a* (**-er**, /-gə(r)/ **-est** /-gɪst/), **-ly** *adv* stark; (*powerful, healthy*) kräftig; (*severe*) streng; (*sturdy*) stabil; (*convincing*) gut

strong: ~hold *n* Festung *f*; (*fig*) Hochburg *f*. **~-room** *n* Tresorraum *m*

strove /strəʊv/ *see* **strive**

struck /strʌk/ *see* **strike**

structural /'strʌktʃərl/ *a*, **-ly** *adv* baulich

structure /'strʌktʃə(r)/ *n* Struktur *f*; (*building*) Bau *m*

struggle /'strʌgl/ *n* Kampf *m*; **with a ~** mit Mühe ● *vt* kämpfen; **~ to do sth** sich abmühen, etw zutun

strum /strʌm/ *v* (*pt/pp* **strummed**) ● *vt* klimpern auf (+ *dat*) ● *vi* klimpern

strung /strʌŋ/ *see* **string**

strut¹ /strʌt/ *n* Strebe *f*

strut² *vi* (*pt/pp* **strutted**) stolzieren

stub /stʌb/ *n* Stummel *m*; (*counterfoil*) Abschnitt *m*. **~ out** *vt* (*pt/pp* **stubbed**) ausdrücken <*cigarette*>

stubble /'stʌbl/ *n* Stoppeln *pl*

stubborn /'stʌbən/ *a*, **-ly** *adv* starrsinnig; <*refusal*> hartnäckig

stubby /'stʌbɪ/ *a*, (**-ier, -iest**) kurz und dick

stuck /stʌk/ *see* **stick²**. **~-'up** *a* [!] hochnäsig

stud /stʌd/ *n* Nagel *m*; (*on clothes*) Niete *f*; (*for collar*) Kragenknopf *m*; (*for ear*) Ohrstecker *m*

student /'stju:dnt/ *n* Student(in) *m(f)*; (*Sch*) Schüler(in) *m(f)*

studio /'stju:dɪəʊ/ *n* Studio *nt*; (*for artist*) Atelier *nt*

studious /'stju:dɪəs/ *a* lerneifrig; (*earnest*) ernsthaft

stud|y /'stʌdɪ/ *n* Studie *f*; (*room*) Arbeitszimmer *nt*; (*investigation*) Untersuchung *f*; **~ies** *pl* Studium *nt* ● *v* (*pt/pp* **studied**) ● *vt* studieren; (*examine*) untersuchen ● *vi* lernen; (*at university*) studieren

stuff /stʌf/ *n* Stoff *m*; ([!] *things*) Zeug *nt* ● *vt* vollstopfen; (*with padding, Culin*) füllen; ausstopfen <*animal*>; (*cram*) [hinein]stopfen. **~ing** *n* Füllung *f*

stuffy /ˈstʌfɪ/ *a* (**-ier, -iest**) stickig; (*old-fashioned*) spießig

stumbl|e /ˈstʌmbl/ *vi* stolpern; **~e across** zufällig stoßen auf (+ *acc*). **~ing-block** *n* Hindernis *nt*

stump /stʌmp/ *n* Stumpf *m* ● **~ up** *vt/i* [!] blechen. **~ed** *a* [!] überfragt

stun /stʌn/ *vt* (*pt/pp* **stunned**) betäuben

stung /stʌŋ/ *see* **sting**

stunk /stʌŋk/ *see* **stink**

stunning /ˈstʌnɪŋ/ *a* [!] toll

stunt /stʌnt/ *n* [!] Kunststück *nt*

stupendous /stju:ˈpendəs/ *a*, **-ly** *adv* enorm

stupid /ˈstju:pɪd/ *a* dumm. **~ity** /-ˈpɪdətɪ/ *n* Dummheit *f*. **~ly** *adv* dumm; **~ly [enough]** dummerweise

sturdy /ˈstɜ:dɪ/ *a* (**-ier, -iest**) stämmig; <*furniture*> stabil; <*shoes*> fest

stutter /ˈstʌtə(r)/ *n* Stottern *nt* ● *vt/i* stottern

sty /staɪ/ *n* (*pl* **sties**) Schweinestall *m*

style /staɪl/ *n* Stil *m*; (*fashion*) Mode *f*; (*sort*) Art *f*; (*hair~*) Frisur *f*; **in ~** in großem Stil

stylish /ˈstaɪlɪʃ/ *a*, -ly *adv* stilvoll

stylist /ˈstaɪlɪst/ *n* Friseur *m*/ Friseuse *f*. **~ic** /-ˈlɪstɪk/ *a*, **-ally** *adv* stilistisch

suave /swɑ:v/ *a* (*pej*) gewandt

subˈconscious /sʌb-/ *a*, **-ly** *adv* unterbewusst ● *n* Unterbewusstsein *nt*

ˈsubdivi|de *vt* unterteilen. **~sion** *n* Unterteilung *f*

subdue /səbˈdju:/ *vt* unterwerfen. **~d** *a* gedämpft; <*person*> still

subject¹ /ˈsʌbdʒɪkt/ *a* **be ~ to sth** etw (*dat*) unterworfen sein ● *n* Staatsbürger(in) *m(f)*; (*of ruler*) Untertan *m*; (*theme*) Thema *nt*; (*of investigation*) Gegenstand *m*; (*Sch*) Fach *nt*; (*Gram*) Subjekt *nt*

subject² /səbˈdʒekt/ *vt* unterwerfen (**to** *dat*); (*expose*) aussetzen (**to** *dat*)

subjective /səbˈdʒektɪv/ *a*, **-ly** *adv* subjektiv

subjunctive /səbˈdʒʌŋktɪv/ *n* Konjunktiv *m*

sublime /səˈblaɪm/ *a*, **-ly** *adv* erhaben

submaˈrine *n* Unterseeboot *nt*

submerge /səbˈmɜ:dʒ/ *vt* untertauchen; **be ~d** unter Wasser stehen ● *vi* tauchen

submission /səbˈmɪʃn/ *n* Unterwerfung *f*

submit /səbˈmɪt/ *v* (*pt/pp* **-mitted**, *pres p* **-mitting**) ● *vt* vorlegen (**to** *dat*); (*hand in*) einreichen ● *vi* sich unterwerfen (**to** *dat*)

subordinate¹ /səˈbɔ:dɪnət/ *a* untergeordnet ● *n* Untergebene(r) *m/f*

subordinate² /səˈbɔ:dɪneɪt/ *vt* unterordnen (**to** *dat*)

subscribe /səbˈskraɪb/ *vi* spenden; **~ to** (*fig*); abonnieren <*newspaper*>. **~r** *n* Spender *m*; Abonnent *m*

subscription /səbˈskrɪpʃn/ *n* (*to club*) [Mitglieds]beitrag *m*; (*to newspaper*) Abonnement *nt*; **by ~** mit Spenden; <*buy*> im Abonnement

subsequent /ˈsʌbsɪkwənt/ *a*, **-ly** *adv* folgend; (*later*) später

subside /səbˈsaɪd/ *vi* sinken; <*ground:*> sich senken; <*storm:*> nachlassen

subsidiary /səbˈsɪdɪərɪ/ *a* untergeordnet ● *n* Tochtergesellschaft *f*

subsid|ize /ˈsʌbsɪdaɪz/ *vt* subventionieren. **~y** *n* Subvention *f*

substance /ˈsʌbstəns/ *n* Substanz *f*

subˈstandard *a* unzulänglich; <*goods*> minderwertig

substantial /səbˈstænʃl/ *a* solide; <*meal*> reichhaltig; (*considerable*) beträchtlich. **~ly** *adv* solide; (*essentially*) im Wesentlichen

substitut|e /ˈsʌbstɪtjuːt/ *n* Ersatz *m*; (*Sport*) Ersatzspieler(in) *m(f)* ● *vt* **~e A for B** B durch A ersetzen ● *vi* **~e for s.o.** jdn vertreten. **~ion** /-ˈtjuːʃn/ *n* Ersetzung *f*

subterranean /sʌbtəˈreɪnɪən/ *a* unterirdisch

ˈsubtitle *n* Untertitel *m*

subtle /ˈsʌtl/ *a* (**-r, -st**), **-tly** *adv* fein; (*fig*) subtil

subtract /səbˈtrækt/ *vt* abziehen, subtrahieren. **~ion** /-ækʃn/ *n* Subtraktion *f*

suburb /ˈsʌbɜːb/ *n* Vorort *m*. **~an** /səˈbɜːbən/ *a* Vorort-. **~ia** /səˈbɜːbɪə/ *n* die Vororte *pl*

ˈsubway *n* Unterführung *f*; (*Amer: railway*) U-Bahn *f*

succeed /səkˈsiːd/ *vi* Erfolg haben; <*plan*:> gelingen; (*follow*) nachfolgen (+ *dat*); **I ~ed** es ist mir gelungen; **he ~ed in escaping** es gelang ihm zu entkommen ● *vt* folgen (+ *dat*)

success /səkˈses/ *n* Erfolg *m*. **~ful** *a*,**-ly** *adv* erfolgreich

succession /səkˈseʃn/ *n* Folge *f*; (*series*) Serie *f*; (*to title, office*) Nachfolge *f*; (*to throne*) Thronfolge *f*; **in ~** hintereinander

successive /səkˈsesɪv/ *a* aufeinander folgend

successor /səkˈsesə(r)/ *n* Nachfolger(in) *m(f)*

succumb /səˈkʌm/ *vi* erliegen (**to** *dat*)

such /sʌtʃ/
● *adjective*
···➤ (*of that kind*) solch. **such a book** ein solches Buch; so ein Buch [!]. **such a person** ein solcher Mensch; so ein Mensch [!]. **such people** solche Leute. **such a thing** so etwas. **no such example** kein solches Beispiel. **there is no such thing** so etwas gibt es nicht; das gibt es gar nicht. **there is no such person** eine solche Person gibt es nicht. **such writers as Goethe and Schiller** Schriftsteller wie Goethe und Schiller
···➤ (*so great*) solch; derartig. **I've got such a headache!** ich habe solche Kopfschmerzen! **it was such fun!** das machte solchen Spaß! **I got such a fright that ...** ich bekam einen derartigen *od* [!] so einen Schrecken, dass ...
···➤ (*with adjective*) so. **such a big house** ein so großes Haus. **he has such lovely blue eyes** er hat so schöne blaue Augen. **such a long time** so lange
● *pronoun*
···➤ **as such** als solcher/solche/solches. **the thing as such** die Sache als solche. (*strictly speaking*) **this is not a promotion as such** dies ist im Grunde genommen keine Beförderung
···➤ **such is**: **such is life** so ist das Leben. **such is not the case** das ist nicht der Fall
···➤ **such as** wie [zum Beispiel]

suchlike /ˈsʌtʃlaɪk/ *pron* [!] dergleichen

suck /ʃʌk/ *vt/i* saugen; lutschen <*sweet*>. **~ up** *vt* aufsaugen ● *vi* **~ up to s.o.** [!] sich bei jdm einschmeicheln

suction /ˈsʌkʃn/ *n* Saugwirkung *f*

sudden /ˈsʌdn/ *a*, **-ly** *adv* plötzlich; (*abrupt*) jäh ● *n* **all of a ~** auf einmal

sue /su:/ *vt* (*pres p* **suing**) verklagen (**for** auf + *acc*) ● *vi* klagen

suede /sweɪd/ *n* Wildleder *nt*

suet /ˈsu:ɪt/ *n* [Nieren]talg *m*

suffer /ˈsʌfə(r)/ *vi* leiden (**from an** + *dat*) ● *vt* erleiden; (*tolerate*) dulden

suffice /səˈfaɪs/ *vi* genügen

sufficient /səˈfɪʃnt/ *a*, **-ly** *adv* genug, genügend; **be ~** genügen

suffocat|e /ˈsʌfəkeɪt/ *vt/i* ersticken. **~ion** /-ˈkeɪʃn/ *n* Ersticken *nt*

sugar /ˈʃʊgə(r)/ *n* Zucker *m* ● *vt* zuckern; (*fig*) versüßen. **~ basin, ~ bowl** *n* Zuckerschale *f*. **~y** *a* süß; (*fig*) süßlich

suggest /səˈdʒest/ *vt* vorschlagen; (*indicate, insinuate*) andeuten. **~ion** /-estʃn/ *n* Vorschlag *m*; Andeutung *f*; (*trace*) Spur *f*. **~ive** /-ɪv/ *a*, **-ly** *adv* anzüglich

suicidal /su:ɪˈsaɪdl/ *a* selbstmörderisch

suicide /ˈsu:ɪsaɪd/ *n* Selbstmord *m*

suit /su:t/ *n* Anzug *m*; (*woman's*) Kostüm *nt*; (*Cards*) Farbe *f*; (*Jur*) Prozess *m* ● *vt* (*adapt*) anpassen (**to** *dat*); (*be convenient for*) passen (+ *dat*); (*go with*) passen zu; <*clothing:*> stehen (**s.o.** *jdm*); **be ~ed for** geeignet sein für; **~ yourself!** wie du willst!

suit|able /ˈsu:təbl/ *a* geeignet; (*convenient*) passend; (*appropriate*) angemessen; (*for weather, activity*) zweckmäßig. **~ably** *adv* angemessen; zweckmäßig

ˈsuitcase *n* Koffer *m*

suite /swi:t/ *n* Suite *f*; (*of furniture*) Garnitur *f*

sulk /sʌlk/ *vi* schmollen. **~y** *a* schmollend

sullen /ˈsʌlən/ *a*, **-ly** *adv* mürrisch

sultry /ˈsʌltrɪ/ *a* (**-ier, -iest**) <*weather*> schwül

sum /sʌm/ *n* Summe *f*; (*Sch*) Rechenaufgabe *f* ● *vt/i* (*pt/pp* **summed**) **~ up** zusammenfassen; (*assess*) einschätzen

summar|ize /ˈsʌməraɪz/ *vt* zusammenfassen. **~y** *n* Zusammenfassung *f* ● *a*, **-ily** *adv* summarisch; <*dismissal*> fristlos

summer /ˈsʌmə(r)/ *n* Sommer *m*. **~time** *n* Sommer *m*

summery /ˈsʌmərɪ/ *a* sommerlich

summit /ˈsʌmɪt/ *n* Gipfel *m*. **~ conference** *n* Gipfelkonferenz *f*

summon /ˈsʌmən/ *vt* rufen; holen <*help*>; (*Jur*) vorladen

summons /ˈsʌmənz/ *n* (*Jur*) Vorladung *f* ● *vt* vorladen

sumptuous /ˈsʌmptjʊəs/ *a*, **-ly** *adv* prunkvoll; <*meal*> üppig

sun /sʌn/ *n* Sonne *f* ● *vt* (*pt/pp* **sunned**) **~ oneself** sich sonnen

sun: ~bathe *vi* sich sonnen. **~bed** *n* Sonnenbank *f*. **~burn** *n* Sonnenbrand *m*

Sunday /ˈsʌndeɪ/ *n* Sonntag *m*

ˈsunflower *n* Sonnenblume *f*

sung /sʌŋ/ *see* **sing**

ˈsunglasses *npl* Sonnenbrille *f*

sunk /sʌŋk/ *see* **sink**

sunny /ˈsʌnɪ/ *a* (**-ier, -iest**) sonnig

sun: ~rise *n* Sonnenaufgang *m*. **~roof** *n* (*Auto*) Schiebedach *nt*. **~set** *n* Sonnenuntergang *m*. **~shade** *n* Sonnenschirm *m*. **~shine** *n* Sonnenschein *m*. **~stroke** *n* Sonnenstich *m*. **~tan** *n* [Sonnen]bräune *f*. **~tanned** *a* braun [gebrannt]. **~tan oil** *n* Sonnenöl *nt*

super /'su:pə(r)/ *a* [!] prima, toll
superb /sʊ'pɜ:b/ *a* erstklassig
superficial /su:pə'fɪʃl/ a, **-ly** *adv* oberflächlich
superfluous /sʊ'pɜ:flʊəs/ *a* überflüssig
superintendent /su:pərɪn'tendənt/ *n* (*of police*) Kommissar *m*
superior /su:'pɪərɪə(r)/ *a* überlegen; (*in rank*) höher ● *n* Vorgesetzte(r) *m/f*. **~ity** /-'ɒrətɪ/ *n* Überlegenheit *f*
superlative /su:'pɜ:lətɪv/ *a* unübertrefflich ● *n* Superlativ *m*
'supermarket *n* Supermarkt *m*
super'natural *a* übernatürlich
supersede /su:pə'si:d/ *vt* ersetzen
superstiti|on /su:pə'stɪʃn/ *n* Aberglaube *m*. **~ous** /-'stɪʃəs/ *a*, **-ly** *adv* abergläubisch
supervis|e /'su:pəvaɪz/ *vt* beaufsichtigen; überwachen <*work*>. **~ion** /-'vɪʒn/ *n* Aufsicht *f*; Überwachung *f*. **~or** *n* Aufseher(in) *m(f)*
supper /'sʌpə(r)/ *n* Abendessen *nt*
supple /'sʌpl/ *a* geschmeidig
supplement /'sʌplɪmənt/ *n* Ergänzung *f*; (*addition*) Zusatz *m*; (*to fare*) Zuschlag *m*; (*book*) Ergänzungsband *m*; (*to newspaper*) Beilage *f* ● *vt* ergänzen. **~ary** /-'mentərɪ/ a zusätzlich
supplier /sə'plaɪə(r)/ *n* Lieferant *m*
supply /sə'plaɪ/ *n* Vorrat *m*; **supplies** *pl* (*Mil*) Nachschub *m* ● *vt* (*pt/pp* **-ied**) liefern; **~ s.o. with sth** jdn mit etw versorgen
support /sə'pɔ:t/ *n* Stütze *f*; (*fig*) Unterstützung *f* ● *vt* stützen; (*bear weight of*) tragen; (*keep*) ernähren; (*give money to*) unterstützen; (*speak in favour of*) befürworten; (*Sport*) Fan sein von. **~er** *n* Anhänger(in) *m(f)*; (*Sport*) Fan *m*
suppose /sə'pəʊz/ *vt* annehmen; (*presume*) vermuten; (*imagine*) sich (*dat*) vorstellen; **be ~d to do sth** etw tun sollen; **not be ~d to** [!] nicht dürfen; **I ~ so** vermutlich. **~dly** /-ɪdlɪ/ *adv* angeblich
supposition /sʌpə'zɪʃn/ *n* Vermutung *f*
suppress /sə'pres/ *vt* unterdrücken. **~ion** /-eʃn/ *n* Unterdrückung *f*
supremacy /su:'preməsɪ/ *n* Vorherrschaft *f*
supreme /su:'pri:m/ *a* höchste(r,s); <*court*> oberste(r,s)
sure /ʃʊə(r)/ *a* (**-r, -st**) sicher; **make ~** sich vergewissern (**of** *gen*); (*check*) nachprüfen ● *adv* (*Amer* [!]) klar; **~ enough** tatsächlich. **~ly** *adv* sicher; (*for emphasis*) doch; (*Amer: gladly*) gern
surf /'sɜ:f/ *n* Brandung *f* ● *vi* (*on Internet*) surfen
surface /'sɜ:fɪs/ *n* Oberfläche *f* ● *vi* (*emerge*) auftauchen
'surfboard *n* Surfbrett *nt*
surfing /'sɜ:fɪŋ/ *n* Surfen *nt*
surge /sɜ:dʒ/ *n* (*of sea*) Branden *nt*; (*fig*) Welle *f* ● *vi* branden; **~ forward** nach vorn drängen
surgeon /'sɜ:dʒən/ *n* Chirurg(in) *m(f)*
surgery /'sɜ:dʒərɪ/ *n* Chirurgie *f*; (*place*) Praxis *f*; (*room*) Sprechzimmer *nt*; (*hours*) Sprechstunde *f*; **have ~** operiert werden
surgical /'sɜ:dʒɪkl/ *a*, **-ly** *adv* chirurgisch
surly /'sɜ:lɪ/ *a* (**-ier, -iest**) mürrisch
surname /'sɜ:neɪm/ *n* Nachname *m*
surpass /sə'pɑ:s/ *vt* übertreffen

surplus /'sɜ:pləs/ *a* überschüssig ● *n* Überschuss *m* (**of** an + *dat*)

surpris|e /sə'praɪz/ *n* Überraschung *f* ● *vt* überraschen; **be ~ed** sich wundern (**at** über + *acc*). **~ing** *a*, **-ly** *adv* überraschend

surrender /sə'rendə(r)/ *n* Kapitulation *f* ● *vi* sich ergeben; (*Mil*) kapitulieren ● *vt* aufgeben

surround /sə'raʊnd/ *vt* umgeben; (*encircle*) umzingeln; **~ed by** umgeben von. **~ing** *a* umliegend. **~ings** *npl* Umgebung *f*

surveillance /sə'veɪləns/ *n* Überwachung *f*; **be under ~** überwacht werden

survey[1] /'sɜ:veɪ/ *n* Überblick *m*; (*poll*) Umfrage *f*; (*investigation*) Untersuchung *f*; (*of land*) Vermessung *f*; (*of house*) Gutachten *nt*

survey[2] /sə'veɪ/ *vt* betrachten; vermessen <*land*>; begutachten <*building*>. **~or** *n* Landvermesser *m*; Gutachter *m*

survival /sə'vaɪvl/ *n* Überleben *nt*; (*of tradition*) Fortbestand *m*

surviv|e /sə'vaɪv/ *vt* überleben ● *vi* überleben; <*tradition:*> erhalten bleiben. **~or** *n* Überlebende(r) *m/f*; **be a ~or** nicht unterzukriegen sein

susceptible /sə'septəbl/ *a* empfänglich/ (*Med*) anfällig (**to** für)

suspect[1] /sə'spekt/ *vt* verdächtigen; (*assume*) vermuten; **he ~s nothing** er ahnt nichts

suspect[2] /'sʌspekt/ *a* verdächtig ● *n* Verdächtige(r) *m/f*

suspend /sə'spend/ *vt* aufhängen; (*stop*) [vorläufig] einstellen; (*from duty*) vorläufig beurlauben. **~ders** *npl* (*Amer: braces*) Hosenträger *pl*

suspense /sə'spens/ *n* Spannung *f*

suspension /sə'spenʃn/ *n* (*Auto*) Federung *f*. **~ bridge** *n* Hängebrücke *f*

suspici|on /sə'spɪʃn/ *n* Verdacht *m*; (*mistrust*) Misstrauen *nt*; (*trace*) Spur *f*. **~ous** /-ɪʃəs/ *a*, **-ly** *adv* misstrauisch; (*arousing suspicion*) verdächtig

sustain /sə'steɪn/ *vt* tragen; (*fig*) aufrechterhalten; erhalten <*life*>; erleiden <*injury*>

sustenance /'sʌstɪnəns/ *n* Nahrung *f*

swagger /'swægə(r)/ *vi* stolzieren

swallow[1] /'swɒləʊ/ *vt/i* schlucken. **~ up** *vt* verschlucken; verschlingen <*resources*>

swallow[2] *n* (*bird*) Schwalbe *f*

swam /swæm/ *see* **swim**

swamp /swɒmp/ *n* Sumpf *m* ● *vt* überschwemmen

swan /swɒn/ *n* Schwan *m*

swank /swæŋk/ *vi* ! angeben

swap /swɒp/ *n* ! Tausch *m* ● *vt/i* (*pt/pp* **swapped**) ! tauschen (**for** gegen)

swarm /swɔ:m/ *n* Schwarm *m* ● *vi* schwärmen; **be ~ing with** wimmeln von

swat /swɒt/ *vt* (*pt/pp* **swatted**) totschlagen

sway /sweɪ/ *vi* schwanken; (*gently*) sich wiegen ● *vt* (*influence*) beeinflussen

swear /sweə(r)/ *v* (*pt* **swore**, *pp* **sworn**) ● *vt* schwören ● *vi* schwören (**by** auf + *acc*); (*curse*) fluchen. **~-word** *n* Kraftausdruck *m*

sweat /swet/ *n* Schweiß *m* ● *vi* schwitzen

sweater /'swetə(r)/ *n* Pullover *m*

Swed|e *n* Schwede *m*/Schwedin *f*. **~en** *n* Schweden *nt*. **~ish** *a* schwedisch

sweep /swi:p/ *n* Schornsteinfeger *m*; (*curve*) Bogen *m*; (*movement*) ausholende Bewegung *f* ● *v* (*pt*/*pp* **swept**) ● *vt* fegen, kehren ● *vi* (*go swiftly*) rauschen; <*wind:*> fegen

sweeping /ˈswi:pɪŋ/ *a* ausholend; <*statement*> pauschal; <*changes*> weit reichend

sweet /swi:t/ *a* (**-er, -est**) süß; **have a ~ tooth** gern Süßes mögen ● *n* Bonbon *m & nt*; (*dessert*) Nachtisch *m*

sweeten /ˈswi:tn/ *vt* süßen

sweet: ~heart *n* Schatz *m*. **~ness** *n* Süße *f*. **~ ˈpea** *n* Wicke *f*. **~-shop** *n* Süßwarenladen *m*

swell /swel/ *n* Dünung *f* ● *v* (*pt* **swelled**, *pp* **swollen** *or* **swelled**) ● *vi* [an]schwellen; <*wood:*> aufquellen ● *vt* anschwellen lassen; (*increase*) vergrößern. **~ing** *n* Schwellung *f*

swelter /ˈsweltə(r)/ *vi* schwitzen

swept /swept/ *see* **sweep**

swerve /swɜ:v/ *vi* einen Bogen machen

swift /swɪft/ *a* (**-er, -est**), **-ly** *adv* schnell

swig /swɪg/ *n* [!] Schluck *m*

swim /swɪm/ *n* **have a ~** schwimmen ● *vi* (**pt swam**, *pp* **swum**) schwimmen; **my head is ~ming** mir dreht sich der Kopf. **~mer** *n* Schwimmer(in) *m(f)*

swimming /ˈswɪmɪŋ/ *n* Schwimmen *nt*. **~-baths** *npl* Schwimmbad *nt*. **~-pool** *n* Schwimmbecken *nt*; (*private*) Swimmingpool *m*

ˈswimsuit *n* Badeanzug *m*

swindle /ˈswɪndl/ *n* Schwindel *m*, Betrug *m* ● *vt* betrügen. **~r** *n* Schwindler *m*

swine /swaɪn/ *n* (*pej*) Schwein *nt*

swing /swɪŋ/ *n* Schwung *m*; (*shift*) Schwenk *m*; (*seat*) Schaukel *f*; **in full ~** in vollem Gange ● (*pt*/*pp* **swung**) ● *vi* schwingen; (*on swing*) schaukeln; (*dangle*) baumeln; (*turn*) schwenken ● *vt* schwingen; (*influence*) beeinflussen

swipe /swaɪp/ *n* [!] Schlag *m* ● *vt* [!] knallen; (*steal*) klauen

swirl /swɜ:l/ *n* Wirbel *m* ● *vt*/*i* wirbeln

Swiss /swɪs/ *a* Schweizer, schweizerisch ● *n* Schweizer(in) *m(f)*; **the ~** *pl* die Schweizer. **~ ˈroll** *n* Biskuitrolle *f*

switch /swɪtʃ/ *n* Schalter *m*; (*change*) Wechsel *m*; (*Amer, Rail*) Weiche *f* ● *vt* wechseln; (*exchange*) tauschen ● *vi* wechseln; **~ to** umstellen auf (+ *acc*). **~ off** *vt* ausschalten; abschalten <*engine*>. **~ on** *vt* einschalten

switchboard *n* [Telefon]zentrale *f*

Switzerland /ˈswɪtsələnd/ *n* die Schweiz

swivel /ˈswɪvl/ *v* (*pt*/*pp* **swivelled**) ● *vt* drehen ● *vi* sich drehen

swollen /ˈswəʊlən/ *see* **swell**

swoop /swu:p/ *n* (*by police*) Razzia *f* ● *vi* **~ down** herabstoßen

sword /sɔ:d/ *n* Schwert *nt*

swore /swɔ:(r)/ *see* **swear**

sworn /swɔ:n/ *see* **swear**

swot /swɒt/ *n* [!] Streber *m* ● *vt* (*pt*/*pp* **swotted**) [!] büffeln

swum /swʌm/ *see* **swim**

swung /swʌŋ/ *see* **swing**

syllable /ˈsɪləbl/ *n* Silbe *f*

syllabus /ˈsɪləbəs/ *n* Lehrplan *m*; (*for exam*) Studienplan *m*

symbol /ˈsɪmbəl/ *n* Symbol *nt* (**of** für). **~ic** /-ˈbɒlɪk/ *a*, **-ally** *adv* symbolisch **~ism** /-ɪzm/ *n*

Symbolik *f*. **~ize** *vt* symbolisieren
symmetr|ical /sɪˈmetrɪkl/ *a*, **-ly** *adv* symmetrisch. **~y** /ˈsɪmətrɪ/ *n* Symmetrie *f*
sympathetic /sɪmpəˈθetɪk/ *a*, **-ally** *adv* mitfühlend; (*likeable*) sympathisch
sympathize /ˈsɪmpəθaɪz/ *vi* mitfühlen
sympathy /ˈsɪmpəθɪ/ *n* Mitgefühl *nt*; (*condolences*) Beileid *nt*
symphony /ˈsɪmfənɪ/ *n* Sinfonie *f*
symptom /ˈsɪmptəm/ *n* Symptom *nt*
synagogue /ˈsɪnəgɒg/ *n* Synagoge *f*
synchronize /ˈsɪŋkrənaɪz/ *vt* synchronisieren
synonym /ˈsɪnənɪm/ *n* Synonym *nt*. **~ous** /-ˈnɒnɪməs/ *a*, **-ly** *adv* synonym
synthesis /ˈsɪnθəsɪs/ *n* (*pl* **-ses** /-si:z/) Synthese *f*
synthetic /sɪnˈθetɪk/ *a* synthetisch
Syria /ˈsɪrɪə/ *n* Syrien *nt*
syringe /sɪˈrɪndʒ/ *n* Spritze *f*
syrup /ˈsɪrəp/ *n* Sirup *m*
system /ˈsɪstəm/ *n* System *nt*. **~atic** /-ˈmætɪk/ *a*, **-ally** *adv* systematisch

Tt

tab /tæb/ *n* (*projecting*) Zunge *f*; (*with name*) Namensschild *nt*; (*loop*) Aufhänger *m*; **pick up the ~** [!] bezahlen
table /ˈteɪbl/ *n* Tisch *m*; (*list*) Tabelle *f*; **at [the] ~** bei Tisch. **~-cloth** *n* Tischdecke *f*. **~spoon** *n* Servierlöffel *m*
tablet /ˈtæblɪt/ *n* Tablette *f*; (*of soap*) Stück *nt*
ˈ**table tennis** *n* Tischtennis *nt*
tabloid /ˈtæblɔɪd/ *n* kleinformatige Zeitung *f*; (*pej*) Boulevardzeitung *f*
taciturn /ˈtæsɪtɜ:n/ *a* wortkarg
tack /tæk/ *n* (*nail*) Stift *m*; (*stitch*) Heftstich *m*; (*Naut & fig*) Kurs *m* ● *vt* festnageln; (*sew*) heften ● *vi* (*Naut*) kreuzen
tackle /ˈtækl/ *n* Ausrüstung *f* ● *vt* angehen <*problem*>; (*Sport*) angreifen
tact /tækt/ *n* Takt *m*, Taktgefühl *nt*. **~ful** *a*, **-ly** *adv* taktvoll
tactic|al /ˈtæktɪkl/ *a*, **-ly** *adv* taktisch. **~s** *npl* Taktik *f*
tactless /ˈtæktlɪs/ *a*, **-ly** *adv* taktlos. **~ness** *n* Taktlosigkeit *f*
tag /tæg/ *n* (*label*) Schild *nt* ● *vi* (*pt/pp* **tagged**) **~ along** mitkommen
tail /teɪl/ *n* Schwanz *m*; **~s** *pl* (*tailcoat*) Frack *m*; **heads or ~s?** Kopf oder Zahl? ● *vt* ([!] *follow*) beschatten ● *vi* **~ off** zurückgehen
tail: ~back *n* Rückstau *m*. **~ light** *n* Rücklicht *nt*
tailor /ˈteɪlə(r)/ *n* Schneider *m*. **~-made** *a* maßgeschneidert
taint /teɪnt/ *vt* verderben
take /teɪk/ *v* (*pt* **took**, *pp* **taken**) ● *vt* nehmen: (*with one*) mitnehmen; (*take to a place*) bringen; (*steal*) stehlen; (*win*) gewinnen; (*capture*) einnehmen; (*require*) brauchen; (*last*) dauern; (*teach*) geben; machen <*exam, subject, holiday, photograph*>; messen <*pulse, temperature*>; **~ sth to the cleaner's** etw in die

Reinigung bringen; **be ~n ill** krank werden; **~ sth calmly** etw gelassen aufnehmen ● *vi* <*plant:*> angehen; **~ after s.o.** jdm nachschlagen; (*in looks*) jdm ähnlich sehen; **~ to** (*like*) mögen; (*as a habit*) sich (*dat*) angewöhnen. **~ away** *vt* wegbringen; (*remove*) wegnehmen; (*subtract*) abziehen; **'to ~ away'** 'zum Mitnehmen'. **~ back** *vt* zurücknehmen; (*return*) zurückbringen. **~ down** *vt* herunternehmen; (*remove*) abnehmen; (*write down*) aufschreiben. **~ in** *vt* hineinbringen; (*bring indoors*) hereinholen; (*to one's home*) aufnehmen; (*understand*) begreifen; (*deceive*) hereinlegen; (*make smaller*) enger machen. **~ off** *vt* abnehmen; ablegen <*coat*>; sich (*dat*) ausziehen <*clothes*>; (*deduct*) abziehen; (*mimic*) nachmachen ● *vi* (*Aviat*) starten. **~ on** *vt* annehmen; (*undertake*) übernehmen; (*engage*) einstellen; (*as opponent*) antreten gegen. **~ out** *vt* hinausbringen; (*for pleasure*) ausgehen mit; ausführen <*dog*>; (*remove*) herausnehmen; (*withdraw*) abheben <*money*>; (*from library*) ausleihen; **~ it out on s.o.** [!] seinen Ärger an jdm auslassen. **~ over** *vt* hinüberbringen; übernehmen <*firm, control*> ● *vi* **~ over from s.o.** jdn ablösen. **~ up** *vt* hinaufbringen; annehmen <*offer*>; ergreifen <*profession*>; sich (*dat*) zulegen <*hobby*>; in Anspruch nehmen <*time*>; einnehmen <*space*>; aufreißen <*floorboards*>; **~ sth up with s.o.** mit jdm über etw (*acc*) sprechen

take: ~-away *n* Essen *nt* zum Mitnehmen; (*restaurant*) Restaurant *nt* mit Straßenverkauf. **~-off** *n* (*Aviat*) Start *m*, Abflug *m*. **~-over** *n* Übernahme *f*

takings /ˈteɪkɪŋz/ *npl* Einnahmen *pl*

talcum /ˈtælkəm/ *n* **~ [powder]** Körperpuder *m*

tale /teɪl/ *n* Geschichte *f*

talent /ˈtælənt/ *n* Talent *nt*

talk /tɔːk/ *n* Gespräch *nt*; (*lecture*) Vortrag *m* ● *vi* reden, sprechen (**to**/**with** mit) ● *vt* reden; **~ s.o. into sth** jdn zu etw überreden. **~ over** *vt* besprechen

talkative /ˈtɔːkətɪv/ *a* gesprächig

tall /tɔːl/ *a* (**-er, -est**) groß; <*building, tree*> hoch. **~ 'story** *n* übertriebene Geschichte *f*

tally /ˈtælɪ/ *vi* übereinstimmen

tame /teɪm/ *a* (**-r, -st**), **-ly** *adv* zahm; (*dull*) lahm [!] ● *vt* zähmen. **~r** *n* Dompteur *m*

tamper /ˈtæmpə(r)/ *vi* **~ with** sich (*dat*) zu schaffen machen an (+ *dat*)

tampon /ˈtæmpɒn/ *n* Tampon *m*

tan /tæn/ *a* gelbbraun ● *n* Gelbbraun *nt*; (*from sun*) Bräune *f* ● *v* (*pt*/*pp* **tanned**) ● *vt* gerben <*hide*> ● *vi* braun werden

tang /tæŋ/ *n* herber Geschmack *m*; (*smell*) herber Geruch *m*

tangible /ˈtændʒɪbl/ *a* greifbar

tangle /ˈtæŋgl/ *n* Gewirr *nt*; (*in hair*) Verfilzung *f* ● *vt* **~ [up]** verheddern ● *vi* sich verheddern

tank /tæŋk/ *n* Tank *m*; (*Mil*) Panzer *m*

tanker /ˈtæŋkə(r)/ *n* Tanker *m*; (*lorry*) Tank[last]wagen *m*

tantrum /ˈtæntrəm/ *n* Wutanfall *m*

tap /tæp/ *n* Hahn *m*; (*knock*) Klopfen *nt*; **on ~** zur Verfügung ● *v* (*pt*/*pp* **tapped**) ● *vt* klopfen an (+ *acc*); anzapfen <*barrel, tree*>; erschließen <*resources*>; abhören <*telephone*> ● *vi*

klopfen. **~-dance** *n* Stepp[tanz] *m* ● *vi* Stepp tanzen, steppen
tape /teɪp/ *n* Band *nt*; (*adhesive*) Klebstreifen *m*; (*for recording*) Tonband *nt* ● *vt* mit Klebstreifen zukleben; (*record*) auf Band aufnehmen
'tape-measure *n* Bandmaß *nt*
taper /'teɪpə(r)/ *vi* sich verjüngen
'tape recorder *n* Tonbandgerät *nt*
tar /tɑ:(r)/ *n* Teer *m* ● *vt* (*pt/pp* **tarred**) teeren
target /'tɑ:gɪt/ *n* Ziel *nt*; (*board*) [Ziel]scheibe *f*
tarnish /'tɑ:nɪʃ/ *vi* anlaufen
tarpaulin /tɑ:'pɔ:lɪn/ *n* Plane *f*
tart[1] /tɑ:t/ *a* (**-er, -est**) sauer
tart[2] *n* ≈ Obstkuchen *m*; (*individual*) Törtchen *nt*; (☒ *prostitute*) Nutte *f* ● *vt* ~ **oneself up** [!] sich auftakeln
tartan /'tɑ:tn/ *n* Schottenmuster *nt*; (*cloth*) Schottenstoff *m*
task /tɑ:sk/ *n* Aufgabe *f*; **take s.o. to ~** jdm Vorhaltungen machen. **~ force** *n* Sonderkommando *nt*
tassel /'tæsl/ *n* Quaste *f*
taste /teɪst/ *n* Geschmack *m*; (*sample*) Kostprobe *f* ● *vt* kosten, probieren; schmecken <*flavour*> ● *vi* schmecken (**of** nach). **~ful** *a*, **-ly** *adv* (*fig*) geschmackvoll. **~less** *a*, **-ly** *adv* geschmacklos
tasty /'teɪstɪ/ *a* (**-ier, -iest**) lecker
tat /tæt/ *see* **tit[2]**
tatters /'tætəz/ *npl* **in ~s** in Fetzen
tattoo /tə'tu:/ *n* Tätowierung *f* ● *vt* tätowieren
tatty /'tætɪ/ *a* (**-ier, -iest**) schäbig; <*book*> zerfleddert
taught /tɔ:t/ *see* **teach**
taunt /tɔ:nt/ *n* höhnische Bemerkung *f* ● *vt* verhöhnen
taut /tɔ:t/ *a* straff
tawdry /'tɔ:drɪ/ *a* (**-ier, -iest**) billig und geschmacklos
tax /tæks/ *n* Steuer *f* ● *vt* besteuern; (*fig*) strapazieren. **~able** /-əbl/ *a* steuerpflichtig. **~ation** /-'seɪʃn/ *n* Besteuerung *f*
taxi /'tæksɪ/ *n* Taxi *nt* ● *vi* (*pt/pp* **taxied**, *pres p* **taxiing**) <*aircraft:*> rollen. **~ driver** *n* Taxifahrer *m*. **~ rank** *n* Taxistand *m*
'taxpayer *n* Steuerzahler *m*
tea /ti:/ *n* Tee *m*. **~-bag** *n* Teebeutel *m*. **~-break** *n* Teepause *f*
teach /ti:tʃ/ *vt/i* (*pt/pp* **taught**) unterrichten; **~ s.o. sth** jdm etw beibringen. **~er** *n* Lehrer(in) *m*(*f*). **~ing** *n* Unterrichten *nt*
tea: ~-cloth *n* (*for drying*) Geschirrtuch *nt*. **~cup** *n* Teetasse *f*
teak /ti:k/ *n* Teakholz *nt*
team /ti:m/ *n* Mannschaft *f*; (*fig*) Team *nt*; (*of animals*) Gespann *nt*
'teapot *n* Teekanne *f*
tear[1] /teə(r)/ *n* Riss *m* ● *v* (*pt* **tore**, *pp* **torn**) ● *vt* reißen; (*damage*) zerreißen; **~ oneself away** sich losreißen ● *vi* [zer]reißen; (*run*) rasen. **~ up** *vt* zerreißen
tear[2] /tɪə(r)/ *n* Träne *f*. **~ful** *a* weinend. **~fully** *adv* unter Tränen. **~gas** *n* Tränengas *nt*
tease /ti:z/ *vt* necken
tea: ~-set *n* Teeservice *nt*. **~ shop** *n* Café *nt*. **~spoon** *n* Teelöffel *m*
teat /ti:t/ *n* Zitze *f*; (*on bottle*) Sauger *m*
'tea-towel *n* Geschirrtuch *nt*
technical /'teknɪkl/ *a* technisch; (*specialized*) fachlich. **~ity** /-'kælətɪ/ *n* technisches Detail *nt*; (*Jur*) Formfehler *m*. **~ly** *adv* technisch; (*strictly*) streng genommen. **~ term** *n* Fachausdruck *m*

technician /tek'nɪʃn/ *n* Techniker *m*

technique /tek'ni:k/ *n* Technik *f*

technological /teknə'lɒdʒɪkl/ *a*, **-ly** *adv* technologisch

technology /tek'nɒlədʒɪ/ *n* Technik *f*

teddy /'tedɪ/ *n* ~ **[bear]** Teddybär *m*

tedious /'ti:dɪəs/ *a* langweilig

tedium /'ti:dɪəm/ *n* Langeweile *f*

teenage /'ti:neɪdʒ/ *a* Teenager-; ~ **boy/girl** Junge *m*/Mädchen *nt* im Teenageralter. **~r** *n* Teenager *m*

teens /ti:nz/ *npl* **the** ~ die Teenagerjahre *pl*

teeter /'ti:tə(r)/ *vi* schwanken

teeth /ti:θ/ *see* **tooth**

teeth|e /ti:ð/ *vi* zahnen. **~ing troubles** *npl* (*fig*) Anfangsschwierigkeiten *pl*

teetotal /ti:'təʊtl/ *a* abstinent. **~ler** *n* Abstinenzler *m*

telebanking /'telɪbæŋkɪŋ/ *n* Telebanking *nt*

telecommunications /telɪkəmju:nɪ'keɪʃnz/ *npl* Fernmeldewesen *nt*

telegram /'telɪgræm/ *n* Telegramm *nt*

telegraph /'telɪgrɑ:f/ **pole** *n* Telegrafenmast *m*

telephone /'telɪfəʊn/ *n* Telefon *nt*; **be on the** ~ Telefon haben; (*be telephoning*) telefonieren ● *vt* anrufen ● *vi* telefonieren

telephone: ~ **booth** *n*, ~ **box** *n* Telefonzelle *f*. ~ **directory** *n* Telefonbuch *nt*. ~ **number** *n* Telefonnummer *f*

tele'photo /telɪ-/ *a* ~ **lens** Teleobjektiv *nt*

telescop|e /'telɪskəʊp/ *n* Teleskop *nt*, Fernrohr *nt*. **~ic** /-'skɒpɪk/ *a* (*collapsible*) ausziehbar

televise /'telɪvaɪz/ *vt* im Fernsehen übertragen

television /'telɪvɪʒn/ *n* Fernsehen *nt*; **watch** ~ fernsehen; ~ **[set]** Fernseher *m* [!]

teleworking *n* Telearbeit *f*

tell /tel/ *vt*/*i* (*pt*/*pp* **told**) sagen (**s.o.** jdm); (*relate*) erzählen; (*know*) wissen; (*distinguish*) erkennen; ~ **the time** die Uhr lesen; **time will** ~ das wird man erst sehen; **his age is beginning to** ~ sein Alter macht sich bemerkbar. ~ **off** *vt* ausschimpfen

telly /'telɪ/ *n* [!] = **television**

temp /temp/ *n* [!] Aushilfssekretärin *f*

temper /'tempə(r)/ *n* (*disposition*) Naturell *nt*; (*mood*) Laune *f*; (*anger*) Wut *f*; **lose one's** ~ wütend werden ● *vt* (*fig*) mäßigen

temperament /'temprəmənt/ *n* Temperament *nt*. **~al** /-'mentl/ *a* temperamentvoll; (*moody*) launisch

temperate /'tempərət/ *a* gemäßigt

temperature /'temprətʃə(r)/ *n* Temperatur *f*; **have** *or* **run a** ~ Fieber haben

temple[1] /'templ/ *n* Tempel *m*

temple[2] *n* (*Anat*) Schläfe *f*

tempo /'tempəʊ/ *n* Tempo *nt*

temporary /'tempərərɪ/ *a*, **-ily** *adv* vorübergehend; <*measure, building*> provisorisch

tempt /tempt/ *vt* verleiten; (*Relig*) versuchen; herausfordern <*fate*>; (*entice*) [ver]locken; **be ~ed** versucht sein (**to** zu). **~ation** /-'teɪʃn/ *n* Versuchung *f*. **~ing** *a* verlockend

ten /ten/ *a* zehn

tenaci|ous /tɪ'neɪʃəs/ *a*, **-ly** *adv* hartnäckig. **~ty** /-'næsətɪ/ *n* Hartnäckigkeit *f*

tenant /'tenənt/ *n* Mieter(in) *m(f)*; (*Comm*) Pächter(in) *m(f)*

tend /tend/ *vi* ~ **to do sth** dazu neigen, etw zu tun

tendency /'tendənsɪ/ *n* Tendenz *f*; (*inclination*) Neigung *f*

tender /'tendə(r)/ *a* zart; (*loving*) zärtlich; (*painful*) empfindlich. **~ly** *adv* zärtlich. **~ness** *n* Zartheit *f*; Zärtlichkeit *f*

tendon /'tendən/ *n* Sehne *f*

tenner /'tenə(r)/ *n* [!] Zehnpfundschein *m*

tennis /'tenɪs/ *n* Tennis *nt*. **~-court** *n* Tennisplatz *m*

tenor /'tenə(r)/ *n* Tenor *m*

tense /tens/ *a* (**-r, -st**) gespannt ● *vt* anspannen <*muscle*>

tension /'tenʃn/ *n* Spannung *f*

tent /tent/ *n* Zelt *nt*

tentative /'tentətɪv/ *a*, **-ly** *adv* vorläufig; (*hesitant*) zaghaft

tenterhooks /'tentəhʊks/ *npl* **be on ~** wie auf glühenden Kohlen sitzen

tenth /tenθ/ *a* zehnte(r,s) ● *n* Zehntel *nt*

tenuous /'tenjʊəs/ *a* schwach

tepid /'tepɪd/ *a* lauwarm

term /tɜ:m/ *n* Zeitraum *m*; (*Sch*) ≈ Halbjahr *nt*; (*Univ*) ≈ Semester *nt*; (*expression*) Ausdruck *m*; **~s** *pl* (*conditions*) Bedingungen *pl*; **in the short/long ~** kurz-/langfristig; **be on good/bad ~s** gut/nicht gut miteinander auskommen

terminal /'tɜ:mɪnl/ *a* End-; (*Med*) unheilbar ● *n* (*Aviat*) Terminal *m*; (*of bus*) Endstation *f*; (*on battery*) Pol *m*; (*Computing*) Terminal *nt*

terminat|e /'tɜ:mɪneɪt/ *vt* beenden; lösen <*contract*>; unterbrechen <*pregnancy*> ● *vi* enden

terminology /tɜ:mɪ'nɒlədʒɪ/ *n* Terminologie *f*

terminus /'tɜ:mɪnəs/ *n* (*pl* **-ni** /-naɪ/) Endstation *f*

terrace /'terəs/ *n* Terrasse *f*; (*houses*) Häuserreihe *f*. **~d house** *n* Reihenhaus *nt*

terrain /te'reɪn/ *n* Gelände *nt*

terrible /'terəbl/ *a*, **-bly** *adv* schrecklich

terrific /tə'rɪfɪk/ *a* [!] (*excellent*) sagenhaft; (*huge*) riesig

terri|fy /'terɪfaɪ/ *vt* (*pt/pp* **-ied**) Angst machen (+ *dat*); **be ~fied** Angst haben. **~fying** *a* Furcht erregend

territorial /terɪ'tɔ:rɪəl/ *a* Territorial-

territory /'terɪtərɪ/ *n* Gebiet *nt*

terror /'terə(r)/ *n* [panische] Angst *f*; (*Pol*) Terror *m*. **~ism** /-ɪzm/ *n* Terrorismus *m*. **~ist** /-ɪst/ *n* Terrorist *m*. **~ize** *vt* terrorisieren

terse /tɜ:s/ *a*, **-ly** *adv* kurz, knapp

test /test/ *n* Test *m*; (*Sch*) Klassenarbeit *f*; **put to the ~** auf die Probe stellen ● *vt* prüfen; (*examine*) untersuchen (**for** auf + *acc*)

testament /'testəmənt/ *n* Testament *nt*

testify /'testɪfaɪ/ *v* (*pt/pp* **-ied**) ● *vt* beweisen; **~ that** bezeugen, dass ● *vi* aussagen

testimonial /testɪ'məʊnɪəl/ *n* Zeugnis *nt*

testimony /'testɪmənɪ/ *n* Aussage *f*

'test-tube *n* Reagenzglas *nt*

tether /'teðə(r)/ *n* **be at the end of one's ~** am Ende seiner Kraft sein ● *vt* anbinden

text /tekst/ *n* Text *m* ● *vt/i* texten. **~book** *n* Lehrbuch *nt*

textile /'tekstaɪl/ *a* Textil- ● *n* **~s** *pl* Textilien *pl*

'text message *n* Textnachricht *f*

texture /'tekstʃə(r)/ *n* Beschaffenheit *f*; (*Tex*) Struktur *f*

Thai /taɪ/ *a* thailändisch. **~land** *n* Thailand *nt*

Thames /temz/ *n* Themse *f*

than /ðən, *betont* ðæn/ *conj* als

thank /θæŋk/ *vt* danken (+ *dat*); **~ you [very much]** danke [schön]. **~ful** *a*, **-ly** *adv* dankbar. **~less** *a* undankbar

thanks /θæŋks/ *npl* Dank *m*; **~!** [!] danke! **~ to** dank (+ *dat or gen*)

that /ðæt/

pl **those**

● *adjective*

····➤ der (*m*), die (*f*), das (*nt*), die (*pl*); (*just seen or experienced*) dieser (*m*), diese (*f*), dieses (*nt*), diese (*pl*). **I'll never forget that day** den Tag werde ich nie vergessen. **I liked that house** dieses Haus hat mir gut gefallen

● *pronoun*

····➤ der (*m*), die (*f*), das (*nt*), die (*pl*). **that is not true** das ist nicht wahr. **who is that in the garden?** wer ist das [da] im Garten? **I'll take that** ich nehme den/die/das. **I don't like those** die mag ich nicht. **is that you?** bist du es? **that is why** deshalb

····➤ **like that** so. **don't be like that!** sei doch nicht so! **a man like that** ein solcher Mann; so ein Mann [!]

····➤ (*after prepositions*) da .... **after that** danach. **with that** damit. **apart from that** außerdem

····➤ (*relative pronoun*) der (*m*), die (*f*), das (*nt*), die (*pl*). **the book that I'm reading** das Buch, das ich lese. **the people that you got it from** die Leute, von denen du es bekommen hast. **everyone that I know** jeder, den ich kenne. **that is all that I have** das ist alles, was ich habe

● *adverb*

····➤ so. **he's not 'that stupid** so blöd ist er [auch wieder] nicht. **it wasn't 'that bad** so schlecht war es auch nicht. **a nail about 'that long** ein etwa so langer Nagel

····➤ (*relative adverb*) der (*m*), die (*f*), das (*nt*), die (*pl*). **the day that I first met her** der Tag, an dem ich sie zum ersten Mal sah. **at the speed that he was going** bei der Geschwindigkeit, die er hatte

● *conjunction*

····➤ dass. **I don't think that he'll come** ich denke nicht, dass er kommt. **we know that you're right** wir wissen, dass du Recht hast. **I'm so tired that I can hardly walk** ich bin so müde, dass ich kaum gehen kann

····➤ **so that** (*purpose*) damit; (*result*) sodass. **he came earlier so that they would have more time** er kam früher, damit sie mehr Zeit hatten. **it was late, so that I had to catch the bus** es war spät, sodass ich den Bus nehmen musste

thatch /θætʃ/ *n* Strohdach *nt*. **~ed** *a* strohgedeckt

thaw /θɔː/ *n* Tauwetter *nt* ● *vt/i* auftauen; **it's ~ing** es taut

the /ðə, *vor einem Vokal* ðɪː/ *def art* der/die/das; (*pl*) die; **play ~ piano/violin** Klavier/Geige spielen ● *adv* **~ more ~ better** je mehr, desto besser; **all ~ better** umso besser

theatre /'θɪətə(r)/ *n* Theater *nt*; (*Med*) Operationssaal *m*

theatrical /θɪ'ætrɪkl/ *a* Theater-; (*showy*) theatralisch

theft /θeft/ *n* Diebstahl *m*

their /ðeə(r)/ *a* ihr

theirs /ðeəz/ *poss pron* ihre(r), ihrs; **a friend of ~** ein Freund von ihnen; **those are ~** die gehören ihnen

them /ðem/ *pron* (*acc*) sie; (*dat*) ihnen
theme /θi:m/ *n* Thema *nt*
them'selves *pron* selbst; (*refl*) sich; **by ~** allein
then /ðen/ *adv* dann; (*at that time in past*) damals; **by ~** bis dahin; **since ~** seitdem; **before ~** vorher; **from ~ on** von da an; **now and ~** dann und wann; **there and ~** auf der Stelle ● *a* damalig
theology /θɪ'ɒlədʒɪ/ *n* Theologie *f*
theoretical /θɪə'retɪkl/ *a*, **-ly** *adv* theoretisch
theory /'θɪərɪ/ *n* Theorie *f*; **in ~** theoretisch
therap|ist /'θerəpɪst/ *n* Therapeut(in) *m(f)*. **~y** *n* Therapie *f*
there /ðeə(r)/ *adv* da; (*with movement*) dahin, dorthin; **down/up ~** da unten/oben; **~ is/are** da ist/sind; (*in existence*) es gibt ● *int* **~, ~!** nun, nun!
there: ~abouts *adv* da [in der Nähe]; **or ~abouts** (*roughly*) ungefähr. **~fore** /-fɔ:(r)/ *adv* deshalb, also
thermometer /θə'mɒmɪtə(r)/ *n* Thermometer *nt*
Thermos (P) /'θɜ:məs/ *n* **~ [flask]** Thermosflasche (P) *f*
thermostat /'θɜ:məstæt/ *n* Thermostat *m*
these /ði:z/ *see* **this**
thesis /'θi:sɪs/ *n* (*pl* **-ses** /-si:z/) Dissertation *f*; (*proposition*) These *f*
they /ðeɪ/ *pron* sie; **~ say** (*generalizing*) man sagt
thick /θɪk/ *a* (**-er, -est**), **-ly** *adv* dick; (*dense*) dicht; <*liquid*> dickflüssig; (🅸 *stupid*) dumm ● *adv* dick ● *n* **in the ~ of** mitten in (+ *dat*). **~en** *vt* dicker machen; eindicken <*sauce*> ● *vi* dicker werden; <*fog:*> dichter werden; <*plot:*> kompliziert werden. **~ness** *n* Dicke *f*; (*density*) Dichte *f*; (*of liquid*) Dickflüssigkeit *f*
thief /θi:f/ *n* (*pl* **thieves**) Dieb(in) *m(f)*
thigh /θaɪ/ *n* Oberschenkel *m*
thimble /'θɪmbl/ *n* Fingerhut *m*
thin /θɪn/ *a* (**thinner, thinnest**), **-ly** *adv* dünn ● *adv* dünn ● *v* (*pt/pp* **thinned**) ● *vt* verdünnen <*liquid*> ● *vi* sich lichten
thing /θɪŋ/ *n* Ding *nt*; (*subject, affair*) Sache *f*; **~s** *pl* (*belongings*) Sachen *pl*; **for one ~** erstens; **just the ~!** genau das Richtige! **how are ~s?** wie gehts? **the latest ~** 🅸 der letzte Schrei
think /θɪŋk/ *vt/i* (*pt/pp* **thought**) denken (**about/of** an + *acc*); (*believe*) meinen; (*consider*) nachdenken; (*regard as*) halten für; **I ~ so** ich glaube schon; **what do you ~ of it?** was halten Sie davon? **~ over** *vt* sich (*dat*) überlegen. **~ up** *vt* sich (*dat*) ausdenken
third /θɜ:d/ *a* dritte(r,s) ● *n* Drittel *nt*. **~ly** *adv* drittens. **~-rate** *a* drittrangig
thirst /θɜ:st/ *n* Durst *m*. **~y** *a*, **-ily** *adv* durstig; **be ~y** Durst haben
thirteen /θɜ:'ti:n/ *a* dreizehn. **~th** *a* dreizehnte(r,s)
thirtieth /'θɜ:tɪɪθ/ *a* dreißigste(r,s)
thirty /'θɜ:tɪ/ *a* dreißig
this /ðɪs/ *a* (*pl* **these**) diese(r,s); (*pl*) diese; **~ one** diese(r,s) da; **I'll take ~** ich nehme diesen/diese/dieses; **~ evening/morning** heute Abend/Morgen; **these days** heutzutage ● *pron* (*pl* **these**) das, dies[es]; (*pl*) die, diese; **~ and that** dies und das; **~ or that** dieses oder das da; **like ~** so; **~ is Peter** das ist Peter; (*Teleph*)

hier [spricht] Peter; **who is ~?** wer ist das? (*Teleph, Amer*) wer ist am Apparat?

thistle /'θɪsl/ *n* Distel *f*

thorn /θɔ:n/ *n* Dorn *m*

thorough /'θʌrə/ *a* gründlich

thoroughbred *n* reinrassiges Tier *nt*; (*horse*) Rassepferd *nt*

thorough|ly /'θʌrəlɪ/ *adv* gründlich; (*completely*) völlig; (*extremely*) äußerst. **~ness** *n* Gründlichkeit *f*

those /ðəʊz/ *see* **that**

though /ðəʊ/ *conj* obgleich, obwohl; **as ~** als ob ● *adv* [!] doch

thought /θɔ:t/ *see* **think** ● *n* Gedanke *m*; (*thinking*) Denken *nt*. **~ful** *a*, **-ly** *adv* nachdenklich; (*considerate*) rücksichtsvoll. **~less** *a*, **-ly** *adv* gedankenlos

thousand /'θaʊznd/ *a* **one**/**a ~** [ein]tausend ● *n* Tausend *nt*. **~th** *a* tausendste(r,s) ● *n* Tausendstel *nt*

thrash /θræʃ/ *vt* verprügeln; (*defeat*) [vernichtend] schlagen

thread /θred/ *n* Faden *m*; (*of screw*) Gewinde *nt* ● *vt* einfädeln; auffädeln <*beads*>. **~bare** *a* fadenscheinig

threat /θret/ *n* Drohung *f*; (*danger*) Bedrohung *f*

threaten /'θretn/ *vt* drohen (+ *dat*); (*with weapon*) bedrohen; **~ s.o. with sth** jdm etw androhen ● *vi* drohen. **~ing** *a*, **-ly** *adv* drohend; (*ominous*) bedrohlich

three /θri:/ *a* drei. **~fold** *a* & *adv* dreifach

thresh /θreʃ/ *vt* dreschen

threshold /'θreʃəʊld/ *n* Schwelle *f*

threw /θru:/ *see* **throw**

thrift /θrɪft/ *n* Sparsamkeit *f*. **~y** *a* sparsam

thrill /θrɪl/ *n* Erregung *f*; [!] Nervenkitzel *m* ● *vt* (*excite*) erregen; **be ~ed with** sich sehr freuen über (+ *acc*). **~er** *n* Thriller *m*. **~ing** *a* erregend

thrive /θraɪv/ *vi* (*pt* **thrived** *or* **throve**, *pp* **thrived** *or* **thriven** /'θrɪvn/) gedeihen (**on** bei); <*business:*> florieren

throat /θrəʊt/ *n* Hals *m*; **cut s.o.'s ~** jdm die Kehle durchschneiden

throb /θrɒb/ *n* Pochen *nt* ● *vi* (*pt*/*pp* **throbbed**) pochen; (*vibrate*) vibrieren

throes /θrəʊz/ *npl* **in the ~ of** (*fig*) mitten in (+ *dat*)

throne /θrəʊn/ *n* Thron *m*

throttle /'θrɒtl/ *vt* erdrosseln

through /θru:/ *prep* durch (+ *acc*); (*during*) während (+ *gen*); (*Amer: up to & including*) bis einschließlich ● *adv* durch; **wet ~** durch und durch nass; **read sth ~** etw durchlesen ● *a* <*train*> durchgehend; **be ~** (*finished*) fertig sein; (*Teleph*) durch sein

throughout /θru:'aʊt/ *prep* **~ the country** im ganzen Land; **~ the night** die Nacht durch ● *adv* ganz; (*time*) die ganze Zeit

throve /θrəʊv/ *see* **thrive**

throw /θrəʊ/ *n* Wurf *m* ● *vt* (*pt* **threw**, *pp* **thrown**) werfen; schütten <*liquid*>; betätigen <*switch*>; abwerfen <*rider*>; ([!] *disconcert*) aus der Fassung bringen; [!] geben <*party*>; **~ sth to s.o.** jdm etw zuwerfen. **~ away** *vt* wegwerfen. **~ out** *vt* hinauswerfen; (**~ away**) wegwerfen; verwerfen <*plan*>. **~ up** *vt* hochwerfen ● *vi* sich übergeben

'throw-away *a* Wegwerf-

thrush /θrʌʃ/ *n* Drossel *f*

thrust /θrʌst/ *n* Stoß *m*; (*Phys*) Schub *m* ● *vt* (*pt*/*pp* **thrust**) stoßen; (*insert*) stecken

thud /θʌd/ *n* dumpfer Schlag *m*

thug /θʌg/ *n* Schläger *m*

thumb /θʌm/ *n* Daumen *m* ● *vt* ~ **a lift** [!] per Anhalter fahren. **~tack** *n* (*Amer*) Reißzwecke *f*

thump /θʌmp/ *n* Schlag *m*; (*noise*) dumpfer Schlag *m* ● *vt* schlagen ● *vi* hämmern; <*heart*:> pochen

thunder /ˈθʌndə(r)/ *n* Donner *m* ● *vi* donnern. **~clap** *n* Donnerschlag *m*. **~storm** *n* Gewitter *nt*. **~y** *a* gewittrig

Thursday /ˈθɜːzdeɪ/ *n* Donnerstag *m*

thus /ðʌs/ *adv* so

thwart /θwɔːt/ *vt* vereiteln; ~ **s.o.** jdm einen Strich durch die Rechnung machen

tick¹ /tɪk/ *n* **on~** [!] auf Pump

tick² *n* (*sound*) Ticken *nt*; (*mark*) Häkchen *nt*; ([!] *instant*) Sekunde *f* ● *vi* ticken ● *vt* abhaken. ~ **off** *vt* abhaken; [!] rüffeln

ticket /ˈtɪkɪt/ *n* Karte *f*; (*for bus, train*) Fahrschein *m*; (*Aviat*) Flugschein *m*; (*for lottery*) Los *nt*; (*for article deposited*) Schein *m*; (*label*) Schild *nt*; (*for library*) Lesekarte *f*; (*fine*) Strafzettel *m*. ~ **collector** *n* Fahrkartenkontrolleur *m*. ~ **office** *n* Fahrkartenschalter *m*; (*for entry*) Kasse *f*

tick|le /ˈtɪkl/ *n* Kitzeln *nt* ● *vt*/*i* kitzeln. **~lish** /ˈtɪklɪʃ/ *a* kitzlig

tidal /ˈtaɪdl/ *a* ~ **wave** Flutwelle *f*

tide /taɪd/ *n* Gezeiten *pl*; (*of events*) Strom *m*; **the ~ is in/out** es ist Flut/Ebbe ● *vt* ~ **s.o. over** jdm über die Runden helfen

tidiness /ˈtaɪdɪnɪs/ *n* Ordentlichkeit *f*

tidy /ˈtaɪdɪ/ *a* (**-ier, -iest**), **-ily** *adv* ordentlich ● *vt* ~ **[up]** aufräumen

tie /taɪ/ *n* Krawatte *f*, Schlips *m*; (*cord*) Schnur *f*; (*fig: bond*) Band *nt*; (*restriction*) Bindung *f*; (*Sport*) Unentschieden *nt*; (*in competition*) Punktgleichheit *f* ● *v* (*pres p* **tying**) ● *vt* binden; machen <*knot*> ● *vi* (*Sport*) unentschieden spielen; (*have equal scores, votes*) punktgleich sein. ~ **up** *vt* festbinden; verschnüren <*parcel*>; fesseln <*person*>; **be ~d up** (*busy*) beschäftigt sein

tier /tɪə(r)/ *n* Stufe *f*; (*of cake*) Etage *f*; (*in stadium*) Rang *m*

tiger /ˈtaɪgə(r)/ *n* Tiger *m*

tight /taɪt/ *a* (**-er, -est**), **-ly** *adv* fest; (*taut*) straff; <*clothes*> eng; <*control*> streng; ([!] *drunk*) blau ● *adv* fest

tighten /ˈtaɪtn/ *vt* fester ziehen; straffen <*rope*>; anziehen <*screw*>; verschärfen <*control*> ● *vi* sich spannen

tightrope *n* Hochseil *nt*

tights /taɪts/ *npl* Strumpfhose *f*

tile /taɪl/ *n* Fliese *f*; (*on wall*) Kachel *f*; (*on roof*) [Dach]ziegel *m* ● *vt* mit Fliesen auslegen; kacheln <*wall*>; decken <*roof*>

till¹ /tɪl/ *prep & conj* = **until**

till² *n* Kasse *f*

tilt /tɪlt/ *n* Neigung *f* ● *vt* kippen; [zur Seite] neigen <*head*> ● *vi* sich neigen

timber /ˈtɪmbə(r)/ *n* [Nutz]holz *nt*

time /taɪm/ *n* Zeit *f*; (*occasion*) Mal *nt*; (*rhythm*) Takt *m*; **~s** (*Math*) mal; **at ~s** manchmal; ~ **and again** immer wieder; **two at a ~** zwei auf einmal; **on ~** pünktlich; **in ~** rechtzeitig; (*eventually*) mit der Zeit; **in no ~** im Handumdrehen; **in a year's ~** in einem Jahr; **behind ~**

verspätet; **behind the ~s** rückständig; **for the ~ being** vorläufig; **what is the ~?** wie spät ist es? wie viel Uhr ist es? **did you have a nice ~?** hat es dir gut gefallen? ● *vt* stoppen <*race*>; **be well ~d** gut abgepaßt sein

time: ~ bomb *n* Zeitbombe *f*. **~less** *a* zeitlos. **~ly** *a* rechtzeitig. **~-switch** *n* Zeitschalter *m*. **~-table** *n* Fahrplan *m*; (*Sch*) Stundenplan *m*

timid /ˈtɪmɪd/ *a*, **-ly** *adv* scheu; (*hesitant*) zaghaft

timing /ˈtaɪmɪŋ/ *n* (*Sport, Techn*) Timing *nt*

tin /tɪn/ *n* Zinn *nt*; (*container*) Dose *f* ● *vt* (*pt/pp* **tinned**) in Dosen konservieren. **~ foil** *n* Stanniol *nt*; (*Culin*) Alufolie *f*

tinge /tɪndʒ/ *n* Hauch *m*

tingle /ˈtɪŋgl/ *vi* kribbeln

tinker /ˈtɪŋkə(r)/ *vi* herumbasteln (**with** an + *dat*)

tinkle /ˈtɪŋkl/ *n* Klingeln *nt* ● *vi* klingeln

tinned /tɪnd/ *a* Dosen-

ˈtin opener *n* Dosenöffner *m*

tinsel /ˈtɪnsl/ *n* Lametta *nt*

tint /tɪnt/ *n* Farbton *m* ● *vt* tönen

tiny /ˈtaɪnɪ/ *a* (**-ier, -iest**) winzig

tip[1] /tɪp/ *n* Spitze *f*

tip[2] *n* (*money*) Trinkgeld *nt*; (*advice*) Rat *m*, [!] Tipp *m*; (*for rubbish*) Müllhalde *f* ● *v* (*pt/pp* **tipped**) ● *vt* (*tilt*) kippen; (*reward*) Trinkgeld geben (**s.o.** jdm) ● *vi* kippen. **~ out** *vt* auskippen. **~ over** *vt/i* umkippen

tipped /tɪpt/ *a* Filter-

tipsy /ˈtɪpsɪ/ *a* [!] beschwipst

tiptoe /ˈtɪptəʊ/ *n* **on ~** auf Zehenspitzen

tiptop /tɪpˈtɒp/ *a* [!] erstklassig

tire /ˈtaɪə(r)/ *vt/i* ermüden. **~d** *a* müde; **be ~d of sth** etw satt haben; **~d out** [völlig] erschöpft. **~less** *a*, **-ly** *adv* unermüdlich. **~some** /-səm/ *a* lästig

tiring /ˈtaɪrɪŋ/ *a* ermüdend

tissue /ˈtɪʃuː/ *n* Gewebe *nt*; (*handkerchief*) Papiertaschentuch *nt*

tit /tɪt/ *n* (*bird*) Meise *f*

ˈtitbit *n* Leckerbissen *m*

title /ˈtaɪtl/ *n* Titel *m*

---

to /tuː, *unbetont* tə/

● *preposition*

····➤ (*destinations: most cases*) zu (+ *dat*). **go to work/the station** zur Arbeit/zum Bahnhof gehen. **from house to house** von Haus zu Haus. **go/come to s.o.** zu jdm gehen/kommen

····➤ (*with name of place or points of compass*) nach. **to Paris/Germany** nach Paris/Deutschland. **to Switzerland** in die Schweiz. **from East to West** von Osten nach Westen. **I've never been to Berlin** ich war noch nie in Berlin

····➤ (*to cinema, theatre, bed*) in (+ *acc*). **to bed with you!** ins Bett mit dir!

····➤ (*to wedding, party, university, the toilet*) auf (+ *acc*).

····➤ (*up to*) bis zu (+ *dat*). **to the end** bis zum Schluss. **to this day** bis heute. **5 to 6 pounds** 5 bis 6 Pfund

····➤ <*give, say, write*> + *dat*. **give/say sth to s.o.** jdm etw geben/sagen. **she wrote to him/the firm** sie hat ihm/an die Firma geschrieben

····➤ <*address, send, fasten*> an (+ *acc*). **she sent it to her brother** sie schickte es an ihren Bruder

····➤ (*in telling the time*) vor. **five to eight** fünf vor acht. **a quarter to ten** Viertel vor zehn

● *before infinitive*
····➤ (*after modal verb*) (*not translated*). **I want to go** ich will gehen. **he is learning to swim** er lernt schwimmen. **you have to** du musst [es tun]
····➤ (*after adjective*) zu. **it is easy to forget** es ist leicht zu vergessen
····➤ (*expressing purpose, result*) um ... zu. **he did it to annoy me** er tat es, um mich zu ärgern. **she was too tired to go** sie war zu müde um zu gehen
● *adverb*
····➤ **be to** <*door, window*> angelehnt sein. **pull a door to** eine Tür anlehnen
····➤ **to and fro** hin und her

toad /təʊd/ *n* Kröte *f*

toast /təʊst/ *n* Toast *m* ● *vt* toasten <*bread*>; (*drink a* ~ *to*) trinken auf (+ *acc*). **~er** *n* Toaster *m*

tobacco /tə'bækəʊ/ *n* Tabak *m*. **~nist's [shop]** *n* Tabakladen *m*

toboggan /tə'bɒgən/ *n* Schlitten *m* ● *vi* Schlitten fahren

today /tə'deɪ/ *n & adv* heute; **~ week** heute in einer Woche

toddler /'tɒdlə(r)/ *n* Kleinkind *nt*

toe /təʊ/ *n* Zeh *m*; (*of footwear*) Spitze *f* ● *vt* **~ the line** spuren. **~nail** *n* Zehennagel *m*

toffee /'tɒfɪ/ *n* Karamell *m & nt*

together /tə'geðə(r)/ *adv* zusammen; (*at the same time*) gleichzeitig

toilet /'tɔɪlɪt/ *n* Toilette *f*. **~ bag** *n* Kulturbeutel *m*. **~ paper** *n* Toilettenpapier *nt*

toiletries /'tɔɪlɪtrɪz/ *npl* Toilettenartikel *pl*

token /'təʊkən/ *n* Zeichen *nt*; (*counter*) Marke *f*; (*voucher*) Gutschein *m* ● *attrib* symbolisch

told /təʊld/ *see* **tell** ● *a* **all ~** insgesamt

tolerable /'tɒlərəbl/ *a*, **-bly** *adv* erträglich; (*not bad*) leidlich

toleran|ce /'tɒlərəns/ *n* Toleranz *f*. **~t** *a*, **-ly** *adv* tolerant

tolerate /'tɒləreɪt/ *vt* dulden, tolerieren; (*bear*) ertragen

toll /təʊl/ *n* Gebühr *f*; (*for road*) Maut *f* (*Aust*); **death ~** Zahl *f* der Todesopfer

tomato /tə'mɑːtəʊ/ *n* (*pl* **-es**) Tomate *f*

tomb /tuːm/ *n* Grabmal *nt*

'tombstone *n* Grabstein *m*

'tom-cat *n* Kater *m*

tomorrow /tə'mɒrəʊ/ *n & adv* morgen; **~ morning** morgen früh; **the day after ~** übermorgen; **see you ~!** bis morgen!

ton /tʌn/ *n* Tonne *f*; **~s of** [!] jede Menge

tone /təʊn/ *n* Ton *m*; (*colour*) Farbton *m* ● *vt* **~ down** dämpfen; (*fig*) mäßigen. **~ up** *vt* kräftigen; straffen <*muscles*>

tongs /tɒŋz/ *npl* Zange *f*

tongue /tʌŋ/ *n* Zunge *f*; **~ in cheek** [!] nicht ernst

tonic /'tɒnɪk/ *n* Tonikum *nt*; (*for hair*) Haarwasser *nt*; (*fig*) Wohltat *f*; **~ [water]** Tonic *nt*

tonight /tə'naɪt/ *n & adv* heute Nacht; (*evening*) heute Abend

tonne /tʌn/ *n* Tonne *f*

tonsil /'tɒnsl/ *n* (*Anat*) Mandel *f*. **~litis** /-sə'laɪtɪs/ *n* Mandelentzündung *f*

too /tuː/ *adv* zu; (*also*) auch; **~ much/little** zu viel/zu wenig

took /tʊk/ *see* **take**

tool /tuːl/ *n* Werkzeug *nt*; (*for gardening*) Gerät *nt*. **~bar** *n* Werkzeugleiste *f*

tooth /tuːθ/ *n* (*pl* **teeth**) Zahn *m*

tooth: ~ache *n* Zahnschmerzen *pl*. **~brush** *n* Zahnbürste *f*.

~less *a* zahnlos. **~paste** *n* Zahnpasta *f*. **~pick** *n* Zahnstocher *m*

top[1] /tɒp/ *n* (*toy*) Kreisel *m*

top[2] *n* oberer Teil *m*; (*apex*) Spitze *f*; (*summit*) Gipfel *m*; (*Sch*) Erste(r) *m/f*; (*top part or half*) Oberteil *nt*; (*head*) Kopfende *nt*; (*of road*) oberes Ende *nt*; (*upper surface*) Oberfläche *f*; (*lid*) Deckel *m*; (*of bottle*) Verschluss *m*; (*garment*) Top *nt*; **at the/on ~** oben; **on ~ of** oben auf (+ *dat/acc*); **on ~ of that** (*besides*) obendrein; **from ~ to bottom** von oben bis unten ● *a* oberste(r,s); (*highest*) höchste(r,s); (*best*) beste(r,s) ● *vt* (*pt/pp* **topped**) an erster Stelle stehen auf (+ *dat*) <*list*>; (*exceed*) übersteigen; (*remove the ~ of*) die Spitze abschneiden von. **~ up** *vt* nachfüllen, auffüllen

top: ~ 'hat *n* Zylinder[hut] *m*. **~-heavy** *a* kopflastig

topic /ˈtɒpɪk/ *n* Thema *nt*. **~al** *a* aktuell

topple /ˈtɒpl/ *vt/i* umstürzen

torch /tɔːtʃ/ *n* Taschenlampe *f*; (*flaming*) Fackel *f*

tore /tɔː(r)/ *see* **tear**[1]

torment[1] /ˈtɔːment/ *n* Qual *f*

torment[2] /tɔːˈment/ *vt* quälen

torn /tɔːn/ *see* **tear**[1] ● *a* zerrissen

torpedo /tɔːˈpiːdəʊ/ *n* (*pl* **-es**) Torpedo *m* ● *vt* torpedieren

torrent /ˈtɒrənt/ *n* reißender Strom *m*. **~ial** /təˈrenʃl/ *a* <*rain*> wolkenbruchartig

tortoise /ˈtɔːtəs/ *n* Schildkröte *f*. **~shell** *n* Schildpatt *nt*

tortuous /ˈtɔːtjʊəs/ *a* verschlungen; (*fig*) umständlich

torture /ˈtɔːtʃə(r)/ *n* Folter *f*; (*fig*) Qual *f* ● *vt* foltern; (*fig*) quälen

toss /tɒs/ *vt* werfen; (*into the air*) hochwerfen; (*shake*) schütteln; (*unseat*) abwerfen; mischen <*salad*>; wenden <*pancake*>; **~ a coin** mit einer Münze losen ● *vi* **~ and turn** (*in bed*) sich [schlaflos] im Bett wälzen

tot[1] /tɒt/ *n* kleines Kind *nt*; (! *of liquor*) Gläschen *nt*

tot[2] *vt* (*pt/pp* **totted**) **~ up** ! zusammenzählen

total /ˈtəʊtl/ *a* gesamt; (*complete*) völlig, total ● *n* Gesamtzahl *f*; (*sum*) Gesamtsumme *f* ● *vt* (*pt/pp* **totalled**); (*amount to*) sich belaufen auf (+ *acc*)

totalitarian /təʊtælɪˈteərɪən/ *a* totalitär

totally /ˈtəʊtəlɪ/ *adv* völlig, total

totter /ˈtɒtə(r)/ *vi* taumeln

touch /tʌtʃ/ *n* Berührung *f*; (*sense*) Tastsinn *m*; (*Mus*) Anschlag *m*; (*contact*) Kontakt *m*; (*trace*) Spur *f*; (*fig*) Anflug *m*; **get/be in ~** sich in Verbindung setzen/in Verbindung stehen (**with** mit) ● *vt* berühren; (*get hold of*) anfassen; (*lightly*) tippen auf/an (+ *acc*); (*brush against*) streifen [gegen]; (*fig: move*) rühren; anrühren <*food, subject*>; **don't ~ that!** fass das nicht an! ● *vi* sich berühren; **~ on** (*fig*) berühren. **~ down** *vi* (*Aviat*) landen. **~ up** *vt* ausbessern

touch|ing /ˈtʌtʃɪŋ/ *a* rührend. **~y** *a* empfindlich

tough /tʌf/ *a* (**-er, -est**) zäh; (*severe, harsh*) hart; (*difficult*) schwierig; (*durable*) strapazierfähig

toughen /ˈtʌfn/ *vt* härten; **~ up** abhärten

tour /tʊə(r)/ *n* Reise *f*, Tour *f*; (*of building, town*) Besichtigung *f*; (*Theat, Sport*) Tournee *f*; (*of duty*) Dienstzeit *f* ● *vt* fahren durch ● *vi* herumreisen

touris|m /ˈtʊərɪzm/ *n* Tourismus *m*, Fremdenverkehr *m*. **~t** /-rɪst/ *n* Tourist(in) *m(f)* ● *attrib*

Touristen-. **~t office** *n* Fremdenverkehrsbüro *nt*
tournament /'tʊənəmənt/ *n* Turnier *nt*
'tour operator *n* Reiseveranstalter *m*
tousle /'taʊzl/ *vt* zerzausen
tow /təʊ/ *n* **give s.o./a car a ~** jdn/ein Auto abschleppen ● *vt* schleppen; ziehen <*trailer*>
toward[s] /tə'wɔ:dz/ *prep* zu (+ *dat*); (*with time*) gegen (+ *acc*); (*with respect to*) gegenüber (+ *dat*)
towel /'taʊəl/ *n* Handtuch *nt*. **~ling** *n* (*Tex*) Frottee *nt*
tower /'taʊə(r)/ *n* Turm *m* ● *vi* **~ above** überragen. **~ block** *n* Hochhaus *nt*. **~ing** *a* hoch aufragend
town /taʊn/ *n* Stadt *f*. **~ 'hall** *n* Rathaus *nt*
tow-rope *n* Abschleppseil *nt*
toxic /'tɒksɪk/ *a* giftig
toy /tɔɪ/ *n* Spielzeug *nt* ● *vi* **~ with** spielen mit; stochern in (+ *dat*) <*food*>. **~shop** *n* Spielwarengeschäft *nt*
trace /treɪs/ *n* Spur *f* ● *vt* folgen (+ *dat*); (*find*) finden; (*draw*) zeichnen; (*with tracing-paper*) durchpausen
track /træk/ *n* Spur *f*; (*path*) [unbefestigter] Weg *m*; (*Sport*) Bahn *f*; (*Rail*) Gleis *nt*; **keep ~ of** im Auge behalten ● *vt* verfolgen. **~ down** *vt* aufspüren; (*find*) finden
'tracksuit *n* Trainingsanzug *m*
tractor /'træktə(r)/ *n* Traktor *m*
trade /treɪd/ *n* Handel *m*; (*line of business*) Gewerbe *nt*; (*business*) Geschäft *nt*; (*craft*) Handwerk *nt*; **by ~** von Beruf ● *vt* tauschen; **~ in** (*give in part exchange*) in Zahlung geben ● *vi* handeln (**in** mit)
'trade mark *n* Warenzeichen *nt*
trader /'treɪdə(r)/ *n* Händler *m*
trade: ~ 'union *n* Gewerkschaft *f*. **~ 'unionist** *n* Gewerkschaftler(in) *m(f)*
trading /'treɪdɪŋ/ *n* Handel *m*
tradition /trə'dɪʃn/ *n* Tradition *f*. **~al** *a*, **-ly** *adv* traditionell
traffic /'træfɪk/ *n* Verkehr *m*; (*trading*) Handel *m*
traffic: ~ circle *n* (*Amer*) Kreisverkehr *m*. **~ jam** *n* [Verkehrs]stau *m*. **~ lights** *npl* [Verkehrs]ampel *f*. **~ warden** *n* ≈ Hilfspolizist *m*; (*woman*) Politesse *f*
tragedy /'trædʒədɪ/ *n* Tragödie *f*
tragic /'trædʒɪk/ *a*, **-ally** *adv* tragisch
trail /treɪl/ *n* Spur *f*; (*path*) Weg *m*, Pfad *m* ● *vi* schleifen; <*plant:*> sich ranken ● *vt* verfolgen, folgen (+ *dat*); (*drag*) schleifen
trailer /'treɪlə(r)/ *n* (*Auto*) Anhänger *m*; (*Amer: caravan*) Wohnwagen *m*; (*film*) Vorschau *f*
train /treɪn/ *n* Zug *m*; (*of dress*) Schleppe *f* ● *vt* ausbilden; (*Sport*) trainieren; (*aim*) richten auf (+ *acc*); erziehen <*child*>; abrichten/(*to do tricks*) dressieren <*animal*>; ziehen <*plant*> ● *vi* eine Ausbildung machen; (*Sport*) trainieren. **~ed** *a* ausgebildet
trainee /treɪ'ni:/ *n* Auszubildende(r) *m/f*; (*Techn*) Praktikant(in) *m(f)*
train|er /'treɪnə(r)/ *n* (*Sport*) Trainer *m*; (*in circus*) Dompteur *m*; **~ers** *pl* Trainingsschuhe *pl*. **~ing** *n* Ausbildung *f*; (*Sport*) Training *nt*; (*of animals*) Dressur *f*
trait /treɪt/ *n* Eigenschaft *f*
traitor /'treɪtə(r)/ *n* Verräter *m*
tram /træm/ *n* Straßenbahn *f*
tramp /træmp/ *n* Landstreicher *m* ● *vi* stapfen; (*walk*) marschieren

trample /'træmpl/ *vt/i* trampeln
trance /trɑ:ns/ *n* Trance *f*
tranquil /'træŋkwɪl/ *a* ruhig. **~lity** /-'kwɪlətɪ/ *n* Ruhe *f*
tranquillizer /'træŋkwɪlaɪzə(r)/ *n* Beruhigungsmittel *nt*
transaction /træn'zækʃn/ *n* Transaktion *f*
transcend /træn'send/ *vt* übersteigen
transfer[1] /'trænsfɜ:(r)/ *n* (*see* **transfer[2]**) Übertragung *f*; Verlegung *f*; Versetzung *f*; Überweisung *f*; (*Sport*) Transfer *m*; (*design*) Abziehbild *nt*
transfer[2] /træns'fɜ:(r)/ *v* (*pt/pp* **transferred**) ● *vt* übertragen; verlegen <*firm, prisoners*>; versetzen <*employee*>; überweisen <*money*>; (*Sport*) transferieren ● *vi* [über]wechseln; (*when travelling*) umsteigen
transform /træns'fɔ:m/ *vt* verwandeln. **~ation** /-fə'meɪʃn/ *n* Verwandlung *f*. **~er** *n* Transformator *m*
transfusion /træns'fju:ʒn/ *n* Transfusion *f*
transistor /træn'zɪstə(r)/ *n* Transistor *m*
transit /'trænsɪt/ *n* Transit *m*; (*of goods*) Transport *m*; **in ~** <*goods*> auf dem Transport
transition /træn'sɪʒn/ *n* Übergang *m*. **~al** *a* Übergangs-
translat|e /træns'leɪt/ *vt* übersetzen. **~ion** /-'leɪʃn/ *n* Übersetzung *f*. **~or** *n* Übersetzer(in) *m(f)*
transmission /trænz'mɪʃn/ *n* Übertragung *f*
transmit /trænz'mɪt/ *vt* (*pt/pp* **transmitted**) übertragen. **~ter** *n* Sender *m*
transparen|cy /træns'pærənsɪ/ *n* (*Phot*) Dia *nt*. **~t** *a* durchsichtig
transplant[1] /'trænsplɑ:nt/ *n* Verpflanzung *f*, Transplantation *f*
transplant[2] /træns'plɑ:nt/ *vt* umpflanzen; (*Med*) verpflanzen
transport[1] /'trænspɔ:t/ *n* Transport *m*
transport[2] /træn'spɔ:t/ *vt* transportieren. **~ation** /-'teɪʃn/ *n* Transport *m*
transpose /træns'pəʊz/ *vt* umstellen
trap /træp/ *n* Falle *f*; (🄿 *mouth*) Klappe *f*; **pony and ~** Einspänner *m* ● *vt* (*pt/pp* **trapped**) [mit einer Falle] fangen; (*jam*) einklemmen; **be ~ped** festsitzen; (*shut in*) eingeschlossen sein. **~'door** *n* Falltür *f*
trash /træʃ/ *n* Schund *m*; (*rubbish*) Abfall *m*; (*nonsense*) Quatsch *m*. **~can** *n* (*Amer*) Mülleimer *m*. **~y** *a* Schund-
trauma /'trɔ:mə/ *n* Trauma *nt*. **~tic** /-'mætɪk/ *a* traumatisch
travel /'trævl/ *n* Reisen *nt* ● *v* (*pt/pp* **travelled**) ● *vi* reisen; (*go in vehicle*) fahren; <*light, sound*:> sich fortpflanzen; (*Techn*) sich bewegen ● *vt* bereisen; fahren <*distance*>. **~ agency** *n* Reisebüro *nt*. **~ agent** *n* Reisebürokaufmann *m*
traveller /'trævələ(r)/ *n* Reisende(r) *m/f*; (*Comm*) Vertreter *m*; **~s** *pl* (*gypsies*) Zigeuner *pl*. **~'s cheque** *n* Reisescheck *m*
trawler /'trɔ:lə(r)/ *n* Fischdampfer *m*
tray /treɪ/ *n* Tablett *nt*; (*for baking*) [Back]blech *nt*; (*for documents*) Ablagekorb *m*
treacher|ous /'tretʃərəs/ *a* treulos; (*dangerous, deceptive*) tückisch. **~y** *n* Verrat *m*
tread /tred/ *n* Schritt *m*; (*step*) Stufe *f*; (*of tyre*) Profil *nt* ● *v* (*pt* **trod**, *pp* **trodden**) ● *vi* (*walk*)

gehen; ~ **on/in** treten auf/ in (+ *acc*) ● *vt* treten
treason /'tri:zn/ *n* Verrat *m*
treasure /'treʒə(r)/ *n* Schatz *m* ● *vt* in Ehren halten. **~r** *n* Kassenwart *m*
treasury /'treʒərɪ/ *n* Schatzkammer *f*; **the T~** das Finanzministerium
treat /tri:t/ *n* [besonderes] Vergnügen *nt* ● *vt* behandeln; **~ s.o. to sth** jdm etw spendieren
treatment /'tri:tmənt/ *n* Behandlung *f*
treaty /'tri:tɪ/ *n* Vertrag *m*
treble /'trebl/ *a* dreifach; **~ the amount** dreimal so viel ● *n* (*Mus*) Diskant *m*; (*voice*) Sopran *m* ● *vt* verdreifachen ● *vi* sich verdreifachen
tree /tri:/ *n* Baum *m*
trek /trek/ *n* Marsch *m* ● *vi* (*pt*/ *pp* **trekked**) latschen
trellis /'trelɪs/ *n* Gitter *nt*
tremble /'trembl/ *vi* zittern
tremendous /trɪ'mendəs/ *a*, **-ly** *adv* gewaltig; (🄸 *excellent*) großartig
tremor /'tremə(r)/ *n* Zittern *nt*; **[earth]** ~ Beben *nt*
trench /trentʃ/ *n* Graben *m*; (*Mil*) Schützengraben *m*
trend /trend/ *n* Tendenz *f*; (*fashion*) Trend *m*. **~y** *a* (**-ier, -iest**) 🄸 modisch
trepidation /trepɪ'deɪʃn/ *n* Beklommenheit *f*
trespass /'trespəs/ *vi* **~ on** unerlaubt betreten
trial /'traɪəl/ *n* (*Jur*) [Gerichts]verfahren *nt*, Prozess *m*; (*test*) Probe *f*; (*ordeal*) Prüfung *f*; **be on ~** auf Probe sein; (*Jur*) angeklagt sein (**for** wegen); **by ~ and error** durch Probieren
triang|le /'traɪæŋgl/ *n* Dreieck *nt*; (*Mus*) Triangel *m*. **~ular** /-'æŋgjʊlə(r)/ *a* dreieckig
tribe /traɪb/ *n* Stamm *m*
tribunal /traɪ'bju:nl/ *n* Schiedsgericht *nt*
tributary /'trɪbjʊtərɪ/ *n* Nebenfluss *m*
tribute /'trɪbju:t/ *n* Tribut *m*; **pay ~** Tribut zollen (**to** *dat*)
trick /trɪk/ *n* Trick *m*; (*joke*) Streich *m*; (*Cards*) Stich *m*; (*feat of skill*) Kunststück *nt* ● *vt* täuschen, 🄸 hereinlegen
trickle /'trɪkl/ *vi* rinnen
trick|ster /'trɪkstə(r)/ *n* Schwindler *m*. **~y** *a* (**-ier, -iest**) *a* schwierig
tricycle /'traɪsɪkl/ *n* Dreirad *nt*
tried /traɪd/ *see* **try**
trifl|e /'traɪfl/ *n* Kleinigkeit *f*; (*Culin*) Trifle *nt*. **~ing** *a* unbedeutend
trigger /'trɪgə(r)/ *n* Abzug *m*; (*fig*) Auslöser *m* ● *vt* **~ [off]** auslösen
trim /trɪm/ *a* (**trimmer, trimmest**) gepflegt ● *n* (*cut*) Nachschneiden *nt*; (*decoration*) Verzierung *f*; (*condition*) Zustand *m* ● *vt* schneiden; (*decorate*) besetzen. **~ming** *n* Besatz *m*; **~mings** *pl* (*accessories*) Zubehör *nt*; (*decorations*) Verzierungen *pl*
trio /'tri:əʊ/ *n* Trio *nt*
trip /trɪp/ *n* Reise *f*; (*excursion*) Ausflug *m* ● *v* (*pt*/*pp* **tripped**) ● *vt* **~ s.o. up** jdm ein Bein stellen ● *vi* stolpern (**on**/**over** über + *acc*)
tripe /traɪp/ *n* Kaldaunen *pl*; (*nonsense*) Quatsch *m*
triple /'trɪpl/ *a* dreifach ● *vt* verdreifachen ● *vi* sich verdreifachen
triplets /'trɪplɪts/ *npl* Drillinge *pl*
triplicate /'trɪplɪkət/ *n* **in ~** in dreifacher Ausfertigung
tripod /'traɪpɒd/ *n* Stativ *nt*
tripper /'trɪpə(r)/ *n* Ausflügler *m*
trite /traɪt/ *a* banal

triumph /'traɪʌmf/ *n* Triumph *m* ● *vi* triumphieren (**over** über + *acc*). **~ant** /-'ʌmfnt/ *a*, **-ly** *adv* triumphierend

trivial /'trɪvɪəl/ *a* belanglos. **~ity** /-'ælətɪ/ *n* Belanglosigkeit *f*

trod, trodden /trɒd, 'trɒdn/ *see* **tread**

trolley /'trɒlɪ/ *n* (*for food*) Servierwagen *m*; (*for shopping*) Einkaufswagen *m*; (*for luggage*) Kofferkuli *m*; (*Amer: tram*) Straßenbahn *f*

trombone /trɒm'bəʊn/ *n* Posaune *f*

troop /tru:p/ *n* Schar *f*; **~s** *pl* Truppen *pl*

trophy /'trəʊfɪ/ *n* Trophäe *f*; (*in competition*) ≈ Pokal *m*

tropic|s /'trɒpɪks/ *npl* Tropen *pl*. **~al** *a* tropisch; <*fruit*> Süd-

trot /trɒt/ *n* Trab *m* ● *vi* (*pt/pp* **trotted**) traben

trouble /'trʌbl/ *n* Ärger *m*; (*difficulties*) Schwierigkeiten *pl*; (*inconvenience*) Mühe *f*; (*conflict*) Unruhe *f*; (*Med*) Beschwerden *pl*; (*Techn*) Probleme *pl*; **get into ~** Ärger bekommen; **take ~** sich (*dat*) Mühe geben ● *vt* (*disturb*) stören; (*worry*) beunruhigen ● *vi* sich bemühen. **~-maker** *n* Unruhestifter *m*. **~some** /-səm/ *a* schwierig; <*flies, cough*> lästig

trough /trɒf/ *n* Trog *m*

troupe /tru:p/ *n* Truppe *f*

trousers /'traʊzəz/ *npl* Hose *f*

trousseau /'tru:səʊ/ *n* Aussteuer *f*

trout /traʊt/ *n inv* Forelle *f*

trowel /'traʊəl/ *n* Kelle *f*

truant /'tru:ənt/ *n* **play ~** die Schule schwänzen

truce /tru:s/ *n* Waffenstillstand *m*

truck /trʌk/ *n* Last[kraft]wagen *m*; (*Rail*) Güterwagen *m*

trudge /trʌdʒ/ *vi* latschen

true /tru:/ *a* (**-r, -st**) wahr; (*loyal*) treu; (*genuine*) echt; **come ~** in Erfüllung gehen; **is that ~?** stimmt das?

truly /'tru:lɪ/ *adv* wirklich; (*faithfully*) treu; **Yours ~** Mit freundlichen Grüßen

trump /trʌmp/ *n* (*Cards*) Trumpf *m* ● *vt* übertrumpfen

trumpet /'trʌmpɪt/ *n* Trompete *f*. **~er** *n* Trompeter *m*

truncheon /'trʌntʃn/ *n* Schlagstock *m*

trunk /trʌŋk/ *n* [Baum]stamm *m*; (*body*) Rumpf *m*; (*of elephant*) Rüssel *m*; (*for travelling*) [Übersee]koffer *m*; (*Amer: of car*) Kofferraum *m*; **~s** *pl* Badehose *f*

trust /trʌst/ *n* Vertrauen *nt*; (*group of companies*) Trust *m*; (*organization*) Treuhandgesellschaft *f*; (*charitable*) Stiftung *f* ● *vt* trauen (+ *dat*), vertrauen (+ *dat*); (*hope*) hoffen ● *vi* vertrauen (**in**/**to** auf + *acc*)

trustee /trʌs'ti:/ *n* Treuhänder *m*

'trust|ful /'trʌstfl/ *a*, **-ly** *adv*, **~ing** *a* vertrauensvoll. **~worthy** *a* vertrauenswürdig

truth /tru:θ/ *n* (*pl* **-s** /tru:ðz/) Wahrheit *f*. **~ful** *a*, **-ly** *adv* ehrlich

try /traɪ/ *n* Versuch *m* ● *v* (*pt/pp* **tried**) ● *vt* versuchen; (*sample, taste*) probieren; (*be a strain on*) anstrengen; (*Jur*) vor Gericht stellen; verhandeln <*case*> ● *vi* versuchen; (*make an effort*) sich bemühen. **~ on** *vt* anprobieren; aufprobieren <*hat*>. **~ out** *vt* ausprobieren

trying /'traɪɪŋ/ *a* schwierig

T-shirt /'ti:-/ *n* T-Shirt *nt*

tub /tʌb/ *n* Kübel *m*; (*carton*) Becher *m*; (*bath*) Wanne *f*

tuba /'tju:bə/ *n* (*Mus*) Tuba *f*

tubby /'tʌbɪ/ *a* (**-ier, -iest**) rundlich
tube /tju:b/ *n* Röhre *f*; (*pipe*) Rohr *nt*; (*flexible*) Schlauch *m*; (*of toothpaste*) Tube *f*; (*Rail* [!]) U-Bahn *f*
tuberculosis /tju:bɜ:kjʊ'ləʊsɪs/ *n* Tuberkulose *f*
tubular /'tju:bjʊlə(r)/ *a* röhrenförmig
tuck /tʌk/ *n* Saum *m*; (*decorative*) Biese *f* ● *vt* (*put*) stecken. ~ **in** *vt* hineinstecken; ~ **s.o. in** *or* **up** jdn zudecken ● *vi* ([!] *eat*) zulangen
Tuesday /'tju:zdeɪ/ *n* Dienstag *m*
tuft /tʌft/ *n* Büschel *nt*
tug /tʌg/ *n* Ruck *m*; (*Naut*) Schleppdampfer *m* ● *v* (*pt/pp* **tugged**) ● *vt* ziehen ● *vi* zerren (**at** an + *dat*)
tuition /tju:'ɪʃn/ *n* Unterricht *m*
tulip /'tju:lɪp/ *n* Tulpe *f*
tumble /'tʌmbl/ *n* Sturz *m* ● *vi* fallen. ~**down** *a* verfallen. ~-**drier** *n* Wäschetrockner *m*
tumbler /'tʌmblə(r)/ *n* Glas *nt*
tummy /'tʌmɪ/ *n* [!] Bauch *m*
tumour /'tju:mə(r)/ *n* Tumor *m*
tumult /'tju:mʌlt/ *n* Tumult *m*
tuna /'tju:nə/ *n* Thunfisch *m*
tune /tju:n/ *n* Melodie *f*; **out of** ~ <*instrument*> verstimmt ● *vt* stimmen; (*Techn*) einstellen. ~ **in** *vt* einstellen: ● *vi* ~ **in to a station** einen Sender einstellen. ~ **up** *vi* (*Mus*) stimmen
tuneful /'tju:nfl/ *a* melodisch
Tunisia /tju:'nɪzɪə/ *n* Tunesien *nt*
tunnel /'tʌnl/ *n* Tunnel *m* ● *vi* (*pt/pp* **tunnelled**) einen Tunnel graben
turban /'tɜ:bən/ *n* Turban *m*
turbine /'tɜ:baɪn/ *n* Turbine *f*
turbulen|ce /'tɜ:bjʊləns/ *n* Turbulenz *f*. ~**t** *a* stürmisch
turf /tɜ:f/ *n* Rasen *m*; (*segment*) Rasenstück *nt*
Turk /tɜ:k/ *n* Türke *m*/Türkin *f*
turkey /'tɜ:kɪ/ *n* Truthahn *m*
Turk|ey *n* die Türkei. ~**ish** *a* türkisch; **the** ~**ish** die Türken
turmoil /'tɜ:mɔɪl/ *n* Aufruhr *m*; (*confusion*) Durcheinander *nt*
turn /tɜ:n/ *n* (*rotation*) Drehung *f*; (*bend*) Kurve *f*; (*change of direction*) Wende *f*; (*Theat*) Nummer *f*; ([!] *attack*) Anfall *m*; **do s.o. a good** ~ jdm einen guten Dienst erweisen; **take** ~**s** sich abwechseln; **in** ~ der Reihe nach; **out of** ~ außer der Reihe; **it's your** ~ du bist an der Reihe ● *vt* drehen; (~ *over*) wenden; (*reverse*) umdrehen; (*Techn*) drechseln <*wood*>; ~ **the page** umblättern; ~ **the corner** um die Ecke biegen ● *vi* sich drehen; (~ *round*) sich umdrehen; <*car:*> wenden; <*leaves:*> sich färben: <*weather:*> umschlagen; (*become*) werden; ~ **right/left** nach rechts/links abbiegen; ~ **to s.o.** sich an jdn wenden. ~ **away** *vt* abweisen ● *vi* sich abwenden. ~ **down** *vt* herunterschlagen <*collar*>; herunterdrehen <*heat, gas*>; leiser stellen <*sound*>; (*reject*) ablehnen; abweisen <*person*>. ~ **in** *vt* einschlagen <*edges*> ● *vi* <*car:*> einbiegen; ([!] *go to bed*) ins Bett gehen. ~ **off** *vt* zudrehen <*tap*>; ausschalten <*light, radio*>; abstellen <*water, gas, engine, machine*> ● *vi* abbiegen. ~ **on** *vt* aufdrehen <*tap*>; einschalten <*light, radio*>; anstellen <*water, gas, engine, machine*>. ~ **out** *vt* (*expel*) vertreiben, [!] hinauswerfen; ausschalten <*light*>; abdrehen <*gas*>; (*produce*) produzieren; (*empty*) ausleeren; [gründlich] aufräumen <*room, cupboard*> ● *vi* (*go out*) hinausgehen; (*transpire*) sich herausstellen. ~ **over** *vt*

umdrehen. ~ **up** *vt* hochschlagen <*collar*>; aufdrehen <*heat, gas*>; lauter stellen <*sound, radio*> ● *vi* auftauchen

turning /ˈtɜːnɪŋ/ *n* Abzweigung *f*. **~-point** *n* Wendepunkt *m*

turnip /ˈtɜːnɪp/ *n* weiße Rübe *f*

turn: ~-out *n* (*of people*) Beteiligung *f*. **~over** *n* (*Comm*) Umsatz *m*; (*of staff*) Personalwechsel *m*. **~pike** *n* (*Amer*) gebührenpflichtige Autobahn *f*. **~table** *n* Drehscheibe *f*; (*on record player*) Plattenteller *m*. **~-up** *n* [Hosen]aufschlag *m*

turquoise /ˈtɜːkwɔɪz/ *a* türkis[farben] ● *n* (*gem*) Türkis *m*

turret /ˈtʌrɪt/ *n* Türmchen *nt*

turtle /ˈtɜːtl/ *n* Seeschildkröte *f*

tusk /tʌsk/ *n* Stoßzahn *m*

tutor /ˈtjuːtə(r)/ *n* [Privat]lehrer *m*

tuxedo /tʌkˈsiːdəʊ/ *n* (*Amer*) Smoking *m*

TV /tiːˈviː/ *abbr of* **television**

tweed /twiːd/ *n* Tweed *m*

tweezers /ˈtwiːzəz/ *npl* Pinzette *f*

twelfth /twelfθ/ *a* zwölfter(r,s)

twelve /twelv/ *a* zwölf

twentieth /ˈtwentɪɪθ/ *a* zwanzigste(r,s)

twenty /ˈtwentɪ/ *a* zwanzig

twice /twaɪs/ *adv* zweimal

twig /twɪg/ *n* Zweig *m*

twilight /ˈtwaɪ-/ *n* Dämmerlicht *nt*

twin /twɪn/ *n* Zwilling *m* ● *attrib* Zwillings-

twine /twaɪn/ *n* Bindfaden *m*

twinge /twɪndʒ/ *n* Stechen *nt*; ~ **of conscience** Gewissensbisse *pl*

twinkle /ˈtwɪŋkl/ *n* Funkeln *nt* ● *vi* funkeln

twin 'town *n* Partnerstadt *f*

twirl /twɜːl/ *vt/i* herumwirbeln

twist /twɪst/ *n* Drehung *f*; (*curve*) Kurve *f*; (*unexpected occurrence*) überraschende Wendung *f* ● *vt* drehen; (*distort*) verdrehen; (! *swindle*) beschummeln; ~ **one's ankle** sich (*dat*) den Knöchel verrenken ● *vi* sich drehen; <*road*:> sich winden. **~er** *n* ! Schwindler *m*

twit /twɪt/ *n* ! Trottel *m*

twitch /twɪtʃ/ *n* Zucken *nt* ● *vi* zucken

twitter /ˈtwɪtə(r)/ *n* Zwitschern *nt* ● *vi* zwitschern

two /tuː/ *a* zwei

two: ~-faced *a* falsch. **~-piece** *a* zweiteilig. **~-way** *a* **~-way traffic** Gegenverkehr *m*

tycoon /taɪˈkuːn/ *n* Magnat *m*

tying /ˈtaɪɪŋ/ *see* **tie**

type /taɪp/ *n* Art *f*, Sorte *f*; (*person*) Typ *m*; (*printing*) Type *f* ● *vt* mit der Maschine schreiben, ! tippen ● *vi* Maschine schreiben, ! tippen. **~writer** *n* Schreibmaschine *f*. **~written** *a* maschinegeschrieben

typical /ˈtɪpɪkl/ *a*, **-ly** *adv* typisch (**of** für)

typify /ˈtɪpɪfaɪ/ *vt* (*pt/pp* **-ied**) typisch sein für

typing /ˈtaɪpɪŋ/ *n* Maschineschreiben *nt*

typist /ˈtaɪpɪst/ *n* Schreibkraft *f*

tyrannical /tɪˈrænɪkl/ *a* tyrannisch

tyranny /ˈtɪrənɪ/ *n* Tyrannei *f*

tyrant /ˈtaɪrənt/ *n* Tyrann *m*

tyre /ˈtaɪə(r)/ *n* Reifen *m*

Uu

ugl|iness /ˈʌglɪnɪs/ *n* Hässlichkeit *f*. **~y** *a* (**-ier, -iest**) hässlich; (*nasty*) übel
UK *abbr see* **United Kingdom**
ulcer /ˈʌlsə(r)/ *n* Geschwür *nt*
ultimate /ˈʌltɪmət/ *a* letzte(r,s); (*final*) endgültig; (*fundamental*) grundlegend, eigentlich. **~ly** *adv* schließlich
ultimatum /ʌltɪˈmeɪtəm/ *n* Ultimatum *nt*
ultraˈviolet *a* ultraviolett
umbrella /ʌmˈbrelə/ *n* [Regen]schirm *m*
umpire /ˈʌmpaɪə(r)/ *n* Schiedsrichter *m* ● *vt/i* Schiedsrichter sein (bei)
umpteen /ʌmpˈtiːn/ *a* [!] zig. **~th** *a* [!] zigste(r,s)
unˈable /ʌn-/ *a* **be ~ to do sth** etw nicht tun können
unaˈbridged *a* ungekürzt
unacˈcompanied *a* ohne Begleitung; <*luggage*> unbegleitet
unacˈcountable *a* unerklärlich
unacˈcustomed *a* ungewohnt; **be ~ to sth** etw (*acc*) nicht gewohnt sein
unˈaided *a* ohne fremde Hilfe
unanimous /juːˈnænɪməs/ *a*, **-ly** *adv* einmütig; <*vote, decision*> einstimmig
unˈarmed *a* unbewaffnet
unasˈsuming *a* bescheiden
unatˈtended *a* unbeaufsichtigt
unˈauthorized *a* unbefugt
unaˈvoidable *a* unvermeidlich
unaˈware *a* **be ~ of sth** sich (*dat*) etw (*gen*) nicht bewusst sein. **~s** /-eəz/ *adv* **catch s.o. ~s** jdn überraschen
unˈbearable *a*, **-bly** *adv* unerträglich
unbeat|able /ʌnˈbiːtəbl/ *a* unschlagbar. **~en** *a* ungeschlagen; <*record*> ungebrochen
unbeˈlievable *a* unglaublich
unˈbiased *a* unvoreingenommen
unˈblock *vt* frei machen
unˈbolt *vt* aufriegeln
unˈbreakable *a* unzerbrechlich
unˈbutton *vt* aufknöpfen
uncalled-for /ʌnˈkɔːldfɔː(r)/ *a* unangebracht
unˈcanny *a* unheimlich
unˈceasing *a* unaufhörlich
unˈcertain *a* (*doubtful*) ungewiss; <*origins*> unbestimmt; **be ~** nicht sicher sein. **~ty** *n* Ungewissheit *f*
unˈchanged *a* unverändert
unˈcharitable *a* lieblos
uncle /ˈʌŋkl/ *n* Onkel *m*
unˈcomfortable *a*, **-bly** *adv* unbequem; **feel ~** (*fig*) sich nicht wohl fühlen
unˈcommon *a* ungewöhnlich
unˈcompromising *a* kompromisslos
unconˈditional *a*, **~ly** *adv* bedingungslos
unˈconscious *a* bewusstlos; (*unintended*) unbewusst; **be ~ of sth** sich (*dat*) etw (*gen*) nicht bewusst sein. **~ly** *adv* unbewusst
unconˈventional *a* unkonventionell
uncoˈoperative *a* nicht hilfsbereit
unˈcork *vt* entkorken
uncouth /ʌnˈkuːθ/ *a* ungehobelt
unˈcover *vt* aufdecken
undeˈcided *a* unentschlossen; (*not settled*) nicht entschieden

undeniable /ʌndɪˈnaɪəbl/ *a*, **-bly** *adv* unbestreitbar
under /ˈʌndə(r)/ *prep* unter (+ *dat/acc*); ~ **it** darunter; ~ **there** da drunter; ~ **repair** in Reparatur; ~ **construction** im Bau; ~ **age** minderjährig ● *adv* darunter
ˈ**undercarriage** *n* (*Aviat*) Fahrwerk *nt*, Fahrgestell *nt*
ˈ**underclothes** *npl* Unterwäsche *f*
underˈcover *a* geheim
ˈ**undercurrent** *n* Unterströmung *f*; (*fig*) Unterton *m*
ˈ**underdog** *n* Unterlegene(r) *m*
underˈdone *a* nicht gar; (*rare*) nicht durchgebraten
underˈestimate *vt* unterschätzen
underˈfed *a* unterernährt
underˈfoot *adv* am Boden
underˈgo *vt* (*pt* **-went**, *pp* **-gone**) durchmachen; sich unterziehen (+ *dat*) <*operation, treatment*>
underˈgraduate *n* Student(in) *m(f)*
underˈground¹ *adv* unter der Erde; <*mining*> unter Tage
ˈ**underground²** *a* unterirdisch; (*secret*) Untergrund- ● *n* (*railway*) U-Bahn *f*. ~ **car park** *n* Tiefgarage *f*
ˈ**undergrowth** *n* Unterholz *nt*
ˈ**underhand** *a* hinterhältig
underˈlie *vt* (*pt* **-lay**, *pp* **-lain**, *pres p* **-lying**) zugrunde liegen (+ *dat*)
underˈline *vt* unterstreichen
underˈlying *a* eigentlich
underˈmine *vt* (*fig*) unterminieren, untergraben
underneath /ʌndəˈniːθ/ *prep* unter (+ *dat/acc*) ● *adv* darunter
ˈ**underpants** *npl* Unterhose *f*
ˈ**underpass** *n* Unterführung *f*
underˈprivileged *a* unterprivilegiert
underˈrate *vt* unterschätzen
ˈ**undershirt** *n* (*Amer*) Unterhemd *nt*
underˈstand *vt/i* (*pt/pp* **-stood**) verstehen; **I** ~ **that ...** (*have heard*) ich habe gehört, dass ... ~**able** /-əbl/ *a* verständlich. ~**ably** /-əblɪ/ *adv* verständlicherweise
underˈstanding *a* verständnisvoll ● *n* Verständnis *nt*; (*agreement*) Vereinbarung *f*; **reach an** ~ sich verständigen
ˈ**understatement** *n* Untertreibung *f*
underˈtake *vt* (*pt* **-took**, *pp* **-taken**) unternehmen; ~ **to do sth** sich verpflichten, etw zu tun
ˈ**undertaker** *n* Leichenbestatter *m*; **[firm of]** ~**s** Bestattungsinstitut *n*
underˈtaking *n* Unternehmen *nt*; (*promise*) Versprechen *nt*
ˈ**undertone** *n* (*fig*) Unterton *m*; **in an** ~ mit gedämpfter Stimme
underˈvalue *vt* unterbewerten
ˈ**underwater¹** *a* Unterwasser-
underˈwater² *adv* unter Wasser
ˈ**underwear** *n* Unterwäsche *f*
underˈweight *a* untergewichtig; **be** ~ Untergewicht haben
ˈ**underworld** *n* Unterwelt *f*
undeˈsirable *a* unerwünscht
unˈdignified *a* würdelos
unˈdo *vt* (*pt* **-did**, *pp* **-done**) aufmachen; (*fig*) ungeschehen machen
unˈdone *a* offen; (*not accomplished*) unerledigt
unˈdoubted *a* unzweifelhaft. ~**ly** *adv* zweifellos
unˈdress *vt* ausziehen; **get** ~**ed** sich ausziehen ● *vi* sich ausziehen
unˈdue *a* übermäßig
undˈuly *adv* übermäßig
unˈearth *vt* ausgraben; (*fig*) zutage bringen. ~**ly** *a*

unheimlich; **at an ~ly hour** [!] in aller Herrgottsfrühe

un'easy *a* unbehaglich

uneco'nomic *a*, **-ally** *adv* unwirtschaftlich

unem'ployed *a* arbeitslos ● *npl* **the ~** die Arbeitslosen

unem'ployment *n* Arbeitslosigkeit *f*

un'ending *a* endlos

un'equal *a* unterschiedlich; <*struggle*> ungleich. **~ly** *adv* ungleichmäßig

unequivocal /ʌnɪ'kwɪvəkl/ *a*, **-ly** *adv* eindeutig

un'ethical *a* unmoralisch; **be ~** gegen das Berufsethos verstoßen

un'even *a* uneben; (*unequal*) ungleich; (*not regular*) ungleichmäßig; <*number*> ungerade

unex'pected *a*, **-ly** *adv* unerwartet

un'fair *a*, **-ly** *adv* ungerecht, unfair. **~ness** *n* Ungerechtigkeit *f*

un'faithful *a* untreu

unfa'miliar *a* ungewohnt; (*unknown*) unbekannt

un'fasten *vt* aufmachen; (*detach*) losmachen

un'favourable *a* ungünstig

un'feeling *a* gefühllos

un'fit *a* ungeeignet; (*incompetent*) unfähig; (*Sport*) nicht fit; **~ for work** arbeitsunfähig

un'fold *vt* auseinander falten, entfalten; (*spread out*) ausbreiten ● *vi* sich entfalten

unfore'seen *a* unvorhergesehen

unforgettable /ʌnfə'getəbl/ *a* unvergesslich

unforgivable /ʌnfə'gɪvəbl/ *a* unverzeihlich

un'fortunate *a* unglücklich; (*unfavourable*) ungünstig; (*regrettable*) bedauerlich; **be ~** <*person*:> Pech haben. **~ly** *adv* leider

un'founded *a* unbegründet

unfurl /ʌn'fɜ:l/ *vt* entrollen

un'furnished *a* unmöbliert

ungainly /ʌn'geɪnlɪ/ *a* unbeholfen

un'grateful *a*, **-ly** *adv* undankbar

un'happiness *n* Kummer *m*

un'happy *a* unglücklich; (*not content*) unzufrieden

un'harmed *a* unverletzt

un'healthy *a* ungesund

un'hurt *a* unverletzt

unification /ju:nɪfɪ'keɪʃn/ *n* Einigung *f*

uniform /'ju:nɪfɔ:m/ *a*, **-ly** *adv* einheitlich ● *n* Uniform *f*

unify /'ju:nɪfaɪ/ *vt* (*pt/pp* **-ied**) einigen

uni'lateral /ju:nɪ-/ *a*, **-ly** *adv* einseitig

uni'maginable *a* unvorstellbar

unim'portant *a* unwichtig

unin'habited *a* unbewohnt

unin'tentional *a*, **-ly** *adv* unabsichtlich

union /'ju:nɪən/ *n* Vereinigung *f*; (*Pol*) Union *f*; (*trade* **~**) Gewerkschaft *f*

unique /ju:'ni:k/ *a* einzigartig. **~ly** *adv* einmalig

unison /'ju:nɪsn/ *n* **in ~** einstimmig

unit /'ju:nɪt/ *n* Einheit *f*; (*Math*) Einer *m*; (*of furniture*) Teil *nt*, Element *nt*

unite /ju:'naɪt/ *vt* vereinigen ● *vi* sich vereinigen

united /ju:'naɪtɪd/ *a* einig. **U~ 'Kingdom** *n* Vereinigtes Königreich *nt*. **U~ 'Nations** *n* Vereinte Nationen *pl*. **U~ States [of America]** *n* Vereinigte Staaten *pl* [von Amerika]

unity /'ju:nətɪ/ *n* Einheit *f*; (*harmony*) Einigkeit *f*
universal /ju:nɪ'vɜ:sl/ *a*, **-ly** *adv* allgemein
universe /'ju:nɪvɜ:s/ *n* [Welt]all *nt*, Universum *nt*
university /ju:nɪ'vɜ:sətɪ/ *n* Universität *f* ● *attrib* Universitäts-
un'just *a*, **-ly** *adv* ungerecht
un'kind *a*, **-ly** *adv* unfreundlich; (*harsh*) hässlich
un'known *a* unbekannt
un'lawful *a*, **-ly** *adv* gesetzwidrig
unleaded /ʌn'ledɪd/ *a* bleifrei
un'leash *vt* (*fig*) entfesseln
unless /ən'les/ *conj* wenn ... nicht; ~ **I am mistaken** wenn ich mich nicht irre
un'like *prep* im Gegensatz zu (+ *dat*)
un'likely *a* unwahrscheinlich
un'limited *a* unbegrenzt
un'load *vt* entladen; ausladen <*luggage*>
un'lock *vt* aufschließen
un'lucky *a* unglücklich; <*day, number*> Unglücks-; **be** ~ Pech haben; <*thing:*> Unglück bringen
un'married *a* unverheiratet. ~ **'mother** *n* ledige Mutter *f*
un'mask *vt* (*fig*) entlarven
unmistakable /ʌnmɪ'steɪkəbl/ *a*, **-bly** *adv* unverkennbar
un'natural *a*, **-ly** *adv* unnatürlich; (*not normal*) nicht normal
un'necessary *a*, **-ily** *adv* unnötig
un'noticed *a* unbemerkt
unob'tainable *a* nicht erhältlich
unob'trusive *a*, **-ly** *adv* unaufdringlich; <*thing*> unauffällig
unof'ficial *a*, **-ly** *adv* inoffiziell
un'pack *vt/i* auspacken
un'paid *a* unbezahlt
un'pleasant *a*, **-ly** *adv* unangenehm
un'plug *vt* (*pt/pp* **-plugged**) den Stecker herausziehen von
un'popular *a* unbeliebt
un'precedented *a* beispiellos
unpre'dictable *a* unberechenbar
unpre'pared *a* nicht vorbereitet
unpre'tentious *a* bescheiden
un'profitable *a* unrentabel
un'qualified *a* unqualifiziert; (*fig: absolute*) uneingeschränkt
un'questionable *a* unbezweifelbar; <*right*> unbestreitbar
unravel /ʌn'rævl/ *vt* (*pt/pp* **-ravelled**) entwirren; (*Knitting*) aufziehen
un'real *a* unwirklich
un'reasonable *a* unvernünftig
unre'lated *a* unzusammenhängend; **be** ~ nicht verwandt sein; <*events:*> nicht miteinander zusammenhängen
unre'liable *a* unzuverlässig
un'rest *n* Unruhen *pl*
un'rivalled *a* unübertroffen
un'roll *vt* aufrollen ● *vi* sich aufrollen
unruly /ʌn'ru:lɪ/ *a* ungebärdig
un'safe *a* nicht sicher
unsatis'factory *a* unbefriedigend
un'savoury *a* unangenehm; (*fig*) unerfreulich
unscathed /ʌn'skeɪðd/ *a* unversehrt
un'screw *vt* abschrauben
un'scrupulous *a* skrupellos
un'seemly *a* unschicklich
un'selfish *a* selbstlos
un'settled *a* ungeklärt; <*weather*> unbeständig; <*bill*> unbezahlt
unshakeable /ʌn'ʃeɪkəbl/ *a* unerschütterlich

unshaven /ʌn'ʃeɪvn/ *a* unrasiert
unsightly /ʌn'saɪtlɪ/ *a* unansehnlich
un'skilled *a* ungelernt; <*work*> unqualifiziert
un'sociable *a* ungesellig
unso'phisticated *a* einfach
un'sound *a* krank, nicht gesund; <*building*> nicht sicher; <*advice*> unzuverlässig; <*reasoning*> nicht stichhaltig
un'stable *a* nicht stabil; (*mentally*) labil
un'steady *a*, **-ily** *adv* unsicher; (*wobbly*) wackelig
un'stuck *a* **come ~** sich lösen; ([!] *fail*) scheitern
unsuc'cessful *a*, **-ly** *adv* erfolglos; **be ~** keinen Erfolg haben
un'suitable *a* ungeeignet; (*inappropriate*) unpassend; (*for weather, activity*) unzweckmäßig
unthinkable /ʌn'θɪŋkəbl/ *a* unvorstellbar
un'tidiness *n* Unordentlichkeit *f*
un'tidy *a*, **-ily** *adv* unordentlich
un'tie *vt* aufbinden; losbinden <*person, boat, horse*>
until /ən'tɪl/ *prep* bis (+ *acc*); **not ~** erst; **~ the evening** bis zum Abend ● *conj* bis; **not ~** erst wenn; (*in past*) erst als
un'told *a* unermesslich
un'true *a* unwahr; **that's ~** das ist nicht wahr
unused[1] /ʌn'ju:zd/ *a* unbenutzt; (*not utilized*) ungenutzt
unused[2] /ʌn'ju:st/ *a* **be ~ to sth** etw nicht gewohnt sein
un'usual *a*, **-ly** *adv* ungewöhnlich
un'veil *vt* enthüllen
un'wanted *a* unerwünscht
un'welcome *a* unwillkommen
un'well *a* **be** *or* **feel ~** sich nicht wohl fühlen
unwieldy /ʌn'wi:ldɪ/ *a* sperrig
un'willing *a*, **-ly** *adv* widerwillig; **be ~ to do sth** etw nicht tun wollen
un'wind *v* (*pt/pp* **unwound**) ● *vt* abwickeln ● *vi* sich abwickeln; ([!] *relax*) sich entspannen
un'wise *a*, **-ly** *adv* unklug
un'worthy *a* unwürdig
un'wrap *vt* (*pt/pp* **-wrapped**) auswickeln; auspacken <*present*>
un'written *a* ungeschrieben
up /ʌp/ *adv* oben; (*with movement*) nach oben; (*not in bed*) auf; <*road*> aufgerissen; <*price*> gestiegen; **be up for sale** zu verkaufen sein; **up there** da oben; **up to** (*as far as*) bis; **time's up** die Zeit ist um; **what's up?** [!] was ist los? **what's he up to?** [!] was hat er vor? **I don't feel up to it** ich fühle mich dem nicht gewachsen; **go up** hinaufgehen; **come up** heraufkommen ● *prep* **be up on sth** [oben] auf etw (*dat*) sein; **up the mountain** oben am Berg; (*movement*) den Berg hinauf; **be up the tree** oben im Baum sein; **up the road** die Straße entlang; **up the river** stromaufwärts; **go up the stairs** die Treppe hinaufgehen
'upbringing *n* Erziehung *f*
up'date *vt* auf den neuesten Stand bringen
up'grade *vt* aufstufen
upheaval /ʌp'hi:vl/ *n* Unruhe *f*; (*Pol*) Umbruch *m*
up'hill *a* (*fig*) mühsam ● *adv* bergauf
up'hold *vt* (*pt/pp* **upheld**) unterstützen; bestätigen <*verdict*>
upholster /ʌp'həʊlstə(r)/ *vt* polstern. **~y** *n* Polsterung *f*
'upkeep *n* Unterhalt *m*
up'market *a* anspruchsvoll
upon /ə'pɒn/ *prep* auf (+ *dat*/*acc*)
upper /'ʌpə(r)/ *a* obere(r,s); <*deck, jaw, lip*> Ober-; **have the**

~ **hand** die Oberhand haben ● *n* (*of shoe*) Obermaterial *nt*
upper 'class *n* Oberschicht *f*
'upright *a* aufrecht
'uprising *n* Aufstand *m*
'uproar *n* Aufruhr *m*
up'set[1] *vt* (*pt/pp* **upset**, *pres p* **upsetting**) umstoßen; (*spill*) verschütten; durcheinander bringen <*plan*>; (*distress*) erschüttern; <*food:*> nicht bekommen (+ *dat*); **get ~ about sth** sich über etw (*acc*) aufregen
'upset[2] *n* Aufregung *f*; **have a stomach ~** einen verdorbenen Magen haben
'upshot *n* Ergebnis *nt*
upside 'down *adv* verkehrt herum; **turn ~** umdrehen
up'stairs[1] *adv* oben; <*go*> nach oben
'upstairs[2] *a* im Obergeschoss
'upstart *n* Emporkömmling *m*
up'stream *adv* stromaufwärts
'uptake *n* **slow on the ~** schwer von Begriff; **be quick on the ~** schnell begreifen
'upturn *n* Aufschwung *m*
upward /'ʌpwəd/ *a* nach oben; <*movement*> Aufwärts-; **~ slope** Steigung *f* ● *adv* **~[s]** aufwärts, nach oben
uranium /jʊ'reɪnɪəm/ *n* Uran *nt*
urban /'ɜ:bən/ *a* städtisch
urge /ɜ:dʒ/ *n* Trieb *m*, Drang *m* ● *vt* drängen; **~ on** antreiben
urgen|cy /'ɜ:dʒənsɪ/ *n* Dringlichkeit *f*. **~ t** *a*, **-ly** *adv* dringend
urine /'jʊərɪn/ *n* Urin *m*, Harn *m*
us /ʌs/ *pron* uns; **it's us** wir sind es
US[A] *abbr* USA *pl*
usable /'ju:zəbl/ *a* brauchbar
usage /'ju:sɪdʒ/ *n* Brauch *m*; (*of word*) [Sprach]gebrauch *m*
use[1] /ju:s/ *n* (*see* **use[2]**) Benutzung *f*, Verwendung *f*; Gebrauch *m*; **be (of) no ~** nichts nützen; **it is no ~** es hat keinen Zweck; **what's the ~?** wozu?
use[2] /ju:z/ *vt* benutzen <*implement, room, lift*>; verwenden <*ingredient, method, book, money*>; gebrauchen <*words, force, brains*>; **~ [up]** aufbrauchen
used[1] /ju:zd/ *a* gebraucht; <*towel*> benutzt; <*car*> Gebraucht-
used[2] /ju:st/ *pt* **be ~ to sth** an etw (*acc*) gewöhnt sein; **get ~ to** sich gewöhnen an (+ *acc*); **he ~ to say** er hat immer gesagt; **he ~ to live here** er hat früher hier gewohnt
useful /'ju:sfl/ *a* nützlich. **~ness** *n* Nützlichkeit *f*
useless /'ju:slɪs/ *a* nutzlos; (*not usable*) unbrauchbar; (*pointless*) zwecklos
user /'ju:zə(r)/ *n* Benutzer(in) *m(f)*
usher /'ʌʃə(r)/ *n* Platzanweiser *m*; (*in court*) Gerichtsdiener *m*
usherette /ʌʃə'ret/ *n* Platzanweiserin *f*
USSR *abbr* (*History*) UdSSR *f*
usual /'ju:ʒʊəl/ *a* üblich. **~ly** *adv* gewöhnlich
utensil /ju:'tensl/ *n* Gerät *nt*
utility /ju:'tɪlətɪ/ *a* Gebrauchs-
utilize /'ju:tɪlaɪz/ *vt* nutzen
utmost /'ʌtməʊst/ *a* äußerste(r,s), größte(r,s) ● *n* **do one's ~** sein Möglichstes tun
utter[1] /'ʌtə(r)/ *a*, **-ly** *adv* völlig
utter[2] *vt* von sich geben <*sigh, sound*>; sagen <*word*>
U-turn /'ju:-/ *n* (*fig*) Kehrtwendung *f*; **'no ~s'** (*Auto*) 'Wenden verboten'

Vv

vacan|cy /'veɪkənsɪ/ *n* (*job*) freie Stelle *f*; (*room*) freies Zimmer *nt*; **'no ~cies'** 'belegt'. **~t** *a* frei; <*look*> [gedanken]leer
vacate /və'keɪt/ *vt* räumen
vacation /və'keɪʃn/ *n* (*Univ & Amer*) Ferien *pl*
vaccinat|e /'væksɪneɪt/ *vt* impfen. **~ion** /-'neɪʃn/ *n* Impfung *f*
vaccine /'væksi:n/ *n* Impfstoff *m*
vacuum /'vækjʊəm/ *n* Vakuum *nt*, luftleerer Raum *m* ● *vt* saugen. **~ cleaner** *n* Staubsauger *m*
vagina /və'dʒaɪnə/ *n* (*Anat*) Scheide *f*
vague /veɪg/ *a* (**-r**, **-st**), **-ly** *adv* vage; <*outline*> verschwommen
vain /veɪn/ *a* (**-er**, **-est**) eitel; <*hope, attempt*> vergeblich; **in ~** vergeblich. **~ly** *adv* vergeblich
valiant /'vælɪənt/ *a*, **-ly** *adv* tapfer
valid /'vælɪd/ *a* gültig; <*claim*> berechtigt; <*argument*> stichhaltig; <*reason*> triftig. **~ity** /və'lɪdətɪ/ *n* Gültigkeit *f*
valley /'vælɪ/ *n* Tal *nt*
valour /'vælə(r)/ *n* Tapferkeit *f*
valuable /'væljʊəbl/ *a* wertvoll. **~s** *npl* Wertsachen *pl*
valuation /væljʊ'eɪʃn/ *n* Schätzung *f*
value /'vælju:/ *n* Wert *m*; (*usefulness*) Nutzen *m* ● *vt* schätzen. **~ 'added tax** *n* Mehrwertsteuer *f*
valve /vælv/ *n* Ventil *nt*; (*Anat*) Klappe *f*; (*Electr*) Röhre *f*
van /væn/ *n* Lieferwagen *m*
vandal /'vændl/ *n* Rowdy *m*. **~ism** /-ɪzm/ *n* mutwillige Zerstörung *f*. **~ize** *vt* demolieren
vanilla /və'nɪlə/ *n* Vanille *f*
vanish /'vænɪʃ/ *vi* verschwinden
vanity /'vænətɪ/ *n* Eitelkeit *f*
vapour /'veɪpə(r)/ *n* Dampf *m*
variable /'veərɪəbl/ *a* unbeständig; (*Math*) variabel; (*adjustable*) regulierbar
variant /'veərɪənt/ *n* Variante *f*
variation /veərɪ'eɪʃn/ *n* Variation *f*; (*difference*) Unterschied *m*
varied /'veərɪd/ *a* vielseitig; <*diet*> abwechslungsreich
variety /və'raɪətɪ/ *n* Abwechslung *f*; (*quantity*) Vielfalt *f*; (*Comm*) Auswahl *f*; (*type*) Art *f*; (*Bot*) Abart *f*; (*Theat*) Varieté *nt*
various /'veərɪəs/ *a* verschieden. **~ly** *adv* unterschiedlich
varnish /'vɑ:nɪʃ/ *n* Lack *m* ● *vt* lackieren
vary /'veərɪ/ *v* (*pt/pp* **-ied**) ● *vi* sich ändern; (*be different*) verschieden sein ● *vt* [ver]ändern; (*add variety to*) abwechslungsreicher gestalten
vase /vɑ:z/ *n* Vase *f*
vast /vɑ:st/ *a* riesig; <*expanse*> weit. **~ly** *adv* gewaltig
vat /væt/ *n* Bottich *m*
VAT /vi:eɪ'ti:, væt/ *abbr* (**value added tax**) Mehrwertsteuer *f*, MwSt.
vault[1] /vɔ:lt/ *n* (*roof*) Gewölbe *nt*; (*in bank*) Tresor *m*; (*tomb*) Gruft *f*
vault[2] *n* Sprung *m* ● *vt/i* **~ [over]** springen über (+ *acc*)
VDU *abbr* (**visual display unit**) Bildschirmgerät *nt*
veal /vi:l/ *n* Kalbfleisch *nt* ● *attrib* Kalbs-

veer /vɪə(r)/ *vi* sich drehen; (*Auto*) ausscheren

vegetable /'vedʒtəbl/ *n* Gemüse *nt*; **~s** *pl* Gemüse *nt* ● *attrib* Gemüse-; <*oil, fat*> Pflanzen-

vegetarian /vedʒɪ'teərɪən/ *a* vegetarisch ● *n* Vegetarier(in) *m(f)*

vegetation /vedʒɪ'teɪʃn/ *n* Vegetation *f*

vehement /'vi:əmənt/ *a*, **-ly** *adv* heftig

vehicle /'vi:ɪkl/ *n* Fahrzeug *nt*

veil /veɪl/ *n* Schleier *m* ● *vt* verschleiern

vein /veɪn/ *n* Ader *f*; (*mood*) Stimmung *f*; (*manner*) Art *f*

velocity /vɪ'lɒsətɪ/ *n* Geschwindigkeit *f*

velvet /'velvɪt/ *n* Samt *m*

vending-machine /'vendɪŋ-/ *n* [Verkaufs]automat *m*

vendor /'vendə(r)/ *n* Verkäufer(in) *m(f)*

veneer /və'nɪə(r)/ *n* Furnier *nt*; (*fig*) Tünche *f*. **~ed** *a* furniert

venerable /'venərəbl/ *a* ehrwürdig

Venetian /və'ni:ʃn/ *a* venezianisch. **v~ blind** *n* Jalousie *f*

vengeance /'vendʒəns/ *n* Rache *f*; **with a ~** gewaltig

Venice /'venɪs/ *n* Venedig *nt*

venison /'venɪsn/ *n* (*Culin*) Reh(fleisch) *nt*

venom /'venəm/ *n* Gift *nt*; (*fig*) Hass *m*. **~ous** /-əs/ *a* giftig

vent /vent/ *n* Öffnung *f*

ventilat|e /'ventɪleɪt/ *vt* belüften. **~ion** /-'leɪʃn/ *n* Belüftung *f*; (*installation*) Lüftung *f*. **~or** *n* Lüftungsvorrichtung *f*; (*Med*) Beatmungsgerät *nt*

ventriloquist /ven'trɪləkwɪst/ *n* Bauchredner *m*

venture /'ventʃə(r)/ *n* Unternehmung *f* ● *vt* wagen ● *vi* sich wagen

venue /'venju:/ *n* (*for event*) Veranstaltungsort *m*

veranda /və'rændə/ *n* Veranda *f*

verb /vɜ:b/ *n* Verb *nt*. **~al** *a*, **-ly** *adv* mündlich; (*Gram*) verbal

verbose /vɜ:'bəʊs/ *a* weitschweifig

verdict /'vɜ:dɪkt/ *n* Urteil *nt*

verge /vɜ:dʒ/ *n* Rand *m* ● *vi* **~ on** (*fig*) grenzen an (+ *acc*)

verify /'verɪfaɪ/ *vt* (*pt/pp* **-ied**) überprüfen; (*confirm*) bestätigen

vermin /'vɜ:mɪn/ *n* Ungeziefer *nt*

vermouth /'vɜ:məθ/ *n* Wermut *m*

versatil|e /'vɜ:sətaɪl/ *a* vielseitig. **~ity** /-'tɪlətɪ/ *n* Vielseitigkeit *f*

verse /vɜ:s/ *n* Strophe *f*; (*of Bible*) Vers *m*; (*poetry*) Lyrik *f*

version /'vɜ:ʃn/ *n* Version *f*; (*translation*) Übersetzung *f*; (*model*) Modell *nt*

versus /'vɜ:səs/ *prep* gegen (+ *acc*)

vertical /'vɜ:tɪkl/ *a*, **-ly** *adv* senkrecht ● *n* Senkrechte *f*

vertigo /'vɜ:tɪgəʊ/ *n* (*Med*) Schwindel *m*

verve /vɜ:v/ *n* Schwung *m*

very /'verɪ/ *adv* sehr; **~ much** sehr; (*quantity*) sehr viel; **~ probably** höchstwahrscheinlich; **at the ~ most** allerhöchstens ● *a* (*mere*) bloß; **the ~ first** der/die/das allererste; **the ~ thing** genau das Richtige; **at the ~ end/beginning** ganz am Ende/Anfang; **only a ~ little** nur ein ganz kleines bisschen

vessel /'vesl/ *n* Schiff *nt*; (*receptacle & Anat*) Gefäß *nt*

vest /vest/ *n* [Unter]hemd *nt*; (*Amer: waistcoat*) Weste *f*

vestige /'vestɪdʒ/ *n* Spur *f*

vestry /'vestrɪ/ *n* Sakristei *f*

vet /vet/ *n* Tierarzt *m* /-ärztin *f* ● *vt* (*pt/pp* **vetted**) überprüfen
veteran /'vetərən/ *n* Veteran *m*
veterinary /'vetərɪnərɪ/ *a* tierärztlich. ~ **surgeon** *n* Tierarzt *m* /-ärztin *f*
veto /'vi:təʊ/ *n* (*pl* **-es**) Veto *nt*
VHF *abbr* (**very high frequency**) UKW
via /'vaɪə/ *prep* über (+ *acc*)
viable /'vaɪəbl/ *a* lebensfähig; (*fig*) realisierbar; <*firm*> rentabel
viaduct /'vaɪədʌkt/ *n* Viadukt *nt*
vibrat|e /vaɪ'breɪt/ *vi* vibrieren. ~**ion** /-'breɪʃn/ *n* Vibrieren *nt*
vicar /'vɪkə(r)/ *n* Pfarrer *m*. ~**age** /-rɪdʒ/ *n* Pfarrhaus *nt*
vice[1] /vaɪs/ *n* Laster *nt*
vice[2] *n* (*Techn*) Schraubstock *m*
vice[3] *a* Vize-; ~ **'chairman** stellvertretender Vorsitzender *m*
vice versa /vaɪsɪ'vɜ:sə/ *adv* umgekehrt
vicinity /vɪ'sɪnətɪ/ *n* Umgebung *f*; **in the ~ of** in der Nähe von
vicious /'vɪʃəs/ *a*, **-ly** *adv* boshaft; <*animal*> bösartig
victim /'vɪktɪm/ *n* Opfer *nt*. ~**ize** *vt* schikanieren
victor /'vɪktə(r)/ *n* Sieger *m*
victor|ious /vɪk'tɔ:rɪəs/ *a* siegreich. ~**y** /'vɪktərɪ/ *n* Sieg *m*
video /'vɪdɪəʊ/ *n* Video *nt*; (*recorder*) Videorecorder *m* ● *attrib* Video-
video: ~ **cas'sette** *n* Videokassette *f*. ~ **game** *n* Videospiel *nt*. ~ **recorder** *n* Videorecorder *m*
Vienn|a /vɪ'enə/ *n* Wien *nt*. ~**ese** /vɪə'ni:z/ *a* Wiener
view /vju:/ *n* Sicht *f*; (*scene*) Aussicht *f*, Blick *m*; (*picture, opinion*) Ansicht *f*; **in my ~** meiner Ansicht nach; **in ~ of** angesichts (+ *gen*); **be on ~** besichtigt werden können ● *vt* sich (*dat*) ansehen; besichtigen <*house*>; (*consider*) betrachten ● *vi* (*TV*) fernsehen. ~**er** *n* (*TV*) Zuschauer(in) *m*(*f*)
view: ~**finder** *n* (*Phot*) Sucher *m*. ~**point** *n* Standpunkt *m*
vigilan|ce /'vɪdʒɪləns/ *n* Wachsamkeit *f*. ~**t** *a*, **-ly** *adv* wachsam
vigorous /'vɪgərəs/ *a*, **-ly** *adv* kräftig; (*fig*) heftig
vigour /'vɪgə(r)/ *n* Kraft *f*; (*fig*) Heftigkeit *f*
vile /vaɪl/ *a* abscheulich
villa /'vɪlə/ *n* (*for holidays*) Ferienhaus *nt*
village /'vɪlɪdʒ/ *n* Dorf *nt*. ~**r** *n* Dorfbewohner(in) *m*(*f*)
villain /'vɪlən/ *n* Schurke *m*; (*in story*) Bösewicht *m*
vindicat|e /'vɪndɪkeɪt/ *vt* rechtfertigen. ~**ion** /-'keɪʃn/ *n* Rechtfertigung *f*
vindictive /vɪn'dɪktɪv/ *a* nachtragend
vine /vaɪn/ *n* Weinrebe *f*
vinegar /'vɪnɪgə(r)/ *n* Essig *m*
vineyard /'vɪnjɑ:d/ *n* Weinberg *m*
vintage /'vɪntɪdʒ/ *a* erlesen ● *n* (*year*) Jahrgang *m*. ~ **'car** *n* Oldtimer *m*
viola /vɪ'əʊlə/ *n* (*Mus*) Bratsche *f*
violat|e /'vaɪəleɪt/ *vt* verletzen; (*break*) brechen; (*disturb*) stören; (*defile*) schänden. ~**ion** /-'leɪʃn/ *n* Verletzung *f*; Schändung *f*
violen|ce /'vaɪələns/ *n* Gewalt *f*; (*fig*) Heftigkeit *f*. ~**t** *a* gewalttätig; (*fig*) heftig. ~**tly** *adv* brutal; (*fig*) heftig
violet /'vaɪələt/ *a* violett ● *n* (*flower*) Veilchen *nt*
violin /vaɪə'lɪn/ *n* Geige *f*, Violine *f*. ~**ist** *n* Geiger(in) *m*(*f*)
VIP *abbr* (**very important person**) Prominente(r) *m*/*f*
viper /'vaɪpə(r)/ *n* Kreuzotter *f*

virgin /ˈvɜːdʒɪn/ *a* unberührt ● *n* Jungfrau *f*. **~ity** /-ˈdʒɪnətɪ/ *n* Unschuld *f*

viril|e /ˈvɪraɪl/ *a* männlich. **~ity** /-ˈrɪlətɪ/ *n* Männlichkeit *f*

virtual /ˈvɜːtjʊəl/ *a* **a ~ ...** praktisch ein ... **~ly** *adv* praktisch

virtu|e /ˈvɜːtjuː/ *n* Tugend *f*; (*advantage*) Vorteil *m*; **by** *or* **in ~e of** auf Grund (+ *gen*)

virtuoso /vɜːtjʊˈəʊzəʊ/ *n* (*pl* **-si** /-ziː/) Virtuose *m*

virtuous /ˈvɜːtjʊəs/ *a* tugendhaft

virus /ˈvaɪərəs/ *n* Virus *nt*

visa /ˈviːzə/ *n* Visum *nt*

visibility /vɪzəˈbɪlətɪ/ *n* Sichtbarkeit *f*; (*Meteorol*) Sichtweite *f*

visible /ˈvɪzəbl/ *a*, **-bly** *adv* sichtbar

vision /ˈvɪʒn/ *n* Vision *f*; (*sight*) Sehkraft *f*; (*foresight*) Weitblick *m*

visit /ˈvɪzɪt/ *n* Besuch *m* ● *vt* besuchen; besichtigen <*town, building*>. **~or** *n* Besucher(in) *m(f)*; (*in hotel*) Gast *m*; **have ~ors** Besuch haben

visor /ˈvaɪzə(r)/ *n* Schirm *m*; (*Auto*) [Sonnen]blende *f*

vista /ˈvɪstə/ *n* Aussicht *f*

visual /ˈvɪzjʊəl/ *a*, **-ly** *adv* visuell. **~ disˈplay unit** *n* Bildschirmgerät *nt*

visualize /ˈvɪzjʊəlaɪz/ *vt* sich (*dat*) vorstellen

vital /ˈvaɪtl/ *a* unbedingt notwendig; (*essential to life*) lebenswichtig. **~ity** /vaɪˈtælətɪ/ *n* Vitalität *f*. **~ly** /ˈvaɪtəlɪ/ *adv* äußerst

vitamin /ˈvɪtəmɪn/ *n* Vitamin *nt*

vivaci|ous /vɪˈveɪʃəs/ *a*, **-ly** *adv* lebhaft. **~ty** /-ˈvæsətɪ/ *n* Lebhaftigkeit *f*

vivid /ˈvɪvɪd/ *a*, **-ly** *adv* lebhaft; <*description*> lebendig

vocabulary /vəˈkæbjʊlərɪ/ *n* Wortschatz *m*; (*list*) Vokabelverzeichnis *nt*; **learn ~** Vokabeln lernen

vocal /ˈvəʊkl/ *a*, **-ly** *adv* stimmlich; (*vociferous*) lautstark

vocalist /ˈvəʊkəlɪst/ *n* Sänger(in) *m(f)*

vocation /vəˈkeɪʃn/ *n* Berufung *f*. **~al** *a* Berufs-

vociferous /vəˈsɪfərəs/ *a* lautstark

vodka /ˈvɒdkə/ *n* Wodka *m*

vogue /vəʊg/ *n* Mode *f*

voice /vɔɪs/ *n* Stimme *f* ● *vt* zum Ausdruck bringen. **~ mail** *n* Voicemail *f*

void /vɔɪd/ *a* leer; (*not valid*) ungültig; **~ of** ohne ● *n* Leere *f*

volatile /ˈvɒlətaɪl/ *a* flüchtig; <*person*> sprunghaft

volcanic /vɒlˈkænɪk/ *a* vulkanisch

volcano /vɒlˈkeɪnəʊ/ *n* Vulkan *m*

volley /ˈvɒlɪ/ *n* (*of gunfire*) Salve *f*; (*Tennis*) Volley *m*

volt /vəʊlt/ *n* Volt *nt*. **~age** /-ɪdʒ/ *n* (*Electr*) Spannung *f*

voluble /ˈvɒljʊbl/ *a*, **-bly** *adv* redselig; <*protest*> wortreich

volume /ˈvɒljuːm/ *n* (*book*) Band *m*; (*Geom*) Rauminhalt *m*; (*amount*) Ausmaß *nt*; (*Radio, TV*) Lautstärke *f*

voluntary /ˈvɒləntərɪ/ *a*, **-ily** *adv* freiwillig

volunteer /vɒlənˈtɪə(r)/ *n* Freiwillige(r) *m/f* ● *vt* anbieten; geben <*information*> ● *vi* sich freiwillig melden

vomit /ˈvɒmɪt/ *n* Erbrochene(s) *nt* ● *vt* erbrechen ● *vi* sich übergeben

voracious /vəˈreɪʃəs/ *a* gefräßig; <*appetite*> unbändig

vot|e /vəʊt/ *n* Stimme *f*; (*ballot*) Abstimmung *f*; (*right*) Wahlrecht

nt ● *vi* abstimmen; (*in election*) wählen. **~er** *n* Wähler(in) *m(f)*
vouch /vaʊtʃ/ *vi* **~ for** sich verbürgen für. **~er** *n* Gutschein *m*
vowel /ˈvaʊəl/ *n* Vokal *m*
voyage /ˈvɔɪɪdʒ/ *n* Seereise *f*; (*in space*) Reise *f*, Flug *m*
vulgar /ˈvʌlgə(r)/ *a* vulgär, ordinär. **~ity** /-ˈgærətɪ/ *n* Vulgarität *f*
vulnerable /ˈvʌlnərəbl/ *a* verwundbar
vulture /ˈvʌltʃə(r)/ *n* Geier *m*

Ww

wad /wɒd/ *n* Bausch *m*; (*bundle*) Bündel *nt*. **~ding** *n* Wattierung *f*
waddle /ˈwɒdl/ *vi* watscheln
wade /weɪd/ *vi* waten
wafer /ˈweɪfə(r)/ *n* Waffel *f*
waffle¹ /ˈwɒfl/ *vi* [!] schwafeln
waffle² *n* (*Culin*) Waffel *f*
waft /wɒft/ *vt/i* wehen
wag /wæg/ *v* (*pt/pp* **wagged**) ● *vt* wedeln mit ● *vi* wedeln
wage /weɪdʒ/ *n*, & **~s** *pl* Lohn *m*
wager /ˈweɪdʒə(r)/ *n* Wette *f*
wagon /ˈwægən/ *n* Wagen *m*; (*Rail*) Waggon *m*
wail /weɪl/ *n* [klagender] Schrei *m* ● *vi* heulen; (*lament*) klagen
waist /weɪst/ *n* Taille *f*. **~coat** /ˈweɪskəʊt/ *n* Weste *f*. **~line** *n* Taille *f*
wait /weɪt/ *n* Wartezeit *f*; **lie in ~ for** auflauern (+ *dat*) ● *vi* warten (**for** auf + *acc*); (*at table*) servieren; **~ on** bedienen ● *vt* **~ one's turn** warten, bis man an der Reihe ist
waiter /ˈweɪtə(r)/ *n* Kellner *m*; **~!** Herr Ober!
waiting: ~-list *n* Warteliste *f*. **~-room** *n* Warteraum *m*; (*doctor's*) Wartezimmer *nt*
waitress /ˈweɪtrɪs/ *n* Kellnerin *f*
waive /weɪv/ *vt* verzichten auf (+ *acc*)
wake¹ /weɪk/ *n* Totenwache *f* ● *v* (*pt* **woke**, *pp* **woken**) **~ [up]** ● *vt* [auf]wecken ● *vi* aufwachen
wake² *n* (*Naut*) Kielwasser *nt*; **in the ~ of** im Gefolge (+ *gen*)
Wales /weɪlz/ *n* Wales *nt*
walk /wɔːk/ *n* Spaziergang *m*; (*gait*) Gang *m*; (*path*) Weg *m*; **go for a ~** spazieren gehen ● *vi* gehen; (*not ride*) laufen, zu Fuß gehen; (*ramble*) wandern; **learn to ~** laufen lernen ● *vt* ausführen <*dog*>. **~ out** *vi* hinausgehen; <*workers:*> in den Streik treten; **~ out on s.o.** jdn verlassen
walker /ˈwɔːkə(r)/ *n* Spaziergänger(in) *m(f)*; (*rambler*) Wanderer *m*/Wanderin *f*
walking /ˈwɔːkɪŋ/ *n* Gehen *nt*; (*rambling*) Wandern *nt*. **~-stick** *n* Spazierstock *m*
wall /wɔːl/ *n* Wand *f*; (*external*) Mauer *f*; **drive s.o. up the ~** [!] jdn auf die Palme bringen ● *vt* **~ up** zumauern
wallet /ˈwɒlɪt/ *n* Brieftasche *f*
ˈwallflower *n* Goldlack *m*
wallop /ˈwɒləp/ *vt* (*pt/pp* **walloped**) [!] schlagen
wallow /ˈwɒləʊ/ *vi* sich wälzen; (*fig*) schwelgen
ˈwallpaper *n* Tapete *f* ● *vt* tapezieren
walnut /ˈwɔːlnʌt/ *n* Walnuss *f*
waltz /wɔːlts/ *n* Walzer *m* ● *vi* Walzer tanzen

wander /ˈwɒndə(r)/ *vi* umherwandern, [!] bummeln; (*fig: digress*) abschweifen. **~ about** *vi* umherwandern

wangle /ˈwæŋgl/ *vt* [!] organisieren

want /wɒnt/ *n* Mangel *m* (**of** an + *dat*); (*hardship*) Not *f*; (*desire*) Bedürfnis *nt* ● *vt* wollen; (*need*) brauchen; **~ [to have] sth** etw haben wollen; **~ to do sth** etw tun wollen; **I ~ you to go** ich will, dass du gehst; **it ~s painting** es müsste gestrichen werden ● *vi* **he doesn't ~ for anything** ihm fehlt es an nichts. **~ed** *a* <*criminal*> gesucht

war /wɔː(r)/ *n* Krieg *m*; **be at ~** sich im Krieg befinden

ward /wɔːd/ *n* [Kranken]saal *m*; (*unit*) Station *f*; (*of town*) Wahlbezirk *m*; (*child*) Mündel *nt* ● *vt* **~ off** abwehren

warden /ˈwɔːdn/ *n* (*of hostel*) Heimleiter(in) *m(f)*; (*of youth hostel*) Herbergsvater *m*; (*supervisor*) Aufseher(in) *m(f)*

warder /ˈwɔːdə(r)/ *n* Wärter(in) *m(f)*

wardrobe /ˈwɔːdrəʊb/ *n* Kleiderschrank *m*; (*clothes*) Garderobe *f*

warehouse /ˈweəhaʊs/ *n* Lager *nt*; (*building*) Lagerhaus *nt*

wares /weəz/ *npl* Waren *pl*

war: ~fare *n* Krieg *m*. **~like** *a* kriegerisch

warm /wɔːm/ *a* (**-er, -est**), **-ly** *adv* warm; <*welcome*> herzlich; **I am ~** mir ist warm ● *vt* wärmen. **~ up** *vt* aufwärmen ● *vi* warm werden; (*Sport*) sich aufwärmen. **~-hearted** *a* warmherzig

warmth /wɔːmθ/ *n* Wärme *f*

warn /wɔːn/ *vt* warnen (**of** vor + *dat*). **~ing** *n* Warnung *f*; (*advance notice*) Vorwarnung *f*; (*caution*) Verwarnung *f*

warp /wɔːp/ *vt* verbiegen ● *vi* sich verziehen

warrant /ˈwɒrənt/ *n* (*for arrest*) Haftbefehl *m*; (*for search*) Durchsuchungsbefehl *m* ● *vt* (*justify*) rechtfertigen; (*guarantee*) garantieren

warranty /ˈwɒrəntɪ/ *n* Garantie *f*

warrior /ˈwɒrɪə(r)/ *n* Krieger *m*

ˈwarship *n* Kriegsschiff *nt*

wart /wɔːt/ *n* Warze *f*

ˈwartime *n* Kriegszeit *f*

wary /ˈweərɪ/ *a* (**-ier, -iest**), **-ily** *adv* vorsichtig; (*suspicious*) misstrauisch

was /wɒz/ *see* **be**

wash /wɒʃ/ *n* Wäsche *f*; (*Naut*) Wellen *pl*; **have a ~** sich waschen ● *vt* waschen; spülen <*dishes*>; aufwischen <*floor*>; **~ one's hands** sich (*dat*) die Hände waschen ● *vi* sich waschen. **~ out** *vt* auswaschen; ausspülen <*mouth*>. **~ up** *vt/i* abwaschen, spülen ● *vi* (*Amer*) sich waschen

washable /ˈwɒʃəbl/ *a* waschbar

wash-basin *n* Waschbecken *nt*

washer /ˈwɒʃə(r)/ *n* (*Techn*) Dichtungsring *m*; (*machine*) Waschmaschine *f*

washing /ˈwɒʃɪŋ/ *n* Wäsche *f*. **~-machine** *n* Waschmaschine *f*. **~-powder** *n* Waschpulver *nt*. **~-ˈup** *n* Abwasch *m*; **do the ~-up** abwaschen, spülen. **~-ˈup liquid** *n* Spülmittel *nt*

wasp /wɒsp/ *n* Wespe *f*

waste /weɪst/ *n* Verschwendung *f*; (*rubbish*) Abfall *m*; **~s** *pl* Öde *f* ● *a* <*product*> Abfall- ● *vt* verschwenden ● *vi* **~ away** immer mehr abmagern

waste: ~ful *a* verschwenderisch. **~ land** *n* Ödland *nt*. **~ ˈpaper** *n* Altpapier *nt*. **~ˈpaper basket** *n* Papierkorb *m*

watch /wɒtʃ/ *n* Wache *f*; (*timepiece*) [Armband]uhr *f* ● *vt* beobachten; sich (*dat*) ansehen <*film, match*>; (*keep an eye on*) achten auf (+ *acc*); ~ **television** fernsehen ● *vi* zusehen. ~ **out** *vi* Ausschau halten (**for** nach); (*be careful*) aufpassen

watch: ~**-dog** *n* Wachhund *m*. ~**ful** *a*, **-ly** *adv* wachsam. ~**man** *n* Wachmann *m*

water /'wɔ:tə(r)/ *n* Wasser *nt*; ~**s** *pl* Gewässer *nt* ● *vt* gießen <*garden, plant*>; (*dilute*) verdünnen ● *vi* <*eyes:*> tränen; **my mouth was** ~**ing** mir lief das Wasser im Munde zusammen. ~ **down** *vt* verwässern

water: ~**-colour** *n* Wasserfarbe *f*; (*painting*) Aquarell *nt*. ~**cress** *n* Brunnenkresse *f*. ~**fall** *n* Wasserfall *m*

'**watering-can** *n* Gießkanne *f*

water: ~**-lily** *n* Seerose *f*. ~**logged** *a* **be** ~**logged** <*ground:*> unter Wasser stehen. ~ **polo** *n* Wasserball *m*. ~**proof** *a* wasserdicht. ~**-skiing** *n* Wasserskilaufen *nt*. ~**tight** *a* wasserdicht. ~**way** *n* Wasserstraße *f*

watery /'wɔ:tərɪ/ *a* wässrig

watt /wɒt/ *n* Watt *nt*

wave /weɪv/ *n* Welle *f*; (*gesture*) Handbewegung *f*; (*as greeting*) Winken *nt* ● *vt* winken mit; (*brandish*) schwingen; wellen <*hair*>; ~ **one's hand** winken ● *vi* winken (**to** *dat*); <*flag:*> wehen. ~**length** *n* Wellenlänge *f*

waver /'weɪvə(r)/ *vi* schwanken

wavy /'weɪvɪ/ *a* wellig

wax /wæks/ *n* Wachs *nt*; (*in ear*) Schmalz *nt* ● *vt* wachsen. ~**works** *n* Wachsfigurenkabinett *nt*

way /weɪ/ *n* Weg *m*; (*direction*) Richtung *f*; (*respect*) Hinsicht *f*; (*manner*) Art *f*; (*method*) Art und Weise *f*; ~**s** *pl* Gewohnheiten *pl*; **on the** ~ auf dem Weg (**to** nach/zu); (*under way*) unterwegs; **a little/long** ~ ein kleines/ganzes Stück; **a long** ~ **off** weit weg; **this** ~ hierher; (*like this*) so; **which** ~ in welche Richtung; (*how*) wie; **by the** ~ übrigens; **in some** ~**s** in gewisser Hinsicht; **either** ~ so oder so; **in this** ~ auf diese Weise; **in a** ~ in gewisser Weise; **lead the** ~ vorausgehen; **make** ~ Platz machen (**for** *dat*); '**give** ~' (*Auto*) 'Vorfahrt beachten'; **go out of one's** ~ (*fig*) sich (*dat*) besondere Mühe geben (**to** zu); **get one's [own]** ~ seinen Willen durchsetzen ● *adv* weit; ~ **behind** weit zurück. ~ '**in** *n* Eingang *m*

way 'out *n* Ausgang *m*; (*fig*) Ausweg *m*

WC *abbr* WC *nt*

we /wi:/ *pron* wir

weak /wi:k/ *a* (**-er, -est**), **-ly** *adv* schwach; <*liquid*> dünn. ~**en** *vt* schwächen ● *vi* schwächer werden. ~**ling** *n* Schwächling *m*. ~**ness** *n* Schwäche *f*

wealth /welθ/ *n* Reichtum *m*; (*fig*) Fülle *f* (**of** an + *dat*). ~**y** *a* (**-ier, -iest**) reich

weapon /'wepən/ *n* Waffe *f*

wear /weə(r)/ *n* (*clothing*) Kleidung *f*; ~ **and tear** Abnutzung *f*, Verschleiß *m* ● *v* (*pt* **wore**, *pp* **worn**) ● *vt* tragen; (*damage*) abnutzen; **what shall I** ~**?** was soll ich anziehen? ● *vi* sich abnutzen; (*last*) halten. ~ **off** *vi* abgehen; <*effect:*> nachlassen. ~ **out** *vt* abnutzen; (*exhaust*) erschöpfen ● *vi* sich abnutzen

weary /'wɪərɪ/ *a* (**-ier, -iest**), **-ily** *adv* müde

weather /'weðə(r)/ *n* Wetter *nt*; **in this** ~ bei diesem Wetter; **under the** ~ [!] nicht ganz auf dem Posten ● *vt* abwettern <*storm*>; (*fig*) überstehen

weather: ~-beaten *a* verwittert; wettergegerbt <*face*>. **~ forecast** *n* Wettervorhersage *f*

weave¹ /wi:v/ *vi* (*pt*/*pp* **weaved**) sich schlängeln (**through** durch)

weave² *n* (*Tex*) Bindung *f* ● *vt* (*pt* **wove**, *pp* **woven**) weben. **~r** *n* Weber *m*

web /web/ *n* Netz *nt*; **the W~** das Web. **~master** *n* Webmaster *m*. **~ page** *n* Webseite *f*. **~site** *n* Website *f*

wed /wed/ *vt*/*i* (*pt*/*pp* **wedded**) heiraten. **~ding** *n* Hochzeit *f*

wedding: ~ day *n* Hochzeitstag *m*. **~ dress** *n* Hochzeitskleid *nt*. **~-ring** *n* Ehering *m*, Trauring *m*

wedge /wedʒ/ *n* Keil *m* ● *vt* festklemmen

Wednesday /ˈwenzdeɪ/ *n* Mittwoch *m*

wee /wi:/ *a* 🅸 klein ● *vi* Pipi machen

weed /wi:d/ *n* & **~s** *pl* Unkraut *nt* ● *vt*/*i* jäten. **~ out** *vt* (*fig*) aussieben

ˈweedkiller *n* Unkrautvertilgungsmittel *nt*

weedy /ˈwi:dɪ/ *a* 🅸 spillerig

week /wi:k/ *n* Woche *f*. **~day** *n* Wochentag *m*. **~end** *n* Wochenende *nt*

weekly /ˈwi:klɪ/ *a* & *adv* wöchentlich ● *n* Wochenzeitschrift *f*

weep /wi:p/ *vi* (*pt*/*pp* **wept**) weinen

weigh /weɪ/ *vt*/*i* wiegen. **~ down** *vt* (*fig*) niederdrücken. **~ up** *vt* (*fig*) abwägen

weight /weɪt/ *n* Gewicht *nt*; **put on/lose ~** zunehmen/abnehmen

weight-lifting *n* Gewichtheben *nt*

weighty /ˈweɪtɪ/ *a* (**-ier, -iest**) schwer; (*important*) gewichtig

weir /wɪə(r)/ *n* Wehr *nt*.

weird /wɪəd/ *a* (**-er, -est**) unheimlich; (*bizarre*) bizarr

welcome /ˈwelkəm/ *a* willkommen; **you're ~!** nichts zu danken! **you're ~ to (have) it** das können Sie gerne haben ● *n* Willkommen *nt* ● *vt* begrüßen

weld /weld/ *vt* schweißen. **~er** *n* Schweißer *m*

welfare /ˈwelfeə(r)/ *n* Wohl *nt*; (*Admin*) Fürsorge *f*. **W ~ State** *n* Wohlfahrtsstaat *m*

well¹ /wel/ *n* Brunnen *m*; (*oil* **~**) Quelle *f*

well² *adv* (**better, best**) gut; **as ~** auch; **as ~ as** (*in addition*) sowohl ... als auch; **~ done!** gut gemacht! ● *a* gesund; **he is not ~** es geht ihm nicht gut; **get ~ soon!** gute Besserung! ● *int* nun, na

well: ~-behaved *a* artig. **~-being** *n* Wohl *nt*

wellingtons /ˈwelɪŋtənz/ *npl* Gummistiefel *pl*

well: ~-known *a* bekannt. **~-off** *a* wohlhabend; **be ~-off** gut dransein. **~-to-do** *a* wohlhabend

Welsh /welʃ/ *a* walisisch ● *n* (*Lang*) Walisisch *nt*; **the ~** *pl* die Waliser. **~man** *n* Waliser *m*

went /went/ *see* **go**

wept /wept/ *see* **weep**

were /wɜ:(r)/ *see* **be**

west /west/ *n* Westen *m*; **to the ~ of** westlich von ● *a* West-, west- ● *adv* nach Westen. **~erly** *a* westlich. **~ern** *a* westlich ● *n* Western *m*

West: ~ ˈGermany *n* Westdeutschland *nt*. **~ ˈIndian** *a* westindisch ● *n* Westinder(in) *m(f)*. **~ ˈIndies** /-ˈɪndɪz/ *npl* Westindische Inseln *pl*

ˈwestward[s] /-wəd[z]/ *adv* nach Westen

wet /wet/ *a* (**wetter, wettest**) nass; <! *person*> weichlich, lasch; **'~ paint'** 'frisch gestrichen' ● *vt* (*pt/pp* **wet** or **wetted**) nass machen

whack /wæk/ *vt* ! schlagen. **~ed** *a* ! kaputt

whale /weɪl/ *n* Wal *m*

wharf /wɔːf/ *n* Kai *m*

---

what /wɒt/

● *pronoun*

····➤ (*in questions*) was. **what is it?** was ist das? **what do you want?** was wollen Sie? **what is your name?** wie heißen Sie? **what?** (! *say that again*) wie?; was? **what is the time?** wie spät ist es? (*indirect*) **I didn't know what to do** ich wusste nicht, was ich machen sollte

> **!** The equivalent of a preposition with **what** in English is a special word in German beginning with *wo-* (*wor-* before a vowel): **for what? what for?** = wofür? wozu? **from what?** wovon? **on what?** worauf? worüber? **under what?** worunter? **with what?** womit? etc. **what do you want the money for?** wozu willst du das Geld? **what is he talking about?** wovon redet er?

····➤ (*relative pronoun*) was. **do what I tell you** tu, was ich dir sage. **give me what you can** gib mir, so viel du kannst. **what little I know** das bisschen, das ich weiß. **I don't agree with what you are saying** ich stimme dem nicht zu, was Sie sagen

····➤ (*in phrases*) **what about me?** was ist mit mir? **what about a cup of coffee?** wie wäre es mit einer Tasse Kaffee? **what if she doesn't come?** was ist, wenn sie nicht kommt? **what of it?** was ist dabei?

● *adjective*

····➤ (*asking for selection*) welcher (*m*), welche (*f*), welches (*nt*), welche (*pl*). **what book do you want?** welches Buch willst du haben? **what colour are the walls?** welche Farbe haben die Wände? **I asked him what train to take** ich habe ihn gefragt, welchen Zug ich nehmen soll

····➤ (*asking how much/many*) **what money does he have?** wie viel Geld hat er? **what time is it?** wie spät ist es? **what time does it start?** um wie viel Uhr fängt es an?

····➤ **what kind of ...?** was für [ein(e)]? **what kind of man is he?** was für ein Mensch ist er?

····➤ (*in exclamations*) was für (+ *nom*). **what a fool you are!** was für ein Dummkopf du doch bist! **what cheek/luck!** was für eine Frechheit/ein Glück! **what a huge house!** was für ein riesiges Haus! **what a lot of people!** was für viele Leute!

---

what'ever *a* [egal] welche(r,s) ● *pron* was ... auch; **~ is it?** was ist das bloß? **~ he does** was er auch tut; **nothing ~** überhaupt nichts

whatso'ever *pron & a* ≈ **whatever**

wheat /wiːt/ *n* Weizen *m*

wheel /wiːl/ *n* Rad *nt*; (*pottery*) Töpferscheibe *f*; (*steering ~*) Lenkrad *nt*; **at the ~** am Steuer ● *vt* (*push*) schieben ● *vi* kehrtmachen; (*circle*) kreisen

wheel: ~barrow *n* Schubkarre *f*. **~chair** *n* Rollstuhl *m*. **~-clamp** *n* Parkkralle *f*

when /wen/ *adv* wann; **the day ~** der Tag, an dem ● *conj* wenn; (*in the past*) als; (*although*) wo ...

doch; ~ **swimming/reading** beim Schwimmen/Lesen

when'ever *conj & adv* [immer] wenn; (*at whatever time*) wann immer; ~ **did it happen?** wann ist das bloß passiert?

where /weə(r)/ *adv & conj* wo; ~ **[to]** wohin; ~ **[from]** woher

whereabouts[1] /weərə'baʊts/ *adv* wo

'whereabouts[2] *n* Verbleib *m*; (*of person*) Aufenthaltsort *m*

where'as *conj* während; (*in contrast*) wohingegen

whereu'pon *adv* worauf[hin]

wher'ever *conj & adv* wo immer; (*to whatever place*) wohin immer; (*from whatever place*) woher immer; (*everywhere*) überall wo; ~ **possible** wenn irgend möglich

whether /'weðə(r)/ *conj* ob

which /wɪtʃ/

● *adjective*

····➤ (*in questions*) welcher (*m*), welche (*f*), welches (*nt*), welche (*pl*). **which book do you need?** welches Buch brauchst du? **which one?** welcher/welche/welches? **which ones?** welche? **which one of you did it?** wer von euch hat es getan? **which way?** (*which direction*) welche Richtung?; (*where*) wohin?; (*how*) wie?

····➤ (*relative*) **he always comes at one, at which time I'm having lunch/by which time I've finished** er kommt immer um ein Uhr; dann esse ich gerade zu Mittag/bis dahin bin ich schon fertig

● *pronoun*

····➤ (*in questions*) welcher (*m*), welche (*f*), welches (*nt*), welche (*pl*). **which is which?** welcher/welche/welches ist welcher/welche/welches? **which of you?** wer von euch?

····➤ (*relative*) der (*m*), die (*f*), das (*nt*), die (*pl*); (*genitive*) dessen (*m, nt*), deren (*f, pl*); (*dative*) dem (*m, nt*), der (*f*), denen (*pl*); (*referring to a clause*) was. **the book which I gave you** das Buch, das ich dir gab. **the trial, the result of which we are expecting** der Prozess, dessen Ergebnis wir erwarten. **the house of which I was speaking** das Haus, von dem *od* wovon ich redete. **after which** wonach; nach dem. **on which** worauf; auf dem. **the shop opposite which we parked** der Laden, gegenüber dem wir parkten. **everything which I tell you** alles, was ich dir sage

which'ever *a & pron* [egal] welche(r,s); ~ **it is** was es auch ist

while /waɪl/ *n* Weile *f*; **a long** ~ lange; **be worth** ~ sich lohnen; **it's worth my** ~ es lohnt sich für mich ● *conj* während; (*as long as*) solange; (*although*) obgleich ● *vt* ~ **away** sich (*dat*) vertreiben

whilst /waɪlst/ *conj* während

whim /wɪm/ *n* Laune *f*

whimper /'wɪmpə(r)/ *vi* wimmern; <*dog:*> winseln

whine /waɪn/ *vi* winseln

whip /wɪp/ *n* Peitsche *f*; (*Pol*) Einpeitscher *m* ● *vt* (*pt/pp* **whipped**) peitschen; (*Culin*) schlagen. **~ped 'cream** *n* Schlagsahne *f*

whirl /wɜ:l/ *vt/i* wirbeln. **~pool** *n* Strudel *m*. **~-wind** *n* Wirbelwind *m*

whirr /wɜ:(r)/ *vi* surren

whisk /wɪsk/ *n* (*Culin*) Schneebesen *m* ● *vt* (*Culin*) schlagen

whisker /'wɪskə(r)/ *n* Schnurrhaar *nt*

whisky /'wɪskɪ/ *n* Whisky *m*

whisper /ˈwɪspə(r)/ *n* Flüstern *nt* ● *vt/i* flüstern

whistle /ˈwɪsl/ *n* Pfiff *m*; (*instrument*) Pfeife *f* ● *vt/i* pfeifen

white /waɪt/ *a* (**-r, -st**) weiß ● *n* Weiß *nt*; (*of egg*) Eiweiß *nt*; (*person*) Weiße(r) *m/f*

white: ~ **ˈcoffee** *n* Kaffee *m* mit Milch. **~-ˈcollar worker** *n* Angestellte(r) *m*. ~ **ˈlie** *n* Notlüge *f*

whiten /ˈwaɪtn/ *vt* weiß machen ● *vi* weiß werden

whiteness /ˈwaɪtnɪs/ *n* Weiß *nt*

Whitsun /ˈwɪtsn/ *n* Pfingsten *nt*

whiz[z] /wɪz/ *vi* (*pt/pp* **whizzed**) zischen. **~-kid** *n* [!] Senkrechtstarter *m*

who /huː/ *pron* wer; (*acc*) wen; (*dat*) wem ● *rel pron* der/die/das, (*pl*) die

whoˈever *pron* wer [immer]; ~ **he is** wer er auch ist; ~ **is it?** wer ist das bloß?

whole /həʊl/ *a* ganz; <*truth*> voll ● *n* Ganze(s) *nt*; **as a** ~ als Ganzes; **on the** ~ im Großen und Ganzen; **the** ~ **of Germany** ganz Deutschland

whole: **~food** *n* Vollwertkost *f*. **~-ˈhearted** *a* rückhaltlos. **~meal** *a* Vollkorn-

ˈwholesale *a* Großhandels- ● *adv* en gros; (*fig*) in Bausch und Bogen. **~r** *n* Großhändler *m*

wholly /ˈhəʊlɪ/ *adv* völlig

whom /huːm/ *pron* wen; **to** ~ wem ● *rel pron* den/die/das, (*pl*) die; (*dat*) dem/der/dem, (*pl*) denen

whopping /ˈwɒpɪŋ/ *a* [!] Riesen-

whore /hɔː(r)/ *n* Hure *f*

whose /huːz/ *pron* wessen; ~ **is that?** wem gehört das? ● *rel pron* dessen/deren/dessen, (*pl*) deren

why /waɪ/ *adv* warum; (*for what purpose*) wozu; **that's** ~ darum

wick /wɪk/ *n* Docht *m*

wicked /ˈwɪkɪd/ *a* böse; (*mischievous*) frech, boshaft

wicker /ˈwɪkə(r)/ *n* Korbgeflecht *nt* ● *attrib* Korb-

wide /waɪd/ *a* (**-r, -st**) weit; (*broad*) breit; (*fig*) groß ● *adv* weit; (*off target*) daneben; ~ **awake** hellwach; **far and** ~ weit und breit. **~ly** *adv* weit; <*known, accepted*> weithin; <*differ*> stark

widen /ˈwaɪdn/ *vt* verbreitern; (*fig*) erweitern ● *vi* sich verbreitern

ˈwidespread *a* weit verbreitet

widow /ˈwɪdəʊ/ *n* Witwe *f*. **~ed** *a* verwitwet. **~er** *n* Witwer *m*

width /wɪdθ/ *n* Weite *f*; (*breadth*) Breite *f*

wield /wiːld/ *vt* schwingen; ausüben <*power*>

wife /waɪf/ *n* (*pl* **wives**) [Ehe]frau *f*

wig /wɪg/ *n* Perücke *f*

wiggle /ˈwɪgl/ *vi* wackeln ● *vt* wackeln mit

wild /waɪld/ *a* (**-er, -est**), **-ly** *adv* wild; <*animal*> wild lebend; <*flower*> wild wachsend; (*furious*) wütend ● *adv* wild; **run** ~ frei herumlaufen ● *n* **in the** ~ wild; **the** **~s** *pl* die Wildnis *f*

wilderness /ˈwɪldənɪs/ *n* Wildnis *f*; (*desert*) Wüste *f*

wildlife *n* Tierwelt *f*

will[1] /wɪl/

● *auxiliary verb*

past **would**

····➤ (*expressing the future*) werden. **she will arrive tomorrow** sie wird morgen ankommen. **he will be there by now** er wird jetzt schon da sein

····➤ (*expressing intention*) (*present tense*) **will you go?** gehst du? **I promise I won't do it again** ich verspreche, ich machs nicht noch mal

····➤ (*in requests*) **will/would you please tidy up?** würdest du bitte aufräumen? **will you be quiet!** willst du ruhig sein!

····➤ (*in invitations*) **will you have/would you like some wine?** wollen Sie/möchten Sie Wein?

····➤ (*negative: refuse to*) nicht wollen. **they won't help me** sie wollen mir nicht helfen. **the car won't start** das Auto will nicht anspringen

····➤ (*in tag questions*) nicht wahr. **you'll be back soon, won't you?** du kommst bald wieder, nicht wahr? **you will help her, won't you?** du hilfst ihr doch, nicht wahr?

····➤ (*in short answers*) **Will you be there? — Yes I will** Wirst du da sein? — Ja

will² *n* Wille *m*; (*document*) Testament *nt*

willing /ˈwɪlɪŋ/ *a* willig; (*eager*) bereitwillig; **be ~** bereit sein. **~ly** *adv* bereitwillig; (*gladly*) gern. **~ness** *n* Bereitwilligkeit *f*

willow /ˈwɪləʊ/ *n* Weide *f*

ˈwill-power *n* Willenskraft *f*

wilt /wɪlt/ *vi* welk werden, welken

wily /ˈwaɪlɪ/ *a* (**-ier, -iest**) listig

win /wɪn/ *n* Sieg *m* ● *v* (*pt/pp* **won**; *pres p* **winning**) ● *vt* gewinnen; bekommen <*scholarship*> ● *vi* gewinnen; (*in battle*) siegen. **~ over** *vt* auf seine Seite bringen

wince /wɪns/ *vi* zusammenzucken

winch /wɪntʃ/ *n* Winde *f* ● *vt* **~ up** hochwinden

wind¹ /wɪnd/ *n* Wind *m*; (**[!]** *flatulence*) Blähungen *pl* ● *vt* **~ s.o.** jdm den Atem nehmen

wind² /waɪnd/ *v* (*pt/pp* **wound**) ● *vt* (*wrap*) wickeln; (*move by turning*) kurbeln; aufziehen <*clock*> *vi* <*road:*> sich winden. **~ up** *vt* aufziehen <*clock*>; schließen <*proceedings*>

wind: ~ farm *n* Windpark *m*. **~ instrument** *n* Blasinstrument *nt*. **~mill** *n* Windmühle *f*

window /ˈwɪndəʊ/ *n* Fenster *nt*; (*of shop*) Schaufenster *nt*

window: ~-box *n* Blumenkasten *m*. **~-cleaner** *n* Fensterputzer *m*. **~-pane** *n* Fensterscheibe *f*. **~-shopping** *n* Schaufensterbummel *m*. **~-sill** *n* Fensterbrett *nt*

ˈwindpipe *n* Luftröhre *f*

ˈwindscreen *n*, (*Amer*) **ˈwindshield** *n* Windschutzscheibe *f*. **~-wiper** *n* Scheibenwischer *m*

wind surfing *n* Windsurfen *nt*

windy /ˈwɪndɪ/ *a* (**-ier, -iest**) windig

wine /waɪn/ *n* Wein *m*

wine: ~-bar *n* Weinstube *f*. **~ glass** *n* Weinglas *nt*. **~-list** *n* Weinkarte *f*

winery /ˈwaɪnərɪ/ *n* (*Amer*) Weingut *nt*

ˈwine-tasting *n* Weinprobe *f*

wing /wɪŋ/ *n* Flügel *m*; (*Auto*) Kotflügel *m*; **~s** *pl* (*Theat*) Kulissen *pl*

wink /wɪŋk/ *n* Zwinkern *nt*; **not sleep a ~** kein Auge zutun ● *vi* zwinkern; <*light:*> blinken

winner /ˈwɪnə(r)/ *n* Gewinner(in) *m(f)*; (*Sport*) Sieger(in) *m(f)*

winning /ˈwɪnɪŋ/ *a* siegreich; <*smile*> gewinnend. **~-post** *n* Zielpfosten *m*. **~s** *npl* Gewinn *m*

wint|er /ˈwɪntə(r)/ *n* Winter *m*. **~ry** *a* winterlich

wipe /waɪp/ *n* **give sth a ~** etw abwischen ● *vt* abwischen; aufwischen <*floor*>; (*dry*) abtrocknen. **~ out** *vt* (*cancel*) löschen; (*destroy*) ausrotten. **~ up** *vt* aufwischen

wire /ˈwaɪə(r)/ *n* Draht *m*

wiring /ˈwaɪərɪŋ/ *n* [elektrische] Leitungen *pl*

wisdom /ˈwɪzdəm/ *n* Weisheit *f*; (*prudence*) Klugheit *f*. **~ tooth** *n* Weisheitszahn *m*

wise /waɪz/ *a* (**-r, -st**), **-ly** *adv* weise; (*prudent*) klug

wish /wɪʃ/ *n* Wunsch *m* ● *vt* wünschen; **~ s.o. well** jdm alles Gute wünschen; **I ~ you could stay** ich wünschte, du könntest hier bleiben ● *vi* sich (*dat*) etwas wünschen. **~ful** *a* **~ful thinking** Wunschdenken *nt*

wistful /ˈwɪstfl/ *a*, **-ly** *adv* wehmütig

wit /wɪt/ *n* Geist *m*, Witz *m*; (*intelligence*) Verstand *m*; (*person*) geistreicher Mensch *m*; **be at one's ~s' end** sich (*dat*) keinen Rat mehr wissen

witch /wɪtʃ/ *n* Hexe *f*. **~craft** *n* Hexerei *f*

with /wɪð/ *prep* mit (+ *dat*); **~ fear/cold** vor Angst/Kälte; **~ it** damit; **I'm going ~ you** ich gehe mit; **take it ~ you** nimm es mit; **I haven't got it ~ me** ich habe es nicht bei mir

withˈdraw *v* (*pt* **-drew**, *pp* **-drawn**) ● *vt* zurückziehen; abheben <*money*> ● *vi* sich zurückziehen. **~al** *n* Zurückziehen *nt*; (*of money*) Abhebung *f*; (*from drugs*) Entzug *m*

wither /ˈwɪðə(r)/ *vi* [ver]welken

withˈhold *vt* (*pt/pp* **-held**) vorenthalten (**from s.o.** jdm)

withˈin *prep* innerhalb (+ *gen*) ● *adv* innen

withˈout *prep* ohne (+ *acc*); **~ my noticing it** ohne dass ich es merkte

withˈstand *vt* (*pt/pp* **-stood**) standhalten (+ *dat*)

witness /ˈwɪtnɪs/ *n* Zeuge *m*/ Zeugin *f* ● *vt* Zeuge/Zeugin sein (+ *gen*); bestätigen <*signature*>

witticism /ˈwɪtɪsɪzm/ *n* geistreicher Ausspruch *m*

witty /ˈwɪtɪ/ *a* (**-ier, -iest**) witzig, geistreich

wives /waɪvz/ *see* **wife**

wizard /ˈwɪzəd/ *n* Zauberer *m*

wizened /ˈwɪznd/ *a* verhutzelt

wobb|le /ˈwɒbl/ *vi* wackeln. **~ly** *a* wackelig

woke, woken /wəʊk, ˈwəʊkn/ *see* **wake**[1]

wolf /wʊlf/ *n* (*pl* **wolves** /wʊlvz/) Wolf *m*

woman /ˈwʊmən/ *n* (*pl* **women**) Frau *f*. **~izer** *n* Schürzenjäger *m*

womb /wu:m/ *n* Gebärmutter *f*

women /ˈwɪmɪn/ *npl see* **woman**

won /wʌn/ *see* **win**

wonder /ˈwʌndə(r)/ *n* Wunder *nt*; (*surprise*) Staunen *nt* ● *vt/i* sich fragen; (*be surprised*) sich wundern; **I ~** da frage ich mich; **I ~ whether she is ill** ob sie wohl krank ist? **~ful** *a*, **-ly** *adv* wunderbar

won't /wəʊnt/ = **will not**

wood /wʊd/ *n* Holz *nt*; (*forest*) Wald *m*; **touch ~!** unberufen!

wood: ~ed /-ɪd/ *a* bewaldet. **~en** *a* Holz-; (*fig*) hölzern. **~pecker** *n* Specht *m*. **~wind** *n* Holzbläser *pl*. **~work** *n* (*wooden parts*) Holzteile *pl*; (*craft*) Tischlerei *f*. **~worm** *n* Holzwurm *m*

wool /wʊl/ *n* Wolle *f* ● *attrib* Woll-. **~len** *a* wollen

woolly /ˈwʊlɪ/ *a* (**-ier, -iest**) wollig; (*fig*) unklar

word /wɜ:d/ *n* Wort *nt*; (*news*) Nachricht *f*; **by ~ of mouth** mündlich; **have a ~ with** sprechen mit; **have ~s** einen Wortwechsel haben. **~ing** *n*

Wortlaut *m*. ~ **processor** *n* Textverarbeitungssystem *nt*

wore /wɔ:(r)/ *see* **wear**

work /wɜ:k/ *n* Arbeit *f*; (*Art, Literature*) Werk *nt*; ~**s** *pl* (*factory, mechanism*) Werk *nt*; **at ~** bei der Arbeit; **out of ~** arbeitslos ● *vi* arbeiten; <*machine, system:*> funktionieren; (*have effect*) wirken; (*study*) lernen; **it won't ~** (*fig*) es klappt nicht ● *vt* arbeiten lassen; bedienen <*machine*>; betätigen <*lever*>. ~ **off** *vt* abarbeiten. ~ **out** *vt* ausrechnen; (*solve*) lösen ● *vi* gut gehen, [!] klappen. ~ **up** *vt* aufbauen; sich (*dat*) holen <*appetite*>; **get ~ed up** sich aufregen

workable /ˈwɜ:kəbl/ *a* (*feasible*) durchführbar

worker /ˈwɜ:kə(r)/ *n* Arbeiter(in) *m(f)*

working /ˈwɜ:kɪŋ/ *a* berufstätig; <*day, clothes*> Arbeits-; **be in ~ order** funktionieren. ~ **class** *n* Arbeiterklasse *f*

work: ~**man** *n* Arbeiter *m*; (*craftsman*) Handwerker *m*. ~**manship** *n* Arbeit *f*. ~**shop** *n* Werkstatt *f*

world /wɜ:ld/ *n* Welt *f*; **in the ~** auf der Welt; **think the ~ of s.o.** große Stücke auf jdn halten. ~**ly** *a* weltlich; <*person*> weltlich gesinnt. ~**-wide** *a & adv* /-ˈ-/ weltweit

worm /wɜ:m/ *n* Wurm *m*

worn /wɔ:n/ *see* **wear** ● *a* abgetragen. ~**-out** *a* abgetragen; <*carpet*> abgenutzt; <*person*> erschöpft

worried /ˈwʌrɪd/ *a* besorgt

worry /ˈwʌrɪ/ *n* Sorge *f* ● *v* (*pt/pp* **worried**) ● *vt* beunruhigen; (*bother*) stören ● *vi* sich beunruhigen, sich (*dat*) Sorgen machen. ~**ing** *a* beunruhigend

worse /wɜ:s/ *a & adv* schlechter; (*more serious*) schlimmer ● *n* Schlechtere(s) *nt*; Schlimmere(s) *nt*

worsen /ˈwɜ:sn/ *vt* verschlechtern ● *vi* sich verschlechtern

worship /ˈwɜ:ʃɪp/ *n* Anbetung *f*; (*service*) Gottesdienst *m* ● *vt* (*pt/pp* **-shipped**) anbeten

worst /wɜ:st/ *a* schlechteste(r,s); (*most serious*) schlimmste(r,s) ● *adv* am schlechtesten; am schlimmsten ● *n* **the ~** das Schlimmste

worth /wɜ:θ/ *n* Wert *m*; **£10's ~ of petrol** Benzin für £10 ● *a* **be ~ £5** £5 wert sein; **be ~ it** (*fig*) sich lohnen. ~**less** *a* wertlos. ~**while** *a* lohnend

worthy /ˈwɜ:ðɪ/ *a* würdig

would /wʊd/ *v aux* **I ~ do it** ich würde es tun, ich täte es; **~ you go?** würdest du gehen? **he said he ~n't** er sagte, er würde es nicht tun; **what ~ you like?** was möchten Sie?

wound¹ /wu:nd/ *n* Wunde *f* ● *vt* verwunden

wound² /waʊnd/ *see* **wind²**

wove, woven /wəʊv, ˈwəʊvn/ *see* **weave²**

wrangle /ˈræŋgl/ *n* Streit *m*

wrap /ræp/ *n* Umhang *m* ● *vt* (*pt/pp* **wrapped**) ~ **[up]** wickeln; einpacken <*present*> ● *vi* ~ **up warmly** sich warm einpacken. ~**per** *n* Hülle *f*. ~**ping** *n* Verpackung *f*

wrath /rɒθ/ *n* Zorn *m*

wreath /ri:θ/ *n* (*pl* **-s** /-ðz/) Kranz *m*

wreck /rek/ *n* Wrack *nt* ● *vt* zerstören; zunichte machen <*plans*>; zerrütten <*marriage*>. ~**age** /-ɪdʒ/ *n* Wrackteile *pl*; (*fig*) Trümmer *pl*

wren /ren/ *n* Zaunkönig *m*

wrench /rentʃ/ *n* Ruck *m*; (*tool*) Schraubenschlüssel *m*; **be a ~** (*fig*) weh tun ● *vt* reißen; **~ sth from s.o.** jdm etw entreißen

wrestl|e /ˈresl/ *vi* ringen. **~er** *n* Ringer *m*. **~ing** *n* Ringen *nt*

wretch /retʃ/ *n* Kreatur *f*. **~ed** /-ɪd/ *a* elend; (*very bad*) erbärmlich

wriggle /ˈrɪgl/ *n* Zappeln *nt* ● *vi* zappeln; (*move forward*) sich schlängeln; **~ out of sth** [!] sich vor etw (*dat*) drücken

wring /rɪŋ/ *vt* (*pt/pp* **wrung**) wringen; (**~** *out*) auswringen; umdrehen <*neck*>; ringen <*hands*>

wrinkle /ˈrɪŋkl/ *n* Falte *f*; (*on skin*) Runzel *f* ● *vt* kräuseln ● *vi* sich kräuseln, sich falten. **~d** *a* runzlig

wrist /rɪst/ *n* Handgelenk *nt*. **~-watch** *n* Armbanduhr *f*

write /raɪt/ *vt/i* (*pt* **wrote**, *pp* **written**, *pres p* **writing**) schreiben. **~ down** *vt* aufschreiben. **~ off** *vt* abschreiben; zu Schrott fahren <*car*>

ˈ**write-off** *n* ≈ Totalschaden *m*

writer /ˈraɪtə(r)/ *n* Schreiber(in) *m(f)*; (*author*) Schriftsteller(in) *m(f)*

writhe /raɪð/ *vi* sich winden

writing /ˈraɪtɪŋ/ *n* Schreiben *nt*; (*handwriting*) Schrift *f*; **in ~** schriftlich. **~-paper** *n* Schreibpapier *nt*

written /ˈrɪtn/ *see* **write**

wrong /rɒŋ/ *a*, **-ly** *adv* falsch; (*morally*) unrecht; (*not just*) ungerecht; **be ~** nicht stimmen; <*person:*> Unrecht haben; **what's ~?** was ist los? ● *adv* falsch; **go ~** <*person:*> etwas falsch machen; <*machine:*> kaputtgehen; <*plan:*> schief gehen ● *n* Unrecht *nt* ● *vt* Unrecht tun (+ *dat*). **~ful** *a* ungerechtfertigt. **~fully** *adv* <*accuse*> zu Unrecht

wrote /rəʊt/ *see* **write**

wrung /rʌŋ/ *see* **wring**

wry /raɪ/ *a* (**-er, -est**) ironisch; <*humour*> trocken

Xx

Xmas /ˈkrɪsməs, ˈeksməs/ *n* [!] Weihnachten *nt*

X-ray /ˈeks-/ *n* (*picture*) Röntgenaufnahme *f*; **~s** *pl* Röntgenstrahlen *pl* ● *vt* röntgen; durchleuchten <*luggage*>

Yy

yacht /jɒt/ *n* Jacht *f*; (*for racing*) Segeljacht *f*. **~ing** *n* Segeln *nt*

yank /jæŋk/ *vt* [!] reißen

Yank *n* [!] Ami *m* [!]

yap /jæp/ *vi* (*pt/pp* **yapped**) <*dog:*> kläffen

yard[1] /jɑːd/ *n* Hof *m*; (*for storage*) Lager *nt*

yard[2] *n* Yard *nt* (= *0,91 m*)

yarn /jɑːn/ *n* Garn *nt*; ([!] *tale*) Geschichte *f*

yawn /jɔːn/ *n* Gähnen *nt* ● *vi* gähnen

year /jɪə(r)/ *n* Jahr *nt*; (*of wine*) Jahrgang *m*; **for ~s** jahrelang. **~ly** *a & adv* jährlich
yearn /jɜːn/ *vi* sich sehnen (**for** nach). **~ing** *n* Sehnsucht *f*
yeast /jiːst/ *n* Hefe *f*
yell /jel/ *n* Schrei *m* ● *vi* schreien
yellow /ˈjeləʊ/ *a* gelb ● *n* Gelb *nt*
yelp /jelp/ *vi* jaulen
yes /jes/ *adv* ja; (*contradicting*) doch ● *n* Ja *nt*
yesterday /ˈjestədeɪ/ *n & adv* gestern; **~'s paper** die gestrige Zeitung; **the day before ~** vorgestern
yet /jet/ *adv* noch; (*in question*) schon; (*nevertheless*) doch; **as ~** bisher; **not ~** noch nicht; **the best ~** das bisher beste ● *conj* doch
Yiddish /ˈjɪdɪʃ/ *n* Jiddisch *nt*
yield /jiːld/ *n* Ertrag *m* ● *vt* bringen; abwerfen <*profit*> ● *vi* nachgeben; (*Amer, Auto*) die Vorfahrt beachten
yoga /ˈjəʊgə/ *n* Yoga *m*
yoghurt /ˈjɒgət/ *n* Joghurt *m*
yoke /jəʊk/ *n* Joch *nt*; (*of garment*) Passe *f*
yolk /jəʊk/ *n* Dotter *m*, Eigelb *nt*
you /juː/ *pron* du; (*acc*) dich; (*dat*) dir; (*pl*) ihr; (*acc, dat*) euch; (*formal*) (*nom & acc, sg & pl*) Sie; (*dat, sg & pl*) Ihnen; (*one*) man; (*acc*) einen; (*dat*) einem; **all of ~** ihr/Sie alle; **I know ~** ich kenne dich/euch/Sie; **I'll give ~ the money** ich gebe dir/euch/Ihnen das Geld; **it does ~ good** es tut einem gut; **it's bad for ~** es ist ungesund
young /jʌŋ/ *a* (**-er**, /-gə(r)/ **-est** /-gɪst/) jung ● *npl* (*animals*) Junge *pl*; **the ~** die Jugend *f*. **~ster** *n* Jugendliche(r) *m/f*; (*child*) Kleine(r) *m/f*
your /jɔː(r)/ *a* dein; (*pl*) euer; (*formal*) Ihr
yours /jɔːz/ *poss pron* deine(r), deins; (*pl*) eure(r), euers; (*formal, sg & pl*) Ihre(r), Ihr[e]s; **a friend of ~** ein Freund von dir/Ihnen/euch; **that is ~** das gehört dir/Ihnen/euch
your'self *pron* (*pl* **-selves**) selbst; (*refl*) dich; (*dat*) dir; (*pl*) euch; (*formal*) sich; **by ~** allein
youth /juːθ/ *n* (*pl* **-s** /-ðːz/) Jugend *f*; (*boy*) Jugendliche(r) *m*. **~ful** *a* jugendlich. **~ hostel** *n* Jugendherberge *f*
Yugoslavia /juːgəˈslɑːvɪə/ *n* Jugoslawien *nt*

Zz

zeal /ziːl/ *n* Eifer *m*
zealous /ˈzeləs/ *a*, **-ly** *adv* eifrig
zebra /ˈzebrə/ *n* Zebra *nt*. **~ ˈcrossing** *n* Zebrastreifen *m*
zero /ˈzɪərəʊ/ *n* Null *f*
zest /zest/ *n* Begeisterung *f*
zigzag /ˈzɪgzæg/ *n* Zickzack *m* ● *vi* (*pt/pp* **-zagged**) im Zickzack laufen/ (*in vehicle*) fahren
zinc /zɪŋk/ *n* Zink *nt*
zip /zɪp/ *n* **~ [fastener]** Reißverschluss *m* ● *vt* **~ [up]** den Reißverschluss zuziehen an (+ *dat*)
ˈzip code *n* (*Amer*) Postleitzahl *f*
zipper /ˈzɪpə(r)/ *n* Reißverschluss *m*
zodiac /ˈzəʊdɪæk/ *n* Tierkreis *m*
zone /zəʊn/ *n* Zone *f*
zoo /zuː/ *n* Zoo *m*
zoological /zuːəˈlɒdʒɪkl/ *a* zoologisch

zoolog|ist /zu:ˈɒlədʒɪst/ *n* Zoologe *m*/gin *f*. **~y** *n* Zoologie *f*

zoom /zu:m/ *vi* sausen. **~ lens** *n* Zoomobjektiv *nt*

German irregular verbs

1st, 2nd, and 3rd person present are given after the infinitive, and past subjunctive after the past indicative, where there is a change of vowel or any other irregularity.

Compound verbs are only given if they do not take the same forms as the corresponding simple verb, e.g. *befehlen*, or if there is no corresponding simple verb, e.g. *bewegen*.

An asterisk (*) indicates a verb which is also conjugated regularly.

Infinitive	Past tense	Past participle
abwägen	wog (wöge) ab	abgewogen
ausbedingen	bedang (bedänge) aus	ausbedungen
backen (du bäckst, er bäckt)	buk (büke)	gebacken
befehlen (du befiehlst, er befiehlt)	befahl (beföhle, befähle)	befohlen
beginnen	begann (begänne)	begonnen
beißen (du/er beißt)	biss (bisse)	gebissen
bergen (du birgst, er birgt)	barg (bärge)	geborgen
bewegen[2]	bewog (bewöge)	bewogen
biegen	bog (böge)	gebogen
bieten	bot (böte)	geboten
binden	band (bände)	gebunden
bitten	bat (bäte)	gebeten
blasen (du/er bläst)	blies	geblasen
bleiben	blieb	geblieben
bleichen*	blich	geblichen
braten (du brätst, er brät)	briet	gebraten
brechen (du brichst, er bricht)	brach (bräche)	gebrochen
brennen	brannte (brennte)	gebrannt

Infinitive	Past tense	Past participle
bringen	brachte (brächte)	gebracht
denken	dachte (dächte)	gedacht
dreschen (du drischst, er drischt)	drosch (drösche)	gedroschen
dringen	drang (dränge)	gedrungen
dürfen (ich/er darf, du darfst)	durfte (dürfte)	gedurft
empfehlen (du empfiehlst, er empfiehlt)	empfahl (empföhle)	empfohlen
erlöschen (du erlischst, er erlischt)	erlosch (erlösche)	erloschen
erschrecken (du erschrickst, er erschrickt)	erschrak (erschäke)	erschrocken
erwägen	erwog (erwöge)	erwogen
essen (du/er isst)	aß (äße)	gegessen
fahren (du fährst, er fährt)	fuhr (führe)	gefahren
fallen (du fällst, er fällt)	fiel	gefallen
fangen (du fängst, er fängt)	fing	gefangen
fechten (du fichtst, er ficht)	focht (föchte)	gefochten
finden	fand (fände)	gefunden
flechten (du flichtst, er flicht)	flocht (flöchte)	geflochten
fliegen	flog (flöge)	geflogen
fliehen	floh (flöhe)	geflohen
fließen (du/er fließt)	floss (flösse)	geflossen
fressen (du/er frisst)	fraß (fräße)	gefressen
frieren	fror (fröre)	gefroren
gären*	gor (göre)	gegoren
gebären (du gebierst, sie gebiert)	gebar (gebäre)	geboren
geben (du gibst, er gibt)	gab (gäbe)	gegeben
gedeihen	gedieh	gediehen
gehen	ging	gegangen
gelingen	gelang (gelänge)	gelungen

Infinitive	Past tense	Past participle
gelten (du giltst, er gilt)	galt (gölte, gälte)	gegolten
genesen (du/er genest)	genas (genäse)	genesen
genießen (du/er genießt)	genoss (genösse)	genossen
geschehen (es geschieht)	geschah (geschähe)	geschehen
gewinnen	gewann (gewönne, gewänne)	gewonnen
gießen (du/er gießt)	goss (gösse)	gegossen
gleichen	glich	geglichen
gleiten	glitt	geglitten
glimmen	glomm (glömme)	geglommen
graben (du gräbst, er gräbt)	grub (grübe)	gegraben
greifen	griff	gegriffen
haben (du hast, er hat)	hatte (hätte)	gehabt
halten (du hältst, er hält)	hielt	gehalten
hängen[2]	hing	gehangen
hauen	haute	gehauen
heben	hob (höbe)	gehoben
heißen (du/er hießt)	hieß	geheißen
helfen (du hilfst, er hilft)	half (hülfe)	geholfen
kennen	kannte (kennte)	gekannt
klingen	klang (klänge)	geklungen
kneifen	kniff	gekniffen
kommen	kam (käme)	gekommen
können (ich/er kann, du kannst)	konnte (könnte)	gekonnt
kriechen	kroch (kröche)	gekrochen
laden (du lädst, er lädt)	lud (lüde)	geladen
lassen (du/er lässt)	ließ	gelassen
laufen (du läufst, er läuft)	lief	gelaufen
leiden	litt	gelitten
leihen	lieh	geliehen
lesen (du/er liest)	las (läse)	gelesen
liegen	lag (läge)	gelegen
lügen	log (löge)	gelogen
mahlen	mahlte	gemahlen

Infinitive	Past tense	Past participle
meiden	mied	gemieden
melken	molk (mölke)	gemolken
messen (du/er misst)	maß (mäße)	gemessen
misslingen	misslang (misslänge)	misslungen
mögen (ich/er mag, du magst)	mochte (möchte)	gemocht
müssen (ich/er muss, du musst)	musste (müsste)	gemusst
nehmen (du nimmst, er nimmt)	nahm (nähme)	genommen
nennen	nannte (nennte)	genannt
pfeifen	pfiff	gepfiffen
preisen (du/er preist)	pries	gepriesen
raten (du rätst, er rät)	riet	geraten
reiben	rieb	gerieben
reißen (du/er reißt)	riss	gerissen
reiten	ritt	geritten
rennen	rannte (rennte)	gerannt
riechen	roch (röche)	gerochen
ringen	rang (ränge)	gerungen
rinnen	rann (ränne)	geronnen
rufen	rief	gerufen
salzen* (du/er salzt)	salzte	gesalzen
saufen (du säufst, er säuft)	soff (söffe)	gesoffen
saugen*	sog (söge)	gesogen
schaffen[1]	schuf (schüfe)	geschaffen
scheiden	schied	geschieden
scheinen	schien	geschienen
scheißen (du/er scheißt)	schiss	geschissen
schelten (du schiltst, er schilt)	schalt (schölte)	gescholten
scheren[1]	schor (schöre)	geschoren
schieben	schob (schöbe)	geschoben
schießen (du/er schießt)	schoss (schösse)	geschossen
schlafen (du schläfst, er schläft)	schlief	geschlafen

Infinitive	Past tense	Past participle
schlagen (du schlägst, er schlägt)	schlug (schlüge)	geschlagen
schleichen	schlich	geschlichen
schleifen[2]	schliff	geschliffen
schließen (du/er schießt)	schloss (schlösse)	geschlossen
schlingen	schlang (schlänge)	geschlungen
schmeißen (du/er schmeißt)	schmiss (schmisse)	geschmissen
schmelzen (du/er schmilzt)	schmolz (schmölze)	geschmolzen
schneiden	schnitt	geschnitten
schrecken* (du schrickst, er schrickt)	schrak (schräke)	geschreckt
schreiben	schrieb	geschrieben
schreien	schrie	geschrie[e]n
schreiten	schritt	geschritten
schweigen	schwieg	geschwiegen
schwellen (du schwillst, er schwillt)	schwoll (schwölle)	geschwollen
schwimmen	schwamm (schwömme)	geschwommen
schwinden	schwand (schwände)	geschwunden
schwingen	schwang (schwänge)	geschwungen
schwören	schwor (schwüre)	geschworen
sehen (du siehst, er sieht)	sah (sähe)	gesehen
sein (ich bin, du bist, er ist, wir sind, ihr seid, sie sind)	war (wäre)	gewesen
senden[1]	sandte (sendete)	gesandt
sieden	sott (sötte)	gesotten
singen	sang (sänge)	gesungen
sinken	sank (sänke)	gesunken
sitzen (du/er sitzt)	saß (säße)	gesessen
sollen (ich/er soll, du sollst)	sollte	gesollt
spalten*	spaltete	gespalten

Infinitive	Past tense	Past participle
spinnen	spann (spönne, spänne)	gesponnen
sprechen (du sprichst, er spricht)	sprach (spräche)	gesprochen
sprießen (du/er sprießt)	spross (sprösse)	gesprossen
springen	sprang (spränge)	gesprungen
stechen (du stichst, er sticht)	stach (stäche)	gestochen
stehen	stand (stünde, stände)	gestanden
stehlen (du stiehlst, er stiehlt)	stahl (stähle)	gestohlen
steigen	stieg	gestiegen
sterben (du stirbst, er stirbt)	starb (stürbe)	gestorben
stinken	stank (stänke)	gestunken
stoßen (du/er stößt)	stieß	gestoßen
streichen	strich	gestrichen
streiten	stritt	gestritten
tragen (du trägst, er trägt)	trug (trüge)	getragen
treffen (du triffst, er trifft)	traf (träfe)	getroffen
treiben	trieb	getrieben
treten (du trittst, er tritt)	trat (träte)	getreten
triefen*	troff (tröffe)	getroffen
trinken	trank (tränke)	getrunken
trügen	trog (tröge)	getrogen
tun (du tust, er tut)	tat (täte)	getan
verderben (du verdirbst, er verdirbt)	verdarb (verdürbe)	verdorben
vergessen (du/er vergisst)	vergaß (vergäße)	vergessen
verlieren	verlor (verlöre)	verloren
verzeihen	verzieh	verziehen
wachsen[1] (du/er wächst)	wuchs (wüchse)	gewachsen
waschen (du wäschst, er wäscht)	wusch (wüsche)	gewaschen
wenden[2]*	wandte (wendete)	gewandt
werben (du wirbst, er wirbt)	warb (würbe)	geworben

Infinitive	Past tense	Past participle
werden (du wirst, er wird)	wurde (würde)	geworden
werfen (du wirfst, er wirft)	warf (würfe)	geworfen
wiegen[1]	wog (wöge)	gewogen
winden	wand (wände)	gewunden
wissen (ich/er weiß, du weißt)	wusste (wüsste)	gewusst
wollen (ich/er will, du willst)	wollte	gewollt
wringen	wrang (wränge)	gewrungen
ziehen	zog (zöge)	gezogen
zwingen	zwang (zwänge)	gezwungen

Englische unregelmäßige Verben

Infinitive *Infinitiv*	Past Tense *Präteritum*	Past Participle *2. Partizip*	Infinitive *Infinitiv*	Past Tense *Präteritum*	Past Participle *2. Partizip*
arise	arose	arisen	**cost**	cost, costed (*vt*)	cost, costed
awake	awoke	awoken	**creep**	crept	crept
be	was	been	**cut**	cut	cut
bear	bore	borne	**deal**	dealt	dealt
beat	beat	beaten	**dig**	dug	dug
become	became	become	**do**	did	done
begin	began	begun	**draw**	drew	drawn
bend	bent	bent	**dream**	dreamt, dreamed	dreamt, dreamed
bet	bet, betted	bet, betted	**drink**	drank	drunk
bid	bade, bid	bidden, bid	**drive**	drove	driven
bind	bound	bound	**dwell**	dwelt	dwelt
bite	bit	bitten	**eat**	ate	eaten
bleed	bled	bled	**fall**	fell	fallen
blow	blew	blown	**feed**	fed	fed
break	broke	broken	**feel**	felt	felt
breed	bred	bred	**fight**	fought	fought
bring	brought	brought	**find**	found	found
build	built	built	**flee**	fled	fled
burn	burnt, burned	burnt, burned	**fling**	flung	flung
burst	burst	burst	**fly**	flew	flown
bust	busted, bust	busted, bust	**forbid**	forbade	forbidden
buy	bought	bought	**forget**	forgot	forgotten
cast	cast	cast	**forgive**	forgave	forgiven
catch	caught	caught	**forsake**	forsook	forsaken
choose	chose	chosen	**freeze**	froze	frozen
cling	clung	clung	**get**	got	got, gotten *Am*
come	came	come	**give**	gave	given
			go	went	gone

Infinitive *Infinitiv*	Past Tense *Präteritum*	Past Participle *2. Partizip*
grind	ground	ground
grow	grew	grown
hang	hung, hanged (*vt*)	hung, hanged
have	had	had
hear	heard	heard
hide	hid	hidden
hit	hit	hit
hold	held	held
hurt	hurt	hurt
keep	kept	kept
kneel	knelt	knelt
know	knew	known
lay	laid	laid
lead	led	led
lean	leaned, leant	leaned, leant
leap	leapt, leaped	leapt, leaped
learn	learnt, learned	learnt, learned
leave	left	left
lend	lent	lent
let	let	let
lie	lay	lain
light	lit, lighted	lit, lighted
lose	lost	lost
make	made	made
mean	meant	meant
meet	met	met
mow	mowed	mown, mowed
overhang	overhung	overhung

Infinitive *Infinitiv*	Past Tense *Präteritum*	Past Participle *2. Partizip*
pay	paid	paid
put	put	put
quit	quitted, quit	quitted, quit
read	read/red/	read/red/
rid	rid	rid
ride	rode	ridden
ring	rang	rung
rise	rose	risen
run	ran	run
saw	sawed	sawn, sawed
say	said	said
see	saw	seen
seek	sought	sought
sell	sold	sold
send	sent	sent
set	set	set
sew	sewed	sewn, sewed
shake	shook	shaken
shed	shed	shed
shine	shone	shone
shit	shit	shit
shoe	shod	shod
shoot	shot	shot
show	showed	shown
shrink	shrank	shrunk
shut	shut	shut
sing	sang	sung
sink	sank	sunk
sit	sat	sat
slay	slew	slain
sleep	slept	slept

Infinitive *Infinitiv*	Past Tense *Präteritum*	Past Participle *2. Partizip*	Infinitive *Infinitiv*	Past Tense *Präteritum*	Past Participle *2. Partizip*
slide	slid	slid	**strive**	strove	striven
sling	slung	slung	**swear**	swore	sworn
slit	slit	slit	**sweep**	swept	swept
smell	smelt, smelled	smelt, smelled	**swell**	swelled	swollen, swelled
sow	sowed	sown, sowed	**swim**	swam	swum
			swing	swung	swung
speak	spoke	spoken	**take**	took	taken
speed	sped, speeded	sped, speeded	**teach**	taught	taught
			tear	tore	torn
spell	spelled, spelt	spelled, spelt	**tell**	told	told
			think	thought	thought
spend	spent	spent	**thrive**	thrived, throve	thrived, thriven
spill	spilt, spilled	spilt, spilled	**throw**	threw	thrown
spin	spun	spun	**thrust**	thrust	thrust
spit	spat	spat	**tread**	trod	trodden
split	split	split	**understand**	understood	understood
spoil	spoilt, spoiled	spoilt, spoiled	**undo**	undid	undone
spread	spread	spread	**wake**	woke	woken
spring	sprang	sprung	**wear**	wore	worn
stand	stood	stood	**weave**	wove	woven
steal	stole	stolen	**weep**	wept	wept
stick	stuck	stuck	**wet**	wet, wetted	wet, wetted
sting	stung	stung			
stink	stank	stunk	**win**	won	won
stride	strode	stridden	**wind**	wound	wound
strike	struck	struck	**wring**	wrung	wrung
string	strung	strung	**write**	wrote	written